To Read Literature

Nov

Dec.

Also by Donald Hall

POETRY

Exiles and Marriages
The Dark Houses
A Roof of Tiger Lilies
The Alligator Bride: Poems New and Selected
The Yellow Room
A Blue Wing Tilts at the Edge of the Sea
The Town of Hill
Kicking the Leaves
The Happy Man
The One Day
Old and New Poems

PROSE

String Too Short to Be Saved
Henry Moore
Writing Well
Dock Ellis in the Country of Baseball
Goatfoot Milktongue Twinbird
Remembering Poets
Ox-Cart Man
To Keep Moving
The Weather for Poetry
The Man Who Lived Alone
Fathers Playing Catch with Sons
The Ideal Bakery
Poetry and Ambition
Seasons at Eagle Pond
Here at Eagle Pond

EDITIONS

Contemporary American Poets
A Choice of Whitman's Verse
The Oxford Book of American Literary Anecdotes
Claims for Poetry
The Oxford Book of Children's Verse in America

PLAYS

An Evening's Frost
Bread and Roses
The Bone Ring

To Read Literature

Fiction Poetry Drama

THIRD EDITION

Donald Hall

Harcourt Brace Jovanovich College Publishers

Fort Worth   Chicago   San Francisco   Philadelphia
Montreal   Toronto   London   Sydney   Tokyo

Publisher	Ted Buchholz
Acquisitions Editor	Michael Rosenberg
Development Editor	Stacy Schoolfield
Design/Project Editor	Publications Development Company
Production Manager	Kathleen Ferguson
Cover Art/Design Supervisor	Serena B. Manning
Cover Design	Pat Sloan
Composition	Publications Development Company

Cover Image: Edward Hopper. *Railroad Sunset.* 1929. Oil on canvas. $28\frac{1}{4} \times 47\frac{3}{4}''$. Collection of Whitney Museum of American Art. Josephine N. Hopper Bequest 70.1170.

Address Editorial Correspondence to: 301 Commerce Street, Suite 3700, Fort Worth, TX 76102

Address Orders to: 6277 Sea Harbor Drive, Orlando, FL 32887
      1-800-782-4479, or 1-800-433-0001. (in Florida)

Acknowledgments start on page 1305.

Printed in the United States of America

Library of Congress Cataloging in Publication Data

Hall, Donald, 1928–
    To read literature, fiction, poetry, drama / [compiled by] Donald Hall.—3rd ed.
        p.   cm.
    Rev. ed. of: To read literature, fiction, poetry, drama. c1987.
    Includes index.
    ISBN 0-03-055542-6
    1. Literature—Collections. I. Hall, Donald, 1928–   . II. To read literature, fiction, poetry, drama.
PN6014.H24   1991
808—dc20   91-5063
                                                  CIP

2 3 4 5   069   9 8 7 6 5 4 3 2 1

for Liam Rector

To the Student . . .

To Read Literature

This book introduces the three principal types or genres of literature: fiction, poetry, and drama. When we learn to read literature, we acquire a pleasure and a resource we never lose. Although literary study is impractical in one sense—few people make their living reading books—in another sense it is almost as practical as breathing. Literature records and embodies centuries of human experience, preserving for us the minds of people who lived before us, who were like us and unlike us, against whom we can measure our common humanity and our historical difference. And, when we read the stories, poems and plays of our contemporaries, they illuminate the world we inhabit together.

When we read great literature, something changes in us that stays changed. Literature remembered becomes material to think with. No one who has read *Othello* with true attention is quite the same again. Reading is an experience that equips us to observe, measure, and judge the people and the properties of our universe.

In the fable of the ant and the grasshopper, the wise ant builds his storehouse against winter and prospers; the foolish grasshopper saves nothing and perishes. Anyone who dismisses the study of literature on the ground that it will not be useful—to a chemist or an engineer, to a foreman or an X-ray technician—imitates the grasshopper. When we shut from our lives everything except food and shelter, part of us starves to death. Food for this hunger is music, painting, film, plays, poems, stories, and novels. Much writing in newspapers, magazines, and popular novels is not literature, if we reserve that word for work of high quality. This reading gives us as little nourishment as most television and most fast food. For the long winters and energetic summers of our lives, we require the sustenance of literature.

Reading literature old and new—taking into ourselves the work of nineteenth-century Russian storytellers, sixteenth-century English dramatists, and contemporary American poets—we acquire a storehouse of knowledge and we entertain ourselves as well. But, to take pleasure and understanding from literature, we have to learn how to read it. No one expects to walk up to a computer and be able to program it without first learning something about computers. For some reason—perhaps because we are familiar with words from childhood and take them for granted—we tend to think that a quick glance at the written word should reward us, and that, if we do not take instant satisfaction, the work is beyond us, or not worth it, or irrelevant. Yet, all our lives, in other skills, we have needed instruction and practice—to be able to ride a bicycle, drive a car, play a guitar, shoot baskets, typewrite, dance.

The knowledge we derive from literature can seem confusing. Equally great works may contradict each other in the generalizations we derive from them. One work may recommend solitude, another society. One may advise us to seize the moment, another to live a life of contemplation. Or, two good readers may disagree about the implication of a work and each argue convincingly, with detailed references to the writing, in support of contrary interpretations. A complex work of literature cannot be reduced to a single, correct meaning. In an elementary arithmetic text, the answers may be printed in the back of the book. No answers are printed in the back of this book or any collection of literature.

Such ambiguity disturbs some students. After an hour's class discussion of a short story, with varying interpretations offered, they want to know "But what *does* it mean?" We must admit that literature is inexact, and its truth is not easily verifiable. Probably the story means several things at once, not *one thing;* and different good readers will always differ, at least a little, in their interpretations and emphasis. This is not to say, however, that the story means anything that anybody finds in it. Although differing and defensible opinions are common, error is common also.

When we speak of truth in the modern world, we usually mean something scientific or tautological. Arithmetic contains the truth of tautology; two and two make four because our definitions of *two* and *four* say so. In laboratories, we encounter the truth of statistics and the truth of observation. If we smoke cigarettes heavily, it is true that we have one chance in four of developing lung cancer. When we heat copper wire over a Bunsen burner, the flame turns blue.

But there is an older sense of truth, in which statements apparently opposite can both be valid. In this older tradition, truth is dependent on context and circumstance, on the agreement of sensible men and women—like the "Guilty" or "Not guilty" verdict of a jury. Because this literary (or philosophical, or legal, or historical) truth is inexact, changeable, and subject to argument, literature can seem nebulous to minds that require certainty.

Let me argue this: If literature is nebulous or inexact; if it is impossible to determine, with scientific precision, the value or the meaning of a work of art, *this inexactness is the price literature pays for representing humanity*. Human beings themselves, in their feelings and thoughts, in the wanderings of their short lives, are ambiguous, ambivalent, shifting mixtures of permanence and change, direction and disorder. Because literature is true to the complexities of human feeling, different people will read the same work with different responses. Literary art will sometimes affirm that opposite things are both true *because they are.*

The Words Themselves

I have talked as if literature were the feelings and thoughts we derive from reading. Whatever literature accomplishes in us, it accomplishes by words. As paint and canvas form the medium of painting, as sequences and combinations of sound different in pitch, duration, and quality form the medium of music, so the best words in the best order make literature.

A Japanese named Basho wrote this haiku about three hundred years ago:

The morning glory—
another thing
that will never be my friend.

Basho reminds us that the natural world is separate from us, that we may not shoulder our way into it, like invading troops of the imagination, and assume that we are intimate with everything. The American poet Robert Bly translated these lines. Here are three other versions:

A. The morning glory
is a separate being
and I can never know it intimately.

B. The morning glory
is yet another object
with which I will never become closely acquainted.

C. The morning glory—
something else
that won't call me companion.

To understand and appreciate how these four versions differ from one another is to become sensitive to the words that make literature. In a general way, they all mean the same thing. After the identical first lines, the translations differ in diction, which is the kinds of words chosen, and in rhythm, which is the pace and tempo of the words. Versions A and B are dry, stiff, and unnatural. *Separate being* sounds pretentious compared to *another thing. Yet another object* is finicky with its *yet another,* and *object* is more scientific-sounding than the casual *thing. With which I will never become closely acquainted* is formal and distant, rhythmically slow. *And I can never know it intimately* lacks interest or surprise in its words. The simplicity of *that will never be my friend,* coming to rest on the surprise of the last word, makes Bly's translation blossom in its final word. In version C, on the other hand, we have a translation nearly as pleasing as the original one. *Something else* has its own casual simplicity, and the little action of *call me companion*—where the morning glory is imagined capable of speech—has some of the surprise that the original translation found in *friend.*

The difference is the words and their order.

Translation and Poetry

When we read literature from past eras and other nations, often we read translation. We could know nothing of Greek tragedy, without translations of the plays, unless we all devoted ourselves to the study of Greek. In order to know the great fiction of Leo Tolstoy or Anton Chekhov, most of us must read translation. But the genres of literature—and, within genres, individual works—translate with different degrees of success. Poetry suffers most in translation. (Robert Frost even defined poetry as "what gets lost in translation.") In reading poetry, we understand most clearly that there are no synonyms, that between any pair of words—meaning approximately the same—there are always real differences. Poems that rely mostly on the image—like Basho's haiku, or like the poem by Pablo Neruda on pages 437–439—translate best; poems of wit and formal intricacy—like those of the Russian, Alexander Pushkin—give little satisfaction in translation.

To Read Literature, for American students, mostly collects works originally written in English—but this book will not deny students their Sophocles nor their Chekhov. When it comes to poetry, I have mostly chosen great works written in English, rather than assembling translations of Tu Fu and Rumi, Baudelaire and Sappho, Lorca and Catullus, Hugo and Dante. The student, learning to read and to love poetry, learns best by studying the real and only words of the poets.

What's Good, What's Bad

The claims I make for literature are large: that it alters and enlarges our minds, our past and present connections with each other, our understanding of our own feelings. These claims apply to excellent literature only. This introduction to literature suggests that some literature is better than other literature, and that some writing is not literature at all. Even if judgments are always subject to reversal, even if there is no way we can be certain of being correct, evaluation lives at the center of literary study.

When I was nineteen, I liked to read everything: science fiction, Russian novels, mystery stories, great poems, adventure magazines. Then, for six months after an accident, sentenced to a hospital bed and a body cast, I compiled a list of all the serious books I had been thinking about reading. Of course, there was a background to this choice: I had been taught by a good teacher who had directed and encouraged and stimulated my reading. I read through Shakespeare, the Bible in the King James version, and novels by Henry James, Ernest Hemingway, and William Faulkner. Toward the end of six months, taking physical therapy, I hurried to finish the books I had assigned myself; I looked forward to taking a vacation among private detectives and adventurers of the twenty-fourth century. I thought I would take a holiday of light reading.

When I tried to read the light things, I experienced one of those "turning points in life" we are asked to describe in freshman composition. I remember the dismay, the abject melancholy that crept over me as I realized—restless, turning from book to book in search of entertainment—that these books bored me; that I was ruined for life, that I would never again lose myself to stick-figure characters and artificial suspense. Literature ruined me for light reading.

To you who begin this book, I give fair warning. If you read these stories and poems and plays with attention, you may lose any taste you have for television sit-coms, for Gothic novels, for Rod McKuen. Something happens.

I don't mean to say that I was able to give reasons why Fyodor Dostoyevsky's novel about a murder was better than Agatha Christie's or why Aldous Huxley's view of the future, though less exciting, was more satisfying than *Astounding Science Fiction*'s. But I began a lifetime of trying to figure out why. What *is* it that makes Shakespeare so valuable to us? The struggle to name reasons for value—to evaluate works of art—is lifelong, and, although we may never arrive at satisfactory explanations, the struggle makes the mind more sensitive, more receptive to the next work of literature it encounters. And, as the mind becomes more sensitive and receptive to literature, it may become more sensitive and receptive to all sorts of things.

. . . and to the Instructor

In making selections and in writing the text for this collection, I have tried to serve one purpose: to help students read literature with pleasure, intelligence, gusto, and discrimination.

This book begins the study of fiction and poetry by examining whole examples, emphasizing that the goal of reading is not the analysis of parts, but the understanding of wholes. For fuller definition of literature's components, later chapters concentrate on parts: on characterization in fiction, for example, and on images in poetry.

Selections are frequently modern or contemporary; students best begin literary study without the distraction of an unfamiliar vocabulary. However, it would be silly to let this principle cheat us of Shakespeare, and *Othello* is included. The drama section begins with translation of Sophocles' *Oedipus Rex* and extends in time through a contemporary play by August Wilson.

I intend the text to be readable and entertaining while it remains serious. Because everyone is curious about the lives of authors we read (whether we ought to be or not), there are biographical notes on all the writers. My emphasis is nevertheless neither biographical nor historical but aesthetic: I mean to examine the way literature works. Discussing characterization, I wish to find the writer's practical means towards characterization—in choice of words, in dialogue, and in description.

Footnotes and glosses translate foreign language material, provide essential identifications, and define words not available in many dictionaries, or words used in archaic sense. In response to suggestions from instructors, we have provided dates where possible for each story, poem and play. These dates are approximate and their provenance varies; when it is known, we give the year of composition; on other occasions, we note the year of copyright, which normally happens a year or two later. For historical thinking, an approximate date is better than none, and 1990 is sufficiently distinct from 1970, not to mention 1870 or 1570. The Appendix, "To Write About Writing," should provide guidance for students preparing papers on literature.

I've taken advice from several hundred American teachers of literature. When this book was only a notion, several years back, many people answered a questionnaire about what it should include. I am grateful; I have followed many suggestions.

Other professors read portions of the manuscript and commented in detail. I should like expecially to thank Sylvan Barnet, R. S. Beal, Gary Blake, John Boni, Larry Champion, Barbara J. Cicardo, Paul Davis, R. H. Deutsch, Richard Dietrich, Donald Drury, John L. Fell, Art Goldsher, Randolph Goodman, William J. Gracie, Jr., Barnett Guttenberg, Nancy J. Hazelton, Michael Hogan, Woodrow L. Holbein, John Huxhold, Henry E. Jacobs, Robert C. Johnson, John J. Keenan, Mike Keene, X. J. Kennedy, Hannah Laipson, Bette B. Lansdown, James MacKillop, James Moody, William W. Nolte II, Anne Pidgeon, Doris Powers, Jules Ryckebusch, H. Miller Solomon, Joe Sperry, William Stull, Cathy Turner, Martha Weathers, and James D. Welch.

Also, I want to thank my own helpers in New Hampshire, in Ann Arbor, and in Santa Monica: Lois Fierro, Sharon Giannotta, Dorothy Foster, Pat Wykes, and Frank Barham—not to mention Jane Kenyon.

Others who read portions of the manuscript and made helpful comments were: Anne C. Armstrong, Walters State Community College; Ellen Bourland, George C. Wallace Community College; William O. Boggs, Robert Morris College; Flynn Brantley, Emory University; Peggy Cole, Arapahoe Community College; Joseph A. Cosenza, St. John's University; James M. Creel, Alvin Community College; Ann B. Dobie, University of Southwestern Louisiana; Linda Dyer Doran, Volunteer State Community College; Terry Frazier, University of North Carolina–Charlotte; Chris Henson, California State University–Fresno; Charles C. Hobbs, Carson-Newman College; Nancy Kensicki, Gallaudet College; Lynn Kloesel, Butler University, Mary Kramer, University of Lowell; Leonard Leff, Oklahoma State University; Zorka Milich, Nassau Community College; Otto Lewis Pfeiff, Arapahoe Community College; Benjamin Saltman, California State University–Northridge; Darlene Harbour Unrue, University of Nevada–Las Vegas; Judith S. VanAlstyne, Broward Community College; John A. Wood, McNeese State University.

I owe a special debt to Dick Maxwell, of Foothill College in Los Altos, California.

For the Third Edition, thanks to those who read portions of the manuscript and made helpful comments: Anne Agee, Anne Arundel Community College; Kitty Chen Dean, Nassau Community College; Bill Hamlin, University of Missouri; Lee Hartman, Howard Community College; Linda Merians, La Salle University; William Nicoloet, Southeastern Massachusetts University; Jill Sessoms, University of South Carolina; Joy Wingersky, Glendale Community College; Sherry Zivley, University of Houston.

At Harcourt Brace Jovanovich, I would like to thank the following people: Michael Rosenberg, Stacy Schoolfield, Molly Shepard and Kathy Ferguson. I would also like to thank Nancy Marcus Land at Publications Development Company.

D. H.

Contents

TO READ A POEM   407

TO READ A PLAY   733

TO READ A

Story

To read a story, we need bifocal vision. Close up, we follow narrative, the story's story, but from a distance, the angle of vision becomes wider even though it remains sharply focused. We follow events performed by characters in settings, put before us by the author's language in fulfillment of the author's vision.

One Modern Short Story

People are story-telling animals. The Bible is full of stories—the history of a people, moral tales, magical tales, parables. An epic like Homer's *Odyssey* is one big story made up of hundreds of little ones, passed from generation to generation by storytellers before there was a written language. These are tales from the youth of our civilization. In our own early youth, we listen to stories and we learn to tell them. On television and movie screens, we watch stories develop before our eyes, as we do in the panels of a comic strip. As we grow up, we read narratives of contemporary events in newspapers. In novels, we read long imaginary narratives. Stories accompany us through our lives.

A story need not be literature, but most literature begins as story or includes story. It thus makes sense to start studying literature by reading one good modern short story, "A Rose for Emily," as a gateway to others. To begin investigating fiction, we will ask twenty questions about the story—and then try to answer them. In the answers, we will touch on critical terms treated at greater length in later chapters. Chapter 4 concentrates on plot; Chapter 5, on character; and Chapter 6, on setting. In this chapter, we will speak briefly about each of these elements of fiction as they appear in "A Rose for Emily."

William Faulkner

William Faulkner (1897–1962) remains one of America's great novelists and storywriters. A chronicler of the South, he was born and raised in Oxford, Mississippi, where he lived most of his life and where he died. Although Faulkner traveled to New York to see his publishers, to Hollywood to write screenplays, and, late in his life, to the University of Virginia to teach, Oxford was the main locus of his life and his fiction. As a young man he attended Ole Miss (The University of Mississippi in Oxford), where he was considered both uppity and shiftless, a combination that earned him the nickname Count No 'Count. He wrote poems without great success and then turned to storytelling, for which he had great talent. His novels began with *Soldier's Pay* (1926) and *Mosquitoes* (1927), which won him attention and little else. With *Sartoris* (1929), he found his great theme, the history of a mythical Southern county called Yoknapatawpha. Faulkner chronicled Yoknapatawpha's inhabitants from its original Native Americans to its rich, plantation-owning families—Compson and Sartoris—then on through rebellion and Reconstruction to a modern era dominated by the shrewd and ignoble Snopes clan. In 1929, he also published *The Sound and the Fury,* which many critics find his best work. The year 1930 brought *As I Lay Dying; Light in August* followed in 1932, *Absalom, Absalom* in 1936. His best later work is comic: *The Hamlet* (1940), *The Town* (1957), and *The Mansion* (1960) further chronicle the unscrupulous Snopeses.

In 1931, *Sanctuary* sold well, but for the most part Faulkner's novels earned him little, and for his living he had to look elsewhere. Even after being awarded the Nobel Prize in 1950, Faulkner needed money from universities and from Hollywood. Earlier, he had supported himself by writing well-crafted short stories for popular magazines. "A Rose for Emily" appeared in *Forum* in 1930.

A Rose for Emily   (1930)

1

When Miss Emily Grierson died, our whole town went to her funeral: the men through a sort of respectful affection for a fallen monument, the women mostly out of curiosity to see the inside of her house, which no one save an old manservant—a combined gardener and cook—had seen in at least ten years.

It was a big, squarish frame house that had once been white, decorated with cupolas and spires and scrolled balconies in the heavily lightsome style of the seventies, set on what had once been our most select street. But garages and cotton gins had encroached and obliterated even the august names of that neighborhood; only Miss Emily's house was left, lifting its stubborn and co-quettish decay above the cotton wagons and the gasoline pumps—an eyesore among eyesores. And now Miss Emily had gone to join the representatives of those august names where they lay in the cedar-bemused cemetery among the ranked and anonymous graves of Union and Confederate soldiers who fell at the battle of Jefferson.

Alive, Miss Emily had been a tradition, a duty and a care; a sort of hereditary obligation upon the town, dating from that day in 1894 when Colonel Sartoris, the mayor—he who fathered the edict that no Negro woman should appear on the streets without an apron—remitted her taxes, the dispensation dating from the death of her father on into perpetuity. Not that Miss Emily would have accepted charity. Colonel Sartoris invented an involved tale to the effect that Miss Emily's father had loaned money to the town, which the town, as a matter of business, preferred this way of repaying. Only a man of Colonel Sartoris' generation and thought could have invented it, and only a woman could have believed it.

When the next generation, with its more modern ideas, became mayors and aldermen, this arrangement created some little dissatisfaction. On the first of the year they mailed her a tax notice. February came, and there was no reply. They wrote her a formal letter, asking her to call at the sheriff's office at her convenience. A week later the mayor wrote her himself, offering to call or send his car for her and received in reply a note on paper of an archaic shape, in a thin flowering calligraphy in faded ink, to the effect that she no longer went out at all. The tax notice was also enclosed, without comment.

5   They called a special meeting of the Board of Aldermen. A deputation waited upon her, knocked at the door through which no visitor had passed since she ceased giving china painting lessons eight or ten years earlier. They were admitted by the old Negro into a dim hall from which a stairway mounted into still more shadow. It smelled of dust and disuse—a close, dank smell. The Negro led them into the parlor. It was furnished in heavy, leather-covered furniture. When the Negro opened the blinds of one window, they could see that the leather was cracked; and when they sat down, a faint dust rose sluggishly about their thighs, spinning with slow motes in the single sun-ray. On a tarnished gilt easel before the fireplace stood a crayon portrait of Miss Emily's father.

They rose when she entered—a small, fat woman in black, with a thin gold chain descending to her waist and vanishing into her belt, leaning on an ebony cane with a tarnished gold head. Her skeleton was small and spare; perhaps that was why what would have been merely plumpness in another was obesity in her. She looked bloated, like a body long submerged in motionless water, and of that pallid hue. Her eyes, lost in the fatty ridges of her face, looked like two small pieces of coal pressed into a lump of dough as they moved from one face to another while the visitors stated their errand.

She did not ask them to sit. She just stood in the door and listened quietly until the spokesman came to a stumbling halt. Then they could hear the invisible watch ticking at the end of the gold chain.

Her voice was dry and cold. "I have no taxes in Jefferson. Colonel Sartoris explained it to me. Perhaps one of you can gain access to the city records and satisfy yourselves."

"But we have. We are the city authorities, Miss Emily. Didn't you get a notice from the sheriff, signed by him?"

10   "I received a paper, yes," Miss Emily said. "Perhaps he considers himself the sheriff . . . I have no taxes in Jefferson."

"But there is nothing on the books to show that, you see. We must go by the—"

"See Colonel Sartoris. I have no taxes in Jefferson."

"But, Miss Emily—"

"See Colonel Sartoris." (Colonel Sartoris had been dead almost ten years.) "I have no taxes in Jefferson. Tobe!" The Negro appeared. "Show these gentlemen out."

2

15 So she vanquished them, horse and foot, just as she had vanquished their fathers thirty years before about the smell. That was two years after her father's death and a short time after her sweetheart—the one we believed would marry her—had deserted her. After her father's death she went out very little; after her sweetheart went away, people hardly saw her at all. A few of the ladies had the temerity to call, but were not received, and the only sign of life about the place was the Negro man—a young man then—going in and out with a market basket.

"Just as if a man—any man—could keep a kitchen properly," the ladies said; so they were not surprised when the smell developed. It was another link between the gross, teeming world and the high and mighty Griersons.

A neighbor, a woman, complained to the mayor, Judge Stevens, eighty years old.

"But what will you have me do about it, madam?" he said.

"Why, send her word to stop it," the woman said. "Isn't there a law?"

20 "I'm sure that won't be necessary," Judge Stevens said. "It's probably just a snake or a rat that nigger of hers killed in the yard. I'll speak to him about it."

The next day he received two more complaints, one from a man who came in diffident deprecation. "We really must do something about it, Judge. I'd be the last one in the world to bother Miss Emily, but we've got to do something." That night the Board of Aldermen met—three graybeards and one younger man, a member of the rising generation.

"It's simple enough," he said. "Send her word to have her place cleaned up. Give her a certain time to do it in, and if she don't . . ."

"Dammit, sir," Judge Stevens said, "will you accuse a lady to her face of smelling bad?"

So the next night, after midnight, four men crossed Miss Emily's lawn and slunk about the house like burglars, sniffing along the base of the brickwork and at the cellar openings while one of them performed a regular sowing motion with his hand out of a sack slung from his shoulder. They broke open the cellar door and sprinkled lime there, and in all the outbuildings. As they recrossed the lawn, a window that had been dark was lighted and Miss Emily sat in it, the light behind her, and her upright torso motionless as that of an idol. They crept quietly across the lawn and into the shadow of the locusts that lined the street. After a week or two the smell went away.

25 That was when people had begun to feel really sorry for her. People in our town, remembering how old lady Wyatt, her great-aunt, had gone completely

crazy at last, believed that the Griersons held themselves a little too high for what they really were. None of the young men were quite good enough for Miss Emily and such. We had long thought of them as a tableau, Miss Emily a slender figure in white in the background, her father a spraddled silhouette in the foreground, his back to her and clutching a horsewhip, the two of them framed by the back-flung front door. So when she got to be thirty and was still single, we were not pleased exactly, but vindicated; even with insanity in the family she wouldn't have turned down all of her chances if they had really materialized.

When her father died, it got about that the house was all that was left to her; and in a way, people were glad. At last they could pity Miss Emily. Being left alone, and a pauper, she had become humanized. Now she too would know the old thrill and the old despair of a penny more or less.

The day after his death all the ladies prepared to call at the house and offer condolence and aid, as is our custom. Miss Emily met them at the door, dressed as usual and with no trace of grief on her face. She told them that her father was not dead. She did that for three days, with the ministers calling on her, and the doctors, trying to persuade her to let them dispose of the body. Just as they were about to resort to law and force, she broke down, and they buried her father quickly.

We did not say she was crazy then. We believed she had to do that. We remembered all the young men her father had driven away, and we knew that with nothing left, she would have to cling to that which had robbed her, as people will.

3

She was sick for a long time. When we saw her again, her hair was cut short, making her look like a girl, with a vague resemblance to those angels in colored church windows—sort of tragic and serene.

30   The town had just let the contracts for paving the sidewalks, and in the summer after her father's death they began the work. The construction company came with niggers and mules and machinery, and a foreman named Homer Barron, a Yankee—a big, dark, ready man, with a big voice and eyes lighter than his face. The little boys would follow in groups to hear him cuss the niggers, and the niggers singing in time to the rise and fall of picks. Pretty soon he knew everybody in town. Whenever you heard a lot of laughing anywhere about the square, Homer Barron would be in the center of the group. Presently we began to see him and Miss Emily on Sunday afternoons driving in the yellow-wheeled buggy and the matched team of bays from the livery stable.

At first we were glad that Miss Emily would have an interest, because the ladies all said, "Of course a Grierson would not think seriously of a Northerner, a day laborer." But there were still others, older people, who said that even grief could not cause a real lady to forget *noblesse oblige*[1]—without calling it *noblesse oblige*. They just said, "Poor Emily. Her kinsfolk should

[1] Duty of the well-born

come to her." She had some kin in Alabama; but years ago her father had fallen out with them over the estate of old lady Wyatt, the crazy woman, and there was no communication between the two families. They had not even been represented at the funeral.

And as soon as the old people said, "Poor Emily," the whispering began. "Do you suppose it's really so?" they said to one another. "Of course it is. What else could . . ." This behind their hands; rustling of craned silk and satin behind jalousies closed upon the sun of Sunday afternoon as the thin, swift clop-clop-clop of the matched team passed: "Poor Emily."

She carried her head high enough—even when we believed that she was fallen. It was as if she demanded more than ever the recognition of her dignity as the last Grierson; as if it had wanted that touch of earthiness to reaffirm her imperviousness. Like when she bought the rat poison, the arsenic. That was over a year after they had begun to say "Poor Emily," and while the two female cousins were visiting her.

"I want some poison," she said to the druggist. She was over thirty then, still a slight woman, though thinner than usual, with cold, haughty black eyes in a face the flesh of which was strained across the temples and about the eye-sockets as you imagine a lighthouse-keeper's face ought to look. "I want some poison," she said.

35   "Yes, Miss Emily. What kind? For rats and such? I'd recom—"

"I want the best you have. I don't care what kind."

The druggist named several. "They'll kill anything up to an elephant. But what you want is—"

"Arsenic," Miss Emily said. "Is that a good one?"

"Is . . . arsenic? Yes, ma'am. But what you want—"

40   "I want arsenic."

The druggist looked down at her. She looked back at him, erect, her face like a strained flag. "Why, of course," the druggist said. "If that's what you want. But the law requires you to tell what you are going to use it for."

Miss Emily just stared at him, her head tilted back in order to look him eye for eye, until he looked away and went and got the arsenic and wrapped it up. The Negro delivery boy brought her the package; the druggist didn't come back. When she opened the package at home there was written on the box, under the skull and bones: "For rats."

4

So the next day we all said, "She will kill herself"; and we said it would be the best thing. When she had first begun to be seen with Homer Barron, we had said, "She will marry him." Then we said, "She will persuade him yet," because Homer himself had remarked—he liked men, and it was known that he drank with the younger men in the Elks' Club—that he was not a marrying man. Later we said, "Poor Emily" behind the jalousies as they passed on Sunday afternoon in the glittering buggy, Miss Emily with her head high and Homer Barron with his hat cocked and a cigar in his teeth, reins and whip in a yellow glove.

Then some of the ladies began to say that it was a disgrace to the town, and a bad example to the young people. The men did not want to interfere, but at last the ladies forced the Baptist minister—Miss Emily's people were Episcopal—to call upon her. He would never divulge what happened during that interview, but he refused to go back again. The next Sunday they again drove about the streets, and the following day the minister's wife wrote to Miss Emily's relations in Alabama.

45 So she had blood-kin under her roof again and we sat back to watch developments. At first nothing happened. Then we were sure they were to be married. We learned that Miss Emily had been to the jeweler's and ordered a man's toilet set in silver, with the letters H.B. on each piece. Two days later we learned that she had bought a complete outfit of men's clothing, including a nightshirt, and we said, "They are married." We were really glad. We were glad because the two female cousins were even more Grierson than Miss Emily had ever been.

So we were not surprised when Homer Barron—the streets had been finished some time since—was gone. We were a little disappointed that there was not a public blowing-off, but we believed that he had gone on to prepare for Miss Emily's coming, or to give her a chance to get rid of the cousins. (By that time it was a cabal, and we were all Miss Emily's allies to help circumvent the cousins.) Sure enough, after another week they departed. And, as we had expected all along, within three days Homer Barron was back in town. A neighbor saw the Negro man admit him at the kitchen door at dusk one evening.

And that was the last we saw of Homer Barron. And of Miss Emily for some time. The Negro man went in and out with the market basket, but the front door remained closed. Now and then we would see her at a window for a moment, as the men did that night when they sprinkled the lime, but for almost six months she did not appear on the streets. Then we knew that this was to be expected too; as if that quality of her father which had thwarted her woman's life so many times had been too virulent and too furious to die.

When we next saw Miss Emily, she had grown fat and her hair was turning gray. During the next few years it grew grayer and grayer until it attained an even pepper-and-salt iron-gray, when it ceased turning. Up to the day of her death at seventy-four it was still that vigorous iron-gray, like the hair of an active man.

From that time on her front door remained closed, save for a period of six or seven years, when she was about forty, during which she gave lessons in china-painting. She fitted up a studio in one of the downstairs rooms, where the daughters and grand-daughters of Colonel Sartoris' contemporaries were sent to her with the same regularity and in the same spirit that they were sent to church on Sundays, with a twenty-five cent piece for the collection plate. Meanwhile her taxes had been remitted.

50 The newer generation became the backbone and the spirit of the town, and the painting pupils grew up and fell away and did not send their children to her with boxes of color and tedious brushes and pictures cut from the ladies' magazines. The front door closed upon the last one and remained

closed for good. When the town got free postal delivery, Miss Emily alone refused to let them fasten the metal numbers above her door and attach a mailbox to it. She would not listen to them.

Daily, monthly, yearly we watched the Negro grow grayer and more stooped, going in and out with the market basket. Each December we sent her a tax notice, which would be returned by the post office a week later, unclaimed. Now and then we would see her in one of the downstairs windows— she had evidently shut up the top floor of the house—like the carven torso of an idol in a niche, looking or not looking at us, we could never tell which. Thus she passed from generation to generation—dear, inescapable, impervious, tranquil, and perverse.

And so she died. Fell ill in the house filled with dust and shadows, with only a doddering Negro man to wait on her. We did not even know she was sick; we had long since given up trying to get any information from the Negro. He talked to no one, probably not even to her, for his voice had grown harsh and rusty, as if from disuse.

She died in one of the downstairs rooms, in a heavy walnut bed with a curtain, her gray head propped on a pillow yellow and moldly with age and lack of sunlight.

5

The Negro met the first of the ladies at the front door and let them in, with their hushed, sibilant voices and their quick, curious glances, and then he disappeared. He walked right through the house and out the back and was not seen again.

55   The two female cousins came at once. They held the funeral on the second day, with the town coming to look at Miss Emily beneath a mass of bought flowers, with the crayon face of her father musing profoundly above the bier and the ladies sibilant and macabre; and the very old men—some in their brushed Confederate uniforms—on the porch and the lawn, talking of Miss Emily as if she had been a contemporary of theirs, believing that they had danced with her and courted her perhaps, confusing time with its mathematical progression, as the old do, to whom all the past is not a diminishing road but, instead, a huge meadow which no winter ever quite touches, divided from them now by the narrow bottleneck of the most recent decade of years.

Already we knew that there was one room in that region above stairs which no one had seen in forty years, and which would have to be forced. They waited until Miss Emily was decently in the ground before they opened it.

The violence of breaking down the door seemed to fill this room with pervading dust. A thin, acrid pall as of the tomb seemed to lie everywhere upon this room decked and furnished as for a bridal: upon the valance curtains of faded rose color, upon the rose-shaded lights, upon the dressing table, upon the delicate array of crystal and the man's toilet things backed with tarnished silver, silver so tarnished that the monogram was obscured. Among them lay a collar and tie, as if they had just been removed, which, lifted, left upon the surface a pale crescent in the dust. Upon a chair hung the suit, carefully folded; beneath it the two mute shoes and the discarded socks.

The man himself lay in the bed.

For a long while we just stood there, looking down at the profound and fleshless grin. The body had apparently once lain in the attitude of an embrace, but now the long sleep that outlasts love, that conquers even the grimace of love, had cuckolded him. What was left of him, rotted beneath what was left of the nightshirt, had become inextricable from the bed in which he lay; and upon him and upon the pillow beside him lay that even coating of the patient and biding dust.

60   Then we noticed that in the second pillow was the indentation of a head. One of us lifted something from it, and leaning forward, that faint and invisible dust dry and acrid in the nostrils, we saw a long strand of iron-gray hair.

Questions for Rereading

1. What happens? Look back at the story and construct the exact sequence of events. When did Homer Barron die? How did he die? Point out the sentences and the paragraphs that let you know what happened.

2. When you first read the story, did you guess how it would end? Were there clues you did not understand? Would you have understood more quickly if the anecdote about buying poison had preceded the anecdote of the odor?

   When you first read about the odor and about buying poison, did it seem that the incidents were told for a purpose? What purpose?

3. People who talk about fiction claim that a story must include **conflict**—some clash between **protagonist** (hero, or character in the forefront) and **antagonist** (some character or force that acts against the protagonist, denying his or her desires). If Miss Emily is the protagonist, who is her antagonist? What is the conflict in the story?

   If you are tempted to think of Homer Barron as antagonist, does it matter that the story continues thirty years after his death? (Remember that conflict does not necessarily occur between individuals.)

4. Notice references to the Civil War in this story. Does that war play a role in this story? Where is it first mentioned? When is it last mentioned? Why is it in the story?

5. In paragraphs 1 and 2, the author speaks of buildings and structures, beginning with an image of Miss Emily herself as a fallen monument. Look through the story for mention of buildings and structures, and comment on Miss Emily as a statue. If she is indeed a fallen monument, what is she a monument *to?*

6. In the plot of the story, an aristocratic Southerner murders a Yankee carpetbagger. Is the story about the triumph of a defeated South over a supposedly triumphant North? What is this story really about?

7. Who tells us this story? What sort of person? What kind of knowledge does the storyteller have? Can the storyteller see into people's minds? Does the storyteller represent any one character in the story? A place? A theme?

8. At the outset, Miss Emily receives a deputation from the Board of Aldermen. We already know her attitude toward taxes. The anecdote does not therefore advance

the plot; it offers no clue to the eventual story of Miss Emily and her lover. Does it nonetheless have a function in the story?

9. How many scenes would you need to turn this story into a play or a film? List the scenes and title them. Is their order essential to Faulkner's telling? Why does he choose this order?

10. In paragraph 15, what does *horse and foot* mean? To what or to whom does this phrase compare Miss Emily?

11. In retrospect, what hint about the plot occurs in paragraph 27?

12. Why does Faulkner use *sidewalks* in paragraph 30?

13. What do you think happened when the Baptist minister called on Miss Emily (paragraph 44)? Why do you think you understand what happened? Is it important that you understand?

14. In paragraph 46, why are we not surprised when Homer disappears? How does the storyteller ensure that we are not surprised?

15. It has been said of this story that "Miss Emily has a shadow, and by this shadow we tell the time of her life." What is her shadow?

16. In paragraph 48, why do we need to know about Miss Emily's hair changing color?

17. In paragraph 51, had she really shut up the top floor of her house? Why *evidently?*

18. In paragraph 54, what purpose is served by telling us that the Negro "walked right through the house and out the back and was not seen again"?

19. The end of paragraph 55 is a lyrical and metaphorical account of the old people's sense of the past, a poetic kind of prose with which a self-indulgent author will sometimes pad out a story or tease us by delaying the resolution of our suspense. Does Faulkner perform this last trick upon us? Does he do anything else as well? Does this image present an alternative or a parallel to anything else in the story?

20. In paragraph 56, why did they wait until after the funeral to open the closed room? What word in the story informs you about the reasons for this delay? Is the delay consistent with the world of this story?

Plot

In "A Rose for Emily," plot—the events that make up the story, linked together in a chain of cause and effect—is of first importance. We feel called upon to examine the plot because the story surprises us. In the last three paragraphs, we learn that Miss Emily murdered Homer Barron and that she slept in bed next to his corpse long after his death. Actually, we receive this shocking information not from the last three paragraphs alone but from these paragraphs together with hints we picked up earlier—long before we suspected murder and necrophilia (an attraction to corpses). For example, we learn that Miss Emily's hair did not begin to turn gray until after Homer Barron's disappearance (paragraph 48) and that it took several years before it turned iron-gray. In the final phrase of the story, "we" discover, on the pillow beside the decayed corpse, "a long strand of iron-gray hair."

Someone legally inclined, reading the paragraph above, might object "But you cannot *say* that the hair is Miss Emily's; lots of people have iron-gray hair. And how do you know she murdered Barron? Yes, she bought arsenic, and he disappeared, and there was the smell, and here is the corpse—but your evidence is merely circumstantial!" *Yes,* we must answer, we do not know beyond all reasonable doubt, as a court of law would have it, that Miss Emily killed Homer Barron. But fiction works with probabilities, and the story creates a network of probabilities. We *know* that Barron died thirty years ago, before the tax anecdote that ends the first section; we know as readers, if not as jurors, that he died from the arsenic Miss Emily bought and administered.

Consider Faulkner's skill in telling this story. He constructs each of the first three sections around one anecdote that furthers the plot. Yet each section contains more than the single incident and advances more than the plot. The opening section foreshadows Miss Emily's death and includes references to the Civil War, a contrast of past and present, and summary narrative—but all these details lead to the action that closes the section. This first section gives us no special clues about the climax, but it sets the story's place and proposes the theme of historical change. And, in its main incident, it advances character. It is also in the first section that we come under the spell of the narrator's point of view.

This first section advances the plot insofar as it establishes character and setting. And it accomplishes one other goal. In a mystery story, an author often tries to outwit readers while remaining fair; the writer gives us clues veiled so that we do not know that they are clues. The first anecdote of Miss Emily reveals character in a way that amuses us, yet gives us no clues about murder and necrophilia. When, in the next two sections, we learn of two more incidents, bizarre and entertaining in themselves, we are led to suspect that each of them is as innocent as the first. But the next two anecdotes—about the smell and about the purchase of rat poison—are essential to our understanding of plot. Because the first incident included nothing sinister, it lightened the later anecdotes—which, had we understood them, would have suggested murder and a decaying corpse.

It is essential in literature that every part perform several functions at once, though the reader may not perceive these simultaneous functions on first reading. In a poem, a word at once contributes to rhythm, to image, to metaphor, to meaning, to overall coherence, to pleasure—making its contribution all at once. In "A Rose for Emily," Faulkner early (in incidents two and three) gives us information about Miss Emily's character, about how the other townspeople see her and react to her, about her changing society, about the setting of her life—and at the same time, like every wily storyteller, he gives us clues to a mystery.

Notice that the story of the smell comes earlier than the story of the rat poison, whereas, in the real sequence, it came afterward. If we first heard that Miss Emily bought rat poison and then heard that her house smelled of rotting flesh, we might smell a rat. By reversing the order, Faulkner gives us the same information, but makes it harder for us to connect the two facts. Most likely, we accept these details as random notes on an eccentric character. At the same time, the unchronological order seems natural enough. From the start, the narration has zipped back and forth in time, as if we were not so much hearing a sequential story as listening to someone's free recollections.

The fourth section of the story covers many years. It begins with a suggestion that Miss Emily might have chosen to commit suicide, presumably because she felt disgraced by her episode with Homer Barron. Yet we accept Homer's disappearance without connecting it to rat poison or bad smells, because the narrator has conditioned us to think of Barron as someone who might run away under the threat of marriage. It is also true (it is the foundation of the story) that we do not consider Miss Emily the murdering kind.

We do not know exactly why Miss Emily murders Homer, even when we have finished the story. We know that she prizes her independence, her dignity, and her status. We know that she does not want to lose anything. (Remember that she wanted to keep her father's body—in itself a foreshadowing of her keeping Homer Barron's.) We know that Homer is not the marrying kind. Worse, he is a vulgar Northerner. Miss Emily's pride drove her to him in the first place, along with the minister's and her cousins' remonstrances. Perhaps we can say that she killed him out of pride, for the sake of her dignity. But we do not know whether Homer finally agreed to marry her or not.

There is no answer to the questions raised in the last paragraph, and no argument about the questions can be won. It is useful to argue about probabilities, when we stick to information supplied to us by the author; by arguing, we concentrate on the story. But it is useless to argue Miss Emily's motives by reference to anything outside the story—like our sense of human nature or our memory of a weekend in a small Mississippi town—because Miss Emily does not exist outside the story.

No probability is conclusive; we are left with mystery, with puzzlement over human behavior. If this dissatisfies us, we should ask ourselves if it would have been a more honest story, or more true to life, if we had finished it knowing exactly why Miss Emily acted as she did. Are human motives for significant actions usually clear and distinct?

Character

In speaking about plot, we had to mention character, because character is revealed by actions. Surely the character of Miss Emily, which we gradually discover through her bizarre actions, is central to the story, and, at the beginning, it is almost Faulkner's whole focus. Notice the different devices with which the storyteller renders character. Take the first sentence: that the whole town went to her funeral tells us that she was important; that to the men she seemed a fallen monument makes her distant, grand, and ruined; and that she aroused the women's curiosity points up Miss Emily's eccentricity. At the beginning, we learn her character from the outside, through reactions to her death. In the second paragraph, Miss Emily's house is described as coquettish in a metaphor that compares a house to a flirtatious woman, perhaps a woman of the Old South. We hear of a grand past and present decay. We learn still more of Miss Emily's character, and of the theme of historical change, from details of architecture and through metaphor.

The third paragraph is a summary; it gives us a brief account of Miss Emily's past, her present sorry circumstances, and her intact if eccentric dignity. Subsequent paragraphs contrast Colonel Sartoris with the town's new governors, and paragraph 5 creates character by describing the interior of the house. That the easel is tarnished confirms one notion; that the sketch is of her father confirms another. In paragraph 6, Miss Emily's physical appearance repels: bloated obesity over a small skeleton. These images of death subliminally prepare us for our eventual discovery. In the next paragraphs, we finally observe Miss Emily for ourselves and watch her win a battle. From the general opinion of others, from summary, from description and setting, from action and speech, we gain a strong sense of her character.

Point of View

In reading a story, we must consider the point of view from which the story is told. Sometimes the author's point of view allows us knowledge of everything, everywhere, all the time, inside brains as well as through walls. Sometimes a story is told by "I," someone who may be a character in the story, or by a narrator who speaks of "he" or "she" and sees everything through one character's eyes. "A Rose for Emily" is told by a narrator who appears in the story only as a citizen of Jefferson. The narrator is not somebody named "I" but a representative "we": "We did not say she was crazy then. We believed she had to do that." This point of view is a collective consensus of townspeople. At the end of the story, the "we" becomes so obviously a substitute for "I" that its use is awkward: "For a long while we just stood there, looking down at the profound and fleshless grin. . . . Then we noticed that in the second pillow was the indentation of a head." At this point, a single individual must perform an act for the sake of the plot; Faulkner might have shifted his point of view from plural to singular and used *I,* but he did not; he used an awkward locution to reduce plural to singular and preserved the tone he had taken pains to create: "One of us lifted something from it. . . ." This is awkward because it requires us to believe that the narrator doesn't care to name the person who lifted the strand of hair. But this awkwardness preserves the anonymous and multiple *we* of the Jefferson citizenry.

Setting

All elements of fiction affect each other. Because the point of view identifiably belongs to the townspeople of Jefferson, point of view and setting affect each other. The setting of Jefferson, over years when memory of the Civil War declines, underscores the historical theme of the story. "A Rose for Emily" (and Faulkner's work in general) is saturated with the heroism, defeat, dignity, and degradation of the Civil War. Like many authors, Faulkner is obsessed with a single subject and takes his power from his obsession. Miss Emily Grierson is the last representative of a family ruined by the war. At the beginning of the story, in the second paragraph, we learn that her house stood in a decaying neighborhood. "And now

> Miss Emily had gone to join the representatives of those august names where they lay in the cedar-bemused cemetery among the ranked and anonymous graves of Union and Confederate soldiers who fell at the battle of Jefferson.

For Faulkner, such a setting provided a strong emotional background against which to narrate his tale. And such a setting led him directly into his theme.

Theme

Faulkner's setting is described in terms of conflict. Now consider the content of the story, its meaning or theme, by way of the particular conflicts suggested and portrayed in it. Reading a story, we are justified in asking "What is it *for?* Does this story leave us with anything beside a moment's entertainment?" (Entertainment is, of course, its own excuse for being. Some stories entertain us *and* instruct us at the same time.) Conflict in "A Rose for Emily" arises between the doomed survivor of the Old South and citizens of the new city that grows out of Reconstruction. Miss Emily's personal conflict with Homer Barron exemplifies the greater (or larger) conflict, because Barron is a Northerner, a carpetbagger come south for work and gain, employed to build Jefferson's first sidewalks, themselves signs of urbanization. Colonel Sartoris, who protected Miss Emily, represented the Old South, as did the later alderman Judge Stevens, when he was outraged at the suggestion that a "lady" be told that her house smelled bad. In the changing habits of the governors, we see a changing Jefferson; in Miss Emily, we see the decadent past attempting to withstand change. Finally, in the story's outrageous climax, Miss Emily's necrophilia is a metaphor of her refusal to change. The Emily-world is graceful, dignified, honorable—but quaint and decayed, and finally morbid. The Barron-world is vital, vulgar, and inevitable. In the story, one feels a conflict within the narrator, perhaps between a heart that loves the old ways and a head that knows them doomed. If the head speaks warning to the heart, it might want to say, "Although the past was attractive, it is sentimental and useless to love the departed past. It is worse than sentimental and useless. It is as if you paid love and devotion, not to a living spouse, but to a corpse."

We find the ultimate lesson of "A Rose for Emily" in Miss Emily's real denial of death, her holding onto the dead—first her father, then Homer Barron. Homer alive was part of the new and progressive society; Miss Emily's retention of his corpse wrests him from one world to another. By using necrophilia as his metaphor, Faulkner chastises the surviving South's wish to hold on to the dead past.

Symbolism

We have not yet mentioned one important character. Miss Emily could not have survived so long as she did without the help of her servant, who grows old along with her, almost as if he were her visible black shadow, aging in public while she stays out of sight. He represents the exploited underclass on whom the aristocratic, impoverished survivor depends. After Miss Emily's death, "The Negro met the first of the ladies at the front door and let them in . . . [and] walked right through the house and out the back and was not seen again." This disappearance is a convenience for the storyteller, who need not deal with another presence who might (or might not) be party to morbid knowledge. However, the disappearance is not improbable—and it is highly appropriate to Faulkner's theme, where Miss Emily and her necrophilia become a symbol of the Old South. A symbol is a sign, something that stands for more than itself. The Negro stands for Miss Emily's connection to the outside world; when Miss Emily ceases to exist, her servant no longer has a connection to this world. It is reasonable that he vanish.

CHAPTER TWO

From Parable to Sketch to Short Story

Fiction has developed over thousands of years—from early stories of heroes, from moral parables and supernatural tales; it has adapted to fit changing religious and secular beliefs, to explain new phenomena, and to record history; it has accommodated fantasy and provided mnemonics for genealogies. Now that we have studied one contemporary story, let's glance backward over fiction's long history.

Stories began before writing, in oral traditions that continue today. Narrative is as old as the first hunter, separated from his tribe, who returned to speak of being treed by lions. He told a *story;* we need not trouble ourselves whether he told the facts. If the telling is proper, we trust the tale. The Old Testament collects stories remembered by the tribes of Israel, written down after centuries of oral transmission, recording the heroes and the history of the tribe—the stories of Moses leading his people out of Egypt, of Abraham and Isaac, of Joseph and his brothers. In Greece, the great stories were preserved in epic poems. Homer's stories centered on the war with Troy and its aftermath, recording the encounters of Hector and Achilles, and of Odysseus and the Sirens.

The Parable

Homer's *Odyssey* teaches the virtues of shrewdness and endurance—and, incidentally, passes along good tips on shipbuilding and seamanship, good manners, politics, piety, cooking, and morals. When Jesus wished to impress a moral point upon his disciples, he told them a story. In these moral stories, or parables, natural objects often stand for ideas. Thus, Mark tells us:

Again he began to teach beside the sea. And a very large crowd gathered about him, so that he got into a boat and sat in it on the sea; and the whole crowd was beside the sea on the land. And he taught them many things in parables, and in his teaching he said to them: "Listen! A sower went out to sow. And as he sowed, some seed fell along the path, and the birds came and devoured it. Other seed fell on rocky ground, where it had not much soil, and immediately it sprang up, since it had no depth of soil; and when the sun rose it was scorched, and since it had no root it withered away. Other seed fell among thorns and the thorns grew up and choked it, and it yielded no grain. And other seeds fell into good soil and brought forth grain, growing up and increasing and yielding thirtyfold and sixtyfold and a hundredfold." And he said, "He who has ears to hear, let him hear."

As often happens in the New Testament, the disciples confess their puzzlement. Mark continues:

And when he was alone, those who were about him with the twelve asked him concerning the parables. And he said to them, "To you has been given the secret of the kingdom of God, but for those outside everything is in parables; so that they may indeed see but not perceive, and may indeed hear but not understand; lest they should turn again, and be forgiven." And he said to them, "Do you not understand this parable? How then will you understand all the parables? The sower sows the word. And these are the ones along the path, where the word is sown; when they hear, Satan immediately comes and takes away the word which is sown in them. And these in like manner are the ones sown upon rocky ground, who, when they hear the word, immediately receive it with joy; and they have no root in themselves, but endure for a while; then, when tribulation or persecution arises on account of the word, immediately they fall away. And others are the ones sown among thorns; they are those who hear the word, but the cares of the world, and the delight in riches, and the desire for other things, enter in and choke the word, and it proves unfruitful. But those that were sown upon the good soil are the ones who hear the word and accept it and bear fruit, thirtyfold and sixtyfold and a hundredfold."

Although the parable tells a story, our interest is not in what will happen next but in interpretation. What *are* the seeds? What do they *stand for?* Mark tells us that the seeds in Jesus' parable stand for words, and shows us Jesus interpreting the different fates of the seeds as different responses to the Word of God.

The Fable

Many old stories teach us how to live. A fable is a tale that sums up an observation of human character in narrative form and leads to a lesson to live by, called a *moral.* A Greek named Aesop is credited with many fables that teach behavior to the young. We say someone cried wolf, often not knowing that we quote Aesop. Probably few of us read the fable, but, at some point in our young lives, if we complained or raised an alarm when we didn't need to, some adult told us this tale invented by a slave in ancient Greece: a boy tricks his elders by warning about wolves when there are no wolves; when a wolf really threatens, no one believes the warning. The fable illustrates an idea and makes a lesson concrete. And if we remember the fox and the sour grapes, we have learned from Aesop another useful generalization about human character.

The Fairy Tale

Another ancient form of narration is the fairy tale, which describes adventures of a hero or heroine who usually encounters magic or the supernatural. Charms, spells, and riddles are common to fairy tales, some of which also include moral lessons or observations. Often, these tales reverse a character's fortunes—like "Cinderella," in which the last becomes the first. Many fairy stories code human secrets into plots that resemble dreams; psychologists study them for clues to human behavior. "Rumpelstiltskin" is a story that occurs in various forms and with changes of the magic name all over Europe. The brothers Jacob and Wilhelm Grimm found four different versions in one area of Germany alone and produced a composite. (This translation was published in England in 1823.)

Rumpelstiltskin

In a certain kingdom once lived a poor miller who had a very beautiful daughter. She was moreover exceedingly shrewd and clever; and the miller was so vain and proud of her, that he one day told the king of the land that his daughter could spin gold out of straw. Now this king was very fond of money; and when he heard the miller's boast, his avarice was excited, and he ordered the girl to be brought before him. Then he led her to a chamber where there was a great quantity of straw, gave her a spinning-wheel, and said, "All this must be spun into gold before morning, as you value your life." It was in vain that the poor maiden declared that she could do no such thing, the chamber was locked and she remained alone.

She sat down in one corner of the room and began to lament over her hard fate, when on a sudden the door opened, and a droll-looking little man hobbled in, and said, "Good morrow to you, my good lass, what are you weeping for?" "Alas!" answered she, "I must spin this straw into gold and I know not how." "What will you give me," said the little man, "to do it for you?" "My necklace," replied the maiden. He took her at her word, and set himself down to the wheel; round about it went merrily, and presently the work was done and the gold all spun.

When the king came and saw this, he was greatly astonished and pleased; but his heart grew still more greedy of gain, and he shut up the poor miller's daughter again with a fresh task. Then she knew not what to do, and sat down once more to weep; but the little man presently opened the door, and said "What will you give me to do your task?" "The ring on my finger," replied she. So her little friend took the ring, and began to work at the wheel, till by the morning all was finished again.

The king was vastly delighted to see all this glittering treasure; but still he was not satisfied, and took the miller's daughter into a yet larger room, and said, "All this must be spun to-night; and if you succeed, you shall be my queen." As soon as she was alone the dwarf came in, and said "What will you give me to spin gold for you this third time?" "I have nothing left," said she.

"Then promise me," said the little man, "your first little child when you are queen." "That may never be," thought the miller's daughter; and as she knew no other way to get her task done, she promised him what he asked, and he spun once more the whole heap of gold. The king came in the morning, and finding all he wanted, married her, and so the miller's daughter really became queen.

5   At the birth of her first little child the queen rejoiced very much, and forgot the little man and her promise; but one day he came into her chamber and reminded her of it. Then she grieved sorely at her misfortune, and offered him all the treasures of the kingdom in exchange; but in vain, till at last her tears softened him, and he said, "I will give you three days' grace, and if during that time you tell me my name, you shall keep your child."

Now the queen lay awake all night, thinking of all the odd names that she had ever heard, and dispatched messengers all over the land to inquire after new ones. The next day the little man came, and she began with Timothy, Benjamin, Jeremiah, and all the names she could remember; but to all of them he said, "That's not my name."

The second day she began with all the comical names she could hear of, Bandy-legs, Hunch-back, Crook-shanks, and so on, but the little gentleman still said to every one of them, "That's not my name."

The third day came back one of the messengers, and said "I can hear of no one other name; but yesterday, as I was climbing a high hill among the trees of the forest where the fox and the hare bid each other good night, I saw a little hut, and before the hut burnt a fire, and round the fire danced a funny little man upon one leg, and sung

'Merrily the feast I'll make,
To-day I'll brew, to-morrow bake;
Merrily I'll dance and sing,
For next day will a stranger bring:
Little does my lady dream
Rumpelstiltskin is my name!'"

When the queen heard this, she jumped for joy, and as soon as her little visitor came, and said "Now, lady, what is my name?" "It is John?" asked she. "No!" "Is it Tom?" "No!"

10   "Can your name be Rumpelstiltskin?"

"Some witch told you that! Some witch told you that!" cried the little man, and dashed his right foot in a rage so deep into the floor, that he was forced to lay hold of it with both hands to pull it out. Then he made the best of his way off, while everybody laughed at him for having had all his trouble for nothing.

This text comes from *The Classic Fairy Tales,* edited by Iona and Peter Opie, who say:

It is a moral tale in that it shows the perils of boasting, though this aspect is not stressed. It is a fairy tale in that the heroine receives supernatural assistance. It is a properly constructed dramatic tale in that to obtain such assistance the heroine has to make the most terrible of pledges, the life of her first-born child. And it is a primitive tale in that it hinges on the belief of the interdependence of name and identity: the dwarf's power is only to be broken if his name can be discovered. It is also a tale possessing genuine folk appeal in that a supernatural creature is outwitted by human cleverness.

"Rumpelstiltskin" is not, then, like Aesop's story about the boy who cried wolf; "Rumpelstiltskin" rouses first our delight in the gnome's outrage and then our fear for the daughter with her two enemies: child-stealing gnome and greedy king. (Note that the greedy king becomes her husband, and consider for a moment woman's relationship to man in this story.) Notice the economy of the fairy tale, how much information is given in the first two sentences. Notice also how qualities of character are fixed, constant, and openly stated. The miller was *vain,* his daughter was *shrewd and clever.* We learn the latter two qualities in the story's course, but the miller's vanity is a given fact; told, not shown. Accident, magic, coincidence mark the fairy story (and the folk tale, the fable, the epic) and separate it from much modern fiction. And, although this tale has its moral (don't brag about your daughter), as a whole it is curiously amoral. We hear that the king is greedy, but he is not judged wrong or wicked or evil. He is as greedy as the miller is vain—as a given fact of character—and because he is king he has the power to kill the miller's daughter if she does not do what he wishes.

In this primitive form, narrative takes precedence over other elements of fiction—narrative without development of character, without complexity of motive, without specified place or setting, without intricacies of time sequence or point of view. Story is everything.

The Folktale

Related to the fairy tale is the folktale, of which we find examples among all cultures and peoples. Folktales entertain, but they also instruct; they preserve the memory of the folk. These stories often concern themselves with means of survival through hard times; often, the supernatural plays a part. This story was told by a Swampy Cree named Andrew Nikumoon and written down by Howard Norman, who grew up in northern Ontario, speaking Cree before he spoke English. A windigo is an evil spirit.

The Wrong-Chill Windigo   (1990)

In a village lived a man named Teal Duck. There was much illness from hunger in his village at that time. Many fevers, in children and others. Teal Duck went out hunting to try to find food to eat. He went out alone. It was when the first ice was breaking up on streams and lakes. "Maybe some ducks will arrive soon," Teal Duck said. It had been a hard winter, with little food.

Some days before, Teal Duck had found a wide stream that was mostly clear of ice. He set out for that stream. It wasn't too far from his village. But when he arrived, the stream was frozen over again! Just then he saw an owl fly down. "Why did you freeze this stream back up?" Teal Duck called to the owl.

"Get out on the ice and shiver, then I'll thaw this stream open again!" answered the owl.

With that, Teal Duck walked out on the stream. He sat down on the ice. He held himself tightly with his arms. Then he began shivering.

5   But the owl said, "No! That's the wrong kind of shivering! You've got the wrong chill in you! That's a chill from a childhood fever!" Then the owl flew away.

Teal Duck stood up. That's when he heard in the distance another ice breakup! He said out loud, "Maybe *that's* where the ducks are!" Teal Duck walked toward that sound. When he arrived at the distant stream, he saw that it too had frozen over! Again he saw the owl. The owl was sitting in a tree. Teal Duck shouted, "Why are you doing this to me?"

Again the owl said, "Get out on that ice!"

Teal Duck, farther away from his village now and starving, walked out on the ice. He sat down. He shivered.

But the owl said, "No, that's not it! That's the shivering from a nightmare dream, when you sit up in fear . . . awake! That's the wrong chill. That's the wrong shivering." Then the owl flew away.

10   So Teal Duck had shivered up the memory of a childhood fever and he had shivered up that other thing—a nightmare. "That's enough for one day!" he called out to the flying owl. But just then ice was cracking in the distance, farther yet from his village.

Again Teal Duck walked in hunger toward cracking ice. Again he arrived at a frozen stream! Again, the owl was there!

The owl said, "The right chill will thaw this ice for ducks to arrive. Then you can get food. Then you won't starve."

So Teal Duck went out on the ice to shiver. He sat down. With his fever he sat. With his nightmare he sat. He shivered. He shivered past those two things, past those days. He was very hungry.

Then a windigo arrived.

15   Teal Duck knew where the chill came from. The windigo sent the chill into him. The windigo did that.

Teal Duck called at the owl, "You've been working for this windigo now you'll do so for me!" With that, Teal Duck conjured all the fevers from his village into that owl! The owl began burning up! Then Teal Duck shouted, "Strike your talons into it!" The owl did so. The owl struck its talons into the windigo's chest. That melted its heart. The windigo was dying. It howled loud in a tremendously fearful way. Then it died.

That howl brought the others all the way from Teal Duck's village. They arrived. Teal Duck said to them, "As the owl is now working for me, I'll make it thaw more ice!"

Teal Duck said, "Owl, get to work!"

With that, the owl thawed open more ice. It had such powers, it cracked open the ice on many lakes and streams. Teal Duck and the others could hear the owl in the distance on the ice, thawing it. The owl, full of those fevers that Teal Duck had conjured into it, was hissing in the water.

20   So that is what happened.

After that, there were ducks to eat.

Jokes

Another ancient form of story is the joke. My grandfather used to tell the tragic tale of the death of his horse Nellie. One summer, in the hottest August in history, he put ears of popcorn on the barn roof for drying, right above the window of Nellie's stall. The day the thermometer hit 112 degrees, the corn got so hot it popped right off the cob, slid down the roof, and fell to the ground past Nellie's window. Poor Nellie thought it was a blizzard and froze to death.

Even this joke tells a story, with characters, props, setting, and action.

The Sketch

Parable, fable, fairy story, folktale, and joke are the ancestors of modern fiction. The sketch is modern and resembles the short story. It is a short prose work that may include narrative, description, dialogue, or characterization but lacks the conflict of a short story. Some sketches, like Ivan Turgenev's great *A Sportsman's Sketches,* may be long and richly textured. Others are more modest, merely capturing the precise tone and atmosphere of a setting; others use psychological observation to form the character sketch. Ernest Hemingway printed brief sketches between the short stories of his first collection, *In Our Time.* Here is one:

> They shot the six cabinet ministers at half-past six in the morning against the wall of a hospital. There were pools of water in the courtyard. There were wet dead leaves on the paving of the courtyard. It rained hard. All the shutters of the hospital were nailed shut. One of the ministers was sick with typhoid. Two soldiers carried him downstairs and out into the rain. They tried to hold him up against the wall but he sat down in a puddle of water. The other five stood very quietly against the wall. Finally the officer told the soldiers it was no good trying to make him stand up. When they fired the first volley he was sitting down in the water with his head on his knees.

Hemingway offers no conflict here, only an unblinking and exact rendering of the scene. Although brief, a sketch can be powerful.

The Short Story

In chapters that follow, under categories like Plot and Character, we look at fiction using examples from the genre of the short story. When we investigate Point of View, or Theme, or Setting, we will note qualities or devices present in most fiction, including novels; but we must always remember that the short story is a literary form in itself. Despite its name, we must not assume that this genre takes its identity from its length alone; a short story is not merely a boiled-down novel.

One of the form's greatest practitioners was the Irishman Frank O'Connor (see his story, pages 325–333), who turned critic to write a book about the short story, *The Lonely Voice* (available in paperback from Colophon Books/ HarperCollins). O'Connor asserts that "even from its beginnings, the short story has functioned in a quite different way from the novel." The short story, he says, always treats of "a submerged population group," and he points out that his own Ireland, which has "failed to produce a single novelist . . . [has] produced four or five storytellers who [are] first-rate." Writers in Russia and the United States also excel at the short story, and O'Connor speculates about why certain nations produce the best storytellers. He praises Hemingway and Porter, among other Americans writing before the time of Flannery O'Connor, or the recent renaissance of American storytelling represented here in the work of Ann Beattie and Raymond Carver.

Among writers, it is commonplace to assert that novels are easier to write than stories. Maybe novels are easier to read also, for stories are as concentrated as poems. Stories work not by accumulation but by sudden revelation and flashes of insight. They work also by their form—a form that must never seem self-conscious. Short stories exemplify the art of appearing artless, but they make great literary art—control and shape leading from observation to understanding.

To enjoy the form, one must first learn how to read it. Before we pay closer attention to the elements of fiction like plot and conflict, let us look briefly at some of the criteria for excellence in fiction, the ways we discriminate between good fiction and bad, between good and better.

Telling Good Fiction from Bad

Like most television, most film, most poetry, and most drama, most fiction is not great literature. Much popular fiction is good entertainment without artistic goals or pretensions. There is nothing evil about entertainment, but our education should reveal the values of literature—which include entertainment and much more. Some people ascribe literary value to a piece of writing in inverse proportion to its popularity; this is snobbery. Anyone who equates popularity with failure will be hard put to explain Dickens and Shakespeare, who were massively popular during their lifetime.

But popularity does not make a writer good, either. Here are the first paragraphs of *Dare to Love* by Jennifer Wilde:

> They still stared and whispered to themselves as I walked down the street. Three years had passed since I was home last, but the village hadn't changed at all, nor had the people. At eighteen, I was no longer a child, but to the villagers I was still the Lawrence girl, the subject of scandal. It pleased me to find that I was not affected by the stares, the whispers. What these people thought simply didn't matter any more. They would never again be able to cause the anger, the pain, the resentment that had marred my childhood.
>
> My blue-black hair fell to my shoulders in waves, and I wore a dusty rose cotton frock trimmed with lace. My manner of dress shocked the villagers, as did my cool, self-possessed attitude.

And here is the end of the same novel:

> "I've never stopped loving you," I whispered.
>
> Pulling me into his arms, he held me loosely for a moment and looked into my eyes. Then he smiled and kissed me with incredible tenderness, murmuring my name as his lips touched mine. This was the way it was meant to be. This was the destiny Inez had foretold for me so many years ago in the gypsy camp. As I put my arms around him, I knew at last that dreams can come true.

If you almost feel that you could write the 548 intervening pages, you are calling this writing predictable. Such excess predictability gives us a place to start. Inferior art pleases, in a mild way, by fulfilling expectations; there are no surprises: the bad will be punished, the detective will get his man. If details are not wholly predictable in *Dare to Love* (we don't know whether there will be a shipwreck in Corsica or a mysterious letter from the Azores), we can be sure that nothing will happen to tax our understanding. Literature, on the other hand, entertains us while it enlarges our awareness of unpredictable human experience.

Popular conventions reveal the state of society and the popular mind. But, while literary study does not neglect history, society, or the human psyche, it looks also at form and theme in a work of art. The literary form in most best sellers is simple, repetitive, and secondhand. Original form takes original reading, which most readers are unprepared to offer. And theme, in most best sellers, is conventional daydream, to beguile our time away and to provide a setting for reverie, which is sometimes about our blue-black hair and sometimes about violence. For example, Mickey Spillane's *Kiss Me, Deadly* begins with this little daydream:

> All I saw was the dame standing there in the glare of the headlights waving her arms like a huge puppet and the curse I spit out filled the car and my own ears. I wrenched the wheel over, felt the rear end start to slide, brought it out with a splash of power and almost ran up the side of the cliff as the car fishtailed. The brakes bit in, gouging a furrow in the shoulder, then jumped to the pavement and held.

Spillane's universe is sexual exploitation and masculine violence. (In Jennifer Wilde, everything in the world is implicitly sexual, but nothing is explicit; in Mickey Spillane, sex is a form of violence.) Here is the ending of the same book:

> She laughed and I heard the insanity in it. The gun pressed into my belt as she kneeled forward, bringing the revulsion with her. "You're going to die now . . . but first you can do it. Deadly . . . deadly . . . kiss me."
>
> The smile never left her mouth and before it was on me I thumbed the lighter and in the moment of time before the scream blossoms into the wild cry of terror she was a mass of flame tumbling on the floor with the blue flames of alcohol turning the white of her hair into black char and her body convulsing under the agony of it. The flames were teeth that ate, ripping and tearing, into scars of other flames and her voice the shrill sound of death on the loose.
>
> I looked, looked away. The door was closed and maybe I had enough left to make it.

Sadism and sentimentality are equally predictable.

Like *Kiss Me, Deadly,* "A Rose for Emily" ends with horror. Then why is "A Rose for Emily" good and *Kiss Me, Deadly* bad? There are many partial answers, beginning with originality, but in the end we must look to theme or content. *Kiss Me, Deadly* has nothing to say beyond affirming its sadism; it is solemn but it is not serious. On the other hand, "A Rose for Emily" says something—about the South, about people who cling to the dead past—that is not common-place. It records observations that are not trite, in language fresh enough to awaken the reader's mind and emotions. We are not speaking of Spillane's intention or purpose, nor of Faulkner's. After all, if Mickey Spillane asserted on a stack of Bibles that his intention was high art, it would not change the value of one word he has written. And if the ghost of William Faulkner rose before us to protest that he wrote "A Rose for Emily" in haste, for money, to meet a mortgage payment, it would not change the value of that story either.

We call some fiction bad when it fails through want of skill; badness like Spillane's or Wilde's derives from the nature of the product. To be good, a thing has to be worth making. One argument for reading good literature is that it educates us to our sensibilities, makes us more sensitive, wiser, broader in understanding and empathy, and more sophisticated. Reading Flannery O'Conner or James Joyce, we see how literature can refine our perceptions. Reading Mickey Spillane, we see something contrary: how writing can equally serve to brutalize and desensitize, to exercise our latent sadism rather than to awaken sensitivity to the suffering of others. If good literature aims to enlarge and enhance our sensibilities, Spillane is bad; *bad* becomes a moral term and not merely a technical one.

CHAPTER FOUR

Plot

P lot is what happens in a story, the story's organized development, usually a chain linking cause and effect. Plot is the first and most obvious quality of a story. When we agree on what happened in a story, we can go on to discuss its significance. To introduce plot, let us rehearse some common terms.

Plot first requires conflict. Conflict may arise between characters; if Sam and Bill are in love with the same woman, their conflict can engender a thousand plots. Conflict may arise between a person and an idea, or a person and an event. A dying protagonist may conflict with antagonist death. Or, an old-fashioned Southern spinster may conflict with the modern world. Such conflict often continues throughout a story, frequently to be resolved at the story's end.

Second, the reader needs to know where and when the story happens, and other information germane to plot. Exposition is the presentation of needed facts; it can occur at any point in the story, but it is usually most necessary at the beginning. An old storyteller might begin:

> On the morning of February 10, 18—, a stranger alighted from the coach in the square of the town of M—. It was a frosty morning, and the stranger appeared ill-dressed for the climate where she chose to take herself, for . . .

To the modern reader, such overt exposition seems too slow, not subtle enough. In "A Rose for Emily," early description of Miss Emily's house and surroundings gives us social and historical background we need to have, while it pretends only to paint a picture.

After exposition, the conflict between protagonist and antagonist un- folds and grows more intense, in a rising action of increasing intensity, until the climax of the story, when we reach the conflict's outcome. Then we have the dénouement (French for untying a knot), which elucidates and concludes the story. At the climax, one of the conflicting forces usually wins out over the other. The dénouement is almost the counterpart of exposition—bookends of the story; it accounts for loose ends, backing us out of the story as the exposition edged us in. With dénouement as with exposition, it is elegant to avoid the obvious. In "A Rose for Emily," the climax occurs when the townspeople break into the locked room; the grisly discovery provides the dénouement.

Some stories lack an obvious climax. It is a writer's joke that to turn an ordinary short story into a story for *The New Yorker,* all you need to do is throw away the last two pages. Sketches lack conflict and climax. Other stories (thrillers, adventure stories) may provide climax after climax, a rising action of peaks with brief valleys.

A story's plot stimulates our wish to know what happens next; suspense keeps us turning the page to find out who killed whom, or who marries whom, or why a character behaves in a bizarre fashion. On the other hand, many writers find it useful to foreshadow, hinting what will happen next. Foreshadowing creates the sense of necessity, inevitability, fate. Many plots use flashback, an ancient and honorable device. In films and novels, in stories and modern plays, we many times enter someone's mind and watch how a present event recalls a past one.

A similar device is the frame: a story begins and ends in the same moment, while the story's middle recalls a past that explains the present. A frame can accommodate foreshadowing; it can present us with a character in a situation —say, on Death Row waiting for execution—and then flash back to childhood to show us the character's progress to condemnation. A frame may create suspense as well as a sense of doom. "A Rose for Emily" begins and ends just after Miss Emily's death, and it is her death that raises the question of her life.

Using terms like plot, we isolate a story's parts. It is worth keeping in mind, however, that a good story is an organic whole: one sentence, or one phrase within a sentence, may advance the plot, indicate character, represent point of view, describe setting, and promote theme or meaning. In literature, everything happens at once.

James Thurber

James Thurber (1894–1961) is associated for most of us with *The New Yorker,* which he helped edit and for which he wrote stories and drew cartoons. Thurber was a comic writer. But, as with many humorists, Thurber's mind has a dark and obsessive side. (Readers interested in pursuing the difficult man behind the stories and cartoons may appreciate Burton Bernstein's biography, *Thurber.*) James Thurber grew up in Columbus, Ohio, and worked for newspapers in Ohio, France, and New York. But not until he joined *The New Yorker*'s staff, when he observed the stylistic devices of E. B. White—with whom he collaborated on *Is Sex Necessary?* (1929)—did he discover and develop the wry manner we cherish.

The Catbird Seat   (1945)

Mr. Martin bought the pack of Camels on Monday night in the most crowded cigar store on Broadway. It was theater time and seven or eight men were buying cigarettes. The clerk didn't even glance at Mr. Martin, who put the pack in his overcoat pocket and went out. If any of the staff at F & S had seen him buy the cigarettes, they would have been astonished, for it was generally known that Mr. Martin did not smoke, and never had. No one saw him.

It was just a week to the day since Mr. Martin had decided to rub out Mrs. Ulgine Barrows. The term "rub out" pleased him because it suggested nothing more than the correction of an error—in this case an error of Mr. Fitweiler. Mr. Martin had spent each night of the past week working out his plan and examining it. As he walked home now he went over it again. For the hundredth time he resented the element of imprecision, the margin of guesswork that entered into the business. The project as he had worked it out was casual and bold, the risks were considerable. Something might go wrong anywhere along the line. And therein lay the cunning of his scheme. No one would ever see in it the cautious, painstaking hand of Erwin Martin, head of the filing department at F & S, of whom Mr. Fitweiler had once said, "Man is fallible but Martin isn't." No one would see his hand, that is, unless it were caught in the act.

Sitting in his apartment, drinking a glass of milk, Mr. Martin reviewed his case against Mrs. Ulgine Barrows, as he had every night for seven nights. He began at the beginning. Her quacking voice and braying laugh had first profaned the halls of F & S on March 7, 1941 (Mr. Martin had a head for dates). Old Roberts, the personnel chief, had introduced her as the newly appointed special adviser to the president of the firm, Mr. Fitweiler. The woman had appalled Mr. Martin instantly, but he hadn't shown it. He had given her his dry hand, a look of studious concentration, and a faint smile. "Well," she had said, looking at the papers on his desk, "are you lifting the oxcart out of the ditch?" As Mr. Martin recalled that moment, over his milk, he squirmed slightly. He must keep his mind on her crimes as a special adviser, not on her peccadillos as a personality. This he found difficult to do, in spite of entering an objection and sustaining it. The faults of the woman as a woman kept chattering on in his mind like an unruly witness. She had, for almost two years now, baited him. In the halls, in the elevator, even in his own office, into which she romped now and then like a circus horse, she was constantly shouting these silly questions at him. "Are you lifting the oxcart out of the ditch? Are you tearing up the pea patch? Are you hollering down the rain barrel? Are you scraping around the bottom of the pickle barrel? Are you sitting in the catbird seat?"

It was Joey Hart, one of Mr. Martin's two assistants, who had explained what the gibberish meant. "She must be a Dodger fan," he had said. "Red Barber announces the Dodger games over the radio and he uses those expressions— picked 'em up down South." Joey had gone on to explain one or two. "Tearing up the pea patch" meant going on a rampage; "sitting in the catbird seat" meant sitting pretty, like a batter with three balls and no strikes on him. Mr. Martin dismissed all this with an effort. It had been annoying, it had driven him near to distraction, but he was too solid a man to be moved to murder by anything so childish. It was fortunate, he reflected as he passed on to the important charges against Mrs. Barrows, that he had stood up under it so well. He had maintained always an outward appearance of polite tolerance. "Why, I even believe you like the woman," Miss Paird, his other assistant, had once said to him. He had simply smiled.

5   A gavel rapped in Mr. Martin's mind and the case proper was resumed. Mrs. Ulgine Barrows stood charged with willful, blatant, and persistent attempts to destroy the efficiency and system of F & S. It was competent, material, and relevant to review her advent and rise to power. Mr. Martin had got the story from Miss Paird, who seemed always able to find things out. According to her, Mrs. Barrows had met Mr. Fitweiler at a party, where she had rescued him from the embraces of a powerfully built drunken man who had mistaken the president of F & S for a famous retired Middle Western football coach. She had led him to a sofa and somehow worked upon him a monstrous magic. The aging gentleman had jumped to the conclusion there and then that this was a woman of singular attainments, equipped to bring out the best in him and in the firm. A week later he had introduced her into F & S as his special adviser. On that day confusion got its foot in the door. After Miss Tyson, Mr. Brundage, and Mr. Bartlett had been fired and Mr. Munson had taken his hat and stalked out, mailing in his resignation later, old Roberts had been emboldened to speak to Mr. Fitweiler. He mentioned that Mr. Munson's department had been "a little disrupted" and hadn't they perhaps better resume the old system there? Mr. Fitweiler had said certainly not. He had the greatest faith in Mrs. Barrows' ideas. "They require a little seasoning, a little seasoning, is all," he had added. Mr. Roberts had given it up. Mr. Martin reviewed in detail all the changes wrought by Mrs. Barrows. She had begun chipping at the cornices of the firm's edifice and now she was swinging at the foundation stones with a pickaxe.

Mr. Martin came now, in his summing up, to the afternoon of Monday, November 2, 1942—just one week ago. On that day, at 3 P.M., Mrs. Barrows had bounced into his office. "Boo!" she had yelled. "Are you scraping around the bottom of the pickle barrel?" Mr. Martin had looked at her from under his green eyeshade, saying nothing. She had begun to wander about the office, taking it in with her great, popping eyes. "Do you really need *all* these filing cabinets?" she had demanded suddenly. Mr. Martin's heart had jumped. "Each of these files," he had said, keeping his voice even, "plays an indispensable part in the system of F & S." She had brayed at him, "Well, don't tear up the pea patch!" and gone to the door. From there she had bawled, "But you sure have got a lot of fine scrap in here!" Mr. Martin could no longer doubt that the finger was on his beloved department. Her pickaxe was on the upswing, poised for the first blow. It had not come yet; he had received no blue memo from the enchanted Mr. Fitweiler bearing nonsensical instructions deriving from the obscene woman. But there was no doubt in Mr. Martin's mind that one would be forthcoming. He must act quickly. Already a precious week had gone by. Mr. Martin stood up in his living room, still holding his milk glass. "Gentlemen of the jury," he said to himself, "I demand the death penalty for this horrible person."

The next day Mr. Martin followed his routine, as usual. He polished his glasses more often and once sharpened an already sharp pencil, but not even Miss

Paird noticed. Only once did he catch sight of his victim; she swept past him in the hall with a patronizing "Hi!" At five-thirty he walked home, as usual, and had a glass of milk, as usual. He had never drunk anything stronger in his life—unless you could count ginger ale. The late Sam Schlosser, the S of F & S, had praised Mr. Martin at a staff meeting several years before for his temperate habits. "Our most efficient worker neither drinks nor smokes," he had said. "The results speak for themselves." Mr. Fitweiler had sat by, nodding approval.

Mr. Martin was still thinking about that red-letter day as he walked over to the Schrafft's on Fifth Avenue near Forty-sixth Street. He got there, as he always did, at eight o'clock. He finished his dinner and the financial page of the *Sun* at a quarter to nine, as he always did. It was his custom after dinner to take a walk. This time he walked down Fifth Avenue at a casual pace. His gloved hands felt moist and warm, his forehead cold. He transferred the Camels from his overcoat to a jacket pocket. He wondered, as he did so, if they did not represent an unnecessary note of strain. Mrs. Barrows smoked only Luckies. It was his idea to puff a few puffs on a Camel (after the rubbing-out), stub it out in the ashtray holding her lipstick-stained Luckies, and thus drag a small red herring across the trail. Perhaps it was not a good idea. It would take time. He might even choke, too loudly.

Mr. Martin had never seen the house on West Twelfth Street where Mrs. Barrows lived, but he had a clear enough picture of it. Fortunately, she had bragged to everybody about her ducky first-floor apartment in the perfectly darling three-story redbrick. There would be no doorman or other attendants; just the tenants on the second and third floors. As he walked along, Mr. Martin realized that he would get there before nine-thirty. He had considered walking north on Fifth Avenue from Schrafft's to a point from which it would take him until ten o'clock to reach the house. At that hour people were less likely to be coming in or going out. But the procedure would have made an awkward loop in the straight thread of his casualness, and he had abandoned it. It was impossible to figure when people would be entering or leaving the house, anyway. There was a great risk at any hour. If he ran into anybody, he would simply have to place the rubbing-out of Ulgine Barrows in the inactive file forever. The same thing would hold true if there were someone in her apartment. In that case he would just say that he had been passing by, recognized her charming house and thought to drop in.

10   It was eighteen minutes after nine when Mr. Martin turned into Twelfth Street. A man passed him, and a man and a woman talking. There was no one within fifty paces when he came to the house, halfway down the block. He was up the steps and in the small vestibule in no time, pressing the bell under the card that said "Mrs. Ulgine Barrows." When the clicking in the lock started, he jumped forward against the door. He got inside fast, closing the door behind him. A bulb in a lantern hung from the hall ceiling on a chain seemed to give a monstrously bright light. There was nobody on the stair, which went up ahead of him along the left wall. A door opened down the hall in the wall on the right. He went toward it swiftly, on tiptoe.

"Well, for God's sake, look who's here!" bawled Mrs. Barrows, and her braying laugh rang out like the report of a shotgun. He rushed past her like a football tackle, bumping her. "Hey, quit shoving!" she said, closing the door behind them. They were in her living room, which seemed to Mr. Martin to be lighted by a hundred lamps. "What's after you?" she said. "You're as jumpy as a goat." He found he was unable to speak. His heart was wheezing in his throat. "I—yes," he finally brought out. She was jabbering and laughing as she started to help him off with his coat. "No, no," he said. "I'll put it here." He took it off and put it on a chair near the door. "Your hat and gloves, too," she said. "You're in a lady's house." He put his hat on top of the coat. Mrs. Barrows seemed larger than he had thought. He kept his gloves on. "I was passing by," he said. "I recognized—is there anyone here?" She laughed louder than ever. "No," she said, "we're all alone. You're as white as a sheet, you funny man. Whatever *has* come over you? I'll mix you a toddy." She started towards a door across the room. "Scotch-and-soda be all right? But say, you don't drink, do you?" She turned and gave him her amused look. Mr. Martin pulled himself together. "Scotch-and-soda will be all right," he heard himself say. He could hear her laughing in the kitchen.

Mr. Martin looked quickly around the living room for the weapon. He had counted on finding one there. There were andirons and a poker and something in a corner that looked like an Indian club. None of them would do. It couldn't be that way. He began to pace around. He came to a desk. On it lay a metal paper knife with an ornate handle. Would it be sharp enough? He reached for it and knocked over a small brass jar. Stamps spilled out of it and it fell to the floor with a clatter. "Hey," Mrs. Barrows yelled from the kitchen, "are you tearing up the pea patch?" Mr. Martin gave a strange laugh. Picking up the knife, he tried its point against his left wrist. It was blunt. It wouldn't do.

When Mrs. Barrows reappeared, carrying two highballs, Mr. Martin, standing there with his gloves on, became acutely conscious of the fantasy he had wrought. Cigarettes in his pocket, a drink prepared for him—it was all too grossly improbable. It was more than that; it was impossible. Somewhere in the back of his mind a vague idea stirred, sprouted. "For heaven's sake, take off those gloves," said Mrs. Barrows. "I always wear them in the house," said Mr. Martin. The idea began to bloom, strange and wonderful. She put the glasses on a coffee table in front of a sofa and sat on the sofa. "Come over here, you odd little man," she said. Mr. Martin went over and sat beside her. It was difficult getting a cigarette out of the pack of Camels, but he managed it. She held a match for him, laughing. "Well," she said, handing him his drink, "this is perfectly marvelous. You with a drink and a cigarette."

Mr. Martin puffed, not too awkwardly, and took a gulp of the highball. "I drink and smoke all the time," he said. He clinked his glass against hers. "Here's nuts to that old windbag, Fitweiler," he said, and gulped again. The stuff tasted awful, but he made no grimace. "Really, Mr. Martin," she said, her voice and posture changing, "you are insulting our employer." Mrs. Barrows was now all special adviser to the president. "I am preparing a bomb," said Mr. Martin, "which will blow the old goat higher than hell." He had only had a little of the drink, which was not strong. It couldn't be that. "Do you take dope or something?" Mrs. Barrows asked coldly. "Heroin," said Mr. Martin. "I'll be coked to the gills when I bump that old buzzard off." "Mr. Martin!"

she shouted, getting to her feet. "That will be all of that. You must go at once." Mr. Martin took another swallow of his drink. He tapped his cigarette out in the ashtray and put the pack of Camels on the coffee table. Then he got up. She stood glaring at him. He walked over and put on his hat and coat. "Not a word about this," he said, and laid an index finger against his lips. All Mrs. Barrows could bring out was "Really!" Mr. Martin put his hand on the doorknob. "I'm sitting in the catbird seat," he said. He stuck his tongue out at her and left. Nobody saw him go.

15   Mr. Martin got to his apartment, walking, well before eleven. No one saw him go in. He had two glasses of milk after brushing his teeth, and he felt elated. It wasn't tipsiness, because he hadn't been tipsy. Anyway, the walk had worn off all effects of the whiskey. He got in bed and read a magazine for a while. He was asleep before midnight.

Mr. Martin got to the office at eight-thirty the next morning, as usual. At a quarter to nine, Ulgine Barrows, who had never before arrived at work before ten, swept into his office. "I'm reporting to Mr. Fitweiler now!" she shouted. "If he turns you over to the police, it's no more than you deserve!" Mr. Martin gave her a look of shocked surprise. "I beg your pardon?" he said. Mrs. Barrows snorted and bounced out of the room, leaving Miss Paird and Joey Hart staring after her. "What's the matter with that old devil now?" asked Miss Paird. "I have no idea," said Mr. Martin, resuming his work. The other two looked at him and then at each other. Miss Paird got up and went out. She walked slowly past the closed door of Mr. Fitweiler's office. Mrs. Barrows was yelling inside, but she was not braying. Miss Paird could not hear what the woman was saying. She went back to her desk.

Forty-five minutes later, Mrs. Barrows left the president's office and went into her own, shutting the door. It wasn't until half an hour later that Mr. Fitweiler sent for Mr. Martin. The head of the filing department, neat, quiet, attentive, stood in front of the old man's desk. Mr. Fitweiler was pale and nervous. He took his glasses off and twiddled them. He made a small, bruffing sound in his throat. "Martin," he said, "you have been with us more than twenty years." "Twenty-two, sir," said Mr. Martin. "In that time," pursued the president, "your work and your—uh—manner have been exemplary." "I trust so, sir," said Mr. Martin. "I have understood, Martin," said Mr. Fitweiler, "that you have never taken a drink or smoked." "That is correct, sir," said Mr. Martin. "Ah, yes." Mr. Fitweiler polished his glasses. "You may describe what you did after leaving the office yesterday, Martin," he said. Mr. Martin allowed less than a second for his bewildered pause. "Certainly, sir," he said. "I walked home. Then I went to Schrafft's for dinner. Afterward I walked home again. I went to bed early, sir, and read a magazine for a while. I was asleep before eleven." "Ah, yes," said Mr. Fitweiler again. He was silent for a moment, searching for the proper words to say to the head of the filing department. "Mrs. Barrows," he said finally, "Mrs. Barrows has worked hard, Martin, very hard. It grieves me to report that she has suffered a severe breakdown. It has taken the form of a persecution complex accompanied by distressing hallucinations." "I am very sorry, sir," said Mr. Martin. "Mrs. Barrows is under the delusion," continued Mr. Fitweiler, "that you visited her last evening and behaved yourself in an—ah—unseemly manner." He raised his hand to silence Mr. Martin's little pained outcry. "It is the nature of these psychological diseases," Mr. Fitweiler said, "to fix upon the least likely and most innocent party as the—uh—source of persecution. These matters are not for the lay mind to grasp, Martin. I've just had my psychiatrist, Dr. Fitch, on the phone. He would not, of course, commit himself, but he made enough generalizations to substantiate my suspicions. I suggested to Mrs. Barrows when she had completed her—uh—story to me this morning, that she visit Dr. Fitch, for I suspected a condition at once. She flew, I regret to say, into a rage, and demanded—uh—requested that I call you on the carpet. You may not know, Martin, but Mrs. Barrows had planned a reorganization of your department—subject to my approval, of course, subject to my approval. This brought you, rather than anyone else, to her mind—but again that is a phenomenon for Dr. Fitch and not for us. So, Martin, I am afraid Mrs. Barrows' usefulness here is at an end." "I am dreadfully sorry, sir," said Mr. Martin.

It was at this point that the door to the office blew open with the suddenness of a gas-main explosion and Mrs. Barrows catapulted through it. "Is the little rat denying it?" she screamed. "He can't get away with that!" Mr. Martin got up and moved discreetly to a point beside Mr. Fitweiler's chair. "You drank and smoked at my apartment," she bawled at Mr. Martin, "and you know it! You called Mr. Fitweiler an old windbag and said you were going to blow him up when you got coked to the gills on your heroin!" She stopped yelling to catch her breath and a new glint came into her popping eyes. "If you weren't such a drab, ordinary little man," she said, "I'd think you'd planned it all. Sticking your tongue out, saying you were sitting in the catbird seat, because you thought no one would believe me when I told it! My God, it's really perfect!" She brayed loudly and hysterically, and the fury was on her again. She glared at Mr. Fitweiler. "Can't you see how he has tricked us, you old fool? Can't you see his little game?" But Mr. Fitweiler had been surreptitiously pressing all the buttons under the top of his desk and employees of F & S began pouring into the room. "Stockton," said Mr. Fitweiler, "you and Fishbein will take Mrs. Barrows to her home. Mrs. Powell, you will go with them." Stockton, who had played a little football in high school, blocked Mrs. Barrows as she made for Mr. Martin. It took him and Fishbein together to force her out of the door into the hall, crowded with stenographers and office boys. She was still screaming imprecations at Mr. Martin, tangled and contradictory imprecations. The hubbub finally died out down the corridor.

"I regret that this has happened," said Mr. Fitweiler. "I shall ask you to dismiss it from your mind, Martin." "Yes, sir," said Mr. Martin, anticipating his chief's "That will be all" by moving to the door. "I will dismiss it." He went out and shut the door, and his step was light and quick in the hall. When he entered his department he had slowed down to his customary gait, and he walked quietly across the room to the W20 file, wearing a look of studious concentration.

Questions on Plot . . .

1. In the opening paragraph, there are details that may seem pointless when you first read them. In retrospect, do these details serve the plot? At what point does Thurber allow you to see their purpose?

2. The last sentence of the first paragraph is brief. What do these four words do for the plot of the story?

3. We learn at the start that Mr. Martin has a plan of action. Later, we learn his motives. What does Thurber gain by organizing his plot backward? Why didn't he start at the beginning and let us see Mr. Martin being provoked into revenge, then developing a plan of action?

4. Where does Thurber's exposition begin? Is it subtle? Is it obvious? Is it necessary?

5. Describe the rising action in Thurber's summary of past events. What is the final straw?

6. Describe Thurber's use of a glass of milk early in the story. Is this detail useful for creating character? Plot?

7. When do we return to the time of the opening paragraph?

8. What is the story's climax? If the story's dénouement is long, is there a reason?

. . . and Other Elements

9. Describe the various means Thurber uses in the first three paragraphs to establish Mr. Martin's character.

10. Is this story implicitly sexist?

Flannery O'Connor

Flannery O'Connor (1925–1964) is another great storyteller from the American South. In her brief life, she completed two novels (*Wise Blood,* 1952; *The Violent Bear It Away,* 1960) and two books of stories, collected with others in *The Complete Stories* (1971). Born in Georgia, she attended the Writers Workshop at the University of Iowa and returned to Georgia to write. She was affected early by the rare disease of lupus and was dying during the years of her mature writing. Flannery O'Connor's stories are often called Gothic—in the old sense of exotic and horrifying. She was a Roman Catholic with strong convictions that often inform or direct the themes of her stories. A collection of her letters, *The Habit of Being,* appeared in 1979.

A Good Man Is Hard to Find   (1955)

The grandmother didn't want to go to Florida. She wanted to visit some of her connections in east Tennessee and she was seizing at every chance to change Bailey's mind. Bailey was the son she lived with, her only boy. He was sitting on the edge of his chair at the table, bent over the orange sports section of the *Journal.* "Now look here, Bailey," she said, "see here, read this," and she stood with one hand on her thin hip and the other rattling the newspaper at his bald head. "Here this fellow that calls himself The Misfit is aloose from the Federal Pen and headed toward Florida and you read here what it says he did to these people. Just you read it. I wouldn't take my children in any direction with a criminal like that aloose in it. I couldn't answer to my conscience if I did."

Bailey didn't look up from his reading so she wheeled around then and faced the children's mother, a young woman in slacks, whose face was as broad and innocent as a cabbage and was tied round with a green head-kerchief that had two points on the top like rabbit's ears. She was sitting on the sofa, feeding the baby his apricots out of a jar. "The children have been to Florida before," the old lady said. "You all ought to take them somewhere else for a change so they would see different parts of the world and be broad. They never have been to east Tennessee."

The children's mother didn't seem to hear her but the eight-year-old boy, John Wesley, a stocky child with glasses, said, "If you don't want to go to Florida, why dontcha stay at home?" He and the little girl, June Star, were reading the funny papers on the floor.

"She wouldn't stay at home to be queen for a day," June Star said without raising her yellow head.

5   "Yes, and what would you do if this fellow, The Misfit, caught you?" the grandmother asked.

"I'd smack his face," John Wesley said.

"She wouldn't stay at home for a million bucks," June Star said. "Afraid she'd miss something. She has to go everywhere we go."

"All right, Miss," the grandmother said. "Just remember that the next time you want me to curl your hair."

June Star said her hair was naturally curly.

10   The next morning the grandmother was the first one in the car, ready to go. She had her big black valise that looked like the head of a hippopotamus in one corner, and underneath it she was hiding a basket with Pitty Sing, the cat, in it. She didn't intend for the cat to be left alone in the house for three days because he would miss her too much and she was afraid he might brush against one of the gas burners and accidentally asphyxiate himself. Her son, Bailey, didn't like to arrive at a motel with a cat.

She sat in the middle of the back seat with John Wesley and June Star on either side of her. Bailey and the children's mother and the baby sat in front and they left Atlanta at eight forty-five with the mileage on the car at 55890. The grandmother wrote this down because she thought it would be interesting to say how many miles they had been when they got back. It took them twenty minutes to reach the outskirts of the city.

The old lady settled herself comfortably, removing her white cotton gloves and putting them up with her purse on the shelf in front of the back window. The children's mother still had on slacks and still had her head tied up in a green kerchief, but the grandmother had on a navy blue straw sailor hat with a bunch of white violets on the brim and a navy blue dress with a small white dot in the print. Her collars and cuffs were white organdy trimmed with lace and at her neckline she had pinned a purple spray of cloth violets containing a sachet. In case of an accident, anyone seeing her dead on the highway would know at once that she was a lady.

She said she thought it was going to be a good day for driving, neither too hot nor too cold, and she cautioned Bailey that the speed limit was fifty-five miles an hour and that the patrolmen hid themselves behind billboards and small clumps of trees and sped out after you before you had a chance to slow down. She pointed out interesting details of the scenery: Stone Mountain; the blue granite that in some places came up to both sides of the highway; the brilliant red clay banks slightly streaked with purple; and the various crops that made rows of green lacework on the ground. The trees were full of silver-white sunlight and the meanest of them sparkled. The children were reading comic magazines and their mother had gone back to sleep.

"Let's go through Georgia fast so we don't have to look at it much," John Wesley said.

15   "If I were a little boy," said the grandmother, "I wouldn't talk about my native state that way. Tennessee has the mountains and Georgia has the hills."

"Tennessee is just a hillbilly dumping ground," John Wesley said, "and Georgia is a lousy state too."

"You said it," June Star said.

"In my time," said the grandmother, folding her thin veined fingers, "children were more respectful of their native states and their parents and everything else. People did right then. Oh look at the cute little pickaninny!" she said and pointed to a Negro child standing in the door of a shack. "Wouldn't that make a picture, now?" she asked and they all turned and looked at the little Negro out of the back window. He waved.

"He didn't have any britches on," June Star said.

20   "He probably didn't have any," the grandmother explained. "Little niggers in the country don't have things like we do. If I could paint, I'd paint that picture," she said.

The children exchanged comic books.

The grandmother offered to hold the baby and the children's mother passed him over the front seat to her. She set him on her knee and bounced him and told him about the things they were passing. She rolled her eyes and screwed up her mouth and stuck her leathery thin face into his smooth bland one. Occasionally he gave her a faraway smile. They passed a large cotton field with five or six graves fenced in the middle of it, like a small island. "Look at the graveyard!" the grandmother said, pointing it out. "That was the old family burying ground. That belonged to the plantation."

"Where's the plantation?" John Wesley asked.

"Gone With the Wind," said the grandmother. "Ha. Ha."

25   When the children finished all the comic books they had brought, they opened the lunch and ate it. The grandmother ate a peanut butter sandwich and an olive and would not let the children throw the box and the paper napkins out the window. When there was nothing else to do they played a game by choosing a cloud and making the other two guess what shape it suggested. John Wesley took one the shape of a cow and June Star guessed a cow and John Wesley said, no, an automobile, and June Star said he didn't play fair, and they began to slap each other over the grandmother.

The grandmother said she would tell them a story if they would keep quiet. When she told a story, she rolled her eyes and waved her head and was very dramatic. She said once when she was a maiden lady she had been courted by a Mr. Edgar Atkins Teagarden from Jasper, Georgia. She said he was a very good-looking man and a gentleman and that he brought her a watermelon every Saturday afternoon with his initials cut in it, E.A.T. Well, one Saturday, she said, Mr. Teagarden brought the watermelon and there was nobody at home and he left it on the front porch and returned in his buggy to Jasper, but she never got the watermelon, she said, because a nigger boy ate it when he saw the initials, E.A.T.! This story tickled John Wesley's funny bone and he giggled and giggled but June Star didn't think it was any good. She said she wouldn't marry a man that just brought her a watermelon on Saturday. The grandmother said she would have done well to marry Mr. Teagarden because he was a gentleman and had bought Coca-Cola stock when it first came out and that he had died only a few years ago, a very wealthy man.

They stopped at The Tower for barbecued sandwiches. The Tower was a part stucco and part wood filling station and dance hall set in a clearing outside of Timothy. A fat man named Red Sammy Butts ran it and there were signs stuck here and there on the building and for miles up and down the

highway saying, TRY RED SAMMY'S FAMOUS BARBEQUE. NONE LIKE FA-
MOUS RED SAMMY'S! RED SAM! THE FAT BOY WITH THE HAPPY LAUGH.
A VETERAN! RED SAMMY'S YOUR MAN!

Red Sammy was lying on the bare ground outside The Tower with his head
under a truck while a gray monkey about a foot high, chained to a small
chinaberry tree, chattered nearby. The monkey sprang back into the tree and
got on the highest limb as soon as he saw the children jump out of the car and
run toward him.

Inside, The Tower was a long dark room with a counter at one end and
tables at the other and dancing space in the middle. They all sat down at a
board table next to the nickelodeon and Red Sam's wife, a tall burnt-brown
woman with hair and eyes lighter than her skin, came and took their order.
The children's mother put a dime in the machine and played "The Tennessee
Waltz," and the grandmother said that tune always made her want to dance.
She asked Bailey if he would like to dance but he only glared at her. He
didn't have a naturally sunny disposition like she did and trips made him
nervous. The grandmother's brown eyes were very bright. She swayed her
head from side to side and pretended she was dancing in her chair. June Star
said play something she could tap to so the children's mother put in another
dime and played a fast number and June Star stepped out onto the dance
floor and did her tap routine.

30   "Ain't she cute?" Red Sam's wife said, leaning over the counter. "Would
you like to come be my little girl?"

"No, I certainly wouldn't," June Star said. "I wouldn't live in a broken-
down place like this for a million bucks!" and she ran back to the table.

"Ain't she cute?" the woman repeated, stretching her mouth politely.

"Aren't you ashamed?" hissed the grandmother.

Red Sam came in and told his wife to quit lounging on the counter and
hurry with these people's order. His khaki trousers reached just to his hip
bones and his stomach hung over them like a sack of meal swaying under his
shirt. He came over and sat down at a table nearby and let out a combination
sigh and yodel. "You can't win," he said. "You can't win," and he wiped his
sweating red face off with a gray handkerchief. "These days you don't know
who to trust," he said. "Ain't that the truth?"

35   "People are certainly not nice like they used to be," said the grandmother.

"Two fellers come in here last week," Red Sammy said, "driving a Chrysler.
It was a old beat-up car but it was a good one and these boys looked all right to
me. Said they worked at the mill and you know I let them fellers charge the gas
they bought? Now why did I do that?"

"Because you're a good man!" the grandmother said at once.

"Yes'm, I suppose so," Red Sam said as if he were struck with the answer.

His wife brought the orders, carrying the five plates all at once without a
tray, two in each hand and one balanced on her arm. "It isn't a soul in this
green world of God's that you can trust," she said. "And I don't count nobody
out of that, not nobody," she repeated, looking at Red Sammy.

40   "Did you read about that criminal, The Misfit, that's escaped?" asked the
grandmother.

"I wouldn't be a bit surprised if he didn't attack this place right here," said the woman. "If he hears about it being here, I wouldn't be none surprised to see him. If he hears it's two cent in the cash register, I wouldn't be a tall surprised if he . . . ."

"That'll do," Red Sam said. "Go bring these people their Co'Colas," and the woman went off to get the rest of the order.

"A good man is hard to find," Red Sammy said. "Everything is getting terrible. I remember the day you could go off and leave your screen door unlatched. Not no more."

He and the grandmother discussed better times. The old lady said that in her opinion Europe was entirely to blame for the way things were now. She said the way Europe acted you would think we were made of money and Red Sam said it was no use talking about it, she was exactly right. The children ran outside into the white sunlight and looked at the monkey in the lacy chinaberry tree. He was busy catching fleas on himself and biting each one carefully between his teeth as if it were a delicacy.

45   They drove off again into the hot afternoon. The grandmother took cat naps and woke up every few minutes with her own snoring. Outside of Toombsboro she woke up and recalled an old plantation that she had visited in this neighborhood once when she was a young lady. She said the house had six white columns across the front and that there was an avenue of oaks leading up to it and two little wooden trellis arbors on either side in front where you sat down with your suitor after a stroll in the garden. She recalled exactly which road to turn off to get to it. She knew that Bailey would not be willing to lose any time looking at an old house, but the more she talked about it, the more she wanted to see it once again and find out if the little twin arbors were still standing. "There was a secret panel in this house," she said craftily, not telling the truth but wishing that she were, "and the story went that all the family silver was hidden in it when Sherman came through but it was never found . . . ."

"Hey!" John Wesley said. "Let's go see it! We'll find it! We'll poke all the woodwork and find it! Who lives there? Where do you turn off at? Hey Pop, can't we turn off there?"

"We never have seen a house with a secret panel!" June Star shrieked. "Let's go to the house with the secret panel! Hey Pop, can't we go see the house with the secret panel!"

"It's not far from here, I know," the grandmother said. "It wouldn't take over twenty minutes."

Bailey was looking straight ahead. His jaw was as rigid as a horseshoe. "No," he said.

50   The children began to yell and scream that they wanted to see the house with the secret panel. John Wesley kicked the back of the front seat and June Star hung over her mother's shoulder and whined desperately into her ear that they never had any fun even on their vacation, that they could never do what THEY wanted to do. The baby began to scream and John Wesley kicked the back of the seat so hard that his father could feel the blows in his kidney.

"All right!" he shouted and drew the car to a stop at the side of the road. "Will you all shut up? Will you all just shut up for one second? If you don't shut up, we won't go anywhere."

"It would be very educational for them," the grandmother murmured.

"All right," Bailey said, "but get this: this is the only time we're going to stop for anything like this. This is the one and only time."

"The dirt road that you have to turn down is about a mile back," the grandmother directed. "I marked it when we passed."

55   "A dirt road," Bailey groaned.

After they had turned around and were headed toward the dirt road, the grandmother recalled other points about the house, the beautiful glass over the front doorway and the candle-lamp in the hall. John Wesley said that the secret panel was probably in the fireplace.

"You can't go inside this house," Bailey said. "You don't know who lives there."

"While you all talk to the people in front, I'll run around behind and get in a window," John Wesley suggested.

"We'll all stay in the car," his mother said.

60   They turned onto the dirt road and the car raced roughly along in a swirl of pink dust. The grandmother recalled the times when there were no paved roads and thirty miles was a day's journey. The dirt road was hilly and there were sudden washes in it and sharp curves on dangerous embankments. All at once they would be on a hill, looking down over the blue tops of trees for miles around, then the next minute, they would be in a red depression with the dust-coated trees looking down on them.

"This place had better turn up in a minute," Bailey said, "or I'm going to turn around."

The road looked as if no one had traveled on it in months.

"It's not much farther," the grandmother said and just as she said it, a horrible thought came to her. The thought was so embarrassing that she turned red in the face and her eyes dilated and her feet jumped up, upsetting her valise in the corner. The instant the valise moved, the newspaper top she had over the basket under it rose with a snarl and Pitty Sing, the cat, sprang onto Bailey's shoulder.

The children were thrown to the floor and their mother, clutching the baby, was thrown out the door onto the ground; the old lady was thrown into the front seat. The car turned over once and landed right side up in a gulch on the side of the road. Bailey remained in the driver's seat with the cat— gray-striped with a broad white face and an orange nose—clinging to his neck like a caterpillar.

65   As soon as the children saw they could move their arms and legs, they scrambled out of the car, shouting, "We've had an ACCIDENT!" The grandmother was curled up under the dashboard, hoping she was injured so that Bailey's wrath would not come down on her all at once. The horrible thought she had had before the accident was that the house she had remembered so vividly was not in Georgia but in Tennessee.

Bailey removed the cat from his neck with both hands and flung it out the window against the side of a pine tree. Then he got out of the car and started looking for the children's mother. She was sitting against the side of the red gutted ditch, holding the screaming baby, but she only had a cut down her face and a broken shoulder. "We've had an ACCIDENT!" the children screamed in a frenzy of delight.

"But nobody's killed," June Star said with disappointment as the grandmother limped out of the car, her hat still pinned to her head but the broken front brim standing up at a jaunty angle and the violet spray hanging off the side. They all sat down in the ditch, except the children, to recover from the shock. They were all shaking.

"Maybe a car will come along," said the children's mother hoarsely.

"I believe I have an injured organ," said the grandmother, pressing her side, but no one answered her. Bailey's teeth were clattering. He had on a yellow sport shirt with bright blue parrots designed on it and his face was as yellow as the shirt. The grandmother decided that she would not mention that the house was in Tennessee.

70 The road was about ten feet above and they could see only the tops of the trees on the other side of it. Behind the ditch they were sitting in there were more woods, tall and dark and deep. In a few minutes they saw a car some distance away on top of a hill, coming slowly as if the occupants were watching them. The grandmother stood up and waved both arms dramatically to attract their attention. The car continued to come on slowly, disappeared around a bend and appeared again, moving even slower, on top of the hill they had gone over. It was a big black battered hearse-like automobile. There were three men in it.

It came to a stop just over them and for some minutes, the driver looked down with a steady expressionless gaze to where they were sitting, and didn't speak. Then he turned his head and muttered something to the other two and they got out. One was a fat boy in black trousers and a red sweat shirt with a silver stallion embossed on the front of it. He moved around on the right side of them and stood staring, his mouth partly open in a kind of loose grin. The other had on khaki pants and a blue striped coat and a gray hat pulled down very low, hiding most of his face. He came around slowly on the left side. Neither spoke.

The driver got out of the car and stood by the side of it, looking down at them. He was an older man than the other two. His hair was just beginning to gray and he wore silver-rimmed spectacles that gave him a scholarly look. He had a long creased-face and didn't have on any shirt or undershirt. He had on blue jeans that were too tight for him and was holding a black hat and a gun. The two boys also had guns.

"We've had an ACCIDENT!" the children screamed.

The grandmother had the peculiar feeling that the bespectacled man was someone she knew. His face was as familiar to her as if she had known him all her life but she could not recall who he was. He moved away from the car and began to come down the embankment, placing his feet carefully so that he wouldn't slip. He had on tan and white shoes and no socks, and his ankles were red and thin. "Good afternoon," he said. "I see you all had you a little spill."

75   "We turned over twice!" said the grandmother.

"Oncet," he corrected. "We seen it happen. Try their car and see will it run, Hiram," he said quietly to the boy with the gray hat.

"What you got that gun for?" John Wesley asked. "Watcha gonna do with that gun?"

"Lady," the man said to the children's mother, "would you mind calling them children to sit down by you? Children make me nervous. I want all you all to sit down right together there where you're at."

"What are you telling US what to do for?" June Star asked.

80   Behind them the line of woods gaped like a dark open mouth. "Come here," said their mother.

"Look here now," Bailey began suddenly, "we're in a predicament! We're in . . . ."

The grandmother shrieked. She scrambled to her feet and stood staring. "You're The Misfit!" she said. "I recognized you at once!"

"Yes'm," the man said, smiling slightly as if he were pleased in spite of himself to be known, "but it would have been better for all of you, lady, if you hadn't of reckernized me."

Bailey turned his head sharply and said something to his mother that shocked even the children. The old lady began to cry and The Misfit reddened.

85   "Lady," he said, "don't you get upset. Sometimes a man says things he don't mean. I don't reckon he meant to talk to you thataway."

"You wouldn't shoot a lady, would you?" the grandmother said and removed a clean handkerchief from her cuff and began to slap at her eyes with it.

The Misfit pointed the toe of his shoe into the ground and made a little hole and then covered it up again. "I would hate to have to," he said.

"Listen," the grandmother almost screamed, "I know you're a good man. You don't look a bit like you have common blood. I know you must come from nice people!"

"Yes mam," he said, "finest people in the world." When he smiled he showed a row of strong white teeth. "God never made a finer woman than my mother and my daddy's heart was pure gold," he said. The boy with the red sweat shirt had come around behind them and was standing with his gun at his hip. The Misfit squatted down on the ground. "Watch them children, Bobby Lee," he said. "You know they make me nervous." He looked at the six of them huddled together in front of him and he seemed to be embarrassed as if he couldn't think of anything to say. "Ain't a cloud in the sky," he remarked, looking up at it. "Don't see no sun but don't see no cloud neither."

90   "Yes, it's a beautiful day," said the grandmother. "Listen," she said, "you shouldn't call yourself The Misfit because I know you're a good man at heart. I can just look at you and tell."

"Hush!" Bailey yelled. "Hush! Everybody shut up and let me handle this!" He was squatting in the position of a runner about to sprint forward but he didn't move.

"I pre-chate that, lady," The Misfit said and drew a little circle in the ground with the butt of his gun.

"It'll take a half a hour to fix this here car," Hiram called, looking over the raised hood of it.

"Well, first you and Bobby Lee get him and that little boy to step over yonder with you," The Misfit said, pointing to Bailey and John Wesley. "The boys want to ask you something," he said to Bailey. "Would you mind stepping back in them woods there with them?"

95   "Listen," Bailey began, "we're in a terrible predicament! Nobody realizes what this is," and his voice cracked. His eyes were as blue and intense as the parrots on his shirt and he remained perfectly still.

The grandmother reached up to adjust her hat brim as if she were going to the woods with him but it came off in her hand. She stood staring at it and after a second she let it fall on the ground. Hiram pulled Bailey up by the arm as if he were assisting an old man. John Wesley caught hold of his father's hand and Bobby Lee followed. They went off toward the woods and just as they reached the dark edge, Bailey turned and supporting himself against a gray naked pine trunk, he shouted, "I'll be back in a minute, Mamma, wait on me!"

"Come back this instant!" his mother shrilled but they all disappeared into the woods.

"Bailey Boy!" the grandmother called in a tragic voice but she found she was looking at The Misfit squatting on the ground in front of her. "I just know you're a good man," she said desperately. "You're not a bit common!"

"Nome, I ain't a good man," The Misfit said after a second as if he had considered her statement carefully, "but I ain't the worst in the world neither. My daddy said I was a different breed of dog from my brothers and sisters. 'You know,' Daddy said, 'it's some that can live their whole life out without asking about it and it's others has to know why it is, and this boy is one of the latters. He's going to be into everything!'" He put on his black hat and looked up suddenly and then away deep into the woods as if he were embarrassed again. "I'm sorry I don't have on a shirt before you ladies," he said, hunching his shoulders slightly. "We buried our clothes that we had on when we escaped and we're just making do until we can get better. We borrowed these from some folks we met," he explained.

100   "That's perfectly all right," the grandmother said. "Maybe Bailey has an extra shirt in his suitcase."

"I'll look and see terrectly," The Misfit said.

"Where are they taking him?" the children's mother screamed.

"Daddy was a card himself," The Misfit said. "You couldn't put anything over on him. He never got in trouble with the Authorities though. Just had the knack of handling them."

"You could be honest too if you'd only try," said the grandmother. "Think how wonderful it would be to settle down and live a comfortable life and not have to think about somebody chasing you all the time."

105   The Misfit kept scratching in the ground with the butt of his gun as if he were thinking about it. "Yes'm, somebody is always after you," he murmured.

The grandmother noticed how thin his shoulder blades were just behind his hat because she was standing up looking down on him. "Do you ever pray?" she asked.

He shook his head. All she saw was the black hat wiggle between his shoulder blades. "Nome," he said.

There was a pistol shot from the woods, followed closely by another. Then silence. The old lady's head jerked around. She could hear the wind move through the tree tops like a long satisfied insuck of breath. "Bailey Boy!" she called.

"I was a gospel singer for a while," The Misfit said. "I been most everything. Been in the arm service, both land and sea, at home and abroad, been twict married, been an undertaker, been with the railroads, plowed Mother Earth, been in a tornado, seen a man burnt alive oncet," and he looked up at the children's mother and the little girl who were sitting close together, their faces white and their eyes glassy; "I even seen a woman flogged," he said.

110   "Pray, pray," the grandmother began, "pray, pray . . ."

"I never was a bad boy that I remember of," The Misfit said in an almost dreamy voice, "but somewheres along the line I done something wrong and got sent to the penitentiary. I was buried alive," and he looked up and held her attention to him by a steady stare.

"That's when you should have started to pray," she said. "What did you do to get sent to the penitentiary that first time?"

"Turn to the right, it was a wall," The Misfit said, looking up again at the cloudless sky. "Turn to the left, it was a wall. Look up it was a ceiling, look down it was a floor. I forgot what I done, lady. I set there and set there, trying to remember what it was I done and I ain't recalled it to this day. Oncet in a while, I would think it was coming to me, but it never come."

"Maybe they put you in by mistake," the old lady said vaguely.

115   "Nome," he said. "It wasn't no mistake. They had the papers on me."

"You must have stolen something," she said.

The Misfit sneered slightly. "Nobody had nothing I wanted," he said. "It was a head-doctor at the penitentiary said what I had done was kill my daddy but I known that for a lie. My daddy died in nineteen ought nineteen of the epidemic flu and I never had a thing to do with it. He was buried in the Mount Hopewell Baptist churchyard and you can go there and see for yourself."

"If you would pray," the old lady said, "Jesus would help you."

"That's right," The Misfit said.

120   "Well then, why don't you pray?" she asked trembling with delight suddenly.

"I don't want no help," he said. "I'm doing all right by myself."

Bobby Lee and Hiram came ambling back from the woods. Bobby Lee was dragging a yellow shirt with bright blue parrots in it.

"Throw me that shirt, Bobby Lee," The Misfit said. The shirt came flying at him and landed on his shoulder and he put it on. The grandmother couldn't name what the shirt reminded her of. "No, lady," The Misfit said while he was buttoning it up, "I found out the crime don't matter. You can do one thing or you can do another, kill a man or take a tire off his car, because sooner or later you're going to forget what it was you done and just be punished for it."

The children's mother had begun to make heaving noises as if she couldn't get her breath. "Lady," he asked, "would you and that little girl like to step off yonder with Bobby Lee and Hiram and join your husband?"

125 "Yes, thank you," the mother said faintly. Her left arm dangled helplessly and she was holding the baby, who had gone to sleep, in the other. "Hep that lady up, Hiram," The Misfit said as she struggled to climb out of the ditch, "and Bobby Lee, you hold onto that little girl's hand."

"I don't want to hold hands with him," June Star said. "He reminds me of a pig."

The fat boy blushed and laughed and caught her by the arm and pulled her off into the woods after Hiram and her mother.

Alone with The Misfit, the grandmother found that she had lost her voice. There was not a cloud in the sky nor any sun. There was nothing around her but woods. She wanted to tell him that he must pray. She opened and closed her mouth several times before anything came out. Finally she found herself saying, "Jesus, Jesus," meaning Jesus will help you, but the way she was saying it, it sounded as if she might be cursing.

"Yes'm," The Misfit said as if he agreed. "Jesus thrown everything off balance. It was the same case with Him as with me except He hadn't committed any crime and they could prove I had committed one because they had the papers on me. Of course," he said, "they never shown me my papers. That's why I sign myself now. I said long ago, you get you a signature and sign everything you do and keep a copy of it. Then you'll know what you done and you can hold up the crime to the punishment and see do they match and in the end you'll have something to prove you ain't been treated right. I call myself The Misfit," he said, "because I can't make what all I done wrong fit what all I gone through in punishment."

130 There was a piercing scream from the woods, followed closely by a pistol report. "Does it seem right to you, lady, that one is punished a heap and another ain't punished at all?"

"Jesus!" the old lady cried. "You got good blood! I know you wouldn't shoot a lady! I know you come from nice people! Pray! Jesus, you ought not to shoot a lady. I'll give you all the money I've got!"

"Lady," The Misfit said, looking beyond her far into the woods, "there never was a body that give the undertaker a tip."

There were two more pistol reports and the grandmother raised her head like a parched old turkey hen crying for water and called, "Bailey Boy, Bailey Boy!" as if her heart would break.

"Jesus was the only One that ever raised the dead," The Misfit continued, "and He shouldn't have done it. He thown everything off balance. If He did what He said, then it's nothing for you to do but thow away everything and follow Him, and if He didn't, then it's nothing for you to do but enjoy the few minutes you got left the best way you can—by killing somebody or burning down his house or doing some other meanness to him. No pleasure but meanness," he said and his voice had become almost a snarl.

135   "Maybe He didn't raise the dead," the old lady mumbled, not knowing what she was saying and feeling so dizzy that she sank down in the ditch with her legs twisted under her.

"I wasn't there so I can't say He didn't," The Misfit said. "I wisht I had of been there," he said, hitting the ground with his fist. "It ain't right I wasn't there because if I had of been there I would of known. Listen lady," he said in a high voice, "if I had of been there I would of known and I wouldn't be like I am now." His voice seemed about to crack and the grandmother's head cleared for an instant. She saw the man's face twisted close to her own as if he were going to cry and she murmured, "Why you're one of my babies. You're one of my own children!" She reached out and touched him on the shoulder. The Misfit sprang back as if a snake had bitten him and shot her three times through the chest. Then he put his gun down on the ground and took off his glasses and began to clean them.

Hiram and Bobby Lee returned from the woods and stood over the ditch, looking down at the grandmother who half sat and half lay in a puddle of blood and with her legs crossed under her like a child's and her face smiling up at the cloudless sky.

Without his glasses, The Misfit's eyes were red-rimmed and pale and defenseless-looking. "Take her off and thow her where you thown the others," he said, picking up the cat that was rubbing itself against his leg.

"She was a talker, wasn't she?" Bobby Lee said, sliding down the ditch with a yodel.

140   "She would of been a good woman," The Misfit said, "if it had been somebody there to shoot her every minute of her life."

"Some fun!" Bobby Lee said.

"Shut up, Bobby Lee," The Misfit said. "It's no real pleasure in life."

Questions on Plot . . .

1. When you first hear of The Misfit, do you expect to meet him? How does this early mention affect the plot?

2. How many different tasks does paragraph 10 perform for this story?

3. What does the conversation with Red Sammy contribute to the plot? Is it part of the complication or the conflict?

4. A lie takes the family onto the dirt road. A lie and an error thus combine to advance the plot. Are these coincidences? Do they arise from character?

5. Notice the *horrible thought* at the start of paragraph 63, completed at the end of paragraph 65. What is accomplished by interrupting this horrible thought with action?

6. How soon do you know that the man we meet is actually The Misfit? Does the lapsed time, before the grandmother names him, further the story's interest?

7. During the conversation between the grandmother and The Misfit, events take place offstage. What is the relationship between the dialogue and the action? What is the effect on the story?

8. Where is the climax of the story?

. . . and Other Elements

9. Who is the deepest thinker among the characters? Does the story emphasize an idea?

10. The protagonist is first identified as the "grandmother," not by a proper name. Does this general name characterize her?

11. Do you ever understand anything in this story before a character does? What is the effect of this device?

12. Remembering the title, look over the grandmother's conversation with Red Sammy and her conversation with The Misfit. Is this story about good and evil? What does it say about good and evil?

13. Do any of the characters change or develop?

14. Who is most morally responsible for the six deaths of this family?

Louise Erdrich

Louise Erdrich (1954–   ) grew up in North Dakota and graduated from Dartmouth College. She did graduate work at Johns Hopkins University. Her first novel was *Love Medicine* (1984), which won a National Book Award. *Beet Queen* followed in 1986 and *Tracks* in 1988. She has also published two books of poems, *Jacklight* in 1984 and *Baptism of Desire* in 1989. (See her poem, "Owls," on page 597.) Her heritage is partly German-American and partly Turtle Mountain Chippewa. She lives in New Hampshire with her husband, the writer Michael Dorris, and their five children. "The Leap" appeared in *Harper's* in 1990.

The Leap   (1990)

My mother is the surviving half of a blindfold trapeze act, not a fact I think about much even now that she is sightless, the result of encroaching and stubborn cataracts. She walks slowly through her house here in New Hampshire, lightly touching her way along walls and running her hands over knickknacks, books, the drift of a grown child's belongings and castoffs. She has never upset an object or as much as brushed a magazine onto the floor. She has never lost her balance or bumped into a closet door left carelessly open.

It has occurred to me that the catlike precision of her movements in old age might be the result of her early training, but she shows so little of the drama or flair one might expect from a performer that I tend to forget the Flying Avalons. She has kept no sequined costume, no photographs, no fliers or posters from that part of her youth. I would, in fact, tend to think that all memory of double somersaults and heart-stopping catches had left her arms and legs were it not for the fact that sometimes, as I sit sewing in the room of the rebuilt house in which I slept as a child, I hear the crackle, catch a whiff of smoke from the stove downstairs, and suddenly the room goes dark, the stitches burn beneath my fingers, and I am sewing with a needle of hot silver, a thread of fire.

I owe her my existence three times. The first was when she saved herself. In the town square a replica tent pole, cracked and splintered, now stands cast in concrete. It commemorates the disaster that put our town smack on the front page of the Boston and New York tabloids. It is from those old newspapers, now historical records, that I get my information. Not from my mother, Anna of the Flying Avalons, nor from any of her in-laws, nor certainly from the other half of her particular act, Harold Avalon, her first husband. In one news account it says, "The day was mildly overcast, but nothing in the air or temperature gave any hint of the sudden force with which the deadly gale would strike."

I have lived in the West, where you can see the weather coming for miles, and it is true that out here we are at something of a disadvantage. When extremes of temperature collide, a hot and cold front, winds generate instantaneously behind a hill and crash upon you without warning. That, I think, was the likely situation on that day in June. People probably commented on the pleasant air, grateful that no hot sun beat upon the striped tent that stretched over the entire center green. They bought their tickets and surrendered them in anticipation. They sat. They ate caramelized popcorn and roasted peanuts. There was time, before the storm, for three acts. The White Arabians of Ali-Khazar rose on their hind legs and waltzed. The Mysterious Bernie folded himself into a painted cracker tin, and the Lady of the Mists made herself appear and disappear in surprising places. As the clouds gathered outside, unnoticed, the ringmaster cracked his whip, shouted his introduction, and pointed to the ceiling of the tent, where the Flying Avalons were perched.

5   They loved to drop gracefully from nowhere, like two sparkling birds, and blow kisses as they threw off their plumed helmets and high-collared capes. They laughed and flirted openly as they beat their way up again on the trapeze bars. In the final vignette of their act, they actually would kiss in midair, pausing, almost hovering as they swooped past one another. On the ground, between bows, Harry Avalon would skip quickly to the front rows and point out the smear of my mother's lipstick, just off the edge of his mouth. They made a romantic pair all right, especially in the blindfold sequence.

That afternoon, as the anticipation increased, as Mr. and Mrs. Avalon tied sparkling strips of cloth onto each other's face and as they puckered their lips in mock kisses, lips destined "never again to meet," as one long breathless article put it, the wind rose, miles off, wrapped itself into a cone, and howled. There came a rumble of electrical energy, drowned out by the sudden roll of drums. One detail not mentioned by the press, perhaps unknown—Anna was pregnant at the time, seven months and hardly showing, her stomach muscles were that strong. It seems incredible that she would work high above the ground when any fall could be so dangerous, but the explanation—I know from watching her go blind—is that my mother lives comfortably in extreme elements. She is one with the constant dark now, just as the air was her home, familiar to her, safe, before the storm that afternoon.

From opposite ends of the tent they waved, blind and smiling, to the crowd below. The ringmaster removed his hat and called for silence, so that the two above could concentrate. They rubbed their hands in chalky powder, then Harry launched himself and swung, once, twice, in huge calibrated beats across space. He hung from his knees and on the third swing stretched wide his arms, held his hands out to receive his pregnant wife as she dove from her shining bar.

It was while the two were in midair, their hands about to meet, that lightning struck the main pole and sizzled down the guy wires, filling the air with a blue radiance that Harry Avalon must certainly have seen through the cloth of his blindfold as the tent buckled and the edifice toppled him forward, the swing continuing and not returning in its sweep, and Harry going down, down into the crowd with his last thought, perhaps, just a prickle of surprise at his empty hands.

My mother once said that I'd be amazed at how many things a person can do within the act of falling. Perhaps, at the time, she was teaching me to dive off a board at the town pool, for I associate the idea with midair somersaults. But I also think she meant that even in that awful doomed second one could think, for she certainly did. When her hands did not meet her husband's, my mother tore her blindfold away. As he swept past her on the wrong side, she could have grasped his ankle, the toe-end of his tights, and gone down clutching him. Instead, she changed direction. Her body twisted toward a heavy wire and she managed to hang on to the braided metal, still hot from the lightning strike. Her palms were burned so terribly that once healed they bore no lines, only the blank scar tissue of a quieter future. She was lowered, gently, to the sawdust ring just underneath the dome of the canvas roof, which did not entirely settle but was held up on one end and jabbed through, torn, and still on fire in places from the giant spark, though rain and men's jackets soon put that out.

10   Three people died, but except for her hands my mother was not seriously harmed until an overeager rescuer broke her arm in extricating her and also, in the process, collapsed a portion of the tent bearing a huge buckle that knocked her unconscious. She was taken to the town hospital, and there she must have hemorrhaged, for they kept her, confined to her bed, a month and a half before her baby was born without life.

Harry Avalon had wanted to be buried in the circus cemetery next to the original Avalon, his uncle, so she sent him back with his brothers. The child, however, is buried around the corner, beyond this house and just down the highway. Sometimes I used to walk there just to sit. She was a girl, but I rarely thought of her as a sister or even as a separate person really. I suppose you could call it the egocentrism of a child, of all young children, but I considered her a less finished version of myself.

When the snow falls, throwing shadows among the stones, I can easily pick hers out from the road, for it is bigger than the others and in the shape of a lamb at rest, its legs curled beneath. The carved lamb looms larger as the years pass, though it is probably only my eyes, the vision shifting, as what is close to me blurs and distances sharpen. In odd moments, I think it is the edge drawing near, the edge of everything, the unseen horizon we do not really speak of in the eastern woods. And it also seems to me, although this is probably an idle fantasy, that the statue is growing more sharply etched, as if, instead of weathering itself into a porous mass, it is hardening on the hillside with each snowfall, perfecting itself.

It was during her confinement in the hospital that my mother met my father. He was called in to look at the set of her arm, which was complicated. He stayed, sitting at her bedside, for he was something of an armchair traveler and had spent his war quietly, at an air force training grounds, where he became a specialist in arms and legs broken during parachute training exercises. Anna Avalon had been to many of the places he longed to visit—Venice, Rome, Mexico, all through France and Spain. She had no family of her own and was taken in by the Avalons, trained to perform from a very young age. They toured Europe before the war, then based themselves in New York. She was illiterate.

It was in the hospital that she finally learned to read and write, as a way of overcoming the boredom and depression of those weeks, and it was my father who insisted on teaching her. In return for stories of her adventures, he graded her first exercises. He bought her her first book, and over her bold letters, which the pale guides of the penmanship pads could not contain, they fell in love.

15   I wonder if my father calculated the exchange he offered: one form of flight for another. For after that, and for as long as I can remember, my mother has never been without a book. Until now, that is, and it remains the greatest difficulty of her blindness. Since my father's recent death, there is no one to read to her, which is why I returned, in fact, from my failed life where the land is flat. I came home to read to my mother, to read out loud, to read long into the dark if I must, to read all night.

Once my father and mother married, they moved onto the old farm he had inherited but didn't care much for. Though he'd been thinking of moving to a larger city, he settled down and broadened his practice in this valley. It still seems odd to me, when they could have gone anywhere else, that they chose to stay in the town where the disaster had occurred, and which my father in the first place had found so constricting. It was my mother who insisted upon it, after her child did not survive. And then, too, she loved the sagging farmhouse with its scrap of what was left of a vast acreage of woods and hidden hay fields that stretched to the game park.

I owe my existence, the second time then, to the two of them and the hospital that brought them together. That is the debt we take for granted since none of us asks for life. It is only once we have it that we hang on so dearly.

I was seven the year the house caught fire, probably from standing ash. It can rekindle, and my father, forgetful around the house and perpetually exhausted from night hours on call, often emptied what he thought were ashes from cold stoves into wooden or cardboard containers. The fire could have started from a flaming box, or perhaps a buildup of creosote inside the chimney was the culprit. It started right around the stove, and the heart of the house was gutted. The baby-sitter, fallen asleep in my father's den on the first floor, woke to find the stairway to my upstairs room cut off by flames. She used the phone, then ran outside to stand beneath my window.

When my parents arrived, the town volunteers had drawn water from the fire pond and were spraying the outside of the house, preparing to go inside after me, not knowing at the time that there was only one staircase and that it was lost. On the other side of the house, the superannuated extension ladder broke in half. Perhaps the clatter of it falling against the walls woke me, for I'd been asleep up to that point.

20 As soon as I awakened, in the small room that I now use for sewing, I smelled the smoke. I followed things by the letter then, was good at memorizing instructions, and so I did exactly what was taught in the second-grade home fire drill. I got up, I touched the back of my door before opening it. Finding it hot, I left it closed and stuffed my rolled-up rug beneath the crack. I did not hide under my bed or crawl into my closet. I put on my flannel robe, and then I sat down to wait.

Outside, my mother stood below my dark window and saw clearly that there was no rescue. Flames had pierced one side wall, and the glare of the fire lighted the massive limbs and trunk of the vigorous old elm that had probably been planted the year the house was built, a hundred years ago at least. No leaf touched the wall, and just one thin branch scraped the roof. From below, it looked as though even a squirrel would have had trouble jumping from the tree onto the house, for the breadth of that small branch was no bigger than my mother's wrist.

Standing there, beside Father, who was preparing to rush back around to the front of the house, my mother asked him to unzip her dress. When he wouldn't be bothered, she made him understand. He couldn't make his hands work, so she finally tore it off and stood there in her pearls and stockings. She directed one of the men to lean the broken half of the extension ladder up against the trunk of the tree. In surprise, he complied. She ascended. She vanished. Then she could be seen among the leafless branches of late November as she made her way up and, along her stomach, inched the length of a bough that curved above the branch that brushed the roof.

Once there, swaying, she stood and balanced. There were plenty of people in the crowd and many who still remember, or think they do, my mother's leap through the ice-dark air toward that thinnest extension, and how she broke the branch falling so that it cracked in her hands, cracked louder than the flames as she vaulted with it toward the edge of the roof, and how it hurtled down end over end without her, and their eyes went up, again, to see where she had flown.

I didn't see her leap through air, only heard the sudden thump and looked out my window. She was hanging by the backs of her heels from the new gutter we had put in that year, and she was smiling. I was not surprised to see her, she was so matter-of-fact. She tapped on the window. I remember how she did it, too. It was the friendliest tap, a bit tentative, as if she was afraid she had arrived too early at a friend's house. Then she gestured at the latch, and when I opened the window she told me to raise it wider and prop it up with the stick so it wouldn't crush her fingers. She swung down, caught the ledge, and crawled through the opening. Once she was in my room, I realized she had on only underclothing, a bra of the heavy stitched cotton women used to wear and step-in, lace-trimmed drawers. I remember feeling light-headed, of course, terribly relieved, and then embarrassed for her to be seen by the crowd undressed.

25   I was still embarrassed as we flew out the window, toward earth, me in her lap, her toes pointed as we skimmed toward the painted target of the fire fighter's net.

I know that she's right. I knew it even then. As you fall there is time to think. Curled as I was, against her stomach, I was not startled by the cries of the crowd or the looming faces. The wind roared and beat its hot breath at our back, the flames whistled. I slowly wondered what would happen if we missed the circle or bounced out of it. Then I wrapped my hands around my mother's hands. I felt the brush of her lips and heard the beat of her heart in my ears, loud as thunder, long as the roll of drums.

Questions on Plot . . .

1. How much exposition does the first sentence give us? Is it awkwardly informative? How can an author use tone to validate the obviousness of an exposition?

2. The last sentence of the second paragraph is long and—when we first read it—mysterious. Why does the author mystify us at this point? Does this mystification accomplish anything for the plot of the story?

3. The first sentence of the third paragraph is short. What does it do for the plot?

4. Is Anna's illiteracy a random detail, probable enough but accidental, or is it woven into the relationships that make the plot of the story? How?

5. When the fire arrives in the last third of the story, has it been expected? Find two earlier items that make us ready for the fire.

. . . and Other Elements

6. Can you find "a random detail" in this story—some bit of information that is irrelevant to plot or character? Bring examples to class for discussion.

7. How does the last image of the story relate to its beginning?

8. One book reviewer has called Louise Erdrich "The most subtle, yet the most powerful of feminist novelists." Could you call "The Leap" a feminist story?

9. The book reviewer in question 8 also claims that Erdrich's work is "dense with competent females and the males who serve them." Comment.

CHAPTER FIVE

Character

A character is an imagined person in a story, whom we know from the words we read on the page.

Plot shows character; character causes plot. In most stories, you cannot speak of the one without evoking the other. In "A Good Man Is Hard to Find," the grandmother's hiding the cat is essential to the plot, yet if her character did not make the act probable, the plot of the story would be flawed. In some stories, characterization is minimal and plot is everything; "action-packed," the advertisers call them, and for characterization we may learn little more than that the cowboy is lean-jawed and the heiress raven-haired. Such descriptions make for stereotypes, thoroughly predictable characters.

Characterization

Fiction writers have many ways to present character, beginning with the names they bestow on characters. When Henry James shows us *May* Bartram in love with John *Marcher,* we may fear that his frosts will chill her flowers. Charles Dickens is a resourceful namer: Mr. Gradgrind, Uriah Heep. But characterization requires more than a name. Let us start with a broad division. If in conversation with friends we try to describe an absent person whom they have never met, we can describe the person directly: the absent friend is five feet ten inches tall, black-haired, stammers, is Irish in ancestry and interested in politics, goes to law school, is loyal, decent, and brave. This method is exposition of character. On the other hand, we may prefer to reveal the person indirectly, by showing action. We then have the choice of *telling* what he is, or of *showing* what he is like. Thus, we can characterize our old friend by telling about a day we went to the roller skating rink to recruit donors for the blood drive, and all of a sudden . . . . This is characterization by action or anecdote.

A slogan of the creative writing class: "Don't tell 'em, show 'em." Writers characterize mostly by *showing* a character in action, but they do both. In "A Rose for Emily," for instance, Miss Emily is characterized first in a summary, a *telling,* and then by a series of anecdotes, a *showing.* This organization— brief telling followed by considerable showing—is common in fiction.

56

Indirect presentation takes various forms. Describing the character's house or clothes or furniture with the objectivity of a camera provides indirect characterization. When some characters talk about others, they help to characterize them—not only by what they say, at its face value, but by what they don't say. For instance, if one character is known to be a sneak and a liar, and praises another character, we are apt to take that praise ironically. We know a character best from what that character *does*. Thus, Miss Emily's independence, eccentricity, and doughtiness show in the way she deals with the aldermen and the pharmacist.

In reading most fiction, we make three related demands on the author's characterization. First, we demand that the characters be *consistent*. We do not demand that they be unchanging; but, if characters change, they must change for a reason. Our second demand is that we must understand that the characters' change is *motivated;* it is usual in the psychology of fiction that characters act from known motives. This psychology serves to make characters *plausible* to us—which is our third requirement: that they be credible, realistic, probable.

These doctrines of realistic characterization apply to most fiction, not all. Stories that differ—with unmotivated acts and implausible or unrealistic characters—often declare themselves deliberate exceptions from the norms of literature.

Characters Round or Flat, Dynamic or Static

The English novelist E. M. Forster, in his book *Aspects of the Novel* (1927), distinguished between "round" characters and "flat" ones. We make much the same metaphor by calling characters "three-dimensional" or "two-dimensional." The round or three-dimensional character in fiction seems more real and more whole than the flat character, the character abstracted into two dimensions. The round character is complex, the flat character simple; the round character can surprise us, remaining unpredictable but probable; the flat character remains predictable, summed up in a few traits. In a novel, we regularly find several round characters and a backdrop of flat ones. In a story, we often find one or two round characters among flat ones. It takes time to develop a round character. In second-rate fiction (and drama, film, and television), all characters are flat, and no one has the complexity Forster describes as round.

The absence of round characters, or the dominance of flat ones, is, therefore, often, but not always, a clear indication of fiction's failure or inferiority. Flat characters may be exactly what a story requires. Some stories concentrate so much on matters *outside* characterization that flat characters do the job. In Thurber's "The Catbird Seat," the characters are two-dimensional, while the story emphasizes ideas and plot above all; the characterization is adequate to the story's purposes. Some novelists (Dickens, for example) show genius in constructing flat characters, dominated by a few traits, with such a richness that we remember them forever.

Flat or two-dimensional characters may be stereotypes. Much television drama relies on stereotypes: the tough, street-wise detective and his sidekick, the idealistic rookie. Everyone recognizes stereotypes and sums them up in clichés: the whore with the heart of gold; the dumb jock; the pompous bank president; the hillbilly. But not all flat characters are stereotypes. In "A Good Man Is Hard to Find," both the grandmother and The Misfit are round; once met, we would know them anywhere. The other characters—The Misfit's henchmen, the father and mother—are flat without dwindling into stereotype. Unlike mere clichés, they are recognizably individual, even though they lack the detail and depth of the round characters.

Usually a round character is dynamic or changing. It is common but not invariable that a short story recount a crisis in a protagonist's life and a subsequent change. Some important event takes place, something is decided or understood: a life alters. If a character's life alters—and we find the change convincing—that character must almost certainly be round. Usually, such change occurs within the character, but it may occur within someone observing the action, and we then grow to understand a character as more complex than we had believed. (Consider "A Rose for Emily.") Other characters remain static or unchanging. Three stories strong in the portrayal of character follow.

James Joyce

James Joyce (1882–1941) was born in Dublin and spent most of his adult life in Paris and Zürich. His long, innovative novel *Ulysses* (1922) is widely considered a major work of our literature. Earlier, Joyce wrote an autobiographical novel, *A Portrait of the Artist as a Young Man* (1916), as well as poems and a play. "Counterparts" comes from *Dubliners,* a collection of short stories that, taken together, makes a portrait of the Dubliner in different guises: male and female, young and old, married and single. Farrington is the Dubliner as an adult, married man.

Counterparts   (1905)

The bell rang furiously and, when Miss Parker went to the tube, a furious voice called out in a piercing North of Ireland accent:

—Send Farrington here!

Miss Parker returned to her machine, saying to a man who was writing at a desk:

—Mr Alleyne wants you upstairs.

5   The man muttered *Blast him!* under his breath and pushed back his chair to stand up. When he stood up he was tall and of great bulk. He had a hanging face, dark wine-coloured, with fair eyebrows and moustache: his eyes bulged forward slightly and the whites of them were dirty. He lifted up the counter and, passing by the clients, went out of the office with a heavy step.

He went heavily upstairs until he came to the second landing, where a door bore a brass plate with the inscription *Mr Alleyne.* Here he halted, puffing with labour and vexation, and knocked. The shrill voice cried:

—Come in!

The man entered Mr Alleyne's room. Simultaneously Mr Alleyne, a little man wearing gold-rimmed glasses on a clean-shaven face, shot his head up over a pile of documents. The head itself was so pink and hairless that it seemed like a large egg reposing on the papers. Mr Alleyne did not lose a moment:

—Farrington? What is the meaning of this? Why have I always to complain of you? May I ask you why you haven't made a copy of that contract between Bodley and Kirwan? I told you it must be ready by four o'clock.

10 —But Mr Shelley said, sir—

—*Mr Shelley said, sir.* . . . Kindly attend to what I say and not to what *Mr Shelley says, sir.* You have always some excuse or another for shirking work. Let me tell you that if the contract is not copied before this evening I'll lay the matter before Mr Crosbie. . . . Do you hear me now?

—Yes, sir.

—Do you hear me now? . . . Ay and another little matter! I might as well be talking to the wall as talking to you. Understand once for all that you get a half an hour for your lunch and not an hour and a half. How many courses do you want, I'd like to know. . . . Do you mind me, now?

—Yes, sir.

15 Mr Alleyne bent his head again upon his pile of papers. The man stared fixedly at the polished skull which directed the affairs of Crosbie & Alleyne, gauging its fragility. A spasm of rage gripped his throat for a few moments and then passed, leaving after it a sharp sensation of thirst. The man recognized the sensation and felt that he must have a good night's drinking. The middle of the month was passed and, if he could get the copy done in time, Mr Alleyne might give him an order on the cashier. He stood still, gazing fixedly at the head upon the pile of papers. Suddenly Mr Alleyne began to upset all the papers, searching for something. Then, as if he had been unaware of the man's presence till that moment, he shot up his head again, saying:

—Eh? Are you going to stand there all day? Upon my word, Farrington, you take things easy!

—I was waiting to see . . .

—Very good, you needn't wait to see. Go downstairs and do your work.

The man walked heavily towards the door and, as he went out of the room, he heard Mr Alleyne cry after him that if the contract was not copied by evening Mr Crosbie would hear of the matter.

20 He returned to his desk in the lower office and counted the sheets which remained to be copied. He took up his pen and dipped it in the ink but he continued to stare stupidly at the last words he had written: *In no case shall the said Bernard Bodley be* . . . The evening was falling and in a few minutes they would be lighting the gas: then he could write. He felt that he must slake the thirst in his throat. He stood up from his desk and, lifting the

counter as before, passed out of the office. As he was passing out the chief clerk looked at him inquiringly.

—It's all right, Mr Shelley, said the man, pointing with his finger to indicate the objective of his journey.

The chief clerk glanced at the hat-rack but, seeing the row complete, offered no remark. As soon as he was on the landing the man pulled a shepherd's plaid cap out of his pocket, put it on his head and ran quickly down the rickety stairs. From the street door he walked on furtively on the inner side of the path towards the corner and all at once dived into a doorway. He was now safe in the dark snug of O'Neill's shop, and, filling up the little window that looked into the bar with his inflamed face, the colour of dark wine or dark meat, he called out:

—Here, Pat, give us a g.p.,[1] like a good fellow.

The curate[2] brought him a glass of plain porter. The man drank it at a gulp and asked for a caraway seed. He put his penny on the counter and, leaving the curate to grope for it in the gloom, retreated out of the snug as furtively as he had entered it.

25   Darkness, accompanied by a thick fog, was gaining upon the dusk of February and the lamps in Eustace Street had been lit. The man went up by the houses until he reached the door of the office, wondering whether he could finish his copy in time. On the stairs a moist pungent odour of perfumes saluted his nose: evidently Miss Delacour had come while he was out in O'Neill's. He crammed his cap back again into his pocket and re-entered the office, assuming an air of absentmindedness.

—Mr Alleyne has been calling for you, said the chief clerk severely. Where were you?

The man glanced at the two clients who were standing at the counter as if to intimate that their presence prevented him from answering. As the clients were both male the chief clerk allowed himself a laugh.

—I know that game, he said. Five times in one day is a little bit. . . . Well, you better look sharp and get a copy of our correspondence in the Delacour case for Mr Alleyne.

This address in the presence of the public, his run upstairs and the porter he had gulped down so hastily confused the man and, as he sat down at his desk to get what was required, he realized how hopeless was the task of finishing his copy of the contract before half past five. The dark damp night was coming and he longed to spend it in the bars, drinking with his friends amid the glare of gas and the clatter of glasses. He got out the Delacour correspondence and passed out of the office. He hoped Mr Alleyne would not discover that the last two letters were missing.

30   The moist pungent perfume lay all the way to Mr Alleyne's room. Miss Delacour was a middle-aged woman of Jewish appearance. Mr Alleyne was said to be sweet on her or on her money. She came to the office often and stayed a long time when she came. She was sitting beside his desk now in an

---

[1] Glass of porter (dark beer, or light stout)   [2] Bartender; ironic reference to an assistant parish priest

aroma of perfumes, smoothing the handle of her umbrella and nodding the great black feather in her hat. Mr Alleyne had swivelled his chair round to face her and thrown his right foot jauntily upon his left knee. The man put the correspondence on the desk and bowed respectfully but neither Mr Alleyne nor Miss Delacour took any notice of his bow. Mr Alleyne tapped a finger on the correspondence and then flicked it towards him as if to say: *That's all right: you can go.*

The man returned to the lower office and sat down again at his desk. He stared intently at the incomplete phrase: *In no case shall the said Bernard Bodley be* . . . and thought how strange it was that the last three words began with the same letter. The chief clerk began to hurry Miss Parker, saying she would never have the letters typed in time for post. The man listened to the clicking of the machine for a few minutes and then set to work to finish his copy. But his head was not clear and his mind wandered away to the glare and rattle of the public-house. It was a night for hot punches. He struggled on with his copy, but when the clock struck five he had still fourteen pages to write. Blast it! He couldn't finish it in time. He longed to execrate aloud, to bring his fist down on something violently. He was so enraged that he wrote *Bernard Bernard* instead of *Bernard Bodley* and had to begin again on a clean sheet.

He felt strong enough to clear out the whole office single-handed. His body ached to do something, to rush out and revel in violence. All the indignities of his life enraged him. . . . Could he ask the cashier privately for an advance? No, the cashier was no good, no damn good: he wouldn't give an advance. . . . He knew where he would meet the boys: Leonard and O'Halloran and Nosey Flynn. The barometer of his emotional nature was set for a spell of riot.

His imagination had so abstracted him that his name was called twice before he answered. Mr Alleyne and Miss Delacour were standing outside the counter and all the clerks had turned round in anticipation of something. The man got up from his desk. Mr Alleyne began a tirade of abuse, saying that two letters were missing. The man answered that he knew nothing about them, that he had made a faithful copy. The tirade continued: it was so bitter and violent that the man could hardly restrain his fist from descending upon the head of the manikin before him.

—I know nothing about any other two letters, he said stupidly.

35 —*You—know—nothing.* Of course you know nothing, said Mr Alleyne. Tell me, he added, glancing first for approval to the lady beside him, do you take me for a fool? Do you think me an utter fool?

The man glanced from the lady's face to the little egg-shaped head and back again; and, almost before he was aware of it, his tongue had found a felicitous moment:

—I don't think, sir, he said, that that's a fair question to put to me.

There was a pause in the very breathing of the clerks. Everyone was astounded (the author of the witticism no less than his neighbours) and Miss Delacour, who was a stout amiable person, began to smile broadly. Mr Alleyne flushed to the hue of a wild rose and his mouth twitched with a dwarf's passion. He shook his fist in the man's face till it seemed to vibrate like the knob of some electric machine:

—You impertinent ruffian! You impertinent ruffian! I'll make short work of you! Wait till you see! You'll apologize to me for your impertinence or you'll quit the office instanter! You'll quit this, I'm telling you, or you'll apologize to me!

40   He stood in a doorway opposite the office watching to see if the cashier would come out alone. All the clerks passed out and finally the cashier came out with the chief clerk. It was no use trying to say a word to him when he was with the chief clerk. The man felt that his position was bad enough. He had been obliged to offer an abject apology to Mr Alleyne for his impertinence but he knew what a hornet's nest the office would be for him. He could remember the way in which Mr Alleyne had hounded little Peake out of the office in order to make room for his own nephew. He felt savage and thirsty and revengeful, annoyed with himself and with everyone else. Mr Alleyne would never give him an hour's rest; his life would be a hell to him. He had made a proper fool of himself this time. Could he not keep his tongue in his cheek? But they had never pulled together from the first, he and Mr Alleyne, ever since the day Mr Alleyne had overheard him mimicking his North of Ireland accent to amuse Higgins and Miss Parker: that had been the beginning of it. He might have tried Higgins for the money, but sure Higgins never had anything for himself. A man with two establishments to keep up, of course he couldn't. . . .

He felt his great body again aching for the comfort of the public-house. The fog had begun to chill him and he wondered could he touch Pat in O'Neill's. He could not touch him for more than a bob—and a bob was no use. Yet he must get money somewhere or other: he had spent his last penny for the g.p. and soon it would be too late for getting money anywhere. Suddenly, as he was fingering his watch-chain, he thought of Terry Kelly's pawn-office in Fleet Street. That was the dart! Why didn't he think of it sooner?

He went through the narrow alley of Temple Bar quickly, muttering to himself that they could all go to hell because he was going to have a good night of it. The clerk in Terry Kelly's said *A crown!* but the consignor held out for six shillings; and in the end the six shillings was allowed him literally. He came out of the pawn-office joyfully, making a little cylinder of the coins between his thumb and fingers. In Westmoreland Street the footpaths were crowded with young men and women returning from business and ragged urchins ran here and there yelling out the names of the evening editions. The man passed through the crowd, looking on the spectacle generally with proud satisfaction and staring masterfully at the office-girls. His head was full of the noises of tram-gongs and swishing trolleys and his nose already sniffed the curling fumes of punch. As he walked on he preconsidered the terms in which he would narrate the incident to the boys:

—So, I just looked at him—coolly, you know, and looked at her. Then I looked back at him again—taking my time, you know. *I don't think that that's a fair question to put to me,* says I.

Nosey Flynn was sitting up in his usual corner of Davy Bryne's and, when he heard the story, he stood Farrington a half-one, saying it was as smart a thing as ever he heard. Farrington stood a drink in his turn. After a while O'Halloran and Paddy Leonard came in and the story was repeated to them. O'Halloran stood tailors of malt, hot, all round and told the story of the retort he had made to the chief clerk when he was in Callan's of Fownes's Street; but, as the retort was after the manner of the liberal shepherds in the eclogues,[3] he had to admit that it was not so clever as Farrington's retort. At this Farrington told the boys to polish off that and have another.

45   Just as they were naming their poisons who should come in but Higgins! Of course he had to join in with the others. The men asked him to give his version of it, and he did so with great vivacity for the sight of five small hot whiskies was very exhilarating. Everyone roared laughing when he showed the way in which Mr Alleyne shook his fist in Farrington's face. Then he imitated Farrington, saying, *And here was my nabs, as cool as you please,* while Farrington looked at the company out of his heavy dirty eyes, smiling and at times drawing forth stray drops of liquor from his moustache with the aid of his lower lip.

When that round was over there was a pause. O'Halloran had money but neither of the other two seemed to have any; so the whole party left the shop somewhat regretfully. At the corner of Duke Street Higgins and Nosey Flynn bevelled off to the left while the other three turned back towards the city. Rain was drizzling down on the cold streets and, when they reached the Ballast Office, Farrington suggested the Scotch House. The bar was full of men and loud with the noise of tongues and glasses. The three men pushed past the whining match-sellers at the door and formed a little party at the corner of the counter. They began to exchange stories. Leonard introduced them to a young fellow named Weathers who was performing at the Tivoli as an acrobat and knock-about *artiste.* Farrington stood a drink all round. Weathers said he would take a small Irish[4] and Apollinaris.[5] Farrington, who had definite notions of what was what, asked the boys would they have an Apollinaris too; but the boys told Tim to make theirs hot. The talk became theatrical. O'Halloran stood a round and then Farrington stood another round, Weathers protesting that the hospitality was too Irish. He promised to get them in behind the scenes and introduce them to some nice girls. O'Halloran said that he and Leonard would go but that Farrington wouldn't go because he was a married man; and Farrington's heavy dirty eyes leered at the company in token that he understood he was being chaffed. Weathers made them all have just one little tincture at his expense and promised to meet them later on at Mulligan's in Poolbeg Street.

When the Scotch House closed they went round to Mulligan's. They went into the parlour at the back and O'Halloran ordered small hot specials all round. They were all beginning to feel mellow. Farrington was just standing another round when Weathers came back. Much to Farrington's relief he

---

[3] In the Roman poet Vergil's *Eclogues,* ten short poems idealizing rural life, the shepherds are gentle and hospitable.   [4] Irish whiskey   [5] A German mineral water

drank a glass of bitter[6] this time. Funds were running low but they had enough to keep them going. Presently two young women with big hats and a young man in a check suit came in and sat at a table close by. Weathers saluted them and told the company that they were out of the Tivoli. Farrington's eyes wandered at every moment in the direction of one of the young women. There was something striking in her appearance. An immense scarf of peacock-blue muslin was wound round her hat and knotted in a great bow under her chin; and she wore bright yellow gloves, reaching to the elbow. Farrington gazed admiringly at the plump arm which she moved very often and with much grace; and when, after a little time, she answered his gaze he admired still more her large dark brown eyes. The oblique staring expression in them fascinated him. She glanced at him once or twice and, when the party was leaving the room, she brushed against his chair and said *O, pardon!* in a London accent. He watched her leave the room in the hope that she would look back at him, but he was disappointed. He cursed his want of money and cursed all the rounds he had stood, particularly all the whiskies and Apollinaris which he had stood to Weathers. If there was one thing that he hated it was a sponge. He was so angry that he lost count of the conversation of his friends.

When Paddy Leonard called him he found that they were talking about feats of strength. Weathers was showing his biceps muscle to the company and boasting so much that the other two had called on Farrington to uphold the national honour. Farrington pulled up his sleeve accordingly and showed his biceps muscle to the company. The two arms were examined and compared and finally it was agreed to have a trial of strength. The table was cleared and the two men rested their elbows on it, clasping hands. When Paddy Leonard said *Go!* each was to try to bring down the other's hand on to the table. Farrington looked very serious and determined.

The trial began. After about thirty seconds, Weathers brought his opponent's hand slowly down on to the table. Farrington's dark wine-coloured face flushed darker still with anger and humiliation at having been defeated by such a stripling.

50   —You're not to put the weight of your body behind it. Play fair, he said.

—Who's not playing fair? said the other.

—Come on again. The two best out of three.

The trial began again. The veins stood out on Farrington's forehead, and the pallor of Weathers' complexion changed to peony. Their hands and arms trembled under the stress. After a long struggle Weathers again brought his opponent's hand slowly on to the table. There was a murmur of applause from the spectators. The curate, who was standing beside the table, nodded his red head toward the victor and said with loutish familiarity:

—Ah! that's the knack!

55   —What the hell do you know about it? said Farrington fiercely, turning on the man. What do you put in your gab for?

---

[6] Ale

—Sh, sh! said O'Halloran, observing the violent expression of Farrington's face. Pony up, boys. We'll have just one little smahan[7] more and then we'll be off.

A very sullen-faced man stood at the corner of O'Connell Bridge waiting for the little Sandymount tram to take him home. He was full of smouldering anger and revengefulness. He felt humiliated and discontented; he did not even feel drunk; and he had only twopence in his pocket. He cursed everything. He had done for himself in the office, pawned his watch, spent all his money; and he had not even got drunk. He began to feel thirsty again and he longed to be back again in the hot reeking public-house. He had lost his reputation as a strong man, having been defeated twice by a mere boy. His heart swelled with fury and, when he thought of the woman in the big hat who had brushed against him and said *Pardon!* his fury nearly choked him.

His tram let him down at Shelbourne Road and he steered his great body along in the shadow of the wall of the barracks. He loathed returning to his home. When he went in by the side-door he found the kitchen empty and the kitchen fire nearly out. He bawled upstairs:

—Ada! Ada!

60   His wife was a little sharp-faced woman who bullied her husband when he was sober and was bullied by him when he was drunk. They had five children. A little boy came running down the stairs.

—Who is that? said the man, peering through the darkness.

—Me, pa.

—Who are you? Charlie?

—No, pa. Tom.

65   —Where's your mother?

—She's out at the chapel.

—That's right. . . . Did she think of leaving any dinner for me?

—Yes, pa. I—

—Light the lamp. What do you mean by having the place in darkness? Are the other children in bed?

70   The man sat down heavily on one of the chairs while the little boy lit the lamp. He began to mimic his son's flat accent, saying half to himself: *At the chapel. At the chapel, if you please!* When the lamp was lit he banged his fist on the table and shouted:

—What's for my dinner?

—I'm going . . . to cook it, pa, said the little boy.

The man jumped up furiously and pointed to the fire.

—On that fire! You let the fire out! By God, I'll teach you to do that again!

75   He took a step to the door and seized the walking-stick which was standing behind it.

—I'll teach you to let the fire out! he said, rolling up his sleeve in order to give his arm free play.

[7] An Irish dialect word for *taste;* a smidgeon

The little boy cried *O, pa!* and ran whimpering round the table, but the man followed him and caught him by the coat. The little boy looked about him wildly but, seeing no way of escape, fell upon his knees.

—Now, you'll let the fire out the next time! said the man, striking at him viciously with the stick. Take that, you little whelp!

The boy uttered a squeal of pain as the stick cut his thigh. He clasped his hands together in the air and his voice shook with fright.

80   —O, pa! he cried. Don't beat me, pa! And I'll . . . I'll say a *Hail Mary* for you. . . . I'll say a *Hail Mary* for you, pa, if you don't beat me. . . . I'll say a *Hail Mary.* . . .

Questions on Character . . .

1. Go through this story, noting Joyce's different methods of conveying Farrington's character. List the methods of characterization you find.

2. Point of view affects characterization. From whose point of view is this story told? When *furiously* and *furious* both turn up in the first paragraph, is this the author's contribution? Or does the character contribute the idea of furiousness?

3. In paragraph 3, how do we know who *a man* is? How does this introduction help the characterization?

4. When do we find the first physical description of Farrington? How does it help characterize him? Is *a heavy step* description of gesture or action? Does it characterize Farrington?

5. In paragraph 8, does the last sentence characterize Mr Alleyne? Farrington? Both? How could it characterize both?

6. Is Farrington a dynamic character? Is he static? Does anything change in the story? Will Farrington be different tomorrow? Do you know more about his character than he does? How can this be so? How do we get this impression?

7. Does Miss Delacour's presence help establish or develop Farrington's character?

8. Farrington makes a witticism. Is it consistent with his character? Contrast Farrington's different reactions to his own witticism. Does this variety indicate a round character?

9. In paragraph 45, is the first sentence the author's way of expressing himself? Who says it? What does it do?

10. How do we begin to understand Weathers's character? Do we observe it objectively? Through Farrington's eyes? Both?

11. Later in the story, we learn a little about Farrington's wife. How much? Does this information contribute to Farrington's characterization?

12. Is Farrington's last action the final touch in his characterization? Is it a climax to the story? Does it resemble other scenes in the story?

13. On the basis of what you know, construct these scenes:

    a. Ada returns and finds Farrington beating her child.

    b. Farrington has breakfast with Ada and the children.

    c. Farrington is summoned to Mr. Alleyne's office the next morning.

. . . and Other Elements

14. What does the title mean?

15. In Farrington's mind, two places are in conflict. Could you describe this story as a conflict of settings?

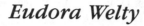

Eudora Welty

Eudora Welty (1909–   ) was born and lives in Jackson, Mississippi, having lived elsewhere only briefly. Her novels include *The Robber Bridegroom* (1942), *Delta Wedding* (1946), *The Ponder Heart* (1954), and *Losing Battles* (1970). This story comes from her first book, a collection of stories called *A Curtain of Green* (1941), which was followed by *The Wide Net* (1943), *The Golden Apple* (1949), and *The Bride of the Innisfallen* (1954). Miss Welty has also published a collection of essays called *The Eye of the Story* (1978), in which she comments on "A Worn Path."

A Worn Path   (1940)

It was December—a bright frozen day in the early morning. Far out in the country there was an old Negro woman with her head tied in a red rag, coming along a path through the pinewoods. Her name was Phoenix Jackson. She was very old and small and she walked slowly in the dark pine shadows, moving a little from side to side in her steps, with the balanced heaviness and lightness of a pendulum in a grandfather clock. She carried a thin, small cane made from an umbrella, and with this she kept tapping the frozen earth in front of her. This made a grave and persistent noise in the still air, that seemed meditative like the chirping of a solitary little bird.

She wore a dark striped dress reaching down to her shoe tops, and an equally long apron of bleached sugar sacks, with a full pocket: all neat and tidy, but every time she took a step she might have fallen over her shoelaces, which dragged from her unlaced shoes. She looked straight ahead. Her eyes were blue with age. Her skin had a pattern all its own of numberless branching wrinkles and as though a whole little tree stood in the middle of her forehead, but a golden color ran underneath, and the two knobs of her cheeks were illumined by a yellow burning under the dark. Under the red rag her hair came down on her neck in the frailest of ringlets, still black, and with an odor like copper.

Now and then there was a quivering in the thicket. Old Phoenix said, "Out of my way, all you foxes, owls, beetles, jack rabbits, coons and wild animals! . . . Keep out from under these feet, little bob-whites. . . . Keep the big wild hogs out of my path. Don't let none of those come running my direction. I got a long way." Under her small black-freckled hand her cane, limber as a buggy whip, would switch at the brush as if to rouse up any hiding things.

On she went. The woods were deep and still. The sun made the pine needles almost too bright to look at, up where the wind rocked. The cones dropped as light as feathers. Down in the hollow was the mourning dove—it was not too late for him.

5   The path ran up a hill. "Seem like there is chains about my feet, time I get this far," she said, in the voice of argument old people keep to use with themselves. "Something always take a hold of me on this hill—pleads I should stay."

After she got to the top she turned and gave a full, severe look behind her where she had come. "Up through pines," she said at length. "Now down through oaks."

Her eyes opened their widest, and she started down gently. But before she got to the bottom of the hill a bush caught her dress.

Her fingers were busy and intent, but her skirts were full and long, so that before she could pull them free in one place they were caught in another. It was not possible to allow the dress to tear. "I in the thorny bush," she said. "Thorns, you doing your appointed work. Never want to let folks pass, no sir. Old eyes thought you was a pretty little *green* bush."

Finally, trembling all over, she stood free, and after a moment dared to stoop for her cane.

10   "Sun so high!" she cried, leaning back and looking, while the thick tears went over her eyes. "The time getting all gone here."

At the foot of this hill was a place where a log was laid across the creek.

"Now comes the trial," said Phoenix.

Putting her right foot out, she mounted the log and shut her eyes. Lifting her skirt, leveling her cane fiercely before her, like a festival figure in some parade, she began to march across. Then she opened her eyes and she was safe on the other side.

"I wasn't as old as I thought," she said.

15   But she sat down to rest. She spread her skirts on the bank around her and folded her hands over her knees. Up above her was a tree in a pearly cloud of mistletoe. She did not dare to close her eyes, and when a little boy brought her a plate with a slice of marble-cake on it she spoke to him. "That would be acceptable," she said. But when she went to take it there was just her own hand in the air.

So she left that tree, and had to go through a barbed-wire fence. There she had to creep and crawl, spreading her knees and stretching her fingers like a baby trying to climb the steps. But she talked loudly to herself: she could not let her dress be torn now, so late in the day, and she could not pay for having her arm or her leg sawed off if she got caught fast where she was.

At last she was safe through the fence and risen up out in the clearing. Big dead trees, like black men with one arm, were standing in the purple stalks of the withered cotton field. There sat a buzzard.

"Who you watching?"

In the furrow she made her way along.

20 "Glad this not the season for bulls," she said, looking sideways, "and the good Lord made his snakes to curl up and sleep in the winter. A pleasure I don't see no two-headed snake coming around that tree, where it come once. It took a while to get by him, back in the summer."

She passed through the old cotton and went into a field of dead corn. It whispered and shook and was taller than her head. "Through the maze now," she said, for there was no path.

Then there was something tall, black, and skinny there, moving before her.

At first she took it for a man. It could have been a man dancing in the field. But she stood still and listened, and it did not make a sound. It was as silent as a ghost.

"Ghost," she said sharply, "who be you the ghost of? For I have heard of nary death close by."

25 But there was no answer—only the ragged dancing in the wind.

She shut her eyes, reached out her hand, and touched a sleeve. She found a coat and inside that emptiness, cold as ice.

"You scarecrow," she said. Her face lighted. "I ought to be shut up for good," she said with laughter. "My senses is gone. I too old. I the oldest people I ever know. Dance, old scarecrow," she said, "while I dancing with you."

She kicked her foot over the furrow, and with mouth drawn down, shook her head once or twice in a little strutting way. Some husks blew down and whirled in streamers about her skirts.

Then she went on, parting her way from side to side with the cane, through the whispering field. At last she came to the end, to a wagon track where the silver grass blew between the red ruts. The quail were walking around like pullets, seeming all dainty and unseen.

30 "Walk pretty," she said. "This the easy place. This the easy going."

She followed the track, swaying through the quiet bare fields, through the little strings of trees silver in their dead leaves, past cabins silver from weather, with the doors and windows boarded shut, all like old women under a spell sitting there. "I walking in their sleep," she said, nodding her head vigorously.

In a ravine she went where a spring was silently flowing through a hollow log. Old Phoenix bent and drank. "Sweet-gum makes the water sweet," she said, and drank more. "Nobody know who made this well, for it was here when I was born."

The track crossed a swampy part where the moss hung as white as lace from every limb. "Sleep on, alligators, and blow your bubbles." Then the track went into the road.

Deep, deep the road went down between the high green-colored banks. Overhead the live-oaks met, and it was as dark as a cave.

35 A black dog with a lolling tongue came up out of the weeds by the ditch. She was meditating, and not ready, and when he came at her she only hit

him a little with her cane. Over she went in the ditch, like a little puff of milkweed.

Down there, her senses drifted away. A dream visited her, and she reached her hand up, but nothing reached down and gave her a pull. So she lay there and presently went to talking. "Old woman," she said to herself, "that black dog come up out of the weeds to stall you off, and now there he sitting on his fine tail, smiling at you."

A white man finally came along and found her—a hunter, a young man, with his dog on a chain.

"Well, Granny!" he laughed. "What are you doing there?"

"Lying on my back like a June-bug waiting to be turned over, mister," she said, reaching up her hand.

40   He lifted her up, gave her a swing in the air, and set her down. "Anything broken, Granny?"

"No sir, them old dead weeds is springy enough," said Phoenix, when she had got her breath. "I thank you for your trouble."

"Where do you live, Granny?" he asked, while the two dogs were growling at each other.

"Away back yonder, sir, behind the ridge. You can't even see it from here."

"On your way home?"

45   "No sir, I going to town."

"Why, that's too far! That's as far as I walk when I come out myself, and I get something for my trouble." He patted the stuffed bag he carried, and there hung down a little closed claw. It was one of the bob-whites, with its beak hooked bitterly to show it was dead. "Now you go on home, Granny!"

"I bound to go to town, mister," said Phoenix. "The time come around."

He gave another laugh, filling the whole landscape. "I know you old colored people! Wouldn't miss going to town to see Santa Claus!"

But something held old Phoenix very still. The deep lines in her face went into a fierce and different radiation. Without warning, she had seen with her own eyes a flashing nickel fall out of the man's pocket onto the ground.

50   How old are you, Granny?" he was saying.

"There is no telling, mister," she said, "no telling."

Then she gave a little cry and clapped her hands and said, "Git on away from here, dog! Look! Look at that dog!" She laughed as if in admiration. "He ain't scared of nobody. He a big black dog." She whispered, "Sic him!"

"Watch me get rid of that cur," said the man. "Sic him, Pete! Sic him!"

Phoenix heard the dogs fighting, and heard the man running and throwing sticks. She even heard a gunshot. But she was slowly bending forward by that time, further and further forward, the lid stretched down over her eyes, as if she were doing this in her sleep. Her chin was lowered almost to her knees. The yellow palm of her hand came out from the fold of her apron. Her fingers slid down and along the ground under the piece of money with the grace and care they would have in lifting an egg from under a setting hen. Then she slowly straightened up, she stood erect, and the nickel was in her apron pocket. A bird flew by. Her lips moved. "God watching me the whole time. I come to stealing."

55 The man came back, and his own dog panted about them. "Well, I scared him off that time," he said, and then he laughed and lifted his gun and pointed it at Phoenix.

She stood straight and faced him.

"Doesn't the gun scare you?" he said, still pointing it.

"No, sir, I seen plenty go off closer by, in my day, and for less than what I done," she said, holding utterly still.

He smiled, and shouldered the gun. "Well, Granny," he said, "you must be a hundred years old, and scared of nothing. I'd give you a dime if I had any money with me. But you take my advice and stay home, and nothing will happen to you."

60 "I bound to go on my way, mister," said Phoenix. She inclined her head in the red rag. Then they went in different directions, but she could hear the gun shooting again and again over the hill.

She walked on. The shadows hung from the oak trees to the road like curtains. Then she smelled wood-smoke, and smelled the river, and she saw a steeple and the cabins on their steep steps. Dozens of little black children whirled around her. There ahead was Natchez shining. Bells were ringing. She walked on.

In the paved city it was Christmas time. There were red and green electric lights strung and crisscrossed everywhere, and all turned on in the daytime. Old Phoenix would have been lost if she had not distrusted her eyesight and depended on her feet to know where to take her.

She paused quietly on the sidewalk where people were passing by. A lady came along in the crowd, carrying an armful of red-, green- and silver-wrapped presents; she gave off perfume like the red roses in hot summer, and Phoenix stopped her.

"Please, missy, will you lace up my shoe?" She held up her foot.

65 "What do you want, Grandma?"

"See my shoe," said Phoenix. "Do all right for out in the country, but wouldn't look right to go in a big building."

"Stand still then, Grandma," said the lady. She put her packages down on the sidewalk beside her and laced and tied both shoes tightly.

"Can't lace 'em with a cane," said Phoenix. "Thank you, missy. I doesn't mind asking a nice lady to tie up my shoe, when I gets out on the street."

Moving slowly and from side to side, she went into the big building, and into a tower of steps, where she walked up and around and around until her feet knew to stop.

70 She entered a door, and there she saw nailed up on the wall the document that had been stamped with the gold seal and framed in the gold frame, which matched the dream that was hung up in her head.

"Here I be," she said. There was a fixed and ceremonial stiffness over her body.

"A charity case, I suppose," said an attendant who sat at the desk before her.

But Phoenix only looked above her head. There was sweat on her face, the wrinkles in her skin shone like a bright net.

"Speak up, Grandma," the woman said. "What's your name? We must have your history, you know. Have you been here before? What seems to be the trouble with you?"

75   Old Phoenix only gave a twitch to her face as if a fly were bothering her.

"Are you deaf?" cried the attendant.

But then the nurse came in.

"Oh, that's just old Aunt Phoenix," she said. "She doesn't come for herself—she has a little grandson. She makes these trips just as regular as clockwork. She lives away back off the Old Natchez Trace." She bent down. "Well, Aunt Phoenix, why don't you just take a seat? We won't keep you standing after your long trip." She pointed.

The old woman sat down, bolt upright in the chair.

80   "Now, how is the boy?" asked the nurse.

Old Phoenix did not speak.

"I said, how is the boy?"

But Phoenix only waited and stared straight ahead, her face very solemn and withdrawn into rigidity.

"Is his throat any better?" asked the nurse. "Aunt Phoenix, don't you hear me? Is your grandson's throat any better since the last time you came for the medicine?"

85   With her hands on her knees, the old woman waited, silent, erect and motionless, just as if she were in armor.

"You mustn't take up our time this way, Aunt Phoenix," the nurse said. "Tell us quickly about your grandson, and get it over. He isn't dead, is he?"

At last there came a flicker and then a flame of comprehension across her face, and she spoke.

"My grandson. It was my memory had left me. There I sat and forgot why I made my long trip."

"Forgot?" The nurse frowned. "After you came so far?"

90   Then Phoenix was like an old woman begging a dignified forgiveness for waking up frightened in the night. "I never did go to school, I was too old at the Surrender," she said in a soft voice. "I'm an old woman without an education. It was my memory fail me. My little grandson, he is just the same, and I forgot it in the coming."

"Throat never heals, does it?" said the nurse, speaking in a loud, sure voice to old Phoenix. By now she had a card with something written on it, a little list. "Yes. Swallowed lye. When was it?—January—two-three years ago—"

Phoenix spoke unasked now. "No, missy, he not dead, he just the same. Every little while his throat begin to close up again, and he not able to swallow. He not get his breath. He not able to help himself. So the time come around, and I go on another trip for the soothing medicine."

"All right. The doctor said as long as you came to get it, you could have it," said the nurse. "But it's an obstinate case."

"My little grandson, he sit up there in the house all wrapped up waiting by himself," Phoenix went on. "We is the only two left in the world. He suffer and it don't seem to put him back at all. He got a sweet look. He going to last.

He wear a little patch quilt and peep out holding his mouth open like a little bird. I remembers so plain now. I not going to forget him again, no, the whole enduring time. I could tell him from all the others in creation."

95 "All right." The nurse was trying to hush her now. She brought her a bottle of medicine. "Charity," she said, making a check mark in her book.

Old Phoenix held the bottle close to her eyes, and then carefully put it into her pocket.

"I thank you," she said.

"It's Christmas time, Grandma," said the attendant. "Could I give you a few pennies out of my purse?"

"Five pennies is a nickel," said Phoenix stiffly.

100 "Here's a nickel," said the attendant.

Phoenix rose carefully and held out her hand. She received the nickel and then fished the other nickel out of her pocket and laid it beside the new one. She stared at her palm closely, with her head on one side.

Then she gave a tap with her cane on the floor.

"This is what come to me to do," she said. "I going to the store and buy my child a little windmill they sells, made out of paper. He going to find it hard to believe there such a thing in the world. I'll march myself back where he waiting, holding it straight up in this hand."

She lifted her free hand, gave a little nod, turned around, and walked out of the doctor's office. Then her slow step began on the stairs, going down.

Questions on Character . . .

1. In the first paragraph, notice how the narrative moves from naming into description and beyond description into metaphor. Do you begin to find characterization in this description? How do the metaphors give you notions of Phoenix's character?

2. Throughout the story, what categories of characterization does Welty use for Phoenix?

3. Most people revise their estimate of Phoenix's age upward as they read the story. What details suggest her age?

4. Why does Phoenix talk to herself? How much do you learn from this one-way conversation? Do you learn different things from her out-loud talk and from her silent thoughts?

5. Pick out the thoughts by which Phoenix reveals most about her character. Do you feel that you know something of Phoenix's past life? Find instances of Phoenix's sense of humor when she is alone.

6. What do you learn of Phoenix's character when she first meets another person?

7. In the hospital, Phoenix forgets everything. Does anything in the story earlier—we could call it plot or character—prepare you for this forgetting? Is it another *hill*?

8. In paragraph 78, we learn about Phoenix from another character. Does it hurt the story that this information comes so late? Would it have been better for the story if we had known earlier? Why?

9. In paragraph 99, why does Phoenix define a nickel? What does this add to her character?

10. Comment on the last sentence of the story. Relate it to the title.

. . . and Other Elements

11. In paragraph 2, we hear about Phoenix's shoelaces; in paragraph 64, we hear of them again. Why repeat this one detail? Does it tell us something about Phoenix, about her character or her situation?

12. What happens to Phoenix in paragraph 15?

13. The plot is a journey and a task. If you were going to make it into a film, how many scenes would you need?

14. In the hospital, we meet a nurse who knows Phoenix and remembers her grandson. Would it be correct to say that the nurse's speeches make the story's climax?

15. In paragraph 95: "'Charity,' she said, making a check mark in a book." Comment on the theme of the story.

Carol Bly

Carol Bly (1930–   ) was born in Duluth and raised in Minnesota and North Carolina. She went to school at Abbot Academy and Wellesley College, then married and spent many years raising a family in a small town in western Minnesota. In 1981, she published a book of essays, *Letters from the Country*. Several of these selections have been reprinted in anthologies. She began publishing fiction late in the 1970s; "The Dignity of Life" was chosen for *The Best American Short Stories 1983,* and collected in *Backbone* (1985). A group of her stories, made into a film by Judith Guest, appeared on public television's American Playhouse in 1989 as *Rachel River.* In 1991, she brought out a second book of stories, *The Tomcat's Wife,* from which we take "After the Baptism." She has taught at the University of Minnesota, Hamline University, McAllister University, and Carleton College.

After the Baptism   (1991)

The Benty family had a beautiful baptism for their baby—when a good deal might have gone wrong. It is hard to run any baptism these days: of all the fifty-odd Episcopalians in Saint Aidan's Church, not to mention the two Lutheran grandparents, who really believes much of what the young priest says? No one with an IQ over one hundred actually supposes that "baptism could never be more truly, truly relevant than it is right now, in our day and age." People may get a kick out of the rhetoric, but that doesn't mean they believe it. If Bill Benty, Senior, the baby's grandfather, tried any of that proclaiming style of Father Geoffrey, if he tried anything like that just once over at the plant, he'd be laughed out to the fence in two minutes.

At least Father Geoffrey was long enough out of seminary now so he'd left off pronouncing Holy Ghost Ha-oly Gha-ost. His delivery was clear and manly. When he took the baby from her godparents, he took hold of her in a no-nonsense way: her mussed, beautiful white skirts billowed over his arm like sail being carried to the water. But the man was vapid. A frank, charming midwestern accent can't bring dead ideas to life. He had been charming about agreeing on the 1928 baptism service, instead of the 1979. Bill's wife, Lois, loved the beautiful old phrasing. Beautiful it was, too, Bill thought now, but on the other hand, how could any realistic person ask those particular three godparents "to renounce the vain pomp and glory of the world"? Where would that crew get any glory from in the first place?

The middle-aged godparent was Bill's long-lost first cousin, Molly Wells. Thirty-odd years ago she had run away to North Carolina to marry. After almost no correspondence in all those years, Molly had shown up widowed— a thin, sad woman with white hair done in what Lois called your bottom-line, body-wave-only permanent. Neither Bill nor Lois had met her husband. Bill had mailed her Dittoed, and later photocopied, Christmas letters, as he did to all his relations, giving news of Lois's work in Episcopal Community Services and whatever of interest there was to say about the chemical plant, and young Will's graduations and accomplishments—Breck School, Reed, the Harvard B School, his first marriage, his job with the arts organization before the snafu, his marriage to Cheryl. Molly and her husband had no children, and her responses to the Benty's news were scarcely more than southern-lady thank-you notes.

Then in July of this long, very hot summer, she announced she was now widowed and would visit. Here she was, a houseguest who kept to her room, considerate enough not to dampen their family joking with her grief. Today, for the baptism, she wore a two-piece pink dress, gloves, and a straw-brimmed hat. Since one expects a young face under a broad-brimmed hat, Bill had had a moment's quake to see Molly, when she came down the staircase that morning. Molly had frankly told them she had not darkened the doorway of a church in thirty years but she would not disgrace them.

5   The other godparents were an oldish young couple whom Will dug up from his remaining high-school acquaintance. Bill had warned Will that you had to give these things time: when a man has been caught embezzling he must allow his friends months, even a year, to keep saying how sorry they are, but the fact is, they can't really ever look at him the same way again. For a good two or three years they will still mention to people that he was caught embezzling or whatever, but in fact they have no rancor left themselves. In about five years, they will again be affectionate friends but never as in the first place. It was only a question of having the sense not to ask them for help getting a job the first two years—and then simply to wait.

Probably Will was lucky to have found this couple, Chad and Jodi Plathe, to stand up for his baby. They were not Episcopalians. They were meditators, and if not actually organic farmers, at least organic eaters. When Will and Cheryl brought them over to Bill and Lois's for dinner earlier in the month, it had been fun to goad them. Each time Chad mentioned an interest of theirs, Bill had said, "Oh, then it follows you must be into organic eating." Or "Oh, then it follows you must be into horoscopes." "Into Sufi dancing, I bet." They were—into all the philosophies he brought up. They looked at him, puzzled, and young Will said, "Very witty, Dad—oh, witty." Once Chad said something hostile back, Bill forgave him everything. In one sense, Bill had rather listen to a non-Christian fallen-away Bay Area Buddhist who is man enough to take offense, at least, than to this Father Geoffrey, with his everlasting love for everything and everybody.

Now Chad and Jodi stood at the font, their backs to the grandparents in the first row and all the congregation in the next rows. They wore their eternal blue jeans, with the tops of plastic sandwich bags sticking out of the back pockets. They wore 1960s-style rebozos with earth-tone embroidery and rust-colored sewn-on doves. Their shoulder-length hair was shiny and combed. At least, Bill thought comfortably, very little evil in the world was generated by vegetarians. He saved up that idea to tell Chad if the conversation dragged at dinner.

Early that morning, Bill had taken his coffee happily out into the little back-kitchen screened porch. The wind was down, and the ivy's thousands of little claws held the screens peacefully. Like all true householders, Bill liked being up while others slept. His wide lawn lay shadowed under four elms the city hadn't had to take down yet. The grass showed a pale gleam of dew and looked more beautiful than it really was. Across the avenue, where the large grounds of Benty Chem started, Bill had ordered a landscaping outfit to put in generous groupings of fine high bushes and hundreds of perennials. He ordered them planted on both sides of the fence. Now that it was August, and everything had taken hold, the grounds looked lavender and gentle.

"You can't make a chemical factory look like an Englishman's estate," Lois had told him last week. "But, darling, darn near! Darn near! If only the protesters would wear battered stovepipe hats and black scarves!"

10   Bill told her that he had heard at a Saint Aidan's Vestry meeting that the protesting or peace-demonstrating community of the Twin Cities definitely regarded Benty Chem as a lot more beautiful place to work around than any one of Honeywell's layouts. "And they should know," Bill added with satisfaction.

At seven-thirty, the usual Sunday contingent of protesters weren't on the job yet. It was generally Sue Ann and Mary, or Sue Ann and Drew, on Sundays. Bill learned their first names automatically, as he learned the first names of new janitorial staff at Benty Chem. Now he gathered himself, got into the car, and was out at Northwest Cargo Recovery on Thirty-fourth Street in good time. He signed for the lobsters. They were moving around a little, safe, greenish-black, in their plastic carrying case. "Hi, fellows and girls!" he said good-naturedly to them. He felt the luggage people smiling at him from behind their counter. Bill knew he was more spontaneous and humorous than most people they dealt with. "For my first grandchild's baptism!" he told them.

When he got home, the caterers had come. Lois was fingering along the bookcases, looking for the extra 1928 prayer books. Molly sat, cool in her silk two-piece dress. "I do believe it's threatening rain," she said in her partly southern accent. "Oh, and rain is just so much needed by our farmers." Her "our farmers" sounded false, feudal even, but Bill said, "Darn right, Molly!"

Now he relaxed in church. He flung an arm around the bench end, a little figure carved in shallow relief. Some Episcopalian in Bill's dad's generation had brought six of these carvings from Norfolk. They all cracked during their first American winter of central heating. Bill and a couple of other vestrymen glued the cracks and set vises; then they mortised in hardwood tholes against the grain, to make them safe forever. Each bench end was a small monk, with robe, hood, and cinch. The medieval sculptor had made the little monks hold their glossy wooden hands up, nearly touching their noses, in prayer. The faces had no particular expression.

Bill sat more informally than other people in Saint Aidan's. He had the peaceful slouch of those who are on the inside, the ones who know the workings behind some occasion, like cooks for a feast, or vestrymen for a service, or grandfathers for a baptism. Bill had done a lot of work and thinking to make this baptism successful, so now his face was pleasant and relaxed. He was aware of the Oppedahls next to him, the baby's other grandparents, sweating out the Episcopal service that they disliked. He thought they were darn good sports. He leaned across Lois at one point and whispered to Merv Oppedahl that a strong Scotch awaited the stalwart fellow that got through all the Smells and Bells. Merv's face broke into a grin, and he made a thumbs-up with the hand that wasn't holding Doreen's hand.

15   All summer the wretched farmers' topsoil had been lifting and lifting, then moving into the suburbs, even into Saint Paul itself. Grit stuck to people's foreheads and screens, even to the woven metal of their fences. But inside Saint Aidan's, the air was high and cool; the clerestory windows, thank heavens, were not the usual dark- and royal-blue and dark-rose stained-glass imitations of Continental cathedral windows—full of symbols of lions for Saint Mark and eagles for Saint John, which a whole generation of Episcopalians didn't know anything about, anyway. Besides, they made churches dark. Saint Aidan's had a good deal of clear glass, and enough gold-stained windows so that all the vaulting looked rather gold and light. It was an oddly watery look. In fact, the church reminded Bill of the insides of the overturned canoe of his childhood. It had been made of varnished ribs and strakes; when the boys turned it over and dove down to come up inside it, madly treading water, they felt transformed by that watery arching. It was a spooky yellow-dark. No matter that at ten their voices must still have been unchanged; they shouted all the rhetoric and bits of poems they knew. They made everything pontifical. They made dire prophecies. They felt portentous about death, even. Not the sissy, capon death they taught you about at Cass Lake Episcopal Camp, but the death that would get you if a giant pried your fists off the thwarts and shoved you down.

Now Father Geoffrey was done with the godparents. He put his thumb into the palm oil and pressed it onto the baby's forehead. Then he cried in a full voice, "I pronounce you, Molly Oppedahl Benty, safe in our Lord Jesus Christ forever!" Tears made some people's eyes brittle. They all sang "Love divine, all loves excel-l-l-ling . . ." using the Hyfrodol tune. Then it was noon, and they could leave.

Everyone tottered across the white, spiky gravel of the parking lot. They called out unnecessary friendly words from car to car. "See you at the Bentys' in five minutes, then!" and "Beautiful service, wasn't it?" "Anyone need a ride? We can certainly take two more!"

The cars full of guests drove companionably across the tacky suburb. People felt happy in different ways, but all of them felt more blessed than the people they passed. They may have been to a sacrament that they didn't much believe in, but they at least had been to one. Then years before, all these streets had been shadowy under the elms. Now, though spindly maple saplings stood guyed in their steel-mesh cages, the town showed itself dispirited in its lidless houses that human beings build and live in. The open garages, with here and there a man pottering about, looked more inviting than the houses. The men tinkered in the hot shadow, handling gigantic mowing and spraying equipment parked there. No one could imagine a passion happening in the houses—not even a mild mid-life crisis. Not even a hobby, past an assembled kit.

Another reason everyone felt contented was that all their troubles with one another had been worked out the week before. Unbeatable, humane, wise, experienced administrator that he was, Bill explained to Lois, he had done the best possible thing to guarantee them all a great baptism Sunday by having Will and Cheryl (and little Molly) over to dinner the week before. There were always tensions about religious occasions. The tensions are all the worse when most of the religion is gone while the custom lives on. Each detail of the custom—what's in good taste and what's the way we've always done it before—is a bloodletting issue. Now, there were two things to do about bloodletting issues, Bill told Lois.

20   "Yes, dear?" she said with a smile.

"If the issues can be solved to anyone's satisfaction, just solve them. But if they can't be solved at all, have the big fight about them a week ahead. Then everybody is sick of fighting by the time you have the occasion itself."

Lois said, "Makes sense. What can't be solved, though?"

He gave her a look. "Our son and our daughter-in-law are not very happily married. They started a baby two months before they married. And you and I will always just have to hope that it was Will's idea to marry Cheryl and not Merv Oppedahl's idea at the end of a magnum. Next: Cheryl wanted the baby to be named Chereen—a combo of Cheryl, for herself, and Doreen, for her mother. Our son thinks Chereen is a disgusting idea. Next: Cheryl puts a descant onto any hymn we sing, including—if I remember correctly, and I am afraid I will never forget—onto 'Jesu, Joy of Man's Desiring' and Beethoven's Ninth, whatever that one is."

"'Hymn to Joy,'" Lois said.

25   "'Hymn to Joy,'" Bill said. "Next: The Oppedahls are probably not very happy that their daughter has married someone who did two years at Sandstone

Federal Prison for embezzlement. Next: You and I are not happy about Will's marrying Cheryl. She is tasteless. He is mean to her. Are you with me so far? Then next is the choice of godparents. Good grief! It is nice that Will wants to honor his second cousin Molly Wells by asking her to stand godparent, but she hasn't gone to church in thirty years. And Cheryl wanted a young couple, not an old great-aunt, for her baby's sponsors. It is obvious Will chose Molly because she gave them seventeen thousand dollars by way of a nest egg. Very handsome thing to do. *Very* handsome, considering Will's record."

Lois said, "Oh, dear, must you?"

"All these things are on people's minds. It's best to have it all out ahead of time. Just because a rich aunt gives someone money is not a reason for having her stand godmother—especially when the baby's mother obviously doesn't want it. Next: The Oppedahls aren't going to be comfortable with the Episcopal Church service, but they'd be a sight *more* comfortable if we used the modern language of 1979—but the baby's grandmother on the other side wants 1928."

Lois said, "Oh, dear. I thought *I* was going to come out of this clean."

Bill laughed, "No one comes out of a family fight clean. Next: Mrs. Oppedahl is a horrible cold fish who doesn't like anybody. She doesn't even like her own daughter very well. In fact—poor Cheryl! Do you know what she told me? She told me the first time she ever felt popular, as she put it, was at Lutheran Bible camp, when all the girls discovered she could harmonize to the hymns. Suddenly it made her part of the group. When they all got back from camp, the girls talked about her as if she were someone that counted, and the boys picked up on it. She was O.K. in high school after that. She told me that just that one Lutheran Bible Camp gave her more nourishment—her word—than she'd ever got from her parents."

30   "You're a wonder, dear," Lois said. "What about the other godparents?"

"The holistic birdseed-eaters? They know perfectly well that the only reason Will chose them was to override any chance of Cheryl's having some couple *she'd* choose. They know that I think their knee-jerk Gaya stuff is silly, and they will feel awkward about the service. I don't know what to do about them."

Lois said, "We will have lobsters. That's not meat! Then they won't bring their plastic bags of whatever."

"Boiled live lobster. Great idea. They will eat it or I will shove it down their throats," Bill said. "I will offend Doreen Oppedahl by offering Merv a strong drink. It'll buck him up, and she's hopeless, anyway."

"Have we thought of everything?" Lois said.

35   Bill turned serious a moment. "I am going to tell Will he can't speak cruelly to his wife in my house."

Lois said, "Well, poor Will! Do you remember how when we were all somewhere, at someone's house, suddenly there was Cheryl telling everyone how she and Will met because they were both at the microfiche in the public library together and they both felt sick from the fiche?"

"Nothing wrong with that," Bill said. "Microfiche does make people feel like throwing up."

"But she went on and on about how nausea had brought them together!"

Bill said, "I remember. Will told her to shut up, too, right in front of everyone."

40 The week before the baptism, therefore, Will and Cheryl and little Molly joined Bill, Lois, and their cousin Molly Wells for dinner. They aired grievances, just as Bill had planned. Then he glanced out the window and said to his son, "Come on out and help me with the protesters, Will."

Everyone looked out. The usual Sunday protesters had been on the opposite sidewalk, near the plant fence. They looked flagged from the heat, but determined. Bill saw it was Sue Ann and Polly this time. They had their signs turned so they could be read from the Benty house. IT IS HARD TO BE PROUD OF CHEMICAL WARFARE was the message for that Sunday. Now the two young people had moved to this side of the avenue, doing the westward reach of their loop on the public sidewalk but taking the eastward reach on Bill and Lois's lawn.

"Not on my lawn they don't," Bill said, smiling equably at the others. "We'll be right back."

Father and son went to the lawn edge and stood side by side, waiting for the protesters to come up abreast of where they were. The women, in the house, could see their backs but couldn't hear what was said. Presently they realized nothing violent seemed likely. They made out the protesters smiling, and Bill turned slightly, apparently calling a parting shot of some civil kind to them. The protesters moved back over to the Benty Chemical side of the street, and Will and Bill came across the lawn toward the house.

Bill had used that time to speak to his son. "I can't stop you from treating your wife rudely in your own home. But in mine, Will, don't you ever swear at her again. And don't tell her to shut up. And stop saying 'For Christ's sake, Cheryl.'"

45 "Dad—my life is going to be some kind of hell."

"I bet it might," Bill said in a speculative tone. "It well might." Just then the sign-bearers came up to them. One said, "Good afternoon, Mr. Benty," to Bill. The other of them said in a very pleasant tone, "There must be some other way human beings can make money besides on contracts for spreading nerve diseases that cause victims five or six hours of agony," and they made to pass on.

"Off the lawn, friends," Bill said levelly. "Sidewalk's public, lawn's private."

"Agony is another word for torture," the first protester said, but they immediately crossed the street.

As Bill and Will came back to the house, Bill said in a low voice, "Go for the pleasant moments, son. Whenever you can."

50 All the difficult conversations took place that could take place: all the permanent grievances—Will's and Cheryl's unhappiness—were hinted at. People felt that they had expressed themselves a little. By the end of the day, they felt gritty and exhausted.

A blessed week passed, and now the baptism party was going off well. The caterers had come, with their white Styrofoam trays. They set out sauces and laid the champagne crooked into its pails of ice. They dropped the lobsters into boiling water. There was lemon mayonnaise and drawn butter, a platter of dark-meat turkey—damper, better than white meat, Lois Benty and the caterers agreed. It is true that as she made her way around the Bentys' dining room table, loading her plate, Doreen Oppedahl whispered to her husband, "It'd never occur to me, I can tell you, to serve dark meat on a company occasion," and Merv whispered back, "No, it never *would* occur to you!" but his tone wasn't malicious. He had spotted the Scotch on the sideboard. That Bill Benty might be pompous, but at least he was as good as his word, and Merv wasn't going to be stuck with that dumb champagne, which tasted like Seven-Up with aspirin. An oblong of pinewood lay piled with ham so thin it wrinkled in waves. The caterers had set parsley here and there, and sprayed mist over everything; they set one tiny chip of ice on each butter pat. "Those caterers just left that chutney preserve that Mrs. Wells brought right in its mason jar," Doreen whispered to Merv. He smiled and whispered, "Shut up, Doreen." She whispered back, "If you get drunk at this party, I will never forgive you."

When all the relations and friends had gathered into the living room, Bill Benty tinkled a glass and asked them to drink to his grandchild. After that, people glanced about, weighing places to sit.

Then the one thing that neither the host nor the hostess had foreseen happened: no one sat in the little groupings Lois had arranged. Nor did people pull up chairs to what free space there was at the dining room table. They gravitated to the messy screened porch off the kitchen. The caterers obligingly swept away all their trays and used foil. People dragged out dining room chairs; other people camped on the old wooden chairs already out there.

The morning's breeze had held. Some of it worked through the gritty screens. People relaxed and felt cheerful. They kept passing the baby about, not letting any one relation get to hold her for too long. Father Geoffrey kept boring people by remarking that it was the most pleasant baptism he could remember. Suddenly Lois Benty pointed across at Chad's and Jodi's plates. "Don't *tell* me you two aren't eating the lobster!" she screamed. "Lobster is not meat, you know!"

55   Both Chad and Jodi gave the smile that experienced vegetarians keep ready for arrogant carnivores. "Well, you see," Jodi said with mock shyness, "we asked the caterers—you see, we did ask. The lobsters weren't stunned first!"

Father Geoffrey said pleasantly, "And delicious they are, too. I've never tasted better."

Jodi said, "They were dropped in alive, you see. . . . So it's a question of their agony." Then Jodi said in a hurried, louder voice, "Mrs. Benty, please don't worry about us! We always bring our own food, so we're all set." She reached into her back jeans pocket and brought out two plastic bags of couscous and sunflower seeds. "We are more than O.K.," she said.

Lois asked people if she could bring them another touch of this or that— the ham, at least? she said, smiling at Mrs. Oppedahl.

"Oh, no!" cried Mrs. Oppedahl. "I've eaten so much! I'd get fat!"

60　　By now Merv had had three quick, life-restoring glasses of Scotch. For once he felt as urbane and witty as Bill Benty, even if he wasn't the boss of a chemical industry.

"Fat!" he shouted. "Afraid you'll get fat! Don't worry! I like a woman fat enough so I can find her in bed!"

He looked around with bright eyes—but there was a pause. Then Bill Benty said in a hearty tone, "Oh, *good* man, Oppedahl! *Good* man!"

Quickly, the baby's great-aunt said to Jodi Plathe, "Those little bags look so interesting! Could you explain what's in them? Is that something we should all be eating?"

Bill said, "Go ahead, Jodi. Convert her. That's what I call a challenge. If you can get her to set down that plate of lobster and eat bulgur wheat instead, you've got something there, Jodi!"

65　　Jodi gave him a look and then said, "No, you tell *me* something, Ms. Wells. I was wondering, why were you crying at the baptism this morning? Somebody said you never went to church at all, and yet . . . I was just wondering."

"Oh," Lois Benty said, getting set to dilute any argument, "I bet you mean during the chrism."

Molly Wells happened to be holding the baby at that moment. Above its dreaming face, hers looked especially tired and conscious. "My dear," she said, "that is a long story. I just know you don't want to hear it."

"Let's have the story, lady," Mr. Oppedahl said. "My wife is always so afraid that I'll tell a story—but the way I look at it is, people like a story. You can always ask 'em, do they mind a little story? And if they don't say no, the way I look at it is, it's O.K. to tell it. So go right ahead. Or I could tell one, if you're too shy."

"Never mind!" cried Bill. "Out with it, Molly!"

70　　Father Geoffrey said gently, "I know I for one would surely like to hear it!"

Molly Wells said, "I have to confess I was mostly daydreaming along through the service, thinking of one thing and another. I never liked church. Unlike Bill here—Bill's my first cousin, you might not know—I was raised in the country, and my dream—my one and my *only* dream—was to get out of the country and marry a prince and live happily ever after.

"The only way I could think to escape at seventeen was to go to Bible camp. So I went—and there, by my great good luck, I met another would-be escaper, Jamie Wells. We cut all the outdoors classes and then used those same places where the classes met to sit and walk together when no one was there. We met in the canoe shed. We sat on the dock near the bin of blue and white hats, depending on how well you swam. We met in the chapel, even, during off times. Wherever we were, we were in love all the time. I recall Jamie said to me, 'There is nothing inside me that wants to go back to the old life, Molly. Is there anything inside you that wants to go back to the old life?' There wasn't, so we ran away. Away meant to stay with his parents and sister, who were at a resort in the Blue Ridge Mountains that summer. We told them we wanted to be married, and they were kind to us. We married, and we lived in love for thirty years.

"It was so pleasant—in the little ways as well as the big ones. Jamie found a hilltop that looked over the valley and across to two mountains—Pisgah and The Rat. He told the workmen how to cut down the laurels and dogwoods and just enough of the armored pine so that you couldn't see the mill down in the valley but you had a clear view to the mountains. We spent hours, hours every day, sitting on our stone terrace. We even had Amos and George bring breakfast out there. I remember best sitting out there in March, when the woods were unleafed except for the horizontal boughs of dogwood everywhere! They looked so unlikely, so vulnerable, out there among all that mountain scrub! The ravines were full of red clay, and the sound of the hounds baying and baying, worrying some rabbit all the time. I remember how we always made a point of taking walks in late afternoon, and I would never stop feeling dazzled by the shards of mica everywhere. And Jamie did have the most wonderful way of putting things. He said mica was bits left over from the first world, back when it was made of pure crystal, when it was made of unbroken love, before God made it over again with clay and trees, ravines, and dogs. I recall when he said that kind of thing my heart used to grow and grow.

"Nothing interrupted us. Now, Jamie's sister, Harriet Jean, always wanted me to do social work for her, but she forgave me when she saw I wasn't going to do it. I expect she understood right off from the very first that I loved her brother, and all a maiden lady really wants from a sister-in-law is that she should really love her brother. We three got along very well. One day, on Amos and George's day off, we had a copperhead on the terrace and Harriet Jean was over there in a flash, and she shot its head right off with her twenty-gauge. She was so good about it, too: I remember she told us very clearly, 'I want you and Jamie to just turn your back now,' and she swept up its head and slung its body over the dustpan handle and carried it off somewhere. She had a good many projects with the black people, and she would have liked me to help her with those . . . but after a while she said to me, 'Molly, I see that you have your hands full with that man, and I mean to stop pestering you,' and she was good as her word. Different occasions came and went—the Vietnam War, I certainly remember that clear as clear. It was in the paper, and when Amos and George came out with the breakfast trays and brought that paper, Jamie said, 'There is a time when a country is in a kind of death agony, the way a person could be,' and I felt a burst of love for him then, too. No one in my family could ever observe and think that clearly."

75   At this point, Mr. Oppedahl said in a loud but respectful voice, "I didn't just get what you said he did for a living."

Molly Wells said, "Oh, that. He had a private income—that whole family did. Of course, he had an office he had to keep to tend his interests with—but it was private income." She shifted the baby, and seemed to rearrange herself a little as she said that. It didn't invite further comment.

She took up her story. "Everything went along all those years, except of course we just wept uncontrollably when George died, and Amos never was so springy serving us after that.

"Then one day we found out that Jamie had inoperable cancer of the lung."

There was a little pause after she said that. They could all hear the footsteps of people on the sidewalk, outside. The wind had cooled a little.

80   "They wanted to do radiation on Jamie, because there were some lung cancer cells in his brain. Well, so we had the radiation treatment. I drove Jamie all the way to Asheville for that, twice a week. It was a very hard time for us: he was often sick. When he wasn't actually sick, he felt sick.

"They managed to kill those lung cells in his brain, and gradually, after many months, he died, but not of brain cancer.

"Well, now," the middle-aged woman said. "Three occasions all came to mind during that baptism service for this beautiful little girl this morning. First, after I had been married not two months, I noticed, the way you gradually get around to noticing everything there is about a man, that the flesh in his upper arm was a little soft, just below the shoulder bulge. I could have expected that, since Jamie just wasn't interested in sports at all and he didn't do any physical work. But still I remember thinking: That bit of softness there will get a little softer all the time, and after twenty years or so it might be very soft and loose from the muscle, the way the upper part of old men's arms are—which kills a woman's feeling just at the moment she notices it. Right away, of course, if it is someone dear to you, you forgive them for that soft upper arm there, for not being young and handsome forever, but still the image of it goes in, and you feel your heart shrink a little. You realize the man will not live forever. Then you love him even better in the next moment, because now—for the first time—you pity him. At least, I felt pity.

"The second occasion is when he was sick having all that radiation. He vomited on our living room floor. It was Sunday evening. We always let Amos go home to his own folks on Sundays, so there wasn't anyone to clean that up—but Harriet Jean was there, and she offered to. Suddenly I remember almost snarling at her—I just bayed at her like a dog. I told her to keep out of it. I would clean up my own husband's mess. Of course she was surprised. She couldn't have been more surprised than I was, though. That night in bed, I went over it carefully, and I realized that the only physical life I had left with Jamie was taking care of him, so his throw-up was a part of my physical life with him. Not lovely—but there it was.

"The last occasion was about a half hour after his death. The hospital people told me I had to leave the room, and I remember I refused. Finally they said I could stay another ten minutes and that was all. Now, you all may know or you may not know that they have their reasons for taking people away from dead bodies. I laid my forehead down on the edge of the bed near Jamie's hip—and then I heard a slight rustling. My mind filled with horror. I lifted my head and looked up to see a slight change in his hand. It had been lying there; now the fist—just the tiniest bit, but I wasn't mistaken—was closing a little. When a person looks back coolly from a distance on a thing like that, you know it is the muscles shrinking or contracting or whatever they do when life has left. To me, though, it was Jamie making the very first move I had ever seen him make in all my life with him in which I had nothing to do with it. He was taking hold of something there—thin air, maybe—but taking hold of it by himself. Now I knew what death was. I stood up and left.

85   "This morning, in church, I was daydreaming about him again. It's a thing I do. I was not going to mention it to any of you.

"I told you about this because I was so surprised to find how my life was not simple at all: it was all tied up in the flesh, this or that about the flesh. And how is flesh ever safe? So when you took that palm oil," she finished, glancing across at Father Geoffrey, "and pronounced our little Molly here safe—*safe!*—in our Lord Jesus Christ forever . . . well, I simply began to cry!"

She sat still a moment and then with her conventional smile looked across at the younger godmother. "Well, you asked the question, and now I have answered you."

In the normal course of things, such a speech would simply bring a family celebration to an absolute stop. People would sit frozen still as crystal for a moment, and then one or another would say, in a forced, light-toned way, "My word, but it's getting late. . . . Dear, we really must . . ." and so forth. But the Benty family were lucky. A simple thing happened: it began to rain finally, the rain people had been wanting all summer. It fell quite swiftly right from the first. It rattled the ivy, and then they could even hear it slamming down on the sidewalks. Footsteps across the avenue picked up and began to run.

They all noticed that odd property of rain: if it has been very dry, the first shower drives the dust upward, so that for a second your nostrils fill with dust.

90   Then the rain continued so strongly it cleaned the air and made the whole family and their friends feel quiet and tolerant. They felt the classic old refreshment we always hope for in water.

Questions on Character . . .

1. Who is quoted in the first paragraph? With whose style of speech does this language belong? Do you know by the content of the language or by its style?

2. An ancient rule for writers is "Show, don't tell." In the second paragraph, Bly tells us about a character ("But the man was vapid.") instead of showing us. Find further examples of Bly's telling about characters—and look for reasons why Bly chooses to violate the old injunction.

3. In the third paragraph, we learn about Molly Wells. Why do we hear so much about her now? When we hear about her through the opinions of others, how do we learn about two characters at once?

4. In the third paragraph—in retrospect—whom does the phrase *before the snafu* characterize?

5. How would you describe the initial characterization of Chad and Jodi Plathe? Do they live up to their characterization, later? Does this characterization have an effect on our understanding of other characters?

6. We hear a good bit about landscaping. Does landscaping speak of character?

7. If Bill Benty is the most rounded character in this story, how is this depth accomplished? Why spend so much time on him, when Molly Wells takes over at the end?

8. What do you learn of the Oppedahls? List the pieces of information that distinguish them from the Bentys according to social class.

9. How does Merv Oppedahl show the influence of Scotch? How do we know? What does it show us of character—his and others? Of theme and of plot?

10. The end of the story is dominated by Molly Wells. How have we been prepared for her speech by glimpses of her character?

. . . and Other Elements

11. How many times does Bly use *beautiful* in the first pages of her story? Why does she use this word so often?

12. Is this a story about social class? Why or why not? If it isn't *about* social class, why is there so much class consciousness in it?

13. What are the protesters protesting and what does it have to do with the story as a whole?

14. Discuss Jodi's statement: ". . . it's a question of their agony."

15. When Merv Oppedahl interrupts Molly's story, what purpose does his question serve as we read the story?

16. Why does it rain? The question is not meteorological.

17. In her book about writing short stories, Bly gives all sorts of advice. Here are some sentences from *The Passionate, Accurate, Short Story*. Relate them to "After the Baptism."

The more we know about the character, the more like one of us the character appears.

Making up stories increases one's love of the universe generally: Everyone knows that.

It is important to drop most of what you have heard about morality spoiling fiction. All the good fiction has moral charge like electric charge.

CHAPTER SIX

Setting

Setting is the place or time of a story—its geography, era, season, and society. In many stories, setting is only the air characters breathe, vital and taken for granted. In others, setting is basic to the theme of a story. Some stories need no background at all. Fables live in a timeless present where crickets talk; usually fantasy happens anywhere and nowhere. But most writers invoke particular places and particular times, and their stories establish these settings precisely. Precise settings help to establish the truth of the story, to persuade the reader of the validity of the tale.

Setting can give us information vital to plot and theme. The two leading characters of Thurber's "The Catbird Seat" grow out of their generalized office life. Faulkner's Miss Emily is shaped by the social details of her changing town. Without these specific historical and social settings, the story would be melodrama; its theme arises from its setting. In "A Good Man Is Hard to Find," the three settings (home, Red Sammy's, the scene of the accident) contrast sordid reality with would-be elevated talk, to ironic effect. In "A Worn Path," the setting is the path itself.

In this last type of setting, landscape fits a subjective mood, and description becomes symbolic. Edgar Allan Poe's "The Fall of the House of Usher" begins with such a description, where physical details represent mental traits:

Shaking off from my spirit what *must* have been a dream, I scanned more narrowly the real aspect of the building. Its principal feature seemed to be that of an excessive antiquity. The discoloration of ages had been great. Minute fungi overspread the whole exterior, hanging in a fine tangled web-work from the eaves. Yet all this was apart from any extraordinary dilapidation. No portion of the masonry had fallen; and there appeared to be a wild inconsistency between its still perfect adaptation of parts, and the crumbling condition of the individual stones. In this there was much that reminded me of the specious totality of old woodwork which has rotted for long years in some neglected vault with no disturbance from the breath of the external air. Beyond this indication of extensive decay, however, the fabric gave little token of instability. Perhaps the eye of a scrutinizing observer might have discovered a barely perceptible fissure, which, extending from the roof of the building in front, made its way down the wall in a zig-zag direction, until it became lost in the sullen waters of the tarn.

The *fissure* is subjective, a representation of the psyche of Roderick Usher, the story's main character and the owner of the house.

We should not forget that, among other reasons, we read to entertain ourselves and we are entertained by the exotic and the unusual. For the same reasons we travel to strange places, we read about strange places.

Margaret Atwood

Margaret Atwood (1939–   ) was born in Ottawa, grew up largely in northern Ontario and Quebec, and now lives in Toronto with her husband and daughter. She is novelist, poet, short story writer, and critic. Her novels include *The Edible Woman* (1969), *Surfacing* (1972), *Lady Oracle* (1976), and *Life Before Man* (1979). She has written a critical book about the themes of Canadian literature, *Survival* (1972), and in 1983 she edited *The New Oxford Book of Canadian Verse in English*. She has published nine books of poems, including *Selected Poems* in 1976, followed by *Two-Headed Poems* (1978) and *True Stories* (1981). For a poem by Margaret Atwood, see page 559.

This story gives the title to a collection of short stories published in 1978.

Dancing Girls   (1977)

The first sign of the new man was the knock on the door. It was the landlady, knocking not at Ann's door, as she'd thought, but on the other door, the one east of the bathroom. Knock, knock, knock; then a pause, soft footsteps, the sound of unlocking. Ann, who had been reading a book on canals, put it down and lit herself a cigarette. It wasn't that she tried to overhear: in this house you couldn't help it.

"Hi!" Mrs. Nolan's voice loud, overly friendly. "I was wondering, my kids would love to see your native costume. You think you could put it on, like, and come down?"

A soft voice, unintelligible.

"Gee, that's great! We'd sure appreciate it!"

5   Closing and locking, Mrs. Nolan slip-slopping along the hall in, Ann knew, her mauve terry-cloth scuffies and flowered housecoat, down the stairs, hollering at her two boys. "You get into this room right now!" Her voice came up through Ann's hot-air register as if the grate were a PA system. It isn't those kids who want to see him, she thought. It's her. She put out the cigarette, reserving the other half for later, and opened her book again. What costume? Which land, this time?

Unlocking, opening, soft feet down the hall. They sounded bare. Ann closed the book and opened her own door. A white robe, the back of a brown head, moving with a certain stealth or caution towards the stairs. Ann went into the bathroom and turned on the light. They would share it; the person in that room always shared her bathroom. She hoped he would be better than the man before, who always seemed to forget his razor and would knock on the door while Ann was having a bath. You wouldn't have to worry about getting raped or anything in this house though, that was one good thing. Mrs. Nolan was better than any burglar alarm, and she was always there.

That one had been from France, studying Cinema. Before him there had been a girl, from Turkey, studying Comparative Literature. Lelah, or that was how it was pronounced. Ann used to find her beautiful long auburn hairs in the washbasin fairly regularly; she'd run her thumb and index finger along them, enviously, before discarding them. She had to keep her own hair chopped off at ear level, as it was brittle and broke easily. Lelah also had a gold tooth, right at the front on the outside where it showed when she smiled. Curiously, Ann was envious of this tooth as well. It and the hair and the turquoise-studded earrings Lelah wore gave her a gypsy look, a wise look that Ann, with her beige eyebrows and delicate mouth, knew she would never be able to develop, no matter how wise she got. She herself went in for "classics," tailored skirts and Shetland sweaters; it was the only look she could carry off. But she and Lelah had been friends, smoking cigarettes in each other's rooms commiserating with each other about the difficulties of their courses and the loudness of Mrs. Nolan's voice. So Ann was familiar with that room; she knew what it looked like inside and how much it cost. It was no luxury suite, certainly, and she wasn't surprised at the high rate of turnover. It had an even more direct pipeline to the sounds of the Nolan family than hers had. Lelah had left because she couldn't stand the noise.

The room was smaller and cheaper than her room, though painted the same depressing shade of green. Unlike hers, it did not have its own tiny refrigerator, sink and stove; you had to use the kitchen at the front of the house, which had been staked out much earlier by a small enclave of mathematicians, two men and one woman, from Hong Kong. Whoever took that room either had to eat out all the time or run the gamut of their conversation, which even when not in Chinese was so rarefied as to be unintelligible. And you could never find any space in the refrigerator, it was always full of mushrooms. This from Lelah; Ann herself never had to deal with them since she could cook in her own room. She could see them, though, as she went in and out. At mealtimes they usually sat quietly at their kitchen table, discussing surds, she assumed. Ann suspected that what Lelah had really resented about them was not the mushrooms: they simply made her feel stupid.

Every morning, before she left for classes, Ann checked the bathroom for signs of the new man—hairs, cosmetics—but there was nothing. She hardly ever heard him; sometimes there was that soft, barefooted pacing, the click of his lock, but there were no radio noises, no coughs, no conversations. For the first couple of weeks, apart from the one glimpse of a tall, billowing figure, she didn't even see him. He didn't appear to use the kitchen, where the mathematicians continued their mysteries undisturbed; or if he did, he cooked while no one else was there. Ann would have forgotten about him completely if it hadn't been for Mrs. Nolan.

10   "He's real nice, not like some you get," she said to Ann in her piercing whisper. Although she shouted at her husband, when he was home, and especially at her children, she always whispered when she was talking to Ann, a hoarse, avid whisper, as if they shared disreputable secrets. Ann was standing in front of her door with the room key in her hand, her usual location during these confidences. Mrs. Nolan knew Ann's routine. It wasn't difficult for her to pretend to be cleaning the bathroom, to pop out and waylay Ann, Ajax and rag in hand, whenever she felt she had something to tell her. She was a short, barrel-shaped woman: the top of her head came only to Ann's nose, so she had to look up at Ann, which at these moments made her seem oddly childlike.

"He's from one of them Arabian countries. Though I thought they wore turbans, or not turbans, those white things, like. He just has this funny hat, sort of like the Shriners. He don't look much like an Arab to me. He's got these tattoo marks on his face. But he's real nice."

Ann stood, her umbrella dripping onto the floor, waiting for Mrs. Nolan to finish. She never had to say anything much; it wasn't expected. "You think you could get me the rent on Wednesday?" Mrs. Nolan asked. Three days early; the real point of the conversation, probably. Still, as Mrs. Nolan had said back in September, she didn't have much of anyone to talk to. Her husband was away much of the time and her children escaped outdoors whenever they could. She never went out herself except to shop, and for Mass on Sundays.

"I'm glad it was you took the room," she'd said to Ann. "I can talk to you. You're not, like, foreign. Not like most of them. It was his idea, getting this big house to rent out. Not that he has to do the work or put up with them. You never know what they'll do."

Ann wanted to point out to her that she was indeed foreign, that she was just as foreign as any of the others, but she knew Mrs. Nolan would not understand. It would be like that fiasco in October. *Wear your native costumes.* She had responded to the invitation out of a sense of duty, as well as one of irony. Wait till they get a load of my native costume, she'd thought, contemplating snowshoes and a parka but actually putting on her good blue wool suit. There was only one thing *native costume* reminded her of: the cover picture on the Missionary Sunday School paper they'd once handed out, which showed children from all the countries of the world dancing in a circle around a smiling white-faced Jesus in a bedsheet. That, and the poem in the *Golden Windows Reader:*

Little Indian, Sioux or Cree,
Oh, don't you wish that you were me?

15   The awful thing, as she told Lelah later, was that she was the only one who'd gone. "She had all this food ready, and not a single other person was there. She was really upset, and I was so embarrassed for her. It was some Friends of Foreign Students thing, just for women: students and the wives of students. She obviously didn't think I was foreign enough, and she couldn't

figure out why no one else came." Neither could Ann, who had stayed for too long and had eaten platefuls of crackers and cheese she didn't want in order to soothe her hostess's thwarted sense of hospitality. The woman, who had tastefully streaked ash-blonde hair and a living room filled with polished and satiny traditional surfaces, had alternately urged her to eat and stared at the door, as if expecting a parade of foreigners in their native costumes to come trooping gratefully through it.

Lelah smiled, showing her wise tooth. "Don't they know any better than to throw those things at night?" she asked. "Those men aren't going to let their wives go out by themselves at night. And the single ones are afraid to walk on the streets alone, I know I am."

"I'm not," Ann said, "as long as you stay on the main ones, where it's lighted."

"Then you're a fool," Lelah said. "Don't you know there was a girl murdered three blocks from here? Left her bathroom window unlocked. Some man climbed through the window and cut her throat."

"I always carry my umbrella," Ann said. Of course there were certain places where you just didn't go. Scollay Square, for instance, where the prostitutes hung out and you might get followed, or worse. She tried to explain to Lelah that she wasn't used to this, to any of this, that in Toronto you could walk all over the city, well, almost anywhere, and never have any trouble. She went on to say that no one here seemed to understand that she wasn't like them, she came from a different country, it wasn't the same; but Lelah was quickly bored by this. She had to get back to Tolstoy, she said, putting out her cigarette in her unfinished cup of instant coffee. (Not strong enough for her, I suppose, Ann thought.)

20   "You shouldn't worry," she said. "You're well off. At least your family doesn't almost disown you for doing what you want to do." Lelah's father kept writing her letters, urging her to return to Turkey, where the family had decided on the perfect husband for her. Lelah had stalled them for one year, and maybe she could stall them for one more, but that would be her limit. She couldn't possibly finish her thesis in that time.

Ann hadn't seen much of her since she'd moved out. You lost sight of people quickly here, in the ever-shifting population of hopeful and despairing transients.

No one wrote her letters urging her to come home, no one had picked out the perfect husband for her. On the contrary. She could imagine her mother's defeated look, the greying and sinking of her face, if she were suddenly to announce that she was going to quit school, trade in her ambitions for fate, and get married. Even her father wouldn't like it. *Finish what you start,* he'd say, *I didn't and look what happened to me.* The bungalow at the top of Avenue Road, beside a gas station, with the roar of the expressway always there, like the sea, and fumes blighting the Chinese elm hedge her mother had planted to conceal the pumps. Both her brothers had dropped out of high school; they weren't the good students Ann had been. One worked in a print shop now and had a wife; the other had drifted to Vancouver, and no one knew what he did. She remembered her first real boyfriend, beefy, easygoing Bill

Decker, with his two-tone car that kept losing the muffler. They'd spent a lot of time parked on side streets, rubbing against each other through all those layers of clothes. But even in that sensual mist, the cocoon of breath and skin they'd spun around each other, those phone conversations that existed as a form of touch, she'd known this was not something she could get too involved in. He was probably flabby by now, settled. She'd had relationships with men since then, but she had treated them the same way. *Circumspect.*

Not that Mrs. Nolan's back room was any step up. Out one window there was a view of the funeral home next door; out the other was the yard, which the Nolan kids had scraped clean of grass and which was now a bog of half-frozen mud. Their dog, a mongrelized German shepherd, was kept tied there, where the kids alternately hugged and tormented it. ("Jimmy! Donny! Now you leave that dog alone!" "Don't do that, he's filthy! Look at you!" Ann covering her ears, reading about underground malls.) She'd tried to fix the room up, she'd hung a madras spread as a curtain in front of the cooking area, she'd put up several prints, Braque still-lifes of guitars and soothing Cubist fruit, and she was growing herbs on her windowsill; she needed surroundings that at least tried not to be ugly. But none of these things helped much. At night she wore earplugs. She hadn't known about the scarcity of good rooms, hadn't realized that the whole area was a student slum, that the rents would be so high, the available places so dismal. Next year would be different; she'd get here early and have the pick of the crop. Mrs. Nolan's was definitely a leftover. You could do much better for the money; you could even have a whole apartment, if you were willing to live in the real slum that spread in narrow streets of three-storey frame houses, fading mustard yellow and soot grey, nearer the river. Though Ann didn't think she was quite up to that. Something in one of the good old houses, on a quiet back street, with a little stained glass, would be more like it. Her friend Jetske had a place like that.

But she was doing what she wanted, no doubt of that. In high school she had planned to be an architect, but while finishing the preliminary courses at university she had realized that the buildings she wanted to design were either impossible—who could afford them?—or futile. They would be lost, smothered, ruined by all the other buildings jammed inharmoniously around them. This was why she had decided to go into Urban Design, and she had come here because this school was the best. Or rumoured to be the best. By the time she finished, she intended to be so well-qualified, so armoured with qualifications, that no one back home would dare turn her down for the job she coveted. She wanted to rearrange Toronto. Toronto would do for a start.

25 She wasn't yet too certain of the specific details. What she saw were spaces, beautiful green spaces, with water flowing through them, and trees. Not big golf-course lawns, though; something more winding, something with sudden turns, private niches, surprising vistas. And no formal flower beds. The houses, or whatever they were, set unobtrusively among the trees, the cars kept where? And where would people shop, and who would live in these places? This was the problem: she could see the vistas, the trees and the

streams or canals, quite clearly, but she could never visualize the people. Her green spaces were always empty.

She didn't see her next-door neighbour again until February. She was coming back from the small local supermarket where she bought the food for her cheap, carefully balanced meals. He was leaning in the doorway of what, at home, she would have called a vestibule, smoking a cigarette and staring out at the rain, through the glass panes at the side of the front door. He should have moved a little to give Ann room to put down her umbrella, but he didn't. He didn't even look at her. She squeezed in, shook her deflated umbrella and checked her mailbox, which didn't have a key. There weren't usually any letters in it, and today was no exception. He was wearing a white shirt that was too big for him and some greenish trousers. His feet were not bare, in fact he was wearing a pair of prosaic brown shoes. He did have tattoo marks, though, or rather scars, a set of them running across his cheek. It was the first time she had seen him from the front. He seemed a little shorter than he had when she'd glimpsed him heading towards the stairs, but perhaps it was because he had no hat on. He was curved so listlessly against the door-frame, it was almost as if he had no bones.

There was nothing to see through the front of Mrs. Nolan's door except the traffic, sizzling by the way it did every day. He was depressed, it must be that. This weather would depress anyone. Ann sympathized with his loneliness, but she did not wish to become involved in it, implicated by it. She had enough trouble dealing with her own. She smiled at him, though since he wasn't looking at her this smile was lost. She went past him and up the stairs.

As she fumbled in her purse for her key, Mrs. Nolan stumped out of the bathroom. "You see him?" she whispered.

"Who?" Ann said.

30   "*Him.*" Mrs. Nolan jerked her thumb. "Standing down there, by the door. He does that a lot. He's bothering me, like. I don't have such good nerves."

"He's not doing anything," Ann said.

"That's what I mean," Mrs. Nolan whispered ominously. "He never does nothing. Far as I can tell, he never goes out much. All he does is borrow my vacuum cleaner."

"Your vacuum cleaner?" Ann said, startled into responding.

"That's what I said." Mrs. Nolan had a rubber plunger which she was fingering. "And there's more of them. They come in the other night, up to his room. Two more, with the same marks and everything, on their faces. It's like some kind of, like, a religion or something. And he never gave the vacuum cleaner back till the next day."

35   "Does he pay the rent?" Ann said, trying to switch the conversation to practical matters. Mrs. Nolan was letting her imagination get out of control.

"Regular," Mrs. Nolan said. "Except I don't like the way he comes down, so quiet like, right into my house. With Fred away so much."

"I wouldn't worry," Ann said in what she hoped was a soothing voice. "He seems perfectly nice."

"It's always that kind," Mrs. Nolan said.

Ann cooked her dinner, a chicken breast, some peas, a digestive biscuit. Then she washed her hair in the bathroom and put it up in rollers. She had to do that, to give it body. With her head encased in the plastic hood of her portable dryer she sat at her table, drinking instant coffee, smoking her usual half cigarette, and attempting to read a book about Roman aqueducts, from which she hoped to get some novel ideas for her current project. (An aqueduct, going right through the middle of the obligatory shopping centre? Would anyone care?) Her mind kept flicking, though, to the problem of the man next door. Ann did not often try to think about what it would be like to be a man. But this particular man . . . Who was he, and what was happening to him? He must be a student, everyone here was a student. And he would be intelligent, that went without saying. Probably on scholarship. Everyone here in the graduate school was on scholarship, except the real Americans, who sometimes weren't. Or rather, the women were, but some of the men were still avoiding the draft, though President Johnson had announced he was going to do away with all that. She herself would never have made it this far without scholarships; her parents could not have afforded it.

40   So he was here on scholarship, studying something practical, no doubt, nuclear physics or the construction of dams, and, like herself and the other foreigners, he was expected to go away again as soon as he'd learned what he'd come for. But he never went out of the house; he stood at the front door and watched the brutish flow of cars, the winter rain, while those back in his own country, the ones who had sent him, were confidently expecting him to return someday, crammed with knowledge, ready to solve their lives. He's lost his nerve, Ann thought. He'll fail. It was too late in the year for him ever to catch up. Such failures, such paralysis, were fairly common here, especially among the foreigners. He was far from home, from the language he shared, the wearers of his native costume; he was in exile, he was drowning. What did he do, alone by himself in his room at night?

Ann switched her hair dryer to COOL and wrenched her mind back to aqueducts. She could see he was drowning but there was nothing she could do. Unless you were good at it you shouldn't even try, she was wise enough to know that. All you could do for the drowning was to make sure you were not one of them.

The aqueduct, now. It would be made of natural brick, an earthy red; it would have low arches, in the shade of which there would be ferns and, perhaps, some delphiniums, in varying tones of blue. She must learn more about plants. Before entering the shopping complex (trust him to assign a shopping complex; before that he had demanded a public housing project), it would flow through her green space, in which, she could now see, there were people walking. Children? *But not children like Mrs. Nolan's.* They would turn her grass to mud, they'd nail things to her trees, their mangy dogs would shit on her ferns, they'd throw bottles and pop cans into her aqueduct. And Mrs. Nolan herself, and her Noah's Ark of seedy, brilliant foreigners, where would she put them? For the houses of the Mrs. Nolans of this world would have to go; that was one of the axioms of Urban Design. She could convert them to small offices, or single-floor apartments; some shrubs and hanging plants and a new coat of paint would do wonders. But she knew this was temporizing. Around her green space, she could see, there was now a high wire fence. Inside it were trees, flowers and grass, outside the dirty snow, the endless rain, the grunting cars and the half-frozen mud of Mrs. Nolan's drab backyard. That was what *exclusive* meant, it meant that some people were excluded. Her parents stood in the rain outside the fence, watching with dreary pride while she strolled about in the eternal sunlight. Their one success.

Stop it, she commanded herself. *They want me to be doing this.* She unwound her hair and brushed it out. Three hours from now, she knew, it would be limp as ever because of the damp.

The next day, she tried to raise her new theoretical problem with her friend Jetske. Jetske was in Urban Design, too. She was from Holland, and could remember running through the devastated streets as a child, begging small change, first from the Germans, later from the American soldiers, who were always good for a chocolate bar or two.

45   "You learn how to take care of yourself," she'd said. "It didn't seem hard at the time, but when you are a child, nothing is that hard. We were all the same, nobody had anything." Because of this background, which was more exotic and cruel than anything Ann herself had experienced (what was growing up next to a gas pump compared with the Nazis?), Ann respected her opinions. She liked her also because she was the only person she'd met here who seemed to know where Canada was. There were a lot of Canadian soldiers buried in Holland. This provided Ann with at least a shadowy identity, which she felt she needed. She didn't have a native costume, but at least she had some heroic dead bodies with which she was connected, however remotely.

"The trouble with what we're doing . . ." she said to Jetske, as they walked towards the library under Ann's umbrella. "I mean, you can rebuild one part, but what do you do about the rest?"

"Of the city?" Jetske said.

"No," Ann said slowly, "I guess I mean of the world."

Jetske laughed. She had what Ann now thought of as Dutch teeth, even and white, with quite a lot of gum showing above them and below the lip. "I didn't know you were a socialist," she said. Her cheeks were pink and healthy, like a cheese ad.

50   "I'm not," Ann said. "But I thought we were supposed to be thinking in total patterns."

Jetske laughed again. "Did you know," she said, "that in some countries you have to get official permission to move from one town to another?"

Ann didn't like this idea at all. "It controls the population flow," Jetske said. "You can't really have Urban Design without that, you know."

"I think that's awful," Ann said.

"Of course you do," Jetske said, as close to bitterness as she ever got. "You've never had to do it. Over here you are soft in the belly, you think you can always have everything. You think there is freedom of choice. The whole world will come to it. You will see." She began teasing Ann again about her plastic headscarf. Jetske never wore anything on her head.

55   Ann designed her shopping complex, putting in a skylight and banks of indoor plants, leaving out the aqueduct. She got an A.

In the third week of March, Ann went with Jetske and some of the others to a Buckminster Fuller lecture. Afterwards they all went to the pub on the corner of the Square for a couple of beers. Ann left with Jetske about eleven o'clock and walked a couple of blocks with her before Jetske turned off towards her lovely old house with the stained glass. Ann continued by herself, warily, keeping to the lighted streets. She carried her purse under her elbow and held her furled umbrella at the ready. For once it wasn't raining.

When she got back to the house and started to climb the stairs, it struck her that something was different. Upstairs, she knew. Absolutely, something was out of line. There was curious music coming from the room next door, a high flute rising over drums, thumping noises, the sound of voices. The man next door was throwing a party, it seemed. Good for him, Ann thought. He might as well do something. She settled down for an hour's reading.

But the noises were getting louder. From the bathroom came the sound of retching. There was going to be trouble. Ann checked her door to make sure it was locked, got out the bottle of sherry she kept in the cupboard next to the oven and poured herself a drink. Then she turned out the light and sat with her back against the door, drinking her sherry in the faint blue light from the funeral home next door. There was no point in going to bed: even with her earplugs in, she could never sleep.

The music and thumpings got louder. After a while there was a banging on the floor, then some shouting, which came quite clearly through Ann's hot-air register. "I'm calling the police! You hear? I'm calling the police! You get them out of here and get out yourself!" The music switched off, the door opened and there was a clattering down the stairs. Then more footsteps— Ann couldn't tell whether they were going up or down—and more shouting. The front door banged and the shouts continued on down the street. Ann undressed and put on her nightgown, still without turning on the light, and crept into the bathroom. The bathtub was full of vomit.

60   This time Mrs. Nolan didn't even wait for Ann to get back from classes. She waylaid her in the morning as she was coming out of her room. Mrs. Nolan was holding a can of Drano and had dark circles under her eyes. Somehow this made her look younger. She's probably not much older than I am, Ann thought. Until now she had considered her middle-aged.

"I guess you saw the mess in there," she whispered.

"Yes, I did," Ann said.

"I guess you heard all that last night." She paused.

"What happened?" Ann asked. In fact she really wanted to know.

65   "He had some dancing girls in there! Three dancing girls, and two other men, in that little room! I thought the ceiling was gonna come right down on our heads!"

"I did hear something like dancing," Ann said.

"Dancing! They was jumping, it sounded like they jumped right off the bed onto the floor. The plaster was coming off. Fred wasn't home, he's not home yet. I was afraid for the kids. Like, with those tattoos, who knows what they was working themselves up to?" Her sibilant voice hinted of ritual murders, young Jimmy and runny-nosed Donny sacrificed to some obscure god.

"What did you do?" Ann asked.

"I called the police. Well, the dancing girls, as soon as they heard I was calling the police, they got out of here, I can tell you. Put on their coats and was down the stairs and out the door like nothing. You can bet they didn't want no trouble with the police. But not the others, they don't seem to know what police means."

70   She paused again, and Ann asked, "Did they come?"

"Who?"

"The police."

"Well, you know around here it always takes the police a while to get there, unless there's some right outside. I know that, it's not the first time I've had to call them. So who knows what they would've done in the meantime? I could hear them coming downstairs, like, so I just grabs the broom and I chased them out. I chased them all the way down the street."

Ann saw that she thought she had done something very brave, which meant that in fact she had. She really believed that the man next door and his friends were dangerous, that they were a threat to her children. She had chased them single-handedly, yelling with fear and defiance. But he had only been throwing a party.

75   "Heavens," she said weakly.

"You can say that again," said Mrs. Nolan. "I went in there this morning, to get his things and put them out front where he could get them without me having to see him. I don't have such good nerves, I didn't sleep at all, even after they was gone. Fred is just gonna have to stop driving nights, I can't take it. But you know? He didn't have no things in there. Not one. Just an old empty suitcase?"

"What about his native costume?" Ann said.

"He had it on," Mrs. Nolan said. "He just went running down the street in it, like some kind of a loony. And you know what else I found in there? In one corner, there was this pile of empty bottles. Liquor. He must've been drinking like a fish for months, and never threw out the bottles. And in another corner, there was this pile of burnt matches. He could've burnt the house down, throwing them on the floor like that. But the worst thing was, you know all the times he borrowed my vacuum cleaner?"

"Yes," Ann said.

80   "Well, he never threw away the dirt. There it all was, in the other corner of the room. He must've just emptied it out and left it there. I don't get it." Mrs. Nolan, by now, was puzzled rather than angry.

"Well," Ann said, "that certainly is strange."

"Strange?" Mrs. Nolan said. "I'll tell you it's strange. He always paid the rent though, right on time. Never a day late. Why would he put the dirt in a corner like that, when he could've put it out in a bag like everyone else? It's not like he didn't know. I told him real clear which were the garbage days, when he moved in."

Ann said she was going to be late for class if she didn't hurry. At the front door she tucked her hair under her plastic scarf. Today it was just a drizzle, not heavy enough for the umbrella. She started off, walking quickly along beside the double line of traffic.

She wondered where he had gone, chased down the street by Mrs. Nolan in her scuffies and flowered housecoat, shouting and flailing at him with a broom. She must have been at least as terrifying a spectacle to him as he was to her, and just as inexplicable. Why would this woman, this fat crazy woman, wish to burst in upon a scene of harmless hospitality, banging and raving? He and his friends could easily have overpowered her, but they would not even have thought about doing that. They would have been too frightened. What unspoken taboo had they violated? What would these cold, mad people do next?

85   Anyway, he did have some friends. They would take care of him, at least for the time being. Which was a relief, she guessed. But what she really felt was a childish regret that she had not seen the dancing girls. If she had known they were there, she might even have risked opening her door. She knew they were not real dancing girls, they were probably just some whores from Scollay Square. Mrs. Nolan had called them that as a euphemism, or perhaps because of an unconscious association with the word *Arabian,* the vaguely Arabian country. She never had found out what it was. Nevertheless, she wished she had seen them. Jetske would find all of this quite amusing, especially the image of her backed against the door, drinking sherry in the dark. It would have been better if she'd had the courage to look.

She began to think about her green space, as she often did during this walk. The green, perfect space of the future. She knew by now that it was cancelled in advance, that it would never come into being, that it was already too late. Once she was qualified, she would return to plan tasteful mixes of residential units and shopping complexes, with a lot of underground malls and arcades to protect people from the snow. But she could allow herself to see it one last time.

The fence was gone now, and the green stretched out endlessly, fields and trees and flowing water, as far as she could see. In the distance, beneath the arches of the aqueduct, a herd of animals, deer or something, was grazing. (She must learn more about animals.) Groups of people were walking happily among the trees, holding hands, not just in twos but in threes, fours, fives. The man from next door was there, in his native costume, and the mathematicians, they were all in their native costumes. Beside the stream a man was playing the flute; and around him, in long flowered robes and mauve scuffies, their auburn hair floating around their healthy pink faces, smiling their Dutch smiles, the dancing girls were sedately dancing.

Questions on Setting . . .

1. Is setting at the heart of this story? Do we understand the characters by means of the setting?

2. In the setting of this story, is anything strange or exotic? From whose standpoint? How do notions of the strange or exotic enter into this story's setting?

3. The list of earlier tenants suggests a variety of backgrounds. Does this variety qualify the setting of the story?

4. What does Ann's subject of study have to do with setting? Is her area of study part of the plot of the story? The theme?

. . . and Other Elements

5. Is Ann a snob? What is her attitude toward Mrs. Nolan? Is Mrs. Nolan a snob?

6. Why doesn't Mrs. Nolan think of Ann as a foreigner?

7. Critics often tell us that, in a short story, someone's life changes. Is Ann's life changed? Can you foresee a change coming?

Alice Munro

Alice Munro (1931–   ) was born and grew up in Wingham, Ontario, then attended the University of Western Ontario. Married, with three daughters, she lived in Vancouver and Victoria before returning to Ontario. In 1968, she won the Governor-General's Award for her first book of short stories, *Dance of the Happy Shades.* Her novel, *Lives of Girls and Women,* appeared in 1971. Other collections of short stories are *Something I've Been Meaning to Tell You* (1974), *The Moons of Jupiter* (1982), *The Progress of Love* (1986), and *Friend of My Youth* (1990).

Friend of My Youth   (1990)

I used to dream about my mother, and though the details in the dream varied, the surprise in it was always the same. The dream stopped, I suppose because it was too transparent in its hopefulness, too easy in its forgiveness.

In the dream I would be the age I really was, living the life I was really living, and I would discover that my mother was still alive. (The fact is, she died when I was in my early twenties and she in her early fifties.) Sometimes I would find myself in our old kitchen, where my mother would be rolling out piecrust on the table, or washing the dishes in the battered cream-colored dishpan with the red rim. But other times I would run into her on the street, in places where I would never have expected to see her. She might be walking through a handsome hotel lobby, or lining up in an airport. She would be looking quite well—not exactly youthful, not entirely untouched by the paralyzing disease that held her in its grip for a decade or more before her death, but so much better than I remembered that I would be astonished. Oh, I just have this little tremor in my arm, she would say, and a little stiffness up this side of my face. It is a nuisance but I get around.

I recovered then what in waking life I had lost—my mother's liveliness of face and voice before her throat muscles stiffened and a woeful, impersonal mask fastened itself over her features. How could I have forgotten this, I would think in the dream—the casual humor she had, not ironic but merry, the lightness and impatience and confidence? I would say that I was sorry I hadn't been to see her in such a long time—meaning not that I felt guilty but that I was sorry I had kept a bugbear in my mind, instead of this reality—and the strangest, kindest thing of all to me was her matter-of-fact reply.

Oh, well, she said, better late than never. I was sure I'd see you someday.

5 When my mother was a young woman with a soft, mischievous face and shiny, opaque silk stockings on her plump legs (I have seen a photograph of her, with her pupils), she went to teach at a one-room school, called Grieves School, in the Ottawa Valley. The school was on a corner of the farm that belonged to the Grieves family—a very good farm for that country. Well-drained fields with none of the Precambrian rock shouldering through the soil, a little willow-edged river running alongside, a sugar bush, log barns, and a large, unornamented house whose wooden walls had never been painted but had been left to weather. And when wood weathers in the Ottawa Valley, my mother said, I do not know why this is, but it never turns gray, it turns black. There must be something in the air, she said. She often spoke of the Ottawa Valley, which was her home—she had grown up about twenty miles away from Grieves School—in a dogmatic, mystified way, emphasizing things about it that distinguished it from any other place on earth. Houses turn black, maple syrup has a taste no maple syrup produced elsewhere can equal, bears amble within sight of farmhouses. Of course I was disappointed when I finally got to see this place. It was not a valley at all, if by that you mean a cleft between hills; it was a mixture of flat fields and low rocks and heavy bush and little lakes—a scrambled, disarranged sort of country with no easy harmony about it, not yielding readily to any description.

The log barns and unpainted house, common enough on poor farms, were not in the Grieveses' case a sign of poverty but of policy. They had the money but they did not spend it. That was what people told my mother. The Grieveses worked hard and they were far from ignorant, but they were very backward. They didn't have a car or electricity or a telephone or a tractor. Some people thought this was because they were Cameronians—they were the only people in the school district who were of that religion—but in fact their church (which they themselves always called the Reformed Presbyterian) did not forbid engines or electricity or any inventions of that sort, just card playing, dancing, movies, and, on Sundays, any activity at all that was not religious or unavoidable.

My mother could not say who the Cameronians were or why they were called that. Some freak religion from Scotland, she said from the perch of her obedient and lighthearted Anglicanism. The teacher always boarded with the Grieveses, and my mother was a little daunted at the thought of going to live in that black board house with its paralytic Sundays and coal-oil lamps and primitive notions. But she was engaged by that time, she wanted to work on her trousseau instead of running around the country having a good time, and she figured she could get home one Sunday out of three. (On Sundays at the Grieveses' house, you could light a fire for heat but not for cooking, you could not even boil the kettle to make tea, and you were not supposed to write a letter or swat a fly. But it turned out that my mother was exempt from these rules. "No, no," said Flora Grieves, laughing at her. "That doesn't mean you. You must just go on as you're used to doing." And after a while my mother had made friends with Flora to such an extent that she wasn't even going home on the Sundays when she'd planned to.)

Flora and Ellie Grieves were the two sisters left of the family. Ellie was married, to a man called Robert Deal, who lived there and worked the farm but had not changed its name to Deal's in anyone's mind. By the way people spoke, my mother expected the Grieves sisters and Robert Deal to be middle-aged at least, but Ellie, the younger sister, was only about thirty, and Flora seven or eight years older. Robert Deal might be in between.

The house was divided in an unexpected way. The married couple didn't live with Flora. At the time of their marriage, she had given them the parlor and the dining room, the front bedrooms and staircase, the winter kitchen. There was no need to decide about the bathroom, because there wasn't one. Flora had the summer kitchen, with its open rafters and uncovered brick walls, the old pantry made into a narrow dining room and sitting room, and the two back bedrooms, one of which was my mother's. The teacher was housed with Flora, in the poorer part of the house. But my mother didn't mind. She immediately preferred Flora, and Flora's cheerfulness, to the silence and sickroom atmosphere of the front rooms. In Flora's domain it was not even true that all amusements were forbidden. She had a crokinole board—she taught my mother how to play.

10   The division had been made, of course, in the expectation that Robert and Ellie would have a family, and that they would need the room. This hadn't happened. They had been married for more than a dozen years and there had not been a live child. Time and again Ellie had been pregnant, but two babies had been stillborn, and the rest she had miscarried. During my mother's first year, Ellie seemed to be staying in bed more and more of the time, and my mother thought that she must be pregnant again, but there was no mention of it. Such people would not mention it. You could not tell from the look of Ellie, when she got up and walked around, because she showed a stretched and ruined though slack-chested shape. She carried a sickbed odor, and she fretted in a childish way about everything. Flora took care of her and did all the work. She washed the clothes and tidied up the rooms and cooked the meals served in both sides of the house, as well as helping Robert with the milking and separating. She was up before daylight and never seemed to tire.

During the first spring my mother was there, a great housecleaning was embarked upon, during which Flora climbed the ladders herself and carried down the storm windows, washed and stacked them away, carried all the furniture out of one room after another so that she could scrub the wood-work and varnish the floors. She washed every dish and glass that was sitting in the cupboards supposedly clean already. She scalded every pot and spoon. Such need and energy possessed her that she could hardly sleep—my mother would wake up to the sound of stovepipes being taken down, or the broom, draped in a dish towel, whacking at the smoky cobwebs. Through the washed uncurtained windows came a torrent of unmerciful light. The cleanliness was devastating. My mother slept now on sheets that had been bleached and starched and that gave her a rash. Sick Ellie complained daily of the smell of varnish and cleansing powders. Flora's hands were raw. But her disposition remained topnotch. Her kerchief and apron and Robert's baggy overalls that she donned for the climbing jobs gave her the air of a comedian— sportive, unpredictable.

My mother called her a whirling dervish.

"You're a regular whirling dervish, Flora," she said, and Flora halted. She wanted to know what was meant. My mother went ahead and explained, though she was a little afraid lest piety should be offended. (Not piety exactly—you could not call it that. Religious strictness.) Of course it wasn't. There was not a trace of nastiness or smug vigilance in Flora's observance of her religion. She had no fear of heathens—she had always lived in the midst of them. She liked the idea of being a dervish, and went to tell her sister.

"Do you know what the teacher says I am?"

Flora and Ellie were both dark-haired, dark-eyed women, tall and narrow-shouldered and long-legged. Ellie was a wreck, of course, but Flora was still superbly straight and graceful. She could look like a queen, my mother said—even riding into town in that cart they had. For church they used a buggy or a cutter, but when they went to town they often had to transport sacks of wool—they kept a few sheep—or of produce, to sell, and they had to bring provisions home. The trip of a few miles was not made often. Robert rode in front, to drive the horse—Flora could drive a horse perfectly well, but it must always be the man who drove. Flora would be standing behind holding on to the sacks. She rode to town and back standing up, keeping an easy balance, wearing her black hat. Almost ridiculous but not quite. A gypsy queen, my mother thought she looked like, with her black hair and her skin that always looked slightly tanned, and her lithe and bold serenity. Of course she lacked the gold bangles and the bright clothes. My mother envied her her slenderness, and her cheekbones.

15 Returning in the fall for her second year, my mother learned what was the matter with Ellie.

"My sister has a growth," Flora said. Nobody then spoke of cancer.

My mother had heard that before. People suspected it. My mother knew many people in the district by that time. She had made particular friends with a young woman who worked in the post office; this woman was going to be one of my mother's bridesmaids. The story of Flora and Ellie and Robert had been told—or all that people knew of it—in various versions. My mother did not feel that she was listening to gossip, because she was always on the alert for any disparaging remarks about Flora—she would not put up with that. But indeed nobody offered any. Everybody said that Flora had behaved like a saint. Even when she went to extremes, as in dividing up the house— that was like a saint.

Robert came to work at Grieveses' some months before the girls' father died. They knew him already, from church. (Oh, that church, my mother said, having attended it once, out of curiosity—that drear building miles on the other side of town, no organ or piano and plain glass in the windows and a doddery old minister with his hours-long sermon, a man hitting a tuning fork for the singing.) Robert had come out from Scotland and was on his way west. He had stopped with relatives or people he knew, members of the scanty congregation. To earn some money, probably, he came to Grieveses'. Soon he and Flora were engaged. They could not go to dances or to card parties like other couples, but they went for long walks. The chaperone— unofficially—was Ellie. Ellie was then a wild tease, a long-haired, impudent, childish girl full of lolloping energy. She would run up hills and smite the mullein stalks with a stick, shouting and prancing and pretending to be a warrior on horseback. That, or the horse itself. This when she was fifteen, sixteen years old. Nobody but Flora could control her, and generally Flora just laughed at her, being too used to her to wonder if she was quite right in the head. They were wonderfully fond of each other. Ellie, with her long skinny body, her long pale face, was like a copy of Flora—the kind of copy you often see in families, in which because of some carelessness or exaggeration of features or coloring, the handsomeness of one person passes into the plainness—or almost plainness—of the other. But Ellie had no jealousy about this. She loved to comb out Flora's hair and pin it up. They had great times, washing each other's hair. Ellie would press her face into Flora's throat, like a colt nuzzling its mother. So when Robert laid claim to Flora, or Flora to him—nobody knew how it was—Ellie had to be included. She didn't show any spite toward Robert, but she pursued and waylaid them on their walks; she sprung on them out of the bushes or sneaked up behind them so softly that she could blow on their necks. People saw her do it. And they heard of her jokes. She had always been terrible for jokes and sometimes it had got her into trouble with her father, but Flora had protected her. Now she put thistles in Robert's bed. She set his place at the table with the knife and fork the wrong way around. She switched the milk pails to give him the old one with the hole in it. For Flora's sake, maybe, Robert humored her.

The father had made Flora and Robert set the wedding day a year ahead, and after he died they did not move it any closer. Robert went on living in the house. Nobody knew how to speak to Flora about this being scandalous, or looking scandalous. Flora would just ask why. Instead of putting the wedding ahead, she put it back—from next spring to early fall, so that there should be a full year between it and her father's death. A year from wedding to funeral—

that seemed proper to her. She trusted fully in Robert's patience and in her own purity.

So she might. But in the winter a commotion started. There was Ellie, vomiting, weeping, running off and hiding in the haymow, howling when they found her and pulled her out, jumping to the barn floor, running around in circles, rolling in the snow. Ellie was deranged. Flora had to call the doctor. She told him that her sister's periods had stopped—could the backup of blood be driving her wild? Robert had had to catch her and tie her up, and together he and Flora had put her to bed. She would not take food, just whipped her head from side to side, howling. It looked as if she would die speechless. But somehow the truth came out. Not from the doctor, who could not get close enough to examine her, with all her thrashing about. Probably, Robert confessed. Flora finally got wind of the truth, through all her high-mindedness. Now there had to be a wedding, though not the one that had been planned.

No cake, no new clothes, no wedding trip, no congratulations. Just a shameful hurry-up visit to the manse. Some people, seeing the names in the paper, thought the editor must have got the sisters mixed up. They thought it must be Flora. A hurry-up wedding for Flora! But no—it was Flora who pressed Robert's suit—it must have been—and got Ellie out of bed and washed her and made her presentable. It would have been Flora who picked one geranium from the window plant and pinned it to her sister's dress. And Ellie hadn't torn it out. Ellie was meek now, no longer flailing or crying. She let Flora fix her up, she let herself be married, she was never wild from that day on.

Flora had the house divided. She herself helped Robert build the necessary partitions. The baby was carried full term—nobody even pretended that it was early—but it was born dead after a long, tearing labor. Perhaps Ellie had damaged it when she jumped from the barn beam and rolled in the snow and beat on herself. Even if she hadn't done that, people would have expected something to go wrong, with that child or maybe one that came later. God dealt out punishment for hurry-up marriages—not just Presbyterians but almost everybody else believed that. God rewarded lust with dead babies, idiots, harelips and withered limbs and clubfeet.

In this case the punishment continued. Ellie had one miscarriage after another, then another stillbirth and more miscarriages. She was constantly pregnant, and the pregnancies were full of vomiting fits that lasted for days, headaches, cramps, dizzy spells. The miscarriages were as agonizing as full-term births. Ellie could not do her own work. She walked around holding on to chairs. Her numb silence passed off, and she became a complainer. If anybody came to visit, she would talk about the peculiarities of her headaches or describe her latest fainting fit, or even—in front of men, in front of unmarried girls or children—go into bloody detail about what Flora called her "disappointments." When people changed the subject or dragged the children away, she turned sullen. She demanded new medicine, reviled the doctor, nagged Flora. She accused Flora of washing the dishes with a great clang and clatter, out of spite, of pulling her—Ellie's—hair when she combed it out, of stingily substituting water-and-molasses for her real medicine. No matter what she said, Flora soothed her. Everybody who came into the house had some story of that kind to tell. Flora said, "Where's my little girl, then? Where's my Ellie? This isn't my Ellie, this is some crosspatch got in here in place of her!"

In the winter evenings after she came in from helping Robert with the barn chores, Flora would wash and change her clothes and go next door to read Ellie to sleep. My mother might invite herself along, taking whatever sewing she was doing, on some item of her trousseau. Ellie's bed was set up in the big dining room, where there was a gas lamp over the table. My mother sat on one side of the table, sewing, and Flora sat on the other side, reading aloud. Sometimes Ellie said, "I can't hear you." Or if Flora paused for a little rest Ellie said, "I'm not asleep yet."

25   What did Flora read? Stories about Scottish life—not classics. Stories about urchins and comic grandmothers. The only title my mother could remember was *Wee Macgregor*. She could not follow the stories very well, or laugh when Flora laughed and Ellie gave a whimper, because so much was in Scots dialect or read with that thick accent. She was surprised that Flora could do it—it wasn't the way Flora ordinarily talked, at all.

(But wouldn't it be the way Robert talked? Perhaps that is why my mother never reports anything that Robert said, never has him contributing to the scene. He must have been there, he must have been sitting there in the room. They would only heat the main room of the house. I see him black-haired, heavy-shouldered, with the strength of a plow horse, and the same kind of sombre, shackled beauty.)

Then Flora would say, "That's all of that for tonight." She would pick up another book, an old book written by some preacher of their faith. There was in it such stuff as my mother had never heard. What stuff? She couldn't say. All the stuff that was in their monstrous old religion. That put Ellie to sleep, or made her pretend she was asleep, after a couple of pages.

All that configuration of the elect and the damned, my mother must have meant—all the arguments about the illusion and necessity of free will. Doom and slippery redemption. The torturing, defeating, but for some minds irresistible pileup of interlocking and contradictory notions. My mother could resist it. Her faith was easy, her spirits at that time robust. Ideas were not what she was curious about, ever.

But what sort of thing was that, she asked (silently), to read to a dying woman? This was the nearest she got to criticizing Flora.

30   The answer—that it was the only thing, if you believed it—never seemed to have occurred to her.

By spring a nurse had arrived. That was the way things were done then. People died at home, and a nurse came in to manage it.

The nurse's name was Audrey Atkinson. She was a stout woman with corsets as stiff as barrel hoops, marcelled hair the color of brass candlesticks, a mouth shaped by lipstick beyond its own stingy outlines. She drove a car into the yard—her own car, a dark-green coupé, shiny and smart. News of Audrey Atkinson and her car spread quickly. Questions were asked. Where did she get the money? Had some rich fool altered his will on her behalf?

Had she exercised influence? Or simply helped herself to a stash of bills under the mattress? How was she to be trusted?

Hers was the first car ever to sit in the Grieveses' yard overnight.

Audrey Atkinson said that she had never been called out to tend a case in so primitive a house. It was beyond her, she said, how people could live in such a way.

35   "It's not that they're poor, even," she said to my mother. "It isn't, is it? That I could understand. Or it's not even their religion. So what is it? They do not care!"

She tried at first to cozy up to my mother, as if they would be natural allies in this benighted place. She spoke as if they were around the same age—both stylish, intelligent women who liked a good time and had modern ideas. She offered to teach my mother to drive the car. She offered her cigarettes. My mother was more tempted by the idea of learning to drive than she was by the cigarettes. But she said no, she would wait for her husband to teach her. Audrey Atkinson raised her pinkish-orange eyebrows at my mother behind Flora's back, and my mother was furious. She disliked the nurse far more than Flora did.

"I knew what she was like and Flora didn't," my mother said. She meant that she caught a whiff of a cheap life, maybe even of drinking establishments and unsavory men, of hard bargains, which Flora was too unworldly to notice.

Flora started into the great housecleaning again. She had the curtains spread out on stretchers, she beat the rugs on the line, she leapt up on the stepladder to attack the dust on the molding. But she was impeded all the time by Nurse Atkinson's complaining.

"I wondered if we could have a little less of the running and clattering?" said Nurse Atkinson with offensive politeness. "I only ask for my patient's sake." She always spoke of Ellie as "my patient" and pretended that she was the only one to protect her and compel respect. But she was not so respectful of Ellie herself. "Allee-oop," she would say, dragging the poor creature up on her pillows. And she told Ellie she was not going to stand for fretting and whimpering. "You don't do yourself any good that way," she said. "And you certainly don't make me come any quicker. What you just as well might do is learn to control yourself." She exclaimed at Ellie's bedsores in a scolding way, as if they were a further disgrace of the house. She demanded lotions, ointments, expensive soap—most of them, no doubt, to protect her own skin, which she claimed suffered from the hard water. (How could it be hard, my mother asked her—sticking up for the household when nobody else would— how could it be hard when it came straight from the rain barrel?)

40   Nurse Atkinson wanted cream, too—she said that they should hold some back, not sell it all to the creamery. She wanted to make nourishing soups and puddings for her patient. She did make puddings, and jellies, from packaged mixes such as had never before entered this house. My mother was convinced that she ate them all herself.

Flora still read to Ellie, but now it was only short bits from the Bible. When she finished and stood up, Ellie tried to cling to her. Ellie wept, sometimes she made ridiculous complaints. She said there was a horned cow outside, trying to get into the room and kill her.

"They often get some kind of idea like that," Nurse Atkinson said. "You mustn't give in to her or she won't let you go day or night. That's what they're like, they only think about themselves. Now, when I'm here alone with her, she behaves herself quite nice. I don't have any trouble at all. But after you been in here I have trouble all over again because she sees you and she gets upset. You don't want to make my job harder for me, do you? I mean, you brought me here to take charge, didn't you?"

"Ellie, now, Ellie dear, I must go," said Flora, and to the nurse she said, "I understand. I do understand that you have to be in charge and I admire you, I admire you for your work. In your work you have to have so much patience and kindness."

My mother wondered at this—was Flora really so blinded, or did she hope by this undeserved praise to exhort Nurse Atkinson to the patience and kindness that she didn't have? Nurse Atkinson was too thick-skinned and self-approving for any trick like that to work.

45   "It is a hard job, all right, and not many can do it," she said. "It's not like those nurses in the hospital, where they got everything laid out for them." She had no time for more conversation—she was trying to bring in "Make-Believe Ballroom" on her battery radio.

My mother was busy with the final exams and the June exercises at the school. She was getting ready for her wedding in July. Friends came in cars and whisked her off to the dressmaker's, to parties, to choose the invitations and order the cake. The lilacs came out, the evenings lengthened, the birds were back and nesting, my mother bloomed in everybody's attention, about to set out on the deliciously solemn adventure of marriage. Her dress was to be appliquéd with silk roses, her veil held by a cap of seed pearls. She belonged to the first generation of young women who saved their money and paid for their own weddings—far fancier than their parents could have afforded.

On her last evening, the friend from the post office came to drive her away, with her clothes and her books and the things she had made for her trousseau and the gifts her pupils and others had given her. There was great fuss and laughter about getting everything loaded into the car. Flora came out and helped. This getting married is even more of a nuisance than I thought, said Flora, laughing. She gave my mother a dresser scarf, which she had crocheted in secret. Nurse Atkinson could not be shut out of an important occasion—she presented a spray bottle of cologne. Flora stood on the slope at the side of the house to wave goodbye. She had been invited to the wedding, but of course she had said she could not come, she could not "go out" at such a time. The last my mother ever saw of her was this solitary, energetically waving figure in her housecleaning apron and bandanna, on the green slope by the black-walled house, in the evening light.

"Well, maybe now she'll get what she should've got the first time round," the friend from the post office said. "Maybe now they'll be able to get married. Is she too old to start a family? How old is she, anyway?"

My mother thought that this was a crude way of talking about Flora and replied that she didn't know. But she had to admit to herself that she had been thinking the very same thing.

50   When she was married and settled in her own home, three hundred miles away, my mother got a letter from Flora. Ellie was dead. She had died firm in her faith, Flora said, and grateful for her release. Nurse Atkinson was staying on for a little while, until it was time for her to go off to her next case. This was late in the summer.

News of what happened next did not come from Flora. When she wrote at Christmas, she seemed to take for granted that information would have gone ahead of her.

"You have in all probability heard," wrote Flora, "that Robert and Nurse Atkinson have been married. They are living on here, in Robert's part of the house. They are fixing it up to suit themselves. It is very impolite of me to call her Nurse Atkinson, as I see I have done. I ought to have called her Audrey."

Of course the post-office friend had written, and so had others. It was a great shock and scandal and a matter that excited the district—the wedding as secret and surprising as Robert's first one had been (though surely not for the same reason), Nurse Atkinson permanently installed in the community, Flora losing out for the second time. Nobody had been aware of any courtship, and they asked how the woman could have enticed him. Did she promise children, lying about her age?

The surprises were not to stop with the wedding. The bride got down to business immediately with the "fixing up" that Flora mentioned. In came the electricity and then the telephone. Now Nurse Atkinson—she would always be called Nurse Atkinson—was heard on the party line lambasting painters and paperhangers and delivery services. She was having everything done over. She was buying an electric stove and putting in a bathroom, and who knew where the money was coming from? Was it all hers, got in her deathbed dealings, in shady bequests? Was it Robert's, was he claiming his share? Ellie's share, left to him and Nurse Atkinson to enjoy themselves with, the shameless pair?

55   All these improvements took place on one side of the house only. Flora's side remained just as it was. No electric lights there, no fresh wallpaper or new venetian blinds. When the house was painted on the outside—cream with dark-green trim—Flora's side was left bare. This strange open statement was greeted at first with pity and disapproval, then with less sympathy, as a sign of Flora's stubbornness and eccentricity (she could have bought her own paint and made it look decent), and finally as a joke. People drove out of their way to see it.

There was always a dance given in the schoolhouse for a newly married couple. A cash collection—called "a purse of money"—was presented to them. Nurse Atkinson sent out word that she would not mind seeing this custom followed, even though it happened that the family she had married into was opposed to dancing. Some people thought it would be a disgrace to gratify her, a slap in the face to Flora. Others were too curious to hold back. They wanted to see how the newlyweds would behave. Would Robert dance? What sort of outfit would the bride show up in? They delayed a while, but finally the dance was held, and my mother got her report.

The bride wore the dress she had worn at her wedding, or so she said. But who would wear such a dress for a wedding at the manse? More than likely it was bought specially for her appearance at the dance. Pure-white satin with a sweetheart neckline, idiotically youthful. The groom was got up in a new dark-blue suit, and she had stuck a flower in his buttonhole. They were a sight. Her hair was freshly done to blind the eye with brassy reflections, and her face looked as if it would come off on a man's jacket, should she lay it against his shoulder in the dancing. Of course she did dance. She danced with every man present except the groom, who sat scrunched into one of the school desks along the wall. She danced with every man present—they all claimed they had to do it, it was the custom—and then she dragged Robert out to receive the money and to thank everybody for their best wishes. To the ladies in the cloakroom she even hinted that she was feeling unwell, for the usual newly-wed reason. Nobody believed her, and indeed nothing ever came of this hope, if she really had it. Some of the women thought that she was lying to them out of malice, insulting them, making them out to be so credulous. But nobody challenged her, nobody was rude to her—maybe because it was plain that she could summon a rudeness of her own to knock anybody flat.

Flora was not present at the dance.

"My sister-in-law is not a dancer," said Nurse Atkinson. "She is stuck in the olden times." She invited them to laugh at Flora, whom she always called her sister-in-law, though she had no right to do so.

60   My mother wrote a letter to Flora after hearing about all these things. Being removed from the scene, and perhaps in a flurry of importance due to her own newly married state, she may have lost sight of the kind of person she was writing to. She offered sympathy and showed outrage, and said blunt disparaging things about the woman who had—as my mother saw it—dealt Flora such a blow. Back came a letter from Flora saying that she did not know where my mother had been getting her information, but that it seemed she had misunderstood, or listened to malicious people, or jumped to unjustified conclusions. What happened in Flora's family was nobody else's business, and certainly nobody needed to feel sorry for her or angry on her behalf. Flora said that she was happy and satisfied in her life, as she always had been, and she did not interfere with what others did or wanted, because such things did not concern her. She wished my mother all happiness in her marriage and hoped that she would soon be too busy with her own responsi-bilities to worry about the lives of people that she used to know.

This well-written letter cut my mother, as she said, to the quick. She and Flora stopped corresponding. My mother did become busy with her own life and finally a prisoner in it.

But she thought about Flora. In later years, when she sometimes talked about the things she might have been, or done, she would say, "If I could have been a writer—I do think I could have been; I could have been a writer—then I would have written the story of Flora's life. And do you know what I would have called it? 'The Maiden Lady.'"

The Maiden Lady. She said these words in a solemn and sentimental tone of voice that I had no use for. I knew, or thought I knew, exactly the value she found in them. The stateliness and mystery. The hint of derision turning to reverence. I was fifteen or sixteen years old by that time, and I believed that I could see into my mother's mind. I could see what she would do with Flora, what she had already done. She would make her into a noble figure, one who accepts defection, treachery, who forgives and stands aside, not once but twice. Never a moment of complaint. Flora goes about her cheerful labors, she cleans the house and shovels out the cow byre, she removes some bloody mess from her sister's bed, and when at last the future seems to open up for her—Ellie will die and Robert will beg forgiveness and Flora will silence him with the proud gift of herself—it is time for Audrey Atkinson to drive into the yard and shut Flora out again, more inexplicably and thoroughly the second time than the first. She must endure the painting of the house, the electric lights, all the prosperous activity next door. "Make-Believe Ballroom," "Amos 'n' Andy." No more Scottish comedies or ancient sermons. She must see them drive off to the dance—her old lover and that coldhearted, stupid, by no means beautiful woman in the white satin wedding dress. She is mocked. (And of course she has made over the farm to Ellie and Robert, of course he has inherited it, and now everything belongs to Audrey Atkinson.) The wicked flourish. But it is all right. It is all right—the elect are veiled in patience and humility and lighted by a certainty that events cannot disturb.

That was what I believed my mother would make of things. In her own plight her notions had turned mystical, and there was sometimes a hush, a solemn thrill in her voice that grated on me, alerted me to what seemed a personal danger. I felt a great fog of platitudes and pieties lurking, an incontestable crippled-mother power, which could capture and choke me. There would be no end to it. I had to keep myself sharp-tongued and cynical, arguing and deflating. Eventually I gave up even that recognition and opposed her in silence.

65   This is a fancy way of saying that I was no comfort and poor company to her when she had almost nowhere else to turn.

I had my own ideas about Flora's story. I didn't think that I could have written a novel but that I would write one. I would take a different tack. I saw through my mother's story and put in what she left out. My Flora would be as black as hers was white. Rejoicing in the bad turns done to her and in her own forgiveness, spying on the shambles of her sister's life. A Presbyterian witch, reading out of her poisonous book. It takes a rival ruthlessness, the comparatively innocent brutality of the thick-skinned nurse, to drive her back, to flourish in her shade. But she is driven back; the power of sex and ordinary greed drive her back and shut her up in her own part of the house with the coal-oil lamps. She shrinks, she caves in, her bones harden and her joints thicken, and—oh, this is it, this is it, I see the bare beauty of the ending I will contrive!—she becomes crippled herself, with arthritis, hardly able to move. Now Audrey Atkinson comes into her full power—she demands the whole house. She wants those partitions knocked out that Robert put up with Flora's help when he married Ellie. She will provide Flora with a room, she will take care of her. (Audrey Atkinson does not wish to be seen as a monster, and perhaps she really isn't one.) So one day Robert carries Flora—for the first and last time he carries her in his arms—to the room that his wife Audrey has prepared for her. And once Flora is settled in her well-lit, well-heated corner Audrey Atkinson undertakes to clean out the newly vacated rooms, Flora's rooms. She carries a heap of old books out into the yard. It's spring again, housecleaning time, the season when Flora herself performed such feats, and now the pale face of Flora appears behind the new net curtains. She has dragged herself from her corner, she sees the light-blue sky with its high skidding clouds over the watery fields, the contending crows, the flooded creeks, the reddening tree branches. She sees the smoke rise out of the incinerator in the yard, where her books are burning. Those smelly old books, as Audrey has called them. Words and pages, the ominous dark spines. The elect, the damned, the slim hopes, the mighty torments—up in smoke. There was the ending.

To me the really mysterious person in the story, as my mother told it, was Robert. He never has a word to say. He gets engaged to Flora. He is walking beside her along the river when Ellie leaps out at them. He finds Ellie's thistles in his bed. He does the carpentry made necessary by his and Ellie's marriage. He listens or does not listen while Flora reads. Finally he sits scrunched up in the school desk while his flashy bride dances by with all the men.

So much for his public acts and appearances. But he was the one who started everything, in secret. He *did it to* Ellie. He did it to that skinny wild girl at a time when he was engaged to her sister, and he did it to her again and again when she was nothing but a poor botched body, a failed childbearer, lying in bed.

He must have done it to Audrey Atkinson, too, but with less disastrous results.

70 Those words, *did it to*—the words my mother, no more than Flora, would never bring herself to speak—were simply exciting to me. I didn't feel any decent revulsion or reasonable indignation. I refused the warning. Not even the fate of Ellie could put me off. Not when I thought of that first encounter—the desperation of it, the ripping and striving. I used to sneak longing looks at men in those days. I admired their wrists and their necks and any bit of their chests a loose button let show, and even their ears and their feet in shoes. I expected nothing reasonable of them, only to be engulfed by their passion. I had similar thoughts about Robert.

What made Flora evil in my story was just what made her admirable in my mother's—her turning away from sex. I fought against everything my mother wanted to tell me on this subject; I despised even the drop in her voice, the gloomy caution, with which she approached it. My mother had grown up in a time and in a place where sex was a dark undertaking for women. She knew that you could die of it. So she honored the decency, the prudery, the frigidity, that might protect you. And I grew up in horror of that very protection, the dainty tyranny that seemed to me to extend to all areas of life, to enforce tea parties and white gloves and all sorts of tinkling inanities. I favored bad words and a breakthrough, I teased myself with the thought of a man's recklessness and domination. The odd thing is that my mother's ideas were in line with some progressive notions of her times, and mine echoed the notions that were favored in my time. This in spite of the fact that we both believed ourselves independent, and lived in backwaters that did not register such changes. It's as if tendencies that seem most deeply rooted in our minds, most private and singular, have come in as spores on the prevailing wind, looking for any likely place to land, any welcome.

Not long before she died, but when I was still at home, my mother got a letter from the real Flora. It came from that town near the farm, the town that Flora used to ride to, with Robert, in the cart, holding on to the sacks of wool or potatoes.

Flora wrote that she was no longer living on the farm.

"Robert and Audrey are still there," she wrote. "Robert has some trouble with his back but otherwise he is very well. Audrey has poor circulation and is often short of breath. The doctor says she must lose weight but none of the diets seem to work. The farm has been doing very well. They are out of sheep entirely and into dairy cattle. As you may have heard, the chief thing nowadays is to get your milk quota from the government and then you are set. The old stable is all fixed up with milking machines and the latest modern equipment, it is quite a marvel. When I go out there to visit I hardly know where I am."

75 She went on to say that she had been living in town for some years now, and that she had a job clerking in a store. She must have said what kind of a store this was, but I cannot now remember. She said nothing, of course, about what had led her to this decision—whether she had in fact been put off her own farm, or had sold out her share, apparently not to much advantage. She stressed the fact of her friendliness with Robert and Audrey. She said her health was good.

"I hear that you have not been so lucky in that way," she wrote. "I ran into Cleta Barnes who used to be Cleta Stapleton at the post office out at home, and she told me that there is some problem with your muscles and she said your speech is affected too. This is sad to hear but they can do such wonderful things nowadays so I am hoping that the doctors may be able to help you."

An unsettling letter, leaving so many things out. Nothing in it about God's will or His role in our afflictions. No mention of whether Flora still went to that church. I don't think my mother ever answered. Her fine legible handwriting, her schoolteacher's writing, had deteriorated, and she had difficulty holding a pen. She was always beginning letters and not finishing them. I would find them lying around the house. *My dearest Mary,* they began. *My darling Ruth, My dear little Joanne (though I realize you are not little anymore), My dear old friend Cleta, My lovely Margaret.* These women were friends from her teaching days, her Normal School days, and from high school. A few were former pupils. I have friends all over the country, she would say defiantly. I have dear, dear friends.

I remember seeing one letter that started out: *Friend of my Youth.* I don't know whom it was to. They were all friends of her youth. I don't recall one that began with *My dear and most admired Flora.* I would always look at them, try to read the salutation and the few sentences she had written, and because I could not bear to feel sadness I would feel an impatience with the flowery language, the direct appeal for love and pity. She would get more of that, I thought (more from myself, I meant), if she could manage to withdraw with dignity, instead of reaching out all the time to cast her stricken shadow.

I had lost interest in Flora by then. I was always thinking of stories, and by this time I probably had a new one on my mind.

80   But I have thought of her since. I have wondered what kind of a store. A hardware store or a five-and-ten, where she has to wear a coverall, or a drugstore, where she is uniformed like a nurse, or a Ladies' Wear, where she is expected to be genteelly fashionable? She might have had to learn about food blenders or chain saws, negligees, cosmetics, even condoms. She would have to work all day under electric lights, and operate a cash register. Would she get a permanent, paint her nails, put on lipstick? She must have found a place to live—a little apartment with a kitchenette, overlooking the main street, or a room in a boarding house. How could she go on being a Cameronian? How could she get to that out-of-the-way church unless she managed to buy a car and learned to drive it? And if she did that she might drive not only to church but to other places. She might go on holidays. She might rent a cottage on a lake for a week, learn to swim, visit a city. She might eat meals in a restaurant, possibly in a restaurant where drinks were served. She might make friends with women who were divorced.

She might meet a man. A friend's widowed brother, perhaps. A man who did not know that she was a Cameronian or what Cameronians were. Who knew nothing of her story. A man who had never heard about the partial painting of the house or the two betrayals, or that it took all her dignity and innocence to keep her from being a joke. He might want to take her dancing, and she would have to explain that she could not go. He would be surprised but not put off—all that Cameronian business might seem quaint to him, almost charming. So it would to everybody. She was brought up in some weird religion, people would say. She lived a long time out on some god-forsaken farm. She is a little bit strange but really quite nice. Nice-looking, too. Especially since she went and got her hair done.

I might go into a store and find her.

No, no. She would be dead a long time now.

But suppose I had gone into a store—perhaps a department store. I see a place with the brisk atmosphere, the straightforward displays, the old-fashioned modern look of the fifties. Suppose a tall, handsome woman, nicely turned out, had come to wait on me, and I had known, somehow, in spite of the sprayed and puffed hair and the pink or coral lips and finger-nails—I had known that this was Flora. I would have wanted to tell her that I knew, I knew her story, though we had never met. I imagine myself trying to tell her. (This is a dream now, I understand it as a dream.) I imagine her listening, with a pleasant composure. But she shakes her head. She smiles at me, and in her smile there is a degree of mockery, a faint, self-assured malice. Weariness, as well. She is not surprised that I am telling her this, but she is weary of it, of me and my idea of her, my information, my notion that I can know anything about her.

85   Of course it's my mother I'm thinking of, my mother as she was in those dreams, saying, It's nothing, just this little tremor; saying with such astonishing lighthearted forgiveness, Oh, I knew you'd come someday. My mother surprising me, and doing it almost indifferently. Her mask, her fate, and most of her affliction taken away. How relieved I was, and happy. But I now recall that I was disconcerted as well. I would have to say that I felt slightly cheated. Yes. Offended, tricked, cheated, by this welcome turnaround, this reprieve. My mother moving rather carelessly out of her old prison, showing options and powers I never dreamed she had, changes more than herself. She changes the bitter lump of love I have carried all this time into a phantom— something useless and uncalled for, like a phantom pregnancy.

The Cameronians, I have discovered, are or were an uncompromising remnant of the Covenanters—those Scots who in the seventeenth century bound themselves, with God, to resist prayer books, bishops, any taint of popery or interference by the King. Their name comes from Richard Cameron, an outlawed, or "field," preacher, soon cut down. The Cameronians—for a long time they have preferred to be called the Reformed Presbyterians—went into battle singing the seventy-fourth and the seventy-eighth Psalms. They hacked the haughty Bishop of St. Andrews to death on the highway and rode their horses over his body. One of their ministers, in a mood of firm rejoicing at his own hanging, excommunicated all the other preachers in the world.

Questions on Setting . . .

1. We said at the beginning of this chapter that, in some stories, "setting is basic." Is "Friend of My Youth" such a story? How? Remember that setting is "geography, era, season, and society."

2. How many different settings does Munro use in this story? How can contrasting settings make statements?

3. We hear much of clothes, when we meet the characters of this story. Note three examples and relate each description of clothes to notions of character.

4. The Grieveses' house is the major setting of this story. How does it set the fiction? How does this setting change?

. . . and Other Subjects

5. In "Friend of My Youth," we have a series of interlocking points of view: a narrator, her mother, a character writing a letter. Do we believe in one point of view more than in others? Does the multiple point of view add a moral complexity to this story? What kind of complexity?

6. Of Robert, the narrator says, "I see him black-haired, heavy-shouldered, with the strength of a plow horse, and the same kind of sombre, shackled beauty." Comment on point of view. What do we learn? Of whom do we learn?

7. We are told at the start of this story that the narrator's mother dies of a paralyzing disease. Why don't we learn the name of the disease? Does the nature of her disease contribute to Munro's theme?

8. Write about the relationship between the narrator and her mother.

9. The last narrative in this story is described as "a dream." Is this a departure from the rest of the story? Is a departure into "dream" satisfying? Disappointing?

Point of View and Irony

A story's **point of view**, our window on its fictional world, gives us our angle of vision. Often, we watch through the viewpoint of one character.

Suppose I met you on the street, having just witnessed a bank robbery and a police shootout with the criminal. I could tell you about my experience from my position as an observer. On the other hand, suppose I met you, having just been mugged and having chased and caught my assailant. I could tell you about it as protagonist of the story. Next, suppose that you continued walking, met someone else you know, and repeated what I told you. You would make one essential change in the telling. No longer would the story be told in the first person (*I* and *we* are first-person pronouns). Because it had not happened to you, you would change *I* to the third-person *he*. "Then he saw a policeman vault over a Porsche, firing his revolver . . . ." If I had told you my thoughts or feelings, you could recount them: "He was scared."

Storytellers use three principal points of view. The first uses an *I* who is an observer or peripheral character. The second uses an *I* who is central to the story either as protagonist or participant. The third (and most common) uses the third person—*he* or *she*—and the storyteller conveys only that one person's thoughts and feelings. We call this point of view **limited omniscience**— "omniscience" because it can read a mind, "limited" because it cannot read all minds.

A less common point of view is **unlimited omniscience**. Suppose that, when you repeated the story I told you, you imagined what the bank robbers and the police were thinking and feeling. You would continue to use the third person, but you would assert your own unlimited omniscience into the minds of others.

There are other variations and combinations, and there are still more possible points of view. On rare occasions, an author may use the second person: "Suppose that *you* continued walking . . . ," but this point of view is rare. Also uncommon is the **objective point of view**, which narrates action but does not report on anyone's ideas or feelings. The reteller of the mugging story, for instance, could tell what happened without speaking of anybody's fear. In the objective point of view, the narrator appears to acknowledge that no one can know what anyone else is thinking. Ernest Hemingway wrote some stories with an objective point of view, never reporting on thoughts or feelings. He also wrote many others that are *largely* objective (reticent about violating privacy), but, at a crucial moment, indicate, in an adverb perhaps, something about a character's feelings. *Objective* is a technical term for a device of fiction, not a critical compliment to an author's disinterest.

We have considered these possibilities:

First-person observer
First-person participant or protagonist
Third person with limited omniscience
Unlimited omniscience
Objective point of view

Now we must look into the distinctive features of each point of view.

The first person grants a sense of immediacy. Sometimes the point-of-view character speaks in the first person as an observer of the action and narrates a story about *him, her,* or *them*—like a narrator, either objective or with limited omniscience. In "A Rose for Emily," the narrator is an observer, a collective bystander who speaks as a plural *we.* The citizenry-as-narrator is rare but not unique to this story; it exemplifies the point of view of first person as observer.

In Tillie Olsen's "I Stand Here Ironing," the *I* is at the center of the story, the mother in a story about mother and daughter. Here, we have an *I* narrator who is a protagonist rather than an observer. We watch everything from her angle of vision. She is our eyes and ears, she is our interpreting brain; we must decide whether we trust her. The character of the narrator qualifies the narration. If you distrust the *I*'s honesty, for instance, you will look behind the words.

Be cautious. Never assume that the *I* of a story is the author. In "I Stand Here Ironing," *I* is not Tillie Olsen; *I* is a character invented by Tillie Olsen.

With the point of view called limited omniscience, everyone except the narrator is presented objectively, without access to thoughts and feelings. We enter only one person's head, and that character may be first- or third-person. The viewpoint character may have *opinions* about somebody else's feelings ("George *looked* terrified"), but does not have *knowledge* ("George *felt* terrified").

The third-person narrator with limited omniscience is the most common point of view in the modern short story. In John Cheever's "The Chaste Clarissa," we know what we know by way of Baxter's thoughts and feelings. Clarissa comes to us through him, and, if we think we understand her, we understand her through Baxter's observations. If we think we understand Baxter himself, it is because the author has given us a "window" through which we watch Baxter's thoughts.

Finally, let us consider unlimited omniscience, in which the narrator has total access to knowledge, thoughts, and feelings. This point of view was common when the novel was new, in the eighteenth century. Novelists then seemed conscious of creating their worlds and felt free to tell us not only what people were saying but what they were thinking. Authors were apt to enter their stories not only as all-knowing voices but also as all-judging moralists. As the novel developed, unlimited omniscience began to seem gross to many novelists. Many preferred the limited omniscience of the third-person narrator. Others switched points of view from chapter to chapter. A common device in both novels and stories keeps *almost* entirely to limited omniscience, but switches, subtly and almost imperceptibly, to unlimited omniscience when the point-of-view character is not on the scene.

With this subtle exception, the short story usually works best with a single and limited point of view. We can read a story (unlike a novel) in one sitting and comprehend it whole. In the short story, unlimited omniscience can seem formally clumsy, untethered, and unsettling—as when, settled into one vantage for observation, we are jerked away to another place by a single sentence. Think of how disturbing it would have been in "A Rose for Emily" if the *we* narrating the story had suddenly claimed to know what *we* couldn't know, saying, "But Miss Emily in her heart never intended to marry Homer Barron." It is not an exaggeration to say that it would ruin the story, and the ruin is not only a ruin in *form*. Limited omniscience owes its popularity neither to form nor to fashion but to human nature; from our own experience, we find *real* the notion that one consciousness and only one consciousness—whether it be represented as *he* or *she* or *I*—observes and interprets the world.

About the objective point of view, there is less to observe. Often, it carries an air of careful reticence, as if the narrator were too noble to gossip or too cool to care. The author must somehow embody feelings in descriptions of gesture and action so that we know how a character feels or responds or changes. The objective point of view is the acme of showing-without-telling.

Deliberately shifting points of view can provide authors opportunities for effects like light and shade, bright sun and dark shadow. Joseph Conrad uses a narrator named Marlowe in a number of stories in which Marlowe speaks in a modern present about the past (for one contrast), addressing a group of rich Londoners about savages in a jungle (for another contrast), with his own observant (*I*) character sharply contrasted with a (*he*) protagonist. Marlowe may tell his story for many pages as if he were an author writing from a limited-omniscience third-person point of view. Then one of his listeners may interrupt him, and the reader is jolted back into the first-person present. The effect gives depth and perspective to a series of contrasts, one scene or time or circumstance illuminated by its opposite.

We have not yet mentioned stream of **consciousness**, the ultimate subjectivity. The author gives us not only the viewpoint character's relevant thought or feeling but also imitates the whole flow of mind, from observation to reverie. In his novel *Ulysses,* James Joyce gives us Leopold Bloom's stream of consciousness:

Nice kind of evening feeling. No more wandering about. Just loll there: quiet dusk: let everything rip. Forget. Tell about places you have been, strange customs. The other one, jar on her head, was getting the supper: fruit, olives, lovely cool water out of the well stonecold like the hole in the wall at Ashtown. Must carry a paper goblet next time I go to the trottingmatches. She listens with big dark soft eyes. Tell her: more and more: all. Then a sigh: silence. Long long long rest.

In "Counterparts," an earlier work, Joyce's acquaintance with Farrington's mind does not extend so far.

Joyce is expert at another device bearing on point of view. He will narrate using style, jargon, or lingo appropriate to the subject of his narration. In "Counterparts," he introduces a narrative passage "Just as they were naming their poisons who should come in but Higgins!" This sentence is *not* James Joyce's own voice—with its cliché for ordering drinks—and it is not a sentence actually spoken. It uses language appropriate to the scene, to characterize both the scene and the people in it. If, in the future, Farrington or one of his barfly friends recounts this pointless evening, he will use this sort of language.

Irony and the Unreliable Narrator

Point of view often contributes to a short story's irony. **Irony** is the perception of incongruity or discrepancy—between words and meanings, between appearances and reality. If I tell you that breaking my leg in three places was enjoyable, I am either ironic or very sick; you perceive the incongruity between statement and meaning. In "The Catbird Seat," it is ironic that a villain gets her come-uppance by being considered a liar when she is telling the truth. In "A Good Man Is Hard to Find," ironic discrepancies between overt statement and implicit meaning color the dialogue between the grandmother and The Misfit. Dramatic irony occurs when a character says more than he means, or when he proclaims as false something that the reader later discovers to be true.

Some ironic effects arise from situations rather than from words; we distinguish verbal irony from **situational irony**. An old burlesque act featured a violinist performing a solo at the front of the stage while a stripper performed behind him, fully visible to the audience. Cooperating, the audience would applaud the stripper, while the violinist pretended to accept the applause as a reward for his own efforts. In literature, we learn situational irony from the narrator's words. But we can distinguish between irony that arises from the author's language and irony implicit in the situation. Both may be present at once. In Flannery O'Connor's "A Good Man Is Hard to Find," the grandmother praises The Misfit, in a desperate attempt at placating him, while it is obvious that other members of the family are being executed. This irony is situational, but the grandmother's pious language adds verbal irony to the irony of situation.

A common ironic device uses a dishonest or stupid narrator who gives the reader an interpretation of the action which the writer expects the reader to distrust. In Joyce's "Counterparts," Farrington is obtuse and unreliable. He thinks it appropriate to pawn his watch for a night's drinking; we know better.

He thinks he beats his son because his son let the fire go out; we know better. Because of the writer's skill, the reader sees through the narrator, or sees more than the narrator sees. This device—the "unreliable narrator"—can work with first person or third. William Faulkner narrated a large portion of *The Sound and the Fury* in the first person, through the mind of an idiot. Henry James achieved some of his finest effects through an obtuse narrator. In "The Beast in the Jungle," John Marcher is cold and reticent, unable to connect with energetic life outside him. In this long story, we see him with his friend May Bartram, and we see her fall in love with him and offer him, in effect, a chance to join humanity. We see everything through the third-person point of view of John Marcher. We realize that he is drying up for want of love, and we see love offered—but we see as well that he does not see it. The effect is extraordinary: *our mountaineering guide cannot see the mountain he walks on.* We want to reach into the book, shake John Marcher by the shoulder, and say "look!"

For practice in thinking about point of view, examine the following samples made up for the occasion:

1. Hopeless and forlorn, the shepherd regarded his prize sheep covered with mud. Meantime, the sheep was thinking of nothing but supper.

2. Harry knew that Gloria was stingy, but this topless convertible was worse than he had expected. He kissed her. She spat into the wind.

   a. I guess she's annoyed, thought Harry.

   b. She was annoyed.

   c. She looked annoyed.

   d. Annoyance crept over her features like a swarm of bees.

3. The grass turned blue in front of Angelique as she stumbled in the hot wind. Black cattle swung their long heads to stare, then bent to graze again. In the distance, a speck of dust grew larger.

4. As I watched, the Mexican reached under the porch and retrieved his salad. I wondered what Maravich would do under such provocation. Before I could imagine the next moment, I heard a shot from somewhere deep in the house and watched Maravich's body twist in the air.

5. I broke the walls myself, and it took a long time. Let me tell you the story from the beginning.

6. While Henry sat at the table, Marge pretended to read comic books. He was praising Verdi's *Otello,* as it happened, when Marge flicked her gum in his hair. Smiling at her youthful exuberance, Henry. . . .

John Cheever

John Cheever (1912–1982) was a novelist (*The Wapshot Chronicle,* 1957; *The Wapshot Scandal,* 1964; *Bullet Park,* 1969; *Falconer,* 1976) who published many volumes of short stories, collected in *The Stories of John Cheever* (1978). Born in Quincy, Massachusetts, he lived in the East all his life and first published most of his stories in *The New Yorker.*

The Chaste Clarissa (1952)

The evening boat for Vineyard Haven was loading freight. In a little while, the warning whistle would separate the sheep from the goats—that's the way Baxter thought of it—the islanders from the tourists wandering through the streets of Woods Hole. His car, like all the others ticketed for the ferry, was parked near the wharf. He sat on the front bumper, smoking. The noise and movement of the small port seemed to signify that the spring had ended and that the shores of West Chop, across the Sound, were the shores of summer, but the implications of the hour and the voyage made no impression on Baxter at all. The delay bored and irritated him. When someone called his name, he got to his feet with relief.

It was old Mrs. Ryan. She called to him from a dusty station wagon, and he went over to speak to her. "I knew it," she said. "I knew that I'd see someone here from Holly Cove. I had that feeling in my bones. We've been traveling since nine this morning. We had trouble with the brakes outside Worcester. Now I'm wondering if Mrs. Talbot will have cleaned the house. She wanted seventy-five dollars for opening it last summer and I told her I wouldn't pay her that again, and I wouldn't be surprised if she's thrown all my letters away. Oh, I hate to have a journey end in a dirty house, but if worse comes to worst, we can clean it ourselves. Can't we, Clarissa?" she asked, turning to a young woman who sat beside her on the front seat. "Oh, excuse me, Baxter!" she exclaimed. "You haven't met Clarissa, have you? This is Bob's wife, Clarissa Ryan."

Baxter's first thought was that a girl like that shouldn't have to ride in a dusty station wagon; she should have done much better. She was young. He guessed that she was about twenty-five. Red-headed, deep-breasted, slender, and indolent, she seemed to belong to a different species from old Mrs. Ryan and her large-boned, forthright daughters. "'The Cape Cod girls, they have no combs. They comb their hair with codfish bones,'" he said to himself but

Clarissa's hair was well groomed. Her bare arms were perfectly white. Woods Hole and the activity on the wharf seemed to bore her and she was not interested in Mrs. Ryan's insular gossip. She lighted a cigarette.

At a pause in the old lady's monologue, Baxter spoke to her daughter-in-law. "When is Bob coming down, Mrs. Ryan?" he asked.

5   "He isn't coming at all," the beautiful Clarissa said. "He's in France. He's—"

"He's gone there for the government," old Mrs. Ryan interrupted, as if her daughter-in-law could not be entrusted with this simple explanation. "He's working on this terribly interesting project. He won't be back until autumn. I'm going abroad myself. I'm leaving Clarissa alone. Of course," she added forcefully, "I expect that she will *love* the island. Everyone does. I expect that she will be kept very busy. I expect that she—"

The warning signal from the ferry cut her off. Baxter said goodbye. One by one, the cars drove aboard, and the boat started to cross the shoal water from the mainland to the resort. Baxter drank a beer in the cabin and watched Clarissa and old Mrs. Ryan, who were sitting on deck. Since he had never seen Clarissa before, he supposed that Bob Ryan must have married her during the past winter. He did not understand how this beauty had ended up with the Ryans. They were a family of passionate amateur geologists and bird-watchers. "We're all terribly keen about birds and rocks," they said when they were introduced to strangers. Their cottage was a couple of miles from any other and had, as Mrs. Ryan often said, "been thrown together out of a barn in 1922." They sailed, hiked, swam in the surf, and organized expeditions to Cuttyhunk and Tarpaulin Cove. They were people who emphasized *corpore sano* unduly, Baxter thought, and they shouldn't leave Clarissa alone in the cottage. The wind had blown a strand of her flame-colored hair across her cheek. Her long legs were crossed. As the ferry entered the harbor, she stood up and made her way down the deck against the light salt wind, and Baxter, who had returned to the island indifferently, felt that the summer had begun.

Baxter knew that in trying to get some information about Clarissa Ryan he had to be careful. He was accepted in Holly Cove because he had summered there all his life. He could be pleasant and he was a good-looking man, but his two divorces, his promiscuity, his stinginess, and his Latin complexion had left with his neighbors a vague feeling that he was unsavory. He learned that Clarissa had married Bob Ryan in November and that she was from Chicago. He heard people say that she was beautiful and stupid. That was all he did find out about her.

He looked for Clarissa on the tennis courts and the beaches. He didn't see her. He went several times to the beach nearest the Ryans' cottage. She wasn't there. When he had been on the island only a short time, he received from Mrs. Ryan, in the mail, an invitation to tea. It was an invitation that he would not ordinarily have accepted, but he drove eagerly that afternoon over to the Ryans' cottage. He was late. The cars of most of his friends and neighbors were parked in Mrs. Ryan's field. Their voices drifted out of the open windows into the garden, where Mrs. Ryan's climbing roses were in bloom. "Welcome aboard!" Mrs. Ryan shouted when he crossed the porch.

"This is my farewell party. I'm going to Norway." She led him into a crowded room.

10   Clarissa sat behind the teacups. Against the wall at her back was a glass cabinet that held the Ryans' geological specimens. Her arms were bare. Baxter watched them while she poured his tea. "Hot? . . . Cold? Lemon? . . . Cream?" seemed to be all she had to say, but her red hair and her white arms dominated that end of the room. Baxter ate a sandwich. He hung around the table.

"Have you ever been to the island before, Clarissa?" he asked.

"Yes."

"Do you swim at the beach at Holly Cove?"

"It's too far away."

15   "When your mother-in-law leaves," Baxter said, "you must let me drive you there in the mornings. I go down at eleven."

"Well, thank you." Clarissa lowered her green eyes. She seemed uncomfortable, and the thought that she might be susceptible crossed Baxter's mind exuberantly. "Well, thank you," she repeated, "but I have a car of my own and—well, I don't know, I don't—"

"What are *you* two talking about?" Mrs. Ryan asked, coming between them and smiling wildly in an effort to conceal some of the force of her interference. "I know it isn't geology," she went on, "and I know that it isn't birds, and I know that it can't be books or music, because those are all things that Clarissa doesn't like, aren't they, Clarissa? Come with me, Baxter," and she led him to the other side of the room and talked to him about sheep raising. When the conversation had ended, the party itself was nearly over. Clarissa's chair was empty. She was not in the room. Stopping at the door to thank Mrs. Ryan and say goodbye, Baxter said that he hoped she wasn't leaving for Europe immediately.

"Oh, but I am," Mrs. Ryan said. "I'm going to the mainland on the six-o'clock boat and sailing from Boston at noon tomorrow."

At half past ten the next morning, Baxter drove up to the Ryans' cottage. Mrs. Talbot, the local woman who helped the Ryans with their housework, answered the door. She said that young Mrs. Ryan was home, and let him in. Clarissa came downstairs. She looked more beautiful than ever, although she seemed put out at finding him there. She accepted his invitation to go swimming, but she accepted it unenthusiastically. "Oh, all right," she said.

20   When she came downstairs again, she had on a bathrobe over her bathing suit, and a broad-brimmed hat. On the drive to Holly Cove, he asked about her plans for the summer. She was noncommittal. She seemed preoccupied and unwilling to talk. They parked the car and walked side by side over the dunes to the beach, where she lay in the sand with her eyes closed. A few of Baxter's friends and neighbors stopped to pass the time, but they didn't stop for long, Baxter noticed. Clarissa's unresponsiveness made it difficult to talk. He didn't care.

He went swimming. Clarissa remained on the sand, bundled in her wrap. When he came out of the water, he lay down near her. He watched his neighbors and their children. The weather had been fair. The women were tanned. They were all married women and, unlike Clarissa, women with children, but the rigors of marriage and childbirth had left them all pretty, agile, and contented. While he was admiring them, Clarissa stood up and took off her bathrobe.

Here was something else, and it took his breath away. Some of the inescapable power of her beauty lay in the whiteness of her skin, some of it in the fact that, unlike the other women, who were at ease in bathing suits, Clarissa seemed humiliated and ashamed to find herself wearing so little. She walked down toward the water as if she were naked. When she first felt the water, she stopped short, for, again unlike the others, who were sporting around the pier like seals, Clarissa didn't like the cold. Then, caught for a second between nakedness and the cold, Clarissa waded in and swam a few feet. She came out of the water, hastily wrapped herself in the robe, and lay down in the sand. Then she spoke, for the first time that morning—for the first time in Baxter's experience—with warmth and feeling.

"You know, those stones on the point have grown a lot since I was here last," she said.

"What?" Baxter said.

25   "Those stones on the point," Clarissa said. "They've grown a lot."

"Stones don't grow," Baxter said.

"Oh yes they do," Clarissa said. "Didn't you know that? Stones grow. There's a stone in Mother's rose garden that's grown a foot in the last few years."

"I didn't know that stones grew," Baxter said.

"Well, they do," Clarissa said. She yawned; she shut her eyes. She seemed to fall asleep. When she opened her eyes again, she asked Baxter the time.

30   "Twelve o'clock," he said.

"I have to go home," she said. "I'm expecting guests."

Baxter could not contest this. He drove her home. She was unresponsive on the ride, and when he asked her if he could drive her to the beach again, she said no. It was a hot, fair day and most of the doors on the island stood open, but when Clarissa said goodbye to Baxter, she closed the door in his face.

Baxter got Clarissa's mail and newspapers from the post office the next day, but when he called with them at the cottage, Mrs. Talbot said that Mrs. Ryan was busy. He went that week to two large parties that she might have attended, but she was not at either. On Saturday night, he went to a barn dance, and late in the evening—they were dancing "Lady of the Lake"—he noticed Clarissa, sitting against the wall.

She was a striking wallflower. She was much more beautiful than any other woman there, but her beauty seemed to have intimidated the men. Baxter dropped out of the dance when he could and went to her. She was sitting on a packing case. It was the first thing she complained about. "There isn't even anything to sit on," she said.

35   "Don't you want to dance?" Baxter asked.

"Oh, I love to dance," she said. "I could dance all night, but I don't think *that's* dancing." She winced at the music of the fiddle and the piano. "I came with the Hortons. They just told me there was going to be a dance. They didn't tell me it was going to be this kind of a dance. I don't like all that skipping and hopping."

"Have your guests left?" Baxter asked.

"What guests?" Clarissa said.

"You told me you were expecting guests on Tuesday. When we were at the beach."

40   "I didn't say they were coming on Tuesday, did I?" Clarissa asked. "They're coming tomorrow."

"Can't I take you home?" Baxter asked.

"All right."

He brought the car around to the barn and turned on the radio. She got in and slammed the door with spirit. He raced the car over the back roads, and when he brought it up to the Ryans' cottage, he turned off the lights. He watched her hands. She folded them on her purse. "Well, thank you very much," she said. "I was having an awful time and you saved my life. I just don't understand this place, I guess. I've always had plenty of partners, but I sat on that hard box for nearly an hour and nobody even spoke to me. You saved my life."

"You're lovely, Clarissa," Baxter said.

45   "Well," Clarissa said, and she sighed. "That's just my outward self. Nobody knows the real me."

That was it, Baxter thought, and if he could only adjust his flattery to what she believed herself to be her scruples would dissolve. Did she think of herself as an actress, he wondered, a Channel swimmer, an heiress? The intimations of susceptibility that came from her in the summer night were so powerful, so heady, that they convinced Baxter that here was a woman whose chastity hung by a thread.

"I think I know the real you," Baxter said.

"Oh no you don't," Clarissa said. "Nobody does."

The radio played some lovelorn music from a Boston hotel. By the calendar, it was still early in the summer, but it seemed, from the stillness and the hugeness of the dark trees, to be much later. Baxter put his arms around Clarissa and planted a kiss on her lips.

50   She pushed him away violently and reached for the door. "Oh, now you've spoiled everything," she said as she got out of the car. "Now you've spoiled everything. I know what you've been thinking. I know you've been thinking it all along." She slammed the door and spoke to him across the window. "Well, you needn't come around here any more, Baxter," she said. "My girl friends are coming down from New York tomorrow on the morning plane and I'll be too busy to see you for the rest of the summer. Good night."

Baxter was aware that he had only himself to blame; he had moved too quickly. He knew better. He went to bed feeling angry and sad, and slept poorly. He was depressed when he woke, and his depression was deepened by the noise of a sea rain, blowing in from the northeast. He lay in bed listening to the rain and the surf. The storm would metamorphose the island. The beaches would be empty. Drawers would stick. Suddenly he got out of bed, went to the telephone, called the airport. The New York plane had been unable to land, they told him, and no more planes were expected that day. The storm seemed to be playing directly into his hands. At noon, he drove in to the village and bought a Sunday paper and a box of candy. The candy was for Clarissa, but he was in no hurry to give it to her.

She would have stocked the icebox, put out the towels, and planned the picnic, but now the arrival of her friends had been postponed, and the lively day that she had anticipated had turned out to be rainy and idle. There were ways, of course, for her to overcome her disappointment, but on the evidence of the barn dance he felt that she was lost without her husband or her mother-in-law, and that there were few, if any, people on the island who would pay her a chance call or ask her over for a drink. It was likely that she would spend the day listening to the radio and the rain and that by the end of it she would be ready to welcome anyone, including Baxter. But as long as the forces of loneliness and idleness were working on his side, it was shrewder, Baxter knew, to wait. It would be best to come just before dark, and he waited until then. He drove to the Ryans' with his box of candy. The windows were lighted. Clarissa opened the door.

"I wanted to welcome your friends to the island," Baxter said. "I—"

"They didn't come," Clarissa said. "The plane couldn't land. They went back to New York. They telephoned me. I had planned such a nice visit. Now everything's changed."

55   "I'm sorry, Clarissa," Baxter said. "I've brought you a present."

"Oh!" She took the box of candy. "What a beautiful box! What a lovely present! What—" Her face and her voice were, for a minute, ingenuous and yielding, and then he saw the force of resistance transform them. "You shouldn't have done it," she said.

"May I come in?" Baxter asked.

"Well, I don't know," she said. "You can't come in if you're just going to sit around."

"We could play cards," Baxter said.

60   "I don't know how," she said.

"I'll teach you," Baxter said.

"No," she said. "No, Baxter, you'll have to go. You just don't understand the kind of woman I am. I spent all day writing a letter to Bob. I wrote and told him that you kissed me last night. I can't let you come in." She closed the door.

From the look on Clarissa's face when he gave her the box of candy, Baxter judged that she liked to get presents. An inexpensive gold bracelet or even a bunch of flowers might do it, he knew, but Baxter was an extremely stingy man, and while he saw the usefulness of a present, he could not bring himself to buy one. He decided to wait.

The storm blew all Monday and Tuesday. It cleared on Tuesday night, and by Wednesday afternoon the tennis courts were dry and Baxter played. He played until late. Then, when he had bathed and changed his clothes, he stopped at a cocktail party to pick up a drink. Here one of his neighbors, a married woman with four children, sat down beside him and began a general discussion of the nature of married love.

65   It was a conversation, with its glances and innuendoes, that Baxter had been through many times, and he knew roughly what it promised. His neighbor was one of the pretty mothers that Baxter had admired on the beach. Her hair was brown. Her arms were thin and tanned. Her teeth were sound. But while he appeared to be deeply concerned with her opinions on love, the white image of Clarissa loomed up in his mind, and he broke off the conversation and left the party. He drove to the Ryans'.

From a distance, the cottage looked shut. The house and the garden were perfectly still. He knocked and then rang. Clarissa spoke to him from an upstairs window.

"Oh, hello, Baxter," she said.

"I've come to say goodbye, Clarissa," Baxter said. He couldn't think of anything better.

"Oh, dear," Clarissa said. "Well, wait just a minute. I'll be down."

70   "I'm going away, Clarissa," Baxter said when she opened the door. "I've come to say goodbye."

"Where are you going?"

"I don't know." He said this sadly.

"Well, come in, then," she said hesitantly. "Come in for a minute. This is the last time that I'll see you, I guess, isn't it? Please excuse the way the place looks. Mr. Talbot got sick on Monday and Mrs. Talbot had to take him to the hospital on the mainland, and I haven't had anybody to help me. I've been all alone."

He followed her into the living room and sat down. She was more beautiful than ever. She talked about the problems that had been presented by Mrs. Talbot's departure. The fire in the stove that heated the water had died. There was a mouse in the kitchen. The bathtub wouldn't drain. She hadn't been able to get the car started.

75   In the quiet house, Baxter heard the sound of a leaky water tap and a clock pendulum. The sheet of glass that protected the Ryans' geological specimens reflected the fading sky outside the window. The cottage was near the water, and he could hear the surf. He noted these details dispassionately and for what they were worth. When Clarissa finished her remarks about Mrs. Talbot, he waited a full minute before he spoke.

"The sun is in your hair," he said.

"What?"

"The sun is in your hair. It's a beautiful color."

"Well, it isn't as pretty as it used to be," she said. "Hair like mine gets dark. But I'm not going to dye it. I don't think that women should dye their hair."

80   "You're so intelligent," he murmured.

"You don't mean that?"

"Mean what?"

"Mean that I'm intelligent."

"Oh, but I do," he said. "You're intelligent. You're beautiful. I'll never forget that night I met you at the boat. I hadn't wanted to come to the island. I'd made plans to go out West."

85   "I can't be intelligent," Clarissa said miserably. "I must be stupid. Mother Ryan says that I'm stupid, and Bob says that I'm stupid, and even Mrs. Talbot

says that I'm stupid, and—" She began to cry. She went to a mirror and dried her eyes. Baxter followed. He put his arms around her. "Don't put your arms around me," she said, more in despair than in anger. "Nobody ever takes me seriously until they get their arms around me." She sat down again and Baxter sat near her. "But you're not stupid, Clarissa," he said. "You have a wonderful intelligence, a wonderful mind. I've often thought so. I've often felt that you must have a lot of very interesting opinions."

"Well, that's funny," she said, "because I do have a lot of opinions. Of course, I never dare say them to anyone, and Bob and Mother Ryan don't ever let me speak. They always interrupt me, as if they were ashamed of me. But I do have these opinions. I mean, I think we're like cogs in a wheel. I've concluded that we're like cogs in a wheel. Do you think we're like cogs in a wheel?"

"Oh, yes," he said. "Oh, yes, I do!"

"I think we're like cogs in a wheel," she said. "For instance, do you think that women should work? I've given that a lot of thought. My opinion is that I don't think married women should work. I mean, unless they have a lot of money, of course, but even then I think it's a full-time job to take care of a man. Or do you think that women should work?"

"What do you think?" he asked. "I'm terribly interested in knowing what you think."

90   "Well, my opinion is," she said timidly, "that you just have to hoe your row. I don't think that working or joining the church is going to change every-thing, or special diets, either. I don't put much stock in fancy diets. We have a friend who eats a quarter of a pound of meat at every meal. He has a scales right on the table and he weighs the meat. It makes the table look awful and I don't see what good it's going to do him. I buy what's reasonable. If ham is reasonable, I buy ham. If lamb is reasonable, I buy lamb. Don't you think that's intelligent?"

"I think that's very intelligent."

"And progressive education," she said. "I don't have a good opinion of progressive education. When we go to the Howards' for dinner, the children ride their tricycles around the table all the time, and it's my opinion that they get this way from progressive schools, and that children ought to be told what's nice and what isn't."

The sun that had lighted her hair was gone, but there was still enough light in the room for Baxter to see that as she aired her opinions, her face suffused with color and her pupils dilated. Baxter listened patiently, for he knew by then that she merely wanted to be taken for something that she was not—that the poor girl was lost. "You're very intelligent," he said, now and then. "You're so intelligent."

It was as simple as that.

Questions on Point of View . . .

1. From whose point of view is this story told? Are there any exceptions?
2. Do we miss being told Clarissa's thoughts?

3. Imagine what would happen if the story were told from Clarissa's point of view. Rewrite a paragraph from Clarissa's point of view.

4. What difference would it make if this story were told in the first person?

5. If you feel that you know what Clarissa thinks, how did you acquire your knowledge?

6. Could this story be told from an objective point of view? What kind of problem would arise?

. . . and Other Elements

7. What is the conflict in this story? The climax? The dénouement?

8. What is the author's attitude toward his characters?

9. Divide the story into scenes to determine the function of each scene to the story as a whole.

10. Is Baxter a round character?

Tillie Olsen

Tillie Olsen (1913–   ) has lived most of her life in San Francisco. As a mother of four children, she had little time for her writing when she was young, and did not publish her first book, *Tell Me a Riddle*, until 1962. *Yonnondio* appeared in 1974. In 1978, she wrote *Silences*, which investigates the problems of writers, especially women, who have written little or stopped writing. "I Stand Here Ironing" comes from *Tell Me a Riddle*.

I Stand Here Ironing   (1956)

I stand here ironing, and what you asked me moves tormented back and forth with the iron.

"I wish you would manage the time to come in and talk with me about your daughter. I'm sure you can help me understand her. She's a youngster who needs help and whom I'm deeply interested in helping."

"Who needs help." . . . Even if I came, what good would it do? You think because I am her mother I have a key, or that in some way you could use me as a key? She has lived for nineteen years. There is all that life that has happened outside of me, beyond me.

And when is there time to remember, to sift, to weigh, to estimate, to total? I will start and there will be an interruption and I will have to gather it all together again. Or I will become engulfed with all I did or did not do, with what should have been and what cannot be helped.

5   She was a beautiful baby. The first and only one of our five that was beautiful at birth. You do not guess how new and uneasy her tenancy in her now-loveliness. You did not know her all those years she was thought homely, or

see her poring over her baby pictures, making me tell her over and over how beautiful she had been—and would be, I would tell her—and was now, to the seeing eye. But the seeing eyes were few or non-existent. Including mine.

I nursed her. They feel that's important nowadays. I nursed all the children, but with her, with all the fierce rigidity of first motherhood, I did like the books then said. Though her cries battered me to trembling and my breasts ached with swollenness, I waited till the clock decreed.

Why do I put that first? I do not even know if it matters, or if it explains anything.

She was a beautiful baby. She blew shining bubbles of sound. She loved motion, loved light, loved color and music and textures. She would lie on the floor in her blue overalls patting the surface so hard in ecstasy her hands and feet would blur. She was a miracle to me, but when she was eight months old I had to leave her daytimes with the woman downstairs to whom she was no miracle at all, for I worked or looked for work and for Emily's father, who "could no longer endure" (he wrote in his good-bye note) "sharing want with us."

I was nineteen, it was the pre-relief, pre-WPA world of the depression. I would start running as soon as I got off the streetcar, running up the stairs, the place smelling sour, and awake or asleep to startle awake, when she saw me she would break into a clogged weeping that could not be comforted, a weeping I can hear yet.

10   After a while I found a job hashing at night so I could be with her days, and it was better. But it came to where I had to bring her to his family and leave her.

It took a long time to raise the money for her fare back. Then she got chicken pox and I had to wait longer. When she finally came, I hardly knew her, walking quick and nervous like her father, looking like her father, thin, and dressed in a shoddy red that yellowed her skin and glared at the pockmarks. All the baby loveliness gone.

She was two. Old enough for nursery school they said, and I did not know then what I know now—the fatigue of the long day, and the lacerations of group life in the kinds of nurseries that are only parking places for children.

Except that it would have made no difference if I had known. It was the only place there was. It was the only way we could be together, the only way I could hold a job.

And even without knowing, I knew. I knew the teacher that was evil because all these years it has curdled into my memory, the little boy hunched in the corner, her rasp, "why aren't you outside, because Alvin hits you? that's no reason, go out, scaredy." I knew Emily hated it even if she did not clutch and implore "don't go Mommy" like the other children, mornings.

15   She always had a reason why we should stay home. Momma, you look sick, Momma, I feel sick. Momma, the teachers aren't there today, they're sick. Momma, we can't go, there was a fire there last night. Momma, it's a holiday today, no school, they told me.

But never a direct protest, never rebellious. I think of our others in their three, four-year-oldness—the explosions, the tempers, the denunciations, the demands—and I feel suddenly ill. I put the iron down. What in me demanded that goodness in her? And what was the cost, the cost to her of such goodness?

The old man living in the back once said in his gentle way: "You should smile at Emily more when you look at her." What was in my face when I looked at her? I loved her. There were all the acts of love.

It was only with the others I remembered what he said, and it was the face of joy, and not of care or tightness or worry I turned to them—too late for Emily. She does not smile easily, let alone almost always as her brothers and sisters do. Her face is closed and sombre, but when she wants, how fluid. You must have seen it in her pantomimes, you spoke of her rare gift for comedy on the stage that rouses a laughter out of the audience so dear they applaud and applaud and do not want to let her go.

Where does it come from, that comedy? There was none of it in her when she came back to me that second time, after I had had to send her away again. She had a new daddy now to learn to love, and I think perhaps it was a better time.

20   Except when we left her alone nights, telling ourselves she was old enough.

"Can't you go some other time, Mommy, like tomorrow?" she would ask. "Will it be just a little while you'll be gone? Do you promise?"

The time we came back, the front door open, the clock on the floor in the hall. She rigid awake. "It wasn't just a little while. I didn't cry. Three times I called you, just three times, and then I ran downstairs to open the door so you could come faster. The clock talked loud. I threw it away, it scared me what it talked."

She said the clock talked loud again that night I went to the hospital to have Susan. She was delirious with fever that comes before red measles but she was fully conscious all the week I was gone and the week after we were home when she could not come near the new baby or me.

She did not get well. She stayed skeleton thin, not wanting to eat, and night after night she had nightmares. She would call for me, and I would rouse from exhaustion to sleepily call back: "You're all right, darling, go to sleep, it's just a dream," and if she still called, in a sterner voice, "now go to sleep, Emily, there's nothing to hurt you." Twice, only twice, when I had to get up for Susan anyhow, I went in to sit with her.

25   Now when it is too late (as if she would let me hold and comfort her like I do the others) I get up and go to her at once at her moan or restless stirring. "Are you awake, Emily? Can I get you something?" And the answer is always the same: "No, I'm all right, go back to sleep, Mother."

They persuaded me at the clinic to send her away to a convalescent home in the country where "she can have the kind of food and care you can't manage for her, and you'll be free to concentrate on the new baby." They still send children to that place. I see pictures on the society page of sleek young women planning affairs to raise money for it, or dancing at the affairs, or decorating Easter eggs or filling Christmas stockings for the children.

They never have a picture of the children so I do not know if the girls still wear those gigantic red bows and the ravaged looks on the every other

Sunday when parents can come to visit "unless otherwise notified"—as we were notified the first six weeks.

Oh it is a handsome place, green lawns and tall trees and fluted flower beds. High up on the balconies of each cottage the children stand, the girls in their red bows and white dresses, the boys in white suits and giant red ties. The parents stand below shrieking up to be heard and the children shriek down to be heard, and between them the invisible wall "Not To Be Contaminated by Parental Germs or Physical Affection."

There was a tiny girl who always stood hand in hand with Emily. Her parents never came. One visit she was gone. "They moved her to Rose Cottage," Emily shouted in explanation. "They don't like you to love anybody here."

30   She wrote once a week, the labored writing of a seven-year old. "I am fine. How is the baby. If I write my leter nicly I will have a star. Love." There never was a star. We wrote every other day, letters she could never hold or keep but only hear read—once. "We simply do not have room for children to keep any personal possessions," they patiently explained when we pieced one Sunday's shrieking together to plead how much it would mean to Emily, who loved so to keep things, to be allowed to keep her letters and cards.

Each visit she looked frailer. "She isn't eating," they told us.

(They had runny eggs for breakfast or mush with lumps, Emily said later, I'd hold it in my mouth and not swallow. Nothing ever tasted good, just when they had chicken.)

It took us eight months to get her released home, and only the fact that she gained back so little of her seven lost pounds convinced the social worker.

I used to try to hold and love her after she came back, but her body would stay stiff, and after a while she'd push away. She ate little. Food sickened her, and I think much of life too. Oh she had physical lightness and brightness, twinkling by on skates, bouncing like a ball up and down up and down over the jump rope, skimming over the hill; but these were momentary.

35   She fretted about her appearance, thin and dark and foreign-looking at a time when every little girl was supposed to look or thought she should look a chubby blonde replica of Shirley Temple. The doorbell sometimes rang for her, but no one seemed to come and play in the house or be a best friend. Maybe because we moved so much.

There was a boy she loved painfully through two school semesters. Months later she told me how she had taken pennies from my purse to buy him candy. "Licorice was his favorite and I brought him some every day, but he still liked Jennifer better'n me. Why, Mommy?" The kind of question for which there is no answer.

School was a worry to her. She was not glib or quick in a world where glibness and quickness were easily confused with ability to learn. To her overworked and exasperated teachers she was an overconscientious "slow learner" who kept trying to catch up and was absent entirely too often.

I let her be absent, though sometimes the illness was imaginary. How different from my now-strictness about attendance with the others. I wasn't working. We had a new baby, I was home anyhow. Sometimes, after Susan grew old enough, I would keep her home from school, too, to have them all together.

Mostly Emily had asthma, and her breathing, harsh and labored, would fill the house with a curiously tranquil sound. I would bring the two old dresser mirrors and her boxes of collections to her bed. She would select beads and single earrings, bottle tops and shells, dried flowers and pebbles, old postcards and scraps, all sorts of oddments; then she and Susan would play Kingdom, setting up landscapes and furniture, peopling them with action.

40   Those were the only times of peaceful companionship between her and Susan. I have edged away from it, that poisonous feeling between them, the terrible balancing of hurts and needs I had to do between the two, and did so badly, those earlier years.

Oh there are conflicts between the others too, each one human, needing, demanding, hurting, taking—but only between Emily and Susan, no, Emily toward Susan that corroding resentment. It seems so obvious on the surface yet it is not obvious. Susan, the second child, Susan, golden- and curly-haired and chubby, quick and articulate and assured, everything in appearance and manner Emily was not; Susan, not able to resist Emily's precious things, losing or sometimes clumsily breaking them; Susan telling jokes and riddles to company for applause while Emily sat silent (to say to me later that was *my* riddle, Mother, I told it to Susan); Susan, who for all the five years' difference in age was just a year behind Emily in developing physically.

I am glad for that slow physical development that widened the difference between her and her contemporaries, though she suffered over it. She was too vulnerable for that terrible world of youthful competition, of preening and parading, of constant measuring of yourself against every other, of envy. "If I had that copper hair," "If I had that skin. . . ." She tormented herself enough about not looking like the others, there was enough of the unsureness, the having to be conscious of words before you speak, the constant caring—what are they thinking of me? without having it all magnified by the merciless physical drives.

Ronnie is calling. He is wet and I change him. It is rare there is such a cry now. That time of motherhood is almost behind me when the ear is not one's own but must always be racked and listening for the child cry, the child call. We sit for a while and I hold him, looking out over the city spread in charcoal with its soft aisles of light. "*Shoogily,*" he breathes and curls closer. I carry him back to bed, asleep. *Shoogily.* A funny word, a family word, inherited from Emily, invented by her to say: *comfort.*

In this and other ways she leaves her seal, I say aloud. And startle at my saying it. What do I mean? What did I start to gather together, to try and make coherent? I was at the terrible, growing years. War years. I do not remember them well. I was working, there were four smaller ones now, there was not time for her. She had to help be a mother, and housekeeper, and shopper. She had to set her seal. Mornings of crisis and near hysteria trying to get lunches packed, hair combed, coats and shoes found, everyone to school or Child Care on time, the baby ready for transportation. And always the paper scribbled on by a smaller one, the book looked at by Susan then mislaid, the homework not done. Running out to that huge school where she was one, she was lost, she was a drop; suffering over the unpreparedness, stammering and unsure in her classes.

45   There was so little time left at night after the kids were bedded down. She would struggle over books, always eating (it was in those years she developed her enormous appetite that is legendary in our family) and I would be ironing, or preparing food for the next day, or writing V-mail to Bill, or tending the baby. Sometimes, to make me laugh, or out of her despair, she would imitate happenings or types at school.

    I think I said once: "Why don't you do something like this in the school amateur show?" One morning she phoned me at work, hardly understandable through the weeping: "Mother, I did it. I won, I won; they gave me first prize; they clapped and clapped and wouldn't let me go."

    Now suddenly she was Somebody, and as imprisoned in her difference as she had been in anonymity.

    She began to be asked to perform at other high schools, even in colleges, then at city and statewide affairs. The first one we went to, I only recognized her that first moment when thin, shy, she almost drowned herself into the curtains. Then: Was this Emily? The control, the command, the convulsing and deadly clowning, the spell, then the roaring, stamping audience, unwilling to let this rare and precious laughter out of their lives.

    Afterwards: You ought to do something about her with a gift like that—but without money or knowing how, what does one do? We have left it all to her, and the gift has as often eddied inside, clogged and clotted, as been used and growing.

50   She is coming. She runs up the stairs two at a time with her light graceful step, and I know she is happy tonight. Whatever it was that occasioned your call did not happen today.

    "Aren't you ever going to finish the ironing, Mother? Whistler painted his mother in a rocker. I'd have to paint mine standing over an ironing board." This is one of her communicative nights and she tells me everything and nothing as she fixes herself a plate of food out of the icebox.

    She is so lovely. Why did you want me to come in at all? Why were you concerned? She will find her way.

    She starts up the stairs to bed. "Don't get me up with the rest in the morning." "But I thought you were having midterms." "Oh, those," she comes back in, kisses me, and says quite lightly, "in a couple of years when we'll all be atom-dead they won't matter a bit."

    She has said it before. She *believes* it. But because I have been dredging the past, and all that compounds a human being is so heavy and meaningful in me, I cannot endure it tonight.

55   I will never total it all. I will never come in to say: She was a child seldom smiled at. Her father left me before she was a year old. I had to work her first six years when there was work, or I sent her home and to his relatives. There were years she had care she hated. She was dark and thin and foreign-looking in a world where the prestige went to blondeness and curly hair and dimples, she was slow where glibness was prized. She was a child of anxious, not

proud, love. We were poor and could not afford for her the soil of easy growth. I was a young mother, I was a distracted mother. There were the other children pushing up, demanding. Her younger sister seemed all that she was not. There were years she did not want me to touch her. She kept too much in herself, her life was such she had to keep too much in herself. My wisdom came too late. She has much to her and probably nothing will come of it. She is a child of her age, of depression, of war, of fear.

Let her be. So all that is in her will not bloom—but in how many does it? There is still enough left to live by. Only help her to know—help make it so there is cause for her to know—that she is more than this dress on the ironing-board, helpless before the iron.

Questions on Point of View . . .

1. What is the point of view in this story? Is it consistent?

2. Who is *you* in the first line? Does the reader know exactly? Does the reader know approximately? Does Olsen's story require that the reader know no more than the reader knows?

3. What kind of speech is this story? Is it spoken out loud? Is the narrator speaking to anyone in particular? When? Why is the story told as it is?

4. The narrator supplies important information in paragraph 18. Did you know it at the time?

5. What do we learn about *you* in paragraph 50?

6. Who speaks in paragraph 51?

7. What does the verb tense tell us in paragraph 52?

8. Does paragraph 53 offer information lacking since paragraph 1? Would this story be better if you had known the information before?

. . . and Other Elements

9. How is Emily characterized?

10. How much do we know of Emily's father? Reconstruct the major events of the mother's life in sequence.

11. How does the final image of the mother ironing, given prominence by the title, bear on the structure and the theme of the story?

Anton Chekhov

Anton Chekhov (1860–1904) trained to be a doctor but abandoned medicine to write stories. Later he became a playwright (see pages 937–975 for a further note on Chekhov and for the text of *The Cherry Orchard*). His grandfather began life as a serf and died a wealthy merchant. Although his father was born to the middle class, he lost his money while Chekhov was in school. If his social and family background was thus confused, Chekhov learned from the confusion. In stories written during the last decades of the Czarist regime, he reached out to all levels of society. Although tuberculosis shortened his life, he virtually invented the modern short story. And he was prolific: The Ecco Press has reprinted thirteen volumes of *The Tales of Chekhov* in paperback.

Gooseberries   (1898)
Translated by Avrahm Yarmolinsky

The sky had been overcast since early morning; it was a still day, not hot, but tedious, as it usually is when the weather is gray and dull, when clouds have been hanging over the fields for a long time, and you wait for the rain that does not come. Ivan Ivanych, a veterinary, and Burkin, a high school teacher, were already tired with walking, and the plain seemed endless to them. Far ahead were the scarcely visible windmills of the village of Mironositzkoe; to the right lay a range of hills that disappeared in the distance beyond the village, and both of them knew that over there were the river, and fields, green willows, homesteads, and if you stood on one of the hills, you could see from there another vast plain, telegraph poles, and a train that from afar looked like a caterpillar crawling, and in clear weather you could even see the town. Now, when it was still and when nature seemed mild and pensive, Ivan Ivanych and Burkin were filled with love for this plain, and both of them thought what a beautiful land it was.

"Last time when we were in Elder Prokofy's barn," said Burkin, "you were going to tell me a story."

"Yes; I wanted to tell you about my brother."

Ivan Ivanych heaved a slow sigh and lit his pipe before beginning his story, but just then it began to rain. And five minutes later there was a downpour, and it was hard to tell when it would be over. The two men halted, at a loss; the dogs, already wet, stood with their tails between their legs and looked at them feelingly.

5   "We must find shelter somewhere," said Burkin. "Let's go to Alyohin's; it's quite near."

"Let's."

They turned aside and walked across a mown meadow, now going straight ahead, now bearing to the right, until they reached the road. Soon poplars came into view, a garden, then the red roofs of barns; the river gleamed, and the view opened on a broad expanse of water with a mill and a white bathing-cabin. That was Sofyino, Alyohin's place.

The mill was going, drowning out the sound of the rain; the dam was shaking. Wet horses stood near the carts, their heads drooping, and men were walking about, their heads covered with sacks. It was damp, muddy, dreary; and the water looked cold and unkind. Ivan Ivanych and Burkin felt cold and messy and uncomfortable through and through; their feet were heavy with mud and when, having crossed the dam, they climbed up to the barns, they were silent as though they were cross with each other.

The noise of a winnowing-machine came from one of the barns, the door was open, and clouds of dust were pouring from within. On the threshold stood Alyohin himself, a man of forty, tall and rotund, with long hair, looking more like a professor or an artist than a gentleman farmer. He was wearing a white blouse, badly in need of washing, that was belted with a rope, and drawers, and his high boots were plastered with mud and straw. His eyes and nose were black with dust. He recognized Ivan Ivanych and Burkin and was apparently very glad to see them.

10   "Please go up to the house, gentlemen," he said, smiling; "I'll be there directly, in a moment."

It was a large structure of two stories. Alyohin lived downstairs in what was formerly the stewards' quarters: two rooms that had arched ceilings and small windows; the furniture was plain, and the place smelled of rye bread, cheap vodka, and harness. He went into the showy rooms upstairs only rarely, when he had guests. Once in the house, the two visitors were met by a chambermaid, a young woman so beautiful that both of them stood still at the same moment and glanced at each other.

"You can't imagine how glad I am to see you, gentlemen," said Alyohin, joining them in the hall. "What a surprise! Pelageya," he said, turning to the chambermaid, "give the guests a change of clothes. And, come to think of it, I will change, too. But I must go and bathe first, I don't think I've had a wash since spring. Don't you want to go into the bathing-cabin? In the meanwhile things will be got ready here."

The beautiful Pelageya, with her soft, delicate air, brought them bath towels and soap, and Alyohin went to the bathing-cabin with his guests.

"Yes, it's a long time since I've bathed," he said, as he undressed. "I've an excellent bathing-cabin, as you see—it was put up by my father—but somehow I never find time to use it." He sat down on the steps and lathered his long hair and neck, and the water around him turned brown.

15   "I say—" observed Ivan Ivanych significantly, looking at his head.

"I haven't had a good wash for a long time," repeated Alyohin, embarrassed, and soaped himself once more; the water about him turned dark-blue, the color of ink.

Ivan Ivanych came out of the cabin, plunged into the water with a splash and swam in the rain, thrusting his arms out wide; he raised waves on which white lilies swayed. He swam out to the middle of the river and dived and a minute later came up in another spot and swam on and kept diving, trying to touch bottom. "By God!" he kept repeating delightedly, "by God!" He swam to the mill, spoke to the peasants there, and turned back and in the middle of the river lay floating, exposing his face to the rain. Burkin and Alyohin were already dressed and ready to leave, but he kept on swimming and diving. "By God!" he kept exclaiming. "Lord, have mercy on me."

"You've had enough!" Burkin shouted to him.

They returned to the house. And only when the lamp was lit in the big drawing room upstairs, and the two guests, in silk dressing-gowns and warm slippers, were lounging in armchairs, and Alyohin himself, washed and combed, wearing a new jacket, was walking about the room, evidently savoring the warmth, the cleanliness, the dry clothes and light footwear, and when pretty Pelageya, stepping noiselessly across the carpet and smiling softly, brought in a tray with tea and jam, only then did Ivan Ivanych begin his story, and it was as though not only Burkin and Alyohin were listening, but also the ladies, old and young, and the military men who looked down upon them, calmly and severely, from their gold frames.

20   "We are two brothers," he began, "I, Ivan Ivanych, and my brother, Nikolay Ivanych, who is two years my junior. I went in for a learned profession and became a veterinary; Nikolay at nineteen began to clerk in a provincial branch of the Treasury. Our father was a *kantonist*,[1] but he rose to be an officer and so a nobleman, a rank that he bequeathed to us together with a small estate. After his death there was a lawsuit and we lost the estate to creditors, but be that as it may, we spent our childhood in the country. Just like peasant children we passed days and nights in the fields and the woods, herded horses, stripped bast from the trees, fished, and so on. And, you know, whoever even once in his life has caught a perch or seen thrushes migrate in the autumn, when on clear, cool days they sweep in flocks over the village, will never really be a townsman and to the day of his death will have a longing for the open. My brother was unhappy in the government office. Years passed, but he went on warming the same seat, scratching away at the same papers, and thinking of one and the same thing: how to get away to the country. And little by little this vague longing turned into a definite desire, into a dream of buying a little property somewhere on the banks of a river or a lake.

"He was a kind and gentle soul and I loved him, but I never sympathized with his desire to shut himself up for the rest of his life on a little property of his own. It is a common saying that a man needs only six feet of earth. But six feet is what a corpse needs, not a man. It is also asserted that if our educated class is drawn to the land and seeks to settle on farms, that's a good thing. But these farms amount to the same six feet of earth. To retire from the city, from the struggle, from the hubbub, to go off and hide on one's own farm—that's not life, it is selfishness, sloth, it is a kind of monasticism, but monasticism without works. Man needs not six feet of earth, not a farm, but the whole globe, all of Nature, where unhindered he can display all the capacities and peculiarities of his free spirit.

"My brother Nikolay, sitting in his office, dreamed of eating his own *shchi*, which would fill the whole farmyard with a delicious aroma, of picknicking

---

[1] The son of a low-ranking soldier, enrolled in a military school

on the green grass, of sleeping in the sun, of sitting for hours on the seat by the gate gazing at field and forest. Books on agriculture and the farming items in almanacs were his joy, the delight of his soul. He liked newspapers too, but the only things he read in them were advertisements of land for sale, so many acres of tillable land and pasture, with house, garden, river, mill, and millpond. And he pictured to himself garden paths, flowers, fruit, bird-houses with starlings in them, crucians in the pond, and all that sort of thing, you know. These imaginary pictures varied with the advertisements he came upon, but somehow gooseberry bushes figured in every one of them. He could not picture to himself a single country-house, a single rustic nook, without gooseberries.

"'Country life has its advantages,' he used to say. 'You sit on the veranda having tea, and your ducks swim in the pond, and everything smells delicious and—the gooseberries are ripening.'

"He would draw a plan of his estate and invariably it would contain the following features: a) the master's house; b) servants' quarters; c) kitchen-garden; d) a gooseberry patch. He lived meagerly: he deprived himself of food and drink; he dressed God knows how, like a beggar, but he kept on saving and salting money away in the bank. He was terribly stingy. It was painful for me to see it, and I used to give him small sums and send him something on holidays, but he would put that away too. Once a man is possessed by an idea, there is no doing anything with him.

25   "Years passed. He was transferred to another province, he was already past forty, yet he was still reading newspaper advertisements and saving up money. Then I heard that he was married. Still for the sake of buying a property with a gooseberry patch he married an elderly, homely widow, without a trace of affection for her, but simply because she had money. After marrying her, he went on living parsimoniously, keeping her half-starved, and he put her money in the bank in his own name. She had previously been the wife of a postmaster, who had got her used to pies and cordials. This second husband did not even give her enough black bread. She began to sicken, and some three years later gave up the ghost. And, of course, it never for a moment occurred to my brother that he was to blame for her death. Money, like vodka, can do queer things to a man. Once in our town a merchant lay on his deathbed; before he died, he ordered a plateful of honey and he ate up all his money and lottery tickets with the honey, so that no one should get it. One day when I was inspecting a drove of cattle at a railway station, a cattle dealer fell under a locomotive and it sliced off his leg. We carried him in to the infirmary, the blood was gushing from the wound—a terrible business, but he kept begging us to find his leg and was very anxious about it: he had twenty rubles in the boot that was on that leg, and he was afraid they would be lost."

"That's a tune from another opera," said Burkin.

Ivan Ivanych paused a moment and then continued:

"After his wife's death, my brother began to look around for a property. Of course, you may scout about for five years and in the end make a mistake, and buy something quite different from what you have been dreaming of.

Through an agent my brother bought a mortgaged estate of three hundred acres with a house, servants' quarters, a park, but with no orchard, no gooseberry patch, no duckpond. There was a stream, but the water in it was the color of coffee, for on one of its banks there was a brickyard and on the other a glue factory. But my brother was not at all disconcerted: he ordered a score of gooseberry bushes, planted them, and settled down to the life of a country gentleman.

"Last year I paid him a visit. I thought I would go and see how things were with him. In his letter to me my brother called his estate 'Chumbaroklov Waste, or Himalaiskoe' (our surname was Chimsha-Himalaisky). I reached the place in the afternoon. It was hot. Everywhere there were ditches, fences, hedges, rows of fir trees, and I was at a loss as to how to get to the yard and where to leave my horse. I made my way to the house and was met by a fat dog with reddish hair that looked like a pig. It wanted to bark, but was too lazy. The cook, a fat, barelegged woman, who also looked like a pig, came out of the kitchen and said that the master was resting after dinner. I went in to see my brother, and found him sitting up in bed, with a quilt over his knees. He had grown older, stouter, flabby; his cheeks, his nose, his lips jutted out: it looked as though he might grunt into the quilt at any moment.

30   "We embraced and dropped tears of joy and also of sadness at the thought that the two of us had once been young, but were now gray and nearing death. He got dressed and took me out to show me his estate.

"Well, how are you getting on here?" I asked.

"'Oh, all right, thank God. I am doing very well.'

"He was no longer the poor, timid clerk he used to be but a real landowner, a gentleman. He had already grown used to his new manner of living and developed a taste for it. He ate a great deal, steamed himself in the bathhouse, was growing stout, was already having a lawsuit with the village commune and the two factories and was very much offended when the peasants failed to address him as 'Your Honor.' And he concerned himself with his soul's welfare too in a substantial, upper-class manner, and performed good deeds not simply, but pompously. And what good works! He dosed the peasants with bicarbonate and castor oil for all their ailments and on his name day he had a thanksgiving service celebrated in the center of the village, and then treated the villagers to a gallon of vodka, which he thought was the thing to do. Oh, those horrible gallons of vodka! One day a fat landowner hauls the peasants up before the rural police officer for trespassing, and the next, to mark a feast day, treats them to a gallon of vodka, and they drink and shout 'Hurrah' and when they are drunk bow down at his feet. A higher standard of living, overeating and idleness develop the most insolent self-conceit in a Russian. Nikolay Ivanych, who when he was a petty official was afraid to have opinions of his own even if he kept them to himself, now uttered nothing but incontrovertible truths and did so in the tone of a minister of state: 'Education is necessary, but the masses are not ready for it; corporal punishment is generally harmful, but in some cases it is useful and nothing else will serve.'

"'I know the common people, and I know how to deal with them,' he would say. 'They love me. I only have to raise my little finger, and they will do anything I want.'

35   "And all this, mark you, would be said with a smile that bespoke kindness and intelligence. Twenty times over he repeated: 'We, of the gentry,' 'I, as a member of the gentry.' Apparently he no longer remembered that our grandfather had been a peasant and our father just a private. Even our surname, 'Chimsha-Himalaisky,' which in reality is grotesque, seemed to him sonorous, distinguished, and delightful.

"But I am concerned now not with him, but with me. I want to tell you about the change that took place in me during the few hours that I spent on his estate. In the evening when we were having tea, the cook served a plateful of gooseberries. They were not bought, they were his own gooseberries, the first ones picked since the bushes were planted. My brother gave a laugh and for a minute looked at the gooseberries in silence, with tears in his eyes—he could not speak for excitement. Then he put one berry in his mouth, glanced at me with the triumph of a child who has at last been given a toy he was longing for and said: 'How tasty!' And he ate the gooseberries greedily, and kept repeating: 'Ah, how delicious! Do taste them!'

"They were hard and sour, but as Pushkin has it,

The falsehood that exalts we cherish more
Than meaner truths that are a thousand strong.

I saw a happy man, one whose cherished dream had so obviously come true, who had attained his goal in life, who had got what he wanted, who was satisfied with his lot and with himself. For some reason an element of sadness had always mingled with my thoughts of human happiness, and now at the sight of a happy man I was assailed by an oppressive feeling bordering on despair. It weighed on me particularly at night. A bed was made up for me in a room next to my brother's bedroom, and I could hear that he was wakeful, and that he would get up again and again, go to the plate of gooseberries and eat one after another. I said to myself: how many contented, happy people there really are! What an overwhelming force they are! Look at life: the insolence and idleness of the strong, the ignorance and brutishness of the weak, horrible poverty everywhere, overcrowding, degeneration, drunkenness, hypocrisy, lying—Yet in all the houses and on all the streets there is peace and quiet; of the fifty thousand people who live in our town there is not one would would cry out, who would vent his indignation aloud. We see the people who go to market, eat by day, sleep by night, who babble nonsense, marry, grow old, good-naturedly drag their dead to the cemetery, but we do not see or hear those who suffer, and what is terrible in life goes on somewhere behind the scenes. Everything is peaceful and quiet and only mute statistics protest: so many people gone out of their minds, so many gallons of vodka drunk, so many children dead from malnutrition—And such a state of things is evidently necessary; obviously the happy man is at ease only because the unhappy ones bear their burdens in silence, and if there were not this silence, happiness would be impossible. It is a general hypnosis. Behind the door of every contented, happy man there ought to be someone standing with a little hammer and continually reminding him with a knock that there are unhappy people, that however happy he may be, life will sooner or later show him its claws, and trouble will come to him—illness, poverty, losses, and then no one will see or hear him, just as now he neither sees nor hears others. But there is no man with a hammer. The happy man lives at his ease, faintly fluttered by small daily cares, like an aspen in the wind—and all is well.

"That night I came to understand that I too had been contented and happy," Ivan Ivanych continued, getting up. "I too over the dinner table or out hunting would hold forth on how to live, what to believe, the right way to govern the people. I too would say that learning was the enemy of darkness, that education was necessary but that for the common people the three R's were sufficient for the time being. Freedom is a boon, I used to say, it is as essential as air, but we must wait awhile. Yes, that's what I used to say, and now I ask: Why must we wait?" said Ivan Ivanych, looking wrathfully at Burkin. "Why must we wait, I ask you? For what reason? I am told that nothing can be done all at once, that every idea is realized gradually, in its own time. But who is it that says so? Where is the proof that it is just? You cite the natural order of things, the law governing all phenomena, but is there law, is there order in the fact that I, a living, thinking man, stand beside a ditch and wait for it to close up of itself or fill up with silt, when I could jump over it or throw a bridge across it? And again, why must we wait? Wait, until we have no strength to live, and yet we have to live and are eager to live!

"I left my brother's place early in the morning, and ever since then it has become intolerable for me to stay in town. I am oppressed by the peace and the quiet, I am afraid to look at the windows, for there is nothing that pains me more than the spectacle of a happy family sitting at table having tea. I am an old man now and unfit for combat, I am not even capable of hating. I can only grieve inwardly, get irritated, worked up, and at night my head is ablaze with the rush of ideas and I cannot sleep. Oh, if I were young!"

40   Ivan Ivanych paced up and down the room excitedly and repeated, "If I were young!"

He suddenly walked up to Alyohin and began to press now one of his hands, now the other.

"Pavel Konstantinych," he said imploringly, "don't quiet down, don't let yourself be lulled to sleep! As long as you are young, strong, alert, do not cease to do good! There is no happiness and there should be none, and if life has a meaning and a purpose, that meaning and purpose is not our happiness but something greater and more rational. Do good!"

All this Ivan Ivanych said with a pitiful, imploring smile, as though he were asking a personal favor.

Afterwards all three of them sat in armchairs in different corners of the drawing room and were silent. Ivan Ivanych's story satisfied neither Burkin nor Alyohin. With the ladies and generals looking down from the golden frames, seeming alive in the dim light, it was tedious to listen to the story of the poor devil of a clerk who ate gooseberries. One felt like talking about elegant people, about women. And the fact that they were sitting in a drawing room where everything—the chandelier under its cover, the armchairs, the carpets underfoot—testified that the very people who were now looking down from the frames had once moved about here, sat and had tea, and the fact that lovely Pelageya was noiselessly moving about—that was better than any story.

45   Alyohin was very sleepy; he had gotten up early, before three o'clock in the morning, to get some work done, and now he could hardly keep his eyes open, but he was afraid his visitors might tell an interesting story in his absence, and he would not leave. He did not trouble to ask himself if what Ivan Ivanych had just said was intelligent or right. The guests were not talking about groats, or hay, or tar, but about something that had no direct bearing on his life, and he was glad of it and wanted them to go on.

"However, it's bedtime," said Burkin, rising. "Allow me to wish you good night."

Alyohin took leave of his guests and went downstairs to his own quarters, while they remained upstairs. They were installed for the night in a big room in which stood two old wooden beds decorated with carvings and in the corner was an ivory crucifix. The wide cool beds which had been made by the lovely Pelageya gave off a pleasant smell of clean linen.

Ivan Ivanych undressed silently and got into bed.

"Lord forgive us sinners!" he murmured, and drew the bedclothes over his head.

50   His pipe, which lay on the table, smelled strongly of burnt tobacco, and Burkin, who could not sleep for a long time, kept wondering where the unpleasant odor came from.

The rain beat against the window panes all night.

Questions on Point of View . . .

1. What point of view do we find in the first paragraph? How long does this last? When does a different point of view take over? In paragraph 9, how does the word *apparently* enforce a point of view? In paragraph 15, can you feel the point of view shifting? Can the story accommodate the change? Why? How? In paragraph 20, how does the point of view change? Name the different points of view.

2. Ivan is a judgmental narrator. Do you take his judgments as valid?

3. In paragraphs 26 and 27, Ivan is interrogated. What happens to the point of view? Does this interrogation further the plot?

4. In paragraph 29, Ivan says that he was "met by a fat dog with reddish hair that looked like a pig . . ." and so on. What would the brother's point of view be?
    How much of Chekhov's theme is accomplished by his strategy in writing "Gooseberries" from different points of view?

5. Summarize Chekhov's use of point of view in "Gooseberries." Connect the story's structure with the story's theme or meaning.

. . . and Other Elements

6. Is the first paragraph's description ironic?

7. Explicate the title.

8. "Once a man is possessed by an idea, there is no doing anything with him." How far will this go as a summary of "Gooseberries"?

9. Does it make sense to speak of "framing" in the plot of this story? How does the story-within-a-story reflect upon the outer story?

10. Before Ivan begins his story, do you know enough of his character to trust him as a storyteller? Do you learn more of his character later? How do you find out about him?

11. In his story, Ivan continually contrasts reality and pretense. Make two columns and see how many contrasts you can find. You could start with "delicious gooseberries" under *Pretense,* and "sour tasting" under *Reality.*

12. Summarize Ivan's opinion of happiness. Are you inclined to accept his ideas? Are you inclined to skepticism? Why?

13. Discuss smells in this story. Does Ivan's pipe stand in for anything else? Does the rain?

CHAPTER EIGHT

Style and Tone

Literary **style** means at least three different things. We speak of a writer's personal style as a particular way of putting things. Some writers are more distinctive than others—more individual or more identifiable—without necessarily being better writers. Some writers, good and bad, show a style as distinctive as a fingerprint because of the way they use diction, syntax, rhythm, imagery, and metaphor. But we also speak of style as belonging to a period, like Elizabethan style—a set of characteristics peculiar to a historical era. In yet another sense, *style* is a word of praise, and a stylist is a writer we honor for meticulous care.

We can begin by identifying distinctive voices. Here is the beginning of a short story by Ernest Hemingway:

> In the fall the war was always there, but we did not go to it any more. It was cold in the fall in Milan and the dark came very early. Then the electric lights came on, and it was pleasant along the streets looking in the windows. There was much game hanging outside the shops, and the snow powdered in the fur of the foxes and the wind blew their tails. The deer hung stiff and heavy and empty, and small birds blew in the wind and the wind turned their feathers.

This distinctive style announces itself as Ernest Hemingway's—with its short sentences, its simplicity of grammar and diction, and its scarcity of adjectives. Here is the very different style of William Faulkner:

> It had not coiled yet and the buzzer had not sounded either, only one thick rapid contraction, one loop cast sideways as though merely for purchase from which the raised head might start slightly backward, not in fright either, not in threat quite yet, more than six feet of it, the head raised higher than his knee and less than his knee's length away, and old, the once-bright markings of its youth dulled now to a monotone concordant too with the wilderness it crawled and lurked: the old one, the ancient and accursed about the earth, fatal and solitary and he could smell it now: the thin sick smell of rotting cucumbers and something else which had no name, evocative of all knowledge and an old weariness and of pariah-hood and of death.

Notice the long and complicated sentences, the abundance of clauses and modifiers. Notice how different are the distinctive styles of Hemingway and Faulkner, writers who flourished in the same decades. For style of the same period, less distinctive but used with equal skill, see Katherine Anne Porter, for instance.

Both a distinctive style and an excellent but general period style will contrast with unskilled writing. Good style connects a right word to another right word to make a right sentence. Bad style uses either the wrong word ("In the fall the fights were still there . . .") or the wrong level of diction for its subject matter ("In the autumn of the year the hostilities continued to ensue . . ."). **Diction** refers to the writer's choice of an individual word: war, fights, hostilities. Diction characterizes the speaker. In Peter Taylor's "A Spinster's Tale," when the protagonist speaks of her scaredness instead of her fear, a word choice helps fix her youth and naïveté without the author's statement of age. **Syntax** is grammar or sentence structure, and is as characteristic of style as word-choice is. Hemingway uses short words in short sentences, or makes long compound sentences by saying *and;* Faulkner writes sentences elongated with dependent clauses.

Using both syntax and diction, Eudora Welty characterizes Phoenix by her style in "A Worn Path" when Phoenix says to herself, "Seems like there is chains about my feet . . . ." Tillie Olsen's unnamed protagonist says to herself, "She blew shining bubbles of sound." Their different speech styles— embodied in diction, syntax, idiom, and metaphor—help establish their characters. Stream of consciousness, like monologue, can also capture a character for us. Third-person narration often characterizes, even if it does not report thoughts. When Joyce wrote "Just as they were naming their poisons . . . ," he characterized not only Farrington but also the whole ambience of Farrington's bar-culture. The grandmother in Flannery O'Connor's "A Good Man Is Hard to Find" speaks clichés of speech and thought that indicate her petty manipulations and little dishonesties. Even her cat's name—Pitty Sing— helps to indicate character by its baby-talk cuteness; the difference between "Pretty Thing" and "Pitty Sing" is style.

It is style that creates **tone**. Tone is the value that style or gesture gives to words. We can say almost anything, in spoken language, and hang varying tones on it by intonation or gesture. If two of us are eating together, one can say "Please pass the salt" so that it is ironic, tender, sarcastic, loving, angry, bored, depressed, joyous, or indifferent. Tone, then, has no simple relation to content. You can imagine a scene—with eye contact, gesture, and context—in which "I hate you" translates as "I love you" or "I love you" as "I hate you."

One can speak in an ironic tone, which calls attention to incongruity by saying words that indicate one thing and reveal another. One can exaggerate irony to the point of sarcasm—another word describing tone. One's tone can be genteel; when a character speaks of someone as wealthy, avoiding the word *rich* because it seems vulgar, that character's tone is genteel. The same genteel character is apt to say that he builds a new home rather than a house, because the word *home* has a comfy tone to it. Both *house* and *home* may denote the same wooden frame or brick structure, but the connotations or associations of the two words differ. We speak of words as having **denotations** or dictionary meanings, by which *rich* and *wealthy* are synonyms. But a good writer, careful of style, uses connotations or associations to characterize; connotations are like gestures of social tone: someone using the word *wealthy* wishes to sound genteel; someone saying *rich* is plain-spoken.

When we read good fiction, we understand the tone by the author's manipulation of language, which is why we speak of tone in connection with style. An unskilled author might use an adverb ("He said, sarcastically") but the best writers seldom need such obvious signposts. We understand the tone, as it were, by gesture—but it is a gesture the author makes in words. When John Updike says that Ace Anderson "flicked on the radio," "flicked" expresses by style or word choice Ace's character; "turned on the radio" would have expressed little. **Metaphors** indicate a character's feelings, ideas, and background. A happy farmer may feel like the cow let out of the barn after winter; a consumer character may feel as if he had free run of Tiffany's.

Style can convey an author's judgment of a character. Instead of saying "For Miss Simmons was vain and silly, unable to tell the difference between . . . ," the author can make Miss Simmons reveal her vanity and silliness in the style and tone of her speech.

John Updike

John Updike (1932–   ) grew up in Pennsylvania, attended Harvard and Oxford, and worked for a while at *The New Yorker,* where his stories and poems first appeared. He writes articles and reviews, stories and poems, and he is best known as a novelist. Some of his many novels are *Rabbit Run* (1960), *The Centaur* (1963), *Couples* (1968), *Rabbit Redux* (1971), and *The Coup* (1978). Updike's fiction is detailed, observant, and exactly constructed. "Ace in the Hole" comes from his earliest collection of stories, *The Same Door* (1959), and gives us an early version of the character Updike developed under another name in *Rabbit Run, Rabbit Redux, Rabbit Is Rich,* and *Rabbit at Rest.* The last two novels won Pulitzer Prizes in 1981 and 1991. See a poem by Updike, "Ex-Basketball Player," on pages 707–708.

Ace in the Hole   (1955)

No sooner did his car touch the boulevard heading home than Ace flicked on the radio. He needed the radio, especially today. In the seconds before the tubes warmed up, he said aloud, doing it just to hear a human voice, "Jesus. She'll pop her lid." His voice, though familiar, irked him; it sounded thin and scratchy, as if the bones in his head were picking up static. In a deeper register Ace added, "She'll murder me." Then the radio came on, warm and strong, so he stopped worrying. The Five Kings were doing "Blueberry Hill"; to hear them made Ace feel so sure inside that from the pack pinched between the car roof and the sun shield he plucked a cigarette, hung it on his lower lip, snapped a match across the rusty place on the dash, held the flame in the instinctive spot near the tip of his nose, dragged, and blew out the match, all in time to the music. He rolled down the window and snapped the match so it spun end-over-end into the gutter. "Two points," he said, and cocked the cigarette toward the roof of the car, sucked powerfully, and exhaled two plumes through his nostrils. He was beginning to feel like himself, Ace Anderson, for the first time that whole day, a bad day. He beat time on the accelerator. The car jerked crazily. "On Blueberry Hill," he sang, "my heart stood still. The wind in the wil-low tree"—he braked for a red light—"played love's suh-*weet* melodee—"

"Go, Dad, bust your lungs!" a kid's voice blared. The kid was riding in a '52 Pontiac that had pulled up beside Ace at the light. The profile of the driver, another kid, was dark over his shoulder.

Ace looked over at him and smiled slowly, just letting one side of his mouth lift a little. "Shove it," he said, good-naturedly, across the little gap of years that separated them. He knew how they felt, young and mean and shy.

But the kid, who looked Greek, lifted his thick upper lip and spat out the window. The spit gleamed on the asphalt like a half-dollar.

5   "Now isn't that pretty?" Ace said, keeping one eye on the light. "You miserable wop. You are *mi*serable." While the kid was trying to think of some smart comeback, the light changed. Ace dug out so hard he smelled burned rubber. In his rear-view mirror he saw the Pontiac lurch forward a few yards, then stop dead, right in the middle of the intersection.

The idea of them stalling their fat tin Pontiac kept him in a good humor all the way home. He decided to stop at his mother's place and pick up the baby, instead of waiting for Evey to do it. His mother must have seen him drive up. She came out on the porch holding a plastic spoon and smelling of cake.

"You're out early," she told him.

"Friedman fired me," Ace told her.

"Good for you," his mother said. "I always said he never treated you right." She brought a cigarette out of her apron pocket and tucked it deep into one corner of her mouth, the way she did when something pleased her.

10   Ace lighted it for her. "Friedman was O.K. personally," he said. "He just wanted too much for his money. I didn't mind working Saturdays, but until eleven, twelve Friday nights was too much. Everybody has a right to some leisure."

"Well, I don't dare think what Evey will say, but I, for one, thank dear God you had the brains to get out of it. I always said that job had no future to it—no future of any kind, Freddy."

"I guess," Ace admitted. "But I wanted to keep at it, for the family's sake."

"Now, I know I shouldn't be saying this, but any time Evey—this is just between us—any time Evey thinks she can do better, there's room for you *and* Bonnie right in your father's house." She pinched her lips together. He could almost hear the old lady think, *There, I've said it.*

"Look, Mom, Evey tries awfully hard, and anyway you know she can't work that way. Not that *that*—I mean, she's a realist, too . . . ." He let the rest of the thought fade as he watched a kid across the street dribbling a basketball around a telephone pole that had a backboard and net nailed on it.

15   "Evey's a wonderful girl of her own kind. But I've always said, and your father agrees, Roman Catholics ought to marry among themselves. Now I know I've said it before, but when they get out in the greater world—"

"*No,* Mom."

She frowned, smoothed herself, and said, "Your name was in the paper today."

Ace chose to let that go by. He kept watching the kid with the basketball. It was funny how, though the whole point was to get the ball up into the air, kids grabbed it by the sides and squeezed. Kids just didn't think.

"Did you hear?" his mother asked.

20   "Sure, but so what?" Ace said. His mother's lower lip was coming at him, so he changed the subject. "I guess I'll take Bonnie."

His mother went into the house and brought back his daughter, wrapped in a blue blanket. The baby looked dopey. "She fussed all day," his mother complained. "I said to your father, 'Bonnie is a dear little girl, but without a doubt she's her mother's daughter.' You were the best-natured boy."

"Well I *had* everything." Ace said with an impatience that made his mother blink. He nicely dropped his cigarette into a brown flowerpot on the edge of the porch and took his daughter into his arms. She was getting heavier, solid. When he reached the end of the cement walk, his mother was still on the porch, waving to him. He was so close he could see the fat around her elbow jiggle, and he only lived a half block up the street, yet here she was, waving to him as if he was going to Japan.

At the door of his car, it seemed stupid to him to drive the measly half block home. His old coach, Bob Behn, used to say never to ride where you could walk. Cars were the death of legs. Ace left the ignition keys in his pocket and ran along the pavement with Bonnie laughing and bouncing at his chest. He slammed the door of his landlady's house open and shut, pounded up the two flights of stairs, and was panting so hard when he reached the door of his apartment that it took him a couple of seconds to fit the key into the lock.

The run must have tuned Bonnie up. As soon as he lowered her into the crib, she began to shout and wave her arms. He didn't want to play with her. He tossed some blocks and a rattle into the crib and walked into the bathroom, where he turned on the hot water and began to comb his hair. Holding the comb under the faucet before every stroke, he combed his hair forward. It was so long, one strand curled under his nose and touched his lips. He whipped the whole mass back with a single pull. He tucked in the tufts around his ears, and ran the comb straight back on both sides of his head. With his fingers he felt for the little ridge at the back where the two sides met. It was there, as it should have been. Finally, he mussed the hair in front enough for one little lock to droop over his forehead, like Alan Ladd. It made the temple seem lower than it was. Every day, his hairline looked higher. He had observed all around him how blond men went bald first. He remembered reading somewhere, though, that baldness shows virility.

25   On his way to the kitchen he flipped the left-hand knob of the television. Bonnie was always quieter with the set on. Ace didn't see how she could

understand much of it, but it seemed to mean something to her. He found a can of beer in the refrigerator behind some brownish lettuce and those hot dogs Evey never got around to cooking. She'd be home any time. The clock said 5:12. She'd pop her lid.

Ace didn't see what he could do but try and reason with her. "Evey," he'd say, "you ought to thank God I got out of it. It had no future to it at all." He hoped she wouldn't get too mad, because when she was mad he wondered if he should have married her, and doubting that made him feel crowded. It was bad enough, his mother always crowding him. He punched the two triangles in the top of the beer can, the little triangle first, and then the big one, the one he drank from. He hoped Evey wouldn't say anything that couldn't be forgotten. What women didn't seem to realize was that there were things you knew but shouldn't say.

He felt sorry he had called the kid in the car a wop.

Ace balanced the beer on a corner where two rails of the crib met and looked under the chairs for the morning paper. He had trouble finding his name, because it was at the bottom of a column on an inside sports page, in a small article about the county basketball statistics:

> "Dusty" Tremwick, Grosvenor Park's sure-fingered center, copped the individual scoring honors with a season's grand (and we do mean grand) total of 376 points. This is within eighteen points of the all-time record of 394 racked up in the 1949–1950 season by Olinger High's Fred Anderson.

Ace angrily sailed the paper into an armchair. Now it was Fred Anderson; it used to be Ace. He hated being called Fred, especially in print, but then the sportswriters were all office boys anyway, Behn used to say.

30   "Do not just ask for shoe polish," a man on television said, "but ask for *Emu Shoe Gloss,* the *only* polish that absolutely *guarantees* to make your shoes look shinier than new." Ace turned the sound off, so that the man moved his mouth like a fish blowing bubbles. Right away, Bonnie howled, so Ace turned it up loud enough to drown her out and went into the kitchen, without knowing what he wanted there. He wasn't hungry; his stomach was tight. It used to be like that when he walked to the gymnasium alone in the dark before a game and could see the people from town, kids and parents, crowding in at the lighted doors. But once he was inside, the locker room would be bright and hot, and the other guys would be there, laughing it up and towel-slapping, and the tight feeling would leave. Now there were whole days when it didn't leave.

A key scratched at the door lock. Ace decided to stay in the kitchen. Let *her* find *him.* Her heels clicked on the floor for a step or two; then the television set went off. Bonnie began to cry. "Shut up, honey," Evey said. There was a silence.

"I'm home," Ace called.

"No kidding. I thought Bonnie got the beer by herself."

Ace laughed. She was in a sarcastic mood, thinking she was Lauren Bacall. That was all right, just so she kept funny. Still smiling, Ace eased

into the living room and got hit with, "What are *you* smirking about? Another question: What's the idea running up the street with Bonnie like she
was a football?"

35   "You saw that?"

"Your mother told me."

"You saw her?"

"Of course I saw her. I dropped by to pick up Bonnie. What the hell do you
think?—I read her tiny mind?"

"Take it easy," Ace said, wondering if Mom had told her about Friedman.

40   "Take it easy? Don't coach *me.* Another question: Why's the car out in front
of her place? You give the car to her?"

"Look, I parked it there to pick up Bonnie, and I thought I'd leave it there."

"Why?"

"Whaddeya mean, why? I just did. I just thought I'd walk. It's not that far,
you know."

"No, I don't know. If you'd be on your feet all day a block would look like
one hell of a long way."

45   "Okay. I'm sorry."

She hung up her coat and stepped out of her shoes and walked around the
room picking up things. She stuck the newspaper in the wastebasket.

Ace said, "My name was in the paper today."

"They spell it right?" She shoved the paper deep into the basket with her
foot. There was no doubt; she knew about Friedman.

"They called me Fred."

50   "Isn't that your name? What *is* your name anyway? Hero J. Great?"

There wasn't any answer, so Ace didn't try any. He sat down on the sofa,
lighted a cigarette, and waited.

Evey picked up Bonnie. "Poor thing stinks. What does your mother do,
scrub out the toilet with her?"

"Can't you take it easy? I know you're tired."

"You should. I'm always tired."

55   Evey and Bonnie went into the bathroom; when they came out, Bonnie
was clean and Evey was calm. Evey sat down in an easy chair beside Ace and
rested her stocking feet on his knees. "Hit me," she said, twiddling her
fingers for the cigarette.

The baby crawled up to her chair and tried to stand, to see what he gave
her. Leaning over close to Bonnie's nose, Evey grinned, smoke leaking
through her teeth, and said, "Only for grownups, honey."

"Eve," Ace began, "there was no future in that job. Working all Saturday,
and then Friday nights on top of it."

"I know. Your mother told *me* all that, too. All I want from you is what
happened."

She was going to take it like a sport, then. He tried to remember how it *did*
happen. "It wasn't my fault," he said. "Friedman told me to back this '51
Chevvy into the line that faces Church Street. He just bought it from an old
guy this morning who said it only had thirteen thousand on it. So in I jump
and start her up. There was a knock in the engine like a machine gun. I

almost told Friedman he'd bought a squirrel, but you know I cut that smart stuff out ever since Palotta laid me off."

60   "You told me that story. What happens in this one?"

"Look, Eve. I *am* telling ya. Do you want me to go out to a movie or something?"

"Suit yourself."

"So I jump in the Chevvy and snap it back in line, and there was a kind of scrape and thump. I get out and look and Friedman's running over, his arms going like *this*"—Ace whirled his own arms and laughed—"and here was the whole back fender of a '49 Merc mashed in. Just look like somebody took a planer and shaved off the bulge, you know, there at the back." He tried to show her with his hands. "The Chevvy, though, didn't have a dent. It even gained some paint. But *Friedman,* to *hear* him—Boy, they can rave when their pocketbook's hit. He said"—Ace laughed again—"never mind."

Evey said, "You're proud of yourself."

65   "No, listen. I'm not happy about it. But there wasn't a thing I could *do.* It wasn't my driving at all. I looked over on the other side, and there was just two or three inches between the Chevvy and a Buick. *Nobody* could have gotten into that hole. Even if it had hair on it." He thought this was pretty good.

She didn't. "You could have looked."

"There just wasn't the *space.* Friedman said stick it in; I stuck it in."

"But you could have looked and moved the other cars to make more room."

"I guess that would have been the smart thing."

70   "I guess, too. Now what?"

"What do you mean?"

"I mean now what? Are you going to give up? Go back to the Army? Your mother? Be a basketball pro? What?"

"You know I'm not tall enough. Anybody under six-six they don't want."

"Is that so? Six-six? Well, please listen to this, Mr. Six-Foot-Five-and-a-Half: I'm fed up. I'm ready as Christ to let you run." She stabbed her cigarette into an ashtray on the arm of the chair so hard the ashtray jumped to the floor. Evey flushed and shut up.

75   What Ace hated most in their arguments was these silences after Evey had said something so ugly she wanted to take it back. "Better ask the priest first," he murmured.

She sat right up. "If there's one thing I don't want to hear about from you it's priests. You let the priests to me. You don't know a damn thing about it. Not a damn thing."

"Hey, look at Bonnie," he said, trying to make a fresh start with his tone.

Evey didn't hear him. "If you think," she went on, "if for one rotten moment you think, Mr. Fred, that the be-all and end-all of my life is you and your hot-shot stunts—"

"Look, Mother," Ace pleaded, pointing at Bonnie. The baby had picked up the ashtray and put it on her head for a hat and was waiting for praise.

80   Evey glanced down sharply at the child. "Cute," she said. "Cute as her daddy."

The ashtray slid from Bonnie's head and she patted where it had been and looked around puzzled.

"Yeah, but watch," Ace said. "Watch her hands. They're really terrific hands."

"You're nuts," Evey said.

"No, honest. Bonnie's great. She's a natural. Get the rattle for her. Never mind, I'll get it." In two steps, Ace was at Bonnie's crib, picking the rattle out of the mess of blocks and plastic rings and beanbags. He extended the rattle toward his daughter, shaking it delicately. Made wary by this burst of attention, Bonnie reached with both hands; like two separate animals they approached from opposite sides and touched the smooth rattle simultaneously. A smile bubbled up on her face. Ace tugged weakly. She held on, and then tugged back. "She's a natural," Ace said, "and it won't do her any good because she's a girl. Baby, we got to have a boy."

85   "I'm not your baby," Evey said, closing her eyes.

Saying "Baby" over and over again, Ace backed up to the radio and, without turning around, switched on the volume knob. In the moment before the tubes warmed, Evey had time to say, "Wise up, Freddy. What shall we do?"

The radio came in on something slow: dinner music. Ace picked Bonnie up and set her in the crib. "Shall we dance?" he asked his wife, bowing.

"I want to talk."

"Baby. It's the cocktail hour."

90   "This is getting us no place," she said, rising from her chair, though.

"Fred Junior. I can see him now," he said, seeing nothing.

"We will have no Juniors."

In her crib, Bonnie whimpered at the sight of her mother being seized. Ace fitted his hand into the natural place on Evey's back and she shuffled stiffly into his lead. When, with a sudden injection of saxophones, the tempo quickened, he spun her out carefully, keeping the beat with his shoulders. Her hair brushed his lips as she minced in, then swung away, to the end of his arm; he could feel her toes dig into the carpet. He flipped his own hair back from his eyes. The music ate through his skin and mixed with the nerves and small veins; he seemed to be great again, and all the other kids were around them, in a ring, clapping time.

Questions on Style . . .

1. Characterize Ace's personal style in both diction and syntax.

2. Looking at the first paragraph alone, list all the details that define Ace's character. How many of these details depend on style?

3. Note the adverb in paragraph 3. Is it an example of too much telling?

4. Discuss the simile in paragraph 4. Whose character does it illustrate?

5. When Ace speaks, does he ever sound as if he is quoting something he picked up, say, from a television ad? Look at paragraph 10. Is this a matter of style?

6. How much of Ace's mother's character do you learn from her speech? Her gestures? Ace's interpretations?

7. In paragraph 24, do we see Ace comb his hair as he would describe it? Does Updike's style characterize Ace here?

8. In paragraph 30, does the author's style change when Ace remembers something from the past? Does this change happen again in the story? What does it mean in the story?

9. Discuss Evey's style. What words characterize her tone?

. . . and Other Elements

10. When do you realize the point of view in the story? What tells you?

11. How much attention does Updike pay to setting?

Ernest Hemingway

Ernest Hemingway (1898–1961) is a great American novelist who began as a poet and short-story writer. Many critics prefer his stories to his novels, even the celebrated *The Sun Also Rises* (1926) and *A Farewell to Arms* (1929). *In Our Time* (1925) alternated short stories with italicized sketches (see page 24). Later novels included *To Have and Have Not* (1937), *For Whom the Bell Tolls* (1940), *Across the River and into the Trees* (1950), *The Old Man and the Sea* (1952), and the posthumous *Islands in the Stream* (1970). During the First World War, Hemingway was an ambulance driver on the Italian front, where he was wounded and hospitalized. Hemingway's individual style colors the world he inhabited: a place of melancholy where codes of behavior protect the hero from madness and dissolution.

A Clean, Well-Lighted Place   (1933)

It was late and every one had left the café except an old man who sat in the shadow the leaves of the tree made against the electric light. In the day time the street was dusty, but at night the dew settled the dust and the old man liked to sit late because he was deaf and now at night it was quiet and he felt the difference. The two waiters inside the café knew that the old man was a little drunk, and while he was a good client they knew that if he became too drunk he would leave without paying, so they kept watch on him.

"Last week he tried to commit suicide," one waiter said.

"Why?"

"He was in despair."

5   "What about?"

"Nothing."

"How do you know it was nothing?"

"He has plenty of money."

They sat together at a table that was close against the wall near the door of the café and looked at the terrace where the tables were all empty except where the old man sat in the shadow of the leaves of the tree that moved slightly in the wind. A girl and a soldier went by in the street. The street light shone on the brass number on his collar. The girl wore no head covering and hurried beside him.

10 "The guard will pick him up," one waiter said.

"What does it matter if he gets what he's after?"

"He had better get off the street now. The guard will get him. They went by five minutes ago."

The old man sitting in the shadow rapped on his saucer with his glass. The younger waiter went over to him.

"What do you want?"

15 The old man looked at him. "Another brandy," he said.

"You'll be drunk," the waiter said. The old man looked at him. The waiter went away.

"He'll stay all night," he said to his colleague. "I'm sleepy now. I never get into bed before three o'clock. He should have killed himself last week."

The waiter took the brandy bottle and another saucer from the counter inside the café and marched out to the old man's table. He put down the saucer and poured the glass full of brandy.

"You should have killed yourself last week," he said to the deaf man. The old man motioned with his finger. "A little more," he said. The waiter poured on into the glass so that the brandy slopped over and ran down the stem into the top saucer of the pile. "Thank you," the old man said. The waiter took the bottle back inside the café. He sat down at the table with his colleague again.

20 "He's drunk now," he said.

"He's drunk every night."

"What did he want to kill himself for?"

"How should I know."

"How did he do it?"

25 "He hung himself with a rope."

"Who cut him down?"

"His niece."

"Why did they do it?"

"Fear for his soul."

30 "How much money has he got?"

"He's got plenty."

"He must be eighty years old."

"Anyway I should say he was eighty."

"I wish he would go home. I never get to bed before three o'clock. What kind of hour is that to go to bed?"

35 "He stays up because he likes it."

"He's lonely. I'm not lonely. I have a wife waiting in bed for me."

"He had a wife once too."

"A wife would be no good to him now."

"You can't tell. He might be better with a wife."

40 "His niece looks after him."

"I know. You said she cut him down."

"I wouldn't want to be that old. An old man is a nasty thing."

"Not always. This old man is clean. He drinks without spilling. Even now, drunk. Look at him."

"I don't want to look at him. I wish he would go home. He has no regard for those who must work."

45 The old man looked from his glass across the square, then over at the waiters.

"Another brandy," he said, pointing to his glass. The waiter who was in hurry came over.

"Finished," he said, speaking with that omission of syntax stupid people employ when talking to drunken people or foreigners. "No more tonight. Close now."

"Another," said the old man.

"No. Finished." The waiter wiped the edge of the table with a towel and shook his head.

50 The old man stood up, slowly counted the saucers, took a leather coin purse from his pocket and paid for the drinks, leaving half a peseta tip.

The waiter watched him go down the street, a very old man walking unsteadily but with dignity.

"Why didn't you let him stay and drink?" the unhurried waiter asked. They were putting up the shutters. "It is not half-past two."

"I want to go home to bed."

"What is an hour?"

55 "More to me than to him."

"An hour is the same."

"You talk like an old man yourself. He can buy a bottle and drink at home."

"It's not the same."

"No, it is not," agreed the waiter with a wife. He did not wish to be unjust. He was only in a hurry.

60 "And you? You have no fear of going home before your usual hour?"

"Are you trying to insult me?"

"No, hombre, only to make a joke."

"No," the waiter who was in a hurry said, rising from pulling down the metal shutters. "I have confidence. I am all confidence."

"You have youth, confidence, and a job," the older waiter said. "You have everything."

65 "And what do you lack?"

"Everything but work."

"You have everything I have."

"No. I have never had confidence and I am not young."

"Come on. Stop talking nonsense and lock up."

70 "I am of those who like to stay late at the café," the older waiter said. "With all those who do not want to go to bed. With all those who need a light for the night."

"I want to go home and into bed."

"We are of two different kinds," the older waiter said. He was now dressed to go home. "It is not only a question of youth and confidence although those things are very beautiful. Each night I am reluctant to close up because there may be some one who needs the café."

"Hombre, there are bodegas open all night long."

"You do not understand. This is a clean and pleasant café. It is well lighted. The light is very good and also, now, there are shadows of the leaves."

75   "Good night," said the younger waiter.

"Good night," the other said. Turning off the electric light he continued the conversation with himself. It is the light of course but it is necessary that the place be clean and pleasant. You do not want music. Certainly you do not want music. Nor can you stand before a bar with dignity although that is all that is provided for these hours. What did he fear? It was not fear or dread. It was a nothing that he knew too well. It was all a nothing and a man was nothing too. It was only that and light was all it needed and a certain cleanness and order. Some lived in it and never felt it but he knew it all was nada y pues nada* y nada y pues nada. Our nada who art in nada, nada be thy name thy kingdom nada thy will be nada in nada as it is in nada. Give us this nada our daily nada and nada us our nada as we nada our nadas and nada us not into nada but deliver us from nada; pues nada. Hail nothing full of nothing, nothing is with thee. He smiled and stood before a bar with a shining steam pressure coffee machine.

"What's yours?" asked the barman.

"Nada."

"Otro loco mas," said the barman and turned away.

80   "A little cup," said the waiter.

The barman poured it for him.

"The light is very bright and pleasant but the bar is unpolished," the waiter said.

The barman looked at him but did not answer. It was too late at night for conversation.

"You want another copita?" the barman asked.

85   "No, thank you," said the waiter and went out. He disliked bars and bodegas. A clean, well-lighted café was a very different thing. Now, without thinking further, he would go home to his room. He would lie in the bed and finally, with daylight, he would go to sleep. After all, he said to himself, it is probably only insomnia. Many must have it.

Questions on Style . . .

1. What is unusual about the style of the first sentence—in construction, punctuation, and word order? Try rephrasing it to contain the same information in other words and in another order.

---

* *Nada y pues nada:* Nothing and more nothing

2. Define the simplicity of Hemingway's style, using the second sentence of his first paragraph as an example.

3. In Hemingway's style, there is much repetition. Find three examples of repeated words. What is the use or effect of this repetition?

4. How does their conversational style help to differentiate the two waiters?

. . . and Other Elements

5. What is the point of view in this story? Does it change? Where? Describe. Does the author bring his own point of view into the story?

6. Is the setting important in this story? How?

7. Some readers find irony in the dialogue: "What about?" "Nothing." Why? Is there irony elsewhere in this story?

8. Is it insomnia?

CHAPTER NINE

Theme

The **theme** of a story is the implicit generality the story supports. Often, we consider that a story's theme is its reason for being. When we speak of a story's theme, we suggest that a tale implies a central insight into human experience. We express the theme of a story not by summarizing its plot but by a sentence or two of generalization. Thus, we might sum up Chekhov's "Gooseberries": people deceive themselves, and their overriding purposes distort their perceptions of reality; we might sum up Joyce's "Counterparts": people, when bullied by someone more powerful than themselves, express their anger by bullying someone weaker than themselves.

These simple summaries of theme are not adequate to describe great short stories. The story is not a problem to which thematic summary provides an answer. However, summaries of plot and of theme can reassure us that we are all reading the same story. Such summaries are always arguable. One of the weaknesses and one of the strengths of literature is that interpretation is never final, but always subject to refinement and alteration. At the same time, one interpretation is *not* as good as another; literature does not resemble clouds in which we can freely imagine shapes. Interpretations will vary, but we must be able to support them by reference to the story. When we compare varying interpretations, they will often both be true and both be limited. By comparing them, we can enlarge our response to the story. And it is possible—even commonplace—for interpretations to be wrong. Reading "Counterparts" after a session in sociology, we might feel that its theme connected drunkenness with child abuse. We would be wrong. Reading "Gooseberries" without full attention, we might take Ivan Ivanych's theme—that happiness is nothing, that only altruism is important—as a theme propounded by the author himself. Again we would be wrong. All in all, theme is harder to argue about than technical matters like plot, character, point of view, and setting. But, difficult or not, theme requires our attention because it is often a story's reason for being.

Not all stories have themes. When Edgar Allan Poe embarks on "The Murders in the Rue Morgue," the purpose of the story is to create suspense and mystery. The story will not lead to an insight into human character.

Generally, stories without themes are inferior art. They can be entertaining, they can be well-written and pleasing, but they lack seriousness. On the other hand, not all stories with themes are serious works of art. Many popular stories develop commonplace or trite themes. Finishing such stories, we say to ourselves, with satisfaction in our wisdom, "How true! It *does* take all kinds to make a world, just as I always said."

There is also the propaganda story, whose theme has designs on us. The author wants to manipulate us into a particular view of the world or into a particular political position. Everyone is familiar with stories about how evil Communists are; in Communist countries, people read the same stories with capitalist villains. Themes and meanings are clear and sharp: hate the wicked _____ and love the noble _____. But, in a political propaganda story (or a didactic tale in the *Sunday School Weekly,* for that matter), we find no subtle characterization, no overview, no genuine insight. Propaganda characters have the simple mindedness we associate with comic books, whether the cause be good (ours) or bad (theirs). When you read a propaganda story, be wary of approving the fiction just because you agree with the politics. Don't swallow bad art for the sake of worthy ideas.

Looking for Themes

It helps, when we investigate stories for their themes, to keep several matters in mind:

1. In looking for a theme, pay attention to the story's title. It may help, as it does in "Counterparts." In "Gooseberries," the title helps as long as we already have some notion of the theme; most of us have our own gooseberries. In "A Good Man Is Hard to Find," the title's irony leads us toward the theme; like many titles, it works as a hint.

2. Remember to state a theme as a complete sentence. "Old people" is not a theme; it's a topic. "Old people continually find the young neglectful" could be a theme.

3. Remember to state a theme as a generalization. "Farrington is bullied, gets drunk, and beats his son" is a plot summary, not a theme.

4. If, in the course of a story, you come to understand a character, or a character comes to understand herself or himself, the discovery probably suggests the story's theme. Joyce constructed his stories to contain **epiphanies**, sudden moments of revelation—either to character or to reader, or to both. In "Counterparts," the epiphany occurs to us as readers when we understand the title, which leads us to the theme.

5. When you write down the generality that is the theme, double-check: does it encompass all the major events of the story? If it doesn't, your understanding of the theme is probably incomplete. Does anything in the story contradict the generality? If anything does, start over again. Do you find your generality in the story, or do you bring to the story some expectation from outside?

6. If you are baffled in finding the theme of a story, reread it one more time, paying special attention to those parts of the story that seem not to

make sense or seem irrelevant or odd. If, for instance, at the end of "Ace in the Hole," you are puzzled by the image Ace imagines, you are probably missing the theme.

Katherine Anne Porter

Katherine Anne Porter (1890–1980) was novelist, essayist, and short-story writer. She grew up in Texas, an independent young woman determined to write. She worked for newspapers, traveled widely, lived in Europe and Mexico, and did not publish a volume until she collected short stories into *Flowering Judas* (1930). Further collections are *Pale Horse, Pale Rider* (1939) and *The Leaning Tower* (1944), followed by her only novel, *Ship of Fools* (1962). Her *Collected Essays* and *Collected Stories* are available in paperback.

Rope (1930)

On the third day after they moved to the country he came walking back from the village carrying a basket of groceries and a twenty-four-yard coil of rope. She came out to meet him, wiping her hands on her green smock. Her hair was tumbled, her nose was scarlet with sunburn; he told her that already she looked like a born country woman. His gray flannel shirt stuck to him, his heavy shoes were dusty. She assured him he looked like a rural character in a play.

Had he brought the coffee? She had been waiting all day long for coffee. They had forgot it when they ordered at the store the first day.

Gosh, no, he hadn't. Lord, now he'd have to go back. Yes, he would if it killed him. He thought, though, he had everything else. She reminded him it was only because he didn't drink coffee himself. If he did he would remember it quick enough. Suppose they ran out of cigarettes? Then she saw the rope. What was that for? Well, he thought it might do to hang clothes on, or something. Naturally she asked him if he thought they were going to run a laundry? They already had a fifty-foot line hanging right before his eyes? Why, hadn't he noticed it, really? It was a blot on the landscape to her.

He thought there were a lot of things a rope might come in handy for. She wanted to know what, for instance. He thought a few seconds, but nothing occurred. They could wait and see, couldn't they? You need all sorts of strange odds and ends around a place in the country. She said, yes, that was so; but she thought just at that time when every penny counted, it seemed funny to buy more rope. That was all. She hadn't meant anything else. She hadn't just seen, not at first, why he felt it was necessary.

5   Well, thunder, he had bought it because he wanted to, and that was all there was to it. She thought that was reason enough, and couldn't understand

why he hadn't said so, at first. Undoubtedly it would be useful, twenty-four yards of rope, there were hundreds of things, she couldn't think of any at the moment, but it would come in. Of course. As he had said, things always did in the country.

But she was a little disappointed about the coffee, and oh, look, look, look at the eggs! Oh, my, they're all running! What had he put on top of them? Hadn't he known eggs mustn't be squeezed? Squeezed, who had squeezed them, he wanted to know. What a silly thing to say. He had simply brought them along in the basket with the other things. If they got broke it was the grocer's fault. He should know better than to put heavy things on top of eggs.

She believed it was the rope. That was the heaviest thing in the pack, she saw him plainly when he came in from the road, the rope was a big package on top of everything. He desired the whole wide world to witness that this was not a fact. He had carried the rope in one hand and the basket in the other, and what was the use of her having eyes if that was the best they could do for her?

Well, anyhow, she could see one thing plain: no eggs for breakfast. They'd have to scramble them now, for supper. It was too damned bad. She had planned to have steak for supper. No ice, meat wouldn't keep. He wanted to know why she couldn't finish breaking the eggs in a bowl and set them in a cool place.

Cool place! if he could find one for her, she'd be glad to set them there. Well, then, it seemed to him they might very well cook the meat at the same time they cooked the eggs and then warm up the meat for tomorrow. The idea simply choked her. Warmed-over meat, when they might as well have had it fresh. Second best and scraps and makeshifts, even to the meat! He rubbed her shoulder a little. It doesn't really matter so much, does it, darling? Sometimes when they were playful, he would rub her shoulder and she would arch and purr. This time she hissed and almost clawed. He was getting ready to say that they could surely manage somehow when she turned on him and said, if he told her they could manage somehow she would certainly slap his face.

10   He swallowed the words red hot, his face burned. He picked up the rope and started to put it on the top shelf. She would not have it on the top shelf, the jars and tins belonged there; positively she would not have the top shelf cluttered up with a lot of rope. She had borne all the clutter she meant to bear in the flat in town, there was space here at least and she meant to keep things in order.

Well, in that case, he wanted to know what the hammer and nails were doing up there? And why had she put them there when she knew very well he needed that hammer and those nails upstairs to fix the window sashes? She simply slowed down everything and made double work on the place with her insane habit of changing things around and hiding them.

She was sure she begged his pardon, and if she had had any reason to believe he was going to fix the sashes this summer she would have left the hammer and nails right where he put them; in the middle of the bedroom floor where they could step on them in the dark. And now if he didn't clear the whole mess out of there she would throw them down the well.

Oh, all right, all right—could he put them in the closet? Naturally not, there were brooms and mops and dustpans in the closet, and why couldn't he find a place for his rope outside her kitchen? Had he stopped to consider there were seven God-forsaken rooms in the house, and only one kitchen?

He wanted to know what of it? And did she realize she was making a complete fool of herself? And what did she take him for, a three-year-old-idiot? The whole trouble with her was she needed something weaker than she was to heckle and tyrannize over. He wished to God now they had a couple of children she could take it out on. Maybe he'd get some rest.

15   Her face changed at this, she reminded him he had forgot the coffee and had bought a worthless piece of rope. And when she thought of all the things they actually needed to make the place even decently fit to live in, well, she could cry, that was all. She looked so forlorn, so lost and despairing he couldn't believe it was only a piece of rope that was causing all the racket. What *was* the matter, for God's sake?

Oh, would he please hush and go away, and *stay* away, if he could, for five minutes? By all means, yes, he would. He'd stay away indefinitely if she wished. Lord, yes, there was nothing he'd like better than to clear out and never come back. She couldn't for the life of her see what was holding him, then. It was a swell time. Here she was, stuck, miles from a railroad, with a half-empty house on her hands, and not a penny in her pocket, and everything on earth to do; it seemed the God-sent moment for him to get out from under. She was surprised he hadn't stayed in town as it was until she had come out and done the work and got things straightened out. It was his usual trick.

It appeared to him that this was going a little far. Just a touch out of bounds, if she didn't mind his saying so. Why the hell had he stayed in town the summer before? To do a half-dozen extra jobs to get the money he had sent her. That was it. She knew perfectly well they couldn't have done it otherwise. She had agreed with him at the time. And that was the only time so help him he had ever left her to do anything by herself.

Oh, he could tell that to his great-grandmother. She had her notion of what had kept him in town. Considerably more than a notion, if he wanted to know. So, she was going to bring all that up again, was she? Well, she could just think what she pleased. He was tired of explaining. It may have looked funny but he had simply got hooked in, and what could he do? It was impossible to believe that she was going to take it seriously. Yes, yes, she knew how it was with a man: if he was left by himself a minute, some woman was certain to kidnap him. And naturally he couldn't hurt her feelings by refusing!

Well, what was she raving about? Did she forget she had told him those two weeks alone in the country were the happiest she had known for four years? And how long had they been married when she said that? All right, shut up! If she thought that hadn't stuck in his craw.

20   She hadn't meant she was happy because she was away from him. She meant she was happy getting the devilish house nice and ready for him. That was what she had meant, and now look! Bringing up something she had said a

year ago simply to justify himself for forgetting her coffee and breaking the eggs and buying a wretched piece of rope they couldn't afford. She really thought it was time to drop the subject, and now she wanted only two things in the world. She wanted him to get that rope from underfoot, and go back to the village and get her coffee, and if he could remember it, he might bring a metal mitt for the skillets, and two more curtain rods, and if there were any rubber gloves in the village, her hands were simply raw, and a bottle of milk of magnesia from the drugstore.

He looked out at the dark blue afternoon sweltering on the slopes, and mopped his forehead and sighed heavily and said, if only she could wait a minute for *anything,* he was going back. He had said so, hadn't he, the very instant they found he had overlooked it?

Oh, yes, well . . . run along. She was going to wash windows. The country was so beautiful! She doubted they'd have a moment to enjoy it. He meant to go, but he could not until he had said that if she wasn't such a hopeless melancholiac she might see that this was only for a few days. Couldn't she remember anything pleasant about the other summers? Hadn't they ever had any fun? She hadn't time to talk about it, and now would he please not leave that rope lying around for her to trip on? He picked it up, somehow it had toppled off the table, and walked out with it under his arm.

Was he going this minute? He certainly was. She thought so. Sometimes it seemed to her he had second sight about the precisely perfect moment to leave her ditched. She had meant to put the mattresses out to sun, if they put them out this minute they would get at least three hours, he must have heard her say that morning she meant to put them out. So of course he would walk off and leave her to it. She supposed he thought the exercise would do her good.

Well, he was merely going to get her coffee. A four-mile walk for two pounds of coffee was ridiculous, but he was perfectly willing to do it. The habit was making a wreck of her, but if she wanted to wreck herself there was nothing he could do about it. If he thought it was coffee that was making a wreck of her, she congratulated him: he must have a damned easy conscience.

25   Conscience or no conscience, he didn't see why the mattresses couldn't very well wait until tomorrow. And anyhow, for God's sake, were they living *in* the house, or were they going to let the house ride them to death? She paled at this, her face grew livid about the mouth, she looked quite dangerous, and reminded him that housekeeping was no more her work than it was his: she had other work to do as well, and when did he think she was going to find time to do it at this rate?

Was she going to start on that again? She knew as well as he did that his work brought in the regular money, hers was only occasional, if they depended on what *she* made—and she might as well get straight on this question once for all!

That was positively not the point. The question was, when both of them were working on their own time, was there going to be a division of the housework, or wasn't there? She merely wanted to know, she had to make her plans. Why, he thought that was all arranged. It was understood that he was to help. Hadn't he always, in summers?

Hadn't he, though? Oh, just hadn't he? And when, and where, and doing what? Lord, what an uproarious joke!

It was such a very uproarious joke that her face turned slightly purple, and she screamed with laughter. She laughed so hard she had to sit down, and finally a rush of tears spurted from her eyes and poured down into the lifted corners of her mouth. He dashed towards her and dragged her up to her feet and tried to pour water on her head. The dipper hung by a string on a nail and he broke it loose. Then he tried to pump water with one hand while she struggled in the other. So he gave it up and shook her instead.

30   She wrenched away, crying out for him to take his rope and go to hell, she had simply given him up: and ran. He heard her high-heeled bedroom slippers clattering and stumbling on the stairs.

He went out around the house and into the lane; he suddenly realized he had a blister on his heel and his shirt felt as if it were on fire. Things broke so suddenly you didn't know where you were. She could work herself into a fury about simply nothing. She was terrible, damn it: not an ounce of reason. You might as well talk to a sieve as that woman when she got going. Damned if he'd spend his life humoring her! Well, what to do now? He would take back the rope and exchange it for something else. Things accumulated, things were mountainous, you couldn't move them or sort them out or get rid of them. They just lay and rotted around. He'd take it back. Hell, why should he? He wanted it. What was it anyhow? A piece of rope. Imagine anybody caring more about a piece of rope than about a man's feelings. What earthly right had she to say a word about it? He remembered all the useless, meaningless things she bought for herself: Why? because I wanted it, that's why! He stopped and selected a large stone by the road. He would put the rope behind it. He would put it in the tool-box when he got back. He'd heard enough about it to last him a life-time.

When he came back she was leaning against the post box beside the road waiting. It was pretty late, the smell of broiled steak floated nose high in the cooling air. Her face was young and smooth and fresh-looking. Her unmanageable funny black hair was all on end. She waved to him from a distance, and he speeded up. She called out that supper was ready and waiting, was he starved?

You bet he was starved. Here was the coffee. He waved it at her. She looked at his other hand. What was that he had there?

Well, it was the rope again. He stopped short. He had meant to exchange it but forgot. She wanted to know why he should exchange it, if it was something he really wanted. Wasn't the air sweet now, and wasn't it fine to be here?

35   She walked beside him with one hand hooked into his leather belt. She pulled and jostled him a little as he walked, and leaned against him. He put his arm clear around her and patted her stomach. They exchanged wary smiles. Coffee, coffee for the Ootsum-Wootsums! He felt as if he were bringing her a beautiful present.

He was a love, she firmly believed, and if she had had her coffee in the morning, she wouldn't have behaved so funny . . . . There was a whippoorwill still coming back, imagine, clear out of season, sitting in the crab-apple tree calling all by himself. Maybe his girl stood him up. Maybe she did. She hoped to hear him once more, she loved whippoorwills . . . He knew how she was, didn't he?

Sure, he knew how she was.

Questions on Theme . . .

1. State the theme of the story. Remember to make it a whole sentence of general-ization, not a plot summary.

2. Does the title "Rope" work like Chekhov's title "Gooseberries?" Does the word help to define this couple? Does the title comment on the story?

3. Does the author present a moral or give us a lesson? What is the story's purpose?

. . . and Other Elements

4. What is the point of view of this story?

5. This story is almost entirely dialogue without direct quotation. What is the effect?

6. Try putting part of this story into direct quotation. How does it change? Try rewrit-ing a portion of the story as a play, with stage directions. How is it different?

7. Does the first sentence present us with information important to the characters' motives?

8. Are these characters flat or round?

9. How much setting do you have in the story? Would you like to have more?

Michelle Cliff

Michelle Cliff (1946–   ) was born in Kingston, Jamaica, and was educated in New York and London. She earned a degree in comparative historical studies of the Renaissance at the Warburg Institute. She has written a book of prose poems, *Claiming an Identity They Taught Me to Despise* (1980), and two novels: *Abeng* (1984) and *No Telephone to Heaven* (1987). "A Hanged Man" comes from her 1990 collection of short fiction, *Bodies of Water*. She lives in California, and, in 1990, won the James Baldwin Award of the Oakland Black Writers Guild and International Black Writers Association.

A Hanged Man   (1990)

This story is based on two historical details. The first is the suicide of a man who hanged himself from his whipping post in a building used for the punishment of slaves. Such whipping houses—removed from the plantations—were not uncom-mon in the years immediately preceding the Civil War, when abolitionists, in groups, came south to investigate reports of the mistreatment of slaves.

The second detail is the life of a man named Peg-leg Joe, a one-legged sailor (we do not know if Joe was black or white or Indian—or a combination thereof), who led slaves to freedom from as far away as Mobile, Alabama. The following verse from an American folk song is one of the only reports we have of Peg-leg Joe: 'De riva's bank am a very good road/ De dead trees show de way/ Lef' foot, peg foot goin' on/ Foller de drinkin' gourd.'

There is a clearing in the woods. A heavy rain has fallen the night before. Water stands around the foundation of a building in the clearing, seeping into brick. The slate roof is washed clean, shingles glint in the early summer sun.

A brick walkway in the form of a cross leads to the front door of the building. It is lined on every side with roses, begun with caution and formality, now loosed, each challenging the fitness of the other; thorns from one cane cut into the cane of another, drawing blood. Musk, Damask, Isfahan, Old Blush, captured on trails blazed by Crusaders, wild scents flashing in the clearing, fetid, fleshy, sweet. An archway of Persian lilac cascades around the entrance to the building.

To the side, by itself, is the sport of the Apothecary, Rosa Mundi, her striped red over pink ground; red from her parent, the rose of Lancaster, about which every schoolchild in those days knew.

The building began life as a station, set in the middle of nowhere, beyond the trees and fields pertinent to the town. *Began life* is not quite right, since the place never actually came to life. Set at the end of a failed spur line where day-trippers had been meant to disembark, admire the roses, the design of the place. Visions of country excursions with parasoled ladies in tasseled carriages held together by chains fell flat. Baskets of sweetmeats and biscuits and chicken legs went unpacked. Jugs of syllabub unpoured. The place seemed too far, not far enough, from home. These people not suited to day trips. The spur line in the end was impractical, not suited to any real cargo.

5   Now, a slender minaret—exotic doodad embellishing the delicate structure—poked up, brushing against the budding branch of an oak. On one balcony a pair of mockingbirds fought and sang, with more repertoire than a muezzin ever had.

The whole establishment became a sort of shame. A waste. Good money poured out. Almost a complete disgrace until someone suggested another use and saved the town's face—in more ways than one.

The building was well-suited to its new found purpose—its setting in a clearing in the woods beyond the town was exactly what was needed, and the architect, dead and gone, was praised as a man of foresight.

Albeit one with a taste for what one town father called the 'Byzantine', referring not only to the minaret, the roses known to Saladin, but to the plaster replica of Power's *Greek Slave,* set on a pedestal in the waiting room, all the rage at the Crystal Palace, the architect had patiently explained.

Noise could not travel to town from this place. Visitors suspect nothing. Sensibilities spared.

10   No one would hear a thing. Not even the Powhatan with his ear to the iron rail.

Anyway the rail had been torn up, interrupted. The Powhatan long gone.

The only ones to hear would be the ones waiting their turn. That was not a bad thing.

He was facing west. Rivers. Smokies. Expanse. Prairie. Monuments.
Behind him was the ocean. Traders. Clippers. One point of a triangle. Cotton. Tobacco.

15 These were at his back.
He was hanging motionless. Drab. Drab in his workclothes. Gray. Brown spots where blood had dried. Hands hung at his sides. Eyes stared. He was rigid. Stiff. Dead weight. Tongue swollen and thick in his mouth.

Beneath him sawdust covered the floor. Stained and wet, it had not been changed in some time. At his side, within arm's reach, were that not absurd, was a rack which held his tools. Cat-o-nine. Rope. Bull. Each suspended by a hand-carved handle, smoothed by sweat and use.

He might hang there for days. Not be found until someone had need of him, his craft. He had no people of his own.

Sunlight passing through the minaret illuminated him. Mockingbirds fought above him, then burst into song. Would they swoop down and peck out his eyes?

20 Early summer. Buds heavy.
The time of the year when Yankees thawed and headed south to investigate. Poking and probing into the 'wrongs', the inquisitive little bands were well-received. (To be impolite would be impolitic.)

Returning home to their mills and factories and righteous societies, their girl-workers twisting filaments on looms, living, if you could call it that, jammed in bleak white-washed rooms, fighting damp and cold—and dust. Clinging to eyebrows, lids, lips, skin whitened, chest heavy—the cotton dust was everywhere, was in the air when Whittier came to speak. Eyes watered.

But they can at least read, a visitor might say. Our nigras, the host might reason, have at least the sun.

Now just where did those Yankees reckon the cotton on those looms came from?

25 India? Egypt?
Blest be the tie that binds, the thread of connection.

Right now, at this very moment, as this hanging man waited on discovery, soul God knows where, if, evensong was being sung in the stone church, for the benefit of women in black and men in black, unused to such elaborate service, severe and shunning any excess.

'To our distinguished visitors,' the pastor spoke, 'brothers and sisters, welcome.'

He paused. 'Let us pray.'

30 Then:

My soul be on thy guard, Ten thousand foes arise;
The hosts of sin are pressing hard To draw thee from the skies.

O watch and fight and pray; The battle ne'er give o'er;
Renew it boldly every day, And help divine implore.

Each recognized the song as theirs. Weighed down by righteousness, they sang their hearts out.

But one woman, black taffeta under a stained-glass window, who wished for something gentler.

After the service there was a somber and sedate dinner, with Bible readings, pan-roasted oysters, watermelon pickle, meat cut high off the hog. A pale old man standing in the shadow of the breakfront, silver salver at the ready. Darkness masking the line running from his eyelid to his jawbone. A lady tinkled Mozart on a spinet.

Over port and cigars the visiting men—the ladies had taken their leave, even now were being helped into their night-things, awkwardly, by women who did not speak, did not respond to them—the men were left the delicate questions, the thing they had come all this way to probe.

35 Upstairs a woman cries out, seized with gripes, wondering if the stories about poisoning are true. Ashamed for wondering. We are their friends, she says to herself, not knowing these dark silent women at all. Don't they realize that? The trichina worms its way into her muscle. She muffles her cry. She lies back in the featherbed, praying for the pain to pass, not wanting to wander around this house, huge and dark, in search of help.

Downstairs the conversation, inquisition, continues.

We have heard . . .

Sir, I beg you . . .

Of brutality . . . branding

Consider your sources . . .

Iron necklaces . . .

Sir, would you wilfully . . .

An excess of punishment . . .

Damage . . .

There are reports . . .

Something on which your livelihood depends?

No.

Well, sir.

We have heard of the lightening of the Africans . . .

Much exaggerated . . .

Their skin . . .

You and your companions . . .

The pale old man, right eye droopy as he tires, as the line to his jawbone tugs at him, pours port.

Are most welcome to look into any nook and cranny on this farm.

Or mine. Or mine. Or mine.

The chorus chimes in.

The company adjourns. The old man replaces the decanter in the breakfront. Thinks again and pours himself a glass. Drinks. Then marks the level on the crystal for the mistress to note where the gentlemen left it. He regards the ruby liquid, himself in it, the line which pains him, then snuffs the candlelight.

Near dawn the figure stiffer than before. A rat sniffs at the leg of the upended stool, moving on to nibble at the dangling thongs. The wind through the minaret imitates human sounds.

The sideboard creaks from the weight of meat. All is laid out in silver. Silver is set on white linen which covers the fine veneer of mahogany. The same pale old man stands against the wall.

The stench of dead humanity is high. The rat has made her way across the floor to where the salt is kept. She licks at the crystals.

40 All hell breaks loose at breakfast. Well, at least temporarily. Temporarily, good manners are suspended. Tempers, held tight last night, loosed. All because a visitor raises the question of Mrs. Stowe and her Uncle Tom.
    The host explodes. Melodrama! Sheer melodrama! Written by a homely woman to buy a black silk dress.
    There is silence at the table.
    Upstairs a woman vomits into a silk pillowslip.

A young woman is standing outside the door of the station, a slip of paper in her hand. She is too frightened to care about the roses. She has not been here before but knows too well the stories. She wears an apron on which she has appliquéd figures, as if they will protect her. Jonah in the belly of the beast. Keep her company. The women at the foot of the cross. Remind her that this life is not all. Shàngó aloft, riding a chariot. Swing low.
45 She knocks. Loud. Then louder.
    Please, marster, don't prolong my agony.
    She does not dare turn the knob.
    She cannot look through the windows. They are painted black.
    She slides the slip of paper underneath the door.
50 Cap'n: fifty lashes and charge to account.
    She sits on a stump to wait.

She sat there for a long time and the door did not open; no one else appeared. In her entire life she had never had this much time when she had been completely alone, not called on. But anticipating punishment robbed her of the use of solitude; she was only frightened.
    The fright built in her over the hours, the tension in her pitching so high that her ears began to ring, and she felt she would explode unless she could move. So she got up and began to walk around, more to relieve her terror than for any other reason.
    At first she explored the grounds, trying to ease her mind with the smell and color of roses. Trying to trace the red stripes of the flesh of one she was

only reminded of the stripes awaiting her, which would make ditches across her back.

55   The only interruption in the stillness was birdsong, and she tried to follow the changes of the two mockingbirds atop the building's tower. Listening, she walked back and forth on the path, toes tracing the moss between the brick. Soon this was as bad as sitting on a stump—she turned to walk away.

Running did not enter her mind; she began to walk away.

When she had walked as long as she had spent by that blasted, haunted building she had the nerve to look behind her, and ahead of her, to her left and to her right. Behind and ahead were woods; to her right, woods. To her left she sensed running water and turned to walk towards it.

It was too sweet. Soaking her feet in this rushing, cold water. Concealed by woods, not a soul to hear her. No break in the stillness here but the breaking of water on rock. She grabbed a bunch of cress from the riverbank and let her mouth enjoy its heat. A cold, wide river was at her side, running— daring her: escape! Bless me, Oshun, she prayed to the *orisha* of sweet water. With that prayer she cast her lot.

She got up, wiped her mouth with the corner of her apron, and walked on. She looked down at the muddy bank and recognized the trace of a track: a human foot beside the circle of a peg-leg. The mark of the journey-man. Spying this she walked forward. There was another track, then another, and after a hundred such tracks she was able to breathe deep, and take heart in this other human presence.

Questions on Theme . . .

1. State Cliff's theme in this story. Or does the story contain two themes? Why or how is Cliff's theme singular?

2. The first paragraph of this story claims to be a note about the story. What does this introduction contribute to the story's theme?

3. Who are "Mrs. Stowe and her Uncle Tom" and why do they make our host explode?

4. The story ends with the phrase, *this other human presence.* Is the phrase ironic? Does the phrase contribute to theme?

5. Why are Yankees relevant to Cliff's purpose in this story?

6. A corpse is treated as a character. What does this do for the theme?

. . . and Other Elements

7. Cliff writes so that the reader must pay close attention, to follow her narrative from paragraph to paragraph, from event to event. Why doesn't she make it easier for us?

8. What is Cliff's point of view?

CHAPTER TEN

Symbolism

A symbol is something that remains itself while it stands for something besides itself—the way a cloth flag is literally fabric while symbolically it stands for our country. The word *symbol,* most simply, means a sign, like a circle containing a cigarette crossed through by a diagonal line. Everybody knows that this sign is a symbol for NO SMOKING. Traffic signs, or national flags, or the logos of sports teams are all **symbols**. These symbols belong to a particular culture or represent it. They are changeable as a culture changes, and often they work by association. A Rolls-Royce, associated with wealth, can act as a conventional symbol of wealth. The homeless person's large, overstuffed plastic bags, an accessory of poverty and homelessness, can be used to stand in for poverty and homelessness.

We also speak of **natural symbols**. These symbols occur in literature but veer toward the cliché: Night is a natural symbol of death and so is autumn. Natural symbols derive from nature, which is why they are pervasive, and why they can become trite. Shakespeare and other geniuses have made great literature from them; Hallmark relies on them in making greeting cards. When Shakespeare compares the process of aging with autumn and the changing of the leaves, and with a dying fire, he is not the only writer to do so; but he uses these natural symbols so well that we do not mind their obviousness.

Natural symbols can give us trouble as writers or readers, because they are trite or obvious. Equally, because they derive from experience, they can be obscure if we do not share the experience. A teacher friend tells me that he had trouble teaching Robert Frost's "Stopping by Woods on a Snowy Evening" when he taught in Hawaii.

In a story, a symbol usually stands for a *class* of events or relationships or suggests something *more* than it is. In "Gooseberries," the fruit literally grows on Ivan Ivanych's brother's estate. As Ivan Ivanych describes the gooseberries, they become a symbol of how a person's dreams promote self-deceit; as Chekhov manipulates his story, we understand that Ivan Ivanych has "gooseberries" of his own—as most of us do. Chekhov uses gooseberries to stand in for something else; he uses gooseberries as a symbol.

Chekhov's gooseberries make a **literary symbol**, a term that needs defining. The existence of literary symbols, in fact, is a reason for literature. When
we talk to somebody who has read what we have read, we can use titles or
names of characters or objects in stories, or we can quote images and lines
from poems, in order to embody the literary symbol that these characters or
properties or images carry to the reader. Talking to friend A about acquaintance B, we can say that, for B, the Jersey Shore in the month of August is
gooseberries. We communicate by a word that encapsulates a literary symbol,
instead of trying to translate that symbol into abstract or philosophical language. In the case of Chekhov's story, maybe the generalized definition
would be: "an object so desired that it is praised whether or not it fulfills the
desire." When a word like *gooseberries* can substitute for such abstraction—
and represent a human emotion more fully than the philosophical language
can—the author of the story has made a literary symbol.

Let us be careful to say what a literary symbol is *not*. It is *not* a type;
Farrington is not a symbol of middle-aged Irish drunkards; Farrington is a
type. He is typical, but he does not stand for anything. A literary symbol signifies something of another class—the way gooseberries stand in for dreaming
and deception. Also, a literary symbol is *not* a translation of an abstract idea
into a concrete image. This device is **allegory**, not symbolism. In the medieval allegorical play called *Everyman,* the hero of the title has acquaintances called Fellowship, Kindred, Goods, Knowledge, Beauty, and Strength.
Summoned by Death, Everyman finds only Good Deeds willing to accompany
him to the grave. In "A Worn Path," Phoenix is another character who undertakes a journey, but Phoenix's journey is not allegorical. A good case might be
made, however, for taking Phoenix's journey as a symbol of the human ability
to endure and survive.

It remains to say what a literary symbol *is*. It is characteristic of the literary
symbol, as opposed to the allegorical device, that it is difficult to name what
the symbol stands for. If it were not difficult, the author could name it
without troubling himself to invent a literary symbol; the French poet
Stéphane Mallarmé called the symbol "the new word," suggesting that the
writer creates in symbols new concepts previously unexpressed. Perhaps we
would call "Gooseberries" a "new word." In the context of his story, Chekhov
makes gooseberries *stand for* something. The attempt to *name* the symbol of
"Gooseberries" feels awkward and inadequate, but the image of gooseberries remains when we have finished the story, resonant in our memories like
a figure from a dream.

Often, a literary symbol seems to bring opposites together. The gooseberries, praised for their excellence, are in reality ghastly. The literary symbol
often acknowledges that the world is complex and ambivalent, and that our
existence is never simple. When Blake writes about a "sick rose," he brings
opposites together in words that seem as if they could never live together—
but they do. The literary symbol becomes antipathetic to the natural symbol
when it avows that dawn has more to do with death than night does; that
autumn is birthlike and spring deathlike; or, as T. S. Eliot put it, "April is the
cruelest month."

When we read a story, certain clues suggest the presence of symbolism; we discover a symbol in a story by its aura of import, its obsessive presence, its inexplicability. Often, but not always, the presence of fantasy suggests symbolism. Here are three symbolic stories that—unlike "A Worn Path" or "Gooseberries"—are dreamlike and fantastic.

Nathaniel Hawthorne

Nathaniel Hawthorne (1804–1864) is the first great author of American literature. One of his ancestors was a judge at the Salem witch trials, and Hawthorne throughout his life expressed ambivalence toward his Puritan past. His father was a sea captain who died on a voyage when Nathaniel was four. Growing up in a small town in Maine, he attended Bowdoin College as a classmate of Longfellow and roommate of Franklin Pierce, who became President. After college, he began to write, mixing his literary pursuits with various government posts. President Pierce made him American consul at Liverpool in 1853, after which he spent some time in Italy. Next to his novels *The Scarlet Letter* (1848) and *The House of the Seven Gables* (1851), Hawthorne's short stories are his best work.

Young Goodman Brown   (1846)

Young Goodman Brown came forth at sunset into the street at Salem village;[1] but put his head back, after crossing the threshold, to exchange a parting kiss with his young wife. And Faith, as the wife was aptly named, thrust her own pretty head into the street, letting the wind play with the pink ribbons of her cap while she called to Goodman Brown.

"Dearest heart," whispered she, softly and rather sadly, when her lips were close to his ear, "prithee put off your journey until sunrise and sleep in your own bed to-night. A lone woman is troubled with such dreams and such thoughts that she's afeared of herself sometimes. Pray tarry with me this night, dear husband, of all nights in the year."

"My love and my Faith," replied young Goodman Brown, "of all nights in the year, this one night must I tarry away from thee. My journey, as thou callest it, forth and back again, must needs be done 'twixt now and sunrise. What, my sweet, pretty wife, dost thou doubt me already, and we but three months married?"

"Then God bless you!" said Faith, with the pink ribbons; "and may you find all well when you come back."

5   "Amen!" cried Goodman Brown. "Say thy prayers, dear Faith, and go to bed at dusk, and no harm will come to thee."

So they parted; and the young man pursued his way until, being about to turn the corner by the meeting-house, he looked back and saw the head of

[1] In 1692 nineteen people were executed in Salem, Massachusetts, after being convicted of witchcraft.

Faith still peeping after him with a melancholy air in spite of her pink ribbons.

"Poor little Faith!" thought he, for his heart smote him. "What a wretch am I to leave her on such an errand! She talks of dreams, too. Methought as she spoke there was trouble in her face, as if a dream had warned her what work is to be done to-night. But no, no; 'twould kill her to think it. Well, she's a blessed angel on earth; and after this one night I'll cling to her skirts and follow her to heaven."

With this excellent resolve for the future, Goodman Brown felt himself justified in making more haste on his present evil purpose. He had taken a dreary road, darkened by all the gloomiest trees of the forest, which barely stood aside to let the narrow path creep through, and closed immediately behind. It was all as lonely as could be; and there is this peculiarity in such a solitude, that the traveller knows not who may be concealed by the innumerable trunks and the thick boughs overhead; so that with lonely footsteps he may yet be passing through an unseen multitude.

"There may be a devilish Indian behind every tree," said Goodman Brown to himself; and he glanced fearfully behind him as he added, "What if the devil himself should be at my very elbow!"

10   His head being turned back, he passed a crook of the road, and, looking forward again, beheld the figure of a man, in grave and decent attire, seated at the foot of an old tree. He arose at Goodman Brown's approach and walked onward side by side with him.

"You are late, Goodman Brown," said he. "The clock of the Old South was striking as I came through Boston, and that is full fifteen minutes agone."

"Faith kept me back a while," replied the young man, with a tremor in his voice, caused by the sudden appearance of his companion, though not wholly unexpected.

It was now deep dusk in the forest, and deepest in that part of it where these two were journeying. As nearly as could be discerned, the second traveller was about fifty years old, apparently in the same rank of life as Goodman Brown, and bearing a considerable resemblance to him, though perhaps more in expression than features. Still they might have been taken for father and son. And yet, though the elder person was as simply clad as the younger, and as simple in manner too, he had an indescribable air of one who knew the world, and who would not have felt abashed at the governor's dinner table or in King William's court, were it possible that his affairs should call him thither. But the only thing about him that could be fixed upon as remarkable was his staff, which bore the likeness of a great black snake, so curiously wrought that it might almost be seen to twist and wriggle itself like a living serpent. This, of course, must have been an ocular deception, assisted by the uncertain light.

"Come, Goodman Brown," cried his fellow-traveller, "this is a dull place for the beginning of a journey. Take my staff, if you are so soon weary."

15   "Friend," said the other, exchanging his slow pace for a full stop, "having kept covenant by meeting thee here, it is my purpose now to return whence I came. I have scruples touching the matter thou wot'st of."

"Sayest thou so?" replied he of the serpent, smiling apart. "Let us walk on, nevertheless, reasoning as we go; and if I convince thee not thou shalt turn back. We are but a little way in the forest yet."

"Too far! too far!" exclaimed the goodman, unconsciously resuming his walk. "My father never went into the woods on such an errand, nor his father before him. We have been a race of honest men and good Christians since the days of the martyrs; and shall I be the first of the name of Brown that ever took this path and kept—"

"Such company, thou wouldst say," observed the elder person, interpreting his pause. "Well said, Goodman Brown! I have been as well acquainted with your family as with ever a one among the Puritans; and that's no trifle to say. I helped your grandfather, the constable, when he lashed the Quaker woman so smartly through the streets of Salem; and it was I that brought your father a pitch-pine knot, kindled at my own hearth, to set fire to an Indian village, in King Philip's war.[2] They were my good friends, both; and many a pleasant walk have we had along this path, and returned merrily after midnight. I would fain be friends with you for their sake."

"If it be as thou sayest," replied Goodman Brown, "I marvel they never spoke of these matters; or, verily, I marvel not, seeing that the least rumor of the sort would have driven them from New England. We are a people of prayer, and good works to boot, and abide no such wickedness."

20 "Wickedness or not," said the traveller with the twisted staff, "I have a very general acquaintance here in New England. The deacons of many a church have drunk the communion wine with me; the selectmen of divers towns make me their chairman; and a majority of the Great and General Court[3] are firm supporters of my interest. The governor and I, too—But these are state secrets."

"Can this be so?" cried Goodman Brown, with a stare of amazement at his undisturbed companion. "Howbeit, I have nothing to do with the governor and council; they have their own ways, and are no rule for a simple husbandman like me. But, were I to go on with thee, how should I meet the eye of that good old man, our minister, at Salem village? Oh, his voice would make me tremble both Sabbath day and lecture[4] day."

Thus far the elder traveller had listened with due gravity; but now burst into a fit of irrepressible mirth, shaking himself so violently that his snakelike staff actually seemed to wriggle in sympathy.

"Ha! ha! ha!" shouted he again and again; then composing himself, "Well, go on, Goodman Brown, go on; but, prithee, don't kill me with laughing."

"Well, then, to end the matter at once," said Goodman Brown, considerably nettled, "there is my wife, Faith. It would break her dear little heart; and I'd rather break my own."

25 "Nay, if that be the case," answered the other, "e'en go thy ways, Goodman Brown. I would not for twenty old women like the one hobbling before us that Faith should come to any harm."

---

[2] The last Indian uprising against the Puritan colonists (1675–1676). King Philip was also known as Metacomet. [3] The colonial legislature of Massachusetts Colony [4] A midweek sermon, often delivered on Thursday

As he spoke he pointed his staff at a female figure on the path, in whom Goodman Brown recognized a very pious and exemplary dame, who had taught him his catechism in youth, and was still his moral and spiritual adviser, jointly with the minister and Deacon Gookin.

"A marvel, truly, that Goody Cloyse[5] should be so far in the wilderness at nightfall," said he. "But with your leave, friend, I shall take a cut through the woods until we have left this Christian woman behind. Being a stranger to you, she might ask whom I was consorting with and whither I was going."

"Be it so," said his fellow-traveller. "Betake you the woods, and let me keep the path."

Accordingly the young man turned aside, but took care to watch his companion, who advanced softly along the road until he had come within a staff's length of the old dame. She, meanwhile, was making the best of her way, with singular speed for so aged a woman, and mumbling some indistinct words—a prayer, doubtless—as she went. The traveller put forth his staff and touched her withered neck with what seemed the serpent's tail.

30   "The devil!" screamed the pious old lady.

"Then Goody Cloyse knows her old friend?" observed the traveller, confronting her and leaning on his writhing stick.

"Ah, forsooth, and is it your worship indeed?" cried the good dame. "Yea, truly it is, and in the very image of my old gossip,[6] Goodman Brown, the grandfather of the silly fellow that now is. But—would your worship believe it?—my broomstick hath strangely disappeared, stolen, as I suspect, by that unhanged witch, Goody Cory, and that, too, when I was all anointed with the juice of smallage, and cinquefoil, and wolf's bane—"

"Mingled with fine wheat and the fat of a new-born babe," said the shape of old Goodman Brown.

"Ah, your worship knows the recipe," cried the old lady, cackling aloud. "So, as I was saying, being all ready for the meeting, and no horse to ride on, I made up my mind to foot it; for they tell me there is a nice young man to be taken into communion to-night. But now your good worship will lend me your arm, and we shall be there in a twinkling."

35   "That can hardly be," answered her friend. "I may not spare you my arm, Goody Cloyse; but here is my staff, if you will."

So saying, he threw it down at her feet, where, perhaps, it assumed life, being one of the rods which its owner had formerly lent to the Egyptian magi.[7] Of this fact, however, Goodman Brown could not take cognizance. He had cast up his eyes in astonishment, and, looking down again, beheld neither Goody Cloyse nor the serpentine staff, but his fellow-traveller alone, who waited for him as calmly as if nothing had happened.

"That old woman taught me my catechism," said the young man; and there was a world of meaning in this simple comment.

They continued to walk onward, while the elder traveller exhorted his companion to make good speed and persevere in the path, discoursing so

---

[5] The real name of a woman condemned in 1692. *Goody* is a contraction of Goodwife, which like Goodman was an epithet for a married person.   [6] Friend   [7] Exodus 7

aptly that his arguments seemed rather to spring up in the bosom of his auditor than to be suggested by himself. As they went, he plucked a branch of maple to serve for a walking stick, and began to strip it of the twigs and little boughs, which were wet with evening dew. The moment his fingers touched them they became strangely withered and dried up as with a week's sunshine. Thus the pair proceeded, at a good free pace, until suddenly, in a gloomy hollow of the road, Goodman Brown sat himself down on the stump of a tree and refused to go any farther.

"Friend," said he, stubbornly, "my mind is made up. Not another step will I budge on this errand. What if a wretched old woman do choose to go to the devil when I thought she was going to heaven: is that any reason why I should quit my dear Faith and go after her?"

40   "You will think better of this by and by," said his acquaintance, composedly. "Sit here and rest yourself a while; and when you feel like moving again, there is my staff to help you along."

Without more words, he threw his companion the maple stick, and was as speedily out of sight as if he had vanished into the deepening gloom. The young man sat a few moments by the roadside, applauding himself greatly, and thinking with how clear a conscience he should meet the minister in his morning walk, nor shrink from the eye of good old Deacon Gookin. And what calm sleep would be his that very night, which was to have been spent so wickedly, but so purely and sweetly now, in the arms of Faith! Amidst these pleasant and praiseworthy meditations, Goodman Brown heard the tramp of horses along the road, and deemed it advisable to conceal himself within the verge of the forest, conscious of the guilty purpose that had brought him thither, though now so happily turned from it.

On came the hoof tramps and the voices of the riders, two grave old voices, conversing soberly as they drew near. These mingled sounds appeared to pass along the road, within a few yards of the young man's hiding-place; but, owing doubtless to the depth of the gloom at that particular spot, neither the travellers nor their steeds were visible. Though their figures brushed the small boughs by the wayside, it could not be seen that they intercepted, even for a moment, the faint gleam from the strip of bright sky athwart which they must have passed. Goodman Brown alternately crouched and stood on tiptoe, pulling aside the branches and thrusting forth his head as far as he durst without discerning so much as a shadow. It vexed him the more, because he could have sworn, were such a thing possible, that he recognized the voices of the minister and Deacon Gookin, jogging along quietly, as they were wont to do, when bound to some ordination or ecclesiastical council. While yet within hearing, one of the riders stopped to pluck a switch.

"Of the two, reverend sir," said the voice like the deacon's, "I had rather miss an ordination dinner than to-night's meeting. They tell me that some of our community are to be here from Falmouth and beyond, and others from Connecticut and Rhode Island, besides several of the Indian powwows,[8] who, after their fashion, know almost as much deviltry as the

[8] Medicine men

best of us. Moreover, there is a goodly young woman to be taken into communion."

"Mighty well, Deacon Gookin!" replied the solemn old tones of the minister. "Spur up, or we shall be late. Nothing can be done, you know, until I get on the ground."

45   The hoofs clattered again; and the voices talking so strangely in the empty air, passed on through the forest, where no church had ever been gathered or solitary Christian prayed. Whither, then, could these holy men be journeying so deep into the heathen wilderness? Young Goodman Brown caught hold of a tree for support, being ready to sink down on the ground, faint and overburdened with the heavy sickness of his heart. He looked up to the sky, doubting whether there really was a heaven above him. Yet there was the blue arch, and the stars brightening in it.

"With heaven above and Faith below, I will stand firm against the devil!" cried Goodman Brown.

While he still gazed upward into the deep arch of the firmament and had lifted his hands to pray, a cloud, though no wind was stirring, hurried across the zenith and hid the brightening stars. The blue sky was still visible, except directly overhead, where this black mass of cloud was sweeping swiftly northward. Aloft in the air, as if from the depths of the cloud, came a confused and doubtful sound of voices. Once the listener fancied that he could distinguish the accents of townspeople of his own, men and women, both pious and ungodly, many of whom he had met at the communion table, and had seen others rioting at the tavern. The next moment, so indistinct were the sounds, he doubted whether he had heard aught but the murmur of the old forest, whispering without a wind. Then came a stronger swell of those familiar tones, heard daily in the sunshine at Salem village, but never until now from a cloud of night. There was one voice, of a young woman, uttering lamentations, yet with an uncertain sorrow, and entreating for some favor, which, perhaps, it would grieve her to obtain; and all the unseen multitude, both saints and sinners, seemed to encourage her onward.

"Faith!" shouted Goodman Brown, in a voice of agony and desperation; and the echoes of the forest mocked him, crying, "Faith! Faith!" as if bewildered wretches were seeking her all through the wilderness.

The cry of grief, rage, and terror was yet piercing the night, when the unhappy husband held his breath for a response. There was a scream, drowned immediately in a louder murmur of voices, fading into far-off laughter, as the dark cloud swept away, leaving the clear and silent sky above Goodman Brown. But something fluttered lightly down through the air and caught on the branch of a tree. The young man seized it, and beheld a pink ribbon.

50   "My Faith is gone!" cried he, after one stupefied moment. "There is no good on earth; and sin is but a name. Come, devil; for to thee is this world given."

And, maddened with despair, so that he laughed loud and long, did Goodman Brown grasp his staff and set forth again, at such a rate that he seemed to fly along the forest path rather than to walk or run. The road grew wilder and drearier and more faintly traced, and vanished at length, leaving him in the heart of the dark wilderness, still rushing onward with the instinct that guides mortal man to evil. The whole forest was peopled with frightful sounds—the creaking of the trees, the howling of wild beasts, and the yell of Indians; while sometimes the wind tolled like a distant church bell, and sometimes gave a broad roar around the traveller, as if all Nature were laughing him to scorn. But he was himself the chief horror of the scene, and shrank not from its other horrors.

"Ha! ha! ha!" roared Goodman Brown when the wind laughed at him. "Let us hear which will laugh loudest. Think not to frighten me with your devil-try. Come witch, come wizard, come Indian powwow, come devil himself, and here comes Goodman Brown. You may as well fear him as he fear you."

In truth, all through the haunted forest there could be nothing more frightful than the figure of Goodman Brown. On he flew among the black pines, brandishing his staff with frenzied gestures, now giving vent to an inspiration of horrid blasphemy, and now shouting forth such laughter as set all the echoes of the forest laughing like demons around him. The fiend in his own shape is less hideous than when he rages in the breast of man. Thus sped the demoniac on his course, until, quivering among the trees, he saw a red light before him, as when the felled trunks and branches of a clearing have been set on fire, and throw up their lurid blaze against the sky, at the hour of midnight. He paused, in a lull of the tempest that had driven him onward, and heard the swell of what seemed a hymn, rolling solemnly from a distance with the weight of many voices. He knew the tune; it was a familiar one in the choir of the village meeting-house. The verse died heavily away, and was lengthened by a chorus, not of human voice, but of all the sounds of the benighted wilderness pealing in awful harmony together. Goodman Brown cried out, and his cry was lost to his own ear by its unison with the cry of the desert.

In the interval of silence he stole forward until the light glared full upon his eyes. At one extremity of an open space, hemmed in by the dark wall of the forest, arose a rock, bearing some rude, natural resemblance either to an altar or a pulpit, and surrounded by four blazing pines, their tops aflame, their stems untouched, like candles at an evening meeting. The mass of foliage that had overgrown the summit of the rock was all on fire, blazing high into the night and fitfully illuminating the whole field. Each pendent twig and leafy festoon was in a blaze. As the red light arose and fell, a numerous congrega-tion alternately shone forth, then disappeared in shadow, and again grew, as it were, out of the darkness, peopling the heart of the solitary woods at once.

55   "A grave and dark-clad company," quoth Goodman Brown.

In truth they were such. Among them, quivering to and fro between gloom and splendor, appeared faces that would be seen next day at the council board of the province, and others which, Sabbath after Sabbath, looked devoutly heavenward, and benignantly over the crowded pews, from the holiest pulpits in the land. Some affirm that the lady of the governor was there. At least there were high dames well known to her, and wives of honored husbands, and widows, a great multitude, and ancient maidens, all of excellent repute, and fair young girls, who trembled lest their mothers should espy them. Either the sudden gleams of light flashing over the obscure field bedazzled Goodman Brown, or he recognized a score of the church members of Salem village famous for their especial sanctity. Good old Deacon Gookin had arrived, and waited at the skirts of that venerable saint, his revered pastor. But, irreverently consorting with these grave, reputable, and pious people, these elders of the church, these chaste dames and dewy virgins, there were men of dissolute lives and women of spotted fame, wretches given over to all mean and filthy vice, and suspected even of horrid crimes. It was strange to see that the good shrank not from the wicked, nor were the sinners abashed by the saints. Scattered also among their pale-faced enemies were the Indian priests, or powwows, who had often scared their native forest with more hideous incantations than any known to English witchcraft.

"But where is Faith?" thought Goodman Brown; and, as hope came into his heart, he trembled.

Another verse of the hymn arose, a slow and mournful strain, such as the pious love, but joined to words which expressed all that our nature can conceive of sin, and darkly hinted at far more. Unfathomable to mere mortals is the lore of fiends. Verse after verse was sung; and still the chorus of the desert swelled between like the deepest tone of a mighty organ; and with the final peal of that dreadful anthem there came a sound, as if the roaring wind, the rushing streams, the howling beasts, and every other voice of the unconcerted wilderness were mingling and according with the voice of guilty man in homage to the prince of all. The four blazing pines threw up a loftier flame, and obscurely discovered shapes and visages of horror on the smoke wreaths above the impious assembly. At the same moment the fire on the rock shot redly forth and formed a glowing arch above its base, where now appeared a figure. With reverence be it spoken, the figure bore no slight similitude, both in garb and manner, to some grave divine of the New England churches.

"Bring forth the converts!" cried a voice that echoed through the field and rolled into the forest.

60   At the word, Goodman Brown stepped forth from the shadow of the trees and approached the congregation, with whom he felt a loathful brotherhood by the sympathy of all that was wicked in his heart. He could have well-nigh sworn that the shape of his own dead father beckoned him to advance, looking downward from a smoke wreath, while a woman, with dim features of despair, threw out her hand to warn him back. Was it his mother? But he had no power to retreat one step, nor to resist, even in thought, when the minister and good old Deacon Gookin seized his arms and led him to the blazing rock. Thither came also the slender form of a veiled female, led between Goody Cloyse, that pious teacher of the catechism, and Martha Carrier, who had received the devil's promise to be queen of hell. A rampant hag was she. And there stood the proselytes beneath the canopy of fire.

"Welcome, my children" said the dark figure, "to the communion of your race. Ye have found thus young your nature and your destiny. My children, look behind you!"

They turned; and flashing forth, as it were, in a sheet of flame, the fiend worshippers were seen; the smile of welcome gleamed darkly on every visage.

"There," resumed the sable form, "are all whom ye have reverenced from youth. Ye deemed them holier than yourselves, and shrank from your own sin, contrasting it with their lives of righteousness and prayerful aspirations heavenward. Yet here are they all in my worshipping assembly. This night it shall be-granted you to know their secret deeds: how hoary-bearded elders of the church have whispered wanton words to the young maids of their households; how many a woman, eager for widows' weeds, has given her husband a drink at bedtime and let him sleep his last sleep in her bosom; how beardless youths have made haste to inherit their fathers' wealth; and how fair damsels—blush not, sweet ones—have dug little graves in the garden, and bidden me, the sole guest, to an infant's funeral. By the sympathy of your human hearts for sin ye shall scent out all the places—whether in church, bed-chamber, street, field, or forest—where crime has been committed, and shall exult to behold the whole earth one stain of guilt, one mighty blood spot. Far more than this. It shall be yours to penetrate, in every bosom, the deep mystery of sin, the fountain of all wicked arts, and which inexhaustibly supplies more evil impulses than human power—than my power at its utmost—can make manifest in deeds. And now, my children, look upon each other."

They did so; and, by the blaze of the hell-kindled torches, the wretched man beheld his Faith, and the wife her husband, trembling before that unhallowed altar.

65 "Lo, there ye stand, my children," said the figure, in a deep and solemn tone, almost sad with its despairing awfulness, as if his once angelic nature could yet mourn for our miserable race. "Depending upon one another's hearts, ye had still hoped that virtue were not all a dream. Now are ye undeceived. Evil is the nature of mankind. Evil must be your only happiness. Welcome again, my children, to the communion of your race."

"Welcome," repeated the fiend worshippers, in one cry of despair and triumph.

And there they stood, the only pair, as it seemed, who were yet hesitating on the verge of wickedness in this dark world. A basin was hallowed, naturally, in the rock. Did it contain water, reddened by the lurid light! or was it blood? or, perchance, a liquid flame? Herein did the shape of evil dip his hand and prepare to lay the mark of baptism upon their foreheads, that they might be partakers of the mystery of sin, more conscious of the secret guilt of others, both in deed and thought, than they could now be of their own. The husband cast one look at his pale wife, and Faith at him. What polluted wretches would the next glance show them to each other, shuddering alike at what they disclosed and what they saw!

"Faith! Faith!" cried the husband, "look up to heaven, and resist the wicked one."

Whether Faith obeyed he knew not. Hardly had he spoken when he found himself amid calm night and solitude, listening to a roar of the wind which died heavily away through the forest. He staggered against the rock, and felt it chill and damp; while a hanging twig, that had been all on fire, besprinkled his cheek with the coldest dew.

70   The next morning young Goodman Brown came slowly into the street of Salem village, staring around him like a bewildered man. The good old minister was taking a walk along the graveyard to get an appetite for breakfast and meditate his sermon, and bestowed a blessing, as he passed, on Goodman Brown. He shrank from the venerable saint as if to avoid anathema. Old Deacon Gookin was at domestic worship, and the holy words of his prayer were heard through the open window. "What God doth the wizard pray to?" quoth Goodman Brown. Goody Cloyse, that excellent old Christian, stood in the early sunshine at her own lattice, catechizing a little girl who had brought her a pint of morning's milk. Goodman Brown snatched away the child as from the grasp of the fiend himself. Turning the corner by the meeting-house, he spied the head of Faith, with the pink ribbons, gazing anxiously forth, and bursting into such joy at sight of him that she skipped along the street and almost kissed her husband before the whole village. But Goodman Brown looked sternly and sadly into her face, and passed on without a greeting.

Had Goodman Brown fallen asleep in the forest and only dreamed a wild dream of a witch-meeting?

Be it so if you will; but, alas! it was a dream of evil omen for young Goodman Brown. A stern, a sad, a darkly meditative, a distrustful, if not a desperate man did he become from the night of that fearful dream. On the Sabbath day, when the congregation were singing a holy psalm, he could not listen because an anthem of sin rushed loudly upon his ear and drowned all the blessed strain. When the minister spoke from the pulpit with power and fervid eloquence, and, with his hand on the open Bible, of the sacred truths of our religion, and of saint-like lives and triumphant deaths, and of future bliss or misery unutterable, then did Goodman Brown turn pale, dreading lest the roof should thunder down upon the gray blasphemer and his hearers. Often, awaking suddenly at midnight, he shrank from the bosom of Faith; and at morning or eventide, when the family knelt down at prayer, he scowled and muttered to himself, and gazed sternly at his wife, and turned away. And when he had lived long, and was borne to his grave a hoary corpse, followed by Faith, an aged woman, and children and grandchildren, a goodly procession, besides neighbors not a few, they carved no hopeful verse upon his tombstone, for his dying hour was gloom.

Questions on Symbolism . . .

1. Is Goodman an allegorical name like Everyman? What sort of a name is Brown? Can names be symbolic? Ironic?

2. Is this tale an allegory? Why?

3. Who is it that Young Goodman Brown meets in the forest? Discuss the staff the man carries. Why does Hawthorne suggest a reasonable explanation for its appearance?

4. Why do Young Goodman Brown and his companion look alike?

5. Is the forest itself a symbol? Is it conventional, natural, traditional, or literary?

6. Does symbolism enhance the theme of this story?

. . . and Other Elements

7. What is the point of view? Who thinks that Faith is aptly named?

8. What happened before the beginning of this story? How do you know about it?

9. Can you find a motif of reversals in this story? List all the reversals you can find.

10. Was it all a dream? What kind of experience has Young Goodman Brown undergone?

Franz Kafka

Franz Kafka (1883–1924) made fantastic and symbolic fictions. In "The
Metamorphosis," the hero is transformed into a gigantic insect. His *Amerika*
(1927) is a symbolic country, and *The Castle* (1926) is a symbolic structure.
Kafka was an insurance clerk who published little in his lifetime and who, when
he died of tuberculosis, requested that his manuscripts be burned. Fortunately
for us, his best friend ignored his request.

A Hunger Artist   (1924)
Translated by Edwin and Willa Muir

During these last decades the interest in professional fasting has markedly
diminished. It used to pay very well to stage such great performances under
one's own management, but today that is quite impossible. We live in a different world now. At one time the whole town took a lively interest in the hunger
artist; from day to day of his fast the excitement mounted; everybody wanted to
see him at least once a day; there were people who bought season tickets for
the last few days and sat from morning till night in front of his small barred
cage; even in the nighttime there were visiting hours, when the whole effect
was heightened by torch flares; on fine days the cage was sent out in the open
air, and then it was the children's special treat to see the hunger artist; for their
elders he was often just a joke that happened to be in fashion, but the children
stood open-mouthed, holding each other's hands for greater security, mar-
veling at him as he sat there pallid in black tights, with his ribs sticking out so
prominently, not even on a seat but down among straw on the ground, sometimes giving a courteous nod, answering questions with a constrained smile, or
perhaps stretching an arm through the bars so that one might feel how thin it
was, and then again withdrawing deep into himself, paying no attention to
anyone or anything, not even to the all-important striking of the clock that was
the only piece of furniture in his cage, but merely staring into vacancy with

half-shut eyes, now and then taking a sip from a tiny glass of water to moisten his lips.

Besides casual onlookers there were also relays of permanent watchers selected by the public, usually butchers, strangely enough, and it was their task to watch the hunger artist day and night, three of them at a time, in case he should have some secret recourse to nourishment. This was nothing but a formality, instituted to reassure the masses, for the initiates knew well enough that during his fast the artist would never in any circumstances, not even under forcible compulsion, swallow the smallest morsel of food; the honor of his profession forbade it. Not every watcher, of course, was capable of understanding this, there were often groups of night watchers who were very lax in carrying out their duties and deliberately huddled together in a retired corner to play cards with great absorption, obviously intending to give the hunger artist the chance of a little refreshment, which they supposed he could draw from some private hoard. Nothing annoyed the artist more than such watchers; they made him miserable; they made his fast seem unendurable; sometimes he mastered his feebleness sufficiently to sing during their watch for as long as he could keep going, to show them how unjust their suspicions were. But that was of little use; they only wondered at his cleverness in being able to fill his mouth even while singing. Much more to his taste were the watchers who sat close up to the bars, who were not content with the dim night lighting of the hall but focused him in the full glare of the electric pocket torch given them by the impresario. The harsh light did not trouble him at all. In any case he could never sleep properly, and he could always drowse a little, whatever the light, at any hour, even when the hall was thronged with noisy onlookers. He was quite happy at the prospect of spending a sleepless night with such watchers; he was ready to exchange jokes with them, to tell them stories out of his nomadic life, anything at all to keep them awake and demonstrate to them again that he had no eatables in his cage and that he was fasting as not one of them could fast. But his happiest moment was when the morning came and an enormous breakfast was brought them, at his expense, on which they flung themselves with the keen appetite of healthy men after a weary night of wakefulness. Of course there were people who argued that this breakfast was an unfair attempt to bribe the watchers, but that was going rather too far, and when they were invited to take on a night's vigil without a breakfast, merely for the sake of the cause, they made themselves scarce, although they stuck stubbornly to their suspicions.

Such suspicions, anyhow, were a necessary accompaniment to the profession of fasting. No one could possibly watch the hunger artist continuously, day and night, and so no one could produce first-hand evidence that the fast had really been rigorous and continuous; only the artist himself could know that; he was therefore bound to be the sole completely satisfied spectator of his own fast. Yet for other reasons he was never satisfied; it was not perhaps mere fasting that had brought him to such skeleton thinness that many people had regretfully to keep away from his exhibitions, because the sight of him was too much for them, perhaps it was dissatisfaction with himself that had worn him down. For he alone knew, what no other initiate knew, how easy it was to fast. It was the easiest thing in the world. He made no secret of this, yet people did not believe him; at the best they set him down as modest, most of them, however, thought he was out for publicity or else was some kind of cheat who found it easy to fast because he had discovered a way of making it easy, and then had the impudence to admit the fact, more or less. He had to put up with all that, and in the course of time had got used to it, but his inner dissatisfaction always rankled, and never yet, after any term of fasting—this must be granted to his credit—had he left the cage of his own free will. The longest period of fasting was fixed by his impresario at forty days, beyond that term he was not allowed to go, not even in great cities, and there was good reason for it, too. Experience had proved that for about forty days the interest of the public could be stimulated by a steadily increasing pressure of advertisement, but after that the town began to lose interest, sympathetic support began notably to fall off; there were of course local variations as between one town and another or one country and another, but as a general rule forty days marked the limit. So on the fortieth day the flower-bedecked cage was opened, enthusiastic spectators filled the hall, a military band played, two doctors entered the cage to measure the results of the fast, which were announced through a megaphone, and finally two young ladies appeared, blissful at having been selected for the honor, to help the hunger artist down the few steps leading to a small table on which was spread a carefully chosen invalid repast. And at this very moment the artist always turned stubborn. True, he would entrust his bony arms to the out-stretched helping hands of the ladies bending over him, but stand up he would not. Why stop fasting at this particular moment, after forty days of it? He had held out for a long time, an illimitably long time; why stop now, when he was in his best fasting form, or rather, not yet quite in his best fasting form? Why should he be cheated of the fame he would get for fasting longer, for being not only the record hunger artist of all time, which presumably he was already, but for beating his own record by a performance beyond human imagination, since he felt that there were no limits to his capacity for fasting? His public pretended to admire him so much, why should it have so little patience with him; he could endure fasting longer, why shouldn't the public endure it? Besides, he was tired, he was comfortable sitting in the straw, and now he was supposed to lift himself to his full height and go down to a meal the very thought of which gave him a nausea that only the presence of the ladies kept him from betraying, and even that with an effort. And he looked up into the eyes of the ladies who were apparently so friendly and in reality so cruel, and shook his head, which felt too heavy on its strengthless neck. But then there happened yet again what always happened. The impresario came forward, without a word—for the band made speech impossible—lifted his arms in the air above the artist, as if inviting Heaven to look down upon its creature here in the straw, this suffering martyr, which indeed he was, although in quite another sense, grasped him round the emaciated waist, with exaggerated caution, so that the frail condition he was in might be appreciated; and committed him to the care of the blenching ladies, not without secretly giving him a shaking so that his legs and body tottered and swayed. The artist now submitted completely; his head lolled on his breast as if it had landed there by chance; his body was hollowed out; his legs in a spasm of self-preservation clung close to each other at the knees, yet scraped on the ground as if it were not really solid ground, as if they were only trying to find solid ground; and the whole weight of his body, a feather-weight after all, relapsed onto one of the ladies, who, looking round for help and panting a little—this post of honor was not at all what she had expected it to be—first stretched her neck as far as she could to keep her face at least free from contact with the artist, then finding this impossible, and her more fortunate companion not coming to her aid but merely holding extended on her own trembling hand the little bunch of knucklebones that was the artist's, to the great delight of the spectators burst into tears and had to be replaced by an attendant who had long been stationed in readiness. Then came the food, a little of which the impresario managed to get between the artist's lips, while he sat in a kind of half-fainting trance, to the accompaniment of cheerful patter designed to distract the public's attention from the artist's condition; after that, a toast was drunk to the public, supposedly prompted by a whisper from the artist in the impresario's ear; the band confirmed it with a mighty flourish, the spectators melted away, and no one had any cause to be dissatisfied with the proceedings, no one except the hunger artist himself, he only, as always.

So he lived for many years, with small regular intervals of recuperation, in visible glory, honored by the world, yet in spite of that troubled in spirit, and all the more troubled because no one would take his trouble seriously. What comfort could he possibly need? What more could he possibly wish for? And if some good-natured person, feeling sorry for him, tried to console him by pointing out that his melancholy was probably caused by fasting, it could happen, especially when he had been fasting for some time, that he reacted with an outburst of fury and to the general alarm began to shake the bars of his cage like a wild animal. Yet the impresario had a way of punishing these outbreaks which he rather enjoyed putting into operation. He would apologize publicly for the artist's behavior, which was only to be excused, he admitted, because of the irritability caused by fasting; a condition hardly to be understood by well-fed people; then by natural transition he went on to mention the artist's equally incomprehensible boast that he could fast for much longer than he was doing; he praised the high ambition, the good will, the great self-denial undoubtedly implicit in such a statement; and then quite simply countered it by bringing out photographs, which were also on sale to the public, showing the artist on the fortieth day of a fast lying in bed almost dead from exhaustion. This perversion of the truth, familiar to the artist though it was, always unnerved him afresh and proved too much for him. What was a consequence of the premature ending of his fast was here presented as the cause of it! To fight against this lack of understanding, against a whole world of nonunderstanding, was impossible. Time and again in good faith he stood by the bars listening to the impresario, but as soon as the photographs appeared he always let go and sank with a groan back on to his straw, and the reassured public could once more come close and gaze at him.

5   A few years later when the witnesses of such scenes called them to mind, they often failed to understand themselves at all. For meanwhile the afore-mentioned change in public interest had set in; it seemed to happen almost overnight; there may have been profound causes for it, but who was going to bother about that; at any rate the pampered hunger artist suddenly found himself deserted one fine day by the amusement seekers, who went stream-ing past him to other more favored attractions. For the last time the impre-sario hurried him over half Europe to discover whether the old interest might still survive here and there; all in vain; everywhere, as if by secret agreement, a positive revulsion from professional fasting was in evidence. Of course it could not really have sprung up so suddenly as all that, and many premoni-tory symptoms which had not been sufficiently remarked or suppressed during the rush and glitter of success now came retrospectively to mind, but it was now too late to take any counter-measures. Fasting would surely come into fashion again at some future date, yet that was no comfort for those living in the present. What, then, was the hunger artist to do? He had been applauded by thousands in his time and could hardly come down to showing himself in a street booth at village fairs, and as for adopting another profes-sion, he was not only too old for that but too fanatically devoted to fasting. So he took leave of the impresario, his partner in an unparalleled career, and hired himself to a large circus; in order to spare his own feelings he avoided reading the conditions of his contract.

A large circus with its enormous traffic in replacing and recruiting men, animals and apparatus can always find a use for people at any time, even for a hunger artist, provided of course that he does not ask too much, and in this particular case anyhow it was not only the artist who was taken on but his famous and long-known name as well; indeed considering the peculiar na-ture of his performance, which was not impaired by advancing age, it could not be objected that here was an artist past his prime, no longer at the height of his professional skill, seeking a refuge in some quiet corner of a circus; on the contrary, the hunger artist averred that he could fast as well as ever, which was entirely credible; he even alleged that if he were allowed to fast as he liked, and this was at once promised him without more ado, he could astound the world by establishing a record never yet achieved, a statement which certainly provoked a smile among the other professionals, since it left out of account the change in public opinion, which the hunger artist in his zeal conveniently forgot.

He had not, however, actually lost his sense of the real situation and took it as a matter of course that he and his cage should be stationed, not in the middle of the ring as a main attraction, but outside, near the animal cages, on a site that was after all easily accessible. Large and gaily painted placards made a frame for the cage and announced what was to be seen inside it. When the public came thronging out in the intervals to see the animals, they could hardly avoid passing the hunger artist's cage and stopping there for a moment, perhaps they might even have stayed longer had not those pressing behind them in the narrow gangway, who did not understand why they should be held up on their way towards the excitements of the menagerie, made it impossible for anyone to stand gazing quietly for any length of time. And that was the reason why the hunger artist, who had of course been looking forward to these visiting hours as the main achievement of his life, began instead to shrink from them. At first he could hardly wait for the intervals; it was exhilarating to watch the crowds come streaming his way, until only too soon—not even the most obstinate self deception, clung to almost consciously, could hold out against the fact—the conviction was borne in upon him that these people, most of them, to judge from their actions, again and again, without exception, were all on their way to the menagerie. And the first sight of them from the distance remained the best. For when they reached his cage he was at once deafened by the storm of shouting and abuse that arose from the two contending factions, which renewed themselves continuously, of those who wanted to stop and stare at him—he soon began to dislike them more than the others—not out of real interest but only out of obstinate self-assertiveness, and those who wanted to go straight on to the animals. When the first great rush was past, the stragglers came along, and these, whom nothing could have prevented from stopping to look at him as long as they had breath, raced past with long strides, hardly even glancing at him, in their haste to get to the menagerie in time. And all too rarely did it happen that he had a stroke of luck, when some father of a family fetched up before him with his children, pointed a finger at the hunger artist and explained at length what the phenomenon meant, telling stories of earlier years when he himself had watched similar but much more thrilling performances, and the children, still rather uncomprehending, since neither inside nor outside school had they been sufficiently prepared for this lesson—what did they care about fasting?—yet showed by the brightness of their intent eyes that new and better times might be coming. Perhaps, said the hunger artist to himself many a time, things would be a little better if his cage were set not quite so near the menagerie. That made it too easy for people to make their choice, to say nothing of what he suffered from the stench of the menagerie, the animals' restlessness by night, the carrying past of raw lumps of flesh for the beasts of prey, the roaring at feeding times, which depressed him continually. But he did not dare to lodge a complaint with the management; after all, he had the animals to thank for the troops of people who passed his cage, among whom there might always be one here and there to take an interest in him, and who could tell where they might seclude him if he called attention to his existence and thereby to the fact that, strictly speaking, he was only an impediment on the way to the menagerie.

A small impediment, to be sure, one that grew steadily less. People grew familiar with the strange idea that they could be expected, in times like these, to take an interest in a hunger artist, and with this familiarity the verdict went out against him. He might fast as much as he could, and he did so; but nothing could save him now, people passed him by. Just try to explain to anyone the art of fasting! Anyone who has no feeling for it cannot be made to understand it. The fine placards grew dirty and illegible, they were torn down; the little notice board telling the number of fast days achieved, which at first was changed carefully every day, had long stayed at the same figure, for after the first few weeks even this small task seemed pointless to the staff; and so the artist simply fasted on and on, as he had once dreamed of doing, and it was no trouble to him, just as he had always foretold, but no one counted the days, no one, not even the artist himself, knew what records he was already breaking, and his heart grew heavy. And when once in a time some leisurely passer-by stopped, made merry over the old figure on the board and spoke of swindling, that was in its way the stupidest lie ever invented by indifference and inborn malice, since it was not the hunger artist who was cheating; he was working honestly, but the world was cheating him of his record.

Many more days went by, however, and that too came to an end. An overseer's eye fell on the cage one day and he asked the attendants why this perfectly good cage should be left standing there unused with dirty straw inside it; nobody knew, until one man, helped out by the notice board, remembered about the hunger artist. They poked into the straw with sticks and found him in it. "Are you still fasting?" asked the overseer. "When on earth do you mean to stop?" "Forgive me, everybody," whispered the hunger artist; only the overseer, who had his ear to the bars, understood him. "Of course," said the overseer, and tapped his forehead with a finger to let the attendants know what state the man was in, "we forgive you." "I always wanted you to admire my fasting," said the hunger artist. "We do admire it," said the overseer, affably. "But you shouldn't admire it," said the hunger artist. "Well, then we don't admire it," said the overseer, "but why shouldn't we admire it?" "Because I have to fast, I can't help it," said the hunger artist. "What a fellow you are," said the overseer, "and why can't you help it?" "Because," said the hunger artist, lifting his head a little and speaking, with his lips pursed, as if for a kiss, right into the overseer's ear, so that no syllable might be lost, "because I couldn't find the food I liked. If I had found it, believe me, I should have made no fuss and stuffed myself like you or anyone else." These were his last words, but in his dimming eyes remained the firm though no longer proud persuasion that he was still continuing to fast.

10   "Well, clear this out now!" said the overseer, and they buried the hunger artist, straw and all. Into the cage they put a young panther. Even the most insensitive felt it refreshing to see this wild creature leaping around the cage that had so long been dreary. The panther was all right. The food he liked was brought him without hesitation by the attendants; he seemed not even to miss his freedom; his noble body, furnished almost to the bursting point with all that it needed, seemed to carry freedom around with it too; somewhere in his jaws it seemed to lurk; and the joy of life streamed with such ardent passion from his throat that for the onlookers it was not easy to stand the shock of it. But they braced themselves, crowded round the cage, and did not want ever to move away.

Questions on Symbolism . . .

1. Is the hunger artist an allegorical figure? What idea would he stand in for?

2. Do you find the hunger artist symbolic? Of what? Is he a "new word"? Do you know anyone who is a hunger artist in matters not related to food and nourishment?

3. Could a writer tell a story of a flagpole sitter or a person who remained in a dark closet for three months and still convey Kafka's theme?

4. What is the relationship between symbol and theme?

5. Is the panther symbolic?

6. What is the point of view of this story? How does the point of view affect the symbolism of the story?

. . . and Other Elements

7. How does the first sentence set the tone for the whole story? Do you suspect irony when you read the first sentence? What word tells you the most?

8. What is the function of the minor characters here?

CHAPTER   ELEVEN

Two Modes of Contemporary Fiction

In the preceding chapter, we concluded our introduction to the elements of fiction. Now it remains to provide further examples of fiction, with notes on particular categories. We will look at Fantasy and Absurdity, and at science fiction.

Fantasy and Absurdity

The fiction of fantasy describes an imagined world where everyday reality is distorted. In literature, works of fantasy are as various as the three stories in the preceding chapter, or as J. R. R. Tolkien's *Lord of the Rings,* and Jonathan Swift's *Gulliver's Travels;* science fiction is fantasy, but so are Shakespeare's *The Tempest,* Lewis Carroll's *Alice's Adventures in Wonderland,* and most of the horror stories of Edgar Allan Poe. The only thing these works have in common is negative: the world they describe does not duplicate our commonsense reality.

Fantastic fiction begins with an improbable basis or a *given* (like an imaginary hypothesis in mathematics) and then becomes probable in terms of that given. It is unlikely that any of us will walk like Alice through a mirror into a land peopled with fantastic creatures, but we demand that Alice behave appropriately under her fantastic circumstances because she is human. Many works mix the human into a fantastic world. But even when all the creatures of fiction are fantastic, they behave according to the character given them by the author. Often, an author uses the unhuman behavior of a fantastic folk— Tolkien's Middle Earthlings—to comment on actual human life and on human character.

Only recently have critics spoken of the absurd in fiction; absurd literature is modern but, like fantasy, its antecedents go back as far as literature does. To the absurdist vision, the ordinary world seems insane and purposeless. In one of his novels, Samuel Beckett spends page after page describing how his protagonist sucks on pebbles and the scheme he develops to switch pebbles among his pockets in order to give them equal attention. We understand that, pointless as his behavior is, it is no sillier than anything else; we understand that the world's habits—its nations and laws and institutions and schools and businesses and customs and morals—are as arbitrary as pebble-sucking. In Albert Camus's novel *The Stranger,* we understand the irrelevance of all behavior, until finally there is no reason for doing anything at all, or for not doing anything at all.

Despite the grimness of its vision—a purposeless world without destiny or divinity—absurdist literature is often comic. If comedy lies in the perception of incongruity, then an absurdist vision, where everything in the world is incongruous, would naturally be comical. Thus, when describing the absurd in literature, critics have spoken of **black comedy**, a combination of despair and laughter that seems peculiarly modern.

In America, Donald Barthelme created in his short stories a world where everything is arbitrary, fantastic, absurd, dark, and usually funny. Other writers also write in this modern tradition—Philip Roth has a man turn into a woman's breast, Robert Coover has the Cat in the Hat run for President, Max Apple imagines a Mr. Howard Johnson.

Donald Barthelme

Donald Barthelme (1933–1990) published two novels, *Snow White* (1967) and *The Dead Father* (1975), and many collections of short fiction. Born in Texas, he lived for many years in New York City, and later taught at the University of Houston. He wrote from a comic, surreal vision of American life and fragmented his perceptions as if he looked at the world through a verbal kaleidoscope. Yet he was one of our most careful and conscious stylists, gathering his fragments into fine sentences.

Some of Us Had Been Threatening Our Friend Colby   (1973)

Some of us had been threatening our friend Colby for a long time, because of the way he had been behaving. And now he'd gone too far, so we decided to hang him. Colby argued that just because he had gone too far (he did not deny that he had gone too far) did not mean that he should be subjected to hanging. Going too far, he said, was something everybody did sometimes. We didn't pay much attention to this argument. We asked him what sort of music he would like played at the hanging. He said he'd think about it but it would take him a while to decide. I pointed out that we'd have to know soon, because Howard, who is a conductor, would have to hire and rehearse the musicians and he couldn't begin until he knew what the music was going to be. Colby said he'd always been fond of Ives' Fourth Symphony. Howard said that this was a "delaying tactic" and that everybody knew that Ives was almost impossible to perform and would involve weeks of rehearsal, and that the size of the orchestra and chorus would put us way over the music budget. "Be reasonable," he said to Colby. Colby said he'd try to think of something a little less exacting.

Hugh was worried about the wording of the invitations. What if one of them fell into the hands of the authorities? Hanging Colby was doubtless against the law, and if the authorities learned in advance what the plan was they would very likely come in and try to mess everything up. I said that although hanging Colby was almost certainly against the law, we had a perfect *moral* right to do so because he was *our* friend, *belonged* to us in various important senses, and he had after all gone too far. We agreed that the invitations would be worded in such a way that the person invited could not know for sure what he was being invited to. We decided to refer to the event as "An Event Involving Mr. Colby Williams." A handsome script was selected from a catalogue and we picked a cream-colored paper. Magnus said he'd see to having the invitations printed, and wondered whether we should serve drinks. Colby said he thought drinks would be nice but was worried about the expense. We told him kindly that the expense didn't matter, that we were after all his dear friends and if a group of his dear friends couldn't get together and do the thing with a little bit of *éclat,* why, what was the world coming to? Colby asked if he would be able to have drinks, too, before the event. We said, "Certainly."

The next item of business was the gibbet. None of us knew too much about gibbet design, but Tomás, who is an architect, said he'd look it up in old books and draw the plans. The important thing, as far as he recollected, was that the trapdoor function perfectly. He said that just roughly, counting labor and materials, it shouldn't run us more than four hundred dollars. "Good God!" Howard said. He said what was Tomás figuring on, rosewood? No, just a good grade of pine, Tomás said. Victor asked if unpainted pine wouldn't look kind of "raw," and Tomás replied that he thought it could be stained a dark walnut without too much trouble.

I said that although I thought the whole thing ought to be done really well, and all, I also thought four hundred dollars for a gibbet, on top of the expense for the drinks, invitations, musicians and everything, was a bit steep, and why didn't we just use a tree—a nice-looking oak, or something? I pointed out that since it was going to be a June hanging the trees would be in glorious leaf and that not only would a tree add a kind of "natural" feeling but it was also strictly traditional, especially in the West. Tomás, who had been sketching gibbets on the backs of envelopes, reminded us that an outdoor hanging always had to contend with the threat of rain. Victor said he liked the idea of doing it outdoors, possibly on the bank of a river, but noted that we would have to hold it some distance from the city, which presented the problem of getting the guests, musicians, etc., to the site and then back to town.

5   At this point everybody looked at Harry, who runs a car-and-truck-rental business. Harry said he thought he could round up enough limousines to

take care of that end but that the drivers would have to be paid. The drivers, he pointed out, wouldn't be friends of Colby's and couldn't be expected to donate their services, any more than the bartender or the musicians. He said that he had about ten limousines, which he used mostly for funerals, and that he could probably obtain another dozen by calling around to friends of his in the trade. He said also that if we did it outside, in the open air, we'd better figure on a tent or awning of some kind to cover at least the principals and the orchestra, because if the hanging was being rained on he thought it would look kind of dismal. As between gibbet and tree, he said, he had no particular preferences, and he really thought that the choice ought to be left up to Colby, since it was his hanging. Colby said that everybody went too far, sometimes, and weren't we being a little Draconian. Howard said rather sharply that all that had already been discussed, and which did he want, gibbet or tree? Colby asked if he could have a firing squad. No, Howard said, he could not. Howard said a firing squad would just be an ego trip for Colby, the blindfold and last-cigarette bit, and that Colby was in enough hot water already without trying to "upstage" everyone with unnecessary theatrics. Colby said he was sorry, he hadn't meant it that way, he'd take the tree. Tomás crumpled up the gibbet sketches he'd been making, in disgust.

Then the question of the hangman came up. Paul said did we really need a hangman? Because if we used a tree, the noose could be adjusted to the appropriate level and Colby could just jump off something—a chair or stool or something. Besides, Paul said, he very much doubted if there were any free-lance hangmen wandering around the country, now that capital punishment has been done away with absolutely, temporarily, and that we'd probably have to fly one in from England or Spain or one of the South American countries, and even if we did that how could we know in advance that the man was a professional, a real hangman, and not just some moneyhungry amateur who might bungle the job and shame us all, in front of everybody? We all agreed that Colby should just jump off something and that a chair was not what he should jump off of, because that would look, we felt, extremely tacky—some old kitchen chair sitting out there under our beautiful tree. Tomás, who is quite modern in outlook and not afraid of innovation, proposed that Colby be standing on a large round rubber ball ten feet in diameter. This, he said, would afford a sufficient "drop" and would also roll out of the way if Colby suddenly changed his mind after jumping off. He reminded us that by not using a regular hangman we were placing an awful lot of the responsibility for the success of the affair on Colby himself, and that although he was sure Colby would perform creditably and not disgrace his friends at the last minute, still, men have been known to get a little irresolute at times like that, and the ten-foot-rubber ball, which could probably be fabricated rather cheaply, would insure a "bang-up" production right down to the wire.

At the mention of "wire," Hank, who had been silent all this time, suddenly spoke up and said he wondered if it wouldn't be better if we used wire instead of rope—more efficient and in the end kinder to Colby, he suggested. Colby began looking a little green, and I didn't blame him, because there is something extremely distasteful in thinking about being hanged with wire instead of rope—it gives you sort of a revulsion, when you think about it. I thought it was really quite unpleasant of Hank to be sitting there talking about wire, just when we had solved the problem of what Colby was going to jump off of so neatly, with Tomás's idea about the rubber ball, so I hastily said that wire was out of the question, because it would injure the tree—cut into the branch it was tied to when Colby's full weight hit it—and that in these days of increased respect for environment, we didn't want that, did we? Colby gave me a grateful look, and the meeting broke up.

Everything went off very smoothly on the day of the event (the music Colby finally picked was standard stuff, Elgar, and it was played very well by Howard and his boys). It didn't rain, the event was well attended, and we didn't run out of Scotch, or anything. The ten-foot rubber ball had been painted a deep green and blended in well with the bucolic setting. The two things I remember best about the whole episode are the grateful look Colby gave me when I said what I said about the wire, and the fact that nobody has ever gone too far again.

Questions

1. How long did it take you to discover the unusual tone or manner of this story?

2. Does Barthelme use language strangely? Is anything unusual about his diction? His syntax? Where does the strangeness come from?

3. What did Colby do? Does the answer to this question suggest a theme for this story?

4. What does it mean to *go too far*? In literature, have you met other characters who went too far? If you have read Greek tragedy, have you encountered characters guilty of this transgression? Were they hanged for it? What happened to them?

5. Barthelme writes sentences like "The next item of business was the gibbet." What kind of phrase is *item of business?* Would a composition teacher praise such a phrase if you used it in a theme? Why or why not? Why does Barthelme use such a phrase?

6. Underline all the clichés in this story.

7. Discuss the dialogue in this story. Do the characters talk as if they were discussing a hanging? Do they sound more as if they were discussing a Rotary lunch? Why?

8. Why would anyone call this story absurd or absurdist?

Science Fiction

Science fiction is popular art, giving us movies ("Star Wars") and television shows ("Star Trek," "Battlestar Galactica") as well as magazines and racks of paperbacks. Historically, science fiction begins in the nineteenth century as a variety of the horror story that combines fantasy with science. When Mary Shelley wrote *Frankenstein,* she made a horror story in which a body was constructed by the scientific Dr. Frankenstein. When Robert Louis Stevenson wrote *Doctor Jekyll and Mr. Hyde,* the transformation was accomplished by a chemical potion.

As science and technology developed, they readily entered fiction. During the past forty or fifty years, science fiction has thrived, from thrillers in pulp magazines to ambitious novels. Some writers have constructed ideal future worlds combining leisure with ethics, Utopias of technology. A Utopia is an imagined ideal country, a way of arguing politics and morals using the fantasy of a perfect model. More important in recent decades has been the anti-Utopia, an inverted ideal describing a world where everything has gone rotten. Writers have set this bad world in the future, making science fiction that is *against* science, or against the uses technology serves. Two famous examples are Aldous Huxley's *Brave New World* and George Orwell's *1984.* Many of the stories published in science-fiction magazines like *Analog* present small anti-Utopias, as does some of the best work of Kurt Vonnegut and Ray Bradbury.

Many reasons have been offered for the popularity of science fiction. One source is our perennial love for the exotic—and for adventure. Some science fiction resembles the old travel books, which told of dragons guarding the ocean's edge. When the Western American frontier still retained its myth, we made it a place for daydream adventures. Now, science fiction imagines a new frontier of the stars.

But some sources are more profound. In religious societies of the past, much popular attention focused on death and the afterlife, on hell and on heaven. In recent secular times, people have looked to the future instead of the afterlife. We read in newspapers and magazines projections of a golden future of leisure, with people served by machines and relieved of drudgery. Where people used to imagine a golden age of the past or project a golden heaven, consumer-readers now daydream a golden age of gadgets. Writers imagine for us a house automatically cleaned, with its food automatically cooked according to a program punched into a keyboard. If this daydream seems paradisal, it finds its dark side in the nightmarish anti-Utopia, for our love of machines is also fear of machines. The (mad) scientist need not consult the devil in his laboratory—but if he goes too far, he oversteps the bounds, and all of us are punished. With this fear of going too far and becoming enslaved by our own slave-machines come a dread and a hope that are virtually religious. It is not fanciful to say that, in much science fiction, we exercise our old religious fears and religious desires, our serious intercourse with the unknown.

Kurt Vonnegut, Jr.

Kurt Vonnegut, Jr. (1922–   ) was a prisoner of war in Germany during the Second World War. In recent years he has combined writing with university teaching. He writes science fiction, fantasy, and political satire. His works include *The Sirens of Titan* (1961), *Cat's Cradle* (1963), *Slaughterhouse Five* (1969), *Breakfast of Champions* (1962), *Slapstick* (1976), and *Jailbird* (1979).

Harrison Bergeron   (1961)

The year was 2081, and everybody was finally equal. They weren't only equal before God and the law. They were equal every which way. Nobody was smarter than anybody else. Nobody was better looking than anybody else. Nobody was stronger or quicker than anybody else. All this equality was due to the 211th, 212th, and 213th Amendments to the Constitution, and to the unceasing vigilance of agents of the United States Handicapper General.

Some things about living still weren't quite right, though. April, for instance, still drove people crazy by not being springtime. And it was in that clammy month that the H-G men took George and Hazel Bergeron's fourteen-year-old son, Harrison, away.

It was tragic, all right, but George and Hazel couldn't think about it very hard. Hazel had a perfectly average intelligence, which meant she couldn't think about anything except in short bursts. And George, while his intelligence was way above normal, had a little mental handicap radio in his ear. He was required by law to wear it at all times. He was tuned to a government transmitter. Every twenty seconds or so, the transmitter would send out some sharp noise to keep people like George from taking unfair advantage of their brains.

George and Hazel were watching television. There were tears on Hazel's cheeks, but she'd forgotten for the moment what they were about.

5   On the television screen were ballerinas.

A buzzer sounded in George's head. His thoughts fled in panic, like bandits from a burglar alarm.

"That was a really pretty dance, that dance they just did," said Hazel.

"Huh?" said George.

"That dance—it was nice," said Hazel.

10   "Yup," said George. He tried to think a little about the ballerinas. They weren't really very good—no better than anybody else would have been, anyway. They were burdened with sash-weights and bags of birdshot, and their faces were masked, so that no one, seeing a free and graceful gesture or a pretty face, would feel like something the cat drug in. George was toying with the vague notion that maybe dancers shouldn't be handicapped. But he didn't get very far with it before another noise in his ear radio scattered his thoughts.

George winced. So did two out of the eight ballerinas.

Hazel saw him wince. Having no mental handicap herself, she had to ask George what the latest sound had been.

"Sounded like somebody hitting a milk bottle with a ball peen hammer," said George.

"I'd think it would be real interesting, hearing all the different sounds," said Hazel, a little envious. "All the things they think up."

15 "Um," said George.

"Only, if I was Handicapper General, you know what I would do?" said Hazel. Hazel, as a matter of fact, bore a strong resemblance to the Handicapper General, a woman named Diana Moon Glampers. "If I was Diana Moon Glampers," said Hazel, "I'd have chimes on Sunday—fast chimes. Kind of in honor of religion."

"I could think, if it was just chimes," said George.

"Well—maybe make 'em real loud," said Hazel. "I think I'd make a good Handicapper General."

"Good as anybody else," said George.

20 "Who knows better'n I do what normal is?" said Hazel.

"Right," said George. He began to think glimmeringly about his abnormal son who was now in jail, about Harrison, but a twenty-one-gun salute in his head stopped that.

"Boy!" said Hazel, "that was a doozy, wasn't it?"

It was such a doozy that George was white and trembling, and tears stood on the rims of his red eyes. Two of the eight ballerinas had collapsed to the studio floor, were holding their temples.

"All of a sudden you look so tired," said Hazel. "Why don't you stretch out on the sofa, so's you can rest your handicap bag on the pillows, honeybunch." She was referring to the forty-seven pounds of birdshot in a canvas bag, which was padlocked around George's neck. "Go on and rest the bag for a little while," she said. "I don't care if you're not equal to me for a while."

25 George weighed the bag with his hands. "I don't mind it," he said. "I don't notice it any more. It's just a part of me."

"You been so tired lately—kind of wore out," said Hazel. "If there was just some way we could make a little hole in the bottom of the bag, and just take out a few of them lead balls. Just a few."

"Two years in prison and two thousand dollars fine for every ball I took out," said George. "I don't call that a bargain."

"If you could just take a few out when you came home from work," said Hazel. "I mean—you don't compete with anybody around here. You just set around."

"If I tried to get away with it," said George, "then other people'd get away with it—and pretty soon we'd be right back to the dark ages again, with everybody competing against everybody else. You wouldn't like that, would you?"

30 "I'd hate it," said Hazel.

"There you are," said George. "The minute people start cheating on laws, what do you think happens to society?"

If Hazel hadn't been able to come up with an answer to this question, George couldn't have supplied one. A siren was going off in his head.

"Reckon it'd fall all apart," said Hazel.

"What would?" said George blankly.

35   "Society," said Hazel uncertainly. "Wasn't that what you just said?"

"Who knows?" said George.

The television program was suddenly interrupted for a news bulletin. It wasn't clear at first as to what the bulletin was about, since the announcer, like all announcers, had a serious speech impediment. For about half a minute, and in a state of high excitement, the announcer tried to say, "Ladies and gentlemen—"

He finally gave up, handed the bulletin to a ballerina to read.

"That's all right—" Hazel said of the announcer, "he tried. That's the big thing. He tried to do the best he could with what God gave him. He should get a nice raise for trying so hard."

40   "Ladies and gentlemen—" said the ballerina, reading the bulletin. She must have been extraordinarily beautiful, because the mask she wore was hideous. And it was easy to see that she was the strongest and most graceful of all the dancers, for her handicap bags were as big as those worn by two-hundred-pound men.

And she had to apologize at once for her voice, which was a very unfair voice for a woman to use. Her voice was a warm, luminous, timeless melody. "Excuse me—" she said, and she began again, making her voice absolutely uncompetitive.

"Harrison Bergeron, age fourteen," she said in a grackle squawk, "has just escaped from jail, where he was held on suspicion of plotting to overthrow the government. He is a genius and an athlete, is under-handicapped, and should be regarded as extremely dangerous."

A police photograph of Harrison Bergeron was flashed on the screen upside down, then sideways, upside down again, then right side up. The picture showed the full length of Harrison against a background calibrated in feet and inches. He was exactly seven feet tall.

The rest of Harrison's appearance was Halloween and hardware. Nobody had ever borne heavier handicaps. He had outgrown hindrances faster than the H-G men could think them up. Instead of a little ear radio for a mental handicap, he wore a tremendous pair of earphones, and spectacles with thick wavy lenses. The spectacles were intended to make him not only half blind, but to give him whanging headaches besides.

45   Scrap metal was hung all over him. Ordinarily, there was a certain symmetry, a military neatness to the handicaps issued to strong people, but Harrison looked like a walking junkyard. In the race of life, Harrison carried three hundred pounds.

And to offset his good looks, the H-G men required that he wear at all times a red rubber ball for a nose, keep his eyebrows shaved off, and cover his even white teeth with black caps at snaggle-tooth random.

"If you see this boy," said the ballerina, "do not—I repeat, do not—try to reason with him."

There was the shriek of a door being torn from its hinges.

Screams and barking cries of consternation came from the television set. The photograph of Harrison Bergeron on the screen jumped again and again, as though dancing to the tune of an earthquake.

50   George Bergeron correctly identified the earthquake, and well he might have—for many was the time his own home had danced to the same crashing tune. "My God—" said George, "that must be Harrison!"

The realization was blasted from his mind instantly by the sound of an automobile collision in his head.

When George could open his eyes again, the photograph of Harrison was gone. A living, breathing Harrison filled the screen.

Clanking, clownish, and huge, Harrison stood in the center of the studio. The knob of the uprooted studio door was still in his hand. Ballerinas, technicians, musicians, and announcers cowered on their knees before him, expecting to die.

"I am the Emperor!" cried Harrison. "Do you hear? I am the Emperor! Everybody must do what I say at once!" He stamped his foot and the studio shook.

55   "Even as I stand here—" he bellowed, "crippled, hobbled, sickened—I am a greater ruler than any man who ever lived! Now watch me become what I *can* become!"

Harrison tore the straps of his handicap harness like wet tissue paper, tore straps guaranteed to support five thousand pounds.

Harrison's scrap-iron handicaps crashed to the floor.

Harrison thrust his thumbs under the bar of the padlock that secured his head harness. The bar snapped like celery. Harrison smashed his headphones and spectacles against the wall.

He flung away his rubber-ball nose, revealed a man that would have awed Thor, the god of thunder.

60   "I shall now select my Empress!" he said, looking down on the cowering people.

"Let the first woman who dares rise to her feet claim her mate and her throne!"

A moment passed, and then a ballerina arose, swaying like a willow.

Harrison plucked the mental handicap from her ear, snapped off her physical handicaps with marvelous delicacy. Last of all, he removed her mask.

She was blindingly beautiful.

"Now—" said Harrison, taking her hand, "shall we show the people the meaning of the word dance? Music!" he commanded.

65   The musicians scrambled back into their chairs, and Harrison stripped them of their handicaps, too. "Play your best," he told them, "and I'll make you barons and dukes and earls."

The music began. It was normal at first—cheap, silly, false. But Harrison snatched two musicians from their chairs, waved them like batons as he sang the music as he wanted it played. He slammed them back into their chairs.

The music began again and was much improved.

Harrison and his Empress merely listened to the music for a while—listened gravely, as though synchronizing their heartbeats with it.

They shifted their weights to their toes.

70   Harrison placed his big hands on the girl's tiny waist, letting her sense the weightlessness that would soon be hers.

And then, in an explosion of joy and grace, into the air they sprang!

Not only were the laws of the land abandoned, but the law of gravity and the laws of motion as well.

They reeled, whirled, swiveled, flounced, capered, gamboled, and spun.

They leaped like deer on the moon.

75 The studio ceiling was thirty feet high, but each leap brought the dancers nearer to it.

It became their obvious intention to kiss the ceiling.

They kissed it.

And then, neutralizing gravity with love and pure will, they remained suspended in air inches below the ceiling, and they kissed each other for a long, long time.

It was then that Diana Moon Glampers, the Handicapper General, came into the studio with a double-barreled ten-gauge shotgun. She fired twice, and the Emperor and the Empress were dead before they hit the floor.

80 Diana Moon Glampers loaded the gun again. She aimed it at the musicians and told them they had ten seconds to get their handicaps back on.

It was then that the Bergerons' television tube burned out.

Hazel turned to comment about the blackout to George. But George had gone out into the kitchen for a can of beer.

George came back in with a beer, paused while a handicap signal shook him up. And then he sat down again. "You been crying?" he said to Hazel.

"Yup," she said.

85 "What about?" he said.

"I forget," she said. "Something real sad on television."

"What was it?" he said.

"It's all kind of mixed up in my mind," said Hazel.

"Forget sad things," said George.

90 "I always do," said Hazel.

"That's my girl," said George. He winced. There was the sound of a riveting gun in his head.

"Gee—I could tell that one was a doozy," said Hazel.

"You can say that again," said George.

"Gee—" said Hazel, "I could tell that one was a doozy."

Questions

1. What does the first paragraph tell you about this story? If it is exposition, do you learn only facts? Do you learn an attitude toward these facts? Do you catch a tone?

2. George's mind is distracted by certain sounds. In choosing and naming these sounds, does the author reveal a satirical purpose?

3. Discuss the point of view in this story. What difference would it have made if you had the story from Harrison's point of view?

4. Do George and Hazel remind you of anybody you know? Despite all the invented hardware they live with, do they seem ordinary? Does their commonness contribute to the story's theme?

5. The story ends with a very old joke. Why?

CHAPTER TWELVE

Longer Fiction: The Short Novel

The difference between a short story and a novel, as the wise tell us, is that the novel is longer. Really, the difference is as much qualitative as quantitative. With its greater space and time in which to develop, the novel tends to take on shapes and purposes different from the short story's. Length allows (and perhaps requires) multiple structures. A typical short story follows a main protagonist through a brief conflict to a conclusion that is also a discovery; it will have space to develop only one or two round characters. In the novel, we usually have several protagonists and more characters, both round and flat. We come to know a novelist's main protagonist well, possibly following him or her throughout life. Or, we may follow whole generations of a family. Either way, we are likely to follow the course of many conflicts, occurring in sequence and simultaneously, that may not be resolved for decades. The plot will take many ups and downs, moving toward a single climax by way of many small climaxes. There may be counterplots and subplots, stories outside the main story, often arranged for contrast or ironic comment. We will not likely find a single change or discovery, but instead, a development through many changes leading to many discoveries. A novel has room for more social and historical complexity, more richness of character, motive, and choice, along with a setting so particular we can draw a map. Finally, in a novel we usually find not the short story's single theme but a woven fabric of themes, complex and interrelated.

The short novel falls between the typical story and the typical novel. In *The Death of Ivan Ilych,* we come to know a single protagonist, as in a story, and we concentrate on a single theme. But the narrative develops character and theme fully, as in a novel.

Leo Tolstoy

Leo Tolstoy (1828–1910) is the author of *War and Peace* (1869), *Anna Karenina* (1877), and the less successful *Resurrection* (1899), novels that place him among the greatest of writers. He also wrote autobiography, drama, and philosophical and religious works—and many stories and short novels, like *The Death of Ivan Ilych* (1886). As he grew older, his religious ideas took possession of his life. An aristocrat, he dressed like a peasant and worked in the fields. He renounced his earlier fiction as too worldly, gave up his royalties, divided his property, and tried to live his conception of the Christian life.

The Death of Ivan Ilych (1886)
Translated by Louise Aylmer Maude

I

During an interval in the Melvinski trial in the large building of the Law Courts, the members and public prosecutor met in Ivan Egorovich Shebek's private room, where the conversation turned on the celebrated Krasovski case. Fëdor Vasilievich warmly maintained that it was not subject to their jurisdiction. Ivan Egorovich maintained the contrary, while Peter Ivanovich, not having entered into the discussion at the start, took no part in it but looked through the *Gazette* which had just been handed in.

"Gentlemen," he said, "Ivan Ilych[1] has died!"

"You don't say so!"

"Here, read it yourself," replied Peter Ivanovich, handing Fëdor Vasilievich the paper still damp from the press. Surrounded by a black border were the words: "Praskovya Fëdorovna Golovina, with profound sorrow, informs relatives and friends of the demise of her beloved husband Ivan Ilych Golovin, Member of the Court of Justice, which occurred on February the 4th of this year 1882. The funeral will take place on Friday at one o'clock in the afternoon."

5   Ivan Ilych had been a colleague of the gentlemen present and was liked by them all. He had been ill for some weeks with an illness said to be incurable. His post had been kept open for him, but there had been conjectures that in case of his death Alexeev might receive his appointment, and that either Vinnikov or Shtabel would succeed Alexeev. So on receiving the news of Ivan Ilych's death the first thought of each of the gentlemen in that private room was of the changes and promotions it might occasion among themselves or their acquaintances.

---

[1] It was customary in Russia for friends to refer to one another by the first two of their three names. Ivan Ilych Golovin would have been known among his peers as Ivan Ilych.

"I shall be sure to get Shtabel's place or Vinnikov's," thought Fëdor Vasilievich. "I was promised that long ago, and the promotion means an extra eight hundred rubles[2] a year for me beside the allowance."

"Now I must apply for my brother-in-law's transfer from Kaluga," thought Peter Ivanovich. "My wife will be very glad, and then she won't be able to say that I never do anything for her relations."

"I thought he would never leave his bed again," said Peter Ivanovich aloud. "It's very sad."

"But what really was the matter with him?"

10 "The doctors couldn't say—at least they could, but each of them said something different. When last I saw him I thought he was getting better."

"And I haven't been to see him since the holidays. I always meant to go."

"Had he any property?"

"I think his wife has a little—but something quite trifling."

"We shall have to go to see her, but they live so terribly far away."

15 "Far away from you, you mean. Everything's far away from your place."

"You see, he can never forgive my living on the other side of the river," said Peter Ivanovich, smiling at Shebek. Then, still talking of the distances between different parts of the city, they returned to the Court.

Besides considerations as to the possible transfers and promotions likely to result from Ivan Ilych's death, the mere fact of the death of a near acquaintance aroused, as usual, in all who heard of it the complacent feeling that, "it is he who is dead and not I."

Each one thought or felt, "Well, he's dead but I'm alive!" But the more intimate of Ivan Ilych's acquaintances, his so-called friends, could not help thinking also that they would now have to fulfil the very tiresome demands of propriety by attending the funeral service and paying a visit of condolence to the widow.

Fëdor Vasilievich and Peter Ivanovich had been his nearest acquaintances. Peter Ivanovich had studied law with Ivan Ilych and had considered himself to be under obligations to him.

20 Having told his wife at dinner-time of Ivan Ilych's death and of his conjecture that it might be possible to get her brother transferred to their circuit, Peter Ivanovich sacrificed his usual nap, put on his evening clothes, and drove to Ivan Ilych's house.

At the entrance stood a carriage and two cabs. Leaning against the wall in the hall downstairs near the cloak-stand was a coffin-lid covered with cloth of gold, ornamented with gold cord and tassels, that had been polished up with metal powder. Two ladies in black were taking off their fur cloaks. Peter Ivanovich recognized one of them as Ivan Ilych's sister, but the other was a stranger to him. His colleague Schwartz was just coming downstairs, but on seeing Peter Ivanovich enter he stopped and winked at him, as if to say, "Ivan Ilych has made a mess of things—not like you and me."

Schwartz's face with his Piccadilly whiskers and his slim figure in evening dress, had as usual an air of elegant solemnity which contrasted with the

[2] A considerable sum in the 1880s

playfulness of his character and had a special piquancy here, or so it seemed to Peter Ivanovich.

Peter Ivanovich allowed the ladies to precede him and slowly followed them upstairs. Schwartz did not come down but remained where he was, and Peter Ivanovich understood that he wanted to arrange where they should play bridge that evening. The ladies went upstairs to the widow's room, and Schwartz with seriously compressed lips but a playful look in his eyes, indicated by a twist of his eyebrows the room to the right where the body lay.

Peter Ivanovich, like everyone else on such occasions, entered feeling uncertain what he would have to do. All he knew was that at such times it is always safe to cross oneself. But he was not quite sure whether one should make obeisances while doing so. He therefore adopted a middle course. On entering the room he began crossing himself and made a slight movement resembling a bow. At the same time, as far as the motion of his head and arm allowed, he surveyed the room. Two young men—apparently nephews, one of whom was a high-school pupil—were leaving the room, crossing themselves as they did so. An old woman was standing motionless, and a lady with strangely arched eyebrows was saying something to her in a whisper. A vigorous, resolute Church Reader, in a frock-coat, was reading something in a loud voice with an expression that precluded any contradiction. The butler's assistant, Gerasim, stepping lightly in front of Peter Ivanovich, was strewing something on the floor. Noticing this, Peter Ivanovich was immediately aware of a faint odour of a decomposing body.

25   The last time he had called on Ivan Ilych, Peter Ivanovich had seen Gerasim in the study. Ivan Ilych had been particularly fond of him and he was performing the duty of a sick nurse.

Peter Ivanovich continued to make the sign of the cross slightly inclining his head in an intermediate direction between the coffin, the Reader, and the icons on the table in a corner of the room. Afterwards, when it seemed to him that this movement of his arm in crossing himself had gone on too long, he stopped and began to look at the corpse.

The dead man lay, as dead men always lie, in a specially heavy way, his rigid limbs sunk in the soft cushions of the coffin, with the head forever bowed on the pillow. His yellow waxen brow with bald patches over his sunken temples was thrust up in the way peculiar to the dead, the protruding nose seeming to press on the upper lip. He was much changed and had grown even thinner since Peter Ivanovich had last seen him, but, as is always the case with the dead, his face was handsomer and above all more dignified than when he was alive. The expression on the face said that what was necessary had been accomplished, and accomplished rightly. Besides this there was in that expression a reproach and a warning to the living. This warning seemed to Peter Ivanovich out of place, or at least not applicable to him. He felt a certain discomfort and so he hurriedly crossed himself once more and turned and went out of the door—too hurriedly and too regardless of propriety, as he himself was aware.

Schwartz was waiting for him in the adjoining room with legs spread wide apart and both hands toying with his top-hat behind his back. The mere sight of that playful, well-groomed, and elegant figure refreshed Peter Ivanovich. He felt that Schwartz was above all these happenings and would not surrender to any depressing influences. His very look said that this incident of a church service for Ivan Ilych could not be a sufficient reason for infringing the order of the session—in other words, that it would certainly not prevent his unwrapping a new pack of cards and shuffling them that evening while a footman placed four fresh candles on the table: in fact, that there was no reason for supposing that this incident would hinder their spending the evening agreeably. Indeed he said this in a whisper as Peter Ivanovich passed him, proposing that they should meet for a game at Fëdor Vasilievich's. But apparently Peter Ivanovich was not destined to play bridge that evening. Praskovya Fëdorovna (a short, fat woman who despite all efforts to the contrary had continued to broaden steadily from her shoulders downwards and who had the same extraordinarily arched eyebrows as the lady who had been standing by the coffin), dressed all in black, her head covered with lace, came out of her own room with some other ladies, conducted them to the room where the dead body lay, and said: "The service will begin immediately. Please go in."

Schwartz, making an indefinite bow, stood still, evidently neither accepting nor declining this invitation. Praskovya Fëdorovna, recognizing Peter Ivanovich, sighed, went close up to him, took his hand, and said: "I know you were a true friend to Ivan Ilych . . ." and looked at him awaiting some suitable response. And Peter Ivanovich knew that, just as it had been the right thing to cross himself in that room, so what he had to do here was to press her hand, sigh, and say, "Believe me. . . ." So he did all this and as he did it felt that the desired result had been achieved: that both he and she were touched.

30   "Come with me. I want to speak to you before it begins," said the widow. "Give me your arm."

Peter Ivanovich gave her his arm and they went to the inner rooms, passing Schwartz, who winked at Peter Ivanovich compassionately.

"That does for our bridge! Don't object if we find another player. Perhaps you can cut in when you do escape," said his playful look.

Peter Ivanovich sighed still more deeply and despondently, and Praskovya Fëdorovna pressed his arm gratefully. When they reached the drawing-room, upholstered in pink cretonne and lighted by a dim lamp, they sat down at the table—she on a sofa and Peter Ivanovich on a low pouffe,[3] the springs of which yielded spasmodically under his weight. Praskovya Fëdorovna had been on the point of warning him to take another seat, but felt that such a warning was out of keeping with her present condition and so changed her mind. As he sat down on the pouffe Peter Ivanovich recalled how Ivan Ilych had arranged this room and had consulted him regarding this pink cretonne with green leaves. The whole room was full of furniture and knickknacks, and on her way to the sofa the lace of the widow's black shawl caught on the carved edge of the table. Peter Ivanovich rose to detach it, and the springs of the pouffe, relieved of his weight, rose also and gave him a push. The widow began detaching her shawl herself, and Peter Ivanovich again sat down,

---

[3] Ottoman or hassock

suppressing the rebellious springs of the pouffe under him. But the widow had not quite freed herself and Peter Ivanovich got up again, and again the pouffe rebelled and even creaked. When this was all over she took out a clean cambric handkerchief and began to weep. The episode with the shawl and the struggle with the pouffe had cooled Peter Ivanovich's emotions and he sat there with a sullen look on his face. This awkward situation was interrupted by Sokolov, Ivan Ilych's butler, who came to report that the plot in the cemetery that Praskovya Fëdorovna had chosen would cost two hundred rubles. She stopped weeping and, looking at Peter Ivanovich with the air of a victim, remarked in French that it was very hard for her. Peter Ivanovich made a silent gesture signifying his full conviction that it must indeed be so.

"Please smoke," she said in a magnanimous yet crushed voice, and turned to discuss with Sokolov the price of the plot for the grave.

35   Peter Ivanovich while lighting his cigarette heard her inquiring very circumstantially into the prices of different plots in the cemetery and finally decide which she would take. When that was done she gave instructions about engaging the choir. Sokolov then left the room.

"I look after everything myself," she told Peter Ivanovich, shifting the albums that lay on the table; and noticing that the table was endangered by his cigarette-ash, she immediately passed him an ash-tray, saying as she did so: "I consider it an affectation to say that my grief prevents my attending to practical affairs. On the contrary, if anything can—I won't say console me, but—distract me, it is seeing to everything concerning him." She again took out her handkerchief as if preparing to cry, but suddenly, as if mastering her feeling, she shook herself and began to speak calmly. "But there is something I want to talk to you about."

Peter Ivanovich bowed, keeping control of the springs of the pouffe, which immediately began quivering under him.

"He suffered terribly the last few days."

"Did he?" said Peter Ivanovich.

40   "Oh, terribly! He screamed unceasingly, not for minutes but for hours. For the last three days he screamed incessantly. It was unendurable. I cannot understand how I bore it; you could hear him three rooms off. Oh, what I have suffered!"

"Is it possible that he was conscious all that time?" asked Peter Ivanovich.

"Yes," she whispered. "To the last moment. He took leave of us a quarter of an hour before he died, and asked us to take Volodya away."

The thought of the sufferings of this man he had known so intimately, first as a merry little boy, then as a school-mate, and later as a grown-up colleague, suddenly struck Peter Ivanovich with horror, despite an unpleasant consciousness of his own and this woman's dissimulation. He again saw that brow, and that nose pressing down on the lip, and felt afraid for himself.

"Three days of frightful suffering and then death! Why, that might suddenly, at any time, happen to me," he thought, and for a moment felt terrified. But—he did not himself know how—the customary reflection at once occurred to him that this had happened to Ivan Ilych and not to him, and that it should not and could not happen to him, and to think that it could would be yielding to depression which he ought not to do, as Schwartz's expression plainly showed. After which reflection Peter Ivanovich felt reassured, and began to ask with interest about the details of Ivan Ilych's death, as though death was an accident natural to Ivan Ilych but certainly not to himself.

45 　　After many details of the really dreadful physical sufferings Ivan Ilych had endured (which details he learnt only from the effect those sufferings had produced on Praskovya Fëdorovna's nerves) the widow apparently found it necessary to get to business.

"Oh, Peter Ivanovich, how hard it is! How terribly, terribly, hard!" and she again began to weep.

Peter Ivanovich sighed and waited for her to finish blowing her nose. When she had done so he said, "Believe me . . ." and she again began talking and brought out what was evidently her chief concern with him— namely, to question him as to how she could obtain a grant of money from the government on the occasion of her husband's death. She made it appear that she was asking Peter Ivanovich's advice about her pension, but he soon saw that she already knew about that to the minutest detail, more even than he did himself. She knew how much could be got out of the government in consequence of her husband's death, but wanted to find out whether she could not possibly extract something more. Peter Ivanovich tried to think of some means of doing so, but after reflecting for a while and, out of propriety, condemning the government for its niggardliness, he said he thought that nothing more could be got. Then she sighed and evidently began to devise means of getting rid of her visitor. Noticing this, he put out his cigarette, rose, pressed her hand, and went out into the anteroom.

In the dining-room where the clock stood that Ivan Ilych had liked so much and had bought at an antique shop, Peter Ivanovich met a priest and a few acquaintances who had come to attend the service, and he recognized Ivan Ilych's daughter, a handsome young woman. She was in black and her slim figure appeared slimmer than ever. She had a gloomy, determined, almost angry expression, and bowed to Peter Ivanovich as though he were in some way to blame. Behind her, with the same offended look, stood a wealthy young man, an examining magistrate, whom Peter Ivanovich also knew and who was her fiancé, as he had heard. He bowed mournfully to them and was about to pass into the death-chamber, when from under the stairs appeared the figure of Ivan Ilych's schoolboy son, who was extremely like his father. He seemed a little Ivan Ilych, such as Peter Ivanovich remembered when they studied law together. His tear-stained eyes had in them the look that is seen in the eyes of boys of thirteen or fourteen who are not pure-minded. When he saw Peter Ivanovich he scowled morosely and shamefacedly. Peter Ivanovich nodded to him and entered the death-chamber. The service began: candles, groans, incense, tears, and sobs. Peter Ivanovich stood looking gloomily down at his feet. He did not look once at the dead man, did not yield to any depressing influence, and was one of the first to leave the room. There was no one in the anteroom, but Gerasim darted out of the dead man's room, rummaged with his strong hands among the fur coats to find Peter Ivanovich's and helped him on with it.

"Well, friend Gerasim," said Peter Ivanovich, so as to say something. "It's a sad affair, isn't it?"

50   "It's God's will. We shall all come to it some day," Gerasim, displaying his teeth—the even, white teeth of a healthy peasant—and, like a man in the thick of urgent work, he briskly opened the front door, called the coachman, helped Peter Ivanovich into the sledge, and sprang back to the porch as if in readiness for what he had to do next.

Peter Ivanovich found the fresh air particularly pleasant after the smell of incense, the dead body, and carbolic acid.

"Where to, sir?" asked the coachman.

"It's not too late even now. . . . . I'll call round on Fëdor Vasilievich."

He accordingly drove there and found them just finishing the first rubber, so that it was quite convenient for him to cut in.

II

55   Ivan Ilych's life had been most simple and most ordinary and therefore most terrible.

He had been a member of the Court of Justice, and died at the age of forty-five. His father had been an official who after serving in various ministries and departments in Petersburg had made the sort of career which brings men to positions from which by reason of their long service they cannot be dismissed, though they are obviously unfit to hold any responsible position, and for whom therefore posts are especially created, which though fictitious carry salaries of from six to ten thousand rubles that are not fictitious, and in receipt of which they live on to a great age.

Such was the Privy Councillor and superfluous member of various superfluous institutions, Ilya Epimovich Golovin.

He had three sons, of whom Ivan Ilych was the second. The eldest son was following in his father's footsteps only in another department, and was already approaching that stage in the service at which a similar sinecure would be reached. The third son was a failure. He had ruined his prospects in a number of positions and was now serving in the railway department. His father and brothers, and still more their wives, not merely disliked meeting him, but avoided remembering his existence unless compelled to do so. His sister had married Baron Greff, a Petersburg official of her father's type. Ivan Ilych was *le phénix de la famille*[4] as people said. He was neither as cold and formal as his elder brother nor as wild as the younger, but was a happy mean between them—an intelligent, polished, lively and agreeable man. He had studied with his younger brother at the School of Law, but the latter had failed to complete the course and was expelled when he was in the fifth class. Ivan Ilych finished the course well. Even when he was at the School of Law he was just what he remained for the rest of his life:

---

[4] His family's darling

a capable, cheerful, good-natured, and sociable man, though strict in the fulfillment of what he considered to be his duty: and he considered his duty to be what was so considered by those in authority. Neither as a boy nor as a man was he a toady, but from early youth was by nature attracted to people of high station as a fly is drawn to the light, assimilating their ways and views of life and establishing friendly relations with them. All the enthusiasms of childhood and youth passed without leaving much trace on him; he succumbed to sensuality, to vanity, and latterly among the highest classes to liberalism, but always within limits which his instinct unfailingly indicated to him as correct.

At school he had done things which had formerly seemed to him very horrid and made him feel disgusted with himself when he did them; but when later on he saw that such actions were done by people of good position and that they did not regard them as wrong, he was able not exactly to regard them as right, but to forget about them entirely or not be at all troubled at remembering them.

60   Having graduated from the School of Law and qualified for the tenth rank of the civil service,[5] and having received money from his father for his equipment, Ivan Ilych ordered himself clothes at Scharmer's, the fashionable tailor, hung a medallion inscribed *respice finem*[6] on his watch-chain, took leave of his professor and the prince who was a patron of the school, had a farewell dinner with his comrades at Donon's first-class restaurant, and with his new and fashionable portmanteau, linen, clothes, shaving and other toilet appliances, and a travelling rug, all purchased at the best shops, he set off for one of the provinces where, through his father's influence, he had been attached to the Governor as an official for special service.

In the province Ivan Ilych soon arranged as easy and agreeable a position for himself as he had had at the School of Law. He performed his official tasks, made his career, and at the same time amused himself pleasantly and decorously. Occasionally he paid official visits to country districts, where he behaved with dignity both to his superiors and inferiors, and performed the duties entrusted to him, which related chiefly to the sectarians,[7] with an exactness and incorruptible honesty of which he could not but feel proud.

In official matters, despite his youth and taste for frivolous gaiety, he was exceedingly reserved, punctilious, and even severe; but in society he was often amusing and witty, and always good-natured, correct in his manner, and *bon enfant*,[8] as the governor and his wife—with whom he was like one of the family—used to say of him.

In the province he had an affair with a lady who made advances to the elegant young lawyer, and there was also a milliner; and there were carousals with aides-de-camp who visited the district, and after-supper visits to a certain outlying street of doubtful reputation; and there was too some obsequiousness to his chief and even to his chief's wife, but all this was done with such a tone of good breeding that no hard names could be applied to it. It all came

---

[5] A good status in the hierarchy at the time   [6] Consider the end   [7] "Old Believers," who dissented from the modern Russian Orthodox Church   [8] Good fellow

under the heading of the French saying: *"Il faut que jeunesse se passe."*[9] It was all done with clean hands, in clean linen, with French phrases, and above all among people of the best society and consequently with the approval of people of rank.

So Ivan Ilych served for five years and then came a change in his official life. The new and reformed judicial institutions were introduced, and new men were needed. Ivan Ilych became such a new man. He was offered the post of examining magistrate, and he accepted it though the post was in another province and obliged him to give up the connexions he had formed and to make new ones. His friends met to give him a send-off; they had a group-photograph taken and presented him with a silver cigarette-case, and he set off to his new post.

65   As examining magistrate Ivan Ilych was just as *comme il faut*[10] and decorous a man, inspiring general respect and capable of separating his official duties from his private life, as he had been when acting as an official on special service. His duties now as examining magistrate were far more interesting and attractive than before. In his former position it had been pleasant to wear an undress uniform made by Scharmer, and to pass through the crowd of petitioners and officials who were timorously awaiting an audience with the governor, and who envied him as with free and easy gait he went straight into his chief's private room to have a cup of tea and cigarette with him. But not many people had then been directly dependent on him—only police officials and the sectarians when he went on special missions—and he liked to treat them politely, almost as comrades, as if he were letting them feel that he who had the power to crush them was treating them in this simple, friendly way. There were then but few such people. But now, as an examining magistrate, Ivan Ilych felt that everyone without exception, even the most important and self-satisfied, was in his power, and that he need only write a few words on a sheet of paper with a certain heading, and this or that important, self-satisfied person would be brought before him in the role of an accused person or a witness, and if he did not choose to allow him to sit down, would have to stand before him and answer his questions. Ivan Ilych never abused his power; he tried on the contrary to soften its expression, but the consciousness of it and of the possibility of softening its effect, supplied the chief interest and attraction of his office. In his work itself, especially in his examinations, he very soon acquired a method of eliminating all considerations irrelevant to the legal aspects of the case, and reducing even the most complicated case to a form in which it would be presented on paper only in its externals, completely excluding his personal opinion of the matter, while above all observing every prescribed formality. The work was new and Ivan Ilych was one of the first men to apply the new Code of 1864.[11]

On taking up the post of examining magistrate in a new town, he made new acquaintances and connexions, placed himself on a new footing, and assumed a somewhat different tone. He took up an attitude of rather

[9] Youth must have its fling   [10] Proper   [11] I.e., appropriately progressive; the new Code followed the 1861 emancipation of the serfs

dignified aloofness towards the provincial authorities, but picked out the best circle of legal gentlemen and wealthy gentry living in the town and assumed a tone of slight dissatisfaction with the government, of moderate liberalism, and of enlightened citizenship. At the same time, without at all altering the elegance of his toilet, he ceased shaving his chin and allowed his beard to grow as it pleased.

Ivan Ilych settled down very pleasantly in this new town. The society there, which inclined towards opposition to the Governor, was friendly, his salary was larger, and he began to play *vint*,[12] which he found added not a little to the pleasure of life, for he had a capacity for cards, played good-humouredly, and calculated rapidly and astutely, so that he usually won.

After living there for two years he met his future wife, Praskovya Fëdorovna Mikhel, who was the most attractive, clever, and brilliant girl of the set in which he moved, and among other amusements and relaxations from his labours as examining magistrate, Ivan Ilych established light and playful relations with her.

While he had been an official on special service he had been accustomed to dance, but now as an examining magistrate it was exceptional for him to do so. If he danced now, he did it as if to show that though he served under the reformed order of things, and had reached the fifth official rank, yet when it came to dancing he could do it better than most people. So at the end of an evening he sometimes danced with Praskovya Fëdorovna, and it was chiefly during these dances that he captivated her. She fell in love with him. Ivan Ilych had at first no definite intention of marrying, but when the girl fell in love with him he said to himself: "Really, why shouldn't I marry?"

70   Praskovya Fëdorovna came of a good family, was not bad looking, and had some little property. Ivan Ilych might have aspired to a more brilliant match, but even this was good. He had his salary, and she, he hoped, would have an equal income. She was well connected, and was a sweet, pretty, and thoroughly correct young woman. To say that Ivan Ilych married because he fell in love with Praskovya Fëdorovna and found that she sympathized with his views of life would be as incorrect as to say that he married because his social circle approved of the match. He was swayed by both these considerations: the marriage gave him personal satisfaction, and at the same time it was considered the right thing by the most highly placed of his associates.

So Ivan Ilych got married.

The preparations for marriage and the beginning of married life, with its conjugal caresses, the new furniture, new crockery, and new linen, were very pleasant until his wife became pregnant — so that Ivan Ilych had begun to think that marriage would not impair the easy, agreeable, gay and always decorous character of his life, approved of by society and regarded by himself as natural, but would even improve it. But from the first months of his wife's pregnancy, something new, unpleasant, depressing, and unseemly, and from which there was no way of escape, unexpectedly showed itself.

[12] A card game somewhat similar to both whist and bridge

His wife, without any reason—*de gaieté de coeur*[13] as Ivan Ilych expressed it to himself—began to disturb the pleasure and propriety of their life. She began to be jealous without any cause, expected him to devote his whole attention to her, found fault with everything, and made coarse and ill-mannered scenes.

At first Ivan Ilych hoped to escape from the unpleasantness of this state of affairs by the same easy and decorous relation to life that had served him heretofore: he tried to ignore his wife's disagreeable moods, continued to live in his usual easy and pleasant way, invited friends to his house for a game of cards, and also tried going out to his club or spending his evenings with friends. But one day his wife began upbraiding him so vigorously, using such coarse words, and continued to abuse him every time he did not fulfil her demands, so resolutely and with such evident determination not to give way till he submitted—that is, till he stayed at home and was bored just as she was—that he became alarmed. He now realized that matrimony—at any rate with Praskovya Fëdorovna—was not always conducive to the pleasures and amenities of life, but on the contrary often infringed both comfort and propriety, and that he must therefore entrench himself against such infringement. And Ivan Ilych began to seek for means of doing so. His official duties were the one thing that imposed upon Praskovya Fëdorovna, and by means of his official work and the duties attached to it he began struggling with his wife to secure his own independence.

75 With the birth of their child, the attempts to feed it and the various failures in doing so, and with the real and imaginary illnesses of mother and child, in which Ivan Ilych's sympathy was demanded but about which he understood nothing, the need of securing for himself an existence outside his family life became still more imperative.

As his wife grew more irritable and exacting and Ivan Ilych transferred the centre of gravity of his life more and more to his official work, so did he grow to like his work better and became more ambitious than before.

Very soon, within a year of his wedding, Ivan Ilych had realized that marriage, though it may add some comforts to life, is in fact a very intricate and difficult affair towards which in order to perform one's duty, that is, to lead a decorous life approved of by society, one must adopt a definite attitude just as towards one's official duties.

And Ivan Ilych evolved such an attitude towards married life. He only required of it those conveniences—dinner at home, housewife, and bed—which it could give him, and above all that propriety of external forms required by public opinion. For the rest he looked for light-hearted pleasure and propriety, and was very thankful when he found them, but if he met with antagonism and querulousness he at once retired into his separate fenced-off world of official duties, where he found satisfaction.

Ivan Ilych was esteemed a good official, and after three years was made Assistant Public Prosecutor. His new duties, their importance, the possibility of indicting and imprisoning anyone he chose, the publicity his speeches

---

[13] Lightheartedly

received, and the success he had in all these things, made his work still more attractive.

80   More children came. His wife became more and more querulous and ill-tempered, but the attitude Ivan Ilych had adopted towards his home life rendered him almost impervious to her grumbling.

After seven years' service in that town he was transferred to another province as Public Prosecutor. They moved, but were short of money and his wife did not like the place they moved to. Though the salary was higher the cost of living was greater, besides which two of their children died and family life became still more unpleasant for him.

Praskovya Fëdorovna blamed her husband for every inconvenience they encountered in their new home. Most of the conversations between husband and wife, especially as to the children's education, led to topics which recalled former disputes, and those disputes were apt to flare up again at any moment. There remained only those rare periods of amorousness which still came to them at times but did not last long. These were islets at which they anchored for a while and then again set out upon that ocean of veiled hostility which showed itself in their aloofness from one another. This aloofness might have grieved Ivan Ilych had he considered that it ought not to exist, but he now regarded the position as normal, and even made it the goal at which he aimed in family life. His aim was to free himself more and more from those unpleasantnesses and to give them a semblance of harmlessness and propriety. He attained this by spending less and less time with his family, and when obliged to be at home he tried to safeguard his position by the presence of outsiders. The chief thing however was that he had his official duties. The whole interest of his life now centered in the official world and that interest absorbed him. The consciousness of his power, being able to ruin anybody he wished to ruin, the importance, even the external dignity of his entry into court, or meetings with his subordinates, his success with superiors and inferiors, and above all his masterly handling of cases, of which he was conscious—all this gave him pleasure and filled his life, together with chats with his colleagues, dinners, and bridge. So that on the whole Ivan Ilych's life continued to flow as he considered it should do—pleasantly and properly.

So things continued for another seven years. His eldest daughter was already sixteen, another child had died, and only one son was left, a schoolboy and a subject of dissension. Ivan Ilych wanted to put him in the School of Law, but to spite him Praskovya Fëdorovna entered him at the High School. The daughter had been educated at home and had turned out well: the boy did not learn badly either.

III

So Ivan Ilych lived for seventeen years after his marriage. He was already a Public Prosecutor of long standing, and had declined several proposed transfers while awaiting a more desirable post, when an unanticipated and unpleasant occurrence quite upset the peaceful course of his life. He was expecting to be offered the post of presiding judge in a University town, but Happe somehow came to the front and obtained the appointment instead. Ivan Ilych became irritable, reproached Happe, and quarrelled both with him and with his immediate superiors—who became colder to him and again passed him over when other appointments were made.

85   This was in 1880, the hardest year of Ivan Ilych's life. It was then that it became evident on the one hand that his salary was insufficient for them to live on, and on the other hand that he had been forgotten, and not only this, but that what was for him the greatest and most cruel injustice appeared to others a quite ordinary occurrence. Even his father did not consider it his duty to help him. Ivan Ilych felt himself abandoned by everyone, and that they regarded his position with a salary of 3,500 rubles as quite normal and even fortunate. He alone knew that with the consciousness of the injustices done him, with his wife's incessant nagging, and with the debts he had contracted by living beyond his means, his position was far from normal.

In order to save money that summer he obtained leave of absence and went with his wife to live in the country at her brother's place.

In the country, without his work, he experienced *ennui*[14] for the first time in his life, and not only *ennui* but intolerable depression, and he decided that it was impossible to go on living like that, and that it was necessary to take energetic measures.

Having passed a sleepless night pacing up and down the veranda, he decided to go to Petersburg and bestir himself, in order to punish those who had failed to appreciate him and to get transferred to another ministry.

Next day, despite many protests from his wife and her brother, he started for Petersburg with the sole object of obtaining a post with a salary of five thousand rubles a year. He was no longer bent on any particular department or tendency, or kind of activity. All he now wanted was an appointment to another post with a salary of five thousand rubles, either in the administration, in the banks, with the railways, in one of the Empress Marya's Institutions,[15] or even in the customs—but it had to carry with it a salary of five thousand rubles and be in a ministry other than that in which they had failed to appreciate him.

90   And this quest of Ivan Ilych's was crowned with remarkable and unexpected success. At Kursk an acquaintance of his, F. I. Ilyin, got into the first-class carriage, sat down beside Ivan Ilych, and told him of a telegram just received by the Governor of Kursk announcing that a change was about to take place in the ministry: Peter Ivanovich was to be superseded by Ivan Semënovich.

The proposed change, apart from its significance for Russia, had a special significance for Ivan Ilych, because by bringing forward a new man, Peter Petrovich, and consequently his friend Zachar Ivanovich, it was highly favorable for Ivan Ilych, since Zachar Ivanovich was a friend and colleague of his.

---

[14] Boredom   [15] A ministry of charitable works

In Moscow this news was confirmed, and on reaching Petersburg Ivan Ilych found Zachar Ivanovich and received a definite promise of an appointment in his former department of Justice.

A week later he telegraphed to his wife: "Zachar in Miller's place. I shall receive appointment on presentation of report."

Thanks to this change of personnel, Ivan Ilych had unexpectedly obtained an appointment in his former ministry which placed him two stages above his former colleagues besides giving him five thousand rubles salary and three thousand five hundred rubles for expenses connected with his removal. All his ill humour towards his former enemies and the whole department vanished, and Ivan Ilych was completely happy.

95 He returned to the country more cheerful and contented than he had been for a long time. Praskovya Fëdorovna also cheered up and a truce was arranged between them. Ivan Ilych told of how he had been fêted by everybody in Petersburg, how all those who had been his enemies were put to shame and now fawned on him, how envious they were of his appointment, and how much everybody in Petersburg had liked him.

Praskovya Fëdorovna listened to all this and appeared to believe it. She did not contradict anything, but only made plans for their life in the town to which they were going. Ivan Ilych saw with delight that these plans were his plans, that he and his wife agreed, and that, after a stumble, his life was regaining its due and natural character of pleasant lightheartedness and decorum.

Ivan Ilych had come back for a short time only, for he had to take up his new duties on the 10th of September. Moreover, he needed time to settle into the new place, to move all his belongings from the province, and to buy and order many additional things: in a word, to make such arrangements as he had resolved on, which were almost exactly what Praskovya Fëdorovna too had decided on.

Now that everything had happened so fortunately, and that he and his wife were at one in their aims and moreover saw so little of one another, they got on together better than they had done since the first years of marriage. Ivan Ilych had thought of taking his family away with him at once, but the insistence of his wife's brother and her sister-in-law, who had suddenly become particularly amiable and friendly to him and his family, induced him to depart alone.

So he departed, and the cheerful state of mind induced by his success and by the harmony between his wife and himself, the one intensifying the other, did not leave him. He found a delightful house, just the thing both he and his wife had dreamt of. Spacious, lofty reception rooms in the old style, a convenient and dignified study, rooms for his wife and daughter, a study for his son—it might have been specially built for them. Ivan Ilych himself superintended the arrangements, chose the wallpapers, supplemented the furniture (preferably with antiques which he considered particularly *comme il faut*), and supervised the upholstering. Everything progressed and progressed and approached the ideal he had set himself: even when things were only half completed they exceeded his expectations. He saw what a refined and elegant character, free from vulgarity, it would all have when it was ready. On falling asleep he pictured to himself how the reception-room would look. Looking at the yet unfinished drawing-room he could see the fireplace, the screen, the what-not, the little chairs dotted here and there, the dishes and plates on the walls, and the bronzes, as they would be when everything was in place. He was pleased by the thought of how his wife and daughter, who shared his taste in this matter, would be impressed by it. They were certainly not expecting as much. He had been particularly successful in finding, and buying cheaply, antiques which gave a particularly aristocratic character to the whole place. But in his letters he intentionally understated everything in order to be able to surprise them. All this so absorbed him that his new duties—though he liked his official work—interested him less than he had expected. Sometimes he even had moments of absentmindedness during the Court Sessions, and would consider whether he should have straight or curved cornices for his curtains. He was so interested in it all that he often did things himself, rearranging the furniture, or rehanging the curtains. Once when mounting a step-ladder to show the upholsterer, who did not understand, how he wanted the hangings draped, he made a false step and slipped, but being a strong and agile man he clung on and only knocked his side against the knob of the window frame. The bruised place was painful but the pain soon passed, and he felt particularly bright and well just then. He wrote: "I feel fifteen years younger." He thought he would have everything ready by September, but it dragged on till mid-October. But the result was charming not only in his eyes but to everyone who saw it.

100   In reality it was just what is usually seen in the houses of people of moderate means who want to appear rich, and therefore succeed only in resembling others like themselves: there were damasks, dark wood, plants, rugs, and dull and polished bronzes—all the things people of a certain class have in order to resemble other people of that class. His house was so like the others that it would never have been noticed, but to him it all seemed to be quite exceptional. He was very happy when he met his family at the station and brought them to the newly furnished house all lit up, where a footman in a white tie opened the door into the hall decorated with plants, and when they went on into the drawing-room and the study uttering exclamations of delight. He conducted them everywhere, drank in their praises eagerly, and beamed with pleasure. At tea that evening, when Praskovya Fëdorovna among other things asked him about his fall, he laughed and showed them how he had gone flying and had frightened the upholsterer.

"It's a good thing I'm a bit of an athlete. Another man might have been killed, but I merely knocked myself, just here; it hurts when it's touched, but it's passing off already—it's only a bruise."

So they began living in their new home—in which, as always happens, when they got thoroughly settled in they found they were just one room short—and with the increased income, which as always was just a little (some five hundred rubles) too little, but it was all very nice.

Things went particularly well at first, before everything was finally arranged and while something had still to be done: this thing bought, that thing ordered, another thing moved, and something else adjusted. Though there were some disputes between husband and wife, they were both so well satisfied and had so much to do that it all passed off without any serious quarrels. When nothing was left to arrange it became rather dull and something seemed to be lacking, but they were then making acquaintances, forming habits, and life was growing fuller.

Ivan Ilych spent his mornings at the law court and came home to dinner, and at first he was generally in a good humour, though he occasionally became irritable just on account of his house. (Every spot on the tablecloth or the upholstery, and every broken window-blind string, irritated him. He had devoted so much trouble to arranging it all that every disturbance of it distressed him.) But on the whole his life ran its course as he believed life should do: easily, pleasantly, and decorously.

105   He got up at nine, drank his coffee, read the paper, and then put on his undress uniform and went to the law courts. There the harness in which he worked had already been stretched to fit him and he donned it without a hitch: petitioners, inquiries at the chancery, the chancery itself, and the sittings public and administrative. In all this the thing was to exclude everything fresh and vital, which always disturbs the regular course of official business, and to admit only official relations with people, and then only on official grounds. A man would come, for instance, wanting some information. Ivan Ilych, as one in whose sphere the matter did not lie, would have nothing to do with him: but if the man had some business with him in his official capacity, something that could be expressed on officially stamped paper, he would do everything, positively everything he could within the limits of such relations, and in doing so would maintain the semblance of friendly human relations, that is, would observe the courtesies of life. As soon as the official relations ended, so did everything else. Ivan Ilych possessed this capacity to separate his real life from the official side of affairs and not mix the two, in the highest degree, and by long practice and natural aptitude had brought it to such a pitch that sometimes, in the manner of a virtuoso, he would even allow himself to let the human and official relations mingle. He let himself do this just because he felt that he could at any time he chose resume the strictly official attitude again and drop the human relation. And he did it all easily, pleasantly, correctly, and even artistically. In the intervals between the sessions he smoked, drank tea, chatted a little about politics, a little about general topics, a little about cards, but most of all about official appointments. Tired, but with the feelings of a virtuoso—one of the first violins who has played his part in an orchestra with precision—he would return home to find that his wife and daughter had been out paying calls, or had a visitor, and that his son had been to school, had done his homework with the tutor, and was duly learning what is taught at High Schools. Everything was as it should be. After dinner, if they had no visitors, Ivan Ilych sometimes read a book that was being much discussed at the time, and in the evening settled down to work, that is, read official papers, compared the depositions of witnesses, and noted paragraphs of the Code applying to them. This was neither dull nor amusing. It was dull when he might have been playing bridge but if no bridge was available it was at any rate

better than doing nothing or sitting with his wife. Ivan Ilych's chief pleasure was giving little dinners to which he invited men and women of good social position, and just as his drawing-room resembled all other drawing-rooms so did his enjoyable little parties resemble all other such parties.

Once they even gave a dance. Ivan Ilych enjoyed it and everything went off well, except that it led to a violent quarrel with his wife about the cakes and sweets. Praskovya Fëdorovna had made her own plans, but Ivan Ilych insisted on getting everything from an expensive confectioner and ordered too many cakes, and the quarrel occurred because some of those cakes were left over and the confectioner's bill came to forty-five rubles. It was a great and disagreeable quarrel. Praskovya Fëdorovna called him "a fool and an imbecile," and he clutched at his head and made angry allusions to divorce.

But the dance itself had been enjoyable. The best people were there, and Ivan Ilych had danced with Princess Trufonova, a sister of the distinguished founder of the Society "Bear my Burden."

The pleasures connected with his work were pleasures of ambition; his social pleasures were those of vanity; but Ivan Ilych's greatest pleasure was playing bridge. He acknowledged that whatever disagreeable incident happened in his life, the pleasure that beamed like a ray of light above everything else was to sit down to bridge with good players, not noisy partners, and of course to four-handed bridge (with five players it was annoying to have to stand out, though one pretended not to mind), to play a clever and serious game (when the cards allowed it) and then to have supper and drink a glass of wine. After a game of bridge, especially if he had won a little (to win a large sum was unpleasant), Ivan Ilych went to bed in specially good humour.

So they lived. They formed a circle of acquaintances among the best people and were visited by people of importance and by young folk. In their views as to their acquaintances, husband, wife and daughter were entirely agreed, and tacitly and unanimously kept at arm's length and shook off the shabby friends and relations who, with much show of affection, gushed into the drawing-room with its Japanese plates on the walls. Soon these shabby friends ceased to obtrude themselves and only the best people remained in the Golovins' set.

Young men made up to Lisa, and Petrishchev, an examining magistrate and Dmitri Ivanovich Petrishchev's son and sole heir, began to be so attentive to her that Ivan Ilych had already spoken to Praskovya Fëdorovna about it, and considered whether they should not arrange a party for them, or get up some private theatricals.

So they lived, and all went well, without change, and life flowed pleasantly.

IV

They were all in good health. It could not be called ill health if Ivan Ilych sometimes said that he had a queer taste in his mouth and felt some discomfort in his left side.

But this discomfort increased and, though not exactly painful, grew into a sense of pressure in his side accompanied by ill humour. And his irritability became worse and worse and began to mar the agreeable, easy, and correct life that had established itself in the Golovin family. Quarrels between husband and wife became more and more frequent, and soon the ease and amenity disappeared and even the decorum was barely maintained. Scenes again became frequent, and very few of those islets remained on which husband and wife could meet without an explosion. Praskovya Fëdorovna now had good reason to say that her husband's temper was trying. With characteristic exaggeration she said he had always had a dreadful temper, and that it had needed all her good nature to put up with it for twenty years. It was true that now the quarrels were started by him. His bursts of temper always came just before dinner, often just as he began to eat his soup. Sometimes he noticed that a plate or dish was chipped, or the food was not right, or his son put his elbow on the table, or his daughter's hair was not done as he liked it, and for all this he blamed Praskovya Fëdorovna. At first she retorted and said disagreeable things to him, but once or twice he fell into such a rage at the beginning of dinner that she realized it was due to some physical derangement brought on by taking food, and so she restrained herself and did not answer, but only hurried to get the dinner over. She regarded this self-restraint as highly praiseworthy. Having come to the conclusion that her husband had a dreadful temper and made her life miserable, she began to feel sorry for herself, and the more she pitied herself the more she hated her husband. She began to wish he would die; yet she did not want him to die because then his salary would cease. And this irritated her against him still more. She considered herself dreadfully unhappy just because not even his death could save her, and though she concealed her exasperation, that hidden exasperation of hers increased his irritation also.

After one scene in which Ivan Ilych had been particularly unfair and after which he had said in explanation that he certainly was irritable but that it was due to his not being well, she said that if he was ill it should be attended to, and insisted on his going to see a celebrated doctor.

115   He went. Everything took place as he had expected and as it always does. There was the usual waiting and the important air assumed by the doctor, with which he was so familiar (resembling that which he himself assumed in court), and the sounding and listening, and the questions which called for answers that were foregone conclusions and were evidently unnecessary, and the look of importance which implied that "if only you put yourself in our hands we will arrange everything—we know indubitably how it has to be done, always in the same way for everybody alike." It was all just as it was in the law courts. The doctor put on just the same air towards him as he himself put on towards an accused person.

The doctor said that so-and-so indicated there was so-and-so inside the patient, but if the investigation of so-and-so did not confirm this, then he must assume that and that. If he assumed that and that, then . . . and so on. To Ivan Ilych only one question was important: was his case serious or not? But the doctor ignored that inappropriate question. From his point of view it was not the one under consideration, the real question was to decide between a floating kidney, chronic catarrh, or appendicitis. It was not a question of Ivan Ilych's life or death, but one between a floating kidney and appendicitis. And that question the doctor solved brilliantly, as it seemed to Ivan Ilych, in favour of the appendix, with the reservation that should an examination of the urine give fresh indications the matter would be reconsidered. All this was just what Ivan Ilych had himself brilliantly accomplished a thousand times in dealing with men on trial. The doctor summed up just as brilliantly, looking over his spectacles triumphantly and even gaily at the accused. From the doctor's summing up Ivan Ilych concluded that things were bad, but that for the doctor, and perhaps for everybody else, it was a matter of indifference, though for him it was bad. And this conclusion struck him painfully, arousing in him a great feeling of pity for himself and of bitterness towards the doctor's indifference to a matter of such importance.

He said nothing of this, but rose, placed the doctor's fee on the table, and remarked with a sigh: "We sick people probably often put inappropriate questions. But tell me, in general, is this complaint dangerous, or not? . . ."

The doctor looked at him sternly over his spectacles with one eye, as if to say: "Prisoner, if you will not keep to the questions put to you, I shall be obliged to have you removed from the court."

"I have already told you what I consider necessary and proper. The analysis may show something more." And the doctor bowed.

120   Ivan Ilych went out slowly, seated himself disconsolately in his sledge, and drove home. All the way home he was going over what the doctor had said, trying to translate those complicated, obscure, scientific phrases into plain language and find in them an answer to the question: "Is my condition bad? Is it very bad? Or is there as yet nothing much wrong?" And it seemed to him that the meaning of what the doctor had said was that it was very bad. Everything in the streets seemed depressing. The cabmen, the houses, the passers-by, and the shops, were dismal. His ache, this dull gnawing ache that never ceased for a moment, seemed to have acquired a new and more serious significance from the doctor's dubious remarks. Ivan Ilych now watched it with a new and oppressive feeling.

He reached home and began to tell his wife about it. She listened, but in the middle of his account his daughter came in with her hat on, ready to go out with her mother. She sat down reluctantly to listen to this tedious story, but could not stand it long, and her mother too did not hear him to the end.

"Well, I am very glad," she said. "Mind now you take your medicine regularly. Give me the prescription and I'll send Gerasim to the chemist's." And she went to get ready to go out.

While she was in the room Ivan Ilych had hardly taken time to breathe, but he sighed deeply when she left it.

"Well," he thought, "perhaps it isn't so bad after all."

125   He began taking his medicine and following the doctor's directions, which had been altered after the examination of the urine. But then it happened that there was a contradiction between the indications drawn from the examination of the urine and the symptoms that showed themselves. It turned out that what was happening differed from what the doctor had told him, and that he had either forgotten, or blundered, or hidden something

from him. He could not, however, be blamed for that, and Ivan Ilych still obeyed his orders implicitly and at first derived some comfort from doing so.

From the time of his visit to the doctor, Ivan Ilych's chief occupation was the exact fulfillment of the doctor's instructions regarding hygiene and the taking of medicine, and the observation of his pain and his excretions. His chief interests came to be people's ailments and people's health. When sickness, deaths, or recoveries were mentioned in his presence, especially when the illness resembled his own, he listened with agitation which he tried to hide, asked questions, and applied what he heard to his own case.

The pain did not grow less, but Ivan Ilych made efforts to force himself to think that he was better. And he could do this so long as nothing agitated him. But as soon as he had any unpleasantness with his wife, or a lack of success in his official work, or held bad cards at bridge, he was at once acutely sensible of his disease. He had formerly borne such mischances, hoping soon to adjust what was wrong, to master it and attain success, or make a grand slam. But now every mischance upset him and plunged him into despair. He would say to himself: "There now, just as I was beginning to get better and the medicine had begun to take effect, comes this accursed misfortune, or unpleasantness . . ." And he was furious with the mishap, or with the people who were causing the unpleasantness and killing him, for he felt that this fury was killing him but could not restrain it. One would have thought that it should have been clear to him that this exasperation with circumstances and people aggravated his illness, and that he ought therefore to ignore unpleasant occurrences. But he drew the very opposite conclusion: he said that he needed peace, and he watched for everything that might disturb it and became irritable at the slightest infringement of it. His condition was rendered worse by the fact that he read medical books and consulted doctors. The progress of his disease was so gradual that he could deceive himself when comparing one day with another— the difference was so slight. But when he consulted the doctors it seemed to him that he was getting worse, and even very rapidly. Yet despite this he was continually consulting them.

That month he went to see another celebrity, who told him almost the same as the first had done but put his questions rather differently, and the interview with this celebrity only increased Ivan Ilych's doubts and fears. A friend of a friend of his, a very good doctor, diagnosed his illness again quite differently from the others, and though he predicted recovery, his questions and suppositions bewildered Ivan Ilych still more and increased his doubts. A homeopathist diagnosed the disease in yet another way, and prescribed medicine which Ivan Ilych took secretly for a week. But after a week, not feeling any improvement and having lost confidence both in the former doctor's treatment and in this one's, he became still more despondent. One day a lady acquaintance mentioned a cure effected by a wonder-working icon. Ivan Ilych caught himself listening attentively and beginning to believe that it had occurred. This incident alarmed him. "Has my mind really weakened to such an extent?" he asked himself. "Nonsense! It's all rubbish. I mustn't give way to nervous fears but having chosen a doctor must keep strictly to his treatment. That is what I will do. Now it's all settled. I won't think about it, but will follow the treatment seriously till summer, and then we shall see. From now there must be no more of this wavering!" This was easy to say but impossible to carry out. The pain in his side oppressed him and seemed to grow worse and more incessant, while the taste in his mouth grew stranger and stranger. It seemed to him that his breath had a disgusting smell, and he was conscious of a loss of appetite and strength. There was no deceiving himself: something terrible, new, and more important than anything before in his life, was taking place within him of which he alone was aware. Those about him did not understand or would not understand it, but thought everything in the world was going on as usual. That tormented Ivan Ilych more than anything. He saw that his household, especially his wife and daughter who were in a perfect whirl of visiting, did not understand anything of it and were annoyed that he was so depressed and so exacting, as if he were to blame for it. Though they tried to disguise it he saw that he was an obstacle in their path, and that his wife had adopted a definite line in regard to his illness and kept to it regardless of anything he said or did. Her attitude was this: "You know," she would say to her friends, "Ivan Ilych can't do as other people do, and keep to the treatment prescribed for him. One day he'll take his drops and keep strictly to his diet and go to bed in good time, but the next day unless I watch him he'll suddenly forget his medicine, eat sturgeon—which is forbidden—and sit up playing cards till one o'clock in the morning."

"Oh, come, when was that?" Ivan Ilych would ask in vexation. "Only once at Peter Ivanovich's."

130   "And yesterday with Shebek."

"Well, even if I hadn't stayed up, this pain would have kept me awake."

"Be that as it may you'll never get well like that, but will always make us wretched."

Praskovya Fëdorovna's attitude to Ivan Ilych's illness, as she expressed it both to others and to him, was that it was his own fault and was another of the annoyances he caused her. Ivan Ilych felt that this opinion escaped her involuntarily—but that did not make it easier for him.

At the law courts too, Ivan Ilych noticed, or thought he noticed, a strange attitude towards himself. It sometimes seemed to him that people were watching him inquisitively as a man whose place might soon be vacant. Then again, his friends would suddenly begin to chaff him in a friendly way about his low spirits, as if the awful, horrible, and unheard-of thing that was going on within him, incessantly gnawing at him and irresistibly drawing him away, was a very agreeable subject for jests. Schwartz in particular irritated him by his jocularity, vivacity, and *savoir-faire,*[16] which reminded him of what he himself had been ten years ago.

135   Friends came to make up a set and they sat down to cards. They dealt, bending the new cards to soften them, and he sorted the diamonds in his hand and found he had seven. His partner said "No trumps" and supported him with two diamonds. What more could be wished for? It ought to be jolly and lively. They would make a grand slam. But suddenly Ivan Ilych

---

[16] Tact; social grace

was conscious of that gnawing pain, that taste in his mouth, and it seemed ridiculous that in such circumstances he should be pleased to make a grand slam.

He looked at his partner Mikhail Mikhaylovich, who rapped the table with his strong hand and instead of snatching up the tricks pushed the cards courteously and indulgently towards Ivan Ilych that he might have the pleasure of gathering them up without the trouble of stretching out his hand for them. "Does he think I am too weak to stretch out my arm?" thought Ivan Ilych, and forgetting what he was doing he over-trumped his partner, missing the grand slam by three tricks. And what was most awful of all was that he saw how upset Mikhail Mikhaylovich was about it but did not himself care. And it was dreadful to realize why he did not care.

They all saw that he was suffering and said: "We can stop if you are tired. Take a rest." Lie down? No, he was not at all tired, and he finished the rubber. All were gloomy and silent. Ivan Ilych felt that he had diffused this gloom over them and could not dispel it. They had supper and went away, and Ivan Ilych was left alone with the consciousness that his life was poisoned and was poisoning the lives of others, and that this position did not weaken but penetrated more and more deeply into his whole being.

With this consciousness, and with physical pain besides that terror, he must go to bed, often to lie awake the greater part of the night. Next morning he had to get up again, dress, go to the law courts, speak, and write; or if he did not go out, spend at home those twenty-four hours a day each of which was a torture. And he had to live thus all alone on the brink of an abyss, with no one who understood or pitied him.

V

So one month passed and then another. Just before the New Year his brother-in-law came to town and stayed at their house. Ivan Ilych was at the law courts and Praskovya Fëdorovna had gone shopping. When Ivan Ilych came home and entered his study he found his brother-in-law there—a healthy, florid man—unpacking his portmanteau himself. He raised his head on hearing Ivan Ilych's footsteps and looked up at him for a moment without a word. That stare told Ivan Ilych everything. His brother-in-law opened his mouth to utter an exclamation of surprise but checked himself, and that action confirmed it all.

"I have changed, eh?"

"Yes, there is a change."

And after that, try as he would to get his brother-in-law to return to the subject of his looks, the latter would say nothing about it. Praskovya Fëdorovna came home and her brother went out to her. Ivan Ilych locked the door and began to examine himself in the glass, first full face, then in profile. He took up a portrait of himself taken with his wife, and compared it with what he saw in the glass. The change in him was immense. Then he bared his arms to the elbow, looked at them, drew the sleeves down again, sat down on an ottoman, and grew blacker than night.

"No, no, this won't do!" he said to himself, and jumped up, went to the table, took up some law papers and began to read them, but could not continue. He unlocked the door and went into the reception-room. The door leading to the drawing-room was shut. He approached it on tiptoe and listened.

"No, you are exaggerating!" Praskovya Fëdorovna was saying.

145   "Exaggerating! Don't you see it ? Why, he's a dead man! Look at his eyes— there's no light in them. But what is it that is wrong with him?"

"No one knows. Nikolaevich [that was another doctor] said something, but I don't know what. And Leshchetitsky [this was the celebrated specialist] said quite the contrary . . ."

Ivan Ilych walked away, went to his own room, lay down, and began musing: "The kidney, a floating kidney." He recalled all the doctors had told him of how it detached itself and swayed about. And by an effort of imagina- tion he tried to catch that kidney and arrest it and support it. So little was needed for this, it seemed to him. "No, I'll go to see Peter Ivanovich again." [That was the friend whose friend was a doctor.] He rang, ordered the car- riage and got ready to go.

"Where are you going, Jean?" asked his wife, with a specially sad and exceptionally kind look.

This exceptionally kind look irritated him. He looked morosely at her.

150   "I must go to see Peter Ivanovich."

He went to see Peter Ivanovich, and together they went to see his friend, the doctor. He was in, and Ivan Ilych had a long talk with him.

Reviewing the anatomical and physiological details of what in the doctor's opinion was going on inside him, he understood it all.

There was something, a small thing, in the vermiform appendix. It might all come right. Only stimulate the energy of one organ and check the activity of another, then absorption would take place and everything would come right. He got home rather late for dinner, ate his dinner, conversed cheer- fully, but could not for a long time bring himself to go back to work in his room. At last, however, he went to his study and did what was necessary, but the consciousness that he had put something aside—an important, intimate matter which he would revert to when his work was done—never left him. When he had finished his work he remembered that this intimate matter was the thought of his vermiform appendix. But he did not give himself up to it, and went to the drawing-room for tea. There were callers there, including the examining magistrate who was a desirable match for his daughter, and they were conversing, playing the piano, and singing. Ivan Ilych, as Praskovya Fëdorovna remarked, spent that evening more cheerfully than usual, but he never for a moment forgot that he had postponed the important matter of the appendix. At eleven o'clock he said good-night and went to his bedroom. Since his illness he had slept alone in a small room next to his study. He undressed and took up a novel by Zola,[17] but instead of reading it fell into thought, and in his imagination that desired improvement in the vermi- form appendix occurred. There was the absorption and evacuation and the

---

[17] The realistic French novelist (1840–1902)

re-establishment of normal activity. "Yes, that's it!" he said to himself. "One need only assist nature, that's all." He remembered his medicine, rose, took it, and lay down on his back watching for the beneficent action of the medicine and for it to lessen the pain. "I need only take it regularly and avoid all injurious influences. I am already feeling better, much better." He began touching his side: it was not painful to the touch. "There, I really don't feel it. It's much better already." He put out the light and turned on his side . . . "The appendix is getting better, absorption is occurring." Suddenly he felt the old, familiar, dull, gnawing pain, stubborn and serious. There was the same familiar loathsome taste in his mouth. His heart sank and he felt dazed. "My God! My God!" he muttered. "Again, again! and it will never cease." And suddenly the matter presented itself in a quite different aspect. "Vermiform appendix! Kidney!" he said to himself. "It's not a question of appendix or kidney, but of life and . . . death. Yes, life was there and now it is going, going and I cannot stop it. Yes. Why deceive myself? Isn't it obvious to everyone but me that I'm dying, and that it's only a question of weeks, days . . . it may happen this moment. There was light and now there is darkness. I was here and now I'm going there! Where?" A chill came over him, his breathing ceased, and he felt only the throbbing of his heart.

"When I am not, what will there be? There will be nothing. Then where shall I be when I am no more? Can this be dying? No, I don't want to!" He jumped up and tried to light the candle, felt for it with trembling hands, dropped candle and candlestick on the floor, and fell back on his pillow.

155 "What's the use? It makes no difference," he said to himself, staring with wide-open eyes into the darkness. "Death. Yes, death. And none of them know or wish to know it, and they have no pity for me. Now they are playing." (He heard through the door the distant sound of a song and its accompaniment.) "It's all the same to them, but they will die too! Fools! I first, and they later, but it will be the same for them. And now they are merry . . . the beasts!"

Anger choked him and he was agonizingly, unbearably, miserable. "It is impossible that all men have been doomed to suffer this awful horror!" He raised himself.

"Something must be wrong. I must calm myself—must think it all over from the beginning." And he began thinking. "Yes, the beginning of my illness: I knocked my side, but I was quite well that day and the next. It hurt a little, then rather more. I saw the doctor, then followed despondency and anguish, more doctors, and I drew nearer to the abyss. My strength grew less and I kept coming nearer and nearer, and now I have wasted away and there is no light in my eyes. I think of the appendix—but this is death! I think of mending the appendix, and all the while here is death! Can it really be death?" Again terror seized him and he gasped for breath. He leant down and began feeling for the matches, pressing with his elbow on the stand beside the bed. It was in the way and hurt him, he grew furious with it, pressed on it still harder, and upset it. Breathless and in despair he fell on his back, expecting death to come immediately.

Meanwhile the visitors were leaving. Praskovya Fëdorovna was seeing them off. She heard something fall and came in.

"What has happened?"

160   "Nothing, I knocked it over accidentally."

She went out and returned with a candle. He lay there panting heavily, like a man who has run a thousand yards, and stared upwards at her with a fixed look.

"What is it, Jean?"

"No . . . o . . . thing. I upset it." ("Why speak of it? She won't understand," he thought.)

And in truth she did not understand. She picked up the stand, lit his candle, and hurried away to see another visitor off. When she came back he still lay on his back, looking upwards.

165   "What is it? Do you feel worse?"

"Yes."

She shook her head and sat down.

"Do you know, Jean, I think we must ask Leshchetitsky to come and see you here."

This meant calling in the famous specialist, regardless of expense. He smiled malignantly and said "No." She remained a little longer and then went up to him and kissed his forehead.

170   While she was kissing him he hated her from the bottom of his soul and with difficulty refrained from pushing her away.

"Good-night, Please God you'll sleep."

"Yes."

VI

Ivan Ilych saw that he was dying, and he was in continual despair.

In the depth of his heart he knew he was dying, but not only was he not accustomed to the thought, he simply did not and could not grasp it.

175   The syllogism he had learnt from Kiezewetter's Logic, "Caius is a man, men are mortal, therefore Caius is mortal," had always seemed to him correct as applied to Caius, but certainly not as applied to himself. That Caius—man in the abstract—was mortal, was perfectly correct, but he was Caius, not an abstract man, but a creature quite, quite separate from all others. He had been little Vanya, with a mamma and papa, with Mitya and Volodya, with the toys, a coachman and a nurse, afterwards with Katenka and with all the joys, griefs, and delights of childhood, boyhood, and youth. What did Caius know of the smell of that striped leather ball Vanya had been so fond of? Had Caius kissed his mother's hand like that, and did the silk of her dress rustle so for Caius? Had he rioted like that at school when the pastry was bad? Had Caius been in love like that? Could Caius preside at a session as he did? "Caius really was mortal, and it was right for him to die; but for me, little Vanya, Ivan Ilych, with all my thoughts and emotions, it's altogether a different matter. It cannot be that I ought to die. That would be too terrible."

Such was his feeling.

"If I had to die like Caius, I should have known it was so. An inner voice would have told me so, but there was nothing of the sort in me and I and all my friends felt that our case was quite different from that of Caius. And now here it is!" he said to himself. "It can't be. It's impossible! But here it is. How is this? How is one to understand it?"

He could not understand it, and tried to drive this false, incorrect, morbid thought away and to replace it by other proper and healthy thoughts. But that thought, and not the thought only but the reality itself, seemed to come and comfort him.

And to replace that thought he called up a succession of others, hoping to find in them some support. He tried to get back into the former current of thoughts that had once screened the thought of death from him. But strange to say, all that had formerly shut off, hidden, and destroyed, his conscious-ness of death, no longer had that effect. Ivan Ilych now spent most of his time in attempting to reestablish that old current. He would say to himself: "I will take up my duties again—after all I used to live by them." And banishing all doubts he would go to the law courts, enter into conversation with his col-leagues, and sit carelessly as was his wont, scanning the crowd with a thoughtful look and leaning both his emaciated arms on the arms of his oak chair; bending over as usual to a colleague and drawing his papers nearer he would interchange whispers with him, and then suddenly raising his eyes and sitting erect would pronounce certain words and open the proceedings. But suddenly in the midst of those proceedings the pain in his side, regard-less of the stage the proceedings had reached, would begin its own gnawing work. Ivan Ilych would turn his attention to it and try to drive the thought of it away, but without success. *It* would come and stand before him and look at him, and he would be petrified and the light would die out of his eyes, and he would again begin asking himself whether *It* alone was true. And his colleagues and subordinates would see with surprise and distress that he, the brilliant and subtle judge, was becoming confused and making mistakes. He would shake himself, try to pull himself together, manage somehow to bring the sitting to a close, and return home with the sorrowful consciousness that his judicial labours could not as formerly hide from him what he wanted them to hide, and could not deliver him from *It*. And what was worst of all was that *It* drew his attention to itself not in order to make him take some action but only that he should look at *It*, look it straight in the face: look at it and without doing anything, suffer inexpressibly.

And to save himself from this condition Ivan Ilych looked for consolations—new screens—and new screens were found and for a while seemed to save him, but then they immediately fell to pieces or rather became transparent as if *It* penetrated them and nothing could veil *It*.

In these latter days he would go into the drawing-room he had arranged—that drawing-room where he had fallen and for the sake of which (how bitterly ridiculous it seemed) he had sacrificed his life—for he knew that his illness originated with that knock. He would enter and see that something had scratched the polished table. He would look for the cause of this and find that it was the bronze ornamentation of an album, that had got bent. He would take up the expensive album which he had lovingly arranged, and feel vexed with his daughter and her friends for their untidiness—for the album was torn here and there and some of the photographs turned upside down. He would put it carefully in order and bend the ornamentation back into position. Then it would occur to him to place all those things in another corner of the room, near the plants. He would call the footman, but his daughter or wife would come to help him. They would not agree, and his wife would contradict him, and he would dispute and grow angry. But that was all right, for then he did not think about *It. It* was invisible.

But then, when he was moving something himself, his wife would say: "Let the servants do it. You will hurt yourself again." And suddenly *It* would flash through the screen and he would see it. It was just a flash, and he hoped it would disappear, but he would involuntarily pay attention to his side. "It sits there as before, gnawing just the same!" And he could no longer forget *It,* but could distinctly see it looking at him from behind the flowers. "What is it all for?"

"It really is so! I lost my life over that curtain as I might have done when storming a fort. Is that possible? How terrible and how stupid. It can't be true! It can't, but it is."

He would go to his study, lie down, and again be alone with *It:* face to face with *It.* And nothing could be done with *It* except to look at it and shudder.

VII

185   How it happened it is impossible to say because it came about step by step, unnoticed, but in the third month of Ivan Ilych's illness, his wife, his daughter, his son, his acquaintances, the doctors, the servants, and above all he himself, were aware that the whole interest he had for other people was whether he would soon vacate his place, and at last release the living from the discomfort caused by his presence and be himself released from his sufferings.

He slept less and less. He was given opium and hypodermic injections of morphine, but this did not relieve him. The dull depression he experienced in a somnolent condition at first gave him a little relief, but only as something new, afterwards it became as distressing as the pain itself or even more so.

Special foods were prepared for him by the doctors' orders, but all those foods became increasingly distasteful and disgusting to him.

For his excretions also special arrangements had to be made, and this was a torment to him every time—a torment from the uncleanliness, the unseemliness, and the smell, and from knowing that another person had to take part in it.

But just through the most unpleasant matter, Ivan Ilych obtained comfort. Gerasim, the butler's young assistant, always came in to carry the things out. Gerasim was a clean, fresh peasant lad, grown stout on town food and always cheerful and bright. At first the sight of him, in his clean Russian peasant costume, engaged in that disgusting task embarrassed Ivan Ilych.

190   Once when he got up from the commode too weak to draw up his trousers, he dropped into a soft armchair and looked with horror at his bare, enfeebled thighs with the muscles so sharply marked on them.

Gerasim with a firm light tread, his heavy boots emitting a pleasant smell of tar and fresh winter air, came in wearing a clean Hessian apron, the sleeves of his print shirt tucked up over his strong bare young arms; and refraining from looking at his sick master out of consideration for his feelings, and restraining the joy of life that beamed from his face, he went up to the commode.

"Gerasim!" said Ivan Ilych in a weak voice.

Gerasim started, evidently afraid he might have committed some blunder, and with a rapid movement turned his fresh, kind, simple young face which just showed the first downy signs of a beard.

"Yes, sir?"

195   "That must be very unpleasant for you. You must forgive me. I am helpless."

"Oh, why, sir," and Gerasim's eyes beamed and he showed his glistening white teeth, "what's a little trouble? It's a case of illness with you, sir."

And his deft strong hands did their accustomed task, and he went out of the room stepping lightly. Five minutes later he as lightly returned.

Ivan Ilych was still sitting in the same position in the armchair.

"Gerasim," he said when the latter had replaced the freshly-washed utensil. "Please come here and help me." Gerasim went up to him. "Lift me up. It is hard for me to get up, and I have sent Dmitri away."

200   Gerasim went up to him, grasped his master with his strong arms deftly but gently, in the same way that he stepped—lifted him, supported him with one hand, and with the other drew up his trousers and would have set him down again, but Ivan Ilych asked to be led to the sofa. Gerasim, without an effort and without apparent pressure, led him, almost lifting him, to the sofa and placed him on it.

"Thank you. How easily and well you do it all!"

Gerasim smiled again and turned to leave the room. But Ivan Ilych felt his presence such a comfort that he did not want to let him go.

"One thing more, please move up that chair. No, the other one—under my feet. It is easier for me when my feet are raised."

Gerasim brought the chair, set it down gently in place, and raised Ivan Ilych's legs on to it. It seemed to Ivan Ilych that he felt better while Gerasim was holding up his legs.

205   "It's better when my legs are higher," he said. "Place that cushion under them."

Gerasim did so. He again lifted his legs and placed them, and again Ivan Ilych felt better while Gerasim held his legs. When he set them down Ivan Ilych fancied he felt worse.

"Gerasim," he said. "Are you busy now?"

"Not at all, sir," said Gerasim, who had learnt from the townfolk how to speak to gentlefolk.

"What have you still to do?"

210   "What have I to do? I've done everything except chopping the logs for tomorrow."

"Then hold my legs up a bit higher, can you?"

"Of course I can. Why not?" And Gerasim raised his master's legs higher and Ivan Ilych thought that in that position he did not feel any pain at all.

"And how about the logs?"

"Don't trouble about that, sir. There's plenty of time."

215   Ivan Ilych told Gerasim to sit down and hold his legs, and began to talk to him. And strange to say it seemed to him that he felt better while Gerasim held his legs up.

After that Ivan Ilych would sometimes call Gerasim and get him to hold his legs on his shoulders, and he liked talking to him. Gerasim did it all easily, willingly, simply, and with a good nature that touched Ivan Ilych. Health, strength, and vitality in other people were offensive to him, but Gerasim's strength and vitality did not mortify but soothed him.

What tormented Ivan Ilych most was the deception, the lie, which for some reason they all accepted, that he was not dying but was simply ill, and that he only need keep quiet and undergo a treatment and then something very good would result. He however knew that do what they would nothing would come of it, only still more agonizing suffering and death. This deception tortured him—their not wishing to admit what they all knew and what he knew, but wanting to lie to him concerning his terrible condition, and wishing and forcing him to participate in that lie. Those lies—lies enacted over him on the eve of his death and destined to degrade this awful, solemn act to the level of their visitings, their curtains, their sturgeon for dinner—were a terrible agony for Ivan Ilych. And strangely enough, many times when they were going through their antics over him he had been within a hair-breath of calling out to them: "Stop lying! You know and I know that I am dying. Then at least stop lying about it!" But he had never had the spirit to do it. The awful, terrible act of his dying was, as he could see, reduced by those about him to the level of a casual, unpleasant, and almost indecorous incident (as if someone entered a drawing room diffusing an unpleasant odour) and this was done by that very decorum which he had served all his life long. He saw that no one felt for him, because no one even wished to grasp his position. Only Gerasim recognized it and pitied him. And so Ivan Ilych felt at ease only with him. He felt comforted when Gerasim supported his legs (sometimes all night long) and refused to go to bed, saying: "Don't you worry, Ivan Ilych. I'll get sleep enough later on," or when he suddenly became familiar and exclaimed: "If you weren't sick it would be another matter, but as it is, why should I grudge a little trouble?" Gerasim alone did not lie; everything showed that he alone understood the facts of the case and did not consider it necessary to disguise them, but simply felt sorry for his emaciated and enfeebled master. Once when Ivan Ilych was sending him away he even said straight out: "We shall all of us die, so why should I grudge a little trouble?"—expressing the fact that he did not think his work burdensome, because he was doing it for a dying man and hoped someone would do the same for him when his time came.

Apart from this lying, or because of it, what most tormented Ivan Ilych was that no one pitied him as he wished to be pitied. At certain moments after prolonged suffering he wished most of all (though he would have been ashamed to confess it) for someone to pity him as a sick child is pitied. He longed to be petted and comforted. He knew he was an important functionary, that he had a beard turning grey, and that therefore what he longed for was impossible, but still he longed for it. And in Gerasim's attitude towards him there was something akin to what he wished for, and so that attitude comforted him. Ivan Ilych wanted to weep, wanted to be petted and cried over, and then his colleague Shebek would come, and instead of weeping and being petted, Ivan Ilych would assume a serious, severe, and profound air, and by force of habit would express his opinion on a decision of the Court of Cassation[18] and would stubbornly insist on that view. The falsity around him and within him did more than anything else to poison his last days.

VIII

It was morning. He knew it was morning because Gerasim had gone, and Peter the footman had come and put out the candles, drawn back one of the curtains, and begun quietly to tidy up. Whether it was morning or evening, Friday or Sunday, made no difference, it was all just the same: the gnawing, unmitigated, agonizing pain, never ceasing for an instant, the consciousness of life inexorably waning but not yet extinguished, the approach of that ever dreadful and hateful Death which was the only reality, and always the same falsity. What were days, weeks, hours, in such a case?

220   "Will you have some tea, sir?"

"He wants things to be regular, and wishes the gentlefolk to drink tea in the morning," thought Ivan Ilych, and only said "No."

"Wouldn't you like to move onto the sofa, sir?"

"He wants to tidy up the room, and I'm in the way. I am uncleanliness and disorder," he thought, and said only:

"No, leave me alone."

225   The man went on bustling about. Ivan Ilych stretched out his hand. Peter came up, ready to help.

"What is it, sir?"

"My watch."

Peter took the watch which was close at hand and gave it to his master.

"Half-past eight. Are they up?"

230   "No sir, except Vladimir Ivanich" (the son) "who has gone to school. Praskovya Fëdorovna ordered me to wake her if you asked for her. Shall I do so?"

"No, there's no need to." "Perhaps I'd better have some tea," he thought, and added aloud: "Yes, bring me some tea."

Peter went to the door, but Ivan Ilych dreaded being left alone. "How can I keep him here? Oh yes, my medicine." "Peter, give me my medicine." "Why not? Perhaps it may still do me some good." He took a spoonful and swallowed it. "No, it won't help. It's all tomfoolery, all deception," he decided as soon as he became aware of the familiar, sickly, hopeless taste. "No, I can't believe in it any longer. But the pain, why this pain? If it would only cease just for a moment!" And he moaned. Peter turned towards him. "It's all right. Go and fetch me some tea."

[18] The highest court of appeals

Peter went out. Left alone Ivan Ilych groaned not so much with pain, terrible though that was, as from mental anguish. Always and for ever the same, always these endless days and nights. If only it would come quicker! If only *what* would come quicker? Death, darkness? . . . No, no! Anything rather than death!

When Peter returned with the tea on a tray, Ivan Ilych stared at him for a time in perplexity, not realizing who and what he was. Peter was disconcerted by that look and his embarrassment brought Ivan Ilych to himself.

235   "Oh, tea! All right, put it down. Only help me to wash and put on a clean shirt."

And Ivan Ilych began to wash. With pauses for rest, he washed his hands and then his face, cleaned his teeth, brushed his hair, and looked in the glass. He was terrified by what he saw, especially by the limp way in which his hair clung to his pallid forehead.

While his shirt was being changed he knew that he would be still more frightened at the sight of his body, so he avoided looking at it. Finally he was ready. He drew on a dressing-gown, wrapped himself in a plaid, and sat down in the armchair to take his tea. For a moment he felt refreshed, but as soon as he began to drink the tea he was again aware of the same taste, and the pain also returned. He finished it with an effort, and then lay down stretching out his legs, and dismissed Peter.

Always the same. Now a spark of hope flashes up, then a sea of despair rages, and always pain; always pain, always despair, and always the same. When alone he had a dreadful and distressing desire to call someone, but he knew beforehand that with others present it would be still worse. "Another dose of morphine—to lose consciousness. I will tell him, the doctor, that he must think of something else. It's impossible, impossible, to go on like this."

An hour and another pass like that. But now there is a ring at the door bell. Perhaps it's the doctor? It is. He comes in fresh, hearty, plump, and cheerful, with that look on his face that seems to say: "There now, you're in a panic about something, but we'll arrange it all for you directly!" The doctor knows this expression is out of place here, but he has put it on once for all and can't take it off—like a man who has put on a frock-coat in the morning to pay a round of calls.

240   The doctor rubs his hands vigorously and reassuringly.

"Brr! How cold it is! There's such a sharp frost; just let me warm myself!" he says, as if it were only a matter of waiting till he was warm, and then he would put everything right.

"Well now, how are you?"

Ivan Ilych feels that the doctor would like to say: "Well, how are your affairs?" but that even he feels that this would not do, and says instead: "What sort of a night have you had?"

Ivan Ilych looks at him as much as to say: "Are you really never ashamed of lying?" But the doctor does not wish to understand this question, and Ivan Ilych says: "Just as terrible as ever. The pain never leaves me and never subsides. If only something . . ."

245   "Yes, you sick people are always like that . . . There, now I think I am warm enough. Even Praskovya Fëdorovna, who is so particular, could find no fault with my temperature. Well, now I can say good-morning," and the doctor presses his patient's hand.

Then, dropping his former playfulness, he begins with a most serious face to examine the patient, feeling his pulse and taking his temperature, and then begins the sounding and auscultation.

Ivan Ilych knows quite well and definitely that all this is nonsense and pure deception, but when the doctor, getting down on his knee, leans over him, putting the ear first higher then lower, and performs various gymnastic movements over him with a significant expression on his face, Ivan Ilych submits to it all as he used to submit to the speeches of the lawyers, though he knew very well that they were all lying and why they were lying.

The doctor, kneeling on the sofa, is still sounding him when Praskovya Fëdorovna's silk dress rustles at the door and she is heard scolding Peter for not having let her know of the doctor's arrival.

She comes in, kisses her husband, and at once proceeds to prove that she has been up a long time already, and only owing to a misunderstanding failed to be there when the doctor arrived.

250   Ivan Ilych looks at her, scans her all over, sets against her the whiteness and plumpness and cleanness of her hands and neck, the gloss of her hair, and the sparkle of her vivacious eyes. He hates her with his whole soul. And the thrill of hatred he feels for her makes him suffer from her touch.

Her attitude towards him and his disease is still the same. Just as the doctor had adopted a certain relation to his patient which he could not abandon, so had she formed one towards him—that he was not doing something he ought to do and was himself to blame, and that she reproached him lovingly for this—and she could not now change that attitude.

"You see he doesn't listen to me and doesn't take his medicine at the proper time. And above all he lies in a position that is no doubt bad for him—with his legs up."

She described how he made Gerasim hold his legs up.

The doctor smiled with a contemptuous affability that said: "What's to be done? These sick people do have foolish fancies of that kind, but we must forgive them."

255   When the examination was over the doctor looked at his watch, and then Praskovya Fëdorovna announced to Ivan Ilych that it was of course as he pleased, but she had sent today for a celebrated specialist who would examine him and have a consultation with Michael Danilovich (their regular doctor).

"Please don't raise any objections. I am doing this for my own sake," she said ironically, letting it be felt that she was doing it all for his sake and only said this to leave him no right to refuse. He remained silent, knitting his brows. He felt that he was so surrounded and involved in a mesh of falsity that it was hard to unravel anything.

Everything she did for him was entirely for her own sake, and she told him she was doing for herself what she actually was doing for herself, as if that was so incredible that he must understand the opposite.

At half-past eleven the celebrated specialist arrived. Again the sounding began and the significant conversations in his presence and in another room, about the kidneys and the appendix, and the questions and answers, with such an air of importance that again, instead of the real question of life and death which now alone confronted him, the question arose of the kidney and appendix which were not behaving as they ought to and would now be attacked by Michael Danilovich and the specialist and forced to mend their ways.

The celebrated specialist took leave of him with a serious though not hopeless look, and in reply to the timid question Ivan Ilych, with eyes glistening with fear and hope, put to him as to whether there was a chance of recovery, said that he could not vouch for it but there was a possibility. The look of hope with which Ivan Ilych watched the doctor out was so pathetic that Praskovya Fëdorovna, seeing it, even wept as she left the room to hand the doctor his fee.

260   The gleam of hope kindled by the doctor's encouragement did not last long. The same room, the same pictures, curtains, wall-paper, medicine bottles, were all there, and the same aching suffering body, and Ivan Ilych began to moan. They gave him a subcutaneous injection and he sank into oblivion.

It was twilight when he came to. They brought him his dinner and he swallowed some beef tea with difficulty, and then everything was the same again and night was coming on.

After dinner, at seven o'clock, Praskovya Fëdorovna came into the room in evening dress, her full bosom pushed up by her corset, and with traces of powder on her face. She had reminded him in the morning that they were going to the theatre. Sarah Bernhardt[19] was visiting the town and they had a box, which he had insisted on their taking. Now he had forgotten about it and her toilet offended him, but he concealed his vexation when he remembered that he had himself insisted on their securing a box and going because it would be an instructive and aesthetic pleasure for the children.

Praskovya Fëdorovna came in, self-satisfied but yet with a rather guilty air. She sat down and asked how he was, but, as he saw, only for the sake of asking and not in order to learn about it, knowing that there was nothing to learn— and then went on to what she really wanted to say: that she would not on any account have gone but that the box had been taken and Helen and their daughter were going, as well as Petrishchev (the examining magistrate, their daughter's financé) and that it was out of the question to let them go alone; but that she would have much preferred to sit with him for a while; and he must be sure to follow the doctor's orders while she was away.

"Oh, and Fëdor Petrovich" (the financé) "would like to come in. May he? And Lisa?"

265   "All right."

Their daughter came in in full evening dress, her fresh young flesh exposed (making a show of that very flesh which in his own case caused so much suffering), strong, healthy, evidently in love, and impatient with illness, suffering, and death, because they interfered with her happiness.

[19] The celebrated French actress (1844–1923), who performed throughout the world, received great acclaim in St. Petersburg in 1882.

Fëdor Petrovich came in too, in evening dress, his hair curled *ä la Capoul,*[20] a tight stiff collar round his long sinewy neck, an enormous white shirt-front and narrow black trousers tightly stretched over his strong thighs. He had one white glove tightly drawn on, and was holding his opera hat in his hand.

Following him the schoolboy crept in unnoticed, in a new uniform, poor little fellow, and wearing gloves. Terribly dark shadows showed under his eyes, the meaning of which Ivan Ilych knew well.

His son had always seemed pathetic to him, and now it was dreadful to see the boy's frightened look of pity. It seemed to Ivan Ilych that Vasya was the only one besides Gerasim who understood and pitied him.

270   They all sat down and again asked how he was. A silence followed. Lisa asked her mother about the opera-glasses, and there was an altercation between mother and daughter as to who had taken them and where they had been put. This occasioned some unpleasantness.

Fëdor Petrovich inquired of Ivan Ilych whether he had ever seen Sarah Bernhardt. Ivan Ilych did not at first catch the question, but then replied: "No, have you seen her before?"

"Yes, in *Adrienne Lecouvreur.*"[21]

Praskovya Fëdorovna mentioned some rôles in which Sarah Bernhardt was particularly good. Her daughter disagreed. Conversation sprang up as to the elegance and realism of her acting—the sort of conversation that is always repeated and is always the same.

In the midst of the conversation Fëdor Petrovich glanced at Ivan Ilych and became silent. Ivan Ilych was staring with glittering eyes straight before him, evidently indignant with them. This had to be rectified, but it was impossible to do so. The silence had to be broken, but for a time no one dared to break it and they all became afraid that the conventional deception would suddenly become obvious and the truth become plain to all. Lisa was the first to pluck up courage and break that silence, but by trying to hide what everybody was feeling, she betrayed it.

275   "Well, if we are going it's time to start," she said, looking at her watch, a present from her father, and with a faint and significant smile at Fëdor Petrovich relating to something known only to them. She got up with a rustle of her dress.

They all rose, said good-night, and went away.

When they had gone it seemed to Ivan Ilych that he felt better; the falsity had gone with them. But the pain remained—that same pain and the same fear that made everything monotonously alike, nothing harder and nothing easier. Everything was worse.

Again minute followed minute and hour followed hour. Everything remained the same and there was no cessation. And the inevitable end of it all became more and more terrible.

"Yes, send Gerasim here," he replied to a question Peter asked.

---

[20] Hairstyle named for French operatic tenor Victor Capoul (1839–1924)   [21] By French playwrights Eugène Scribe (1791–1861) and Ernest Legouvé (1807–1903)

IX

His wife returned late at night. She came in on tiptoe, but he heard her, opened his eyes, and made haste to close them again. She wished to send Gerasim away and sit with him herself, but he opened his eyes and said: "No, go away."

"Are you in great pain?"

"Always the same."

"Take some opium."

He agreed and took some. She went away.

Till about three in the morning he was in a state of stupefied misery. It seemed to him that he and his pain were being thrust into a narrow, deep black sack, but though they were pushed further and further in they could not be pushed to the bottom. And this, terrible enough in itself, was accompanied by suffering. He struggled but yet cooperated. And suddenly he broke through, fell, and regained consciousness. Gerasim was sitting at the foot of the bed dozing quietly, while he himself lay with his emaciated stockinged legs resting on Gerasim's shoulders; the same shaded candle was there and the same unceasing pain.

"Go away, Gerasim," he whispered.

"It's all right, sir. I'll stay a while."

"No, Go away."

He removed his legs from Gerasim's shoulders, turned sideways onto his arm, and felt sorry for himself. He only waited till Gerasim had gone into the next room and then restrained himself no longer but wept like a child. He wept on account of his helplessness, his terrible loneliness, the cruelty of man, the cruelty of God, and the absence of God.

"Why hast Thou done all this? Why hast Thou brought me here? Why, why dost Thou torment me so terribly?"

He did not expect an answer and yet wept because there was no answer and could be none. The pain again grew more acute, but he did not stir and did not call. He said to himself: "Go on! Strike me! But what is it for? What have I done to Thee? What is it for?"

Then he grew quiet and not only ceased weeping but even held his breath and became all attention. It was as though he were listening not to an audible voice but to the voice of his soul, to the current of thoughts arising within him.

"What is it you want?" was the first clear conception capable of expression in words, that he heard.

"What do you want? What do you want?" he repeated to himself.

"What do I want? To live and not to suffer," he answered.

And again he listened with such concentrated attention that even his pain did not distract him.

"To live? How?" asked the inner voice.

"Why, to live as I used to—well and pleasantly."

"As you lived before, well and pleasantly?" the voice repeated.

And in imagination he began to recall the best moments of his pleasant life. But strange to say none of those best moments of his pleasant life now seemed at all what they had then seemed—none of them except the first recollections of childhood. There, in childhood, there had been something really pleasant with which it would be possible to live if it could return. But the child who had experienced that happiness existed no longer, it was like a reminiscence of somebody else.

As soon as the period began which had produced the present Ivan Ilych, all that had then seemed joys now melted before his sight and turned into something trivial and often nasty.

And the further he departed from childhood and the nearer he came to the present the more worthless and doubtful were the joys. This began with the School of Law. A little that was really good was still found there—there was light-heartedness, friendship, and hope. But in the upper classes there had already been fewer of such good moments. Then during the first years of his official career, when he was in the service of the Governor, some pleasant moments again occurred: they were the memories of love for a woman. Then all became confused and there was still less of what was good; later on again there was still less that was good, and the further he went the less there was. His marriage, a mere accident, then the disenchantment that followed it, his wife's bad breath and the sensuality and hypocrisy: then that deadly official life and those preoccupations about money, a year of it, and two, and ten, and twenty, and always the same thing. And the longer it lasted the more deadly it became. "It is as if I had been going downhill while I imagined I was going up. And that is really what it was. I was going up in public opinion, but to the same extent life was ebbing away from me. And now it is all done and there is only death."

"Then what does it mean? Why? It can't be that life is so senseless and horrible. But if it really has been so horrible and senseless, why must I die and die in agony? There is something wrong!"

"Maybe I did not live as I ought to have done," it suddenly occurred to him. "But how could that be, when I did everything properly?" he replied, and immediately dismissed from his mind this, the sole solution of all the riddles of life and death, as something quite impossible.

305   "Then what do you want now? To live? Live how? Live as you lived in the law courts when the usher proclaimed 'The judge is coming!' The judge is coming, the judge!" he repeated to himself. "Here he is, the judge. But I am not guilty!" he exclaimed angrily. "What is it for?" And he ceased crying, but turning his face to the wall continued to ponder on the same question: Why, and for what purpose, is there all this horror? But however much he pondered he found no answer. And whenever the thought occurred to him, as it often did, that it all resulted from his not having lived as he ought to have done, he at once recalled the correctness of his whole life and dismissed so strange an idea.

X

Another fortnight passed. Ivan Ilych now no longer left his sofa. He would not lie in bed but lay on the sofa, facing the wall nearly all the time. He suffered ever the same unceasing agonies and in his loneliness pondered always on the same insoluble question: "What is this? Can it be that it is death?" And the inner voice answered: "Yes, it is Death."

"Why these sufferings?" And the voice answered, "For no reason—they just are so." Beyond and besides this there was nothing.

From the very beginning of his illness, ever since he had first been to see the doctor, Ivan Ilych's life had been divided between two contrary and alternating moods: now it was despair and the expectation of this uncomprehended and terrible death, and now hope and an intently interested observation of the functioning of his organs. Now before his eyes there was only a kidney or an intestine that temporarily evaded its duty, and now only that incomprehensible and dreadful death from which it was impossible to escape.

These two states of mind had alternated from the very beginning of his illness, but the further it progressed the more doubtful and fantastic became the conception of the kidney, and the more real the sense of impending death.

310   He had but to call to mind what he had been three months before and what he was now, to call to mind with what regularity he had been going downhill, for every possibility of hope to be shattered.

Latterly during that loneliness in which he found himself as he lay facing the back of the sofa, a loneliness in the midst of a populous town and surrounded by numerous acquaintances and relations but that yet could not have been more complete anywhere—either at the bottom of the sea or under the earth—during that terrible loneliness Ivan Ilych had lived only in memories of the past. Pictures of his past rose before him one after another. They always began with what was nearest in time and then went back to what was the most remote—to his childhood—and rested there. If he thought of the stewed prunes that had been offered him that day, his mind went back to the raw shrivelled French plums of his childhood, their peculiar flavour and the flow of saliva when he sucked their stones, and along with the memory of that taste came a whole series of memories of those days: his nurse, his brother, and their toys. "No, I mustn't think of that . . . It is too painful," Ivan Ilych said to himself, and brought himself back to the present—to the button on the back of the sofa and the creases in its morocco. "Morocco is expensive, but it does not wear well: there had been a quarrel about it. It was a different kind of quarrel and a different kind of morocco that time when we tore father's portfolio and were punished, and Mamma brought us some tarts . . ." And again his thoughts dwelt on his childhood, and again it was painful and he tried to banish them and fix his mind on something else.

Then again together with that chain of memories another series passed through his mind—of how his illness had progressed and grown worse. There also the further back he looked the more life there had been. There had been more of what was good life and more of life itself. The two merged together. "Just as the pain went on getting worse and worse, so my life grew worse and worse," he thought. "There is one bright spot there at the back, at the beginning of life, and afterwards all becomes blacker and blacker and proceeds more and more rapidly—in inverse ratio to the square of the distance from death," thought Ivan Ilych. And the example of a stone falling downwards with increasing velocity entered his mind. Life, a series of increasing sufferings, flies further and further towards its end—the most terrible suffering. "I am fly-ing . . . ." He shuddered, shifted himself, and tried to resist, but was already aware that resistance was impossible, and again with eyes weary of gazing but unable to cease seeing what was before them, he stared at the back of the sofa and waited—awaiting that dreadful fall and shock and destruction.

"Resistance is impossible!" he said to himself. "If I could only understand what it is all for! But that too is impossible. An explanation would be possible if it could be said that I have not lived as I ought to. But it is impossible to say that," and he remembered all the legality, correctitude, and propriety of his life. "That at any rate can certainly not be admitted," he thought, and his lips smiled ironically as if someone could see that smile and be taken in by it. "There is no explanation! Agony, death . . . What for?"

XI

Another two weeks went by in this way and during that fortnight an event occurred that Ivan Ilych and his wife had desired. Petrishchev formally pro-posed. It happened in the evening. The next day Praskovya Fëdorovna came into her husband's room considering how best to inform him of it, but that very night there had been a fresh change for the worse in his condition. She found him still lying on the sofa but in a different position. He lay on his back, groaning and staring fixedly in front of him.

315   She began to remind him of his medicines, but he turned his eyes towards her with such a look that she did not finish what she was saying; so great an animosity, to her in particular, did that look express.

"For Christ's sake let me die in peace!" he said.

She would have gone away, but just then their daughter came in and went up to say good morning. He looked at her as he had done at his wife, and in reply to her inquiry about his health said dryly that he would soon free them all of himself. They were both silent and after sitting with him for a while went away.

"Is it our fault?" Lisa said to her mother. "It's as if we were to blame! I am sorry for papa, but why should we be tortured?"

The doctor came at his usual time. Ivan Ilych answered "Yes" and "No," never taking his angry eyes from him, and at last said: "You know you can do nothing for me, so leave me alone."

320   "We can ease your sufferings."

The doctor went into the drawing-room and told Praskovya Fëdorovna that the case was very serious and that the only resource left was opium to allay her husband's sufferings, which must be terrible.

It was true, as the doctor said, that Ivan Ilych's physical sufferings were terrible, but worse than the physical sufferings were his mental sufferings, which were his chief torture.

His mental sufferings were due to the fact that that night, as he looked at Gerasim's sleepy, good-natured face with its prominent cheek-bones, the question suddenly occurred to him: "What if my whole life has really been wrong?"

It occurred to him that what had appeared perfectly impossible before, namely that he had not spent his life as he should have done, might after all be true. It occurred to him that his scarcely perceptible attempts to struggle against what was considered good by the most highly placed people, those scarcely noticeable impulses which he had immediately suppressed, might have been the real thing, and all the rest false. And his professional duties and the whole arrangement of his life and of his family, and all his social and official interests, might all have been false. He tried to defend all those things to himself and suddenly felt the weakness of what he was defending. There was nothing to defend.

325 "But if that is so," he said to himself, "and I am leaving this life with the consciousness that I have lost all that was given me and it is impossible to rectify it—what then?"

He lay on his back and began to pass his life in review in quite a new way. In the morning when he saw first his footman, then his wife, then his daughter, and then the doctor, their every word and movement confirmed to him the awful truth that had been revealed to him during the night. In them he saw himself—all that for which he had lived—and saw clearly that it was not real at all, but a terrible and huge deception which had hidden both life and death. This consciousness intensified his physical suffering tenfold. He groaned and tossed about, and pulled at his clothing which choked and stifled him. And he hated them on that account.

He was given a large dose of opium and became unconscious, but at noon his sufferings began again. He drove everybody away and tossed from side to side.

His wife came to him and said:

"Jean, my dear, do this for me. It can't do any harm and often helps. Healthy people often do it."

330 He opened his eyes wide.

"What? Take communion? Why? It's unnecessary! However . . . ." She began to cry.

"Yes, do, my dear. I'll send for our priest. He is such a nice man."

"All right. Very well," he muttered.

When the priest came and heard his confession, Ivan Ilych was softened and seemed to feel a relief from his doubts and consequently from his sufferings, and for a moment there came a ray of hope. He again began to think of the vermiform appendix and the possibility of correcting it. He received the sacrament with tears in his eyes.

335 When they laid him down again afterwards he felt a moment's ease, and the hope that he might live awoke in him again. He began to think of the operation that had been suggested to him. "To live! I want to live!" he said to himself.

His wife came to congratulate him after his communion, and when uttering the usual conventional words she added:

"You feel better, don't you?"

Without looking at her he said "Yes."

Her dress, her figure, the expression of her face, the tone of her voice, all revealed the same thing. "This is wrong, it is not as it should be. All you have lived for and still live for is falsehood and deception, hiding life and death from you." And as soon as he admitted that thought, his hatred and his agonizing physical suffering again sprang up, and with that suffering a consciousness of the unavoidable, approaching end. And to this was added a new sensation of grinding shooting pain and a feeling of suffocation.

340 The expression of his face when he uttered that "yes" was dreadful. Having uttered it, he looked her straight in the eyes, turned on his face with a rapidity extraordinary in his weak state and shouted:

"Go away! Go away and leave me alone!"

XII

From that moment the screaming began that continued for three days, and was so terrible that one could not hear it through two closed doors without horror. At the moment he answered his wife he realized that he was lost, that there was no return, that the end had come, the very end, and his doubts were still unsolved and remained doubts.

"Oh! Oh! Oh!" he cried in various intonations. He had begun by screaming "I won't!" and continued screaming on the letter O.

For three whole days, during which time did not exist for him, he struggled in that black sack into which he was being thrust by an invisible resistless force. He struggled as a man condemned to death struggles in the hands of the executioner, knowing that he cannot save himself. And every moment he felt that despite all his efforts he was drawing nearer and nearer to what terrified him. He felt that his agony was due to his being thrust into that black hole and still more to his not being able to get right into it. He was hindered from getting into it by his conviction that his life had been a good one. That very justification of his life held him fast and prevented his moving forward, and it caused him most torment of all.

345 Suddenly some force struck him in the chest and side, making it still harder to breathe, and he fell through the hole and there at the bottom was a light. What had happened to him was like the sensation one sometimes experiences in a railway carriage when one thinks one is going backwards while one is really going forwards and suddenly becomes aware of the real direction.

"Yes, it was all not the right thing," he said to himself, "but that's no matter. It can be done. But what *is* the right thing?" he asked himself, and suddenly grew quiet.

This occurred at the end of the third day, two hours before his death. Just then his schoolboy son had crept softly in and gone up to the bedside. The dying man was still screaming and waving his arms. His hand fell on the boy's head, and the boy caught it, pressed it to his lips, and began to cry.

At that very moment Ivan Ilych fell through and caught sight of the light, and it was revealed to him that though his life had not been what it should have been, this could still be rectified. He asked himself, "What *is* the right thing?" and grew still, listening. Then he felt that someone was kissing his hand. He opened his eyes, looked at his son, and felt sorry for him. His wife came up to him and he glanced at her. She was gazing at him openmouthed, with undried tears on her nose and cheek and a despairing look on her face. He felt sorry for her too.

"Yes, I am making them wretched," he thought. "They are sorry, but it will be better for them when I die." He wished to say this but had not the strength to utter it. "Besides, why speak? I must act," he thought. With a look at his wife he indicated his son and said: "Take him away . . . sorry for him . . . sorry for you too . . ." He tried to add, "forgive me," but said "forgo" and waved his hand, knowing that He whose understanding mattered would understand.

350   And suddenly it grew clear to him that what had been oppressing him and would not leave him was dropping away at once from two sides, from ten sides, and from all sides. He was sorry for them, he must act so as not to hurt them and free himself from these sufferings. "How good and how simple!" he thought. "And the pain?" he asked himself. "What has become of it? Where are you, pain?"

He turned his attention to it.

"Yes, here it is. Well, what of it? Let the pain be."

"And death . . . where is it?"

He sought his former accustomed fear of death and did not find it. "Where is it? What death?" There was no fear because there was no death.

355   In place of death there was light.

"So that's what it is!" he suddenly exclaimed aloud. "What joy!"

To him all this happened in a single instant, and the meaning of that instant did not change. For those present his agony continued for another two hours. Something rattled in his throat, his emaciated body twitched, then the gasping and rattle became less and less frequent.

"It is finished!" said someone near him.

He heard these words and repeated them in his soul.

360   "Death is finished," he said to himself. "It is no more!"

He drew in a breath, stopped in the midst of a sigh, stretched out, and died.

Questions

1. Consider the point of view in the first section of this short novel. Is it necessary at the start? Why? When and why does the point of view change? Is it consistent thereafter?

2. Discuss the chronological sequence. We know from the start that Ivan Ilych will die. Why does Tolstoy remove the suspense? If we moved the first section to the end, how would it affect Tolstoy's theme?

3. From reading the story, what do you know of upper-middle-class life in Czarist Russia? How important is the setting of this story? Do you need to know as much as you know?

4. Ivan Ilych's house-fixing gets much attention. It seems to him that he dies because of it. Why does Tolstoy make it so important?

5. Do you feel the author present in this story, offering his own ideas and judgments, his morality? Discuss.

6. How many characters do you feel you know well in this story? Are the characters particularized? Could you imagine a reason that (to a given author and a given story) individual characters could seem important?

7. What is Tolstoy's theme? Do you agree with the commentator who compared this story to the book of Job, calling it "an exploration of the problem of undeserved suffering"? Is this story symbolic?

8. Find ironies in this story. Is the story generally ironic?

9. The name "Ivan Ilych" is like "John Smith" in the United States. Can a character's name help to characterize him? Does Ivan Ilych himself resemble any Americans you know, despite the obvious differences of time and place?

10. Is this story ever funny?

11. What is Gerasim's function in this story?

Stories for Further Reading

Chinua Achebe

Chinua Achebe (1930–   ) was born in Nigeria, where he continues to live, the most eminent of African fiction writers in English. His books begin with *Things Fall Apart* (1959) and continue with *Arrow of God* (1964), *A Man of the People* (1986), and *Anthills of the Savannah* (1987).

The Madman   (1973)

He was drawn to markets and straight roads. Not any tiny neighbourhood market where a handful of garrulous women might gather at sunset to gossip and buy ogili for the evening's soup, but a huge, engulfing bazaar beckoning people familiar and strange from far and near. And not any dusty, old footpath beginning in this village, and ending in that stream, but broad, black, mysterious highways without beginning or end. After much wandering he had discovered two such markets linked together by such a highway; and so ended his wandering. One market was Afo, the other Eke. The two days between them suited him very well: before setting out for Eke he had ample time to wind up his business properly at Afo. He passed the night there putting right again his hut after a day of defilement by two fat-bottomed market women who said it was their market-stall. At first he had put up a fight but the women had gone and brought their men-folk—four hefty beasts of the bush—to whip him out of the hut. After that he always avoided them, moving out on the morning of the market and back in at dusk to pass the night. Then in the morning he rounded off his affairs swiftly and set out on that long, beautiful boa-constrictor of a road to Eke in the distant town of Ogbu. He held his staff and cudgel at the ready in his right hand, and with the left he steadied the basket of his belongings on his head. He had got himself this cudgel lately to deal with little beasts on the way who threw stones at him and made fun of their mothers' nakedness, not his own.

He used to walk in the middle of the road, holding it in conversation. But one day the driver of a mammy-wagon and his mate came down on him shouting, pushing and slapping his face. They said their lorry very nearly ran over their mother, not him. After that he avoided those noisy lorries too, with the vagabonds inside them.

Having walked one day and one night he was now close to the Eke market-place. From every little side-road crowds of market people poured into the big highway to join the enormous flow to Eke. Then he saw some young ladies with water-pots on their heads coming towards him, unlike all the rest, away from the market. This surprised him. Then he saw two more water-pots rise out of a sloping footpath leading off his side of the highway. He felt thirsty then and stopped to think it over. Then he set down his basket on the roadside and turned into the sloping footpath. But first he begged his high-way not to be offended or continue the journey without him. "I'll get some for you too," he said coaxingly with a tender backward glance. "I know you are thirsty."

Nwibe was a man of high standing in Ogbu and was rising higher; a man of wealth and integrity. He had just given notice to all the ozo men of the town that he proposed to seek admission into their honoured hierarchy in the coming initiation season.

5   "Your proposal is excellent," said the men of title. "When we see we shall believe." Which was their dignified way of telling you to think it over once again and make sure you have the means to go through with it. For ozo is not a child's naming ceremony; and where is the man to hide his face who begins the ozo dance and then is foot-stuck to the arena? But in this instance the caution of the elders was no more than a formality for Nwibe was such a sensible man that no one could think of him beginning something he was not sure to finish.

On that Eke day Nwibe had risen early so as to visit his farm beyond the stream and do some light work before going to the market at midday to drink a horn or two of palm-wine with his peers and perhaps buy that bundle of roofing thatch for the repair of his wives' huts. As for his own hut he had a couple of years back settled it finally by changing his thatch-roof to zinc. Sooner or later he would do the same for his wives. He could have done Mgboye's hut right away but decided to wait until he could do the two together, or else Udenkwo would set the entire compound on fire. Udenkwo was the junior wife, by three years, but she never let that worry her. Happily

Mgboye was a woman of peace who rarely demanded the respect due to her from the other. She would suffer Udenkwo's provoking tongue sometimes for a whole day without offering a word in reply. And when she did reply at all her words were always few and her voice low.

That very morning Udenkwo had accused her of spite and all kinds of wickedness on account of a little dog.

"What has a little dog done to you?" she screamed loud enough for half the village to hear. "I ask you, Mgboye, what is the offence of a puppy this early in the day?"

"What your puppy did this early in the day," replied Mgboye, "is that he put his shit-mouth into my soup-pot."

10   "And then?"

"And then I smacked him."

"You smacked him! Why don't you cover your soup-pot? Is it easier to hit a dog than cover a pot? Is a small puppy to have more sense than a woman who leaves her soup-pot about . . . ?"

"Enough from you, Udenkwo."

"It is not enough, Mgboye, it is not enough. If that dog owes you any debt I want to know. Everything I have, even a little dog I bought to eat my infant's excrement keeps you awake at nights. You are a bad woman, Mgboye, you are a very bad woman!"

15   Nwibe had listened to all of this in silence in his hut. He knew from the vigour in Udenkwo's voice that she could go on like this till market-time. So he intervened, in his characteristic manner by calling out to his senior wife.

"Mgboye! Let me have peace this early morning!"

"Don't you hear all the abuses Udenkwo . . ."

"I hear nothing at all from Udenkwo and I want peace in my compound. If Udenkwo is crazy must everybody else go crazy with her? Is one crazy woman not enough in my compound so early in the day?"

"The great judge has spoken," sang Udenkwo in a sneering sing-song. "Thank you, great judge. Udenkwo is mad. Udenkwo is always mad, but those of you who are sane let . . ."

20   "Shut your mouth, shameless woman, or a wild beast will lick your eyes for you this morning. When will you learn to keep your badness within this compound instead of shouting it to all Ogbu to hear? I say shut your mouth!"

There was silence then except for Udenkwo's infant whose yelling had up till then been swallowed up by the larger noise of the adults.

"Don't cry, my father," sang Udenkwo to him. "They want to kill your dog, but our people say the man who decides to chase after a chicken, for him is the fall . . ."

By the middle of the morning Nwibe had done all the work he had to do on his farm and was on his way again to prepare for market. At the little stream he decided as he always did to wash off the sweat of work. So he put his cloth on a huge boulder by the men's bathing section and waded in. There was nobody else around because of the time of day and because it was market day. But from instinctive modesty he turned to face the forest away from the approaches.

The madman watched him for quite a while. Each time he bent down to carry water in cupped hands from the shallow stream to his head and body the madman smiled at his parted behind. And then remembered. This was the same hefty man who brought three others like him and whipped me out of my hut in the Afo market. He nodded to himself. And he remembered again: this was the same vagabond who descended on me from the lorry in the middle of my highway. He nodded once more. And then he remembered yet again: this was the same fellow who set his children to throw stones at me and make remarks about their mothers' buttocks, not mine. Then he laughed.

25   Nwibe turned sharply round and saw the naked man laughing, the deep grove of the stream amplifying his laughter. Then he stopped as suddenly as he had begun; the merriment vanished from his face.

"I have caught you naked," he said.

Nwibe ran a hand swiftly down his face to clear his eyes of water.

"I say I have caught you naked, with your thing dangling about."

"I can see you are hungry for a whipping," said Nwibe with quiet menace in his voice, for a madman is said to be easily scared away by the very mention of a whip. "Wait till I get up there. . . . What are you doing? Drop it at once . . . I say drop it!"

30   The madman had picked up Nwibe's cloth and wrapped it round his own waist. He looked down at himself and began to laugh again.

"I will kill you," screamed Nwibe as he splashed towards the bank, maddened by anger. "I will whip that madness out of you today!"

They ran all the way up the steep and rocky footpath hedged in by the shadowy green forest. A mist gathered and hung over Nwibe's vision as he ran, stumbled, fell, pulled himself up again and stumbled on, shouting and cursing. The other, despite his unaccustomed encumbrance steadily increased his lead, for he was spare and wiry, a thing made for speed. Furthermore, he did not waste his breath shouting and cursing; he just ran. Two girls going down to the stream saw a man running up the slope towards them pursued by a stark-naked madman. They threw down their pots and fled, screaming.

When Nwibe emerged into the full glare of the highway he could not see his cloth clearly any more and his chest was on the point of exploding from the fire and torment within. But he kept running. He was only vaguely aware of crowds of people on all sides and he appealed to them tearfully without stopping: "Hold the madman, he's got my cloth!" By this time the man with the cloth was practically lost among the much denser crowds far in front so that the link between him and the naked man was no longer clear.

Now Nwibe continually bumped against people's backs and then laid flat a frail old man struggling with a stubborn goat on a leash. "Stop the madman," he shouted hoarsely, his heart tearing to shreds, "he's got my cloth!" Everyone looked at him first in surprise and then less surprise because strange sights are common in a great market. Some of them even laughed.

35   "They've got his cloth he says."

"That's a new one I'm sure. He hardly looks mad yet. Doesn't he have people, I wonder."

"People are so careless these days. Why can't they keep proper watch over their sick relation, especially on the day of the market?"

Farther up the road on the very brink of the market-place two men from Nwibe's village recognized him and, throwing down the one his long basket of yams, the other his calabash of palm-wine held on a loop, gave desperate chase, to stop him setting foot irrevocably within the occult territory of the powers of the market. But it was in vain. When finally they caught him it was well inside the crowded square. Udenkwo in tears tore off her topcloth which they draped on him and led him home by the hand. He spoke just once about a madman who took his cloth in the stream.

"It is all right," said one of the men in the tone of a father to a crying child. They led and he followed blindly, his heavy chest heaving up and down in silent weeping. Many more people from his village, a few of his in-laws and one or two others from his mother's place had joined the grief-stricken party. One man whispered to another that it was the worst kind of madness, deep and tongue-tied.

40   "May it end ill for him who did this," prayed the other.

The first medicine man his relatives consulted refused to take him on, out of some kind of integrity.

"I could say yes to you and take your money," he said. "But that is not my way. My powers of cure are known throughout Olu and Igbo but never have I professed to bring back to life a man who has sipped the spirit-waters of ani-mmo. It is the same with a madman who of his own accord delivers himself to the divinities of the market-place. You should have kept better watch over him."

"Don't blame us too much," said Nwibe's relative. "When he left home that morning his senses were as complete as yours and mine now. Don't blame us too much."

"Yes, I know. It happens that way sometimes. And they are the ones that medicine will not reach. I know."

45   "Can you do nothing at all then, not even to untie his tongue?"

"Nothing can be done. They have already embraced him. It is like a man who runs away from the oppression of his fellows to the grove of an alusi and says to him: Take me, oh spirit, I am your osu. No man can touch him thereafter. He is free and yet no power can break his bondage. He is free of men but bonded to a god."

The second doctor was not as famous as the first and not so strict. He said the case was bad, very bad indeed, but no one folds his arms because the condition of his child is beyond hope. He must still grope around and do his best. His hearers nodded in eager agreement. And then he muttered into his own inward ear: If doctors were to send away every patient whose cure they were uncertain of, how many of them would eat one meal in a whole week from their practice?

Nwibe was cured of his madness. That humble practitioner who did the miracle became overnight the most celebrated mad-doctor of his generation.

They called him Sojourner to the Land of the Spirits. Even so it remains true that madness may indeed sometimes depart but never with all his clamorous train. Some of these always remain—the trailers of madness you might call them—to haunt the doorway of the eyes. For how could a man be the same again of whom witnesses from all the lands of Olu and Igbo have once reported that they saw today a fine, hefty man in his prime, stark naked, tearing through the crowds to answer the call of the market-place? Such a man is marked for ever.

Nwibe became a quiet, withdrawn man avoiding whenever he could the boisterous side of the life of his people. Two years later, before another initiation season, he made a new inquiry about joining the community of titled men in his town. Had they received him perhaps he might have become at least partially restored, but those ozo men, dignified and polite as ever, deftly steered the conversation away to other matters.

Toni Cade Bambara

Toni Cade Bambara (1939–   ) published her first book of short stories in 1972, under the title *Gorilla, My Love. The Sea Birds Are Still Alive* (1977) collected all her stories. Born and brought up in New York, she studied in Italy and France, and she has taught at Rutgers University and Duke University; she lived in Atlanta for some time, and now resides in Philadelphia. Her novel *The Salt Eaters* appeared in 1980.

The Lesson   (1960)

Back in the days when everyone was old and stupid or young and foolish and me and Sugar were the only ones just right, this lady moved on our block with nappy hair and proper speech and no makeup. And quite naturally we laughed at her, laughed the way we did at the junk man who went about his business like he was some big-time president and his sorry-ass horse his secretary. And we kinda hated her too, hated the way we did the winos who cluttered up our parks and pissed on our handball walls and stank up our hallways and stairs so you couldn't halfway play hide-and-seek without a goddamn gas mask. Miss Moore was her name. The only woman on the block with no first name. And she was black as hell, cept for her feet, which were fish-white and spooky. And she was always planning these boring-ass things for us to do, us being my cousin, mostly, who lived on the block cause we all moved North the same time and to the same apartment then spread out gradual to breathe. And our parents would yank our heads into some kinda shape and crisp up our clothes so we'd be presentable for travel with Miss Moore, who always looked like she was going to church, though she never did. Which is just one of the things the grownups talked about when they talked behind her back like a dog. But when she came calling with some sachet she'd sewed up or some gingerbread she'd made or some book, why then they'd all be too embarrassed to turn her down and we'd get handed over all spruced up. She'd been to college and said it was only right that she should take responsibility for the young ones' education, and she not even related by marriage or blood. So they'd go for it. Specially Aunt Gretchen. She was the main gofer in the family. You got some old dumb shit foolishness you want somebody to go for, you send for Aunt Gretchen. She been screwed into the go-along for so long, it's a blood-deep natural thing with her. Which is how she got saddled with me and Sugar and Junior in the first place while our mothers were in a la-de-da apartment up the block having a good ole time.

So this one day Miss Moore rounds us all up at the mailbox and it's pure-dee hot and she's knocking herself out about arithmetic. And school suppose to let up in summer I heard, but she don't never let up. And the starch in my pinafore scratching the shit outta me and I'm really hating this nappy-head bitch and her goddamn college degree. I'd much rather go to the pool or to the show where it's cool. So me and Sugar leaning on the mailbox being surly, which is a Miss Moore word. And Flyboy checking out what everybody brought for lunch. And Fat Butt already wasting his peanut-butter-and-jelly sandwich like the pig he is. And Junebug punchin on Q.T.'s arm for potato chips. And Rosie Giraffe shifting from one hip to the other waiting for some-body to step on her foot or ask her if she from Georgia so she can kick ass, preferably Mercedes'. And Miss Moore asking us do we know what money is, like we a bunch of retards. I mean real money, she say, like it's only poker chips or monopoly papers we lay on the grocer. So right away I'm tired of this and say so. And would much rather snatch Sugar and go to the Sunset and terrorize the West Indian kids and take their hair ribbons and their money too. And Miss Moore files that remark away for next week's lesson on brother-hood, I can tell. And finally I say we oughta get to the subway cause it's cooler and besides we might meet some cute boys. Sugar done swiped her mama's lipstick, so we ready.

So we heading down the street and she's boring us silly about what things cost and what our parents make and how much goes for rent and how money ain't divided up right in this country. And then she gets to the part about we all poor and live in the slums, which I don't feature. And I'm ready to speak on that, but she steps out in the street and hails two cabs just like that. Then she hustles half the crew in with her and hands me a five-dollar bill and tells me to calculate 10 percent tip for the driver. And we're off. Me and Sugar and Junebug and Flyboy hangin out the window and hollering to everybody, putting lipstick on each other cause Flyboy a faggot anyway, and making farts with our sweaty armpits. But I'm mostly trying to figure how to spend this money. But they all fascinated with the meter ticking and Junebug starts laying bets as to how much it'll read when Flyboy can't hold his breath no more. Then Sugar lays bets as to how much it'll be when we get there. So I'm stuck. Don't nobody want to go for my plan, which is to jump out at the next light and run off to the first bar-b-que we can find. Then the driver tells us to get the hell out cause we there already. And the

meter reads eighty-five cents. And I'm stalling to figure out the tip and
Sugar say give him a dime. And I decide he don't need it bad as I do, so later
for him. But then he tries to take off with Junebug foot still in the door so
we talk about his mama something ferocious. Then we check out that we on
Fifth Avenue and everybody dressed up in stockings. One lady in a fur coat,
hot as it is. White folks crazy.

"This is the place," Miss Moore say, presenting it to us in the voice she uses
at the museum. "Let's look in the windows before we go in."

5   "Can we steal?" Sugar asks very serious like she's getting the ground rules
squared away before she plays. "I beg your pardon," says Miss Moore, and we
fall out. So she leads us around the windows of the toy store and me and
Sugar screamin, "This is mine, that's mine, I gotta have that, that was made
for me, I was born for that," till Big Butt drowns us out.

"Hey, I'm goin to buy that there."

"That there? You don't even know what it is, stupid."

"I do so," he say punchin on Rosie Giraffe. "It's a microscope."

"Whatcha gonna do with a microscope, fool?"

10   "Look at things."

"Like what, Ronald?" asks Miss Moore. And Big Butt ain't got the first notion.
So here go Miss Moore gabbing about the thousands of bacteria in a drop of
water and the somethinorother in a speck of blood and the million and one
living things in the air around us is invisible to the naked eye. And what she say
that for? Junebug go to town on that "naked" and we rolling. Then Miss Moore
ask what it cost. So we all jam into the window smudgin it up and the price tag
say $300. So then she ask how long'd take for Big Butt and Junebug to save up
their allowances. "Too long," I say. "Yeh," adds Sugar, "outgrown it by that
time." And Miss Moore say no, you never outgrow learning instruments. "Why,
even medical students and interns and," blah, blah, blah. And we ready to
choke Big Butt for bringing it up in the first damn place.

"This here costs four hundred eighty dollars," say Rosie Giraffe. So we pile
up all over her to see what she pointin out. My eyes tell me it's a chunk of
glass cracked with something heavy, and different-color inks dripped into
the splits, then the whole thing put into a oven or something. But for $480 it
don't make sense.

"That's a paperweight made of semi-precious stones fused together under
tremendous pressure," she explains slowly, with her hands doing the mining
and all the factory work.

"So what's a paperweight?" asks Rosie Giraffe.

15   "To weigh paper with, dumbbell," say Flyboy, the wise man from the East.

"Not exactly," say Miss Moore, which is what she say when you warm or way
off too. "It's to weigh paper down so it won't scatter and make your desk
untidy." So right away me and Sugar curtsy to each other and then to Mercedes
who is more the tidy type.

"We don't keep paper on top of the desk in my class," say Junebug, figuring Miss Moore crazy or lyin one.

"At home, then," she say. "Don't you have a calendar and a pencil case
and a blotter and a letter-opener on your desk at home where you do your

homework?" And she know damn well what our homes look like cause she
nosys around in them every chance she gets.

"I don't even have a desk," say Junebug. "Do we?"

20   "No. And I don't get no homework neither," say Big Butt.

"And I don't even have a home," say Flyboy like he do at school to keep the
white folks off his back and sorry for him. Send this poor kid to camp posters,
is his specialty.

"I do," says Mercedes. "I have a box of stationery on my desk and a picture
of my cat. My godmother bought the stationery and the desk. There's a big
rose on each sheet and the envelopes smell like roses."

"Who wants to know about your smelly-ass stationery," say Rosie Giraffe
fore I can get my two cents in.

"It's important to have a work area all your own so that . . ."

25   "Will you look at this sailboat, please," say Flyboy, cuttin her off and pointin
to the thing like it was his. So once again we tumble all over each other to gaze
at this magnificent thing in the toy store which is just big enough to maybe sail
two kittens across the pond if you strap them to the posts tight. We all start
reciting the price tag like we in assembly. "Handcrafted sailboat of fiberglass
at one thousand one hundred ninety-five dollars."

"Unbelievable," I hear myself say and am really stunned. I read it again for
myself just in case the group recitation put me in a trance. Same thing. For
some reason this pisses me off. We look at Miss Moore and she looking at us,
waiting for I dunno what.

Who'd pay all that when you can buy a sailboat set for a quarter at Pop's, a
tube of glue for a dime, and a ball of string for eight cents? "It must have a motor
and a whole lot else besides," I say. "My sailboat cost me about fifty cents."

"But will it take water?" says Mercedes with her smart ass.

"Took mine to Alley Pond Park once," say Flyboy. "String broke. Lost it. Pity."

30   "Sailed mine in Central Park and it keeled over and sank. Had to ask my
father for another dollar."

"And you got the strap," laugh Big Butt. "The jerk didn't even have a string
on it. My old man wailed on his behind."

Little Q.T. was staring hard at the sailboat and you could see he wanted it
bad. But he too little and somebody'd just take it from him. So what the hell.
"This boat for kids, Miss Moore?"

"Parents silly to buy something like that just to get all broke up," say Rosie
Giraffe.

"That much money it should last forever," I figure.

35   "My father'd buy it for me if I wanted it."

"Your father, my ass," say Rosie Giraffe getting a chance to finally push
Mercedes.

"Must be rich people shop here," say Q.T.

"You are a very bright boy," say Flyboy. "What was your first clue?" And he
rap him on the head with the back of his knuckles, since Q.T. the only one he
could get away with. Though Q.T. liable to come up behind you years later
and get his licks in when you half expect it.

"What I want to know is," I says to Miss Moore though I never talk to her, I wouldn't give the bitch that satisfaction, "is how much a real boat costs? I figure a thousand'd get you a yacht any day."

40   "Why don't you check that out," she says, "and report back to the group?" Which really pains my ass. If you gonna mess up a perfectly good swim day least you could do is have some answers. "Let's go in," she say like she got something up her sleeve. Only she don't lead the way. So me and Sugar turn the corner to where the entrance is, but when we get there I kinda hang back. Not that I'm scared, what's there to be afraid of, just a toy store. But I feel funny, shame. But what I got to be shamed about? Got as much right to go in as anybody. But somehow I can't seem to get hold of the door, so I step away for Sugar to lead. But she hangs back too. And I look at her and she looks at me and this is ridiculous. I mean, damn, I have never ever been shy about doing nothing or going nowhere. But then Mercedes steps up and then Rosie Giraffe and Big Butt crowd in behind and shove, and next thing we all stuffed into the doorway with only Mercedes squeezing past us, smoothing out her jumper and walking right down the aisle. Then the rest of us tumble in like a glued-together jigsaw done all wrong. And people lookin at us. And it's like the time me and Sugar crashed into the Catholic church on a dare. But once we got in there and everything so hushed and holy and the candles and the bowin and the handkerchiefs on all the drooping heads, I just couldn't go through with the plan. Which was for me to run up to the altar and do a tap dance while Sugar played the nose flute and messed around in the holy water. And Sugar kept givin me the elbow. Then later teased me so bad I tied her up in the shower and turned it on and locked her in. And she'd be there till this day if Aunt Gretchen hadn't finally figured I was lyin about the boarder taking a shower.

Same thing in the store. We all walkin on tiptoe and hardly touchin the games and puzzles and things. And I watched Miss Moore who is steady watchin us like she waiting for a sign. Like Mama Drewery watches the sky and sniffs the air and takes note of just how much slant is in the bird formation. Then me and Sugar bump smack into each other, so busy gazing at the toys, 'specially the sailboat. But we don't laugh and go into our fat-lady bump-stomach routine. We just stare at that price tag. Then Sugar run a finger over the whole boat. And I'm jealous and want to hit her. Maybe not her, but I sure want to punch somebody in the mouth.

"Watcha bring us here for, Miss Moore?"

"You sound angry, Sylvia. Are you mad about something?" Givin me one of them grins like she tellin a grown-up joke that never turns out to be funny. And she's lookin very closely at me like maybe she plannin to do my portrait from memory. I'm mad, but I won't give her that satisfaction. So I slouch around the store bein very bored and say, "Let's go."

Me and Sugar at the back of the train watchin the tracks whizzin by large then small then gettin gobbled up in the dark. I'm thinkin about this tricky toy I saw in the store. A clown that somersaults on a bar then does chin-ups just cause you yank lightly at his leg. Cost $35. I could see me askin my mother for a $35 birthday clown. "You wanna who that costs what?" she'd say, cocking her head to the side to get a better view of the hole in my head. Thirty-five dollars could buy new bunk beds for Junior and Gretchen's boy. Thirty-five dollars and the whole household could go visit Granddaddy Nelson in the country. Thirty-five dollars would pay for the rent and the piano bill too. Who are these people that spend that much for performing clowns and $1,000 for toy sailboats? What kinda work they do and how they live and how come we ain't in on it? Where we are is who we are, Miss Moore always pointing out. But it don't necessarily have to be that way, she always adds then waits for somebody to say that poor people have to wake up and demand their share of the pie and don't none of us know what kind of pie she talkin about in the first damn place. But she ain't so smart cause I still got her four dollars from the taxi and she sure ain't getting it. Messin up my day with this shit. Sugar nudges me in my pocket and winks.

45   Miss Moore lines us up in front of the mailbox where we started from, seem like years ago, and I got a headache for thinkin so hard. And we lean all over each other so we can hold up under the draggy-ass lecture she always finishes us off with at the end before we thank her for borin us to tears. But she just looks at us like she readin tea leaves. Finally she say, "Well, what did you think of F.A.O. Schwartz?"

Rosie Giraffe mumbles, "White folks crazy."

"I'd like to go there again when I get my birthday money," says Mercedes, and we shove her out the pack so she has to lean on the mailbox by herself.

"I'd like a shower. Tiring day," say Flyboy.

Then Sugar surprises me by sayin, "You know, Miss Moore, I don't think all of us here put together eat in a year what that sailboat costs." And Miss Moore lights up like somebody goosed her. "And?" she say, urging Sugar on. Only I'm standin on her foot so she don't continue.

50   "Imagine for a minute what kind of society it is in which some people can spend on a toy what it would cost to feed a family of six or seven. What do you think?"

"I think," say Sugar pushing me off her feet like she never done before, cause I whip her ass in a minute, "that this is not much of a democracy if you ask me. Equal chance to pursue happiness means an equal crack at the dough, don't it?" Miss Moore is besides herself and I am disgusted with Sugar's treachery. So I stand on her foot one more time to see if she'll shove me. She shuts up, and Miss Moore looks at me, sorrowfully I'm thinkin. And somethin weird is goin on, I can feel it in my chest.

"Anybody else learn anything today?" lookin dead at me. I walk away and Sugar has to run to catch up and don't even seem to notice when I shrug her arm off my shoulder.

"Well, we got four dollars anyway," she says.

"Uh hunh."

55   "We could go to Hascombs and get half a chocolate layer and then go to the Sunset and still have plenty money for potato chips and ice-cream sodas."

"Uh hunh."

"Race you to Hascombs," she say.

We start down the block and she gets ahead which is O.K. by me cause I'm goin to the West End and then over to the Drive to think this day through. She can run if she want to and even run faster. But ain't nobody gonna beat me at nuthin.

Jorge Luis Borges

Jorge Luis Borges (1899–1986) was born and lived in Buenos Aires, Argentina. At a time when the literature of South America is extraordinarily rich and lively, Borges has been known as perhaps the foremost writer of the continent. Enigmatic and fantastic, his work has influenced writers all over the world.

The Secret Miracle   (1962)
Translated by Harriet de Onis

And God had him die for a hundred years and then revived him and said:
  "How long have you been here?"
  "A day or a part of a day," he answered.

—Koran, II, 261

The night of March 14, 1943, in an apartment in the Zeltnergasse of Prague, Jaromir Hladik, the author of the unfinished drama entitled *The Enemies,* of *Vindication of Eternity* and of a study of the indirect Jewish sources of Jakob Böhme,[1] had a dream of a long game of chess. The players were not two persons, but two illustrious families; the game had been going on for centuries. Nobody could remember what the stakes were, but it was rumored that they were enormous, perhaps infinite; the chessmen and the board were in a secret tower. Jaromir (in his dream) was the first-born of one of the contending families. The clock struck the hour for the game, which could not be postponed. The dreamer raced over the sands of a rainy desert, and was unable to recall either the pieces or the rules of chess. At that moment he awoke. The clangor of the rain and of the terrible clocks ceased. A rhythmic, unanimous noise, punctuated by shouts of command, arose from the Zeltnergasse. It was dawn, and the armored vanguard of the Third Reich[2] was entering Prague.

On the nineteenth the authorities received a denunciation; that same nineteenth, toward evening, Jaromir Hladik was arrested. He was taken to an aseptic, white barracks on the opposite bank of the Moldau. He was unable to refute a single one of the Gestapo's charges; his mother's family name was Jaroslavski, he was of Jewish blood, his study on Böhme had marked Jewish

---

[1] German mystic and philosopher (1575–1624)   [2] Hitler's Germany. On 15 March 1939 German armies took over Prague, in Czechoslovakia, by *Anschluss* (annexation); the Gestapo was the secret police.

emphasis, his signature had been one more on the protest against the *Anschluss.* In 1928 he had translated the *Sepher Yezirah*[3] for the publishing house of Hermann Barsdorf. The fulsome catalogue of the firm had exaggerated, for publicity purposes, the translator's reputation, and the catalogue had been examined by Julius Rothe, one of the officials who held Hladik's fate in his hands. There is not a person who, except in the field of his own specialization, is not credulous; two or three adjectives in Gothic type were enough to persuade Julius Rothe of Hladik's importance, and he ordered him sentenced to death *pour encourager les autres.*[4] The execution was set for March 29th, at 9:00 A.M. This delay (whose importance the reader will grasp later) was owing to the desire on the authorities' part to proceed impersonally and slowly, after the manner of vegetables and plants.

Hladik's first reaction was mere terror. He felt he would not have shrunk from the gallows, the block, or the knife, but that death by a firing squad was unbearable. In vain he tried to convince himself that the plain, unvarnished fact of dying was the fearsome thing, not the attendant circumstances. He never wearied of conjuring up these circumstances, senselessly trying to exhaust all their possible variations. He infinitely anticipated the process of his dying, from the sleepless dawn to the mysterious volley. Before the day set by Julius Rothe he died hundreds of deaths in courtyards whose forms and angles strained geometrical probabilities, machine-gunned by variable soldiers in changing numbers, who at times killed him from a distance, at others from close by. He faced these imaginary executions with real terror (perhaps, with real bravery); each simulacrum lasted a few seconds. When the circle was closed, Jaromir returned once more and interminably to the tremulous vespers of his death. Then he reflected that reality does not usually coincide with our anticipation of it; with a logic of his own he inferred that to foresee a circumstantial detail is to prevent its happening. Trusting in this weak magic, he invented, *so that they would not happen,* the most gruesome details. Finally, as was natural, he came to fear that they were prophetic. Miserable in the night, he endeavored to find some way to hold fast to the fleeting substance of time. He knew that it was rushing headlong toward the dawn of the twenty-ninth. He reasoned aloud: "I am now in the night of the twenty-second; while this night lasts (and for six nights more), I am invulnerable, immortal." The nights of sleep seemed to him deep, dark pools in which he could submerge himself. There were moments when he longed impatiently for the final burst of fire that would free him, for better or for worse, from the vain compulsion of his imaginings. On the twenty-eighth, as the last sunset was reverberating from the high barred windows, the thought of his drama, *The Enemies,* deflected him from these abject considerations.

Hladik had rounded forty. Aside from a few friendships and many habits, the problematic exercise of literature constituted his life. Like all writers, he measured the achievements of others by what they had accomplished, asking of them that they measure him by what he envisaged or planned. All the

---

[3] Ancient Jewish mystical writings   [4] To encourage others

books he had published had left him with a complex feeling of repentance. His studies of the work of Böhme, of Ibn Erza,[5] and of Fludd[6] had been characterized essentially by mere application; his translation of the *Sepher Yezirah,* by carelessness, fatigue, and conjecture. *Vindication of Eternity* perhaps had fewer shortcomings. The first volume gave a history of man's various concepts of eternity, from the immutable Being of Parmenides[7] to the modifiable Past of Hinton.[8] The second denied (with Francis Bradley)[9] that all the events of the universe make up a temporal series, arguing that the number of man's possible experiences is not infinite, and that a single "repetition" suffices to prove that time is a fallacy . . . . Unfortunately, the arguments that demonstrate this fallacy are equally fallacious. Hladik was in the habit of going over them with a kind of contemptuous perplexity. He had also composed a series of Expressionist poems; to the poet's chagrin they had been included in an anthology published in 1924, and no subsequent anthology but inherited them. From all this equivocal, uninspired past Hladik had hoped to redeem himself with his drama in verse, *The Enemies.* (Hladik felt the verse form to be essential because it makes it impossible for the spectators to lose sight of irreality, one of art's requisites.)

5   The drama observed the unities of time, place, and action. The scene was laid in Hradčany, in the library of Baron von Roemerstadt, on one of the last afternoons of the nineteenth century. In the first scene of the first act a strange man visits Roemerstadt. (A clock was striking seven, the vehemence of the setting sun's rays glorified the windows, a passionate, familiar Hungarian music floated in the air.) This visit is followed by others; Roemerstadt does not know the people who are importuning him, but he has the uncomfortable feeling that he has seen them somewhere, perhaps in a dream. They all fawn upon him, but it is apparent—first to the audience and then to the Baron—that they are secret enemies, in league to ruin him. Roemerstadt succeeds in checking or evading their involved schemings. In the dialogue mention is made of his sweetheart, Julia von Weidenau, and a certain Jaroslav Kubin, who at one time pressed his attentions on her. Kubin has now lost his mind, and believes himself to be Roemerstadt. The dangers increase; Roemerstadt, at the end of the second act, is forced to kill one of the conspirators. The third and final act opens. The incoherencies gradually increase; actors who had seemed out of the play reappear; the man Roemerstadt killed returns for a moment. Someone points out that evening has not fallen; the clock strikes seven, the high windows reverberate in the western sun, the air carries an impassioned Hungarian melody. The first actor comes on and repeats the lines he had spoken in the first scene of the first act. Roemerstadt speaks to him without surprise; the audience understands that Roemerstadt is the miserable Jaroslav Kubin. The drama has never taken place; it is the circular delirium that Kubin lives and relives endlessly.

[5] Jewish philosopher (1090?–1164) born in Spain   [6] Sir Robert Fludd (1574–1637), English mystical philosopher and physician   [7] Greek philosopher who lived six centuries before the birth of Christ   [8] James Hinton (1822–1875), English philosopher and physician   [9] Francis H. Bradley (1846–1924), English philosopher and logician

Hladik had never asked himself whether this tragicomedy of errors was preposterous or admirable, well thought out or slipshod. He felt that the plot I have just sketched was best contrived to cover up his defects and point up his abilities and held the possibility of allowing him to redeem (symbolically) the meaning of his life. He had finished the first act and one or two scenes of the third; the metrical mixtures of the work made it possible for him to keep working it over, changing the hexameters, without the manuscript in front of him. He thought how he still had two acts to do, and that he was going to die very soon. He spoke with God in the darkness: "If in some fashion I exist, if I am not one of Your repetitions and mistakes, I exist as the author of *The Enemies*. To finish this drama, which can justify me and justify You, I need another year. Grant me these days, You to whom the centuries and time belong." This was the last night, the most dreadful of all, but ten minutes later sleep flooded over him like a dark water.

Toward dawn he dreamed that he had concealed himself in one of the naves of the Clementine Library. A librarian wearing dark glasses asked him: "What are you looking for?" Hladik answered: "I am looking for God." The librarian said to him: "God is in one of the letters on one of the pages of one of the four hundred thousand volumes of the Clementine. My fathers and the fathers of my fathers have searched for this letter; I have grown blind seeking it." He removed his glasses, and Hladik saw his eyes, which were dead. A reader came in to return an atlas. "This atlas is worthless," he said, and handed it to Hladik, who opened it at random. He saw a map of India as in a daze. Suddenly sure of himself, he touched one of the tiniest letters. A ubiquitous voice said to him: "The time of your labor has been granted." At this point Hladik awoke.

He remembered that men's dreams belong to God, and that Maimonides[10] had written that the words heard in a dream are divine when they are distinct and clear and the person uttering them cannot be seen. He dressed: two soldiers came into the cell and ordered him to follow them.

From behind the door, Hladik had envisaged a labyrinth of passageways, stairs, and separate buildings. The reality was less spectacular: they descended to an inner court by a narrow iron stairway. Several soldiers—some with uniform unbuttoned—were examining a motorcycle and discussing it. The sergeant looked at the clock; it was 8:44. They had to wait until it struck nine. Hladik, more insignificant than pitiable, sat down on a pile of wood. He noticed that the soldiers' eyes avoided his. To ease his wait, the sergeant handed him a cigarette. Hladik did not smoke; he accepted it out of politeness or humility. As he lighted it, he noticed that his hands were shaking. The day was clouding over; the soldiers spoke in a low voice as though he were already dead. Vainly he tried to recall the woman of whom Julia von Weidenau was the symbol.

10   The squad formed and stood at attention. Hladik, standing against the barracks wall, waited for the volley. Someone pointed out that the wall was going to be stained with blood; the victim was ordered to step forward a few

---

[10] Moses Maimonides (1135–1204), a philosopher born in Spain, collected Jewish oral law into a written code.

paces. Incongruously, this reminded Hladik of the fumbling preparations of photographers. A big drop of rain struck one of Hladik's temples and rolled slowly down his cheek; the sergeant shouted the final order.

The physical universe came to a halt.

The guns converged on Hladik, but the men who were to kill him stood motionless. The sergeant's arm eternized an unfinished gesture. On a paving stone of the courtyard a bee cast an unchanging shadow. The wind ceased, as in a picture. Hladik attempted a cry, a word, a movement of the hand. He realized that he was paralyzed. Not a sound reached him from the halted world. He thought: "I am in hell, I am dead." He thought: "I am mad." He thought: "Time has stopped." Then he reflected that if that was the case, his mind would have stopped too. He wanted to test this; he repeated (without moving his lips) Vergil's mysterious fourth Eclogue.[11] He imagined that the now remote soldiers must be sharing his anxiety; he longed to be able to communicate with them. It astonished him not to feel the least fatigue, not even the numbness of his protracted immobility. After an indeterminate time he fell asleep. When he awoke the world continued motionless and mute. The drop of water still clung to his cheek, the shadow of the bee to the stone. The smoke from the cigarette he had thrown away had not dispersed. Another "day" went by before Hladik understood.

He had asked God for a whole year to finish his work; His omnipotence had granted it. God had worked a secret miracle for him; German lead would kill him at the set hour, but in his mind a year would go by between the order and its execution. From perplexity he passed to stupor, from stupor to resignation, from resignation to sudden gratitude.

He had no document but his memory; the training he had acquired with each added hexameter gave him a discipline unsuspected by those who set down and forget temporary, incomplete paragraphs. He was not working for posterity or even for God, whose literary tastes were unknown to him. Meticulously, motionlessly, secretly, he wrought in time his lofty, invisible labyrinth. He worked the third act over twice. He eliminated certain symbols as overobvious, such as the repeated striking of the clock, the music. Nothing hurried him. He omitted, he condensed, he amplified. In certain instances he came back to the original version. He came to feel an affection for the courtyard, the barracks; one of the faces before him modified his conception of Roemerstadt's character. He discovered that the wearying cacophonies that bothered Flaubert[12] so much are mere visual superstitions, weakness and limitation of the written word, not the spoken. . . . He concluded his drama. He had only the problem of a single phrase. He found it. The drop of water slid down his cheek. He opened his mouth in a maddened cry, moved his face, dropped under the quadruple blast.

15 Jaromir Hladik died on March 29, at 9:02 A.M.

---

[11] The fourth Eclogue (see note on page 000) of the Roman epic poet Publius Vergilius Maro (70–19 B.C.) is sometimes read as a prophecy of Christ. [12] The novelist Gustave Flaubert (1821–1880), a magnificent stylist of the French language, contended that every word in a piece of fiction must have precision and harmony.

Raymond Carver

Raymond Carver (1938–1988) attended Humboldt State University in California and did post-graduate work in writing at the University of Iowa. He taught at several universities, received a Guggenheim Fellowship, and, in 1983, was given a Strauss Living Award from the American Academy and Institute of Arts and Letters. He has published many volumes of poetry and stories, the latter collected in *Will You Please Be Quiet, Please?* (1976), *What We Talk About When We Talk About Love* (1981), and *Cathedral* (1983). We take this story from the latter work; an earlier version appeared in the 1981 collection.

A Small, Good Thing   (1983)

Saturday afternoon she drove to the bakery in the shopping center. After looking through a loose-leaf binder with photographs of cakes taped onto the pages, she ordered chocolate, the child's favorite. The cake she chose was decorated with a space ship and launching pad under a sprinkling of white stars, and a planet made of red frosting at the other end. His name, SCOTTY, would be in green letters beneath the planet. The baker, who was an older man with a thick neck, listened without saying anything when she told him the child would be eight years old next Monday. The baker wore a white apron that looked like a smock. Straps cut under his arms, went around in back and then to the front again, where they were secured under his heavy waist. He wiped his hands on his apron as he listened to her. He kept his eyes down on the photographs and let her talk. He let her take her time. He'd just come to work and he'd be there all night, baking, and he was in no real hurry.

She gave the baker her name, Ann Weiss, and her telephone number. The cake would be ready on Monday morning, just out of the oven, in plenty of time for the child's party that afternoon. The baker was not jolly. There were no pleasantries between them, just the minimum exchange of words, the necessary information. He made her feel uncomfortable, and she didn't like that. While he was bent over the counter with the pencil in his hand, she studied his coarse features and wondered if he'd ever done anything else with his life besides be a baker. She was a mother and thirty-three years old, and it seemed to her that everyone, especially someone the baker's age—a man old enough to be her father—must have children who'd gone through this special time of cakes and birthday parties. There must be that between them, she thought. But he was abrupt with her—not rude, just abrupt. She gave up trying to make friends with him. She looked into the back of the bakery and could see a long, heavy wooden table with aluminum pie pans stacked at one end; and beside the table a metal container filled with empty racks. There was an enormous oven. A radio was playing country-Western music.

The baker finished printing the information on the special order card and closed up the binder. He looked at her and said, "Monday morning." She thanked him and drove home.

On Monday morning, the birthday boy was walking to school with another boy. They were passing a bag of potato chips back and forth and the birthday boy was trying to find out what his friend intended to give him for his birthday that afternoon. Without looking, the birthday boy stepped off the curb at an intersection and was immediately knocked down by a car. He fell on his side with his head in the gutter and his legs out in the road. His eyes were closed, but his legs moved back and forth as if he were trying to climb over something. His friend dropped the potato chips and started to cry. The car had gone a hundred feet or so and stopped in the middle of the road. The man in the driver's seat looked back over his shoulder. He waited until the boy got unsteadily to his feet. The boy wobbled a little. He looked dazed, but okay. The driver put the car into gear and drove away.

5   The birthday boy didn't cry, but he didn't have anything to say about anything either. He wouldn't answer when his friend asked him what it felt like to be hit by a car. He walked home, and his friend went on to school. But after the birthday boy was inside his house and was telling his mother about it—she sitting beside him on the sofa, holding his hands in her lap, saying, "Scotty, honey, are you sure you feel all right, baby?" thinking she would call the doctor anyway—he suddenly lay back on the sofa, closed his eyes, and went limp. When she couldn't wake him up, she hurried to the telephone and called her husband at work. Howard told her to remain calm, remain calm, and then he called an ambulance for the child and left for the hospital himself.

Of course, the birthday party was canceled. The child was in the hospital with a mild concussion and suffering from shock. There'd been vomiting, and his lungs had taken in fluid which needed pumping out that afternoon. Now he simply seemed to be in a very deep sleep—but no coma, Dr. Francis had emphasized, no coma, when he saw the alarm in the parents' eyes. At eleven o'clock that night, when the boy seemed to be resting comfortably enough after the many X-rays and the lab work, and it was just a matter of his waking up and coming around, Howard left the hospital. He and Ann had been at the hospital with the child since that afternoon, and he was going home for a short while to bathe and change clothes. "I'll be back in an hour," he said. She nodded. "It's fine," she said. "I'll be right here." He kissed her on the forehead, and they touched hands. She sat in the chair beside the bed and looked at the child. She was waiting for him to wake up and be all right. Then she could begin to relax.

Howard drove home from the hospital. He took the wet, dark streets very fast, then caught himself and slowed down. Until now, his life had gone smoothly and to his satisfaction—college, marriage, another year of college for the advanced degree in business, a junior partnership in an investment firm. Fatherhood. He was happy and, so far, lucky—he knew that. His parents were still living, his brothers and his sister were established, his friends from college had gone out to take their places in the world. So far, he had kept away from any real harm, from those forces he knew existed and that could cripple or bring down a man if the luck went bad, if things suddenly turned. He pulled into the driveway and parked. His left leg began to tremble. He sat in the car for a minute and tried to deal with the present situation in a rational manner. Scotty had been hit by a car and was in the hospital, but he was going to be all right. Howard closed his eyes and ran his hand over his face. He got out of the car and went up to the front door. The dog was barking inside the house. The telephone rang and rang while he unlocked the door and fumbled for the light switch. He shouldn't have left the hospital, he shouldn't have. "Goddamn it!" he said. He picked up the receiver and said, "I just walked in the door!"

"There's a cake here that wasn't picked up," the voice on the other end of the line said.

"What are you saying?" Howard asked.

10   "A cake," the voice said. "A sixteen-dollar cake."

Howard held the receiver against his ear, trying to understand. "I don't know anything about a cake," he said. "Jesus, what are you talking about?"

"Don't hand me that," the voice said.

Howard hung up the telephone. He went into the kitchen and poured himself some whiskey. He called the hospital. But the child's condition remained the same; he was still sleeping and nothing had changed there. While water poured into the tub, Howard lathered his face and shaved. He'd just stretched out in the tub and closed his eyes when the telephone rang again. He hauled himself out, grabbed a towel, and hurried through the house, saying, "Stupid, stupid," for having left the hospital. But when he picked up the receiver and shouted, "Hello!" there was no sound at the other end of the line. Then the caller hung up.

He arrived back at the hospital a little after midnight. Ann still sat in the chair beside the bed. She looked up at Howard, and then she looked back at the child. The child's eyes stayed closed, the head was still wrapped in bandages. His breathing was quiet and regular. From an apparatus over the bed hung a bottle of glucose with a tube running from the bottle to the boy's arm.

15   "How is he?" Howard said. "What's all this?" waving at the glucose and the tube.

"Dr. Francis's orders," she said. "He needs nourishment. He needs to keep up his strength. Why doesn't he wake up, Howard? I don't understand, if he's all right."

Howard put his hand against the back of her head. He ran his fingers through her hair. "He's going to be all right. He'll wake up in a little while. Dr. Francis knows what's what."

After a time, he said, "Maybe you should go home and get some rest. I'll stay here. Just don't put up with this creep who keeps calling. Hang up right away."

"Who's calling?" she asked.

20   "I don't know who, just somebody with nothing better to do than call up people. You go on now."

She shook her head. "No," she said, "I'm fine."

"Really," he said. "Go home for a while, and then come back and spell me in the morning. It'll be all right. What did Dr. Francis say? He said Scotty's going to be all right. We don't have to worry. He's just sleeping now, that's all."

A nurse pushed the door open. She nodded at them as she went to the bedside. She took the left arm out from under the covers and put her fingers on the wrist, found the pulse, then consulted her watch. In a little while, she put the arm back under the covers and moved to the foot of the bed, where she wrote something on a clipboard attached to the bed.

"How is he?" Ann said. Howard's hand was a weight on her shoulder. She was aware of the pressure from his fingers.

25   "He's stable," the nurse said. Then she said, "Doctor will be in again shortly. Doctor's back in the hospital. He's making rounds right now."

"I was saying maybe she'd want to go home and get a little rest," Howard said. "After the doctor comes," he said.

"She could do that," the nurse said. "I think you should both feel free to do that, if you wish." The nurse was a big Scandinavian woman with blond hair. There was the trace of an accent in her speech.

"We'll see what the doctor says," Ann said. "I want to talk to the doctor. I don't think he should keep sleeping like this. I don't think that's a good sign." She brought her hand up to her eyes and let her head come forward a little. Howard's grip tightened on her shoulder, and then his hand moved up to her neck, where his fingers began to knead the muscles there.

"Dr. Francis will be here in a few minutes," the nurse said. Then she left the room.

30   Howard gazed at his son for a time, the small chest quietly rising and falling under the covers. For the first time since the terrible minutes after Ann's telephone call to him at his office, he felt a genuine fear starting in his limbs. He began shaking his head. Scotty was fine, but instead of sleeping at home in his own bed, he was in a hospital bed with bandages around his head and a tube in his arm. But this help was what he needed right now.

Dr. Francis came in and shook hands with Howard, though they'd just seen each other a few hours before. Ann got up from the chair. "Doctor?"

"Ann," he said and nodded. "Let's just first see how he's doing," the doctor said. He moved to the side of the bed and took the boy's pulse. He peeled back one eyelid and then the other. Howard and Ann stood beside the doctor and watched. Then the doctor turned back the covers and listened to the boy's heart and lungs with his stethoscope. He pressed his fingers here and there on the abdomen. When he was finished, he went to the end of the bed and studied the chart. He noted the time, scribbled something on the chart, and then looked at Howard and Ann.

"Doctor, how is he?" Howard said. "What's the matter with him exactly?"

"Why doesn't he wake up?" Ann said.

35   The doctor was a handsome, big-shouldered man with a tanned face. He wore a three-piece blue suit, a striped tie, and ivory cufflinks. His gray hair was combed along the sides of his head, and he looked as if he had just come from a concert. "He's all right," the doctor said. "Nothing to shout about, he

could be better, I think. But he's all right. Still, I wish he'd wake up. He should wake up pretty soon." The doctor looked at the boy again. "We'll know some more in a couple of hours, after the results of a few more tests are in. But he's all right, believe me, except for the hairline fracture of the skull. He does have that."

"Oh, no," Ann said.

"And a bit of a concussion, as I said before. Of course, you know he's in shock," the doctor said. "Sometimes you see this in shock cases. This sleeping."

"But he's out of any real danger?" Howard said. "You said before he's not in a coma. You wouldn't call this a coma, then—would you, doctor?" Howard waited. He looked at the doctor.

"No, I don't want to call it a coma," the doctor said and glanced over at the boy once more. "He's just in a very deep sleep. It's a restorative measure the body is taking on its own. He's out of any real danger, I'd say that for certain, yes. But we'll know more when he wakes up and the other tests are in," the doctor said.

40   "It's a coma," Ann said. "Of sorts."

"It's not a coma yet, not exactly," the doctor said. "I wouldn't want to call it coma. Not yet, anyway. He's suffered shock. In shock cases, this kind of reaction is common enough; it's a temporary reaction to bodily trauma. Coma. Well, coma is a deep, prolonged unconsciousness, something that could go on for days, or weeks even. Scotty's not in that area, not as far as we can tell. I'm certain his condition will show improvement by morning. I'm betting that it will. We'll know more when he wakes up, which shouldn't be long now. Of course, you may do as you like, stay here or go home for a time. But by all means feel free to leave the hospital for a while if you want. This is not easy, I know." The doctor gazed at the boy again, watching him, and then he turned to Ann and said, "You try not to worry, little mother. Believe me, we're doing all that can be done. It's just a question of a little more time now." He nodded at her, shook hands with Howard again, and then he left the room.

Ann put her hand over the child's forehead. "At least he doesn't have a fever," she said. Then she said, "My God, he feels so cold, though. Howard? Is he supposed to feel like this? Feel his head."

Howard touched the child's temples. His own breathing had slowed. "I think he's supposed to feel this way right now," he said. "He's in shock, re-member? That's what the doctor said. The doctor was just in here. He would have said something if Scotty wasn't okay."

Ann stood there a while longer, working her lip with her teeth. Then she moved over to her chair and sat down.

45   Howard sat in the chair next to her chair. They looked at each other. He wanted to say something else and reassure her, but he was afraid, too. He took her hand and put it in his lap, and this made him feel better, her hand being there. He picked up her hand and squeezed it. Then he just held her hand. They sat like that for a while, watching the boy and not talking. From time to time, he squeezed her hand. Finally, she took her hand away.

"I've been praying," she said.

He nodded.

She said, "I almost thought I'd forgotten how, but it came back to me. All I had to do was close my eyes and say, 'Please God, help us—help Scotty,' and then the rest was easy. The words were right there. Maybe if you prayed, too," she said to him.

"I've already prayed," he said. "I prayed this afternoon—yesterday afternoon, I mean—after you called, while I was driving to the hospital. I've been praying," he said.

50 "That's good," she said. For the first time, she felt they were together in it, this trouble. She realized with a start that, until now, it had only been happening to her and to Scotty. She hadn't let Howard into it, though he was there and needed all along. She felt glad to be his wife.

The same nurse came in and took the boy's pulse again and checked the flow from the bottle hanging above the bed.

In an hour, another doctor came in. He said his name was Parsons, from Radiology. He had a bushy mustache. He was wearing loafers, a Western shirt, and a pair of jeans.

"We're going to take him downstairs for more pictures," he told them. "We need to do some more pictures, and we want to do a scan."

"What's that?" Ann said. "A scan?" She stood between this new doctor and the bed. "I thought you'd already taken all your X-rays."

55 "I'm afraid we need some more," he said. "Nothing to be alarmed about. We just need some more pictures, and we want to do a brain scan on him."

"My God," Ann said.

"It's perfectly normal procedure in cases like this," this new doctor said. "We just need to find out for sure why he isn't back awake yet. It's normal medical procedure, and nothing to be alarmed about. We'll be taking him down in a few minutes," this doctor said.

In a little while, two orderlies came into the room with a gurney. They were black-haired, dark-complexioned men in white uniforms, and they said a few words to each other in a foreign tongue as they unhooked the boy from the tube and moved him from his bed to the gurney. Then they wheeled him from the room. Howard and Ann got on the same elevator. Ann gazed at the child. She closed her eyes as the elevator began its descent. The orderlies stood at either end of the gurney without saying anything, though once one of the men made a comment to the other in their own language, and the other man nodded slowly in response.

Later that morning, just as the sun was beginning to lighten the windows in the waiting room outside the X-ray department, they brought the boy out and moved him back up to his room. Howard and Ann rode up on the elevator with him once more, and once more they took up their places beside the bed.

60 They waited all day, but still the boy did not wake up. Occasionally, one of them would leave the room to go downstairs to the cafeteria to drink coffee and then, as if suddenly remembering and feeling guilty, get up from the table and hurry back to the room. Dr. Francis came again that afternoon and

examined the boy once more and then left after telling them he was coming along and could wake up at any minute now. Nurses, different nurses from the night before, came in from time to time. Then a young woman from the lab knocked and entered the room. She wore white slacks and a white blouse and carried a little tray of things which she put on the stand beside the bed. Without a word to them, she took blood from the boy's arm. Howard closed his eyes as the woman found the right place on the boy's arm and pushed the needle in.

"I don't understand this," Ann said to the woman.

"Doctor's orders," the woman said. "I do what I'm told. They say draw that one, I draw. What's wrong with him, anyway?" she said. "He's a sweetie."

"He was hit by a car," Howard said. "A hit-and-run."

The young woman shook her head and looked again at the boy. Then she took her tray and left the room.

65   "Why won't he wake up?" Ann said. "Howard? I want some answers from these people."

Howard didn't say anything. He sat down again in the chair and crossed one leg over the other. He rubbed his face. He looked at his son and then he settled back in the chair, closed his eyes, and went to sleep.

Ann walked to the window and looked out at the parking lot. It was night, and cars were driving into and out of the parking lot with their lights on. She stood at the window with her hands gripping the sill, and knew in her heart that they were into something now, something hard. She was afraid, and her teeth began to chatter until she tightened her jaws. She saw a big car stop in front of the hospital and someone, a woman in a long coat, get into the car. She wished she were that woman and somebody, anybody, was driving her away from here to somewhere else, a place where she would find Scotty waiting for her when she stepped out of the car, ready to say *Mom* and let her gather him in her arms.

In a little while, Howard woke up. He looked at the boy again. Then he got up from the chair, stretched, went over to stand beside her at the window. They both started out at the parking lot. They didn't say anything. But they seemed to feel each other's insides now, as though the worry had made them transparent in a perfectly natural way.

The door opened and Dr. Francis came in. He was wearing a different suit and tie this time. His gray hair was combed along the sides of his head, and he looked as if he had just shaved. He went straight to the bed and examined the boy. "He ought to have come around by now. There's just no good reason for this," he said. "But I can tell you we're all convinced he's out of any danger. We'll just feel better when he wakes up. There's no reason, absolutely none, why he shouldn't come around. Very soon. Oh, he'll have himself a dilly of a headache when he does, you can count on that. But all of his signs are fine. They're as normal as can be."

70   "It is a coma, then?" Ann said.

The doctor rubbed his smooth cheek. "We'll call it that for the time being, until he wakes up. But you must be worn out. This is hard. Feel free to go out for a bite," he said. "It would do you good. I'll put a nurse in here while

you're gone if you'll feel better about going. Go and have yourselves something to eat."

"I couldn't eat anything," Ann said.

"Do what you need to do, of course," the doctor said. "Anyway, I wanted to
tell you that all the signs are good, the tests are negative, nothing showed up
at all, and just as soon as he wakes up he'll be over the hill."

"Thank you, doctor," Howard said. He shook hands with the doctor again.
The doctor patted Howard's shoulder and went out.

75   "I suppose one of us should go home and check on things," Howard said.
"Slug needs to be fed, for one thing."

"Call one of the neighbors," Ann said. "Call the Morgans. Anyone will feed
a dog if you ask them to."

"All right," Howard said. After a while, he said, "Honey, why don't *you* do it?
Why don't you go home and check on things, and then come back? It'll do you
good. I'll be right here with him. Seriously," he said. "We need to keep up our
strength on this. We'll want to be here for a while even after he wakes up."

"Why don't *you* go?" she said. "Feed Slug. Feed yourself."

"I already went," he said. "I was gone for exactly an hour and fifteen
minutes. You go home for an hour and freshen up. Then come back."

80   She tried to think about it, but she was too tired. She closed her eyes and
tried to think about it again. After a time, she said, "Maybe I *will* go home for
a few minutes. Maybe if I'm not just sitting right here watching him every
second, he'll wake up and be all right. You know? Maybe he'll wake up if I'm
not here. I'll go home and take a bath and put on clean clothes. I'll feed Slug.
Then I'll come back."

"I'll be right here," he said. "You go on home, honey. I'll keep an eye on
things here." His eyes were bloodshot and small, as if he'd been drinking for a
long time. His clothes were rumpled. His beard had come out again. She
touched his face, and then she took her hand back. She understood he wanted
to be by himself for a while, not have to talk or share his worry for a time. She
picked her purse up from the nightstand, and he helped her into her coat.

"I won't be gone long," she said.

"Just sit and rest for a little while when you get home," he said. "Eat something. Take a bath. After you get out of the bath, just sit for a while and rest. It'll
do you a world of good, you'll see. Then come back," he said. "Let's try not to
worry. You heard what Dr. Francis said."

She stood in her coat for a minute trying to recall the doctor's exact words,
looking for any nuances, any hint of something behind his words other than
what he had said. She tried to remember if his expression had changed any
when he bent over to examine the child. She remembered the way his features had composed themselves as he rolled back the child's eyelids and
then listened to his breathing.

85   She went to the door, where she turned and looked back. She looked at the
child, and then she looked at the father. Howard nodded. She stepped out of
the room and pulled the door closed behind her.

She went past the nurses' station and down to the end of the corridor,
looking for the elevator. At the end of the corridor, she turned to her right and

entered a little waiting room where a Negro family sat in wicker chairs. There was a middle-aged man in a khaki shirt and pants, a baseball cap pushed back on his head. A large woman wearing a housedress and slippers was slumped in one of the chairs. A teenaged girl in jeans, hair done in dozens of little braids, lay stretched out in one of the chairs smoking a cigarette, her legs crossed at the ankles. The family swung their eyes to Ann as she entered the room. The little table was littered with hamburger wrappers and Styrofoam cups.

"Franklin," the large woman said as she roused herself. "Is it about Franklin?" Her eyes widened. "Tell me now, lady," the woman said. "Is it about Franklin?" She was trying to rise from her chair, but the man had closed his hand over her arm.

"Here, here," he said. "Evelyn."

"I'm sorry," Ann said. "I'm looking for the elevator. My son is in the hospital, and now I can't find the elevator."

90   "Elevator is down that way, turn left," the man said as he aimed a finger.

The girl drew on her cigarette and stared at Ann. Her eyes were narrowed to slits, and her broad lips parted slowly as she let the smoke escape. The Negro woman let her head fall on her shoulder and looked away from Ann, no longer interested.

"My son was hit by a car," Ann said to the man. She seemed to need to explain herself. "He has a concussion and a little skull fracture, but he's going to be all right. He's in shock now, but it might be some kind of coma, too. That's what really worries us, the coma part. I'm going out for a little while, but my husband is with him. Maybe he'll wake up while I'm gone."

"That's too bad," the man said and shifted in the chair. He shook his head. He looked down at the table, and then he looked back at Ann. She was still standing there. He said, "Our Franklin, he's on the operating table. Somebody cut him. Tried to kill him. There was a fight where he was at. At this party. They say he was just standing and watching. Not bothering nobody. But that don't mean nothing these days. Now he's on the operating table. We're just hoping and praying, that's all we can do now." He gazed at her steadily.

Ann looked at the girl again, who was still watching her, and at the older woman, who kept her head down, but whose eyes were now closed. Ann saw the lips moving silently, making words. She had an urge to ask what those words were. She wanted to talk more with these people who were in the same kind of waiting she was in. She was afraid, and they were afraid. They had that in common. She would have liked to have said something else about the accident, told them more about Scotty, that it had happened on the day of his birthday, Monday, and that he was still unconscious. Yet she didn't know how to begin. She stood looking at them without saying anything more.

95   She went down the corridor the man had indicated and found the elevator. She waited a minute in front of the closed doors, still wondering if she was doing the right thing. Then she put out her finger and touched the button.

She pulled into the driveway and cut the engine. She closed her eyes and leaned her head against the wheel for a minute. She listened to the ticking sounds the engine made as it began to cool. Then she got out of the car. She could hear the dog barking inside the house. She went to the front door, which was unlocked. She went inside and turned on lights and put on a kettle of water for tea. She opened some dogfood and fed Slug on the back porch. The dog ate in hungry little smacks. It kept running into the kitchen to see that she was going to stay. As she sat down on the sofa with her tea, the telephone rang.

"Yes!" she said as she answered. "Hello!"

"Mrs. Weiss," a man's voice said. It was five o'clock in the morning, and she thought she could hear machinery or equipment of some kind in the background.

"Yes, yes! What is it?" she said. "This is Mrs. Weiss. This is she. What is it, please?" She listened to whatever it was in the background. "Is it Scotty, for Christ's sake?"

100   "Scotty," the man's voice said. "It's about Scotty, yes. It has to do with Scotty, that problem. Have you forgotten about Scotty?" the man said. Then he hung up.

She dialed the hospital's number and asked for the third floor. She demanded information about her son from the nurse who answered the telephone. Then she asked to speak to her husband. It was, she said, an emergency.

She waited, turning the telephone cord in her fingers. She closed her eyes and felt sick at her stomach. She would have to make herself eat. Slug came in from the back porch and lay down near her feet. He wagged his tail. She pulled at his ear while he licked her fingers. Howard was on the line.

"Somebody just called here," she said. She twisted the telephone cord. "He said it was about Scotty," she cried.

"Scotty's fine," Howard told her. "I mean, he's still sleeping. There's been no change. The nurse has been in twice since you've been gone. A nurse or else a doctor. He's all right."

105   "This man called. He said it was about Scotty," she told him.

"Honey, you rest for a little while, you need the rest. It must be that same caller I had. Just forget it. Come back down here after you've rested. Then we'll have breakfast or something."

"Breakfast," she said. "I don't want any breakfast."

"You know what I mean," he said. "Juice, something. I don't know. I don't know anything, Ann. Jesus, I'm not hungry, either. Ann, it's hard to talk now. I'm standing here at the desk. Dr. Francis is coming again at eight o'clock this morning. He's going to have something to tell us then, something more definite. That's what one of the nurses said. She didn't know any more than that. Ann? Honey, maybe we'll know something more then. At eight o'clock. Come back here before eight. Meanwhile, I'm right here and Scotty's all right. He's still the same," he added.

"I was drinking a cup of tea," she said, "when the telephone rang. They said it was about Scotty. There was a noise in the background. Was there a noise in the background on that call you had, Howard?"

110   "I don't remember," he said. "Maybe the driver of the car, maybe he's a psychopath and found out about Scotty somehow. But I'm here with him. Just rest like you were going to do. Take a bath and come back by seven or so, and

we'll talk to the doctor together when he gets here. It's going to be all right, honey. I'm here, and there are doctors and nurses around. They say his condition is stable."

"I'm scared to death," she said.

She ran water, undressed, and got into the tub. She washed and dried quickly, not taking the time to wash her hair. She put on clean underwear, wool slacks, and a sweater. She went into the living room, where the dog looked up at her and let its tail thump once against the floor. It was just starting to get light outside when she went out to the car.

She drove into the parking lot of the hospital and found a space close to the front door. She felt she was in some obscure way responsible for what had happened to the child. She let her thoughts move to the Negro family. She remembered the name Franklin and the table that was covered with hamburger papers, and the teenaged girl staring at her as she drew on her cigarette. "Don't have children," she told the girl's image as she entered the front door of the hospital. "For God's sake, don't."

She took the elevator up to the third floor with two nurses who were just going on duty. It was Wednesday morning, a few minutes before seven. There was a page for a Dr. Madison as the elevator doors slid open on the third floor. She got off behind the nurses, who turned in the other direction and continued the conversation she had interrupted when she'd gotten into the elevator. She walked down the corridor to the little alcove where the Negro family had been waiting. They were gone now, but the chairs were scattered in such a way that it looked as if people had just jumped up from them the minute before. The tabletop was cluttered with the same cups and papers, the ashtray was filled with cigarette butts.

115   She stopped at the nurses' station. A nurse was standing behind the counter, brushing her hair and yawning.

"There was a Negro boy in surgery last night," Ann said. "Franklin was his name. His family was in the waiting room. I'd like to inquire about his condition."

A nurse who was sitting at a desk behind the counter looked up from a chart in front of her. The telephone buzzed and she picked up the receiver, but she kept her eyes on Ann.

"He passed away," said the nurse at the counter. The nurse held the hairbrush and kept looking at her. "Are you a friend of the family or what?"

"I met the family last night," Ann said. "My own son is in the hospital. I guess he's in shock. We don't know for sure what's wrong. I just wondered about Franklin, that's all. Thank you." She moved down the corridor. Elevator doors the same color as the walls slid open and a gaunt, bald man in white pants and white canvas shoes pulled a heavy cart off the elevator. She hadn't noticed these doors last night. The man wheeled the cart out into the corridor and stopped in front of the room nearest the elevator and consulted a clipboard. Then he reached down and slid a tray out of the cart. He rapped lightly on the door and entered the room. She could smell the unpleasant odors of warm food as she passed the cart. She hurried on without looking at any of the nurses and pushed open the door to the child's room.

120   Howard was standing at the window with his hands behind his back. He turned around as she came in.

"How is he?" she said. She went over to the bed. She dropped her purse on the floor beside the nightstand. It seemed to her she had been gone a long time. She touched the child's face. "Howard?"

"Dr. Francis was here a little while ago," Howard said. She looked at him closely and thought his shoulders were bunched a little.

"I thought he wasn't coming until eight o'clock this morning," she said quickly.

"There was another doctor with him. A neurologist."

125   "A neurologist," she said.

Howard nodded. His shoulders were bunching, she could see that. "What'd they say, Howard? For Christ's sake, what'd they say? What is it?"

"They said they're going to take him down and run more tests on him, Ann. They think they're going to operate, honey. Honey, they *are* going to operate. They can't figure out why he won't wake up. It's more than just shock or concussion, they know that much now. It's in his skull, the fracture, it has something, something to do with that, they think. So they're going to operate. I tried to call you, but I guess you'd already left the house."

"Oh, God," she said. "Oh, please, Howard, please," she said, taking his arms.

"Look!" Howard said. "Scotty! Look, Ann!" He turned her toward the bed.

130   The boy had opened his eyes, then closed them. He opened them again now. The eyes stared straight ahead for a minute, then moved slowly in his head until they rested on Howard and Ann, then traveled away again.

"Scotty," his mother said, moving to the bed.

"Hey, Scott," his father said. "Hey, son."

They leaned over the bed. Howard took the child's hand in his hands and began to pat and squeeze the hand. Ann bent over the boy and kissed his forehead again and again. She put her hands on either side of his face. "Scotty, honey, it's Mommy and Daddy," she said. "Scotty?"

The boy looked at them, but without any sign of recognition. Then his mouth opened, his eyes scrunched closed, and he howled until he had no more air in his lungs. His face seemed to relax and soften then. His lips parted as his last breath was puffed through his throat and exhaled gently through his clenched teeth.

135   The doctors called it a hidden occlusion and said it was a one-in-a-million circumstance. Maybe if it could have been detected somehow and surgery undertaken immediately, they could have saved him. But more than likely not. In any case, what would they have been looking for? Nothing had shown up in the tests or in the X-rays.

Dr. Francis was shaken. "I can't tell you how badly I feel. I'm so very sorry, I can't tell you," he said as he led them into the doctors' lounge. There was a doctor sitting in a chair with his legs hooked over the back of another chair, watching an early-morning TV show. He was wearing a green delivery-room outfit, loose green pants and green blouse, and a green cap that covered his hair. He looked at Howard and Ann and then looked at Dr. Francis. He got to his feet and turned off the set and went out of the room. Dr. Francis guided Ann to the sofa, sat down beside her, and began to talk in a low, consoling voice. At one point, he leaned over and embraced her. She could feel his chest rising and falling evenly against her shoulder. She kept her eyes open and let him hold her. Howard went into the bathroom, but he left the door open. After a violent fit of weeping, he ran water and washed his face. Then he came out and sat down at the little table that held a telephone. He looked at the telephone as though deciding what to do first. He made some calls. After a time, Dr. Francis used the telephone.

"Is there anything else I can do for the moment?" he asked them.

Howard shook his head. Ann stared at Dr. Francis as if unable to comprehend his words.

The doctor walked them to the hospital's front door. People were entering and leaving the hospital. It was eleven o'clock in the morning. Ann was aware of how slowly, almost reluctantly, she moved her feet. It seemed to her that Dr. Francis was making them leave when she felt they should stay, when it would be more the right thing to do to stay. She gazed out into the parking lot and then turned around and looked back at the front of the hospital. She began shaking her head. "No, no," she said. "I can't leave him here, no." She heard herself say that and thought how unfair it was that the only words that came out were the sort of words used on TV shows where people were stunned by violent or sudden deaths. She wanted her words to be her own. "No," she said, and for some reason the memory of the Negro woman's head lolling on the woman's shoulder came to her. "No," she said again.

140   "I'll be talking to you later in the day," the doctor was saying to Howard. "There are still some things that have to be done, things that have to be cleared up to our satisfaction. Some things that need explaining."

"An autopsy," Howard said.

Dr. Francis nodded.

"I understand," Howard said. Then he said, "Oh, Jesus. No, I don't understand, doctor. I can't, I can't. I just can't."

Dr. Francis put his arm around Howard's shoulders. "I'm sorry. God, how I'm sorry." He let go of Howard's shoulders and held out his hand. Howard looked at the hand, and then he took it. Dr. Francis put his arms around Ann once more. He seemed full of some goodness she didn't understand. She let her head rest on his shoulder, but her eyes stayed open. She kept looking at the hospital. As they drove out of the parking lot, she looked back at the hospital.

145 At home, she sat on the sofa with her hands in her coat pockets. Howard closed the door to the child's room. He got the coffee-maker going and then he found an empty box. He had thought to pick up some of the child's things that were scattered around the living room. But instead he sat down beside her on the sofa, pushed the box to one side, and leaned forward, arms

between his knees. He began to weep. She pulled his head over into her lap and patted his shoulder. "He's gone," she said. She kept patting his shoulder. Over his sobs, she could hear the coffee-maker hissing in the kitchen. "There, there," she said tenderly. "Howard, he's gone. He's gone and now we'll have to get used to that. To being alone."

In a little while, Howard got up and began moving aimlessly around the room with the box, not putting anything into it, but collected some things together on the floor at one end of the sofa. She continued to sit with her hands in her coat pockets. Howard put the box down and brought coffee into the living room. Later, Ann made calls to relatives. After each call had been placed and the party had answered, Ann would blurt out a few words and cry for a minute. Then she would quietly explain, in a measured voice, what had happened and tell them about arrangements. Howard took the box out to the garage, where he saw the child's bicycle. He dropped the box and sat down on the pavement beside the bicycle. He took hold of the bicycle awkwardly so that it leaned against his chest. He held it, the rubber pedal sticking into his chest. He gave the wheel a turn.

Ann hung up the telephone after talking to her sister. She was looking up another number when the telephone rang. She picked it up on the first ring.

"Hello," she said, and she heard something in the background, a humming noise. "Hello!" she said. "For God's sake," she said. "Who is this? What is it you want?"

"Your Scotty, I got him ready for you," the man's voice said. "Did you forget him?"

150 "You evil bastard!" she shouted into the receiver. "How can you do this, you evil son of a bitch?"

"Scotty," the man said. "Have you forgotten about Scotty?" Then the man hung up on her.

Howard heard the shouting and came in to find her with her head on her arms over the table, weeping. He picked up the receiver and listened to the dial tone.

Much later, just before midnight, after they had dealt with many things, the telephone rang again.

"You answer it," she said. "Howard, it's him, I know." They were sitting at the kitchen table with coffee in front of them. Howard had a small glass of whiskey beside his cup. He answered on the third ring.

155 "Hello," he said. "Who is this? Hello! Hello!" The line went dead. "He hung up," Howard said. "Whoever it was."

"It was him," she said. "That bastard. I'd like to kill him," she said. "I'd like to shoot him and watch him kick," she said.

"Ann, my God," he said.

"Could you hear anything?" she said. "In the background? A noise, machinery, something humming?"

"Nothing, really. Nothing like that," he said. "There wasn't much time. I think there was some radio music. Yes, there was a radio going, that's all I could tell. I don't know what in God's name is going on," he said.

160   She shook her head. "If I could, could get my hands on him." It came to her then. She knew who it was. Scotty, the cake, the telephone number. She pushed the chair away from the table and got up. "Drive me down to the shopping center," she said. "Howard."

"What are you saying?"

"The shopping center. I know who it is who's calling. I know who it is. It's the baker, the son-of-a-bitching baker, Howard. I had him bake a cake for Scotty's birthday. That's who's calling. That's who has the number and keeps calling us. To harass us about that cake. The baker, that bastard."

They drove down to the shopping center. The sky was clear and stars were out. It was cold, and they ran the heater in the car. They parked in front of the bakery. All of the shops and stores were closed, but there were cars at the far end of the lot in front of the movie theater. The bakery windows were dark, but when they looked through the glass they could see a light in the back room and, now and then, a big man in an apron moving in and out of the white, even light. Through the glass, she could see the display cases and some little tables with chairs. She tried the door. She rapped on the glass. But if the baker heard them, he gave no sign. He didn't look in their direction.

They drove around behind the bakery and parked. They got out of the car. There was a lighted window too high up for them to see inside. A sign near the back door said THE PANTRY BAKERY, SPECIAL ORDERS. She could hear faintly a radio playing inside and something creak—an oven door as it was pulled down? She knocked on the door and waited. Then she knocked again, louder. The radio was turned down and there was a scraping sound now, the distinct sound of something, a drawer, being pulled open and then closed.

165   Someone unlocked the door and opened it. The baker stood in the light and peered out at them. "I'm closed for business," he said. "What do you want at this hour? It's midnight. Are you drunk or something?"

She stepped into the light that fell through the open door. He blinked his heavy eyelids as he recognized her. "It's you," he said.

"It's me," she said. "Scotty's mother. This is Scotty's father. We'd like to come in."

The baker said, "I'm busy now. I have work to do."

She had stepped inside the doorway anyway. Howard came in behind her. The baker moved back. "It smells like a bakery in here. Doesn't it smell like a bakery in here, Howard?"

170   "What do you want?" the baker said. "Maybe you want your cake? That's it, you decided you want your cake. You ordered a cake, didn't you?"

"You're pretty smart for a baker," she said. "Howard, this is the man who's been calling us." She clenched her fists. She stared at him fiercely. There was a deep burning inside her, an anger that made her feel larger than herself, larger than either of these men.

"Just a minute here," the baker said. "You want to pick up your three-day-old cake? That it? I don't want to argue with you, lady. There it sits over there, getting stale. I'll give it to you for half of what I quoted you. No. You want it? You can have it. It's no good to me, no good to anyone now. It cost me time and money to make that cake. If you want it, okay, if you don't, that's okay, too. I have to get back to work." He looked at them and rolled his tongue behind his teeth.

"More cakes," she said. She knew she was in control of it, of what was increasing in her. She was calm.

"Lady, I work sixteen hours a day in this place to earn a living," the baker said. He wiped his hands on his apron. "I work night and day in here, trying to make ends meet." A look crossed Ann's face that made the baker move back and say, "No trouble, now." He reached to the counter and picked up a rolling pin with his right hand and began to tap it against the palm of his other hand. "You want the cake or not? I have to get back to work. Bakers work at night," he said again. His eyes were small, mean-looking, she thought, nearly lost in the bristly flesh around his cheeks. His neck was thick with fat.

175   "I know bakers work at night," Ann said. "They make phone calls at night, too. You bastard," she said.

The baker continued to tap the rolling pin against his hand. He glanced at Howard. "Careful, careful," he said to Howard.

"My son's dead," she said with a cold, even finality. "He was hit by a car Monday morning. We've been waiting with him until he died. But, of course, you couldn't be expected to know that, could you? Bakers can't know everything—can they, Mr. Baker? But he's dead. He's dead, you bastard!" Just as suddenly as it had welled in her, the anger dwindled, gave way to something else, a dizzy feeling of nausea. She leaned against the wooden table that was sprinkled with flour, put her hands over her face, and began to cry, her shoulders rocking back and forth. "It isn't fair," she said. "It isn't, isn't fair."

Howard put his hand at the small of her back and looked at the baker. "Shame on you," Howard said to him. "Shame."

The baker put the rolling pin back on the counter. He undid his apron and threw it on the counter. He looked at them, and then he shook his head slowly. He pulled a chair out from under the card table that held papers and receipts, an adding machine, and a telephone directory. "Please sit down," he said. "Let me get you a chair," he said to Howard. "Sit down now, please." The baker went into the front of the shop and returned with two little wrought-iron chairs. "Please sit down, you people."

180   Ann wiped her eyes and looked at the baker. "I wanted to kill you," she said. "I wanted you dead."

The baker had cleared a space for them at the table. He shoved the adding machine to one side, along with the stacks of notepaper and receipts. He pushed the telephone directory onto the floor, where it landed with a thud. Howard and Ann sat down and pulled their chairs up to the table. The baker sat down, too.

"Let me say how sorry I am," the baker said, putting his elbows on the table. "God alone knows how sorry. Listen to me. I'm just a baker. I don't claim to be anything else. Maybe once, maybe years ago, I was a different kind of human being. I've forgotten, I don't know for sure. But I'm not any longer, if I ever was. Now I'm just a baker. That don't excuse my doing what I did, I know. But I'm deeply sorry. I'm sorry for your son, and sorry for my part in this," the baker said. He spread his hands out on the table and turned them over to reveal his palms. "I don't have any children myself, so I can only imagine what you must be feeling. All I can say to you now is that I'm sorry. Forgive me, if you can," the baker said. "I'm not an evil man, I don't think. Not evil, like you said on the phone. You got to understand what it comes down to is I don't know how to act anymore, it would seem. Please," the man said, "let me ask you if you can find it in your hearts to forgive me?"

It was warm inside the bakery. Howard stood up from the table and took off his coat. He helped Ann from her coat. The baker looked at them for a minute and then nodded and got up from the table. He went to the oven and turned off some switches. He found cups and poured coffee from an electric coffee-maker. He put a carton of cream on the table, and a bowl of sugar.

"You probably need to eat something," the baker said. "I hope you'll eat some of my hot rolls. You have to eat and keep going. Eating is a small, good thing in a time like this," he said.

185   He served them warm cinnamon rolls just out of the oven, the icing still runny. He put butter on the table and knives to spread the butter. Then the baker sat down at the table with them. He waited. He waited until they each took a roll from the platter and began to eat. "It's good to eat something," he said, watching them. "There's more. Eat up. Eat all you want. There's all the rolls in the world in here."

They ate rolls and drank coffee. Ann was suddenly hungry, and the rolls were warm and sweet. She ate three of them, which pleased the baker. Then he began to talk. They listened carefully. Although they were tired and in anguish, they listened to what the baker had to say. They nodded when the baker began to speak of loneliness, and of the sense of doubt and limitation that had come to him in his middle years. He told them what it was like to be childless all these years. To repeat the days with the ovens endlessly full and endlessly empty. The party food, the celebrations he'd worked over. Icing knuckle-deep. The tiny wedding couples stuck into cakes. Hundreds of them, no, thousands by now. Birthdays. Just imagine all those candles burning. He had a necessary trade. He was a baker. He was glad he wasn't a florist. It was better to be feeding people. This was a better smell anytime than flowers.

"Smell this," the baker said, breaking open a dark loaf. "It's a heavy bread, but rich." They smelled it, then he had them taste it. It had the taste of molasses and coarse grains. They listened to him. They ate what they could. They swallowed the dark bread. It was like daylight under the fluorescent trays of light. They talked into the early morning, the high, pale cast of light in the windows, and they did not think of leaving.

Kate Chopin

Kate Chopin (1852–1904) grew up in St. Louis, then lived for more than thirty
years in New Orleans and on a cotton plantation in Louisiana. When she returned
to her hometown, after the death of her husband, she began to write the work for
which she is best known. Her last novel was *The Awakening* (1899), a scandal in
its time for its frankness.

The Story of an Hour   (1894)

Knowing that Mrs. Mallard was afflicted with a heart trouble, great care was
taken to break to her as gently as possible the news of her husband's death.

It was her sister Josephine who told her, in broken sentences, veiled hints
that revealed in half concealing. Her husband's friend Richards was there,
too, near her. It was he who had been in the newspaper office when intelligence of the railroad disaster was received, with Brently Mallard's name
leading the list of "killed." He had only taken the time to assure himself of its
truth by a second telegram, and had hastened to forestall any less careful,
less tender friend in bearing the sad message.

She did not hear the story as many women have heard the same, with a
paralyzed inability to accept its significance. She wept at once, with sudden,
wild abandonment, in her sister's arms. When the storm of grief had spent
itself she went away to her room alone. She would have no one follow her.

There stood, facing the open window, a comfortable, roomy armchair.
Into this she sank, pressed down by a physical exhaustion that haunted her
body and seemed to reach into her soul.

5   She could see in the open square before her house the tops of trees that
were all aquiver with the new spring life. The delicious breath of rain was in
the air. In the street below a peddler was crying his wares. The notes of a
distant song which some one was singing reached her faintly, and countless
sparrows were twittering in the eaves.

There were patches of blue sky showing here and there through the clouds
that had met and piled above the other in the west facing her window.

She sat with her head thrown back upon the cushion of the chair quite
motionless, except when a sob came up into her throat and shook her, as a
child who has cried itself to sleep continues to sob in its dreams.

She was young, with a fair, calm face, whose lines bespoke repression and
even a certain strength. But now there was a dull stare in her eyes, whose gaze
was fixed away off yonder on one of those patches of blue sky. It was not a
glance of reflection, but rather indicated a suspension of intelligent thought.

There was something coming to her and she was waiting for it, fearfully.
What was it? She did not know; it was too subtle and elusive to name. But she
felt it, creeping out of the sky, reaching toward her through the sounds, the
scents, the color that filled the air.

10   Now her bosom rose and fell tumultuously. She was beginning to recognize this thing that was approaching to possess her, and she was striving to

beat it back with her will—as powerless as her two white slender hands would have been.

When she abandoned herself a little whispered word escaped her slightly parted lips. She said it over and over under her breath: "Free, free, free!" The vacant stare and the look of terror that had followed it went from her eyes. They stayed keen and bright. Her pulses beat fast, and the coursing blood warmed and relaxed every inch of her body.

She did not stop to ask if it were not a monstrous joy that held her. A clear and exalted perception enabled her to dismiss the suggestion as trivial.

She knew that she would weep again when she saw the kind, tender hands folded in death; the face that had never looked save with love upon her, fixed and gray and dead. But she saw beyond that bitter moment a long procession of years to come that would belong to her absolutely. And she opened and spread her arms out to them in welcome.

There would be no one to live for during those coming years; she would live for herself. There would be no powerful will bending her in that blind persistence with which men and women believe they have a right to impose a private will upon a fellow creature. A kind intention or a cruel intention made the act seem no less a crime as she looked upon it in that brief moment of illumination.

15 And yet she had loved him—sometimes. Often she had not. What did it matter! What could love, the unsolved mystery, count for in face of this possession of self-assertion which she suddenly recognized as the strongest impulse of her being.

"Free! Body and soul free!" she kept whispering.

Josephine was kneeling before the closed door with her lips to the keyhole, imploring for admission. "Louise, open the door! I beg; open the door—you will make yourself ill. What are you doing, Louise? For heaven's sake open the door."

"Go away. I am not making myself ill." No; she was drinking in a very elixir of life through that open window.

Her fancy was running riot along those days ahead of her. Spring days, and summer days, and all sorts of days that would be her own. She breathed a quick prayer that life might be long. It was only yesterday she had thought with a shudder that life might be long.

20 She arose at length and opened the door to her sister's importunities. There was a feverish triumph in her eyes, and she carried herself unwittingly like a goddess of Victory. She clasped her sister's waist, and together they descended the stairs. Richards stood waiting for them at the bottom

Some one was opening the front door with a latchkey. It was Brently Mallard who entered, a little travel-stained, composedly carrying his grip-sack and umbrella. He had been far from the scene of accident, and did not even know there had been one. He stood amazed at Josephine's piercing cry; at Richards' quick motion to screen him from the view of his wife.

But Richards was too late.

When the doctors came they said she had died of heart disease—of joy that kills.

Ralph Ellison

Ralph Ellison (1914–   ) was born in Oklahoma and has lived in recent years in New York City. His one novel, *The Invisible Man* (1952), won him immediate recognition as a leading black American writer. In 1964, he published a collection of essays, *Shadow and Act.*

Battle Royal   (1948)

It goes a long way back, some twenty years. All my life I had been looking for something, and everywhere I turned someone tried to tell me what it was. I accepted their answers too, though they were often in contradiction and even self-contradictory. I was naïve. I was looking for myself and asking everyone except myself questions which I, and only I, could answer. It took me a long time and much painful boomeranging of my expectations to achieve a realization everyone else appears to have been born with: That I am nobody but myself. But first I had to discover that I am an invisible man!

And yet I am no freak of nature, nor of history. I was in the cards, other things having been equal (or unequal) eighty-five years ago. I am not ashamed of my grandparents for having been slaves. I am only ashamed of myself for having at one time been ashamed. About eighty-five years ago they were told that they were free, united with others of our country in everything pertaining to the common good, and, in everything social, separate like the fingers of the hand. And they believed it. They exulted in it. They stayed in their place, worked hard, and brought up my father to do the same. But my grandfather is the one. He was an odd old guy, my grandfather, and I am told I take after him. It was he who caused the trouble. On his deathbed he called my father to him and said, "Son, after I'm gone I want you to keep up the fight. I never told you, but our life is a war and I have been a traitor all my born days, a spy in the enemy's country ever since I give up my gun back in the Reconstruction. Live with your head in the lion's mouth. I want you to overcome 'em with yeses, undermine 'em with grins, agree 'em to death and destruction, let 'em swoller you till they vomit or bust wide open." They thought the old man had gone out of his mind. He had been the meekest of men. The younger children were rushed from the room, the shades drawn and the flame of the lamp turned so low that it sputtered on the wick like the old man's breathing. "Learn it to the younguns," he whispered fiercely; then he died.

But my folks were more alarmed over his last words than over his dying. It was as though he had not died at all, his words caused so much anxiety. I was warned emphatically to forget what he had said and, indeed, this is the first time it has been mentioned outside the family circle. It had a tremendous effect upon me, however. I could never be sure of what he meant. Grandfather had been a quiet old man who never made any trouble, yet on his deathbed he had called himself a traitor and a spy, and he had spoken of his meekness as a dangerous activity. It became a constant puzzle which lay unanswered in the back of my mind. And whenever things went well for me I remembered my grandfather and felt guilty and uncomfortable. It was as though I was carrying out his advice in spite of myself. And to make it worse, everyone loved me for it. I was praised by the most lily-white men of the town. I was considered an example of desirable conduct—just as my grandfather had been. And what puzzled me was that the old man had defined it as *treachery*. When I was praised for my conduct I felt a guilt that in some way I was doing something that was really against the wishes of the white folks, that if they had understood they would have desired me to act just the opposite, that I should have been sulky and mean, and that that really would have been what they wanted, even though they were fooled and thought they wanted me to act as I did. It made me afraid that some day they would look upon me as a traitor and I would be lost. Still I was more afraid to act any other way because they didn't like that at all. The old man's words were like a curse. On my graduation day I delivered an oration in which I showed that humility was the secret, indeed, the very essence of progress. (Not that I believed this—how could I, remembering my grandfather?—I only believed that it worked.) It was a great success. Everyone praised me and I was invited to give the speech at a gathering of the town's leading white citizens. It was a triumph for our whole community.

It was in the main ballroom of the leading hotel. When I got there I discovered that it was on the occasion of a smoker, and I was told that since I was to be there anyway I might as well take part in the battle royal to be fought by some of my schoolmates as part of the entertainment. The battle royal came first.

5   All of the town's big shots were there in their tuxedos, wolfing down the buffet foods, drinking beer and whiskey and smoking black cigars. It was a large room with a high ceiling. Chairs were arranged in neat rows around three sides of a portable boxing ring. The fourth side was clear, revealing a gleaming space of polished floor. I had some misgivings over the battle royal, by the way. Not from a distaste for fighting, but because I didn't care too much for the other fellows who were to take part. They were tough guys who seemed to have no grandfather's curse worrying their minds. No one could mistake their toughness. And besides, I suspected that fighting a battle royal might detract from the dignity of my speech. In those pre-invisible days I visualized myself as a potential Booker T. Washington.[1] But the other fellows didn't care too much for me either, and there were nine of them. I felt

---

[1] Black American teacher and leader (1856–1915)

superior to them in my way, and I didn't like the manner in which we were all crowded together into the servants' elevator. Nor did they like my being there. In fact, as the warmly lighted floors flashed past the elevator we had words over the fact that I, by taking part in the fight, had knocked one of their friends out of a night's work.

We were led out of the elevator through a rococo hall into an anteroom and told to get into our fighting togs. Each of us was issued a pair of boxing gloves and ushered out into the big mirrored hall, which we entered looking cautiously about us and whispering, lest we might accidentally be heard above the noise of the room. It was foggy with cigar smoke. And already the whiskey was taking effect. I was shocked to see some of the most important men of the town quite tipsy. They were all there—bankers, lawyers, judges, doctors, fire chiefs, teachers, merchants. Even one of the more fashionable pastors. Something we could not see was going on up front. A clarinet was vibrating sensuously and the men were standing up and moving eagerly forward. We were a small tight group, clustered together, our bare upper bodies touching and shining with anticipatory sweat; while up front the big shots were becoming increasingly excited over something we still could not see. Suddenly I heard the school superintendent, who had told me to come, yell, "Bring up the shines, gentlemen! Bring up the little shines!"

We were rushed up to the front of the ballroom, where it smelled even more strongly of tobacco and whiskey. Then we were pushed into place. I almost wet my pants. A sea of faces, some hostile, some amused, ringed around us, and in the center, facing us, stood a magnificent blonde—stark naked. There was a dead silence. I felt a blast of cold air chill me. I tried to back away, but they were behind me and around me. Some of the boys stood with lowered heads, trembling. I felt a wave of irrational guilt and fear. My teeth chattered, my skin turned to goose flesh, my knees knocked. Yet I was strongly attracted and looked in spite of myself. Had the price of looking been blindness, I would have looked. The hair was yellow like that of a circus kewpie doll, the face heavily powdered and rouged, as though to form an abstract mask, the eyes hollow and smeared a cool blue, the color of a baboon's butt. I felt a desire to spit upon her as my eyes brushed slowly over her body. Her breasts were firm and round as the domes of East Indian temples, and I stood so close as to see the fine skin texture and beads of pearly perspiration glistening like dew around the pink and erected buds of her nipples. I wanted at one and the same time to run from the room, to sink through the floor, or go to her and cover her from my eyes and the eyes of the others with my body; to feel the soft thighs, to caress her and destroy her, to love her and murder her, to hide from her, and yet to stroke where below the small American flag tattooed upon her belly her thighs formed a capital V. I had a notion that of all in the room she saw only me with her impersonal eyes.

And then she began to dance, a slow sensuous movement; the smoke of a hundred cigars clinging to her like the thinnest of veils. She seemed like a fair bird-girl girdled in veils calling to me from the angry surface of some gray and threatening sea. I was transported. Then I became aware of the clarinet playing and the big shots yelling at us. Some threatened us if we looked and others if we did not. On my right I saw one boy faint. And now a man grabbed a silver pitcher from a table and stepped close as he dashed ice water upon him and stood him up and forced two of us to support him as his head hung and moans issued from his thick bluish lips. Another boy began to plead to go home. He was the largest of the group, wearing dark red fighting trunks much too small to conceal the erection which projected from him as though in answer to the insinuating low-registered moaning of the clarinet. He tried to hide himself with his boxing gloves.

And all the while the blonde continued dancing, smiling faintly at the big shots who watched her with fascination, and faintly smiling at our fear. I noticed a certain merchant who followed her hungrily, his lips loose and drooling. He was a large man who wore diamond studs in a shirtfront which swelled with the ample paunch underneath, and each time the blonde swayed her undulating hips he ran his hand through the thin hair of his bald head and, with his arms upheld, his posture clumsy like that of an intoxicated panda, wound his belly in a slow and obscene grind. This creature was completely hypnotized. The music had quickened. As the dancer flung herself about with a detached expression on her face, the men began reaching out to touch her. I could see their beefy fingers sink into the soft flesh. Some of the others tried to stop them and she began to move around the floor in graceful circles, as they gave chase, slipping and sliding over the polished floor. It was mad. Chairs went crashing, drinks were spilt, as they ran laughing and howling after her. They caught her just as she reached a door, raised her from the floor, and tossed her as college boys are tossed at a hazing, and above her red, fixed-smiling lips I saw the terror and disgust in her eyes, almost like my own terror and that which I saw in some of the other boys. As I watched, they tossed her twice and her soft breasts seemed to flatten against the air and her legs flung wildly as she spun. Some of the more sober ones helped her to escape. And I started off the floor, heading for the anteroom with the rest of the boys.

10   Some were still crying and in hysteria. But as we tried to leave we were stopped and ordered to get into the ring. There was nothing to do but what we were told. All ten of us climbed under the ropes and allowed ourselves to be blindfolded with broad bands of white cloth. One of the men seemed to feel a bit sympathetic and tried to cheer us up as we stood with our backs against the ropes. Some of us tried to grin. "See that boy over there?" one of the men said. "I want you to run across at the bell and give it to him right in the belly. If you don't get him, I'm going to get you. I don't like his looks." Each of us was told the same. The blindfolds were put on. Yet even then I had been going over my speech. In my mind each word was as bright as flame. I felt the cloth pressed into place, and frowned so that it would be loosened when I relaxed.

But now I felt a sudden fit of blind terror. I was unused to darkness. It was as though I had suddenly found myself in a dark room filled with poisonous cottonmouths. I could hear the bleary voices yelling insistently for the battle royal to begin.

"Get going in there!"

"Let me at the big nigger!"

I strained to pick up the school superintendent's voice, as though to squeeze some security out of that slightly more familiar sound.

15   "Let me at those black sonsabitches!" someone yelled.

"No, Jackson, no!" another voice yelled. "Here, somebody, help me hold Jack."

"I want to get at that ginger-colored nigger. Tear him limb from limb," the first voice yelled.

I stood against the ropes trembling. For in those days I was what they called ginger-colored, and he sounded as though he might crunch me between his teeth like a crisp ginger cookie.

Quite a struggle was going on. Chairs were being kicked about and I could hear voices grunting as with a terrific effort. I wanted to see, to see more desperately than ever before. But the blindfold was as tight as a thick skin-puckering scab and when I raised my gloved hands to push the layers of white aside a voice yelled, "Oh, no you don't, black bastard! Leave that alone!"

20   "Ring the bell before Jackson kills him a coon!" someone boomed in the sudden silence. And I heard the bell clang and the sound of feet scuffling forward.

A glove smacked against my head. I pivoted, striking out stiffly as someone went past, and felt the jar ripple along the length of my arm to my shoulder. Then it seemed as though all nine of the boys had turned upon me at once. Blows pounded me from all sides while I struck out as best I could. So many blows landed upon me that I wondered if I were not the only blindfolded fighter in the ring, or if the man called Jackson hadn't succeeded in getting me after all.

Blindfolded, I could no longer control my motions. I had no dignity. I stumbled about like a baby or a drunken man. The smoke had become thicker and with each new blow it seemed to sear and further restrict my lungs. My saliva became like hot bitter glue. A glove connected with my head, filling my mouth with warm blood. It was everywhere. I could not tell if the moisture I felt upon my body was sweat or blood. A blow landed hard against the nape of my neck. I felt myself going over, my head hitting the floor. Streaks of blue light filled the black world behind the blindfold. I lay prone, pretending that I was knocked out, but felt myself seized by hands and yanked to my feet. "Get going, black boy! Mix it up!" My arms were like lead, my head smarting from blows. I managed to feel my way to the ropes and held on, trying to catch my breath. A glove landed in my midsection and I went over again, feeling as though the smoke had become a knife jabbed into my guts. Pushed this way and that by the legs milling around me, I finally pulled erect and discovered that I could see the black, sweat-washed forms weaving in the smoky-blue atmosphere like drunken dancers weaving to the rapid drumlike thuds of blows.

Everyone fought hysterically. It was complete anarchy. Everybody fought everybody else. No group fought together for long. Two, three, four, fought one, then turned to fight each other, were themselves attacked. Blows landed below the belt and in the kidney, with the gloves open as well as closed, and with my eye partly opened now there was not so much terror. I moved carefully, avoiding blows, although not too many to attract attention, fighting from group to group. The boys groped about like blind, cautious crabs crouching to protect their mid-sections, their heads pulled in short against their shoulders, their arms stretched nervously before them, with their fists testing the smoke-filled air like the knobbed feelers of hypersensitive snails. In the corner I glimpsed a boy violently punching the air and heard him scream in pain as he smashed his hand against a ring post. For a second I saw him bent over holding his hand, then going down as a blow caught his unprotected head. I played one group against the other, slipping in and throwing a punch then stepped out of range while pushing the others into the melee to take the blows blindly aimed at me. The smoke was agonizing and there were no rounds, no bells at three minute intervals to relieve our exhaustion. The room spun around me, a swirl of lights, smoke, sweating bodies surrounded by tense white faces. I bled from both nose and mouth, the blood spattering upon my chest.

The men kept yelling, "Slug him, black boy! Knock his guts out!"

25   "Uppercut him! Kill him! Kill that big boy!"

Taking a fake fall, I saw a boy going down heavily beside me as though we were felled by a single blow, saw a sneaker-clad foot shoot into his groin as the two who had knocked him down stumbled upon him. I rolled out of range, feeling a twinge of nausea.

The harder we fought the more threatening the men became. And yet, I had begun to worry about my speech again. How would it go? Would they recognize my ability? What would they give me?

I was fighting automatically when suddenly I noticed that one after another of the boys was leaving the ring. I was surprised, filled with panic, as though I had been left alone with an unknown danger. Then I understood. The boys had arranged it among themselves. It was custom for the two men left in the ring to slug it out for the winner's prize. I discovered this too late. When the bell sounded two men in tuxedos leaped into the ring and removed the blindfold. I found myself facing Tatlock, the biggest of the gang. I felt sick at my stomach. Hardly had the bell stopped ringing in my ears than it clanged again and I saw him moving swiftly toward me. Thinking of nothing else to do I hit him smash on the nose. He kept coming, bringing the rank sharp violence of stale sweat. His face was a black blank of a face, only his eyes alive—with hate of me and aglow with a feverish terror from what had happened to us all. I became anxious. I wanted to deliver my speech and he came at me as though he meant to beat it out of me. I smashed him again and again, taking his blows as they came. Then on a sudden impulse I struck him lightly and as we clinched, I whispered, "Fake like I knocked you out, you can have the prize."

"I'll break your behind," he whispered hoarsely.

30   "For *them*?"

"For *me,* sonofabitch."

They were yelling for us to break it up and Tatlock spun me half around with a blow, and as a joggled camera sweeps in a reeling scene, I saw the howling red faces crouching tense beneath the cloud of blue-gray smoke. For a moment the world wavered, unraveled, flowed, then my head cleared and Tatlock bounced before me. The fluttering shadow before my eyes was his jabbing left hand. Then falling forward, my head against his damp shoulder, I whispered.

"I'll make it five dollars more."

"Go to hell!"

35   But his muscles relaxed a trifle beneath my pressure and I breathed, "Seven?"

"Give it to your ma," he said, ripping me beneath the heart.

And while I still held him I butted him and moved away. I felt myself bombarded with punches. I fought back with hopeless desperation. I wanted to deliver my speech more than anything else in the world, because I felt only these men could judge truly my ability, and now this stupid clown was ruining my chances. I began fighting carefully now, moving in to punch him and out again with my greater speed. A lucky blow to his chin and I had him going too—until I heard a loud voice yell, "I got my money on the big boy."

Hearing this, I almost dropped my guard. I was confused: Should I try to win against the voice out there? Would not this go against my speech, and was not this a moment for humility, for nonresistance? A blow to my head as I danced about sent my right eye popping like a jack-in-the-box and settled my dilemma. The room went red as I fell. It was a dream fall, my body languid and fastidious as to where to land, until the floor became impatient and smashed up to meet me. A moment later I came to. An hypnotic voice said FIVE emphatically. And I lay there, hazily watching a dark red spot of my own blood shaping itself into a butterfly, glistening and soaking into the soiled gray world of the canvas.

When the voice drawled TEN I was lifted up and dragged to a chair. I sat dazed. My eye pained and swelled with each throb of my pounding heart and I wondered if now I would be allowed to speak. I was wringing wet, my mouth still bleeding. We were grouped along the wall now. The other boys ignored me as they congratulated Tatlock and speculated as to how much they would be paid. One boy whimpered over his smashed hand. Looking up front, I saw attendants in white jackets rolling the portable ring away and placing a small square rug in the vacant space surrounded by chairs. Perhaps, I thought, I will stand on the rug to deliver my speech.

40   Then the M.C. called to us, "Come on up here boys and get your money."

We ran forward to where the men laughed and talked in their chairs, waiting. Everyone seemed friendly now.

"There it is on the rug," the man said. I saw the rug covered with coins of all dimensions and a few crumpled bills. But what excited me, scattered here and there, were the gold pieces.

"Boys, it's all yours," the man said. "You get all you grab."

"That's right, Sambo," a blond man said, winking at me confidentially.

45   I trembled with excitement, forgetting my pain. I would get the gold and the bills, I thought. I would use both hands. I would throw my body against the boys nearest me to block them from the gold.

"Get down around the rug now," the man commanded, "and don't anyone touch it until I give the signal."

"This ought to be good," I heard.

As told, we got around the square rug on our knees. Slowly the man raised his freckled hand as we followed it upward with our eyes.

I heard, "These niggers look like they're about to pray!"

50   Then, "Ready," the man said. "Go!"

I lunged for a yellow coin lying on the blue design on the carpet, touching it and sending a surprised shriek to join those rising around me. I tried frantically to remove my hand but could not let go. A hot, violent force tore through my body, shaking me like a wet rat. The rug was electrified. The hair bristled up on my head as I shook myself free. My muscles jumped, my nerves jangled, writhed. But I saw that this was not stopping the other boys. Laughing in fear and embarrassment, some were holding back and scooping up the coins knocked off by the painful contortions of the others. The men roared above us as we struggled.

"Pick it up, goddamnit, pick it up!" someone called like a bass-voiced parrot. "Go on, get it!"

I crawled rapidly around the floor, picking up the coins, trying to avoid the coppers and to get greenbacks and the gold. Ignoring the shock by laughing, as I brushed the coins off quickly, I discovered that I could contain the electricity—a contradiction, but it works. Then the men began to push us onto the rug. Laughing embarrassedly, we struggled out of their hands and kept after the coins. We were all wet and slippery and hard to hold. Suddenly I saw a boy lifted into the air, glistening with sweat like a circus seal, and dropped, his wet back landing flush upon the charged rug, heard him yell and saw him literally dance upon his back, his elbows beating a frenzied tattoo upon the floor, his muscles twitching like the flesh of a horse stung by many flies. When he finally rolled off, his face was gray and no one stopped him when he ran from the floor amid booming laughter.

"Get the money," the M.C. called. "That's good hard American cash!"

55   And we snatched and grabbed, snatched and grabbed. I was careful not to come too close to the rug now, and when I felt the hot whiskey breath descend upon me like a cloud of foul air I reached out and grabbed the leg of a chair. It was occupied and I held on desperately.

"Leggo nigger! Leggo!"

The huge face wavered down to mine as he tried to push me free. But my body was slippery and he was too drunk. It was Mr. Colcord, who owned a chain of movie houses and "entertainment palaces." Each time he grabbed me I slipped out of his hands. It became a real struggle. I feared the rug more than I did the drunk, so I held on, surprising myself for a moment by trying to topple *him* upon the rug. It was such an enormous idea that I found myself actually carrying it out. I tried not to be obvious, yet when I grabbed his leg, trying to tumble him out of the chair, he raised up roaring with laughter, and, looking at me with soberness dead in the eye, kicked me viciously in the chest. The chair leg flew out of my hand and I felt myself going and rolled. It was as though I had rolled through a bed of hot coals. It seemed a whole century would pass before I would roll free, a century in which I was seared through the deepest levels of my body to the fearful breath within me and the breath seared and heated to the point of explosion. It'll all be over in a flash, I thought as I rolled clear. It'll all be over in a flash.

But not yet, the men on the other side were waiting, red faces swollen as though from apoplexy as they bent forward in their chairs. Seeing their fingers coming toward me I rolled away as a fumbled football rolls off the receiver's fingertips, back into the coals. That time I luckily sent the rug sliding out of place and heard the coins ringing against the floor and the boys scuffling to pick them up and the M.C. calling, "All right, boys, that's all. Go get dressed and get your money."

I was limp as a dish rag. My back felt as though it had been beaten with wires.

60   When we had dressed the M.C. came in and gave us each five dollars, except Tatlock, who got ten for being last in the ring. Then he told us to leave. I was not to get a chance to deliver my speech, I thought. I was going out into the dim alley in despair when I was stopped and told to go back. I returned to the ballroom, where the men were pushing back their chairs and gathering in groups to talk.

The M.C. knocked on a table for quiet. "Gentlemen," he said, "we almost forgot an important part of the program. A most serious part, gentlemen. This boy was brought here to deliver a speech which he made at his graduation yesterday . . ."

"Bravo!"

"I'm told that he is the smartest boy we've got out there in Greenwood. I'm told that he knows more big words than a pocket-sized dictionary."

Much applause and laughter.

65   "So now, gentlemen, I want you to give him your attention."

There was still laughter as I faced them, my mouth dry, my eye throbbing. I began slowly, but evidently my throat was tense, because they began shouting, "Louder! Louder!"

"We of the younger generation extol the wisdom of that great leader and educator," I shouted, "who first spoke these flaming words of wisdom. 'A ship lost at sea for many days suddenly sighted a friendly vessel. From the mast of the unfortunate vessel was seen a signal: "Water, water; we die of thirst!" The answer from the friendly vessel came back: "Cast down your bucket where you are." The captain of the distressed vessel, at last heeding the injunction, cast down his bucket, and it came up full of fresh sparkling water from the mouth of the Amazon River.' And like him I say, and in his words, 'To those of my race who depend upon bettering their condition in a foreign land, or who underestimate the importance of cultivating friendly relations with the Southern white man, who is his next-door neighbor, I would say: "Cast down your bucket where you are"—cast it down in making friends in every manly way of the people of all races by whom we are surrounded. . . .'"

I spoke automatically and with such fervor that I did not realize that the men were still talking and laughing until my dry mouth, filling up with blood from the cut, almost strangled me. I coughed, wanting to stop and go to one of the tall brass, sand-filled spittoons to relieve myself, but a few of the men, especially the superintendent, were listening and I was afraid. So I gulped it down, blood, saliva, and all, and continued. (What powers of endurance I had during those days! What enthusiasm! What a belief in the rightness of things!) I spoke even louder in spite of the pain. But still they talked and still they laughed, as though deaf with cotton in dirty ears. So I spoke with greater emotional emphasis. I closed my ears and swallowed blood until I was nauseated. The speech seemed a hundred times as long as before, but I could not leave out a single word. All had to be said, each memorized nuance considered, rendered. Nor was that all. Whenever I uttered a word of three or more syllables a group of voices would yell for me to repeat it. I used the phrase "social responsibility" and they yelled:

"What's that word you say, boy?"

70   "Social responsibility," I said.

"What?"

"Social . . ."

"Louder."

". . . responsibility."

75   "More!"

"Respon—"

"Repeat!"

"—sibility."

The room filled with the uproar of laughter until, no doubt, distracted by having to gulp down my blood, I made a mistake and yelled a phrase I had often seen denounced with newspaper editorials, heard debated in private.

80   "Social . . ."

"What?" they yelled. ". . . equality—"

The laughter hung smokelike in the sudden stillness. I opened my eyes, puzzled. Sounds of displeasure filled the room. The M.C. rushed forward. They shouted hostile phrases at me. But I did not understand.

A small dry mustached man in the front row blared out, "Say that slowly, son!"

85   "What sir?"

"What you just said!"

"Social responsibility, sir," I said.

"You weren't being smart, were you, boy?" he said, not unkindly.

"No sir!"

90   "You sure that about 'equality' was a mistake?"

"Oh, yes, sir," I said. "I was swallowing blood."

"Well, you had better speak more slowly so we can understand. We mean to do right by you, but you've got to know your place at all times. All right, now, go on with your speech."

I was afraid. I wanted to leave but I wanted also to speak and I was afraid they'd snatch me down.

"Thank you, sir," I said, beginning where I had left off, and having them ignore me as before.

95   Yet when I finished there was a thunderous applause. I was surprised to see the superintendent come forth with a package wrapped in white tissue paper, and, gesturing for quiet, address the men.

"Gentlemen, you see that I did not overpraise this boy. He makes a good speech and some day he'll lead his people in the proper paths. And I don't have to tell you that that is important in these days and times. This is a good, smart boy, and so to encourage him in the right direction, in the name of the Board of Education I wish to present him a prize in the form of this . . ."

He paused, removing the tissue paper and revealing a gleaming calfskin brief case.

". . . in the form of this first-class article from Shad Whitmore's shop."

"Boy," he said, addressing me, "take this prize and keep it well. Consider it a badge of office. Prize it. Keep developing as you are and some day it will be filled with important papers that will help shape the destiny of your people."

100   I was so moved that I could hardly express my thanks. A rope of bloody saliva forming a shape like an undiscovered continent drooled upon the leather and I wiped it quickly away. I felt an importance that I had never dreamed.

"Open it and see what's inside," I was told.

My fingers a-tremble, I complied, smelling the fresh leather and finding an official-looking document inside. It was a scholarship to the state college for Negroes. My eyes filled with tears and I ran awkwardly off the floor.

I was so overjoyed; I did not even mind when I discovered that the gold pieces I had scrambled for were brass pocket tokens advertising a certain make of automobile.

When I reached home everyone was excited. Next day the neighbors came to congratulate me. I even felt safe from grandfather, whose deathbed curse usually spoiled my triumphs. I stood beneath his photograph with my brief case in hand and smiled triumphantly into his stolid black peasant's face. It was a face that fascinated me. The eyes seemed to follow everywhere I went.

105   That night I dreamed I was at a circus with him and that he refused to laugh at the clowns no matter what they did. Then later he told me to open my brief case and read what was inside and I did, finding an official envelope stamped with the state seal; and inside the envelope I found another and another, endlessly, and I thought I would fall of weariness. "Them's years," he said. "Now open that one." And I did and in it I found an engraved document containing a short message in letters of gold. "Read it," my grand-father said. "Out loud."

"To Whom It May Concern," I intoned. "Keep This Nigger Boy Running."

I awoke with the old man's laughter ringing in my ears.

(It was a dream I was to remember and dream again for many years after. But at that time I had no insight into its meaning. First I had to attend college.)

Nadine Gordimer

Nadine Gordimer (1923–   ) was born and lives in
South Africa, one of many excellent writers who have
emerged from that violent country. Her novels include
A Guest of Honor (1970), *The Conservationist* (1974),
Burger's Daughter (1979), and *A Sport of Nature* (1986).
She is admired even more for her short stories, gathered in
a *Selected Stories* available from Penguin Books. Her latest
work is *My Son's Story* (1990).

The Train from Rhodesia   (1952)

The train came out of the red horizon and bore down towards them over the
single straight track.

The stationmaster came out of his little brick station with its pointed
chalet roof, feeling the creases in his serge uniform in his legs as well. A stir
of preparedness rippled through the squatting native venders waiting in the
dust; the face of a carved wooden animal, eternally surprised, stuck out of a
sack. The stationmaster's barefoot children wandered over. From the grey
mud huts with the untidy heads that stood within a decorated mud wall,
chickens, and dogs with their skin stretched like parchment over their bones,
followed the piccanins down to the track. The flushed and perspiring west
cast a reflection, faint, without heat, upon the station, upon the tin shed
marked 'Goods', upon the walled kraal, upon the grey tin house of the
stationmaster and upon the sand, that lapped all around, from sky to sky, cast
little rhythmical cups of shadow, so that the sand became the sea, and closed
over the children's black feet softly and without imprint.

The stationmaster's wife sat behind the mesh of her veranda. Above her
head the hunk of a sheep's carcass moved slightly, dangling in a current of air.

They waited.

5   The train called out, along the sky; but there was no answer; and the cry
hung on: I'm coming . . . I'm coming . . .

The engine flared out now, big, whisking a dwindling body behind it; the
track flared out to let it in.

Creaking, jerking, jostling, gasping, the train filled the station.

Here, let me see that one—the young woman curved her body farther out of
the corridor window. Missus? smiled the old man, looking at the creatures he
held in his hand. From a piece of string on his grey finger hung a tiny woven
basket; he lifted it, questioning. No, no, she urged, leaning down towards

him, across the height of the train towards the man in the piece of old rug; that one, that one, her hand commanded. It was a lion, carved out of soft dry wood that looked like spongecake; heraldic, black and white, with impressionistic detail burnt in. The old man held it up to her still smiling, not from the heart, but at the customer. Between its vandyke teeth, in the mouth opened in an endless roar too terrible to be heard, it had a black tongue. Look, said the young husband, if you don't mind! And round the neck of the thing, a piece of fur (rat? rabbit? meerkat?); a real mane, majestic, telling you somehow that the artist had delight in the lion.

All up and down the length of the train in the dust the artists sprang, walking bent, like performing animals, the better to exhibit the fantasy held towards the faces on the train. Buck, startled and stiff, staring with round black and white eyes. More lions, standing erect, grappling with strange, thin, elongated warriors who clutched spears and showed no fear in their slits of eyes. How much, they asked from the train, how much?

10   Give me penny, said the little ones with nothing to sell. The dogs went and sat, quite still, under the dining car, where the train breathed out the smell of meat cooking with onion.

A man passed beneath the arch of reaching arms meeting grey-black and white in the exchange of money for the staring wooden eyes, the stiff wooden legs sticking up in the air; went along under the voices and the bargaining, interrogating the wheels. Past the dogs; glancing up at the dining car where he could stare at the faces, behind glass, drinking beer, two by two, on either side of a uniform railway vase with its pale dead flower. Right to the end, to the guard's van, where the stationmaster's children had just collected their mother's two loaves of bread; to the engine itself, where the stationmaster and the driver stood talking against the steaming complaint of the resting beast.

The man called out to them, something loud and joking. They turned to laugh, in a twirl of steam. The two children careered over the sand, clutching the bread, and burst through the iron gate and up the path through the garden in which nothing grew.

Passengers drew themselves in at the corridor windows and turned into compartments to fetch money, to call someone to look. Those sitting inside looked up: suddenly different, caged faces, boxed in, cut off after the contact of outside. There was an orange a piccanin would like . . . What about that chocolate? It wasn't very nice . . .

A girl had collected a handful of the hard kind, that no one liked, out of the chocolate box, and was throwing them to the dogs, over at the dining car. But the hens darted in and swallowed the chocolates, incredibly quick and accurate, before they had even dropped in the dust, and the dogs, a little bewildered, looked up with their brown eyes, not expecting anything.

15   —No, leave it, said the young woman, don't take it . . .

Too expensive, too much, she shook her head and raised her voice to the old man, giving up the lion. He held it high where she had handed it to him. No, she said, shaking her head. Three-and-six? insisted her husband, loudly. Yes baas! laughed the old man. *Three-and-six?*—the young man was incredulous. Oh leave it—she said. The young man stopped. Don't you want it? he said, keeping his face closed to the old man. No, never mind, she said, leave it. The old native kept his head on one side, looking at them sideways, holding the lion. Three-and-six, he murmured, as old people repeat things to themselves.

The young woman drew her head in. She went into the coupé and sat down. Out of the window, on the other side, there was nothing: sand and bush; a thorn tree. Back through the open doorway, past the figure of her husband in the corridor, there was the station, the voices, wooden animals waving, running feet. Her eye followed the funny little valance of scrolled wood that outlined the chalet roof of the station; she thought of the lion and smiled. That bit of fur round the neck. But the wooden buck, the hippos, the elephants, the baskets that already bulked out of their brown paper under the seat and on the luggage rack! How will they look at home? Where will you put them? What will they mean away from the places you found them? Away from the unreality of the last few weeks? The young man outside. But he is not part of the unreality; he is for good now. Odd . . . somewhere there was an idea that he, that living with him, was part of the holiday, the strange places.

Outside, a bell rang. The stationmaster was leaning against the end of the train, green flag rolled in readiness. A few men who had got down to stretch their legs sprang on to the train, clinging to the observation platforms, or perhaps merely standing on the iron step, holding the rail; but on the train, safe from the now dusty platform, the one tin house, the empty sand.

There was a grunt. The train jerked. Through the glass the beer drinkers looked out, as if they could not see beyond it. Behind the fly-screen, the stationmaster's wife sat facing back at them beneath the darkening hunk of meat.

20   There was a shout. The flag drooped out. Joints not yet coordinated, the segmented body of the train heaved and bumped back against itself. It began to move slowly the scrolled chalet moved past it, the yells of the natives, running alongside jetted up into the air, fell back at different levels. Staring wooden faces waved drunkenly, there, then gone, questioning for the last time at the windows. Here one-and-six baas!—As one automatically opens a hand to catch a thrown ball, a man fumbled wildly down his pocket, brought up the shilling and sixpence and threw them out; the old native, gasping, his skinny toes splaying the sand, flung the lion.

The piccanins were waving, the dogs stood, tails uncertain, watching the train go: past the mud huts, where a woman turned to look up from the smoke of the fire, her hand pausing on her hip.

The stationmaster went slowly in under the chalet.

The old native stood, breath blowing out the skin between his ribs, feet tense, balanced in the sand, smiling and shaking his head. In his opened palm, held in the attitude of receiving, was the retrieved shilling and sixpence.

The blind end of the train was being pulled helplessly out of the station.

25   The young man swung in from the corridor, breathless. He was shaking his head with laughter and triumph. Here! he said. And waggled the lion at her. One-and-six!

What? she said.

He laughed. I was arguing with him for fun, bargaining—when the train had pulled out already, he came tearing after. . . . One-and-six Baas! So there's your lion.

She was holding it away from her, the head with the open jaws, the pointed teeth, the black tongue, the wonderful ruff of fur facing her. She was looking at it with an expression of not seeing, of seeing something different. Her face was drawn up, wryly, like the face of a discomforted child. Her mouth lifted nervously at the corner. Very slowly, cautious, she lifted her finger and touched the mane, where it was joined to the wood.

But how could you, she said. He was shocked by the dismay of her face.

30 Good Lord, he said, what's the matter?

If you wanted the thing, she said, her voice rising and breaking with the shrill impotence of anger, why didn't you buy it in the first place? If you wanted it, why didn't you pay for it? Why didn't you take it decently, when he offered it? Why did you have to wait for him to run after the train with it, and give him one-and-six? One-and-six!

She was pushing it at him, trying to force him to take the lion. He stood astonished, his hands hanging at his sides.

But you wanted it! You liked it so much?

—It's a beautiful piece of work, she said fiercely, as if to protect it from him.

35 You liked it so much! You said yourself it was too expensive—

Oh *you*—she said, hopeless and furious. *You* . . . She threw the lion onto the seat.

He stood looking at her.

She sat down again in the corner and her face slumped in her hands, stared out of the window. Everything was turning round inside her. One-and-six. One-and-six. One-and-six for the wood and the carving and the sinews of the legs and the switch of the tail. The mouth open like that and the teeth. The black tongue, rolling, like a wave. The mane round the neck. To give one-and-six for that. The heat of shame mounted through her legs and body and sounded in her ears like the sound of sand pouring. Pouring, pouring. She sat there, sick. A weariness, a tastelessness, the discovery of a void made her hands slacken their grip, atrophy emptily, as if the hour was not worth their grasp. She was feeling like this again. She had thought it was something to do with singleness, with being alone and belonging too much to oneself.

She sat there not wanting to move or speak, or to look at anything even; so that the mood should be associated with nothing, no object, word or sight that might recur and so recall the feeling again. . . . Smuts blew in grittily, settled on her hands. Her back remained at exactly the same angle, turned against the young man sitting with his hands drooping between his sprawled legs, and the lion, fallen on its side in the corner.

The train had cast the station like a skin. It called out to the sky, I'm coming, I'm coming; and again, there was no answer.

Langston Hughes

Langston Hughes (1902–1967) was born in Joplin, Missouri. He came to New York, where he was a leading spirit in the Harlem renaissance of black American writers in the 1920s and 1930s. Best known as a poet—*Shakespeare in Harlem* (1942), *One Way Ticket* (1949), *Selected Poems* (1959)—he also wrote children's books, plays, and novels. See also page 629.

On the Road   (1952)

He was not interested in the snow. When he got off the freight, one early evening during the depression, Sargeant never even noticed the snow. But he must have felt it seeping down his neck, cold, wet, sopping in his shoes. But if you had asked him, he wouldn't have known it was snowing. Sargeant didn't see the snow, not even under the bright lights of the main street, falling white and flaky against the night. He was too hungry, too sleepy, too tired.

The Reverend Mr. Dorset, however, saw the snow when he switched on his porch light, opened the front door of his parsonage, and found standing there before him a big black man with snow on his face, a human piece of night with snow on his face—obviously unemployed.

Said the Reverend Mr. Dorset before Sargeant even realized he'd opened his mouth: "I'm sorry. No! Go right on down this street four blocks and turn to your left, walk up seven and you'll see the Relief Shelter. I'm sorry. No!" He shut the door.

Sargeant wanted to tell the holy man that he had already been to the Relief Shelter, been to hundreds of relief shelters during the depression years, the beds were always gone and supper was over, the place was full, and they drew the color line anyhow. But the minister said, "No," and shut the door. Evidently he didn't want to hear about it. And he *had* a door to shut.

5   The big black man turned away. And even yet he didn't see the snow, walking right into it. Maybe he sensed it, cold, wet, sticking to his jaws, wet on his black hands, sopping in his shoes. He stopped and stood on the sidewalk hunched over—hungry, sleepy, cold—looking up and down. Then he looked right where he was—in front of a church. Of course! A church! Sure, right next to a parsonage, certainly a church.

It had *two* doors.

Broad white steps in the night all snowy white. Two high arched doors with slender stone pillars on either side. And way up, a round lacy window with a stone crucifix in the middle and Christ on the crucifix in stone. All this was pale in the street lights, solid and stony pale in the snow.

Sargeant blinked. When he looked up, the snow fell into his eyes. For the first time that night he *saw* the snow. He shook his head. He shook the snow from his coat sleeves, felt hungry, felt lost, felt not lost, felt cold. He walked up the steps of the church. He knocked at the door. No answer. He tried the handle. Locked. He put his shoulder against the door and his long black body slanted like a ramrod. He pushed. With loud rhythmic grunts, like the grunts in a chain-gang song, he pushed against the door.

"I'm tired . . . Huh! . . . Hongry . . . Uh! . . . I'm sleepy . . . Huh! I'm cold . . . I got to sleep somewheres," Sargeant said. "This here is a church, ain't it? Well, uh!"

10   He pushed against the door.

Suddenly, with an undue cracking and screaking, the door began to give way to the tall black Negro who pushed ferociously against it.

By now two or three white people had stopped in the street, and Sargeant was vaguely aware of some of them yelling at him concerning the door. Three or four more came running, yelling at him.

"Hey!" they said. "Hey!"

"Uh-huh," answered the big tall Negro, "I know it's a white folks' church, but I got to sleep somewhere." He gave another lunge at the door. "Huh!"

15   And the door broke open.

But just when the door gave way, two white cops arrived in a car, ran up the steps with their clubs, and grabbed Sargeant. But Sargeant for once had no intention of being pulled or pushed away from the door.

Sargeant grabbed, but not for anything so weak as a broken door. He grabbed for one of the tall stone pillars beside the door, grabbed at it and caught it. And held it. The cops pulled Sargeant pulled. Most of the people in the street got behind the cops and helped them pull.

"A big black unemployed Negro holding onto our church!" thought the people. "The idea!"

The cops began to beat Sargeant over the head, and nobody protested. But he held on.

20   And then the church fell down.

Gradually, the big stone front of the church fell down, the walls and the rafters, the crucifix and the Christ. Then the whole thing fell down, covering the cops and the people with bricks and stones and debris. The whole church fell down in the snow.

Sargeant got out from under the church and went walking on up the street with the stone pillar on his shoulder. He was under the impression that he had buried the parsonage and the Reverend Mr. Dorset who said, "No!" So he laughed, and threw the pillar six blocks up the street and went on.

Sargeant thought he was alone, but listening to the *crunch, crunch, crunch* on the snow of his own footsteps, he heard other footsteps, too, doubling his own. He looked around, and there was Christ walking along beside him, the same Christ that had been on the cross on the church—still stone with a rough stone surface, walking along beside him just like he was broken off the cross when the church fell down.

"Well, I'll be dogged," said Sargeant. "This here's the first time I ever seed you off the cross."

25   "Yes," said Christ, crunching his feet in the snow. "You had to pull the church down to get me off the cross."

"You glad?" said Sargeant.

"I sure am," said Christ.

They both laughed.

"I'm a hell of a fellow, ain't I?" said Sargeant. "Done pulled the church down!"

30   "You did a good job," said Christ. "They have kept me nailed on a cross for nearly two thousand years."

"Whee-ee-e!" said Sargeant. "I know you are glad to get off."

"I sure am," said Christ.

They walked on in the snow. Sargeant looked at the man of stone.

"And you have been up there two thousand years?"

35   "I sure have," Christ said.

"Well, if I had a little cash," said Sargeant, "I'd show you around a bit."

"I been around," said Christ.

"Yeah, but that was a long time ago."

"All the same," said Christ, "I've been around."

40   They walked on in the snow until they came to the railroad yards. Sargeant was tired, sweating and tired.

"Where you goin'?" Sargeant said, stopping by the tracks. He looked at Christ. Sargeant said, "I'm just a bum on the road. How about you? Where you goin'?"

"God knows," Christ said, "but I'm leavin' here."

They saw the red and green lights of the railroad yard half veiled by the snow that fell out of the night. Away down the track they saw a fire in a hobo jungle.

"I can go there and sleep," Sargeant said.

45   "You can?"

"Sure," said Sargeant. "That place ain't got no doors."

Outside the town, along the tracks, there were barren trees and bushes below the embankment, snow-gray in the dark. And down among the trees and bushes there were makeshift houses made out of boxes and tin and old pieces of wood and canvas. You couldn't see them in the dark, but you knew they were there if you'd ever been on the road, if you had ever lived with the homeless and hungry in a depression.

"I'm side-tracking," Sargeant said. "I'm tired."

"I'm gonna make it on to Kansas City," said Christ.

50   "O.K.," Sargeant said. "So long!"

He went down into the hobo jungle and found himself a place to sleep. He never did see Christ no more. About 6:00 A.M. a freight came by. Sargeant scrambled out of the jungle with a dozen or so more hobos and ran along the track, grabbing at the freight. It was dawn, early dawn, cold and gray.

"Wonder where Christ is by now?" Sargeant thought. "He musta gone on way on down the road. He didn't sleep in this jungle."

Sargeant grabbed the train and started to pull himself up into a moving coal car, over the edge of a wheeling coal car. But strangely enough, the car was full of cops. The nearest cop rapped Sargeant soundly across the knuckles with his night stick. Wham! Rapped his big black hands for clinging to the top of the car. Wham! But Sargeant did not turn loose. He clung on and tried to pull himself into the car. He hollered at the top of his voice, "Damn it, lemme in this car!"

"Shut up," barked the cop. "You crazy coon!" He rapped Sargeant across the knuckles and punched him in the stomach. "You ain't out in no jungle now. This ain't no train. You in jail."

55   Wham! across his bare black fingers clinging to the bars of his cell. Wham! between the steel bars low down against his shins.

Suddenly Sargeant realized that he really was in jail. He wasn't on no train. The blood of the night before had dried on his face, his head hurt terribly, and a cop outside in the corridor was hitting him across the knuckles for holding onto the door, yelling and shaking the cell door.

"They musta took me to jail for breaking down the door last night," Sargeant thought, "that church door."

Sargeant went over and sat on a wooden bench against the cold stone wall. He was emptier than ever. His clothes were wet, clammy cold wet, and shoes sloppy with snow water. It was just about dawn. There he was, locked up behind a cell door, nursing his bruised fingers.

The bruised fingers were his, but not the *door.*

60   Not the *club,* but the fingers.

"You wait," mumbled Sargeant, black against the jail wall. "I'm gonna break down this door, too."

"Shut up—or I'll paste you one," said the cop.

"I'm gonna break down this door," yelled Sargeant as he stood up in his cell.

Then he must have been talking to himself because he said, "I wonder where Christ's gone? I wonder if he's gone to Kansas City?"

Jamaica Kincaid

Jamaica Kincaid (1949–   ) was born in St. John's, Antigua, in the West Indies. She is author of two novels, *Annie John* (1985) and *Lucy* (1990). "What I Have Been Doing Lately" comes from a collection of short stories, *At the Bottom of the River* (1983). She works as a staff writer on *The New Yorker* and lives in New York.

What I Have Been Doing Lately   (1983)

What I have been doing lately: I was lying in bed and the doorbell rang. I ran downstairs. Quick. I opened the door. There was no one there. I stepped outside. Either it was drizzling or there was a lot of dust in the air and the dust was damp. I stuck out my tongue and the drizzle or the damp dust tasted like government school ink. I looked north. I looked south. I decided to start walking north. While walking north, I noticed that I was barefoot. While walking north, I looked up and saw the planet Venus. I said, "It must be almost morning." I saw a monkey in a tree. The tree had no leaves. I said, "Ah, a monkey. Just look at that. A monkey." I walked for I don't know how long before I came up to a big body of water. I wanted to get across it but I couldn't swim. I wanted to get across it but it would take me years to build a boat. I wanted to get across it but it would take me I didn't know how long to build a bridge. Years passed and then one day, feeling like it, I got into my boat and rowed across. When I got to the other side, it was noon and my shadow was small and fell beneath me. I set out on a path that stretched out straight ahead. I passed a house, and a dog was sitting on the verandah but it looked the other way when it saw me coming. I passed a boy tossing a ball in the air but the boy looked the other way when he saw me coming. I walked and I walked but I couldn't tell if I walked a long time because my feet didn't feel as if they would drop off. I turned around to see what I had left behind me but nothing was familiar. Instead of the straight path, I saw hills. Instead of the boy with his ball, I saw tall flowering trees. I looked up and the sky was without clouds and seemed near, as if it were the ceiling in my house and, if I stood on a chair, I could touch it with the tips of my fingers. I turned around and looked ahead of me again. A deep hole had opened up before me. I looked in. The hole was deep and dark and I couldn't see the bottom. I thought, What's down there?, so on purpose I fell in. I fell and I fell, over and over, as if I were an old suitcase. On the sides of the deep hole I could see things written, but perhaps it was in a foreign language because I couldn't read them. Still I fell, for I don't know how long. As I fell I began to see that I didn't like the way falling made me feel. Falling made me feel sick and I missed all the people I had loved. I said, I don't want to fall anymore, and I reversed myself. I was standing again on the edge of the deep hole. I looked at the deep hole and I said, You can close up now, and it did. I walked some more without knowing distance. I only knew that I passed through days and nights, I only knew that I passed through rain and shine, light and darkness. I was never thirsty and I felt no pain. Looking at the horizon, I made a joke for myself: I said, "The earth has thin lips," and I laughed.

Looking at the horizon again, I saw a lone figure coming toward me, but I wasn't frightened because I was sure it was my mother. As I got closer to the figure, I could see that it wasn't my mother, but still I wasn't frightened because I could see that it was a woman.

When this woman got closer to me, she looked at me hard and then she threw up her hands. She must have seen me somewhere before because she said, "It's you. Just look at that. It's you. And just what have you been doing lately?"

I could have said, "I have been praying not to grow any taller."

5   I could have said, "I have been listening carefully to my mother's words, so as to make a good imitation of a dutiful daughter."

I could have said, "A pack of dogs, tired from chasing each other all over town, slept in the moonlight."

Instead, I said, What I have been doing lately: I was lying in bed on my back, my hands drawn up, my fingers interlaced lightly at the nape of my neck. Someone rang the doorbell. I went downstairs and opened the door but there was no one there. I stepped outside. Either it was drizzling or there was a lot of dust in the air and the dust was damp. I stuck out my tongue and the drizzle or the damp dust tasted like government school ink. I looked north and I looked south. I started walking north. While walking north, I wanted to move fast, so I removed the shoes from my feet. While walking north, I looked up and saw the planet Venus and I said, "If the sun went out, it would be eight minutes before I would know it." I saw a monkey sitting in a tree that had no leaves and I said, "A monkey. Just look at that. A monkey." I picked up a stone and I threw it at the monkey. The monkey, seeing the stone, quickly moved out of its way. Three times I threw a stone at the monkey and three times it moved away. The fourth time I threw the stone, the monkey caught it and threw it back at me. The stone struck me on my forehead over my right eye, making a deep gash. The gash healed immediately but now the skin on my forehead felt false to me. I walked for I don't know how long before I came to a big body of water. I wanted to get across, so when the boat came I paid my fare. When I got to the other side, I saw a lot of people sitting on the beach and they were having a picnic. They were the most beautiful people I had ever seen. Everything about them was black and shiny. Their skin was black and shiny. Their shoes were black and shiny. Their hair was black and shiny. The clothes they wore were black and shiny. I could hear them laughing and chatting and I said, I would like to be with these people, so I started to walk toward them, but when I got up close to them I saw that they weren't at a picnic and they weren't beautiful and they weren't chatting and laughing. All around me was black mud and the people all looked as if they had been made up out of the black mud. I looked up and saw that the sky seemed far away and nothing I could stand on would make me able to touch it with my fingertips. I thought, If only I could get out of this, so I started to walk. I must have walked for a long time because my feet hurt and felt as if they would drop off. I thought, If only just around the bend I would see my house and inside my house I would find my bed, freshly made at that, and in the kitchen I would find my mother or anyone else that I loved making me a custard. I thought, If only it was a Sunday and I was sitting in a church and I had just heard someone sing a psalm. I felt very sad so I sat down. I felt so sad that I rested my head on my own knees and smoothed my own head. I felt so sad I couldn't imagine feeling any other way again. I said, I don't like this. I don't want to do this anymore. And I went back to lying in bed, just before the doorbell rang.

D. H. Lawrence

D. H. (David Herbert) Lawrence (1885–1930) was the son of a coalminer. He graduated from a teachers' college, taught school for a time, and wrote poems and novels with a prolific energy. In 1912, he began living with a German noblewoman, Frieda von Richthofen Weekley. Married two years later, they were objects of suspicion during the First World War in England, because of Frieda's nationality and Lawrence's pacifism. After the war, they moved restlessly around the world: Italy, Ceylon, Australia, New Mexico, Mexico. Lawrence excelled at writing travel literature—together with criticism, philosophical essays, and almost every literary form. Examples of his poems are printed in this volume on pages 633–634. Among his most famous novels are *Sons and Lovers* (1913), *The Rainbow* (1915), *Women in Love* (1921), and *Lady Chatterley's Lover* (1928).

The Rocking-Horse Winner   (1926)

There was a woman who was beautiful, who started with all the advantages, yet she had no luck. She married for love, and the love turned to dust. She had bonny children, yet she felt they had been thrust upon her, and she could not love them. They looked at her coldly, as if they were finding fault with her. And hurriedly she felt she must cover up some fault in herself. Yet what it was that she must cover up she never knew. Nevertheless, when her children were present, she always felt the centre of her heart go hard. This troubled her, and in her manner she was all the more gentle and anxious for her children, as if she loved them very much. Only she herself knew that at the centre of her heart was a hard little place that could not feel love, no, not for anybody. Everybody else said of her: "She is such a good mother. She adores her children." Only she herself, and her children themselves, knew it was not so. They read it in each other's eyes.

There were a boy and two little girls. They lived in a pleasant house, with a garden, and they had discreet servants, and felt themselves superior to anyone in the neighbourhood.

Although they lived in style, they felt always an anxiety in the house. There was never enough money. The mother had a small income, and the father had a small income, but not nearly enough for the social position which they had to keep up. The father went into town to some office. But though he had good prospects, these prospects never materialized. There was always the grinding sense of the shortage of money, though the style was always kept up.

At last the mother said: "I will see if I can't make something." But she did not know where to begin. She racked her brains, and tried this thing and the other, but could not find anything successful. The failure made deep lines come into her face. Her children were growing up, they would have to go to school. There must be more money, there must be more money. The father, who was always very handsome and expensive in his tastes, seemed as if he never would be able to do anything worth doing. And the mother, who had a great belief in herself, did not succeed any better, and her tastes were just as expensive.

5   And so the house came to be haunted by the unspoken phrase: There must be more money! There must be more money! The children could hear it all the time, though nobody said it aloud. They heard it at Christmas, when the expensive and splendid toys filled the nursery. Behind the shining modern rocking horse, behind the smart doll's-house, a voice would start whispering: "There must be more money! There must be more money!" And the children would stop playing, to listen for a moment. They would look into each other's eyes, to see if they had all heard. And each one saw in the eyes of the other two that they too had heard. "There must be more money! There must be more money!"

It came whispering from the springs of the still-swaying rocking horse, and even the horse, bending his wooden, champing head, heard it. The big doll, sitting so pink and smirking in her new pram, could hear it quite plainly, and seemed to be smirking all the more self-consciously because of it. The foolish puppy, too, that took the place of the Teddy bear, he was looking so extraordinarily foolish for no other reason but that he heard the secret whisper all over the house: "There must be more money!"

Yet nobody ever said it aloud. The whisper was everywhere, and therefore no one spoke it. Just as no one ever says: "We are breathing!" in spite of the fact that breath is coming and going all the time.

"Mother," said the boy Paul one day, "why don't we keep a car of our own? Why do we always use uncle's, or else a taxi?"

"Because we're the poor members of the family," said the mother.

10   "But why are we, mother?"

"Well—I suppose," she said slowly and bitterly, "it's because your father has no luck."

The boy was silent for some time.

"Is luck money, mother?" he asked, rather timidly.

"No, Paul. Not quite. It's what causes you to have money."

15   "Oh!" said Paul vaguely. "I thought when Uncle Oscar said filthy lucker, it meant money."

"Filthy lucre does mean money," said the mother. "But it's lucre, not luck."

"Oh!" said the boy. "Then what is luck, mother?"

"It's what causes you to have money. If you're lucky you have money. That's why it's better to be born lucky than rich. If you're rich, you may lose your money. But if you're lucky, you will always get more money."

"Oh! Will you? And is father not lucky?"

20   "Very unlucky, I should say," she said bitterly.

The boy watched her with unsure eyes.

"Why?" he asked.

"I don't know. Nobody ever knows why one person is lucky and another unlucky."

"Don't they? Nobody at all? Does nobody know?"

25   "Perhaps God. But He never tells."

"He ought to, then. And aren't you lucky either, mother?"

"I can't be, if I married an unlucky husband."

"But by yourself, aren't you?"

"I used to think I was, before I married. Now I think I am very unlucky indeed."

30   "Why?"

"Well—never mind! Perhaps I'm not really," she said.

The child looked at her, to see if she meant it. But he saw, by the lines of her mouth, that she was only trying to hide something from him.

"Well, anyhow," he said stoutly, "I'm a lucky person."

"Why?" said his mother, with a sudden laugh.

35   He stared at her. He didn't even know why he had said it.

"God told me," he asserted, brazening it out.

"I hope He did, dear!" she said, again with a laugh, but rather bitter.

"He did, mother!"

"Excellent!" said the mother, using one of her husband's exclamations.

40   The boy saw she did not believe him; or, rather, that she paid no attention to his assertion. This angered him somewhat; and made him want to compel her attention.

He went off by himself, vaguely, in a childish way, seeking for the clue to "luck." Absorbed, taking no heed of other people, he went about with a sort of stealth, seeking inwardly for luck. He wanted luck, he wanted it, he wanted it. When the two girls were playing dolls in the nursery, he would sit on his big rocking horse, charging madly into space, with a frenzy that made the little girls peer at him uneasily. Wildly the horse careered, the waving dark hair of the boy tossed, his eyes had a strange glare in them. The little girls dared not speak to him.

When he had ridden to the end of his mad little journey, he climbed down and stood in front of his rocking horse, staring fixedly into its lowered face. Its red mouth was slightly open, its big eye was wide and glassy-bright.

"Now!" he would silently command the snorting steed. "Now, take me to where there is luck! Now take me!"

And he would slash the horse on the neck with the little whip he had asked Uncle Oscar for. He knew the horse could take him to where there was luck, if only he forced it. So he would mount again, and start on his furious ride, hoping at last to get there. He knew he could get there.

45   "You'll break your horse, Paul!" said the nurse.

"He's always riding like that! I wish he'd leave off!" said his elder sister Joan.

But he only glared down on them in silence. Nurse gave him up. She could make nothing of him. Anyhow he was growing beyond her.

One day his mother and his Uncle Oscar came in when he was on one of his furious rides. He did not speak to them.

"Hallo, you young jockey! Riding a winner?" said his uncle.

50   "Aren't you growing too big for a rocking horse? You're not a very little boy any longer, you know," said his mother.

But Paul only gave a blue glare from his big, rather close-set eyes. He would speak to nobody when he was in full tilt. His mother watched him with an anxious expression on her face.

At last he suddenly stopped forcing his horse into the mechanical gallop, and slid down.

"Well, I got there!" he announced fiercely, his blue eyes still flaring, and his sturdy long legs straddling apart.

"Where did you get to?" asked his mother.

55   "Where I wanted to go," he flared back at her.

"That's right, son!" said Uncle Oscar. "Don't you stop till you get there. What's the horses's name?"

"He doesn't have a name," said the boy.

"Gets on without all right?" asked the uncle.

"Well, he has different names. He was called Sansovino last week."

60   "Sansovino, eh? Won the Ascot. How did you know his name?"

"He always talks about horse races with Bassett," said Joan.

The uncle was delighted to find that his small nephew was posted with all the racing news. Bassett, the young gardener, who had been wounded in the left foot in the war and had got his present job through Oscar Cresswell, whose batman he had been, was a perfect blade of the "turf." He lived in the racing events, and the small boy lived with him.

Oscar Cresswell got it all from Bassett.

"Master Paul comes and asks me, so I can't do more than tell him, sir," said Bassett, his face terribly serious, as if he were speaking of religious matters.

65   "And does he ever put anything on a horse he fancies?"

"Well—I don't want to give him away—he's a young sport, a fine sport, sir. Would you mind asking him yourself? He sort of takes a pleasure in it, and perhaps he'd feel I was giving him away, sir, if you don't mind."

Bassett was serious as a church.

The uncle went back to his nephew, and took him off for a ride in the car.

"Say, Paul, old man, do you ever put anything on a horse?" the uncle asked.

70   The boy watched the handsome man closely.

"Why, do you think I oughtn't to?" he parried.

"Not a bit of it! I thought perhaps you might give me a tip for the Lincoln."

The car sped on into the country, going down to Uncle Oscar's place in Hampshire.

"Honour bright?" said the nephew.

75   "Honour bright, son!" said the uncle.

"Well, then, Daffodil."

"Daffodil! I doubt it, sonny. What about Mirza?"

"I only know the winner," said the boy. "That's Daffodil."

"Daffodil, eh?"

80   There was a pause. Daffodil was an obscure horse comparatively.

"Uncle!"

"Yes, son?"

"You won't let it go any further, will you? I promised Bassett."

"Bassett be damned, old man! What's he got to do with it?"

85   "We're partners. We've been partners from the first. Uncle, he lent me my first five shillings, which I lost. I promised him, honour bright, it was only between me and him; only you gave me that ten-shilling note I started winning with, so I thought you were lucky. You won't let it go any further, will you?"

The boy gazed at his uncle from those big, hot, blue eyes, set rather close together. The uncle stirred and laughed uneasily.

"Right you are, son! I'll keep your tip private. Daffodil, eh? How much are you putting on him?"

"All except twenty pounds," said the boy. "I keep that in reserve."

The uncle thought it a good joke.

90   "You keep twenty pounds in reserve, do you, you young romancer. What are you betting, then?"

"I'm betting three hundred," said the boy gravely. "But it's between you and me, Uncle Oscar! Honour bright?"

The uncle burst into a roar of laughter.

"It's between you and me all right, you young Nat Gould," he said, laughing. "But where's your three hundred?"

"Bassett keeps it for me. We're partners."

95   "You are, are you! And what is Bassett putting on Daffodil?"

"He won't go quite so high as I do, I expect. Perhaps he'll go a hundred and fifty."

"What, pennies?" laughed the uncle.

"Pounds," said the child, with a surprised look at his uncle. "Bassett keeps a bigger reserve than I do."

Between wonder and amusement Uncle Oscar was silent. He pursued the matter no further, but he determined to take his nephew with him to the Lincoln races.

100   "Now, son," he said, "I'm putting twenty on Mirza, and I'll put five for you on any horse you fancy. What's your pick?"

"Daffodil, uncle."

"No, not the fiver on Daffodil!"

"I should if it was my own fiver," said the child.

"Good! Good! Right you are! A fiver for me and a fiver for you on Daffodil."

105 The child had never been to a race meeting before, and his eyes were blue fire. He pursed his mouth tight, and watched. A Frenchman just in front had put his money on Lancelot. Wild with excitement, he flayed his arms up and down, yelling "Lancelot! Lancelot!" in his French accent.

Daffodil came in first, Lancelot second. Mizra third. The child, flushed and with eyes blazing, was curiously serene. His uncle brought him four five-pound notes, four to one.

"What am I to do with these?" he cried, waving them before the boy's eyes.

"I suppose we'll talk to Bassett," said the boy. "I expect I have fifteen hundred now; and twenty in reserve; and this twenty."

His uncle studied him for some moments.

110 "Look here, son!" he said. "You're not serious about Bassett and that fifteen hundred, are you?"

"Yes, I am. But it's between you and me, uncle. Honour bright!"

"Honour bright all right, son! But I must talk to Bassett."

"If you'd like to be a partner, uncle, with Bassett and me, we could all be partners. Only, you'd have to promise, honour bright, uncle, not to let it go beyond us three. Bassett and I are lucky, and you must be lucky, because it was your ten shillings I started winning with. . . ."

Uncle Oscar took both Bassett and Paul into Richmond Park for an afternoon, and there they talked.

115 'It's like this, you see, sir," Bassett said. "Master Paul would get me talking about racing events, spinning yarns, you know, sir. And he was always keen on knowing if I'd made or if I'd lost. It's about a year since, now, that I put five shillings on Blush of Dawn for him—and we lost. Then the luck turned, with that ten shillings he had from you, that we put on Singhalese. And since that time, it's been pretty steady, all things considering. What do you say, Master Paul?"

"We're all right when we're sure," said Paul. "It's when we're not quite sure that we go down."

"Oh, but we're careful then," said Bassett.

"But when are you sure?" smiled Uncle Oscar.

"It's Master Paul, sir," said Bassett, in a secret, religious voice. "It's as if he had it from heaven. Like Daffodil, now, for the Lincoln. That was as sure as eggs."

120 "Did you put anything on Daffodil?" asked Oscar Cresswell.

"Yes, sir, I made my bit."

"And my nephew?"

Bassett was obstinately silent, looking at Paul.

"I made twelve hundred, didn't I, Bassett? I told uncle, I was putting three hundred on Daffodil."

125 "That's right," said Bassett, nodding.

"But where's the money?" asked the uncle.

"I keep it safe locked up, sir. Master Paul he can have it any minute he likes to ask for it."

"What, fifteen hundred pounds?"

"And twenty! and forty, that is, with the twenty he made on the course."

130   "It's amazing!" said the uncle.

"If Master Paul offers you to be partners, sir, I would, if I were you; if you'll excuse me," said Bassett.

Oscar Cresswell thought about it.

"I'll see the money," he said.

They drove home again, and sure enough, Bassett came round to the gardenhouse with fifteen hundred pounds in notes. The twenty pounds reserve was left with Joe Glee, in the Turf Commission deposit.

135   "You see, it's all right, uncle, when I'm sure! Then we go strong, for all we're worth. Don't we, Bassett?"

"We do at that, Master Paul."

"And when are you sure?" said the uncle, laughing.

"Oh, well, sometimes I'm absolutely sure, like about Daffodil," said the boy; "and sometimes I have an idea; and sometimes I haven't even an idea, have I, Bassett? Then we're careful, because we mostly go down."

"You do, do you? And when you're sure, like about Daffodil, what makes you sure, sonny?"

140   "Oh, well, I don't know," said the boy uneasily. "I'm sure, you know, uncle; that's all."

"It's as if he had it from heaven, sir," Bassett reiterated.

"I should say so!" said the uncle.

But he became a partner. And when the Leger was coming on, Paul was "sure" about Lively Spark, which was a quite inconsiderable horse. The boy insisted on putting a thousand on the horse. Bassett went for five hundred, and Oscar Cresswell two hundred. Lively Spark came in first, and the betting had been ten to one against him. Paul had made ten thousand.

"You see," he said, "I was absolutely sure of him."

145   Even Oscar Cresswell had cleared two thousand.

"Look here, son," he said, "this sort of thing makes me nervous."

"It needn't, uncle! Perhaps I shan't be sure again for a long time."

"But what are you going to do with your money?" asked the uncle.

"Of course," said the boy, "I started it for mother. She said she had no luck, because father is unlucky, so I thought if I was lucky, it might stop whispering."

150   "What might stop whispering?"

"Our house. I hate our house for whispering."

"What does it whisper?"

"Why—why"—the boy fidgeted—"why, I don't know. But it's always short of money, you know, uncle."

"I know it, son, I know it."

155   "You know people send mother writs, don't you, uncle?"

"I'm afraid I do," said the uncle.

"And then the house whispers, like people laughing at you behind your back, it's awful, that is! I thought if I was lucky. . . ."

"You might stop it," added the uncle.

The boy watched him with big blue eyes that had an uncanny cold fire in them, and he said never a word.

160   "Well, then!" said the uncle. "What are we doing?"

"I shouldn't like mother to know I was lucky," said the boy.

"Why not, son?"

"She'd stop me."

"I don't think she would."

165   "Oh!"—and the boy writhed in an odd way—"I don't want her to know, uncle."

"All right, son! We'll manage it without her knowing."

They managed it very easily. Paul, at the other's suggestion, handed over five thousand pounds to his uncle, who deposited it with the family lawyer, who was then to inform Paul's mother that a relative had put five thousand pounds into his hands, which sum was to be paid out a thousand pounds at a time, on the mother's birthday, for the next five years.

"So she'll have a birthday present of a thousand pounds for five successive years," said Uncle Oscar. "I hope it won't make it all the harder for her later."

Paul's mother had her birthday in November. The house had been "whispering" worse than ever lately, and, even in spite of his luck, Paul could not bear up against it. He was very anxious to see the effect of the birthday letter, telling his mother about the thousand pounds.

170   When there were no visitors, Paul now took his meals with his parents, as he was beyond the nursery control. His mother went into town nearly every day. She had discovered that she had an odd knack of sketching furs and dress materials, so she worked secretly in the studio of a friend who was the chief "artist" for the leading drapers. She drew the figures of ladies in furs and ladies in silk and sequins for the newspaper advertisements. This young woman artist earned several thousand pounds a year, but Paul's mother only made several hundreds, and she was again dissatisfied. She so wanted to be first in something, and she did not succeed, even in making sketches for drapery advertisements.

She was down to breakfast on the morning of her birthday. Paul watched her face as she read her letters. He knew the lawyer's letter. As his mother read it, her face hardened and became more expressionless. Then a cold, determined look came on her mouth. She hid the letter under the pile of others and said not a word about it.

"Didn't you have anything nice in the post for your birthday, mother?" said Paul.

"Quite moderately nice," she said, her voice cold and absent.

She went away to town without saying more.

175   But in the afternoon Uncle Oscar appeared. He said Paul's mother had had a long interview with the lawyer, asking if the whole five thousand could be advanced at once, as she was in debt.

"What do you think, uncle?" said the boy.

"I leave it to you, son."

"Oh, let her have it, then! We can get some more with the other," said the boy.

"A bird in the hand is worth two in the bush, laddie!" said Uncle Oscar.

180   "But I'm sure to know for the Grand National; or the Lincolnshire; or else the Derby. I'm sure to know for one of them," said Paul.

So Uncle Oscar signed the agreement, and Paul's mother touched the whole five thousand. Then something very curious happened. The voice in the house suddenly went mad, like a chorus of frogs on a spring evening. There were certain new furnishings, and Paul had a tutor. He was really going to Eton, his father's school, in the following autumn. There were flowers in the winter, and a blossoming of the luxury Paul's mother had been used to. And yet the voices in the house, behind the sprays of mimosa and almond blossom, and from under the piles of iridescent cushions, simply trilled and screamed in a sort of ecstasy: "There must be more money! Oh-h, there must be more money. Oh, now, now-w! Now-w-w—there must be more money!— more than ever! More than ever!"

It frightened Paul terribly. He studied away at his Latin and Greek with his tutors. But his intense hours were spent with Bassett. The Grand National had gone by: he had not "known," and that had lost a hundred pounds. Summer was at hand. He was in agony for the Lincoln. But even for the Lincoln he didn't "know" and he lost fifty pounds. He became wild-eyed and strange, as if something were going to explode in him.

"Let it alone, son! Don't you bother about it!" urged Uncle Oscar. But it was as if the boy couldn't really hear what his uncle was saying.

"I've got to know for the Derby! I've got to know for the Derby!" the child reiterated, his big eyes blazing with a sort of madness.

185   His mother noticed how overwrought he was.

"You'd better go to the seaside. Wouldn't you like to go now to the seaside, instead of waiting? I think you'd better," she said, looking down at him anxiously, her heart curiously heavy because of him.

But the child lifted his uncanny blue eyes.

"I couldn't possibly go before the Derby, mother!" he said. "I couldn't possibly!"

"Why not?" she said, her voice becoming heavy when she was opposed. "Why not? You can still go from the seaside to see the Derby with your Uncle Oscar, if that's what you wish. No need for you to wait here. Besides, I think you care too much about these races. It's a bad sign. My family has been a gambling family, and you won't know till you grow up how much damage it has done. But it has done damage. I shall have to send Bassett away, and ask Uncle Oscar not to talk racing to you, unless you promise to be reasonable about it; go away to the seaside and forget it. You're all nerves!"

190   "I'll do what you like, mother, so long as you don't send me away till after the Derby," the boy said.

"Send you away from where? Just from this house?"

"Yes," he said, gazing at her.

"Why, you curious child, what makes you care about this house so much, suddenly? I never knew you loved it."

He gazed at her without speaking. He had a secret within a secret, something he had not divulged, even to Bassett or to his Uncle Oscar.

195   But his mother, after standing undecided and a little bit sullen for some
moments, said:

"Very well, then! Don't go to the seaside till after the Derby, if you don't
wish it. But promise me you won't let your nerves go to pieces. Promise you
won't think so much about horse racing and events, as you call them!"

"Oh, no," said the boy casually. "I won't think much about them, mother.
You needn't worry. I wouldn't worry, mother, if I were you."

"If you were me and I were you," said his mother, "I wonder what we
should do!"

"But you know you needn't worry, mother, don't you?" the boy repeated.

200   "I should be awfully glad to know it," she said wearily.

"Oh, well, you can, you know. I mean, you ought to know you needn't
worry," he insisted.

"Ought I? Then I'll see about it," she said.

Paul's secret of secrets was in his wooden horse, that which had no name.
Since he was emancipated from a nurse and a nursery-governess, he had had
his rocking horse removed to his own bedroom at the top of the house.

"Surely, you're too big for a rocking horse!" his mother had remonstrated.

205   "Well, you see, mother, till I can have a real horse, I like to have some sort
of animal about," had been his quaint answer.

"Do you feel he keeps you company?" she laughed.

"Oh, yes! He's very good, he always keeps me company, when I'm there,"
said Paul.

So the horse, rather shabby, stood in an arrested prance in the boy's
bedroom.

The Derby was drawing near, and the boy grew more and more tense. He
hardly heard what was spoken to him, he was very frail, and his eyes were
really uncanny. His mother had sudden seizures of uneasiness about him.
Sometimes, for half-an-hour, she would feel a sudden anxiety about him
that was almost anguish. She wanted to rush to him at once, and know he
was safe.

210   Two nights before the Derby, she was at a big party in town, when one of
her rushes of anxiety about her boy, her first-born, gripped her heart till she
could hardly speak. She fought with the feeling, might and main, for she
believed in common sense. But it was too strong. She had to leave the dance
and go downstairs to telephone to the country. The children's nursery-
governess was terribly surprised and startled at being rung up in the night.

"Are the children all right, Miss Wilmot?"

"Oh, yes, they are quite all right."

"Master Paul? Is he all right?"

"He went to bed as right as a trivet. Shall I run up and look at him?"

215   "No," said Paul's mother reluctantly. "No! Don't trouble. It's all right. Don't
sit up. We shall be home fairly soon." She did not want her son's privacy
intruded upon.

"Very good," said the governess.

It was about one o'clock when Paul's mother and father drove up to their
house. All was still. Paul's mother went to her room and slipped off her white

fur coat. She had told her maid not to wait up for her. She heard her husband downstairs, mixing a whisky-and-soda.

And then, because of the strange anxiety at her heart, she stole upstairs to her son's room. Noiselessly she went along the upper corridor. Was there a faint noise? What was it?

She stood, with arrested muscles, outside his door, listening. There was a strange, heavy, and yet not loud noise. Her heart stood still. It was a soundless noise, yet rushing and powerful. Something huge, in violent, hushed motion. What was it? What in God's name was it? She ought to know. She felt that she knew the noise. She knew what it was.

220   Yet she could not place it. She couldn't say what it was. And on and on it went, like a madness.

Softly, frozen with anxiety and fear, she turned the door handle.

The room was dark. Yet in the space near the window, she heard and saw something plunging to and fro. She gazed in fear and amazement.

Then suddenly she switched on the light, and saw her son, in his green pyjamas, madly surging on the rocking horse. The blaze of light suddenly lit him up, as he urged the wooden horse, and lit her up, as she stood, blonde, in her dress of pale green and crystal, in the doorway.

"Paul!" she cried. "Whatever are you doing?"

225   "It's Malabar!" he screamed, in a powerful, strange voice. "It's Malabar."

His eyes blazed at her for one strange and senseless second, as he ceased urging his wooden horse. Then he fell with a crash to the ground, and she, all her tormented motherhood flooding upon her, rushed to gather him up.

But he was unconscious, and unconscious he remained, with some brain-fever. He talked and tossed, and his mother sat stonily by his side.

"Malabar! It's Malabar! Bassett, Bassett, I know! It's Malabar!"

So the child cried, trying to get up and urge the rocking horse that gave him his inspiration.

230   "What does he mean by Malabar?" asked the heart-frozen mother.

"I don't know," said the father stonily.

"What does he mean by Malabar?" she asked her brother Oscar.

"It's one of the horses running for the Derby," was the answer.

And, in spite of himself, Oscar Cresswell spoke to Bassett, and himself put a thousand on Malabar: at fourteen to one.

235   The third day of the illness was critical: they were waiting for a change. The boy, with his rather long, curly hair, was tossing ceaselessly on the pillow. He neither slept nor regained consciousness, and his eyes were like blue stones. His mother sat, feeling her heart had gone, turned actually into stone.

In the evening, Oscar Cresswell did not come, but Bassett sent a message, saying could he come up for one moment, just one moment? Paul's mother was very angry at the intrusion, but on second thought she agreed. The boy was the same. Perhaps Bassett might bring him to consciousness.

The gardener, a shortish fellow with a little brown moustache, and sharp little brown eyes, tiptoed into the room, touched his imaginary cap to Paul's mother, and stole to the bedside, staring with glittering, smallish eyes, at the tossing, dying child.

"Master Paul!" he whispered. "Master Paul! Malabar came in first all right, a clean win. I did as you told me. You've made over seventy thousand pounds, you have; you've got over eighty thousand. Malabar came in all right, Master Paul."

"Malabar! Malabar! Did I say Malabar, mother? Did I say Malabar? Do you think I'm lucky, mother? I knew Malabar, didn't I? Over eighty thousand pounds! I call that lucky, don't you, mother? Over eighty thousand pounds! I knew, didn't I know I knew? Malabar came in all right. If I ride my horse till I'm sure, then I tell you, Bassett, you can go as high as you like. Did you go for all you were worth, Bassett?"

240   "I went a thousand on it, Master Paul."

"I never told you, mother, that if I can ride my horse, and get there, then I'm absolutely sure—oh, absolutely! Mother, did I ever tell you? I am lucky."

"No, you never did," said the mother.

But the boy died in the night.

And even as he lay dead, his mother heard her brother's voice saying to her: "My God, Hester, you're eighty-odd thousand to the good and a poor devil of a son to the bad. But, poor devil, poor devil, he's best gone out of a life where he rides his rocking horse to find a winner."

Alice Mattison

Alice Mattison (1942–   ) grew up in New York City and earned a Ph.D. at Harvard before getting married and raising her three sons. She teaches and lives in New Haven, Connecticut. In 1979, she published a book of poems, *Animals,* and, in 1988, a book of stories called *Great Wits,* from which we take "The Middle Ages."

The Middle Ages   (1988)

The mysterious knight, who has known the playwright since she entered the day-care center he attended when she was two, easily slays the dragon and wins the admiration of the princess, whom he has known slightly since she moved into his neighborhood in third grade. The queen makes a congratulatory speech. The knight's mother and the queen's mother exchange looks; they first met eleven years ago, at the screening of the prepared-childbirth film that was to help ready them for the births of the knight and the queen.

The knight asks for a private conference with the king, who shoos the queen and the princess away. The queen, a short white girl, ushers out, in matronly fashion, her tall black daughter. The knight's mother wonders, not for the first time, why the playwright, the strong daughter of a strong mother, writes scenes that depict weak women. Or is this moment in the play because she simply needs to get half her characters off the stage?

The knight, now alone with the king, who has been in this class with him for two years, confesses that he is not a knight but only a squire. Deeply moved by the courage of his confession, the king does not behead him for impersonation but dubs him a knight "in Christ's name"—a phrase that momentarily startles the knight's Jewish mother, and also, she notes, the playwright's Jewish mother and stepfather. The line seems to go right past the playwright's divorced, non-Jewish father, who is visiting from California. Before the play, he shook hands nostalgically with parents out of his daughter's babyhood, proud to remember their names.

The play ends, and there are congratulations and applause for everyone, including the children who made the costumes and the props. The knight's mother finds her son trying to take off his costume in a corner of the classroom, and goes to help him and hug him. He is noncommittal but seems satisfied with his performance. The group of parents, trooping back into the classroom from the makeshift theater in the school library, address further compliments to the two young teachers—a black man, a white woman—of this Talented and Gifted Class, which has convened on Thursday afternoons all year, gathering children from half the city. It's surprising to the knight's mother, though, how many of them she recognizes, and there are several more whose names she can't remember but who look familiar. The parents move around the room, not sure what is expected of them but happy to catch up on news, to admire the projects on the walls and tables (all connected with the Middle Ages), to smile shyly and exchange pleasantries with the families they do not know.

5   The knight's mother walks slowly around the tables, looking at the castles. They are made of plain cardboard and corrugated cardboard, along with toilet-paper rolls, paper-towel rolls, string, tape, and sections of egg cartons. One has a drawbridge with string cables to draw it up. Crouching, she sees that another castle has been divided into rooms. The labor is intricate. She sees little clay sheep and geese in a courtyard; there is a tilting clay woman mounting a cardboard staircase, which seems to want to straighten itself. The knight's castle is the smallest in the classroom and one of the simplest, but it has crenellated walls, meticulously cut.

The man teacher comes to talk to her about the castles. The children worked in groups, he explains. The groups were varied, and the teachers were careful to place children with classmates they didn't know very well. The knight worked with one other child, a girl, which must not have been easy for him. They agree that the knight is shy with girls. At first, he was in a larger group, the teacher explains, but one child was difficult, and the teachers thought it best to divide this group. The mother remembers that the knight talked about the difficult child, and about the castle, but not about a girl.

The teacher is proud of the way the castles were made. He explains that one of the children, on her end-of-the-year Program Evaluation Sheet, actually wrote that it was her favorite project because she learned to work with different kinds of children. The mother and the teacher agree that this result was indeed praiseworthy.

The knight's mother now introduces the knight's grandmother to the director of the Talented and Gifted Program, a woman famous for her memory, who mentions the occasion on which she met the grandmother before, at another Medieval Fair, three years ago, when the knight's older brother was in fifth grade. No, the brother is not here tonight; he is playing the cello in an ensemble at the music school. His father dropped him off and was almost late for the play. The older brother did not seem to mind that his parents were missing his concert. They have attended others—long, earnest performances by a succession of small groups. Each time, the father wondered whether some young virtuoso might save the occasion.

But now the knight's mother begins to worry, imagining the music-school concert over and the audience dispersed, her son alone in the dark with his cello outside a locked building, or perhaps being conscientiously kept company by the already exhausted teacher.

10   The knight explains that they cannot leave. He may be allowed to take his castle home. At the last class, the teachers asked the children in each group to draw lots for the group's castle. He and his co-worker, Jonquil McMahon, drew lots and Jonquil won. But she is not present. "If the first person doesn't come by a quarter to nine, the second person can take the castle," the knight says. "I'm the second person, because there isn't anybody else." It is now eight-twenty. Families are beginning to leave. The fathers, supervised by anxious sons and daughters, carefully detach large medieval figures painted on brown wrapping paper from the wall—knights, ladies, monks—loosening the Scotch tape piece by piece and trying to keep the arms and legs from tearing.

Each student has made a coat of arms, a cardboard shield divided into four sections. The knight explains that one quarter of each coat of arms represents the present, one the future, one something he is proud of, and one something he enjoys. To show the present, he has drawn his family, including the cat and dog. A scroll surprisingly lettered PH.D. IN LITERATURE denotes his future. He is proud of his certificate for cooperation, from summer day camp. Pleasure is shown by a hockey stick. The knight's mother picks out herself, with dark hair, in the row of family members. She cannot remember ever making anything like this coat of arms, a work that might acknowledge and unite the parts of her life.

By the time the coat of arms has been taken down and examined, it is eight-thirty. One of the teachers thinks the knight might take the castle now, but the other teacher says they should not deviate from the announced plan. The knight, in any case, has no wish to break the rules. He sits at a table in the library with his mother and grandmother. The father stays in the classroom, restlessly moving around, picking up books about the Middle Ages. The mother can see him through the doorway. She recognizes the book he has been looking at. When she passed the table and glanced at it, it was opened to a detailed description of medieval warfare, including the use of boiling oil.

"Is Jonquil a black girl?" asks the grandmother.

"Yes."

15   "I like the name Jonquil," says the mother.

"She looks like what you'd think," the knight says.

"Delicate?"

"Sort of."

"I feel sorry for her," says the grandmother. "Maybe she wanted to come but she couldn't."

20   "I don't think she wanted to come," says the knight.

At twenty-five to nine, the mother goes back into the classroom. Two or three families are left. The teachers are starting to take down from the walls the work of the children who didn't show up. The playwright's father has gone, taking with him the playwright's life-size cutout on brown paper of a lady in a conical hat; perhaps he means to take it back to California with him. Now the playwright's mother and stepfather take their leave with the playwright, the mother carrying the playwright's new baby brother, the stepfather balancing one of the largest castles, which he tilts carefully to fit it through the door.

The knight has come back into the classroom. He is watching the clock. The mother sits down on the corner of a table. She thinks she should keep the grandmother company in the library, but she isn't wearing a watch and wants to know what time it is. Across the room, the father has found something to read. It looks like a storybook, with a colorful cover. He is leaning with one shoulder against a blackboard, holding the book a little away from him, as if he means to be able to drop it at any moment.

"Six and a half minutes," the knight says.

"That's *you*," says the woman teacher, smiling at the knight. "You really are a stickler for rules. Everything just so. But you're such a good judge. You make us all be fair in class. And you never take anything you're not entitled to."

25   The knight shrugs. He does not recognize himself in the description.

"Four minutes," says the knight. The father is impatient. He closes the book and puts it down. Obviously, Jonquil is not coming. The fair is over. They discuss carrying the castle out to the car. Or should he drive around to the door? No, he answers himself, they can carry the castle easily. But the bottom is paper, not cardboard. Will the walls make it rigid enough? Can they carry it without hurting it?

"I really think you can take it now," says the woman teacher.

"No. A minute to go," the knight says.

"You're a little crazy," she says. "But it's a good kind of crazy."

30   The knight is staring at the clock. The mother is standing up, tired, her face empty. A last family is leaving. Another family is walking into the classroom—a woman, a teenage girl, a younger girl: a black family. They look calm, as if they are doing something ordinary.

The mother sees that this is not a family that has been here all evening, returning for a forgotten picture or jacket. This is Jonquil.

The woman teacher, her eyes startled, is greeting the teenage sister— another former student, it seems. The knight's family does not wait to see Jonquil—who is expressionless and sturdy, not delicate—take up the castle. The mother feels the knight yank at her arm. They hurry the grandmother out to the car.

"It would have been worse if we'd met them in the street and had to deal with an ethical dilemma," says the mother as they start down the steps outside the building.

"They looked cynical," says the father. "This was terrible. This was truly terrible."

35   The grandmother says that maybe the family had no choice but to come late, that they had to be somewhere else. It is the end of the school year. There are many celebrations and performances. The concert, for example.

"That's not how they looked," says the mother. She tries to picture the woman's businesslike face wearing the expression that all mothers—housewives or working women, black or white—wear when they rush in late to claim a child or to applaud and admire: the exasperated eyes, the frustrated headshake that says "Of *course* I care. It was traffic, responsibility, necessity that kept me away—not ease, not whim."

The face, in the mother's mind, will not hold the expression. The woman did not want to make the usual half-humorous claim of membership in the guild of the conscientious, or did not know she could. Or perhaps for her an avowal of fellowship would be a mad luxury, courtly protocol in the midst of battle.

The mother doesn't know how to explain this to the boy but reaches out a hand, as they approach the car, to touch the back of his neck. He brushes his head against her palm, and she thinks he may turn and cry, but he does not.

"Still," says the grandmother, "now you know how to make castles."

40   "I couldn't get the wall to stand up straight," says the boy. "Mr. Evans had to glue it for me, and then he told me it came apart after I went home and he had to glue it again. I didn't know what to do. It kept on falling."

Bharati Mukherjee

Bharati Mukherjee (1940–   ) was born in Calcutta, India, where she began her education. Years later, she earned a Ph.D. at the University of Iowa. She has published two novels, two nonfiction books, and an earlier book of stories, *Darkness* (1985). This story comes from *The Middleman and Other Stories* (1987), which won the National Book Critics Circle Award in fiction. She has received grants from the National Endowment for the Arts and the Guggenheim Foundation.

Jasmine   (1988)

Jasmine came to Detroit from Port-of-Spain, Trinidad, by way of Canada. She crossed the border at Windsor in the back of a gray van loaded with mattresses and a box springs. The plan was for her to hide in an empty mattress box if she heard the driver say, "All bad weather seems to come down from Canada, doesn't it?" to the customs man. But she didn't have to crawl into a box and hold her breath. The customs man didn't ask to look in.

The driver let her off at a scary intersection on Woodward Avenue and gave her instructions on how to get to the Plantations Motel in Southfield. The trick was to keep changing vehicles, he said. That threw off the immigration guys real quick.

Jasmine took money for cab fare out of the pocket of the great big raincoat that the van driver had given her. The raincoat looked like something that nuns in Port-of-Spain sold in church bazaars. Jasmine was glad to have a coat with wool lining, though; and anyway, who would know in Detroit that she was Dr. Vassanji's daughter?

All the bills in her hand looked the same. She would have to be careful when she paid the cabdriver. Money in Detroit wasn't pretty the way it was back home, or even in Canada, but she liked this money better. Why should money be pretty, like a picture? Pretty money is only good for putting on your walls maybe. The dollar bills felt businesslike, serious. Back home at work, she used to count out thousands of Trinidad dollars every day and not even think of them as real. Real money was worn and green, American dollars. Holding the bills in her fist on a street corner meant she had made it in okay. She'd outsmarted the guys at the border. Now it was up to her to use her wits to do something with her life. As her Daddy kept saying, "Girl, is opportunity come only once." The girls she'd worked with at the bank in Port-of-Spain had gone green as bananas when she'd walked in with her ticket on Air Canada. Trinidad was too tiny. That was the trouble. Trinidad was an island stuck in the middle of nowhere. What kind of place was that for a girl with ambition?

5   The Plantations Motel was run by a family of Trinidad Indians who had come from the tuppenny-ha'penny country town, Chaguanas. The Daboos were nobodies back home. They were lucky, that's all. They'd gotten here before the rush and bought up a motel and an ice cream parlor. Jasmine felt very superior when she saw Mr. Daboo in the motel's reception area. He was a pumpkin-shaped man with very black skin and Elvis Presley sideburns turning white. They looked like earmuffs. Mrs. Daboo was a bumpkin, too; short, fat, flapping around in house slippers. The Daboo daughters seemed very American, though. They didn't seem to know that they were nobodies, and kept looking at her and giggling.

She knew she would be short of cash for a great long while. Besides, she wasn't sure she wanted to wear bright leather boots and leotards like Viola and Loretta. The smartest move she could make would be to put a down payment on a husband. Her Daddy had told her to talk to the Daboos first chance. The Daboos ran a service fixing up illegals with islanders who had made it in legally. Daddy had paid three thousand back in Trinidad, with the Daboos and the mattress man getting part of it. They should throw in a good-earning husband for that kind of money.

The Daboos asked her to keep books for them and to clean the rooms in the new wing, and she could stay in 16B as long as she liked. They showed her 16B. They said she could cook her own roti; Mr. Daboo would bring in a stove, two gas rings that you could fold up in a metal box. The room was quite grand, Jasmine thought. It had a double bed, a TV, a pink sink and matching bathtub. Mrs. Daboo said Jasmine wasn't the big-city Port-of-Spain type she'd expected. Mr. Daboo said that he wanted her to stay because it was nice to have a neat, cheerful person around. It wasn't a bad deal, better than stories she'd heard about Trinidad girls in the States.

All day every day except Sundays Jasmine worked. There wasn't just the bookkeeping and the cleaning up. Mr. Daboo had her working on the match-up marriage service. Jasmine's job was to check up on social security cards, call clients' bosses for references, and make sure credit information wasn't false. Dermatologists and engineers living in Bloomfield Hills, store owners on Canfield and Woodward: she treated them all as potential liars. One of the first things she learned was that Ann Arbor was a magic word. A boy goes to Ann Arbor and gets an education, and all the barriers come crashing down. So Ann Arbor was the place to be.

She didn't mind the work. She was learning about Detroit, every side of it. Sunday mornings she helped unload packing crates of Caribbean spices in a shop on the next block. For the first time in her life, she was working for a black man, an African. So what if the boss was black? This was a new life, and she wanted to learn everything. Her Sunday boss, Mr. Anthony, was a courtly, Christian, church-going man, and paid her the only wages she had in her pocket. Viola and Loretta, for all their fancy American ways, wouldn't go out with blacks.

10   One Friday afternoon she was writing up the credit info on a Guyanese Muslim who worked in an assembly plant when Loretta said that enough was enough and that there was no need for Jasmine to be her father's drudge.

"Is time to have fun," Viola said. "We're going to Ann Arbor."

Jasmine filed the sheet on the Guyanese man who probably now would never get a wife and got her raincoat. Loretta's boyfriend had a Cadillac parked out front. It was the longest car Jasmine had ever been in and louder than a country bus. Viola's boyfriend got out of the front seat. "Oh, oh, sweet things," he said to Jasmine. "Get in front." He was a talker. She'd learned that much from working on the matrimonial match-ups. She didn't believe him for a second when he said that there were dudes out there dying to ask her out.

Loretta's boyfriend said, "You have eyes I could leap into, girl."

Jasmine knew he was just talking. They sounded like Port-of-Spain boys of three years ago. It didn't surprise her that these Trinidad country boys in Detroit were still behind the times, even of Port-of-Spain. She sat very stiff between the two men, hands on her purse. The Daboo girls laughed in the back seat.

15   On the highway the girls told her about the reggae night in Ann Arbor. Kevin and the Krazee Islanders. Malcolm's Lovers. All the big reggae groups in the Midwest were converging for the West Indian Students Association fall

bash. The ticket didn't come cheap but Jasmine wouldn't let the fellows pay. She wasn't that kind of girl.

The reggae and steel drums brought out the old Jasmine. The rum punch, the dancing, the dreadlocks, the whole combination. She hadn't heard real music since she got to Detroit, where music was supposed to be so famous. The Daboos girls kept turning on rock stuff in the motel lobby whenever their father left the area. She hadn't danced, really *danced,* since she'd left home. It felt so good to dance. She felt hot and sweaty and sexy. The boys at the dance were more than sweet talkers; they moved with assurance and spoke of their futures in America. The bartender gave her two free drinks and said, "Is ready when you are, girl." She ignored him but she felt all hot and good deep inside. She knew Ann Arbor was a special place.

When it was time to pile back into Loretta's boyfriend's Cadillac, she just couldn't face going back to the Plantations Motel and to the Daboos with their accounting books and messy files.

"I don't know what happen, girl," she said to Loretta. "I feel all crazy inside. Maybe is time for me to pursue higher studies in this town."

"This Ann Arbor, girl, they don't just take you off the street. It *cost* like hell."

20   She spent the night on a bashed-up sofa in the Student Union. She was a well-dressed, respectable girl, and she didn't expect anyone to question her right to sleep on the furniture. Many others were doing the same thing. In the morning, a boy in an army parka showed her the way to the Placement Office. He was a big, blond, clumsy boy, not bad-looking except for the blond eyelashes. He didn't scare her, as did most Americans. She let him buy her a Coke and a hotdog. That evening she had a job with the Moffitts.

Bill Moffitt taught molecular biology and Lara Hatch-Moffitt, his wife, was a performance artist. A performance artist, said Lara, was very different from being an actress, though Jasmine still didn't understand what the difference might be. The Moffitts had a little girl, Muffin, whom Jasmine was to look after, though for the first few months she might have to help out with the housework and the cooking because Lara said she was deep into performance rehearsals. That was all right with her, Jasmine said, maybe a little too quickly. She explained she came from a big family and was used to heavy-duty cooking and cleaning. This wasn't the time to say anything about Ram, the family servant. Americans like the Moffitts wouldn't understand about keeping servants. Ram and she weren't in similar situations. Here mother's helpers, which is what Lara had called her—Americans were good with words to cover their shame—seemed to be as good as anyone.

Lara showed her the room she would have all to herself in the finished basement. There was a big, old TV, not in color like the motel's and a portable typewriter on a desk which Lara said she would find handy when it came time to turn in her term papers. Jasmine didn't say anything about not being a student. She was a student of life, wasn't she? There was a scary moment after they'd discussed what she could expect as salary, which was three times more than anything Mr. Daboo was supposed to pay her but hadn't. She thought Bill Moffitt was going to ask her about her visa or her green card number and social security. But all Bill did was smile and smile at her—he had a wide, pink, baby face—and play with a button on his corduroy jacket. The button would need sewing back on, firmly.

Lara said, "I think I'm going to like you, Jasmine. You have a something about you. A something real special. I'll just bet you've acted, haven't you?" The idea amused her, but she merely smiled and accepted Lara's hug. The interview was over.

Then Bill opened a bottle of Soave and told stories about camping in northern Michigan. He'd been raised there. Jasmine didn't see the point in sleeping in tents; the woods sounded cold and wild and creepy. But she said, "Is exactly what I want to try out come summer, man. Campin and huntin."

25   Lara asked about Port-of-Spain. There was nothing to tell about her hometown that wouldn't shame her in front of nice white American folk like the Moffitts. The place was shabby, the people were grasping and cheating and lying and life was full of despair and drink and wanting. But by the time she finished, the island sounded romantic. Lara said, "It wouldn't surprise me one bit if you were a writer, Jasmine."

Ann Arbor was a huge small town. She couldn't imagine any kind of school the size of the University of Michigan. She meant to sign up for courses in the spring. Bill brought home a catalogue bigger than the phonebook for all of Trinidad. The university had courses in everything. It would be hard to choose; she'd have to get help from Bill. He wasn't like a professor, not the ones back home where even high school teachers called themselves professors and acted like little potentates. He wore blue jeans and thick sweaters with holes in the elbows and used phrases like "in vitro" as he watched her curry up fish. Dr. Parveen back home—he called himself "doctor" when everybody knew he didn't have even a Master's degree—was never seen without his cotton jacket which had gotten really ratty at the cuffs and lapel edges. She hadn't learned anything in the two years she'd put into college. She'd learned more from working in the bank for two months than she had at college. It was the assistant manager, Personal Loans Department, Mrs. Singh, who had turned her on to the Daboos and to smooth, bargain-priced emigration.

Jasmine liked Lara. Lara was easygoing. She didn't spend the time she had between rehearsals telling Jasmine how to cook and clean American-style. Mrs. Daboo did that in 16D. Mrs. Daboo would barge in with a plate of stale samosas and snoop around giving free advice on how mainstream Americans did things. As if she were dumb or something! As if she couldn't keep her own eyes open and make her mind up for herself. Sunday mornings she had to share the butcher-block workspace in the kitchen with Bill. He made the Sunday brunch from new recipes in *Gourmet* and *Cuisine*. Jasmine hadn't seen a man cook who didn't have to or wasn't getting paid to do it. Things were topsy-turvy in the Moffitt house. Lara went on two- and three-day road trips and Bill stayed home. But even her Daddy, who'd never poured himself a cup of tea, wouldn't put Bill down as a woman. The mornings Bill tried out something complicated, a Cajun shrimp, sausage, and beans dish, for instance, Jasmine skipped church services. The Moffitts didn't go to church, though they seemed to be good Christians. They just didn't talk church talk, which suited her fine.

Two months passed. Jasmine knew she was lucky to have found a small, clean, friendly family like the Moffitts to build her new life around. "Man!" she'd exclaim as she vacuumed the wide-plank wood floors or ironed (Lara wore pure silk or pure cotton). "In this country Jesus givin out good luck only!" By this time they knew she wasn't a student, but they didn't care and said they wouldn't report her. They never asked if she was illegal on top of it.

To savor her new sense of being a happy, lucky person, she would put herself through a series of "what ifs": what if Mr. Singh in Port-of-Spain hadn't turned her on to the Daboos and loaned her two thousand! What if she'd been ugly like the Mintoo girl and the manager hadn't even offered! What if the customs man had unlocked the door of the van! Her Daddy liked to say, "You is a helluva girl, Jasmine."

30   "Thank you, Jesus," Jasmine said, as she carried on.

Christmas Day the Moffitts treated her just like family. They gave her a red cashmere sweater with a V neck so deep it made her blush. If Lara had worn it, her bosom wouldn't hang out like melons. For the holiday weekend Bill drove her to the Daboos in Detroit. "You work too hard," Bill said to her. "Learn to be more selfish. Come on, throw your weight around." She'd rather not have spent time with the Daboos, but that first afternoon of the interview she'd told Bill and Lara that Mr. Daboo was her mother's first cousin. She had thought it shameful in those days to have no papers, no family, no roots. Now Loretta and Viola in tight, bright pants seemed trashy like girls at Two-Johnny Bissoondath's Bar back home. She was stuck with the story of the Daboos being family. Village bumpkins, ha! She would break out. Soon.

Jasmine had Bill drop her off at the RenCen. The Plantations Motel, in fact, the whole Riverfront area, was too seamy. She'd managed to cut herself off mentally from anything too islandy. She loved her Daddy and Mummy, but she didn't think of them that often anymore. Mummy had expected her to be homesick and come flying right back home. "Is blowin sweat-of-brow money is what you doin, Pa," Mummy had scolded. She loved them, but she'd become her own person. That was something that Lara said: "I am my own person."

The Daboos acted thrilled to see her back. "What you drinkin, Jasmine girl?" Mr. Daboo kept asking. "You drinkin sherry or what?" Pouring her little glasses of sherry instead of rum was a sure sign he thought she had become whitefolk-fancy. The Daboo sisters were very friendly, but Jasmine considered them too wild. Both Loretta and Viola had changed boyfriends. Both were seeing black men they'd danced with in Ann Arbor. Each night at bedtime, Mr. Daboo cried. "In Trinidad we stayin we side, they stayin they side. Here, everything mixed up. Is helluva confusion, no?"

On New Year's Eve the Daboo girls and their black friends went to a dance. Mr. and Mrs. Daboo and Jasmine watched TV for a while. Then Mr. Daboo got out a brooch from his pocket and pinned it on Jasmine's red sweater. It was a Christmasy brooch, a miniature sleigh loaded down with snowed-on mistletoe. Before she could pull away, he kissed her on the lips.

"Good luck for the New Year!" he said. She lifted her head and saw tears. "Is year for dreams comin true."

35   Jasmine started to cry, too. There was nothing wrong, but Mr. Daboo, Mrs. Daboo, she, everybody was crying.

What for? This is where she wanted to be. She'd spent some damned uncomfortable times with the assistant manager to get approval for her loan. She thought of Daddy. He would be playing poker and fanning himself with a magazine. Her married sisters would be rolling out the dough for stacks and stacks of roti, and Mummy would be steamed purple from stirring the big pot of goat curry on the stove. She missed them. But. It felt strange to think of anyone celebrating New Year's Eve in summery clothes.

In March Lara and her performing group went on the road. Jasmine knew that the group didn't work from scripts. The group didn't use a stage, either; instead, it took over supermarkets, senior citizens' centers, and school halls, without notice. Jasmine didn't understand the performance world. But she was glad that Lara said, "I'm not going to lay a guilt trip on myself. Muffie's in super hands," before she left.

Muffie didn't need much looking after. She played Trivial Pursuit all day, usually pretending to be two persons, sometimes Jasmine, whose accent she could imitate. Since Jasmine didn't know any of the answers, she couldn't help. Muffie was a quiet, precocious child with see-through blue eyes like her dad's, and red braids. In the early evenings Jasmine cooked supper, something special she hadn't forgotten from her island days. After supper she and Muffie watched some TV, and Bill read. When Muffie went to bed, Bill and she sat together for a bit with their glasses of Soave. Bill, Muffie, and she were a family, almost.

Down in her basement room that late, dark winter, she had trouble sleeping. She wanted to stay awake and think of Bill. Even when she fell asleep it didn't feel like sleep because Bill came barging into her dreams in his funny, loose-jointed, clumsy way. It was mad to think of him all the time, and stupid and sinful; but she couldn't help it. Whenever she put back a book he'd taken off the shelf to read or whenever she put his clothes through the washer and dryer, she felt sick in a giddy, wonderful way. When Lara came back things would get back to normal. Meantime she wanted the performance group miles away.

40   Lara called in at least twice a week. She said things like, "We've finally obliterated the margin between realspace and performancespace." Jasmine filled her in on Muffie's doings and the mail. Bill always closed with, "I love you. We miss you, hon."

One night after Lara had called—she was in Lincoln, Nebraska—Bill said to Jasmine, "Let's dance."

She hadn't danced since the reggae night she'd had too many rum punches. Her toes began to throb and clench. She untied her apron and the fraying, knotted-up laces of her running shoes.

Bill went around the downstairs rooms turning down lights. "We need atmosphere," he said. He got a small, tidy fire going in the living room

grate and pulled the Turkish scatter rug closer to it. Lara didn't like anybody walking on the Turkish rug, but Bill meant to have his way. The hissing logs, the plants in the dimmed light, the thick patterned rug: everything
was changed. This wasn't the room she cleaned every day.

He stood close to her. She smoothed her skirt down with both hands.
45 "I want you to choose the record," he said.
"I don't know your music."
She brought her hand high to his face. His skin was baby smooth.
"I want *you* to pick," he said. "You are your own person now."
"You got island music?"
50 He laughed, "What do you think?" The stereo was in a cabinet with albums
packed tight alphabetically into the bottom three shelves. "Calypso has not
been a force in my life."
She couldn't help laughing. "Calypso? Oh, man." She pulled dust jackets
out at random. Lara's records. The Flying Lizards. The Violent Fems. There
was so much still to pick up on!
"This one," she said, finally.
He took the record out of her hand. "God!" he laughed. "Lara must have
found this in a garage sale!" He laid the old record on the turntable. It was
"Music for Lovers," something the nuns had taught her to foxtrot to way
back in Port-of-Spain.
They danced so close that she could feel his heart heaving and crashing
against her head. She liked it, she liked it very much. She didn't care what
happened.
55 "Come on," Bill whispered. "If it feels right, do it." He began to take her
clothes off.
"Don't, Bill," she pleaded.
"Come on, baby," he whispered again. "You're a blossom, a flower."
He took off his fisherman's knit pullover, the corduroy pants, the blue
shorts. She kept pace. She'd never had such an effect on a man. He nearly
flung his socks and Adidas into the fire. "You feel so good," he said. "You
smell so good. You're really something, flower of Trinidad."
"Flower of Ann Arbor," she said, "not Trinidad."
60 She felt so good she was dizzy. She'd never felt this good on the island
where men did this all the time, and girls went along with it always for
favors. You couldn't feel really good in a nothing place. She was thinking
this as they made love on the Turkish carpet in front of the fire: she was a
bright, pretty girl with no visa, no papers, and no birth certificate. No nothing other than what she wanted to invent and tell. She was a girl rushing
wildly into the future.
His hand moved up her throat and forced her lips apart and it felt so
good, so right, that she forgot all the dreariness of her new life and gave
herself up to it.

Frank O'Connor

Frank O'Connor (1903–1966) was born Michael Francis O'Donovan, in County
Cork, Ireland. He wrote two novels, some literary criticism including his study of
the short story, *The Lonely Voice* (1962), translations from the Irish, two volumes
of autobiography, and many collections of short stories. *The Stories of Frank
O'Connor* preserves the work of this master.

Guests of the Nation   (1931)

At dusk the big Englishman, Belcher, would shift his long legs out of the ashes
and say "Well, chums, what about it?" and Noble or me would say "All right,
chum" (for we had picked up some of their curious expressions), and the little
Englishman, Hawkins, would light the lamp and bring out the cards. Sometimes Jeremiah Donovan would come up and supervise the game and get excited over Hawkins's cards, which he always played badly, and shout at him as
if he was one of our own "Ah, you divil, you, why didn't you play the tray?"

But ordinarily Jeremiah was a sober and contented poor devil like the big
Englishman, Belcher, and was looked up to only because he was a fair hand
at documents, though he was slow enough even with them. He wore a
small cloth hat and big gaiters over his long pants, and you seldom saw him
with his hands out of his pockets. He reddened when you talked to him,
tilting from toe to heel and back, and looking down all the time at his big
farmer's feet. Noble and me used to make fun of his broad accent, because
we were from the town.

I couldn't at the time see the point of me and Noble guarding Belcher
and Hawkins at all, for it was my belief that you could have planted that pair
down anywhere from this to Claregalway and they'd have taken root there
like a native weed. I never in my short experience seen two men to take to
the country as they did.

They were handed on to us by the Second Battalion when the search for
them became too hot, and Noble and myself, being young, took over with a
natural feeling of responsibility, but Hawkins made us look like fools when
he showed that he knew the country better than we did.

5   "You're the bloke they calls Bonaparte," he says to me. "Mary Brigid
O'Connell told me to ask you what you done with the pair of her brother's
socks you borrowed."

For it seemed, as they explained it, that the Second used to have little
evenings, and some of the girls of the neighbourhood turned in, and, seeing
they were such decent chaps, our fellows couldn't leave the two Englishmen
out of them. Hawkins learned to dance "The Walls of Limerick," "The Siege
of Ennis," and "The Waves of Tory" as well as any of them, though, naturally,
he couldn't return the compliment, because our lads at that time did not
dance foreign dances on principle.

So whatever privileges Belcher and Hawkins had with the Second they
just naturally took with us, and after the first day or two we gave up all

pretence of keeping a close eye on them. Not that they could have got far, for they had accents you could cut with a knife and wore khaki tunics and overcoats with civilian pants and boots. But it's my belief that they never had any idea of escaping and were quite content to be where they were.

It was a treat to see how Belcher got off with the old woman of the house where we were staying. She was a great warrant to scold, and cranky even with us, but before ever she had a chance of giving our guests, as I may call them, a lick of her tongue, Belcher had made her his friend for life. She was breaking sticks, and Belcher, who hadn't been more than ten minutes in the house, jumped up from his seat and went over to her.

"Allow me, madam," he says, smiling his queer little smile, "please allow me"; and he takes the bloody hatchet. She was struck too paralytic to speak, and after that, Belcher would be at her heels, carrying a bucket, a basket, or a load of turf, as the case might be. As Noble said, he got into looking before she leapt, and hot water, or any little thing she wanted, Belcher would have it ready for her. For such a huge man (and though I am five foot ten myself I had to look up at him) he had an uncommon shortness—or should I say lack?—of speech. It took us some time to get used to him, walking in and out, like a ghost, without a word. Especially because Hawkins talked enough for a platoon, it was strange to hear big Belcher with his toes in the ashes come out with a solitary "Excuse me, chum," or "That's right, chum." His one and only passion was cards, and I will say for him that he was a good card-player. He could have fleeced myself and Noble, but whatever we lost to him Hawkins lost to us, and Hawkins played with the money Belcher gave him.

10   Hawkins lost to us because he had too much old gab, and we probably lost to Belcher for the same reason. Hawkins and Noble would spit at one another about religion into the early hours of the morning, and Hawkins worried the soul out of Noble, whose brother was a priest, with a string of questions that would puzzle a cardinal. To make it worse, even in treating of holy subjects, Hawkins had a deplorable tongue. I never in all my career met a man who could mix such a variety of cursing and bad language into an argument. He was a terrible man, and a fright to argue. He never did a stroke of work, and when he had no one else to talk to, he got stuck in the old woman.

He met his match in her, for one day when he tried to get her to complain profanely of the drought, she gave him a great come-down by blaming it entirely on Jupiter Pluvius (a deity neither Hawkins nor I had ever heard of, though Noble said that among the pagans it was believed that he had something to do with the rain). Another day he was swearing at the capitalists for starting the German war when the old lady laid down her iron, puckered up her little crab's mouth, and said: "Mr. Hawkins, you can say what you like about the war, and think you'll deceive me because I'm only a simple poor countrywoman, but I know what started the war. It was the Italian Count that stole the heathen divinity out of the temple in Japan. Believe me, Mr. Hawkins, nothing but sorrow and want can follow the people that disturb the hidden powers."

A queer old girl, all right.

II

We had our tea one evening, and Hawkins lit the lamp and we all sat into cards. Jeremiah Donovan came in too, and sat down and watched us for a while, and it suddenly struck me that he had no great love for the two Englishmen. It came as a great surprise to me, because I hadn't noticed anything about him before.

Late in the evening a really terrible argument blew up between Hawkins and Noble, about capitalists and priests and love of your country.

15   "The capitalists," says Hawkins with an angry gulp, "pays the priests to tell you about the next world so as you won't notice what the bastards are up to in this."

"Nonsense, man!" says Noble, losing his temper. "Before ever a capitalist was thought of, people believed in the next world."

Hawkins stood up as though he was preaching a sermon.

"Oh, they did, did they?" he says with a sneer. "They believed all the things you believe, isn't that what you mean? And you believe that God created Adam, and Adam created Shem, and Shem created Jehoshaphat. You believe all that silly old fairytale abut Eve and Eden and the apple. Well, listen to me, chum. If you're entitled to hold a silly belief like that, I'm entitled to hold my silly belief—which is that the first thing your God created was a bleeding capitalist, with morality and Rolls-Royce complete. Am I right, chum?" he says to Belcher.

"You're right, chum," says Belcher with his amused smile, and got up from the table to stretch his long legs into the fire and stroke his moustache. So, seeing that Jeremiah Donovan was going, and that there was no knowing when the argument about religion would be over, I went out with him. We strolled down to the village together, and then he stopped and started blushing and mumbling and saying I ought to be behind, keeping guard on the prisoners. I didn't like the tone he took with me, and anyway I was bored with life in the cottage, so I replied by asking him what the hell we wanted guarding them at all for. I told him I'd talked it over with Noble, and that we'd both rather be out with a fighting column.

20   "What use are those fellows to us?" says I.

He looked at me in surprise and said: "I thought you knew we were keeping them as hostages."

"Hostages?" I said.

"The enemy have prisoners belonging to us," he says, "and now they're talking of shooting them. If they shoot our prisoners, we'll shoot theirs."

"Shoot them?" I said.

25   "What else did you think we were keeping them for?" he says.

"Wasn't it very unforeseen of you not to warn Noble and myself of that in the beginning?" I said.

"How was it?" says he. "You might have known it."

"We couldn't know it, Jeremiah Donovan," says I. "How could we when they were on our hands so long?"

"The enemy have our prisoners as long and longer," says he.

30   "That's not the same thing at all," says I.

"What difference is there?" says he.

I couldn't tell him, because I knew he wouldn't understand. If it was only an old dog that was going to the vet's, you'd try and not get too fond of him, but Jeremiah Donovan wasn't a man that would ever be in danger of that.

"And when is this thing going to be decided?" says I.

"We might hear tonight," he says. "Or tomorrow or the next day at latest. So if it's only hanging round here that's a trouble to you, you'll be free soon enough."

35   It wasn't the hanging round that was a trouble to me at all by this time. I had worse things to worry about. When I got back to the cottage the argument was still on. Hawkins was holding forth in his best style, maintaining that there was no next world, and Noble was maintaining that there was; but I could see that Hawkins had had the best of it.

"Do you know what, chum?" he was saying with a saucy smile. "I think you're just as big a bleeding unbeliever as I am. You say you believe in the next world, and you know just as much about the next world as I do, which is sweet damn-all. What's heaven? You don't know. Where's heaven? You don't know. You know sweet damn-all! I ask you again, do they wear wings?"

"Very well, then," says Noble, "they do. Is that enough for you? They do wear wings."

"Where do they get them, then? Who makes them? Have they a factory for wings? Have they a sort of store where you hands in your chit and takes your bleeding wings?"

"You're an impossible man to argue with," says Noble. "Now, listen to me—" And they were off again.

40   It was long after midnight when we locked up and went to bed. As I blew out the candle I told Noble what Jeremiah Donovan was after telling me. Noble took it very quietly. When we'd been in bed about an hour he asked me did I think we ought to tell the Englishmen. I didn't think we should, because it was more than likely that the English wouldn't shoot our men, and even if they did, the brigade officers, who were always up and down with the Second Battalion and knew the Englishmen well, wouldn't be likely to want them plugged. "I think so too," says Noble. "It would be great cruelty to put the wind up them now."

"It was very unforeseen of Jeremiah Donovan anyhow," says I.

It was next morning that we found it so hard to face Belcher and Hawkins. We went about the house all day scarcely saying a word. Belcher didn't seem to notice; he was stretched into the ashes as usual, with his usual look of waiting in quietness for something unforeseen to happen, but Hawkins noticed and put it down to Noble's being beaten in the argument of the night before.

"Why can't you take a discussion in the proper spirit?" he says severely. "You and your Adam and Eve! I'm a Communist, that's what I am. Communist or anarchist, it all comes to much the same thing." And for hours he went round the house, muttering when the fit took him. "Adam and Eve! Adam and Eve! Nothing better to do with their time than picking bleeding apples!"

III

I don't know how we got through that day, but I was very glad when it was over, the tea things were cleared away, and Belcher said in his peaceable way: "Well, chums, what about it?" We sat round the table and Hawkins took out the cards, and just then I heard Jeremiah Donovan's footstep on the path and a dark presentiment crossed my mind. I rose from the table and caught him before he reached the door.

45   "What do you want?" I asked.

"I want those two soldier friends of yours," he says, getting red.

"Is that the way, Jeremiah Donovan?" I asked.

"That's the way. There were four of our lads shot this morning, one of them a boy of sixteen."

"That's bad," I said.

50   At that moment Noble followed me out, and the three of us walked down the path together, talking in whispers. Feeney, the local intelligence officer, was standing by the gate.

"What are you going to do about it?" I asked Jeremiah Donovan.

"I want you and Noble to get them out; tell them they're being shifted again; that'll be the quietest way."

"Leave me out of that," says Noble under his breath.

Jeremiah Donovan looks at him hard.

55   "All right," he says. "You and Feeney get a few tools from the shed and dig a hole by the far end of the bog. Bonaparte and myself will be after you. Don't let anyone see you with the tools. I wouldn't like it to go beyond ourselves."

We saw Feeney and Noble go round to the shed and went in ourselves. I left Jeremiah Donovan to do the explanations. He told them that he had orders to send them back to the Second Battalion. Hawkins let out a mouthful of curses, and you could see that though Belcher didn't say anything, he was a bit upset too. The old woman was for having them stay in spite of us, and she didn't stop advising them until Jeremiah Donovan lost his temper and turned on her. He had a nasty temper, I noticed. It was pitch-dark in the cottage by this time, but no one thought of lighting the lamp, and in the darkness the two Englishmen fetched their topcoats and said good-bye to the old woman.

"Just as a man makes a home of a bleeding place, some bastard at headquarters thinks you're too cushy and shunts you off," says Hawkins, shaking her hand.

"A thousand thanks, madam," says Belcher. "A thousand thanks for everything"—as though he'd made it up.

We went round to the back of the house and down towards the bog. It was only then that Jeremiah Donovan had told them. He was shaking with excitement.

60   "There were four of our fellows shot in Cork this morning and now you're to be shot as a reprisal."

"What are you talking about?" snaps Hawkins. "It's bad enough being mucked about as we are without having to put up with your funny jokes."

"It isn't a joke," says Donovan. "I'm sorry, Hawkins, but it's true," and begins on the usual rigmarole about duty and how unpleasant it is.

I never noticed that people who talk a lot about duty find it much of a trouble to them.

"Oh, cut it out!" says Hawkins.

65 "Ask Bonaparte," says Donovan, seeing that Hawkins isn't taking him seriously. "Isn't it true, Bonaparte?"

"It is," I say, and Hawkins stops.

"Ah, for Christ's sake, chum!"

"I mean it, chum," I say.

"You don't sound as if you meant it."

70 "If he doesn't mean it, I do," says Donovan, working himself up.

"What have you against me, Jeremiah Donovan?"

"I never said I had anything against you. But why did your people take out four of our prisoners and shoot them in cold blood?"

He took Hawkins by the arm and dragged him on, but it was impossible to make him understand that we were in earnest. I had the Smith and Wesson in my pocket and I kept fingering it and wondering what I'd do if they put up a fight for it or ran, and wishing to God they'd do one or the other. I knew if they did run for it, that I'd never fire on them. Hawkins wanted to know was Noble in it, and when we said yes, he asked us why Noble wanted to plug him. Why did any of us want to plug him? What had he done to us? Weren't we all chums? Didn't we understand him and didn't he understand us? Did we imagine for an instant that he'd shoot us for all the so-and-so officers in the so-and-so British Army?

By this time we'd reached the bog, and I was so sick I couldn't even answer him. We walked along the edge of it in the darkness, and every now and then Hawkins would call a halt and begin all over again, as if he was wound up, about our being chums, and I knew that nothing but the sight of the grave would convince him that we had to do it. And all the time I was hoping that something would happen; that they'd run for it or that Noble would take over the responsibility from me. I had the feeling that it was worse on Noble than on me.

IV

75 At last we saw the lantern in the distance and made towards it. Noble was carrying it, and Feeney was standing somewhere in the darkness behind him, and the picture of them so still and silent in the bogland brought it home to me that we were in earnest, and banished the last bit of hope I had.

Belcher, on recognizing Noble, said: "Hallo, chum," in his quiet way, but Hawkins flew at him at once, and the argument began all over again, only this time Noble had nothing to say for himself and stood with his head down, holding the lantern between his legs.

It was Jeremiah Donovan who did the answering. For the twentieth time, as though it was haunting his mind, Hawkins asked if anybody thought he'd shoot Noble.

"Yes, you would," says Jeremiah Donovan.

"No, I wouldn't damn you!"

80   "You would, because you'd know you'd be shot for not doing it."

"I wouldn't, not if I was to be shot twenty times over. I wouldn't shoot a pal. And Belcher wouldn't—isn't that right, Belcher?"

"That's right, chum," Belcher said, but more by way of answering the question than of joining in the argument. Belcher sounded as though whatever unforeseen thing he'd always been waiting for had come at last.

"Anyway, who says Noble would be shot if I wasn't? What do you think I'd do if I was in his place, out in the middle of a blasted bog?"

"What would you do?" asks Donovan.

85   "I'd go with him wherever he was going, of course. Share my last bob with him and stick by him through thick and thin. No one can ever say of me that I let down a pal."

"We had enough of this," says Jeremiah Donovan, cocking his revolver. "Is there any message you want to send?"

"No, there isn't."

"Do you want to say your prayers?"

Hawkins came out with a cold-blooded remark that even shocked me and turned on Noble again.

90   "Listen to me, Noble," he says. "You and me are chums. You can't come over to my side, so I'll come over to your side. That show you I mean what I say? Give me a rifle and I'll go along with you and the other lads."

Nobody answered him. We knew that was no way out.

"Hear what I'm saying?" he says. "I'm through with it. I'm a deserter or anything else you like. I don't believe in your stuff, but it's no worse than mine. That satisfy you?"

Noble raised his head, but Donovan began to speak and he lowered it again without replying.

"For the last time, have you any messages to send?" says Donovan in a cold, excited sort of voice.

95   "Shut up, Donovan! You don't understand me, but these lads do. They're not the sort to make a pal and kill a pal. They're not the tools of any capitalist."

I alone of the crowd saw Donovan raise his Webley to the back of Hawkins's neck, and as he did so I shut my eyes and tried to pray. Hawkins had begun to say something else when Donovan fired, and as I opened my eyes at the bang, I saw Hawkins stagger at the knees and lie out flat at Noble's feet, slowly and as quiet as a kid falling asleep, with the lantern-light on his lean legs and bright farmer's boots. We all stood very still, watching him settle out in the last agony.

Then Belcher took out a handkerchief and began to tie it about his own eyes (in our excitement we'd forgotten to do the same for Hawkins), and, seeing it wasn't big enough, turned and asked for the loan of mine. I gave it to him and he knotted the two together and pointed with his foot at Hawkins.

"He's not quite dead," he says. "Better give him another."

Sure enough, Hawkins's left knee is beginning to rise. I bend down and put my gun to his head; then, recollecting myself, I get up again. Belcher understands what's in my mind.

100   "Give him his first," he says. "I don't mind. Poor bastard, we don't know what's happening to him now."

I knelt and fired. By this time I didn't seem to know what I was doing. Belcher, who was fumbling a bit awkwardly with the handkerchiefs, came out with a laugh as he heard the shot. It was the first time I heard him laugh and it sent a shudder down my back; it sounded so unnatural.

"Poor bugger!" he said quietly. "And last night he was so curious about it all. It's very queer, chums, I always think. Now he knows as much about it as they'll ever let him know, and last night he was all in the dark."

Donovan helped him to tie the handkerchiefs about his eyes. "Thanks, chum," he said. Donovan asked if there were any messages he wanted sent.

"No, chum," he says. "Not for me. If any of you would like to write to Hawkins's mother, you'll find a letter from her in his pocket. He and his mother were great chums. But my missus left me eight years ago. Went away with another fellow and took the kid with her. I like the feeling of a home, as you may have noticed, but I couldn't start again after that."

105   It was an extraordinary thing, but in those few minutes Belcher said more than in all the weeks before. It was just as if the sound of the shot had started a flood of talk in him and he could go on the whole night like that, quite happily, talking about himself. We stood round like fools now that he couldn't see us any longer. Donovan looked at Noble, and Noble shook his head. Then Donovan raised his Webley, and at that moment Belcher gives his queer laugh again. He may have thought we were talking about him, or perhaps he noticed the same thing I'd noticed and couldn't understand it.

"Excuse me, chums," he says. "I feel I'm talking the hell of a lot, and so silly, about my being so handy about a house and things like that. But this thing came on me suddenly. You'll forgive me, I'm sure."

"You don't want to say a prayer?" asks Donovan.

"No, chum," he says. "I don't think it would help. I'm ready and you boys want to get it over."

"You understand that we're only doing our duty?" says Donovan.

110   Belcher's head was raised like a blind man's, so that you could only see his chin and the tip of his nose in the lantern-light.

"I never could make out what duty was myself," he said. "I think you're all good lads, if that's what you mean. I'm not complaining."

Noble, just as if he couldn't hear any more of it, raised his fist at Donovan, and in a flash Donovan raised his gun and fired. The big man went over like a sack of meal, and this time there was no need of a second shot.

I don't remember much about the burying, but that it was worse than all the rest because we had to carry them to the grave. It was all mad lonely with nothing but a patch of lantern-light between ourselves and the dark, and birds hooting and screeching all round, disturbed by the guns. Noble went through Hawkins's belongings to find the letter from his mother, and then joined his hands together. He did the same with Belcher. Then, when we'd filled in the grave, we separated from Jeremiah Donovan and Feeney and took our tools back to the shed. All the way we didn't speak a word. The kitchen was dark and cold as we'd left it, and the old woman was sitting over the hearth, saying her beads. We walked past her into the room, and Noble struck a match to light the lamp. She rose quietly and came to the doorway with all her cantankerousness gone.

"What did ye do with them?" she asked in a whisper, and Noble started so that the match went out in his hand.

115 "What's that?" he asked without turning round.

"I heard ye," she said.

"What did you hear?" asked Noble.

"I heard ye. Do ye think I didn't hear ye, putting the spade back in the houseen?"

Noble struck another match and this time the lamp lit for him.

120 "Was that what ye did to them?" she asked.

Then, by God, in the very doorway, she fell on her knees and began praying, and after looking at her for a minute or two Noble did the same by the fireplace. I pushed my way out past her and left them at it. I stood at the door, watching the stars and listening to the shrieking of the birds dying out over the bogs. It is so strange what you feel at times like that that you can't describe it. Noble says he saw everything ten times the size, as though there were nothing in the whole world but that little patch of bog with the two Englishmen stiffening into it, but with me it was as if the patch of bog where the Englishmen were was a million miles away, and even Noble and the old woman, mumbling behind me, and the birds and the bloody stars were all far away, and I was somehow very small and very lost and lonely like a child astray in the snow. And anything that happened to me afterwards, I never felt the same about again.

Edgar Allan Poe

Edgar Allan Poe (1809–1849) is known for his macabre, grotesque, and mysterious stories and poems. He invented the detective story with tales like "The Purloined Letter" and "The Murders in the Rue Morgue." Poe's short life was unsettled and tempestuous. He attended the University of Virginia for a few months, leaving when he quarreled with his grandfather over gambling debts he had contracted. He was expelled from West Point for breaking rules, married his thirteen-year-old cousin, and struggled to earn enough money by his writing to support himself and his family. He is one of the first great American authors, and his literary criticism is as original as his stories and poems. For a poem by Poe, see page 666.

The Murders in the Rue Morgue   (1841)

What song the Syrens sang, or what name Achilles assumed when he hid himself among women, although puzzling questions, are not beyond *all* conjecture.
—*Sir Thomas Browne,* Urn-Burial

The mental features discoursed of as the analytical, are, in themselves, but little susceptible of analysis. We appreciate them only in their effects. We know of them, among other things, that they are always to their possessor, when inordinately possessed, a source of the liveliest enjoyment. As the strong man exults in his physical ability, delighting in such exercises as call his muscles into action, so glories the analyst in that moral activity which *disentangles.* He derives pleasure from even the most trivial occupations bringing his talents into play. He is fond of enigmas, of conundrums, of hieroglyphics; exhibiting in his solutions of each a degree of *acumen* which appears to the ordinary apprehension preternatural. His results, brought about by the very soul and essence of method, have, in truth, the whole air of intuition. The faculty of re-solution is possibly much invigorated by mathematical study, and especially by that highest branch of it which, unjustly, and merely on account of its retrograde operations, has been called, as if *par excellence,* analysis. Yet to calculate is not in itself to analyze. A chess-player, for example, does the one without effort at the other. It follows that the game of chess, in its effects upon mental character, is greatly misunderstood. I am not now writing a treatise, but simply prefacing a somewhat peculiar narrative by observations very much at random; I will, therefore, take occasion to assert that the higher powers of the reflective intellect are more decidedly and more usefully tasked by the unostentatious game of draughts than by all the elaborate frivolity of chess. In this latter, where the pieces have different and *bizarre* motions, with various and variable values, what is only complex is mistaken (a not unusual error) for what is profound. The *attention* is here called powerfully into play. If it flag for an instant, an oversight is committed, resulting in injury or defeat. The possible moves being not only manifold but involute, the chances of such oversights are multiplied; and in nine cases out of ten it is the more concentrative rather than the more acute player who conquers. In draughts, on the contrary, where the moves are *unique* and have but little variation, the probabilities of inadvertence are diminished, and the mere attention being left comparatively unemployed, what advantages are obtained by either party are obtained by superior *acumen.* To be less abstract—Let us suppose a game of draughts where the pieces are reduced to four kings, and where, of course, no oversight is to be expected. It is obvious that here the victory can be decided (the players being at all equal) only by some *recherche* movement, the result of some strong exertion of the intellect. Deprived of ordinary resources, the analyst throws himself into the spirit of his opponent, identifies himself therewith, and not unfrequently sees thus, at a glance, the sole methods (sometimes indeed absurdly simple ones) by which he may seduce into error or hurry into miscalculation.

Whist has long been noted for its influence upon what is termed the calculating power; and men of the highest order of intellect have been known to take an apparently unaccountable delight in it, while eschewing chess as frivolous. Beyond doubt there is nothing of a similar nature so greatly tasking the faculty of analysis. The best chess-player in Christendom *may* be little more than the best player of chess; but proficiency in whist implies capacity for success in all these more important undertakings where mind struggles with mind. When I say proficiency, I mean that perfection in the game which includes a comprehension of *all* the sources whence legitimate advantage may be derived. These are not only manifold but multiform, and lie frequently among recesses of thought altogether inaccessible to the ordinary understanding. To observe attentively is to remember distinctly; and, so far, the concentrative chess-player will do very well at whist; while the rules of Hoyle (themselves based upon the mere mechanism of the game) are sufficiently and generally comprehensible. Thus to have a retentive memory, and to proceed by "the book," are points commonly regarded as the sum total of good playing. But it is in matters beyond the limits of mere rule that the skill of the analyst is evinced. He makes, in silence, a host of observations and inferences. So, perhaps, do his companions; and the difference in the extent of the information obtained, lies not so much in the validity of the inference as in the quality of the observation. The necessary knowledge is that of *what* to observe. Our player confines himself not at all; nor, because the game is the object, does he reject deductions from things external to the game. He examines the countenance of his partner, comparing it carefully with that of each of his opponents. He considers the mode of assorting the cards in each hand; often counting trump by trump, and honor by honor, through the glances bestowed by their holders upon each. He notes every variation of face as the play progresses, gathering a fund of thought from the differences in the expression of certainty, of surprise, of triumph, or chagrin. From the manner of gathering up a trick he judges whether the person taking it can make another in the suit. He recognizes what is played through feint, by the air with which it is thrown upon the table. A casual or inadvertent word; the accidental dropping or turning of a card, with the accompanying anxiety or carelessness in regard to its concealment; the counting of the tricks, with the order of their arrangement; embarrassment, hesitation, eagerness or trepidation—all afford, to his apparently intuitive perception, indications of the true state of affairs. The first two or three rounds having been played, he is in full possession of the contents of each hand, and thenceforward puts down his cards with as absolute a precision of purpose as if the rest of the party had turned outward the faces of their own.

The analytical power should not be confounded with simple ingenuity; for while the analyst is necessarily ingenious, the ingenious man is often remarkably incapable of analysis. The consecutive or combining power, by which ingenuity is usually manifested, and to which the phrenologists (I believe erroneously) have assigned a separate organ, supposing it a primitive faculty, has been so frequently seen in those whose intellect bordered otherwise upon idiocy, as to have attracted general observation among writers on morals. Between ingenuity and the analytic ability there exists a difference far greater, indeed, than that between the fancy and the imagination, but of a character very strictly analogous. It will be found, in fact, that the ingenious are always fanciful, and the *truly* imaginative never otherwise than analytic.

The narrative which follows will appear to the reader somewhat in the light of a commentary upon the propositions just advanced.

5   Residing in Paris during the spring and part of the summer of 18—, I there became acquainted with a Monsieur C. Auguste Dupin. This young gentleman was of an excellent—indeed of an illustrious family, but, by a variety of

untoward events, had been reduced to such poverty that the energy of his character succumbed beneath it, and he ceased to bestir himself in the world, or to care for the retrieval of his fortunes. By courtesy of his creditors, there still remained in his possession a small remnant of his patrimony; and, upon the income arising from this, he managed, by means of a rigorous economy, to procure the necessaries of life, without troubling himself about its superfluities. Books, indeed, were his sole luxuries, and in Paris these are easily obtained.

Our first meeting was at an obscure library in the Rue Montmartre, where the accident of our both being in search of the same very rare and very remarkable volume, brought us into closer communion. We saw each other again and again. I was deeply interested in the little family history which he detailed to me with all that candor which a Frenchman indulges whenever mere self is the theme. I was astonished, too, at the vast extent of his reading; and, above all, I felt my soul enkindled within me by the wild fervor, and the vivid freshness of his imagination. Seeking in Paris the objects I then sought, I felt that the society of such a man would be to me a treasure beyond price; and this feeling I frankly confided to him. It was at length arranged that we should live together during my stay in the city; and as my worldly circumstances were somewhat less embarrassed than his own, I was permitted to be at the expense of renting, and furnishing in a style which suited the rather fantastic gloom of our common temper, a time-eaten and grotesque mansion, long deserted through superstitions into which we did not inquire, and tottering to its fall in a retired and desolate portion of the Faubourg St. Germain.

Had the routine of our life at this place been known to the world, we should have been regarded as madmen—although, perhaps, as madmen of a harmless nature. Our seclusion was perfect. We admitted no visitors. Indeed the locality of our retirement had been carefully kept a secret from my own former associates; and it had been many years since Dupin had ceased to know or be known in Paris. We existed within ourselves alone.

It was a freak of fancy in my friend (for what else shall I call it?) to be enamored of the Night, for her own sake; and into this *bizarrerie,* as into all his others, I quietly fell; giving myself up to his wild whims with a perfect *abandon.* The sable divinity would not herself dwell with us always; but we could counterfeit her presence. At the first dawn of the morning we closed all the massy shutters of our old building; lighted a couple of tapers which, strongly perfumed, threw out only the ghastliest and feeblest of rays. By the aid of these we then busied our souls in dreams—reading, writing, or conversing; until warned by the clock of the advent of the true Darkness. Then we sallied forth into the streets, arm and arm, continuing the topics of the day, or roaming far and wide until a late hour, seeking, amid the wild lights and shadows of the populous city, that infinity of mental excitement which quiet observation can afford.

At such times I could not help remarking and admiring (although from his rich ideality I had been prepared to expect it) a peculiar analytic ability in Dupin. He seemed, too, to take an eager delight in this exercise—if not exactly in its display—and did not hesitate to confess the pleasure thus derived.

He boasted to me, with a low chuckling laugh, that most men, in respect to himself, wore windows in their bosoms, and was wont to follow up such assertions by direct and very startling proof of his intimate knowledge of my own. His manner at these moments was frigid and abstract; his eyes were vacant in expression; while his voice, usually a rich tenor, rose into a treble which would have sounded petulantly but for the deliberateness and entire distinctness of the enunciation. Observing him in these moods, I often dwelt meditatively upon the old philosophy of the Bi-Part Soul, and amused myself with the fancy of a double Dupin—the creative and the resolvent.

10   Let it not be supposed, from what I have just said, that I am detailing any mystery, or penning any romance. What I have described in the Frenchman was merely the result of an excited, or perhaps of a diseased, intelligence. But of the character of his remarks at the periods in question an example will best convey the idea.

We were strolling one night down a long dirty street, in the vicinity of the Palais Royal. Being both, apparently, occupied with thought, neither of us had spoken a syllable for fifteen minutes at least. All at once Dupin broke forth with these words:

"He is a very little fellow, that's true, and would do better for the *Théâtre des Variétés.*"

"There can be no doubt of that," I replied unwittingly, and not at first observing (so much had I been absorbed in reflection) the extraordinary manner in which the speaker had chimed in with my meditations. In an instant afterwards I recollected myself, and my astonishment was profound.

"Dupin," said I, gravely, "this is beyond my comprehension. I do not hesitate to say that I am amazed, and can scarcely credit my senses. How was it possible you should know I was thinking of ———?" Here I paused, to ascertain beyond a doubt whether he really knew of whom I thought.

15   "——— of Chantilly," said he, "why do you pause? You were remarking to yourself that his diminutive figure unfitted him for tragedy."

This was precisely what had formed the subject of my reflections. Chantilly was a *quondam*[1] cobbler of the Rue St. Denis, who, becoming stage-mad, had attempted the *rôle* of Xerxes, in Crébillon's tragedy so called, and been notoriously Pasquinaded[2] for his pains.

"Tell me, for Heaven's sake," I exclaimed, "the method—if method there is—by which you have been enabled to fathom my soul in this matter." In fact I was even more startled than I would have been willing to express.

"It was the fruiterer," replied my friend, "who brought you to the conclusion that the mender of soles was not of sufficient height for Xerxes *et id genus omne.*"[3]

"The fruiterer!—you astonish me—I know no fruiterer whomsoever."

20   "The man who ran up against you as we entered the street—it may have been fifteen minutes ago."

I now remembered that, in fact, a fruiterer, carrying upon his head a large basket of apples, had nearly thrown me down, by accident, as we passed from

---

[1] Former   [2] Mocked, ridiculed   [3] And everything of this kind

the Rue C——— into the thoroughfare where we stood; but what this had to do with Chantilly I could not possibly understand.

There was not a particle of *charlatanerie* about Dupin. "I will explain," he said, "and that you may comprehend all clearly, we will first retrace the course of your meditations, from the moment in which I spoke to you until that of the *rencontre*[4] with the fruiterer in question. The larger links of the chain run thus—Chantilly, Orion, Dr. Nichols, Epicurus, Stereotomy, the street stones, the fruiterer."

There are few persons who have not, at some period of their lives, amused themselves in retracing the steps by which particular conclusions of their own minds have been attained. The occupation is often full of interest; and he who attempts it for the first time is astonished by the apparently illim-itable distance and incoherence between the starting-point and the goal. What, then, must have been my amazement when I heard the Frenchman speak what he had just spoken, and when I could not help acknowledging that he had spoken the truth. He continued:

"We had been talking of horses, if I remember aright, just before leaving the Rue C———. This was the last subject we discussed. As we crossed into the street, a fruiterer, with a large basket upon his head, brushing quickly past us, thrust you upon a pile of paving-stones collected at a spot where the causeway is undergoing repair. You stepped upon one of the loose frag-ments, slipped, slightly strained your ankle, appeared vexed or sulky, mut-tered a few words, turned to look at the pile, and then proceeded in silence. I was not particularly attentive to what you did; but observation has become with me, of late, a species of necessity.

25 "You kept your eyes upon the ground—glancing, with a petulant expres-sion, at the holes and ruts in the pavement (so that I saw you were still thinking of the stones), until we reached the little alley called Lamartine, which has been paved, by way of experiment, with the overlapping and riveted blocks. Here your countenance brightened up, and, perceiving your lips move, I could not doubt that you murmured the word 'stereotomy,' a term very affectedly applied to this species of pavement. I knew that you could not say to yourself 'stereotomy' without being brought to think of atomies, and thus of the theories of Epicurus; and since, when we discussed this subject not very long ago, I mentioned to you how singularly, yet with how little notice, the vague guesses of that noble Greek had met with confir-mation in the late nebular cosmogony, I felt that you could not avoid casting your eyes upwards to the great *nebula* in Orion, and I certainly expected that you would do so. You did look up; and I was now assured that I had correctly followed your steps. But in that bitter *tirade* upon Chantilly, which appeared in yesterday's '*Musée*,' the satirist, making some disgraceful allusions to the cobbler's change of name upon assuming the buskin, quoted a Latin line about which we have often conversed, I mean the line

Perdidit antiquum litera prima sonum[5]

---

[4] Meeting, encounter [5] "The first letter has lost its original sound."

I had told you that this was in reference to Orion, formerly written Urion; and, from certain pungencies connected with this explanation, I was aware that you could not have forgotten it. It was clear, therefore, that you would not fail to combine the two ideas of Orion and Chantilly. That you did combine them I saw by the character of the smile which passed over your lips. You thought of the poor cobbler's immolation. So far, you had been stooping in your gait; but now I saw you draw yourself up to your full height. I was then sure that you reflected upon the diminutive figure of Chantilly. At this point I interrupted your meditations to remark that as, in fact, he *was* a very little fellow—that Chantilly—he would do better at the *Théâtre des Variétés.*"

Not long after this, we were looking over an evening edition of the "Gazette des Tribunaux," when the following paragraphs arrested our attention.

"EXTRAORDINARY MURDERS.—This morning, about three o'clock, the inhabitants of the Quartier St. Roch were aroused from sleep by a succession of terrific shrieks, issuing, apparently, from the fourth story of a house in the Rue Morgue, known to be in the sole occupancy of one Madame L'Espanaye, and her daughter, Mademoiselle Camille L'Espanaye. After some delay, occasioned by a fruitless attempt to procure admission in the usual manner, the gateway was broken in with a crowbar, and eight or ten of the neighbors entered, accompanied by two *gendarmes.* By this time the cries had ceased; but, as the party rushed up the first flight of stairs, two or more rough voices, in angry contention, were distinguished, and seemed to proceed from the upper part of the house. As the second landing was reached, these sounds, also, had ceased, and everything remained perfectly quiet. The party spread themselves, and hurried from room to room. Upon arriving at a large back chamber in the fourth story (the door of which, being found locked, with the key inside, was forced open), a spectacle presented itself which struck every one present not less with horror than with astonishment.

"The apartment was in the wildest disorder—the furniture broken and thrown about in all directions. There was only one bedstead; and from this the bed had been removed, and thrown into the middle of the floor. On a chair lay a razor, besmeared with blood. On the hearth were two or three long and thick tresses of gray human hair, also dabbled in blood, and seeming to have been pulled out by the roots. Upon the floor were found four Napoleons,[6] an earring of topaz, three large silver spoons, three smaller of *métal d'Alger,*[7] and two bags, containing nearly four thousand francs in gold. The drawers of a *bureau,* which stood in one corner, were open, and had been, apparently, rifled, although many articles still remained in them. A small iron safe was discovered under the *bed* (not under the bedstead). It was open, with the key still in the door. It had no contents beyond a few old letters, and other papers of little consequence.

"Of Madame L'Espanaye no traces were here seen; but an unusual quantity of soot being observed in the fireplace, a search was made in the chimney, and (horrible to relate!) the corpse of the daughter, head downwards, was dragged therefrom; it having been thus forced up the narrow aperture for a considerable distance. The body was quite warm. Upon examining it, many excoriations were perceived, no doubt occasioned by the violence with which it had been thrust up and disengaged. Upon the face were many severe scratches, and, upon the throat,

[6] A twenty-franc piece bearing Napoleon's image   [7] A silvered-colored alloy of tin, lead, and antimony.

dark bruises, and deep indentations of finger-nails, as if the deceased had been throttled to death.

30 "After a thorough investigation of every portion of the house, without farther discovery, the party made its way into a small paved yard in the rear of the building, where lay the corpse of the old lady, with her throat so entirely cut that, upon an attempt to raise her, the head fell off. The body, as well as the head, was fearfully mutilated—the former so much so as scarcely to retain any semblance of humanity.

"To this horrible mystery there is not as yet, we believe, the slightest clue."

The next day's paper had these additional particulars.

"*The Tragedy in the Rue Morgue*. Many individuals have been examined in relation to this most extraordinary and frightful affair" (the word '*affaire*' has not yet, in France, that levity of import which it conveys with us), "but nothing whatever has transpired to throw light upon it. We give below all the material testimony elicited.

"*Pauline Dubourg,* laundress, deposes that she has known both the deceased for three years, having washed for them during that period. The old lady and her daughter seemed on good terms—very affectionate towards each other. They were excellent pay. Could not speak in regard to their mode or means of living. Believed that Madame L. told fortunes for a living. Was reputed to have money put by. Never met any persons in the house when she called for the clothes or took them home. Was sure that they had no servant in employ. There appeared to be no furniture in any part of the building except in the fourth story.

35 "*Pierre Moreau,* tobacconist, deposes that he had been in the habit of selling small quantities of tobacco and snuff to Madame L'Espanaye for nearly four years. Was born in the neighborhood, and has always resided there. The deceased and her daughter had occupied the house in which the corpses were found, for more than six years. It was formerly occupied by a jeweler, who under-let the upper rooms to various persons. The house was the property of Madame L. She became dissatisfied with the abuse of the premises by her tenant, and moved into them herself, refusing to let any portion. The old lady was childish. Witness had seen the daughter some five or six times during the six years. The two lived an exceedingly retired life—were reputed to have money. Had heard it said among the neighbors that Madame L. told fortunes—did not believe it. Had never seen any person enter the door except the old lady and her daughter, porter once or twice, and a physician some eight or ten times.

"Many other persons, neighbors, gave evidence to the same effect. No one was spoken of as frequenting the house. It was not known whether there were any living connections of Madame L. and her daughter. The shutters of the front windows were seldom opened. Those in the rear were always closed, with the exception of the large back room, fourth story. The house was a good house—not very old.

"*Isidore Musèt, gendarme,* deposes that he was called to the house about three o'clock in the morning, and found some twenty or thirty persons at the gateway, endeavoring to gain admittance. Forced it open, at length, with a bayonet—not with a crowbar. Had but little difficulty in getting it open, on account of its being a double or folding gate, and bolted neither at bottom nor top. The shrieks were continued until the gate was forced—and then suddenly ceased. They seemed to be screams of some person (or persons) in great agony—were loud and drawn out, not short and quick. Witness led the way upstairs. Upon reaching the first landing, heard two voices in loud and angry contention—the one a gruff voice, the other much shriller—a very strange voice. Could distinguish some words of the former, which was that of a Frenchman. Was positive that it was not a woman's voice. Could distinguish the words '*sacré*' and '*diable.*' The shrill voice was that of a foreigner. Could not be sure whether it was the voice of a man or of a woman. Could not make out what was said, but believed the language to be Spanish. The state of the room and of the bodies was described by this witness as we described them yesterday.

"*Henry Duval,* a neighbor, and by trade a silversmith, deposes that he was one of the party who first entered the house. Corroborates the testimony of Musèt in general. As soon as they forced an entrance, they reclosed the door, to keep out the crowd, which collected very fast, notwithstanding the lateness of the hour. The shrill voice, the witness thinks, was that of an Italian. Was certain it was not French. Could not be sure that it was a man's voice. It might have been a woman's. Was not acquainted with the Italian language. Could not distinguish the words, but was convinced by the intonation that the speaker was an Italian. Knew Madame L. and her daughter. Had conversed with both frequently. Was sure that the shrill voice was not that of either of the deceased.

"———*Odenheimer, restaurateur.* This witness volunteered his testimony. Not speaking French, was examined through an interpreter. Is a native of Amsterdam. Was passing the house at the time of the shrieks. They lasted for several minutes—probably ten. They were long and loud—very awful and distressing. Was one of those who entered the building. Corroborated the previous evidence in every respect but one. Was sure that the shrill voice was that of a man—of a Frenchman. Could not distinguish the words uttered. They were loud and quick—unequal—spoken apparently in fear as well as in anger. The voice was harsh—not so much shrill as harsh. Could not call it a shrill voice. The gruff voice said repeatedly '*sacré,*' '*diable*' and once '*mon Dieu.*'

40   "*Jules Mignaud,* banker, of the firm of Mignaud et Fils, Rue Deloraine. Is the elder Mignaud. Madame L'Espanaye had some property. Had opened an account with his banking house in the spring of the year—(eight years previously). Made frequent deposits in small sums. Had checked for nothing until the third day before her death, when she took out in person the sum of 4000 francs. This sum was paid in gold, and a clerk sent home with the money.

"*Adolphe Le Bon,* clerk to Mignaud et Fils, deposes that on the day in question, about noon, he accompanied Madame L'Espanaye to her residence with the 4000 francs, put up in two bags. Upon the door being opened, Mademoiselle L. appeared and took from his hands one of the bags, while the old lady relieved him of the other. He then bowed and departed. Did not see any person in the street at the time. It is a bye-street—very lonely.

"*William Bird,* tailor, deposes that he was one of the party who entered the house. Is an Englishman. Has lived in Paris two years. Was one of the first to ascend the stairs. Heard the voices in contention. The gruff voice was that of a Frenchman. Could make out several words, but cannot now remember all. Heard distinctly '*sacré*' and '*mon Dieu.*' There was a sound at the moment as if of several persons struggling—a scraping and scuffling sound. The shrill voice was very loud—louder than the gruff one. Is sure that it was not the voice of an Englishman. Appeared to be that of a German. Might have been a woman's voice. Does not understand German.

"Four of the above-named witnesses, being recalled, deposed that the door of the chamber in which was found the body of Mademoiselle L. was locked on the inside when the party reached it. Everything was perfectly silent—no groans or noises of any kind. Upon forcing the door no person was seen. The windows, both of the back and front room, were down and firmly fastened from within. A door between the two rooms was closed, but not locked. The door leading from the front room into the passage was locked, with the key on the inside. A small room in the front of the house, on the fourth story, at the head of the passage, was open, the door being ajar. This room was crowded with old beds, boxes, and so forth. These were carefully removed and searched. There was not an inch of any portion of the house which was not carefully searched. Sweeps were sent up and down the chimneys. The house was a four-story one, with garrets (*mansardes*). A trap-door on the roof was nailed down very securely—did not appear to have been opened for years. The time elapsing between the hearing of the voices in contention and the breaking open of the room door, was variously stated by the witnesses. Some made it as short as three minutes—some as long as five. The door was opened with difficulty.

"*Alfonzo Garcio,* undertaker, deposes that he resides in the Rue Morgue. Is a native of Spain. Was one of the party who entered the house. Did not proceed upstairs. Is nervous, and was apprehensive of the consequences of agitation. Heard the voices in contention. The gruff voice was that of a Frenchman. Could not distinguish what was said. The shrill voice was that of an Englishman—is sure of this. Does not understand the English language, but judges by the intonation.

45   "*Alberto Montani,* confectioner, deposes that he was among the first to ascend the stairs. Heard the voices in question. The gruff voice was that of a Frenchman. Distinguished several words. The speaker appeared to be expostulating. Could not make out the words of the shrill voice. Spoke quick and unevenly. Thinks it the voice of a Russian. Corroborates the general testimony. Is an Italian. Never conversed with a native of Russia.

"Several witnesses, recalled, here testified that the chimneys of all the rooms on the fourth story were too narrow to admit the passage of a human being. By 'sweeps' were meant cylindrical sweeping-brushes, such as are employed by those who clean chimneys. These brushes were passed up and down every flue in the house. There is no back passage by which any one could have descended while the party proceeded upstairs. The body of Mademoiselle L'Espanaye was so firmly wedged in the chimney that it could not be got down until four or five of the party united their strength.

"*Paul Dumas,* physician, deposes that he was called to view the bodies about daybreak. They were both then lying on the sacking of the bedstead in the chamber where Mademoiselle L. was found. The corpse of the young lady was much bruised and excoriated. The fact that it had been thrust up the chimney would sufficiently account for these appearances. The throat was greatly chafed. There were several deep scratches just below the chin, together with a series of livid spots which were evidently the impression of fingers. The face was fearfully discolored, and the eyeballs protruded. The tongue had been partially bitten through. A large bruise was discovered upon the pit of the stomach, produced, apparently, by the pressure of a knee. In the opinion of M. Dumas, Mademoiselle L'Espanaye had been throttled to death by some person or persons unknown. The corpse of the mother was horribly mutilated. All the bones of the right leg and arm were more or less shattered. The left *tibia* much splintered, as well as all the ribs of the left side. Whole body dreadfully bruised and discolored. It was not possible to say how the injuries had been inflicted. A heavy club of wood, or a broad bar of iron—a chair—any large, heavy, and obtuse weapon would have produced such results, if wielded by the hands of a very powerful man. No woman could have inflicted the blows with any weapon. The head of the deceased, when seen by witness, was entirely separated from the body, and was also greatly shattered. The throat had evidently been cut with some very sharp instrument—probably with a razor.

"*Alexandre Etienne,* surgeon, was called with M. Dumas to view the bodies. Corroborated the testimony, and the opinions of M. Dumas.

"Nothing farther of importance was elicited, although several other persons were examined. A murder so mysterious, and so perplexing in all its particulars, was never before committed in Paris—if indeed a murder has been committed at all. The police are entirely at fault —an unusual occurrence in affairs of this nature. There is not, however, the shadow of a clue apparent."

50   The evening edition of the paper stated that the greatest excitement still continued in the Quartier St. Roch—that the premises in question had been carefully researched, and fresh examinations of witnesses instituted, but all to no purpose. A postscript, however, mentioned that Adolphe Le Bon had been arrested and imprisoned—although nothing appeared to criminate him, beyond the facts already detailed.

Dupin seemed singularly interested in the progress of this affair—at least so I judged from his manner, for he made no comments. It was only after the announcement that Le Bon had been imprisoned, that he asked me my opinion respecting the murders.

I could merely agree with all Paris in considering them an insoluble mystery. I saw no means by which it would be possible to trace the murderer.

"We must not judge of the means," said Dupin, "by this shell of an examination. The Parisian police, so much extolled for *acumen,* are cunning, but no more. There is no method in their proceedings, beyond the method of the moment. They make a vast parade of measures; but, not unfrequently, these are so ill adapted to the objects proposed, as to put us in mind of Monsieur Jourdain's calling for his *robe-de-chambre—pour mieux entendre la musique.*[8] The results attained by them are not unfrequently surprising, but, for the most part, are brought about by simple diligence and activity. When these qualities are unavailing, their schemes fail. Vidocq, for example, was a good guesser, and a persevering man. But, without educated thought, he erred continually by the very intensity of his investigations. He impaired his vision by holding the object too close. He might see, perhaps, one or two points with unusual clearness, but in so doing he, necessarily, lost sight of the matter as a whole. Thus there is such a thing as being too profound. Truth is not always in a well. In fact, as regards the more important knowledge, I do believe that she is invariably superficial. The depth lies in the valleys where we seek her, and not upon the mountain-tops where she is found. The modes and sources of this kind of error are well typified in the contemplation of the heavenly bodies. To look at a star by glances—to view it in a side-long way, by turning towards it the exterior portions of the *retina* (more susceptible of feeble impressions of light than the interior), is to behold the star distinctly— is to have the best appreciation of its luster—a luster which grows dim just in proportion as we turn our vision *fully* upon it. A greater number of rays actually fall upon the eye in the latter case, but in the former, there is the more

[8] In Molière's comedy *The Bourgeois Gentleman,* M. Jourdain believes he can hear music better when he wears his bathrobe.

refined capacity for comprehension. By undue profundity we perplex and enfeeble thought; and it is possible to make even Venus herself vanish from the firmament by a scrutiny too sustained, too concentrated, or too direct.

"As for these murders, let us enter into some examinations for ourselves, before we make up an opinion respecting them. An inquiry will afford us amusement" (I thought this an odd term, so applied, but said nothing), "and, besides, Le Bon once rendered me a service for which I am not ungrateful. We will go and see the premises with our own eyes. I know G——, the Prefect of Police, and shall have no difficulty in obtaining the necessary permission."

55 The permission was obtained, and we proceeded at once to the Rue Morgue. This is one of those miserable thoroughfares, which intervene between the Rue Richelieu and the Rue St. Roch. It was late in the afternoon when we reached it; as this quarter is at a great distance from that in which we resided. The house was readily found; for there were still many persons gazing up at the closed shutters, with an objectless curiosity, from the opposite side of the way. It was an ordinary Parisian house, with a gateway, on one side of which was a glazed watchbox, with a sliding panel in the window, indicating a *loge de concierge*. Before going in we walked up the street, turned down an alley, and then, again turning, passed in the rear of the building—Dupin, meanwhile, examining the whole neighborhood, as well as the house, with a minuteness of attention for which I could see no possible object.

Retracing our steps, we came again to the front of the dwelling, rang, and, having shown our credentials, were admitted by the agents in charge. We went upstairs—into the chamber where the body of Mademoiselle L'Espanaye had been found, and where both the deceased still lay. The disorders of the room had, as usual, been suffered to exist. I saw nothing beyond what had been stated in the "Gazette des Tribunaux." Dupin scrutinized everything—not excepting the bodies of the victims. We then went into the other rooms, and into the yard: a *gendarme* accompanying us throughout. The examination occupied us until dark, when we took our departure. On our way home my companion stopped in for a moment at the office of the daily papers.

I have said that the whims of my friend were manifold, and that *Je les ménageais:*—for this phrase there is no English equivalent. It was his humor, now, to decline all conversation on the subject of the murder, until about noon the next day. He then asked me, suddenly, if I had observed anything *peculiar* at the scene of the atrocity.

There was something in his manner of emphasizing the word "peculiar," which caused me to shudder, without knowing why.

"No, nothing *peculiar*," I said; "nothing more, at least, than we both saw stated in the paper."

60 "The 'Gazette,'" he replied, "has not entered, I fear, into the unusual horror of the thing. But dismiss the idle opinions of this print. It appears to me that this mystery is considered insoluble, for the very reason which should cause it to be regarded as easy of solution—I mean for the *outré* character of its features. The police are confounded by the seeming absence of motive—not for the murder itself—but for the atrocity of the murder. They are puzzled, too, by the seeming impossibility of reconciling the voices

heard in contention, with the facts that no one was discovered upstairs but the assassinated Mademoiselle L'Espanaye, and that there were no means of egress without the notice of the party ascending. The wild disorder of the room; the corpse thrust, with the head downwards, up the chimney; the frightful mutilation of the body of the old lady; these considerations, with those just mentioned, and others which I need not mention, have suffered to paralyze the powers, by putting completely at fault the boasted *acumen,* of the government agents. They have fallen into the gross but common error of confounding the unusual with the abstruse. But it is by these deviations from the plane of the ordinary, that reason feels its way, if at all, in its search for the true. In investigations such as we are now pursuing, it should not be so much asked 'what has occurred,' as 'what has occurred that has never occurred before.' In fact, the facility with which I shall arrive, or have arrived, at the solution of this mystery, is in the direct ratio of its apparent insolubility in the eyes of the police."

I stared at the speaker in mute astonishment.

"I am now awaiting," continued he, looking towards the door of our apartment—"I am now awaiting a person who, although perhaps not the perpetrator of these butcheries, must have been in some measure implicated in their perpetration. Of the worst portion of the crimes committed, it is probable that he is innocent. I hope that I am right in this supposition; for upon it I build my expectation of reading the entire riddle. I look for the man here—in this room—every moment. It is true that he may not arrive; but the probability is that he will. Should he come, it will be necessary to detain him. Here are pistols; and we both know how to use them when occasion demands their use."

I took the pistols, scarcely knowing what I did, or believing what I heard, while Dupin went on, very much as if in a soliloquy. I have already spoken of his abstract manner at such times. His discourse was addressed to myself; but his voice, although by no means loud, had that intonation which is commonly employed in speaking to some one at a great distance. His eyes, vacant in expression, regarded only the wall.

"That the voices heard in contention," he said, "by the party upon the stairs, were not the voices of the women themselves, was fully proved by the evidence. This relieves us of all doubt upon the question whether the old lady could have first destroyed the daughter, and afterward have committed suicide, I speak of this point chiefly for the sake of method; for the strength of Madame L'Espanaye would have been utterly unequal to the task of thrusting her daughter's corpse up the chimney as it was found; and the nature of the wounds upon her own person entirely preclude the idea of self-destruction. Murder, then, has been committed by some third party; and the voices of this third party were those heard in contention. Let me now advert—not to the whole testimony respecting these voices—but to what was *peculiar* in that testimony. Did you observe anything peculiar about it?"

65   I remarked that, while all the witnesses agreed in supposing the gruff voice to be that of a Frenchman, there was much disagreement in regard to the shrill, or, as one individual termed it, the harsh voice.

"That was the evidence itself," said Dupin, "but it was not the peculiarity of the evidence. You have observed nothing distinctive. Yet there *was* something to be observed. The witnesses, as you remark, agreed about the gruff voice; they were here unanimous. But in regard to the shrill voice, the peculiarity is—not that they disagreed—but that, while an Italian, an Englishman, a Spaniard, a Hollander, and a Frenchman attempted to describe it, each one spoke of it as that *of a foreigner.* Each is sure that it was not the voice of one of his own countrymen. Each likens it—not to the voice of an individual of any nation with whose language he is conversant—but the converse. The Frenchman supposes it the voice of a Spaniard, and 'might have distinguished some words *had he been acquainted with the Spanish.*' The Dutchman maintains it to have been that of a Frenchman; but we find it stated that '*not understanding French this witness was examined through an interpreter.*' The Englishman thinks it the voice of a German, and '*does not understand German.*' The Spaniard 'is sure' that it was that of an Englishman, but 'judges by the intonation' altogether, '*as he has no knowledge of the English.*' The Italian believes it the voice of a Russian, but '*has never conversed with a native of Russia.*' A second Frenchman differs, moreover, with the first, and is positive that the voice was that of an Italian; but, *not being cognizant of that tongue,* is, like the Spaniard, 'convinced by the intonation.' Now, how strangely unusual must that voice have really been, about which such testimony as this *could* have been elicited!—in whose *tones,* even, denizens of the five great divisions of Europe could recognize nothing familiar! You will say that it might have been the voice of an Asiatic—of an African. Neither Asiatics nor Africans abound in Paris; but, without denying the inference, I will now merely call your attention to three points. The voice is termed by one witness 'harsh rather than shrill.' It is represented by two others to have been 'quick and *unequal.*' No words—no sounds resembling words—were by any witness mentioned as distinguishable.

"I know not," continued Dupin, "what impression I may have made, so far, upon your own understanding; but I do not hesitate to say that legitimate deductions even from this portion of the testimony—the portion respecting the gruff and shrill voices—are in themselves sufficient to engender a suspicion which should give direction to all farther progress in the investigation of the mystery. I said 'legitimate deductions'; but my meaning is not thus fully expressed. I designed to imply that the deductions are the *sole* proper ones, and that the suspicion arises *inevitably* from them as the single result. What the suspicion is, however, I will not say just yet. I merely wish you to bear in mind that, with myself, it was sufficiently forcible to give a definite form—a certain tendency—to my inquiries in the chamber.

"Let us now transport ourselves, in fancy, to this chamber. What shall we first seek here? The means of egress employed by the murderers. It is not too much to say that neither of us believe in præternatural events. Madame and Mademoiselle L'Espanaye were not destroyed by spirits. The doers of the deed were material, and escaped materially. Then how? Fortunately, there is but one mode of reasoning upon the point, and that mode *must* lead us to a definite decision.—Let us examine, each by each, the possible means of egress. It is clear that the assassins were in the room where Mademoiselle L'Espanaye was found, or at least in the room adjoining, when the party ascended the stairs. It is then only from these two apartments that we have to seek issues. The police have laid bare the floors, the ceilings, and the masonry of the walls, in every direction. No *secret* issues could have escaped their vigilance. But not trusting to *their* eyes, I examined with my own. There were, then, *no* secret issues. Both doors leading from the rooms into the passage were securely locked, with the keys inside. Let us turn to the chimneys. These, although of ordinary width for some eight or ten feet above the hearths, will not admit, throughout their extent, the body of a large cat. The impossibility of egress, by means already stated, being thus absolute, we are reduced to the windows. Through those of the front room no one could have escaped without notice from the crowd in the street. The murderers *must* have passed, then, through those of the back room. Now, brought to this conclusion in so unequivocal a manner as we are, it is not our part, as reasoners, to reject it on account of apparent impossibilities. It is only left for us to prove that these apparent 'impossibilities' are, in reality, not such.

"There are two windows in the chamber. One of them is unobstructed by furniture, and is wholly visible. The lower portion of the other is hidden from view by the head of the unwieldy bedstead which is thrust close up against it. The former was found securely fastened from within. It resisted the utmost force of those who endeavored to raise it. A large gimlet-hole had been pierced in its frame to the left, and a very stout nail was found fitted therein, nearly to the head. Upon examining the other window, a similar nail was seen similarly fitted in it; and a vigorous attempt to raise this sash, failed also. The police were now entirely satisfied that egress had not been in these directions. And, *therefore,* it was thought a matter of supererogation to withdraw the nails and open the windows.

70   "My own examination was somewhat more particular, and was so for the reason I have just given—because here it was, I knew, that all apparent impossibilities *must* be proved to be not such in reality.

"I proceeded to think thus—*à posteriori.*[9] The murderers *did* escape from one of these windows. This being so, they could not have refastened the sashes from the inside, as they were found fastened;—the consideration which put a stop, through its obviousness, to the scrutiny of the police in this quarter. Yet the sashes *were* fastened. They *must,* then, have the power of fastening themselves. There was no escape from this conclusion. I stepped to the unobstructed casement, withdrew the nail with some difficulty, and attempted to raise the sash. It resisted all my efforts, as I had anticipated. A concealed spring must, I now knew, exist; and this corroboration of my idea convinced me that my premises, at least, were correct, however mysterious still appeared the circumstances attending the nails. A careful search soon brought to light the hidden spring. I pressed it, and, satisfied with the discovery, forbore to upraise the sash.

[9] Reasoning from effect back to cause

"I now replaced the nail and regarded it attentively. A person passing out through this window might have reclosed it, and the spring would have caught—but the nail could not have been replaced. The conclusion was plain, and again narrowed in the field of my investigations. The assassins *must* have escaped through the other window. Supposing, then, the springs upon each sash to be the same, as was probable, there *must* be found a difference between the nails, or at least between the modes of their fixture. Getting upon the sacking of the bedstead, I looked over the head-board minutely at the second casement. Passing my hand down behind the board, I readily discovered and pressed the spring, which was, as I had supposed, identical in character with its neighbor. I now looked at the nail. It was as stout as the other, and apparently fitted in the same manner—driven in nearly up to the head.

"You will say that I was puzzled; but, if you think so, you must have misunderstood the nature of the inductions. To use a sporting phrase, I had not been once 'at fault.' The scent had never for an instant been lost. There was no flaw in any link of the chain. I had traced the secret to its ultimate result,—and that result was *the nail*. It had, I say, in very respect, the appearance of its fellow in the other window; but this fact was an absolute nullity (conclusive as it might seem to be) when compared with the consideration that here, at this point, terminated the clue. 'There *must* be something wrong,' I said, 'about the nail.' I touched it; and the head, with about a quarter of an inch of the shank, came off in my fingers. The rest of the shank was in the gimlet-hole, where it had been broken off. The fracture was an old one (for its edges were incrusted with rust), and had apparently been accomplished by the blow of a hammer, which had partially imbedded, in the top of the bottom sash, the head portion of the nail. I now carefully replaced this head portion in the indentation whence I had taken it, and the resemblance to a perfect nail was complete—the fissure was invisible. Pressing the spring, I gently raised the sash for a few inches; the head went up with it, remaining firm in its bed. I closed the window, and the semblance of the whole nail was again perfect.

"The riddle, so far, was now unriddled. The assassin had escaped through the window which looked upon the bed. Dropping of its own accord upon his exit (or perhaps purposely closed), it had become fastened by the spring; and it was the retention of this spring which had been mistaken by the police for that of the nail,—farther inquiry being thus considered unnecessary.

75   "The next question is that of the mode of descent. Upon this point I had been satisfied in my walk with you around the building. About five feet and a half from the casement in question there runs a lightning-rod. From this rod it would have been impossible for any one to reach the window itself, to say nothing of entering it. I observed, however, that the shutters of the fourth story were of the peculiar kind called by Parisian carpenters *ferrades*—a kind rarely employed at the present day, but frequently seen upon very old mansions at Lyons and Bordeaux. They are in the form of an ordinary door (a single, not a folding door), except that the upper half is latticed or worked in open trellis—thus affording an excellent hold for the hands. In the present instance these shutters are fully three feet and a half broad. When we saw them from the rear of the house, they were both about half open—that is to

say, they stood off at right angles from the wall. It is possible that the police, as well as myself, examined the back of the tenement; but, if so, in looking at these *ferrades* in the line of their breadth (as they must have done), they did not perceive this great breadth itself, or, at all events, failed to take it into due consideration. In fact, having once satisfied themselves that no egress could have been made in this quarter, they would naturally bestow here a very cursory examination. It was clear to me, however, that the shutter belonging to the window at the head of the bed, would, if swung fully back to the wall, reach to within two feet of the lightning-rod. It was also evident that, by exertion of a very unusual degree of activity and courage, an entrance into the window, from the rod, might have been thus effected.—By reaching to the distance of two feet and a half (we now suppose the shutter open to its whole extent) a robber might have taken a firm grasp upon the trellis-work. Letting go, then, his hold upon the rod, placing his feet securely against the wall, and springing boldly from it, he might have swung the shutter so as to close it, and, if we imagine the window open at the time, might even have swung himself into the room.

"I wish you to bear especially in mind that I have spoken of a *very* unusual degree of activity as requisite to success in so hazardous and so difficult a feat. It is my design to show you, first, that the thing might possibly have been accomplished:—but, secondly and *chiefly*, I wish to impress upon your understanding the *very extraordinary*—the almost præternatural character of that agility which could have accomplished it.

"You will say, no doubt, using the language of the law, that 'to make out my case' I should rather undervalue, than insist upon a full estimation of the activity required in this matter. This may be the practice in law, but it is not the usage of reason. My ultimate object is only the truth. My immediate purpose is to lead you to place in juxtaposition that *very unusual* activity of which I have just spoken, with that *very peculiar* shrill (or harsh) and *unequal* voice, about whose nationality no two persons could be found to agree, and in whose utterance no syllabification could be detected."

At these words a vague and half-formed conception of the meaning of Dupin flitted over my mind. I seemed to be upon the verge of comprehension, without power to comprehend—as men, at times, find themselves upon the brink of rememberance, without being able, in the end, to remember. My friend went on with his discourse.

"You will see," he said, "that I have shifted the question from the mode of egress to that of ingress. It was my design to suggest that both were effected in the same manner, at the same point. Let us now revert to the interior of the room. Let us survey the appearances here. The drawers of the bureau, it is said, had been rifled, although many articles of apparel still remained within them. The conclusion here is absurd. It is a mere guess—a very silly one— and no more. How are we to know that the articles found in the drawers were not all these drawers had originally contained? Madame L'Espanaye and her daughter lived an exceedingly retired life—saw no company—seldom went out—had little use for numerous changes of habiliment. Those found were at least of as good quality as any likely to be possessed by these ladies. If a thief had taken any, why did he not take the best—why did he not take all? In a word, why did he abandon four thousand francs in gold to encumber himself with a bundle of linen? The gold *was* abandoned. Nearly the whole sum mentioned by Monsieur Mignaud, the banker, was discovered, in bags, upon the floor. I wish you, therefore, to discard from your thoughts the blundering idea of *motive,* engendered in the brains of the police by that portion of the evidence which speaks of money delivered at the door of the house. Coincidences ten times as remarkable as this (the delivery of the money, and murder committed within three days upon the party receiving it), happen to all of us every hour of our lives, without attracting even momentary notice. Coincidences, in general, are great stumbling-blocks in the way of that class of thinkers who have been educated to know nothing of the theory of probabilities—that theory to which the most glorious objects of human research are indebted for the most glorious of illustration. In the present instance, had the gold been gone, the fact of its delivery three days before would have formed something more than a coincidence. It would have been corroborative of this idea of motive. But, under the real circumstances of the case, if we are to suppose gold the motive of this outrage, we must also imagine the perpetrator so vacillating an idiot as to have abandoned his gold and his motive together.

80   "Keeping now steadily in mind the points to which I have drawn your attention—that peculiar voice, that unusual agility, and that startling absence of motive in a murder so singularly atrocious as this—let us glance at the butchery itself. Here is a woman strangled to death by manual strength, and thrust up a chimney, head downwards. Ordinary assassins employ no such modes of murder as this. Least of all, do they thus dispose of the murdered. In the manner of thrusting the corpse up the chimney, you will admit that there was something *excessively outré*—something altogether irreconcilable with our common notions of human action, even when we suppose the actors the most depraved of men. Think, too, how great must have been that strength which could have thrust the body *up* such an aperture so forcibly that the united vigor of several persons was found barely sufficient to drag it *down*!

"Turn, now, to other indications of the employment of a vigor most marvelous. On the hearth were thick tresses—very thick tresses—of gray human hair. These had been torn out by the roots. You are aware of the great force necessary in tearing thus from the head even twenty or thirty hairs together. You saw the locks in question as well as myself. Their roots (a hideous sight!) were clotted with fragments of the flesh of the scalp—sure token of the prodigious power which had been exerted in uprooting perhaps half a million of hairs at a time. The throat of the old lady was not merely cut, but the head absolutely severed from the body: the instrument was a mere razor. I wish you also to look at the *brutal* ferocity of these deeds. Of the bruises upon the body of Madame L'Espanaye I do not speak. Monsieur Dumas, and his worthy coadjutor Monsieur Etienne, have pronounced that they were inflicted by some obtuse instrument; and so far these gentlemen are very correct. The obtuse instrument was clearly the stone pavement in the yard, upon which the victim had fallen from the window which looked in upon the bed. This idea, however simple it may now seem, escaped the police for the same reason that the breadth of the shutters escaped them—because, by the affair of the nails, their perceptions had been hermetically sealed against the possibility of the windows having ever been opened at all.

"If now, in addition to all these things, you have properly reflected upon the odd disorder of the chamber, we have gone so far as to combine the ideas of an agility astounding, a strength superhuman, a ferocity brutal, a butchery without motive, a *grotesquerie* in horror absolutely alien from humanity, and a voice foreign in tone to the ears of men of many nations, and devoid of all distinct or intelligible syllabification. What result, then, has ensued? What impression have I made upon your fancy?"

I felt a creeping of the flesh as Dupin asked me the question. "A madman," I said, "has done this deed—some raving maniac, escaped from a neighboring *Maison de Santé*."

"In some respects," he replied, "your idea is not irrelevant. But the voices of madmen, even in their wildest paroxysms, are never found to tally with that peculiar voice heard upon the stairs. Madmen are of some nation, and their language, however incoherent in its words, has always the coherence of syllabification. Besides, the hair of a madman is not such as I now hold in my hand. I disentangled this little tuft from the rigidly clutched fingers of Madame L'Espanaye. Tell me what you can make of it."

85   "Dupin!" I said, completely unnerved; "this hair is most unusual—this is no *human* hair."

"I have not asserted that it is," said he; "but, before we decide this point, I wish you to glance at the little sketch I have here traced upon this paper. It is a *facsimile* drawing of what has been described in one portion of the testimony as 'dark bruises, and deep indentations of fingernails,' upon the throat of Mademoiselle L'Espanaye, and in another (by Messrs. Dumas and Etienne), as a 'series of livid spots, evidently the impression of fingers.'

"You will perceive," continued my friend, spreading out the paper upon the table before us, "that this drawing gives the idea of a firm and fixed hold. There is no *slipping* apparent. Each finger has retained—possibly until the death of the victim—the fearful grasp by which it originally imbedded itself. Attempt, now, to place all your fingers, at the same time, in the respective impressions as you see them."

I made the attempt in vain.

"We are possibly not giving this matter a fair trial," he said. "The paper is spread out upon a plane surface; but the human throat is cylindrical. Here is a billet of wood, the circumference of which is about that of the throat. Wrap the drawing around it, and try the experiment again."

90   I did so; but the difficulty was even more obvious than before.

"This," I said, "is the mark of no human hand."

"Read now," replied Dupin, "this passage from Cuvier."

It was a minute anatomical and generally descriptive account of the large fulvous Orang-Outang of the East Indian Islands. The gigantic stature, the prodigious strength and activity, the wild ferocity, and the imitative propensities of these mammalia are sufficiently well known to all. I understood the full horrors of the murder at once.

"The description of the digits," said I, as I made an end of reading, "is in exact accordance with this drawing. I see that no animal but an Orang-Outang, of the species here mentioned, could have impressed the indentations as you have traced them. This tuft of tawny hair, too, is identical in character with that of the beast of Cuvier. But I cannot possibly comprehend the particulars of this frightful mystery. Besides, there were *two* voices heard in contention, and one of them was unquestionably the voice of a Frenchman."

95   "True; and you will remember an expression attributed almost unanimously, by the evidence, to this voice,—the expression, *'mon Dieu!'* This, under the circumstances, has been justly characterized by one of the witnesses (Montani, the confectioner), as an expression of remonstrance or expostulation. Upon these two words, therefore, I have mainly built my hopes of a full solution of the riddle. A Frenchman was cognizant of the murder. It is possible—indeed it is far more than probable—that he was innocent of all participation in the bloody transactions which took place. The Orang-Outang may have escaped from him. He may have traced it to the chamber; but, under the agitating circumstances which ensued, he could never have recaptured it. It is still at large. I will not pursue these guesses— for I have no right to call them more—since the shades of reflection upon which they are based are scarcely of sufficient depth to be appreciable by my own intellect, and since I could not pretend to make them intelligible to the understanding of another. We will call them guesses then, and speak of them as such. If the Frenchman in question is indeed, as I suppose, innocent of this atrocity, this advertisement, which I left last night, upon our return home, at the office of 'Le Monde' (a paper devoted to the shipping interest, and much sought by sailors), will bring him to our residence."

He handed me a paper, and I read thus:

CAUGHT—*In the Bois de Boulogne, early in the morning of the* ——— *inst.* (the morning of the murder), *a very large tawny Orang-Outang of the Bornese species. The owner (who is ascertained to be a sailor, belonging to a Maltese vessel), may have the animal again, upon identifying it satisfactorily, and paying a few charges arising from its capture and keeping. Call at No.* ———, *Rue* ———, *Faubourg St. Germain—au troisième.*

"How was it possible," I asked, "that you should know the man to be a sailor, and belonging to a Maltese vessel?"

"I do *not* know it," said Dupin. "I am not *sure* of it. Here, however, is a small piece of ribbon, which from its form, and from its greasy appearance, has evidently been used in tying the hair in one of those long *queues* of which sailors are so fond. Moreover, this knot is one which few besides sailors can tie, and is peculiar to the Maltese. I picked the ribbon up at the foot of the lightning-rod. It could not have belonged to either of the deceased. Now if, after all, I am wrong in my induction from this ribbon, that the Frenchman was a sailor belonging to a Maltese vessel, still I can have done no harm in saying what I did in the advertisement. If I am in error, he will merely suppose that I have been misled by some circumstance into which he will not take the trouble to inquire. But if I am right, a great point is gained. Cognizant although innocent of the murder, the Frenchman will naturally hesitate about replying to the advertisement—about demanding the Orang-Outang. He will reason thus:—'I am innocent; I am poor; my Orang-Outang is of great value—to one in my circumstances a fortune of itself—why should I lose it through idle apprehensions of danger? Here it is, within my grasp. It was found in the Bois de Boulogne—at a vast distance from the scene of that butchery. How can it ever be suspected that a brute beast should have done the deed? The police are at fault—they have failed to procure the slightest clue. Should they even trace the animal, it would be impossible to prove me cognizant of the murder, or to implicate me in guilt on account of that cognizance. Above all, *I am known.* The advertiser designates me as the possessor of the beast. I am not sure to what limit his knowledge may extend. Should I avoid claiming a property of so great value, which it is known that I possess, I will render the animal, at least, liable to suspicion. It is not my policy to attract attention either to myself or to the beast. I will answer the advertisement, get the Orang-Outang, and keep it close until this matter has blown over.'"

100   At this moment we heard a step upon the stairs.

    "Be ready," said Dupin, "with your pistols, but neither use them nor show them until at a signal from myself."

    The front door of the house had been left open, and the visitor had entered, without ringing, and advanced several steps upon the staircase. Now, however, he seemed to hesitate. Presently we heard him descending. Dupin was moving quickly to the door, when we again heard him coming up. He did not turn back a second time, but stepped up with decision and rapped at the door of our chamber.

    "Come in," said Dupin, in a cheerful and hearty tone.

    A man entered. He was a sailor, evidently,—a tall, stout, and muscular-looking person, with a certain dare-devil expression of countenance, not altogether unprepossessing. His face, greatly sunburnt, was more than half hidden by whisker and *mustachio.* He had with him a huge oaken cudgel, but appeared to be otherwise unarmed. He bowed awkwardly, and bade us "good evening," in French accents, which, although somewhat Neufchatel-ish, were still sufficiently indicative of a Parisian origin.

105   "Sit down, my friend," said Dupin. "I suppose you have called about the Orang-Outang. Upon my word, I almost envy you the possession of him; a remarkably fine, and no doubt a very valuable animal. How old do you suppose him to be?"

    The sailor drew a long breath, with the air of a man relieved of some intolerable burthen, and then replied, in an assured tone:

    "I have no way of telling—but he can't be more than four or five years old. Have you got him here?"

    "Oh no; we had no conveniences for keeping him here. He is at a livery stable in the Rue Dubourg, just by. You can get him in the morning. Of course you are prepared to identify the property?"

    "To be sure I am, sir."

110 "I shall be sorry to part with him," said Dupin.

"I don't mean that you should be at all this trouble for nothing, sir," said the man. "Couldn't expect it. Am very willing to pay a reward for the finding of the animal—that is to say, anything in reason."

"Well," replied my friend, "that is all very fair, to be sure. Let me think!—what should I have? Oh! I will tell you. My reward shall be this. You shall give me all the information in your power about these murders in the Rue Morgue."

Dupin said the last words in a very low tone, and very quietly. Just as quickly, too, he walked towards the door, locked it, and put the key in his pocket. He then drew a pistol from his bosom and placed it, without the least flurry, upon the table.

The sailor's face flushed up as if he were struggling with suffocation. He started to his feet and grasped his cudgel; but the next moment he fell back into his seat, trembling violently, and with the countenance of death itself. He spoke not a word. I pitied him from the bottom of my heart.

115 "My friend," said Dupin, in a kind tone, "you are alarming yourself unnecessarily—you are indeed. We mean you no harm whatever. I pledge you the honor of a gentleman, and of a Frenchman, that we intend you no injury. I perfectly well know that you are innocent of the atrocities in the Rue Morgue. It will not do, however, to deny that you are in some measure implicated in them. From what I have already said, you must know that I have had means of information about this matter—means of which you could never have dreamed. Now the thing stands thus. You have done nothing which you could have avoided—nothing, certainly, which renders you culpable. You were not even guilty of robbery, when you might have robbed with impunity. You have nothing to conceal. You have no reason for concealment. On the other hand you are bound by every principle of honor to confess all you know. An innocent man is now imprisoned, charged with that crime of which you can point out the perpetrator."

The sailor had recovered his presence of mind, in a great measure, while Dupin uttered these words; but his original boldness of bearing was all gone.

"So help me God," said he, after a brief pause, "I *will* tell you all I know about this affair;—but I do not expect you to believe one half I say—I would be a fool indeed if I did. Still, I *am* innocent, and I will make a clean breast if I die for it."

What he stated was, in substance, this. He had lately made a voyage to the Indian Archipelago. A party, of which he formed one, landed at Borneo, and passed into the interior on an excursion of pleasure. Himself and a companion had captured the Orang-Outang. This companion dying, the animal fell into his own exclusive possession. After great trouble, occasioned by the intractable ferocity of his captive during the home voyage, he at length succeeded in lodging it safely at his own residence in Paris, where, not to attract towards himself the unpleasant curiosity of his neighbors, he kept it carefully secluded, until such time as it should recover from a wound in the foot, received from a splinter on board ship. His ultimate design was to sell it.

Returning home from some sailors' frolic on the night, or rather in the morning of the murder, he found the beast occupying his own bedroom, into which it had broken from a closet adjoining, where it had been, as was thought, securely confined. Razor in hand, and fully lathered, it was sitting before a looking-glass, attempting the operation of shaving, in which it had no doubt previously watched its master through the keyhole of the closet. Terrified at the sight of so dangerous a weapon in the possession of an animal so ferocious, and so well able to use it, the man, for some moments, was at a loss what to do. He had been accustomed, however, to quiet the creature, even in its fiercest moods, by the use of a whip, and to this he now resorted. Upon sight of it, the Orang-Outang sprang at once through the door of the chamber, down the stairs, and thence, through a window, unfortunately open, into the street.

120   The Frenchman followed in despair; the ape, razor still in hand, occasionally stopping to look back and gesticulate at its pursuer, until the latter had nearly come up with it. It then again made off. In this manner the chase continued for a long time. The streets were profoundly quiet, as it was nearly three o'clock in the morning. In passing down an alley in the rear of the Rue Morgue, the fugitive's attention was arrested by a light gleaming from the open window of Madame L'Espanaye's chamber, in the fourth story of her house. Rushing to the building, it perceived the lightning-rod, clambered up with inconceivable agility, grasped the shutter, which was thrown fully back against the wall, and, by its means swung itself directly upon the headboard of the bed. The whole feat did not occupy a minute. The shutter was kicked open again by the Orang-Outang as it entered the room.

The sailor, in the meantime, was both rejoiced and perplexed. He had strong hopes of now recapturing the brute, as it could scarcely escape from the trap into which it had ventured, except by the rod, where it might be intercepted as it came down. On the other hand, there was much cause for anxiety as to what it might do in the house. This latter reflection urged the man still to follow the fugitive. A lightning-rod is ascended without difficulty, especially by a sailor; but, when he had arrived as high as the window, which lay far to his left, his career was stopped; the most that he could accomplish was to reach over so as to obtain a glimpse of the interior of the room. At this glimpse he nearly fell from his hold through excess of horror. Now it was that those hideous shrieks arose upon the night, which had startled from slumber the inmates of the Rue Morgue. Madame L'Espanaye and her daughter, habited in their night clothes, had apparently been arranging some papers in the iron chest already mentioned, which had been wheeled into the middle of the room. It was open, and its contents lay beside it on the floor. The victims must have been sitting with their backs toward the window; and, from the time elapsing between the ingress of the beast and the screams, it seems probable that it was not immediately perceived. The flapping-to of the shutter would naturally have been attributed to the wind.

As the sailor looked in, the gigantic animal had seized Madame L'Espanaye by the hair (which was loose, as she had been combing it), and was flourishing the razor about her face, in imitation of the motions of a barber. The daughter lay prostrate and motionless; she had swooned. The screams and struggles of the old lady (during which the hair was torn from her head) had the effect of changing the probably pacific purposes of the Orang-Outang into those of wrath. With one determined sweep of its muscular arm it nearly severed her head from her body. The sight of blood inflamed its anger into frenzy. Gnashing its teeth, and flashing fire from its eyes, it flew upon the body of the girl, and imbedded its fearful talons in her throat, retaining its grasp until she expired. Its wandering and wild glances fell at this moment upon the head of the bed, over which the face of its master, rigid with horror, was just discernible. The fury of the beast, who no doubt bore still in mind the dreaded whip, was instantly converted into fear. Conscious of having deserved punishment, it seemed desirous of concealing its bloody deeds, and skipped about the chamber in an agony of nervous agitation; throwing down and breaking furniture as it moved, and dragging the bed from the bedstead. In conclusion, it seized first the corpse of the daughter, and thrust it up the chimney, as it was found; then that of the old lady, which it immediately hurled through the window headlong.

As the ape approached the casement with its mutilated burthen, the sailor shrank aghast to the rod, and, rather gliding than clambering down it, hurried at once home—dreading the consequences of the butchery, and gladly abandoning, in his terror, all solicitude about the fate of the Orang-Outang. The words heard by the party upon the staircase were the Frenchman's exclamations of horror and affright, comingled with the fiendish jabberings of the brute.

I have scarcely anything to add. The Orang-Outang must have escaped from the chamber, by the rod, just before the breaking of the door. It must have closed the window as it passed through it. It was subsequently caught by the owner himself, who obtained for it a very large sum at the *Jardin des Plantes.* Le Bon was instantly released, upon our narration of the circumstances (with some comments from Dupin) at the *bureau* of the Prefect of Police. This functionary, however well disposed to my friend, could not altogether conceal his chagrin at the turn which affairs had taken, and was fain to indulge in a sarcasm or two, about the propriety of every person minding his own business.

125   "Let them talk," said Dupin, who had not thought it necessary to reply. "Let him discourse; it will ease his conscience. I am satisfied with having defeated him in his own castle. Nevertheless, that he failed in the solution of this mystery, is by no means that matter for wonder which he supposes it; for, in truth, our friend the Prefect is somewhat too cunning to be profound. In his wisdom is no *stamen*. It is all head and no body, like the pictures of the Goddess Laverna,—or, at best, all head and shoulders, like a codfish. But he is a good creature after all. I like him especially for one master stroke of cant, by which he has attained his reputation for ingenuity. I mean the way he had '*de nier ce qui est, et d'expliquer ce qui n'est pas.*'"[10]

[10] "To deny the existence of what is, and to explain the notion of what isn't."—Rousseau, *Nouvelle Héloïse*

Leslie Marmon Silko

Leslie Marmon Silko (1948–   ) is a poet and fiction writer—a storyteller—who grew up on a Laguna Pueblo Reservation in New Mexico, in a house of rock and adobe. She attended the University of New Mexico and taught at Navajo Community College in Arizona before spending two years studying the Eskimo-Aleut culture in Alaska. Besides her poetry, she has written the screen play for the Marlon Brando film, *Black Elk,* a book of short stories (*Storyteller,* 1981), and a novel (*Ceremony,* 1977). See her poem on page 686.

Storyteller   (1975)

Every day the sun came up a little lower on the horizon, moving more slowly until one day she got excited and started calling the jailer. She realized she had been sitting there for many hours, yet the sun had not moved from the center of the sky. The color of the sky had not been good lately; it had been pale blue, almost white, even when there were no clouds. She told herself it wasn't a good sign for the sky to be indistinguishable from the river ice, frozen solid and white against the earth. The tundra rose up behind the river but all the boundaries between the river and hills and sky were lost in the density of the pale ice.

She yelled again, this time some English words which came randomly into her mouth, probably swear words she'd heard from the oil drilling crews last winter. The jailer was an Eskimo, but he would not speak Yupik[1] to her. She had watched people in other cells, when they spoke to him in Yupik he ignored them until they spoke English.

He came and stared at her. She didn't know if he understood what she was telling him until he glanced behind her at the small high window. He looked at the sun, and turned and walked away. She could hear the buckles on his heavy snowmobile boots jingle as he walked to the front of the building.

It was like the other buildings that white people, the Gussucks,[2] brought with them: BIA[3] and school buildings, portable buildings that arrived sliced in halves, on barges coming up the river. Squares of metal panelling bulged out with the layers of insulation stuffed inside. She had asked once what it was and someone told her it was to keep out the cold. She had not laughed then, but she did now. She walked over to the small double-pane window and she laughed out loud. They thought they could keep out the cold with stringy yellow wadding. Look at the sun. It wasn't moving; it was frozen,

---

[1] An Eskimo-Aleut language   [2] A term for "the whites"   [3] Bureau of Indian Affairs

caught in the middle of the sky. Look at the sky, solid as the river with ice which had trapped the sun. It had not moved for a long time; in a few more hours it would be weak, and heavy frost would begin to appear on the edges and spread across the face of the sun like a mask. Its light was pale yellow, worn thin by the winter.

5   She could see people walking down the snow-packed roads, their breath steaming out from their parka hoods, faces hidden and protected by deep ruffs of fur. There were no cars or snowmobiles that day; the cold had silenced their machines. The metal froze; it split and shattered. Oil hardened and moving parts jammed solidly. She had seen it happen to their big yellow machines and the giant drill last winter when they came to drill their test holes. The cold stopped them, and they were helpless against it.

Her village was many miles upriver from this town, but in her mind she could see it clearly. Their house was not near the village houses. It stood alone on the bank upriver from the village. Snow had drifted to the eaves of the roof on the north side, but on the west side, by the door, the path was almost clear. She had nailed scraps of red tin over the logs last summer. She had done it for the bright red color, not for added warmth the way the village people had done. This final winter had been coming even then; there had been signs of its approach for many years.

She went because she was curious about the big school where the Government sent all the other girls and boys. She had not played much with the village children while she was growing up because they were afraid of the old man, and they ran when her grandmother came. She went because she was tired of being alone with the old woman whose body had been stiffening for as long as the girl could remember. Her knees and knuckles were swollen grotesquely, and the pain had squeezed the brown skin of her face tight against the bones; it left her eyes hard like river stone. The girl asked once what it was that did this to her body, and the old woman had raised up from sewing a sealskin boot, and stared at her.

"The joints," the old woman said in a low voice, whispering like wind across the roof, "the joints are swollen with anger."

Sometimes she did not answer and only stared at the girl. Each year she spoke less and less, but the old man talked more—all night sometimes, not to anyone but himself; in a soft deliberate voice, he told stories, moving his smooth brown hands above the blankets. He had not fished or hunted with the other men for many years, although he was not crippled or sick. He stayed in his bed, smelling like dry fish and urine, telling stories all winter; and when warm weather came, he went to his place on the river bank. He sat with a long willow stick, poking at the smoldering moss he burned against the insects while he continued with the stories.

10   The trouble was that she had not recognized the warnings in time. She did not see what the Gussuck school would do to her until she walked into the dormitory and realized that the old man had not been lying about the place. She thought he had been trying to scare her as he used to when she was very small and her grandmother was outside cutting up fish. She hadn't believed

what he told her about the school because she knew he wanted to keep her there in the log house with him. She knew what he wanted.

The dormitory matron pulled down her underpants and whipped her with a leather belt because she refused to speak English.

"Those backwards village people," the matron said, because she was an Eskimo who had worked for the BIA a long time, "they kept this one until she was too big to learn." The other girls whispered in English. They knew how to work the showers, and they washed and curled their hair at night. They ate Gussuck food. She lay on her bed and imagined what her grandmother might be sewing, and what the old man was eating in his bed. When summer came, they sent her home.

The way her grandmother had hugged her before she left for school had been a warning too, because the old woman had not hugged or touched her for many years. Not like the old man, whose hands were always hunting, like ravens circling lazily in the sky, ready to touch her. She was not surprised when the priest and the old man met her at the landing strip, to say that the old lady was gone. The priest asked her where she would like to stay. He referred to the old man as her grandfather, but she did not bother to correct him. She had already been thinking about it; if she went with the priest, he would send her away to a school. But the old man was different. She knew he wouldn't send her back to school. She knew he wanted to keep her.

He told her one time, that she would get too old for him faster than he got too old for her; but again she had not believed him because sometimes he lied. He had lied about what he would do with her if she came into his bed. But as the years passed, she realized what he said was true. She was restless and strong. She had no patience with the old man who had never changed his slow smooth motions under the blankets.

15   The old man was in his bed for the winter; he did not leave it except to use the slop bucket in the corner. He was dozing with his mouth open slightly; his lips quivered and sometimes they moved like he was telling a story even while he dreamed. She pulled on the sealskin boots, the mukluks with the bright red flannel linings her grandmother had sewn for her, and she tied the bright red yarn tassels around her ankles over the gray wool pants. She zipped the wolfskin parka. Her grandmother had worn it for many years, but the old man said that before she died, she instructed him to bury her in an old black sweater, and to give the parka to the girl. The wolf pelts were creamy colored and silver, almost white in some places, and when the old lady had walked across the tundra in the winter, she was invisible in the snow.

She walked toward the village, breaking her own path through the deep snow. A team of sled dogs tied outside a house at the edge of the village leaped against their chains to bark at her. She kept walking, watching the dusky sky for the first evening stars. It was warm and the dogs were alert. When it got cold again, the dogs would lie curled and still, too drowsy from the cold to bark or pull at the chains. She laughed loudly because it made them howl and snarl. Once the old man had seen her tease the dogs and he shook his head. "So that's the kind of woman you are," he said, "in the wintertime the two of us are no different from those dogs. We wait in the cold for someone to bring us a few dry fish."

She laughed out loud again, and kept walking. She was thinking about the Gussuck oil drillers. They were strange; they watched her when she walked near their machines. She wondered what they looked like underneath their quilted goose-down trousers; she wanted to know how they moved. They would be something different from the old man.

The old man screamed at her. He shook her shoulders so violently that her head bumped against the log wall. "I smelled it!" he yelled, "as soon as I woke up! I am sure of it now. You can't fool me!" His thin legs were shaking inside the baggy wool trousers; he stumbled over her boots in his bare feet. His toenails were long and yellow like bird claws; she had seen a gray crane last summer fighting another in the shallow water on the edge of the river. She laughed out loud and pulled her shoulder out of his grip. He stood in front of her. He was breathing hard and shaking; he looked weak. He would probably die next winter.

"I'm warning you," he said, "I'm warning you." He crawled back into his bunk then, and reached under the old soiled feather pillow for a piece of dry fish. He lay back on the pillow, staring at the ceiling and chewed dry strips of salmon. "I don't know what the old woman told you," he said, "but there will be trouble." He looked over to see if she was listening. His face suddenly relaxed into a smile, his dark slanty eyes were lost in wrinkles of brown skin. "I could tell you, but you are too good for warnings now. I can smell what you did all night with the Gussucks."

20   She did not understand why they came there, because the village was small and so far upriver that even some Eskimos who had been away to school did not want to come back. They stayed downriver in the town. They said the village was too quiet. They were used to the town where the boarding school was located, with electric lights and running water. After all those years away at school, they had forgotten how to set nets in the river and where to hunt seals in the fall. When she asked the old man why the Gussucks bothered to come to the village, his narrow eyes got bright with excitement.

"They only come when there is something to steal. The fur animals are too difficult for them to get now, and the seals and fish are hard to find. Now they come for oil deep in the earth. But this is the last time for them." His breathing was wheezy and fast; his hands gestured at the sky. "It is approaching. As it comes, ice will push across the sky." His eyes were open wide and he stared at the low ceiling rafters for hours without blinking. She remembered all this clearly because he began the story that day, the story he told from that time on. It began with a giant bear which he described muscle by muscle, from the curve of the ivory claws to the whorls of hair at the top of the massive skull. And for eight days he did not sleep, but talked continuously of the giant bear whose color was pale blue glacier ice.

The snow was dirty and worn down in a path to the door. On either side of the path, the snow was higher than her head. In front of the door there were jagged yellow stains melted into the snow where men had urinated. She stopped in the entry way and kicked the snow off her boots. The room was dim; a kerosene lantern by the cash register was burning low. The long wooden shelves were jammed with cans of beans and potted meats. On the bottom shelf a jar of mayonnaise was broken open, leaking oily white clots on the floor. There was no one in the room except the yellowish dog sleeping in the front of the long glass display case. A reflection made it appear to be lying on the knives and ammunition inside the case. Gussucks kept dogs inside their houses with them; they did not seem to mind the odors which seeped out of the dogs. "They tell us we are dirty for the food we eat—raw fish and fermented meat. But we do not live with dogs," the old man once said. She heard voices in the back room, and the sound of bottles set down hard on tables.

They were always confident. The first year they waited for the ice to break up on the river, and then they brought their big yellow machines up river on barges. They planned to drill their test holes during the summer to avoid the freezing. But the imprints and graves of their machines were still there, on the edge of the tundra above the river, where the summer mud had swallowed them before they ever left sight of the river. The village people had gathered to watch the white men, and to laugh as they drove the giant machines, one by one, off the steel ramp into the bogs; as if sheer numbers of vehicles would somehow make the tundra solid. But the old man said they behaved like desperate people, and they would come back again. When the tundra was frozen solid, they returned.

Village women did not even look through the door to the back room. The priest had warned them. The storeman was watching her because he didn't let Eskimos or Indians sit down at the tables in the back room. But she knew he couldn't throw her out if one of his Gussuck customers invited her to sit with him. She walked across the room. They stared at her, but she had the feeling she was walking for someone else, not herself, so their eyes did not matter. The red-haired man pulled out a chair and motioned for her to sit down. She looked back at the storeman while the red-haired man poured her a glass of red sweet wine. She wanted to laugh at the storeman the way she laughed at the dogs, straining against the chains, howling at her.

25   The red-haired man kept talking to the other Gussucks sitting around the table, but he slid one hand off the top of the table to her thigh. She looked over at the storeman to see if he was still watching her. She laughed out loud at him and the red-haired man stopped talking and turned to her. He asked if she wanted to go. She nodded and stood up.

Someone in the village had been telling him things about her, he said as they walked down the road to his trailer. She understood that much of what he was saying, but the rest she did not hear. The whine of the big generators at the construction camp sucked away the sound of his words. But English was of no concern to her anymore, and neither was anything the Christians in the village might say about her or the old man. She smiled at the effect of the subzero air on the electric lights around the trailers; they did not shine. They left only flat yellow holes in the darkness.

It took him a long time to get ready, even after she had undressed for him. She waited in the bed with the blankets pulled close, watching him. He adjusted the thermostat and lit candles in the room, turning out the electric lights. He searched through a stack of record albums until he found the right one. She was not sure about the last thing he did: he taped something on the wall behind the bed where he could see it while he lay on top of her. He was shriveled and white from the cold; he pushed against her body for warmth. He guided her hands to his thighs; he was shivering.

She had returned a last time because she wanted to know what it was he stuck on the wall above the bed. After he finished each time, he reached up and pulled it loose, folding it carefully so that she could not see it. But this time she was ready; she waited for his fast breathing and sudden collapse on top of her. She slid out from under him and stood up beside the bed. She looked at the picture while she got dressed. He did not raise his face from the pillow, and she thought she heard teeth rattling together as she left the room.

She heard the old man move when she came in. After the Gussuck's trailer, the log house felt cool. It smelled like dry fish and cured meat. The room was dark except for the blinking yellow flame in the mica window of the oil stove. She squatted in front of the stove and watched the flames for a long time before she walked to the bed where her grandmother had slept. The bed was covered with a mound of rags and fur scraps the old woman had saved. She reached into the mound until she felt something cold and solid wrapped in a wool blanket. She pushed her fingers around it until she felt smooth stone. Long ago, before the Gussucks came, they had burned whale oil in the big stone lamp which made light and heat as well. The old woman had saved everything they would need when the time came.

30   In the morning, the old man pulled a piece of dry caribou meat from under the blankets and offered it to her. While she was gone, men from the village had brought a bundle of dry meat. She chewed it slowly, thinking about the way they still came from the village to take care of the old man and his stories. But she had a story now, about the red-haired Gussuck. The old man knew what she was thinking, and his smile made his face seem more round than it was.

"Well," he said, "what was it?"

"A woman with a big dog on top of her."

He laughed softly to himself and walked over to the water barrel. He dipped the tin cup into the water.

"It doesn't surprise me," he said.

35   "Grandma," she said, "there was something red in the grass that morning. I remember." She had not asked about her parents before. The old woman stopped splitting the fish bellies open for the willow drying racks. Her jaw muscles pulled so tightly against her skull, the girl thought the old woman would not be able to speak.

"They bought a tin can full of it from the storeman. Late at night. He told them it was alcohol safe to drink. They traded a rifle for it." The old woman's voice sounded like each word stole strength from her. "It made no difference about the rifle. That year the Gussuck boats had come, firing big guns at the walrus and seals. There was nothing left to hunt after that anyway. So," the old lady said, in a low soft voice the girl had not heard for a long time, "I didn't say anything to them when they left that night."

"Right over there," she said, pointing at the fallen poles, half buried in the river sand and tall grass, "in the summer shelter. The sun was high half the night then. Early in the morning when it was still low, the policeman came around. I told the interpreter to tell him that the storeman had poisoned them." She made outlines in the air in front of her, showing how their bodies lay twisted on the sand; telling the story was like laboring to walk through deep snow; sweat shone in the white hair around her forehead. "I told the priest too, after he came. I told him the storeman lied." She turned away from the girl. She held her mouth even tighter, set solidly, not in sorrow or anger, but against the pain, which was all that remained. "I never believed," she said, "not much anyway. I wasn't surprised when the priest did nothing."

The wind came off the river and folded the tall grass into itself like river waves. She could feel the silence the story left, and she wanted to have the old woman go on.

"I heard sounds that night, grandma. Sounds like someone was singing. It was light outside. I could see something red on the ground." The old woman did not answer her; she moved to the tub full of fish on the ground beside the workbench. She stabbed her knife into the belly of a whitefish and lifted it onto the bench. "The Gussuck storeman left the village right after that," the old woman said as she pulled the entrails from the fish, "otherwise, I could tell you more." The old woman's voice flowed with the wind blowing off the river; they never spoke of it again.

40   When the willows got their leaves and the grass grew tall along the river banks and around the sloughs, she walked early in the morning. While the sun was still low on the horizon, she listened to the wind off the river; its sound was like the voice that day long ago. In the distance, she could hear the engines of the machinery the oil drillers had left the winter before, but she did not go near the village or the store. The sun never left the sky and the summer became the same long day, with only the winds to fan the sun into brightness or allow it to slip into twilight.

She sat beside the old man at his place on the river bank. She poked the smoky fire for him, and felt herself growing wide and thin in the sun as if she had been split from belly to throat and strung on the willow pole in preparation for the winter to come. The old man did not speak anymore. When men from the village brought him fresh fish he hid them deep in the river grass where it was cool. After he went inside, she split the fish open and spread them to dry on the willow frame the way the old woman had done. Inside, he dozed and talked to himself. He had talked all winter, softly and incessantly, about the giant polar bear stalking a lone hunter across Bering Sea ice. After all the months the old man had been telling the story, the bear was within a hundred feet of the man; but the ice fog had closed in on them now and the man could only smell the sharp ammonia odor of the bear, and hear the edge of the snow crust crack under the giant paws.

One night she listened to the old man tell the story all night in his sleep, describing each crystal of ice and the slightly different sounds they made under each paw; first the left and then the right paw, then the hind feet. Her grandmother was there suddenly, a shadow around the stove. She spoke in her low wind voice and the girl was afraid to sit up to hear more clearly. Maybe what she said had been to the old man because he stopped telling the story and began to snore softly the way he had long ago when the old woman had scolded him for telling his stories while others in the house were trying to sleep. But the last words she heard clearly: "It will take a long time, but the story must be told. There must not be any lies." She pulled the blankets up around her chin, slowly, so that her movements would not be seen. She thought her grandmother was talking about the old man's bear story; she did not know about the other story then.

She left the old man wheezing and snoring in his bed. She walked through river grass glistening with frost; the bright green summer color was already fading. She watched the sun move across the sky, already lower on the horizon, already moving away from the village. She stopped by the fallen poles of the summer shelter where her parents had died. Frost glittered on the river sand too; in a few more weeks there would be snow. The predawn light would be the color of an old woman. An old woman sky full of snow. There had been something red lying on the ground the morning they died. She looked for it again, pushing aside the grass with her foot. She knelt in the sand and looked under the fallen structure for some trace of it. When she found it, she would know what the old woman had never told her. The wind made her shiver.

The summer rain had washed the mud from between the logs; the sod blocks stacked as high as her belly next to the log walls had lost their square-cut shape and had grown into soft mounds of tundra moss and stiff-bladed grass bending with clusters of seed bristles. She looked at the northwest, in the direction of the Bering Sea. The cold would come down from there to find narrow slits in the mud, rainwater holes in the outer layer of sod which protected the log house. The dark green tundra stretched away flat and continuous. Somewhere the sea and the land met; she knew by their dark green colors there were no boundaries between them. That was how the cold would come: when the boundaries were gone the polar ice would range across the land into the sky. She watched the horizon for a long time. She would stand in that place on the north side of the house and she would keep watch on the northwest horizon, and eventually she would see it come. She would watch for its approach in the stars, and hear it come with the wind. These preparations were unfamiliar, but gradually she recognized them as she did her own footprints in the snow.

45   She emptied the slop jar beside his bed twice a day and kept the barrel full of water melted from river ice. He did not recognize her anymore, and when he spoke to her, he called her by her grandmother's name and talked about people and events from long ago, before he went back to telling the story. The giant bear was creeping across the new snow on its belly, close enough now that the man could hear the rasp of its breathing. On and on in a soft

singing voice, the old man caressed the story, repeating the words again and again like gentle strokes.

The sky was gray like a river crane's egg; its density curved into the thin crust of frost already covering the land. She looked at the bright red color of the tin against the ground and the sky and she told the village men to bring the pieces for the old man and her. To drill the test holes in the tundra, the Gussucks had used hundreds of barrels of fuel. The village people split open the empty barrels that were abandoned on the river bank, and pounded the red tin into flat sheets. The village people were using the strips of tin to mend walls and roofs for winter. But she nailed it on the log walls for its color. When she finished, she walked away with the hammer in her hand, not turning around until she was far away, on the ridge above the river banks, and then she looked back. She felt a chill when she saw how the sky and the land were already losing their boundaries, already becoming lost in each other. But the red tin penetrated the thick white color of earth and sky; it defined the boundaries like a wound revealing the ribs and heart of a great caribou about to bolt and be lost to the hunter forever. That night the wind howled and when she scratched a hole through the heavy frost on the inside of the window, she could see nothing but the impenetrable white; whether it was blowing snow or snow that had drifted as high as the house, she did not know.

It had come down suddenly, and she stood with her back to the wind looking at the river, its smoky water clotted with ice. The wind had blown the snow over the frozen river, hiding thin blue streaks where fast water ran under ice translucent and fragile as memory. But she could see shadows of boundaries, outlines of paths which were slender branches of solidity reaching out from the earth. She spent days walking on the river, watching the colors of ice that would safely hold her, kicking the heel of her boot into the snow crust, listening for a solid sound. When she could feel the paths through the soles of her feet, she went to the middle of the river where the fast gray water churned under a thin pane of ice. She looked back. On the river bank in the distance she could see the red tin nailed to the log house, something not swallowed up by the heavy white belly of the sky or caught in the folds of the frozen earth. It was time.

The wolverine fur around the hood of her parka was white with the frost from her breathing. The warmth inside the store melted it, and she felt tiny drops of water on her face. The storeman came in from the back room. She unzipped the parka and stood by the oil stove. She didn't look at him, but stared instead at the yellowish dog, covered with scabs of matted hair, sleeping in front of the stove. She thought of the Gussuck's picture, taped on the wall above the bed and she laughed out loud. The sound of her laughter was piercing; the yellow dog jumped to its feet and the hair bristled down its back. The storeman was watching her. She wanted to laugh again because he didn't know about the ice. He did not know that it was prowling the earth, or that it had already pushed its way into the sky to seize the sun. She sat down in the chair by the stove and shook her long hair loose. He was like a dog tied up all winter, watching while the others got fed. He remembered how she had gone with the old drillers, and his blue eyes moved like flies crawling over her body. He held his thin pale lips like he wanted to spit on her. He hated the people because they had something of value, the old man said, something which the Gussucks could never have. They thought they could take it, suck it out of the earth or cut it from the mountains; but they were fools.

There was a matted hunk of dog hair on the floor by her foot. She thought of the yellow insulation coming unstuffed: their defense against the freezing going to pieces as it advanced on them. The ice was crouching on the northwest horizon like the old man's bear. She laughed out loud again. The sun would be down now; it was time.

50   The first time he spoke to her, she did not hear what he said, so she did not answer or even look up at him. He spoke to her again but his words were only noises coming from his pale mouth, trembling now as his anger began to unravel. He jerked her up and the chair fell over behind her. His arms were shaking and she could feel his hands tense up, pulling the edges of the parka tighter. He raised his fist to hit her, his thin body quivering with rage; but the fist collapsed with the desire he had for the valuable things, which, the old man had rightly said, was the only reason they came. She could hear his heart pounding as he held her close and arched his hips against her, groaning and breathing in spasms. She twisted away from him and ducked under his arms.

She ran with a mitten over her mouth, breathing through the fur to protect her lungs from the freezing air. She could hear him running behind her, his heavy breathing, the occasional sound of metal jingling against metal. But he ran without his parka or mittens, breathing the frozen air; its fire squeezed the lungs against the ribs and it was enough that he could not catch her near his store. On the river bank he realized how far he was from his stove, and the wads of yellow stuffing that held off the cold. But the girl was not able to run very fast through the deep drifts at the edge of the river. The twilight was luminous and he could still see clearly for a long distance; he knew he could catch her so he kept running.

When she neared the middle of the river she looked over her shoulder. He was not following her tracks; he went straight across the ice, running the shortest distance to reach her. He was close then; his face was twisted and scarlet from the exertion and the cold. There was satisfaction in his eyes; he was sure he could outrun her.

She was familiar with the river, down to the instant ice flexed into hairline fractures, and the cracking bone-sliver sounds gathered momentum with the opening ice until the churning gray water was set free. She stopped and turned to the sound of the river and the rattle of swirling ice fragments where he fell through. She pulled off a mitten and zipped the parka to her throat. She was conscious then of her own rapid breathing.

She moved slowly, kicking the ice ahead with the heel of her boot, feeling for sinews of ice to hold her. She looked ahead and all around herself; in the twilight, the dense white sky had merged into the flat snow-covered tundra. In the frantic running she had lost her place on the river. She stood still. The east bank of the river was lost in the sky; the boundaries had been swallowed by the freezing white. But then, in the distance, she saw something red, and suddenly it was as she had remembered it all those years.

55   She sat on her bed and while she waited, she listened to the old man. The hunter had found a small jagged knoll on the ice. He pulled his beaver fur cap off his head; the fur inside it steamed with his body heat and sweat. He left it upside down on the ice for the great bear to stalk, and he waited downwind on top of the ice knoll; he was holding the jade knife.

She thought she could see the end of his story in the way he wheezed out the words; but still he reached into his cache of dry fish and dribbled water into his mouth from the tin cup. All night she listened to him describe each breath the man took, each motion of the bear's head as it tried to catch the sound of the man's breathing, and tested the wind for his scent.

The state trooper asked her questions, and the woman who cleaned house for the priest translated them into Yupik. They wanted to know what happened to the storeman, the Gussuck who had been seen running after her down the road onto the river late last evening. He had not come back, and the Gussuck boss in Anchorage was concerned about him. She did not answer for a long time because the old man suddenly sat up in his bed and began to talk excitedly, looking at all of them—the trooper in his dark glasses and the housekeeper in her corduroy parka. He kept saying, "The story! The story! Eh-ya! The great bear! The hunter!"

They asked her again, what happened to the man from the Northern Commercial store. "He lied to them. He told them it was safe to drink. But I will not lie." She stood up and put on the gray wolfskin parka. "I killed him," she said, "but I don't lie."

The attorney came back again, and the jailer slid open the steel doors and opened the cell to let him in. He motioned for the jailer to stay to translate for him. She laughed when she saw how the jailer would be forced by this Gussuck to speak Yupik to her. She liked the Gussuck attorney for that, and for the thinning hair on his head. He was very tall, and she liked to think about the exposure of his head to the freezing; she wondered if he would feel the ice descending from the sky before the others did. He wanted to know why she told the state trooper she had killed the storeman. Some village children had seen it happen, he said, and it was an accident. "That's all you have to say to the judge: it was an accident." He kept repeating it over and over again to her, slowly in a loud but gentle voice: "It was an accident. He was running after you and he fell through the ice. That's all you have to say in court. That's all. And they will let you go home. Back to your village." The jailer translated the words sullenly, staring down at the floor. She shook her head. "I will not change the story, not even to escape this place and go home. I intended that he die. The story must be told as it is." The attorney exhaled loudly; his eyes looked tired. "Tell her that she could not have killed him that way. He was a white man. He ran after her without a parka or mittens. She could not have planned that." He paused and turned toward the cell door. "Tell her I will do all I can for her. I will explain to the judge that her mind is confused." She laughed out loud when the jailer translated what the attorney said. The Gussucks did not understand the story; they could not see the way it must be told, year after year as the old man had done, without lapse or silence.

60   She looked out the window at the frozen white sky. The sun had finally broken loose from the ice but it moved like a wounded caribou running on strength which only dying animals find, leaping and running on bullet-shattered lungs. Its light was weak and pale; it pushed dimly through the clouds. She turned and faced the Gussuck attorney.

"It began a long time ago," she intoned steadily, "in the summertime. Early in the morning, I remember, something red in the tall river grass. . . ."

The day after the old man died, men from the village came. She was sitting on the edge of her bed, across from the woman the trooper hired to watch her. They came into the room slowly and listened to her. At the foot of her bed they left a king salmon that had been slit open wide and dried last summer. But she did not pause or hesitate; she went on with the story, and she never stopped, not even when the woman got up to close the door behind the village men.

The old man would not change the story even when he knew the end was approaching. Lies could not stop what was coming. He thrashed around on the bed, pulling the blankets loose, knocking bundles of dried fish and meat on the floor. The hunter had been on the ice for many hours. The freezing winds on the ice knoll had numbed his hands in the mittens, and the cold had exhausted him. He felt a single muscle tremor in his hand that he could not stop, and the jade knife fell; it shattered on the ice, and the blue glacier bear turned slowly to face him.

Isaac Bashevis Singer

Isaac Bashevis Singer (1904–1991) was born in Poland and came to the United States in 1935, becoming a U.S. citizen in 1943. He writes in Yiddish. His work is then translated into English. He lives in Manhattan and draws frequently on the remembered past of Jewish communities in Poland. His novels include *The Family Moskat,* which appeared in English in 1950, *Satan in Goray* (1955), *The Magician of Lublin* (1960), and *Sosha* (1979). He has collected his short stories, which are probably his best work, in *Gimpel the Fool* (1957), *The Spinoza of Market Street* (1961), *Short Friday* (1964), and *The Seance and Other Stories* (1968). In 1978, he was awarded the Nobel Prize for Literature.

Gimpel the Fool   (1953)

I

I am Gimpel the fool. I don't think myself a fool. On the contrary. But that's what folks call me. They gave me the name while I was still in school. I had seven names in all: imbecile, donkey, flax-head, dope, glump, ninny, and fool. The last name stuck. What did my foolishness consist of? I was easy to take in. They said, "Gimpel, you know the rabbi's wife has been brought to childbed?" So I skipped school. Well, it turned out to be a lie. How was I supposed to know? She hadn't had a big belly. But I never looked at her belly. Was that really so foolish? The gang laughed and hee-hawed, stomped and danced and chanted a good-night prayer. And instead of the raisins they give when a woman's lying in, they stuffed my hand full of goat turds. I was no weakling. If I slapped someone he'd see all the way to Cracow. But I'm really not a slugger by nature. I think to myself: Let it pass. So they take advantage of me.

I was coming home from school and heard a dog barking. I'm not afraid of dogs, but of course I never want to start up with them. One of them may be mad, and if he bites there's not a Tartar in the world who can help you. So I made tracks. Then I looked around and saw the whole market-place wild with laughter. It was no dog at all but Wolf-Leib the Thief. How was I supposed to know it was he? It sounded like a howling bitch.

When the pranksters and leg-pullers found that I was easy to fool, every one of them tried his luck with me. "Gimpel, the Czar is coming to Frampol; Gimpel, the moon fell down in Turbeen; Gimpel, little Hodel Furpiece found a treasure behind the bathhouse." And I like a golem[1] believed everyone. In the first place, everything is possible, as it is written in the Wisdom of the Fathers. I've forgotten just how. Second, I had to believe when the whole town came down on me! If I ever dared to say, "Ah, you're kidding!" there was trouble. People got angry. "What do you mean! You want to call everyone a liar?" What was I to do? I believed them, and I hope at least that did them some good.

I am an orphan. My grandfather who brought me up was already bent toward the grave. So they turned me over to a baker, and what a time they gave me there! Every woman or girl who came to bake a batch of noodles had to fool me at least once. "Gimpel, there's a fair in heaven; Gimpel, the rabbi gave birth to a calf in the seventh month; Gimpel, a cow flew over the roof and laid brass eggs." A student from the yeshiva[2] came once to buy a roll, and he said, "You, Gimpel, while you stand here scraping with your baker's shovel the Messiah has come. The dead have arisen." "What do you mean?" I said. "I heard no one blowing the ram's horn!" He said, "Are you deaf?" And all began to cry. "We heard it, we heard!" Then in came Rietze the Candle-dipper and called out in her hoarse voice, "Gimpel, your father and mother have stood up from the grave. They're looking for you."

5   To tell the truth, I knew very well that nothing of the sort had happened, but all the same, as folks were talking, I threw on my wool vest and went out. Maybe something had happened. What did I stand to lose by looking? Well, what a cat music went up! And then I took a vow to believe nothing more. But that was no go either. They confused me so that I didn't know the big end from the small.

[1] Stupid person   [2] School of Jewish thought and tradition

I went to the rabbi to get some advice. He said, "It is written, better to be a fool all your days than for one hour to be evil. You are not a fool. They are the fools. For he who causes his neighbor to feel shame loses Paradise himself." Nevertheless the rabbi's daughter took me in. As I left the rabbinical court she said, "Have you kissed the wall yet?" I said, "No, what for?" She answered, "It's the law; you've got to do it after every visit." Well, there didn't seem to be any harm in it. And she burst out laughing. It was a fine trick. She put one over on me all right.

I wanted to go off to another town, but then everyone got busy matchmaking, and they were after me so they nearly tore my coat tails off. They talked at me and talked until I got water on the ear. She was no chaste maiden, but they told me she was a virgin pure. She had a limp, and they said it was deliberate, from coyness. She had a bastard, and they told me the child was her little brother. I cried, "You're wasting your time. I'll never marry that whore." But they said indignantly, "What a way to talk! Aren't you ashamed of yourself? We can take you to the rabbi and have you fined for giving her a bad name." I saw then that I wouldn't escape them so easily and I thought: They're set on making me their butt. But when you're married the husband's the master, and if that's all right with her it's agreeable to me too. Besides, you can't pass through life unscathed, nor expect to.

I went to her clay house, which was built on the sand, and the whole gang, hollering and chorusing, came after me. They acted like bear-baiters. When we came to the well they stopped all the same. They were afraid to start anything with Elka. Her mouth would open as if it were on a hinge, and she had a fierce tongue. I entered the house. Lines were strung from wall to wall and clothes were drying. Barefoot she stood by the tub, doing the wash. She was dressed in a worn hand-me-down gown of plush. She had her hair up in braids and pinned across her head. It took my breath away, almost, the reek of it all.

Evidently she knew who I was. She took a look at me and said, "Look who's here! He's come, the drip. Grab a seat."

10 I told her all; I denied nothing. "Tell me the truth," I said, "are you really a virgin, and is that mischievous Yechiel actually your little brother? Don't be deceitful with me, for I'm an orphan."

"I'm an orphan myself," she answered, "and whoever tries to twist you up, may the end of his nose take a twist. But don't let them think they can take advantage of me. I want a dowry of fifty guilders, and let them take up a collection besides. Otherwise they can kiss my you-know-what." She was very plainspoken. I said, "It's the bride and not the groom who gives a dowry." Then she said, "Don't bargain with me. Either a flat 'yes' or a flat 'no'—Go back where you came from."

I thought: No bread will ever be baked from *this* dough. But ours is not a poor town. They consented to everything and proceeded with the wedding. It so happened that there was a dysentery epidemic at the time. The ceremony was held at the cemetery gates, near the little corpse-washing hut. The fellows got drunk. While the marriage contract was being drawn up I heard the most pious high rabbi ask, "Is the bride a widow or a divorced woman?"

And the sexton's wife answered for her, "Both a widow and divorced." It was a black moment for me. But what was I to do, run away from under the marriage canopy?

There was singing and dancing. An old granny danced opposite men, hugging a braided white *chalah*.[3] The master of revels made a "God 'a mercy" in memory of the bride's parents. The schoolboys threw burrs, as on Tishe b'Av[4] fast day. There were a lot of gifts after the sermon: a noodle board, a kneading trough, a bucket, brooms, ladles, household articles galore. Then I took a look and saw two strapping young men carrying a crib. "What do we need this for?" I asked. So they said, "Don't rack your brains about it. It's all right, it'll come in handy." I realized I was going to be rooked. Take it another way though, what did I stand to lose? I reflected: I'll see what comes of it. A whole town can't go altogether crazy.

II

At night I came where my wife lay, but she wouldn't let me in. "Say, look here, is this what they married us for?" I said. And she said, "My monthly has come." "But yesterday they took you to the ritual bath, and that's afterward, isn't it supposed to be?" "Today isn't yesterday," said she, "and yesterday's not today. You can beat it if you don't like it." In short, I waited.

15   Not four months later she was in childbed. The townsfolk hid their laughter with their knuckles. But what could I do? She suffered intolerable pains and clawed at the walls. "Gimpel," she cried, "I'm going. Forgive me!" The house filled with women. They were boiling pans of water. The screams rose to the welkin.

The thing to do was to go to the House of Prayer to repeat Psalms, and that was what I did.

The townsfolk liked that, all right. I stood in a corner saying Psalms and prayers, and they shook their heads at me. "Pray, pray!" they told me. "Prayer never made any woman pregnant." One of the congregation put a straw to my mouth and said, "Hay for the cows." There was something to that too, by God!

She gave birth to a boy. Friday at the synagogue the sexton stood up before the Ark,[5] pounded on the reading table, and announced, "The wealthy Reb Gimpel invites the congregation to a feast in honor of the birth of a son." The whole House of Prayer rang with laughter. My face was flaming. But there was nothing I could do. After all, I *was* the one responsible for the circumcision honors and rituals.

Half the town came running. You couldn't wedge another soul in. Women brought peppered chick-peas, and there was a keg of beer from the tavern. I ate and drank as much as anyone, and they all congratulated me. Then there was a circumcision, and I named the boy after my father, may he rest in peace. When all were gone and I was left with my wife alone, she thrust her head through the bed-curtain and called me to her.

---

[3] Loaf of bread eaten on the Sabbath and other holidays   [4] A day of fasting and deep mourning   [5] Container of the holy books of the Torah

20   "Gimpel," said she, "why are you silent? Has your ship gone and sunk?"

"What shall I say?" I answered. "A fine thing you've done to me! If my mother had known of it she'd have died a second time."

She said, "Are you crazy, or what?"

"How can you make such a fool," I said, "of one who should be the lord and master?"

"What's the matter with you?" she said. "What have you taken it into your head to imagine?"

25   I saw that I must speak bluntly and openly. "Do you think this the way to use an orphan?" I said. "You have borne a bastard."

She answered, "Drive this foolishness out of your head. The child is yours."

"How can he be mine?" I argued. "He was born seventeen weeks after the wedding."

She told me then that he was premature. I said, "Isn't he a little too premature?" She said she had had a grandmother who carried just as short a time and she resembled this grandmother of hers as one drop of water does another. She swore to it with such oaths that you would have believed a peasant at the fair if he had used them. To tell the plain truth, I didn't believe her; but when I talked it over next day with the schoolmaster he told me that the very same thing had happened to Adam and Eve. Two they went up to bed, and four they descended.

"There isn't a woman in the world who is not the granddaughter of Eve," he said.

30   That was how it was; they argued me dumb. But then, who really knows how such things are?

I began to forget my sorrow. I loved the child madly, and he loved me too. As soon as he saw me he'd wave his little hands and want me to pick him up, and when he was colicky I was the only one who could pacify him. I bought him a little bone teething ring and a little gilded cap. He was forever catching the evil eye from someone, and then I had to run to get one of those abra-cadabras for him that would get him out of it. I worked like an ox. You know how expenses go up when there's an infant in the house. I don't want to lie about it; I didn't dislike Elka either, for that matter. She swore at me and cursed, and I couldn't get enough of her. What strength she had! One of her looks could rob you of the power of speech. And her orations! Pitch and sulphur, that's what they were full of, and yet somehow also full of charm. I adored her every word. She gave me bloody wounds though.

In the evening I brought her a white loaf as well as a dark one, and also poppyseed rolls I baked myself. I thieved because of her and swiped every-thing I could lay my hands on: macaroons, raisins, almonds, cakes. I hope I may be forgiven for stealing from the Saturday pots the women left to warm in the baker's oven. I would take out scraps of meat, a chunk of pudding, a chicken leg or head, a piece of tripe, whatever I could nip quickly. She ate and became fat and handsome.

I had to sleep away from home all during the week, at the bakery. On Friday nights when I got home she always made an excuse of some sort. Either she had heartburn, or a stitch in the side or hiccups, or headaches. You know what women's excuses are. I had a bitter time of it. It was rough. To add to it, this little brother of hers, the bastard, was growing bigger. He'd put lumps on me, and when I wanted to hit back she'd open her mouth and curse so powerfully I saw a green haze floating before my eyes. Ten times a day she threatened to divorce me. Another man in my place would have taken French leave and disappeared. But I'm the type that bears it and says nothing. What's one to do? Shoulders are from God, and burdens too.

One night there was a calamity in the bakery; the oven burst, and we almost had a fire. There was nothing to do but go home, so I went home. Let me, I thought, also taste the joy of sleeping in bed in mid-week. I didn't want to wake the sleeping mite and tiptoed into the house. Coming in, it seemed to me that I heard not the snoring of one but, as it were, a double snore, one a thin enough snore and the other like the snoring of a slaughtered ox. Oh, I didn't like that! I didn't like it at all. I went up to the bed, and things suddenly turned black. Next to Elka lay a man's form. Another in my place would have made an uproar, and enough noise to rouse the whole town, but the thought occurred to me that I might wake the child. A little thing like that—why frighten a little swallow, I thought. All right then, I went back to the bakery and stretched out on a sack of flour and till morning I never shut an eye. I shivered as if I had malaria. "Enough of being a donkey," I said to myself. "Gimpel isn't going to be a sucker all his life. There's a limit even to the foolishness of a fool like Gimpel."

35   In the morning I went to the rabbi to get advice, and it made a great commotion in the town. They sent the beadle for Elka right away. She came, carrying the child. And what do you think she did? She denied it, denied everything, bone and stone! "He's out of his head," she said. "I know nothing of dreams or divinations." They yelled at her, warned her, hammered on the table, but she stuck to her guns: it was a false accusation, she said.

The butchers and the horse-traders took her part. One of the lads from the slaughterhouse came by and said to me, "We've got our eye on you, you're a marked man." Meanwhile the child started to bear down and soiled itself. In the rabbinical court there was an Ark of the Covenant,[6] and they couldn't allow that, so they sent Elka away.

I said to the rabbi, "What shall I do?"

"You must divorce her at once," said he.

"And what if she refuses?" I asked.

40   He said, "You must serve the divorce. That's all you have to do."

I said, "Well, all right, Rabbi. Let me think about it."

"There's nothing to think about," said he. "You mustn't remain under the same roof with her."

"And if I want to see the child?" I asked.

"Let her go, the harlot," said he, "and her brood of bastards with her."

45   The verdict he gave me was that I mustn't even cross her threshold—never again, as long as I should live.

---

[6] Box holding the Ten Commandments

During the day it didn't bother me so much. I thought: It was bound to happen, the abscess had to burst. But at night when I stretched out upon the sacks I felt it all very bitterly. A longing took me, for her and for the child. I wanted to be angry, but that's my misfortune exactly, I don't have it in me to be really angry. In the first place—this was how my thoughts went—there's bound to be a slip sometimes. You can't live without errors. Probably that lad who was with her led her on and gave her presents and what not, and women are often long on hair and short on sense, and so he got around her. And then since she denies it so, maybe I was only seeing things? Hallucinations do happen. You see a figure or a mannikin or something, but when you come up closer it's nothing, there's not a thing there. And if that's so, I'm doing her an injustice. And when I got so far in my thoughts I started to weep. I sobbed so that I wet the flour where I lay. In the morning I went to the rabbi and told him that I had made a mistake. The rabbi wrote on with his quill, and he said that if that were so he would have to reconsider the whole case. Until he had finished I wasn't to go near my wife, but I might send her bread and money by messenger.

III

Nine months passed before all the rabbis could come to an agreement. Letters went back and forth. I hadn't realized that there could be so much erudition about a matter like this.

Meanwhile Elka gave birth to still another child, a girl this time. On the Sabbath I went to the synagogue and invoked a blessing on her. They called me up to the Torah, and I named the child for my mother-in-law—may she rest in peace. The louts and loudmouths of the town who came into the bakery gave me a going over. All Frampol refreshed its spirits because of my trouble and grief. However, I resolved that I would always believe what I was told. What's the good of *not* believing? Today it's your wife you don't believe; tomorrow it's God Himself you won't take stock in.

By an apprentice who was her neighbor I sent daily a corn or a wheat loaf, or a piece of pastry, rolls or bagels, or, when I got the chance, a slab of pudding, a slice of honeycake, or wedding strudel—whatever came my way. The apprentice was a goodhearted lad, and more than once he added something on his own. He had formerly annoyed me a lot, plucking my nose and digging me in the ribs, but when he started to be a visitor to my house he became kind and friendly. "Hey, you, Gimpel," he said to me, "you have a very decent little wife and two fine kids. You don't deserve them."

50   "But the things people say about her," I said.

"Well, they have long tongues," he said, "and nothing to do with them but babble. Ignore it as you ignore the cold of last winter."

One day the rabbi sent for me and said, "Are you certain, Gimpel, that you were wrong about your wife?"

I said, "I'm certain."

"Why, but look here! You yourself saw it."

55   "It must have been a shadow," I said.

"The shadow of what?"

"Just one of the beams, I think."

"You can go home then. You owe thanks to the Yanover rabbi. He found an obscure reference in Maimonides[7] that favored you."

I seized the rabbi's hand and kissed it.

60   I wanted to run home immediately. It's no small thing to be separated for so long a time from wife and child. Then I reflected: I'd better go back to work now, and go home in the evening. I said nothing to anyone, although as far as my heart was concerned it was like one of the Holy Days. The women teased and twitted me as they did every day, but my thought was: Go on, with your loose talk. The truth is out, like the oil upon the water. Maimonides says it's right, and therefore it is right!

At night, when I had covered the dough to let it rise, I took my share of bread and a little sack of flour and started homeward. The moon was full and the stars were glistening, something to terrify the soul. I hurried onward, and before me darted a long shadow. It was winter, and a fresh snow had fallen. I had a mind to sing, but it was growing late and I didn't want to wake the householders. Then I felt like whistling, but I remembered that you don't whistle at night because it brings the demons out. So I was silent and walked as fast as I could.

Dogs in the Christian yards barked at me when I passed, but I thought: Bark your teeth out! What are you but mere dogs? Whereas I am a man, the husband of a fine wife, the father of promising children.

As I approached the house my heart started to pound as though it were the heart of a criminal. I felt no fear, but my heart went thump! thump! Well, no drawing back. I quietly lifted the latch and went in. Elka was asleep. I looked at the infant's cradle. The shutter was closed, but the moon forced its way through the cracks. I saw the newborn child's face and loved it as soon as I saw it—immediately—each tiny bone.

Then I came nearer to the bed. And what did I see but the apprentice lying there beside Elka. The moon went out all at once. It was utterly black, and I trembled. My teeth chattered. The bread fell from my hands, and my wife waked and said, "Who is that, ah?"

65   I muttered, "It's me."

"Gimpel?" she asked. "How come you're here? I thought it was forbidden."

"The rabbi said," I answered and shook as with a fever.

"Listen to me, Gimpel," she said, "go out to the shed and see if the goat's all right. It seems she's been sick." I have forgotten to say that we had a goat. When I heard she was unwell I went into the yard. The nannygoat was a good little creature. I had a nearly human feeling for her.

With hesitant steps I went up to the shed and opened the door. The goat stood there on her four feet. I felt her everywhere, drew her by the horns, examined her udders, and found nothing wrong. She had probably eaten too much bark. "Good night, little goat," I said. "Keep well." And the little beast answered with a "Maa" as though to thank me for the good will.

[7] See note 10, page 260.

70   I went back. The apprentice had vanished.

"Where," I asked, "is the lad?"

"What lad?" my wife answered.

"What do you mean?" I said. "The apprentice. You were sleeping with him."

"The things I have dreamed this night and the night before," she said, "may they come true and lay you low, body and soul! An evil spirit has taken root in you and dazzles your sight." She screamed out, "You hateful creature! You moon calf! You spook! You uncouth man! Get out, or I'll scream all Frampol out of bed!"

75   Before I could move, her brother sprang out from behind the oven and struck me a blow on the back of the head. I thought he had broken my neck. I felt that something about me was deeply wrong, and I said, "Don't make a scandal. All that's needed now is that people should accuse me of raising spooks and *dybbuks*."[8] For that was what she had meant. "No one will touch bread of my baking."

In short, I somehow calmed her.

"Well," she said, "that's enough. Lie down, and be shattered by wheels."

Next morning I called the apprentice aside. "Listen here, brother!" I said. And so on and so forth. "What do you say?" He stared at me as though I had dropped from the roof or something.

"I swear," he said, "you'd better go to an herb doctor or some healer. I'm afraid you have a screw loose, but I'll hush it up for you." And that's how the thing stood.

80   To make a long story short, I lived twenty years with my wife. She bore me six children, four daughters and two sons. All kinds of things happened, but I neither saw nor heard. I believed, and that's all. The rabbi recently said to me, "Belief in itself is beneficial. It is written that a good man lives by his faith."

Suddenly my wife took sick. It began with a trifle, a little growth upon the breast. But she evidently was not destined to live long; she had no years. I spent a fortune on her. I have forgotten to say that by this time I had a bakery of my own and in Frampol was considered to be something of a rich man. Daily the healer came, and every witch doctor in the neighborhood was brought. They decided to use leeches, and after that to try cupping. They even called a doctor from Lublin, but it was too late. Before she died she called me to her bed and said, "Forgive me, Gimpel."

I said, "What is there to forgive? You have been a good and faithful wife."

"Woe, Gimpel!" she said. "It was ugly how I deceived you all these years. I want to go clean to my Maker, and so I have to tell you that the children are not yours."

If I had been clouted on the head with a piece of wood it couldn't have bewildered me more.

85   "Whose are they?" I asked.

"I don't know," she said. "There were a lot . . . but they're not yours." And as she spoke she tossed her head to the side, her eyes turned glassy, and it was all up with Elka. On her whitened lips there remained a smile.

---

[8] Evil spirits

I imagined that, dead as she was, she was saying, "I deceived Gimpel. That was the meaning of my brief life."

VI

One night, when the period of mourning was done, as I lay dreaming on the flour sacks, there came the Spirit of Evil himself and said to me, "Gimpel, why do you sleep?"

I said, "What should I be doing? Eating *kreplach*?"[9]

90   "The whole world deceives you," he said, "and you ought to deceive the world in your turn."

"How can I deceive all the world?" I asked him.

He answered, "You might accumulate a bucket of urine every day and at night pour it into the dough. Let the sages of Frampol eat filth."

"What about the judgment in the world to come?" I said.

"There is no world to come," he said. "They've sold you a bill of goods and talked you into believing you carried a cat in your belly. What nonsense!"

95   "Well then," I said, "and is there a God?"

He answered, "There is no God either."

"What," I said, "*is* there, then?"

"A thick mire."

He stood before my eyes with a goatish beard and horn, long-toothed, and with a tail. Hearing such words, I wanted to snatch him by the tail, but I tumbled from the flour sacks and nearly broke a rib. Then it happened that I had to answer the call of nature, and, passing, I saw the risen dough, which seemed to say to me, "Do it." In brief, I let myself be persuaded.

100   At dawn the apprentice came. We kneaded the bread, scattered caraway seeds on it, and set it to bake. Then the apprentice went away, and I was left sitting in the little trench by the oven on a pile of rags. Well, Gimpel, I thought, you've revenged yourself on them for all the shame they've put on you. Outside the frost glittered, but it was warm beside the oven. The flames heated my face. I bent my head and fell into a doze.

I saw in a dream at once, Elka in her shroud. She called to me, "What have you done, Gimpel?"

I said to her, "It's all your fault," and started to cry.

"You fool!" she said. "You fool! Because I was false is everything false too? I never deceived anyone but myself. I'm paying for it all, Gimpel. They spare you nothing here."

I looked at her face. It was black; I was startled and waked, and remained sitting dumb. I sensed that everything hung in the balance. A false step now and I'd lose Eternal Life. But God gave me His help. I seized the long shovel and took out the loaves, carried them into the yard, and started to dig a hole in the frozen earth.

105   My apprentice came back as I was doing it. "What are you doing boss?" he said, and grew pale as a corpse.

[9] A dumpling filled with cheese or meat

"I know what I'm doing," I said and I buried it all before his eyes.

Then I went home, and took my hoard from its hiding place, and divided it among the children. "I saw your mother tonight," I said. "She's turning black, poor thing."

They were so astounded they couldn't speak a word.

"Be well," I said, "and forget that such a one as Gimpel ever existed." I put on my short coat, a pair of boots, took the bag that held my prayer shawl in one hand, my stock in the other, and kissed the *mezzuzah*.[10] When people saw me in the street they were greatly surprised.

110   "Where are you going?" they said.

I answered, "Into the world." And so I departed from Frampol.

I wandered over the land, and good people did not neglect me. After many years I became old and white; I heard a great deal, many lies and falsehoods, but the longer I lived the more I understood that there were really no lies. Whatever doesn't really happen is dreamed at night. It happens to one if it doesn't happen to another, tomorrow if not today, or a century hence if not next year. What difference can it make? Often I heard tales of which I said, "Now this is a thing that cannot happen." But before a year had elapsed I heard that it actually had come to pass somewhere.

Going from place to place, eating at strange tables, it oftens happens that I spin yarns—improbable things that could never have happened—about devils, magicians, windmills, and the like. The children run after me, calling, "Grandfather, tell us a story." Sometimes they ask for particular stories, and I try to please them. A fat young boy once said to me, "Grandfather, it's the same story you told us before." The little rogue, he was right.

So it is with dreams too. It is many years since I left Frampol, but as soon as I shut my eyes I am there again. And whom do you think I see? Elka. She is standing by the washtub, as at our first encounter, but her face is shining and her eyes are as radiant as the eyes of a saint, and she speaks outlandish words to me, strange things. When I wake I have forgotten it all. But while the dream lasts I am comforted. She answers all my queries, and what comes out is that all is right. I weep and implore, "Let me be with you." And she consoles me and tells me to be patient. The time is nearer than it is far. Sometimes she strokes and kisses me and weeps upon my face. When I awaken I feel her lips and taste the salt of her tears.

115   No doubt the world is entirely an imaginary world, but it is only once removed from the true world. At the door of the hovel where I lie, there stands the plank on which the dead are taken away. The gravedigger Jew has his spade ready. The grave waits and the worms are hungry; the shrouds are prepared—I carry them in my beggar's sack. Another *shnorrer*[11] is waiting to inherit my bed of straw. When the time comes I will go joyfully. Whatever may be there, it will be real, without complication, without ridicule, without deception. God be praised: there even Gimpel cannot be deceived.

---

[10] A container for texts from Deuteronomy (6:4–9, 11:13–21) that is affixed to doorposts by Orthodox Jews   [11] Beggar

John Steinbeck

John Steinbeck (1902–1968) was a Californian, born in Salinas, who studied at
Stanford University. *The Grapes of Wrath* (1939), probably his best-known novel,
describes the migrant workers who fled the Dust Bowl for the fields of California.
In *Tortilla Flat* (1935), his characters are Mexican-Americans in Monterey.
Steinbeck wrote many novels, stories, screenplays, and travelogues. In 1962, he
was awarded the Nobel Prize for Literature.

The Chrysanthemums   (1938)

The high grey-flannel fog of winter closed off the Salinas Valley from the sky
and from all the rest of the world. On every side it sat like a lid on the
mountains and made of the great valley a closed pot. On the broad, level land
floor the gang ploughs bit deep and left the black earth shining like metal
where the shares had cut. On the foot-hill ranches across the Salinas River,
the yellow stubble fields seemed to be bathed in pale cold sunshine, but
there was no sunshine in the valley now in December. The thick willow
scrub along the river flamed with sharp and positive yellow leaves.

It was a time of quiet and of waiting. The air was cold and tender. A light
wind blew up from the southwest so that the farmers were mildly hopeful of
a good rain before long; but fog and rain do not go together.

Across the river, on Henry Allen's foot-hill ranch there was little work to
be done, for the hay was cut and stored and the orchards were ploughed up
to receive the rain deeply when it should come. The cattle on the higher
slopes were becoming shaggy and rough-coated.

Elisa Allen, working in her flower garden, looked down across the yard and
saw Henry, her husband, talking to two men in business suits. The three of
them stood by the tractor-shed, each man with one foot on the side of the little
Fordson. They smoked cigarettes and studied the machine as they talked.

5   Elisa watched them for a moment and then went back to her work. She was
thirty-five. Her face was lean and strong and her eyes were as clear as water.
Her figure looked blocked and heavy in her gardening costume, a man's black
hat pulled low down over her eyes, clod-hopper shoes, a figured print dress
almost completely covered by a big corduroy apron with four big pockets to
hold the snips, the trowel and scratcher, the seeds and the knife she worked
with. She wore heavy leather gloves to protect her hands while she worked.

She was cutting down the old year's chrysanthemum stalks with a pair of
short and powerful scissors. She looked down toward the men by the tractor-
shed now and then. Her face was eager and mature and handsome; even her
work with the scissors was over-eager, over-powerful. The chrysanthemum
stems seemed too small and easy for her energy.

She brushed a cloud of hair out of her eyes with the back of her glove, and
left a smudge of earth on her cheek in doing it. Behind her stood the neat
white farmhouse with red geraniums close-banked around it as high as the
windows. It was a hard-swept-looking little house, with hard-polished windows, and a clean mud-mat on the front steps.

Elisa cast another glance toward the tractor-shed. The strangers were getting into their Ford coupé. She took off a glove and put her strong fingers down into the forest of new green chrysanthemum sprouts that were growing around the old roots. She spread the leaves and looked down among the close-growing stems. No aphids were there, no sow bugs or snails or cutworms. Her terrier fingers destroyed such pests before they could get started.

Elisa started at the sound of her husband's voice. He had come near quietly, and he leaned over the wire fence that protected her flower garden from cattle and dogs and chickens.

10   "At it again," he said. "You've got a strong new crop coming."

Elisa straightened her back and pulled on the gardening glove again. "Yes. They'll be strong this coming year." In her tone and on her face there was a little smugness.

"You've got a gift with things," Henry observed. "Some of those yellow chrysanthemums you had this year were ten inches across. I wish you'd work out in the orchard and raise some apples that big."

Her eyes sharpened. "Maybe I could do it, too. I've got a gift with things, all right. My mother had it. She could stick anything in the ground and make it grow. She said it was having planters' hands that knew how to do it."

"Well, it sure works with flowers," he said.

15   "Henry, who were those men you were talking to?"

"Why, sure, that's what I came to tell you. They were from the Western Meat Company. I sold those thirty head of three-year-old steers. Got nearly my own price, too."

"Good," she said. "Good for you."

"And I thought," he continued, "I thought how it's Saturday afternoon, and we might go into Salinas for dinner at a restaurant, and then to a picture show—to celebrate, you see."

"Good," she repeated. "Oh, yes. That will be good."

20   Henry put on his joking tone. "There's fights tonight. How'd you like to go to the fights?"

"Oh, no," she said breathlessly. "No, I wouldn't like fights."

"Just fooling, Elisa. We'll go to a movie. Let's see. It's two now. I'm going to take Scotty and bring down those steers from the hill. It'll take us maybe two hours. We'll go in town about five and have a dinner at the Cominos Hotel. Like that?"

"Of course I'll like it. It's good to eat away from home."

"All right, then. I'll go get up a couple of horses."

25   She said: "I'll have plenty of time to transplant some of these sets, I guess."

She heard her husband calling Scotty down by the barn. And a little later she saw the two men ride up the pale yellow hillside in search of the steers.

There was a little square sandy bed kept for rooting the chrysanthemums. With her trowel she turned the soil over and over, and smoothed it and patted it firm. Then she dug ten parallel trenches to receive the sets. Back at the chrysanthemum bed she pulled out the little crisp shoots, trimmed off the leaves of each one with her scissors and laid it on a small orderly pile.

A squeak of wheels and plod of hoofs came from the road. Elisa looked up. The country road ran along the dense bank of willows and cottonwoods that bordered the river, and up this road came a curious vehicle, curiously drawn. It was an old spring-wagon, with a round canvas top on it like the cover of a prairie schooner. It was drawn by an old bay horse and a little grey-and-white burro. A big stubble-bearded man sat between the cover flaps and drove the crawling team. Underneath the wagon, between the hind wheels, a lean and rangy mongrel dog walked sedately. Words were painted on the canvas, in clumsy, crooked letters. "Pots, pans, knives, sisors, lawn mores, Fixed." Two rows of articles, and the triumphantly definitive "Fixed" below. The black paint had run down in little sharp points beneath each letter.

Elisa, squatting on the ground, watched to see the crazy, loose-jointed wagon pass by. But it didn't pass. It turned into the farm road in front of her house, crooked old wheels skirling and squeaking. The rangy dog darted from between the wheels and ran ahead. Instantly the two ranch shepherds flew out at him. Then all three stopped, and with stiff and quivering tails, with taut straight legs, with ambassadorial dignity, they slowly circled, sniffing daintily. The caravan pulled up to Elisa's wire fence and stopped. Now the newcomer dog, feeling outnumbered, lowered his tail and retired under the wagon with raised hackles and bared teeth.

30   The man on the wagon seat called out: "That's a bad dog in a fight when he gets started."

Elisa laughed. "I see he is. How soon does he generally get started?"

The man caught up her laughter and echoed it heartily. "Sometimes not for weeks and weeks," he said. He climbed stiffly down, over the wheel. The horse and the donkey drooped like unwatered flowers.

Elisa saw that he was a very big man. Although his hair and beard were greying, he did not look old. His worn black suit was wrinkled and spotted with grease. The laughter had disappeared from his face and eyes the moment his laughing voice ceased. His eyes were dark, and they were full of the brooding that gets in the eyes of teamsters and of sailors. The calloused hands he rested on the wire fence were cracked, and every crack was a black line. He took off his battered hat.

"I'm off my general road, ma'am," he said. "Does this dirt road cut over across the river to the Los Angeles highway?"

35   Elisa stood up and shoved the thick scissors in her apron pocket. "Well, yes, it does, but it winds around and then fords the river. I don't think your team could pull through the sand."

He replied with some asperity: "It might surprise you what them beasts can pull through."

"When they get started?" she asked.

He smiled for a second. "Yes. When they get started."

"Well," said Elisa, "I think you'll save time if you go back to the Salinas road and pick up the highway there."

40   He drew a big finger down the chicken wire and made it sing. "I ain't in any hurry, ma'am. I go from Seattle to San Diego and back every year. Takes all my time. About six months each way. I aim to follow nice weather."

Elisa took off her gloves and stuffed them in the apron pocket with the scissors. She touched the under edge of her man's hat, searching for fugitive hairs. "That sounds like a nice kind of way to live," she said.

He leaned confidentially over the fence. "Maybe you noticed the writing on my wagon. I mend pots and sharpen knives and scissors. You got any of them things to do?"

"Oh, no," she said quickly. "Nothing like that." Her eyes hardened with resistance.

"Scissors is the worst thing," he explained. "Most people just ruin scissors trying to sharpen 'em, but I know how. I got a special tool. It's a little bobbit kind of thing, and patented. But it sure does the trick."

45   "No. My scissors are all sharp."

"All right, then. Take a pot," he continued earnestly, "a bent pot, or a pot with a hole. I can make it like new so you don't have to buy no new ones. That's a saving for you."

"No," she said shortly. "I tell you I have nothing like that for you to do."

His face fell to an exaggerated sadness. His voice took on a whining undertone. "I ain't had a thing to do today. Maybe I won't have no supper tonight. You see I'm off my regular road. I know folks on the highway clear from Seattle to San Diego. They save their things for me to sharpen up because they know I do it so good and save them money."

"I'm sorry," Elisa said irritably. "I haven't anything for you to do."

50   His eyes left her face and fell to searching the ground. They roamed about until they came to the chrysanthemum bed where she had been working. "What's them plants, ma'am?"

The irritation and resistance melted from Elisa's face. "Oh, those are chrysanthemums, giant whites and yellows. I raise them every year, bigger than anybody around here."

"Kind of a long-stemmed flower? Looks like a quick puff of colored smoke?" he asked.

"That's it. What a nice way to describe them."

"They smell kind of nasty till you get used to them," he said.

55   "It's a good bitter smell," she retorted, "not nasty at all."

He changed his tone quickly. "I like the smell myself."

"I had ten-inch blooms this year," she said.

The man leaned farther over the fence. "Look. I know a lady down the road a piece, has got the nicest garden you ever seen. Got nearly every kind of flower but no chrysanthemums. Last time I was mending a copper-bottom washtub for her (that's a hard job but I do it good), she said to me: 'If you ever run acrost some nice chrysanthemums I wish you'd try to get me a few seeds.' That's what she told me."

Elisa's eyes grew alert and eager. "She couldn't have known much about chrysanthemums. You can raise them from seed, but it's much easier to root the little sprouts you see there."

60   "Oh," he said. "I s'pose I can take none to her, then."

"Why yes you can," Elisa cried. "I can put some in damp sand, and you can carry them right along with you. They'll take root in the pot if you keep them damp. And then she can transplant them."

"She'd sure like to have some, ma'am. You say they're nice ones?"

"Beautiful," she said. "Oh, beautiful." Her eyes shone. She tore off the battered hat and shook out her dark pretty hair. "I'll put them in a flowerpot, and you can take them right with you. Come into the yard."

While the man came through the picket gate Elisa ran excitedly along the geranium-bordered path to the back of the house. And she returned carrying a big red flowerpot. The gloves were forgotten now. She kneeled on the ground by the starting bed and dug up the sandy soil with her fingers and scooped it into the bright new flowerpot. Then she picked up the little pile of shoots she had prepared. With her strong fingers she pressed them into the sand and tamped around them with her knuckles. The man stood over her. "I'll tell you what to do," she said. "You remember so you can tell the lady."

65   "Yes, I'll try to remember."

"Well, look. These will take root in about a month. Then she must set them out, about a foot apart in good rich earth like this, see?" She lifted a handful of dark soil for him to look at. "They'll grow fast and tall. Now remember this: In July tell her to cut them down, about eight inches from the ground."

"Before they bloom?" he asked.

"Yes, before they bloom." Her face was tight with eagerness. "They'll grow right up again. About the last of September the buds will start."

She stopped and seemed perplexed. "It's the budding that takes the most care," she said hesitantly. "I don't know how to tell you." She looked deep into his eyes, searchingly. Her mouth opened a little, and she seemed to be listening. "I'll try to tell you," she said. "Did you ever hear of planting hands?"

70   "Can't say I have, ma'am."

"Well, I can only tell you what it feels like. It's when you're picking off the buds you don't want. Everything goes right down into your fingertips. You watch your fingers work. They do it themselves. You can feel how it is. They pick and pick the buds. They never make a mistake. They're with the plant. Do you see? Your fingers and the plant. You can feel that, right up your arm. They know. They never make a mistake. You can feel it. When you're like that you can't do anything wrong. Do you see that? Can you understand that?"

She was kneeling on the ground looking up at him. Her breast swelled passionately.

The man's eyes narrowed. He looked away self-consciously. "Maybe I know," he said. "Sometimes in the night in the wagon there—"

Elisa's voice grew husky. She broke in on him: "I've never lived as you do, but I know what you mean. When the night is dark—why, the stars are sharp-pointed, and there's quiet. Why, you rise up and up! Every pointed star gets driven into your body. It's like that. Hot and sharp and—lovely."

75   Kneeling there, her hand went out toward his legs in the greasy black trousers. Her hesitant fingers almost touched the cloth. Then her hand dropped to the ground. She crouched low like a fawning dog.

He said: "It's nice, just like you say. Only when you don't have no dinner, it ain't."

She stood up then, very straight, and her face was ashamed. She held the flowerpot out to him and placed it gently in his arms. "Here. Put it in your wagon, on the seat, where you can watch it. Maybe I can find something for you to do."

At the back of the house she dug in the can pile and found two old and battered aluminum saucepans. She carried them back and gave them to him. "Here, maybe you can fix these."

His manner changed. He became professional. "Good as new I can fix them." At the back of his wagon he set a little anvil, and out of an oily toolbox dug a small machine hammer. Elisa came through the gate to watch him while he pounded out the dents in the kettles. His mouth grew sure and knowing. At a difficult part of the work he sucked his underlip.

80   "You sleep right in the wagon?" Elisa asked.

"Right in the wagon, ma'am. Rain or shine. I'm dry as a cow in there."

"It must be nice," she said. "It must be very nice. I wish women could do such things."

"It ain't the right kind of a life for a woman."

Her upper lip raised a little, showing her teeth. "How do you know? How can you tell?" she said.

85   "I don't know, ma'am," he protested. "Of course, I don't know. Now here's your kettles, done. You don't have to buy no new ones."

"How much?"

"Oh, fifty cents'll do. I keep my prices down and my work good. That's why I have all them satisfied customers up and down the highway."

Elisa brought him a fifty-cent piece from the house and dropped it in his hand. "You might be surprised to have a rival some time. I can sharpen scissors, too. And I can beat the dents out of little pots. I could show you what a woman might do."

He put his hammer back in the oily box and shoved the little anvil out of sight. "It would be a lonely life for a woman, ma'am, and a scarey life, too, with animals creeping under the wagon all night." He climbed over the single-tree, steadying himself with a hand on the burro's white rump. He settled himself in the seat, picked up the lines. "Thank you kindly ma'am," he said. "I'll do like you told me; I'll go back and catch the Salinas road."

90   "Mind," she called, "if you're long in getting there, keep the sand damp."

"Sand, ma'am? . . . Sand? Oh, sure. You mean around the chrysanthemums. Sure I will." He clucked his tongue. The beasts leaned luxuriously into their collars. The mongrel dog took his place between the back wheels. The wagon turned and crawled out the entrance road and back the way it had come, along the river.

Elisa stood in front of her wire fence watching the slow progress of the caravan. Her shoulders were straight, her head thrown back, her eyes half-closed, so that the scene came vaguely into them. Her lips moved silently, forming the words "Good-bye—good-bye." Then she whispered: "That's a bright direction. There's a glowing there." The sound of her whisper startled her. She shook herself free and looked about to see whether anyone had been listening. Only the dogs had heard. They lifted their heads toward her from their sleeping in the dust, and then stretched out their chins and settled asleep again. Elisa turned and ran hurriedly into the house.

In the kitchen she reached behind the stove and felt the water tank. It was full of hot water from the noonday cooking. In the bathroom she tore off her soiled clothes and flung them into the corner. And then she scrubbed herself with a little block of pumice, legs and thighs, loins and chest and arms, until her skin was scratched and red. When she had dried herself she stood in front of a mirror in her bedroom and looked at her body. She tightened her stomach and threw out her chest. She turned and looked over her shoulder at her back.

After a while she began to dress, slowly. She put on her newest under-clothing and her nicest stockings and the dress which was the symbol of her prettiness. She worked carefully on her hair, pencilled her eyebrows and rouged her lips.

95   Before she was finished she heard the little thunder of hoofs and the shouts of Henry and his helper as they drove the red steers into the corral. She heard the gate bang shut and set herself for Henry's arrival.

His step sounded on the porch. He entered the house calling: "Elisa, where are you?"

"In my room, dressing. I'm not ready. There's hot water for your bath. Hurry up. It's getting late."

When she heard him splashing in the tub, Elisa laid his dark suit on the bed, and shirt and socks and tie beside it. She stood his polished shoes on the floor beside the bed. Then she went to the porch and sat primly and stiffly down. She looked toward the river road where the willow-line was still yellow with frosted leaves so that under the high grey fog they seemed a thin band of sunshine. This was the only color in the grey afternoon. She sat unmoving for a long time. Her eyes blinked rarely.

Henry came banging out of the door, shoving his tie inside his vest as he came. Elisa stiffened and her face grew tight. Henry stopped short and looked at her. "Why—why, Elisa. You look so nice!"

100   "Nice? You think I look nice? What do you mean by 'nice'?"

Henry blundered on. "I don't know. I mean you look different, strong and happy."

"I am strong? Yes, strong. What do you mean by 'strong'?"

He looked bewildered. "You're playing some kind of a game," he said helplessly. "It's a kind of a play. You look strong enough to break a calf over your knee, happy enough to eat it like a watermelon."

For a second she lost her rigidity. "Henry! Don't talk like that. You didn't know what you said." She grew complete again. "I'm strong," she boasted. "I never knew before how strong."

105   Henry looked down toward the tractor-shed, and when he brought his eyes back to her, they were his own again. "I'll get out the car. You can put on your coat while I'm starting."

Elisa went into the house. She heard him drive to the gate and idle down his motor, and then she took a long time to put on her hat. She pulled it here and pressed it there. When Henry turned the motor off she slipped into her coat and went out.

The little roadster bounced along on the dirt road by the river, raising the birds and driving the rabbits into the brush. Two cranes flapped heavily over the willow-line and dropped into the river-bed.

Far ahead on the road Elisa saw a dark speck. She knew.

She tried not to look as they passed it, but her eyes would not obey. She whispered to herself sadly: "He might have thrown them off the road. That wouldn't have been much trouble, not very much. But he kept the pot," she explained. "He had to keep the pot. That's why he couldn't get them off the road."

110 The roadster turned a bend and she saw the caravan ahead. She swung full around toward her husband so she could not see the little covered wagon and the mis-matched team as the car passed them.

In a moment it was over. The thing was done. She did not look back.

She said loudly, to be heard above the motor: "It will be good, tonight, a good dinner."

"Now you've changed again," Henry complained. He took one hand from the wheel and patted her knee. "I ought to take you in to dinner oftener. It would be good for both of us. We get so heavy out on the ranch."

"Henry," she asked, "could we have wine at dinner?"

115 "Sure we could. Say! That will be fine."

She was silent for a while; then she said: "Henry, at those prizefights, do the men hurt each other very much?"

"Sometimes a little, not often. Why?"

"Well, I've read how they break noses, and blood runs down their chests. I've read how the fighting gloves get heavy and soggy with blood."

He looked around at her. "What's the matter, Elisa? I didn't know you read things like that." He brought the car to a stop, then turned to the right over the Salinas River bridge.

120 "Do any women ever go to the fights?" she asked.

"Oh, sure, some. What's the matter, Elisa? Do you want to go? I don't think you'd like it, but I'll take you if you really want to go."

She relaxed limply in the seat. "Oh, no. No. I don't want to go. I'm sure I don't." Her face was turned away from him. "It will be enough if we can have wine. It will be plenty." She turned up her coat collar so he could not see that she was crying weakly—like an old woman.

Amy Tan

Amy Tan (1952–   ) was born in Oakland, California. Her parents had settled there after leaving China. She attended college, first in Oregon, then at California State University in San Jose, California, where she earned a master's degree in linguistics. She attended a fiction workshop in 1985—at the Squaw Valley Community of Writers—and wrote her first novel, *The Joy Luck Club* (1989), from which we take "Two Kinds." In 1991 she published her second novel, *The Kitchen God's Wife*.

Two Kinds   (1989)

My mother believed you could be anything you wanted to be in America. You could open a restaurant. You could work for the government and get good retirement. You could buy a house with almost no money down. You could become rich. You could become instantly famous.

"Of course, you can be prodigy, too," my mother told me when I was nine. "You can be best anything. What does Auntie Lindo know? Her daughter, she is only best tricky."

America was where all my mother's hopes lay. She had come to San Francisco in 1949 after losing everything in China: her mother and father, her family home, her first husband, and two daughters, twin baby girls. But she never looked back with regret. Things could get better in so many ways.

We didn't immediately pick the right kind of prodigy. At first my mother thought I could be a Chinese Shirley Temple. We'd watch Shirley's old movies on TV as though they were training films. My mother would poke my arm and say, "*Ni kan.* You watch." And I would see Shirley tapping her feet, or singing a sailor song, or pursing her lips into a very round O while saying "Oh, my goodness."

5   "*Ni kan,*" my mother said, as Shirley's eyes flooded with tears. "You already know how. Don't need talent for crying!"

Soon after my mother got this idea about Shirley Temple, she took me to the beauty training school in the Mission District and put me in the hands of a student who could barely hold the scissors without shaking. Instead of getting big fat curls, I emerged with an uneven mass of crinkly black fuzz. My mother dragged me off to the bathroom and tried to wet down my hair.

"You look like Negro Chinese," she lamented, as if I had done this on purpose.

The instructor of the beauty training school had to lop off these soggy clumps to make my hair even again. "Peter Pan is very popular these days," the instructor assured my mother. I now had hair the length of a boy's, with curly bangs that hung at a slant two inches above my eyebrows. I liked the haircut, and it made me actually look forward to my future fame.

In fact, in the beginning I was just as excited as my mother, maybe even more so. I pictured this prodigy part of me as many different images, and I tried each one on for size. I was a dainty ballerina girl standing by the curtain, waiting to hear the music that would send me floating on my tiptoes. I was like the Christ child lifted out of the straw manger, crying with holy indignity. I was Cinderella stepping from her pumpkin carriage with sparkly cartoon music filling the air.

10   In all of my imaginings I was filled with a sense that I would soon become perfect. My mother and father would adore me. I would be beyond reproach. I would never feel the need to sulk, or to clamor for anything.

But sometimes the prodigy in me became impatient. "If you don't hurry up and get me out of here, I'm disappearing for good," it warned. "And then you'll always be nothing."

Every night after dinner my mother and I would sit at the Formica-topped kitchen table. She would present new tests, taking her examples from stories of amazing children that she had read in *Ripley's Believe It or Not* or *Good Housekeeping, Reader's Digest,* or any of a dozen other magazines she kept in a pile in our bathroom. My mother got these magazines from people whose houses she cleaned. And since she cleaned many houses each week, we had a great assortment. She would look through them all, searching for stories about remarkable children.

The first night she brought out a story about a three-year-old boy who knew the capitals of all the states and even of most of the European countries. A teacher was quoted as saying that the little boy could also pronounce the names of the foreign cities correctly. "What's the capital of Finland?" my mother asked me, looking at the story.

All I knew was the capital of California, because Sacramento was the name of the street we lived on in Chinatown. "Nairobi!" I guessed, saying the most foreign word I could think of. She checked to see if that might be one way to pronounce *Helsinki* before showing me the answer.

15   The tests got harder—multiplying numbers in my head, finding the queen of hearts in a deck of cards, trying to stand on my head without using my hands, predicting the daily temperatures in Los Angeles, New York, and London. One night I had to look at a page from the Bible for three minutes and then report everything I could remember. "Now Jehoshaphat had riches and honor in abundance and . . . that's all I remember, Ma," I said.

And after seeing, once again, my mother's disappointed face, something inside me began to die. I hated the tests, the raised hopes and failed expectations. Before going to bed that night I looked in the mirror above the bathroom sink, and when I saw only my face staring back—and understood that it would always be this ordinary face—I began to cry. Such a sad, ugly girl! I made high-pitched noises like a crazed animal, trying to scratch out the face in the mirror.

And then I saw what seemed to be the prodigy side of me—a face I had never seen before. I looked at my reflection, blinking so that I could see more clearly. The girl staring back at me was angry, powerful. She and I were the same. I had new thoughts, willful thoughts—or, rather, thoughts filled with lots of won'ts. I won't let her change me, I promised myself. I won't be what I'm not.

So now when my mother presented her tests, I performed listlessly, my head propped on one arm. I pretended to be bored. And I was. I got so bored that I started counting the bellows of the foghorns out on the bay while my mother drilled me in other areas. The sound was comforting and reminded me of the cow jumping over the moon. And the next day I played a game with myself, seeing if my mother would give up on me before eight bellows. After a while I usually counted only one bellow, maybe two at most. At last she was beginning to give up hope.

Two or three months went by without any mention of my being a prodigy. And then one day my mother was watching the *Ed Sullivan Show* on TV. The TV was old and the sound kept shorting out. Every time my mother got halfway up from the sofa to adjust the set, the sound would come back on and Sullivan would be talking. As soon as she sat down, Sullivan would go silent again. She got up—the TV broke into loud piano music. She sat down—silence. Up and down, back and forth, quiet and loud. It was like a stiff, embraceless dance between her and the TV set. Finally, she stood by the set with her hand on the sound dial.

20   She seemed entranced by the music, a frenzied little piano piece with a mesmerizing quality, which alternated between quick, playful passages and teasing, lilting ones.

"*Ni kan,*" my mother said, calling me over with hurried hand gestures. "Look here."

I could see why my mother was fascinated by the music. It was being pounded out by a little Chinese girl, about nine years old, with a Peter Pan haircut. The girl had the sauciness of a Shirley Temple. She was proudly modest, like a proper Chinese child. And she also did a fancy sweep of a curtsy, so that the fluffy skirt of her white dress cascaded to the floor like the petals of a large carnation.

In spite of these warning signs, I wasn't worried. Our family had no piano and we couldn't afford to buy one, let alone reams of sheet music and piano lessons. So I could be generous in my comments when my mother bad-mouthed the little girl on TV.

"Play note right, but doesn't sound good!" my mother complained. "No singing sound."

25   "What are you picking on her for?" I said carelessly. "She's pretty good. Maybe she's not the best, but she's trying hard." I knew almost immediately that I would be sorry I had said that.

"Just like you," she said. "Not the best. Because you not trying." She gave a little huff as she let go of the sound dial and sat down on the sofa.

The little Chinese girl sat down also, to play an encore of "Anitra's Tanz," by Grieg.[1] I remember the song, because later on I had to learn how to play it.

Three days after watching the *Ed Sullivan Show* my mother told me what my schedule would be for piano lessons and piano practice. She had talked to Mr. Chong, who lived on the first floor of our apartment building. Mr. Chong was a retired piano teacher, and my mother had traded housecleaning services for weekly lessons and a piano for me to practice on every day, two hours a day, from four until six.

When my mother told me this, I felt as though I had been sent to hell. I whined, and then kicked my foot a little when I couldn't stand it anymore.

30   "Why don't you like me the way I am?" I cried. "I'm *not* a genius! I can't play the piano. And even if I could, I wouldn't go on TV if you paid me a million dollars!"

My mother slapped me. "Who ask you to be genius?" she shouted. "Only ask you be your best. For you sake. You think I want you to be genius? Hnnh! What for! Who ask you!"

"So ungrateful," I heard her mutter in Chinese. "If she had as much talent as she has temper, she'd be famous now."

Mr. Chong, whom I secretly nicknamed Old Chong, was very strange, always tapping his fingers to the silent music of an invisible orchestra. He looked ancient in my eyes. He had lost most of the hair on the top of his head, and he wore thick glasses and had eyes that always looked tired. But he must have been younger than I thought, since he lived with his mother and was not yet married.

I met Old Lady Chong once, and that was enough. She had a peculiar smell, like a baby that had done something in its pants, and her fingers felt like a dead person's, like an old peach I once found in the back of the refrigerator; its skin just slid off the flesh when I picked it up.

35   I soon found out why Old Chong had retired from teaching piano. He was deaf. "Like Beethoven!" he shouted to me. "We're both listening only in our head!" And he would start to conduct his frantic silent sonatas.

Our lessons went like this. He would open the book and point to different things, explaining their purpose: "Key! Treble! Bass! No sharps or flats! So this is C major! Listen now and play after me!"

And then he would play the C scale a few times, a simple chord, and then, as if inspired by an old unreachable itch, he would gradually add more notes and running trills and a pounding bass until the music was really something quite grand.

I would play after him, the simple scale, the simple chord, and then just play some nonsense that sounded like a cat running up and down on top of

---

[1] A section from the incidental music that Edvard Grieg (1843–1907) wrote for *Peer Gynt,* a play by Henrik Ibsen

garbage cans. Old Chong would smile and applaud and say, "Very good! But now you must learn to keep time!"

So that's how I discovered that Old Chong's eyes were too slow to keep up with the wrong notes I was playing. He went through the motions in half time. To help me keep rhythm, he stood behind me and pushed down on my right shoulder for every beat. He balanced pennies on top of my wrists so that I would keep them still as I slowly played scales and arpeggios. He had me curve my hand around an apple and keep that shape when playing chords. He marched stiffly to show me how to make each finger dance up and down, staccato, like an obedient little soldier.

40   He taught me all these things, and that was how I also learned I could be lazy and get away with mistakes, lots of mistakes. If I hit the wrong notes because I hadn't practiced enough, I never corrected myself. I just kept playing in rhythm. And Old Chong kept conducting his own private reverie.

So maybe I never really gave myself a fair chance. I did pick up the basics pretty quickly, and I might have become a good pianist at that young age. But I was so determined not to try, not to be anybody different, that I learned to play only the most ear-splitting preludes, the most discordant hymns.

Over the next year I practiced like this, dutifully in my own way. And then one day I heard my mother and her friend Lindo Jong both talking in a loud, bragging tone of voice so that others could hear. It was after church, and I was leaning against a brick wall, wearing a dress with stiff white petticoats. Auntie Lindo's daughter, Waverly, who was my age, was standing farther down the wall, about five feet away. We had grown up together and shared all the closeness of two sisters, squabbling over crayons and dolls. In other words, for the most part, we hated each other. I thought she was snotty. Waverly Jong had gained a certain amount of fame as "Chinatown's Littlest Chinese Chess Champion."

"She bring home too many trophy," Auntie Lindo lamented that Sunday. "All day she play chess. All day I have no time do nothing but dust off her winnings." She threw a scolding look at Waverly, who pretended not to see her.

"You lucky you don't have this problem," Auntie Lindo said with a sigh to my mother.

45   And my mother squared her shoulders and bragged: "Our problem worser than yours. If we ask Jing-mei wash dish, she hear nothing but music. It's like you can't stop this natural talent."

And right then I was determined to put a stop to her foolish pride.

A few weeks later Old Chong and my mother conspired to have me play in a talent show that was to be held in the church hall. By then my parents had saved up enough to buy me a secondhand piano, a black Wurlitzer spinet with a scarred bench. It was the showpiece of our living room.

For the talent show I was to play a piece called "Pleading Child," from Schumann's *Scenes From Childhood.*[2] It was a simple, moody piece that

[2] Piano work by Robert Schumann (1810-56) with twelve titled sections and an epilogue

sounded more difficult than it was. I was supposed to memorize the whole thing. But I dawdled over it, playing a few bars and then cheating, looking up to see what notes followed. I never really listened to what I was playing. I daydreamed about being somewhere else, about being someone else.

The part I liked to practice best was the fancy curtsy: right foot out, touch the rose on the carpet with a pointed foot, sweep to the side, bend left leg, look up, and smile.

50   My parents invited all the couples from their social club to witness my debut. Auntie Lindo and Uncle Tin were there. Waverly and her two older brothers had also come. The first two rows were filled with children either younger or older than I was. The littlest ones got to go first. They recited simple nursery rhymes, squawked out tunes on miniature violins, and twirled hula hoops in pink ballet tutus, and when they bowed or curtsied, the audience would sigh in unison, "*Awww,*" and then clap enthusiastically.

When my turn came, I was very confident. I remember my childish excitement. It was as if I knew, without a doubt, that the prodigy side of me really did exist. I had no fear whatsoever, no nervousness. I remember thinking, This is it! This is it! I looked out over the audience, at my mother's blank face, my father's yawn, Auntie Lindo's stiff-lipped smile, Waverly's sulky expression. I had on a white dress, layered with sheets of lace, and a pink bow in my Peter Pan haircut. As I sat down, I envisioned people jumping to their feet and Ed Sullivan rushing up to introduce me to everyone on TV.

And I started to play. Everything was so beautiful. I was so caught up in how lovely I looked that I wasn't worried about how I would sound. So I was surprised when I hit the first wrong note. And then I hit another, and another. A chill started at the top of my head and began to trickle down. Yet I couldn't stop playing, as though my hands were bewitched. I kept thinking my fingers would adjust themselves back, like a train switching to the right track. I played this strange jumble through to the end, the sour notes staying with me all the way.

When I stood up, I discovered my legs were shaking. Maybe I had just been nervous, and the audience, like Old Chong, had seen me go through the right motions and had not heard anything wrong at all. I swept my right foot out, went down on my knee, looked up, and smiled. The room was quiet, except for Old Chong, who was beaming and shouting, "Bravo! Bravo! Well done!" But then I saw my mother's face, her stricken face. The audience clapped weakly, and as I walked back to my chair, with my whole face quivering as I tried not to cry, I heard a little boy whisper loudly to his mother, "That was awful," and the mother whispered, "Well, she certainly tried."

And now I realized how many people were in the audience—the whole world, it seemed. I was aware of eyes burning into my back. I felt the shame of my mother and father as they sat stiffly through the rest of the show.

55   We could have escaped during intermission. Pride and some strange sense of honor must have anchored my parents to their chairs. And so we watched it all: The eighteen-year-old boy with a fake moustache who did a magic show and juggled flaming hoops while riding a unicycle. The breasted girl with white makeup who sang an aria from *Madame Butterfly*

and got an honorable mention. And the eleven-year-old boy who won first prize playing a tricky violin song that sounded like a busy bee.

After the show the Hsus, the Jongs, and the St. Clairs, from the Joy Luck Club, came up to my mother and father.

"Lots of talented kids," Auntie Lindo said vaguely, smiling broadly.

"That was somethin' else," my father said, and I wondered if he was referring to me in a humorous way, or whether he even remembered what I had done.

Waverly looked at me and shrugged her shoulders. "You aren't a genius like me," she said matter-of-factly. And if I hadn't felt so bad, I would have pulled her braids and punched her stomach.

60   But my mother's expression was what devastated me: a quiet, blank look that said she had lost everything. I felt the same way, and everybody seemed now to be coming up, like gawkers at the scene of an accident, to see what parts were actually missing.

When we got on the bus to go home, my father was humming the busy-bee tune and my mother was silent. I kept thinking she wanted to wait until we got home before shouting at me. But when my father unlocked the door to our apartment, my mother walked in and went straight to the back, into the bedroom. No accusations. No blame. And in a way, I felt disappointed. I had been waiting for her to start shouting, so that I could shout back and cry and blame her for all my misery.

I had assumed that my talent-show fiasco meant that I would never have to play the piano again. But two days later, after school, my mother came out of the kitchen and saw me watching TV.

"Four clock," she reminded me, as if it were any other day. I was stunned, as though she were asking me to go through the talent-show torture again. I planted myself more squarely in front of the TV.

"Turn off TV," she called from the kitchen five minutes later.

65   I didn't budge. And then I decided. I didn't have to do what my mother said anymore. I wasn't her slave. This wasn't China. I had listened to her before, and look what happened. She was the stupid one.

She came out of the kitchen and stood in the arched entryway of the living room. "Four clock," she said once again, louder.

"I'm not going to play anymore," I said nonchalantly. "Why should I? I'm not a genius."

She stood in front of the TV. I saw that her chest was heaving up and down in an angry way.

"No!" I said, and I now felt stronger, as if my true self had finally emerged. So this was what had been inside me all along.

70   "No! I won't!" I screamed.

She snapped off the TV, yanked me by the arm and pulled me off the floor. She was frighteningly strong, half pulling, half carrying me toward the piano and kicked the throw rugs under my feet. She lifted me up and onto the hard bench. I was sobbing by now, looking at her bitterly. Her chest was heaving even more and her mouth was open, smiling crazily as if she were pleased that I was crying.

"You want me to be someone that I'm not!" I sobbed. "I'll never be the kind of daughter you want me to be!"

"Only two kinds of daughters," she shouted in Chinese. "Those who are obedient and those who follow their own mind! Only one kind of daughter can live in this house. Obedient daughter!"

"Then I wish I weren't your daughter. I wish you weren't my mother," I shouted. As I said these things I got scared. It felt like worms and toads and slimy things crawling out of my chest, but it also felt good, that this awful side of me had surfaced, at last.

75   "Too late change this," my mother said shrilly.

And I could sense her anger rising to its breaking point. I wanted to see it spill over. And that's when I remembered the babies she had lost in China, the ones we never talked about. "Then I wish I'd never been born!" I shouted. "I wish I were dead! Like them."

It was as if I had said magic words. Alakazam!—her face went blank, her mouth closed, her arms went slack, and she backed out of the room, stunned, as if she were blowing away like a small brown leaf, thin, brittle, lifeless.

It was not the only disappointment my mother felt in me. In the years that followed, I failed her many times, each time asserting my will, my right to fall short of expectations. I didn't get straight As. I didn't become class president. I didn't get into Stanford. I dropped out of college.

Unlike my mother, I did not believe I could be anything I wanted to be. I could only be me.

80   And for all those years we never talked about the disaster at the recital or my terrible declarations afterward at the piano bench. Neither of us talked about it again, as if it were a betrayal that was now unspeakable. So I never found a way to ask her why she had hoped for something so large that failure was inevitable.

And even worse, I never asked her about what frightened me the most: Why had she given up hope? For after our struggle at the piano, she never mentioned my playing again. The lessons stopped. The lid to the piano was closed, shutting out the dust, my misery, and her dreams.

So she surprised me. A few years ago she offered to give me the piano, for my thirtieth birthday. I had not played in all those years. I saw the offer as a sign of forgiveness, a tremendous burden removed.

"Are you sure?" I asked shyly. "I mean, won't you and Dad miss it?"

"No, this your piano," she said firmly. "Always your piano. You only one can play."

85   "Well, I probably can't play anymore," I said. "It's been years."

"You pick up fast," my mother said, as if she knew this was certain. "You have natural talent. You could be genius if you want to."

"No, I couldn't."

"You just not trying," my mother said. And she was neither angry nor sad. She said it as if announcing a fact that could never be disproved. "Take it," she said.

But I didn't at first. It was enough that she had offered it to me. And after that, every time I saw it in my parents' living room, standing in front of the bay window, it made me feel proud, as if it were a shiny trophy that I had won back.

90   Last week I sent a tuner over to my parents' apartment and had the piano reconditioned, for purely sentimental reasons. My mother had died a few months before, and I had been getting things in order for my father, a little bit at a time. I put the jewelry in special silk pouches. The sweaters she had knitted in yellow, pink, bright orange—all the colors I hated—I put in moth-proof boxes. I found some old Chinese silk dresses, the kind with little slits up the sides. I rubbed the old silk against my skin, and then wrapped them in tissue and decided to take them home with me.

After I had the piano tuned, I opened the lid and touched the keys. It sounded even richer than I remembered. Really, it was a very good piano. Inside the bench were the same exercise notes with handwritten scales, the same secondhand music books with their covers held together with yellow tape.

I opened up the Schumann book to the dark little piece I had played at the recital. It was on the left-hand page, "Pleading Child." It looked more diffi-cult than I remembered. I played a few bars, surprised at how easily the notes came back to me.

And for the first time, or so it seemed, I noticed the piece on the right-hand side. It was called "Perfectly Contented." I tried to play this one as well. It had a lighter melody but with the same flowing rhythm and turned out to be quiet easy. "Pleading Child" was shorter but slower; "Perfectly Con-tented" was longer but faster. And after I had played them both a few times, I realized they were two halves of the same song.

Alice Walker

Alice Walker (1944–   ) is a poet and fiction writer, born in Georgia, who went to college at Sarah Lawrence and later taught at Wellesley and Yale. Her best-known work is the novel *The Color Purple* (1982), which won the Pulitzer Prize in 1983. Her poems are collected in *Revolutionary Petunias* (1973) and *"Goodnight, Willie Lee, I'll See You in the Morning"* (1979). She published her essays in *In Search of Our Mothers' Gardens* (1983), and she has made two collections of short stories: *In Love and Trouble* (1973) and *You Can't Keep a Good Woman Down* (1981).

Nineteen Fifty-Five   (1981)

1955

The car is a brandnew red Thunderbird convertible, and it's passed the house more than once. It slows down real slow now, and stops at the curb. An older gentleman dressed like a Baptist deacon gets out on the side near the house, and a young fellow who looks about sixteen gets out on the driver's side. They are white, and I wonder what in the world they doing in this neighborhood.

Well, I say to J. T., put your shirt on, anyway, and let me clean these glasses offa the table.

We had been watching the ballgame on TV. I wasn't actually watching, I was sort of daydreaming, with my foots up in J. T.'s lap.

I seen 'em coming on up the walk, brisk, like they coming to sell something, and then they rung the bell, and J. T. declined to put on a shirt but instead disappeared into the bedroom where the other television is. I turned down the one in the living room; I figured I'd be rid of these two double quick and J. T. could come back out again.

5   Are you Gracie Mae Still? asked the old guy, when I opened the door and put my hand on the lock inside the screen.

And I don't need to buy a thing, said I.

What makes you think we're sellin'? he asks, in that hearty Southern way that makes my eyeballs ache.

Well, one way or another and they're inside the house and the first thing the young fellow does is raise the TV a couple of decibels. He's about five feet nine, sort of womanish looking, with real dark white skin and a red pouting mouth. His hair is black and curly and he looks like a Loosianna creole.

About one of your songs, says the deacon. He is maybe sixty, with white hair and beard, white silk shirt, black linen suit, black tie and black shoes. His cold gray eyes look like they're sweating.

10   One of my songs?

Traynor here just *loves* your songs. Don't you, Traynor? He nudges Traynor with his elbow. Traynor blinks, says something I can't catch in a pitch I don't register.

The boy learned to sing and dance livin' round you people out in the country. Practically cut his teeth on you.

Traynor looks up at me and bites his thumbnail.

I laugh.

15   Well, one way or another they leave with my agreement that they can record one of my songs. The deacon writes me a check for five hundred dollars, the boy grunts his awareness of the transaction, and I am laughing all over myself by the time I rejoin J. T.

Just as I am snuggling down beside him though I hear the front door bell going off again.

Forgit his hat? asks J. T.

I hope not, I say.

The deacon stands there leaning on the door frame and once again I'm thinking of those sweaty-looking eyeballs of his. I wonder if sweat makes your eyeballs pink because his are sure pink. Pink and gray and it strikes me that nobody I'd care to know is behind them.

20   I forgot one little thing, he says pleasantly. I forgot to tell you Traynor and I would like to buy up all of those records you made of the song. I tell you we sure do love it.

Well, love it or not, I'm not so stupid as to let them do that without making 'em pay. So I says, Well, that's gonna cost you. Because, really, that song never did sell all that good, so I was glad they was going to buy it up. But on the other hand, them two listening to my song by themselves, and nobody else getting to hear me sing it, give me a pause.

Well, one way or another the deacon showed me where I would come out ahead on any deal he had proposed so far. Didn't I give you five hundred dollars? he asked. What white man—and don't even need to mention colored— would give you more? We buy up all your records of that particular song: first, you git royalties. Let me ask you, how much you sell that song for in the first place? Fifty dollars? A hundred, I say. And no royalties from it yet, right? Right. Well, when we buy up all of them records you gonna git royalties. And that's gonna make all them race record shops sit up and take notice of Gracie Mae Still. And they gonna push all them other records of yourn they got. And you no doubt will become one of the big name colored recording artists. And then we can offer you another five hundred dollars for letting us do all this for you. And by God you'll be sittin' pretty! You can go out and buy you the kind of outfit a star should have. Plenty sequins and yards of red satin.

I had done unlocked the screen when I saw I could get some more money out of him. Now I held it wide open while he squeezed through the opening between me and the door. He whipped out another piece of paper and I signed it.

He sort of trotted out to the car and slid in beside Traynor, whose head was back against the seat. They swung around in a u-turn in front of the house and then they was gone.

25   J. T. was putting his shirt on when I got back to the bedroom. Yankees beat the Orioles 10–6, he said. I believe I'll drive out to Paschal's pond and go fishing. Wanta go?

While I was putting on my pants J. T. was holding the two checks.

I'm real proud of a woman that can make cash money without leavin' home, he said. And I said *Umph*. Because we met on the road with me singing in first one little low-life jook after another, making ten dollars a night for myself if I was lucky, and sometimes bringin' home nothing but my life. And J. T. just loved them times. The way I was fast and flashy and always on the go from one time to another. He loved the way my singin' made the dirt farmers cry like babies and the womens shout Honey, hush! But that's mens. They loves any style to which you can get 'em accustomed.

1956

My little grandbaby called me one night on the phone: Little Mama, Little Mama, there's a white man on the television singing one of your songs! Turn on channel 5.

Lord, if it wasn't Traynor. Still looking half asleep from the neck up, but kind of awake in a nasty way from the waist down. He wasn't doing too bad with my song either, but it wasn't just the song the people in the audience was screeching and screaming over, it was that nasty little jerk he was doing from the waist down.

30   Well, Lord have mercy, I said, listening to him. If I'da closed my eyes, it could have been me. He had followed every turning of my voice, side streets, avenues, red lights, train crossing and all. It give me a chill.

Everywhere I went I heard Traynor singing my song, and all the little white girls just eating it up. I never had so many ponytails switched across my line of vision in my life. They was so *proud*. He was a *genius*.

Well, all that year I was trying to lose weight anyway and that and high blood pressure and sugar kept me pretty well occupied. Traynor had made a smash from a song of mine, I still had seven hundred dollars of the original one thousand dollars in the bank, and I felt if I could just bring my weight down, life would be sweet.

1957

I lost ten pounds in 1956. That's what I give myself for Christmas. And J. T. and me and the children and their friends and grandkids of all description had just finished dinner—over which I had put on nine and a half of my lost ten—when who should appear at the front door but Traynor. Little Mama, Little Mama! It's that white man who sings ———— ———— ————. The children didn't call it my song anymore. Nobody did. It was funny how that happened. Traynor and the deacon had bought up all my records, true, but on his record he had put "written by Gracie Mae Still." But that was just another name on the label, like "produced by Apex Records."

On the TV he was inclined to dress like the deacon told him. But now he looked presentable.

35   Merry Christmas, said he.

And same to you, Son.

I don't know why I called him Son. Well, one way or another they're all our sons. The only requirement is that they be younger than us. But then again, Traynor seemed to be aging by the minute.

You looks tired, I said. Come on in and have a glass of Christmas cheer.

J. T. ain't never in his life been able to act decent to a white man he wasn't working for, but he poured Traynor a glass of bourbon and water, then he took all the children and grandkids and friends and whatnot out to the den. After while I heard Traynor's voice singing the song, coming from the stereo console. It was just the kind of Christmas present my kids would consider cute.

40   I looked at Traynor, complicit. But he looked like it was the last thing in the world he wanted to hear. His head was pitched forward over his lap, his hands holding his glass and his elbows on his knees.

I done sung that song seem like a millions times this year, he said. I sung it on the Grand Ole Opry, I sung it on the Ed Sullivan show. I sung it on Mike Douglas, I sung it at the Cotton Bowl, the Orange Bowl. I sung it at Festivals. I sung it at Fairs. I sung it overseas in Rome, Italy, and once in a submarine *underseas.* I've sung it and sung it, and I'm making forty thousand dollars a day offa it, and you know what, I don't have the faintest notion what that song means.

Whatchumean, what do it mean? It mean what it says. All I could think was: These suckers is making forty thousand a *day* offa my song and now they gonna come back and try to swindle me out of the original thousand.

It's just a song, I said. Cagey. When you fool around with a lot of no count mens you sing a bunch of 'em. I shrugged.

Oh, he said. Well. He started brightening up. I just come by to tell you I think you are a great singer.

45   He didn't blush, saying that. Just said it straight out.

And I brought you a little Christmas present too. Now you take this little box and you hold it until I drive off. Then you take it outside under that first streetlight back up the street aways in front of that green house. Then you open the box and see . . . Well, just *see.*

What had come over this boy, I wondered, holding the box. I looked out the window in time to see another white man come up and get in the car with him and then two more cars full of white mens start out behind him. They was all in long black cars that looked like a funeral procession.

Little Mama, Little Mama, what is it? One of my grandkids come running up and started pulling at the box. It was wrapped in gay Christmas paper— the thick, rich kind that it's hard to picture folks making just to throw away.

J. T. and the rest of the crowd followed me out the house, up the street to the streetlight and in front of the green house. Nothing was there but somebody's gold-grilled white Cadillac. Brandnew and most distracting. We got to looking at it so till I almost forgot the little box in my hand. While the others were busy making 'miration I carefully took off the paper and ribbon and folded them up and put them in my pants pocket. What should I see but a pair of genuine solid gold caddy keys.

50   Dangling the keys in front of everybody's nose, I unlocked the caddy, motioned for J. T. to git in on the other side, and us didn't come back home for two days.

1960

Well, the boy was sure nuff famous by now. He was still a mite shy of twenty but already they was calling him the Emperor of Rock and Roll.

Then what should happen but the draft.

Well, says J. T. There goes all this Emperor of Rock and Roll business.

But even in the army the womens was on him like white on rice. We watched it on the News.

55   *Dear Gracie Mae* [he wrote from Germany],

How you? Fine I hope as this leaves me doing real well. Before I come in the army I was gaining a lot of weight and gitting jittery from making all them dumb movies. But now I exercise and eat right and get plenty of rest. I'm more awake than I been in ten years.

I wonder if you are writing any more songs?

Sincerely,
Traynor

I wrote him back:

Dear Son,

We is all fine in the Lord's good grace and hope this finds you the same. J. T. and me be out all times of the day and night in that car you give me—which you know you didn't have to do. Oh, and I do appreciate the mink and the new self-cleaning oven. But if you send anymore stuff to eat from Germany I'm going to have to open up a store in the neighborhood just to get rid of it. Really, we have more than enough of everything. The Lord is good to us and we don't know Want.

Glad to here you is well and gitting your right rest. There ain't nothing like exercising to help that along. J. T. and me work some part of every day that we don't go fishing in the garden.

Well, so long Soldier.

Sincerely,
Gracie Mae

He wrote:

Dear Gracie Mae,

I hope you and J. T. like that automatic power tiller I had one of the stores back home send you. I went through a mountain of catalogs looking for it—I wanted something that even a woman could use.

I've been thinking about writing some songs of my own but every time I finish one it don't seem to be about nothing I've actually lived myself. My agent keeps sending me other people's songs but they just sound mooney. I can hardly git through 'em without gagging.

Everybody still loves that song of yours. They ask me all the time what do I think it means, really. I mean, they want to know just what I want to know. Where out of your life did it come from?

Sincerely,
Traynor

1968

I didn't see the boy for seven years. No. Eight. Because just about everybody was dead when I saw him again. Malcolm X, King, the president and his brother, and even J. T. J. T. died of a head cold. It just settled in his head like a block of ice, he said, and nothing we did moved it until one day he just leaned out the bed and died.

His good friend Horace helped me put him away, and then about a year later Horace and me started going together. We was sitting out on the front porch swing one summer night, dusk-dark, and I saw this great procession of lights winding to a stop.

60   Holy Toledo! said Horace. (He's got a real sexy voice like Ray Charles.) Look *at* it. He meant the long line of flashy cars and the white men in white summer suits jumping out on the drivers' sides and standing at attention. With wings they could pass for angels, with hoods they could be the Klan.

Traynor comes waddling up the walk.

And suddenly I know what it is he could pass for. An Arab like the ones you see in storybooks. Plump and soft and with never a care about weight. Because with so much money, who cares? Traynor is almost dressed like someone from a storybook too. He has on, I swear, about ten necklaces. Two sets of bracelets on his arms, at least one ring on every finger, and some kind of shining buckles on his shoes, so that when he walks you get quite a few twinkling lights.

Gracie Mae, he says, coming up to give me a hug. J. T.

I explain that J. T. passed. That this is Horace.

65   Horace, he says, puzzled but polite, sort of rocking back on his heels, Horace.

That's it for Horace. He goes in the house and don't come back.

Looks like you and me is gained a few, I say.

He laughs. The first time I ever heard him laugh. It don't sound much like a laugh and I can't swear that it's better than no laugh a'tall.

He's gitting fat for sure, but he's still slim compared to me. I'll never see three hundred pounds again and I've just about said (excuse me) fuck it. I got to thinking about it one day an' I thought: aside from the fact that they say it's unhealthy, my fat ain't never been no trouble. Mens always have loved me. My kids ain't never complained. Plus they's fat. And fat like I is I looks distinguished. You see me coming and know somebody's *there*.

70   Gracie Mae, he says, I've come with a personal invitation to you to my house tomorrow for dinner. He laughed. What did it sound like? I couldn't

place it. See them men out there? he asked me. I'm sick and tired of eating with them. They don't never have nothing to talk about. That's why I eat so much. But if you come to dinner tomorrow we can talk about the old days. You can tell me about that farm I bought you.

I sold it, I said.

You did?

Yeah, I said, I did. Just cause I said I liked to exercise by working in a garden didn't mean I wanted five hundred acres! Anyhow, I'm a city girl now. Raised in the country it's true. Dirt poor—the whole bit—but that's all behind me now.

Oh well, he said, I didn't mean to offend you.

75   We sat a few minutes listening to the crickets.

Then he said: You wrote that song while you was still on the farm, didn't you, or was it right after you left?

You had somebody spying on me? I asked.

You and Bessie Smith got into a fight over it once, he said.

You *is* been spying on me!

80   But I don't know what the fight was about, he said. Just like I don't know what happened to your second husband. Your first one died in the Texas electric chair. Did you know that? Your third one beat you up, stole your touring costumes and your car and retired with a chorine to Tuskegee. He laughed. He's still there.

I had been mad, but suddenly I calmed down. Traynor was talking very dreamily. It was dark but seems like I could tell his eyes weren't right. It was like some*thing* was sitting there talking to me but not necessarily with a person behind it.

You gave up on marrying and seem happier for it. He laughed again. I married but it never went like it was supposed to. I never could squeeze any of my own life either into it or out of it. It was like singing somebody else's record. I copied the way it was sposed to be *exactly* but I never had a clue what marriage meant.

I bought her a diamond ring big as your fist. I bought her clothes. I built her a mansion. But right away she didn't want the boys to stay there. Said they smoked up the bottom floor. Hell, there were *five* floors.

No need to grieve, I said. No need to. Plenty more where she comes from.

85   He perked up. That's part of what that song means, ain't it? No need to grieve. Whatever it is, there's plenty more down the line.

I never really believed that way back when I wrote that song, I said. It was all bluffing then. The trick is to live long enough to put your young bluffs to use. Now if I was to sing that song today I'd tear it up. 'Cause I done lived long enough to know it's *true*. Them words could hold me up.

I ain't lived that long, he said.

Look like you on your way, I said. I don't know why, but the boy seemed to need some encouraging. And I don't know, seem like one way or another you talk to rich white folks and you end up reassuring *them*. But what the hell, by now I feel something for the boy. I wouldn't be in his bed all alone in the middle of the night for nothing. Couldn't be nothing worse than being famous the world over for something you don't even understand. That's what I tried to tell Bessie. She wanted that same song. Overheard me practicing it one day, said, with her hands on her hips: Gracie Mae, I'ma sing your song tonight. I *likes* it.

Your lips be too swole to sing, I said. She was mean and she was strong, but I trounced her.

90   Ain't you famous enough with your own stuff? I said. Leave mine alone. Later on, she thanked me. By then she was Miss Bessie Smith to the World, and I was still Miss Gracie Mae Nobody from Notasulga.

The next day all these limousines arrived to pick me up. Five cars and twelve bodyguards. Horace picked that morning to start painting the kitchen.

Don't paint the kitchen, fool, I said. The only reason that dumb boy of ours is going to show me his mansion is because he intends to present us with a new house.

What you gonna do with it? he asked me, standing there in his shirtsleeves stirring the paint.

Sell it. Give it to the children. Live in it on weekends. It don't matter what I do. He sure don't care.

95   Horace just stood there shaking his head. Mama you sure looks *good,* he says. Wake me up when you git back.

Fool, I say, and pat my wig in front of the mirror.

The boy's house is something else. First you come to this mountain, and then you commence to drive and drive up this road that's lined with magnolias. Do magnolias grow on mountains? I was wondering. And you come to lakes and you come to ponds and you come to deer and you come up on some sheep. And I figure these two is sposed to represent England and Wales. Or something out of Europe. And you just keeping on coming to stuff. And it's all pretty. Only the man driving my car don't look at nothing but the road. Fool. And then *finally,* after all this time, you begin to go up the driveway. And there's more magnolias—only they're not in such good shape. It's sort of cool up this high and I don't think they're gonna make it. And then I see this building that looks like if it had a name it would be The Tara Hotel. Columns and steps and outdoor chandeliers and rocking chairs. Rocking chairs? Well, and there's the boy on the steps dressed in a dark green satin jacket like you see folks wearing on TV late at night, and he looks sort of like a fat dracula with all that house rising behind him, and standing beside him there's this little white vision of loveliness that he introduces as his wife.

He's nervous when he introduces us and he says to her: This is Gracie Mae Still, I want you to know me. I mean . . . and she gives him a look that would fry meat.

Won't you come in, Gracie Mae, she says, and that's the last I see of her.

100   He fishes around for something to say or do and decides to escort me to the kitchen. We go through the entry and the parlor and the breakfast room and the dining room and the servants' passage and finally get there. The first

thing I notice is that, altogether, there are five stoves. He looks about to introduce me to one.

Wait a minute, I say. Kitchens don't do nothing for me. Let's go sit on the front porch.

Well, we hike back and we sit in the rocking chairs rocking until dinner.

Gracie Mae, he says down the table, taking a piece of fried chicken from the woman standing over him, I got a little surprise for you.

It's a house, ain't it? I ask, spearing a chitlin.

105   You're getting *spoiled,* he says. And the way he says *spoiled* sounds funny. He slurs it. It sounds like his tongue is too thick for his mouth. Just that quick he's finished the chicken and is now eating chitlins *and* a pork chop. *Me* spoiled, I'm thinking.

I already got a house. Horace is right this minute painting the kitchen. I bought that house. My kids feel comfortable in that house.

But this one I bought you is just like mine. Only a little smaller.

I still don't need no house. And anyway who would clean it?

He looks surprised.

110   Really, I think, some peoples advance *so* slowly.

I hadn't thought of that. But what the hell, I'll get you somebody to live in.

I don't want other folks living 'round me. Makes me nervous.

You *don't?* It *do?*

What I want to wake up and see folks I don't even know for?

115   He just sits there downtable staring at me. Some of that feeling is in the song, ain't it? Not the words, the *feeling.* What I want to wake up and see folks I don't even know for? But I see twenty folks a day I don't even know, including my wife.

This food wouldn't be bad to wake up to though, I said. The boy had found the genius of corn bread.

He looked at me real hard. He laughed. Short. They want what you got but they don't want you. They want what I got only it ain't mine. That's what makes 'em so hungry for me when I sing. They getting the flavor of something but they ain't getting the thing itself. They like a pack of hound dogs trying to gobble up a scent.

You talking 'bout your fans?

Right. Right. He says.

120   Don't worry 'bout your fans, I say. They don't know their asses from a hole in the ground. I doubt there's a honest one in the bunch.

That's the point. Dammit, that's the point! He hits the table with his fist. It's so solid it don't even quiver. You need a honest audience! You can't have folks that's just gonna lie right back to you.

Yeah, I say, it was small compared to yours, but I had one. It would have been worth my life to try to sing 'em somebody else's stuff that I didn't know nothing about.

He must have pressed a buzzer under the table. One of his flunkies zombies up.

Git Johnny Carson, he says.

125   On the phone? asks the zombie.

On the phone, says Traynor, what you think I mean, git him offa the front porch? Move your ass.

So two weeks later we's on the Johnny Carson show.

Traynor is all corseted down nice and looks a little bit fat but mostly good. And all the women that grew up on him and my song squeal and squeal. Traynor says: The lady who wrote my first hit record is here with us tonight, and she's agreed to sing it for all of us, just like she sung it forty-five years ago. Ladies and Gentlemen, the great Gracie Mae Still!

Well, I had tried to lose a couple of pounds my own self, but failing that I had me a very big dress made. So I sort of rolls over next to Traynor, who is dwarfted by me, so that when he puts his arm around back of me to try to hug me it looks funny to the audience and they laugh.

130   I can see this pisses him off. But I smile out there at 'em. Imagine squealing for twenty years and not knowing why you're squealing? No more sense of endings and beginnings than hogs.

It don't matter, Son, I say. Don't fret none over me.

I commence to sing. And I sound—wonderful. Being able to sing good ain't all about having a good singing voice a'tall. A good singing voice helps. But when you come up in the Hard Shell Baptist church like I did you understand early that the fellow that sings is the singer. Them that waits for programs and arrangements and letters from home is just good voices occupying body space.

So there I am singing my own song, my own way. And I give it all I got and enjoy every minute of it. When I finish Traynor is standing up clapping and clapping and beaming at first me and then the audience like I'm his mama for true. The audience claps politely for about two seconds.

Traynor looks disgusted.

135   He comes over and tries to hug me again. The audience laughs.

Johnny Carson looks at us like we both weird.

Traynor is mad as hell. He's supposed to sing something called a love ballad. But instead he takes the mike, turns to me and says: Now see if my imitation still holds up. He goes into the same song, *our* song, I think, looking out at his flaky audience. And he sings it just the way he always did. My voice, my tone, my inflection, everything. But he forgets a couple of lines. Even before he's finished the matronly squeals begin.

He sits down next to me looking whipped.

It don't matter, Son, I say, patting his hand. You don't even know those people. Try to make the people you know happy.

140   Is that in the song? he asks.

Maybe. I say.

1977

For a few years I hear from him, then nothing. But trying to lose weight takes all the attention I got to spare. I finally faced up to the fact that my fat is the hurt I don't admit, not even to myself, and that I been trying to bury it from the day I was born. But also when you git real old, to tell the truth, it ain't as pleasant. It gits lumpy and slack. Yuck. So one day I said to Horace, I'ma git this shit offa me.

And he fell in with the program like he always try to do and Lord such a procession of salads and cottage cheese and fruit juice!

One night I dreamed Traynor had split up with his fifteenth wife. He said: *You meet 'em for no reason. You date 'em for no reason. You marry 'em for no reason. I do it all but I swear it's just like somebody else doing it. I feel like I can't remember Life.*

145   The boy's in trouble, I said to Horace.

You've always said that, he said.

I have?

Yeah. You always said he looked asleep. You can't sleep through life if you wants to live it.

You not such a fool after all, I said, pushing myself up with my cane and hobbling over to where he was. Let me sit down on your lap, I said, while this salad I ate takes effect.

150   In the morning we heard Traynor was dead. Some said fat, some said heart, some said alcohol, some said drugs. One of the children called from Detroit. Them dumb fans of his is on a crying rampage, she said. You just ought to turn on the TV.

But I didn't want to see 'em. They was crying and crying and didn't even know what they was crying for. One day this is going to be a pitiful country, I thought.

TO READ A

Poem

To read a poem, we must concentrate on its particular words and on the way its words connect with each other.

When we read a story, we fix our attention on character and plot, conflict and resolution. Some poems use plots and characters, but these elements are secondary to poetry's images, metaphors, tones of voice, and allusions.

When we pay close attention to words, we understand poems and take pleasure in them. For the sake of that ultimate pleasure, most of this section of the book explores the elements, types, and forms of poetry. By collecting many poems by four poets—John Keats, Emily Dickinson, Robert Frost, and Adrienne Rich—we can look at these poets in depth. We then gather a few poems by many poets, for a wider sampling of the poetry of our language.

Before we look into the elements of poetry one at a time, we will discuss poems as a whole, the way "To Read a Story" began with William Faulkner's "A Rose for Emily." Because poems are shorter, we can look at more.

CHAPTER ONE

Good Poems

Robert Frost, "Stopping by Woods on a Snowy Evening"

Here is a detailed reading of a poem by Robert Frost, "Stopping by Woods on a Snowy Evening." A close reading is called an **explication**, which someone has defined as "an explanation with complications." A pure explanation might first paraphrase the poem, turning its lines into words of prose. An explication goes further: it tries to account for the whole poem by attending to its sounds, its minute suggestions of meaning, its shapeliness. No explication will equal the poem itself, but in a good explication we can feel that we have come close to noticing and naming everything in the poem that affects us.

Stopping by Woods on a Snowy Evening   (1923)

Whose woods these are I think I know.
His house is in the village though;
He will not see me stopping here
To watch his woods fill up with snow.

My little horse must think it queer
To stop without a farmhouse near
Between the woods and frozen lake
The darkest evening of the year.

He gives his harness bells a shake
10 To ask if there is some mistake.
The only other sound's the sweep
Of easy wind and downy flake.

The woods are lovely, dark and deep,
But I have promises to keep,
And miles to go before I sleep,
And miles to go before I sleep.

Read this poem aloud, separating the lines with slight pauses but keeping your sense of whole sentences. Different lengths of pause between the lines affect a poem's rhythm. The pause you make at the end of the first line, where Frost ends the sentence with a period, should be longer than the pauses between lines in the second stanza, where there is no punctuation until the end. When we hear a poem or read it aloud, we encounter its body. Unless we feel a poem in our own bodies, we are apt to consider it merely an idea; we are apt to confuse a poem with its paraphrase.

Still, a good way to begin talking about a poem is to paraphrase or summarize it, to see if we are discussing the same poem. (A paraphrase finds different words for each of the poem's phrases. A **summary** is a short, simple report of the plot, like *TV Guide*'s descriptions of television shows.) Once we have paraphrased or summarized the poem, we can talk about its body and its soul. Here, summary is easy: *A man driving a horse-drawn cart or sleigh pauses beside a forest to watch the snow falling on it; the horse seems to want to keep moving, and the man decides he ought to move on, although the scene is pretty, and even inviting.*

Frost used to define poetry as what gets left out in a translation. You might as well say, instead, what gets left out in a summary; there's a gap the size of New Hampshire between Frost's sixteen lines and my forty-four words. But a summary helps at the start of an explication. When you've read a poem two or three times—slowly and quickly, silently and aloud—and when you have arrived at a tentative paraphrase, you are ready to go back to the poem and look at it bit by bit, as if you were taking apart a machine in order to understand how it works.

Start with the title. Sometimes titles give information we need to understand a poem's wholeness. This title, "Stopping by Woods on a Snowy Evening," is a description or label; it tells us what we're going to see, and then gives us the means to see it. This particular title requires little work on the reader's part.

In his first line—"Whose woods these are I think I know"—Frost switches the normal word order, which would have us say something like "I think I know whose woods these are." By moving *woods* to the start of the sentence, Frost gives it more prominence or power. We might say "What *nerve* you've got, heaven only knows!" for a similar emphasis.

In the second line, "His house is in the village though," the last word makes no logical sense; *though* or *although* should make some sort of contradiction or qualification to the statement that *I* know who owns this woodlot. But Frost writes as we usually speak—and *though* qualifies something left out. To understand *though,* we might paraphrase the whole statement, bracketing what is implicit: "I know who owns this land [and I would feel self-conscious if the owner saw me standing and staring into space this way] but he doesn't live out here, and therefore he won't see me pausing to gaze idly." The word *though* implies more than its one syllable would seem able to contain.

At the same time *though* implies something, it rhymes with the word that ends the first line. A rhyme word must feel natural or the poet will seem to have chosen it for the sake of rhyming. Looking to the rest of the stanza, we see that Frost doesn't rhyme the next line with anything nearby but rhymes the fourth line with the first and the second, tying the stanza together. Because we have the word *snowy* in the title, the idea of snow is important to this poem before we start reading it. Then the word *snow* ends a three-line sentence that makes snow the object of our attention. The last two lines of the stanza are a natural, inevitable journey to the culminating word *snow*. As soon as we get there, we realize that this is where we had to go, all the time. This inevitability is underlined by the rhyme, where *know* and *though* build up a sound-expectancy to culminate in *snow*.

Maybe the speaker's self-consciousness is the most important element in the first stanza. (I say "the speaker"—though it feels awkward—because I don't want to say "Robert Frost." *I* in a poem does not necessarily mean the poet.) To sense some embarrassment is to catch the tone of voice.* We all learn to catch the tone of people talking, when we understand the hundreds of small signals that tell us whether the person's tone is ironic or straightforward, conniving or sincere. *Voyeur → sneaking a look at...*

As the stanza ends, we learn something besides the speaker's embarrassment; we learn the motive for stopping: "To watch his woods fill up with snow." Frost's language here is plain, but it could be plainer or flatter still; *I* could have said "to see it snow on his trees" or "to look at the snow falling on his forest." Saying *fill up* contributes to the image* or picture made by the poet; *his woods* becomes a container—empty or partly empty—which *snow* can fill.

As mentioned before, *here* doesn't rhyme with anything around it. If we hold the sound of the word in our ears, however, we are rewarded when we read the first line of the second stanza. We find pleasure in linking with something begun earlier; the experience is similar to the moment in a piece of music when a theme (or a phrase or a chord) returns. Rhyme holds parts of this poem together, linking stanzas more firmly than many poems try to do. The third line of each stanza, unrhymed to the lines near it, rhymes with three of the lines in the stanza following. The first three stanzas together are like groups of four dancers doing the same dance, with one member of each foursome holding hands with the group beyond it.

If it's a dance, it must move to a tune. **Rhythm** is an approximate recurrence or repetition in the pacing of sound; rhythm can be fast or slow, staccato or flowing. **Meter**, which is a measure or count of something, puts its own mark on certain rhythms. "Stopping by Woods" is written in meter, and this meter helps define the rhythm of the poem. If we pronounce *evening* as two syllables, we have, in every line, even-numbered syllables (two, four, six, and eight) that are louder than the odd-numbered syllables. Not all the even syllables are loud, but they are louder than the one, three, five, seven syllables. In *promises, prom-* is louder than the *have* before it, and *-ses* is louder than the *-i-* (just barely louder; you cannot say *prom-*IH-*ses*). This alternation of louder and softer syllables is the meter of the poem. Meter is not the only contributor to differing lengths of pause at lines' ends. A poet can manipulate punctuation

---

meter

* Tone and image as elements of poetry are subjects of later chapters.

to accelerate rhythm or to slow it down. In prose, if we said that we stopped between the woods and a frozen lake, the darkest evening of the year, we would put a comma after *lake*, as I do in this sentence. But Frost uses the line's pause and avoids a comma, which would slow the stanza down more than he wants it slowed. On the other hand, in prose he wouldn't need a comma if he were telling us that he had promises to keep and miles to go before he slept— but here the poet slows his rhythm at the measured ending of the poem, and he puts a comma after *keep*. Notice that Frost manipulates commas only where commas in prose would be optional.

The second stanza, picking up the *here* rhyme, tells us that the *little* horse (*little* sounds affectionate; this person seems to care about his horse's feel-ings) *must think it queer*. Consider the word *must* as we use it in speech. If we know that it's raining, we say "It's raining"; if we only think so—because of forecasts or the distant sound of falling water—we say "It *must* be raining." We claim that something must be true only if we don't know it for certain. When Frost writes "My little horse must think it queer," he uses the doubtful *must;* he knows a human cannot mindread his horse. The speaker in the poem at-tributes doubts to his horse because he himself believes it weird or eccentric to stop one's horse for no good reason, out in the middle of nowhere, to watch snow falling in the darkness. This man's uneasiness shows in his self-mockery: even his horse *must* think he's crazy.

As this stanza continues, ostensibly telling what the horse must think queer, the poet gives us more information, in images that carry feelings on their backs. The road, we learn, passes between *the woods*—which are like a container filled with snow—and the *frozen lake*. Sometimes an image in-forms us by what it omits. *Frozen* adds cold to the poem (an image records not just pictures but *any* experience of the senses, like cold). The line also increases the solitude of the scene: the lane runs between wood and lake only; no houses or factories here, no inns or filling stations; just these cold and natural things, on "The darkest evening of the year."

This last detail (if we read clearly enough, looking for the implications of words) is strange if we take it literally—and when we read a poem, we ought to try at first to take the wording literally. We cannot conclude that this man has determined scientifically, using some instrument that measures light, that this clouded, moonless, starless night contains fewer candlepower units than any other night in the preceding twelve months. We could take it, in a roundabout way, that tonight is December 22, the longest night of the year, and insist with some logic that the length of its darkness aggregates more darkness and that therefore this is indeed the "darkest evening of the year." But poetry usually works by common sense, not on riddles that ingenuity must solve. It's just too complicated to explain this line as telling us that tonight is the winter solstice. Probably we do best to take the line as an expressive exaggeration, the way people always talk about the weather: "There's enough snow out there to bury the barn." "It hasn't rained so much since Noah." "It's the darkest night of the whole damned year."

In the third stanza, the little horse does what horses do; he shudders or shakes, standing still in the cold night. To the driver, who still feels foolish pausing to gaze at snow in the woods, the horse's jingling harness bells seem like the horse's reproach. The jingling is another image—so far we've had images of sight (*to watch*), of touch (*frozen lake*), and of sound (*bells*)— and now the sound images multiply: "the sweep / Of easy wind and downy flake." Notice that images often appeal to more than one sense. If *frozen* is an image of cold in *frozen lake,* it is also an image of sight and touch, because we know what a frozen lake looks like and feels like. And *the sweep* is a swooshing sound, but it's also (at least distantly) a visual broom moving.

The phrase *easy wind* is not an image at all. We could not draw (or play on an instrument, or hear) an easy wind as opposed to a difficult wind or an uneasy one. Does it mean anything at all to call the wind easy? First, let us paraphrase, using alternative words. Perhaps this wind is light and gentle— *easy* as "full of ease," like the softness of *downy* that *easy* is parallel to. If this paraphrase is accurate, someone might ask why the poet doesn't call the wind "light and gentle" or, to keep line length the same, just "gentle." We answer that *gentle* is not the same as *easy* and *easy* does it better; the para-phrase is only intellectual, and *easy* says it better because of its sound. It is a long and luxuriant word. That long *e* stretches itself out like a big cat on a sofa, and then the *z*-sound (spelled with an *s*) slinks sensuously and stretches again into the shorter *e*-sound of the *y*. These two syllables take longer to say than half a line elsewhere in the poem.

I would not argue that, in this word, "sound imitates sense" the way the sound of *drop* or *squish* is similar to the meanings of those words. (When sound imitates sense, we call it **onomatopoeia**.) I am not sure that a light wind speaks in long *e*s or in *z*s. But I am sure that the grateful tongue delights in this word, picking up the long *e* of *sweep* and looking ahead to the long *e* that ends *downy,* and that these words, giving us in our minds the qualities of the scene, at the same time give us a sound-pleasure. We have two pleasures at once, one in our minds as we assent to a description, the other in our mouths as the poet arranges vowels and consonants, much as a chef arranges flavors for our pleasure.

We have concentrated on *easy. Downy* gives pleasure also. The *y* picks up the line's earlier *e* sound; the *ow* picks up a vowel from *sounds* in the line before. (This repetition of vowel sounds is called **assonance**.) If you don't know the word *downy,* look it up. (Always look up words you are not certain of.) *Down* means a good many things; among others it means goosefeathers, soft and white, and *downy* is an adjective made from the noun *down.* Be-cause down is soft (touch) and white (vision), it gives us two kinds of image at once, and perhaps also distantly gives us an image of the snow as a great white bird. It is also a rural image, connected with barnyard and countryside. If Frost had tried comparing the whiteness of the snow to the whiteness of a sailboat's sails, his comparison would have gone far from the poem's world. Finally, the word *down* works its power on us for at least one more reason: it reminds us of the direction in which, relentlessly, snow must fall.

By the end of the third stanza, the poem has erected a dramatic conflict, like a story or a play. The conflict lives in the mind of the speaker, who attributes one side of his feeling to his horse; of course, it is the speaker who thinks it queer to pause where he pauses; at the same time, it is the speaker who stops to gaze into the *lovely* beauty of the wood, exercising the other side of his feeling. He is "of two minds about it," in the old expression. In the final stanza, mind 1 writes the first line and mind 2 answers with the second, third, and fourth; the mind with the most lines has the last word.

In our daily lives, we are often ambivalent—of two minds, and sometimes of three or four—about what we do. Often, two desires are in conflict; the woods are lovely, but I have duties; the scoop of ice cream will taste good, but I will get fat; I want to see this movie, but I want to pass that test. Human beings are ambivalent by nature: we often find ourselves headed in two directions at the same time. In our deepest selves, we are never one-hundred percent *anything,* neither loving nor hating, and if we tell ourselves we are pure, we fool ourselves.

Poetry expresses human ambivalence. That's one reason poetry is complicated—because people are complicated, and because poetry is true to people. Bad poems are often bad—lying, distorted, phony, sentimental—exactly because they deny ambivalent feeling. This poem is excellent (here is one criterion for excellence in poetry) because it embodies with honest clarity true human ambivalence. This poem is almost *about* ambivalence and its conflicts; at least it acts out a particular ambivalence with so much clarity that the poem in the reader's mind can stand for other conflicts. What for Frost's speaker was a quarrel between woods and duties can translate, in our lives, into a quarrel between birdwatching or writing a letter. When one set of particulars can stand in for another set of relationships, we have a **symbol**.

Symbols raise another subject: in interpreting a poem, where does the reader stop? Many people find further complexities—"levels," "meanings"—in this poem. Some readers have found this poem suicidal and claimed that it contains a wish to die. People have often tended to look for a death wish in Frost's work because, in his lifetime, Frost spoke about suicidal feelings. But should we *therefore* consider that when Frost's speaker looks into the woods, he takes the woods as a symbol for death and longs for the darkness of his own death? Not *therefore,* at any rate, for then we would be leaping from life to poem as if it were always possible to make equations between the facts of the life and the facts of the poem.

What can we say, finally, about the meaning of this poem—looking only at the poem itself? Meaning is not paraphrase, nor is it singling out words for their special effects, nor is it accounting for rhythm and form. It is all these things, and it is more. Meaning is what we try to explicate: the whole impression of a poem on our minds, our emotions, and our bodies. We can never wholly explicate a poem, any more than we can explicate ourselves, or another person—but we can try to come close. The only way to stretch and exercise our ability to read a poem is to try to understand and to name our whole response.

Then how shall we understand this last stanza, and the implications of the whole poem? Implication is the word I want to use. Although I may understand what is said on the surface, another voice speaks from underneath the poem—not a "hidden meaning," implying that the poet is a riddler or an Easter-egg-hider, but a second language of the poem, which exists underneath the first language. This is the quiet voice of implication, the poet's psyche speaking to the reader's psyche in a language just underneath the common-sense words, a language only these words in this order could manage to imply.

A poet makes a contract with the reader: I agree to use words as thoroughly as I can; you agree to read them the same way. Because this is a poem, we shall do well to examine even the simplest words. First, we have the bald statement of attraction: "The woods are lovely, dark, and deep." The word *lovely* has the word *love* in it, as *downy* included *down*. So the woods pertain somehow to love. *Dark* and *deep* go together, not just for their **alliteration** (the repetition of initial consonants). The woods are dark in this evening, filling up with snow (by definition, white); and they are deep, like a vessel with room for the filling. The woods are mysterious, perhaps a place suitable for hiding, and this sensation of mystery has an attraction like the attraction people feel for each other; so the woods are *lovely. Dark and deep* work together as a double adjective, explaining the *kind* of "lovely." How different the line would be if Frost had punctuated it differently and used a comma after *dark.* "The woods are lovely, dark, and deep"—pronounced as punctuated—makes a different sound, and even a different *meaning:* the extra comma makes the three adjectives enumerate separate qualities of the woods; in the line as Frost wrote it, instead of enumerated qualities we have a rush of feeling. Such difference a comma makes!

Apparently, the feelings in this poem are universal, and all of us find in ourselves, on occasion, a desire to abandon the track of everyday duty and embrace the peace of nothingness. Perhaps I go too far, in trying to name the unnameable, with the paraphrase "the peace of nothingness." My naming is not so good as Frost's naming and some readers will prefer their own different naming. "The peace of nothingness" attempts to paraphrase a feeling that, for some people, apparently seems suicidal—and for others merely sleepy. My inadequate phrase attempts to bring together the two sides.

Different readings can be valid—but *not all readings.* There are limits to the validity of interpretations, and these limits are set by the poem. One reader tells me that the poem indicates a desire to put a bullet through one's head. Another says the poem implies that Frost wants to move to Arizona and escape the winter. The suicidal reading is only a little askew. If all of us sometimes desire what we might call peace or oblivion, such feeling is not entirely alien to the desire to die. Perhaps sleep—"death's second self," as Shakespeare called it—will satisfy the desire. The speaker in this poem expresses a taste for darkness that resembles the wish to die but does not duplicate it; to find a death wish in this poem is only an exaggeration, like calling the pain of a stubbed toe "excruciating agony." On the other hand, the reader who finds Frost on his way to Arizona simply misreads; there is nothing like it in the poem. Presumably, the cold of the poem made the reader think of a warm climate and then attribute the thought to Frost's poem. To avoid misinterpretation, always take care to distinguish the source of a notion: does Phoenix happen in the poem or in your own head?

After talking about one poem for so many pages, I think of Whitman's little poem about listening to the "Learn'd Astronomer," who spoke in scientific terms about astronomical data. Whitman's response is to go outside the lecture hall and look up "in perfect silence at the stars." Read again Robert Frost's simple, pleasurable, universal poem:

Stopping by Woods on a Snowy Evening

Whose woods these are I think I know.
His house is in the village though;
He will not see me stopping here
To watch his woods fill up with snow.

My little horse must think it queer
To stop without a farmhouse near
Between the woods and frozen lake
The darkest evening of the year.

He gives his harness bells a shake
10 To ask if there is some mistake.
The only other sound's the sweep
Of easy wind and downy flake.

The woods are lovely, dark and deep,
But I have promises to keep,
And miles to go before I sleep,
And miles to go before I sleep.

Questions and Exercises

1. What happens when Frost repeats a line?

2. Whose feet these are I think I know.
   His head's beneath a T-shirt though.
   He will not mind an ice cube here . . .

   Complete a fourth line.

3. Rewrite the poem, staying as close to the original as you can, but change all the important words. Use a thesaurus or a dictionary of synonyms, if you like. Let *whose* and *I* and *his* remain; change *woods, know, horse,* and so forth. You could begin "Whose forest this is, I recognize . . . ." Compare different versions in class, deciding which is closest to the original, and which most ingenious. Compare the class versions with Frost's original. (Sometimes it works best to concentrate on one stanza only or to divide the class into four sections, each doing one stanza.)

William Carlos Williams, "so much depends"

Robert Frost was a traditional poet, writing in rhyme and meter. During Frost's lifetime, the slightly younger William Carlos Williams made a different sort of poem. Williams was born in Rutherford, New Jersey, where he practiced medicine for more than forty years, after his education in Switzerland, at the University of Pennsylvania, and in Germany. He wrote free verse, lines of poetry strong in rhythm but free of the regular repetitions of meter. He is another good poet; his poems force us to acknowledge kinds of excellence foreign to Frost's excellence. Williams invents original shapes in his poems and forces us to become aware of a poem as a made object. He was a poet of images, of the *eye;* but, as we will see, he wrote also for the *ear* and placed his words for our maximum pleasure in their sound.

> So much depends upon a red wheelbarrow, glazed with rainwater, beside the white chickens.

This sentence is unlikely to elicit much response. It seems nonsensical, unworthy of attention. In a way, attention is exactly the problem. This poem by William Carlos Williams is printed above not as a poem but as a one-sentence paragraph in which the words have not been *attended to. Attention,* which Williams brings to bear by his use of *lines,* is exactly what we miss.

When someone asks the difference between poetry and prose, I like to answer: "Poetry is jagged on the right-hand side of the page." Poetry is written in lines, and lines make a big difference. Lines act like musicians' notations. They tell us how to say a poem aloud, or how to hear it. Yet, most beginning readers of poetry read either as if lines didn't exist at all or as if the sense always stopped at the lines' ends.

Knowing that the wheelbarrow sentence is really a poem, let us try putting it into lines, starting with the most obvious arrangement:

> So much depends upon
> a red wheelbarrow
> glazed with rainwater
> beside the white chickens.

I call this arrangement obvious, because the lines break where the phrases pause. If you were saying the prose sentence aloud and had to pause three times because you were out of breath, you would pause where these lines end. As it happens, these linebreaks are not the poet's—but if they were, let us see what we could find in them. Putting the sentence into these lines must affect the meaning of the sentence, if we take "meaning" to be the words' total impact on the reader. In search of meaning, let us first try paraphrase: "These things are really important: a small red cart with wheels on it, with water on it from a rainshower, next to the poultry." (I cannot paraphrase the simplicities of *red* and *white.*) When I asserted that meaning must be changed by the line arrangement, my claim was not grand; putting these clauses into lines slows down the sentence, adding pauses greater than the pauses we would make if we spoke the sentence as prose. The pauses isolate the clauses within brackets of time, made visible on poetry's page by the white spaces around the poem. The results are focus, intensity, concentration, and emphasis.

In the lines quoted, the last three make visual images, and the first line insists on the importance of what follows—therefore, on the importance of the visual. To isolate these lines, by pauses and spaces, is to emphasize the singularity of each unit and to draw closer attention to the redness of the wheelbarrow, to the wetness of the rain, to the whiteness of the chickens. The greater emphasis of these lines *intensifies* meaning.

But not sufficiently for William Carlos Williams. Here is the poem as he actually wrote it:

so much depends
upon

a red wheel
barrow

glazed with rain
water

beside the white
chickens

By this arrangement, meaning is further enhanced, sound is released, and the poem is made exact, fixed, permanent—like a carving. The prose sentence from page 417 is repeated exactly, but, by breaking the words into these lines, Williams makes an object; and his object enforces a meaning.

First, *look* at the poem William Carlos Williams wrote. Look at its shape on the page, without reading or understanding a word; the poem already begins to make a statement, saying "I am orderly; I am arranged on purpose; there is nothing sloppy or careless or inadvertent in me; I will reward careful reading." The visual statement of a poem on the page may be the least of poetry's sensuous qualities, but it exists.

The visual shape suggests an audible performance, behaving like musical notation. In its true form, the poem has more pauses than it had in the four-line version, and more variety in the pauses; generally, the pause between the lines of each two-line stanza is short—like the pause between *wheel* and *barrow*—and the pause that leaps the larger white space between stanzas is longer. But there are degrees of difference within this generalization. Syntax and sense require that the pause between *rain* and *water* be shorter than the pause between *white* and *chickens*. With seven places for pauses at line-ends, the poem calls for seven different degrees of pause.

More pause creates still more emphasis, a more concentrated focus. We see this most clearly in *wheelbarrow: wheel / barrow,* where a linebreak gives us two nouns for one, shows us the original parts of a compound word, and makes a statement about the importance of observing the physical world. This linebreak gives us twice as much *thingness,* making us recognize wheels as separate, barrow as separate, and wheelbarrow as a synthesis of the two, which is also a third thing. In *rainwater,* we see the same act repeated. The first line's *depend / upon* splits a verb phrase into its parts (like the later splitting of compound nouns) and hangs the preposition from a verb that originally meant "hang from." In the last stanza, splitting *white* from *chickens* gives us at least a little more attention to the quality of the color than we get if *white chickens* is printed on one line.

But the poem's arrangement does more than intensify meaning and more than make a pretty shape. It releases varied sounds, two assonances in particular, that grant the reader a pleasure equivalent to the eye's pleasure in seeing *red, rain,* and *white.* In the four-line arrangement, the third line was "glazed with rainwater." When the poet did it his way, the fifth line of the poem becomes "glazed with rain," and the long diphthong *āi* bursts twice into bloom. The flowering of the diphthong alters the pace of the line, for when the reader comes to *rain* and tastes the pleasure of the repeated sound, he or she stretches it a little; the *n* of "rain" allows the sound to be held on the tongue and savored.

The next pair of lines gives the same pleasure to the mouth alerted to assonance. The long-*i* diphthong in the second syllable of *beside* finds itself mirrored and repeated in the vowel of *white,* buried midline in the earlier version. Both times the word stretched and exalted is a sensuous and meaningful word, *rain* describing the sources of *water, white* the color of chickens; insofar as sound specifies more attention given to a word, assonance impinges upon our understanding, and the coincidence of vowel sounds contributes to meaning.

This little poem by William Carlos Williams is not a vessel loaded with philosophical or intellectual content; it does not resemble the works of Plato or Thomas Jefferson. The poem does have meaning, but its statement belongs more to the area of sensation than to the area of thought.

Feelings and ideas happen at the same time; ideas carry feelings with them, and feelings imply ideas. If Williams's poem insists on the importance of the physical world, the *insistence* is an emotional value placed on a philosophical idea. And the poem makes its statement not by generalizing but by giving a particular example—something of the world, visible, stared at, and held to. The visual details are perceived with passion and necessity, as if they were railings on a narrow bridge, onto which we hold in order not to fall into the chasm below. The intensity of this experience, which makes the poem valuable, derives largely from the poet's skill in manipulating sounds. Here it is again:

so much depends
upon

a red wheel
barrow

glazed with rain
water

beside the white
chickens

Exercise

Using different words, imitate the shape and sound of Williams's poem. A form is anything done a second time. The first time somebody wrote a sonnet, it was not a sonnet; the second time somebody wrote one, and the third—then we began to call them sonnets. Consider that you are writing a newly discovered form of poetry called a wheelbarrow. You can define a wheelbarrow as four two-line stanzas; each first line has three words, each second line has one word; each one-word second line has two syllables; each three-word first line has either three or four syllables.

Here's one student's wheelbarrow:

it is extremely
serious

to watch the
teacher

writing long words
in chalk

on blackboards
all morning

Which lines fit the form? Which don't?

Wallace Stevens, "Disillusionment of Ten O'Clock"

A third example of a good poem is one by Wallace Stevens, who was a friend of William Carlos Williams when they were both young and who met Robert Frost in Florida when both poets were old. After graduation from Harvard and the New York University Law School, Stevens practiced law in New York City; he lived in Greenwich Village and spent much time with other writers who gathered there. In his late thirties, he became associated with the Hartford Accident and Indemnity Company, serving as a vice-president for the last decade of his life.

Disillusionment of Ten O'Clock   (1915)

The houses are haunted
By white night-gowns.
None are green,
Or purple with green rings,
Or green with yellow rings,
Or yellow with blue rings.
None of them are strange,
With socks of lace
And beaded ceintures.
10 People are not going
To dream of baboons and periwinkles.
Only, here and there, an old sailor,
Drunk and asleep in his boots,
Catches tigers
In red weather.

With this poem I will not provide an explication; instead, I will ask questions, hoping to suggest ways of arriving at an explication. Read the poem several times, slowly, before you begin to read the questions.

Questions

1. In the title, is *ten o'clock* A.M. or P.M.? What in the poem suggests one or the other?

2. Think of the word *disillusionment.* Take it apart. What might this word have to do with the hour of ten o'clock? Are there illusions or disillusions in the body of the poem?

3. Does *haunted* tell you anything about the title? How?

4. There is a ghost in the word *haunted.* Ordinarily, there would be no ghost in the word *night-gown.* What word makes *haunted* go with *night-gown?*

5. Do you know whether there are bodies inside these nightgowns?

6. In lines 3 through 6, the poet presents images in the negative. Can we learn anything from being told that something does *not* exist? What do these negatives imply? What is missing from these houses?

7. In line 7, *strange* can be a vague and imprecise word; in this context, do other words define *strange* and make it less vague?

8. A *ceinture* is a belt, and the word was already unusual when Stevens published the poem in 1915. Why would a poet use a word most readers would have to look up? Can a poet mean something simply by using an outlandish word?

9. In line 10, we finally hear of people. Are these the people whose houses are haunted by white nightgowns? How can you tell?

10. Stevens could have broken his lines differently:

People are not
Going to dream of baboons . . .

or:

People are not going to dream
Of baboons . . .

Can you think of why it was a good idea to break the line where Stevens broke it?

11. In this poem, baboons and periwinkles are examples that are parallel to other examples. What words in this poem are they parallel to? Why?

12. What is the relationship of the last four lines of the poem to the lines that came earlier?

13. Why is the sailor drunk? What is he doing? How do these details contrast with the main scene of the poem?

14. Someone has said that in this poem Stevens was eating his cake and having it too. Comment.

15. Frost's poem was written in metrical four-line stanzas. Williams's poem was tightly structured free verse. Characterize sound and rhythm in this poem, pointing out particular effects. Can you find assonance? Alliteration?

To find other poems by these poets, check the index.

Poems Are Made of Words

A poem is single, whole, and seamless, but, to discuss it, we need to treat it as if we could take it apart and examine its elements as we can examine elements of a machine: this is a carburetor, which mixes air and fuel; this is a spark plug. . . . The parts of an internal-combustion engine, however, are genuinely separate; in a poem, you cannot detach rhythm from imagery except by paying attention to the one element rather than to the other; within a poem, rhythm and imagery are properties of the same words.

Before we concentrate on the elements of poetry, let us look at the medium of poetry, which is words. Many people assume that poetry's materials are emotions and ideas. Emotions and ideas exist *in* poems or *through* poems, and we must account for them in paraphrase when we explicate, but they are not poetry's material. If we argued that emotions and ideas are poetry's material, we would have to claim that trees and mountains are the medium of landscape painting. Canvas and paint are the painter's material, and poems are made of words.

Reading poetry, we read words used with the greatest *energy* and *fixity.*

Fixity is the unique correctness and immovability of a word in its place. If you change almost any word in a long novel, you change the novel very little; if you change a word in a good poem, you change the poem considerably: "His house is in the hamlet though" would change Frost's poem by substituting *hamlet* for *village.* This fixity is partly a function of size, but not entirely; it is a measure of relative exactness in use. Poetry does not acknowledge synonyms. *Roget's Thesaurus* or any other dictionary of synonyms lists words that resemble each other in their meaning, but a poet makes poems by manipulating the small differences in meaning between synonyms; think of the differences between *hamlet* and *village,* or the many differences among *hide, conceal, cover up, secrete, screen, obscure, suppress, veil, disguise, camouflage, shroud.*

Energy comes from the efficiency with which the poet uses language; poems are made of words used efficiently. When I write this sentence, I sound like an engineer—and I want to. An efficient machine turns energy received into a nearly equal amount of energy put out. Sloppy language wastes energy, often by failing to say what it means; at best, it uses more words than are necessary, perhaps three vague words in place of the precise one. "Glazed with rain / water" is better than "covered all over with dampness as a result of precipitation." *Good poetry is the perfect machine of language.*

To use words most efficiently, the writer must be aware of their wholeness, of their dictionary senses or **denotations**, and of **connotations**—the associations not usually found in a dictionary. The poet uses the history of a word, its family, its origins, its associations. *Snow* carries "whiteness" with it, a connotation. Other connotations for snow include cold and winter. Further associations can become less universal and more particular. For a Northerner, *snow* may include "skiing"; for a Sun Belt resident, *snow* may include the notion of travel. If the associations of *snow* include not only travel but a three-day drive in a Plymouth that uses too much oil, connotation has given way to private association. Much connotation is public enough for use not only by poets and not only for literature. Real estate agents do not sell *houses;* they sell *homes*—the same buildings, but connoting comfort, warmth, and a dog sleeping in front of the fireplace. A *sanitation engineer* may do the same work a plumber used to do, but the title sounds more impressive. If poets use connotations to tell us honest feelings, politicians and lobbyists can use connotations for deceit. *Honorarium* sounds better than *payment, payment* better than *bribe*. All three words are heavy with connotation.

Concepts of denotation and connotation are useful, but we need to understand that they don't tell us everything. The *con*notation of *wheelbarrow* does not include its compoundness, revealed only when a poet splits it back into two words: *wheel barrow*. And when a word has different *de*notations or dictionary meanings, the peripheral definitions of the word in the poem hover around the central ones.

Poets do not always use every potential meaning of a word. By their context, they can employ some connotations or unused denotations and shut off others. Thomas Hardy's poem "During Wind and Rain" includes the line

How the sick leaves reel down in throngs.

A dictionary may tell us that to reel is to be thrown off balance, to stagger, to move in a circle, to dance a reel, or to pull in a fishing line. In the context of the poem, not every meaning becomes active. Because the word before *leaves* is *sick, reel,* as in "stagger"—like a sick person too weak to walk—becomes strengthened by context. Earlier in this poem, Hardy speaks of music: "They sing their dearest songs . . . / Treble and tenor and bass / And one to play . . . ," and although the songs may be hymns or folk songs, the "dance" part of *reel* shows signs of life. (All of these meanings are related: *reel* originally meant a kind of spool, and evolved into all sorts of circular motions.) Connotations interweave, and peripheral denotations act like connotations. In this poem's context, the stagger-meaning is foremost, the dance-meaning acts like a strong connotation, and the fishing-meaning hovers unused in the distance. If a reader, when first glancing at this line, thought of *reel* as fishing reel, the line would remain obscure until the reader looked for another denotation of *reel.*

When leaves are compared to dancers, the poet has made a metaphor. We should mention one other matter connecting word and metaphor. Many readers leap to interpret a word as metaphor when the poet has used it literally. The insistence on the fanciful, at the expense of the plain, is a common source of misreading. Edwin Arlington Robinson begins a stanza about a dying man

> Blind, with but a wandering hour to live . . .

Many readers see the word *blind* and think that Robinson means "obtuse" in the common metaphorical use of the word—as in "Good grief! Are you *blind?*" But the rest of the stanza reveals that the man is sightless. Readers who hold on to the "obtuse" meaning find the poem highly obscure. It is wise to remember a rule of thumb: take poems literally until they make you take them figuratively. "Sightless" is the denotation of the word *blind. Blind* has meant "sightless" for a long time; the first citation in the *Oxford English Dictionary* (*OED,* that wonderful, enormous dictionary that quotes words in contexts as they change over history) is dated A.D. 1000. The first citation of *blind* as "obtuse" is also A.D. 1000; the metaphorical use is as ancient as the literal.

Reading old poems, we need the *OED* to let us know how poets used words—efficiently, with energy and fixity—in their own times, for words change. When the eighteenth-century poet Alexander Pope spoke of *science* he did not mean physics or chemistry but knowledge in general; our word *science* comes from *scio,* Latin for "I know."

Reading new poems, we can use the *OED* also, because many poets—seeking the energy that comes from using words in their wholeness—refer by their context to a word's history, its old or original meanings. Richard Wilbur is a contemporary American who likes to play with **etymology**, the study of word origins and history. In his poem "Lamarck Elaborated," he pretends to believe genetic theories that say that genes transmit acquired characteristics.* The theory is untrue, but, with his imagination, Wilbur tries out a world in which the things of the world created our bodies. The sun, for instance, made our eyes. Wilbur writes a stanza of complicated wordplay:

> The yielding water, the repugnant stone,
> The poisoned berry and the flaring rose
> Attired in sense the tactless finger-bone
> And set the taste-buds and inspired the nose.

Paraphrased, the stanza says that we acquired touch, taste, and smell by acts of touching, tasting, and smelling. Water, which gives to the touch, and stone,

---

* French naturalist Jean Baptiste Pierre Antoine de Monet, Chevalier de Lamarck (1744–1829). His flawed theory of evolution was nevertheless an important forerunner of the work of Charles Darwin.

which doesn't—which pushes it back, which is what *repugnant* means—
attired (clothed) *in sense* (in our senses) *the finger-bone,* which had formerly
been clumsy or without tact; *tact* comes from the word for "touch," as in
tactile, so *tactless* by etymology means "untouching": before it was clothed in
sensation, the fingerbone was without touch. The *berry* that poisons us, which
we distinguish by taste, *sets* our taste buds, the way a gardener sets out plants.
The flaring rose (flared like a nostril to smell) *inspired* our noses. *Inspired,* in
one common usage, means "invented" ("Monday Night Football was the inspiration of Roone Arledge") but actually comes from a Latin word that means "to
breathe in."

Here are a few poems—with questions intended to sharpen your sensitivity
to the manipulation of words.

Hogwash (1944)

The tongue that mothered such a metaphor
Only the purest purist could despair of.

Nobody ever called swill sweet but isn't
Hogwash a daisy in a field of daisies?

What beside sports and flowers could you find
To praise better than the American language?

Bruised by American foreign policy
What shall I soothe me, what defend me with

But a handful of clean unmistakable words—
10 Daisies, daisies, in a field of daisies?
                              —*Robert Francis**

Questions

1. In the first line, what happens if you remove *mothered* and substitute "fathered"?
   "conjured"? "created"? "gathered"? "mounted"? "built up"? "constructed"? What
   are the associations of *mothered* and of the substitute words?

2. How does the word *swill* find its way into this poem? Would "junk" be just as
   good? "Garbage"?

3. Look up the word *daisy* to check on its ancestry. What are the insides of *daisy?* If
   you used "tulip," how would its different history match the rest of the poem? Is
   daisy better for this poem, or just different? If the word were "flower," would the
   poem be less than it is?

* See page 600 for a note about Robert Francis. Brief biographical notes on poets whose
work is included in this book precede their poems in "A Gathering of Poems," which begins on
page 555. For rapid location of dates and other information about any author represented in this
volume, look for the italicized page number following the entry for his or her name in the index.

4. Does *defend,* in its associations, relate to other words in this poem?

5. In the last stanza, what sort of *handful* would you have if your hand were full of words? A handful of swill? What does the poet compare words to?

During Wind and Rain   (1917)

They sing their dearest songs—
He, she, all of them—yea,
Treble and tenor and bass,
     And one to play;
With the candles mooning each face. . . .
     Ah, no; the years O!
How the sick leaves reel down in throngs!

They clear the creeping moss—
Elders and juniors—aye,
Making the pathway neat
     And the garden gay;
And they build a shady seat. . . .
     Ah, no; the years, the years;
See, the white storm-birds wing across!

They are blithely breakfasting all—
Men and maidens—yea,
Under the summer tree,
     With a glimpse of the bay,
While pet fowl come to the knee. . . .
     Ah, no; the years O!
And the rotten rose is ript from the wall.

They change to a high new house,
He, she, all of them—aye,
Clocks and carpets and chairs
     On the lawn all day,
And brightest things that are theirs. . . .
     Ah, no; the years, the years;
Down their carved names the rain-drop ploughs.
                                        —*Thomas Hardy*

Questions

1. Consider the associations of *creeping.* Which are used? Which unused? Does the word make a comparison?

2. In line 21, Hardy uses the word *ript.* Substitute *pulled* and consider the differences. Substitute "descends" for *is ript.* Discuss the differing associations of the words. Discuss the differing grammar.

3. In line 22, try these substitutes for *high:* "tall," "white," "brand," "dark," and "low." Is difference in image a difference in value?

4. The last word of the poem is *ploughs*. How do its denotation, connotations, sound, and grammar—the whole word, family associations and all—contribute to this poem? Does the whole word *conclude* the poem?

good times   (1969)

my daddy has paid the rent
and the insurance man is gone
and the lights is back on
and my uncle brud has hit
for one dollar straight
and they is good times
good times
good times

10 my mama has made bread
and grampaw has come
and everybody is drunk
and dancing in the kitchen
and singing in the kitchen
oh these is good times
good times
good times

oh children think about the
good times
        —Lucille Clifton

Questions

1. The speaker in *good times* uses a different English. Discuss the import of *is* instead of *are*.

2. How do words change when we repeat them? What is the effect of repeating *good times?*

3. Does this poem make you think of music? How?

Silence   (1935)

My father used to say,
"Superior people never make long visits,
have to be shown Longfellow's grave
or the glass flowers at Harvard.
Self-reliant like the cat—
that takes its prey to privacy,
the mouse's limp tail hanging like a shoelace from its mouth—
they sometimes enjoy solitude,
and can be robbed of speech
10 by speech which has delighted them.

The deepest feeling always shows itself in silence;
not in silence, but restraint."
Nor was he insincere in saying, "Make my house your inn."
Inns are not residences.

—Marianne Moore

Questions

1. In the second line, the poet uses the word *superior.* Make a list of words that might be considered synonyms and that would make sense in this context. Discuss the difference each substitution would make to the poem.

2. Longfellow's grave is in Cambridge, Massachusetts, a city that also contains Harvard University, which shows in a museum some remarkably realistic glass reproductions of flowers—a favorite stop for tourists. What is the connection of the sentence containing these objects with the sentences that make the rest of this poem? In lines 3 and 4, what words provide the implicit connection?

3. In this poem, where does the idea of silence enter, after the title?

4. What do you make of this cat? Have you known cats who liked to show off their prey, who are not reticent at all? If you have, does the knowledge bother you in reading this poem? Do you feel that the cat somehow seems more important to the poem than its use as an illustrative simile could warrant? How?

5. How does the author show that although *Superior people* enjoy being by themselves, they are equipped to encounter others?

6. "Not in silence, but restraint." What is the difference? Why does the author say one thing and then correct it? What is the effect of using two words instead of one?

7. The last two lines make a distinction by means of definitions. How does this verbal contrast grow out of earlier lines of the poem?

When President John F. Kennedy was inaugurated in 1961, he invited Robert Frost to read a poem as part of the ceremony. Frost recited this poem, which he had written years before.

The Gift Outright   (1942)

The land was ours before we were the land's.
She was our land more than a hundred years
Before we were her people. She was ours
In Massachusetts, in Virginia,
But we were England's, still colonials,
Possessing what we still were unpossessed by,
Possessed by what we now no more possessed.
Something we were withholding made us weak
Until we found out that it was ourselves
10 We were withholding from our land of living,
And forthwith found salvation in surrender.
Such as we were we gave ourselves outright
(The deed of gift was many deeds of war)
To the land vaguely realizing westward,

But still unstoried, artless, unenhanced,
Such as she was, such as she would become.

Questions

1. Frost *almost* recited the poem as written. For the next-to-last word, he said *will* instead of *would.* How did this alter the meaning of the poem?

2. Distinguish different sorts of possession. Why does Frost use the same word when the reader must learn to distinguish different meanings for it? What allows you to find different meanings for one word in a single poem?

3. What sort of a phrase is *salvation in surrender?*

4. Does *realize* usually take an object? Does it here? How does the grammar help to define this use of the word?

5. Notice the many balances throughout the poem. List them.

Here's an old poem, written during Queen Elizabeth I's reign, with its spelling modernized. Ben Jonson was a great playwright, a rival and friend of Shakespeare. He wrote on the death of his firstborn son.

On My First Son   (1603)

Farewell, thou child of my right hand, and joy;
My sin was too much hope of thee, loved boy.
Seven years thou wert lent to me, and I thee pay,
Exacted by thy fate, on the just day.
O, could I lose all father now. For why
Will man lament the state he should envy?
To have so soon 'scaped° world's, and flesh's, rage,   escaped
And if no other misery, yet age?
Rest in soft peace, and, asked, say here doth lie
10 Ben Jonson, his° best piece of poetry.   Jonson's
For whose sake, henceforth, all his vows be such,
As what he loves may never like too much.

Questions

1. In the third line, Jonson's word order puts *I* next to *thee,* which we would not do. *Thee* is the object of *pay,* and we would say "And I pay thee" or "And I pay you." In what sense is *pay* used?

2. How can Jonson call the day *just?* What other words—or what ideas carried by what words—support *just?*

3. How would you paraphrase *all father?*

4. Look up the word *poetry* in an etymological dictionary. How can Jonson use the word to stand in for his son?

5. The poem works by a series of contrasted words. What does *lament* contrast with? *rage? world's?*

6. Describe the contrast in the last line.

CHAPTER THREE

Images

An **image** is language that speaks to our senses, recording a sensuous experience. Poetry abounds in visual images, directed to the sense of sight, like "white chickens" or ". . . woods fill up with snow." Poetry also includes images of touch, taste, smell, and hearing. Hot-and-cold is tactile, a form of touch; here is a poem made of images for heat:

Heat   (1925)

O wind, rend open the heat,
cut apart the heat,
rend it to tatters.

Fruit cannot drop
through this thick air—
fruit cannot fall into heat
that presses up and blunts
the points of pears
and rounds the grapes.

10 Cut the heat—
plough through it,
turning it on either side
of your path.

                              —*H.D.*

The American poet H.D. (Hilda Doolittle) was one of the Imagist poets, a group dedicated to writing vivid and precise natural description. When H.D. asks the wind to *rend open the heat,* she gives the invisible heat a bulk that can be *cut apart,* therefore making an image of heat as something thick, substantial. Then she tells us how bulky it is: "Fruit cannot drop / through this thick air." These lines imply a natural scene with fruit trees, and air so heavy that even a falling apple cannot penetrate it. H.D. communicates feeling through exaggeration; she does not merely render like a snapshot. She describes the heat as a pressure, antigravitational and upward, blunting the pears that would otherwise be sharp-angled; heat acts, by its constant pressure, to make the grapes round. Then the poet ends her poem by returning implicitly to the wind for help—meteorological reality, because breezes blow away hot air—and when she asks the wind to become a plow, she again evokes the thickness, weight, and density of the heat, comparing it to earth a plow turns.

Images of touch like H.D.'s are not as common as visual images. In this old poem, a male poet describes the appearance of a woman:

Upon Julia's Clothes   (1648)

Whenas in silks my Julia goes,
Then, then, methinks, how sweetly flows
That liquefaction of her clothes.

Next, when I cast mine eyes, and see
That brave vibration, each way free,
O, how that glittering taketh me!
                    —*Robert Herrick*

Herrick describes something seen, and his images are visual. We are invited to *see* Julia in motion, wearing a silk dress. We don't know the color of the silk, and we know nothing of Julia's appearance except for her dress. We have the watery image of *flows* and *liquefaction,* and, later, her sway from side to side and the silk's glitter. The poem gives us only a partial picture of Julia, but we feel Herrick's whole delight: the visual images embody Herrick's feeling.

Poets use images to embody feelings; they use images instead of abstract explanations. Here's a poem by Allen Ginsberg:

First Party at Ken Kesey's with Hell's Angels   (1968)

Cool black night thru redwoods
cars parked outside in shade
behind the gate, stars dim above
the ravine, a fire burning by the side
porch and a few tired souls hunched over
in black leather jackets. In the huge
wooden house, a yellow chandelier
at 3 A.M. the blast of loudspeakers
hi-fi Rolling Stones Ray Charles Beatles
10 Jumping Joe Jackson and twenty youths
dancing to the vibration thru the floor,
a little weed in the bathroom, girls in scarlet
tights, one muscular smooth skinned man
sweating dancing for hours, beer cans
bent littering the yard, a hanged man
sculpture dangling from a high creek branch,
children sleeping softly in bedroom bunks,

And 4 police cars parked outside the painted
gate, red lights revolving in the leaves.
                                                    —*Allen Ginsberg*

The poem starts with a word of skin-feelings, *cool,* and ends with a compelling
visual image. With the phrases *cool black, shade, stars dim,* and *fire burning,*
Ginsberg sets a scene of contrasts. Then the poet speaks of *souls hunched
over,* and we feel a tiredness. Next in the poem we have an image of sound,
then dancing; the dancing comes as a visual image, but the word's associations contain muscular feeling as well. Then the poem leads us through everything seen, in a list of images—litter, a sculpture, children sleeping—with a
cinematic effect, as if a camera panned slowly over a static scene, recording
frame after frame of reality. Finally, the camera settles on the ominous image
of the police cars with lights revolving. The poem's effect comes entirely from
its images; there is no commentary at all.

The reader is *shown,* not *told.* Modern poets usually avoid abstract language, using concrete details instead. At the end of this poem, Ginsberg
might have written about fear or apprehensiveness or dread or ominousness.
Using instead the images *police cars parked* and *red lights revolving,* he
communicates feeling directly; abstractions would have communicated the
names of feelings, or *ideas* about feelings, not the feelings themselves.

H.D.'s heat was tactile, using images of touch. Ginsberg's poem is mostly
visual but also uses images of touch and hearing. When Robert Frost, in
"Stopping by Woods on a Snowy Evening," wrote about "the sweep / Of easy
wind . . . ," he used an image of sound. Poets use images of smell more
rarely ("the acrid odor of maple") and also images of taste: when Keats longs
for wine, he calls it "a draught of vintage that hath been / Cool'd a long
time . . ."; he appeals to the touch-sense of the tongue, or taste.

Read this brief poem by Rita Dove.

Lint   (1989)

Beneath the brushed wing of the mallard
an awkward loveliness.

Under the cedar lid a mirror
and a box in a box.

Blue is all around
like an overturned bowl.

What to do with this noise
and persistent lint,

the larder filled past caring?
10 How good to revolve

on the edge of a system—
small, unimaginable, cold.

                                                    —*Rita Dove*

Notice how she starts her poem with a visual image, in the first line, before she tells us about "awkward loveliness" in the second line. The image props up the words about the image; the poem expresses sensuous love for the physical world. Without images that embody beauty and the love of beauty—"Blue is all around/ like an overturned bowl."—the poem would merely editorialize.

Images describe real things, and these poems come from the world we live in. Here are more poems of our world, with questions that mostly call attention to their images.

Nantucket   (1938)

Flowers through the window
lavender and yellow

changed by white curtains—
Smell of cleanliness—

Sunshine of late afternoon—
On the glass tray

a glass pitcher, the tumbler
turned down, by which

a key is lying—And the
10 immaculate white bed
      —*William Carlos Williams*

Questions

1. Most of these images are visual. Is there an exception?

2. Is *changed* an image? Is it an idea?

3. Do these images carry feeling? Can you name the feeling?

4. Can you paraphrase this poem for its ideas?

Denise Levertov is an American poet who takes great pleasure in observation of the world outside: sight, sound, coolness—and soot from chimneys.

The World Outside   (1964)

i

On the kitchen wall a flash
of shadow:
          swift pilgrimage
of pigeons, a spiral
celebration of air, of sky-deserts.
And on tenement windows
a blaze
          of lustred watermelon:

stain of the sun
10 westering somewhere back of Hoboken.

ii

The goatherd upstairs! Music
from his sweet flute
roves from summer to summer
in the dusty air of airshafts
and among the flakes
of soot that float
in a daze from chimney
to chimney—notes
remote, cool, speaking of slender
20 shadows under olive-leaves. A silence.

iii

Groans, sighs, in profusion,
with coughing, muttering, orchestrate
solitary grief; the crash of glass, a low voice
repeating over and over, 'No.
      No. I want my key. No you did not.
      No.'—a commonplace.
And in counterpoint, from other windows,
the effort to be merry—ay, maracas!
—sibilant, intricate—the voices wailing pleasure,
30   arriving perhaps at joy, late, after sets
have been switched off, and silences
are dark windows?
                                    —Denise Levertov

Questions

1. How many images can you find in this poem, appealing to how many senses?

2. When the poet says *pilgrimage,* what world does she enter? Is it figurative or literal? What other words go with *pilgrimage?*

3. Is there any sort of connection between "a blaze / of . . . watermelon" and "notes / remote, cool . . ."?

Latin Night at the Pawnshop   (1987)
Chelsea, Massachusetts
Christmas, 1987

The apparition of a salsa band
gleaming in the Liberty Loan
pawnshop window:

Golden trumpet,
silver trombone,
congas, maracas, tambourine,

all with price tags dangling
like the city morgue ticket
on a dead man's toe.
                    —*Martín Espada*

Questions

1. The poet begins this imagistic poem with an abstraction, *apparition*. Does this
word influence the way you see the musical instruments?

2. This poem ends with a simile. Or is it an image? Or both?

3. What does the poet accomplish by his final comparison?

We have been reading poems that describe realities. Allen Ginsberg's
dancers and police cars are really there—we accept his word for it. Herrick's
Julia wears silk clothing. H.D.'s poem exaggerates, but it does not invent a
bizarre world. William Carlos Williams and Denise Levertov describe an
objective world in language that specifies the way they take it in. Martín
Espada's pawnshop is real.

But some poems use fantastic images to create worlds previously uncre-
ated, as if the poet were recounting a dream. Here's a dreamy poem by
Gregory Orr called "Washing My Face":

Last night's dreams disappear.
They are like the sink draining:
a transparent rose swallowed by its stem.

The last image conjures up something imaginary—*a transparent rose*. Because we know what roses look like, and because we know what transparency
means, we can assemble these words into an image of a transparent rose.
Then we understand that the transparent rose resembles the water in the
sink, when we wash our faces at waking; the water makes a swirling shape
like petals, as it disappears down the drain. The tenuousness of last night's
dreams makes *transparent* feel right; the pleasant word *rose* implies that
these disappearing dreams were happy ones.

Many contemporary Americans write poems that include realistic as well as
fantastic images. These poems may move back and forth from one sort of
concrete detail to another, from the seen to the dreamed and back again.
James Wright wrote many poems that combined the two ways of seeing—
looking out and looking in. Here is one:

Lying in a Hammock at William Duffy's Farm in Pine Island, Minnesota   (1961)

Over my head, I see the bronze butterfly,
Asleep on the black trunk,
Blowing like a leaf in green shadow.

Down the ravine behind the empty house,
The cowbells follow one another
Into the distances of the afternoon.
To my right,
In a field of sunlight between two pines,
The droppings of last year's horses
10   Blaze up into golden stones.
I lean back, as the evening darkens and comes on.
A chicken hawk floats over, looking for home.
I have wasted my life.
                                —*James Wright*

The first time one reads the poem, the last line is a shock. Some people feel that the last line is not earned, that it comes out of nowhere, that the poem fails because of a trick ending. Other readers report that, although they are shocked by the ending, it feels right. The issue is whether the last line grows naturally out of what goes before. Granted that it is a surprise, is it a cheap surprise or is it a surprise that leads to clear understanding?

Look back at what the poet sees, as he lies in the hammock at William Duffy's farm in Pine Island, Minnesota.* Notice the lethargy and passivity, not only of lying in a hammock but also of the many enclosures of space—in a hammock which is on a farm, which is in a town, which is named after an island, which is in a state. There are many layers to this cocoon.

First, the poet sees a butterfly colored bronze. But bronze is not only a color, it is a metal. If a butterfly were bronze, it would be permanent and inorganic. One of the connotations of *butterfly,* on the other hand, is the fragility of a brief life. In the phrase *bronze butterfly,* fantastic when we think of the metal bronze, we find the paradox of evanescence and solidity, change and permanence. We also see the color of bronze in contrast to the tree trunk's color, and then we see the butterfly move, "Blowing like a leaf in green shadow," as if its fragility returned quickly and the vision of permanence were brief. In the dream world, images can change quickly. The first three lines give us an extended image of clear contrasting colors—and contrasting senses of permanence and change. In the next three lines we cannot see the cows but, hearing the cowbells, we can visualize the ravine where they walk. Some of these words carry feeling without carrying images. "Into the distances of the afternoon" is not a visual image, nor is it addressed to any other sense, but the line takes the cows away from us, and the increasing distance—together with the emptiness of the house in the line before—introduces loneliness. The next four lines give us another scene and an absence of horses. We begin to realize that most things in this poem are gone. The horses have left behind only their manure.

In this poem, nothing goes down and stays down; nothing comes up without going down again. Any perception calls forth its opposite; if a butterfly is bronze, it is also moving in the wind. Even when the poet talks of the

---

* This poem comes from a tradition and an historical moment when the reader properly assumes the identity of "I" and the poet.

cowbells (more frail and distant than cows) he has them *follow one another* (which is warm and companionable) *into the distances,* which are far, lonely, and separate. Now, like a playwright keeping our attention with dramatic contrast, the poet has built to something glorious—and shocks us with horse manure; then he shocks us again by making horse manure glorious: it blazes up "into golden stones," an image of fantasy. The more we look at these words, the more we realize the complications of feeling that control them. The poem is not intellectually complex; it is complex in feeling, an emotional density embodied in images.

In the next line, the poet at first departs from imaging the world around him, and says *I lean back,* as if in passive withdrawal. Then he observes the world again, *as the evening darkens and comes on.* This is not the absence of light but the gathering of darkness, something coming close to him as everything else leaves. Loneliness slides toward something more desperate, and the poet writes the line that brings everything together. The next-to-last line is the climax of the poem and the skeleton key to the feelings of the poem: "A chicken hawk floats over, looking for home." In the mind of this lonely speaker, the bird is going home; even this predator, killer of the homely chicken, has a home to look for. By implication of the whole poem, and especially of the last line, the speaker does not have a home to go to. Instead, he lies in a hammock on somebody else's farm, and everything he looks at reminds him of his solitude and his unworthiness. We sense that wherever the poet looks in the landscape, he cannot help but see his own troubles.

Once you have understood the psychological state of the poem's speaker, its images make their melancholy point. At first sight, the butterfly was transformed into solidity and value—the speaker *wants* his life to change—then it becomes fragile and transitory again; but it remains beautiful in its sleep, as he does not, in his passivity. The *empty house* is the home the speaker is exiled from, as he is exiled from cows' company. Wherever the cowbells move, we know that eventually in the afternoon the cows will go home to be milked; the bells remind us of a destination. While the speaker remains static, passive, unchanging, even horse droppings are glorified! All the speaker can think to do, under the ominous pressure of darkness, is give up.

Other poetry goes further into fantasy than James Wright's, Sometimes a poet will use wholly bizarre images—without even the connection of rose to sink, or horse droppings to gold—to tell the truth of feeling. Chilean poet Pablo Neruda received the gift of a pair of socks hand-knitted by a peasant woman. He was pleased at this tribute, and wrote a poem that embodied his pleasure. Robert Bly translated it from the Spanish.

Ode to My Socks   (tr. 1974)

Maru Mori brought me
a pair
of socks
which she knitted herself
with her sheep-herder's hands,

two socks as soft
as rabbits.
I slipped my feet
into them
10 as though into
two
cases
knitted
with threads of
twilight
and goatskin.
Violent socks,
my feet were
two fish made
20 of wool,
two long sharks
seablue, shot
through
by one golden thread,
two immense blackbirds,
two cannons,
my feet
were honored
in this way
30 by
these
heavenly
socks.
They were
so handsome
for the first time
my feet seemed to me
unacceptable
like two decrepit
40 firemen, firemen
unworthy
of that woven
fire,
of those glowing
socks.

Nevertheless
I resisted
the sharp temptation
to save them somewhere
50 as schoolboys
keep
fireflies,
as learned men
collect
sacred texts,

I resisted
the mad impulse
to put them
in a golden
60 cage
and each day give them
birdseed
and pieces of pink melon.
Like explorers
in the jungle who hand
over the very rare
green deer
to the spit
and eat it
70 with remorse,
I stretched out
my feet
and pulled on
the magnificent
socks
and then my shoes.

The moral
of my ode is this:
beauty is twice
80 beauty
and what is good is doubly
good
when it is a matter of two socks
made of wool
in winter.

> —*Pablo Neruda*

Questions

1. When Neruda writes that he "resisted / the mad impulse / to put them / in a golden / cage . . . ," is he using an image to describe the socks? Did this help you know what they look like? If an image does not describe an object, what else can it describe?

2. In rapid succession, Neruda says that his feet were "two fish made / of wool," "two long sharks," "two immense blackbirds," and "two cannons." What does this do to advice about trying to take poems literally?

3. Find other examples of the fantastic image in this poem and interpret them.

4. Contrast:

   Dear Maru Mori,

   Thank you ever so much for your kind gift of a pair of socks. They are very pretty. They are warm. They fit me perfectly. I will wear them all the time. Mrs. Neruda likes them too. Thank you again.

   Yours truly,
   Pablo Neruda

CHAPTER FOUR

Figures of Speech, Especially Metaphors

Figures of speech are extraordinary, original, nonliteral uses of language, common to lively speech and literature. It would be literal to say "She walked slowly across the field." To say "She walked across the field as slowly as a snail with a pulled muscle" uses a figure of speech called a **simile**, which makes an explicit comparison using *like* or *as* or a verb like *seems* or *appears.* A **metaphor**, like a simile, talks about one thing in terms of another, but a metaphor's comparison is implicit; it does not use *like* or *as, seems* or *appears:* "She snailed her painful way across the field." Poems abound in metaphors. This chapter deals mainly with metaphors and similes, but includes a few other figures of speech.

Here is another poem by Gregory Orr that uses simile:

All Morning   (1975)

All morning the dream lingers.
I am like thick grass
in a meadow, still
soaked with dew at noon.
            —*Gregory Orr*

The poet compares himself to grass, declaring that he shares a quality with it. The simile works through a visual image—we *see* grass soaked with dew—but it is not the picture that does the comparing: a set of relationships makes the comparison work. This simile, like many, can be expressed as an equation: dew is to grass as dreams are to me. The comparison *states* that my dreams remain with me for a while, the way dew clings to a blade of grass. Besides this statement, there are two implications to the simile: eventually the dream/dew will vanish/evaporate; because dew brings nourishment to grass, dreaming has value for me.

If we omitted *like* from Orr's poem, we would have:

All morning the dream lingers.
I am thick grass
in a meadow, still
soaked with dew at noon.

The last three lines would make a metaphor, not a simile. The terms compared —*I* to *thick grass,* dreams to persistent dew—would remain the same, but the manner of the comparison would change. The reader is led by the simile: "I am *like* thick grass"; when the line becomes "I am thick grass," the guiding hand disappears and the reader may not know where to go.

Often, metaphor is more powerful than simile. Apparently it is older and more primitive, and derives from "primary process thinking," as psychologists describe it, in which dissimilar things are perceived as identical. Metaphor is the poetic mode of thought, flying across barriers of logic to assert identities. When small children speak of the leg of a table or the hand of a clock, they perceive a flesh-and-blood leg and a hand; the table, in their language, has power to walk, the clock can gesture and point. For the child, such metaphors are alive; for the adult they are dead. When the adult mind thinks in metaphor, it regains lost power misplaced in the pursuit of maturity.

All language began as metaphor, and in many of our words is buried an image that unites dissimilar things: a daisy was once a day's eye. In casual speech, we use continual **personification** (a figure of speech by which we humanize the nonhuman): clouds frown, fires rage, distant mountains glower, meadows look cheerful, zippers prove recalcitrant, the sun smiles, and the horizon looks inviting.

Metaphors in poems often happen quickly; we are moved without knowing what has touched us; unless we are explicating, we do not even notice that the poet has used metaphor. One of Robert Frost's best poems, "To Earthward" (page 542), begins by saying that, when he was young, feelings came easily; a tiny stimulus produced a strong response: "The petal of the rose," he says, "It was that stung." We understand *stung* as "gave pain," with the consciousness that this pain derives from pleasure too exquisite; the pang of beauty is overwhelming and therefore painful. If we think about it, *stung* is a metaphor, because a rose does not ordinarily sting anything. What stings us? A thorn pricks, but it does not sting. When Frost writes "The petal of the rose / It was that stung," he compares the soft petal of a flower to the harsh sting of a bee. Metaphors work by contrast as well as by comparison; things compared in a metaphor must be unlike, and the poet makes them alike. Usually, difference affects us more than similarity; a poet who compares the seemingly incomparable wins us with energy of resolved contrast.

It is easy to see how *sting* and *petal* contrast. But how do they come together? A bee—never named, yet part of the connotations of *sting*—belongs in a garden. A poem often finds its metaphors within an area, and Frost's poem moves among flowers and gardens for its images and metaphors. Bees work in gardens for pollen. If Frost had substituted for *stung* an image of a dentist's office—"The petal of the rose / It was that drilled"—we would not have been able to follow him in his feeling. Coherence of metaphor makes Frost's words operate upon us, even if we do not know that we are operated upon. Coherence of *rose* and *stung,* by way of an unstated bee, develops the metaphor.

Many metaphors in poetry work almost subliminally, like Frost's *stung,* but we also find extended metaphors. In the following poem, William Shakespeare starts by asking if he might make a comparison:

(1609)

Shall I compare thee to a summer's day?
Thou art more lovely and more temperate:
Rough winds do shake the darling buds of May,
And summer's lease hath all too short a date.
Sometime too hot the eye of heaven shines,
And often is his gold complexion dimm'd;
And every fair° from fair sometime declines,   beautiful thing
By chance or nature's changing course untrimm'd.
But thy eternal summer shall not fade
10 Nor lose possession of that fair thou ow'st.°   ownest: possess
Nor shall Death brag thou wand'rest in his shade,
When in eternal lines to time thou grow'st;
    So long as men can breathe or eyes can see,
    So long lives this and this gives life to thee.
                                        —*William Shakespeare*

This poem follows the common poetic form of the **sonnet**, fourteen lines of rhymed iambic pentameter (see pages 496–498). In the course of his fourteen lines, Shakespeare compares relentlessly, always to the effect that A is greater than B. No, you are not like a summer's day, you are better. To prove his conclusion, he compares parts of wholes. He breaks a summer's day down into weather, temperature, and temperament. Weather is more changeable than you are; you remain the same when the weather does not. Even in May, when blossoms begin to show, the weather can be unpleasant—but not you. Summer is a tenant who has rented an estate for a short time only (Shakespeare's sonnets and plays are full of legal and financial metaphor) but your tenancy of beauty is longer than a mere summer. Notice that by the fourth line Shakespeare has established his comparison of *thee* and *summer* so thoroughly that he can introduce the further metaphor of tenancy without confusion.

If summer leases, summer resembles a human being. The fifth line introduces another personification, when we hear of *the eye of heaven,* and we identify the *eye* with the sun when we hear that this eye *shines.* Having established the sun, without speaking of it directly, Shakespeare describes *his gold complexion,* as if the yellow sun had skin, and makes a cloudy day the sun's loss. In contrast, his love is never lessened or dimmed. Notice how the connotations of precious metal work to flatter the day, and thus flatter the love that is greater than the day.

The first eight lines of the poem—the **octave** of a sonnet—carry out its implications. The **sestet**—the sonnet's last six lines—expands upon the unchanging quality of the love and ends by praising itself. Death shall not brag of keeping this person-summer's day in shade, because these lines of poetry give eternal life. Shakespeare is able to bring Death into his metaphor, because shade treats sun as death treats life.

Shakespeare's poem extends a series of linked metaphors through fourteen lines. Here is another example of a single-word metaphor, like Frost's *stung,* which I use in order to move on to another subject. At the end of "During Wind and Rain" (page 426), Thomas Hardy writes:

> Down their carved names the rain-drop ploughs.

A plow is a natural object in the rural scene of this poem—and thus belongs in this poem's metaphorical area—but this is not a literal plow; metaphor turns a raindrop into an agricultural implement: raindrop is to gravestone as plow is to earth. The metaphor of *ploughs* has implications central to the poem: if raindrop acts on granite as plow on meadow, by implication many years have passed. If, however, we read the line lazily, taking *ploughs* as if it meant "moves vigorously forward"—as in a dead metaphor like "the fullback plows through the line" or "the tugboat plows through the waves"—nothing happens at all.

We constantly use figures of speech that once enjoyed freshness and vitality but that we no longer hear as figures of speech. Declaring we feel immovable, we say "I am glued to my chair." If we picture what we have said, we have a comical scene. But with dead metaphors, neither speaker nor hearer pictures anything at all. In a dead metaphor, the old comparison or assertion of identity is what is dead. If we did not say that we were glued to the chair, we might have said that we were anchored to the spot and no one would see the old schooner in the harbor, its anchor played out behind it, caught in the coral of the harbor bottom. For that matter, "dead metaphor" is a dead metaphor; and if I say that the old comparison is buried, I make the same morbid assertion. Once these metaphors were alive; now they are decayed corpses. The first time anyone used the metaphor of "dead metaphor," he implied that a hole had been dug—six feet deep, six feet long, three feet across—in the dirt of the phrase, and that somebody had placed the body of a comparison in this hole and heaped dirt over the body.

Live metaphors embody feelings. Dead metaphors embody stock responses, clichés, and lethargy. Bad poetry uses dead metaphors as commonly as we do in speech. Good poetry invents new metaphors, making vivid comparisons.

People often mix their dead metaphors. "Then the hand of God stepped in . . ." makes a wonderful anatomical mixture. Of course *the hand of God* was used as if it meant "fortuitous circumstance," and *stepped in* as if it meant "happened next." When I first taught writing, one of my students wrote in a poem "The door yawned and beckoned." By *yawned* she meant that it opened, by *beckoned* that it looked inviting. But the two dead metaphors together made an impossible anatomy again, in which a door was an open mouth from which a hand suddenly extended. (Journalists as well as poets are experts at

mixing dead metaphors. Take this example: "Mushrooming insurance and energy costs represent a double-barreled shotgun pointed at New England's ski
areas." The writer of this sentence developed the ability *not* to see, or the
writer could not have turned a soft vegetable into a steel weapon.)

Forming the habit of taking things literally, a reader becomes increasingly
sensitive to language. Reading literally, we do not read the word *blind* automatically as if it means "obtuse"—which is to use *blind* as a dead metaphor.
When we read *blind,* we take it to mean "sightless" until we find out otherwise. Then we do not write a sentence like this one recently printed in a
country weekly: "'American optometrists are blind to the advantages of small
town living,' said Dr. Harvey Bagnold to the Rotary Club last Tuesday."

Taking words as literally as possible—until the poem forces us to understand that we are reading a metaphor—we read the metaphor that is there.
When Hamlet talks about his problems, he says that one possibility is to "take
arms against a sea of troubles." The *Encyclopaedia Britannica,* in an otherwise sensible entry on "Metaphor," cites this figure as a mixed metaphor
because people do not bear weapons against the ocean. It is not a mixed
metaphor. It is visual metaphor embodying an idea and the emotions appropriate to that idea. Hamlet acknowledges that his problems are as soluble as
the sea is vulnerable to his assault. The image expresses his feelings of
futility. Shakespeare has Hamlet reveal his feelings by making a metaphor
that provides an image of someone taking arms—in the context of the play, a
sword or dagger—against an ocean.

Besides personification, a subdivision of metaphor mentioned on page 441,
and hyperbole, or extreme exaggeration ("That room was two miles wide!"),
we need mention only two other forms of figurative language, not quite so
common as metaphor and simile. In **synechdoche** we speak of something by
naming only a part of it. A poet might refer to a naval fleet as "two hundred
keels," for instance, and his audience would understand that *keel* stood for
boat. It is a way of referring to boats without using the word, which has perhaps lost freshness through overuse. We use synechdoche in everyday speech
if we say that, during the summer, Gloria acquired wheels—she bought a used
Oldsmobile. The part of the car stands in for the whole of the car.

In **metonomy** we speak of the object in terms of something closely connected with it—not a part of it as in synechdoche, but a thing closely and
legitimately associated with it. Thus we can refer to a stove as its heat, for heat
is not a part of the stove but a quality of it, or an association. Charles Reznikoff
writes:

> Holding the stem of the
> beauty she had
> as if it were still
> a rose.

The poet first uses *beauty* by metonomy, as a quality of flowers; then he
makes the flower particular.

Here are some poems followed by questions about metaphor and other figures of speech.

(1609)

That time of year thou mayst in me behold
When yellow leaves, or none, or few, do hang
Upon those boughs which shake against the cold,
Bare ruin'd choirs[1] where late the sweet birds sang.
In me thou seest the twilight of such day
As after sunset fadeth in the west,
Which by and by black night doth take away,
Death's second self, that seals up all in rest.
In me thou seest the glowing of such fire
10   That on the ashes of his youth doth lie,
As the death-bed whereon it must expire,
Consumed with that which it was nourish'd by.
　　This thou perceiv'st which makes thy love more strong,
　　To love that well which thou must leave ere long.
　　　　　　　　　　　　　　　—William Shakespeare

Questions

1. Paraphrase the poem, summarize the content, and discern the structure.

2. Where do you find the first figure of speech? What sort of figure is it?

3. How are the three quatrains linked in idea? Is there metaphorical coherence? Imagistic coherence?

4. In the fourth line, are the birds literal or figurative or both?

5. In the eleventh and twelfth lines, does the analogy make a complex idea simpler? Or does it make a simple idea more difficult?

6. List and name all figures of speech in this sonnet.

The Hill   (1962)

It is sometime since I have been
to what it was had once turned me backwards,
and made my head into
a cruel instrument.

It is simple
to confess. Then done,
to walk away, walk away,
to come again.

---

[1] Choir lofts, the part of the church building where the choirboys sang during religious services

But that form, I must answer,
10 is dead in me, completely,
and I will not allow it
to reappear—

Saith perversity, the willful,
the magnanimous cruelty,
which is in me
like a hill.

—Robert Creeley

Questions

1. What are the connotations of *instrument?* Is the word a metaphor?
2. Note all the metaphors in this poem. Is there a dead metaphor here? A personification?
3. Note other figures of speech.
4. Does the final figure of speech have impact on the earlier word *me?*

November and Aunt Jemima (1990)

We sit at the table and that is grace,
the way one commits the prelude to kowtowing
by folding into the chair.

Usually we eat as if on a subway,
among strangers, standing to avoid the
toilet seat. Today, though, is Thanksgiving

so guilt bibs us, an extra place
is set for Aunt Jemima, the pancake box
occupies the chair, the family resemblance

10 unmistakeable. Hips full as Southern Baptist
tents but of a different doctrine.
Teeth white as the shock of lynching, thirty-two

tombstones. Despite the headrag
neither she nor her sister that bore me
are mistaken for gypsies.

The color of corrosion, she is not called
classic. The syrup that is the liquid
version of her skin flows like the promised

milk and honey so once a year we welcome
20 her. Even Christ would not be welcome every
day. Especially Christ who cannot come

without judgment just as she cannot come
without pancakes, flat, humane stones
still thrown at her by those whose sins

being white are invisible as her pain, the
mix in the box after the grinding of bones.
                                        —*Thylias Moss*

Questions

1. How are the verbs of the first stanza—including participles—related to each other?

2. In the twelfth line, do you like the construction of the simile? Why?

3. What is "the color of corrosion"? What does this phrase imply?

4. Discuss the final metaphor here. Is it also an image? How does it conclude the poem?

CHAPTER FIVE

Tone, with a
Note on Intentions

Apoem's **tone**, in common definition, reveals the writer's attitude toward a subject, an attitude that could include sarcasm or irony or awe. In conversation, we indicate tone by our manner of speaking or by our facial expression: "Great!" can be pronounced so that it is a compliment or an insult. When we discuss a poem's tone, we discuss the value we attribute to its statements. Wallace Stevens, in "Disillusionment of Ten O'Clock," wrote:

> People are not going
> To dream of baboons and periwinkles.

In the context of this poem, which has already told us about "houses . . . haunted / By white night-gowns," we hear the speaker's tone as ironic. **Irony** is the perception of incongruity of discrepancy—between statement and meaning, for instance. Because we know that these unimaginative people will dream colorless dreams, it is ironic to name the exotic *baboons and periwinkles* as possible subjects of their dreams. Other poems are explosive and angry in tone, like John Donne's line beginning "The Canonization":

> For Godsake hold your tongue and let me love!

Other poems reveal sarcasm, as in E. E. Cummings's lines from "Poem, or Beauty Hurts Mr. Vinal":

> take it from me kiddo
> believe me
> my country, 'tis of
>
> you, land of the Cluett
> Shirt Boston Garter and Spearmint
> Girl With The Wrigley Eyes (of you
> land of the Arrow Ide
> and Earl &

Wilson
10   Collars) of you i
     sing: land of Abraham Lincoln and Lydia E. Pinkham,
     land above all of Just Add Hot Water and Serve—
     from every B. V. D.

     let freedom ring

These examples are relatively simple. Because most poems are complex, many-sided, and ambivalent, the tone of many poems is hard to name and easy to mistake.

When we speak of a poem's tone, we make a metaphor, speaking of a poem as if it were a person and could voice its own words. It can help, studying tone in poetry, to try out the analogy of poems-as-people. If we sometimes misunderstand tone in poems, it is also true that we can misunderstand personal tones of voice, even when we have body, pitch, gesture, and eyebrows to help us understand. In everyday life, we interpret people's tones every hour of the day, without noticing that we do it. When we are offended by someone, or when we are touched or pleased, it is often the tone that does the offending or the pleasing. Perhaps we live with someone, and after dinner one night someone says "I'll do the dishes." These four words, depending on their tone, could mean a great many things. They could mean "Of course I'm getting stuck with doing the dishes, you slob, the way I always do, and the way I get stuck with taking out the garbage and picking up the biology notes from Gerry and standing in line for the football tickets." Or, they could mean "I want to do the dishes because you look so tired, and I'm always happy to take on a little work on your behalf, because you do so much for me, and I'm grateful for you getting that book from the library." Or, they could mean "I'm about to ask a favor," or "I think you're mad at me," or "I'll get points this way," or "Here is something I can do in order to avoid doing homework," or "When you wash the dishes, they never get clean."

Usually, we can decode the tone of somebody's voice. For that matter, we decode the way someone crosses a room or closes a door or drinks a Coke. Decoding a roommate, we use a glossary of behavior that we have been learning since birth. Door slams mean anger, says this dictionary; deep sighs mean frustration. We receive signals through gestures and through words, and we respond in kind; we communicate by tones.

Readers of poetry learn a system of signals by which they understand the tone of a poem, just as everybody learns the tones of personal pitch and gesture. One of the contracts that a poet makes with readers stipulates that tone shall be ascertainable: an assured tone is one of the criteria of excellence in poetry. Sometimes, poems fail by not making tone clear enough. For instance, here is a portion of a poem by a talented student:

    . . . on sour air, the bells
    chimed season's greetings
    to the departed host
    of Christmas . . .

If you cannot decode the tone of this fragment, you are not alone. What is the poet's attitude toward the subject? The poet intended *season's greetings* to be highly ironic, even sarcastic. Reading it, one could not be certain; a potential irony floated, unanchored, two inches above the page. The poet might have anchored irony any number of ways, but it is worth saying that ironic clichés are difficult to control; sometimes a context that demands irony provides control, sometimes it will come from a structure that repeats and varies the same irony. This fragment fails to make the irony seem intentional.

A Note on Intentions

When most of us speak about poetry, we refer to an author's intentions without even noticing that we do it. Speaking of diction and idiom, metaphor and image, we couch our discoveries in terms of the poet's presumed wishes and endeavors. Interpreting meaning, we say "This is what the poet was trying to say." The last phrase is especially common—and it is unfortunate: it promotes a picture of the poet as a fumbling, inarticulate slob, unable to say what is meant. The expression suggests that we will help out the dolt standing there with mouth open; let us inform the grateful poet of what he or she was trying and failing to say.

Whenever we begin to speak of a poet's intentions, we ought to consider what we are *really* talking about. Surely, no one is so presumptuous as to believe that he or she *really* knows what was in Milton's mind before he wrote *Paradise Lost*—or what was in Robert Frost's mind before he wrote "Stopping by Woods on a Snowy Evening," for that matter. Common sense reveals our ignorance; we need no degrees in psychology. Everything that ever happened to Robert Frost—every poem he ever read, every conversation he ever took part in, every winter he ever lived through, every horse he ever drove—entered his poem. Or so I am free to suppose.

We never know, with anything like certainty, why we make important decisions in our own lives. If ignorance prevails about our own intentions, how can we possibly presume to know someone else's? The formula What was he trying to do? How well did he accomplish his purposes? presupposes a sort of knowledge we cannot claim. It is true that some poets have revealed their intentions to us—in autobiography, in letters to editors or to friends, and in answer to questions. I suggest that we should not believe them. We should *listen* to what they say—if the poem is good, the poet's talk about it is bound to be interesting, even if only for what the poet leaves out. But we should listen skeptically, with our minds alert for falsity; we should not listen naïvely, as if we were getting the words from the horse's mouth. Often, the most sophisticated people become naïve when artists claim to explain their work. When politicians explain that their motives are noble and selfless, nobody believes them. When poets do the same, people nod their heads. Really, there is every reason for artists to lie to us when they tell us about their work—because they have every reason to lie to themselves. Good poems by their nature reveal many sides of a person, including sides poets may wish to conceal. Robert Frost, for instance, revealed a dark side in many poems—fears of madness, longings for oblivion, notions of evil, intimations of meaninglessness—which was not the self he chose to reveal on the lecture platform. In speaking about his poems, he denied their darkness.

Some poets have the illusion that they intend whatever takes place in their poems. They are like people who, in an argument, defend the rightness of everything they have ever said or done. Other poets admit that they wrote this phrase, or that whole poem, without knowing exactly what they were saying. T. S. Eliot, for instance, proclaimed his innocence of intention in much of "The Waste Land." Probably more often, a writer will consciously intend something on the surface—and write something else underneath the surface. The writer may not be aware of the subsurface meaning until later, when somebody points it out. Some writers deny it even after it is pointed out. Some students and teachers talk in classrooms about "hidden meanings" in a poem, an unfortunate phrase that makes reading poems sound like detective work. If we must speak of "hidden meanings," we ought to acknowledge that poets frequently hide meanings from themselves, and not just from readers.

Maybe the word *intention* should be stricken from our critical vocabulary; we speak sometimes of "unconscious intentions," a phrase in which the noun contradicts the adjective. In our lives, we tend to judge by actions or results rather than intentions; if someone breaks our jaw while "only trying to help," we are smarter to remember the broken jaw than to warm ourselves over the avowed intention. With poems, we must pay no attention to intentions, or even to the idea of intentions, but look for actions and results. We must attend to what is there, *really there on the page,* and to the impingements of the words upon us.

Tone is easy to miss or misinterpret. Many readers seize on one notion of tone in a quick reading, and ignore or cannot accept alternative readings. Assuming one tone, they eliminate the possibility of others, or of tonal variation. This short poem, alive with tone, requires thoughtful reading.

Transformations   (1917)

Portion of this yew
Is a man my grandsire knew,
Bosomed here at its foot:
This branch may be his wife,
A ruddy human life
Now turned to a green shoot.

These grasses must be made
Of her who often prayed,
Last century, for repose;
10 And the fair girl long ago
Whom I often tried to know
May be entering this rose.

So, they are not underground,
But as nerves and veins abound
In the growths of upper air,
And they feel the sun and rain,
And the energy again
That made them what they were!
—*Thomas Hardy*

First, let us agree on a summary. A man walks among the graves of people he has heard about or has known in life. He observes that all these bodies endure, at least as particles in graveyard plants.

This summary is as pale as a government bulletin, because I am trying to sanitize the tone of it. What, then, is the tone of Hardy's poem? Is it melancholy? Is the visitor happy in the graveyard? Does Hardy announce molecular immortality as a discovery of vast scientific and spiritual importance? At first glance, he may seem to do the last. One student, writing about this poem, said, at the end of a paper, "So after this depression about everybody dying Thos. Hardy shakes himself out of it. He decides to look on the bright side of things so he notices that everybody really lives and nobody really dies because the roses etcetera go on blooming year after year after year after year." These sentences run into trouble as a paraphrase, and describe a poem which, if Hardy had written it, would have been dishonest; this student has Hardy turn himself away from sadness by lying to himself and to his readers. And this poem is *almost* the one Hardy wrote; I don't think that this student's interpretation is far off. Still, it mistakes Hardy's tone.

"Transformations" begins with a physical scene. An old man—many clues, like trying to know a fair girl, and an acquaintance with someone "last century," hint that the speaker is male and is getting on—walks musing in a graveyard. At the beginning, he thinks of deaths remote from him, and the tone is quiet and contemplative. As the old man moves forward in time, closer to his own end, the tone shifts.

Notice that Hardy begins by implying that he is certain, and modifies his tone of certainty as the poem develops. The change in the degree and in the type of assertion makes the change in tone. The first two lines are plain statement: "Portion of this yew / Is a man my grandsire knew. . . ." Obviously, the speaker knows the truth of what he says, and we believe him; the yew tree must be adjacent to the grave, and we can accept this assertion scientifically. If someone is buried next to a tree, after a number of years it must be true that some of the tree's molecules contain atoms that were earlier part of that person's body. When the speaker goes on "Bosomed here at its foot," he moves into metaphor. The metaphor has resonance and secondary implication, but it also carries information: the man my grandsire knew is buried (his burial compared to a baby snuggled up to a breast) at the base of the tree.

The speaker then takes certainty as a starting point and adds fancy: "This branch *may be* his wife . . ." He plays straight with us: he *admits* that when he begins to think of a particular part of the tree as composed of a particular person, he is *playing* with the possibilities of his scientific commonplace. If the wife (as we can assume) is buried beside her husband "here at its foot," it is common sense to assume that she also participates in the tree's molecules, but it is fanciful to think of her as a special new branch. (That she's thought of as a *green shoot* implies that she died more recently than her husband.) The speaker modestly admits a lack of knowledge or certainty, admits his playful fancy, by using the verb form *may be.*

The first line of the second stanza appears at first glance to make a definite assertion: "These grasses must be made . . ." If *must be* in our usage meant "absolutely, incontrovertibly has to be," we would have a statement of certainty. But, with the typical oddity of our speech, *must be* encodes a lack of certainty. When Hardy writes "These grasses must be made," he uses *must be* the way we do when we say "It must be six o'clock." (Robert Frost, as we have seen, used the same idiom when he wrote "My little horse must think it queer. . . .") In Hardy's poem, we are allowed to understand that a woman (who "prayed / Last century for repose") is buried hereabouts, so her remains may well be part of the grasses here; on the other hand, the lines say, possibly they are not (because of the length of time? because of possible error about the gravesite?). In the second part of this stanza, Hardy reverts to the *may be* form of possibility, making the metaphor that is the high point of the poem: "the fair girl . . . / May be entering this rose." Her molecules promenade through the stem to the blossom. In the metaphor, the rose has doors or portals, like a house or church, and the pretty young woman in the shape of her molecules walks through the door.

So far the tone has been simple. Hardy told us a certainty followed by fancies and probabilities. We walk beside an old man though a churchyard, where he ruminates on the persistence of matter translated from one organism to another. In the third stanza, the tone changes entirely. We can perceive the change in the poem's grammar. In his verb forms, Hardy reverts from *must be* and *may be* to direct assertion. "So," the poem tells us, as a result of what has just been said, "they [the dead] *are* not underground."

But they are. Yes, some molecules of decay may have escaped, but the dead are not *really* "as nerves or veins" abounding "In the growths of upper air." We know that the poem tells us false when it says that they *abound* and that "they *feel* the sun and rain / And the energy again / That made them what they were!" The *tone* of this assertion is made loud by the exclamation point, a triumphant, almost ecstatic assertion of the survival of the dead. It is the *tone* of the exclamation that must concern the reader. The poem seems to argue that it has proved survival after death by what it has observed of plant life. The poem began by winning our trust with its scrupulous use of verbs moving from *is* to *may be* and *must be.* Now it seems to violate the trust, by asserting *are* when we must be aware that the idea depends on speculation, on fantasy, and on a scientific notion that deals with particles of human flesh, not with whole human beings.

Because the leap to assertion is such a grand leap, and because we have learned to trust the implicit reasonableness of the speaker, the leap to false assertion creates a tone of strong and urgent feeling, which speaks to us like unwritten lines of poetry, saying "I know this assertion to be false; I make it only because I must, because the mortality of bodies is unacceptable to me!" The poem, through its tone—accomplished mostly by variations in verbs— speaks to us eloquently of the dread and fear of death.

Hardy's intention, in writing the poem, is not known to the reader—not to me, not to you, not to Hardy's most devoted student or scholar. But, in its own words and in its slow and steady motion down the page, the poem makes its shape inevitable—if we read with a steady care, with attention, and with the sensitivity we use interpreting the gesture and pitch of a person we love.

Here are some poems to read for their tone.

Museum Piece   (1950)

The good grey guardians of art
Patrol the halls on spongy shoes,
Impartially protective, though
Perhaps suspicious of Toulouse.[1]

Here dozes one against the wall,
Disposed upon a funeral chair.
A Degas[2] dancer pirouettes
Upon the parting of his hair.

See how she spins! The grace is there,
10 But strain as well is plain to see.
Degas loved the two together:
Beauty joined to energy.

Edgar Degas purchased once
A fine El Greco,[3] which he kept
Against the wall beside his bed
To hang his pants on while he slept.
                          —Richard Wilbur

Questions

1. In the first line, what is the tone of the word *good?*

2. Alliteration is the repetition of consonant sounds, as in *good gray guardians.* Does alliteration in the first line contribute to the tone of the line?

3. Notice the rhyme in the first stanza. Can a rhyme contribute to tone? Does this rhyme?

[1] Henri de Toulouse-Lautrec Monfa (1864–1901) made notable paintings of Parisian life and characters, but is best known for his posters of nightclubs and entertainers.   [2] Edgar Degas (1834–1917), one of the important French impressionists, is best known for his paintings and pastels of ballerinas.   [3] El Greco (1548?–1614?), native of Crete and student of the Venetian master Titian, lived in Toledo from his late twenties and was the leading sixteenth-century mystical Spanish painter. His work often distorts the human form by elongating it.

4. Does the first stanza introduce a tone that remains the same throughout the poem? Where does the poem's tone change? How do you know?

5. What is the tone of the last line of the poem? Does it resolve the differing tones earlier in the poem?

Hay for the Horses   (1959)

He had driven half the night
From far down San Joaquin
Through Mariposa, up the
Dangerous mountain roads,
And pulled in at eight A.M.
With his big truckload of hay behind the barn.
With winch and ropes and hooks
We stacked the bales up clean
To splintery redwood rafters
10   High in the dark, flecks of alfalfa
Whirling through shingle-cracks of light,
Itch of haydust in the sweaty shirt and shoes.
At lunchtime under Black oak
Out in the hot corral,
—The old mare nosing lunchpails,
Grasshoppers crackling in the weeds—
'I'm sixty-eight,' he said,
'I first bucked hay when I was seventeen.
I thought, that day I started,
20   I sure would hate to do this all my life.
And dammit, that's just what
I've gone and done.'
                         —Gary Snyder

Questions

1. How would you characterize the tone of the first sentence of this poem? Do you trust it to be straightforward? Why?

2. In the poem's middle, does the tone change at all? Do you sense any change in the speaker's attitude toward the subject?

3. In the last part of the poem, the poet quotes another speaker. Does this new speaker have a characteristic tone? What do you know of him from his tone? What does the poet do to reveal his tone?

What I Heard at the Discount Department Store   (1988)

Don't touch that. And stop your whining too.
Stop it. I mean it. You know I do.
If you don't stop, I'll give you fucking something
to cry about right here
and don't you think I won't either.

So she did. She slapped him across the face.
And you could hear the snap of flesh against the flesh
halfway across the store. Then he wasn't whining anymore.
Instead, he wept. His little body heaved and shivered and wept.
10 He was seven or eight. She was maybe thirty.
Above her left breast, the pin said: Nurse's Aide.

Now they walk hand in hand down the aisle
between the tables piled with tennis shoes
and underpants and plastic bags of socks.

I told you I would. You knew I would.
You can't get away with shit like that with me,
you know you can't.
You're not in school anymore.
You're with your mother now.
20 You can get away with fucking murder there,
but you can't get away with shit like that with me.
Stop that crying now I say
or I'll give you another little something
like I did before.

Stop that now. You'd better stop.

That's better. That's a whole lot better.
You know you can't do that with me.
You're with your mother now.

                                        —David Budbill

Questions

1. How soon do you understand that a character, other than the poet, speaks this poem? What is her tone and how do you know it?

2. How can a title contribute to the tone of a poem?

3. Do you ever find this poem departing from the tone established at the start? Where?

CHAPTER SIX

Symbols and Allusions

In "To Read a Story," a symbol was defined as a person, object, place, or event that comes to stand for something other than it is, usually something more than it is, and for a class of events or relationships. This definition can serve as a starter here. Again, we must make distinctions among kinds of symbolism: the **conventional** (or **traditional**) **symbol**, the **natural symbol**, and the **literary symbol**. We must speak as well about allusion and reference in poetry, devices that overlap when a poet refers or alludes to a traditional symbol and that resemble each other in the difficulty they cause for students.

It is easiest to speak first of *natural symbols,* which occur in literature but which tend toward cliché: night is a natural symbol of death, and so is autumn. Shakespeare and other geniuses have made great literature using natural symbols; remember "That time of year thou mayst in me behold . . ." (page 445), where both night and autumn are symbols of death. Because natural symbols tend to be trite, modern writers seldom use them, or use them in the negative, setting up the expectation of a stock response, and then disappointing it. The great modern poet T. S. Eliot began one of his first poems, "The Love Song of J. Alfred Prufrock," with

> Let us go then, you and I,
> When the evening is spread out against the sky . . .

appealing to stock responses, and to the natural symbolism of sunset as beauty or fulfillment. His audience, when he wrote the poem in 1911, might have expected him to go on:

> Like veils of painted gossamer on high . . .

Instead, he turned this expectation upside down with his actual third line:

> Like a patient etherized upon a table.

A natural symbol underwent a radical alteration.

The word *symbol* begins by meaning a simple sign, like a circle containing a cigarette, with a diagonal line crossing out the cigarette; everybody knows the sign or the symbol for NO SMOKING. We speak of *conventional symbols* like these signs and like national flags or the logos of sports teams. Another sort of conventional symbol (it would be better perhaps to speak of these as *traditional symbols*) are images or phrases that have acquired meaning over centuries of history or association, like the cross and the Star of David. A poet who uses an image of a cross can hardly avoid reference to Christ, Christianity, and suffering. Therefore, reference allies itself to traditional (and conventional) symbolism. We speak of conventional and traditional symbols together because the distinction between them is quantitative; "conventional" symbols are simple signs; "traditional" symbols are signs with long and complex associations.

Finally, there is the *literary symbol,* of which a fictional example was Chekhov's "Gooseberries." Here is a poem by William Blake:

The Sick Rose   (1794)

O Rose, thou art sick!
The invisible worm
That flies in the night,
In the howling storm,

Has found out thy bed
Of crimson joy,
And his dark secret love
Does thy life destroy.
        —*William Blake*

Reading this poem, let us as always first try the literal. A sick rose could suffer from a plant bacterium. But the second line of the poem reveals that we cannot continue to read on a literal level, because invisible worms fly only in the imagination. Back to the first line, then. *Rose* is capitalized, which may give us the sense that this flower is more than a flower, or that a real flower is addressed as if it embodied something beyond itself. To connect this flower with the notion of sickness seems a violation of the natural, as if we said that a mountain squeaked like a mouse. The contrast between *rose* and *sick* occurs at the levels of both sound and idea, as the full *o*s of the first two syllables dwindle into the quick short *i*s of *sick* and *invisible*.

"The Sick Rose" makes a literary symbol. When we ask what it is a symbol *of,* we ask the wrong sort of question. A literary symbol is not a figure or a riddle to which there exists a simple answer, or a correct interpretation. Instead, it is a series of words—creating image or event or character or fantasy or plot or scene—that is irreducible, that in itself is a formula for a complex set of feelings and ideas never before rendered in the same way. *The literary symbol cannot be translated or identified.* We can talk about it and we can talk around it, but the symbol will always sit in the center of our words, smiling enigmatically, content to be itself. A great French symbolist poet, Stéphane Mallarmé, made a metaphor for the symbol: he said it was "the new word." We can find this metaphor useful to our thinking about the literary symbol, because it cannot be defined or named by anything except itself. It resembles, then, a "new word," as if the poet invented the word *chair* for the first time, and there were no other word for chair but *chair*.

William Blake makes a symbol for a new thing. *The invisible worm* is not described in terms of horns and claws; it is a general "worm," with the particular attribute of invisibility—and with other attributes that associate feelings with this *new word*. This is a worm gifted with flight like a dragon, and gifted especially to fly in a darkness (night as a natural symbol is frightening, possibly the place of evil) and through a storm (destruction, possibly divine wrath) that makes a noise like the cries of someone in pain. The sick rose and its worm live in a place of terror and fear, are themselves instruments and victims of terror and fear. Syntax of subject and object, predator and victim, locates a scene in the second stanza. The worm has found "thy bed / Of crimson joy . . ." The word *joy* seems unambivalent, but it is not: crimson is blood-color, one of sin's colors, and dangerous; at least violent and extreme. One would expect malice from such a worm, and one hears *love* instead, but it is a *dark, secret* love, and it is a love that rhymes *joy* with *destroy*. When love is both dark and secret, adjectives like crimson complicate the wholeness of the noun; if they do not reverse love into hate, or joy into pain, or fondness into malice, they introduce elements of the negative into the positive; they make by their complexity a wholeness. It is a wholeness that is also a new, single thing: symbolist poem or "new word."

Many poems speak of roses, in many different ways—sometimes as traditional or literary symbols and sometimes not. Theodore Roethke's great contemporary poem, "The Rose" (pages 677–680), makes a literary symbol, another new word like William Blake's. But in Charles Reznikoff's four-line poem,

> Holding the stem of the
> beauty she had
> as if it were still
> a rose.

rose is not a symbol but a type, "a thing of beauty." When Shakespeare says "A rose by any other name would smell as sweet," or when Gertrude Stein tells us "A rose is a rose is a rose," these writers do not make new words, but, like Reznikoff, they use the rose as a type: a flower beautiful in its odor; a thing of this world.

The Problem of Allusion

Blake's "The Sick Rose" carries countless associations for the student of literature. If a contemporary poet wrote now about "the rose's worm"—he or she would make an **allusion** to "The Sick Rose," almost a quotation. Allusion works with ideas as well as with words. One critic reading Blake's "The Sick

Rose" believed that he found an allusion to Shakespeare's line "Lilies that fester smell far worse than weeds." It is now time for us to focus on allusion. Poems can allude to other poems and to history, to ideas, to fact, and to myth. All poems retelling old stories are allusive; a new version of "Casey at the Bat" would be an allusion to the old ballad; a new poem that tells about Oedipus or Hamlet must be based on allusions to the old plays.

Allusion has become a problem for modern readers, because people no longer share the same backgrounds. A century ago, an allusion to the Bible supposed no special knowledge; a century ago, among literate people, it was not obscure to speak of Greek deities like Apollo or Aphrodite; a century ago, even scientific knowledge was commonly held, partly because there was relatively little of it. Now we not only specialize in fields; we find specialties within specialties. The high-energy physicist cannot understand the physicist who studies the behavior of particles at low temperatures.

Allusion is common in poetry, and acts as a barrier to understanding. Sensitivity to allusion in poetry can only grow with extended reading. It is not an element of poetry that can be studied by exercise and thought; it is an element of poetry that can be named and introduced—but then it must be learned and practiced by much reading. No shortcut will solve the problem of allusion.

But one shortcut, obvious enough, will *help* with certain poems. Here is an epigram (a short, pithy poem; see pages 510–511) by Louise Bogan:

To an Artist, to Take Heart   (1941)

Slipping in blood, by his own hand, through pride,
Hamlet, Othello, Coriolanus fall.
Upon his bed, however, Shakespeare died,
Having endured them all.

                                        —*Louise Bogan*

Bogan alludes to three Shakespearean heroes. The names of Hamlet and Othello will be familiar to most American students, though not always the stories that their names allude to. The name of Coriolanus will be new to most. Reading this poem, the student is forced to a dictionary or a reference book.* The

---

* Earlier, this book urged the use of the *Oxford English Dictionary* (page 424). In the pursuit of allusions, the student can use the whole reference room. For help with the proper names in Bogan's poem, the *Oxford Companion to English Literature* would perhaps be the best resource, in which entries for these names summarize plots and tell the tragic flaws of heroes. Oxford also prints a *Companion to American Literature,* and *Companions* to the literatures of other languages. The *Oxford Classical Dictionary* is very good on mythology, and there are classical dictionaries and companions from other publishers. The *Readers' Encyclopedia* is a useful volume, as are more specialized volumes of reference: the *Encyclopedia of American Biography. Webster's Biographical Dictionary, An Encyclopedia of World History,* and the *Encyclopaedia Britannica.* The *New Columbia Encyclopedia* is an excellent resource in one volume. Reference librarians will often point researchers in the right direction. With certain poets, especially highly allusive poets of the eighteenth century who refer to their own contemporaries by name and by pseudonym, it is useful to consult the notes of a scholarly edition of the poet's work, where the research has been done for us.

problem of allusion is often a problem of vocabulary, especially when it is a matter of proper names. To know that Hamlet is the hero of a play by Shakespeare called *Hamlet*—as a dictionary might tell us—would not help, even with this brief poem. But if we know enough of the story to remember that Hamlet died young and by violence, we can begin to understand the allusion and the poem. We cannot understand the poem without understanding the allusions.

Checking allusions in Louise Bogan's four lines, we learn that Coriolanus's tragic flaw was pride; we add this fact to Othello's suicide and Hamlet's death in a duel. We notice that the three phrases of Bogan's first line follow the order of the three heroes' names in the second line. We understand that the playwright who conceived them lived longer then they did, even if he suffered (*endured* has the connotation of survival with difficulty) and ended by dying in bed.

Because of the difficulties of allusion, certain great and allusive poets are underrepresented in this book, among them Milton, Dryden, and Pope. For the same reason, it is hard to choose poems that can give fair exercise in uncovering allusions. The poems that follow, and the questions that go with them, raise issues largely of symbolism. But not entirely.

Proust's Madeleine   (1949)

Somebody has given my
Baby daughter a box of
Old poker chips to play with.
Today she hands me one while
I am sitting with my tired
Brain at my desk. It is red.
On it is a picture of
An elk's head and the letters
B.P.O.E.—a chip from
10 A small town Elks' Club. I flip
It idly in the air and
Catch it and do a coin trick
To amuse my little girl.
Suddenly everything slips aside.
I see my father
Doing the very same thing,
Whistling "Beautiful Dreamer,"
His breath smelling richly
Of whiskey and cigars. I can
20 Hear him coming home drunk
From the Elk's Club in Elkhart
Indiana, bumping the
Chairs in the dark. I can see
Him dying of cirrhosis
Of the liver and stomach
Ulcers and pneumonia,

Or, as he said on his deathbed, of
Crooked cards and straight whiskey,
Slow horses and fast women.
                    —*Kenneth Rexroth*

Questions

1. Where does allusion begin in this poem? List and explain its allusions.

2. Does this poem use any sort of symbol?

The Draft Horse   (1962)

With a lantern that wouldn't burn
In too frail a buggy we drove
Behind too heavy a horse
Through a pitch-dark limitless grove.

And a man came out of the trees
And took our horse by the head
And reaching back to his ribs
Deliberately stabbed him dead.

The ponderous beast went down
10 With a crack of a broken shaft.
And the night drew through the trees
In one long invidious draft.

The most unquestioning pair
That ever accepted fate
And the least disposed to ascribe
Any more than we had to to hate,

We assumed that the man himself
Or someone he had to obey
Wanted us to get down
20 And walk the rest of the way.
                    —*Robert Frost*

Questions

1. Do you take this action literally?

2. Are there natural symbols here? Traditional or conventional symbols?

3. Does this poem make a "new word"? What in this poem gives you the suggestion that it might be symbolic?

The Monument   (1939)

Now can you see the monument? It is of wood
built somewhat like a box. No. Built
like several boxes in descending sizes
one above the other.
Each is turned half-way round so that
its corners point toward the sides
of the one below and the angles alternate.
Then on the topmost cube is set
a sort of fleur-de-lys of weathered wood,
10 long petals of board, pierced with odd holes,
four-sided, stiff, ecclesiastical.
From it four thin, warped poles spring out,
(slanted like fishing-poles or flag-poles)
and from them jig-saw work hangs down,
four lines of vaguely whittled ornament
over the edges of the boxes
to the ground.
The monument is one-third set against
a sea; two-thirds against a sky.
20 The view is geared
(that is, the view's perspective)
so low there is no "far away,"
and we are far away within the view.
A sea of narrow, horizontal boards
lies out behind our lonely monument,
its long grains alternating right and left
like floor-boards—spotted, swarming-still,
and motionless. A sky runs parallel,
and it is palings, coarser than the sea's:
30 splintery sunlight and long-fibred clouds.
"Why does that strange sea make no sound?
Is it because we're far away?
Where are we? Are we in Asia Minor,
or in Mongolia?"
                An ancient promontory,
an ancient principality whose artist-prince
might have wanted to build a monument
to mark a tomb or boundary, or make
a melancholy or romantic scene of it . . .
40 "But that queer sea looks made of wood,
half-shining, like a driftwood sea.
And the sky looks wooden, grained with cloud.
It's like a stage-set; it is all so flat!
Those clouds are full of glistening splinters!
What is that?"
                It is the monument.
"It's piled-up boxes,
outlined with shoddy fret-work, half-fallen off,
cracked and unpainted. It looks old."

50   —The strong sunlight, the wind from the sea,
      all the conditions of its existence,
      may have flaked off the paint, if ever it was painted,
      and made it homelier than it was.
      "Why did you bring me here to see it?
      A temple of crates in cramped and crated scenery,
      what can it prove?
      I am tired of breathing this eroded air,
      this dryness in which the monument is cracking."

      It is an artifact
60   of wood. Wood holds together better
      than sea or cloud or sand could by itself,
      much better than real sea or sand or cloud.
      It chose that way to grow and not to move.
      The monument's an object, yet those decorations,
      carelessly nailed, looking like nothing at all,
      give it away as having life, and wishing;
      wanting to be a monument, to cherish something.
      The crudest scroll-work says "commemorate,"
      while once each day the light goes around it
70   like a prowling animal,
      or the rain falls on it, or the wind blows into it.
      It may be solid, may be hollow.
      The bones of the artist-prince may be inside
      or far away on even drier soil.
      But roughly but adequately it can shelter
      what is within (which after all
      cannot have been intended to be seen).
      It is the beginning of a painting,
      a piece of sculpture, or poem, or monument,
80   and all of wood. Watch it closely.
                                          —*Elizabeth Bishop*

Questions

1. Is this a symbolist poem? What lines or words help you decide?

2. What sorts of symbol can you discover in this poem?

Facing It   (1988)

My black face fades,
hiding inside the black granite.
I said I wouldn't,
dammit: No tears.
I'm stone. I'm flesh.
My clouded reflection eyes me
like a bird of prey, the profile of night
slanted against morning. I turn

this way—the stone lets me go.
10 I turn that way—I'm inside
the Vietnam Veterans Memorial
again, depending on the light
to make a difference.
I go down the 58,022 names,
half-expecting to find
my own in letters like smoke.
I touch the name Andrew Johnson;
I see the booby trap's white flash.
Names shimmer on a woman's blouse
20 but when she walks away
the names stay on the wall.
Brushstrokes flash, a red bird's
wings cutting across my stare.
The sky. A plane in the sky.
A white vet's image floats
closer to me, then his pale eyes
look through mine. I'm a window.
He's lost his right arm
inside the stone. In the black mirror
30 a woman's trying to erase names:
No, she's brushing a boy's hair.
                    —*Yusef Komunyakaa*

Questions

1. This African-American poet fought in Viet Nam. Did you understand as much from the poem? How do we judge true autobiographical anecdote from fiction or even from symbol? Can we be sure?

2. Can we take a real object and turn it into a symbol? Are some real objects created to be symbols? Does this poet turn a symbol into a symbol? How?

The Apparitions   (1940)

Because there is safety in derision
I talked about an apparition,
I took no trouble to convince,
Or seem plausible to a man of sense,
Distrustful of that popular eye
Whether it be bold or sly.
Fifteen apparitions have I seen;
The worst a coat upon a coat-hanger.

I have found nothing half so good
10 As my long-planned half solitude,
Where I can sit up half the night
With some friend that has the wit
Not to allow his looks to tell

When I am unintelligible.
Fifteen apparitions have I seen;
The worst a coat upon a coat-hanger.

When a man grows old his joy
Grows more deep day after day,
His empty heart is full at length,
20 But he has need of all that strength
Because of the increasing Night
That opens her mystery and fright.
Fifteen apparitions have I seen;
The worst a coat upon a coat-hanger.
                    —William Butler Yeats

Questions

1. Note any use of conventional or traditional symbols.

2. Does the image of *a coat upon a coat-hanger* change its implications as it is repeated?

3. Does the poem make a literary symbol?

The Return   (1912)

See, they return; ah, see the tentative
            Movements, and the slow feet,
            The trouble in the pace and the uncertain
            Wavering!

See they return, one, and by one,
With fear, as half-awakened;
As if the snow should hesitate
And murmur in the wind,
            and half turn back;
10 These were the 'Wing'd-with-Awe,'
            Inviolable.

Gods of the wingèd shoe!
With them the silver hounds,
            sniffing the trace of air!

Haie! Haie!

            These were the swift to harry;
These the keen-scented;
These were the souls of blood.

Slow on the leash,
20   pallid the leash-men!
                    —Ezra Pound

Questions

1. Can you find any allusions in this poem?

2. Can you identify *they* in this poem? If you cannot name a definite identity, can you name a kind of action that *they* embody?

3. If the poem is symbolic, what kind of symbol does it make?

CHAPTER SEVEN

The Sound of Poems

When we explicate a poem, we investigate its sound as well as its symbol, its shape and architecture as well as its paraphrase and implication. Talking about William Carlos Williams's wheelbarrow poem, we looked at the poem as artifact, as made object. This chapter concentrates on the pleasures poems make by their sound.

We derive at least two distinct pleasures from the sound of language in poetry. One is the pleasure of *rhythm,* of words in motion, uncoiling in sentences from poetic line to line. Here is the beginning of *Paradise Lost* by John Milton:

> Of man's first disobedience, and the fruit
> Of that forbidden tree, whose mortal taste
> Brought death into the world, and all our woe,
> With loss of Eden, till one greater Man
> Restore us, and regain the blissful seat,
> Sing, Heavenly Muse . . .

The pleasure of rhythm is like the pleasure of dancing, or of tapping our feet to keep time with music. Rhythm recalls primitive origins of poetry where song and poem and dance happened together. This rhythm-pleasure of poetry's sound connects with our pleasure in bodily motion.

The other pleasure is the delight that we take in adjacent sounds rubbing together, vowels held and savored, consonants clicking together. Here are some lines from "To Autumn" by John Keats:

> Then in a wailful choir the small gnats mourn
> Among the river sallows,° borne aloft   willows
> Or sinking as the light wind lives or dies; . . .

Rhythm and Linebreak

First, let us look at rhythm. The lines of a poem are essential to its signature and its identity. Milton broke some of his lines where the meaning paused, as with

Brought death into the world, and all our woe . . .

When the sense pauses or stops at the end of a line, we call it **end-stopped**. Most of the time, Milton broke his lines in the middle of a phrase, so that the sense of the sentence ran over into the line following, as with

> With loss of Eden, till one greater Man
> Restore us . . .

When the sense runs over the end of a line, we call the line enjambed, and the practice **enjambment**.

Even when a line is enjambed, it retains its identity as a line of poetry; reading it aloud, we make a slight pause at the end. Or, we show the line-end in another way, by raising our voice perhaps, or by holding on to the last syllable. We do not pause evenly—we pause longer when the line is end-stopped—but we find some means to show with our voice that we have come to the end of a line. If we do not, we might was well be reading prose. One eighteenth-century critic with no ear suggested that we print Milton as prose or that we rebreak his lines according to phrases of sense, which could make the first lines of *Paradise Lost* look like this:

> Of man's first disobedience
> and the fruit
> of that forbidden tree
> whose mortal taste
> brought death
> into the world
> and all our woe,
> with loss of Eden,
> till one greater Man
> restore us,
> and regain
> the blissful seat,
> sing
> Heavenly Muse . . .

How boring and flat the lines become! There can be little attention to pauses within lines, because the critic would break the line wherever there might be a pause. There is no tension; music and sense become identical, which results in the disappearance of music.

We must develop a sense of the poetic line, if we are to take pleasure in poetry. Here are lines by Louis Simpson:

> Caesar Augustus
> In his time lay
> Dying, and just as
> Cold as they,
> On the cold morning
> Of a cold day.

These lines lose their pleasure, as well as their dance and their power, if we space them according to the phrases of their sense:

Caesar Augustus
In his time lay dying
And just as cold as they
On the cold morning
Of a cold day.

As prose, pleasure, dance, and power disappear completely: "Caesar Augustus in his time lay dying and just as cold as they on the cold morning of a cold day." (The complete poem is on page 492.)

The examples we have looked at use rhyme and meter, the subjects of the next chapter. With free verse, which lacks any regular beat, the line becomes the major way of organizing sound. Here is a stanza from a free-verse poem by John Haines, "And When the Green Man Comes," revised into phrase-unit lines:

His eyes are blind with April,
his breath distilled
of butterflies and bees,
and in his beard the maggot sings.

Here it is with lines broken arbitrarily; *not* as the poet broke them in his finished poem:

His eyes are
blind with April, his
breath
distilled of
butterflies and
bees, and in
his beard the
maggot sings.

The first version is boring, the second jagged or nervous. Here is the stanza as Haines actually wrote it:

His eyes are blind
with April,
his breath distilled
of butterflies
and bees, and in his beard
the maggot sings.

Notice how the organized rhythm of the last version calls attention to sound; putting *eyes* and *blind* together in a short line, for instance, repeats the long *ai*s. Notice as well the repetition of *l*s, in the last syllable of each of the first four lines.

Sounds can exist for their own sake—and, because they can, sounds organize emphasis. *blind / with April* and *distilled / of butterflies* share a syntactic structure, but, instead of ending at the same place, one of the two clauses continues *of butterflies / and bees*. Syntax and linebreak combine to isolate, in the last line of the stanza, the significant conclusion: *the maggot sings*. My earlier linebreaks, falsifying the poem, obscured or invalidated these possibilities.

Some free-verse poems use a long line in which the linebreak seldom interrupts the sense. They are all end-stopped. Take these lines by Walt Whitman, from "Song of Myself":

> I think I could turn and live with animals, they're so placid and self-contain'd,
> I stand and look at them long and long.
>
> They do not sweat and whine about their condition,
> They do not lie awake in the dark and weep for their sins,
> They do not make me sick discussing their duty to God,
> Not one is dissatisfied, not one is demented with the mania of owning things,
> Not one kneels to another, or to his kind that lived thousands of years ago,
> Not one is respectable or unhappy over the whole earth.

If one printed these lines as prose, in paragraph form, one would lose the slow pace that the long lines give. On the other hand, one could slow the pace into absolute boredom by breaking the lines at the commas, making them shorter:

> I think I could turn and live
> with animals,
> they're so placid
> and self-contain'd.
> I stand and look at them
> long and long.
>
> They do not sweat and whine
> about their condition.
> They do not lie awake in the dark
> and weep for their sins.
> They do not make me sick
> discussing their duty to God.
> Not one is dissatisfied.
> Not one is demented
> with the mania
> of owning things.
> Not one kneels to another
> nor to his kind
> that lived thousands of years ago.
> Not one is respectable
> or unhappy
> over the whole earth.

In this mistreatment, I have reduced the various pauses—commas, shorter pauses between whole phrases, long line-end pauses—into one sort of pause. We should be grateful for Whitman's generous line, which makes a satisfying rhythm within itself—and not only by its motion from line to line. A pause within the line is called a **caesura**, and is shown when we mark it by a pair of vertical lines ‖. Whitman's lines include many pauses or caesuras. In a shorter line like Milton's, we do not have so many, but we can often find an obvious place to pause, sometimes shown by punctuation:

Of man's first disobedience, ‖ and the fruit

and sometimes not, as in Keats's line:

Or sinking ‖ as the light wind lives or dies . . .

Poets work with a variety of pauses, at the ends of lines and inside them, and the variety contributes to the rhythm of the poetic line.

Here are some exercises that may be suitable for out-loud performance in the classroom.

Exercises

1. Following is a passage from *Antony and Cleopatra,* done Shakespeare's way (a.) and as two actors with differing interpretations might have done it (b. and c.). Notice which lines are enjambed, which end-stopped, in the first presentation. Discuss the difference the linebreaks make in the three versions.

    a. The barge she sat in, like a burnished throne,
    Burned on the water: the poop was beaten gold;
    Purple the sails, and so perfumèd that
    The winds were love-sick with them; the oars were silver,
    Which to the tune of flutes kept stroke, and made
    The water which they beat to follow faster.

    b. The barge she sat in
    like a burnished throne
    burned on the water.
    The poop was beaten gold,
    purple the sails,
    and so perfumèd
    that the winds
    were love-sick with them.
    The oars were silver,
    which to the flutes kept stroke
    and made the water
    which they beat
    to follow faster.

c. The barge
   she sat in like
   a burnished throne burned on the
   water the poop was
   beaten
   gold purple the
   sails and so perfumèd that the winds
   were love-

   . . .

   sick
   with
   them
   the oars were silver which to the tune of flutes kept stroke and made the water
   which they beat to
   follow
   faster.

2. Here are three versions of a free-verse poem by William Carlos Williams. Which
   do you think is the poet's? Which is the least pleasing lineation?

   a. As the cat climbed
      over the top of

      the jamcloset first
      the right forefoot

      carefully then the
      hind stepped down

      into the pit of the
      empty flower pot

   b. As the cat
      climbed over
      the top of

      the jamcloset
      first the right
      forefoot

      carefully
      then the hind
      stepped down

      into the pit of
      the empty
      flowerpot

   c. As the cat climbed
      over the top

of the jamcloset
first the right
forefoot carefully
then the hind
stepped down
into the pit
of the empty
flower pot.

Vowels and Consonants

To enjoy the intimate sounds of poems, we take pleasure in savoring words and parts of words. This pleasure does not exclude meanings, but it can exist for its own sake. Sometimes we enjoy tripping along with nonsense sounds, as when Yeats makes a line of "fol, de rol, de rolly o," or Shakespeare mixes words and sounds: "With a hey, ho, the wind and the rain."

Alliteration is the repetition of consonant sounds, especially at the beginning of words. When Wallace Stevens writes "In kitchen cups concupiscent curds," he keeps our tongues flicking at the roofs of our mouths.

Assonance is the repetition of vowel sounds—"beside the white"; "glazed with rain." We take pleasure in holding onto vowels that remind us of each other. The last line of Hardy's "During Wind and Rain" shows interlocking assonance and alliteration:

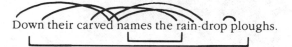

The two syllables at the beginning and end of the line contain the same *ow* vowel sound; in the middle of the line, there is the long *a* of *names* and the long *a* of *rain*. In addition, the line repeats the *n* of *down, names,* and *rain;* the *r* of *carved, rain,* and *drop;* the *p* of *drop* and *ploughs;* the *d* of *down* and *drop.*

Poets typically ascend to assonance, holding long vowels, when their poems are most exalted, as when Hardy ends his lyric with the line above. When Keats wrote his odes, he especially delighted in repeating vowels and consonants—more than in his other poems. This stanza is from "Ode to a Nightingale":

> I cannot see what flowers are at my feet,
>   Nor what soft incense hangs upon the boughs,
> But, in embalmèd darkness, guess each sweet
>   Wherewith the seasonable month endows
> The grass, the thicket, and the fruit-tree wild—
> White hawthorn, and the pastoral eglantine;
>   Fast-fading violets covered up in leaves;
>   And mid-May's eldest child,
> The coming musk-rose, full of dewy wine,
>   The murmurous haunt of flies on summer eves.

In the first line, Keats mixes assonance and alliteration. The vowels of *see* and *feet* are identical, while *flowers* and *feet* begin with the same consonant. The consonant sound of *th* repeats softly through lines 4 to 6: *Wherewith, the* (five times), *month, thicket,* and *hawthorn.* Two sets of rhyme words have the same long *ai:* wild, eglantine, child, wine. The identical diphthong (a double vowel, this one composed of *ah* and *ee*) occurs elsewhere in: *While, violets, flies.*

It is not a requirement of great poetry that sounds be so gorgeous. Frost is *never* so ornate, in his alliteration or his assonance, as Keats in the odes. Frost's attention dotes on rhythm, linebreak, and the happy and continuous tension between sentence and line. Here are poems for sound study.

New Year's Day   (1946)

Again and then again . . . the year is born

To ice and death, and it will never do

To skulk behind storm-windows by the stove

To hear the postgirl sounding her French horn

When the thin tidal ice is wearing through.

Here is the understanding not to love

Each other, or tomorrow that will sieve

Our resolutions. While we live, we live

To snuff the smoke of victims. In the snow

10   The kitten heaved its hindlegs, as if fouled,

And died. We bent it in a Christmas box

And scattered blazing weeds to scare the crow

Until the snake-tailed sea-winds coughed and howled

For alms outside the church whose double locks

Wait for St. Peter, the distorted key.

Under St. Peter's bell the parish sea

Swells with its smelt into the burlap shack

Where Joseph plucks his hand-lines like a harp,

And hears the fearful *Puer natus est*[1]

20   Of Circumcision, and relives the wrack

And howls of Jesus whom he holds. How sharp

The burden of the Law before the beast:

Time and the grindstone and the knife of God.

The Child is born in blood, O child of blood.

—Robert Lowell

Questions

1. At the end of each line, write either S (for end-stopped) or E (for enjambed).
2. What one consonant is most often repeated at the beginning of words in this poem? Can you discover further alliteration?
3. In the next-to-last line, what vowel sound dominates?

I Wake and Feel the Fell of Dark   (1877)

I wake and feel the fell of dark, not day.

What hours, O what black hours we have spent

This night! what sights you, heart, saw; ways you went!

And more must, in yet longer light's delay.

With witness I speak this. But where I say

Hours I mean years, mean life. And my lament

Is cries countless, cries like dead letters sent

To dearest him that lives alas! away.

I am gall, I am heartburn. God's most deep decree

10   Bitter would have me taste: my taste was me;

Bones built in me, flesh filled, blood brimmed the curse.

Selfyeast of spirit a dull dough sours. I see

---

[1] The Child is born

The lost are like this, and their scourge to be

As I am mine, their sweating selves; but worse.
                              —*Gerard Manley Hopkins*

Questions

   1. Underline the alliteration in this poem.

   2. Letter each line as end-stopped (S) or enjambed (E).

The Dalliance of the Eagles   (1880)

Skirting the river road, (my forenoon walk, my rest,)

Skyward in air a sudden muffled sound, the dalliance of the eagles,

The rushing amorous contact high in space together,

The clinching interlocking claws, a living, fierce, gyrating wheel,

Four beating wings, two beaks, a swirling mass tight grappling,

In tumbling turning clustering loops, straight downward falling,

Till o'er the river pois'd, the twain yet one, a moment's lull,

A motionless still balance in the air, then parting, talons loosing,

Upward again on slow-firm pinions slanting, their separate diverse flight,

10 She hers, he his, pursuing.
                              —*Walt Whitman*

Questions

   1. In this poem, mark the pauses within the lines with caesuras (‖).

   2. Note any alliteration or assonance.

Eating Alone   (1985)

I've pulled the last of the year's young onions.
The garden is bare now. The ground is cold,
brown and old. What is left of the day flames
in the maples at the corner of my
eye. I turn, a cardinal vanishes.
By the cellar door, I wash the onions,
then drink from the icy metal spigot.

Once, years back, I walked beside my father
among the windfall pears. I can't recall
10 our words. We may have strolled in silence. But
I still see him bend that way—left hand braced
on knee, creaky—to lift and hold to my
eye a rotten pear. In it, a hornet
spun crazily, glazed in slow, glistening juice.

It was my father I saw this morning
waving to me from the trees. I almost
called to him, until I came close enough
to see the shovel, leaning where I had
left it, in the flickering, deep green shade.

20 White rice steaming, almost done. Sweet green peas
fried in onions. Shrimp braised in sesame
oil and garlic. And my own loneliness.
What more could I, a young man, want.

—Li-Young Lee

Questions

1. In the first line, two adjacent words almost rhyme. Find them. How do you describe this phenomenon? Is there anything like it later in the poem?

2. Find assonance. Find alliteration.

3. Find different degrees of enjambment in this poem, and describe its various effects.

4. The last line could end in a question mark but it doesn't. What are the consequences for the sound of the poem?

To Autumn   (1819)

I

Season of mists and mellow fruitfulness,

Close bosom friend of the maturing sun,

Conspiring with him how to load and bless

With fruit the vines that round the thatch-eaves run:

To bend with apples the mossed cottage-trees,

And fill all fruit with ripeness to the core;

To swell the gourd, and plump the hazel shells

With a sweet kernel; to set budding more,

And still more, later flowers for the bees,

10   Until they think warm days will never cease,

For summer has o'er-brimmed their clammy cells.

II

Who hath not seen thee oft amid thy store?

Sometimes whoever seeks abroad may find

Thee sitting careless on a granary floor,

Thy hair soft-lifted by the winnowing wind;

Or on a half-reaped furrow sound asleep,

Drowsed with the fume of poppies, while thy hook

Spares the next swath and all its twinèd flowers;

And sometimes like a gleaner thou dost keep

20   Steady thy laden head across a brook;

Or by a cider-press, with patient look,

Thou watchest the last oozings, hours by hours.

III

Where are the songs of spring? Ay, where are they?

Think not of them, thou hast thy music too—

While barrèd clouds bloom the soft-dying day,

And touch the stubble-plains with rosy hue.

Then in a wailful choir the small gnats mourn

Among the river sallows,° borne aloft   willows

Or sinking as the light wind lives or dies;

30   And full-grown lambs loud bleat from hilly bourn;

Hedge-crickets sing; and now with treble soft

The redbreast whistles from a garden-croft;

And gathering swallows twitter in the skies.
                                        —*John Keats*

Question

1. Make curved marks over each line of verse, to show the interconnections of alliteration; underneath each line, connect the assonances with horizontal brackets. (See the markings on the line by Thomas Hardy, page 474.)

CHAPTER EIGHT

Meter and Rhyme

Meter and rhyme is examined separately from "The Sound of Poetry" to make a point. From all poems, we demand pleasing sound. All good poems are formal: the poem's words, and their order and arrangement, must seem inevitable and immovable. In some poems, meter and rhyme provide specialized means toward these ends. First we will define meter, distinguishing it from rhythm, and exemplifying its use by poets in the English tradition. Because rhyme is a separate device, and because meter and rhyme can each occur without the other, we will treat rhyme separately, later in the chapter.

Meter

English meter is a count of syllables. Usually, the syllables come in pairs, and one is louder than the other.

Meter is not the same as rhythm. Meter is numbers or counting; rhythm, a vaguer word, implies an approximate recurrence or repetition in the pacing of sound; rhythm, as we saw earlier, is fast or slow, staccato or flowing. Words describing rhythm are imprecise, because rhythm cannot accept precise description. We compare rhythm to a liquid when we call it flowing, or to a broken solid when we call it jagged. The previous chapter devoted space to rhythm in the poetic line, and contrasted the rhythm of Milton's metrical line with the rhythm of the same words broken into different lines; then it made the same contrast with free verse, using poems by John Haines and Walt Whitman (pages 470–472). In each example, the poet's rhythms, deployed in lines, were pleasing to the ear. The same words, broken into other lines, made monotonous or unpleasing rhythms. When we read poems, we invariably perceive rhythm: in a good poem, the rhythm is pleasurable and can even be expressive. In a bad poem, the rhythm tends to be weak, prosaic, boring, and without expressive function. Poems in free verse and poems in meter both have rhythm and, in either type of verse, rhythms may be good or bad.

Meter is numbers, or counting, as we have noted. The word comes from a Greek word, *metron,* which means "measure." In poetry, meter is a count of something we can hear.

In English language poetry, the common meter (known by various names) counts relative loudness and softness of syllables.

Relative Stress

To hear English meter, you must be able to distinguish relative loudness, which is also called *stress* or *accent*. Within a word that has more than one syllable, one syllable is louder than the rest. We speak of proNOUNcing a word, not of PROnouncing or of pronounCING it. In pronouncing the words of our own language, we have memorized a pattern of loudness. When we say conTENT our listeners know we are not speaking of CONtent, because we make two different words, depending on which of the syllables we pronounce more prominently.

Practice your sense of relative loudness. Everyone knows how to pronounce the words that follow; everyone saying them aloud will put the **accent** at the right place. (Accent means prominence; in our language, accent is mostly achieved by relative volume. Sometimes greater length or pitch variation is *added* to volume for the sake of accentuation.) But not everyone can name what is happening when words are pronounced correctly. Pronounce each of these two-syllable words; then decide which of the two syllables is louder.

depict	necktie
hammer	destroy
cowbell	dispatch
rampart	debris
nugget	dental
neglect	

Try these words of three and more syllables:

memory	implement
rambunctious	implementation
reputation	compliment
dangerous	comprehend

Three-syllable words that take their major accent on the first or the third syllable carry a minor accent on the syllable at the word's other end. In MEM-or-y, *mem* is the accentuated syllable, but the little *-y* at the end is louder, at least, than the *-or-* in the middle. The opposite arrangement works with com-pre-HEND. A word like ar-RANGE-ment, with the accent in the middle, shows no minor accent. (Minor accent is sometimes called secondary stress.) These habits of three-syllable words become important in metrical poems.

Iambic Pentameter: The Foot

For examples, let's start with the English ten-syllable line, arranged as **iambic pentameter**, the most common meter in great English poems. An **iambic foot** in English is a softer syllable followed by a louder one. *Pentameter* translates as "five-measure." Therefore, typical iambic pentameter is five groups of two syllables, the second syllable in each group louder than the first. When we scan—or put marks to indicate the meter of a line—we put bars to separate the feet of the line, making the typical line ˘´| ˘´| ˘´| ˘´ | ˘´ |. These bars erect a figurative barrier between the feet, to emphasize that stress is relative (and relevant) *only within the foot.*

The ˘´ | ˘´ | ˘´ | ˘´ | ˘´ | shows the counting that remains constant, which assures that the verse remains metrical. But, while the counting, or **scansion**, stays the same, the rhythm can vary considerably. After all, ˘´ | ˘´ | ˘´ | ˘´ | ˘´ | could contain ten monosyllables or two polysyllables; it could be fast, it could be slow; it could contain a period, the end of one sentence and the start of another; it could contain many commas, caesuras slowing the line; or it could contain no punctuation at all, and move more quickly. The ˘´ | ˘´ | ˘´ | ˘´ | ˘´ | tells us very little of what the line will sound like; it shows meter, not rhythm, in five relative hills and five relative valleys. The hills at one point in the line may be lower in elevation than the valleys in another part of the line. "Bang *bang,* bang *bang,* bang *bang,* bang *bang,* bang *bang*" fulfills the pattern. (We can bang this out on the desk top, every even bang louder than every odd one.) But "The University of Michigan" also fulfills the pattern. Say it slowly, exaggerating a little, and you can hear it: "The U-ni-VER-sit-Y of MICH-i-GAN." If you try saying "THE u-NI-ver-SI-ty OF Mich-I-gan," you do not pronounce our language.

The scansion ˘´ | ˘´ | ˘´ | ˘´ | ˘´ |, common to many lines different in rhythm, describes an expectation the mind develops from reading thousands of lines of poetry. *Iambic pentameter* means, or translates to, "the only thing *all* these lines have in common."

Terms for Feet and for Length of Line

In the examples, we shall continue to concentrate on the iambic foot, most often in the pentameter line. Because we occasionally encounter other meters, it is useful to know terms for the most common feet and lengths of lines.

Some types of feet:
Iambic: a softer syllable followed by a louder: *des*PAIR ˘´
Trochaic: a louder syllable followed by a softer: HAPP*y* ´ ˘
Dactylic: a louder syllable followed by two softer ones: CHANGE*able* ´ ˘ ˘
Anapestic: two softer syllables followed by a louder one: *in the* HOUSE ˘˘ ´

Some lengths of lines:
Monometer: one foot
Dimeter: two feet
Trimeter: three feet
Tetrameter: four feet
Pentameter: five feet
Hexameter (or the Alexandrine): six feet

Rhythmical Variety within Metrical Regularity

Within absolute metrical regularity, where every line scans as ˘´ | ˘´ | ˘´ | ˘´ | ˘´ |, iambic pentameter offers all the variety a poet wants or needs. No departure from this scheme is needed for variety's sake. Iambic pentameter finds most of its variety in playing upon the relativity of stress. Seldom in our literature do you find a line as evenly stressed as bang *bang* × 5, or as "The man who stole the bread was making toast." "The University of Michigan," which has only two really loud noises, is more typical of iambic pentameter. Here is the beginning of Keats's "The Eve of St. Agnes":

Sĭ. Ág | nĕs Éve— | Aȟ, bít | tĕr chíll | ĭt wás . . . .

This line scans exactly as our example does, ⌣‒ | ⌣‒ | ⌣‒ | ⌣‒ | ⌣‒ |. There is a pause after the fourth syllable, a rhythmical fact the meter does not count. All the even-numbered syllables are louder than all the odd-numbered syllables, and the "louder" sounds are almost equal to each other. The last syllable, *was,* is probably a little softer than the second, fourth, sixth, or eighth syllables—a fact that is part of the rhythm of the line but is irrelevant to its meter. The second line reads:

Tȟe oẃl, | fŏr aĺl | hĭs feáth | eȓs, wás | ă-cóld;

which again scans like the pattern. Two caesuras, after the second and the seventh syllables, contribute rhythmical variation. Of the five relatively loud syllables, creating the five feet, three are *quite* loud; two are not so loud as the other three, but still louder than their proximate neighbors *for* and *-ers.* So the variations in true loudness, small as they are, make rhythmical variety, while the sameness of relative loudness makes metrical identity. In the third line,

Tȟe haȓe | limȟp'd trémb | lĭng thȓough | tȟe fȓo | zĕn gráss,

we have another line that scans typically—but this line varies considerably in rhythm from the earlier two. For instance, *through* is louder than the *-ing* of *trembling,* and thus *-ing through* makes a regular foot of relative stress, but *through* is not truly loud at all; its softness—which remains louder than its neighbor—is *metrically* irrelevant, and *rhythmically* pleasing by providing variety. In the first half of this line, the second, third, and fourth syllables are all quite loud. Bang, bang, bang. I do not mean that they are *equally* loud; it would be absurd to suggest that they were each pronounced with an equal number of decibels. But they are all louder than the *through* that takes metrical stress later in the line.

But they cannot be louder than each other. English meter uses *relative* stress, and we can expect that the first loud syllable (the second syllable in the line) is louder than the first soft syllable; the line begins with a regular iamb. Then we have two loud syllables together, *limp'd tremb-,* and in English we would expect that one of the two—the second, if the poem appears iambic— can easily and naturally be spoken more loudly than the first. And so it can.

The order of these four syllables, as a reader says them, may climb four steps of increasing volume, each syllable a little louder than the one before it. If that is so, then *limp'd*—a softer syllable in the meter of the line—would in fact be louder than *hare*—a louder syllable in the meter of the whole line. *Because an invisible foot-separator comes between the two syllables, the relative loudness of* hare *and* limp'd *is metrically irrelevant.*

Keats's fourth line is more like his second line:

Aṅd sí | leṅt wás | tħe flóck | iṅ wóol | lÿ fóld . . .

Was is not very loud, but it is relatively loud. Nowhere else in the line is there metrical ambiguity or a rhythmical variation.

Thus, English meter, by shrewd use of relativity, can find rhythmical variation without changing the number of syllables in a line, and without changing the order of louder and softer syllables. Once we have read a few thousand lines with a typical swing of louder and softer, we have an expectation in our heads through which we perceive and sort out the syllables on the page. Meter is what lines have in common. If you were asked to scan the single line:

Rocks, caves, lakes, fens, bogs, dens, and shades of death

you would be right to refuse. But if you came upon this line deep in Milton's *Paradise Lost,* when you had learned to step to the tune of iambic pentameter, you would sort it by twos, giving a sharp beat like a foot tap to the even-numbered syllables:

Rocks, *caves,* lakes, *fens,* bogs, *dens,* and *shades* of *death* . . .

You would not sort it (as you could have done if the words had turned up in a prose paragraph) by threes, for instance:

Rocks, caves, *lakes,* bogs, fens, *dens,* and *shades* of *death* . . .

The reading dictated by meter allows large latitude—there can be different heights to these peaks and valleys—but meter imposes limits to its latitude: a peak remains peakish, relative to an adjacent valley.

The Miltonic line gives us an example of iambic pentameter that finds rhythmic variation by adding more volume. It has *more* loud noises in the line than we expect, though it retains only five relative stresses. More commonly, lines like "The University of Michigan" contain *fewer* loud noises than five. Scholars tell us that Shakespeare's pentameter averages about three loud noises a line—and, *not by average but always,* five relative stresses. In *Macbeth*

Tomorrow and tomorrow and tomorrow . . .

makes a typical Shakespearean line. The three *-mor*-s, middles of three *tomorrows,* make three loud noises, each louder than the syllable in front of it, the three *to*s. The two *and*s are not loud, but they are louder than the *-ow*s which come before them, thus adding up to the five iambics of the pentameter.

Metrical Variations

There are several common departures from the ⌣⌢ | ⌣⌢ | ⌣⌢ | ⌣⌢ | ⌣⌢ | scheme. These departures are not irregularities; they are variations *within* meter, not outside. We call them metrical variations, and we will talk about them in the order of their frequency. As they are used, they contribute to the variety of metrical verse.

Initial inversion

The most common metrical variation is reversal of the order of louder and softer syllables in one foot. This happens most frequently in the first foot in the line and is called **initial inversion.**

Suppose you have read a hundred lines that share ⌣⌢ | ⌣⌢ | ⌣⌢ | ⌣⌢ | ⌣⌢ |. Then you come on a line beginning with a loud syllable—maybe a two-syllable word that can only be pronounced with the louder syllable first, like *studies*. The beginning of this line reverses for one second the order of louder and softer, only to return immediately to the old and expected order. This line with initial inversion scans ⌢⌣ | ⌣⌢ | ⌣⌢ | ⌣⌢ | ⌣⌢ |. Look at this sample:

> Thĕ Ú | nĭvér | sĭtý | ŏf Mích | ĭgán
> Stúdiĕs | thĕ pó | ĕtŕy | ŏf Keáts | ańd Fróst.

The little rhythmical turn at the beginning of the second line becomes a familiar dance step in the motion of metrical poetry in English: a little whirl, a sudden tipping-over and recovery, *bang* bang-bang *bang*. This metrical turn resembles the motion of a large inflated toy that is heavily weighted on its rounded bottom surface. When a child pushes it over, the toy immediately rights itself. When Macbeth has said "Tomorrow and tomorrow and tomorrow," he continues,

> Creéps ĭn | thĭs pét | tў páce | frŏm dáy | tŏ dáy . . .

and it is clear that *in* is softer than *Creeps*. Although the remainder of this line scans like the pattern, the first foot is inverted—and the expectation that this foot *may* be inverted lurks in the head of the reader. Shakespeare, Milton, Keats, and Frost, all metrical poets, use initial inversion frequently. After Keats wrote "And silent was the flock in woolly fold," his next line made the dance-step of initial inversion:

> Numb wĕre | thĕ beáds | mań's fińg | eŕs, whíle | hĕ tóld . . .

and in the next lines returned to regular motion:

> His rosary, and while his frosted breath
> Like pious incense from a censor old . . .

Medial inversion

Less frequent than initial inversion is inversion elsewhere in the line, which is called **medial inversion** wherever it comes. Medial inversion makes its own pause, wherever it happens in the line; most medial inversions therefore take place after natural caesuras, often indicated by commas or other marks of punctuation:

> She said to me: open your book and read!

Open your book is that little dance-step of inversion again, now in the middle of the line. In "The Eve of St. Agnes," Keats makes this line:

> Frŏm húr | rў tó | aňd fro. | Soón, ŭp | ălóft . . .

Soon is louder than its neighboring *up.* After the pause for the end of the preceding sentence, Keats has started a new thought with a medial inversion.

Even if the line lacks a natural caesura, medial inversion will make a pause. In Theodore Roethke's "My Papa's Waltz," the poet makes a sudden medial inversion (with an iambic trimeter line; three feet, not five):

> Yŏu béat | tíme ŏn | mў heád . . .

The slight awkwardness of the enforced pause between *beat* and *time* sounds just right for the rhythm of someone beating time on a small boy's head.

Feminine endings

After inversion, the most common metrical variation is the extra syllable. Shakespeare's line

> Tomorrow and tomorrow and tomorrow . . .

is regular iambic. But it has eleven syllables, with an extra syllable at the end of the line. This pattern is called a **feminine ending**. The extra syllable dangles into the pause at the end of the line. It does not feel like a variation, although it varies in fact from the basic scheme. We scan it ⌣ ⁄ | ⌣ ⁄ | ⌣ ⁄ | ⌣ ⁄ | ⌣ ⁄ ⌣ |. Robert Frost's blank verse has many feminine endings, as in "The Death of the Hired Man":

> Hĕ búnd | lĕs év | erў fork | fŭl ín | tŏ pláce
> Aňd tágs | aňd númb | eřs ít | fŏr fúr | thĕr réfereňce
> Sŏ hé | căn fínd | aňd eás | ĭlý | dĭslódge ĭt.

The last two lines have feminine endings, if you pronounce *reference* with two syllables, as Frost did.

Extra syllables

An extra syllable elsewhere in the line—or in the final foot *before* the last stress—is a palpable metrical variation. The extra syllable, a second softer syllable, makes a foot of three syllables, which scans ⌣⌣ ⌐. In "The Death of the Hired Man," Frost writes:

> You never see him standing on the hay
> He's trying to lift, straining to lift himself.

Practice scanning these lines. In the second line, the meter begins easily enough with an iambic, *Hĕ's trý-*; the line ends with three feet that start with a medial inversion: *stráining | tŏ líft | hĭmsélf*. In between these two clumps, we have the three syllables of an extra-syllabic foot: *-ĭng tŏ líft*. You may notice that these three syllables are quick to say, occupying no more elapsed time than two syllables elsewhere in the line. Three-syllable feet in an iambic poem tend to be quick to say.

When metrical poetry sounds most conversational and speechlike (in later Shakespeare, in Robert Frost) we find most extra syllables and feminine endings.

Exercises

1. To mark the meter of a line, as we have done in the text, is to *scan;* the result is called *scansion.* Scan the following poems, drawing vertical lines to separate the feet, and showing which syllables are louder, which softer.

from Richard II   (1595)

Let's talk of graves, of worms, and epitaphs,

Make dust our paper, and with rainy eyes

Write sorrow on the bosom of the earth . . .

For God's sake, let us sit upon the ground,

And tell sad stories of the death of kings:

How some have been deposed; some slain in war;

Some haunted by the ghosts they have deposed;

Some poisoned by their wives; some sleeping killed;

All murdered: for within the hollow crown

10 That rounds the mortal temples of a king

Keeps Death his court; and there the antick sits,

Scoffing his state, and grinning at his pomp;

Allowing him a breath, a little scene,

To monarchize, be feared, and kill with looks;

Infusing him with self and vain conceit—

As if this flesh which walls about our life,

Were brass impregnable; and humoured thus,

Comes at the last, and with a little pin

Bores through his castle-wall, and—farewell king!
                    —*William Shakespeare*

To the Western World   (1957)

A siren sang, and Europe turned away

From the high castle and the shepherd's crook.

Three caravels went sailing to Cathay

On the strange ocean, and the captains shook

Their banners out across the Mexique Bay.

And in our early days we did the same.

Remembering our fathers in their wreck

We crossed the sea from Palos where they came

And saw, enormous to the little deck,

10 A shore in silence waiting for a name.

The treasures of Cathay were never found.

In this America, this wilderness

Where the axe echoes with a lonely sound,

The generations labor to possess

And grave by grave we civilize the ground.
                        —Louis Simpson

  2. The following examples, fabricated for this text, include metrical errors. Assume
     that they come from poems that have established themselves as iambic pentameter.

     a. Ridiculous impoverishments of gold
         Adorn her throat, where jealousy was often told.

     b. The dance of death, begun in August air,
         Regales the Autumn and the fair.

     c. Harsh moments fail the resplendent flesh of
         Doorjambs heavy, gilt, worn, and repulsive.

Rhyme

Rhyme is a feature common to many metrical poems, not to all. **Blank verse** is iambic pentameter without rhyme; rhyme is what it is blank of. (Do not confuse blank verse with free verse. Free verse, which is free of meters, occasionally has rhyme.) The most common rhyme is the exact repetition, in two or more words, of the final vowel and consonants of a word. *Love,* as we all know, rhymes with *dove.* Here *-ove* is the unity, *l* and *d* the variety.

Direct Rhyme

Look at a rhyming dictionary, and you may be astonished at the variety of rhymes available. Suppose I am writing a rhymed poem and am stuck for a rhyme with the word *decrease.* I could look in *The Complete Rhyming Dictionary and Poet's Craft Book,* edited by Clement Wood, and find under the sound *ees* fifty-nine possible words, beginning: afterpiece/ambergris/battlepiece/Bereneice/Bernice/cantatrice/caprice/cease/surrice/chimney-piece/Clarisse/coulease/crease . . . . If I were rhyming a word like *deletion* on two or more syllables (**feminine rhyme**), I would find another list: accretion/completion/concretion; for a three-syllable rhyme, for *credulous,* for instance, I could find sedulous on another list. These examples are **direct rhyme**.

Indirect Rhyme

Some poets use **indirect rhyme** or **off-rhyme**, almost-but-not-quite directly rhyming. Rhyme/line, for instance, is indirect because the consonants, though similar, are not the same. In rhyme/spice, the vowels rhyme but the consonants differ; this example is also indirect rhyme, but the degree of indirectness is greater. Another poet might rhyme consonants and let the vowels fend for themselves: rhyme/lame/: goat/bleat. Emily Dickinson often used indirect rhyme, sometimes rhyming open vowels that are similar but not the same:

The Silence condescended—
Creation stopped—for Me—
But awed beyond my errand—
I worshipped—did not "pray"—

If you hold on to the vowel ending of *pray,* its diphthong separates into an *a* and an *e.* The ending *e* rhymes with *Me.* Dickinson also rhymes consonants:

I cannot live with You—
It would be Life—
And Life is over there—
Behind the Shelf.

Cliché Rhyme

When poets rhyme *love* with *dove,* they make a **cliché rhyme**. Other cliché rhymes include fire/desire, breath/death, and womb/tomb. Occasionally, good poets get away with cliché rhyme, because their syntax or sense makes the second of the cliché rhymes somehow unexpected. Most cliché rhymes are flaws in a poem. Finding cliché rhymes is not an important tool in evaluating poems; rather, it is a way to look at what happens in rhyming. The pairs of rhymes listed above are cliché not only because they have been used so often, but also because the words resemble each other: each of the examples can be a noun, and all but one are monosyllables. Each belongs to the same level of diction. Most important, each recalls its mate by similarity or opposition of meaning. Fire is a symbol of desire. Breath is ended by death. What begins in the womb ends in the tomb. For all these reasons, the first word of each pair leads one to expect the second, and when expectation is exactly fulfilled, the result is boredom. A poem must balance the predictable with the unpredictable, expectation with surprise, unity with variety.

Original Rhyme

In a rhyme, the unity is the repetition of sound; the variety is all the other differences two words can muster. For instance, words can differ in length, and we can rhyme a monosyllable with a polysyllable, like *tracks* with *haversacks.* We can rhyme words spelled differently, like *tracks* with *axe.* We can rhyme different parts of speech, a verb *hacks* with a noun *jacks.* We can rhyme words of different backgrounds, like *egomaniacs* with *humpbacks,* or *kleptomaniacs* with *packs.* We can rhyme combinations of alien words: *Jack's/ hypochondriacs/kayaks/quacks.* In feminine rhyme, we can pair two words with one, rhyming *pluck it* with *Nantucket.*

The further apart the words are, the more original the rhyme. At extremes, rhyme can be witty or comic. In one of his poems, Ogden Nash uses a *boomerang* for hunting in order to cook a *kangaroo meringue.* Witty rhyme would be inappropriate to many poems, in which neither poet nor reader would want rhyme to stand out and be noticeable apart from the poem's other qualities. Highly original rhyme is appropriate in this poem:

Early in the Morning   (1950)

Early in the morning
The dark Queen said,
"The trumpets are warning
There's trouble ahead."
Spent with carousing,
With wine-soaked wits,
Antony drowsing
Whispered, "It's
Too cold a morning
10 To get out of bed."

The army's retreating,
The fleet has fled,
Caesar is beating
His drums through the dead.
"Antony, horses!
We'll get away,
Gather our forces
For another day . . ."
"It's a cold morning,"
20 Antony said.

Caesar Augustus
Cleared his phlegm.
"Corpses disgust us.
Cover them."
Caesar Augustus
In his time lay
Dying, and just as
Cold as they,
On the cold morning
30 Of a cold day.
                —Louis Simpson

Line length contributes to the wit of rhyming here; with only two feet to a line, rhyming becomes a stunt. Who would have expected *drowsing* to rhyme with *carousing,* or *Augustus* with *just as* and *disgust us?*

Natural Rhyme

In this poem by Thomas Hardy, rhyme is neither cliché nor witty. Through the skill of the poet, the rhyme appears natural in the poem while it adds its particular music:

The Oxen   (1915)

Christmas Eve, and twelve of the clock.
    "Now they are all on their knees,"
An elder said as we sat in a flock
    By the embers in hearthside ease.

We pictured the meek mild creatures where
    They dwelt in their strawy pen,
Nor did it occur to one of us there
    To doubt they were kneeling then.

So fair a fancy few would weave
10   In these years! Yet, I feel,
If someone said on Christmas Eve,
    "Come; see the oxen kneel

"In the lonely barton° by yonder coomb°   farmyard; a hollow
    Our childhood used to know,"
I should go with him in the gloom,
    Hoping it might be so.
                —*Thomas Hardy*

This rhyme helps fix the poem's form, click the lid of its box; it neither stands out as a stunt of wit nor bores us with the overly predictable.

Rhymed Stanzas

"The Oxen" is written in **stanzas**; a stanza is an arrangement of metrical lines, sometimes different in length, with a repeated order of rhyme, a **rhyme-scheme**. We indicate rhyme-schemes by letters. For "The Oxen," the rhyme-scheme is ABAB, because the first and third lines rhyme, and the second and fourth. Sometimes poets invent stanzas and rhyme schemes of great complexity, varying line length and the arrangements of rhyme.

Tywater   (1947)

Death of Sir Nihil, book the *nth,*

Upon the charred and clotted sward,

Lacking the lily of our Lord,

Alases of the hyacinth.

Could flicker from behind his ear

A whistling silver throwing knife

And with a holler punch the life

Out of a swallow in the air.

Behind the lariat's butterfly

10 Shuttled his white and gritted grin,

And cuts of sky would roll within

The noose-hole, when he spun it high.

The violent, neat and practised skill

Was all he loved and all he learned;

When he was hit, his body turned

To clumsy dirt before it fell.

And what to say of him, God knows.

Such violence. And such repose.
                             —*Richard Wilbur*

God's Love   (1990)

God loves us all, I'm pleased to say—

Or those who love him anyway—

Or those who love him and are good.

Or so they say. Or so he should.
                             —*Vikram Seth*

Questions

1. Scan each poem. Mark the rhyme schemes with the appropriate letters.
2. Discriminate between direct and indirect rhymes in the two poems. Find different types of off-rhyme.
3. In these poems, look for examples of cliché rhyme, original rhyme, and natural rhyme. Can you find all of them?
4. To practice scansion, mark the poems double-spaced on pages 475–480. Which poems are free-verse?

CHAPTER NINE

Forms and Types of Poetry

P oetic forms are traditional arrangements of line and rhyme-scheme, like the sonnet. (When we use the word *forms* for these arrangements, we are not calling other poetry—like free verse or blank verse—formless. *Form* is merely a traditional word for this sort of arrangement.)

By types of poetry, we mean distinctions between narrative and dramatic poetry on the one hand and, on the other, subdivisions like the epigram and the prose poem. These forms and types do not exhaust poetry's possibilities; they are exemplary and suggestive.

Poetic Forms

The Limerick

Each form of poetry demands a particular number of lines, of certain length, rhyming in a certain way. In a *limerick,* for instance, two rhyming trimeter lines are followed by two dimeter lines, which also rhyme, and then by a fifth trimeter line, which rhymes with the first two. The rhyme-scheme is AABBA, and the BB lines are often indented. A limerick's feet are usually three syllables long, each an **anapest**: softer, softer, louder, or ⌣⌣ ´. (Authors of limericks sometimes substitute iambs for anapests.) Here is an example by a modern master of the form, Edward Gorey (born 1925):

> Each night Father fills me with dread
> When he sits on the foot of my bed;
>   I'd not mind that he speaks
>   In gibbers and squeaks,
> But for seventeen years he's been dead.

These anonymous limericks can provide a refresher course in meter:

> There was a young man of Japan
> Whose verses would never scan.
>   When he was asked why
>   He would reply
> Well, I simply try to get as many syllables into the last line as I possibly can.

There was a young man of China
Whose aesthetic was somewhat fina.
   It was his design
   To make the last line
Short.

So much for limericks, which can serve as an example of many poetic forms using particular line lengths and rhyme schemes.*

The Haiku

Many American students have written haikus in school. When English haiku-writers follow the Japanese syllable count, they use lines of five, seven, and five syllables. The **haiku**, an imagistic poem, usually includes two images, of which the second is a surprise, a leap from the first. At a minimum, the two images conflict. Here is a translation from a sixteenth-century Japanese poet named Moritaki:

A falling petal
drops upward, back to the branch;
it's a butterfly.

Many poets writing haikus in English, aware of differences between English and Japanese, ignore syllable count and concentrate on images.

The Sonnet

The poetic form of the sonnet has remained at the center of English poetry from the sixteenth century onward. English poets from Thomas Wyatt (1503–1542) to the present have found the sonnet a congenial form, mostly for emotional statement. In one of his own sonnets, Wordsworth spoke of the sonnet as the key with which Shakespeare unlocked his heart. Shakespeare wrote a sequence of sonnets, as did many other poets in the sixteenth and seventeenth centuries. Even when it is a part of a sequence, a sonnet is a whole and individual poem, of a certain length, with several possible internal structures whereby a poet can entertain and conclude a whole, small subject. Early sonnets and sonnet sequences were mostly concerned with love. John Donne's "Holy Sonnets" are religious, as are many of Milton's sonnets. More recently, sonnets have extended themselves to all sorts of feelings.

The sonnet is fourteen lines long, and written in iambic pentameter. (We can find poems called sonnets that are exceptions to these rules; the word originally meant "little song" and some poets have interpreted the word broadly.) Sonnets have three main traditional structures and rhyme schemes. One is the **Italian** or **Petrarchan sonnet**, which is divided into two parts.

---

* Readers interested in the many poetic forms not mentioned here may consult Lewis Turco's *A Book of Forms,* which defines and exemplifies widely among special forms, or look at the pages about poetic forms in Clement Wood's *Complete Rhyming Dictionary.*

The octave, the first eight lines, uses only two rhymes: ABBAABBA. The sestet in an Italian or Petrarchan sonnet can rhyme in several ways—CDECDE is common; so is CDCDCD—so long as it does not end in a couplet. Many English poets, notably Milton and Wordsworth, have practiced the Italian sonnet with success.

The English language, however, is noted for the paucity of its rhyme, especially compared to the Italian richness in rhyme-words. The octave of the Italian sonnet can make trouble for the English poet, because it uses only two rhyme-sounds for eight words. The **English sonnet**, more commonly called the **Shakespearean sonnet**, began a little earlier than Shakespeare—it was first used by Henry Howard, Earl of Surrey (1517–1547)—and uses a rhyme scheme more adapted to the English language: ABAB CDCD EFEF GG. Edmund Spenser, finding the Italian sonnet not suited to English but the English sonnet too loose, invented a third rhyme scheme that is a compromise between the two: ABAB BCBC CDCD EE. This arrangement makes the **Spenserian sonnet**.

Rhyme-schemes are probably less important to sonnets than structures of thought, but rhyme-schemes seem to suggest such structures. In the Italian sonnet, the octave and the sestet usually make a two-part structure not further subdivided. Frequently, an octave will set forth a problem, or tell a story, to which the sestet may provide a solution, a counterdirection, a commentary, or a surprise. There are exceptions; some Italian sonnets are indivisible fourteen-line poems.

The English or Shakespearean sonnet, which often breaks down into eight and six, may also break in other places. It may subdivide into four and four, plus four and two; or into four, four, four, and two; or into eight, four, and two. The Shakespearean sonnet, structurally more adaptable, is a less precise form.

Quoted throughout this text are sonnets by Shakespeare (see pages 442 and 445). Here is another:

Let me not to the marriage of true minds   (1609)

Let me not to the marriage of true minds
Admit impediments. Love is not love
Which alters when it alteration finds,
Or bends with the remover to remove.
O no, it is an ever-fixèd mark
That look on tempests and is never shaken;
It is the star to every wand'ring bark,
Whose worth's unknown, although his height be taken.
Love's not Time's fool, though rosy lips and cheeks
10 Within his bending sickle's compass come;
Love alters not with his brief hours and weeks,
But bears it out even to the edge of doom.
   If this be error and upon me proved,
    I never writ, nor no man ever loved.
                    —*William Shakespeare*

Notice the rhyme scheme in this sonnet by John Milton:

On the Late Massacre in Piedmont[1]   (1655)

Avenge, O Lord, thy slaughtered saints, whose bones
Lie scattered on the Alpine mountains cold;
Ev'n them who kept thy truth so pure of old,
When all our fathers worshipped stocks and stones,
Forget not: in thy book record their groans
Who were thy sheep, and in their ancient fold
Slain by the bloody Piedmontese, that rolled
Mother with infant down the rocks. Their moans
The vales redoubled to the hills, and they
10 To heav'n. Their martyred blood and ashes sow
O'er all th' Italian fields, where still doth sway
The triple[2] Tyrant that from these may grow
A hundredfold, who, having learnt thy way,
Early may fly the Babylonian woe.[3]

—John Milton

Wordsworth, Keats, Tennyson, Frost—most great poets have turned to the sonnet during their lives. Examples of the sonnet may be found throughout this book. See, for instance, pages 476, 544, 585–586, 683, 687, and 722.

Poetic Types

Ballad

A ballad is almost a form—at least, there are typical stanzas, and even ballads we can call typical—but the word *ballad* does not represent a form as codified as the sonnet. Although ballads tell stories, we separate them from the later category of narrative poetry, because they form a great body of anonymous literature, and from the later, sophisticated imitation of the ballad. Here is an anonymous Scots ballad, with some old Scottish words footnoted:

Edward

"Why dois[1] your brand[2] sae[3] drap[4] wi bluid,[5]
    Edward, Edward,
Why dois your brand sae drap wi bluid,
    And why sae sad gang[6] yee O?"
"O I hae[7] killed my hauke[8] sae guid,[9]
    Mither, mither,
O I hae killed my hauke sae guid,
    And I had nae mair[10] but hee O."

---

[1] In 1655 the Protestant Waldenses of southern France were suppressed for refusing to adhere to Roman Catholicism.   [2] A reference to the papal crown.   [3] See Revelation 14:1–3,8.

[1] does   [2] sword   [3] so   [4] drip   [5] blood   [6] go   [7] have   [8] hawk   [9] good   [10] more

"Your haukis bluid was nevir sae reid,[11]
10   Edward, Edward,
Your haukis bluid was nevir sae reid,
    My deir son I tell thee O."
"O I hae killed my reid roan steid,[12]
    Mither, mither,
O I hae killed my reid roan steid,
    That erst [13] was sae fair and free O."

"Your steid was auld,[14] and ye hae gat mair,
    Edward, Edward,
Your steid was auld, and ye hae gat mair,
20   Sum other dule[15] ye drie[16] O."
"O I hae killed my fadir[17] deir,
    Mither, mither,
O I hae killed my fadir deir,
    Alas, and wae[18] is mee O!"

"And whatten penance wul[19] ye drie for that,
    Edward, Edward?
And whatten penance wul ye drie for that?
    My deir son, now tell me O."
"Ile set my feet in yonder boat,
30   Mither, mither,
Ile set me feet in yonder boat,
    And Ile fare ovir the sea O."

"And what wul ye doe wi your towirs and your ha,[20]
    Edward, Edward?
And what wul ye doe wi your towirs and your ha,
    That were sae fair to see O?"
"Ile let thame stand tul they doun fa,
    Mither, mither,
Ile let thame stand tul they doun fa,
40   For here nevir mair maun[21] I bee O."

"And what wul ye leive to your bairns[22] and your wife,
    Edward, Edward?
And what wul ye leive to your bairns and your wife,
    Whan ye gang ovir the sea O?"
"The warldis[23] room, let them beg thrae[24] life,
    Mither, mither,
The warldis room, let them beg thrae life,
    For thame nevir mair wul I see O."

"And what wul ye leive to your ain[25] mither deir?
50   Edward, Edward?

---

[11] red [12] steed [13] formerly [14] old [15] grief [16] suffer [17] father [18] woe [19] will [20] hall
[21] must [22] children [23] world's [24] through [25] own

And what wul ye leive to your ain mither dier?
    My deir son, now tell me O."
"The curse of hell frae[26] me sall[27] ye beir,[28]
    Mither, mither,
The curse of hell frae me sall ye beir,
    Sic[29] counseils[30] ye gave to me O."

                                   —*Anonymous*

A ballad tells a story. In "Edward," the story is told in dialogue, as if the poem were a tiny play, with the speeches organized into stanzas. In the tight and musical stanzas of this ballad, we hear a son reluctantly telling his mother that he has killed his father, and finally cursing his mother for having urged him to patricide. When a harrowing story is told in rhymed and delicate verses, the tension between form and content, story and music makes a dreadful energy.

Later poets imitated old ballad forms in writing narrative poems. One of the most famous literary ballads in English is by John Keats:

La Belle Dame sans Merci[1]   (1820)

Oh, what can ail thee, knight-at-arms,
    Alone and palely loitering?
The sedge has withered from the lake,
    And no birds sing!

Oh, what can ail thee, knight-at-arms,
    So haggard and so woe-begone?
The squirrel's granary is full,
    And the harvest's done.

I see a lily on thy brow,
10   With anguish moist and fever-dew,
And on thy cheek a fading rose
    Fast withereth too.

I met a lady in the meads
    Full beautiful, a fairy's child.
Her hair was long, her foot was light,
    And her eyes were wild.

I made a garland for her head,
    And bracelets too, and fragrant zone;
She looked at me as she did love,
20   And made sweet moan.

I set her on my pacing steed,
    And nothing else saw all day long;

---

[26] from   [27] shall   [28] bear   [29] such   [30] advice

[1] The beautiful, pitiless woman

For sidelong would she bend, and sing
    A fairy's song.

She found me roots of relish sweet,
    And honey wild, and manna dew;
And sure in language strange she said,
    "I love thee true."

She took me to her elfin grot,
30   And there she wept, and sighed full sore,
And there I shut her wild wild eyes
    With kisses four.

And there she lullèd me asleep
    And there I dreamed—Ah! woe betide!—
The latest dream I ever dreamed
    On the cold hill side.

I saw pale kings and princes too,
    Pale warriors, death-pale were they all;
The cried—"La belle Dame sans merci
40   Hath thee in thrall!"

I saw their starved lips in the gloam
    With horrid warning gapèd wide,
And I awoke and found me here,
    On the cold hill side.

And this is why I sojourn here,
    Alone and palely loitering,
Though the sedge is withered from the lake,
    And no birds sing.
                    —*John Keats*

The verse here is smoother and more literary than the old ballads, and the language is closer to our own, but the poem makes its ancestry clear.

Narrative, Epic, Dramatic

Many poems, including ballads, tell stories and are therefore narrative. The earliest surviving poetry is narrative, ancient epics originally chanted or sung to a form of musical accompaniment. *Gilgamesh* is the oldest surviving poem, composed in Sumeria about five thousand years ago; Homer's *Iliad* and *Odyssey* are a mere three thousand years old. These epics were composed orally, before the invention of writing; they were memorized, and changed ("revised") by generations of reciter-poets. (There was no single, innovative, sole-author Homer, though it is possible that one blind bard assembled and organized the *Iliad* and the *Odyssey* more thoroughly than any of his predecessors.)

Prehistoric Greeks remembered and celebrated their past by memorizing Homer. Epics are historical records of the heroes of the tribe, combining fact and legend. Centuries after these oral epics were composed, professional poets made sophisticated epics in imitation of the old collective style. The Roman Virgil, wishing to write a patriotic poem in service to his emperor Augustus, followed the pattern of Homer when he composed *The Aeneid.*

In the Christian era, Dante's *Divine Comedy* is a sophisticated epic. Its embodiment of Christian theology makes it a vast departure from classical forms, but the ghost who guides Dante through hell to purgatory is Virgil himself. In English, the great epic is *Paradise Lost,* Milton's seventeenth-century account of creation and the war between good and evil.

Many poems are narrative tales, comic or tragic, without being epic. The great narrative poet in English is Geoffrey Chaucer. His language is archaic, and best saved for advanced study. *The Canterbury Tales* is a lengthy series of different stories told by and about ordinary people—not, like an epic, tales of gods and heroes making history.

After Chaucer, to the present time, many poets have written stories in rhyme and meter (less often in free verse). Some of the stories take dramatic form, most often as monologues by a speaker who reveals himself as he tells his story (see Robert Browning's "My Last Duchess," pages 573–574). One example of modern narrative is a story poem by Robert Frost:

"Out, Out—"   (1916)

The buzz saw snarled and rattled in the yard
And made dust and dropped stove-length sticks of wood,
Sweet-scented stuff when the breeze drew across it.
And from there those that lifted eyes could count
Five mountain ranges one behind the other
Under the sunset far into Vermont.
And the saw snarled and rattled, snarled and rattled,
As it ran light, or had to bear a load.
And nothing happened: day was all but done.
10 Call it a day, I wish they might have said
To please the boy by giving him the half hour
That a boy counts so much when saved from work.
His sister stood beside them in her apron
To tell them "Supper." At the word, the saw,
As if to prove saws knew what supper meant,
Leaped out at the boy's hand, or seemed to leap—
He must have given the hand. However it was,
Neither refused the meeting. But the hand!
The boy's first outcry was a rueful laugh,
20 As he swung toward them holding up the hand
Half in appeal, but half as if to keep
The life from spilling. Then the boy saw all—
Since he was old enough to know, big boy
Doing a man's work, though a child at heart—
He saw all spoiled. "Don't let him cut my hand off—
The doctor, when he comes. Don't let him, sister!"

So. But the hand was gone already.
The doctor put him in the dark of ether.
He lay and puffed his lips out with his breath.
30 And then—the watcher at his pulse took fright.
No one believed. They listened at his heart.
Little—less—nothing!—and that ended it.
No more to build on there. And they, since they
Were not the one dead, turned to their affairs.

                            —*Robert Frost*

Many younger American poets are returning to poems of narrative and character; their poems might almost be short stories, except that they are written in lines. Here's a story about a Puerto Rican barber in New York, written (we are told in a subtitle) by his daughter remembering her father's talk.

Valentino's Hair   (1987)
1960—my father cannot help but tell

It's been almost thirty-five years.
I can scarcely believe it, niña.
Time trusts no one and so it disappears
before us like the smoke from my
        cigarette.
In 1925 I was young, I was a part
of a world eating at its own edges
without being satisfied.
The Roaring Twenties didn't roar.
10 They swelled with passions.
They danced, and I danced with them.

I had a barber shop in a Manhattan
        hotel.
It is not there anymore.
It burned down during World War II.
But in its time it was elegant, private.
My shop was small, only one chair.
Every comb, every lotion, every towel
        perfect:
20 like the stars which burn in the sky,
everything shined.
The barber chair was gold-leafed
and made of the softest leather.
A man could fall asleep in that chair
with lather still fresh on his face.
There were four large oval mirrors,
two on one wall, two on the opposite
        wall.
They faced each other like distant
30   lovers,
never permitted to kiss,

only permitted to greet each other
with their cool but receptive stares.

The walls had cloth wallpaper.
The wallpaper too had gold leaf
with a blue and brown background of
        leaves
and trees and ocean in the distance.
And it reminded me of my town
40   Aguadilla,
the great stretches of beach,
the lush rain forests of Puerto Rico.
Anyway, fate had been good to me,
and I was owner of the barber shop
in the hotel, and I made good money,
and the times looked good,
and I lost a lot of money
before the Twenties were gone.
But that's not why I'm telling you this.

50 One day in 1926, early afternoon, 1:00
        P.M.,
things were slow, and I was reading
        the paper,
studying the horse racing sheet.
Mangual had come by, picked up a
        couple of bets
from me and got a haircut.
He had hair in those days.
It was just after he had left,
60 and I remember thinking what a hot
        summer

we were having, and I was tipped back
in my barber chair,
almost sleeping, almost dreaming.
You know how it is when you're
    between
sleep and dream and a slight push
can send you into one world or the
    other.
70 Well, suddenly the wall phone rang.
I thought for sure it was Mangual.
Sometimes he'd call and try to get me
to change my bets. He'd tell me
I was wasting my money,
and he had a tip on a horse
so fast you'd think it had six legs.

The phone rang a second time.
I did not hurry. I don't quite know why,
but I waited until the fourth ring
80 and snapped forward in the chair
and lifted the phone receiver off the
    hook.
The front desk at the hotel was calling.
A guest wanted a haircut and shave.
I had no customers in the shop, except
maybe a fly seeking decay in summer
    heat.
I said I was available, asked for the
    room number.
90 That was that. Just another customer,
I remember thinking. Possibly a
    stockbroker,
a businessman, maybe Mafia.
I'd given them haircuts and shaves too.

I took my best tools.
I had recently purchased them
and had a special black leather box
    made.
Like a doctor.
100 In a way I was a kind of doctor.
What I did helped people ride a stream
to slow recovery, to arrive on the shore
of something new, something hidden.
A secret place. A secret person.
Well, so I went. I closed my shop,
putting a note on the door saying
I'd be back in an hour, and then I
    strutted down
the wine-red carpeted hallway into the
110   lobby,
past the front desk and into the elevator.

I pressed the button for the eighth floor
and rode up alone to my destiny.

There was a small mirror on the
    elevator wall,
just above the button panel.
It was there for the ladies and
    gentlemen,
on their way to parties,
120 to look one last time at the present.
And so I did. I stared into the face
of a twenty-seven-year-old man
who knew little about the ways of this
    world.
And for that moment I thought I saw
    someone else.
Someone who was walking towards me
from another place we held in common.
The elevator door opened
130 to wake me from my daydream.

Room 808 was my customer,
and I found myself at the door
tapping lightly on its face.
The rooms were spacious,
and the windows faced Central Park.
I could hear the sound of an electric
    fan
as the door opened, and I was greeted
by a fair-haired, frail-looking man.
140 He was in a dark suit,
and he was smoking a cigarette in a
    holder.
Quite a dandy. He greeted me warmly,
thanked me for being so prompt.
His employer was absolutely desperate
to be ready for an evening engagement
and had little time or desire to walk
the busy streets looking for a barber
    shop,
150 and if he did walk the streets,
he probably would be mobbed by
    admirers,
and he would definitely make my time
    worthwhile,
and I had come highly recommended.

Well, all these things came quickly
out of this amiable, high-strung
    American
as he led me to a room where the light
160   was good

and which had been prepared
with a chair, table, and large mirror.
The sink was to the left of the table.
I began setting the tools on the table
and emptying my satchel of hair and
　　skin products,
which I had also brought with me.
As I did, I looked up at the mirror,
more so to see if it was clean than
170　　anything else.
When I did, I saw the reflection,
a dark-haired man in the mirror
standing in the doorway behind me.
It was the ladykiller.
It was Rudolph Valentino.
He looked drawn and tired.
He had obviously not shaved
for his face was already darkening with
　　whiskers.
180　He was wearing a very white
　　undershirt
and a pair of dark pants.
By his side was a very slim, exotic
　　looking woman.
They were arguing, but very quietly,
in whispers like lovers separated
by a thin wall from their neighbors.
The woman kept insisting on
　　something,
190　and she called him Rudy.
He finally looked at me staring at him
in the mirror and smiled slightly,
　　stopping the woman
in her sentence by simply saying,
　　"Enough!"
He closed the door behind him,
　　walked towards me,
his hand out to shake my hand.

And to my surprise he said my name.
200　"I'm glad to meet you, Señor Sapia."
The look of amazement must have
　　been on my face.
I suddenly began to feel flushed.
In the mirror I could see how red my
　　cheeks were.
And then he apologized and told me
his secretary had a bad habit
of never informing people who their
　　customer was.
210　One time in California
he needed a manicure and a pedicure.

The hotel sent up an elderly lady
to give him what he requested.
But she was never told who her client
　　was.
When Valentino walked out to greet
　　her,
his pants leg rolled up, barefoot,
the woman drew in a long hard look
220　and fainted on the royal blue rug,
her silver hair perfectly in place.
Valentino tried to revive her
and members of his party called
for the house doctor and all was panic.
And the strange thing was
they couldn't revive her.
They declared the woman dead,
Valentino concluded, remorse in his
　　voice.
230　The hotel cooperated,
reported the woman died of a heart
　　attack
in the hallway, not Valentino's room.
He had enough of scandal.
This would have been too cruel,
too bizarre, he confessed.
I was struck by Valentino's story.
Why should he tell me,
Facundo Sapia, a simple barber?

240　My girl, I was suddenly caught
between laughing and crying.
The poor man had a power
he couldn't control,
and here I was absolving him
of his sin, listening to his confession
like a priest in my white smock.
And now he was to do penance,
he was to give something up to me.
I would raise my chalice of shaving
250　　cream
and lift my silver razor to the light.

"Sapia means wisdom, doesn't it?" he
　　asked.
"Yes," I told him. "My mother's name
　　was Inocencia."
"Ah," he said. "What a beautiful name,
　　Innocent Wisdom."
And he sat down in the chair,
looked into the mirror, and asked me
260　to help him with this man in the mirror,
meaning, of course, himself.

I covered him with the white apron.
And I began to apply the shaving cream
to his face while his eyes stared directly
into the eyes of the pitiful man
he thought he saw in the mirror.
I began to lather and disguise
that perfect face, slowly, with
    compliance,
270 like an accomplice to the development
of the belief in one god.
Perhaps her god was what
the elderly lady thought she saw
before she fainted into death.

As I shaved Rudolph Valentino,
he remained silent, and I remained
    silent.
My hands had to be steady,
for they guided the instrument
280 and I simply followed.
Valentino noticed my hands.
They looked like his father's hands,
the way the fingers naturally curved
when the hand relaxed.
I began to cut his hair;
he trained his eyes on my hands.
"You do not realize it," he said,
"but you are cutting away at my life too,
time leaving me like moments
290 falling to the floor."

Suddenly, I was afraid of a man
I could easily destroy
with one swerve of my razor,
with one jolt of my scissors.
A man who was a great lover,
not philosopher.
I didn't want to hear philosophy.
I wanted to know about the desert at
    night,
300 the ride of the four horsemen,
the posture of the tango.
But he was speaking about death,
his own death.
And he was implicating me.
But most frightening of all,
I had this disturbing feeling he was
    right.
He was dying. I was dying.
We were all dying at this moment,
310 in this place, where his hair fell calmly
to the floor like our simple desires.

Somehow I gathered my courage
and told him he had something
all men wished they had.
It was not his money or his appearance.
He immediately turned directly to me,
causing my scissor to glance
slightly off of his left ear.
He just stared at me.
320 Didn't say one word.
He just looked and looked into my face.
I felt like a broken fish under the eye
    of God;
he was waiting for the answer.
What he had was a way with women.
I told him about the woman I was in
    love with
but who did not even care if I lived or
    died.
330 She did not even know I existed.
Oh, she was a friend of a friend,
and we talked, but I could sense
she had no fascination for me.
It was odd to tell this to Rudolph
    Valentino,
a man never scorned by a woman,
a man who had probably made love
to every woman he touched.

Well, we continued in silence.
340 I trimming his hair,
which was in need of a haircut,
and he turned toward the mirror,
staring into his own eyes,
then once or twice stealing
a quick, deliberate glance at me.
The silence in the room
made everything else around us so
    loud.

My scissors clipping steadily.
350 The car horns from down on the street.
Suddenly I could hear the young man
and the exotic looking woman
in the next room arguing,
at first with quick exchanges and long
    pauses.
Then their voices grew more intense,
    more hateful,
until finally I heard a crash or a fall,
I really wasn't sure which.
360 But I could hear someone crying and
    gasping

and trying to talk, trying to defend.
It was the young man's voice.
I think she had hit him with something.   390
Valentino's eyes changed.
"Damn it, damn it," he started saying.
"Yes, I'm lucky," he said to me,
"and I'll probably be lucky in hell too."

He suddenly laughed, as if he realized
370 something ridiculous
far beyond his reach,
distant as his past.
By then I had begun putting talcum
      powder
around his neck, ready to remove   400
the white apron covered with his hair.
His image in the mirror was the image
I had seen in the dark theatre.
Valentino gave the mirror his famous
380   profile,
the delicate ears, the high forehead,
      the angular nose.
"Señor Sapia," he said, very
      conclusively,
"your reputation is not exaggerated."   410
With that, he gave me a one hundred
      dollar bill

from a money clip he had in his
      pocket,
and he walked ceremoniously out the
      door.

Something happened to me, mi
      muchacha.
Something seized my senses.
He had said it himself.
"You are cutting away at my life too."
We all take something from each
      other.
It was then I got down on my knees,
began gathering with these hands his
      hair,
hurrying like a mad man,
afraid someone would open the door,
      catch me,
afraid someone would see my
      uncontrollable frenzy.
One month later he died and I
      discovered
the magical power of the hair.
It was then when I used that power.
I used it to seduce a woman I loved.
The woman who didn't love me.

                              —*Yvonne Sapia*

Here's a poem more of character than of narrative. David Dooley takes on the voice of an old writer submitting to an interview:

How I Wrote It   (1988)

What the goddamn hell are you talking about, boy,
I never did one thing in my life on account of a theory—
look here: do you breathe theory? do you piss theory? do you fuck theory?
When I was living in Paris with Olga, if you've read me
you know about Olga, Polish whore and a damn good one,
claimed to be a Russian countess, that was her theory,
but she forgot she was a countess, even forgot she was a whore,
she liked it so much you see, opened her legs, dark thick hair,
rich-cunted—one point I will make for your tape recorder,
10 you can't be an artist without a sense of smell,
nights when I'd stagger home to Olga, I'd stop in the alley
and get a whiff of the beer, the piss, rotting vegetables,
some nights vomit, before I hauled upstairs and put it to her,
a woman who made use of a man's efforts,
not like that Oriental whore, she's in one of the books too,
who started chewing an apple when I was ready to explode.
So I'd give her the kind of fucking she was meant for
and afterwards sometimes I'd go to the typewriter buck naked

and start writing till she bitched about the noise
20 though more than once she fell asleep and honked like a flight of geese
but she'd bitch so I'd open a notebook and while she slept,
on summer nights the windows open and she lay there naked asleep
the covers tangled down at her knees till I wouldn't know
if I were writing with my pen or my cock, I'd use
whatever tool I needed. There were no answers
because there were never any questions. If you write,
you don't need answers. That's where you fellows go wrong.
You need books and paper and food and cunt and drink
and that's it. By daybreak there'd be pages of Olga in the typewriter,
30 pages of Olga in the notebook, and squirming in the bed
she'd be rubbing the yellow muck out of her big cow eyes.
Pages of Olga, and growing up in Baltimore,
the train ride to Marseille in the dead of winter,
Kontarsky and the pimples on his ass, the baptistery doors in Florence.
And I bought this great roll of wrapping paper
from a butcher shop, and on it I wrote plans, ideas, images.
Then I hung these scrolls of wrapping paper on the walls,
all around me were the books I was going to write.
Olga would have preferred pictures of milkmaids,
40 things she could sell for whiskey when times were bad.
The novel, how to write the novel, I heard that guff
in *caves,* bars, cafés, from writers who drank when
they should have been writing, and some, as Prescott said,
who wrote when they should have been drinking.
Art, Prescott went on and on about art, significant form,
he and his nancy-boy friends over from Oxford.
You mean writing, I said? Writing means getting your hands dirty,
writing means getting filthy all over. Holy men like dirt.
A holy man told me that once. Gurudev, surely you've heard the name.
50 Gurudev told me that in my room, Anneke's room actually,
I was living with Anneke then, she had a razor scar that long
across her left cheek where a crazy pimp cut her,
and the damnedest thing was, it made her sexier than before.
Every writer in Paris wanted to bang her, and a lot of them did.
One evening Gurudev was sitting cross-legged on the floor
so I decided to try it too, turned out I was a natural at it,
and Anneke got mad and pitched one of her crazy fits,
she could throw fits the way sows piss, so she was raving about men,
what pigs they were, how life was *merde* and God was a wad of snot.
60 Before I could swear at her, Gurudev leaned toward her, grinned,
and said, "I couldn't agree more!" Even Anneke had to laugh at that,
although she had absolutely no sense of humor and was drunk,
if he hadn't been a holy man she'd have ripped off his cotton pajamas,
damn near did it anyway—if a vixen in heat trapped in quicksand
could laugh, that was how she barked and howled with laughter.
Then she calmed down, tried to sit cross-legged and fell over backwards.
Gurudev taught us some of his chanting, and I was inspired to sing
"Don't Sit Under the Apple Tree with Anyone Else but Me,"
which Anneke thought was funny, and clapped her hands like a baby,

70 then I sang "I'll Take You Home Again, Kathleen" like an Irish tenor,
which sounds like when you began to sing, someone grabbed your balls
and twisted. Gurudev giggled. Indian holy men have fine giggles.
That night I explained to Gurudev how to be a writer. What was it
you said to me earlier, something about the form of the novel having failed
so that only the not-novel could be the novel? Horseshit!
Horseshit! It's the volcano inside you that has to erupt.
The lava doesn't care where it burns. If the book is bleeding chunks,
so is life. The blood lets you recognize the source.
What became of Anneke? What happened when she was with me
80 is in the books. After that, who knows? Now Prescott,
Prescott jumped into the Seine and hit his head on a piling.
He was in a coma for months and two of the nuns
fell in love with him. Then he recovered. Young man,
could your generation satisfy a whore? I doubt it.
I knew how to live with the grime, you see.
The grime on a tenement is as beautiful as the sunrise.

—David Dooley

Lyric and Song

We have come to use lyric to mean a short poem, usually emotional or
descriptive. The term is perhaps too general to be useful. Originally derived
from the word for lyre (a musical instrument) the word indicated a poem
composed for singing. Many old poems were originally written as songs.
Here is one of Shakespeare's songs, from *Love's Labour's Lost*:

Winter   (1595)

When icicles hang by the wall,
    And Dick the shepherd blows his nail,
And Tom bears logs into the hall,
    And milk comes frozen home in pail,
When blood is nipp'd, and ways be foul,
Then nightly sings the staring owl,
                    Tu-who;

Tu-whit, tu-who—a merry note,
While greasy Joan doth keel the pot.

10 When all aloud the wind doth blow,
    And coughing drowns the parson's saw,
And birds sit brooding in the snow,
    And Marian's nose looks red and raw,
When roasted crabs hiss in the bowl,
Then nightly sings the staring owl,
                    Tu-who;

Tu-whit, tu-who—a merry note,
While greasy Joan doth keel the pot.
                    —William Shakespeare

Epigrams

An epigram is short, pithy, witty, and conclusive. Here is one by Thomas Hardy:

Epitaph on a Pessimist   (1925)

I'm Smith of Stoke, aged sixty-odd,
   I've lived without a dame
From youth-time on; and would to God
   My Dad had done the same.
                —Thomas Hardy

(An **epitaph** is an inscription for a gravestone; some epitaphs are also epigrams. Note that there is a third word sometimes confused with epigram and epitaph; an **epigraph** is a quotation an author places at the start of a work.)

Countee Cullen, a leader of the Harlem renaissance in the 1920s, wrote this epigram:

For a Lady I Know   (1925)

She even thinks that up in heaven
Her class lies late and snores,
While poor black cherubs rise at seven
To do celestial chores.
                —Countee Cullen

J. V. Cunningham wrote most of his work in epigrammatic form, some of it funny:

(1950)

Naked I came, naked I leave the scene,
And naked was my pastime in between.

some not:

(1950)

On a cold night I came through the cold rain
And false snow to the wind shrill on your pane
With no hope and no anger and no fear:
Who are you? and with whom do you sleep here?

Most epigrams rhyme. We call a short free-verse poem an epigram only when brevity combines with wit:

The Bath Tub   (1916)

As a bathtub lined with white porcelain,
When the hot water gives out or goes tepid,
So is the slow cooling of our chivalrous passion,
O my much praised but-not-altogether-satisfactory lady.

—Ezra Pound

Visual Poetry

While most poetry appeals to the ear, some poetry arranges itself for the pleasure of the eye. Early in the seventeenth century, George Herbert wrote:

Easter Wings   (1633)

> Lord, who createdst man in wealth and store,
> Though foolishly he lost the same,
> Decaying more and more
> Till he became
> Most poor:
> With thee
> O let me rise
> As larks, harmoniously,
> And sing this day thy victories:
10 Then shall the fall further the flight in me.

> My tender age in sorrow did begin;
> And still with sicknesses and shame
> Thou didst so punish sin,
> That I became
> Most thin.
> With thee
> Let me combine,
> And feel this day thy victory;
> For, if I imp my wing on thine,
20 Affliction shall advance the flight in me.

—George Herbert

This poem is a pleasure both to ear and to eye. If you heard the poem read aloud, you would be aware of lines becoming shorter, then longer again—a closing in, an opening up—but you would not be aware that the poem created on the page the visual shape of an angel's wings. Reading and seeing the poem are separate pleasures. Herbert's "Easter Wings" is a **concrete poem** because a portion of its creation is visual.

Modern poems sometimes exist to the eye and not to the ear. When E. E. Cummings makes

(1958)

l(a

le
af
fa
ll

s)
one
l
iness

there is no way to pronounce the poem except by spelling it and indicating marks of punctuation. (Even then, the voicing will detract from the poem; the voice will have to decide whether the first character is *ell* or *one*. (It is *ell*, in terms of the words *loneliness* and *a leaf falls*, but the meaning of the poem is underscored by the visual pun on *ell* and *one*.) The poem exists, not to the eye and ear together, nor to both eye and ear separately, but to the eye alone.

Concrete poetry is a blend of poetry and painting, or visual art. Ian Hamilton Finlay is a contemporary leader among concretists. Here is his "Homage to Malevich"—the painter who tilted a white square on a white background in "White on White":

(1971)

lackblockblackb
lockblackblockb
lackblockblackb
lockblackblockb
lackblockblackb
lockblackblockb
lackblockblackb
lockblackblockb

lackblockblackb   lackblockblackb   lackblockblackb
lockblackblockb   lockblackblockb   lockblackblockb
lackblockblackb   lackblockblackb   lackblockblackb
lockblackblockb   lockblackblockb   lockblackblockb
lackblockblackb   lackblockblackb   lackblockblackb
lockblackblockb   lockblackblockb   lockblackblockb
lackblockblackb   lackblockblackb   lackblockblackb
lockblackblockb   lockblackblockb   lockblackblockb

                       lackblockblackb
                       lockblackblockb
                       lackblockblackb
                       lockblackblockb
                       lackblockblackb
                       lockblackblockb
                       lackblockblackb
                       lockblackblockb

—*Ian Hamilton Finlay*

Some poems assembled as concrete are less like pictures and more like collections of letters for the mind to dwell on—like the French movement *lettrism.* Aram Saroyan has composed poems of a single word like *oxygen,* or a single nonword like *blod* (immortalized by the *Guinness Book of Records* as the world's shortest poem). These poems are not so interesting in their own sensuous shape as they are in the thoughts they lead to. They resemble conceptual sculpture, like Yoko Ono's row of empty flowerpots titled *Imagining Flowers.*

Prose Poems

Poems written in paragraphs have been a part of literature for more than a hundred years. Usually, a prose poem shares most of the qualities we associate with poetry—images, metaphor, figures, controlled rhythm, and fantasy— except for lines and linebreaks.

Russell Edson is a contemporary American who writes prose poems. He writes tiny narratives—which might be called fables, or novels-to-read-through-a-microscope—that other people call prose poems. When it becomes difficult to decide whether a piece of writing is a story, a poem, a play, or an essay, then the task is useless. Here is a prose poem—I'll call it—by Russell Edson:

Bringing a Dead Man Back into Life   (1976)

The dead man is introduced back into life. They take him to a country fair, to a French restaurant, a round of late night parties . . . He's beginning to smell.
They give him a few days off in bed.

He's taken to a country fair again; a second engagement at the French restaurant; another round of late night parties . . . No response . . . They brush the maggots away . . . That terrible smell! . . . No use . . .
What's wrong with you?
. . . No use . . .
They slap his face. His cheek comes off; bone underneath, jaws and teeth . . .

10   Another round of late night parties . . . Dropping his fingers . . . An ear falls off . . . Loses a foot in a taxi . . . No use . . . The smell . . . Maggots everywhere!

Another round of late night parties. His head comes off, rolls on the floor. A woman stumbles on it, an eye rolls out. She screams.
No use . . . Under his jacket nothing but maggots and ribs . . . No use . . .
—*Russell Edson*

CHAPTER TEN

Versions of the Same

This chapter gathers different versions of the same texts: poets' revisions of their own work, variant translations of one original, and a pedagogic paraphrase. Saying that different words express the same content, we beg questions; when two texts differ in their wording, by definition nothing is truly the same. Still, revisions and variant translations can give us multiple examples of phrases that resemble each other and are *not* the same, thus providing opportunity to examine differences of diction, rhythm, image, metaphor, sound, and (often) meter. By noticing these differences, we can review the study of poetry and sharpen our ability to tell better from good, best from better.

Poets' Revisions

William Butler Yeats revised his poems many times. He published his first volume in 1885, and by 1895 he had revised some of these poems in a new collection of his work. When he was in his sixties, he rewrote some poems he had written in his twenties. When people objected, he answered:

> The friends that have it I do wrong
> Whenever I remake a song,
> Should know what issue is at stake:
> It is myself that I remake.

With his early revisions, he remade style, not self. He changed:

> In three days' time he stood up with a moan
> And he went down to the long sands alone.

to:

> In three days' time, Cuchulain[1] with a moan
> Stood up, and came to the long sands alone.

[1] *Cuchulain* is pronounced cuh-HULL-an.

In this revision, a proper name replaces a pronoun, and a boring rhythm becomes varied and expressive: *Stood up,* with a pause after it, then eight syllables of walking, seems to imitate in its rhythm the action it describes.

In 1892, in the first version of a famous poem called "When You Are Old," Yeats wrote the couplet:

> Murmur, a little sad, "From us fled Love.
> He paced upon the mountains far above . . ."

The adjective *sad* goes strangely with the verb *murmur,* and the normal word order at the end of the first line would have been *Love fled from us.* Dissatisfied six years later, Yeats rewrote the lines to read:

> Murmur, a little sadly, how Love fled
> And paced upon the mountains overhead . . .

Now this line approaches natural speech, without affectation or awkwardness.

Four versions of the last stanza of "Cradle Song" show Yeats growing in simplicity and directness:

1889

> My darling I kiss you,
>   With arms round my own.
> Ah, how I shall miss you
>   When heavy and grown.

1892

> I kiss you and kiss you
>   With arms round my own.
> Ah, how I shall miss you
>   When, dear, you have grown.

1901

> I kiss you and kiss you
> My pigeon, my own.
> Ah, how I shall miss you,
> When you have grown.

1925

> I sigh that kiss you
> For I must own
> That I shall miss you
> When you have grown.

In the 1889 stanza, the first line lacks the energy it picked up when Yeats paced the line with two verbs. In the last line, the word *heavy* is unfortunate— the kind of error any writer can make, where a word brings in an irrelevant association the writer is blind to. *Heavy* for Yeats probably implied ponderous and slow-moving, an end to youth; unfortunately, it is a euphemism for obesity. In 1892, he improved the first line and in the fourth line got rid of *heavy* but substituted the rhythmically awkward *dear,* chopping the line up with commas. In 1901, he repaired the fourth line—finally—but left behind the decorative *pigeon* and the decorative *Ah.* By 1925, he was all for spareness. In judging among these "versions of the same," there is room for difference of opinion, but I like the last version best. This 1925 change comes close to remaking the self.

Yeats was not the only great poet to revise his work. William Blake in "London" (page 570), originally wrote:

> But most the midnight Harlot's curse
> From every dismal street I hear,
> Weaves around the Marriage hearse
> And blasts the new born Infant's tear.

A year later, he revised these lines into:

> But most thro' midnight streets I hear
> How the youthful Harlot's curse
> Blasts the new-born Infant's tear
> And blights with plagues the Marriage hearse.

Notice that the elements of the first stanza—midnight, harlot's curse, street, marriage hearse, blasts, infant, tear—turn up again in the later stanza. We lose *dismal* and we gain another adjective, *youthful.* We lose the pretty word *weave* —to weave is to create, to turn thread into cloth; in this context the pretty word is oddly used for destructive purpose—and we have in return the far more powerful *blights with plagues,* combining diseases of plants and animals. Although the first stanza was powerful, the revision increases the poem's power, intensity, and density, adding a new area of meaning in the metaphor of diseases. Before, death entered with *hearse,* but we lacked the cause of death. The order of things is changed in the second version, and the order itself makes the poetry more powerful. It moves from the innocent streets to the prostitute and her oath, to the damnation of the infant's weeping, and finally to the disease and death of the institution of marriage.

Exercise

In "La Belle Dame sans Merci," Keats originally wrote the stanza:

> She took me to her elfin grot,
>   And there she wept, and sighed full sore,
> And there I shut her wild wild eyes
>   With kisses four.

He changed these lines—three out of four—into:

> She took me to her elfin grot,
>   And there she gazed and sighèd deep,
> And there I shut her wild sad eyes—
>   So kissed to sleep.

Many critics feel that Keats's revision is inferior to the original. What do you think, and why?

Robert Frost kept most of his variant versions from the public. He liked to give the impression that he revised little. Still, he published a number of poems in an early version, tinkered with them, and published them in revised form. His most remarkable printed revision is that of "Design," one of his greatest poems. In 1912 he included in a letter this poem:

In White   (1912)

A dented spider like a snowdrop white
On a white Heal-all,[1] holding up a moth
Like a white piece of lifeless satin cloth—
Saw ever curious eye so strange a sight?
Portent in little, assorted death and blight
Like the ingredients of a witches' broth?
The beady spider, the flower like a froth,
And the moth carried like a paper kite.

What had that flower to do with being white,
10   The blue Brunella,[2] every child's delight?
What brought the kindred spider to that height?
(Make we no thesis of the miller's° plight.)   moth
What but design of darkness and of night?
Design, design! Do I use the word aright?
                                                        —Robert Frost

Not until 1922 did "In White" turn up again, retitled:

Design   (1922)

I found a dimpled spider, fat and white,
On a white heal-all, holding up a moth
Like a white piece of rigid satin cloth—
Assorted characters of death and blight
Mixed ready to begin the morning right,
Like the ingredients of a witches' broth—

---

[1] A flower, normally blue, reported to have healing qualities   [2] Another name for the heal-all

A snow-drop spider, a flower like a froth,
And dead wings carried like a paper kite.

What had that flower to do with being white,
10 The wayside blue and innocent heal-all?
What brought the kindred spider to that height,
Then steered the white moth thither in the night?
What but design of darkness to appall?—
If design govern in a thing so small.

—Robert Frost

It is useful with this poem, or these two poems, to compare them line by line. Here "In White" is in roman type, "Design" in italic:

1. A dented spider like a snowdrop white
   1. *I found a dimpled spider, fat and white,*

2. On a white Heal-all, holding up a moth
   2. *On a white heal-all, holding up a moth*

3. Like a white piece of lifeless satin cloth—
   3. *Like a white piece of rigid satin cloth—*

4. Saw ever curious eye so strange a sight?
   4. *Assorted characters of death and blight*

5. Portent in little, assorted death and blight
   5. *Mixed ready to begin the morning right,*

6. Like the ingredients of a witches' broth?
   6. *Like the ingredients of a witches' broth—*

7. The beady spider, the flower like a froth,
   7. *A snow-drop spider, a flower like a froth,*

8. And the moth carried like a paper kite.
   8. *And dead wings carried like a paper kite.*

9. What had that flower to do with being white,
   9. *What had that flower to do with being white,*

10. The blue Brunella every child's delight?
    10. *The wayside blue and innocent heal-all?*

11. What brought the kindred spider to that height?
    11. *What brought the kindred spider to that height,*

12. (Make we no thesis of the miller's plight.)
    12. *Then steered the white moth thither in the night?*

13. What but design of darkness and of night?
    13. *What but design of darkness to appall?—*

14. Design, design! Do I use the word aright?
    14. *If design govern in a thing so small.*

Exercises

1. In 1/*1*, compare *dented* with *dimpled*. What kind of object do you associate with *dented?* What kind with *dimpled?* Is either association preferable to the other in the context of the whole poem?

2. In 3/*3*, could you defend *lifeless* against *rigid?* Is either of these adjectives more specific than the other? More physical?

3. Paraphrase 3/*4*. How does the sentence work? Does *3/4* say something similar? Different? Does the grammar help in the later version?

4. In 7/*7*, compare *beady* and *snow-drop*.

5. In 8/*8*, compare the rhythms of the two lines at the beginning. What are the changes? Do you like them? Can you say why?

6. The second stanzas or sestets of these two versions differ in a number of ways. List all the differences you can see. Decide whether you approve of the changes made. Imagine why Robert Frost might have wanted to make them. Look up the history of *appall* and decide how it is used in this poem. Which of the two poems is clearer? Which of the two poems is better? Why?

Different Translations

Different translations of the same poem can offer us an opportunity to compare style, rhythm, and diction—even when we do not know the original. We can turn translations to our purposes by deciding which version we prefer, and why. We can sharpen our wits by defining our choices. Here is the Twenty-third Psalm, translated from the Hebrew of the Old Testament, in the seventeenth-century King James version:

> The Lord is my shepherd;
> I shall not want.
> He maketh me to lie down in green pastures: he leadeth me beside the still
>   waters.
>   He restoreth my soul: he leadeth me in the paths of righteousness for his
>   name's sake.
> Yea, though I walk through the valley of the shadow of death, I will fear no evil:
>   for thou art with me; thy rod and thy staff they comfort me.
>   Thou preparest a table before me in the presence of mine enemies:
> 10   Thou annointest my head with oil; my cup runneth over.
>   Surely goodness and mercy shall follow me all the days of my life:
> And I will dwell in the house of the Lord forever.

Here is the Revised Standard Version, which came out first in 1952—very close, but not the same:

> The Lord is my shepherd, I shall not want;
>   he makes me lie down in green pastures.
> He leads me beside still waters;
>   he restores my soul.

He leads me in paths of righteousness
    for his name's sake.

Even though I walk through the valley of the shadow of death,
    I fear no evil; for thou art with me;
    thy rod and thy staff,
10   they comfort me.
Thou preparest a table before me
in the presence of my enemies;
thou anointest my head with oil,
    my cup overflows.
Surely goodness and mercy shall follow me
    all the days of my life;
and I shall dwell in the house of the LORD
      for ever.

Here is the same Psalm in a version from *The Book of Psalms* copyrighted by the American Bible Society in 1976:

    The LORD is my shepherd;
        I have everything I need.
He lets me rest in fields of green grass
    and leads me to quiet pools of fresh water.
He gives me new strength.
He guides me in the right paths,
    as he has promised.
Even if I go through deepest darkness,
    I will not be afraid, LORD,
10   for you are with me.
Your shepherd's rod and staff protect me.

You prepare a banquet for me,
    where all my enemies can see me;
You welcome me as an honored guest
    and fill my cup to the brim.
I know that your goodness and love
    will be with me all my life;
    and your house will be my home as long as I live.

Finally, here is a version by David Rosenberg, an American poet who is translating the Bible, book by book, in his "A Poet's Bible." This modern version is taken from *Blues of the Sky,* Rosenberg's selection from the Psalms:

The Lord is my shepherd
and keeps me from wanting
what I can't have

lush green grass is set
around me and crystal water
to graze by

there I revive with my soul
find the way that love makes
for his name

10   and though I pass through cities of pain, through death's living shadow
I'm not afraid to touch
to know what I am

your shepherd's staff is always there
to keep me calm
in my body

you set a table before me
in the presence of my enemies
you give me grace to speak

to quiet them
20   to be full with humanness
to be warm in my soul's lightness

to feel contact every day
in my hand and in my belly
love coming down to me

in the air of your name, Lord
in your house
in my life

Shakespeare in Paraphrase

Let us end with a gross example of paraphrase. Recently, a publisher issued four
Shakespearean tragedies with the original lines on the left-hand page and line-
by-line paraphrases on the right. The editors—or translators—intended to
provide pedagogical help for contemporary students, changing archaic words
into modern synonyms. At the same time, they often turned Shakespeare's
metaphors into plain speech. At the beginning of *Hamlet,* when the guards,
Francisco and Bernardo, challenge each other, Francisco says "Stand and unfold yourself." In the paraphrase, the sentence reads "Stand still and tell me
who you are."

When we remove metaphor in favor of plain speech, we remove images—
and those images often carry feelings on their backs. When Francisco asked
Bernardo "Stand and unfold yourself," he thought of Bernardo physically like a
butterfly expanding vulnerable wings or perhaps like a flag unfurling. But when
Francisco asks Bernardo in the paraphrase "Stand still and tell me who you are,"
we have a mere request for identification. We have no picture, no image, no
sense of something vulnerable or formerly closed in on itself, now opening up.

Here is a well-known speech, with Shakespeare's text in roman type. In
italic, after each Shakespearean line, is the modern paraphrase. You can read
each speech as a whole or read one line at a time, first the original and then the
paraphrase.

1. To be, or not to be: that is the question:
   1. To be, or not to be: that is what really matters.

2. Whether 'tis nobler in the mind to suffer
   2. Is it nobler to accept passively

3. The slings and arrows of outrageous fortune,
   3. the trials and tribulations that unjust fate sends.

4. Or to take arms against a sea of troubles,
   4. or to resist an ocean of troubles,

5. And by opposing end them. To die, to sleep—
   5. and, by our own effort, defeat them? To die, to fall asleep—

6. No more—and by a sleep to say we end
   6. perhaps that's all there is to it—and by that sleep suppose we put an end to

7. The heartache, and the thousand natural shocks
   7. the heartache and the thousands of pains and worries

8. That flesh is heir to! 'Tis a consummation
   8. that are a part of being human! That's an end

9. Devoutly to be wished. To die, to sleep—
   9. we could all look forward to. To die, to sleep—

10. To sleep—perchance to dream: ay, there's the rub,
    10. to sleep—maybe to dream: yes, that's the catch.

11. For in that sleep of death what dreams may come
    11. For in that sleep of death the nightmares that may come

12. When we have shuffled off this mortal coil,
    12. when we have freed ourselves from the turmoil of this mortal life

13. Must give us pause. There's the respect
    13. must make us hesitate. There's the thought

14. That makes calamity of so long life:
    14. that makes a disaster out of living to a ripe old age.

15. For who would bear the whips and scorns of time,
    15. After all, who wants to put up with the lashes and insults of this world,

16. Th' oppressor's wrong, the proud man's contumely,
    16. the tyrant's injustice and contempt of arrogant men,

17. The pangs of despised love, the law's delay,
    17. the pains of rejected love, the law's frustrating slowness,

18. The insolence of office, and the spurns
    18. insults from our superiors, and the snubs

19. That patient merit of th' unworthy takes,
    19. that deserving and hopeful people have to take from powerful inferiors,

20. When he himself might his quietus make
    20. when he could end the whole process by killing himself

> 21. With a bare bodkin? . . .
>   *21. with a bare dagger? . . .*

In Shakespeare's first line, Hamlet speaks of *the question,* which, as he thinks out loud, becomes a true, unanswerable question—not a question in the abstracted sense of problem, like "the Middle East question." Instead of using *question,* the paraphraser speaks of *what really matters,* which is empty language. The difference is small, because Shakespeare's *question* is not a word of great importance in Hamlet's speech. Yet, the difference in the two words is typical: *question* is concrete, in the form of a real question; *what really matters* has neither "reality" nor "matter" in its syllabic bones.

When the paraphraser substitutes *to accept passively* for *in the mind to suffer,* one wants to argue. Shakespeare distinguishes between inaction, which includes mental suffering, and external action against huge forces. The paraphraser includes the notion of passivity but excludes mental suffering; Shakespeare seems mistranslated. In *trials and tribulations* we find a cliché to substitute for an image of weapons. Although the *slings and arrows* may be abstracted into *trials and tribulations* in our minds—almost like calling them "nuisances and annoyances"—the cliché is pale; we lose the implication of pain and death carried in *slings and arrows.* Paraphrasing *outrageous* as *unjust* is another diminishment. *Outrageous* retains in modern speech most of its old character, especially when we denounce something with the noun *outrage. Unjust* is less emotional, more intellectual. We begin to see that the paraphrase, by draining the language of particularity in metaphor and image, drains the poetry of feeling.

So much for the first five lines. The rest of this speech can bear more attention.

Exercises

1. In 7/7, discuss the removal of *natural.* Is anything missing that Shakespeare may have felt essential?

2. In 8/8, what is the first metaphor removed? Does the missing metaphor have any general relevance to this play?

3. In 9/9, is *devoutly* paraphrased?

4. 12/12. Using a large dictionary (the *Oxford English Dictionary,* usually in a college library, would be the best) consider the metaphor of *shuffle . . . coil.* Does *the turmoil of this mortal life* paraphrase parts of Shakespeare's line? Does it paraphrase the whole?

5. In 14/14, find a new metaphor added by the paraphraser. Is it good poetry?

6. 15/15, are the substitute words examples of the occasional usefulness of paraphrases in reading older authors? Do you find other good examples of paraphrase in this passage from *Hamlet?*

CHAPTER ELEVEN

Four Poets

We have been studying elements of poetry, with examples as brief as a line and as long as a single poem. It will be useful to concentrate next on a group of poems by a single poet. This chapter has selections from the work of one English and three American poets, each represented by characteristic poems. The Englishman, John Keats, was born in 1795; when he died at the age of twenty-five, he had written several of the best poems of the language. The Americans are two women and a man, born in 1830, 1929, and 1874. Emily Dickinson was an Easterner who lived most of her life in one town; Robert Frost, a Californian, became the great poet of New England; and Adrienne Rich, a woman from the East, now lives and writes in California.

John Keats

John Keats (1795–1821) trained to become a physician, then gave up his medical studies to devote himself to poetry. Among his friends were the critic William Hazlitt and the older poet Liegh Hunt. Keats published his first book of poems in 1817. In the nineteenth century, literary criticism was frequently affected by political beliefs or associations, and Keats's poems were attacked viciously because of his associations with the liberal thinkers of his day. He developed tuberculosis early. In the space of a few months he wrote his best work, his poems on a Grecian Urn, to a Nightingale, to Autumn. He went to Italy for his health in September 1820 but died on February 23 of the next year. Carved on his tomb at his request were the words "Here lies one whose name was writ in water." Keats's letters contain superb speculations on the nature of poetry. See also pages 478–480 and 500–501.

On First Looking into Chapman's Homer   (1816)

Much have I travelled in the realms of gold,
    And many goodly states and kingdoms seen;
    Round many western islands have I been
Which bards in fealty to Apollo hold.
Oft of one wide expanse had I been told
    That deep-browed Homer ruled as his demesne;
    Yet did I never breathe its pure serene
Till I heard Chapman speak out loud and bold.
Then felt I like some watcher of the skies
10   When a new planet swims into his ken;
Or like stout Cortez when with eagle eyes
    He stared at the Pacific, and all his men
Looked at each other with a wild surmise—
    Silent, upon a peak in Darien.

When I have fears that I may cease to be   (1818)

When I have fears that I may cease to be
    Before my pen has gleaned my teeming brain,
Before high-pilèd books, in charactery,
    Hold like rich garners the full ripened grain;
When I behold, upon the night's starred face,
    Huge cloudy symbols of a high romance,
And think that I may never live to trace
    Their shadows with the magic hand of chance;
And when I feel, fair creature of an hour,
10   That I shall never look upon thee more,
Never have relish in the fairy power
    Of unreflecting love; then on the shore

Of the wide world I stand alone and think
Till love and fame to nothingness do sink.

Ode to a Nightingale   (1819)

I

My heart aches, and a drowsy numbness pains
    My sense, as though of hemlock[1] I had drunk,
Or emptied some dull opiate to the drains
    One minute past, and Lethe-wards[2] had sunk.
'Tis not through envy of thy happy lot,
    But being too happy in thine happiness,—
        That thou, light-wingèd Dryad° of the trees,   nymph
            In some melodious plot
Of beechen green, and shadows numberless,
10   Singest of summer in full-throated ease.

II

O for a draught of vintage that hath been
    Cooled a long age in the deep-delvèd earth,
Tasting of Flora[3] and the country green,
    Dance, and Provençal song,[4] and sunburnt mirth!
O for a beaker full of the warm South,
    Full of the true, the blushful Hippocrene,[5]
        With beaded bubbles winking at the brim,
            And purple-stainèd mouth,
That I might drink, and leave the world unseen,
20   And with thee fade away into the forest dim.

III

Fade far away, dissolve, and quite forget
    What thou among the leaves hast never known,
The weariness, the fever, and the fret
    Here, where men sit and hear each other groan;
Where palsy shakes a few, sad, last gray hairs,
    Where youth grows pale, and spectre-thin, and dies;
        Where but to think is to be full of sorrow
            And leaden-eyed despairs;
Where Beauty cannot keep her lustrous eyes,
30   Or new Love pine at them beyond to-morrow.

[1] Poison hemlock, a lethally poisonous herb of the carrot family, was used in ancient Greece to execute criminals.   [2] In Greek mythology, Lethe was the river in the underworld from which the shades of the dead drank to obtain forgetfulness of the past.   [3] Roman goddess of flowers and spring   [4] Provence, the South of France, was famous for the songs of love and adventure constructed or repeated by its medieval troubadors.   [5] The "Fountain of the Horse" on Mount Helicon, sacred to the Muses

IV

Away! away! for I will fly to thee,
  Not charioted by Bacchus and his pards,[6]
But on the viewless° wings of Poesy,   invisible
  Though the dull brain perplexes and retards.
Already with thee! tender is the night,
  And haply the Queen-Moon is on her throne,
    Clustered around by all her starry fays;°   fairies
      But here there is no light,
Save what from heaven is with the breezes blown
40   Through verdurous glooms and winding mossy ways.

V

I cannot see what flowers are at my feet,
  Nor what soft incense hangs upon the boughs,
But, in embalmèd° darkness, guess each sweet   fragrant
  Wherewith the seasonable month endows
The grass, the thicket, and the fruit-tree wild—
  White hawthorn, and the pastoral eglantine;
    Fast-fading violets covered up in leaves;
      And mid-May's eldest child,
The coming musk-rose, full of dewy wine,
50   The murmurous haunt of flies on summer eves.

VI

Darkling° I listen, and for many a time   In darkness
  I have been half in love with easeful Death,
Called him soft names in many a musèd rhyme,
  To take into the air my quiet breath;
Now more than ever seems it rich to die,
  To cease upon the midnight with no pain,
    While thou art pouring forth thy soul abroad
      In such an ecstasy.
Still wouldst thou sing, and I have ears in vain—
60   To thy high requiem become a sod.

VII

Thou wast not born for death, immortal bird!
  No hungry generations tread thee down;
The voice I hear this passing night was heard
  In ancient days by emperor and clown:
Perhaps the self-same song that found a path
  Through the sad heart of Ruth,[7] when, sick for home,
    She stood in tears amid the alien corn;°   wheat
      The same that oft-times hath

---

[6] Bacchus, the Roman god of wine, was sometimes portrayed riding in a chariot drawn by leopards.   [7] A reference to the Moabite widow whose story is told in the Old Testament book of Ruth

Charmed magic casements, opening on the foam
70   Of perilous seas, in faery lands forlorn.

VIII

Forlorn! the very word is like a bell
    To toll me back from thee to my sole self!
Adieu! the fancy cannot cheat so well
    As she is famed to do, deceiving elf.
Adieu! adieu! thy plaintive anthem fades
    Past the near meadows, over the still stream,
        Up the hill-side; and now 'tis buried deep
          In the next valley-glades:
Was it a vision, or a waking dream?
80   Fled is that music . . . Do I wake or sleep?

Ode on a Grecian Urn   (1819)

I

Thou still unravished bride of quietness,
    Thou foster-child of silence and slow time,
Sylvan historian, who canst thus express
    A flowery tale more sweetly than our rhyme!
What leaf-fringed legend haunts about thy shape
    Of deities or mortals, or of both,
        In Tempe or the dales of Arcady?[1]
What men or gods are these? What maidens loth?
    What mad pursuit? What struggle to escape?
10   What pipes and timbrels? What wild ecstasy?

II

Heard melodies are sweet, but those unheard
    Are sweeter; therefore, ye soft pipes, play on;
Not to the sensual° ear, but, more endeared,   sensuous
    Pipe to the spirit ditties of no tone.
Fair youth beneath the trees, thou canst not leave
    Thy song, nor ever can those trees be bare;
        Bold lover, never, never canst thou kiss,
Though winning near the goal—yet do not grieve:
    She cannot fade, though thou hast not thy bliss,
20   For ever wilt thou love, and she be fair!

III

Ah, happy, happy boughs, that cannot shed
    Your leaves, nor ever bid the spring adieu;
And, happy melodist, unwearièd,
    For ever piping songs for ever new!

---

[1] Tempe and the glens of Arcady are landscapes of legendary beauty.

More happy love, more happy, happy love!
    For ever warm and still to be enjoyed,
        For ever panting, and for ever young—
All breathing human passion far above,
    That leaves a heart high-sorrowful and cloyed,
30   A burning forehead, and a parching tongue.

IV

Who are these coming to the sacrifice?
    To what green altar, O mysterious priest,
Lead'st thou that heifer lowing at the skies,
    And all her silken flanks with garlands drest?
What little town by river or sea shore,
    Or mountain built with peaceful citadel,
        Is emptied of this folk, this pious morn?
And, little town, thy streets for evermore
    Will silent be; and not a soul to tell
40   Why thou art desolate can e'er return.

V

O Attic² shape! Fair attitude! With brede°   pattern, design
    Of marble men and maidens overwrought,
With forest branches and the trodden weed—
    Thou, silent form, dost tease us out of thought
As doth eternity. Cold pastoral!
    When old age shall this generation waste,
        Thou shalt remain, in midst of other woe
Than ours, a friend to man, to whom thou say'st,
    "Beauty is truth, truth beauty"—that is all
50   Ye know on earth, and all ye need to know.

This Living Hand   (1820)

This living hand, now warm and capable
Of earnest grasping, would, if it were cold
And in the icy silence of the tomb,
So haunt thy days and chill thy dreaming nights
That thou would wish thine own heart dry of blood
So in my veins red life might stream again,
And thou be conscience-calmed. See here it is—
I hold it towards you.

---

² Attic equals Athenian and therefore classic grace and simplicity.

Emily Dickinson

Emily Dickinson (1830–1886) grew up in Amherst, Massachusetts, where her family was associated with Amherst College. She attended school with other young women but, as she grew older, became reclusive, until she rarely left her own room. When she was young, she made attempts to print her poems and she placed a few in obscure publications. Then she apparently renounced this notion of fame and wrote, so far as we know, for herself. Her eccentricities of punctuation, not to mention the strangeness of her metaphors and rhymes, may derive from her sense that she was her own and only audience. Yet power and insight accumulated in her isolation. She is probably the greatest female poet of our language, and every year her audience grows wider.

He put the Belt around my life   (1861)

He put the Belt around my life—
I heard the Buckle snap—
And turned away, imperial,
My Lifetime folding up—
Deliberate, as a Duke would do
A Kingdom's Title Deed—
Henceforth, a Dedicated sort—
A Member of the Cloud.

Yet not too far to come at call—
10 And do the little Toils
That make the Circuit of the Rest—
And deal occasional smiles
To lives that stoop to notice mine—
And kindly ask it in—
Whose invitation, know you not
For Whom I must decline?

He fumbles at your Soul   (1862)

He fumbles at your Soul
As Players at the Keys
Before they drop full Music on—
He stuns you by degrees—
Prepares your brittle Nature
For the Ethereal Blow
By fainter Hammers—further heard—
Then nearer—Then so slow

Your Breath has time to straighten—
10 Your Brain—to bubble Cool—
Deals—One—imperial—Thunderbolt—
That scalps your naked Soul—

When Winds take Forests in their
Paws— The Universe—is still—

After great pain, a formal feeling comes—   (1862)

After great pain, a formal feeling
    comes—
The Nerves sit ceremonious, like
    Tombs—
The stiff Heart questions was it He,
    that bore,
And Yesterday, or Centuries before?

The Feet, mechanical, go round—
Of Ground, or Air, or Ought—

10 A Wooden way
Regardless grown,
A Quartz contentment, like a stone—

This is the Hour of Lead—
Remembered, if outlived,
As Freezing persons, recollect the
    Snow—
First—Chill—then Stupor—then the
    letting go—

The first Day's Night had come—   (1862)

The first Day's Night had come—
And grateful that a thing
So terrible—had been endured—
I told my Soul to sing—

She said her Strings were snapt—
Her Bow   to Atoms blown—
And so to mend her—gave me work
Until another Morn—

And then—a Day as huge
10 As Yesterdays in pairs,

Unrolled its horror in my face—
Until it blocked my eyes—

My Brain—begun to laugh—
I mumbled—like a fool—
And tho' 'tis Years ago—that Day—
My Brain keeps giggling—still.

And Something's odd—within—
That person that I was—
And this One—do not feel the same—
20 Could it be Madness—this?

Much Madness is divinest Sense—   (1862)

Much Madness is divinest Sense—
To a discerning Eye—
Much Sense—the starkest Madness—
'Tis the Majority

In this, as All, prevail—
Assent—and you are sane—
Demur—you're straightway dangerous—
And handled with a Chain—

I heard a Fly buzz—when I died—   (1862)

I heard a Fly buzz—when I died—
The Stillness in the Room
Was like the Stillness in the Air—
Between the Heaves of Storm—

The Eyes around—had wrung them
     dry—
And Breaths were gathering firm
For that last Onset—when the King
Be witnessed—in the Room—

10 I willed my Keepsakes—Signed away
What portion of me be
Assignable—and then it was
There interposed a Fly—

With Blue—uncertain stumbling
     Buzz—
Between the light—and me—
And then the Windows failed—and then
I could not see to see—

I would not paint—a picture—   (1862)

I would not paint—a picture—
I'd rather be the One
Its bright impossibility
To dwell—delicious—on—
And wonder how the fingers feel
Whose rare—celestial—stir—
Evokes so sweet a Torment—
Such sumptuous—Despair—

I would not talk, like Cornets—
10 I'd rather be the One
Raised softly to the Ceilings—
And out, and easy on—

Through Villages of Ether—
Myself endued Balloon
By but a lip of Metal—
The pier to my Pontoon—

Nor would I be a Poet—
It's finer—own the Ear—
Enamored—impotent—content—
20 The License to revere,
A privilege so awful
What would the Dower be,
Had I the Art to stun myself
With Bolts of Melody!

I'm ceded—I've stopped being Theirs—   (1862)

I'm ceded—I've stopped being
   Theirs—
The name They dropped upon my face
With water, in the country church
Is finished using, now,
And They can put it with my Dolls,
My childhood, and the string of spools,
I've finished threading—too—

Baptized, before, without the choice,
10 But this time, consciously, of Grace—
Unto supremest name—

Called to my Full—The Crescent
   dropped—
Existence's whole Arc, filled up,
With one small Diadem.

My second Rank—too small the first—
Crowned—Crowing—on my Father's
   breast—
A half unconscious Queen—
20 But this time—Adequate—Erect,
With Will to choose, or to reject,
And I choose, just a Crown—

The Soul has Bandaged moments—   (1862)

The Soul has Bandaged moments—
When too appalled to stir—
She feels some ghastly Fright come up
And stop to look at her—

Salute her—with long fingers—
Caress her freezing hair—
Sip, Goblin, from the very lips
The Lover—hovered—o'er—
Unworthy, that a thought so mean
10 Accost a Theme—so—fair—

The soul has moments of Escape—
When bursting all the doors—

She dances like a Bomb, abroad,
And swings upon the Hours,

As do the Bee—delirious borne—
Long Dungeoned from his Rose—
Touch Liberty—then know no more,
But Noon, and Paradise—
The Soul's retaken moments—
20 When, Felon led along,
With shackles on the plumed feet,
And staples, in the Song,

The Horror welcomes her, again,
These, are not brayed of Tongue—

The Province of the Saved   (1862)

The Province of the Saved
Should be the Art—To save—
Through Skill obtained in Themselves—
The Science of the Grave

No Man can understand
But He that hath endured

The Dissolution—in Himself—
That Man—be qualified

To qualify Despair
10 To Those who failing new—
Mistake Defeat for Death—Each time—
Till acclimated—to—

A still—Volcano—Life— (1862)

A still—Volcano—Life—
That flickered in the night—
When it was dark enough to do
Without erasing sight—

A quiet—Earthquake Style—
Too subtle to suspect

By natures this side Naples—
The North cannot detect

The Solemn—Torrid—Symbol—
10 The lips that never lie—
Whose hissing Corals part—and shut—
And Cities—ooze away—

I cannot live with You— (1862)

I cannot live with You—
It would be Life—
And Life is over there—
Behind the Shelf

The Sexton keeps the Key to—
Putting up
Our Life—His Porcelain—
Like a Cup—

Discarded of the Housewife—
10 Quaint—or Broke—
A newer Sevres pleases—
Old Ones crack—

I could not die—with You—
For One must wait
To shut the Other's Gaze down—
You—could not—

And I—Could I stand by
And see You—freeze—
Without my Right of Frost—
20 Death's privilege?

Nor could I rise—with You—
Because Your Face
Would put out Jesus'—
That New Grace

Glow plain—and foreign
On my homesick Eye—

Except that You than He
Shone closer by—

They'd judge Us—How—
30 For You—served Heaven—You know,
Or sought to—
I could not—

Because You saturated Sight—
And I had no more Eyes
For sordid excellence
As Paradise

And were You lost, I would be—
Though My Name
Rang loudest
40 On the Heavenly fame—

And were You—saved—
And I—condemned to be
Where You were not—
That self—were Hell to Me—

So We must meet apart—
You there—I—here—
With just the Door ajar
That Oceans are—and Prayer—
And that White Sustenance—
50 Despair—

Me from Myself—to banish—   (1862)

Me from Myself—to banish—
Had I Art—
Impregnable my Fortress
Unto All Heart—

But since Myself—assault Me—
How have I peace

Except by subjugating
Consciousness?

And since We're mutual Monarch
10 How this be
Except by Abdication—
Me—of Me?

Because I could not stop for Death—   (1863)

Because I could not stop for Death—
He kindly stopped for me—
The Carriage held but just Ourselves—
And Immortality.

We slowly drove—He knew no haste
And I had put away
My labor and my leisure too,
For His Civility—

We passed the School, where Children
10   strove
At Recess—in the Ring—
We passed the Fields of Gazing Grain—
We passed the Setting Sun—

Or rather—He passed Us—
The Dews drew quivering and chill—
For only Gossamer, my Gown—
My Tippet—only Tulle—

We paused before a House that seemed
A Swelling of the Ground—
20 The Roof was scarcely visible—
The Cornice—in the Ground—

Since then—'tis Centuries—and yet
Feels shorter than the Day
I first surmised the Horse's Heads
Were toward Eternity—

My Life had stood—a Loaded Gun—   (1863)

My Life had stood—a Loaded Gun—
In Corners—till a Day
The Owner passed—identified—
And carried Me away—

And now We roam in Sovereign
     Woods—
And now We hunt the Doe—
And every time I speak for Him—
The Mountains straight reply—

10 And do I smile, such cordial light
Upon the Valley glow—
It is as a Vesuvian face
Had let its pleasure through—

And when at Night—Our good Day
     done—
I guard My Master's Head—
'Tis better than the Eider-Duck's
Deep Pillow—to have shared—

To foe of His—I'm deadly foe—
20 None stir the second time—
On whom I lay a Yellow Eye—
Or an emphatic Thumb—

Though I than He—may longer live
He longer must—than I—
For I have but the power to kill,
Without—the power to die—

Severer Service of myself   (1863)

Severer Service of myself
I—hastened to demand
To fill the awful Vacuum
Your life had left behind—

I worried Nature with my Wheels
When Hers had ceased to run—
When she had put away Her Work
My own had just begun.

I strove to weary Brain and Bone—
10 To harass to fatigue
The glittering Retinue of nerves—
Vitality to clog

To some dull comfort Those obtain
Who put a Head away
They knew the Hair to—
And forget the color of the Day—

Affliction would not be appeased—
The Darkness braced as firm
As all my stratagem had been
20 The Midnight to confirm—

No Drug for Consciousness—can be—
Alternative to die
Is Nature's only Pharmacy
For Being's Malady—

I felt a Cleaving in my Mind—   (1864)

I felt a Cleaving in my Mind—
As if my Brain had split—
I tried to match it—Seam by Seam—
But could not make them fit.

The thought behind, I strove to join
Unto the thought before—
But Sequence ravelled out of Sound
Like Balls—upon a Floor.

A narrow Fellow in the Grass   (1865)

A narrow Fellow in the Grass
Occasionally rides—
You may have met Him—did you not
His notice sudden is—

The Grass divides as with a Comb—
A spotted shaft is seen—
And then it closes at your feet
And opens further on—

He likes a Boggy Acre
10 A Floor too cool for Corn—
Yet when a Boy, and Barefoot—
I more than once at Noon

Have passed, I thought, a Whip lash
Unbraiding in the Sun
When stooping to secure it
It wrinkled, and was gone—

Several of Nature's People
I know, and they know me—
I feel for them a transport
20 Of cordiality—

But never met this Fellow
Attended, or alone
Without a tighter breathing
And Zero at the Bone—

Robert Frost

Robert Frost (1874–1963) was born in California and died
in New England at the age of eighty-eight. The New
England countryside, its people, and their speech take
center stage in his poems. Frost's father died when he was
ten, and his mother took him back East. He attended high
school in Massachusetts, went to Dartmouth briefly,
worked in mills, and, after marriage, spent two years at
Harvard without taking a degree. He tried his hand at
farming while he wrote poems, but his poems did not win
acceptance from American editors. In 1912, he took his
family to England, where a London publisher recognized
the quality of the work; *A Boy's Will* appeared in 1913.
When Frost returned to the United States in 1915, he
found America ready for him. He won the Pulitzer Prize
four times. Two years before he died, he read a poem at
the inauguration of President John F. Kennedy. Other
poems by Robert Frost appear on pages 409, 428, 462, 502–503, and 517–518.

The Pasture   (1913)

I'm going out to clean the pasture spring;
I'll only stop to rake the leaves away
(And wait to watch the water clear, I may)
I sha'n't be gone long.—You come too.

I'm going out to fetch the little calf
That's standing by the mother. It's so young
It totters when she licks it with her tongue.
I sha'n't be gone long.—You come too.

Mowing   (1913)

There was never a sound beside the wood but one,
And that was my long scythe whispering to the ground.
What was it it whispered? I knew not well myself;
Perhaps it was something about the heat of the sun,
Something, perhaps, about the lack of sound—
And that was why it whispered and did not speak.
It was no dream of the gift of idle hours,
Or easy gold at the hand of fay or elf:
Anything more than the truth would have seemed too weak
10 To the earnest love that laid the swale in rows,
Not without feeble-pointed spikes of flowers
(Pale orchises), and scared a bright green snake.
The fact is the sweetest dream that labor knows.
My long scythe whispered and left the hay to make.

Home Burial   (1914)

He saw her from the bottom of the stairs
Before she saw him. She was starting down,
Looking back over her shoulder at some fear.
She took a doubtful step and then undid it
To raise herself and look again. He spoke
Advancing toward her: 'What is it you see
From up there always—for I want to know.'
She turned and sank upon her skirts at that,
And her face changed from terrified to dull.
10 He said to gain time: 'What is it you see,'
Mounting until she cowered under him.
'I will find out now—you must tell me, dear.'
She, in her place, refused him any help
With the least stiffening of her neck and silence.
She let him look, sure that he wouldn't see,
Blind creature; and awhile he didn't see.
But at last he murmured, 'Oh,' and again, 'Oh.'

'What is it—what?' she said.

                         'Just that I see.'

20 'You don't,' she challenged. 'Tell me what it is.'

'The wonder is I didn't see at once.
I never noticed it from here before.
I must be wonted to it—that's the reason.
The little graveyard where my people are!
So small the window frames the whole of it.
Not so much larger than a bedroom, is it?
There are three stones of slate and one of marble,
Broad-shouldered little slabs there in the sunlight
On the sidehill. We haven't to mind *those*.
30 But I understand: it is not the stones,
But the child's mound—'

                    'Don't, don't, don't, don't,' she cried.

She withdrew shrinking from beneath his arm
That rested on the bannister, and slid downstairs;
And turned on him with such a daunting look,
He said twice over before he knew himself:
'Can't a man speak of his own child he's lost?'

'Not you! Oh, where's my hat? Oh, I don't need it!
I must get out of here. I must get air.
40 I don't know rightly whether any man can.'

'Amy! Don't go to someone else this time.
Listen to me. I won't come down the stairs.'
He sat and fixed his chin between his fists.
'There's something I should like to ask you, dear.'

'You don't know how to ask it.'

                   'Help me, then.'

Her fingers moved the latch for all reply.

'My words are nearly always an offense.
I don't know how to speak of anything
50 So as to please you. But I might be taught
I should suppose. I can't say I see how.
A man must partly give up being a man
With women-folk. We could have some arrangement
By which I'd bind myself to keep hands off
Anything special you're a-mind to name.
Though I don't like such things 'twixt those that love.
Two that don't love can't live together without them.
But two that do can't live together with them.'
She moved the latch a little. 'Don't—don't go.
60 Don't carry it to someone else this time.
Tell me about it if it's something human.
Let me into your grief. I'm not so much
Unlike other folks as your standing there
Apart would make me out. Give me my chance.
I do think, though, you overdo it a little.
What was it brought you up to think it the thing
To take your mother-loss of a first child
So inconsolably—in the face of love.
You'd think his memory might be satisfied—'

70 'There you go sneering now!'

                      'I'm not, I'm not!

You make me angry. I'll come down to you.
God, what a woman! And it's come to this,
A man can't speak of his own child that's dead.'

'You can't because you don't know how to speak.
If you had any feelings, you that dug
With your own hand—how could you?—his little grave;
I saw you from that very window there,
Making the gravel leap and leap in air,
80 Leap up, like that, like that, and land so lightly
And roll back down the mound beside the hole.
I thought, Who is that man? I didn't know you.
And I crept down the stairs and up the stairs

To look again, and still your spade kept lifting.
Then you came in. I heard your rumbling voice
Out in the kitchen, and I don't know why,
But I went near to see with my own eyes.
You could sit there with the stains on your shoes
Of the fresh earth from your own baby's grave
90 And talk about your everyday concerns.
You had stood the spade up against the wall
Outside there in the entry, for I saw it.'

'I shall laugh the worst laugh I ever laughed.
I'm cursed. God, if I don't believe I'm cursed.'

'I can repeat the very words you were saying.
"Three foggy mornings and one rainy day
Will rot the best birch fence a man can build."
Think of it, talk like that at such a time!
What had how long it takes a birch to rot
100 To do with what was in the darkened parlor.
You *couldn't* care! The nearest friends can go
With anyone to death, comes so far short
They might as well not try to go at all.
No, from the time when one is sick to death,
One is alone, and he dies more alone.
Friends make pretense of following to the grave,
But before one is in it, their minds are turned
And making the best of their way back to life
And living people, and things they understand.
110 But the world's evil. I won't have grief so
If I can change it. Oh, I won't, I won't!'

'There, you have said it all and you feel better.
You won't go now. You're crying. Close the door.
The heart's gone out of it: why keep it up.
Amy! There's someone coming down the road!'

'*You*—oh, you think the talk is all. I must go—
Somewhere out of this house. How can I make you—'

'If—you—do!' She was opening the door wider.
'Where do you mean to go? First tell me that.
120 I'll follow and bring you back by force. I *will!*—'

After Apple-Picking   (1914)

My long two-pointed ladder's sticking through a tree
Toward heaven still,
And there's a barrel that I didn't fill
Beside it, and there may be two or three
Apples I didn't pick upon some bough.

But I am done with apple-picking now.
Essence of winter sleep is on the night,
The scent of apples: I am drowsing off.
I cannot rub the strangeness from my sight
10 I got from looking through a pane of glass
I skimmed this morning from the drinking trough
And held against the world of hoary grass.
It melted, and I let it fall and break.
But I was well
Upon my way to sleep before it fell,
And I could tell
What form my dreaming was about to take.
Magnified apples appear and disappear,
Stem end and blossom end,
20 And every fleck of russet showing clear.
My instep arch not only keeps the ache,
It keeps the pressure of a ladder round.
I feel the ladder sway as the boughs bend.
And I keep hearing from the cellar bin
The rumbling sound
Of load on load of apples coming in.
For I have had too much
Of apple-picking: I am overtired
Of the great harvest I myself desired.
30 There were ten thousand thousand fruit to touch,
Cherish in hand, lift down, and not let fall.
For all
That struck the earth,
No matter if not bruised or spiked with stubble,
Went surely to the cider-apple heap
As of no worth.
One can see what will trouble
This sleep of mine, whatever sleep it is.
Were he not gone,
40 The woodchuck could say whether it's like his
Long sleep, as I describe its coming on,
Or just some human sleep.

The Road Not Taken   (1916)

Two roads diverged in a yellow wood,
And sorry I could not travel both
And be one traveler, long I stood
And looked down one as far as I could
To where it bent in the undergrowth;

Then took the other, as just as fair,
And having perhaps the better claim,
Because it was grassy and wanted wear;
Though as for that the passing there
10 Had worn them really about the same,

And both that morning equally lay
In leaves no step had trodden black.
Oh, I kept the first for another day!
Yet knowing how way leads on to way,
I doubted if I should ever come back.

I shall be telling this with a sigh
Somewhere ages and ages hence:
Two roads diverged in a wood, and I—
I took the one less traveled by,
20 And that has made all the difference.

Birches   (1915)

When I see birches bend to left and right
Across the lines of straighter darker trees,
I like to think some boy's been swinging them.
But swinging doesn't bend them down to stay
As ice-storms do. Often you must have seen them
Loaded with ice a sunny winter morning
After a rain. They click upon themselves
As the breeze rises, and turn many-colored
As the stir cracks and crazes their enamel.
10 Soon the sun's warmth makes them shed crystal shells
Shattering and avalanching on the snow-crust—
Such heaps of broken glass to sweep away
You'd think the inner dome of heaven had fallen.
They are dragged to the withered bracken by the load,
And they seem not to break; though once they are bowed
So low for long, they never right themselves:
You may see their trunks arching in the woods
Years afterwards, trailing their leaves on the ground
Like girls on hands and knees that throw their hair
20 Before them over their heads to dry in the sun.
But I was going to say when Truth broke in
With all her matter-of-fact about the ice-storm
I should prefer to have some boy bend them
As he went out and in to fetch the cows—
Some boy too far from town to learn baseball,
Whose only play was what he found himself,
Summer or winter, and could play alone.
One by one he subdued his father's trees
By riding them down over and over again
30 Until he took the stiffness out of them,
And not one but hung limp, not one was left
For him to conquer. He learned all there was
To learn about not launching out too soon
And so not carrying the tree away
Clear to the ground. He always kept his poise
To the top branches, climbing carefully
With the same pains you use to fill a cup
Up to the brim, and even above the brim.
Then he flung outward, feet first, with a swish,
40 Kicking his way down through the air to the ground.
So was I once myself a swinger of birches.
And so I dream of going back to be.
It's when I'm weary of considerations,
And life is too much like a pathless wood
Where your face burns and tickles with the cobwebs
Broken across it, and one eye is weeping
From a twig's having lashed across it open.
I'd like to get away from earth awhile
And then come back to it and begin over.
50 May no fate willfully misunderstand me

And half grant what I wish and snatch me away
Not to return. Earth's the right place for love:
I don't know where it's likely to go better.
I'd like to go by climbing a birch tree,
And climb black branches up a snow-white trunk
Toward heaven, till the tree could bear no more,
But dipped its top and set me down again.
That would be good both going and coming back.
One could do worse than be a swinger of birches.

To Earthward   (1923)

Love at the lips was touch
As sweet as I could bear;
And once that seemed too much;
I lived on air

That crossed me from sweet things
The flow of—was it musk
From hidden grapevine springs
Down hill at dusk?

10 I had the swirl and ache
From sprays of honeysuckle
That when they're gathered shake
Dew on the knuckle.

I craved strong sweets, but those
Seemed strong when I was young;
The petal of the rose
It was that stung.

20 Now no joy but lacks salt
That is not dashed with pain
And weariness and fault;
I crave the stain

Of tears, the aftermark
Of almost too much love,
The sweet of bitter bark
And burning clove.

When stiff and sore and scarred
I take away my hand
From leaning on it hard
In grass and sand,

30 The hurt is not enough:
I long for weight and strength
To feel the earth as rough
To all my length.

The Need of Being Versed in Country Things   (1920)

The house had gone to bring again
To the midnight sky a sunset glow.
Now the chimney was all of the house that stood,
Like a pistil after the petals go.

The barn opposed across the way,
That would have joined the house in flame
Had it been the will of the wind, was left
To bear forsaken the place's name.

No more it opened with all one end
10 For teams that came by the stony road
To drum on the floor with scurrying hoofs
And brush the mow with the summer load.

The birds that came to it through the air
At broken windows flew out and in,
Their murmur more like the sigh we sigh
From too much dwelling on what has been.

Yet for them the lilac renewed its leaf,
And the aged elm, though touched with fire;
And the dry pump flung up an awkward arm;
20 And the fence post carried a strand of wire.

For them there was really nothing sad.
But though they rejoiced in the nest they kept,
One had to be versed in country things
Not to believe the phoebes wept.

Once by the Pacific   (1926)

The shattered water made a misty din.
Great waves looked over others coming in,
And thought of doing something to the shore
That water never did to land before.
The clouds were low and hairy in the skies,
Like locks blown forward in the gleam of eyes.
You could not tell, and yet it looked as if
The shore was lucky in being backed by cliff,
The cliff in being backed by continent;
10 It looked as if a night of dark intent
Was coming, and not only a night, an age.
Someone had better be prepared for rage.
There would be more than ocean-water broken
Before God's last *Put out the Light* was spoken.

Acquainted with the Night   (1928)

I have been one acquainted with the night.
I have walked out in rain—and back in rain.
I have outwalked the furthest city light.

I have looked down the saddest city lane.
I have passed by the watchman on his beat
And dropped my eyes, unwilling to explain.

I have stood still and stopped the sound of feet
When far away an interrupted cry
Came over houses from another street,

10 But not to call me back or say good-by;
And further still at an unearthly height,
One luminary clock against the sky

Proclaimed the time was neither wrong nor right.
I have been one acquainted with the night.

The Silken Tent   (1939)

She is as in a field a silken tent
At midday when a sunny summer breeze
Has dried the dew and all its ropes relent,
So that in guys it gently sways at ease,
And its supporting central cedar pole,
That is its pinnacle to heavenward
And signifies the sureness of the soul,
Seems to owe naught to any single cord,
But strictly held by none, is loosely bound
10   By countless silken ties of love and thought
To everything on earth the compass round,
And only by one's going slightly taut
In the capriciousness of summer air
Is of the slightest bondage made aware.

The Most of It   (1942)

He thought he kept the universe alone;
For all the voice in answer he could wake
Was but the mocking echo of his own
From some tree-hidden cliff across the lake.
Some morning from the boulder-broken beach
He would cry out on life, that what it wants
Is not its own love back in copy speech,
But counter-love, original response.
And nothing ever came of what he cried
10   Unless it was the embodiment that crashed
In the cliff's talus on the other side,
And then in the far distant water splashed.
But after a time allowed for it to swim,
Instead of proving human when it neared
And someone else additional to him,
As a great buck it powerfully appeared,
Pushing the crumpled water up ahead,
And landed pouring like a waterfall,
And stumbled through the rocks with horny tread,
20   And forced the underbrush—and that was all.

Adrienne Rich

Adrienne Rich (1929–   ) grew up in Baltimore and attended Radcliffe College. She published her first book, *A Change of World,* as Yale Younger Poet in her senior year at college, and two years later received a Guggenheim Fellowship. Her second volume, *The Diamond Cutters* (1955), was followed by a gap of some years, during which she had three sons in quick succession. Over the years, her work has changed considerably, diminishing in decorativeness, becoming starker, tighter, tougher, and more emotional. Her prose book, *Of Woman Born* (1977), is a monument of the feminist movement. Most of the poems reproduced here come from *The Fact of a Doorframe,* which selects among her poems from 1950 to 1984. Long a resident of the northeast—Massachusetts, New York, Vermont—Rich now lives in California.

Aunt Jennifer's Tigers   (1951)

Aunt Jennifer's tigers prance across a screen,
Bright topaz denizens of a world of green.
They do not fear the men beneath the tree;
They pace in sleek chivalric certainty.

Aunt Jennifer's fingers fluttering through her wool
Find even the ivory needle hard to pull.
The massive weight of Uncle's wedding band
Sits heavily upon Aunt Jennifer's hand.

When Aunt is dead, her terrified hands will lie
10 Still ringed with ordeals she was mastered by.
The tigers in the panel that she made
Will go on prancing, proud and unafraid.

Women   (1968)
   —for C.R.G.

My three sisters are sitting
on rocks of black obsidian.
For the first time, in this light, I can see who they are.

My first sister is sewing her costume for the procession.
She is going as the Transparent Lady
and all her nerves will be visible.

My second sister is also sewing,
at the seam over her heart which has never healed entirely.
At last, she hopes, this tightness in her chest will ease.

10 My third sister is gazing
   at a dark-red crust spreading westward far out on the sea.
   Her stockings are torn but she is beautiful.

After Twenty Years   (1971)
   —for A.P.C.

Two women sit at a table by a window. Light breaks
unevenly on both of them.
Their talk is a striking of sparks
which passers-by in the street observe
as a glitter in the glass of that window.
Two women in the prime of life.
Their babies are old enough to have babies.
Loneliness has been part of their story for twenty years,
the dark edge of the clever tongue,
10 the obscure underside of the imagination.
It is snow and thunder in the street.
While they speak the lightning flashes purple.
It is strange to be so many women,
eating and drinking at the same table,
those who bathed their children in the same basin
who kept their secrets from each other
walked the floors of their lives in separate rooms
and flow into history now as the woman of their time
living in the prime of life
20 as in a city where nothing is forbidden
and nothing permanent.

From an Old House in America   (1974)

1.

Deliberately, long ago
the carcasses

of old bugs crumbled
into the rut of the window

and we started sleeping here
Fresh June bugs batter this June's

screens, June-lightning batters
the spiderweb

10 I sweep the wood-dust
from the wood-box

the snout of the vacuum cleaner
sucks the past away

2.

Other lives were lived here:
mostly un-articulate

yet someone left her creamy signature
in the trail of rusticated

narcissus straggling up
20 through meadowgrass and vetch

Families breathed close
boxed-in from the cold

hard times, short growing season
the old rainwater cistern

hulks in the cellar

3.

Like turning through the contents of a
    drawer:
these rusted screws, this empty vial

30 useless, this box of watercolor paints
dried to insolubility—

but this—
this pack of cards with no card missing

still playable
and three good fuses

and this toy: a little truck
scarred red, yet all its wheels still turn

The humble tenacity of things
waiting for people, waiting for months,
40   for years

4.

*Often rebuked, yet always back
    returning*
I place my hand on the hand

of the dead, invisible palm-print
on the doorframe

spiked with daylilies, green leaves
catching in the screen door

or I read the backs of old postcards
50 curling from thumbtacks, winter and
    summer

fading through cobweb-tinted panes—
white church in Norway

Dutch hyacinths bleeding azure
red beach on Corsica

set-pieces of the world
stuck to this house of plank

I flash on wife and husband
embattled, in the years

60 that dried, dim ink was wet
those signatures

5.

If they call me man-hater, you
would have known it for a lie

but the *you* I want to speak to
has become your death

If I dream of you these days
I know my dreams are mine and not of
    you

70 yet something hangs between us
older and stranger than ourselves

like a translucent curtain, a sheet of
    water
a dusty window

the irreducible, incomplete connection
between the dead and living

or between man and woman in this
savagely fathered and unmothered
    world

80 **6.**

The other side of a translucent
curtain, a sheet of water

a dusty window, Non-being
utters its flat tones

the speech of an actor learning his lines
phonetically

the final autistic statement
of the self-destroyer

All my energy reaches out tonight
90 to comprehend a miracle beyond

raising the dead: the undead to watch
back on the road of birth

7.

I am an American woman:
I turn that over

like a leaf pressed in a book
I stop and look up from

into the coals of the stove
or the black square of the window

100 Foot-slogging through the Bering Strait
jumping from the *Arbella* to my death

chained to the corpse beside me
I feel my pains begin

I am washed up on this continent
shipped here to be fruitful

my body a hollow ship
bearing sons to the wilderness

sons who ride away
on horseback, daughters

110 whose juices drain like mine
into the *arroyo* of stillbirths, massacres

Hanged as witches, sold as
      breeding-wenches
my sisters leave me

I am not the wheatfield
nor the virgin forest

I never chose this place
yet I am of it now

In my decent collar, in the
120   daguerrotype
I pierce its legend with my look

my hands wring the necks of prairie
      chickens
I am used to blood

When the men hit the hobo track
I stay on with the children

my power is brief and local
but I know my power

I have lived in isolation
130 from other women, so much

in the mining camps, the first cities
the Great Plains winters

Most of the time, in my sex, I was
      alone

8.

Tonight in this northeast kingdom
striated iris stand in a jar with daisies

the porcupine gnaws in the shed
fireflies beat and simmer

140 caterpillars begin again
their long, innocent climb

the length of leaves of burdock
or webbing of a garden chair

plain and ordinary things
speak softly

the light square on old wallpaper
where a poster has fallen down

Robert Indiana's LOVE
leftover of a decade

150 ## 9.

I do not want to simplify
Or: I would simplify

by naming the complexity
It was made over-simple all along

the separation of powers
the allotment of sufferings

her spine cracking in labor
his plow driving across the Indian
      graves

160 her hand unconscious on the cradle,
      her mind
with the wild geese

his mother-hatred driving him
into exile from the earth

the refugee couple with their
      cardboard luggage
standing on the ramshackle
      landing-stage

he with fingers frozen around his Law
170 she with her down quilt sewn through
    iron nights

—the weight of the old world, plucked
drags after them, a random feather-bed

10.

Her children dead of diphtheria, she
set herself on fire with kerosene

(O Lord I was unworthy
Thou didst find me out)

she left the kitchen scrubbed
180 down to the marrow of its boards

"The penalty for barrenness
is emptiness

my punishment is my crime
what I have failed to do, is me . . ."

—Another month without a show
and this the seventh year

O Father let this thing pass out of me
I swear to You

I will live for the others, asking nothing
190 *I will ask nothing, ever, for myself*

11.

Out back of this old house
datura tangles with a gentler weed

its spiked pods smelling
of bad dreams and death

I reach through the dark, groping
past spines of nightmare

to brush the leaves of sensuality
A dream of tenderness

200 wrestles with all I know of history
I cannot now lie down

with a man who fears my power
or reaches for me as for death

or with a lover who imagines
we are not in danger

12.

If it was lust that had defined us—
their lust and fear of our deep places

we have done our time
210 as faceless torsos licked by fire

we are in the open, on our way—
our counterparts

the pinyon jay, the small
gilt-winged insect

the Cessna throbbing level
the raven floating in the gorge

the rose and violet vulva of the earth
filling with darkness

yet deep within a single sparkle
220 of red, a human fire

and near and yet above the western
    planet
calmly biding her time

13.

They were the distractions, lust and fear
but are

themselves a key
Everything that can be used, will be:

the fathers in their ceremonies
230 the genital contests

the cleansing of blood from pubic hair
the placenta buried and guarded

their terror of blinding
by the look of her who bore them

If you do not believe
that fear and hatred

read the lesson again
in the old dialect

14.

240 *But can't you see me as a human being*
he said

What is a human being
she said

I try to understand
he said

what will you undertake
she said

will you punish me for history
he said

250 *what will you undertake*
she said

do you believe in collective guilt
he said

let me look in your eyes
she said

15.

Who is here. The Erinyes.
One to sit in judgment.

One to speak tenderness.
260 One to inscribe the verdict on the
        canyon wall.

If you have not confessed
the damage

if you have not recognized
the Mother of reparations

if you have not come to terms
with the women in the mirror

if you have not come to terms
with the inscription

270 the terms of the ordeal
the discipline   the verdict

if still you are on your way
still She awaits your coming

16.

"Such women are dangerous
to the order of things"

and yes, we will be dangerous
to ourselves

groping through spines of nightmare
280 (*datura* tangling with a simpler herb)

because the line dividing
lucidity from darkness

is yet to be marked out

Isolation, the dream
of the frontier woman

leveling her rifle along
the homestead fence

still snares our pride
—a suicidal leaf

290 laid under the burning-glass
in the sun's eye

Any woman's death diminishes me

from Twenty-One Love Poems   (1976)

II

I wake up in your bed. I know I have been dreaming.
Much earlier, the alarm broke us from each other,
you've been at your desk for hours. I know what I dreamed:
our friend the poet comes into my room

where I've been writing for days,
drafts, carbons, poems are scattered everywhere,
and I want to show her one poem
which is the poem of my life. But I hesitate,
and wake. You've kissed my hair
10 to wake me. *I dreamed you were a poem,*
I say, *a poem I wanted to show someone* . . .
and I laugh and fall dreaming again
of the desire to show you to everyone I love,
to move openly together
in the pull of gravity, which is not simple,
which carries the feathered grass a long way down the upbreathing air.

XII

Sleeping, turning in turn like planets
rotating in their midnight meadow:
a touch is enough to let us know
20 we're not alone in the universe, even in sleep:
the dream-ghosts of two worlds
walking their ghost-towns, almost address each other.
I've wakened to your muttered words
spoken light- or dark-years away
as if my own voice had spoken.
But we have different voices, even in sleep,
and our bodies, so alike, are yet so different
and the past echoing through our bloodstreams
is freighted with different language, different meanings—
30 though in any chronicle of the world we share
it could be written with new meaning
we were two lovers of one gender,
we were two women of one generation.

Living Memory   (1988)

Open the book of tales you knew by heart,
begin driving the old roads again,
repeating the old sentences, which have changed
minutely from the wordings you remembered.
A full moon on the first of May
drags silver film on the Winooski River.
The villages are shut
for the night, the woods are open
and soon you arrive at a crossroads
10 where late, late in time you recognize
part of yourself is buried.   Call it Danville,
village of water-witches.

From here on instinct is uncompromised and clear:
the tales come crowding like the Kalevala
longing to burst from the tongue.   Under the trees

of the backroad you rumor the dark
with houses, sheds, the long barn
moored like a barge on the hillside.
Chapter and verse.   A mailbox.   A dooryard.
20 A drink of springwater from the kitchen tap.
An old bed, old wallpaper.   Falling asleep like a child
in the heart of the story.

Reopen the book.   A light mist soaks the page,
blunt naked buds tip the wild lilac scribbled
at the margin of the road, no one knows when.
Broken stones of drywall mark the onset
of familiar paragraphs slanting up and away
each with its own version, nothing ever
has looked the same from anywhere.
30 We came like others to a country of farmers—
Puritans, Catholics, Scotch Irish, Québecois:
bought a failed Yankee's empty house and barn
from a prospering Yankee,
Jews following Yankee footprints,
prey to many myths but most of all
that Nature makes us free.   That the land can save us.
Pioneer, indigenous; we were neither.

You whose stories these farms secrete,
you whose absence these fields publish,
40 all you whose lifelong travail
took as given this place and weather
who did what you could with the means you had—
it was pick and shovel work
done with a pair of horses, a stone boat
a strong back, and an iron bar: clearing pasture—
Your memories crouched, foreshortened in our text.
Pages torn.   New words crowding the old.

I knew a woman whose clavicle was smashed
inside a white clapboard house with an apple tree
50 and a row of tulips by the door.   I had a friend
with six children and a tumor like a seventh
who drove me to my driver's test and in exchange
wanted to see Goddard College, in Plainfield.   She'd heard
women without diplomas could study there.
I knew a woman who walked
straight across cut stubble in her bare feet away,
women who said, *He's a good man, never*
laid a hand to me as living proof.
A man they said fought death
60 to keep fire for his wife for one more winter, leave
a woodpile to outlast him.
I was left the legacy of a pile of stovewood

split by a man in the mute chains of rage.
The land he loved as landscape
could not unchain him.   There are many,
Gentile and Jew, it has not saved.   Many hearts have burst
over these rocks, in the shacks
on the failure sides of these hills.   Many guns
turned on brains already splitting
70 in silence.   Where are those versions?
Written-across like nineteenth-century letters
or secrets penned in vinegar, invisible
till the page is held over flame.

I was left the legacy of three sons
—as if in an old legend of three brothers
where one changes into a rufous hawk
one into a snowy owl
one into a whistling swan
and each flies to the mother's side
80 as she travels, bringing something she has lost,
and she sees their eyes are the eyes of her children
and speaks their names and they become her sons.
But there is no one legend and one legend only.

This month the land still leafless, out from snow
opens in all directions, the transparent woods
with sugar-house, pond, cellar-hole unscreened.
Winter and summer cover the closed roads
but for a few weeks they lie exposed,
the old nervous-system of the land.   It's the time
90 when history speaks in a row of crazy fence-poles
a blackened chimney, houseless, a spring
soon to be choked in second growth
a stack of rusting buckets, a rotting sledge.
It's the time when your own living
laid open between seasons
ponders clues like the *One Way* sign defaced
to *Bone Way,* the stones
of a graveyard in Vermont, a Jewish cemetery
in Birmingham, Alabama.
100 How you have needed these places,
as a tall gaunt woman used to need to sit
at the knees of bronze-hooded *Grief*
by Clover Adams' grave.
But you will end somewhere else, a sift of ashes
awkwardly flung by hands you have held and loved
or, nothing so individual, bones reduced
with, among, other bones, anonymous,
or wherever the Jewish dead
have to be sought in the wild grass overwhelming
110 the cracked stones.   Hebrew spelled in wilderness.

All we can read is life.   Death is invisible.
A yahrzeit candle belongs
to life.   The sugar skulls
eaten on graves for the Day of the Dead
belong to life.   To the living.   The Kaddish is to the living,
the Day of the Dead, for the living.   Only the living
invent these plumes, tombs, mounds, funeral ships,
living hands turn the mirrors to the walls,
tear the boughs of yew to lay on the casket,
120   rip the clothes of mourning.   Only the living
decide death's color: is it white or black?
The granite bulkhead
incised with names, the quilt of names, were made
by the living, for the living.
                              I have watched
films from a Pathé camera, a picnic
in sepia, I have seen my mother
tossing an acorn into the air;
my grandfather, alone in the heart of his family;
my father, young, dark, theatrical;
130   myself, a six-month child.
Watching the dead we see them living
their moments, they were at play, nobody thought
they would be watched so.
                              When Selma threw
her husband's ashes into the Hudson
and they blew back on her and on us, her friends,
it was life.   Our blood raced in that gritty wind.

Such details get bunched, packed, stored
in these cellar-holes of memory
140   so little is needed
to call on the power, though you can't name its name:
It has its ways of coming back:
a truck going into gear on the crown of the road
the white-throat sparrow's notes
the moon in her fullness standing
right over the concrete steps the way
she stood the night they landed there.
                              From here
nothing has changed, and everything.

150   The scratched and treasured photograph Richard showed me
taken in '29, the year I was born:
it's the same road I saw
strewn with the Perseids one August night,
looking older, steeper than now
and rougher, yet I knew it.   Time's
power, the only just power—would you
give it away?

A Gathering of Poems

A. R. Ammons

Archie Randolph Ammons (1926–   ) worked in business for many years before he became a professor of English. He teaches at Cornell.

Working with Tools   (1971)

I make a simple assertion
like a nice piece of stone
and you
alert to presence and entrance
man your pick and hammer

and by chip and deflection
distract simplicity
and cut my assertion
back to mangles, little heaps:

10 well, baby, that's the way
you get along: it's all right,
I understand such
ways of being afraid:
sometimes you want my come-on

hard, something to
take in and be around:
sometimes you want
a vaguer touch: I understand
and won't give assertion up.

Matthew Arnold

Matthew Arnold (1822–1888) comes after Tennyson and Browning as a poet of the
Victorian age; as a man of letters, he comes after no one. His father was headmaster
of Rugby, and Arnold was educated at Rugby, at Winchester, and at Oxford, where
he won the Newdigate Prize for Poetry. For many years, he inspected schools for
the government. He lectured on poetry at Oxford. He wrote his poems mostly in
early life; as he grew older, he concentrated on the essay.

Dover Beach   (1851)

The sea is calm tonight,
The tide is full, the moon lies fair
Upon the straits;—on the French coast the light
Gleams and is gone; the cliffs of England stand,
Glimmering and vast, out in the tranquil bay.
Come to the window, sweet is the night-air!
Only, from the long line of spray
Where the sea meets the moon-blanched land,
Listen! you hear the grating roar
10 Of pebbles which the waves draw back, and fling,
At their return, up the high strand,
Begin and cease, and then again begin,
With tremulous cadence slow, and bring
The eternal note of sadness in.

Sophocles long ago
Heard it on the Aegean, and it brought
Into his mind the turbid ebb and flow
Of human misery; we
Find also in the sound a thought,
20 Hearing it by this distant northern sea.

The Sea of Faith
Was once, too, at the full, and round earth's shore
Lay like the folds of a bright girdle furled.
But now I only hear
Its melancholy, long, withdrawing roar,
Retreating, to the breath
Of the night-wind, down the vast edges drear
And naked shingles of the world.

Ah, love, let us be true
30 To one another! for the world, which seems
To lie before us like a land of dreams,
So various, so beautiful, so new,
Hath really neither joy, nor love, nor light,
Nor certitude, nor peace, nor help for pain;
And we are here as on a darkling plain
Swept with confused alarms of struggle and flight,
Where ignorant armies clash by night.

(See also "The Dover Bitch," page 612.)

John Ashbery

John Ashbery (1927–   ) attended Harvard, overlapping with Robert Creeley, Robert Bly, Adrienne Rich, and Frank O'Hara. He spent ten years in Paris, writing for an American newspaper there, and later worked for *Art News* in New York. For many years, his poetry attracted a small but enthusiastic group of readers. In 1975, he won the Pulitzer Prize, the National Book Award, and the award of the National Book Critics Circle. His *Selected Poems* appeared in 1985.

Rivers and Mountains   (1962)

On the secret map the assassins
Cloistered, the Moon River was marked
Near the eighteen peaks and the city
Of humiliation and defeat—wan ending
Of the trail among dry, papery leaves
Gray-brown quills like thoughts
In the melodious but vast mass of today's
Writing through fields and swamps
Marked, on the map, with little bunches of weeds.
10 Certainly squirrels lived in the woods
But devastation and dull sleep still
Hung over the land, quelled
The rioters turned out of sleep in the peace of prisons
Singing on marble factory walls
Deaf consolation of minor tunes that pack
The air with heavy invisible rods
Pent in some sand valley from
Which only quiet walking ever instructs.
The bird flew over and
20 Sat—there was nothing else to do.
Do not mistake its silence for pride or strength
Or the waterfall for a harbor
Full of light boats that is there
Performing for thousands of people
In clothes some with places to go
Or games. Sometimes over the pillar
Of square stones its impact
Makes a light print.
So going around cities
30 To get to other places you found
It all on paper but the land
Was made of paper processed
To look like ferns, mud or other
Whose sea unrolled its magic
Distances and then rolled them up
Its secret was only a pocket
After all but some corners are darker
Than these moonless nights spent as on a raft
In the seclusion of a melody heard
40 As though through trees

And you can never ignite their touch
Long but there were homes
Flung far out near the asperities
Of a sharp, rocky pinnacle
And other collective places
Shadows of vineyards whose wine
Tasted of the forest floor
Fisheries and oyster beds
Tides under the pole
50 Seminaries of instruction, public
Places for electric light
And the major tax assessment area
Wrinkled on the plan
Of election to public office
Sixty-two years old bath and breakfast
The formal traffic, shadows
To make it not worth joining
After the ox had pulled away the cart.

Your plan was to separate the enemy into two groups
60 With the razor-edged mountains between.
It worked well on paper
But their camp had grown
To be the mountains and the map
Carefully peeled away and not torn
Was the light, a tender but tough bark
On everything. Fortunately the war was solved
In another way by isolating the two sections
Of the enemy's navy so that the mainland
Warded away the big floating ships.
70 Light bounced off the ends
Of the small gray waves to tell
Them in the observatory
About the great drama that was being won
To turn off the machinery
And quietly move among the rustic landscape
Scooping snow off the mountains rinsing
The coarser ones that love had
Slowly risen in the night to overflow
Wetting pillow and petal
80 Determined to place the letter
On the unassassinated president's desk
So that a stamp could reproduce all this
In detail, down to the last autumn leaf
And the affliction of June ride
Slowly out into the sun-blackened landscape.

Margaret Atwood

For a note on Margaret Atwood, see page 88.

You Are Happy   (1974)

The water turns
a long way down over the raw stone,
ice crusts around it

We walk separately
along the hill to the open
beach, unused
picnic tables, wind
shoving the brown waves, erosion,
    gravel
10 rasping on gravel.

In the ditch a deer
carcass, no head. Bird
running across the glaring
road against the low pink sun.

When you are this
cold you can think about
nothing but the cold, the images

hitting into your eyes
like needles, crystals, you are happy.

W. H. Auden

Wystan Hugh Auden (1907–1973) began to publish at the end of the 1920s and,
in the next decade, became the spokesman of a generation. Marxist and
psychological, he wrote a poetry of ideas; then his ideas changed. Just before
the Second World War he emigrated to America and lived in New York for most
of the remainder of his life, becoming an Anglo-Catholic and altering his old
political concepts.

Musée des Beaux Arts[1]   (1938)

About suffering they were never wrong,
The Old Masters: how well they understood
Its human position; how it takes place
While someone else is eating or opening a window or just walking dully along;
How, when the aged are reverently, passionately waiting
For the miraculous birth, there always must be
Children who did not specially want it to happen, skating
On a pond at the edge of the wood:
They never forgot
10 That even the dreadful martyrdom must run its course
Anyhow in a corner, some untidy spot
Where the dogs go on with their doggy life and the torturer's horse
Scratches its innocent behind on a tree.

[1] Museum of Fine Arts

In Brueghel's *Icarus*,[2] for instance: how everything turns away
Quite leisurely from the disaster; the ploughman may
Have heard the splash, the forsaken cry,
But for him it was not an important failure; the sun shone
As it had to on the white legs disappearing into the green
Water; and the expensive delicate ship that must have seen
20 Something amazing, a boy falling out of the sky,
Had somewhere to get to and sailed calmly on.

In Memory of W. B. Yeats   (1939)
  (d. Jan. 1939)

1

He disappeared in the dead of winter:
The brooks were frozen, the airports almost deserted,
And snow disfigured the public statues;
The mercury sank in the mouth of the dying day.
O all the instruments agree
The day of his death was a dark cold day.

Far from his illness
The wolves ran on through the evergreen forests,
The peasant river was untempted by the fashionable quays;
10 By mourning tongues
The death of the poet was kept from his poems.

But for him it was his last afternoon as himself,
An afternoon of nurses and rumors;
The provinces of his body revolted,
The squares of his mind were empty,
Silence invaded the suburbs,
The current of his feeling failed: he became his admirers.

Now he is scattered among a hundred cities
And wholly given over to unfamiliar affections;
20 To find his happiness in another kind of wood
And be punished under a foreign code of conscience.
The words of a dead man
Are modified in the guts of the living.

But in the importance and noise of tomorrow
When the brokers are roaring like beasts on the floor of the Bourse,
And the poor have the sufferings to which they are fairly accustomed,
And each in the cell of himself is almost convinced of his freedom;
A few thousand will think of this day
As one thinks of a day when one did something slightly unusual.

---

[2] Pieter Brueghel the Elder (1520?–1569) was a major sixteenth-century Flemish painter. His *The Fall of Icarus,* to which Auden alludes here, is in the Musée des Beaux Arts in Brussels.

30 O all the instruments agree
The day of his death was a dark cold day.

2

You were silly like us; your gift survived it all;
The parish of rich women, physical decay,
Yourself; mad Ireland hurt you into poetry.
Now Ireland has her madness and her weather still,
For poetry makes nothing happen: it survives
In the valley of its saying where executives
Would never want to tamper; it flows south
From ranches of isolation and the busy griefs,
40 Raw towns that we believe and die in; it survives,
A way of happening, a mouth.

3

Earth, receive an honored guest;
William Yeats is laid to rest:
Let the Irish vessel lie
Emptied of its poetry.

Time that is intolerant
Of the brave and innocent,
And indifferent in a week
To a beautiful physique,

50 Worships language and forgives
Everyone by whom it lives;
Pardons cowardice, conceit,
Lays its honors at their feet.

Time that with this strange excuse
Pardoned Kipling[1] and his views,
And will pardon Paul Claudel,[2]
Pardons him for writing well.

In the nightmare of the dark
All the dogs of Europe bark,
60 And the living nations wait,
Each sequestered in its hate;

Intellectual disgrace
Stares from every human face,
And the seas of pity lie
Locked and frozen in each eye.

---

[1] Rudyard Kipling (1865–1936), British writer born in Bombay and author of the *Jungle Books, Kim,* novels, short stories, and many poems, wrote much about the British Empire.
[2] Paul Claudel (1868–1955), French dramatist, poet, and diplomat, produced works that were highly mystical and often symbolist.

Follow, poet, follow right
To the bottom of the night,
With your unconstraining voice
Still persuade us to rejoice;

70 With the farming of a verse
Make a vineyard of the curse,
Sing of human unsuccess
In a rapture of distress;

In the deserts of the heart
Let the healing fountain start,
In the prison of his days
Teach the free man how to praise.

The Unknown Citizen (1939)

To JS/07/M/378
This Marble Monument is Erected by the State

He was found by the Bureau of Statistics to be
One against whom there was no official complaint,
And all the reports on his conduct agree
That, in the modern sense of an old-fashioned word, he was a saint,

For in everything he did he served the Greater Community.
Except for the War till the day he retired
He worked in a factory and never got fired,
But satisfied his employers, Fudge Motors Inc.
Yet he wasn't a scab or odd in his views,
10 For his Union reports that he paid his dues,
(Our report on his Union shows it was sound)
And our Social Psychology workers found
That he was popular with his mates and liked a drink.
The Press are convinced that he bought a paper every day
And that his reactions to advertisements were normal in every way.

Policies taken out in his name prove that he was fully insured,
And his Health-card shows he was once in hospital but left it cured.

Both Producers Research and High-Grade Living declare
He was fully sensible to the advantages of the Installment Plan
20 And had everything necessary to the Modern Man,
A gramophone, a radio, a car and a frigidaire.
Our researchers into Public Opinion are content
That he held the proper opinions for the time of year;
When there was peace, he was for peace; when there was war, he went.

He was married and added five children to the population.
Which our Eugenist says was the right number for a parent of his generation.

And our teachers report that he never interfered with their education.

Was he free? Was he happy? The question is absurd:
Had anything been wrong, we should certainly have heard.

Jimmy Santiago Baca

Jimmy Santiago Baca (1952–   ) is author of *Martin and Meditations on the South Valley* (1987), which won the American Book Award of the Before Columbus Foundation, and *Black Mesa Poems* (1990), among other works.

Perfecto Flores   (1989)
for Perfecto

We banter
back and forth
the price
for laying brick.
"You people only pay
the rich, those who
already have money.
I have a whole yard of bricks
collected over thirty years
10 working as a mason.
I offer you a good price,
load them on the truck,
bring sand and gravel,
do the work almost for nothing,
and you won't pay me
half what Hunter charges."
He was right, I relented,
paid him seventy cents a block.
The next day
20 he brought them,
towing cement mixer
behind his old truck.
He rounded the weeping willow
trunk with blocks
left over from apartments
he worked on
six years ago,
then poured cement
and troweled it smooth.
30 After he was done, he asked,
"Can I have that roll of wire back there?"
He lives by scraps, built three houses

for his daughter with construction site
scraps.
In English
his name is Perfect Flower.
Brawny man with bull shoulders,
who forty years ago came from Mexico,
tired of the mines, the somnolent
40 spirit of Mexicans. ". . . I was the first one
to say I wouldn't ride the old bus.
It was falling apart. I refused, and
the rest followed, and soon a new bus
was brought up the mountain."
I gave him our old Falcon
for pouring cement floor
in the guest cottage,
jar of blessed black-purple
Acoma corn kernels
50 for helping me uproot a tree,
gave him seven rabbits
and a box of chickens
for helping me cut adobe arches.
We curse and laugh as we work.
He proudly hefts a wheelbarrow
brimmed with cement. "Ah! Sixty-two, *cabrón!*
And you, naa! You would break your back!"
He ribs me, proud of his strength.
He has nothing that glows his face
60 so much as stories of his working years,
feats of courage in the mines
when he was called upon to defuse dynamite
that didn't explode. Short, stocky
gray-haired man, always in his yard
scattering chicken seed, nailing, sawing,
always in jean overalls.
Chews a ground weed,
carries a stub pencil and grimy wad of paper
for figuring, and
70 always turns to me when I drive
or walk into his yard
with a roguish grin,
his love of telling stories
competing with mine.
He growls with laughter
at the blisters on my hands,
takes his gloves off,
spreads his palms up—
a gallery owner who strips black cloth
80 off his prized Van Gogh painting,
"Look! You could sharpen a file
on these hands," he grins proudly.

Imamu Amiri Baraka

Imamu Amiri Baraka (LeRoi Jones) (1934–   ) is a leading black playwright
and poet. He has also published short stories and polemical prose. He began
publishing as an integrated black writer and edited a magazine in collaboration
with white editors. In later years his politics have moved from black separatism
to Marxism-Leninism.

Careers   (1979)

What is the life
of the old lady
standing
on the stair
print flowered
housedress
gray and orange
hair
bent
10 on a rail
eyes open for
jr.
bobby
jb, somebody
to come, and carry her
wish
slow
cripple woman, still does
white folks work
20 in the mornings she get up
creeps into a cadillac
up into the florient lilac titty valleys
of blind ugliness, you think the woman loves
the younger white woman
the woman she ladles soup for
the radio she turns on when the white lady nods
she carries them in her bowed back hunched face
my grandmother workd the same
but stole things for jesus' sake
30 we wore boss rags in grammar school
straight off the backs of straight up americans
used but groovy and my grandmother when she returned at night
with mason jars and hat boxes full of goods
probably asked for forgiveness on the bus
i think the lady across from me must do the same
though she comes back in a cab, so times, it seems,
have changed.

Wendell Berry

Wendell Berry (1934–   ) was born in Kentucky, lived in New York briefly, and returned to his home state, where he taught at the University of Kentucky. Increasingly, Berry has turned to farming his own land and to writing about "culture and agriculture." He has written novels and books of essays as well as poems. With Gary Snyder, he is a poet whose work and life serve to preserve the planet.

The Wild Geese   (1971)

Horseback on Sunday morning,
harvest over, we taste persimmon
and wild grape, sharp sweet
of summer's end. In time's maze
over the fall fields, we name names
that went west from here, names
that rest on graves. We open
a persimmon seed to find the tree
that stands in promise,
10 pale, in the seed's marrow.

Geese appear high over us,
pass, and the sky closes. Abandon,
as in love or sleep, holds
them to their way, clear,
in the ancient faith: what we need
is here. And we pray, not
for new earth or heaven, but to be
quiet in heart, and in eye
clear. What we need is here.

John Berryman

John Berryman (1914–1972) wrote with great ambition and intensity (fiction and essays as well as poetry) and is best known for *Homage to Mistress Bradstreet* (1954) and *The Dream Songs* (1969).

from The Dream Songs   (1964)

14

Life, friends, is boring. We must not say so.
After all, the sky flashes, the great sea yearns,
we ourselves flash and yearn,
and moreover my mother told me as a boy
(repeatingly) 'Ever to confess you're bored
means you have no

Inner Resources.' I conclude now I have no
inner resources, because I am heavy bored.
Peoples bore me,
10 literature bores me, especially great literature,
Henry bores me, with his plights & gripes
as bad as achilles,

who loves people and valiant art, which bores me.
And the tranquil hills, & gin, look like a drag

and somehow a dog
has taken itself & its tail considerably away
into mountains or sea or sky, leaving
behind: me, wag.

16

Henry's pelt was put on sundry walls
20   where it did much resemble Henry and
them persons was delighted.
Especially his long & glowing tail
by all them was admired, and visitors.
They whistled: This is *it!*

Golden, whilst your frozen daiquiris
whir at midnight, gleams on you his fur
& silky & black.
Mission accomplished, pal.
My molten yellow & moonless bag,
30   drained, hangs at rest.

Collect in the cold depths barracuda. Ay,
In Sealdah Station some possessionless
children survive to die.
The Chinese communes hum. Two daiquiris
withdrew into a corner of the gorgeous room
and one told the other a lie.

312

I have moved to Dublin to have it out with you,
majestic Shade,[1] You whom I read so well
so many years ago,
40   did I read your lesson right? did I see through
your phases to the real? your heaven, your hell
did I enquire properly into?
For years then I forgot you, I put you down,
ingratitude is the necessary curse
of making things new:
I brought my family to see me through,
I brought my homage & my soft remorse,
I brought a book or two

only, including in the end your last
50   strange poems made under the shadow of death
Your high figures float
again across my mind and all your past
fills my walled garden with your honey breath
wherein I move, a mote.

[1] A reference to William Butler Yeats

Elizabeth Bishop

Elizabeth Bishop (1911–1979) was born in Massachusetts, attended Vassar, and lived for many years in Brazil. Critics noticed the influence of Marianne Moore on her first book of poems, *North and South* (1946). She won a Pulitzer Prize in 1956 for *Poems,* and later published *Questions of Travel* (1965) and *Geography III* (1977). *The Complete Poems 1927–1979* appeared in 1983. See also pages 463–464.

The Fish (1939)

I caught a tremendous fish
and held him beside the boat
half out of water, with my hook
fast in a corner of his mouth.
He didn't fight.
He hadn't fought at all.
He hung a grunting weight,
battered and venerable
and homely. Here and there
10 his brown skin hung in strips
like ancient wallpaper,
and its pattern of darker brown
was like wallpaper:
shapes like full-blown roses
stained and lost through age.
He was speckled with barnacles,
fine rosettes of lime,
and infested
with tiny white sea-lice,
20 and underneath two or three
rags of green weed hung down.
While his gills were breathing in
the terrible oxygen
—the frightening gills,
fresh and crisp with blood,
that can cut so badly—
I thought of the coarse white flesh
packed in like feathers,
the big bones and the little bones,
30 the dramatic reds and blacks
of his shiny entrails,
and the pink swim-bladder
like a big peony.
I looked into his eyes
which were far larger than mine
but shallower, and yellowed,
the irises backed and packed
with tarnished tinfoil

seen through the lenses
40 of old scratched isinglass.
They shifted a little, but not
to return my stare.
—It was more like the tipping
of an object toward the light.
I admired his sullen face,
the mechanism of his jaw,
and then I saw
that from his lower lip
—if you could call it a lip—
50 grim, wet, and weaponlike,
hung five old pieces of fish-line,
or four and a wire leader
with the swivel still attached,
with all their five big hooks
grown firmly in his mouth.
A green line, frayed at the end
where he broke it, two heavier lines,
and a fine black thread
still crimped from the strain and snap
60 when it broke and he got away.
Like medals with their ribbons
frayed and wavering,
a five-haired beard of wisdom
trailing from his aching jaw.
I stared and stared
and victory filled up
the little rented boat,
from the pool of bilge
where oil had spread a rainbow
70 around the rusted engine
to the bailer rusted orange,
the sun-cracked thwarts,
the oarlocks on their strings,
the gunnels—until everything
was rainbow, rainbow, rainbow!
And I let the fish go.

William Blake

William Blake (1757–1827) called his first major work *Songs of Innocence and Experience*. This sequence included many pairings of poems, the one viewed under the aspect of innocence and the other under the aspect of experience. Some of Blake's paired poems have the same names; in another pairing, we have the lamb and the tiger. His later work is obscure, difficult—and superbly rewarding. He was an engraver by trade, and executed his own etchings and engravings. Like Campion, Blake was master of two arts. He was a mystic, and told how some of his poems were dictated to him by voices. See also pages 458 and 516.

The Lamb   (1789)

Little Lamb, who made thee?
Dost thou know who made thee;
Gave thee life and bid thee feed
By the stream and o'er the mead;
Gave thee clothing of delight,
Softest clothing, woolly, bright;
Gave thee such a tender voice
Making all the vales rejoice?
Little Lamb, who made thee?
10 Dost thou know who made thee?

Little Lamb, I'll tell thee,
Little Lamb, I'll tell thee:
He is callèd by thy name,
For He calls Himself a Lamb.
He is meek and He is mild:
He became a little child.
I a child and thou a lamb,
We are callèd by His name.
Little Lamb, God bless thee.
20 Little Lamb, God bless thee.

The Tyger   (1794)

Tyger! Tyger! burning bright
In the forests of the night,
What immortal hand or eye
Could frame thy fearful symmetry?

In what distant deeps or skies
Burnt the fire of thine eyes?
On what wings dare he aspire?
What the hand dare seize the fire?

And what shoulder, and what art,
10 Could twist the sinews of thy heart?
And when thy heart began to beat,
What dread hand? and what dread feet?

What the hammer? what the chain?
In what furnace was thy brain?
What the anvil? what dread grasp
Dare its deadly terrors clasp?

When the stars threw down their spears
And watered heaven with their tears,
Did he smile his work to see?
20 Did he who made the Lamb make thee?

Tyger! Tyger! burning bright
In the forests of the night,
What immortal hand or eye
Dare frame thy fearful symmetry?

The Garden of Love   (1794)

I went to the Garden of Love,
And saw what I never had seen:
A Chapel was built in the midst,
Where I used to play on the green.

And the gates of this Chapel were shut,
And "Thou shalt not" writ over the door;
So I turned to the Garden of Love
That so many sweet flowers bore;

10 And I saw it was filled with graves,
And tomb-stones where flowers should
be,

And Priests in black gowns were
walking their rounds,
And binding with briars my joys and
desires.

London   (1794)

I wander thro' each chartered street,
Near where the chartered Thames
does flow,
And mark in every face I meet
Marks of weakness, marks of woe.

In every cry of every Man,
In every Infant's cry of fear,
In every voice, in every ban,
The mind-forged manacles I hear.

10 How the Chimney-sweeper's cry
Every black'ning Church appalls;
And the hapless Soldier's sigh
Runs in blood down Palace walls.

But most thro' midnight streets I hear
How the youthful Harlot's curse
Blasts the new-born Infant's tear,
And blights with plagues the Marriage
hearse.

Robert Bly

Robert Bly (1926–   ) comes from a farm in western Minnesota. After some
time in the Navy, he attended Harvard, from which he graduated in 1950. Editor
of an influential literary magazine—variously called *The Fifties, The Sixties,* and
The Seventies—he has championed modernist poets of other literatures and has
extended great influence on a younger generation of American poets. His own
poems have been collected in *Silence in the Snowy Fields* (1962), *The Light
Around the Body* (1967)—which won a National Book Award—and in many
other collections, including a *Selected Poems* in 1986. See also Bly's translation,
pages 437–439.

Hunting Pheasants in a Cornfield   (1960)

I

What is so strange about a tree alone in an open field?
It is a willow tree. I walk around and around it.
The body is strangely torn, and cannot leave it.
At last I sit down beneath it.

II

It is a willow tree alone in acres of dry corn.
Its leaves are scattered around its trunk, and around me,
Brown now, and speckled with delicate black.
Only the cornstalks now can make a noise.

III

The sun is cold, burning through the frosty distances of space.
10 The weeds are frozen to death long ago.

Why then do I love to watch
The sun moving on the chill skin of the branches?

IV

The mind has shed leaves alone for years.
It stands apart with small creatures near its roots.
I am happy in this ancient place,
A spot easily caught sight of above the corn,
If I were a young animal ready to turn home at dusk.

Louise Bogan

Louise Bogan (1897–1970) was born in Maine and lived most of her life in New
York City. She was an excellent critic. Her letters and journals were extraordinary,
and her poems were few, spare, and perfect. See also page 460.

Cartography   (1941)

As you lay in sleep
I saw the chart
Of artery and vein
Running from your heart,

Plain as the strength
Marked upon the leaf
Along the length,
Mortal and brief,

Of your gaunt hand.
10 I saw it clear:
The wiry brand
Of the life we bear

Mapped like the great
Rivers that rise
Beyond our fate
And distant from our eyes.

Emily Brontë

Emily Brontë (1818–1848) was sister of Charlotte and Anne; all were novelists
and poets in their youth. Emily wrote *Wuthering Heights.*

No Coward Soul Is Mine   (1846)

No coward soul is mine,
No trembler in the world's storm-troubled sphere:
I see Heaven's glories shine,
And faith shines equal, arming me from fear.

O God within my breast,
Almighty, ever-present Deity!
Life, that in me hast rest
As I, undying life, have power in Thee!

Vain are the thousand creeds
10 That move men's hearts; unutterably vain;
Worthless as withered weeds,
Or idlest froth amid the boundless main,

To waken doubt in one
Holding so fast by Thy infinity,
So surely anchored on
The steadfast rock of immortality.
With wide embracing love
Thy spirit animates eternal years,
Pervades and broods above,
20 Changes, sustains, dissolves, creates, and rears.

Though earth and moon were gone,
And suns and universes cease to be,
And Thou wert left alone,
Every existence would exist in Thee.

There is not room for death,
Nor atom that his might could render void:
Since Thou art Being and Breath
And what Thou art may never be destroyed.

Gwendolyn Brooks

Gwendolyn Brooks (1917–   ) is a leading black American poet, born in
Kansas and long resident of Chicago, who began publishing with *A Street in
Bronzeville* in 1945. *Annie Allen,* published in 1949, received a Pulitzer Prize.
Brooks took a new life from the vitality of the black movement of the 1960s.

The Bean Eaters   (1959)

They eat beans mostly, this old yellow pair.
Dinner is a casual affair.
Plain chipware on a plain and creaking wood,
Tin flatware.

Two who are Mostly Good.
Two who have lived their day,
But keep on putting on their clothes
And putting things away.

And remembering . . .
10 Remembering, with twinklings and twinges,
As they lean over the beans in their rented back room that is full of beads and
receipts and dolls and cloths, tobacco crumbs, vases and fringes.

We Real Cool   (1959)

The Pool Players.
Seven at the Golden Shovel.

We real cool. We
Left school. We

Lurk late. We
Strike straight. We

Sing sin. We
Thin gin. We

Jazz June. We
Die soon.

Robert Browning

Robert Browning (1812–1889) was three years younger than Tennyson and
shared with him first rank among Victorian poets. In 1846, he and Elizabeth
Barrett were married. They wrote poems together for fifteen years, until she died
in 1861. He is most celebrated for his dramatic monologues. He is buried in
Westminster Abbey.

My Last Duchess   (1842)

FERRARA

That's my last Duchess painted on the wall,
Looking as if she were alive. I call
That piece a wonder, now: Frà Pandolf's hands
Worked busily a day, and there she stands.
Will't please you sit and look at her? I said
"Frà Pandolf" by design, for never read
Strangers like you that pictured countenance,
The depth and passion of its earnest glance,
But to myself they turned (since none puts by
10 The curtain I have drawn for you, but I)
And seemed as they would ask me, if they durst,
How such a glance came there; so, not the first
Are you to turn and ask thus. Sir, 'twas not
Her husband's presence only, called that spot
Of joy into the Duchess' cheek: perhaps
Frà Pandolf chanced to say, "Her mantle laps
Over my lady's wrist too much," or "Paint
Must never hope to reproduce the faint
Half-flush that dies along her throat." Such stuff
20 Was courtesy, she thought, and cause enough
For calling up that spot of joy. She had
A heart—how shall I say?—too soon made glad,
Too easily impressed; she liked whate'er
She looked on, and her looks went everywhere.
Sir, 'twas all one! My favour at her breast,
The dropping of the daylight in the West,

The bough of cherries some officious fool
Broke in the orchard for her, the white mule
She rode with round the terrace—all and each
30 Would draw from her alike the approving speech,
Or blush, at least. She thanked men,—good! but thanked
Somehow—I know not how—as if she ranked
My gift of a nine-hundred-years-old name
With anybody's gift. Who'd stoop to blame
This sort of trifling? Even had you skill
In speech—(which I have not)—to make your will
Quite clear to such an one, and say, "Just this
"Or that in you disgusts me; here you miss,
"Or there exceed the mark"—and if she let
40 Herself be lessoned so, nor plainly set
Her wits to yours, forsooth, and made excuse,
—E'en then would be some stooping; and I choose
Never to stoop. Oh sir, she smiled, no doubt,
Whene'er I passed her; but who passed without
Much the same smile? This grew; I gave commands;
Then all smiles stopped together. There she stands
As if alive. Will't please you rise? We'll meet
The company below, then. I repeat,
The Count your master's known munificence
50 Is ample warrant that no just pretense
Of mine for dowry will be disallowed;
Though his fair daughter's self, as I avowed
At starting, is my object. Nay, we'll go
Together down, sir. Notice Neptune, though,
Taming a sea-horse, thought a rarity,
Which Claus of Innsbruck cast in bronze for me!

David Budbill

David Budbill (1940–   ) lives in Vermont and has published four books of poems, books for young adults, and plays that have been produced in San Francisco and Princeton, New Jersey. In 1991 he published his *Collected Poems*.

Robert Burns

Robert Burns (1759–1796), after the medieval poets, is the great poet of
Scotland. He is one of the few British poets to arise from the working classes,
having begun life as a farm laborer. Much of his work derives from a folk
tradition and from anonymous Scots songs.

John Anderson My Jo   (1790)

John Anderson my jo,° John,   darling
    When we were first acquent,
Your locks were like the raven,
    Your bonnie brow was brent;°   straight, steep
But now your brow is beld,° John,   bald
    Your locks are like the snaw,
But blessings on your frosty pow,°   head
    John Anderson, my jo.
John Anderson my jo, John,
10   We clamb° the hill thegither,   climbed
And monie a cantie° day, John,   merry
    We've had wi' ane anither:
Now we maun° totter down, John,   must
    And hand in hand we'll go,
And sleep thegither at the foot,
    John Anderson my jo.

George Gordon, Lord Byron

George Gordon, Lord Byron (1788–1824) in his life was the stereotype of the
romantic poet—handsome, promiscuous, daring. His most romantic poems,
valuing emotion above all things, were not his best work, which was satirical and
comic and shared attitudes, though not form or diction, with the poets of the
eighteenth century. In 1823 Byron joined a Greek revolutionary movement striving
to establish freedom for the Greek people; he died of a fever at Missolonghi in
April 1824.

Stanzas   (1820)
(When a man hath no freedom to fight for at home)

When a man hath no freedom to fight for at home,
    Let him combat for that of his neighbors;
Let him think of the glories of Greece and of Rome,
    And get knocked on the head for his labors.

To do good to mankind is the chivalrous plan,
    And is always as nobly requited;
Then battle for freedom wherever you can,
    And, if not shot or hanged, you'll get knighted.

Thomas Campion

Thomas Campion (1567–1620) composed music for his lyrics, one of the few artists to become master of two arts. Although he could rhyme well enough when he wanted to, he despised English rhyming as vulgar, and argued for the establishment of Greek and Roman meters in English verse.

Rose-Cheeked Laura   (1610)

Rose-cheeked Laura, come,
Sing thou smoothly with thy beauty's
Silent music, either other
    Sweetly gracing.

Lovely forms do flow
From concent° divinely framèd;   sounds in harmony
Heaven is music, and thy beauty's
    Birth is heavenly.

These dull notes we sing
10 Discords need for helps to grace them;
Only beauty purely loving
    Knows no discord,

But still moves delight,
Like clear springs renewed by flowing,
Ever perfect, ever in them-
    Selves eternal.

Lewis Carroll

Lewis Carroll was the pen name of Charles Lutwidge Dodgson (1832–1898), a distinguished mathematician, when he wrote *Alice's Adventures in Wonderland* and other works of fantasy and nonsense. On the faculty at Oxford, amateur photographer as well as writer, Carroll made up numerous words when he composed "Jabberwocky"; some of them have taken their place in the language.

Jabberwocky   (1871)

'Twas brillig, and the slithy toves
    Did gyre and gimble in the wabe:
All mimsy were the borogoves,
    And the mome raths outgrabe.

"Beware the Jabberwock, my son!
    The jaws that bite, the claws that catch!
Beware the Jubjub bird, and shun
    The frumious Bandersnatch!"

He took his vorpal sword in hand;
10   Long time the manxome foe he sought—
So rested he by the Tumtum tree,
    And stood awhile in thought.

And, as in uffish thought he stood,
    The Jabberwock, with eyes of flame,
Came whiffling through the tulgey wood,
    And burbled as it came!
One, two! One, two! And through and through
    The vorpal blade went snicker-snack!
He left it dead, and with its head
20   He went galumphing back.

"And hast thou slain the Jabberwock?
    Come to my arms, my beamish boy!
O frabjous day! Callooh, Callay!"
    He chortled in his joy.

'Twas brillig, and the slithy toves
    Did gyre and gimble in the wabe:
All mimsy were the borogoves,
    And the mome raths outgrabe.

John Clare

John Clare (1793–1864) was an agricultural laborer who went insane in 1837 but continued to write poems in the asylum.

I Am   (1848)

I am: yet what I am none cares or knows,
    My friends forsake me like a memory lost;
I am the self-consumer of my woes,
    They rise and vanish in oblivious host,
Like shades in love and death's oblivion lost,
And yet I am, and live with shadows tost

Into the nothingness of scorn and noise,
    Into the living sea of waking dreams,
Where there is neither sense of life nor joys,
10   But the vast shipwreck of my life's esteems;
And e'en the dearest—that I loved the best—
Are strange—nay, rather stranger than the rest.

I long for scenes where man has never trod,
    A place where woman never smiled or wept;

There to abide with my Creator, God,
    And sleep as I in childhood sweetly slept:
Untroubling and untroubled where I lie,
The grass below—above the vaulted sky.

Tom Clark

Tom Clark (1941–   ) was born in Illinois, attended the University of Michigan, and studied at Cambridge University in England. He writes books on baseball: *Champagne and Baloney* about Charles Finley, *No Big Deal* about Mark Fidrych.

Poem   (1969)

Like musical instruments
Abandoned in a field
The parts of your feelings

Are starting to know a quiet
The pure conversion of your
Life into art seems destined

Never to occur
You don't mind
You feel spiritual and alert

10 As the air must feel
Turning into sky aloft and blue
You feel like

You'll never feel like touching
            anything or anyone
Again
And then you do

Lucille Clifton

Lucille Clifton (1936–   ) grew up in New York State and now teaches at the University of California at Santa Cruz. She has published six books of poems, beginning with *Good Times* in 1969. More recently, *Good Woman: Poems and a Memoir 1969–1980,* and *Next* appeared, both in 1987. Clifton has also written works for children. See also page 427.

my dream about the cows   (1987)

and then i see the cattle of my own town,
rustled already,
prodded by pale cowboys with a foreign smell
into dark pens built to hold them forever,
and then i see a few of them
rib thin and weeping low over
sparse fields and milkless lives but
standing somehow standing,
and then i see how all despair is

10 thin and weak and personal and
    then i see it's only
    the dream about the cows.

my dream about the poet   (1987)

a man.
i think it is a man.
sits down with wood.
i think he's holding wood.
he carves.
he is making a world
he says
as his fingers cut citizens
trees and things
10 which he perceives to be a world
    but someone says that is
    only a poem.
    he laughs.
    i think he is laughing.

Hart Crane

Hart Crane (1899–1932) published his first book of poems, *White Buildings*, in 1926. *The Bridge* (1930), a long poem centering on the Brooklyn Bridge, was an attempt to provide a myth of America. Alcoholic and homosexual, prone to binges and fights, Crane lived a short and turbulent life, ended by suicide when he jumped from a ship taking him from Mexico back to New York in 1932.

from The Bridge   (1930)
To Brooklyn Bridge

How many dawns, chill from his rippling rest
The seagull's wings shall dip and pivot him,
Shedding white rings of tumult, building high
Over the chained bay waters Liberty—

Then, with inviolate curve, forsake our eyes
As apparitional as sails that cross
Some page of figures to be filed away;
—Till elevators drop us from our day . . .

I think of cinemas, panoramic sleights
10 With multitudes bent toward some flashing scene
    Never disclosed, but hastened to again,
    Foretold to other eyes on the same screen;

And Thee, across the harbor, silver-paced
As though the sun took step of thee, yet left
Some motion ever unspent in thy stride,—
Implicitly thy freedom staying thee!

Out of some subway scuttle, cell or loft
A bedlamite speeds to thy parapets,
Tilting there momently, shrill shirt ballooning,
20 A jest falls from the speechless caravan.

Down Wall, from girder into street noon leaks,
A rip-tooth of the sky's acetylene;
All afternoon the cloud-flown derricks turn . . .
Thy cables breathe the North Atlantic still.

And obscure as that heaven of the Jews,
Thy guerdon . . . Accolade thou dost bestow
Of anonymity time cannot raise:
Vibrant reprieve and pardon thou dost show.

O harp and altar, of the fury fused,
30 (How could mere toil align thy choiring strings!)
Terrific threshold of the prophet's pledge,
Prayer of pariah, and the lover's cry,—

Again the traffic lights that skim thy swift
Unfractioned idiom, immaculate sigh of stars,
Beading thy path—condense eternity:
And we have seen night lifted in thine arms.

Under thy shadow by the piers I waited;
Only in darkness is thy shadow clear.
The City's fiery parcels all undone,
40 Already snow submerges an iron year . . .

O Sleepless as the river under thee,
Vaulting the sea, the prairies' dreaming sod,
Unto us lowliest sometime sweep, descend
And of the curveship lend a myth to God.

from Voyages   (1926)

II

And yet this great wink of eternity,
Of rimless floods, unfettered leewardings,
Samite sheeted and processioned where
Her undinal vast belly moonward bends,
Laughing the wrapt inflections of our love;

Take this Sea, whose diapason knells
On scrolls of silver snowy sentences,
The sceptred terror of whose sessions rends
As her demeanors motion well or ill,
10 All but the pieties of lovers' hands.

And onward, as bells off San Salvador
Salute the crocus lustres of the stars,
In these poinsettia meadows of her tides,—
Adagios of islands, O my Prodigal,
Complete the dark confessions her veins spell.

Mark how her turning shoulders wind the hours,
And hasten while her penniless rich palms
Pass superscription of bent foam and wave,—
Hasten, while they are true,—sleep, death, desire,
20 Close round one instant in one floating flower.

Bind us in time, O Seasons clear, and awe.
O minstrel galleons of Carib fire,
Bequeath us to no earthly shore until
Is answered in the vortex of our grave
The seal's wide spindrift gaze toward paradise.

Robert Creeley

Robert Creeley (1926–   ) grew up in New England, and attended Harvard,
after which he tried chicken farming in New Hampshire, then lived on the
Spanish island of Majorca. Most recently, he has alternated between Waldoboro,
Maine, and the University of Buffalo, in New York. Creeley taught at Black
Mountain College and edited the *Black Mountain Review,* contributing to the
formation of the Black Mountain school of poetry. His *Collected Poems* appeared
in 1982. See also pages 445–446.

The Rain   (1962)

All night the sound had
come back again,
and again falls
this quiet, persistent rain.

What am I to myself
that must be remembered,
insisted upon
so often? Is it

10 that never the ease,
even the hardness,
of rain falling
will have for me

something other than this,
something not so insistent—
am I to be locked in this
final uneasiness.

Love, if you love me,
lie next to me.
Be for me, like rain,
20 the getting out

of the tiredness, the fatuousness, the semi-
lust of intentional indifference.
Be wet
with a decent happiness.

Countee Cullen

Countee Cullen (1903–1946) was a leader in the Harlem renaissance of the 1920s. He wrote many books of poems, and edited a black magazine called *Opportunity* as well as an influential anthology called *Caroling Dusk* (1927). Anchor Books has published his collected works in paperback.

E. E. Cummings

Edward Estlin Cummings (1894–1962) grew up in Cambridge, Massachusetts, and attended Harvard before becoming a volunteer ambulance driver in the First World War. He wrote a prose book about this experience, *The Enormous Room*, and began to publish books of poems in 1923. His typographical innovations tended to conceal a diction which, much of the time, was traditional and romantic. The bitter humor of his satires proved his best work in poetry. See also pages 448–449 and 512.

Poem, or Beauty Hurts Mr. Vinal   (1926)

take it from me kiddo
believe me
my country, 'tis of

you, land of the Cluett
Shirt Boston Garter and Spearmint
Girl With The Wrigley Eyes(of you
land of the Arrow Ide
and Earl &
Wilson
10 Collars) of you i
sing: land of Abraham Lincoln and Lydia E. Pinkham,
land above all of Just Add Hot Water And Serve—
from every B.V.D.

let freedom ring

amen. i do however protest, anent the un
-spontaneous and otherwise scented merde which
greets one (Everywhere Why) as divine poesy per
that and this radically defunct periodical. i would
suggest that certain ideas gestures
20 rhymes, like Gillette Razor Blades
having been used and reused
to the mystical moment of dullness emphatically are
Not To Be Resharpened. (Case in point

if we are to believe these gently O sweetly
melancholy trillers amid the thrillers

these crepuscular violinists among my and your
skyscrapers—Helen & Cleopatra were Just Too Lovely,
The Snail's On The Thorn enter Morn and God's
In His andsoforth

30 do you get me?)according
to such supposedly indigenous
throstles Art is O World O Life
a formula: example, Turn Your Shirttails Into
Drawers and If It Isn't An Eastman It Isn't A
Kodak therefore my friends let
us now sing each and all fortissimo A-
mer
i
ca, I
40 love,
You. And there're a
hun-dred-mil-lion-oth-ers, like
all of you successfully if
delicately gelded(or spaded)
gentlemen(and ladies)—pretty

littleliverpill-
hearted-Nujolneeding-There's-A-Reason
americans(who tensetendoned and with
upward vacant eyes, painfully
50 perpetually crouched, quivering, upon the
sternly allotted sandpile
—how silently
emit a tiny violetflavored nuisance:Odor?

ono.
comes out like a ribbon lies flat on the brush

J. V. Cunningham

J V Cunningham (1911–1985) was a Professor of English at Brandeis University,
a scholar and critic as well as a poet. His *Collected Poems and Epigrams* came out
in 1971.

James Dickey

James Dickey (1923–   ) was an All-Southern halfback and then a fighter pilot
during the Second World War and the Korean War. He tried teaching and
advertising and, after publishing volumes of poetry, returned to teaching again. His
Buckdancer's Choice won the National Book Award in 1966. His novel *Deliverance*
became a successful motion picture.

The Heaven of Animals   (1961)

Here they are. The soft eyes open.
If they have lived in a wood
It is a wood.
If they have lived on plains
It is grass rolling
Under their feet forever.

Having no souls, they have come,
Anyway, beyond their knowing.
Their instincts wholly bloom
10 And they rise.
The soft eyes open.

To match them, the landscape flowers,
Outdoing, desperately
Outdoing what is required:
The richest wood,
The deepest field.

For some of these,
It could not be the place
It is, without blood.
20 These hunt, as they have done,
But with claws and teeth grown perfect,

More deadly than they can believe.
They stalk more silently,
And crouch on the limbs of trees,
And their descent
Upon the bright backs of their prey

May take years
In a sovereign floating of joy.
And those that are hunted
30 Know this as their life,
Their reward: to walk

Under such trees in full knowledge
Of what is in glory above them,
And to feel no fear,
But acceptance, compliance.
Fulfilling themselves without pain

At the cycle's center,
They tremble, they walk
Under the tree,
40 They fall, they are torn,
They rise, they walk again.

Emily Dickinson   *(1830–1886)*

See pages 530–535.

John Donne

John Donne (1572–1631) was chief of the "Metaphysical Poets." It was his wit, and
that of other metaphysicals, to speak of one thing in terms of another far removed,
as when the parting of husband and wife is compared to the two feet of a geometric
compass. In his youth, he wrote playful and complex erotic poetry; after he became
an Anglican priest in 1615, his poetry became increasingly religious, thus
providing literary observers with a division into two poets, Jack Donne and Dr.
Donne. His devotional prose, including his sermons, ranks among the best English
prose of the seventeenth century. From 1621 until he died, he was Dean of St.
Paul's in London. He preached his final sermon wearing a shroud.

The Canonization   (1633)

For Godsake hold your tongue, and let me love,
    Or chide my palsy, or my gout,

My five grey hairs, or ruined fortune flout;
    With wealth your state, your mind with arts improve,
        Take you a course, get you a place,
        Observe his Honor, or his Grace;
Or the king's real, or his stampèd face[1] Contemplate; what you will, approve,
    So you will let me love.

10 Alas, alas, who's injured by my love?
    What merchant's ships have my sighs drowned?
Who says my tears have overflowed his ground?
    When did my colds a forward spring remove?
        When did the heats which my veins fill
        Add one more to the plaguy bill?[2]
Soldiers find wars, and lawyers find out still
    Litigious men, which quarrels move,
    Though she and I do love.

Call us what you will, we are made such by love;
20   Call her one, me another fly,
We're tapers too, and at our own cost die,
    And we in us find the eagle and the dove.
        The phoenix riddle hath more wit
        By us; we two being one are it.
So to one neutral thing both sexes fit,
    We die and rise the same, and prove
    Mysterious by this love.

We can die by it, if not live by love,
    And if unfit for tombs and hearse
30 Our legend be, it will be fit for verse;
    And if no piece of chronicle we prove,
        We'll build in sonnets pretty rooms;
        As well a well-wrought urn becomes
The greatest ashes, as half-acre tombs,
    And by these hymns all shall approve
    Us canonized for love:

And thus invoke us; You, whom reverend love
    Made one another's hermitage;
You, to whom love was peace, that now is rage;
40   Who did the whole world's soul contract, and drove
        Into the glasses of your eyes—
        So made such mirrors, and such spies,
That they did all to you epitomize,
    Countries, towns, courts: beg from above
    A pattern of your love!

---

[1] On coins   [2] List of those dead of plague

Death, Be Not Proud   (1610)

Death, be not proud, though some have callèd thee
Mighty and dreadful, for thou are not so;
For those whom thou think'st thou dost overthrow
Die not, poor Death; nor yet canst thou kill me.
From rest and sleep, which but thy pictures be,
Much pleasure; then from thee much more must flow;
And soonest our best men with thee do go—
Rest of their bones and souls' delivery!
Thou'rt slave to fate, chance, kings, and desperate men,
10 And dost with poison, war, and sickness dwell;
And poppy or charms can make us sleep as well
And better than thy stroke. Why swell'st thou then?
One short sleep past, we wake eternally,
And Death shall be no more: Death, thou shalt die.

David Dooley

David Dooley (1947–   ) grew up in Tennessee and
took his B.A. at Johns Hopkins University. He works as a
legal assistant in San Antonio, Texas, and has published a
book of poems, *The Volcano Inside* (1988).

Edward Dorn

Edward Dorn (1929–   ) attended Black Mountain College and studied with
Robert Creeley and Charles Olson. One of Olson's didactic pamphlets is a
bibliography addressed to Ed Dorn. Perhaps his best work is the long poem
originally called *Gunslinger,* now shortened to *Slinger.*

On the Debt My Mother Owed to Sears Roebuck   (1964)

Summer was dry, dry the garden
our beating hearts, on that farm, dry

with the rows of corn the grasshoppers
came happily to strip, in hordes, the first
thing I knew about locust was they came
dry under the foot like the breaking of
a mechanical bare heart which collapses
from an unkind an incessant word whispered
in the house of the major farmer
10   and the catalogue company,
from no fault of anyone
my father coming home tired
and grinning down the road, turning in
is the tank full? thinking of the horse
and my lazy arms thinking of the water
so far below the well platform.

On the debt my mother owed to sears roebuck
we brooded, she in the house, a little heavy
from too much corn meal, she
20   a little melancholy from the dust of the fields
in her eye, the only title she ever had to lands—
and man's ways winged their way to her through the mail
saying so much per month
so many months, this is yours, take it
take it, take it, take it
and in the corncrib, like her lives in that house
the mouse nibbled away at the cob's yellow grain
until six o'clock when her sorrows grew less
and my father came home

30   On the debt my mother owed to sears roebuck?
I have nothing to say, it gave me clothes to
wear to school,
and my mother brooded
in the rooms of the house, the kitchen, waiting
for the men she knew, her husband, her son
from work, from school, from the air of locusts
and dust masking the hedges of fields she knew
in her eye as a vague land where she lived,
boundaries, whose tractors chugged pulling harrows
40   pulling discs, pulling great yields from the earth
pulse for the armies in two hemispheres, 1943
and she was part of that *stay at home army* to keep
things going, owing that debt.

Rita Dove

Rita Dove (1952–   ) won the Pulitzer Prize in 1987 for *Thomas and Beulah,* her third book of poems. This lyric comes from her fourth collection, *Grace Notes* (1989). She teaches at the University of Virginia. See also page 432.

Horse and Tree   (1989)

Everybody who's anybody longs to be a tree—
or ride one, hair blown to froth.
That's why horses were invented, and saddles
tooled with singular stars.

This is why we braid their harsh manes
as if they were children, why children
might fear a carousel at first for the way
it insists that life is round. No,

we reply, there is music and then it stops;
10   the beautiful is always rising and falling.
We call and the children sing back *one more time.*
In the tree the luminous sap ascends.

John Dryden

John Dryden (1631–1700) was a prolific writer, a great literary man, Milton's successor, and Pope's predecessor—without being quite so great a poet as either of them. He wrote many of his plays in rhymed couplets. The heroic couplet is Dryden's particular measure: pairs of end-stopped pentameter lines, rhymed directly, usually forming a complete two-line unit of thought or narrative; Dryden codified the form. Chaucer had written in couplets, as had Ben Jonson. Dryden made the form more rigid while retaining great vigor and force. Pope, with unprecedented dexterity and skill, carried it even further, but some feel that Dryden's verse is more vigorous than Pope's. Most of his best work is in long poems—philosophical or satirical, allusive, and difficult to read without study of the age. This short poem shows Dryden's finish and his energy.

To the Memory of Mr. Oldham   (1684)

Farewell, too little and too lately known,
Whom I began to think and call my own;
For sure our souls were near allied, and thine
Cast in the same poetic mold with mine.
One common note on either lyre did strike,
And knaves and fools we both abhorred alike.
To the same goal did both our studies drive:
The last set out the soonest did arrive.
Thus Nisus[1] fell upon the slippery place,
10 Whilst his young friend performed and won the race.
O early ripe! to thy abundant store
What could advancing age have added more?
It might (what nature never gives the young)
Have taught the numbers° of thy native tongue.   poetic meters
But satire needs not those, and wit will shine
Through the harsh cadence of a rugged line.
A noble error, and but seldom made,
When poets are by too much force betrayed.
Thy gen'rous fruits, though gathered ere their prime,
20 Still shewed a quickness; and maturing time
But mellows what we write to the dull sweets of rhyme.
Once more, hail, and farewell! farewell, thou young,
But ah! too short, Marcellus[2] of our tongue!
Thy brows with ivy and with laurels bound;
But fate and gloomy night encompass thee around.

---

[1] In Vergil's *Aeneid* Nisus is beaten in a race by a younger friend.   [2] Marcus Claudius Marcellus, nephew and adopted son of Augustus Caesar, died at twenty and is lamented by Vergil in the sixth book of the *Aeneid*.

Alan Dugan

Alan Dugan (1923–   ) was Yale Younger Poet in 1961, with *Poems,* his first
book, which won both the Pulitzer Prize and the National Book Award. His *New
and Collected Poems (1961–1983)* appeared in 1983. He was born in Brooklyn,
attended Queens College, spent World War II in the Air Force, and lives in
Provincetown, Massachusetts.

On Hurricane Jackson   (1961)

Now his nose's bridge is broken, one
    eye
will not focus and the other is a stray;
trainers whisper in his mouth while
    one ear
listens to itself, clenched like a fish;
generally shadowboxing in a smoky
    room,

his mind hides like the aching boys
10 who lost a contest in the Panhellenic
    games
and had to take the back roads home,
but someone else, his perfect youth,
laureled in newsprint and dollar bills,
triumphs forever on the great white way
to the statistical Sparta of the champs.

Robert Duncan

Robert Duncan (1919–1990) born in Oakland, was a San Francisco poet for most
of his life, associated with the Black Mountain group of poets. Erudite and
prolific, Duncan was a source of energy for other poets, especially in the Bay
Area, in ideas and example.

Poetry, a Natural Thing   (1960)

    Neither our vices nor our virtues
further the poem. "They came up
    and died
just like they do every year
    on the rocks."
    The poem
feeds upon thought, feeling, impulse,
    to breed itself,
a spiritual urgency at the dark ladders leaping.

10 This beauty is an inner persistence
    toward the source
striving against (within) down-rushet of the river,
    a call we heard and answer
in the lateness of the world
    primordial bellowings
from which the youngest world might spring,

salmon not in the well where the
    hazelnut falls
but at the falls battling, inarticulate,
20   blindly making it.

This is one picture apt for the mind.

A second: a moose painted by Stubbs,[1]
where last year's extravagant antlers
    lie on the ground.
The forlorn moosey-faced poem wears
    new antler-buds,
      the same,

"a little heavy, a little contrived,"

his only beauty to be
30   all moose.

Richard Eberhart

Richard Eberhart (1904–   ) attended Dartmouth College in New Hampshire
and went from there to Cambridge University in England, where he first
published. He taught at a preparatory school, served in the Navy (some of his
poems of the Second World War are deservedly famous), and for many years
taught at Dartmouth.

The Groundhog   (1932)

In June, amid the golden fields,
I saw a groundhog lying dead.
Dead lay he; my senses shook,
And mind outshot our naked frailty.
There lowly in the vigorous summer
His form began its senseless change,
And made my senses waver dim
Seeing nature ferocious in him.
Inspecting close his maggots' might
10 And seething cauldron of his being,
Half with loathing, half with a strange
    love,
I poked him with an angry stick.
The fever arose, became a flame
And Vigour circumscribed the skies,

Immense energy in the sun,
And through my frame a sunless
    trembling.
My stick had done nor good nor harm.
20 Then stood I silent in the day
Watching the object, as before;
And kept my reverence for knowledge
Trying for control, to be still,
To quell the passion of the blood;
Until I had bent down on my knees
Praying for joy in the sight of decay.
And so I left; and I returned
In Autumn strict of eye, to see
The sap gone out of the groundhog,
30 But the bony sodden hulk remained.

[1] George Stubbs (1724–1806), an English artist, is best known for his animal paintings.

But the year had lost its meaning,
And in intellectual chains
I lost both love and loathing,
Mured up in the wall of wisdom.
Another summer took the fields again
Massive and burning, full of life,
But when I chanced upon the spot
There was only a little hair left,
And bones bleaching in the sunlight
40 Beautiful as architecture;

I watched them like a geometer,
And cut a walking stick from a birch.
It has been three years, now.
There is no sign of the groundhog.
I stood there in the whirling summer,
My hand capped a withered heart,
And thought of China and of Greece,
Of Alexander in his tent;
Of Montaigne in his tower,
50 Of Saint Theresa in her wild lament.

T. S. Eliot

Thomas Stearns Eliot (1888–1965) was born in St. Louis, Missouri, into a family two generations removed from Boston that had created its own small Boston in St. Louis. Eliot went to prep school in Massachusetts, to Harvard, and then abroad. After some time in Europe on fellowships (he expected to finish a doctorate in philosophy at Harvard), he married an Englishwoman and settled in England, dedicating himself to the life of a poet. For a time, he taught school; for a longer time, he worked in a bank, and finally he became a publisher, overseer of the best poetry list in England, at Faber & Faber. His early work, derived largely from French sources, was notable for its irony and for the desolation of its landscape. This work culminated in the great modernist poem *The Waste Land,* in 1922. Toward the end of the 1920s, Eliot converted to Anglo-Catholicism, and most of the rest of his poetry was dedicated to exploring the implications of conversion. "Journey of the Magi" is one record. *Four Quartets* is the last of his great work in poetry, though he wrote verse plays for the West End and Broadway afterward, with success more commercial than poetical. He was awarded the Nobel Prize in 1948, was widely celebrated as a critic, and was the leading literary figure of the English-speaking world during the first half of the twentieth century.

The Love Song of J. Alfred Prufrock   (1911)

S'io credesse che mia resposta fosse
A persona che mai tornasse al mondo,
Questa fiamma staria senza piu scosse.
Ma perciocche giammai di questo fondo
Non torno vivo alcun, s'i'odo il vero,
Senza tema d'infamia ti rispondo.[1]

Let us go then, you and I,
When the evening is spread out against the sky

---

[1] The Italian epigraph, from Dante's *Inferno,* is the speech of one who is dead and damned, whose punishment is to be wrapped in a constantly burning flame. He believes his hearer also will remain in Hell and thus says: "If I thought my reply were to someone who could ever return to the world, this flame would waver no more [i.e., I would speak no more]. But since, I'm told, nobody ever escapes from this pit, I'll tell you without fear of ill fame."

Like a patient etherized upon a table;
Let us go, through certain half-deserted streets,
The muttering retreats
Of restless nights in one-night cheap hotels
And sawdust restaurants with oyster-shells:
Streets that follow like a tedious argument
Of insidious intent
10 To lead you to an overwhelming question . . .
Oh, do not ask, "What is it?"
Let us go and make our visit.

    In the room the women come and go
Talking of Michelangelo.

    The yellow fog that rubs its back upon the window-panes,
The yellow smoke that rubs its muzzle on the window-panes
Licked its tongue into the corners of the evening,
Lingered upon the pools that stand in drains,
Let fall upon its back the soot that falls from chimneys,
20 Slipped by the terrace, made a sudden leap,
And seeing that it was a soft October night,
Curled once about the house, and fell asleep.

    And indeed there will be time
For the yellow smoke that slides along the street,
Rubbing its back upon the window-panes;
There will be time, there will be time
To prepare a face to meet the faces that you meet;
There will be time to murder and create,
And time for all the works and days of hands
30 That lift and drop a question on your plate;
Time for you and time for me,
And time yet for a hundred indecisions,
And for a hundred visions and revisions,
Before the taking of a toast and tea.

    In the room the women come and go
Talking of Michelangelo.

    And indeed there will be time
To wonder, "Do I dare?" and, "Do I dare?"
Time to turn back and descend the stair,
40 With a bald spot in the middle of my hair—
[They will say: "How his hair is growing thin!"]
My morning coat, my collar mounting firmly to the chin,
My necktie rich and modest, but asserted by a simple pin—
[They will say: "But how his arms and legs are thin!"]
Do I dare
Disturb the universe?
In a minute there is time
For decisions and revisions which a minute will reverse.

For I have known them all already, known them all:—
50 Have known the evenings, mornings, afternoons,
I have measured out my life with coffee spoons;
I know the voices dying with a dying fall
Beneath the music from a farther room.
    So how should I presume?

And I have known the eyes already, known them all—
The eyes that fix you in a formulated phrase,
And when I am formulated, sprawling on a pin,
When I am pinned and wriggling on the wall,
Then how should I begin
60 To spit out all the butt-ends of my days and ways?
    And how should I presume?

And I have known the arms already, known them all—
Arms that are braceleted and white and bare
[But in the lamplight, downed with light brown hair!]
Is it perfume from a dress
That makes me so digress?
Arms that lie along a table, or wrap about a shawl.
    And should I then presume?
    And how should I begin?
                 . . . .

70 Shall I say, I have gone at dusk through narrow streets
And watched the smoke that rises from the pipes
Of lonely men in shirt-sleeves, leaning out of windows? . . .

    I should have been a pair of ragged claws
Scuttling across the floors of silent seas.
                 . . . .

And the afternoon, the evening, sleeps so peacefully!
Smoothed by long fingers,
Asleep . . . tired . . . or it malingers,
Stretched on the floor, here beside you and me.
Should I, after tea and cakes and ices,
80 Have the strength to force the moment to its crisis?
But though I have wept and fasted, wept and prayed,
Though I have seen my head [grown slightly bald] brought in upon a platter,
I am no prophet—and here's no great matter;
I have seen the moment of my greatness flicker,
And I have seen the eternal Footman hold my coat, and snicker,
And in short, I was afraid.

    And would it have been worth it, after all,
After the cups, the marmalade, the tea,
Among the porcelain, among some talk of you and me,
90 Would it have been worth while,
To have bitten off the matter with a smile,
To have squeezed the universe into a ball

To roll it toward some overwhelming question,
To say: "I am Lazarus, come from the dead,
Come back to tell you all, I shall tell you all"—
If one, settling a pillow by her head,
 Should say: "That is not what I meant at all.
 That is not it, at all."

 And would it have been worth it, after all,
100 Would it have been worth while,
After the sunsets and the dooryards and the sprinkled streets,
After the novels, after the teacups, after the skirts that trail along the floor—
And this, and so much more?—
It is impossible to say just what I mean!
But as if a magic lantern threw the nerves in patterns on a screen:
Would it have been worth while
If one, settling a pillow or throwing off a shawl,
And turning toward the window, should say:
 "That is not it at all,
110 That is not what I meant, at all."
    . . . .

No! I am not Prince Hamlet, nor was meant to be;
Am an attendant lord, one that will do
To swell a progress, start a scene or two,
Advise the prince; no doubt, an easy tool,
Deferential, glad to be of use,
Politic, cautious, and meticulous;
Full of high sentence, but a bit obtuse;
At times, indeed, almost ridiculous—
Almost, at times, the Fool.

120 I grow old . . . I grow old . . .
I shall wear the bottoms of my trousers rolled.

 Shall I part my hair behind? Do I dare to eat a peach?
I shall wear white flannel trousers, and walk upon the beach.
I have heard the mermaids singing, each to each.

 I do not think that they will sing to me.

 I have seen them riding seaward on the waves
Combing the white hair of the waves blown back
When the wind blows the water white and black.

 We have lingered in the chambers of the sea
130 By sea-girls wreathed with seaweed red and brown
Till human voices wake us, and we drown.

Journey of the Magi   (1927)

'A cold coming we had of it,
Just the worst time of the year
For a journey, and such a long journey:
The ways deep and the weather sharp,
The very dead of winter.'
And the camels galled, sore-footed, refractory,
Lying down in the melting snow.
There were times we regretted
The summer palaces on slopes, the terraces,
10 And the silken girls bringing sherbet.
Then the camel men cursing and grumbling
And running away, and wanting their liquor and women,
And the night-fires going out, and the lack of shelters,
And the cities hostile and the towns unfriendly
And the villages dirty and charging high prices:
A hard time we had of it.
At the end we preferred to travel all night,
Sleeping in snatches,
With the voices singing in our ears, saying
20 That this was all folly.

Then at dawn we came down to a temperate valley,
Wet, below the snow line, smelling of vegetation;
With a running stream and a water-mill beating the darkness,
And three trees on the low sky,
And an old white horse galloped away in the meadow.
Then we came to a tavern with vine-leaves over the lintel,
Six hands at an open door dicing for pieces of silver,
And feet kicking the empty wine-skins.
But there was no information, and so we continued
30 And arrived at evening, not a moment too soon
Finding the place; it was (you may say) satisfactory.

All this was a long time ago, I remember,
And I would do it again, but set down
This set down
This: were we led all that way for
Birth or Death? There was a Birth, certainly,
We had evidence and no doubt. I had seen birth and death,
But had thought they were different; this Birth was
Hard and bitter agony for us, like Death, our death.
40 We returned to our places, these Kingdoms,
But no longer at ease here, in the old dispensation,
With an alien people clutching their gods.
I should be glad of another death.

Louise Erdrich

Owls* (1989)

The barred owls scream in the black pines,
searching for mates. Each night
the noise wakes me, a death
rattle, everything in sex that wounds.
There is nothing in the sound but raw need
of one feathered body for another.
Yet, even when they find one another,
there is no peace.

In Ojibwa, the owl is Kokoko, and not
10 even the smallest child loves the gentle sound
of the word. Because the hairball
of bones and vole teeth can be hidden
under snow, to kill the man who walks over it.
Because the owl looks behind itself to see you coming,
the vane of the feather does not disturb
air, and the barb is ominously soft.

Have you ever seen, at dusk,
an owl take flight from the throat of a dead tree?
Mist, troubled spirit.
20 You will notice only after
its great silver body has turned to bark.
The flight was soundless.

That is how we make love,
when there are people in the halls around us,
clashing dishes, filling their mouths
with air, with debris, pulling
switches and filters as the whole machinery
of life goes on, eliminating and eliminating
until there are just the two bodies
30 fiercely attached, the feathers
floating down and cleaving to their shapes.

* See the note on Louise Erdrich, page 50 and her story, "The Leap."

Martín Espada

Martín Espada (1957–   ), who was born in Brooklyn, has become a leader among Latino poets in the United States. He lives in Boston and works as a tenant lawyer and supervisor of a legal services program called Su Clinica. Most recently, he has published three collections: *The Immigrant Iceboy's Bolero* (1982), *Trumpets from the Islands of Their Eviction* (1987), and *Rebellion is the Circle of a Lover's Hands* (1990) from which we reprint these poems. See also pages 434–435.

The Savior is Abducted in Puerto Rico   (1990)
Adjuntas, Puerto Rico, 1985

At a place in the mountains,
where the road skids
into tangled trees
and stacks of rock,
a single white cross leans.

The name has dissolved,
obscured in a century of storms
that asphyxiated shacks
with mud, yanking
10   the stone vertebrae
from bridges.

On the cross,
the dark absence of Christ
spreads and hangs,
a crucified shadow
where thieves
tore the brass body down,
leaving amputated feet and hands
still nailed,
20   and the accidental dead
without a guide
on the mountain roads
of the underworld.

Edward Fitzgerald

Edward Fitzgerald (1809–1883) first translated the *Rubáiyát* of Omar Khayyám in 1859 and continued to revise it the rest of his life. His other poems and translations have attracted little attention, but this translation—more adaptation than translation—has endured like no other foreign poem done into English.

from The Rubáiyát of Omar Khayyám   (tr. 1859)

1

Wake! for the Sun, who scattered into flight
The Stars before him from the Field of Night,
    Drives Night along with them from Heav'n, and strikes
The Sultán's Turret with a Shaft of Light.

7

Come, fill the Cup, and in the fire of Spring
Your Winter-garment of Repentance fling:
    The Bird of Time has but a little way
To flutter—and the Bird is on the Wing.

12

A Book of Verses underneath the Bough,
A Jug of Wine, a Loaf of Bread—and Thou
    Beside me singing in the Wilderness—
Oh, Wilderness were Paradise enow!

13

Some for the Glories of This World; and some
Sigh for the Prophet's Paradise to come;
    Ah, take the Cash, and let the Credit go,
Nor heed the rumble of a distant Drum!

19

I sometimes think that never blows so red
The Rose as where some buried Caesar bled;
    That every Hyacinth the Garden wears
Dropt in her Lap from some once lovely Head.

22

For some we loved, the loveliest and the best
That from his Vintage rolling Time hath prest,
    Have drunk their Cup a Round or two before,
And one by one crept silently to rest.

27

Myself when young did eagerly frequent
Doctor and Saint, and heard great argument
    About it and about: but evermore
Came out by the same door where in I went.

71

The Moving Finger writes; and, having writ,
Moves on: nor all your Piety nor Wit
    Shall lure it back to cancel half a Line,
Nor all your Tears wash out a Word of it.

100

Yon rising Moon that looks for us again—
How oft hereafter will she wax and wane;
    How oft hereafter rising look for us
Through this same Garden—and for *one* in vain!

101

And when like her, oh Sákí, you shall pass
Among the Guests Star-scatter'd on the Grass,
    And in your joyous errand reach the spot
Where I made One—turn down an empty Glass!

Robert Francis

Robert Francis (1901–1987) lived most of his life in Massachusetts, mostly in a house called Fort Juniper in the countryside outside Amherst. He wrote an autobiography, some fiction, and some satirical prose. A poet of reticence and quiet, he lived without much attention from critics and prizegivers, writing his finished poems one at a time. See also page 425.

Three Woodchoppers   (1944)

Three woodchoppers walk up the
    road.
Day after day it is the same.
The short man always takes the lead
Limping like one a trifle lame.

And number two leans as he goes
And number three walks very straight.
I do not time them but I know
They're never early, never late.

10 So I have seen them for a week,
Have seen them but have heard no
    sound.
I never saw one turn to speak.
I never saw one look around.

Out of a window to the south
I watch them come against the light.
I cross the room and to the north
I watch till they are out of sight.

Robert Frost   *(1874–1963)*

See pages 536–544.

Allen Ginsberg

Allen Ginsberg (1926–   ) was born in New Jersey and attended Columbia University in New York City, but became known as a San Francisco poet with the publication of *Howl* in 1956. At the forefront of the Beat Generation (he appears in several novels by Jack Kerouac, under different names), Ginsberg has been a leader, spiritual and political as well as poetic. See also pages 431–432.

America   (1956)

America I've given you all and now I'm nothing.
America two dollars and twentyseven cents January 17, 1956.
I can't stand my own mind.
America when will we end the human war?
Go fuck yourself with your atom bomb.
I don't feel good don't bother me.

I won't write my poem till I'm in my right mind.
America when will you be angelic?
When will you take off your clothes?
10 When will you look at yourself through the grave?
When will you be worthy of your million Trotskyites?
America why are your libraries full of tears?
America when will you send your eggs to India?
I'm sick of your insane demands.
When can I go into the supermarket and buy what I need with my good looks?
America after all it is you and I who are perfect not the next world.
Your machinery is too much for me.
You made me want to be a saint.
There must be some other way to settle this argument.
20 Burroughs is in Tangiers I don't think he'll come back it's sinister.
Are you being sinister or is this some form of practical joke?
I'm trying to come to the point.
I refuse to give up my obsession.
America stop pushing I know what I'm doing.
America the plum blossoms are falling.
I haven't read the newspapers for months, everyday somebody goes on trial for
     murder.
America I feel sentimental about the Wobblies.
America I used to be a communist when I was a kid I'm not sorry.
30 I smoke marijuana every chance I get.
I sit in my house for days on end and stare at the roses in the closet.
When I go to Chinatown I get drunk and never get laid.
My mind is made up there's going to be trouble.
You should have seen me reading Marx.
My psychoanalyst thinks I'm perfectly right.
I won't say the Lord's Prayer.
I have mystical visions and cosmic vibrations.
America I still haven't told you what you did to Uncle Max after he came over from
     Russia.

40 I'm addressing you.
Are you going to let your emotional life be run by Time Magazine?
I'm obsessed by Time Magazine.
I read it every week.
Its cover stares at me every time I slink past the corner candystore.
I read it in the basement of the Berkeley Public Library.
It's always telling me about responsibility. Businessmen are serious.
     Movie producers are serious. Everybody's serious but me.
It occurs to me that I am America.
I am talking to myself again.

50 Asia is rising against me.
I haven't got a chinaman's chance.
I'd better consider my national resources.
My national resources consist of two joints of marijuana millions of genitals
     an unpublishable private literature that goes 1400 miles an hour and
     twentyfive-thousand mental institutions.

I say nothing about my prisons nor the millions of underprivileged who live in
    my flowerpots under the light of five hundred suns.
I have abolished the whorehouses of France, Tangiers is the next to go.
My ambition is to be President despite the fact that I'm a Catholic.

60 America how can I write a holy litany in your silly mood?
I will continue like Henry Ford my strophes are as individual as his automobiles
    more so they're all different sexes.
America I will sell you strophes $2500 apiece $500 down on your old strophe
America free Tom Mooney
America save the Spanish Loyalists
America Sacco & Vanzetti must not die
America I am the Scottsboro boys.
America when I was seven momma took me to Communist Cell meetings
    they sold us garbanzos a handful per ticket a ticket costs a nickel and the
70   speeches were free everybody was angelic and sentimental about the
    workers it was all so sincere you have no idea what a good thing the party
    was in 1835 Scott Nearing was a grand old man a real mensch Mother
    Bloor made me cry I once saw Israel Amter plain. Everybody must have
    been a spy.
America you don't really want to go to war.
America it's them bad Russians.
Them Russians them Russians and them Chinamen. And them Russians.
The Russia wants to eat us alive. The Russia's power mad. She wants to take
    our cars from out our garages.
80 Her wants to grab Chicago. Her needs a Red Readers' Digest. Her wants our
    auto plants in Siberia. Him big bureaucracy running our fillingstations.
That no good. Ugh. Him make Indians learn read. Him need big black
    niggers. Hah. Her make us all work sixteen hours a day. Help.
America this is quite serious.
America this is the impression I get from looking in the television set.
America is this correct?
I'd better get right down to the job.
It's true I don't want to join the Army or turn lathes in precision parts factories,
    I'm nearsighted and psychopathic anyway.
90 America I'm putting my queer shoulder to the wheel.

Louise Glück

Louise Glück (1943–   ) lives in Vermont and has published five collections of
her poems; the latest is *Ararat* (1990).

Gratitude (1975)

Do not think I am not grateful for your small
kindness to me.
I like small kindnesses.

In fact I actually prefer them to the more
substantial kindness, that is always eying you,
like a large animal on a rug,
until your whole life reduces
to nothing but waking up morning after morning
cramped, and the bright sun shining on its tusks.

Robert Graves

Robert Graves (1895–1986) fought in the First World War directly upon
graduation from English public school. He was one of the survivors, and later
wrote, in his autobiographical *Good-Bye to All That,* one of the great accounts of
that war. He wrote many novels, including *I, Claudius,* and collections of essays
and humor, but he was first and foremost a poet throughout a long and prolific
career. His mythic system, concerned with the muse of poetry, was described in
The White Goddess, and he remained faithful to his Muse through many poems,
revised many times, in the many volumes of his *Collected Poems.*

In Broken Images   (1947)

He is quick, thinking in clear images;
I am slow, thinking in broken images.
He becomes dull, trusting to his clear images;
I become sharp, mistrusting my broken images.

Trusting his images, he assumes their relevance;
Mistrusting my images, I question their relevance.

Assuming their relevance, he assumes the fact;
Questioning their relevance, I question the fact.

When the fact fails him, he questions his senses;
10 When the fact fails me, I approve my senses.

He continues quick and dull in his clear images;
I continue slow and sharp in my broken images.

He in a new confusion of his understanding;
I in a new understanding of my confusion.

Thom Gunn

Thom Gunn (1929–   ) grew up in England, son of a successful journalist, attended Cambridge, and came to California in 1954. He lives in San Francisco, where he has spent most of the time since leaving England.

On the Move   (1957)
'Man, you gotta Go.'

The blue jay scuffling in the bushes follows
Some hidden purpose, and the gust of birds
That spurts across the field, the wheeling swallows,
Have nested in the trees and undergrowth.
Seeking their instinct, or their poise, or both,
One moves with an uncertain violence
Under the dust thrown by a baffled sense
Or the dull thunder of approximate words.

On motorcycles, up the road, they come:
10 Small, black, as flies hanging in heat, the Boys,
Until the distance throws them forth, their hum
Bulges to thunder held by calf and thigh.
In goggles, donned impersonality,
In gleaming jackets trophied with the dust,
They strap in doubt—by hiding it, robust—
And almost hear a meaning in their noise.

Exact conclusion of their hardiness
Has no shape yet, but from known whereabouts
They ride, direction where the tires press.
20 They scare a flight of birds across the field:
Much that is natural, to the will must yield.
Men manufacture both machine and soul,
And use what they imperfectly control
To dare a future from the taken routes.

It is a part solution, after all.
One is not necessarily discord
On earth; or damned because, half animal,
One lacks direct instinct, because one wakes
Afloat on movement that divides and breaks.
30 One joins the movement in a valueless world,
Choosing it, till, both hurler and the hurled,
One moves as well, always toward, toward.

A minute holds them, who have come to go:
The self-defined, astride the created will
They burst away; the towns they travel through
Are home for neither bird nor holiness,
For birds and saints complete their purposes.
At worst, one is in motion; and at best,
Reaching no absolute, in which to rest,
40 One is always nearer by not keeping still.

H.D. (Hilda Doolittle)

Hilda Doolittle (1886–1961) attended Bryn Mawr College and knew William Carlos Williams and Ezra Pound when all three poets were young. (It was at Pound's suggestion that she began signing her poems with her initials only.) She began as an imagist poet; later in life she wrote long philosophic poems. See also page 430.

Sea Rose   (1916)

Rose, harsh rose,
marred and with stint of petals,
meagre flower, thin,
sparse of leaf,

more precious
than a wet rose,
single on a stem—
you are caught in the drift.

Stunted, with small leaf,
10   you are flung on the sand,
you are lifted
in the crisp sand
that drives in the wind.

Can the spice-rose
drip such acrid fragrance
hardened in a leaf?

John Haines

John Haines (1924–   ) was a homesteader in Alaska for fifteen years and now divides his time between Alaska and the continental United States.

Thomas Hardy

Thomas Hardy (1840–1928) is better known as a novelist than as a poet, but many devoted readers find the poetry even better than the fiction. He began life as an architect and published his first novel when he was thirty-two. For many years Hardy wrote few poems and concentrated on novels, of which the best known are *The Return of the Native, The Mayor of Casterbridge, Tess of the D'Urbervilles,* and *Jude the Obscure. Jude* appeared in 1896, and was denounced as obscene. Perhaps using that denunciation as an excuse, Hardy renounced fiction, and—now freed by the success of his fiction from the necessity to make money—devoted himself to poetry, as he had always wanted to do. He was almost sixty when his first book of poems appeared. Between 1898 and his death at eighty-eight in 1928 he published the fifteen hundred poems that appear in his *Collected Poems.* He is a poet admired by other poets. See also pages 426, 451–452, 492–493, and 510.

The Ruined Maid   (1866)

"O' Melia, my dear, this does everything crown!
Who could have supposed I should meet you in Town?

And whence such fair garments, such prosperi-ty?"—
"O didn't you know I'd been ruined?" said she.

—"You left us in tatters, without shoes or socks,
Tired of digging potatoes, and spudding up docks;°   digging weeds
And now you've gay bracelets and bright feathers three!"—
"Yes: that's how we dress when we're ruined," said she.

—"At home in the barton° you said 'thee' and 'thou,'   farmyard
10 And 'thik oon,' and 'theäs oon,' and 't'other'; but now
Your talking quite fits 'ee for high compa-ny!"—
"Some polish is gained with one's ruin," said she.

—"Your hands were like paws then, your face blue and bleak
But now I'm bewitched by your delicate cheek.
And your little gloves fit as on any la-dy!"—
"We never do work when we're ruined," said she.

—"You used to call home-life a hag-ridden dream,
And you'd sigh, and you'd sock; but at present you seem
To know not of megrims° or melancho-ly!"—   depressions
20 "True. One's pretty lively when ruined," said she.
—"I wish I had feathers, a fine sweeping gown,
And a delicate face, and could strut about Town!"—
"My dear—a raw country girl, such as you be,
Cannot quite expect that. You ain't ruined," said she.

Robert Hayden

Robert Hayden (1913–1980) grew up in Detroit, where he attended Wayne State
University, later studying at the University of Michigan. He taught at Fisk in
Nashville for many years, and then returned to teach at Michigan. In 1976 he
went to Washington as Poetry Consultant at the Library of Congress. His poems
explored areas of the black American experience, and in a time of militancy
Hayden avoided militancy. He became an adherent of the Bahá'i faith when he
was a young man and remained true to it.

Middle Passage   (1970)

I

Jesús, Estrella, Esperanza, Mercy:

Sails flashing to the wind like weapons,
sharks following the moans the fever and the dying;
horror the corposant and compass rose.

Middle Passage:
      voyage through death
          to life upon these shores.

      "10 April 1800—
      Blacks rebellious. Crew uneasy. Our linguist says
10   their moaning is a prayer for death,
      ours and their own. Some try to starve themselves.
      Lost three this morning leaped with crazy laughter
      to the waiting sharks, sang as they went under."

Desire, Adventure, Tartar, Ann:

      Standing to America, bringing home
      black gold, black ivory, black seed.
         Deep in the festering hold thy father lies,
         of his bones New England pews are made,
         those are altar lights that were his eyes.

20 Jesus   Saviour   Pilot   Me
      Over   Life's   Tempestuous   Sea
      We pray that Thou wilt grant, O Lord,
      safe passage to our vessels bringing
      heathen souls unto Thy chastening.

      Jesus Saviour
         "8 bells. I cannot sleep, for I am sick
         with fear, but writing eases fear a little
         since still my eyes can see these words take shape
         upon the page & so I write, as one
30   would turn to exorcism. 4 days scudding,
         but now the sea is calm again. Misfortune
         follows in our wake like sharks (our grinning
         tutelary gods). Which one of us
         has killed an albatross? A plague among
         our blacks—Ophthalmia: blindness—& we
         have jettisoned the blind to no avail.
         It spreads, the terrifying sickness spreads.
         Its claws have scratched sight from the Capt.'s eyes
         & there is blindness in the fo'c'sle
40   & we must sail 3 weeks before we come
         to port."

         What port awaits us, Davy Jones'
         or home? I've heard of slavers drifting, drifting,
         playthings of wind and storm and chance, their crews
         gone blind, the jungle hatred
         crawling up on deck.

Thou   Who   Walked   On   Galilee

"Deponent further sayeth *The Bella J*
left the Guinea Coast
50   with cargo of five hundred blacks and odd
for the barracoons of Florida:

"That there was hardly room 'tween-decks for half
the sweltering cattle stowed spoon-fashion there;
that some went mad of thirst and tore their flesh
and sucked the blood:

"That Crew and Captain lusted with the comeliest
of the savage girls kept naked in the cabins;
that there was one they called The Guinea Rose
and they cast lots and fought to lie with her:

60   "That when the Bo's'n piped all hands, the flames
spreading from starboard already were beyond
control, the negroes howling and their chains
entangled with the flames:
"That the burning blacks could not be reached,
that the Crew abandoned ship,
leaving their shrieking negresses behind,
that the Captain perished drunken with the wenches:

"Further Deponent sayeth not."

Pilot   Oh   Pilot   Me

II

70   Aye, lad, and I have seen those factories,
Gambia, Rio Pongo, Calabar;
have watched the artful mongos baiting traps
of war wherein the victor and the vanquished

Were caught as prizes for our barracoons.
Have seen the nigger kings whose vanity
and greed turned wild black hides of Fellatah,
Mandingo, Ibo, Kru to gold for us.

And there was one—King Anthracite we named him—
fetish face beneath French parasols
80   of brass and orange velvet, impudent mouth
whose cups were carven skulls of enemies:

He'd honor us with drum and feast and conjo
and palm-oil-glistening wenches deft in love,
and for tin crowns that shone with paste,
red calico and German-silver trinkets

Would have the drums talk war and send
his warriors to burn the sleeping villages
and kill the sick and old and lead the young
in coffles to our factories.

90 Twenty years a trader, twenty years,
for there was wealth aplenty to be harvested
from those black fields, and I'd be trading still
but for the fevers melting down my bones.

III

Shuttles in the rocking loom of history,
the dark ships move, the dark ships move,
their bright ironical names
like jests of kindness on a murderer's mouth;
plough through thrashing glister toward
fata morgana's lucent melting shore,
100 weave toward New World littorals that are
mirage and myth and actual shore.
Voyage through death,
                        voyage whose chartings are unlove.

A charnel stench, effluvium of living death
spreads outward from the hold,
where the living and the dead, the horribly dying,
lie interlocked, lie foul with blood and excrement.

> *Deep in the festering hold thy father lies,*
> *the corpse of mercy rots with him,*
110 > *rats eat love's rotten gelid eyes.*

> *But, oh, the living look at you*
> *with human eyes whose suffering accuses you,*
> *whose hatred reaches through the swill of dark*
> *to strike you like a leper's claw.*

> *You cannot stare that hatred down*
> *or chain the fear that stalks the watches*
> *and breathes on you its fetid scorching breath;*
> *cannot kill the deep immortal human wish,*
> *the timeless will.*

120 > "But for the storm that flung up barriers
> of wind and wave, *The Amistad,* señores,
> would have reached the port of Príncipe in two,
> three days at most; but for the storm we should
> have been prepared for what befell.
> Swift as the puma's leap it came. There was
> that interval of moonless calm filled only
> with the water's and the rigging's usual sounds,
> then sudden movement, blows and snarling cries

and they had fallen on us with machete
130   and marlinspike. It was as though the very
air, the night itself were striking us.
Exhausted by the rigors of the storm,
we were no match for them. Our men went down
before the murderous Africans. Our loyal
Celestino ran from below with gun
and lantern and I saw, before the cane-
knife's wounding flash, Cinquez,
that surly brute who calls himself a prince,
directing, urging on the ghastly work.
140   He hacked the poor mulatto down, and then
he turned on me. The decks were slippery
when daylight finally came. It sickens me
to think of what I saw, of how these apes
threw overboard the butchered bodies of
our men, true Christians all, like so much jetsam.
Enough, enough. The rest is quickly told:
Cinquez was forced to spare the two of us
You see to steer the ship to Africa,
and we like phantoms doomed to rove the sea
150   voyaged east by day and west by night,
deceiving them, hoping for rescue,
prisoners on our own vessel, till
at length we drifted to the shores of this
your land, America, where we were freed
from our unspeakable misery. Now we
demand, good sirs, the extradition of
Cinquez and his accomplices to La
Havana. And it distresses us to know
there are so many here who seem inclined
160   to justify the mutiny of these blacks.
We find it paradoxical indeed
that you whose wealth, whose tree of liberty
are rooted in the labor of your slaves
should suffer the august John Quincy Adams
to speak with so much passion of the right
of chattel slaves to kill their lawful masters
and with his Roman rhetoric weave a hero's
garland for Cinquez. I tell you that
we are determined to return to Cuba
170   with our slaves and there see justice done. Cinquez—
or let us say 'the Prince'—Cinquez shall die."

The deep immortal human wish,
the timeless will:

Cinquez its deathless primaveral image,
life that transfigures many lives.

Voyage through death

                    to life upon these shores.

Seamus Heaney

Seamus Heaney (1939–   ) was born in County Derry in Northern Ireland, and
now lives in Dublin with his wife and three children. He has visited the United
States on many occasions and currently teaches one term a year at Harvard University.
Field Work (1979) was his fourth book of poems. In 1980 he published *Preoccupations:
Selected Prose* and reissued his first three books as *Poems 1965–1975*. *Station Island*
appeared in 1984. In 1990 he published a *Selected Poems.*

A Drink of Water   (1976)

She came every morning to draw water
Like an old bat staggering up the field:
The pump's whooping cough, the bucket's clatter
And slow diminuendo as it filled,
Announced her. I recall
Her grey apron, the pocked white enamel
Of the brimming bucket, and the treble
Creak of her voice like the pump's handle.
Nights when a full moon lifted past her gable
10 It fell back through her window and would lie
Into the water set out on the table.
Where I have dipped to drink again, to be
Faithful to the admonishment on her cup,
Remember the Giver fading off the lip.

Song   (1979)

A rowan like a lipsticked girl.
Between the by-road and the main road
Alder trees at a wet and dripping distance
Stand off among the rushes.

There are the mud-flowers of dialect
And the immortelles of perfect pitch
And that moment when the bird sings very close
To the music of what happens.

Iron Spike   (1985)

So like a harrow pin
I hear harness creaks and the click
of stones in a ploughed-up field.
But it was the age of steam

at Eagle Pond, New Hampshire,
when this rusted spike I found there
was aimed and driven in
to fix a cog on the line.

What guarantees things keeping
10 if a railway can be lifted
like a long briar out of ditch growth?
I felt I had come on myself

in the grassy silent path
where I drew the iron like a thorn
or a word I had thought my own
out of a stranger's mouth.

And the sledge-head that sank it
with a last opaque report
deep into the creosoted
20 sleeper, where is that?

And the sweat-cured haft?
Ask the ones on the buggy,
inaudible and upright
and sped along without shadows.

Anthony Hecht

Anthony Hecht (1923–   ) fought in the infantry in the Second World War and
has taught at American universities for most of his life. He is not prolific, finishes
few poems, and finishes them with an extraordinarily high gloss. In 1990 he
published *Collected Earlier Poems* together with a new collection called *The
Transparent Man*.

The Dover Bitch: A Criticism of Life   (1967)
(for Andrews Wanning)

So there stood Matthew Arnold and this girl
With the cliffs of England crumbling away behind them,
And he said to her, "Try to be true to me,
And I'll do the same for you, for things are bad
All over, etc., etc."
Well now, I knew this girl. It's true she had read
Sophocles in a fairly good translation
And caught that bitter allusion to the sea,
But all the time he was talking she had in mind
10 The notion of what his whiskers would feel like
On the back of her neck. She told me later on
That after a while she got to looking out
At the lights across the channel, and really felt sad,
Thinking of all the wine and enormous beds
And blandishments in French and the perfumes.
And then she got really angry. To have been brought
All the way down from London, and then be addressed
As a sort of mournful cosmic last resort
Is really tough on a girl, and she was pretty.
20 Anyway, she watched him pace the room
And finger his watch-chain and seem to sweat a bit,
And then she said one or two unprintable things.
But you mustn't judge her by that. What I mean to say is,
She's really all right. I still see her once in a while
And she always treats me right. We have a drink
And I give her a good time, and perhaps it's a year
Before I see her again, but there she is,
Running to fat, but dependable as they come.
And sometimes I bring her a bottle of *Nuit d'Amour*.

George Herbert

George Herbert (1593–1633) was an English priest and author of great religious poetry. He attended Cambridge University and died as a country parson. See also page 511.

Church Monuments   (1633)

While that my soul repairs to her devotion,
Here I intomb my flesh, that it betimes
May take acquaintance of this heap of dust;
To which the blast of death's incessant motion,
Fed with the exhalation of our crimes,
Drives all at last. Therefore I gladly trust

My body to this school, that it may learn
To spell his elements, and find his birth
Written in dusty heraldry and lines;
10 Which dissolution sure doth best discern,
Comparing dust with dust, and earth with earth.
These laugh at jet and marble, put for signs,

To sever the good fellowship of dust,
And spoil the meeting. What shall point out them
When they shall bow, and kneel, and fall down flat
To kiss those heaps, which now they have in trust?
Dear flesh, while I do pray, learn here thy stem
And true descent, that when thou shalt grow fat,

And wanton in thy cravings, thou mayst know,
20 That flesh is but the glass which holds the dust
That measures all our time; which also shall
Be crumbled into dust. Mark here below
How tame these ashes are, how free from lust—
That thou mayst fit thyself against thy fall.

Robert Herrick

Robert Herrick (1591–1674) is among the most playful of English poets. An admirer of Ben Jonson, he wrote short poems, sacred and profane, in a variety of forms. See also page 431.

Delight in Disorder   (1648)

A sweet disorder in the dress
Kindles in clothes a wantonness:

A lawn° about the shoulders thrown — a thin fabric
Into a fine distraction;
An erring lace, which here and there
Enthralls the crimson stomacher,° — decorative garment, often embroidered
A cuff neglectful, and thereby
Ribands to flow confusedly;
A winning wave, deserving note,
10 In the tempestuous petticoat;
A careless shoe-string, in whose tie
I see a wild civility,—
Do more bewitch me, than when art
Is too precise in every part.

Geoffrey Hill

Geoffrey Hill (1932–   ) grew up in a small town in the English Midlands,
where his father was the policeman. He attended Oxford, and, after earning his
degree, went to Leeds University, where he lectured and taught. After several
years of teaching at Cambridge University, he moved to the United States in 1988
and is now at Boston University. In 1985, he brought out his *Collected Poems*.

Merlin   (1959)

I will consider the outnumbering dead:
For they are the husks of what was rich seed.
Now, should they come together to be fed,
They would outstrip the locusts' covering tide.

Arthur, Elaine, Mordred; they are all gone
Among the raftered galleries of bone.
By the long barrows of Logres they are made one,
And over their city stands the pinnacled corn.

Orpheus and Eurydice   (1959)

Though there are wild dogs
   Infesting the roads
We have recitals, catalogues
   Of protected birds;

And the rare pale sun
   To water our days.
Men turn to savagery now or turn
   To the laws'

Immutable black and red.
10   To be judged for his song,
Traversing the still-moist dead,
   The newly-stung,

Love goes, carrying compassion
   To the rawly-difficult;
His countenance, his hands' motion,
   Serene even to a fault.

Linda Hogan

Linda Hogan (1947–   ) is a Chickasaw Native American who has written many books of poetry, short stories, and essays. She has taught at the University of Minnesota and received fellowships from the National Endowment for the Arts as well as fellowships from Colorado and Minnesota. Some of her books include *The New Native American Novel* (1986) and *Savings* (1988).

The Rainy Season   (1985)

The women are walking to town
beneath black umbrellas
and the roofs are leaking.
Oh, let them be,
let the buckled wood give way this once
and the mildew rot the plaster,
the way it happens with age
when a single thought of loneliness
is enough to bring collapse.

10 See, here they come,
the witches are downstairs
undermining the foundations.
The skeletal clothes hanger
has unwound from its life at last,
hidden in a dark coat
thrown over its shoulders.
Nothing is concealed,
not silver moths
falling out the empty sleeves
20 or the old cat with shining fur
covering his bony spine,
that string of knots
for keeping track of this mouse
and that.

Even the mice have their days of woe.
In the field and in the world
there are unknown sorrows.
Every day collapses

despite the women
30 walking to town with black umbrellas
holding up the sky.

Garrett Hongo

Garrett Hongo (1951–   ) was born in Volcano, Hawaii,
and grew up mostly in California. After graduating from
Pomona College, he attended the University of Michigan,
where he won a Hopwood Award. He has published two
books of his poems, *Yellow Light* (1982) and *The River of
Heaven* (1988). He teaches at the University of Oregon.

The Legend   (1988)

In Chicago, it is snowing softly
and a man has just done his wash for the week.
He steps into the twilight of early evening,
carrying a wrinkled shopping bag
full of neatly folded clothes,
and, for a moment, enjoys
the feel of warm laundry and crinkled paper,
flannellike against his gloveless hands.
There's a Rembrandt glow on his face,
10 a triangle of orange in the hollow of his cheek
as a last flash of sunset
blazes the storefronts and lit windows of the street.

He is Asian, Thai or Vietnamese,
and very skinny, dressed as one of the poor
in rumpled suit pants and a plaid mackinaw,
dingy and too large.
He negotiates the slick of ice
on the sidewalk by his car,
opens the Fairlane's back door,
20 leans to place the laundry in,
and turns, for an instant,
toward the flurry of footsteps
and cries of pedestrians

as a boy—that's all he was—
backs from the corner package store
shooting a pistol, firing it,
once, at the dumbfounded man
who falls forward,
grabbing at his chest.

30 A few sounds escape from his mouth,
a babbling no one understands
as people surround him
bewildered at his speech.
The noises he makes are nothing to them.
The boy has gone, lost
in the light array of foot traffic
dappling the snow with fresh prints.
Tonight, I read about Descartes'
grand courage to doubt everything
40 except his own miraculous existence
and I feel so distinct
from the wounded man lying on the concrete
I am ashamed.

Let the night sky cover him as he dies.
Let the weaver girl cross the bridge of heaven
and take up his cold hands.

IN MEMORY OF JAY KASHIWAMURA

Gerard Manley Hopkins

Gerard Manley Hopkins (1844–1889) attended Oxford. In his early twenties, he converted to Roman Catholicism, becoming a Jesuit in 1868. He corresponded with Robert Bridges and Coventry Patmore and devoted himself considerably to his poetry insofar as such devotion was consistent with his calling. But he did not publish, and he was not known until Robert Bridges collected his poems after Hopkins's death and edited and published them. He has been a major influence on modern poets. See also pages 476–477.

Spring and Fall   (1877)
To a Young Child

Márgarét, are you grîeving
Over Goldengrove unleaving?
Leáves, lîke the things of man, you
With your fresh thoughts care for, can you?
Áh! ás the heart grows older
It will come to such sights colder

By and by, nor spare a sigh
Though worlds of wanwood leafmeal lie;
And yet you wíll weep and know why.
10 Now no matter, child, the name:
Sórrow's spríngs áre the same.
Nor mouth had, no nor mind, expressed
What heart heard of, ghost guessed:
Is ís the blight man was born for,
It is Margaret you mourn for.

The Windhover   (1877)
To Christ Our Lord

I caught this morning morning's minion, king-
    dom of daylight's dauphin, dapple-dawn-drawn Falcon, in his riding
Of the rolling level underneath him steady air, and striding
High there, how he rung upon the rein of a wimpling wing
In his ecstacy! then off, off forth on swing,
    As a skate's heel sweeps smooth on a bow-bend; the hurl and gliding
    Rebuffed the big wind. My heart in hiding
Stirred for a bird,—the achieve of, the mastery of the thing!

Brute beauty and valor and act, oh, air, pride, plume, here
10   Buckle! AND the fire that breaks from thee then, a billion
Times told lovelier, more dangerous, O my chevalier!

    No wonder of it: shéer plód makes plough down sillion
Shine, and blue-bleak embers, ah my dear,
    Fall, gall themselves, and gash gold-vermilion.

A. E. Housman

Alfred Edward Housman (1859–1936) was a classical scholar and professor of
Latin at Cambridge University. He wrote little poetry, notably *A Shropshire Lad* in
1896 and *Last Poems* in 1922, but what he wrote was extraordinarily fine and
finished, if lacking in range and depth.

To an Athlete Dying Young   (1896)

The time you won your town the race
We chaired you through the
    marketplace;
Man and boy stood cheering by,
And home we brought you
    shoulder-high.

To-day, the road all runners come,
Shoulder-high we bring you home,
And set you at your threshold down,
10 Townsman of a stiller town.

Smart lad, to slip betimes away
From fields where glory does not stay
And early though the laurel grows
It withers quicker than the rose.

Eyes the shady night has shut
Cannot see the record cut,
And silence sounds no worse than
    cheers
After earth has stopped the ears:

20 Now you will not swell the rout
Of lads that wore their honors out,

Runners whom renown outran
And the name died before the man.
So set, before its echoes fade,
The fleet foot on the sill of shade,
And hold to the low lintel up
The still-defended challenge-cup.

And round that early-laurelled head
Will flock to gaze the strengthless
30   dead,
And find unwithered on its curls
The garland briefer than a girl's.

Langston Hughes

Langston Hughes (1902–1967), a leader of the Harlem renaissance of black
American literature, often used folk sources in his poetry, especially the forms,
diction, and rhythm of blues. He also wrote fiction, essays, and drama. See also
page 296.

Hope   (1942)

Sometimes when I'm lonely,
Don't know why,
Keep thinkin' I won't be lonely
By and by.

Bad Luck Card   (1927)

Cause you don't love me
Is awful, awful hard.
Gypsy done showed me
My bad luck card.

There ain't no good left
In this world for me.

Gypsy done tole me—
Unlucky as can be.

I don't know what
10 Po' weary me can do.
Gypsy says I'd kill my self
If I was you.

Homecoming   (1959)

I went back in the alley
And I opened up my door.
All her clothes was gone:
She wasn't home no more.

I pulled back the covers,
I made down the bed.
A *whole* lot of room
Was the only thing I had.

Ted Hughes

Ted Hughes (1930–   ) attended Cambridge University, where he met and
married Sylvia Plath. His poems have been continually difficult, obdurate, and
violent, often about animals—real or mythical. He is concerned to discover and
explore instinctual life. In 1984, he became Poet Laureate of England.

Thrushes   (1959)

Terrifying are the attent sleek thrushes on the lawn,
More coiled steel than living—a poised
Dark deadly eye, those delicate legs
Triggered to stirrings beyond sense—with a start, a bounce, a stab
Overtake the instant and drag out some writhing thing.
No indolent procrastinations and no yawning stares,
No sighs or head-scratchings. Nothing but bounce and stab
And a ravening second.

Is it their single-mind-sized skulls, or a trained
10 Body, or genius, or a nestful of brats
Gives their days this bullet and automatic
Purpose? Mozart's brain had it, and the shark's mouth
That hungers down the blood-smell even to a leak of its own
Side and devouring of itself: efficiency which
Strikes too streamlined for any doubt to pluck at it
Or obstruction deflect.

With a man it is otherwise. Heroisms on horseback,
Outstripping his desk-diary at a broad desk,
Carving at a tiny ivory ornament
20 For years: his act worships itself—while for him,
Though he bends to be blent in the prayer, how loud and above what
Furious spaces of fire do the distracting devils
Orgy and hosannah, under what wilderness
Of black silent waters weep.

Richard Hugo

Richard Hugo (1923–1982) was born in Seattle and lived much of his adult life in Montana. The Northwest and the Rocky Mountains form the background of much of his poetry. After his first collection, *A Run of Jacks* (1961), he published eight more books of poems before he died, and his posthumous *Collected Poems* is widely available. *The Triggering Town* (1979) collects essays and lectures on poetry. He also wrote a detective story called *Death and the Good Life* (1981).

Degrees of Gray in Philipsburg   (1973)

You might come here Sunday on a whim.
Say your life broke down. The last good kiss
you had was years ago. You walk these streets
laid out by the insane, past hotels
that didn't last, bars that did, the tortured try
of local drivers to accelerate their lives.
Only churches are kept up. The jail
turned 70 this year. The only prisoner
is always in, not knowing what he's done.

10 The principal supporting business now
is rage. Hatred of the various grays
the mountain sends, hatred of the mill,
The Silver Bill repeal, the best liked girls
who leave each year for Butte. One good
restaurant and bars can't wipe the boredom out.
The 1907 boom, eight going silver mines,
a dance floor built on springs—
all memory resolves itself in gaze,
in panoramic green you know the cattle eat
20 or two stacks high above the town,
two dead kilns, the huge mill in collapse
for fifty years that won't fall finally down.

Isn't this your life? That ancient kiss
still burning out your eyes? Isn't this defeat
so accurate, the church bell simply seems
a pure announcement: ring and no one comes?
Don't empty houses ring? Are magnesium
and scorn sufficient to support a town,
not just Philipsburg, but towns
30 of towering blondes, good jazz and booze
the world will never let you have
until the town you came from dies inside?

Say no to yourself. The old man, twenty
when the jail was built, still laughs
although his lips collapse. Someday soon,
he says, I'll go to sleep and not wake up.

You tell him no. You're talking to yourself.
The car that brought you here still runs.
The money you buy lunch with,
40   no matter where it's mined, is silver
and the girl who serves your food
is slender and her red hair lights the wall.

Randall Jarrell

Randall Jarrell (1914–1965) was born in Tennessee and studied at Vanderbilt. He
taught at Kenyon College as a young man, along with John Crowe Ransom.
Robert Lowell and Peter Taylor were students there, and from this concentration
of talent emerged much American literature. Jarrell served in World War II and
wrote about it. In the last decades of his life, he lived in North Carolina, where he
taught, and he wrote criticism that was possibly better known during his lifetime
than his poetry.

Eighth Air Force[1]   (1947)

If, in an odd angle of the hutment,
A puppy laps the water from a can
Of flowers, and the drunk sergeant shaving
Whistles *O Paradiso!*[2]—shall I say that man
Is not as men have said: a wolf to man?

The other murderers troop in yawning;
Three of them play Pitch, one sleeps, and one
Lies counting missions, lies there sweating
Till even his heart beats: One; One; One.
10   *O murderers!* . . . Still, this is how it's done:

This is war. . . . But since these play, before they die,
Like puppies with their puppy; since, a man,
I did as these have done, but did not die—
I will content the people as I can
And give up these to them: Behold the man![3]

I have suffered, in a dream, because of him,
Many things;[4] for this last saviour, man,
I have lied as I lie now. But what is lying?
Men wash their hands, in blood, as best they can:
20   I find no fault in this just man.

[1] In World War II, the U.S. Eighth Air Force bombed Germany and occupied Europe from
bases in England.   [2] An aria from Meyerbeer's *L'Africaine*   [3] John 19:4–5   [4] Matthew 27:19

Robinson Jeffers

Robinson Jeffers (1887–1962) settled with his family in California when he was sixteen years old. His third book, *Tamar and Other Poems* (1924), brought him to readers' attention. As he grew older, he became progressively more misanthropic, with a passionate and romantic love for the natural world. He found man pathetic and inadequate in comparison to natural grandeurs. He built his own house out of stone in Carmel.

Hurt Hawks   (1928)

I

The broken pillar of the wing jags from the clotted shoulder,
The wing trails like a banner in defeat,
No more to use the sky forever but live with famine
And pain a few days: cat nor coyote
Will shorten the week of waiting for death, there is game without talons.
He stands under the oak-bush and waits
The lame feet of salvation; at night he remembers freedom
And flies in a dream, the dawns ruin it.
He is strong and pain is worse to the strong, incapacity is worse.
10 The curs of the day come and torment him
At distance, no one but death the redeemer will humble that head,
The intrepid readiness, the terrible eyes.
The wild God of the world is sometimes merciful to those
That ask mercy, not often to the arrogant,
You do not know him, you communal people, or you have forgotten him;
Intemperate and savage, the hawk remembers him;
Beautiful and wild, the hawks, and men that are dying, remember him.

II

I'd sooner, except the penalties, kill a man than a hawk; but the great redtail[1]
Had nothing left but unable misery
20 From the bone too shattered for mending, the wing that trailed under his talons
    when he moved.
We had fed him six weeks, I gave him freedom,
He wandered over the foreland hill and returned in the evening, asking for death,
Not like a beggar, still eyed with the old
Implacable arrogance. I gave him the lead gift in the twilight. What fell was relaxed,
Owl-downy, soft feminine feathers; but what
Soared: the fierce rush: the night-herons by the flooded river cried fear at its rising
Before it was quite unsheathed from reality.

[1] Red-tailed hawk

Ben Jonson

Ben Jonson (1572–1637) was actor as well as playwright, and his great plays rank
second only to Shakespeare's. In 1598, he killed another actor in a duel but
avoided execution by pleading benefit of clergy—at least he spoke Latin. Although
his plays remain at the center of his work, he mastered the art of poetry in all
forms, and his works are voluminous and superb in range and in accomplishment.
See also page 429.

To Heaven   (1616)

Good and great God! can I not think of Thee,
   But it must straight my melancholy be?
Is it interpreted in me disease,
   That, laden with my sins, I seek for ease?
O be Thou witness, that the reins dost know
   And hearts of all, if I be sad for show;
And judge me after, if I dare pretend
   To aught but grace, or aim at other end.
As Thou art all, so be Thou all to me,
10   First, midst, and last, converted One and Three!
My faith, my hope, my love; and, in this state,
   My judge, my witness, and my advocate!
Where have I been this while exiled from Thee,
   And whither rapt, now Thou but stoop'st to me?
Dwell, dwell here still! O, being everywhere,
   How can I doubt to find Thee ever here?
I know my state, both full of shame and scorn,
   Conceived in sin, and unto labor born,
Standing with fear, and must with horror fall,
20   And destined unto judgment, after all.
I feel my griefs too, and there scarce is ground
   Upon my flesh t'inflict another wound;
Yet dare I not complain or wish for death
   With holy Paul, lest it be thought the breath
Of discontent; or that these prayers be
   For weariness of life, not love of Thee.

Donald Justice

Donald Justice (1925–   ) grew up in Florida and attended the Writers
Workshop at Iowa, where he taught for some years before returning to his home
state and the University of Florida. His *Selected Poems* appeared in 1979.

Counting the Mad   (1957)

This one was put in a jacket,
This one was sent home,
This one was given bread and meat
But would eat none,
And this one cried No No No No
All day long.

This one looked at the window
As though it were a wall,
This one saw things that were not
10   there,

This one things that were,
And this one cried No No No No
All day long.

This one thought himself a bird,
This one a dog,
And this one thought himself a man,
An ordinary man,
And cried and cried No No No No
All day long.

John Keats   *(1795–1821)*

See pages 525–529.

X. J. Kennedy

X. J. Kennedy (1929–   ) was named Joseph Kennedy, but he felt that there
had been enough Joseph Kennedys in the news. He is the author of poems for
children, successful textbooks, and many collections of poems.

In a Prominent Bar in Secaucus One Day   (1961)
(To the tune of 'The Old Orange Flute' or the tune of 'Sweet Betsy from Pike')

In a prominent bar in Secaucus one day
Rose a lady in skunk with a topheavy sway,
Raised a knobby red finger—all turned from their beer—
While with eyes bright as snowcrust she sang high and clear:

'Now who of you'd think from an eyeload of me
That I once was a lady as proud as could be?
Oh I'd never sit down by a tumbledown drunk
If it wasn't, my dears, for the high cost of junk.

'All the gents used to swear that the white of my calf
10 Beat the down of the swan by a length and a half.
In the kerchief of linen I caught to my nose
Ah, there never fell snot, but a little gold rose.

'I had seven gold teeth and a toothpick of gold,
My Virginia cheroot was a leaf of it rolled
And I'd light it each time with a thousand in cash—
Why the bums used to fight if I flicked them an ash.

'Once the toast of the Biltmore, the belle of the Taft,
I would drink bottle beer at the Drake, never draught,
And dine at the Astor on Salisbury steak
20 With a clean tablecloth for each bite I did take.

'In a car like the Roxy I'd roll to the track,
A steel-guitar trio, a bar in the back,
And the wheels made no noise, they turned over so fast,
Still it took you ten minutes to see me go past.

'When the horses bowed down to me that I might choose,
I bet on them all, for I hated to lose.
Now I'm saddled each night for my butter and eggs
And the broken threads race down the backs of my legs.

'Let you hold in mind, girls, that your beauty must pass
30 Like a lovely white clover that rusts with its grass.
Keep your bottoms off bar stools and marry you young
Or be left—an old barrel with many a bung.

'For when time takes you out for a spin in his car
You'll be hard-pressed to stop him from going too far
And be left by the roadside, for all your good deeds,
Two toadstools for tits and a face full of weeds.'

All the house raised a cheer, but the man at the bar
Made a phonecall and up pulled a red patrol car
And she blew us a kiss as they copped her away
40 From that prominent bar in Secaucus, N.J.

Galway Kinnell

Galway Kinnell (1927–   ) grew up in Rhode Island and attended Princeton University. For many years, he supported himself by teaching correspondence courses. He spent a year teaching in Iran and an occasional term at an American university while he devoted himself to literary work. He has published one novel, and translations of Villon and the contemporary French poet Yves Bonnefoy. The *Book of Nightmares,* probably his best-known book of poems, appeared in 1971. His *Selected Poems* appeared in 1982 and won the Pulitzer Prize. In 1985, he published *The Past,* and in 1990 *When One Has Lived a Long Time Alone.*

The Bear   (1967)

1

In late winter
I sometimes glimpse bits of steam
coming up from
some fault in the old snow
and bend close and see it is lung-colored
and put down my nose
and know
the chilly, enduring odor of bear.

2

I take a wolf's rib and whittle
10 it sharp at both ends
and coil it up
and freeze it in blubber and place it out
on the fairway of the bears.

And when it has vanished
I move out on the bear tracks,
roaming in circles
until I come to the first, tentative, dark
splash on the earth.

And I set out
20 running, following the splashes
of blood wandering over the world.
At the cut, gashed resting places
I stop and rest,
at the crawl-marks
where he lay out on his belly
to overpass some stretch of bauchy ice
I lie out
dragging myself forward with bear-knives in my fists.

3

On the third day I begin to starve,
30   at nightfall I bend down as I knew I would
at a turd sopped in blood,
and hesitate, and pick it up,
and thrust it in my mouth, and gnash it down,
and rise
and go on running.

4

On the seventh day,
living by now on bear blood alone,
I can see his upturned carcass far out ahead, a scraggled,
steamy hulk,
40   the heavy fur riffling in the wind.

I come up to him
and stare at the narrow-spaced, petty eyes,
the dismayed
face laid back on the shoulder, the nostrils
flared, catching
perhaps the first taint of me as he
died.

I hack
a ravine in his thigh, and eat and drink,
50   and tear him down his whole length
and open him and climb in
and close him up after me, against the wind
and sleep.

5

And dream
of lumbering flatfooted
over the tundra,
stabbed twice from within,
splattering a trail behind me,
splattering it out no matter which way I lurch,
60   no matter which parabola of bear-transcendence,
which dance of solitude I attempt,
which gravity-clutched leap,
which trudge, which groan.

6

Until one day I totter and fall—
fall on this
stomach that has tried so hard to keep up,
to digest the blood as it leaked in,
to break up

and digest the bone itself: and now the breeze
70 blows over me, blows off
the hideous belches of ill-digested bear blood
and rotted stomach
and the ordinary, wretched odor of bear,

blows across
my sore, lolled tongue a song
or screech, until I think I must rise up
and dance. And I lie still.

7

I awaken I think. Marshlights
reappear, geese
80 come trailing again up the flyway.
In her ravine under old snow the dam-bear
lies, licking
lumps of smeared fur
and drizzly eyes into shapes

with her tongue. And one
hairy-soled trudge stuck out before me,
the next groaned out,
the next,
the next,
90 the rest of my days I spend
wandering: wondering
what, anyway,
was that sticky infusion, that rank flavor of blood, that poetry, by which I lived?

Etheridge Knight

Etheridge Knight (1933–1991) fought in the Korean War and later became
addicted to heroin. He supported his habit by stealing, which landed him in the
Indiana State Prison. He began to write poems in prison, where Gwendolyn
Brooks visited and encouraged him. His first volume was called *Poems from
Prison.* After his release, he taught poetry at various colleges and conducted
workshops all over the United States.

Hard Rock Returns to Prison from the Hospital for the Criminal Insane   (1968)

Hard Rock was "known not to take no shit
From nobody," and he had the scars to prove it:
Split purple lips, lumped ears, welts above
His yellow eyes, and one long scar that cut

Across his temple and plowed through a thick
Canopy of kinky hair.

The WORD was that Hard Rock wasn't a mean nigger
Anymore, that the doctors had bored a hole in his head,
Cut out part of his brain, and shot electricity
10   Through the rest. When they brought Hard Rock back,
Handcuffed and chained, he was turned loose,
Like a freshly gelded stallion, to try his new status.
And we all waited and watched, like indians at a corral,
To see if the WORD was true.

As we waited we wrapped ourselves in the cloak
Of his exploits: "Man, the last time, it took eight
Screws to put him in the Hole." "Yeah, remember when he
Smacked the captain with his dinner tray?" "He set
The record for time in the Hole—67 straight days!"
20   "Ol Hard Rock! man, that's one crazy nigger."
And then the jewel of a myth that Hard Rock had once bit
A screw on the thumb and poisoned him with syphilitic spit.

The testing came, to see if Hard Rock was really tame.
A hillbilly called him a black son of a bitch
And didn't lose his teeth, a screw who knew Hard Rock
From before shook him down and barked in his face.
And Hard Rock did *nothing*. Just grinned and looked silly,
His eyes empty like knot holes in a fence.

And even after we discovered that it took Hard Rock
30   Exactly 3 minutes to tell you his first name,
We told ourselves that he had just wised up,
Was being cool; but we could not fool ourselves for long,
And we turned away, our eyes on the ground. Crushed.
He had been our Destroyer, the doer of things
We dreamed of doing but could not bring ourselves to do,
The fears of years, like a biting whip,
Had cut grooves too deeply across our backs.

Yusef Komunyakaa

Yusef Komunyakaa (1947–   ) has written three books of poems—*Copasetic*
(1984), *I Apologize for the Eyes in My Head* (1986), and *Dien Cai Dau* (1989).
At Indiana University he teaches both Afro-American studies and creative
writing. He served in 1969 and 1970 with the Army in Vietnam.

Walter Savage Landor

Walter Savage Landor (1775–1864) wrote short poems over a long life. He was famous for his violent temper; according to one often-repeated anecdote, he took out his anger on a servant by throwing her through a window onto a garden. He was best at the epigram and short, pointed verse.

I Strove with None   (1849)

I strove with none, for none was worth my strife.
    Nature I loved and, next to Nature, Art:
I warmed both hands before the fire of life;
    It sinks, and I am ready to depart.

Philip Larkin

Philip Larkin (1922–1985) attended Oxford, wrote two early novels, and chose the life of a professional librarian. He wrote little, but his work was finished and fine. In the eyes of most observers, he was the best English poet of his time. He was librarian of the University at Hull. His volumes are *The Less Deceived* (1955), *The Whitsun Weddings* (1964), and *High Windows* (1974). His *Collected Poems* was issued in the United States in 1989.

Mr. Bleaney   (1964)

'This was Mr. Bleaney's room. He stayed
The whole time he was at the Bodies, till
They moved him.' Flowered curtains, thin and frayed,
Fall to within five inches of the sill,
Whose window shows a strip of building land,
Tussocky, littered. 'Mr. Bleaney took
My bit of garden properly in hand.'
Bed, upright chair, sixty-watt bulb, no hook

Behind the door, no room for books or bags—
10 'I'll take it.' So it happens that I lie
Where Mr. Bleaney lay, and stub my fags
On the same saucer-souvenir, and try

Stuffing my ears with cotton-wool, to drown
The jabbering set he egged her on to buy.
I know his habits—what time he came down,
His preference for sauce to gravy, why

He kept on plugging at the four aways[1]—
Likewise their yearly frame: the Frinton folk
Who put him up for summer holidays,
20 And Christmas at his sister's house in Stoke.

But if he stood and watched the frigid wind
Tousling the clouds, lay on the fusty bed
Telling himself that this was home, and grinned,
And shivered, without shaking off the dread

That how we live measures our own nature,
And at his age having no more to show
Than one hired box should make him pretty sure
He warranted no better, I don't know.

Aubade   (1978)

I work all day, and get half drunk at night.
Waking at four to soundless dark, I stare.
In time the curtain-edges will grow light.
Till then I see what's really always there:
Unresting death, a whole day nearer now,
Making all thought impossible but how
And where and when I shall myself die.
Arid interrogation: yet the dread
Of dying, and being dead,
10 Flashes afresh to hold and horrify.

The mind blanks at the glare. Not in remorse
—The good not done, the love not given, time
Torn off unused—nor wretchedly because
An only life can take so long to climb
Clear of its wrong beginnings, and may never;
But at the total emptiness for ever,
The sure extinction that we travel to
And shall be lost in always. Not to be here,
Not to be anywhere,
20 And soon; nothing more terrible, nothing more true.

This is a special way of being afraid
No trick dispels. Religion used to try,
That vast moth-eaten musical brocade
Created to pretend we never die,
And specious stuff that says *No rational being
Can fear a thing it will not feel*, not seeing
That this is what we fear—no sight, no sound,
No touch or taste or smell, nothing to think with,
Nothing to love or link with,
30 The anaesthetic from which none come round.

[1] A form of betting on English professional soccer games

And so it stays just on the edge of vision,
A small unfocused blur, a standing chill
That slows each impulse down to indecision.
Most things may never happen: this one will,
And realisation of it rages out
In furnace-fear when we are caught without
People or drink. Courage is no good:
It means not scaring others. Being brave
Lets no one off the grave.
40 Death is no different whined at than withstood.

Slowly light strengthens, and the room takes shape.
It stands plain as a wardrobe, what we know,
Have always known, know that we can't escape,
Yet can't accept. One side will have to go.
Meanwhile telephones crouch, getting ready to ring
In locked-up offices, and all the uncaring
Intricate rented world begins to rouse.
The sky is white as clay, with no sun.
Work has to be done.
50 Postmen like doctors go from house to house.

D. H. Lawrence

David Herbert Lawrence (1885–1930) was the son of a coalminer, born in a
working-class district of England. He wrote from an early age, and with the aid of
scholarships wrested himself away from his background to become a writer. Best
known as a novelist, especially for *The Rainbow, Women in Love,* and *Lady
Chatterley's Lover,* he was a great essayist, literary critic, writer of travel books,
letter-writer—and to some critics best of all as a poet. He died of tuberculosis,
having accomplished an enormous volume of work, before he turned forty-five.
See page 302, for a short story by D. H. Lawrence.

The Song of a Man Who Has Come Through   (1914)

Not I, not I, but the wind that blows through me!
A fine wind is blowing the new direction of Time.
If only I let it bear me, carry me, if only it carry me!
If only I am sensitive, subtle, oh, delicate, a winged gift!
If only, most lovely of all, I yield myself and am borrowed
By the fine, fine wind that takes its course through the chaos of the world
Like a fine, an exquisite chisel, a wedge-blade inserted;
If only I am keen and hard like the sheer tip of a wedge
Driven by invisible blows,
10 The rock will split, we shall come at the wonder, we shall find the Hesperides.[1]

---

[1] In Greek mythology, sisters who protected a garden in which grew a tree bearing golden
apples

Oh, for the wonder that bubbles into my soul,
I would be a good fountain, a good well-head,
Would blur no whisper, spoil no expression.

What is the knocking?
What is the knocking at the door in the night?
It is somebody wants to do us harm.

No, no, it is the three strange angels.
Admit them, admit them.

Bavarian Gentians   (1929)

Not every man has gentians in his house
In soft September, at slow, sad Michaelmas.

Bavarian gentians, tall and dark, but dark
darkening the daytime torch-like with the smoking blueness of Pluto's gloom,
ribbed hellish flowers erect, with their blaze of darkness spread blue,
blown flat into points, by the heavy white draught of the day.

Torch-flowers of the blue-smoking darkness, Pluto's dark-blue blaze
black lamps from the halls of Dis,[1] smoking dark blue
giving off darkness, blue darkness, upon Demeter's yellow-pale day
10   whom have you come for, here in the white-cast day?
Reach me a gentian, give me a torch!
let me guide myself with the blue, forked torch of a flower
down the darker and darker stairs, where blue is darkened on blueness
down the way Persephone goes, just now, in first-frosted September
to the sightless realm where darkness is married to dark
and Persephone herself is but a voice, as a bride,
a gloom invisible enfolded in the deeper dark
of the arms of Pluto as he ravishes her once again
and pierces her once more with his passion of the utter dark
20   among the splendour of black-blue torches, shedding fathomless darkness on the
      nuptials.

Give me a flower on a tall stem, and three dark flames,
for I will go to the wedding, and be wedding-guest
at the marriage of the living dark.

---

[1] Dis, Dispater, the Roman name for a deity who was the same as the Greek Pluto, god of the underworld

Li-Young Lee

Li-Young Lee (1957–   ) was born of Chinese parents in Indonesia, where his father was a political prisoner. Escaping from Indonesia in 1959, the family wandered among Hong Kong, Macau, and Japan and finally arrived in the United States in 1964. With his wife and children, Li-Young Lee lives in Chicago, where he works as a commercial artist. He has published two collections of his poetry: *Rose* (1986) and *The City in Which I Love You* (1990). See also pages 477–478.

From Blossoms   (1986)

From blossoms comes
this brown paper bag of peaches
we bought from the boy
at the bend in the road where we turned toward
signs painted *Peaches.*

From laden boughs, from hands,
from sweet fellowship in the bins,
comes nectar at the roadside, succulent
peaches we devour, dusty skin and all,
10 comes the familiar dust of summer, dust we eat.
O, to take what we love inside,
to carry within us an orchard, to eat
not only the skin, but the shade,
not only the sugar, but the days, to hold
the fruit in our hands, adore it, then bite into
the round jubilance of peach.

There are days we live
as if death were nowhere
in the background; from joy
20 to joy to joy, from wing to wing,
from blossom to blossom to
impossible blossom, to sweet impossible blossom.

Denise Levertov

Denise Levertov (1923–   ), who was born in England, came to the United States when she married an American soldier. Her early poems were collected in England. After her move to the United States, she became affiliated with the Black Mountain group of poets and her style changed considerably. She was a leader in the antiwar movement during the Vietnam years. See also pages 433–434.

October   (1961)

Certain branches cut
certain leaves fallen
the grapes
        cooked and put up
for winter

mountains without one
shrug of cloud

no feint of blurred
wind-willow leaf-light

10 their chins up
in blue of the eastern sky
their red cloaks
wrapped tight to the bone

Philip Levine

Philip Levine (1928–   ) grew up in Detroit and attended the Writers Workshop at Iowa. His work was formal at the beginning, restrained and delicate, and has acquired strength and vitality as he has grown older. His volumes include a *Selected Poems* (1984).

Salami   (1972)

Stomach of goat, crushed
sheep balls, soft full
pearls of pig eyes,
snout gristle, fresh earth,
worn iron of trotter, slate
of Zaragoza, dried cat heart,
cock claws. She grinds
them with one hand and
with the other fists
10 mountain thyme, basil,
paprika, and knobs of garlic.
And if a tooth of stink thistle
pulls blood from the round
blue marbled hand
all the better for
this ruby of Pamplona,
this bright jewel of Vich,
this stained crown
of Solsona, this
20 salami.

        The daughter
of mismatched eyes,
36 year old infant smelling
of milk. Mama, she cries, mama,
but mama is gone,
and the old stone cutter
must wipe the drool
from her jumper. His puffed fingers
unbutton and point her
30 to toilet. Ten, twelve hours
a day, as long as the winter sun
holds up he rebuilds
the unvisited church
of San Martin. Cheep cheep
of the hammer high above
the town, sparrow cries
lost in the wind or lost
in the mind. At dusk he leans
to the coal dull wooden Virgin
40 and asks for blessings on

the slow one and peace
on his grizzled head, asks
finally and each night
for the forbidden, for
the knowledge of every
mysterious stone, and
the words go out on
the overwhelming incense
of salami.
50   A single crow
passed high over the house,
I wakened out of nightmare.
The winds had changed,
the Tremontana was tearing
out of the Holy Mountains
to meet the sea winds
in my yard, burning and
scaring the young pines.
The single poplar wailed
60 in terror. With salt,

with guilt, with the need
to die, the vestments
of my life flared, I
was on fire, a stranger
staggering through my house
butting walls and falling
over furniture, looking
for a way out. In the last room
where moonlight slanted
70 through a broken shutter
I found my smallest son
asleep or dead, floating
on a bed of colorless light.
When I leaned closer
I could smell the small breaths
going and coming, and each
bore its prayer for me,
the true and earthy prayer
of salami.

Vachel Lindsay

Vachel Lindsay (1879–1931) is best known for the long poems—like "General William Booth Enters into Heaven" and "The Congo"—which he recited on platforms with energy, showmanship, and pizzaz. His readings were popular, his poetry successful for many years. Toward the end of his life, during the Great Depression, he found it difficult to make a living. He had perhaps published too much, too uncritically.

The Flower-Fed Buffaloes   (1926)

The flower-fed buffaloes of the spring
In the days of long ago,
Ranged where the locomotives sing
And the prairie flowers lie low.—
The tossing, blooming, perfumed
     grass
Is swept away by the wheat,
Wheels and wheels and wheels spin by
In the spring that still is sweet.

But the flower-fed buffaloes of the
10   spring
Left us, long ago.
They gore no more, they bellow no
     more,
They trundle around the hills no more:—
With the Blackfeet, lying low,
With the Pawnees, lying low,
Lying low.

John Logan

John Logan (1923–1987) was born in Red Oak, Iowa, and went to school in the
Midwest. In more recent years, he lived in California, in upstate New York, and in
Hawaii, writing his poems and editing *Choice*.

The Picnic   (1960)

It is the picnic with Ruth in the spring.
Ruth was third on my list of seven girls
But the first two were gone (Betty) or else
Had someone (Ellen has accepted Doug).
Indian Gully the last day of school;
Girls make the lunches for the boys too.
I wrote a note to Ruth in algebra class
Day before the test. She smiled, and nodded.
We left the cars and walked through the young corn
10 The shoots green as paint and the leaves like tongues
Trembling. Beyond the fence where we stood
Some wild strawberry flowered by an elm tree
And Jack-in-the-pulpit was olive ripe.
A blackbird fled as I crossed, and showed
A spot of gold or red under its quick wing.
I held the wire for Ruth and watched the whip
Of her long, striped skirt as she followed.
Three freckles blossomed on her thin, white back
Underneath the loop where the blouse buttoned.
20 We went for our lunch away from the rest,
Stretched in the new grass, our heads close
Over unknown things wrapped up in wax papers.
Ruth tried for the same, I forget what it was,
And our hands were together. She laughed,
And a breeze caught the edge of her little
Collar and the edge of her brown, loose hair
That touched my cheek. I turned my face in-
to the gentle fall. I saw how sweet it smelled.
She didn't move her head or take her hand.
30 I felt a soft caving in my stomach
As at the top of the highest slide
When I had been a child, but was not afraid,
And did not know why my eyes moved with wet
As I brushed her cheek with my lips and brushed
Her lips with my own lips. She said to me
Jack, Jack, different than I had ever heard,
Because she wasn't calling me, I think,
Or telling me. She used my name to
Talk in another way I wanted to know.
40 She laughed again and then she took her hand;
I gave her what we both had touched—can't
Remember what it was, and we ate the lunch.

Afterward we walked in the small, cool creek
Our shoes off, her skirt hitched, and she smiling,
My pants rolled, and then we climbed up the high
Side of Indian Gully and looked
Where we had been, our hands together again.
It was then some bright thing came in my eyes,
Starting at the back of them and flowing
50 Suddenly through my head and down my arms
And stomach and my bare legs that seemed not
To stop in feet, not to feel the red earth
Of the Gully, as though we hung in a
Touch of birds. There was a word in my throat
With the feeling and I knew the first time
What it meant and I said, it's beautiful.
Yes, she said, and I felt the sound and word
In my hand join the sound and word in hers
As in one name said, or in one cupped hand.
60 We put back on our shoes and socks and we
Sat in the grass awhile, crosslegged, under
A blowing tree, not saying anything.
And Ruth played with shells she found in the creek,
As I watched. Her small wrist which was so sweet
To me turned by her breast and the shells dropped
Green, white, blue, easily into her lap,
Passing light through themselves. She gave the pale
Shells to me, and got up and touched her hips
With her light hands, and we walked down slowly
70 To play the school games with the others.

Audre Lorde

Audre Lorde (1934–   ) was born in New York City. She has edited
magazines, written books of poems, and received a grant from the National
Endowment for the Arts. She now teaches at New York's Hunter College.

Hanging Fire   (1978)

I am fourteen
and my skin has betrayed me
the boy I cannot live without
still sucks his thumb
in secret
how come my knees are
always so ashy
what if I die
before morning
10 and momma's in the bedroom
with the door closed.

I have to learn how to dance
in time for the next party
my room is too small for me
suppose I die before graduation
they will sing sad melodies
but finally
tell the truth about me
There is nothing I want to do
20 and too much
that has to be done

and momma's in the bedroom
with the door closed.

Nobody even stops to think
about my side of it
I should have been on Math Team
my marks were better than his
why do I have to be

the one
30 wearing braces
I have nothing to wear tomorrow
will I live long enough
to grow up
and momma's in the bedroom
with the door closed.

Robert Lowell

Robert Lowell (1917–1977) was born in Massachusetts into the eminent literary
and academic family of the Lowells, related to the poets Amy and James Russell
Lowell and to a president of Harvard. After attending Harvard for several terms,
he transferred to Kenyon College in Ohio, where he studied with John Crowe
Ransom and made the acquaintance of Allen Tate and Randall Jarrell. His first
book, *Land of Unlikeness,* published in a small edition in 1944, was followed by
Lord Weary's Castle in 1947, which won the Pulitzer Prize. With *Life Studies* in
1959, his work took an abrupt turn away from the formal stanzas and couplets of
his early poetry into the painful confessional verse that came to characterize
him. In his last years, he wrote with a prolixity he had lacked as a young man and
perhaps with less success. He published nine volumes in the last twelve years of
his life, before he died of a heart attack at the age of sixty. See also pages 475–476.

After the Surprising Conversions   (1946)

September twenty-second, Sir: today
I answer. In the latter part of May,
Hard on our Lord's Ascension, it began
To be more sensible. A gentleman
Of more than common understanding, strict
In morals, pious in behavior, kicked
Against our goad. A man of some renown,
An useful, honored person in the town,
He came of melancholy parents; prone
10 To secret spells, for years they kept alone—
His uncle, I believe, was killed of it:
Good people, but of too much or little wit.
I preached one Sabbath on a text from Kings;
He showed concernment for his soul. Some things
In his experience were hopeful. He
Would sit and watch the wind knocking a tree
And praise this countryside our Lord has made.
Once when a poor man's heifer died, he laid
A shilling on the doorsill; though a thirst
20 For loving shook him like a snake, he durst
Not entertain much hope of his estate
In heaven. Once we saw him sitting late
Behind his attic window by a light

That guttered on his Bible; through that night
He meditated terror, and he seemed
Beyond advice or reason, for he dreamed
That he was called to trumpet Judgment Day
To Concord. In the latter part of May
He cut his throat. And though the coroner
30 Judged him delirious, soon a noisome stir
Palsied our village. At Jehovah's nod
Satan seemed more let loose amongst us: God
Abandoned us to Satan, and he pressed
Us hard, until we thought we could not rest
Till we had done with life. Content was gone.
All the good work was quashed. We were undone.
The breath of God had carried out a planned
And sensible withdrawal from this land;
The multitude, once unconcerned with doubt,
40 Once neither callous, curious nor devout,
Jumped at broad noon, as though some peddler groaned
At it in its familiar twang: "My friend,
Cut your own throat. Cut your own throat. Now! Now!"
September twenty-second, Sir, the bough
Cracks with the unpicked apples, and at dawn
The small-mouth bass breaks water, gorged with spawn.

Skunk Hour   (1957)
(For Elizabeth Bishop)

Nautilus Island's hermit
heiress still lives through winter in her Spartan cottage;
her sheep still graze above the sea.
Her son's a bishop. Her farmer
is first selectman in our village;
she's in her dotage.

Thirsting for
the hierarchic privacy
of Queen Victoria's century,
10 she buys up all
the eyesores facing her shore,
and lets them fall.

The season's ill—
we've lost our summer millionaire,
who seemed to leap from an L. L. Bean[1]
catalogue. His nine-knot yawl
was auctioned off to lobstermen.
A red fox stain covers Blue Hill.

---

[1] A Maine store that specializes in outdoor gear and country clothing; its label is popular among affluent city people who summer in the country.

And now our fairy
20 decorator brightens his shop for fall;
his fishnet's filled with orange cork,
orange, his cobbler's bench and awl;
there is no money in his work,
he'd rather marry.

One dark night,
my Tudor Ford climbed the hill's skull;
I watched for love-cars. Lights turned down,
they lay together, hull to hull,
where the graveyard shelves on the town. . . .
30 My mind's not right.

A car radio bleats,
"Love, O careless Love. . . ." I hear
my ill-spirit sob in each blood cell,
as if my hand were at its throat. . . .
I myself am hell;
nobody's here—

only skunks, that search
in the moonlight for a bite to eat.
They march on their soles up Main Street:
40 white stripes, moonstruck eyes' red fire
under the chalk-dry and spar spire
of the Trinitarian Church.

I stand on top
of our back steps and breathe the rich air—
a mother skunk with her column of kittens swills the garbage pail.
She jabs her wedge-head in a cup
of sour cream, drops her ostrich tail,
and will not scare.

For the Union Dead   (1960)
"Relinquunt Omnia Servare Rem Publicam."[1]

The old South Boston Aquarium stands
in a Sahara of snow now. Its broken windows are boarded.
The bronze weathervane cod has lost half its scales.
The airy tanks are dry.

Once my nose crawled like a snail on the glass;
my hand tingled
to burst the bubbles
drifting from the noses of the cowed, compliant fish.

[1] "They sacrifice everything to serve the republic."

My hand draws back. I often sigh still
10 for the dark downward and vegetating kingdom
of the fish and reptile. One morning last March,
I pressed against the new barbed and galvanized

fence on the Boston Common. Behind their cage,
yellow dinosaur steamshovels were grunting
as they cropped up tons of mush and grass
to gouge their underworld garage.

Parking spaces luxuriate like civic
sandpiles in the heart of Boston.
A girdle of orange, Puritan-pumpkin colored girders
20 braces the tingling Statehouse,

shaking over the excavations, as it faces Colonel Shaw
and his bell-cheeked Negro infantry
on St. Gaudens'[2] shaking Civil War relief,
propped by a plank splint against the garage's earthquake.

Two months after marching through Boston,
half the regiment was dead;
at the dedication,
William James[3] could almost hear the bronze Negroes breathe.

Their monument sticks like a fishbone
30 in the city's throat.
Its Colonel is as lean
as a compass-needle.

He has an angry wrenlike vigilance,
a greyhound's gentle tautness;
he seems to wince at pleasure,
and suffocate for privacy.

He is out of bounds now. He rejoices in man's lovely,
peculiar power to choose life and die—
when he leads his black soldiers to death,
40 he cannot bend his back.

On a thousand small town New England greens,
the old white churches hold their air
of sparse, sincere rebellion; frayed flags
quilt the graveyards of the Grand Army of the Republic.

The stone statues of the abstract Union Soldier
grow slimmer and younger each year—

[2] Sculptor Augustus Saint-Gaudens (1848–1907) made a bronze relief of Colonel Robert
Shaw (1837–1863), who led a regiment during the Civil War. [3] William James (1842–1910),
American psychologist and philosopher, professor at Harvard

wasp-waisted, they doze over muskets
and muse through their sideburns . . .

Shaw's father wanted no monument
50 except the ditch,
where his son's body was thrown
and lost with his "niggers."

The ditch is nearer.
There are no statues for the last war here;
on Boylston Street, a commercial photograph
shows Hiroshima boiling

over a Mosler Safe, the "Rock of Ages"
that survived the blast. Space is nearer.
When I crouch to my television set,
60 the drained faces of Negro school-children rise like balloons.

Colonel Shaw
is riding on his bubble,
he waits
for the blessèd break.

The Aquarium is gone. Everywhere,
giant finned cars nose forward like fish;
a savage servility
slides by on grease.

Derek Mahon

Derek Mahon (1941–   ) was born in Belfast, a northerner like many important
Irish poets of our time. He has published many books of poems, of which *Poems
1962–1978* is available in the United States from the Oxford University Press, and
They Hunt by Night from the Wake Forest University Press. He has lived much of
his adult life in London, and has spent time in the United States.

The Chinese Restaurant in Portrush   (1979)

Before the holidaymakers comes the spring
Softening the sharp air of the coast
In time for the first 'invasion'.
Today the place is as it might have been,
Gentle and almost hospitable. A girl
Strides past the Northern Counties Hotel,
Light-footed, swinging a book-bag,
And the doors that were shut all winter
Against the north wind and the sea-mist

10 Lie open to the street, where one
  By one the gulls go window-shopping
  And an old wolfhound dozes in the sun.

  While I sit with my paper and prawn chow-mein
  Under a framed photograph of Hong Kong
  The proprietor of the Chinese restaurant
  Stands at the door as if the world were young
  Watching the first yacht hoist a sail—
  An ideogram on sea-cloud—and the light
  Of heaven upon the mountains of Donegal;
20 And whistles a little tune, dreaming of home.

Christopher Marlowe

Christopher Marlowe (1564–1593) born the same year as Shakespeare, was a
great playwright who helped establish English poetry upon the stage. Two of his
best plays were *Tragedy of Doctor Faustus* and *Edward II*. He was murdered in a
tavern at Deptford by a man named Ingram Frisar.

The Passionate Shepherd to His Love   (1600)

Come live with me and be my love,
And we will all the pleasures prove
That hills and valleys, dale and field,
And all the craggy mountains yield!

There will we sit upon the rocks
And see the shepherds feed their
    flocks,
By shallow rivers, to whose falls
Melodious birds sing madrigals.

10 There will I make thee beds of roses
With a thousand fragrant posies,
A cap of flowers, and a kirtle
Embroider'd all with leaves of myrtle;

A gown made of the finest wool
Which from our pretty lambs we pull;

Fair lined slippers for the cold,
With buckles of the purest gold;

A belt of straw and ivy buds,
With coral clasps and amber studs:
20 And if these pleasures may thee move,
Come live with me and be my love!

Thy silver dishes, for thy meat
As precious as the gods do eat,
Shall on an ivory table be
Prepared each day for thee and me.

The shepherd swains shall dance and
    sing
For thy delight each May morning.
If these delights thy mind may move,
30 Then live with me and be my love!

Sir Walter Ralegh (see also page 672) wrote an answer for the Nymph to
address to the Shepherd:

The Nymph's Reply to the Shepherd   (1600)

If all the world and love were young,
And truth in every shepherd's tongue,
These pretty pleasures might me move
To live with thee and be thy love.

Time drives the flocks from field to fold
When rivers rage and rocks grow cold,
And Philomel° becometh dumb;   the nightingale
The rest complains of care to come.

The flowers do fade, and wanton fields
10 To wayward winter reckoning yields;
A honey tongue, a heart of gall,
Is fancy's spring, but sorrow's fall.

Thy gowns, thy shoes, thy beds of roses,
Thy cap, thy kirtle,° and thy posies   underdress
Soon break, soon wither, soon forgotten—
In folly ripe, in reason rotten.

Thy belt of straw and ivy buds,
Thy coral clasps and amber studs,
All these in me no means can move
20 To come to thee and be thy love.

But could youth last and love still breed,
Had joys no date nor age no need,
Then these delights my mind might move
To live with thee and be thy love.

Andrew Marvell

Andrew Marvell (1621–1678) was a poet in youth but, as he grew older, became
increasingly more political than poetical. A defender of Cromwell and Milton,
after the restoration of the monarchy he joined Parliament and represented his
birthplace, Hull.

The Garden   (1652)

How vainly men themselves amaze
To win the palm, the oak, or bays;[1]
And their incessant labours see
Crowned from some single herb or tree,

Whose short and narrow-vergèd shade
Does prudently their toils upbraid;
While all flowers and all trees do close
To weave the garlands of repose.

[1] Laurel wreaths, symbolizing achievement in sport, politics, and poetry

Fair Quiet, have I found thee here,
10 And Innocence, thy sister dear!
Mistaken long, I sought you then
In busy companies of men.
Your sacred plants, if here below,
Only among the plants will grow:
Society is all but rude
To this delicious solitude.

No white nor red was ever seen
So amorous as this lovely green.
Fond lovers, cruel as their flame,
20 Cut in these trees their mistress' name:
Little, alas, they know or heed,
How far these beauties hers exceed!
Fair trees! wheres'e'er your barks I
    wound,
No name shall but your own be found.

When we have run our passion's
    heat,
Love hither makes his best retreat.
The gods, that mortal beauty chase,
30 Still in a tree did end their race.
Apollo hunted Daphne so,
Only that she might laurel grow;
And Pan did after Syrinx speed,
Not as a nymph, but for a reed.

What wondrous life is this I lead!
Ripe apples drop about my head;
The luscious clusters of the vine
Upon my mouth do crush their wine;
The nectarine, and curious peach,
40 Into my hands themselves do reach;
Stumbling on melons, as I pass,
Ensnared with flowers, I fall on grass.

Meanwhile the mind, from pleasure
    less,
Withdraws into its happiness:
The mind, that ocean where each kind

Does straight its own resemblance find;
Yet it creates, transcending these,
Far other worlds, and other seas;
50 Annihilating all that's made
To a green thought in a green shade.

Here at the fountain's sliding foot,
Or at some fruit-tree's mossy root,
Casting the body's vest aside,
My soul into the boughs does glide:
There like a bird it sits and sings,
Then whets, and combs its silver wings;
And, till prepared for longer flight,
Waves in its plumes the various light.

60 Such was that happy garden-state,
While man there walked without a
    mate:
After a place so pure and sweet,
What other help could yet be meet?
But 'twas beyond a mortal's share
To wander solitary there:
Two Paradises 'twere in one,
To live in Paradise alone.

How well the skilful gardener drew
70 Of flowers and herbs this dial new!
Where, from above, the milder sun
Does through a fragrant zodiac run;
And, as it works, the industrious bee
Computes its time as well as we.
How could such sweet and wholesome
    hours
Be reckoned but with herbs and
    flowers?

To His Coy Mistress (1652)

Had we but world enough, and time,
This coyness, Lady, were no crime.
We would sit down, and think which way
To walk, and pass our long love's day.
Thou by the Indian Ganges' side
Shouldst rubies find; I by the tide
Of Humber would complain. I would
Love you ten years before the Flood;
And you should, if you please, refuse
10 Till the conversion of the Jews.
My vegetable° love should grow   vegetative
Vaster than empires, and more slow.
An hundred years should go to praise
Thine eyes, and on thy forehead gaze;
Two hundred to adore each breast;
But thirty thousand to the rest:
An age, at least, to every part,
And the last age should show your heart.
For, Lady, you deserve this state,
20 Nor would I love at lower rate.
      But, at my back, I always hear
Time's wingèd chariot hurrying near:
And yonder, all before us lie
Deserts of vast eternity.
Thy beauty shall no more be found;
Nor, in thy marble vault, shall sound
My echoing song. Then worms shall try
That long preserved virginity:
And your quaint honour turn to dust;
30 And into ashes all my lust.
The grave's a fine and private place,
But none, I think, do there embrace.
      Now, therefore, while the youthful hue
Sits on thy skin like morning dew,
And while thy willing soul transpires
At every pore with instant fires,
Now let us sport us while we may;
And now, like amorous birds of prey,
Rather at once our time devour,
40 Than languish in his slow-chapt° power.   slow-jawed
Let us roll all our strength, and all
Our sweetness, up into one ball;
And tear our pleasures, with rough strife,
Thorough° the iron gates of life.   through
      Thus, though we cannot make our sun
Stand still, yet we will make him run.

Wesley McNair

Wesley McNair (1941–   ) was born in New Hampshire and has written most of his poems out of his sense of character connected to region. He attended the University of New Hampshire in Keene, and has held a Fulbright Lectureship in Chile, two National Endowment grants, and a Guggenheim fellowship. His first book of poems, *The Faces of Americans in 1953* (1984) won the Devins Award; *The Town of No* followed in 1989.

Mina Bell's Cows   (1983)

O where are Mina Bell's cows who gave no milk
and grazed on her dead husband's farm?
Each day she walked with them into the field,
loving their swayback dreaminess more
than the quickness of any dog or chicken.
Each night she brought them grain in the dim barn,
holding their breath in her hands.
O when the lightning struck Daisy and Bets,
her son dug such great holes in the yard
10 she could not bear to watch him.
And when the baby, April, growing old
and wayward, fell down the hay chute,
Mina just sat in the kitchen, crying "Ape,
Ape," as if she called all three cows,
her walleyed girls who never would come home.

Where I Live   (1983)

You will come into an antique town
whose houses move apart
as if you'd interrupted
a private discussion. This is the place
you must pass through to get there.
Imagining lives tucked in
like china plates, continue driving.
Beyond the landscaped streets,
beyond the last colonial gas station
10 and unsolved by zoning,
is a road. It will take you
to old farmhouses and trees
with car-tire swings.
Signs will announce hairdressing
and nightcrawlers.
The timothy grass will run beside you
all the way to where I live.

Archibald MacLeish

Archibald MacLeish (1892–1982) attended Yale, went to law school at Harvard, practiced law briefly, and then moved to France as an American expatriate in the 1920s. When the Great Depression hit the United States he returned to this country, where he became increasingly political. He worked for *Fortune,* wrote on political subjects, and eventually allied himself with President Franklin D. Roosevelt. He was Librarian of Congress, and, toward the end of Roosevelt's life, became an Assistant Secretary of State. When Roosevelt died, MacLeish left government. He taught at Harvard for some years, beginning in 1949, and returned to the writing of poetry.

You, Andrew Marvell   (1928)

And here face down beneath the sun
And here upon earth's noonward height
To feel the always coming on
The always rising of the night:

To feel creep up the curving east
The earthy chill of dusk and slow
Upon those under lands the vast
And ever climbing shadow grow

And strange at Ecbatan the trees
10 Take leaf by leaf the evening strange
The flooding dark about their knees
The mountains over Persia change

And now at Kermanshah the gate
Dark empty and the withered grass
And through the twilight now the late
Few travelers in the westward pass

And Baghdad darken and the bridge
Across the silent river gone

And through Arabia the edge
20 Of evening widen and steal on

And deepen on Palmyra's street
The wheel rut in the ruined stone
And Lebanon fade out and Crete
High through the clouds and overblown

And over Sicily the air
Still flashing with the landward gulls
And loom and slowly disappear
The sails above the shadowy hulls

And Spain go under and the shore
30 Of Africa the gilded sand
And evening vanish and no more
The low pale light across that land

Nor now the long light on the sea:

And here face downward in the sun
To feel how swift how secretly
The shadow of the night comes on . . .

Louis MacNeice

Louis MacNeice (1907–1963) was an English poet associated during the 1930s with W. H. Auden, who collaborated with him on *Letters from Iceland.* Born in Ireland, he lived most of his life in London, where he was a producer for the BBC.

The Sunlight on the Garden   (1937)

The sunlight on the garden
Hardens and grows cold,
We cannot cage the minute

Within its nets of gold,
When all is told
We cannot beg for pardon.

Our freedom as free lances
Advances towards its end;
The earth compels, upon it
10 Sonnets and birds descend;
And soon, my friend,
We shall have no time for dances.

The sky was good for flying
Defying the church bells
And every evil iron

Siren and what it tells:
The earth compels,
We are dying, Egypt, dying

And not expecting pardon,
20 Hardened in heart anew,
But glad to have sat under
Thunder and rain with you,
And grateful too
For sunlight on the garden.

James Merrill

James Merrill (1926–   ) attended Amherst and now alternates between a
house in Greece and a house in Connecticut. He has published two novels; his
books of poems have won the National Book Award and other prizes.

After Greece   (1962)

Light into the olive entered
And was oil. Rain made the huge pale stones
Shine from within. The moon turned his hair white
Who next stepped from between the columns,
Shielding his eyes. All through
The countryside were old ideas
Found lying open to the elements.
Of the gods' houses only
A minor premise here and there
10 Would be balancing the heaven of fixed stars
Upon a Doric capital. The rest
Lay spilled, their fluted drums half sunk in cyclamen
Or deep in water's biting clarity
Which just barely upheld me
The next week, when I sailed for home.
But where is home   these walls?
These limbs? The very spaniel underfoot
Races in sleep, toward what?
It is autumn. I did not invite
20 Those guests, windy and brittle, who drink my liquor.
Returning from a walk I find
The bottles filled with spleen, my room itself
Smeared by reflection on to the far hemlocks.
I some days flee in dream
Back to the exposed porch of the maidens
Only to find my great-great-grandmothers
Erect there, peering
Into a globe of red Bohemian glass.

As it swells and sinks, I call up
30 Graces, Furies, Fates, removed
To my country's warm, lit halls, with rivets forced
Through drapery, and nothing left to bear.
They seem anxious to know
What holds up heaven nowadays.
I start explaining how in that vast fire
Were other irons—well, Art, Public Spirit,
Ignorance, Economics, Love of Self,
Hatred of Self, a hundred more,
Each burning to be felt, each dedicated
40 To sparing us the worst; how I distrust them
As I should have done those ladies; how I want
Essentials: salt, wine, olive, the light, the scream—
No! I have scarcely named you,
And look, in a flash you stand full-grown before me,
Row upon row, Essentials,
Dressed like your sister caryatids
Or tombstone angels jealous of their dead,
With undulant coiffures, lips weathered, cracked by grime,
And faultless eyes gone blank beneath the immense
50 Zinc and gunmetal northern sky . . .
Stay then. Perhaps the system
Calls for spirits. This first glass I down
To the last time
I ate and drank in that old world. May I
Also survive its meanings, and my own.

John Milton

John Milton (1608–1674) was a precocious poet. He prepared himself assiduously
for his poetic vocation, and in 1637 wrote the remarkable elegy "Lycidas" for a
young man he had known at Cambridge. During the next twenty years he wrote a
few sonnets—excellent poems—but largely he substituted politics and political
action for poetry, working as Cromwell's Latin secretary. His first marriage was
tempestuous, and he wrote prose works advocating divorce, which earned him
considerable denunciation. He became blind while he was still Cromwell's
secretary, and was assisted by several helpers, notably Andrew Marvell. After
Cromwell's death and the restoration of the monarchy, he was imprisoned,
released, and lived in poverty. He had begun his great work, the religious epic
Paradise Lost, while he was chiefly engaged in politics, but he completed it in
blindness and poverty. Afterward he wrote "Paradise Regained" and "Samson
Agonistes." In prose, his "Areopagitica" (on freedom of the press) is his most
celebrated work. See also page 498.

On His Blindness   (1655)

When I consider how my light is spent
Ere half my days in this dark world and wide,

And that one talent which is death to hide
Lodged with me useless, though my soul more bent
To serve therewith my Maker, and present
My true account, lest He returning chide,
"Doth God exact day-labor, light denied?"
I fondly ask. But Patience, to prevent
That murmur, soon replies, "God doth not need
10 Either man's work or his own gifts. Who best
Bear His mild yoke, they serve Him best. His state
Is kingly: thousands at His bidding speed,
And post o'er land and ocean without rest;
They also serve who only stand and wait."

Marianne Moore

Marianne Moore (1887–1972) was born in St. Louis, graduated from Bryn Mawr,
and taught school in Pennsylvania, but lived most of her life in Brooklyn. As
editor of *The Dial* from 1925 to 1929 she published many of the best modern
poets. Her own poems are original and even eccentric. Her intricate descriptions
are scrupulous in detail, shaped into prosaic lines that achieve a singular music.
See also pages 427–428.

A Grave   (1935)

Man looking into the sea,
taking the view from those who have as much right to it as you have to it yourself,
it is human nature to stand in the middle of a thing,
but you cannot stand in the middle of this;
the sea has nothing to give but a well excavated grave.
The firs stand in a procession, each with an emerald turkey foot at the top,
reserved as their contours, saying nothing;
repression, however, is not the most obvious characteristic of the sea;
the sea is a collector, quick to return a rapacious look.
10 There are others besides you who have worn that look—
whose expression is no longer a protest; the fish no longer investigate them
for their bones have not lasted;
men lower nets, unconscious of the fact that they are desecrating a grave,
and row quickly away—the blades of the oars
moving together like the feet of water spiders as if there were no such thing as death.
The wrinkles progress among themselves in a phalanx—beautiful under networks of
       foam,
and fade breathlessly while the sea rustles in and out of the seaweed;
20 the birds swim through the air at top speed, emitting catcalls as heretofore—
the tortoise shell scourges about the feet of the cliffs, in motion beneath them;
and the ocean, under the pulsation of lighthouses and noise of bell buoys,
advances as usual, looking as if it were not that ocean in which dropped things are
       bound to sink—
in which if they turn and twist, it is neither with volition nor consciousness.

Thylias Moss

Thylias Moss (1954–   ) has published three books of poems including
Hosiery Seams on a Bowlegged Woman (1983), *Pyramid of Bone* (1989), and
At Redbone's (1990). She graduated from Oberlin College and did graduate
work at the University of New Hampshire. She teaches at Phillips Academy in
Andover, Massachusetts.

Sunrise Comes to Second Avenue   (1990)

Daylight announces
the start of day six hours old.

We all have thankless
jobs to do. Consider
the devotion of fishes singing
hymns without voices.

The clock's hands searching
for the lost face, a place

for the Eucharist. The man
10 bedded down on the roadway,

the asphalt pope out of bread,
breath and blessings.

The streetcleaner
sweeping up confessions.

Edwin Muir

Edwin Muir (1887–1959) was born in the Orkneys, off the coast of Scotland.
After his father was evicted from an island farm, young Muir grew up in the slums
of Glasgow. His poetry built upon the contrast between the pastoral and the
industrial. He and his wife Willa lived by their wits most of their lives, and are
Kafka's translators. Muir is author of an excellent *Autobiography* as well as the
neglected *Collected Poems*.

The Horses   (1952)

Barely a twelvemonth after
The seven days war that put the world to sleep,
Late in the evening the strange horses came.
By then we had made our covenant with silence,
But in the first few days it was so still
We listened to our breathing and were afraid.
On the second day
The radios failed; we turned the knobs; no answer.
On the third day a warship passed us, heading north,
10 Dead bodies piled on the deck. On the sixth day
A plane plunged over us into the sea. Thereafter
Nothing. The radios dumb;
And still they stand in corners of our kitchens,
And stand, perhaps, turned on, in a million rooms

All over the world. But now if they should speak,
If on a sudden they should speak again,
If on the stroke of noon a voice should speak,
We would not listen, we would not let it bring
That old bad world that swallowed its children quick
20 At one great gulp. We would not have it again.
Sometimes we think of the nations lying asleep,
Curled blindly in impenetrable sorrow,
And then the thought confounds us with its strangeness.
The tractors lie about our fields; at evening
They look like dank sea-monsters couched and waiting.
We leave them where they are and let them rust:
'They'll moulder away and be like other loam.'
We make our oxen drag our rusty ploughs,
Long laid aside. We have gone back
30 Far past our fathers' land.
                              And then, that evening
Late in the summer the strange horses came.
We heard a distant tapping on the road,
A deepening drumming; it stopped, went on again
And at the corner changed to hollow thunder.
We saw the heads
Like a wild wave charging and were afraid.
We had sold our horses in our fathers' time
To buy new tractors. Now they were strange to us
40 As fabulous steeds set on an ancient shield
Or illustrations in a book of knights.
We did not dare go near them. Yet they waited,
Stubborn and shy, as if they had been sent
By an old command to find our whereabouts
And that long-lost archaic companionship.
In the first moment we had never a thought
That they were creatures to be owned and used.
Among them were some half-a-dozen colts
Dropped in some wilderness of the broken world,
50 Yet new as if they had come from their own Eden.
Since then they have pulled our ploughs and borne our loads
But that free servitude still can pierce our hearts.
Our life is changed; their coming our beginning.

David Mura

David Mura (1952–   ) is a *sansei* (third generation Japanese-American)
who lives in St. Paul, Minnesota, where he is married to a pediatrician and
teaches at The Loft: A Place for Literature. He has published a book of poems,
After We Lost Our Way, and a long essay called *A Male Grief: Notes on
Pornography and Addiction.*

Grandfather and Grandmother in Love   (1989)

Now I will ask for one true word beyond
betrayal, that creaks and buoys like the bedsprings
used by the bodies that begot the bodies that begot me.
Now I will think of the moon bluing the white
sheets soaked in sweat, that heard him whisper
haiku of clover, azalea, the cry of the cuckoo;
complaints of moles and beetles,
blight and bad debts, as the *biwa*'s[1] spirit
bubbled up between them, its song quavering.
10 Now I take this word, crack it, like a seed
between the teeth, spit it out in the world
to root in the loam of his greenhouse roses;
let it leave the sweet taste of *teriyaki,*
a grain of her rice lodged in my molars;
in my nostrils, a faint hot breath of *sake.*

Now as *otoo-san*[2], *okaa-san*[3], drift towards
each other, there reverberates the *ran*[4]
of lovers, and the ship of the past bursts
into that other world; and she, still teasing,
20 pushes him away, swats his hand, a pesky,
tickling fly, then turns to his face that
cries out laughing, as he hauls her in,
trawling the currents, gathering
a sea that seems endless, depths a boy dreams of,
where flounder, dolphin, fluorescent fins, fish
with wings spill before him glittering scales,
and letting slip the net, he dives under,
and night washes over them, slipping from
sight, just the soft shush of waves, drifting ground
30 swells, echoing the knocking tide of morning.

---

[1] *Biwa:* a Japanese stringed instrument.   [2] *Otoo-san:* father.   [3] *Okaa-san:* mother (Japanese
couples call each other Father and Mother).   [4] *Ran:* chaos.

Thomas Nashe

Thomas Nashe (1567–1601) was a literary jack-of-all-trades—pamphleteer, playwright, poet, and author of the first adventure novel in English. Ever contentious, he wrote a comedy called "The Isle of Dogs" which attacked the government so thoroughly that Nashe spent some months in jail. This poem is said to have been written during the plague that afflicted London from 1592 to 1594.

Adieu! Farewell Earth's Bliss!   (1592)

Adieu! farewell earth's bliss!
This world uncertain is:
Fond are life's lustful joys,
Death proves them all but toys,
None from his darts can fly:
I am sick, I must die.
    Lord, have mercy on us!

Rich men, trust not in wealth!
Gold cannot buy you health;
10 Physic himself must fade,
All things to end are made,
The plague full swift goes by:
I am sick, I must die.
    Lord, have mercy on us!

Beauty is but a flower
Which wrinkles will devour;
Brightness falls from the air,
Queens have died young and fair,
Dust hath closed Helen's eye:
20 I am sick, I must die.
    Lord, have mercy on us!

Strength stoops unto the grave:
Worms feed on Hector brave;
Swords may not fight with fate;
Earth still holds ope her gate;
'Come! come!' the bells do cry.
I am sick, I must die.
    Lord, have mercy on us!

Wit with his wantonness
30 Tasteth death's bitterness;
Hell's executioner
Hath no ears for to hear
What vain art can reply:
I am sick, I must die.
    Lord, have mercy on us!

Haste, therefore, each degree,
To welcome destiny:
Heaven is our heritage,
Earth but a player's stage,
40 Mount we unto the sky:
I am sick, I must die.
    Lord, have mercy on us!

Frank O'Hara

Frank O'Hara (1926–1966) was a poet of vast influence; the naturalness of O'Hara's language has earned him many followers. He attended Harvard and then worked at the Museum of Modern Art in New York, where he held an important position at the time of his accidental death in 1966. His *Collected Poems* came out in 1971.

The Day Lady Died   (1964)

It is 12:20 in New York a Friday
three days after Bastille day, yes
it is 1959 and I go get a shoeshine

because I will get off the 4:19 in Easthampton
at 7:15 and then go straight to dinner
and I don't know the people who will feed me

I walk up the muggy street beginning to sun
and have a hamburger and a malted and buy
an ugly NEW WORLD WRITING to see what the poets
10   in Ghana are doing these days
                              I go on to the bank
and Miss Stillwagon (first name Linda I once heard)
doesn't even look up my balance for once in her life
and in the GOLDEN GRIFFIN I get a little Verlaine
for Patsy with drawings by Bonnard although I do
think of Hesiod, trans. Richmond Lattimore or
Brendan Behan's new play or *Le Balcon* or *Les Nègres*

of Genet, but I don't, I stick with Verlaine
after practically going to sleep with quandariness

20   and for Mike I just stroll into the PARK LANE
Liquor Store and ask for a bottle of Strega and
then I go back where I came from to 6th Avenue
and the tobacconist in the Ziegfeld Theatre and
casually ask for a carton of Gauloises and a carton
of Picayunes, and a NEW YORK POST with her face on it

and I am sweating a lot by now and thinking of
leaning on the john door in the 5 SPOT
while she whispered a song along the keyboard
to Mal Waldron and everyone and I stopped breathing

Sharon Olds

Sharon Olds (1942–   ), born in San Francisco, went to Stanford and Columbia, and now teaches at New York University. Her books include *Satan Says* (1980), *The Dead and the Living* (1984), and *The Gold Cell* (1987).

Sex without Love   (1984)

How do they do it, the ones who make love
without love? Beautiful as dancers,
gliding over each other like ice skaters
over the ice, fingers hooked
inside each other's bodies, faces
red as steak, wine, wet as the
children at birth whose mothers are going to
give them away. How do they come to the
come to the   come to the   God   come to the
10   still waters, and not love

the one who came there with them, light
rising slowly as steam off their joined
skin? These are the true religious,
the purists, the pros, the ones who will not
accept a false Messiah, love the
priest instead of the God. They do not
mistake the lover for their own pleasure,
they are like great runners: they know they are alone
with the road surface, the cold, the wind,
20 the fit of their shoes, their over-all cardio-
vascular health—just factors, like the partner
in the bed, and not the truth, which is the
single body alone in the universe
against its own best time.

Charles Olson

Charles Olson (1910–1970) was highly influential as a poet and literary thinker. His
first publication was critical, a book about *Moby Dick* called *Call Me Ishmael.* He
wrote an essay on "Projective Verse" which may be regarded as the manifesto of the
Black Mountain School of American poets, loosely derived from Pound and from
Zukofsky's Objectivism. His long series of *Maximus Poems* is his major poetic work.

Maximus, to Gloucester, Sunday, July 19   (1960)

and they stopped before that bad sculpture of a fisherman

—"as if one were to talk to a man's house,
knowing not what gods or heroes are"—
not knowing what a fisherman is
instead of going straight to the Bridge
and doing no more than—saying no more than—
in the Charybdises of the
Cut waters the flowers tear off
the wreathes

10 the flowers
turn
the character of the sea   The sea jumps
the fate of the flower   The drowned men are undrowned
in the eddies
of the eyes
of the flowers
opening
the sea's eyes

The disaster
20 is undone

What was received as alien
—the flower
on the water, that a man drowns
that he dies in water as he dies on earth, the impossible
        that this gross fact can return to us
                in this upset
on a summer day
of a particular tide

that the sensation is true,
30 that the transformations of fire are, first of all, sea—
        "as gold for wares wares for gold"

        Let them be told who stopped first
        by a bronze idol

        A fisherman is not a successful man,
        he is not a famous man he is not a man
        of power, these are the damned by God

whose surface bubbles
with these gimlets
which screw-in like

40 potholes, caustic
caked earth of painted
pools, Yellowstone

Park of holes
is death the diseased
presence on us, the spilling lesion
of the brilliance
it is to be alive: to walk onto it,
as Jim Bridger the first into it,

it is more true a scabious
50 field than it is a pretty
meadow

        When a man's coffin is the sea
        the whole of creation shall come to his funeral,

        it turns out; the globe
        is below, all lapis

        and its blue surface golded
        by what happened

        this afternoon: there are eyes
        in this water

60 the flowers
    from the shore,

    awakened
    the sea

            Men are so sure they know very many things,
            they don't even know night and day are one

            A fisherman works without reference to
            that difference. It is possible he also

            by lying there when he does lie, jowl
            to the sea, has another advantage: it is said,

70 'You rectify what can be rectified,' and when a man's heart
    cannot see this, the door of his divine intelligence is shut

            let you who paraded to the Cut today
            to hold memorial services to all fishermen
            who have been lost at sea in a year
            when for the first time not one life was lost

                    radar sonar radio telephone good engines
                    bed-check seaplanes goodness over and under us

            no difference
            when men come back

Gregory Orr

Gregory Orr (1947–   ) published two books of poems, *Burning the Empty Nests* and *Gathering the Bones Together,* while still in his twenties. He was born in upstate New York and attended Antioch College and Columbia University. He teaches at the University of Virginia. See also pages 435 and 440.

The Sweater   (1975)

I will lose you. It is written
into this poem the way
the fisherman's wife knits
his death into the sweater.

Wilfred Owen

Wilfred Owen (1893–1918) was a poet of the First World War. Like most young
Englishmen in 1914, he had cherished a romantic notion of battle. He lived long
enough—the war killed him, just a few days before the armistice—to write bitter
and antiromantic poems of real modern war.

Dulce et Decorum Est[1]   (1918)

Bent double, like old beggars under sacks,
Knock-kneed, coughing like hags, we cursed through sludge,
Till on the haunting flares we turned our backs,
And towards our distant rest began to trudge.
Men marched asleep. Many had lost their boots,
But limped on, blood-shod. All went lame, all blind;
Drunk with fatigue; deaf even to the hoots
Of gas-shells dropping softly behind.

Gas! Gas! Quick, boys!—An ecstasy of fumbling,
10 Fitting the clumsy helmets just in time,
But someone still was yelling out and stumbling
And floundering like a man in fire or lime.—
Dim through the misty panes and thick green light,
As under a green sea, I saw him drowning.
In all my dreams before my helpless sight
He plunges at me, guttering, choking, drowning.

If in some smothering dreams, you too could pace
Behind the wagon that we flung him in,
And watch the white eyes writhing in his face,
20 His hanging face, like a devil's sick of sin;
If you could hear, at every jolt, the blood
Come gargling from the froth-corrupted lungs,
Bitter as the cud
Of vile, incurable sores on innocent tongues,—
My friend, you would not tell with such high zest
To children ardent for some desperate glory,
The old Lie: Dulce et decorum est
Pro patria mori.

---

[1] The Roman poet Horace wrote that it "is sweet and fitting" (*dulce et decorum est*) "to die
for one's country" (*pro patria mori*). Compare Pound's poem on page 669.

Joyce Peseroff

Joyce Peseroff (1948–   ) grew up in New York City, studied writing at the
University of California at Irvine, and lives outside Boston. Her most recent book
is *Dog in a Lifeboat* (1991).

The Hardness Scale   (1977)

Diamonds are forever so I gave you quartz
which is #7 on the hardness scale
and it's hard enough to get to know anybody these days
if only to scratch the surface
and quartz will scratch six other mineral surfaces:
it will scratch glass
it will scratch gold
it will even
scratch your eyes out one morning—you can't be
10 too careful.
Diamonds are industrial so I bought
a ring of topaz
which is #8 on the hardness scale.
I wear it on my right hand, the way it was
supposed to be, right? No tears and fewer regrets
for reasons smooth and clear as glass. Topaz will scratch glass,
it will scratch your quartz,
and all your radio crystals. You'll have to be silent
the rest of your days
20 not to mention your nights. Not to mention
the night you ran away very drunk very
very drunk and you tried to cross the border
but couldn't make it across the lake.
Stirring up geysers with the oars you drove the red canoe
in circles, tried to pole it but
your left hand didn't know
what the right hand was doing. You fell asleep
and let everyone know it when you woke up.
30 In a gin-soaked morning (hair of the dog) you went
hunting for geese,
shot three lake trout in violation of the game laws,
told me to clean them and that
my eyes were bright as sapphires
which is #9 on the hardness scale.
A sapphire will cut a pearl
it will cut stainless steel
it will cut vinyl and mylar and will probably
cut a record this fall
40 to be released on an obscure label known only to aficionados.
I will buy a copy.
I may buy you a copy
depending on how your tastes have changed.

I will buy copies for my friends
we'll get a new needle,
a diamond needle,
which is #10 on the hardness scale
and will cut anything.
It will cut wood and mortar,
50 plaster and iron,
it will cut the sapphires in my eyes and I will bleed
blind as 4 A.M. in the subways when even degenerates
are dreaming, blind as the time
you shot up the room with a new hunting rifle
blind drunk
as you were.
You were #11 on the hardness scale
later that night
apologetic as
60 you worked your way up
slowly from the knees
and you worked your way down
from the open-throated blouse.
Diamonds are forever so I give you softer things.

Sylvia Plath

Sylvia Plath (1932–1963) attended Smith College, and wrote with a professional
skill from an early age. She attended Cambridge University on a fellowship, where
she met and married the English poet Ted Hughes. After the birth of their second
child, when Plath and Hughes were separated, her work abandoned its skillful
surfaces and became profoundly emotional, angry, brilliant, and disturbing. There
was a brief moment of great poetry, ended by her suicide. The posthumous *Ariel*
(1965) collects her best poetry.

Lady Lazarus   (1963)

I have done it again.
One year in every ten
I manage it—

A sort of walking miracle, my skin
Bright as a Nazi lampshade,
My right foot

A paperweight,
My face a featureless, fine
Jew linen.

10 Peel off the napkin
O my enemy.
Do I terrify?—

The nose, the eye pits, the full set of
    teeth?
The sour breath
Will vanish in a day.

Soon, soon the flesh
The grave cave ate will be
At home on me

20 And I a smiling woman.
I am only thirty.
And like the cat I have nine times to
      die.

This is Number Three.
What a trash
To annihilate each decade.

What a million filaments.
The peanut-crunching crowd
Shoves in to see

30 Them unwrap me hand and foot—
The big strip tease.
Gentleman, ladies,

These are my hands,
My knees.
I may be skin and bone,

Nevertheless, I am the same, identical
      woman.
The first time it happened I was ten.
It was an accident.

40 The second time I meant
To last it out and not come back at all.
I rocked shut

As a seashell.
They had to call and call
And pick the worms off me like sticky
      pearls.

Dying
Is an art, like everything else.
I do it exceptionally well.

50 I do it so it feels like hell.
I do it so it feels real.
I guess you could say I've a call.

It's easy enough to do it in a cell.
It's easy enough to do it and stay put.
It's the theatrical

Comeback in broad day
To the same place, the same face, the
      same brute

Amused shout:
60 "A miracle!"
That knocks me out.
There is a charge

For the eyeing of my scars, there is a
      charge
For the hearing of my heart—
It really goes.

And there is a charge, a very large
      charge,
For a word or a touch
70 Or a bit of blood

Or a piece of my hair or my clothes.
So, so, Herr Doktor.
So, Herr Enemy.

I am your opus,
I am your valuable,
The pure gold baby

That melts to a shriek.
I turn and burn.
Do not think I underestimate your
80   great concern.

Ash, ash—
You poke and stir.
Flesh, bone, there is nothing there—

A cake of soap,
A wedding ring,
A gold filling.

Herr God, Herr Lucifer,
Beware
Beware.

90 Out of the ash
I rise with my red hair
And I eat men like air.

Edgar Allan Poe

For a note on Edgar Allan Poe, see page 333.

The City in the Sea (1827)

Lo! Death has reared himself a throne
In a strange city lying alone
Far down within the dim West,
Where the good and the bad and the
    worst and the best
Have gone to their eternal rest.
There shrines and palaces and towers
(Time-eaten towers that tremble not!)
Resemble nothing that is ours.
10 Around, by lifting winds forgot,
Resignedly beneath the sky
The melancholy waters lie.

No rays from the holy heaven come
    down
On the long night-time of that town;
But light from out the lurid sea
Streams up the turrets silently—
Gleams up the pinnacles far and free—
Up domes—up spires—up kingly
20   halls—
Up fanes—up Babylon-like walls—
Up shadowy long-forgotten bowers
Of sculptured ivy and stone flowers—
Up many and many a marvellous
    shrine
Whose wreathèd friezes intertwine
The viol, the violet, and the vine.

Resignedly beneath the sky
The melancholy waters lie:

30 So blend the turrets and shadows there
That all seem pendulous in air,
While from a proud tower in the town
Death looks gigantically down.

There open fanes and gaping graves
Yawn level with the luminous waves;
But not the riches there that lie
In each idol's diamond eye—
Not the gaily-jewelled dead
Tempt the waters from their bed;
40 For no ripples curl, alas!
Along that wilderness of glass—
No swellings tell that winds may be
Upon some far-off happier sea—
No heavings hint that winds have been
On seas less hideously serene.
But lo, a stir is in the air!
The wave—there is a movement there!
As if the towers had thrust aside,
In slightly sinking, the dull tide—
50 As if their tops had feebly given
A void within the filmy Heaven.
The waves have now a redder glow—
The hours are breathing faint and low—
And when, amid no earthly moans,
Down, down that town shall settle
    hence,
Hell, rising from a thousand thrones,
Shall do it reverence.

Alexander Pope

Alexander Pope (1688–1744), crippled by a childhood disease, was unusually small. He was precocious, beginning to write with considerable excellence at sixteen. Much of the greater work is highly allusive. Although the poetry becomes more subtle and wise, the witwork of the young Pope was never surpassed. Pope was so proficient at the couplet that he was able to translate the entire *Iliad* and *Odyssey* into these twenty-syllable units. These lines are excerpted from "An Epistle to Dr. Arbuthnot." They begin by referring to some bad poets whom Pope earlier attacked, "all such." Then Pope draws a sketch of "Atticus," by whom he intended his contemporaries to understand his admired contemporary and rival, Joseph Addison, author of essays, poems, and a tragedy called *Cato.*

Atticus   (1723)

Peace to all such! but were there one whose fires
True genius kindles, and fair fame inspires;
Blest with each talent, and each art to please,
And born to write, converse, and live with ease,
Should such a man, too fond to rule alone,
Bear, like the Turk, no brother near the throne,
View him with scornful, yet with jealous eyes,
And hate for arts that caused himself to rise;
Damn with faint praise, assent with civil leer,
10 And, without sneering, teach the rest to sneer;
Willing to wound, and yet afraid to strike,
Just hint a fault, and hesitate dislike;
Alike reserved to blame, or to commend,
A timorous foe, and a suspicious friend;
Dreading e'en fools, by flatterers besieged,
And so obliging, that he ne'er obliged;
Like Cato, give his little Senate laws,
And sit attentive to his own applause:
While wits and Templars every sentence raise,
20 And wonder with a foolish face of praise—
Who but must laugh, if such a man there be?
Who would not weep, if Atticus were he?

Ezra Pound

Ezra Pound (1885–1972) was born in Idaho, but left as an infant and grew up in the suburbs of Philadelphia. From an early age, he determined to become a great poet and he set out to educate himself to that end. After graduate work at the University of Pennsylvania, he taught briefly at Wabash College in Crawfordsville, Indiana. He was fired when he afforded a night's shelter to a homeless dancing girl and left almost immediately for Europe, where he spent most of the rest of his life. A young man of extraordinary generosity, he discovered or promoted writers as diverse as Lawrence, Eliot, Joyce, and Frost. He was determinedly esthetic. After the First World War killed off many friends—young artists of great promise—he became increasingly embittered about social matters and turned paranoid. This development led to his admiration for Benito Mussolini, the Italian dictator, and to the act of broadcasting on Italian radio to American troops during the Second World War. After the war, he was accused of treason but was judged mentally unfit to stand trial. After many years in St. Elizabeth's Hospital in Washington, DC, under guard, he was released as an old man to return to Italy, where he lived out his long life. See also pages 466 and 511.

The River-Merchant's Wife: A Letter (1915)

While my hair was still cut straight across my forehead
I played about the front gate, pulling flowers.
You came by on bamboo stilts, playing horse,
You walked about my seat, playing with blue plums.
And we went on living in the village of Chokan:
Two small people, without dislike or suspicion.

At fourteen I married My Lord you.
I never laughed, being bashful.
Lowering my head, I looked at the wall.
10 Called to, a thousand times, I never looked back.

At fifteen I stopped scowling,
I desired my dust to be mingled with yours
For ever and for ever and for ever.
Why should I climb the look out?

At sixteen you departed,
You went into far Ku-to-yen, by the river of swirling eddies,
And you have been gone five months.
The monkeys make sorrowful noise overhead.
You dragged your feet when you went out.
20 By the gate now, the moss is grown, the different mosses,
Too deep to clear them away!
The leaves fall early this autumn, in wind.
The paired butterflies are already yellow with August
Over the grass in the West garden;
They hurt me. I grow older.

If you are coming down through the narrows of the river Kiang,
Please let me know beforehand,
And I will come out to meet you
                    As far as Cho-fu-Sa.   (*By Rihaku*)[1]

from Hugh Selwyn Mauberley   (1920)

IV

These fought in any case,
and some believing,
        pro domo,[1] in any case . . .

Some quick to arm,
some for adventure,
some from fear of weakness,
some from fear of censure,
some for love of slaughter, in imagination,
learning later . . .
10   some in fear, learning love of slaughter;

Died some, pro patria,[2]
        non 'dulce' non 'et decor'[3] . . .
walked eye-deep in hell
believing in old men's lies, then unbelieving
came home, home to a lie,
home to many deceits,
home to old lies and new infamy;
usury age-old and age-thick
and liars in public places.

20   Daring as never before, wastage as never before.
Young blood and high blood,
fair cheeks, and fine bodies;

fortitude as never before
frankness as never before,
disillusions as never told in the old days,
hysterias, trench confessions,
laughter out of dead bellies.

---

[1] The Japanese name for Chinese poet Li Po, who wrote the original

[1] In Latin *pro domo* means "for home." Pound is alluding to a poem by the Roman poet Horace, whom he quotes (and later contradicts), who wrote that is is "sweet and fitting" [2] (*Dulce et decor [um]*) to die "for one's country" [3] (*pro patria*). Compare Wilfred Owen's poem on page 662.

V

There died a myriad,
And of the best, among them,
30 For an old bitch gone in the teeth,
For a botched civilization,

Charm, smiling at the good mouth,
Quick eyes gone under earth's lid,

For two gross of broken statues,
For a few thousand battered books.

John Crowe Ransom

John Crowe Ransom (1888–1974) grew up in Tennessee and was a Rhodes Scholar
at Oxford. A leader in the Agrarian movement (a group of Southern writers in the
late 1920s and the 1930s) he went to Kenyon College as a professor in 1937, edited
the highly successful *Kenyon Review,* and wrote criticism as well as poetry.

Captain Carpenter   (1924)

Captain Carpenter rose up in his prime
Put on his pistols and went riding out
But had got wellnigh nowhere at that time
Till he fell in with ladies in a rout.

It was a pretty lady and all her train
That played with him so sweetly but before
An hour she'd taken a sword with all her main
And twined him of his nose for evermore.

Captain Carpenter mounted up one day
10 And rode straightway into a stranger rogue
That looked unchristian but be that as may
The Captain did not wait upon prologue.

But drew upon him out of his great heart
The other swung against him with a club
And cracked his two legs at the shinny part
And let him roll and stick like any tub.
Captain Carpenter rode many a time
From male and female took he sundry harms
He met the wife of Satan crying "I'm
20 The she-wolf bids you shall bear no more arms."

Their strokes and counters whistled in the wind
I wish he had delivered half his blows
But where she should have made off like a hind
The bitch bit off his arms at the elbows.

And Captain Carpenter parted with his ears
To a black devil that used him in this wise
O Jesus ere his threescore and ten years
Another had plucked out his sweet blue eyes.

Captain Carpenter got up on his roan
30 And sallied from the gate in hell's despite
I heard him asking in the grimmest tone
If any enemy yet there was to fight?

"To any adversary it is fame
If he risk to be wounded by my tongue
Or burnt in two beneath my red heart's flame
Such are the perils he is cast among.

"But if he can he has a pretty choice
From an anatomy with little to lose
Whether he cut my tongue and take my voice
40 Or whether it be my round red heart he choose."

It was the neatest knave that ever was seen
Stepping in perfume from his lady's bower
Who at this word put in his merry mien
And fell on Captain Carpenter like a tower.

I would not knock old fellows in the dust
But there lay Captain Carpenter on his back
His weapons were the old heart in his bust
And a blade shook between rotten teeth alack.

The rogue in scarlet and grey soon knew his mind
50 He wished to get his trophy and depart
With gentle apology and touch refined
He pierced him and produced the Captain's heart.

God's mercy rest on Captain Carpenter now
I thought him Sirs an honest gentleman
Citizen husband soldier and scholar enow
Let jangling kites eat of him if they can.

Sir Walter Ralegh

Sir Walter Ralegh (1552?–1618) is the same man who was alleged to have spread his cloak over a puddle that his queen might walk dry-shod. More reliably, we know of Ralegh as adventurer, explorer, and prisoner. He was a man of action who fought in France and who led several voyages to the New World. Three times, on various charges, he was committed to the Tower, where he probably wrote most of his poetry. After a failed expedition to the Orinoco, during which a Spanish colony was raided, Ralegh was executed (a major cause of death among Elizabethan poets). See also page 646.

Verses Written the Night Before His Execution   (1618)

Even such is time, that takes in trust
Our youth, our joys, our all we have,
And pays us but with age and dust;
Who in the dark and silent grave,
When we have wandered all our ways,
Shuts up the story of our days:
But from this earth, this grave, this dust,
My God shall raise me up, I trust.

Liam Rector

Liam Rector (1949–   ) grew up in Virginia and studied at Johns Hopkins University. He has taught at schools and universities, directed the poetry program at the Folger Shakespeare Library, worked for the National Endowment for the Arts, and directed Associated Writing Programs. He now lives in Norfolk, Virginia. His first book of poems, *The Sorrows of Architecture,* appeared in 1984.

Showing   (1984)

They showed up for awhile and they died.
They showed up for some while and they died.
They smoked a few cigarettes and were remembered
by others who showed up and died.
They played the piano; they sat reading.
They had dinner and went to the ocean.
They stared into the hospital they were born into
and they died. They remembered
years which were lost to them
10 unless they concentrated and they died.
All their fear died. All that concern over death
died for a moment and they died. All their curly hair
and the wide sky and their many walks shot up
into a memory remembered
by others who died.
All their photographs and their staring curiosity,
all their wake up and lie down, died. I knock
twice on your door, old boy.

Kenneth Rexroth

Kenneth Rexroth (1905–1982) was born in Indiana and lived for many years in San Francisco, where he was an elder figure behind the Beat Generation. Anarchist in politics and broad in learning, he published essays and translations as well as original poems. See also pages 461–462.

The Signature of All Things   (1949)

My head and shoulders, and my book
In the cool shade, and my body
Stretched bathing in the sun, I lie
Reading beside the waterfall—
Boehme's "Signature of all Things."[1]
Through the deep July day the leaves
Of the laurel, all the colors
Of gold, spin down through the moving
Deep laurel shade all day. They float
10 On the mirrored sky and forest
For a while, and then, still slowly
Spinning, sink through the crystal deep
Of the pool to its leaf gold floor.
The saint saw the world as streaming
In the electrolysis of love.
I put him by and gaze through shade
Folded into shade of slender
Laurel trunks and leaves filled with sun.
The wren broods in her moss domed
20   nest.
A newt struggles with a white moth
Drowning in the pool. The hawks
      scream,
Playing together on the ceiling
Of heaven. The long hours go by.
I think of those who have loved me,
Of all the mountains I have climbed,
Of all the seas I have swum in.
The evil of the world sinks.
30 My own sin and trouble fall away
Like Christian's bundle, and I watch
My forty summers fall like falling
Leaves and falling water held
Eternally in summer air.

Deer are stamping in the glades,
Under the full July moon.
There is a smell of dry grass
In the air, and more faintly,
The scent of a far off skunk.
40 As I stand at the wood's edge,
Watching the darkness, listening
To the stillness, a small owl
Comes to the branch above me,
On wings more still than my breath.
When I turn my light on him,
His eyes glow like drops of iron,
And he perks his head at me,
Like a curious kitten.
The meadow is bright as snow.
50 My dog prowls the grass, a dark
Blur in the blur of brightness.
I walk to the oak grove where
The Indian village was once.
There, in blotched and cobwebbed light
And dark, dim in the blue haze,
Are twenty Holstein heifers,
Black and white, all lying down,
Quietly together, under
The huge trees rooted in the graves.

—

60 When I dragged the rotten log
From the bottom of the pool,
It seemed heavy as stone.
I let it lie in the sun

---

[1] *The Signature of All Things* is one of the major works of German religious mystic writer Jakob Boehme (1575–1624), whose thought influenced such later philosophers as Hegel and Schopenhauer.

For a month; and then chopped it
Into sections, and split them
For kindling, and spread them out
To dry some more. Late that night,
After reading for hours,
While moths rattled at the lamp—
70 The saints and the philosophers
On the destiny of man—
I went out on my cabin porch,

And looked up through the black forest
At the swaying islands of stars.
Suddenly I saw at my feet,
Spread on the floor of night, ingots
Of quivering phosphorescence,
And all about were scattered chips
Of pale cold light that was alive.

Charles Reznikoff

Charles Reznikoff (1894–1975), a leading Objectivist poet, was born in New York City, where he lived most of his life. He wrote poems about the people he observed in the place where he lived. He also wrote some excellent poems out of his reading about American labor history, about the holocaust, and about biblical subjects.

Adrienne Rich

See pages 545–554.

Edwin Arlington Robinson

Edwin Arlington Robinson (1869–1935) was born in Maine, and many of his poems use the background of small towns in New England. Most of his adult life, he spent the summers in New Hampshire at the MacDowell Colony and the rest of the year in a New York apartment. He wrote many book-length poems, some of them on subjects like *Merlin* and *Lancelot*. For most readers, the best of his work is the shorter poems of character and narrative.

Eros Turannos[1]   (1916)

She fears him, and will always ask
   What fated her to choose him;
She meets in his engaging mask
   All reasons to refuse him;
But what she meets and what she fears

Are less than are the downward years,
Drawn slowly to the foamless weirs
   Of age, were she to lose him.

Between a blurred sagacity
10   That once had power to sound him,

---

[1] Love, the Tyrant

And Love, that will not let him be
   The Judas that she found him,
Her pride assuages her almost,
As if it were alone the cost.—
He sees that he will not be lost,
   And waits and looks around him.

A sense of ocean and old trees
   Envelops and allures him;
Tradition, touching all he sees,
20   Beguiles and reassures him;
And all her doubts of what he says
Are dimmed with what she knows of
   days—
Till even prejudice delays
   And fades, and she secures him.

The falling leaf inaugurates
   The reign of her confusion:
The pounding wave reverberates
   The dirge of her illusion;
30 And home, where passion lived and
   died,

Becomes a place where she can hide,
While all the town and harbor side
   Vibrate with her seclusion.

We tell you, tapping on our brows,
   The story as it should be,—
As if the story of a house
   Were told, or ever could be;
We'll have no kindly veil between
40 Her visions and those we have seen,—
As if we guessed what hers have been,
   Or what they are or would be.

Meanwhile we do no harm; for they
   That with a god have striven,
Not hearing much of what we say,
   Take what the god has given;
Though like waves breaking it may be,
Or like a changed familiar tree,
Or like a stairway to the sea
50   Where down the blind are driven.

Mr. Flood's Party (1921)

Old Eben Flood, climbing alone one night
Over the hill between the town below
And the forsaken upland hermitage
That held as much as he should ever know
On earth again of home, paused warily.
The road was his with not a native near;
And Eben, having leisure, said aloud,
For no man else in Tilbury Town to hear:

"Well, Mr. Flood, we have the harvest moon
10 Again, and we may not have many more;
The bird is on the wing, the poet says,
And you and I have said it here before.
Drink to the bird." He raised up to the light
The jug that he had gone so far to fill,
And answered huskily: "Well, Mr. Flood,
Since you propose it, I believe I will."

Alone, as if enduring to the end
A valiant armor of scarred hopes outworn,
He stood there in the middle of the road
20 Like Roland's[1] ghost winding a silent horn.

    [1] A hero of French medieval romances who died, ambushed by Saracens, after summoning
help by blowing his famous horn

Below him, in the town among the trees,
Where friends of other days had honored him,
A phantom salutation of the dead
Rang thinly till old Eben's eyes were dim.

Then, as a mother lays her sleeping child
Down tenderly, fearing it may awake,
He set the jug down slowly at his feet
With trembling care, knowing that most things break;
And only when assured that on firm earth
30　It stood, as the uncertain lives of men
Assuredly did not, he paced away,
And with his hand extended paused again:

"Well, Mr. Flood, we have not met like this
In a long time; and many a change has come
To both of us, I fear, since last it was
We had a drop together. Welcome home!"
Convivially returning with himself,
Again he raised the jug up to the light;
And with an acquiescent quaver said:
40　"Well, Mr. Flood, if you insist, I might.

"Only a very little, Mr. Flood—
For auld lang syne. No more, sir; that will do."
So, for the time, apparently it did,
And Eben evidently thought so too;
For soon amid the silver loneliness
Of night he lifted up his voice and sang,
Secure, with only two moons listening,
Until the whole harmonious landscape rang—
"For auld lang syne." The weary throat gave out,
50　The last word wavered, and the song was done.
He raised again the jug regretfully
And shook his head, and was again alone.
There was not much that was ahead of him,
And there was nothing in the town below—
Where strangers would have shut the many doors
That many friends had opened long ago.

Theodore Roethke

Theodore Roethke (1908–1963) was born in Saginaw, Michigan, where his father kept the greenhouse that figures so prominently in his poems. He attended the University of Michigan and spent his last sixteen years in Seattle, where he was a professor at the University of Washington. He began by writing tight, formal stanzas and later broadened his repertoire to include a wide variety of tones and manners. Possibly no other major poet has traveled so widely in the realms of style. When he died, he had recently written his best work, notably "The Rose."

My Papa's Waltz   (1948)

The whiskey on your breath
Could make a small boy dizzy;
But I hung on like death:
Such waltzing was not easy.

We romped until the pans
Slid from the kitchen shelf;
My mother's countenance
Could not unfrown itself.

10 The hand that held my wrist
Was battered on one knuckle;
At every step you missed
My right ear scraped a buckle.

You beat time on my head
With a palm caked hard by dirt,
Then waltzed me off to bed
Still clinging to your shirt.

The Rose   (1963)

1

There are those to whom place is unimportant,
But this place, where sea and fresh water meet,
Is important—
Where the hawks sway out into the wind,
Without a single wingbeat,
And the eagles sail low over the fir trees,
And the gulls cry against the crows
In the curved harbors,
And the tide rises up against the grass
10 Nibbled by sheep and rabbits.
A time for watching the tide,
For the heron's hieratic fishing,
For the sleepy cries of the towhee,
The morning birds gone, the twittering finches,
But still the flash of the kingfisher, the wingbeat of the scoter,
The sun a ball of fire coming down over the water,
The last geese crossing against the reflected afterlight,
The moon retreating into a vague cloud-shape
To the cries of the owl, the eerie whooper.
20 The old log subsides with the lessening waves,
And there is silence.

I sway outside myself
Into the darkening currents,

Into the small spillage of driftwood,
The waters swirling past the tiny headlands.
Was it here I wore a crown of birds for a moment
While on a far point of the rocks
The light heightened,
And below, in a mist out of nowhere,
30 The first rain gathered?

2

As when a ship sails with a light wind—
The waves less than the ripples made by rising fish,
The lacelike wrinkles of the wake widening, thinning out,
Sliding away from the traveler's eye,
The prow pitching easily up and down,
The whole ship rolling slightly sideways,
The stern high, dipping like a child's boat in a pond—
Our motion continues.

But this rose, this rose in the sea-wind,
40 Stays,
Stays in its true place,
Flowering out of the dark,
Widening at high noon, face upward,
A single wild rose, struggling out of the white embrace of the morning-glory,
Out of the briary hedge, the tangle of matted underbrush,
Beyond the clover, the ragged hay,
Beyond the sea pine, the oak, the wind-tipped madrona,
Moving with the waves, the undulating driftwood,
Where the slow creek winds down to the black sand of the shore
50 With its thick grassy scum and crabs scuttling back into their glistening craters.

And I think of roses, roses,
White and red, in the wide six-hundred-foot greenhouses,
And my father standing astride the cement benches,
Lifting me high over the four-foot stems, the Mrs. Russells, and his own elaborate
     hybrids.
And how those flowerheads seemed to flow toward me, to beckon me, only a child,
     out of myself.

What need for heaven, then,
With that man, and those roses?

3

60 What do they tell us, sound and silence?
I think of American sounds in this silence:
On the banks of the Tombstone, the wind-harps having their say,
The thrush singing alone, that easy bird,
The killdeer whistling away from me,
The mimetic chortling of the catbird
Down in the corner of the garden, among the raggedy lilacs,

The bobolink skirring from a broken fencepost,
The bluebird, lover of holes in old wood, lilting its light song,
And that thin cry, like a needle piercing the ear, the insistent cicada,
70 And the ticking of snow around oil drums in the Dakotas,
The thin whine of telephone wires in the wind of a Michigan winter,
The shriek of nails as old shingles are ripped from the top of a roof,
The bulldozer backing away, the hiss of the sandblaster,
And the deep chorus of horns coming up from the streets in early morning.
I return to the twittering of swallows above water,
And that sound, that single sound,
When the mind remembers all,
And gently the light enters the sleeping soul,
A sound so thin it could not woo a bird,

80 Beautiful my desire, and the place of my desire.

I think of the rock singing, and light making its own silence,
At the edge of a ripening meadow, in early summer,
The moon lolling in the close elm, a shimmer of silver,
Or that lonely time before the breaking of morning
When the slow freight winds along the edge of the ravaged hillside,
And the wind tries the shape of a tree,
While the moon lingers,
And a drop of rain water hangs at the tip of a leaf
Shifting in the wakening sunlight
90 Like the eye of a new-caught fish.

4

I live with the rocks, their weeds,
Their filmy fringes of green, their harsh
Edges, their holes
Cut by the sea-slime, far from the crash
Of the long swell,
The oily, tar-laden walls
Of the toppling waves,
Where the salmon ease their way into the kelp beds,
And the sea rearranges itself among the small islands.
100 Near this rose, in this grove of sun-parched, wind-warped madronas,
Among the half-dead trees, I came upon the true ease of myself,
As if another man appeared out of the depths of my being,
And I stood outside myself,
Beyond becoming and perishing,
A something wholly other,
As if I swayed out on the wildest wave alive,
And yet was still.
And I rejoiced in being what I was:
In the lilac change, the white reptilian calm,
110 In the bird beyond the bough, the single one
With all the air to greet him as he flies,
The dolphin rising from the darkening waves;

And in this rose, this rose in the sea-wind,
Rooted in stone, keeping the whole of light,
Gathering to itself sound and silence—
Mine and the sea-wind's.

The Meadow Mouse (1963)

1

In a shoe box stuffed in an old nylon stocking
Sleeps the baby mouse I found in the meadow,
Where he trembled and shook beneath a stick
Till I caught him up by the tail and brought him in,
Cradled in my hand,
A little quaker, the whole body of him trembling,
His absurd whiskers sticking out like a cartoon-mouse,
His feet like small leaves,
Little lizard-feet,
10   Whitish and spread wide when he tried to struggle away,
Wriggling like a miniscule puppy.

Now he's eaten his three kinds of cheese and drunk from his bottle-cap
        watering-trough—
So much he just lies in one corner,
His tail curled under him, his belly big
As his head: his bat-like ears
Twitching, tilting toward the least sound.

Do I imagine he no longer trembles
When I come close to him?
20   He seems no longer to tremble.

2

But this morning the shoe-box house on the back porch is empty.
Where has he gone, my meadow mouse,
My thumb of a child that nuzzled in my palm?—
To run under the hawk's wing,
Under the eye of the great owl watching from the elm-tree,
To live by courtesy of the shrike, the snake, the tom-cat.

I think of the nestling fallen into the deep grass,
The turtle gasping in the dusty rubble of the highway,
The paralytic stunned in the tub, and the water rising,—
30   All things innocent, hapless, forsaken.

Carl Sandburg

Carl Sandburg (1878–1967) became known as a poet in 1914, when *Poetry* published "Chicago," later reprinted in *Chicago Poems*. Deriving from Whitman, populist, a celebrator of the commonplace, Sandburg was a popular poet who became the biographer of Abraham Lincoln (six volumes, awarded a Pulitzer Prize in 1939) and toward the end of his life the author of a long novel called *Remembrance Rock*.

Chicago   (1916)

Hog Butcher for the World,
Tool Maker, Stacker of Wheat,
Player with Railroads and the Nation's Freight Handler;
Stormy, husky, brawling,
City of the Big Shoulders:
They tell me you are wicked and I believe them, for I have seen your painted
    women under the gas lamps luring the farm boys.
And they tell me you are crooked and I answer: Yes, it is true I have seen the
    gunman kill and go free to kill again.
10 And they tell me you are brutal and my reply is: On the faces of women and
    children I have seen the marks of wanton hunger.
And having answered so I turn once more to those who sneer at this my city, and I
    give them back the sneer and say to them:
Come and show me another city with lifted head singing so proud to be alive and
    coarse and strong and cunning.
Flinging magnetic curses amid the toil of piling job on job, here is a tall bold
    slugger set vivid against the little soft cities;
Fierce as a dog with tongue lapping for action, cunning as a savage pitted against
    the wilderness,
20   Bareheaded,
        Shoveling,
        Wrecking,
        Planning,
        Building, breaking, rebuilding,
Under the smoke, dust all over his mouth, laughing with white teeth,
Under the terrible burden of destiny laughing as a young man laughs,
Laughing even as an ignorant fighter laughs who has never lost a battle,
Bragging and laughing that under his wrist is the pulse, and under his ribs the heart
    of the people,
30   Laughing!
Laughing the stormy, husky, brawling laughter of Youth, half-naked, sweating, proud
    to be Hog Butcher, Tool Maker, Stacker of Wheat, Player with Railroads and
    Freight Handler to the Nation.

Yvonne Sapia

Yvonne Sapia (1946–   ) was born in New York City and moved to Florida when she was ten. She has published two collections of her poetry, *The Fertile Crescent* (1983) and *Valentino's Hair* (1987). She teaches at Lake City Community College in Florida.

Vikram Seth

Vikram Seth (1952–   ), born in India, has spent much of his life in England, the United States, and China. He is an economist as well as a poet and essayist. He has written a novel in verse called *The Golden Gate* (1987), and two collections of briefer poems—*The Humble Administrator's Garden* (1985) and *All You Who Sleep Tonight* (1990).

Anne Sexton

Anne Sexton (1928–1974) did not begin to write poems until she was in her late twenties, attending poetry workshops. Then she wrote prolifically and with great energy for many years, combating psychosis and an urge to suicide. Her books include *To Bedlam and Part Way Back* (1960), *Live or Die* (1967), and *The Awful Rowing Towards God* (1975).

Wanting to Die   (1966)

Since you ask, most days I cannot remember.
I walk in my clothing, unmarked by that voyage.
Then the almost unnameable lust returns.

Even then I have nothing against life.
I know well the grass blades you mention,
the furniture you have placed under the sun.

But suicides have a special language.
Like carpenters they want to know *which tools*.
They never ask *why build*.

10   Twice I have so simply declared myself,
have possessed the enemy, eaten the enemy,
have taken on his craft, his magic.

In this way, heavy and thoughtful,
warmer than oil or water,
I have rested, drooling at the mouth-hole.

I did not think of my body at needle point.
Even the cornea and the leftover urine were gone.
Suicides have already betrayed the body.

Still-born, they don't always die,
20 but dazzled, they can't forget a drug so sweet
that even children would look on and smile.

To thrust all that life under your tongue!—
that, all by itself, becomes a passion.
Death's a sad bone; bruised, you'd say,

and yet she waits for me, year after year,
to so delicately undo an old wound,
to empty my breath from its bad prison.

Balanced there, suicides sometimes meet,
raging at the fruit, a pumped-up moon,
30 leaving the bread they mistook for a kiss,
leaving the page of the book carelessly open,
something unsaid, the phone off the hook
and the love, whatever it was, an infection.

William Shakespeare

For a note on William Shakespeare, see page 798. For other poems, see pages 442, 445, and 509.

They that have power to hurt and will do none   (1609)

They that have power to hurt and will do none,
That do not do the thing they most do show,
Who, moving others, are themselves as stone,
Unmoved, cold, and to temptation slow,—
They rightly do inherit heaven's graces
And husband nature's riches from expense;
They are the lords and owners of their faces,
Others but stewards of their excellence.
The summer's flower is to the summer sweet,
10 Though to itself it only live and die:
But if that flower with base infection meet,
The basest weed outbraves his dignity:
   For sweetest things turn sourest by their deeds;
   Lilies that fester smell far worse than weeds.

Percy Bysshe Shelley

Percy Bysshe Shelley (1792–1822) was expelled from Oxford in 1811 for writing
a pamphlet in defense of atheism. That year he married his first wife, who was
sixteen, from whom he separated three years later. She killed herself. He married
Mary Wollstonecraft—author of *Frankenstein*—in 1814 and spent much of the
rest of his life in Italy. He was friendly with Byron and acquainted with Keats. In
Italy, in the last three years of his life, he wrote his best poems, including "Ode
to the West Wind." On July 8, 1822, he was shipwrecked in a storm while sailing
off the Italian coast and drowned.

Ode to the West Wind   (1820)

1

O wild West Wind, thou breath of Autumn's being,
Thou, from whose unseen presence the leaves dead
Are driven, like ghosts from an enchanter fleeing,
Yellow, and black, and pale, and hectic red,
Pestilence-striken multitudes: O thou,
Who chariotest to their dark wintry bed

The wingèd seeds, where they lie cold and low,
Each like a corpse within its grave, until
Thine azure sister of the Spring shall blow

10 Her clarion o'er the dreaming earth, and fill
(Driving sweet buds like flocks to feed in air)
With living hues and odours plain and hill:

Wild Spirit, which art moving everywhere;
Destroyer and preserver; hear, oh, hear!

2

Thou on whose stream, 'mid the steep sky's commotion,
Loose clouds like earth's decaying leaves are shed,
Shook from the tangled boughs of Heaven and Ocean,

Angels of rain and lightning: there are spread
On the blue surface of thine airy surge,
20 Like the bright hair uplifted from the head

Of some fierce Mænad, even from the dim verge
Of the horizon to the zenith's height,
The locks of the approaching storm. Thou dirge

Of the dying year, to which this closing night
Will be the dome of a vast sepulchre,
Vaulted with all thy congregated might

Of vapours, from whose solid atmosphere
Black rain, and fire, and hail will burst: oh, hear!

3

Thou who didst waken from his summer dreams
30 The blue Mediterranean, where he lay,
Lulled by the coil of his crystálline streams,

Beside a pumice isle in Baiæ's bay,
And saw in sleep old palaces and towers
Quivering within the wave's intenser day,

All overgrown with azure moss and flowers
So sweet, the sense faints picturing them! Thou
For whose path the Atlantic's level powers
Cleave themselves into chasms, while far below
The sea-blooms and the oozy woods which wear
40 The sapless foliage of the ocean, know

Thy voice, and suddenly grow gray with fear,
And tremble and despoil themselves: oh, hear!

4

If I were a dead leaf thou mightest bear;
If I were a swift cloud to fly with thee;
A wave to pant beneath thy power, and share

The impulse of thy strength, only less free
Than thou, O uncontrollable! If even
I were as in my boyhood, and could be

The comrade of thy wanderings over Heaven,
50 As then, when to outstrip thy skyey speed
Scarce seemed a vision; I would ne'er have striven

As thus with thee in prayer in my sore need.
Oh, lift me as a wave, a leaf, a cloud!
I fall upon the thorns of life! I bleed!

A heavy weight of hours has chained and bowed
One too like thee: tameless, and swift, and proud.

5

Make me thy lyre, even as the forest is:
What if my leaves are falling like its own!
The tumult of thy mighty harmonies

60 Will take from both a deep, autumnal tone,
Sweet though in sadness. Be thou, Spirit fierce,
My spirit! Be thou me, impetuous one!

Drive my dead thoughts over the universe
Like withered leaves to quicken a new birth!
And, by the incantation of this verse,

Scatter, as from an unextinguished hearth
Ashes and sparks, my words among mankind!
Be through my lips to unawakened earth

The trumpet of a prophecy! O, wind,
70 If Winter comes, can Spring be far behind?

Sir Philip Sidney

Sir Philip Sidney (1554–1586) died fighting for England against Spain, and none
of his considerable work appeared until after his death. In his generation he was
widely admired and became the subject of several elegies, most notably
Spenser's. He was loved not only for his talent and his intelligence but also for
the nobility of his character. According to legend, while he was dying he refused
a cup of water, sending it to the wounded man beside him, claiming "Thy
necessity is greater than mine."

from Astrophel and Stella   (1591)

With how sad steps, O Moon! thou climb'st the skies!
How silently, and with how wan a face!
What! may it be, that even in heavenly place
That busy archer° his sharp arrows tries?   Cupid
Sure, if that long-with-love-acquainted eyes
Can judge of love, thou feel'st a lover's case;
I read it in thy looks; thy languish'd grace,
To me that feel the like, thy state descries.
Then, even of fellowship, O Moon, tell me,
10 Is constant love deem'd there but want of wit?
Are beauties there as proud as here they be?
Do they above love to be loved, and yet
    Those lovers scorn whom that love doth possess?
    Do they call virtue there ungratefulness?

Leslie Marmon Silko*

Where Mountain Lion Lay Down with Deer   (1973)

I climb the black rock mountain
    stepping from day to day
                    silently.

* For a note on Silko, see page 357.

I smell the wind for my ancestors
      pale blue leaves
       crushed wild mountain smell.
Returning
    up the gray stone cliff
    where I descended
10   a thousand years ago.
Returning to faded black stone.
    where mountain lion lay down with deer.
It is better to stay up here
          watching wind's reflection
          in tall yellow flowers.
The old ones who remember me are gone
      the old songs are all forgotten
and the story of my birth.
How I danced in snow-frost moonlight
20   distant stars to the end of the Earth,
How I swam away
       in freezing mountain water
       narrow mossy canyon tumbling down
          out of the mountain
            out of the deep canyon stone
     down
       the memory
          spilling out
          into the world.

Charles Simic

Charles Simic (1938–   ) was born in Yugoslavia and came to the United States in 1949. He lives in New Hampshire and has published many books of poems. *The World Doesn't End* (1989) received the Pulitzer Prize in 1990, when he published his most recent volume, *Gods and Devils*.

Fork   (1971)

This strange thing must have crept
Right out of hell.
It resembles a bird's foot
Worn around the cannibal's neck.

As you hold it in your hand,
As you stab with it into a piece of meat,
It is possible to imagine the rest of the bird:
Its head which like your fist
Is large, bald, beakless and blind.

Shelley   (1990)
for M. Follain

Poet of the dead leaves driven like ghosts,
Driven like pestilence-stricken multitudes,
I read you first
One rainy evening in New York City,

In my atrocious Slavic accent,
Saying the mellifluous verses
From a battered, much-stained volume
I had bought earlier that day
In a second-hand bookstore on Fourth Avenue
10 Run by an initiate of the occult masters.

The little money I had being almost spent,
I walked the streets my nose in the book.
I sat in a dingy coffee shop
With last summer's dead flies on the table.
The owner was an ex-sailor
Who had grown a huge hump on his back
While watching the rain, the empty street.
He was glad to have me sit and read.
He'd refill my cup with a liquid dark as river Styx.

20 Shelley spoke of a mad, blind, dying king;
Of rulers who neither see, nor feel, nor know;
Of graves from which a glorious Phantom may
Burst to illumine our tempestuous day.

I too felt like a glorious phantom
Going to have my dinner
In a Chinese restaurant I knew so well.
It had a three-fingered waiter
Who'd bring my soup and rice each night
Without ever saying a word.

30 I never saw anyone else there.
The kitchen was separated by a curtain
Of glass beads which clicked faintly
Whenever the front door opened.
The front door opened that evening
To admit a pale little girl with glasses.

The poet spoke of the everlasting universe
Of things . . . of gleams of a remoter world
Which visit the soul in sleep . . .
Of a desert peopled by storms alone . . .

40 The streets were strewn with broken umbrellas
Which looked like funereal kites

This little Chinese girl might have made.
The bars on MacDougal Street were emptying.
There had been a fist fight.
A man leaned against a lamp post arms extended
    as if crucified,
The rain washing the blood off his face.

In a dimly lit side street,
Where the sidewalk shone like a ballroom mirror
50 At closing time—
A well-dressed man without any shoes
Asked me for money.
His eyes shone, he looked triumphant
Like a fencing master
Who had just struck a mortal blow.

How strange it all was . . . The world's raffle
That dark October night . . .
The yellowed volume of poetry
With its Splendors and Glooms
60 Which I studied by the light of storefronts:
Drugstores and barbershops,
Afraid of my small windowless room
Cold as a tomb of an infant emperor.

Louis Simpson

Louis Simpson (1923–   ) was born in Jamaica and grew up there, coming to
the United States when he was seventeen. He left Columbia College to enter
the U.S. Army during the Second World War and received his citizenship at
Berchtesgaden. He has published a novel, a textbook, several volumes of
criticism, and numerous books of poems. *At the End of the Open Road* (1963)
won a Pulitzer Prize. His *Collected Poems* appeared in 1988, and a *Selected Prose*
in 1989. See also pages 489–490 and 492.

Walt Whitman at Bear Mountain   (1960)

". . . life which does not give the preference to any other life, of any previous
period, which therefore prefers its own existence . . ."

—*Ortega y Gasset*

Neither on horseback nor seated,
But like himself, squarely on two feet,
The poet of death and lilacs
Loafs by the footpath. Even the bronze looks alive
Where it is folded like cloth. And he seems friendly.

'Where is the Mississippi panorama
And the girl who played the piano?
Where are you, Walt?
The Open Road goes to the used-car lot.

10 'Where is the nation you promised?
These houses built of wood sustain
Colossal snows,
And the light above the street is sick to death.

'As for the people—see how they neglect you!
Only a poet pauses to read the inscription.'

'I am here,' he answered.
'It seems you have found me out.
Yet, did I not warn you that it was Myself
I advertised? Were my words not sufficiently plain?

20 'I gave no prescriptions,
And those who have taken my moods for prophecies
Mistake the matter.'
Then, vastly amused—'Why do you reproach me?
I freely confess I am wholly disreputable.
Yet I am happy, because you have found me out.'

A crocodile in wrinkled metal loafing . . .

Then all the realtors,
Pickpockets, salesmen, and the actors performing
Official scenarios,
30 Turned a deaf ear, for they had contracted
American dreams.

But the man who keeps a store on a lonely road,
And the housewife who knows she's dumb,
And the earth, are relieved.

All that grave weight of America
Cancelled! Like Greece and Rome.
The future in ruins!
The castles, the prisons, the cathedrals
Unbuilding, and roses
40 Blossoming from the stones that are not there . . .

The clouds are lifting from the high Sierras,
The Bay mists clearing;
And the angel in the gate, the flowering plum,
Dances like Italy, imagining red.

In the Suburbs   (1963)

There's no way out.
You were born to waste your life.
You were born to this middleclass life

As others before you
Were born to walk in procession
To the temple, singing.

Christopher Smart

Christopher Smart (1722–1771) wrote the long poem excerpted below when he
was insane. It was his habit, in his madness, to go down on his knees in a crowded
street and ask other people to pray with him. Samuel Johnson, apprised of Smart's
eccentricities, avowed that he would as soon pray with Kit Smart as with any man.

from Jubilate Agno[1]   (1763)

For I will consider my Cat Jeoffry.
For he is the servant of the Living God, duly and daily serving him.
For at the first glance of the glory of God in the East he worships in his way.
For is this done by wreathing his body seven times round with elegant
    quickness.
For then he leaps up to catch the musk,° which is the blessing of   catnip (?)
    God upon his prayer.
For he rolls upon prank to work it in.
For having done duty and received blessing he begins to consider himself.
10 For this he performs in ten degrees.
For first he looks upon his fore-paws to see if they are clean.
For secondly he kicks up behind to clear away there.
For thirdly he works it upon stretch with the fore-paws extended.
For fourthly he sharpens his paws by wood.
For fifthly he washes himself.
For sixthly he rolls upon wash.
For seventhly he fleas himself, that he may not be interrupted upon the beat.
For eighthly he rubs himself against a post.
For ninthly he looks up for his instructions.
20 For tenthly he goes in quest of food.
For having considered God and himself he will consider his neighbor.
For if he meets another cat he will kiss her in kindness.
For when he takes his prey he plays with it to give it chance.
For one mouse in seven escapes by his dallying.
For when his day's work is done his business more properly begins.

[1] Rejoice in the Lamb

For he keeps the Lord's watch in the night against the adversary.
For he counteracts the powers of darkness by his electrical skin and glaring
    eyes.
For he counteracts the Devil, who is death, by brisking about the life.
30 For in his morning orisons he loves the sun and the sun loves him.
For he is of the tribe of Tiger.
For the Cherub Cat is a term of the Angel Tiger.
For he has the subtlety and hissing of a serpent, which in goodness he
    suppresses.
For he will not do destruction if he is well-fed, neither will he spit without
    provocation.
For he purrs in thankfulness, when God tells him he's a good Cat.
For he is an instrument for the children to learn benevolence upon.
For every house is incomplete without him and a blessing is lacking in the
40   spirit.
For the Lord commanded Moses concerning the cats at the departure of the
    Children of Israel from Egypt.
For every family had one cat at least in the bag.
For the English Cats are the best in Europe.

W. D. Snodgrass

William DeWitt Snodgrass (1926–   ) was born in Pennsylvania and attended
the Writer's Workshop at Iowa, where he wrote his first book, *Heart's Needle*
(1959), which won the 1960 Pulitzer Prize. Credited by Robert Lowell with the
invention of confessional verse, Snodgrass in his own work has moved on to the
dramatic monologue. In 1987 he published his *Selected Poems*.

Lobsters in the Window   (1963)

First, you think they are dead.
Then you are almost sure
One is beginning to stir.
Out of the crushed ice, slow
As the hands of a schoolroom clock,
He lifts his one great claw
And holds it over his head;
Now, he is trying to walk.

But like a run-down toy;
10 Like the backward crabs we boys
Splashed after in the creek,
Trapped in jars or a net,
And then took home to keep.
Overgrown, retarded, weak,
He is fumbling yet
From the deep chill of his sleep

As if, in a glacial thaw
Some ancient thing might wake
Sore and cold and stiff
20 Struggling to raise one claw
Like a defiant fist;
Yet wavering, as if
Starting to swell and ache
With that thick peg in the wrist.

I should wave back, I guess.
But still in his permanent clench
He's fallen back with the mass
Heaped in their common trench
Who stir, but do not look out
30 Through the rainstreaming glass,
Hear what the newsboys shout,
Or see the raincoats pass.

Gary Snyder

Gary Snyder (1930–   ) grew up on the West Coast and attended Reed College. He did graduate work in Oriental languages at Berkeley and has lived many years in Japan, studying Zen Buddhism in Kyoto. Now he lives in a house of his own construction called Kitkitdizze, north of Sacramento, and practices the life he preaches. See also page 455.

Above Pate Valley   (1959)

We finished clearing the last
Section of trail by noon,
High on the ridge-side
Two thousand feet above the creek—
Reached the pass, went on
Beyond the white pine groves,
Granite shoulders, to a small
Green meadow watered by the snow,
Edged with Aspen—sun
10 Straight high and blazing
But the air was cool.
Ate a cold fried trout in the
Trembling shadows. I spied
A glitter, and found a flake

Black volcanic glass—obsidian—
By a flower. Hands and knees
Pushing the Bear grass, thousands
Of arrowhead leavings over a
Hundred yards. Not one good
20 Head, just razor flakes
On a hill snowed all but summer,
A land of fat summer deer.
They came to camp. On their
Own trails. I followed my own
Trail here. Picked up the cold-drill,
Pick, singlejack, and sack
Of dynamite.
Ten thousand years.

Cathy Song

Cathy Song (1955–   ) lives in Honolulu, Hawaii, where she was born. A graduate of Wellesley College and Boston University, she has published two collections of her poems. *Picture Bride* appeared in the Yale Younger Poets Series in 1983, and *Frameless Windows, Square of Light* in 1988.

A Small Light   (1988)

When the man comes home he takes off his hat
and looks up at the leaves of the tree.
The light annoints each leaf as it sinks into the sea.
The tree shimmers like a thousand mirrors,
the suddenness of birds in flight.
A child is sleeping in the house.
The house rises and falls with each breath
as if the house were made of cloth.
Tacked to the walls is the sound of the clock
10 which keeps the house from floating away.
A curtain divides the bed and the sink.
A woman lies on the bed and feels

the house fall into itself, the window fill with leaves.
Her body fills with sleep
as if sleep were a dream of water.
The sound of the clock grows smaller
like a light in a window you pass at night.
The child opens her eyes to a dream of water.
A web in the window is sunlight
20 seen from the inside of water.
Floating in the window, it is barely there,
like her breath, like hair.
She understands what can't be seen
can still be broken.
She holds her breath as though her breath
could break. When the tree hauls its leaves
in shadows across the room,
the web stretches like an accordian,
but silent, elastic, made of skin.
30 A dead stream is a river of leaves.
All day the wind stirs a parched soup,
a kindling of matchsticks and leaves,
the size of the child's hand.
Some part of the tree is always dying.
Somewhere it is always raining leaves
and a child, closing the door on the falling
walls of a house, walks away,
her slight dress sinking into the dry river,
hair, a small light, touching each leaf.

Robert Southwell

Robert Southwell (1561?–1595), a Catholic, wrote most of his devotional poetry
in prison, where he was tortured and finally executed.

The Burning Babe   (1592)

As I in hoary winter's night stood shivering in the snow,
Surprised I was with sudden heat, which made my heart to glow;
And lifting up a fearful eye to view what fire was near,
A pretty Babe all burning bright, did in the air appear,
Who scorchèd with excessive heat, such floods of tears did shed,
As though His floods should quench His flames which with His tears were fed;
Alas! quoth He, but newly born, in fiery heats I fry,
Yet none approach to warm their hearts or feel my fire but I!
My faultless breast the furnace is, the fuel wounding thorns,
10 Love is the fire, and sighs the smoke, the ashes shame and scorns;
The fuel Justice layeth on, and Mercy blows the coals,
The metal in this furnace wrought are men's defilèd souls,

For which, as now on fire I am to work them to their good,
So will I melt into a bath to wash them in My blood:
With this He vanished out of sight, and swiftly shrank away,
And straight I callèd unto mind that it was Christmas-day.

William Stafford

William Stafford (1914–   ) was born in Kansas and has lived most of his life in the Pacific Northwest. His *Stories That Could Be True: Poems New and Collected* appeared in 1977, only fifteen years after his first collection, *Travelling Through the Dark,* won the National Book Award. His poetry is quiet, reticent, reserved, compassionate, and ultimately happy.

Travelling Through the Dark   (1960)

Travelling through the dark I found a deer
dead on the edge of the Wilson River road.
It is usually best to roll them into the canyon:
that road is narrow; to swerve might make more dead.

By glow of the tail-light I stumbled back of the car
and stood by the heap, a doe, a recent killing;
she had stiffened already, almost cold.
I dragged her off; she was large in the belly.

My fingers touching her side brought me the reason—
10   her side was warm; her fawn lay there waiting,
alive, still, never to be born.
Beside that mountain road I hesitated.

The car aimed ahead its lowered parking lights;
under the hood purred the steady engine.
I stood in the glare of the warm exhaust turning red;
around our group I could hear the wilderness listen.

I thought hard for us all—my only swerving—,
then pushed her over the edge into the river.

Wallace Stevens

Wallace Stevens (1879–1955) is one of the finest of American poets. He attended
Harvard, tried his luck as a journalist, and went to New York University Law School.
After practicing some years in New York City, he took a job with the legal
department of Hartford Accident and Indemnity, an insurance company, and
eventually moved to Hartford, thus becoming known as "the insurance man who is
a poet." His poetry has a delicacy, a Frenchified elegance, and a nice concern for
matters epistemological. There seemed to be a clear and sustained break between
the poetry he wrote and the life he lived. Perhaps they came together in Florida,
which like many Connecticut businessmen he visited and which entered his poems
as a place of unsurpassable bright lushness. See also page 420.

The Emperor of Ice-Cream   (1922)

Call the roller of big cigars,
The muscular one, and bid him whip
In kitchen cups concupiscent curds.
Let the wenches dawdle in such dress
As they are used to wear, and let the boys
Bring flowers in last month's newspapers.
Let be be finale of seem.
The only emperor is the emperor of ice-cream.

Take from the dresser of deal,
10 Lacking the three glass knobs, that sheet
On which she embroidered fantails once
And spread it so as to cover her face.
If her horny feet protrude, they come
To show how cold she is, and dumb.
Let the lamp affix its beam.
The only emperor is the emperor of ice-cream.

The Snow Man   (1921)

One must have a mind of winter
To regard the frost and the boughs
Of the pine-trees crusted with snow;

And have been cold a long time
To behold the junipers shagged with ice,
The spruces rough in the distant glitter

Of the January sun; and not to think
Of any misery in the sound of the wind,
In the sound of a few leaves,

10 Which is the sound of the land
Full of the same wind
That is blowing in the same bare place

For the listener, who listens in the snow,
And, nothing himself, beholds
Nothing that is not there and the nothing that is.

Sunday Morning   (1915)

I

Complacencies of the peignoir, and late
Coffee and oranges in a sunny chair,
And the green freedom of a cockatoo
Upon a rug mingle to dissipate
The holy hush of ancient sacrifice.
She dreams a little, and she feels the dark
Encroachment of that old catastrophe,
As a calm darkens among water-lights.
The pungent oranges and bright, green wings
10 Seem things in some procession of the dead,
Winding across wide water, without sound.
The day is like wide water, without sound,
Stilled for the passing of her dreaming feet
Over the seas, to silent Palestine,
Dominion of the blood and sepulchre.

II

Why should she give her bounty to the dead?
What is divinity if it can come
Only in silent shadows and in dreams?
Shall she not find in comforts of the sun,
20 In pungent fruit and bright, green wings, or else
In any balm or beauty of the earth,
Things to be cherished like the thought of heaven?
Divinity must live within herself:
Passions of rain, or moods in falling snow;
Grievings in loneliness, or unsubdued
Elations when the forest blooms; gusty
Emotions on wet roads on autumn nights;
All pleasures and all pains, remembering
The bough of summer and the winter branch.
30 These are the measures destined for her soul.

III

Jove in the clouds had his inhuman birth.
No mother suckled him, no sweet land gave
Large-mannered motions to his mythy mind
He moved among us, as a muttering king,
Magnificent, would move among his hinds,
Until our blood, commingling, virginal,
With heaven, brought such requital to desire
The very hinds discerned it, in a star.

Shall our blood fail? Or shall it come to be
40 The blood of paradise? And shall the earth
Seem all of paradise that we shall know?
The sky will be much friendlier then than now,
A part of labor and a part of pain,
And next in glory to enduring love,
Not this dividing and indifferent blue.

IV

She says, "I am content when wakened birds,
Before they fly, test the reality
Of misty fields, by their sweet questionings;
But when the birds are gone, and their warm fields
50 Return no more, where, then, is paradise?"
There is not any haunt of prophecy,
Nor any old chimera of the grave,
Neither the golden underground, nor isle
Melodious, where spirits gat them home,
Nor visionary south, nor cloudy palm
Remote on heaven's hill, that has endured
As April's green endures; or will endure
Like her remembrance of awakened birds,
Or her desire for June and evening, tipped
60 By the consummation of the swallow's wings.

V

She says, "But in contentment I still feel
The need of some imperishable bliss."
Death is the mother of beauty; hence from her,
Alone, shall come fulfilment to our dreams
And our desires. Although she strews the leaves
Of sure obliteration on our paths,
The path sick sorrow took, the many paths
Where triumph rang its brassy phrase, or love
Whispered a little out of tenderness,
70 She makes the willow shiver in the sun
For maidens who were wont to sit and gaze
Upon the grass, relinquished to their feet.
She causes boys to pile new plums and pears
On disregarded plate. The maidens taste
And stray impassioned in the littering leaves.

VI

Is there no change of death in paradise?
Does ripe fruit never fall? Or do the boughs
Hang always heavy in that perfect sky,
Unchanging, yet so like our perishing earth,
80 With rivers like our own that seek for seas

They never find, the same receding shores
That never touch with inarticulate pang?
Why set the pear upon those river-banks
Or spice the shores with odors of the plum?
Alas, that they should wear our colors there,
The silken weavings of our afternoons,
And pick the strings of our insipid lutes!
Death is the mother of beauty, mystical,
Within whose burning bosom we devise
90   Our earthly mothers waiting, sleeplessly.

VII

Supple and turbulent, a ring of men
Shall chant in orgy on a summer morn
Their boisterous devotion to the sun,
Not as a god, but as a god might be,
Naked among them, like a savage source.
Their chant shall be a chant of paradise,
Out of their blood, returning to the sky;
And in their chant shall enter, voice by voice,
The windy lake wherein their lord delights,
100   The trees, like serafin, and echoing hills,
That choir among themselves long afterward.
They shall know well the heavenly fellowship
Of men that perish and of summer morn.
And whence they came and whither they shall go
The dew upon their feet shall manifest.

VIII

She hears, upon that water without sound,
A voice that cries, "The tomb in Palestine
Is not the porch of spirits lingering.
It is the grave of Jesus, where he lay."
110   We live in an old chaos of the sun,
Or old dependency of day and night,
Or island solitude, unsponsored, free,
Of that wide water, inescapable.
Deer walk upon our mountains, and the quail
Whistle about us their spontaneous cries;
Sweet berries ripen in the wilderness;
And, in the isolation of the sky,
At evening, casual flocks of pigeons make
Ambiguous undulations as they sink,
120   Downward to darkness, on extended wings.

Mark Strand

Mark Strand (1934–   ) was born in Canada and went to college in the United
States, where he has settled. He lives in Salt Lake City and teaches at the
University of Utah. In 1990–1991 he was Poet Laureate of the United States and,
in 1990, republished his *Selected Poems* as well as a new collection called *The
Continuous Life*. He has also written books of art criticism, short stories, and
children's books.

Always   (1990)
for Charles Simic

Always so late in the day
In their rumpled clothes, sitting
Around a table lit by a single bulb,
The great forgetters were hard at work.
They tilted their heads to one side, closing their eyes.
Then a house disappeared, and a man in his yard
With all his flowers in a row.
The great forgetters wrinkled their brows.
Then Florida went and San Francisco
10 Where tugs and barges leave
Small gleaming scars across the Bay.
One of the great forgetters struck a match.
Gone were the harps of beaded lights
That vault the rivers of New York.
Another filled his glass
And that was it for crowds at evening
Under sulphur yellow streetlamps coming on.
And afterwards Bulgaria was gone, and then Japan.
"Where will it stop?" one of them said.
20 "Such difficult work, pursuing the fate
Of everything known," said another.
"Down to the last stone," said a third,
"And only the cold zero of perfection
Left for the imagination." And gone
Were North and South America,
And gone as well the moon.
Another yawned, another gazed at the window:
No grass, no trees . . .
The blaze of promise everywhere.

The End   (1990)

Not every man knows what he shall sing at the end,
Watching the pier as the ship sails away, or what it will seem like
When he's held by the sea's roar, motionless, there at the end,
Or what he shall hope for once it is clear that he'll never go back.

When the time has passed to prune the rose or caress the cat,
When the sunset torching the lawn and the full moon icing it down
No longer appear, not every man knows what he'll discover instead.
When the weight of the past leans against nothing, and the sky

Is no more than remembered light, and the stories of cirrus
10   And cumulus come to a close, and all the birds are suspended in flight,
Not every man knows what is waiting for him, or what he shall sing
When the ship he is on slips into darkness, there at the end.

Alfred, Lord Tennyson

Alfred, Lord Tennyson (1809–1892), who began to publish poems before he was twenty, matured in technical accomplishment early. After his great friend Arthur Hallam died in 1833, Tennyson matured in other ways, beginning his long, elegiac "In Memoriam." In Tennyson's character, there was a quarrel between a personal predilection for melancholy and the Victorian duty to be optimistic and progressive. For much of his life, Victorian optimism won out; he is the poet of his age. When he speaks the philosophy of imperialism, as in "Ulysses," he speaks it with eloquence and vigor. In his more private poems, sweetness and fire remain as public gusto vanishes.

Ulysses   (1833)

It little profits that an idle king,
By this still hearth, among these barren crags,
Matched with an agèd wife, I mete and dole
Unequal laws unto a savage race,
That hoard, and sleep, and feed, and know not me.
I cannot rest from travel: I will drink
Life to the lees: all times I have enjoyed
Greatly, have suffered greatly, both with those
That loved me, and alone; on shore, and when
10   Through scudding drifts the rainy Hyades
Vext the dim sea: I am become a name;
For always roaming with a hungry heart
Much have I seen and known; cities of men
And manners, climates, councils, governments,
Myself not least, but honored of them all;
And drunk delight of battle with my peers,
Far on the ringing plains of windy Troy.
I am a part of all that I have met;
Yet all experience is an arch wherethro'
20   Gleams that untraveled world, whose margin fades
For ever and for ever when I move.
How dull it is to pause, to make an end,
To rust unburnished, not to shine in use!

As though to breathe were life. Life piled on life
Were all too little, and of one to me
Little remains: but every hour is saved
From that eternal silence, something more,
A bringer of new things; and vile it were
For some three suns to store and hoard myself,
30   And this gray spirit yearning in desire
To follow knowledge like a sinking star,
Beyond the utmost bound of human thought.

This is my son, mine own Telemachus,
To whom I leave the scepter and the isle—
Well-loved of me, discerning to fulfill
This labor, by slow prudence to make mild
A rugged people, and through soft degrees
Subdue them to the useful and the good.
Most blameless is he, centered in the sphere
40   Of common duties, decent not to fail
In offices of tenderness, and pay
Meet adoration to my household gods,
When I am gone. He works his work, I mine.

There lies the port; the vessel puffs her sail:
There gloom the dark broad seas. My mariners,
Souls that have toiled, and wrought, and thought with me—
That ever with a frolic welcome took
The thunder and the sunshine, and opposed
Free hearts, free foreheads—you and I are old;
50   Old age hath yet his honor and his toil;
Death closes all: but something ere the end,
Some work of noble note, may yet be done,
Not unbecoming men that strove with Gods.
The lights begin to twinkle from the rocks:
The long day wanes: the slow moon climbs: the deep
Moans round with many voices. Come, my friends,
'Tis not too late to seek a newer world.
Push off, and sitting well in order smite
The sounding furrows; for my purpose holds
60   To sail beyond the sunset, and the baths
Of all the western stars, until I die.
It may be that the gulfs will wash us down:
It may be we shall touch the Happy Isles,
And see the great Achilles, whom we knew.
Though much is taken, much abides; and though
We are not now that strength which in old days
Moved earth and heaven; that which we are, we are;
One equal temper of heroic hearts,
Made weak by time and fate, but strong in will
70   To strive, to seek, to find, and not to yield.

The Eagle   (1851)

He clasps the crag with crooked hands;
Close to the sun in lonely lands,
Ringed with the azure world, he stands.

The wrinkled sea beneath him crawls;
He watches from his mountain walls,
And like a thunderbolt he falls.

Dylan Thomas

Dylan Thomas (1914–1953) grew up in Wales and wrote prose and poetry about his
childhood. He began early to write excellent lyrical poetry, and published his first
book when he was only nineteen. At least half of his *Collected Poems* was written
or drafted before he was twenty-two. Continually in debt and an alcoholic, he lived
a life with less and less poetry in it. The sparse later work remained high in quality,
like the play *Under Milk Wood,* finished just as he died at the age of thirty-nine.

This Bread I Break   (1939)

This bread I break was once the oat,
This wine upon a foreign tree
Plunged in its fruit;
Man in the day or wind at night
Laid the crops low, broke the grape's joy.

Once in this wind the summer blood
Knocked in the flesh that decked the vine,
Once in this bread
The oat was merry in the wind;
10   Man broke the sun, pulled the wind down.

This flesh you break, this blood you let
Make desolation in the vein,
Were oat and grape
Born of the sensual root and sap;
My wine you drink, my bread you snap.

Fern Hill   (1946)

Now as I was young and easy under the apple boughs
About the lilting house and happy as the grass was green,
     The night above the dingle starry,
          Time let me hail and climb

    Golden in the heydays of his eyes,
And honoured among wagons I was prince of the apple towns
And once below a time I lordly had the trees and leaves
      Trail with daisies and barley
Down the rivers of the windfall light.

10 And as I was green and carefree, famous among the barns
About the happy yard and singing as the farm was home,
    In the sun that is young once only,
      Time let me play and be
    Golden in the mercy of his means,
And green and golden I was huntsman and herdsman, the calves
Sang to my horn, the foxes on the hills barked clear and cold,
      And the sabbath rang slowly
    In the pebbles of the holy streams.

    All the sun long it was running, it was lovely, the hay
20 Fields high as the house, the tunes from the chimneys, it was air
    And playing, lovely and watery
      And fire green as grass.
    And nightly under the simple stars
As I rode to sleep the owls were bearing the farm away,
All the moon long I heard, blessed among stables, the night-jars
    Flying with the ricks, and the horses
      Flashing into the dark.

    And then to awake, and the farm, like a wanderer white
With the dew, come back, the cock on his shoulder: it was all
30   Shining, it was Adam and maiden,
      The sky gathered again
    And the sun grew round that very day.
So it must have been after the birth of the simple light
In the first, spinning place, the spellbound horses walking warm
    Out of the whinnying green stable
      On to the fields of praise.

    And honoured among foxes and pheasants by the gay house
Under the new made clouds and happy as the heart was long,
    In the sun born over and over,
40   I ran my heedless ways,
    My wishes raced through the house high hay
And nothing I cared, at my sky blue trades, that time allows
In all his tuneful turning so few and such morning songs
    Before the children green and golden
      Follow him out of grace,

    Nothing I cared, in the lamb white days, that time would take me
Up to the swallow thronged loft by the shadow of my hand,
    In the moon that is always rising,
      Nor that riding to sleep
50   I should hear him fly with the high fields

And wake to the farm forever fled from the childless land.
Oh as I was young and easy in the mercy of his means,
    Time held me green and dying
  Though I sang in my chains like the sea.

Do not go gentle into that good night   (1952)

Do not go gentle into that good night,
Old age should burn and rave at close of day;
Rage, rage against the dying of the light.

Though wise men at their end know dark is right,
Because their words had forked no lightning they
Do not go gentle into that good night.

Good men, the last wave by, crying how bright
Their frail deeds might have danced in a green bay,
Rage, rage against the dying of the light.

10 Wild men who caught and sang the sun in flight,
And learn, too late, they grieved it on its way,
Do not go gentle into that good night.

Grave men, near death, who see with blinding sight
Blind eyes could blaze like meteors and be gay,
Rage, rage against the dying of the light.

And you, my father, there on the sad height,
Curse, bless, me now with your fierce tears, I pray.
Do not go gentle into that good night.
Rage, rage against the dying of the light.

Edward Thomas

Edward Thomas (1878–1917) was Robert Frost's great English friend, a freelance
writer of prose whom Frost teased and encouraged into poetry. Thomas came to
poetry late, wrote furiously in his brief poetic life, and was killed in World War I.

The Owl   (1915)

Downhill I came, hungry, and yet not starved;
Cold, yet had heat within me that was proof
Against the North wind; tired, yet so that rest
Had seemed the sweetest thing under a roof.

Then at the inn I had food, fire, and rest,
Knowing how hungry, cold, and tired was I.
All of the night was quite barred out except
An owl's cry, a most melancholy cry

Shaken out long and clear upon the hill,
10 No merry note, nor cause of merriment,
But one telling me plain what I escaped
And others could not, that night, as in I went.

And salted was my food, and my repose,
Salted and sobered, too, by the bird's voice
Speaking for all who lay under the stars,
Soldiers and poor, unable to rejoice.

Charles Tomlinson

Charles Tomlinson (1927–) was born in an industrial English town and
attended Cambridge. He teaches at Bristol and is a painter as well as a poet. In
some of his poetry he has learned from American sources, especially Wallace
Stevens and the Black Mountain poets.

Paring the Apple (1958)

There are portraits and still-lifes.

And there is paring the apple.

And then? Paring it slowly,
From under cool-yellow
Cold-white emerging. And. . . ?

The spring of concentric peel
Unwinding off white,
The blade hidden, dividing.

There are portraits and still-lifes
10 And the first, because 'human'

Does not excel the second, and
Neither is less weighted
With a human gesture, than paring the
apple
With a human stillness.

The cool blade
Severs between coolness, apple-rind
Compelling a recognition.

Jean Toomer

Jean Toomer (1894–1967) wrote in *Cane* a combination of poetry and prose that was an early contribution to the literature of the black American.

Reapers   (1923)

Black reapers with the sound of steel on stones
Are sharpening scythes. I see them place the hones
In their hip-pockets as a thing that's done,
And start their silent swinging, one by one.
Black horses drive a mower through the weeds,
And there, a field rat, startled, squealing bleeds,
His belly close to ground. I see the blade,
Blood-stained, continue cutting weeds and shade.

*John Updike

Ex-Basketball Player   (1958)

Pearl Avenue runs past the high-school lot,
Bends with the trolley tracks, and stops, cut off
Before it has a chance to go two blocks,
At Colonel McComsky Plaza. Berth's Garage
Is on the corner facing west, and there,
Most days, you'll find Flick Webb, who helps Berth out.

Flick stands tall among the idiot pumps—
Five on a side, the old bubble-head style,
Their rubber elbows hanging loose and low.
10   One's nostrils are two S's, and his eyes
An E and O. And one is squat, without
A head at all—more of a football type.

Once Flick played for the high-school team, the Wizards.
He was good: in fact, the best. In '46
He bucketed three hundred ninety points,
A county record still. The ball loved Flick.
I saw him rack up thirty-eight or forty
In one home game. His hands were like wild birds.

He never learned a trade, he just sells gas,
20   Checks oil, and changes flats. Once in a while,

* For a note on John Updike, see page 147.

As a gag, he dribbles an inner tube,
But most of us remember anyway.
His hands are fine and nervous on the lug wrench.
It makes no difference to the lug wrench, though.

Off work, he hangs around Mae's luncheonette.
Grease-gray and kind of coiled, he plays pinball,
Smokes those thin cigars, nurses lemon phosphates.
Flick seldom says a word to Mae, just nods
Beyond her face toward bright applauding tiers
30   Of Necco Wafers, Nibs, and Juju Beads.

Derek Walcott

Derek Walcott (1930–   ) was born in Saint Lucia in the
West Indies, and now lives in Massachusetts. He teaches at
Boston University. Walcott has published many collections,
including a *Collected Poems: 1948–1984* and, most recently,
Omeros (1990).

Sea Grapes   (1971)

That sail in cloudless light
which tires of islands,
a schooner beating up the Caribbean

for home, could be Odysseus
home-bound through the Aegean,
just as that husband's

sorrow under the sea-grapes, repeats
the adulterer's hearing Nausicaa's name
in every gull's outcry.

10   But whom does this bring peace? The classic war
between a passion and responsibility
is never finished, and has been the same

to the sea-wanderer and the one on shore,
now wriggling on his sandals to walk home,
since Troy sighed its last flame,

and the blind giant's boulder heaved the trough
from which The Odyssey's hexameters come
to finish up as Caribbean surf.

The classics can console. But not enough.

Robert Penn Warren

Robert Penn Warren (1905–   ) attended Vanderbilt University and then
Oxford University as a Rhodes scholar. He was the youngest member of the
Fugitive Group of Southern writers, along with Allen Tate and John Crowe
Ransom. Author with Cleanth Brooks of *Understanding Poetry,* a most influential
textbook, he is an eminent critic and novelist—*All the King's Men* won the
Pulitzer Prize for fiction in 1947—as well as a poet. His books of poems have
earned him Pulitzer Prizes and a National Book Award.

Gold Glade   (1957)

Wandering, in autumn, the woods of boyhood,
Where cedar, black, thick, rode the ridge,
Heart aimless as rifle, boy-blankness of mood,
I came where ridge broke, and the great ledge,
Limestone, set the toe high as treetop by dark edge

Of a gorge, and water hid, grudging and grumbling,
And I saw, in mind's eye, foam white on
Wet stone, stone wet-black, white water tumbling,
And so went down, and with some fright on
10 Slick boulders, crossed over. The gorge-depth drew night on,

But high over high rock and leaf-lacing, sky
Showed yet bright, and declivity wooed
My foot by the quietening stream, and so I
Went on, in quiet, through the beech wood:
There, in gold light, where the glade gave, it stood.

The glade was geometric, circular, gold,
No brush or weed breaking that bright gold of leaf-fall.
In the center it stood, absolute and bold
Beyond any heart-hurt, or eye's grief-fall.
20 Gold-massy in air, it stood in gold light-fall,

No breathing of air, no leaf now gold-falling,
No tooth-stitch of squirrel, or any far fox bark,

No woodpecker coding, or late jay calling.
Silence: gray-shagged, the great shagbark
Gave forth gold light. There could be no dark.

But of course dark came, and I can't recall
What county it was, for the life of me.
Montgomery, Todd, Christian—I know them all.
Was it even Kentucky or Tennessee?
30 Perhaps just an image that keeps haunting me.

No, no! in no mansion under earth,
Nor imagination's domain of bright air,
But solid in soil that gave it its birth,
It stands, wherever it is, but somewhere.
I shall set my foot, and go there.

Walt Whitman

Walt Whitman (1819–1892) is the first great American poet. He is also one of the greatest innovators in the history of the art. His long, loose rhythms derive in part from the King James version of the Bible and in part from the expansive gestures of nineteenth-century political oratory. But largely they seem Whitman's own creation.

Born on Long Island, son of a carpenter who was also a farmer, Whitman was sporadically educated, became a newspaper editor, and created himself as a poet. The first edition of *Leaves of Grass,* which through subsequent editions became a collection of his life's work, appeared in 1855. Emerson praised him, but few other early readers had the imagination to understand that his writing was poetry at all. Not only was his work innovative; in its broad sensuality and in its hints at homoeroticism, it was shocking. Emily Dickinson's comment, in a letter to Thomas Wentworth Higginson, tells the tale: "You speak of Mr. Whitman—I never read his Book—but was told that he was disgraceful—"

Out of the Cradle Endlessly Rocking   (1881)

Out of the cradle endlessly rocking,
Out of the mocking-bird's throat, the musical shuttle,
Out of the Ninth-month midnight,
Over the sterile sands and the fields beyond, where the child leaving his bed
        wandered alone, bareheaded, barefoot,
Down from the showered halo,
Up from the mystic play of shadows twining and twisting as if they were alive,
Out from the patches of briers and blackberries,
From the memories of the bird that chanted to me,
10 From your memories sad brother, from the fitful risings and fallings I heard,
From under that yellow half-moon late-risen and swollen as if with tears,
From those beginning notes of yearning and love there in the mist,
From the thousand responses of my heart never to cease,

From the myriad thence-aroused words,
From the word stronger and more delicious than any,
From such as now they start the scene revisiting,
As a flock, twittering, rising, or overhead passing,
Borne hither, ere all eludes me, hurriedly,
A man, yet by these tears a little boy again,
20 Throwing myself on the sand, confronting the waves,
I, chanter of pains and joys, uniter of here and hereafter,
Taking all hints to use them, but swiftly leaping beyond them,
A reminiscence sing.

Once Paumanok,
When the lilac-scent was in the air and Fifth-month grass was growing,
Up this seashore in some briers,
Two feathered guests from Alabama, two together,
And their nest, and four light-green eggs spotted with brown,
And every day the he-bird to and fro near at hand,
30 And every day the she-bird crouched on her nest, silent, with bright eyes,
And every day I, a curious boy, never too close, never disturbing them,
Cautiously peering, absorbing, translating.

Shine! shine! shine!
Pour down your warmth, great sun!
While we bask, we two together.

Two together!
Winds blow south, or winds blow north.
Day come white, or night come black,
Home, or rivers and mountains from home,
40 *Singing all time, minding no time,*
While we two keep together.

Till of a sudden,
May-be killed, unknown to her mate,
One forenoon the she-bird crouched not on the nest,
Nor returned that afternoon, nor the next,
Nor ever appeared again.

And thenceforward all summer in the sound of the sea,
And at night under the full of the moon in calmer weather,
Over the hoarse surging of the sea,
50 Or flitting from brier to brier by day,
I saw, I heard at intervals the remaining one, the he-bird,
The solitary guest from Alabama.

Blow! blow! blow!
Blow up sea-winds along Paumanok's shore:
I wait and I wait till you blow my mate to me.

Yes, when the stars glistened,
All night long on the prong of a moss-scalloped stake,

Down almost amid the slapping waves,
Sat the lone singer wonderful causing tears.

60 He called on his mate,
He poured forth the meanings which I of all men know.

Yes my brother I know,
The rest might not, but I have treasured every note,
For more than once dimly down to the beach gliding,
Silent, avoiding the moonbeams, blending myself with the shadows,
Recalling now the obscure shapes, the echoes, the sounds and sights after their
    sorts,
The white arms out in the breakers tirelessly tossing,
I, with bare feet, a child, the wind wafting my hair,
70 Listened long and long.

Listened to keep, to sing, now translating the notes,
Following you my brother.

Soothe! soothe! soothe!
Close on its wave soothes the wave behind.
And again another behind embracing and lapping, every one close,
But my love soothes not me, not me.

Low hangs the moon, it rose late.
It is lagging—O I think it is heavy with love, with love.
O madly the sea pushes upon the land,
80 *With love, with love.*

O night! do I not see my love fluttering out among the breakers?
What is that little black thing I see there in the white?

Loud! loud! loud!
Loud I call to you, my love!

High and clear I shoot my voice over the waves,
Surely you must know who is here, is here,
You must know who I am, my love.

Low-hanging moon!
What is that dusky spot in your brown yellow?
90 *O it is the shape, the shape of my mate!*
O moon do not keep her from me any longer.

Land! land! O land!
Whichever way I turn, O I think you could give me my mate back again if you only
    would.
For I am almost sure I see her dimly whichever way I look.

O rising stars!
Perhaps the one I want so much will rise, will rise with some of you.

O throat! O trembling throat!
Sound clearer through the atmosphere!
100　Pierce the woods, the earth,
Somewhere listening to catch you must be the one I want.

Shake out carols!
Solitary here, the night's carols!
Carols of lonesome love! death's carols!
Carols under that lagging, yellow, waning moon!
O under that moon where she droops almost down into the sea!
O reckless despairing carols.

But soft! sink low!
Soft! let me just murmur.
110　And do you wait a moment you husky-noised sea,
For somewhere I believe I heard my mate responding to me,
So faint, I must be still, be still to listen,
But not altogether still, for then she might not come immediately to me.

Hither my love!
Here I am! Here!
With this just-sustained note I announce myself to you.
This gentle call is for you my love, for you.

Do not be decoyed elsewhere,
That is the whistle of the wind, it is not my voice,
120　That is the fluttering, the fluttering of the spray.
Those are the shadows of leaves.

O darkness! O in vain!
O I am very sick and sorrowful.

O brown halo in the sky near the moon, drooping upon the sea!
O troubled reflection in the sea!
O throat! O throbbing heart!
And I singing uselessly, uselessly all the night.

O past! O happy life! O songs of joy!
In the air, in the woods, over fields,
130　Loved! loved! loved! loved! loved!
But my mate no more, no more with me!
We two together no more.

The aria sinking,
All else continuing, the stars shining,
The winds blowing, the notes of the bird continuous echoing,
With angry moans the fierce old mother incessantly moaning,
On the sands of Paumanok's shore gray and rustling,
The yellow half-moon enlarged, sagging down, drooping, the face of the sea almost
　　　touching,
140　The boy ecstatic, with his bare feet the waves, with his hair the atmosphere dallying,

The love in the heart long pent, now loose, now at last tumultuously bursting,
The aria's meaning, the ears, the soul, swiftly depositing,
The strange tears down the cheeks coursing,
The colloquy there, the trio, each uttering,
The undertone, the savage old mother incessantly crying,
To the boy's soul's questions sullenly timing, some drowned secret hissing,
To the outsetting bard.

Demon or bird! (said the boy's soul,)
Is it indeed toward your mate you sing? or is it really to me?
150 For I, that was a child, my tongue's use sleeping, now I have heard you,
Now in a moment I know what I am for, I awake,
And already a thousand singers, a thousand songs, clearer, louder and more
     sorrowful than yours,
A thousand warbling echoes have started to life within me, never to die.

O you singer solitary, singing by yourself, projecting me,
O solitary me listening, never more shall I cease perpetuating you,
Never more shall I escape, never more the reverberations,
Never more the cries of unsatisfied love be absent from me,
Never again leave me to be the peaceful child I was before what there in the night,
160 By the sea under the yellow and sagging moon,
The messenger there aroused, the fire, the sweet hell within,
The unknown want, the destiny of me.

O give me the clue! (it lurks in the night here somewhere,)
O if I am to have so much, let me have more!

A word then, (for I will conquer it,)
The word final, superior to all,
Subtle, sent up—what is it?—I listen;
Are you whispering it, and have been all the time, you sea-waves?
Is that it from your liquid rims and wet sands?

170 Whereto answering, the sea,
Delaying not, hurrying not,
Whispered me through the night, and very plainly before daybreak,
Lisped to me the low and delicious word death,
And again death, death, death, death,
Hissing melodious, neither like the bird nor like my aroused child's heart,
But edging near as privately for me rustling at my feet,
Creeping thence steadily up to my ears and laving me softly all over,
Death, death, death, death, death.

Which I do not forget,
180 But fuse the song of my dusky demon and brother,
That he sang to me in the moonlight on Paumanok's gray beach,
With the thousand responsive songs at random,
My own songs awaked from that hour,
And with thèm the key, the word up from the waves,
The word of the sweetest song and all songs,

That strong and delicious word which, creeping to my feet,
(Or like some old crone rocking the cradle, swathed in sweet garments, bending
    aside,)
The sea whispered me.

A Farm Picture   (1865)

Through the ample open door of the peaceful country barn,
A sunlit pasture field with cattle and horses feeding,
And haze and vista, and the far horizon fading away.

Cavalry Crossing a Ford   (1865)

A line in long array where they wind betwixt green islands,
They take a serpentine course, their arms flash in the sun—hark to the musical
    clank,
Behold the silvery river, in it the splashing horses loitering stop to drink,
Behold the brown-faced men, each group, each person a picture, the negligent rest
    on the saddles,
Some emerge on the opposite bank, others are just entering the ford—while,
Scarlet and blue and snowy white,
The guidon flags flutter gayly in the wind.

Richard Wilbur

Richard Wilbur (1921–   ) was born in New Jersey and has lived in the eastern
United States. During World War II, he fought in Italy and France; he began
writing poems in the Army. His work is decorative, skillful, aimed to please and
to enlighten rather than to shock or to overwhelm. He is one of the few poets of
his generation who has not undergone violent change, in work and private life,
which has earned him the disapproval of critics. In 1988, he published his *New
and Collected Poems,* which won him his second Pulitzer Prize. See also pages
454 and 493–494.

Still, Citizen Sparrow   (1950)

Still, citizen sparrow, this vulture which you call
Unnatural, let him but lumber again to air
Over the rotten office, let him bear
The carrion ballast up, and at the tall

Tip of the sky lie cruising. Then you'll see
That no more beautiful bird is in heaven's height,
No wider more placid wings, no watchfuller flight;
He shoulders nature there, the frightfully free,

The naked-headed one. Pardon him, you
10 Who dart in the orchard aisles, for it is he
Devours death, mocks mutability,
Has heart to make an end, keeps nature new.

Thinking of Noah, childheart, try to forget
How for so many bedlam hours his saw
Soured the song of birds with its wheezy gnaw,
And the slam of his hammer all the day beset

The people's ears. Forget that he could bear
To see the towns like coral under the keel,
And the fields so dismal deep. Try rather to feel
20 How high and weary it was, on the waters where

He rocked his only world, and everyone's.
Forgive the hero, you who would have died
Gladly with all you knew; he rode that tide
To Ararat;[1] all men are Noah's sons.

William Carlos Williams

William Carlos Williams (1883–1963) knew Ezra Pound at the University of
Pennsylvania when they were students. Williams went on to become a medical
doctor, living most of his life in suburban Rutherford, New Jersey, where he
practiced medicine, specializing in obstetrics. His poetry was resolute in its use
of the American idiom. Followers have turned his theory and his practice into
one of the main schools of contemporary American poetry. See also pages 418,
433, and 473–474.

This Is Just to Say   (1938)

I have eaten
the plums
that were in
the icebox

and which
you were probably

saving
for breakfast

Forgive me
10 they were delicious
so sweet
and so cold

[1] The mountain on which Noah's Ark landed

Spring and All   (1922)

By the road to the contagious hospital
under the surge of the blue
mottled clouds driven from the
northeast—a cold wind. Beyond, the
waste of broad, muddy fields
brown with dried weeds, standing and
    fallen

patches of standing water
the scattering of tall trees

10 All along the road the reddish
purplish, forked, upstanding, twiggy
stuff of bushes and small trees
with dead, brown leaves under them
leafless vines—

Lifeless in appearance, sluggish
dazed spring approaches—

They enter the new world naked,
cold, uncertain of all
save that they enter. All about them
20 the cold, familiar wind—

Now the grass, tomorrow
the stiff curl of wildcarrot leaf

One by one objects are defined—
It quickens: clarity, outline of leaf

But now the stark dignity of
entrance—Still, the profound change
has come upon them: rooted they
grip down and begin to awaken

William Wordsworth

William Wordsworth (1770–1850) attended Cambridge, afterward touring Europe
on foot and living for a year in France when the revolutionary society was at its
most exciting. Back in England, he continued to write poems, and in 1795 began
his long and close friendship with Samuel Taylor Coleridge. The two poets, with
Wordsworth's sister Dorothy and with Coleridge's wife, lived near each other for
a time, and Wordsworth and Coleridge published *Lyrical Ballads* in 1798, a
collection of poetry by both of them, including Coleridge's "Rime of the Ancient
Mariner" and Wordsworth's "Lines Written Above Tintern Abbey." The year of
publication provides as good a date as any for the beginning of the romantic
movement in English literature. Two years later, reprinting the volume,
Wordsworth added prose "observations" in which he defended his own theory of
poetry, deriving his language from rustic life. His imagery also derived from
rustic life, and his poems were at first denounced as obscure and meaningless.
Later, he became one of the most popular poets of the English tradition. In his
long life, he wrote prolifically; most of his best work is early.

Ode: Intimations of Immortality from
Recollections of Early Childhood   (1806)

The Child is father of the Man;
And I could wish my days to be
Bound each to each by natural piety.

I

There was a time when meadow, grove, and stream,
The earth, and every common sight,
        To me did seem
        Apparelled in celestial light,
The glory and the freshness of a dream.
It is not now as it hath been of yore;—
        Turn whereso'er I may,
            By night or day,
The things which I have seen I now can see no more.

II

10   The Rainbow comes and goes,
        And lovely is the Rose,
        The moon doth with delight
Look round her when the heavens are bare,
        Waters on a starry night
        Are beautiful and fair;
The sunshine is a glorious birth;
    But yet I know, where'er I go,
That there hath past away a glory from the earth.

III

Now, while the birds thus sing a joyous song,
20   And while the young lambs bound
            As to the tabor's sound,
To me alone there came a thought of grief:
A timely utterance gave that thought relief,
        And I again am strong:
The cataracts blow their trumpets from the steep;
No more shall grief of mine the season wrong;
I hear the Echoes through the mountains throng,
The Winds come to me from the fields of sleep,
        And all the earth is gay;
30   Land and sea
    Give themselves up to jollity,
        And with the heart of May
    Doth every Beast keep holiday;—
        Thou Child of Joy,
Shout round me, let me hear thy shouts, thou happy
        Shepherd-boy!

IV

Ye blessed Creatures, I have heard the call
    Ye to each other make; I see
The heavens laugh with you in your jubilee;
40   My heart is at your festival,
        My head hath its coronal,
The fulness of your bliss, I feel—I feel it all.
        Oh evil day! if I were sullen

While Earth herself is adorning,
   This sweet May-morning,
And the Children are culling
   On every side,
In a thousand valleys far and wide,
Fresh flowers; while the sun shines warm,
50 And the Babe leaps up on his Mother's arm:—
   I hear, I hear, with joy I hear!
   —But there's a Tree, of many, one,
A single Field which I have looked upon,
Both of them speak of something that is gone:
   The Pansy at my feet
   Doth the same tale repeat:
Whither is fled the visionary gleam?
Where is it now, the glory and the dream?

V

Our birth is but a sleep and a forgetting:
60 The Soul that rises with us, our life's Star,
   Hath had elsewhere its setting,
     And cometh from afar:
   Not in entire forgetfulness,
   And not in utter nakedness,
But trailing clouds of glory do we come
   From God, who is our home:
Heaven lies about us in our infancy!
Shades of the prison-house begin to close
   Upon the growing Boy,
70 But He beholds the light, and whence it flows,
   He sees it in his joy;
The Youth, who daily farther from the east
   Must travel, still is Nature's Priest,
   And by the vision splendid
   Is on his way attended;
At length the Man perceives it die away,
And fade into the light of common day.

VI

Earth fills her lap with pleasures of her own;
Yearnings she hath in her own natural kind,
80 And, even with something of a Mother's mind,
   And no unworthy aim,
   The homely Nurse doth all she can
To make her Foster-child, her Inmate Man,
   Forget the glories he hath known,
And that imperial palace whence he came.

VII

Behold the Child among his new-born blisses,
A six years' Darling of a pigmy size!
See, where 'mid work of his own hand he lies,

Fretted by sallies of his mother's kisses,
90 With light upon him from his father's eyes!
See, at his feet, some little plan or chart,
Some fragment from his dream of human life,
Shaped by himself with newly-learnèd art;
           A wedding or a festival,
           A mourning or a funeral;
              And this hath now his heart,
              And unto this he frames his song.
              Then will he fit his tongue
To dialogues of business, love, or strife;
100   But it will not be long
              Ere this be thrown aside,
              And with new joy and pride
The little Actor cons another part;
Filling from time to time his "humorous stage"
With all the Persons, down to palsied Age,
That Life brings with her in her equipage;
              As if his whole vocation
              Were endless imitation.

VIII

Thou, whose exterior semblance doth belie
110   Thy Soul's immensity;
Thou best Philosopher, who yet dost keep
Thy heritage, thou Eye among the blind,
That, deaf and silent, read'st the eternal deep,
Haunted for ever by the eternal mind,—
              Mighty Prophet! Seer blest!
              On whom those truths do rest,
Which we are toiling all our lives to find,
In darkness lost, the darkness of the grave,
Thou, over whom thy Immortality
120 Broods like the Day, a Master o'er a Slave,
A Presence which is not to be put by;
Thou little Child, yet glorious in the might
Of heaven-born freedom on thy being's height,
Why with such earnest pains dost thou provoke
The years to bring the inevitable yoke,
Thus blindly with thy blessedness at strife?
Full soon thy Soul shall have her earthly freight,
And custom lie upon thee with a weight,
Heavy as frost, and deep almost as life!

IX

130   O joy! that in our embers
              Is something that doth live,
              That nature yet remembers
              What was so fugitive!
The thought of our past years in me doth breed

Perpetual benediction: not indeed
For that which is most worthy to be blest;
Delight and liberty, the simple creed
Of Childhood, whether busy or at rest,
With new-fledged hope still fluttering in his breast:—
140   Not for these I raise
          The song of thanks and praise;
            But for those obstinate questionings
            Of sense and outward things,
            Fallings from us, vanishings;
            Blank misgivings of a Creature
Moving about in worlds not realised,
High instincts before which our mortal Nature
Did tremble like a guilty Thing surprised:
            But for those first affections,
150   Those shadowy recollections,
       Which, be they what they may,
Are yet the fountain-light of all our day,
Are yet a master-light of all our seeing;
      Uphold us, cherish, and have power to make
Our noisy years seem moments in the being
Of the eternal Silence: truths that wake,
           To perish never:
Which neither listlessness, nor mad endeavour,
           Nor Man nor Boy,
160 Nor all that is at enmity with joy,
Can utterly abolish or destroy!
      Hence in a season of calm weather
        Though inland far we be,
Our Souls have sight of that immortal sea
        Which brought us hither,
       Can in a moment travel thither,
And see the Children sport upon the shore,
And hear the mighty waters rolling evermore.

X

Then sing, ye Birds, sing, sing a joyous song!
170   And let the young Lambs bound
         As to the tabor's sound!
We in thought will join your throng,
        Ye that pipe and ye that play,
        Ye that through your hearts today
        Feel the gladness of the May!
What though the radiance which was once so bright
Be now for ever taken from my sight,
      Though nothing can bring back the hour
Of splendour in the grass, of glory in the flower
180   We will grieve not, rather find
        Strength in what remains behind;
        In the primal sympathy
        Which having been must ever be;

In the soothing thoughts that spring
Out of human suffering;
In the faith that looks through death,
In years that bring the philosophic mind.

XI

And O, ye Fountains, Meadows, Hills, and Groves,
Forebode not any severing of our loves!
190 Yet in my heart of hearts I feel your might;
I only have relinquished one delight
To live beneath your more habitual sway.
I love the Brooks which down their channels fret,
Even more than when I tripped lightly as they;
The innocent brightness of a new-born Day
        Is lovely yet;
The Clouds that gather round the setting sun
Do take a sober colouring from an eye
That hath kept watch o'er man's mortality;
200 Another race hath been, and other palms are won.
Thanks to the human heart by which we live,
Thanks to its tenderness, its joys, and fears,
To me the meanest flower that blows can give
Thoughts that do often lie too deep for tears.

The World Is Too Much with Us   (1807)

The world is too much with us; late and soon,
Getting and spending, we lay waste our powers:
Little we see in Nature that is ours;
We have given our hearts away, a sordid boon!
The sea that bares her bosom to the moon;
The winds that will be howling at all hours,
And are up-gathered now like sleeping flowers;
For this, for everything, we are out of tune;
It moves us not.—Great God! I'd rather be
10 A pagan suckled in a creed outworn;
So might I, standing on this pleasant lea,
Have glimpses that would make me less forlorn;
Have sight of Proteus rising from the sea;
Or hear old Triton blow his wreathèd horn.

James Wright

James Wright (1927–1980) grew up among the coal mines and steel mills of Ohio and attended Kenyon College, where he studied with John Crowe Ransom. His first book was *The Green Wall,* which made him the Yale Younger Poet in 1957. *This Journey* appeared posthumously in 1982. In 1990, his publishers issued his collected poems under the title *Above the River.* See also pages 435–436.

The First Days   (1974)
Optima dies prima fugit[1]

The first thing I saw in the morning
Was a huge golden bee ploughing
His burly right shoulder into the belly
Of a sleek yellow pear
Low on a bough.
Before he could find that sudden black honey
That squirms around in there
Inside the seed, the tree could not bear any more.
The pear fell to the ground
10 With the bee still half alive
Inside its body.
He would have died if I hadn't knelt down
And sliced the pear gently
A little more open.
The bee shuddered, and returned.
Maybe I should have left him alone there,
Drowning in his own delight.
The best days are the first
To flee, sang the lovely
20 Musician born in this town
So like my own.
I let the bee go
Among the gasworks at the edge of Mantua.

---

[1] "The best day is the first to flee," a line from the Roman poet Virgil, who was born near Mantua

Jay Wright

Jay Wright (1935–   ) was born in New Mexico and lives in New Hampshire, which he sometimes leaves to teach at Yale University. His *Selected Poems* was published by Princeton University Press in 1987, and *Elaine's Book* in 1988. He has received a Fellowship from the MacArthur Foundation.

Meta-A and the A of Absolutes   (1976)

I write my God in blue.
I run my gods upstream on flimsy rafts.
I bathe my goddesses in foam, in moonlight.
I take my reasons from my mother's snuff breath,
or from an old woman, sitting with a lemonade,
at twilight, on the desert's steps.
Brown by day and black by night,
my God has wings that open to no reason.
He scutters from the touch of old men's eyes,
10 scutters from the smell of wisdom, an orb
of light leaping from a fire.
Press him he bleeds.
When you take your hand to sacred water,
there is no sign of any wound.
And so I call him supreme, great artist,
judge of time, scholar of all living event,
the possible prophet of the possible event.
Blind men, on bourbon, with guitars,
blind men with their scars dulled by kola,
20 blind men seeking the shelter of a raindrop,
blind men in corn, blind men in steel,
reason by their lights that our tongues
are free, our tongues will redeem us.
Speech is the fact, and the fact is true.
What is moves, and what is moving is.
We cling to these contradictions.
We know we will become our contradictions,
our complex body's own desire.
Yet speech is not the limit of our vision.
30 The ear entices itself with any sound.
The skin will caress whatever tone
or temperament that rises or descends.
The bones will set themselves to a dance.
The blood will argue with a bird in flight.
The heart will scale the dew from an old chalice,
brush and thrill to an old bone.
And yet there is no sign to arrest us
                        from the possible.
We remain at rest there, in transit
40 from our knowing to our knowledge.
So I would set a limit where I meet my logic.

I would clamber from my own cave
into the curve of sign, an alphabet
of transformation, the clan's cloak of reason.
I am good when I am in motion,
when I think of myself at rest
in the knowledge of my moving,
when I have the vision of my mother at rest,
in moonlight, her lap the cradle of my father's head.
50 I am good when I trade my shells,
and walk from boundary to boundary,
unarmed and unafraid of another's speech.
I am good when I learn the world
through the touch of my present body.
I am good when I take the cove of a cub
                    into my care.
I am good when I hear the changes in my body
echo all my changes down the years,
when what I know indeed is what I would
60   know in deed.
I am good when I know the darkness of all light,
and accept the darkness, not as sign, but as my body.
This is the A of absolutes,
the logbook of judgments,
the good sign.

Thomas Wyatt

Sir Thomas Wyatt (1503–1542) was ambassador for Henry VIII—and several
times imprisoned by him in the Tower of London for alleged offenses. Wyatt
brought the sonnet to England, imitating the form used by Italian poets. When
the music of English verse had vanished for a hundred years after Chaucer's
death, Wyatt's lyrics and sonnets began its restoration.

They Flee from Me   (1535)

They flee from me, that sometime did me seek,
With naked foot, stalking in my chamber.
I have seen them, gentle, tame, and meek,
That now are wild, and do not remember
That sometime they put themselves in danger
To take bread at my hand, and now they range,
Busily seeking with a continual change.

Thankèd be fortune, it hath been otherwise
Twenty times better; but once, in special,
10 In thin array, after a pleasant guise,
When her loose gown from her shoulders did fall,

And she me caught in her arms long and small,
Therewithal sweetly did me kiss,
And softly said, "Dear heart, how like you this?"

It was no dream; I lay broad waking.
But all is turned, thorough my gentleness,
Into a strange fashion of forsaking;
And I have leave to go, of her goodness,
And she also to use new-fangledness.
20 But since that I so kindely° am served,   naturally
I would fain know what she hath deserved.

William Butler Yeats

William Butler Yeats (1865–1939), born in Dublin, grew up largely in Ireland in
an Anglo-Irish family. Both his father and his brother were well-known artists.
Yeats published his first collection of poetry when he was twenty-four and wrote
continually until his death fifty years later. Considered by many the greatest of
modern poets, Yeats was a leader in the Irish renaissance, playwright and
founder of the Abbey Theatre, an Irish patriot and a denouncer of nationalism, a
mystic and skeptic—a man of passion and conflict whose poetry derived from
passionate conflict. In 1919, he acquired Thoor Ballylee, an ancient Norman
tower in the west of Ireland that became a feature and a fixture in his poetry. He
became a senator of independent Ireland and was awarded the Nobel Prize for
literature in 1923. He made his best books of poems after receiving the prize:
The Tower in 1928 and the posthumous *Last Poems* in 1940.

The Magi   (1914)

Now as at all times I can see in the mind's eye,
In their stiff, painted clothes, the pale unsatisfied ones
Appear and disappear in the blue depth of the sky
With all their ancient faces like rain-beaten stones,
And all their helms of silver hovering side by side,
And all their eyes still fixed, hoping to find once more,
Being by Calvary's turbulence unsatisfied,
The uncontrollable mystery on the bestial floor.

The Second Coming   (1921)

Turning and turning in the widening gyre°   spiral
The falcon cannot hear the falconer;
Things fall apart; the centre cannot hold;
Mere anarchy is loosed upon the world,
The blood-dimmed tide is loosed, and everywhere
The ceremony of innocence is drowned;

The best lack all conviction, while the worst
Are full of passionate intensity.

10   Surely some revelation is at hand;
    Surely the Second Coming is at hand.
The Second Coming! Hardly are those words out
When a vast image out of *Spiritus Mundi*°   soul of the world
Troubles my sight: somewhere in sands of the desert
A shape with lion body and the head of a man,
A gaze blank and pitiless as the sun,
Is moving its slow thighs, while all about it
Reel shadows of the indignant desert birds.
The darkness drops again; but now I know
That twenty centuries of stony sleep
20   Were vexed to nightmare by a rocking cradle,
    And what rough beast, its hour come round at last,
Slouches towards Bethlehem to be born?

Sailing to Byzantium   (1927)

I

That is no country for old men. The young
In one another's arms, birds in the trees
—Those dying generations—at their song,
The salmon-falls, the mackerel-crowded seas,
Fish, flesh, or fowl, commend all summer long
Whatever is begotten, born, and dies.
Caught in that sensual music all neglect
Monuments of unageing intellect.

II

An aged man is but a paltry thing,
10   A tattered coat upon a stick, unless
    Soul clap its hands and sing, and louder sing
For every tatter in its mortal dress,
Nor is there singing school but studying
Monuments of its own magnificence;
And therefore I have sailed the seas and come
To the holy city of Byzantium.

III

O sages standing in God's holy fire
As in the gold mosaic of a wall,
Come from the holy fire, perne° in a gyre,   wind or unwind
20   And be the singing-masters of my soul.
    Consume my heart away; sick with desire
And fastened to a dying animal
It knows not what it is; and gather me
Into the artifice of eternity.

IV

Once out of nature I shall never take
My bodily form from any natural thing,
But such a form as Grecian goldsmiths make
Of hammered gold and gold enamelling
To keep a drowsy Emperor awake;
30 Or set upon a golden bough to sing
To lords and ladies of Byzantium
Of what is past, or passing, or to come.

Leda and the Swan   (1924)

A sudden blow: the great wings beating still
Above the staggering girl, her thighs caressed
By the dark webs, her nape caught in his bill,
He holds her helpless breast upon his breast.

How can those terrified vague fingers push
The feathered glory from her loosening thighs?
And how can body, laid in that white rush,
But feel the strange heart beating where it lies?

A shudder in the loins engenders there
10 The broken wall, the burning roof and tower
And Agamemnon dead.
                          Being so caught up,
So mastered by the brute blood of the air,
Did she put on his knowledge with his power
Before the indifferent beak could let her drop?

Among School Children   (1928)

I

I walk through the long schoolroom questioning;
A kind old nun in a white hood replies;
The children learn to cipher and to sing,
To study reading-books and history,
To cut and sew, be neat in everything
In the best modern way—the children's eyes
In momentary wonder stare upon
A sixty-year-old smiling public man.

II

I dream of a Ledaean body, bent
10 Above a sinking fire, a tale that she
Told of a harsh reproof, or trivial event
That changed some childish day to tragedy—
Told, and it seemed that our two natures blent

Into a sphere from youthful sympathy,
Or else, to alter Plato's parable,
Into the yolk and white of the one shell.

III

And thinking of that fit of grief or rage
I look upon one child or t'other there
And wonder if she stood so at that age—
20 For even daughters of the swan can share
Something of every paddler's heritage—
And had that color upon cheek or hair,
And thereupon my heart is driven wild:
She stands before me as a living child.

IV

Her present image floats into the mind—
Did Quattrocento finger fashion it
Hollow of cheek as though it drank the wind
And took a mess of shadows for its meat?
And I though never of Ledaean kind
30 Had pretty plumage once—enough of that,
Better to smile on all that smile, and show
There is a comfortable kind of old scarecrow.

V

What youthful mother, a shape upon her lap
Honey of generation had betrayed,
And that must sleep, shriek, struggle to escape
As recollection or the drug decide,
Would think her son, did she but see that shape
With sixty or more winters on its head,
A compensation for the pang of his birth,
40 Or the uncertainty of his setting forth?

VI

Plato thought nature but a spume that plays
Upon a ghostly paradigm of things;
Solider Aristotle played the taws
Upon the bottom of a king of kings;[1]
World-famous golden-thighed Pythagoras
Fingered upon a fiddle-stick or strings
What a star sang and careless Muses heard:
Old clothes upon old sticks to scare a bird.

VII

Both nuns and mothers worship images,
50 But those the candles light are not as those

[1] Aristotle tutored Alexander the Great.

That animate a mother's reveries,
But keep a marble or a bronze repose.
And yet they too break hearts—O Presences
That passion, piety or affection knows,
And that all heavenly glory symbolize—
O self-born mockers of man's enterprise;

VIII

Labor is blossoming or dancing where
The body is not bruised to pleasure soul,
Nor beauty born out of its own despair,
60 Nor blear-eyed wisdom out of midnight oil.
O chestnut-tree, great-rooted blossomer,
Are you the leaf, the blossom or the bole?
O body swayed to music, O brightening glance,
How can we know the dancer from the dance?

Crazy Jane Talks with the Bishop   (1933)

I met the Bishop on the road
And much said he and I.
'Those breasts are flat and fallen now,
Those veins must soon be dry;
Live in a heavenly mansion,
Not in some foul sty.'

'Fair and foul are near of kin,
And fair needs foul,' I cried.
'My friends are gone, but that's a truth

10 Nor grave nor bed denied,
Learned in bodily lowliness
And in the heart's pride.

'A woman can be proud and stiff
When on love intent;
But Love has pitched his mansion in
The place of excrement;
For nothing can be sole or whole
That has not been rent.'

Louis Zukofsky

Louis Zukofsky (1904–1978) is one of the founders of Objectivism, a school of
poets that declared the poem itself an object, and natural objects the material of
poetry. He began as a follower of Ezra Pound, published widely in the 1930s, and
then survived in obscurity until a group of younger poets, following a similar
esthetic, rediscovered him in the 1960s.

"In Arizona"   (1965)

In Arizona
          (how many years in the mountains)
The small stumped bark of a tree
Looks up
          in the shape of an adored pup

The indians do not approach it
The round indian tents
                remain where they are
The tanned whites
10   are never seen by it
And one can imagine its imploring eyes

The skies
           it seems to look up to
                    blue
The same sun that warms the desert
Warms what one
                can imagine to be its ears.

TO READ A

Play

To read a play is different from reading a story or poem. Oral performance of poetry and fiction is optional, and not the primary form by which we experience poems and stories. For plays, performance is primary; performance *is* the play.

Silent reading is secondary, but it provides opportunity for our imagination to become director, actor, costumer, and scene designer. No other form of literary reading demands so much participation and mental action from us as readers. Reading a play, we must attend to character and narrative, to language and symbol—and, with the help of stage directions, we must also dress the characters, set them in a place, and move them around. In our best reading of drama, we imagine actors' voices rolling out the lines.

To prepare for the silent reading of plays, we need to begin, not with the analysis of an example, as we did for stories and poems, but with understanding the parts of the theatrical whole—components of our mental theater.

The Mental Theater

Each genre of literature suggests its own style of reading. We usually read fiction and poetry silently, in private. When we read plays, privacy and silence may impoverish the genre, for a play comes alive only when it is performed before an audience. In a theater, actors' voices may sink to a whisper, rise to a shout, or tremble with emotion: bodies gesture, eyes weep; flowing robes sweep beneath elegant wigs in front of painted mountains, while a bird sings offstage. Characters with names like Othello and Hedda Gabler walk, leap, wheel about; others dance, strut, collapse on a stage that (we are instructed) is a street in Venice or a drawing room in Norway. Characters hold objects in their hands: the skull of an old jester, a philosopher's manuscript. When we read drama* in silence and in private, we must make up for the absence of sight and sound.

The playwright,† the poet, and the novelist have different powers at their disposal. Neither playwright nor novelist can expect focused attention on particular words as the poet can. Nor can the playwright declaim onstage his own psychological analysis of character the way the novelist sometimes does. The play we read is a script (dialogue and stage directions) in which the playwright provides the means for a production that will *show* characters in action. In this showing, drama discovers its power: the dramatist has the advantage of employing actual bodies and voices of skilled actors, costumed by expert designers, directed and coached and rehearsed for performance. With the movements of bodies, occupying space, surrounded by objects, the playwright's words engage the playwright's audience.

The distinguishing fact about the genre of drama is that to experience it fully we must experience it communally. An audience responds to language, spectacle, motion, and gesture as a community, and each of us is affected by the responses—laughter, tears, coughs, intaken breaths—of people around us.

---

* Drama can mean several things. It means the entire genre of plays, as in "An Introduction to Drama." It means a historical segment of the genre, as in "Greek drama." *A* drama is a single play—"*Hamlet* is Shakespeare's greatest drama." We also use the word as a metaphor to describe exciting events: "a real-life drama."

† A *playwright* writes plays; do not spell the word *playwrite*.

Actors are aware of audience, too, and partly because no audience is identical to another, no two performances of a play are ever quite the same—even when the same actors perform the same drama twice in one day. The uniqueness of each performance is a product of the interaction of actors and watchers.

Reading drama in private, we can, to a degree, supply what is missing by making a mental theater as we read. We can supply the missing voice, gesture, motion, and spectacle. The more we have experienced theater, the more vividly we can populate the brain's stage with imagined actors.

Sometimes, knowing what we are doing, we may turn off the lights of the mental stage and read plays as if they were stories or poems. Shakespeare's plays *are* poetry as well as drama, and they reward the close attention to language that poetry demands of us. Chekhov's plays, with their psychological curiosities, invite us to investigate and understand character, as if we were reading Katherine Anne Porter's or William Faulkner's fiction. When we read closet drama—works written in the form of plays but intended for reading rather than for production—we read as if we were reading fiction or poetry.

But we do not read drama fully without knowing particularities of staging and performance. To prepare the way for reading plays, let us start by listing Aristotle's classic components of drama and then the common features of the theater like direction, acting, costuming, blocking, and lighting.

Elements of Drama

The first critic to analyze plays was the ancient Greek philosopher Aristotle, in his *Poetics.* Aristotle based his analysis only on Greek plays, but his description of drama's elements remains useful. He discussed them in an order of importance: plot, character, thought, diction, spectacle, and song. Many modern playwrights and directors depart from Aristotle's sequence. Some elevate character over plot, others put thought above both plot and character; still others emphasize one or two qualities to the exclusion of others. **Melodramas**, for instance, are plays in which action and suspense dominate the stage at the expense of thought, character, and all other qualities; musicals emphasize spectacle and song.

Plot

Plot is the sequence of events in narration, the structure of action and incident by which the playwright tells a story. Usually, a play's plot divides into acts, which are the main divisions of plays, traditionally signaled by the lowering of the curtain (if one is used) and raising of the house lights, followed by an intermission. Modern plays are usually divided into three or two acts; older plays often have five. Both the Greeks and the Elizabethans performed plays without interruption, like today's films, but modern editors and directors have divided old plays into acts for modern audiences and readers. Acts are often subdivided into scenes, separate episodes of dialogue among groups of characters.

Acts and scenes are the blocks out of which the playwright constructs the plot. A commonplace example of plot is "Boy meets girl, boy loses girl, boy gets girl" (boy/girl are reversible). The cliché describes a brief union, then a crisis or conflict of separation, and finally a resolution of conflict joining girl and boy. It makes a stick-figure story, which exemplifies the **unified** or **symmetrical plot**. In a unified plot, the audience finds formal satisfaction in the raising and resolution of **suspense** and expectation. If an issue is raised or a problem is stated early in the play, we know that the plot will return to this issue or problem. Suspense raises tension when it asks whether something desired or feared will happen. In a **conflict** (often between characters, sometimes between character and circumstance or idea or fate), we need to discover who will prevail and how. When the play's end answers the questions suspense had raised, our tension is resolved. As audience we are first excited, then we are relaxed. Along with our emotional response, we take esthetic pleasure in resolution of tension, as we do in the tension and release of a piece of music, when we enjoy a theme's return.

All plays include conflict, tension, suspense, resolution. But plots need not be unified or symmetrical. Sometimes a plot is **linear** or **episodic**, thrusting a narrative forward scene by scene. The episodic plot emphasizes time and sequence, and it can be seen mainly in the pageants or panoramas by which townspeople sometimes present the history of their town at its centennial. Such linear plots proceed chronologically without attention to symmetries or balances. They may retain conflict, tension, resolution: they tend to proceed by a series of conflicts resolved and new conflicts encountered; the township survives a flood only to be ravaged by cholera. A linear or episodic structure requires other dramatic qualities, if it is to achieve a pleasing sense of wholeness. Unity may largely derive from character or from idea while plot remains linear and episodic.

Oedipus Rex, Othello, The Importance of Being Earnest, Hedda Gabler, and *Death of a Salesman* are all plays with a unified or symmetrical plot. For familiar examples of each plot type at its extreme, we need look no further than a television play. A soap opera is episodic, interweaving different plot lines like braided hair. A half-hour situation comedy is unified, even predictable in shape—with a goal (raise money for the school band) and a conflict (against the school board's rules) and a crisis (a student ruse is defeated) and a resolution (alternate funding discovered).

In many plays, more than one plot occupies the stage; if one plot dominates, anything else is considered a **subplot**. In an episodic play, a subplot may be a story told and completed in one episode; in a unified play it is likely to be ongoing; in either case, the subplot tells a story in tandem with the main story (often plots touch each other, as characters meet or overlap from one plot to another) that usually acts as commentary on the main story. In the heroic plays of the eighteenth century, the main plot was often a highly serious tale of love and honor; underneath the story of lords and ladies, servants or commoners played out a love story, less honorable and more funny, that cast an ironic reflection on the main plot. In Shakespeare's *A Midsummer Night's Dream,* the love-quarrels of the nobility and the love-quarrels of the fairy king and queen interweave to our delight; the workers' stage company, rehearsing a play about tragic lovers, makes a third set of characters interwoven with the other two.

It is helpful to know certain terms used in discussing plot. Often, at the beginning of a play, the author needs to present information on which the plot is based. Sophocles starts *Oedipus Rex* with essential information about disaster in the city of Thebes. Shakespeare establishes Iago's anger at Othello in the play's first scene. **Exposition** is the presentation of necessary background information. We find exposition in fiction and in poetry, but on the stage it gives the playwright a particular problem; the poet or storyteller can speak as narrator, but the playwright cannot speak so directly. (Occasionally, plays use narrators. Shakespeare occasionally used a **prologue**—lines spoken by an actor to introduce a play—and Thornton Wilder's Stage Manager in *Our Town* narrates background and provides commentary, but the device is uncommon.) A skillful playwright gives us necessary information through the dialogue of the characters—so cleverly that we are not aware that we are being informed. A less experienced writer may begin a play with the butler and the maid, otherwise unimportant to the story, letting us know that Lord and Lady Redesworth are expected home soon from the bridge tournament, that their spendthrift nephew will arrive for supper, and that the murder trial of Sir Humphrey's niece begins in the morning.

Clumsy exposition is faulty plotting. Plays without conflict or tension bore us; so do plays in which the motives for action seem arbitrary; many a poor playwright has killed an innocent character merely to lower the first-act curtain. On the other hand, some second-rate theater is skillful in plotting—and we associate its inferiority with the slickness of its skill. Skillful construction is essential to the theater, but if a play shows nothing but formal skill, we belittle it with the label **well-made play**. The expression refers to a type of theater piece developed by the French playwright Eugène Scribe (1791–1861) and his followers, a play constructed on an ingenious pattern, sure to satisfy the box office—often rather shallow in situation and character. Ibsen (who directed nearly a hundred light French plays as an apprentice) broke away from the formula but kept elements like the "obligatory scene"—as when Hedda Gabler's idealistic illusions are destroyed. George Bernard Shaw inverted the tricks of the well-made play to disguise his satire of Victorian complacency.

If exposition tells us what has already happened or can be expected to happen, **foreshadowing** predicts, hints, warns, or threatens what *may* happen. Oedipus warns what will happen to the guilty party (whom the audience knows to be Oedipus himself, thus contributing to the play's tension). As the complexities and complications build, we speak of **rising action**—as if it toiled uphill through small conflicts and minor crises toward a supreme crisis, a final conflict. This is the play's **climax**, its answer to the **dramatic question** posed by the conflict: Will Othello trust the lying Iago? After the climax, there are often smaller questions left to be answered, problems to be solved; the play's conclusion, a **falling action** generally swifter than its rising action, may be called its **resolution**, or its **conclusion**, or its **dénouement**—from a French word that means the untying of a knot. If the dénouement drags on too long, though, we grow displeased or frustrated and call it **anticlimax**.

Character

A character is an imagined person, created by the playwright in dialogue and stage direction, made particular by the director and actor. A character begins in the script—a potential, an outline, a series of possibilities noted in dialogue—and can be realized in different ways (and with different degrees of success) by different directors and actors.

We may divide characters, as we find them in reading drama, as realistic, nonrealistic, and stereotyped. A realistic character is a person presented with background or history that discloses motivation for actions and feelings. Usually, in a realistic drama, we **empathize** with the character; empathy allows us to *feel* ourselves *into* a character; imaginatively, we become that character. A nonrealistic character may be nonhuman, a talking fish or a leprechaun. When medieval playwrights wrote allegory for the theater, characters on the stage would take the roles of abstractions like Christian or Lust. In contemporary pageants, we sometimes find allegorical figures standing in for abstractions like Liberty or Totalitarianism. But allegory is only one form of nonrealism. Samuel Beckett invents an old man named Krapp with a collection of audiotapes of himself. He cannot be reduced to an abstraction like *Loneliness;* neither is he the chap next door.

The **stereotype** is a familiar kind of character. When we use the word *stereotype* about modern drama, we are usually being critical, as when we criticize a poet for using clichés or stock language. In a television show about a police department, we often find stereotypes like the old street-wise detective paired with the young idealistic detective. In the classic American western movie, we expect the figure of the hero's loyal sidekick.

In earlier times, many dramatists wrote parts for characters their audience expected. When we speak of such characters as stereotypes, we speak of expected features of a kind of drama; we are not being critical. In Roman comedy, audiences laughed at a bragging, vainglorious military man; English comedy from Shakespeare's time onward invented variants on the stereotype of the fop—generally overdressed peacocks with pretensions to valor and to success with women—whose lies and stratagems are comically exposed. A stereotype is a collection of characteristics. A fully drawn character may be expected to change within a play; a stereotype remains a sum of qualities unchanged and unchanging. Even exposed, the fop will remain a fop.

In great drama, we find characters who enter as stereotypes but soon transcend their expected roles. One stereotype is the **ingénue**—the innocent or naïve young woman—but to call *Hamlet's* Ophelia an ingénue, while true enough, tells us little about her. Shakespeare creates Ophelia's character with Ophelia's distinctive language, and she becomes a fully realized character, as when she says, observing Hamlet when he appears insane:

> O, what a noble mind is here o'erthrown!
> The courtier's, soldier's, scholar's, eye, tongue, sword,
> Th'expectancy and rose of the fair state,
> The glass of fashion, and the mould of form,
> Th'observed of all observers, quite quite down,
> And I of ladies most deject and wretched,
> That sucked the honey of his music vows,
> Now see that noble and most sovereign reason
> Like sweet bells jangled, out of tune and harsh,
> That unmatched form and feature of blown youth,
> Blasted with ecstasy!

No essayist could *tell* of devotion and grief more eloquently than Shakespeare *shows* us in Ophelia's words.

Frequently, conflict, mentioned in discussing plot, flares up between the characters of a play. We call the hero of a play, especially a tragedy, the play's **protagonist**, and sometimes he finds himself in conflict with an enemy or **antagonist** who seeks to thwart his purpose. Not all plays are so neat in their opposition of characters. If Oedipus is clearly the protagonist of the play bearing his name, his early conflict with Kreon would seem to name Kreon an antagonist; but surely Oedipus's ultimate antagonist is Fate. In *Othello,* the villain is Iago, but Othello's jealousy also derives from his own human fallibility.

In a modern play, the playwright may indicate character by writing **stage directions** in the script, lines describing character or scene or action. When Willy Loman returns home at the start of *Death of a Salesman,* we understand his fatigue, as we understand his wife's compassion with the help of stage directions: *"He sits on the bed beside her, a little numb." "She is taking off his shoes." "He presses two fingers against his eyes."*

Stage business, the gesture or nonverbal action of actors on the stage, contributes to characterization. Although the modern playwright supplies business in the stage directions, no author describes every minute action or expression of every character. In any production of a play, characterization is developed by further stage business, facial expression, gesture, and move-ment—hundreds of particulars not specified in any script. These expressions of the text are the province of the play's **director**—the person who oversees the play's performance, controlling interpretations, movement, pacing, light-ing, and scenery, and integrating all the dramatic ingredients. When we stage a play in our mental theater, we are our own director.

Through the director's efforts, we pass from characterization as a quality of the script to characterization as a product of performance. Stage business, in practice, is partly the playwright's doing and partly the director's. This division of labor marks the modern theater; until the eighteenth century, authors did not supply stage directions, and directors as such were unknown. Plays were produced under *somebody's* leadership—perhaps the chief actor of the company, perhaps the playwright, perhaps the stage manager. A mod-ern director who takes on an old play feels free to invent the staging. Many directors feel considerable freedom to make new interpretations of a mod-ern play, even to departing from the playwright's indicated interpretation.

If the director is the emperor of characterization in the play's world, actors are the lieutenants who control the realm. The actor's skills, acquired over years of training and experience, cover the range of feelings that voice and body can express. Volume, pitch, timbre, and accent of voice combine with the vocabulary of body language in gesture, gait, and posture. But actors' skills must work in service to the whole production, and it is the director's job to set the overall tone and to make the production cohere. A single text is subject to many interpretations. Readers and critics of *Othello* differ widely in their understanding of the play, and different productions reflect these differences. Laurence Olivier's film production of *Othello* (1966) has been called a psychoanalytic interpretation, dwelling on the Moorish general's emotional constitution: it is a painful and excellent production unusual in its inwardness. The play's fine Broadway production of 1982, starring James Earl Jones as Othello and Christopher Plummer as Iago, achieved its power by a more traditional and outward approach, characterizing Othello as a military genius unsophisticated in matters of the heart. To fit varying interpretations of the protagonist, each production required a different Desdemona, a different Iago.

The director begins production with a script from which he or she derives a notion of character. Under ideal circumstances, the director chooses actors who fulfill the requirements of the interpretation. One director might want a muscular, vigorous lead actor; another might want someone lean and ascetic.

Director and actor are also subject to the **theatrical conventions** of their day. Stereotypes are conventions of theater. In the Greek theater, it was a convention that the players speak from behind masks; women's parts in Elizabethan theater were taken by boys. The usual realism of the modern play is itself a series of conventions; in most modern plays, we take it as realistic that a drawing room or a bedroom should have one open side, through which we can view the proceedings, and that most of the actors face that open side as they speak to each other. Although it is easy enough to notice conventions alien to our own, like masks, we seldom notice the conventions we are used to.

Perhaps nothing dates so quickly as theatrical styles and conventions. For example, on the Elizabethan stage, where boys played women's roles, love scenes were understandably stylized. In the late seventeenth century, women began to play women's roles, and love scenes became more realistic; yet from the Restoration until recent times, an actor and actress in a passionate love scene would wait for applause after an eloquent embrace, as if they had just sung an operatic duet. Only in the late nineteenth century and the early twentieth did actors begin to imitate feeling, not from the gesture book but from their own psyches and their director's ideas of human character.

Some actors are highly technical, learning by study what to do with body, voice, and expression, and reproducing feeling by expertise. Others draw from their own feelings, improvising dramatic movement and gesture out of private emotion. Konstantin Stanislavsky (1865–1938) proposed in his book *An Actor Prepares* (1926) that actors perform by summoning their own feelings. In his Moscow Art Theater, he trained his actors to search their own psyches for their characters' emotions, and then to act on stage as the character would.

Thought

For most readers, the thought of a play, its theme, its ideas, will take precedence over other elements. Thought is drama's summation, what remains in the mind when the theater is dark again or the book is closed. Aristotle placed thought third, recognizing it as product of plot and character. For Aristotle, thought is the statement about human life that the play's action exemplifies. It resides largely in dialogue, Aristotle tells us, and can be subsumed under three headings: first, "proof and refutation"; second, "the excitation of the feelings, such as pity, fear, anger . . ."; third, "the suggestion of importance or its opposite."

These three categories suggest different sorts of thought in drama, or different uses of thought. If a play offers "proof and refutation" the play is argumentative, and its design is **didactic**. To be didactic is to teach. There is a long tradition of plays that teach, that have a design on our thoughts and actions. George Bernard Shaw's plays are almost always didactic as well as entertaining; they make persuasive statements about politics and society. If a didactic play does not otherwise engage us, it will not convince us by its arguments or persuade us by its teaching; finding it *merely* didactic, we will dismiss it as propaganda.

Aristotle's second category of thought implies a response to script and production observable in the audience: "the excitation of the feelings. . . ." Aristotle does not separate idea from feeling: he includes emotions *within* his category of thought or theme. Finally, Aristotle speaks of values— "importance or its opposite." Thought ascribes value—or lack of value—to a drama's action. Sophocles's subject in *Oedipus*—the welfare of a people, the fated guilt of their king, his punishment—has a magnitude to which his characters in their speech and actions are adequate. The "opposite" of importance, on the other hand, can result from the triviality of a subject or from the inadequate treatment of a serious subject. The themes of popular dramatic art can often be justly summarized by a cliché: "It takes all kinds to make a world" or "There's a little bit of good in just about everybody."

In most plays, the protagonist's conflicts embody the play's thought. Although we cannot reduce *Othello*'s themes to an easy paraphrase, we can observe Shakespeare's thought in his matching of characters—Desdemona's utter goodness, for instance, against Iago's thorough evil—and in his ironic use of the key words *honest* and *honesty.* We understand that the play's insights about the human psyche center on Iago's gradual corruption of Othello.

The reader does well to observe the minor characters as well as major ones; in theater, everything coalesces to create the play's thought. Thinking about a play, we should draw back from the emotional crises of the plot to ask ourselves, for instance, about Cassio's function in *Othello:* What does his presence mean to the play's ideas, as well as to its structure? If Lopahin were not onstage in *The Cherry Orchard,* what would be lacking in Chekhov's play? By analyzing the intellectual function of a play's characters, we analyze the content of the play.

Sometimes a play or a film includes physical objects important to its thought. If a playwright continually reminds us of a place or a thing, onstage or off, we should consider its function and meaning in the play with as much attention as if it were another character. The cherry orchard itself in Chekhov's play is not listed among the performers and remains invisible to the audience, but it is essential to the play's theme and thought; Chekhov suggests as much by taking it for his title. By contrast, the comic title of *The Importance of Being Earnest* assures us of its own opposite.

Language

Aristotle's fourth element of drama is usually translated "diction." In the *Poetics,* Aristotle defines the style appropriate to Greek drama, writing from a theatrical tradition other than ours. The importance he grants to language may serve to remind us that plays are language first, that they begin as dialogue, and that great dialogue is words arranged in the best order. (Exceptions like the one-actor play—Samuel Beckett's *Krapp's Last Tape,* for instance—give us theatrical language without dialogue, although Krapp converses with his own taped voice. Wordless **mime theater**, sometimes one-actor performances like Marcel Marceau's, remains a portion of theater outside literature.) The greatest playwrights are great *writers:* Shakespeare and Sophocles are poets, Chekhov and Shaw are masters of prose. It is no coincidence that, if Shakespeare had written no plays, his sonnets and long poems would earn him prominence in the history of literature, or that Chekhov is often considered literature's greatest master of the short story.

The "best words" for a particular play depend on the subject undertaken. If we did not feel that the characters in *Death of a Salesman* speak in an American idiom, we would not believe in them. If poetic language were attributed to the salesman Willy Loman, we would find the play intolerably confusing. Good plays range wide in their language, from the poetic choruses of Sophocles to the natural non sequiturs of Chekhov's characters in *The Cherry Orchard.* In comedy, characters often speak with a wit— balanced phrases, paradox, epigram—few of us can manage in everyday life; and as their language is, so is their witty construction of plot.

To remind yourself of the difference language makes, glance back at the Shakespeare/Shakespearean paraphrase on pages 521–523.

Spectacle

The Physical Stage

Spectacle is what the audience sees, the play as it exists to the eye, the visual theater. The first element of spectacle is the theater itself and its physical stage. When we read *Oedipus Rex* and *Othello,* it helps to know about the actual theaters Sophocles and Shakespeare wrote for. Beginning with the mid-seventeenth century, the most common western theater shape (almost universal until recent years) has been the **proscenium stage**. The stage with which modern Americans are most familiar is a slight variant, which we will call the **picture stage**: at the front of an auditorium is a framed, rectangular space—the proscenium arch—across which we may draw a **stage curtain**. At the bottom of the stage's front are **footlights** for low illumination; at the top of the frame are lights that cast illumination downward. This framed, rectangular, lighted space is the box within which the actors act, and it extends to various depths from the **stage front** to **stage rear**.

The original proscenium stages of the seventeenth century featured a **forestage**, a platform thrust into the audience before the proscenium arch.

Most of the acting was done on this forward deck. Gradually, in the eighteenth and early nineteenth centuries, the forestage grew smaller, and acting tended to concentrate itself behind the proscenium arch, where lighting could be better controlled, where scenery could be varied, where **stage machinery** could raise and lower painted scenes on pulleys, for instance, or slide them on rails laterally from the wings.

Although most theaters and auditoriums, from high schools to Broadway, still feature the picture stage, its shape may vary. In the later nineteenth century, some theatrical producers began to experiment with the return of the forestage, often building a platform over the **orchestra pit** (a sunken area, below the level of the audience, between the picture stage and the first row of seats, where musicians play their instruments in productions of musical plays and opera). Some more modern theaters, especially those built for the production of Shakespearean plays, extend a narrowing forestage (sometimes called the **thrust stage**) into the audience, with rows of seats on three sides. Some theatrical spaces are constructed with the audience seated on all sides—called the **arena stage**, or **theater in the round**. For this physical theater, plays must be directed to be seen on all sides and must do largely without scenery. Still other experimental theaters feature actors who wander among the spectators.

Scenery, Set, and Props

A director typically relies on a **set** or **scenic designer**; the set is the scenery and furniture the audience sees. The setting for a play may include a realistic painted **backdrop** of forest or castle, or the back of the set may be the wall of a room, with real wallpaper and a real window in it. The designer submits sketches to the director for approval; carpenters and painters then turn these designs into furniture and scenery. In the most realistic interpretations of plays, rooms look like rooms we live in and forests as much like forests as a designer's skills can make them. A production may require many changes of scene, if the play's plot moves from battleground to commander's tent to king's palace. Often, the curtain is drawn while the set is changed. A production may use backdrops painted on sliding wings and stored out of sight to left and right until they are needed. Sets may be lifted to hang above the stage, then lowered by stage machinery when they are needed. Stage machinery needed for such equipment is expensive and bulky. Some modern stages are equipped with a **revolving stage**, a circular platform cut into the stage floor, rotated by hand or by machine; this revolving stage is divided into segments, and each segment can be rotated to face the audience with a different set.

Many modern directors use a nonrealistic set, even for scripts and productions that have realistic characters. On a relatively bare stage, the designer may create a **unit set**, perhaps a platform with steps leading to it, and a few black boxes; as the script requires, a box may become a throne or a tree trunk, the platform a balcony or a bedroom. Such staging requires imagination from director and audience; it is cheaper in production and it allows the play to move faster because no set changes are required.

In nonrealistic modern theater, a nonrealistic setting is often specified in stage directions: a curtain, a rug, a screen. Samuel Beckett's nonrealistic *Waiting for Godot* specifies only "A Country Road. A tree"; few designers have been tempted to realism. Taking the playwright's general indication, the designer makes the set particular.

Props are properties, or portable pieces of scenery, not attached to walls or screens. Sofas and chairs, or objects characters carry in their hands, are typical props.

Costume

Only in the past century and a half has costuming attempted realism. When Elizabethans took on the roles of Romans, they dressed in high Elizabethan fashion (a practice used as an argument for performing old plays in the dress of our own day). Actors tended to strut the stage in their greatest finery, their clothing contributing to theatrical spectacle. In the middle of the nineteenth century, as the theater moved further toward the illusion of reality, actors began to wear clothes considered appropriate to the historical time of the script, and Romans looked as we believe Romans to have looked.

The play's director collaborates with the **costume designer** or **costumer** as closely as with the set designer. For many productions, settings and costumes are created by a single designer.

Makeup

On the Greek stage, actors wore masks that made their faces look larger and more powerful, from the distant perspective of the Greek auditorium. On the modern realistic stage, makeup is a portion of spectacle—and frequently it uses artifice to appear natural. The bright lighting of most stage productions can give a healthy actor the pallor of a corpse, unless the actor first applies a ruddy base makeup, accents lips, and emphasizes eyes. Made-up eyes look larger; eyes tend to disappear without makeup, especially when seen from the rear of the second balcony.

Lighting

The ancient stage, from the Greeks to the Elizabethans, used no light but the sun. The only variations of light occurred when an actor entered a shaded area of the stage, as when an Elizabethan hid or conspired under the small balcony at stage rear. When the theater moved indoors in the seventeenth century, only candles illuminated the stage, casting a dim and fitful light even when massed in candelabra. Successive technological innovations gradually improved stage lighting. Oil lamps afforded more control than candles and could cast bright light on a single part of the stage by the use of reflecting mirrors; colored glass in front of the flame could cast tinted light to imitate sunlight or fire. Early in the nineteenth century came the gas light—brighter than oil lamps and more controllable. Late in the nineteenth century, theaters began to use electric lights, which could go on and off without the use of matches—a miracle.

Today, directors planning productions write **light cues** into their texts and work with lighting engineers to realize their intentions.* Options are many: light can be general and uniform all over the stage; light can illuminate one character or one group of characters, keeping the rest of the stage dark or dim; lights can emphasize the finality of a scene by turning off all at once (a **blackout**); lights can shine on an actor from the theater ceiling in front of the stage, or from a balcony, or from banks of lights at the theater's sides; light can come from below (footlights) or behind (backlighting) or beside (from the wings).

Lighting can further the plot, as in the weird contrasts of melodrama, or the thought, as when it delineates part of the stage as a dream area or a reality area. Lights can be used for character; one actor can wear a virtual halo of **follow spots**. Lights can turn one character sallow and another ruddy. They can indicate the lapse of time by suggesting twilight or dawn. The rear of the stage may be occupied by a **cyclorama**—a curved white surface that readily accepts lighting, useful for sunrises, sunsets, rainbows, or the abstract play of color and shadow. With actors positioned behind gauze or **scrim**, a sidelight will render the gauze opaque and the actors invisible; a front light will reverse the vision—actors visible and gauze transparent; still another arrangement of lights will show the actors as shadows against the scrim.

Because light can create illusions of movement—when actors move out of light into dimness, for instance, they appear to move farther than they do—lighting is integral to the planning of the play's movement and gesture. The more subtle the play, the more subtle the lighting it requires. Melodramas tend to be higher in contrast of dark and light, and musicals more bright, than *Othello* or *Death of a Salesman*. In the didactic theater of Berthold Brecht and others, the playwright may specify an even light—like the light in a classroom or lecture hall.

Blocking

When directors plan a production, they plan the movement of players on the stage: this control of movement is called **blocking**. The audience looks at actors placed on stage in relationship to one another, and the director's blocking creates and continually recreates the relationships the audience perceives. Moving or standing still, bodies in relationship to each other can express character, further plot, or contribute to the expression of idea. If character A walks nervously up and down during an interview with character B, who sits still, we observe in spectacle an enactment of character and conflict. Nowhere are directors more active or are their presences more felt than in this spectacle of bodies in relationship to others.

Dance

A final element of spectacle is dance. In a musical play, its presence is obvious and necessitates the use of a **choreographer** or dance director. These plays

---

* A **lighting designer** is sometimes one of a three-member design team (with scenic and costume designers) who work with each other and with the director to mount a theater production.

are entertainment, and spectacle remains spectacle. In other plays, like Peter Shaffer's *Equus,* dance or dancelike movement is essential to plot, character, and thought.

Music and Sound

When Aristotle incorporated music in his list of drama's components, he was writing about an ancient theater in which speech was probably sung or chanted. In theater as we know it, sound is part of the total effect: first as spoken dialogue, in its manner of speaking; then as nonverbal utterance by actors—laughs and grunts and cries of pain; then as noises made by props, like a chair scraping or a radio turned on, or Hedda Gabler's piano-playing; then as silence; then as sound effects, like train whistles and a mysterious snapping sound in *The Cherry Orchard* or a telephone ringing or an offstage gunshot.

Assembling the Elements

Theatrical genius can be defined as the ability to make all these elements of theater work at once. The proportions of responsibility differ—playwright largely responsible for language and director largely responsible for specta-cle—but the results are interdependent. In good productions, plot is not sacrificed to spectacle or sound to character, but all cohere to make the single masterpiece. In the plays that follow, we must gauge the possibilities of coherence in a script. Thinking of Aristotle's six categories, we can ob-serve their potential interaction or integration. When Iago and Roderigo plot against Cassio in *Othello,* the language provides us with plot, character, thought, and language; but the playwright has also allowed us, by his power of imaginative seeing, to make a mental theater.

Some Suggestions for Studying Drama

Reading the plays that follow, students may study characterization and inter-pretation by reading scenes aloud in class, different students using the same words for different ideas of character. In discussion, a class may simulate a production, down to details of gesture, costuming, and lighting. Still, it is good to practice not only at directing but at our most familiar role—being an audience. If a class is able to attend a performance of any drama on any level of competence, it can profit by discussing the production in the terms used in this chapter. Excerpts from a recorded play heard in the classroom will provide no examples of spectacle but, for that very reason, may prove useful to consideration of plot, character, thought, voice-acting, and sound. A film will allow discussion of spectacle. Or, the class may agree to watch the same television show (a dramatic show would be best) for discussions of dramatic ingredients. Some profit may even be discovered in analysis of the plot structure of a thirty-second commercial.

CHAPTER THREE

Greek Drama, Tragedy, and Sophocles

History

About the origins of Greek theater we can only speculate; by the time we are able to speak of probable fact, we are only a century earlier than Sophocles's *Oedipus Rex,* which was first produced about 430 or 425 B.C. Apparently, by 535 B.C., the citizens of Athens watched tragedies during the festival of Dionysus— a Greek fertility god and the god of wine, worshiped in late winter and early spring at ceremonies called the Dionysia. One part of the Dionysia was a contest among playwrights, in which three authors each entered a tragic trilogy (three plays) accompanied by a short comedy or satire.

Drama seems to have evolved from religious worship in which a chorus of voices spoke hymns to Dionysus. We are told that a man named Thespis added to the chorus the figure of a single speaker who addressed the group and thus invented drama. Although further speakers or characters were added, the chorus always remained part of Greek drama, speaking as the collective voice of a people. In some plays, the chorus leader detaches himself from the group, almost becoming another individual character, to engage in dialogue.

The great playwright Aeschylus (ca. 524–456 B.C.) wrote the earliest plays that survive. According to Aristotle, it was Aeschylus who added a second speaker to Thespis's first, and Sophocles (ca. 496–406 B.C.) who added the third actor and fixed the fluctuating size of the chorus at fifteen speakers. The surviving plays of Aeschylus are great works of the ancient world, notably the *Oresteia* trilogy (*Agamemnon, Choephoroe,* and *Eumenides*) and *Seven Against Thebes.* It is testimony to drama's ritual origins that Aeschylus was accused of revealing in his plays religious secrets he had learned in a private initiation. Among the Greek gods, only Dionysus took possession of his worshipers; the actors at the Dionysia, shedding their personal identities to act, could be regarded as possessed by Dionysus.

We do know a little about the staging of Greek drama. At the back of the stage was a row of decorative columns, suggestive of a palace, before which the play took place. Behind this facade stood a small room where the actors

The classic Greek theater at Epidaurus, constructed in the fourth century B.C.,
seated fourteen thousand spectators on fifty-five tiers. Today, as in Hellenistic
times, audiences throng there for performances of the tragedies of Sophocles and
other masterworks.

could retire. The front of this room, visible between the columns, was probably decorated with scenery; this facade was called the *skene,* ancestor of our
word *scene.* In front of the *skene* and the columns, the actors spoke their
roles. As a voice of the citizenry, the chorus occupied an intermediary place
in the *orchestron,* an area for dancing and choral speaking midway between
actors and audience.

Greek theater thus placed distance between actors and audience, perhaps
because of the drama's religious nature. Actors were magnified, their faces
enlarged and made rigid by masks that apparently also functioned as mega-
phones, enlarging voice as well as face. The voice needed amplification
because Greek theaters were huge: at Epidaurus, the amphitheater seated
fourteen thousand people. Each stage was built below a small hill. The
audience sat in tiers rising in horseshoe shape uphill from the stage. Actors'
voices boomed from the wall of the *skene* and rose up the hillside.

Aristotle's *Poetics*

The Greek philosopher Aristotle (384–322 B.C.), writing shortly after the great age of the playwrights, investigated their work in his *Poetics,* which remains history's most influential work of literary criticism. Earlier, we noted his six elements of drama. We need to touch now on Aristotle's larger idea of art as imitation of nature, on his definition of tragedy, on his notions of the psychological functions of tragedy, and on a few of his formal observations.

For us, the word *imitation* sounds negative; an imitation is inferior, second-hand, derivative. But the Greeks attached no negative connotation to *mimesis* or imitation: to imitate nature meant to be true to life. Truth was not defined historically (what *really* happened) or morally (what *ought* to happen), but philosophically (what *would happen according to the laws of probability and human nature*). If Sophocles's Oedipus howls with anguish when he learns his dreadful secret, it is probable or true to nature that he would do so. If his mother-wife hangs herself when she learns the horrid truth, it is probable or true to nature that she would do so.

Aristotle tells us *Literature is more probable than history.* Historical fact gives us the actions of one person on one day under the accidental conditions of that day. If a reporter were recording the events of a historic Thebes, maybe we would learn that it was raining or that a messenger fell asleep in a ditch and was late or that Kreon pulled a muscle and needed help climbing stairs. These historical particulars would be irrelevant to the general truth to nature that Greek playwrights imitated.

This notion of probability helps explain the clear line of plot in Greek drama. If the playwright's task is to imitate nature's probability, the playwright may dispense with local particulars and concentrate on essences. This directness helps account for the inevitability we sense in Greek tragedy as events follow each other, not at random or by accident but because one event leads to the next by inexorable laws.

When Aristotle defined tragedy, he was a critic telling us what it had been, not a theorist saying what it ought to be. He described the features of tragedy as he observed them, like a naturalist describing a species of fish. "Tragedy, then," he summarizes, "is the imitation of an action that is serious, complete, and of a certain magnitude . . . in the form of action, not of narrative; through pity and fear effecting the proper purgation of these emotions." Defining terms within this famous definition, he tells us that "an action implies personal agents, who necessarily possess certain distinctive qualities both of character and thought . . . the two natural causes from which accidents spring. . . . But most important of all is the structure of the incident. For Tragedy is an imitation, not of men, but of an action and of life. . . ." Aristotle places plot foremost in his hierarchy of elements. Probability of the plot, built on causation rather than accident, becomes a requirement of form—it leads to the clarity with which we perceive the whole "complete" and "serious" action.

Becoming more particular, Aristotle tells us that a tragedy, by its nature, must tell of a *downfall,* and that the hero must be a virtuous man of some eminence, brought down by "some error or frailty." The unmerited fall of someone perfectly virtuous would merely shock us; the fall of a villain "would inspire neither pity nor fear." For the Greek words usually translated "fear" and "pity," commentators have suggested that we might better understand Aristotle's ideas if we read *dread* and *compassion.* Dread is the emotion that confronts inevitable misery; if pity seems to elevate the audience and separate it from the character of the drama, compassion identifies the audience with the protagonist in his downfall; without some manner of empathy or identification, it is difficult to argue for the presence of dread.

Aristotle asserts that the audience—as a result of experiencing these emotions in witnessing tragedy—undergoes an emotional purging or catharsis. This idea has puzzled commentators for hundreds of years. The notion of catharsis, most people agree, is Aristotle's defense of drama's social value and therefore a reply to Plato, who banned poets from his ideal Republic for promoting irrationality. Catharsis does not simply imply that tragedy is a safety valve for dangerous feelings, the way American football is sometimes defended as relieving spectators of their aggression. Aristotle's idea implies that art first arouses emotions and then directs and controls them, not removing them but shaping them. Plato's complaint that poetry "feeds and waters the passions instead of starving them" is countered by the notion that the emotions need not be (perhaps *can*not be) starved, but that they may be directed by intelligence and by the formal control of the dramatic artist.

A few other points from Aristotle's *Poetics:* The protagonist is "of high estate" and is frequently a king. Remember that a Greek king was not a symbolic monarch but a leader and protector of his people. We should think of Greek kings in terms of power and the state. When the dramatic protagonist is royal, like Oedipus, his downfall is a calamity for his people. And tragedy deals not with *any* king, but with kings who have displayed special courage or nobility or intelligence. Oedipus came to Thebes a stranger without title or wealth, then by his wit solved the riddle of the Sphinx and saved the city.

People commonly speak of the tragic protagonist as possessed of a "tragic flaw"—like a flaw in a diamond. Aristotle himself speaks of the tragic hero's "error or frailty." In later tragedies, we can often speak of flaws like Macbeth's ambition or Hamlet's indecisiveness—though one-word summations remain superficial. If we look for such a fatal weakness in Oedipus, we might point to his violent temper, his killing a stranger at a crossroads. But *Oedipus Rex* is clearly more than a play about someone who should have controlled his temper. It is a play about someone of whom it was prophesied at birth that he would kill his father—and who killed his father, despite everybody's attempts to keep it from happening. *Oedipus* is a play about fate or inevitability. Although some tragic heroes possess a moral Achilles' heel, it is more correct to understand Oedipus's frailty as being intrinsic to all human beings, not avoidable by exercise of will to virtue. These errors or frailties are fated and ineluctable; the dread with which we watch them work their way to the hero's downfall is a religious dread. Greek tragedies are saturated with awe for the gods and with a sense of the distinction between mortals and the divine. Remember that Dionysus was a god of fertility. For the food we eat, we rely on the fated, necessary, ineluctable death and rebirth of the year. Nature must die in the autumn in order to be born again in the spring. Many primitive peoples felt that, unless they enacted the ritual of dying, using their king as a sacrifice or scapegoat, some year the spring would not return.

In discussing the plots of Greek tragedies, Aristotle emphasized formal features: **reversal of intention** and **recognition**. These features are usually interrelated; Aristotle says that they must "form the internal structure of the plot, so that what follows should be the necessary or probable result. . . ." In reversal of intention, the audience watches a character take an action intended to accomplish one thing, and, as the audience continues to watch, this action accomplishes the opposite of what the character intends. "Thus in the *Oedipus* a messenger came to cheer Oedipus and free him from his alarms about his mother, but by revealing who he is, he produces the opposite effect." Recognition is revelation, something previously unknown coming to light. The messenger's reversal, in the paragraph above, affords Oedipus a terrible recognition: his wife Jocasta is also his mother.

Many critics have noticed that an almost pervasive concern of the theater is to question appearance and reality, perhaps because in watching a drama we are aware that the stage is occupied by actors who pretend to be what they are not. Central to the theater as we know it is the act of unmasking—a form of recognition—and we should notice that the mask itself was a property of the Greek stage. Tragic recognition is shocking or painful; comic recognition is often funny and satirical, as in *The Importance of Being Earnest*.

More Terms of Tragedy

Later critics have named other features of tragedy. **Dramatic irony** is sometimes called **tragic irony** because it is so common to tragedy. It often results from reversal of intention. Dramatic irony runs throughout *Oedipus Rex,* where the hero unwittingly denounces himself when he denounces the evildoer. In dramatic irony, the audience understands the consequences of the character's speech or act, but the character understands nothing until too late. We may want to rise in our chairs like a naïve watcher of a melodrama, to shout at the hero "Look out! Behind you!" We may want to say "Oedipus, *think* about what you're saying!" But no matter what we wish to say, the story will act itself out, as it has acted itself out over the centuries. Dramatic irony supports a sense of tragic inevitability and therefore supports and intensifies our dread and our awe.

Inevitable and inexorable is our sense of our own death and the deaths of people close to us—and possibly the deaths of our country, culture, or kind. The Sphinx's riddle that Oedipus solved was the identity of the creature that had four legs in morning, two legs at noon, and three at nightfall. Oedipus answered: humankind, that crawls as a baby, stands up as an adult, and hobbles with a cane in old age. Moreover, the riddle prefigures the play.

Although we see nothing of baby Oedipus on stage, the plot relies on accounts of Oedipus's infancy; the play starts with a strong, upright, powerful, two-legged king of his country; it ends with Oedipus a pitiful wreck, self-aged by his self-blinding, being led off the stage in disgrace, impotence, and exile. The hero's downfall has moved him from noon to night.

If catharsis is an idea difficult to understand, we know it is Aristotle's attempt to explain the exaltation or relief with which audiences and readers have responded to tragedy over the centuries. Why does a spectacle so depressing exalt us, or leave us better than we were? People have put forward all sorts of explanations. In a poem he called "Lapis Lazuli," William Butler Yeats suggests something that may help us understand Aristotle's catharsis. The poet describes a world in which civilization may be destroyed at any moment, and then asserts that every human figure acts out a tragic role; he describes the world as if it were a play. Moving back from individual to group, he says that every culture or civilization *will* die, as we all know. Finally, he imagines people carved in lapis lazuli (a hard stone known for its long endurance) who regard the world's scene from a distance while they listen to a skilled artist performing tragic art. When we see the characters of the world through the spectacles of tragedy, he tells us, our deaths and downfalls become acceptable; Yeats even claims that we may accept the tragic world with gaiety if we view human life and death through the form of tragedy. He answers Plato firmly. We may regard catharsis as tragic art's ability to reconcile us, through its inevitable form, to the dread of our own ending.

Sophocles

Sophocles was born at Colonus about 496 B.C. As a young man, he was musician, dancer, poet, and actor—roles the Greeks did not differentiate so much as we do. Like Shakespeare, he learned stagecraft by performing as an actor. We are told that he wrote 123 plays by which he won twenty-four victories in the playwrights' contest at the Dionysia. Only seven of his plays survive entire: after *Oedipus Rex,* the best known are *Antigone* and *Oedipus at Colonus*—Sophocles's final play, performed after his death at the age of ninety.

When the first audience witnessed the first production of *Oedipus Rex* around 430 to 425 B.C., they already knew the myth of Oedipus, which Homer recounted briefly in the *Odyssey.* Born to the king and queen of Thebes, Oedipus was sent to be exposed on a hillside because a prophecy warned that he would kill his father. By a series of believable events, the baby was not killed, and Oedipus was raised in another city thinking himself the true son of another couple. Traveling as a stranger, he killed a man at a crossroads; coming to Thebes thereafter he saved the city from the scourge of the Sphinx by answering the Sphinx's riddle. He then married the widowed queen. At the beginning of the play, many years have passed since the encounter at the crossroads, the triumph over the Sphinx, and the marriage, but a plague has infested the city, the result of an impious act at first unknown. In the course of the play, Oedipus discovers that he killed his father and married his mother.

Sophocles

Oedipus Rex (c. 430 B.C., tr. 1939)
Translated by Dudley Fitts and Robert Fitzgerald

Persons Represented

OEDIPUS	MESSENGER
A PRIEST	SHEPHERD OF LAÏOS
CREON	SECOND MESSENGER
TEIRESIAS	CHORUS OF THEBAN ELDERS
IOCASTE	

The Scene. *Before the palace of Oedipus, King of Thebes. A central door and two lateral doors open onto a platform which runs the length of the façade. On the platform, right and left, are altars; and three steps lead down into the "orchestra," or chorus-ground. At the beginning of the action these steps are crowded by suppliants who have brought branches and chaplets of olive leaves and who lie in various attitudes of despair.* OEDIPUS *enters.*

Prologue

OEDIPUS My children, generations of the living
In the line of Kadmos, nursed at his ancient hearth:
Why have you strewn yourselves before these altars
In supplication, with your boughs and garlands?
The breath of incense rises from the city
With a sound of prayer and lamentation.

                              Children,
I would not have you speak through messengers,
And therefore I have come myself to hear you—
10 I, Oedipus, who bear the famous name.   [*To a* PRIEST]
You, there, since you are eldest in the company,
Speak for them all, tell me what preys upon you,

Whether you come in dread, or crave some blessing:
Tell me, and never doubt that I will help you
In every way I can; I should be heartless
Were I not moved to find you suppliant here.
    PRIEST   Great Oedipus, O powerful King of Thebes!
You see how all the ages of our people
Cling to your altar steps: here are boys
20 Who can barely stand alone, and here are priests
By weight of age, as I am a priest of God,
And young men chosen from those yet unmarried;
As for the others, all that multitude,
They wait with olive chaplets in the squares,
At the two shrines of Pallas, and where Apollo
Speaks in the glowing embers.

                               Your own eyes
Must tell you: Thebes is in her extremity
And can not lift her head from the surge of death.
30 A rust consumes the buds and fruits of the earth;
The herds are sick; children die unborn,
And labor is vain. The god of plague and pyre
Raids like detestable lightning through the city,
And all the house of Kadmos is laid waste,
All emptied, and all darkened: Death alone
Battens upon the misery of Thebes.

You are not one of the immortal gods, we know;
Yet we have come to you to make our prayer
As to the man of all men best in adversity
40 And wisest in the ways of God. You saved us
From the Sphinx, that flinty singer, and the tribute
We paid to her so long; yet you were never
Better informed than we, nor could we teach you:
It was some god breathed in you to set us free.

Therefore, O mighty King, we turn to you:
Find us our safety, find us a remedy,
Whether by counsel of the gods or men.
A king of wisdom tested in the past
Can act in a time of troubles, and act well.
50 Noblest of men, restore
Life to your city! Think how all men call you
Liberator for your triumph long ago;
Ah, when your years of kingship are remembered,
Let them not say *We rose, but later fell*—
Keep the State from going down in the storm!
Once, years ago, with happy augury,
You brought us fortune; be the same again!

No man questions your power to rule the land:
But rule over men, not over a dead city!
60 Ships are only hulls, citadels are nothing,
When no life moves in the empty passageways.
 OEDIPUS Poor children! You may be sure I know
All that you longed for in your coming here.
I know that you are deathly sick; and yet,
Sick as you are, not one is as sick as I.
Each of you suffers in himself alone
His anguish, not another's; but my spirit
Groans for the city, for myself, for you.

I was not sleeping, you are not waking me.
70 No, I have been in tears for a long while
And in my restless thought walked many ways.
In all my search, I found one helpful course,
And that I have taken: I have sent Creon,
Son of Menoikeus, brother of the Queen,
To Delphi, Apollo's place of revelation,
To learn there, if he can,
What act or pledge of mine may save the city.
I have counted the days, and now, this very day,
I am troubled, for he has overstayed his time.
80 What is he doing? He has been gone too long.
Yet whenever he comes back, I should do ill
To scant whatever hint the god may give.
 PRIEST It is a timely promise. At this instant
They tell me Creon is here.
 OEDIPUS   O Lord Apollo!
May his news be fair as his face is radiant!
 PRIEST It could not be otherwise: he is crowned with bay,
The chaplet is thick with berries.
 OEDIPUS   We shall soon know;
90 He is near enough to hear us now.   [*Enter* CREON]
      O Prince:
Brother: son of Menoikeus:
What answer do you bring us from the god?
 CREON It is favorable. I can tell you, great afflictions
Will turn out well, if they are taken well.
 OEDIPUS What was the oracle? These vague words
Leave me still hanging between hope and fear.
 CREON Is it your pleasure to hear me with all these
Gathered around us? I am prepared to speak,
100 But should we not go in?
 OEDIPUS   Let them all hear it.
It is for them I suffer, more than for myself.
 CREON Then I will tell you what I heard at Delphi.

In plain words
The god commands us to expel from the land of Thebes
An old defilement that it seems we shelter.
It is a deathly thing, beyond expiation.
We must not let it feed upon us longer.
    OEDIPUS What defilement? How shall we rid ourselves of it?
110   CREON By exile or death, blood for blood. It was
Murder that brought the plague-wind on the city.
    OEDIPUS Murder of whom? Surely the god has named him?
    CREON My lord: long ago Laïos was our king,
Before you came to govern us.
    OEDIPUS   I know;
I learned of him from others; I never saw him.
    CREON He was murdered; and Apollo commands us now
To take revenge upon whoever killed him.
    OEDIPUS Upon whom? Where are they? Where shall we find a clue
120 To solve that crime, after so many years?
    CREON Here in this land, he said.
                                      If we make enquiry,
We may touch things that otherwise escape us.
    OEDIPUS Tell me: Was Laïos murdered in his house,
Or in the fields, or in some foreign country?
    CREON He said he planned to make a pilgrimage.
He did not come home again.
    OEDIPUS   And was there no one,
No witness, no companion, to tell what happened?
130   CREON They were all killed but one, and he got away
So frightened that he could remember one thing only.
    OEDIPUS What was that one thing? One may be the key
To everything, if we resolve to use it.
    CREON He said that a band of highwaymen attacked them,
Outnumbered them, and overwhelmed the King.
    OEDIPUS Strange, that a highwayman should be so daring—
Unless some faction here bribed him to do it.
    CREON We thought of that. But after Laïos' death
New troubles arose and we had no avenger.
140   OEDIPUS What troubles could prevent your hunting down the killers?
    CREON The riddling Sphinx's song
Made us deaf to all mysteries but her own.
    OEDIPUS Then once more I must bring what is dark to light.
It is most fitting that Apollo shows,
As you do, this compunction for the dead.
You shall see how I stand by you, as I should,
To avenge the city and the city's god,
And not as though it were for some distant friend,
But for my own sake, to be rid of evil.
150 Whoever killed King Laïos might—who knows?—

Decide at any moment to kill me as well.
By avenging the murdered king I protect myself.
Come, then, my children: leave the altar steps,
Lift up your olive boughs!
                            One of you go
And summon the people of Kadmos to gather here.
I will do all that I can; you may tell them that.   [*Exit a* PAGE]
So, with the help of God,
We shall be saved—or else indeed we are lost.

160   PRIEST Let us rise, children. It was for this we came,
And now the King has promised it himself.
Phoibos has sent us an oracle; may he descend
Himself to save us and drive out the plague.

[*Exeunt* OEDIPUS *and* CREON *into the palace by the central door. The* PRIEST *and the*
SUPPLIANTS *disperse R and L. After a short pause the* CHORUS *enters the orchestra.*]

Párodos

     CHORUS What is the god singing in his profound   [*Strophe 1*]
Delphi of gold and shadow?
What oracle for Thebes, the sunwhipped city?

Fear unjoints me, the roots of my heart tremble.

Now I remember, O Healer, your power, and wonder:
Will you send doom like a sudden cloud, or weave it
Like nightfall of the past?

Ah no: be merciful, issue of holy sound:
Dearest to our expectancy: be tender!

10 Let me pray to Athenê, the immortal daughter of Zeus,   [*Antistrophe 1*]
And to Artemis her sister
Who keeps her famous throne in the market ring,
And to Apollo, bowman at the far butts of heaven—

O gods, descend! Like three streams leap against
The fires of our grief, the fires of darkness;
Be swift to bring us rest!

As in the old time from the brilliant house
Of air you stepped to save us, come again!

Now our afflictions have no end,   [*Strophe 2*]
20 Now all our stricken host lies down
And no man fights off death with his mind;

The noble plowland bears no grain,
And groaning mothers can not bear—

See, how our lives like birds take wing,
Like sparks that fly when a fire soars,
To the shore of the god of evening.

The plague burns on, it is pitiless,   [*Antistrophe 2*]
Though pallid children laden with death
Lie unwept in the stony ways,

30   And old gray women by every path
Flock to the strand about the altars

There to strike their breasts and cry
Worship of Zeus in wailing prayers:
Be kind, God's golden child!

There are no swords in this attack by fire,   [*Strophe 3*]
No shields, but we are ringed with cries.

Send the besieger plunging from our homes
Into the vast sea-room of the Atlantic
Or into the waves that foam eastward of Thrace—
40   For the day ravages what the night spares—

Destroy our enemy, lord of the thunder!
Let him be riven by lightning from heaven!

Phoibos Apollo, stretch the sun's bowstring,   [*Antistrophe 3*]
That golden cord, until it sing for us,
Flashing arrows in heaven!
                              Artemis, Huntress,
Race with flaring lights upon our mountains!

O scarlet god, O golden-banded brow,
O Theban Bacchos in a storm of Maenads,

[*Enter* OEDIPUS, *C.*]

50   Whirl upon Death, that all the Undying hate!
Come with blinding cressets, come in joy!

Scene I

OEDIPUS   Is this your prayer? It may be answered. Come,
Listen to me, act as the crisis demands,
And you shall have relief from all these evils.

Until now I was a stranger to this tale,
As I had been a stranger to the crime.
Could I track down the murderer without a clue?
But now, friends,
As one who became a citizen after the murder,
I make this proclamation to all Thebans:
10 If any man knows by whose hand Laïos, son of Labdakos,
Met his death, I direct that man to tell me everything,
No matter what he fears for having so long withheld it.
Let it stand as promised that no further trouble
Will come to him, but he may leave the land in safety.

Moreover: If anyone knows the murderer to be foreign,
Let him not keep silent: he shall have his reward from me.
However, if he does conceal it; if any man
Fearing for his friend or for himself disobeys this edict,
Hear what I propose to do:

20 I solemnly forbid the people of this country,
Where power and throne are mine, ever to receive that man
Or speak to him, no matter who he is, or let him
Join in sacrifice, lustration, or in prayer.
I decree that he be driven from every house,
Being, as he is, corruption itself to us: the Delphic
Voice of Zeus has pronounced this revelation.
Thus I associate myself with the oracle
And take the side of the murdered king.

As for the criminal, I pray to God—
30 Whether it be a lurking thief, or one of a number—
I pray that that man's life be consumed in evil and wretchedness.
And as for me, this curse applies no less
If it should turn out that the culprit is my guest here,
Sharing my hearth.
                    You have heard the penalty.
I lay it on you now to attend to this
For my sake, for Apollo's, for the sick
Sterile city that heaven has abandoned.
Suppose the oracle had given you no command:
40 Should this defilement go uncleansed for ever?
You should have found the murderer: your king,
A noble king, had been destroyed!
                    Now I,
Having the power that he held before me,
Having his bed, begetting children there
Upon his wife, as he would have, had he lived—
Their son would have been my children's brother,

If Laïos had had luck in fatherhood!
(But surely ill luck rushed upon his reign) —
50 I say I take the son's part, just as though
I were his son, to press the fight for him
And see it won! I'll find the hand that brought
Death to Labdakos' and Polydoros' child,
Heir of Kadmos' and Agenor's line.
And as for those who fail me,
May the gods deny them the fruit of the earth,
Fruit of the womb, and may they rot utterly!
Let them be wretched as we are wretched, and worse!

For you, for loyal Thebans, and for all
60 Who find my actions right, I pray the favor
Of justice, and of all the immortal gods.
    CHORAGOS   Since I am under oath, my lord, I swear
I did not do the murder, I can not name
The murderer. Might not the oracle
That has ordained the search tell where to find him?
    OEDIPUS   An honest question. But no man in the world
Can make the gods do more than the gods will.
    CHORAGOS   There is one last expedient—
    OEDIPUS   Tell me what it is.
70 Though it seem slight, you must not hold it back.
    CHORAGOS   A lord clairvoyant to the lord Apollo,
As we all know, is the skilled Teiresias.
One might learn much about this from him, Oedipus.
    OEDIPUS   I am not wasting time:
Creon spoke of this, and I have sent for him—
Twice, in fact; it is strange that he is not here.
    CHORAGOS   The other matter—that old report—seems useless.
    OEDIPUS   Tell me. I am interested in all reports.
    CHORAGOS   The King was said to have been killed by highwaymen.
80   OEDIPUS   I know. But we have no witnesses to that.
    CHORAGOS   If the killer can feel a particle of dread,
Your curse will bring him out of hiding!
    OEDIPUS   No.
The man who dared that act will fear no curse.

[*Enter the blind seer* TEIRESIAS, *led by a* PAGE]

    CHORAGOS   But there is one man who may detect the criminal.
This is Teiresias, this is the holy prophet
In whom, alone of all men, truth was born.
    OEDIPUS   Teiresias: seer: student of mysteries,
Of all that's taught and all that no man tells,
90 Secrets of Heaven and secrets of the earth:

Blind though you are, you know the city lies
Sick with plague; and from this plague, my lord,
We find that you alone can guard or save us.

Possibly you did not hear the messengers?
Apollo, when we sent to him,
Sent us back word that this great pestilence
Would lift, but only if we established clearly
The identity of those who murdered Laïos.
They must be killed or exiled.

100   Can you use
Birdflight or any art of divination
To purify yourself, and Thebes, and me
From this contagion? We are in your hands.
There is no fairer duty
Than that of helping others in distress.

  TEIRESIAS How dreadful knowledge of the truth can be
When there's no help in truth! I knew this well,
But did not act on it: else I should not have come.

  OEDIPUS What is troubling you? Why are your eyes so cold?

110 TEIRESIAS Let me go home. Bear your own fate, and I'll
Bear mine. It is better so: trust what I say.

  OEDIPUS What you say is ungracious and unhelpful
To your native country. Do not refuse to speak.

  TEIRESIAS When it comes to speech, your own is neither temperate
Nor opportune. I wish to be more prudent.

  OEDIPUS In God's name, we all beg you—

  TEIRESIAS   You are all ignorant.
No; I will never tell you what I know.
Now it is my misery; then, it would be yours.

120 OEDIPUS What! You do know something, and will not tell us?
You would betray us all and wreck the State?

  TEIRESIAS I do not intend to torture myself, or you.
Why persist in asking? You will not persuade me.

  OEDIPUS What a wicked old man you are! You'd try a stone's
Patience! Out with it! Have you no feeling at all?

  TEIRESIAS You call me unfeeling. If you could only see
The nature of your own feelings . . .

  OEDIPUS   Why,
Who would not feel as I do? Who could endure

130 Your arrogance toward the city?

  TEIRESIAS   What does it matter!
Whether I speak or not, it is bound to come.

  OEDIPUS Then, if "it" is bound to come, you are bound to tell me.

  TEIRESIAS No, I will not go on. Rage as you please.

  OEDIPUS Rage? Why not!
                              And I'll tell you what I think:

You planned it, you had it done, you all but
Killed him with your own hands: if you had eyes,
I'd say the crime was yours, and yours alone.

140   TEIRESIAS   So? I charge you, then,
Abide by the proclamation you have made:
From this day forth
Never speak again to these men or to me;
You yourself are the pollution of this country.

    OEDIPUS   You dare say that! Can you possibly think you have
Some way of going free, after such insolence?

    TEIRESIAS   I have gone free. It is the truth sustains me.

    OEDIPUS   Who taught you shamelessness? It was not your craft.

    TEIRESIAS   You did. You made me speak. I did not want to.

150   OEDIPUS   Speak what? Let me hear it again more clearly.

    TEIRESIAS   Was it not clear before? Are you tempting me?

    OEDIPUS   I did not understand it. Say it again.

    TEIRESIAS   I say that you are the murderer whom you seek.

    OEDIPUS   Now twice you have spat out infamy. You'll pay for it!

    TEIRESIAS   Would you care for more? Do you wish to be really angry?

    OEDIPUS   Say what you will. Whatever you say is worthless.

    TEIRESIAS   I say that you live in hideous love with her
Who is nearest you in blood. You are blind to the evil.

    OEDIPUS   It seems you can go on mouthing like this for ever.

160   TEIRESIAS   I can, if there is power in truth.

    OEDIPUS   There is:
But not for you, not for you,
You sightless, witless, senseless, mad old man!

    TEIRESIAS   You are the madman. There is no one here
Who will not curse you soon, as you curse me.

    OEDIPUS   You child of endless night! You can not hurt me
Or any other man who sees the sun.

    TEIRESIAS   True: it is not from me your fate will come.
That lies within Apollo's competence,

170   As it is his concern.

    OEDIPUS   Tell me:
Are you speaking for Creon, or for yourself?

    TEIRESIAS   Creon is no threat. You weave your own doom.

    OEDIPUS   Wealth, power, craft of statesmanship!
Kingly position, everywhere admired!
What savage envy is stored up against these,
If Creon, whom I trusted, Creon my friend,
For this great office which the city once
Put in my hands unsought—if for this power

180   Creon desires in secret to destroy me!

He has bought this decrepit fortune-teller, this
Collector of dirty pennies, this prophet fraud—

Why, he is no more clairvoyant than I am!
Tell us:

Has your mystic mummery ever approached the truth?
When that hellcat the Sphinx was performing here,
What help were you to these people?
Her magic was not for the first man who came along:
It demanded a real exorcist. Your birds—
190 What good were they? or the gods, for the matter of that?
But I came by,
Oedipus, the simple man, who knows nothing—
I thought it out for myself, no birds helped me!
And this is the man you think you can destroy,
That you may be close to Creon when he's king!
Well, you and your friend Creon, it seems to me,
Will suffer most. If you were not an old man,
You would have paid already for your plot.

    CHORAGOS We can not see that his words or yours
200 Have been spoken except in anger, Oedipus,
And of anger we have no need. How can God's will
Be accomplished best? That is what most concerns us.

    TEIRESIAS You are a king. But where argument's concerned
I am your man, as much a king as you.
I am not your servant, but Apollo's.
I have no need of Creon to speak for me.
Listen to me. You mock my blindness, do you?
But I say that you, with both your eyes, are blind:
You can not see the wretchedness of your life,
210 Nor in whose house you live, no, nor with whom.
Who are your father and mother? Can you tell me?
You do not even know the blind wrongs
That you have done them, on earth and in the world below.
But the double lash of your parents' curse will whip you
Out of this land some day, with only night
Upon your precious eyes.
Your cries then—where will they not be heard?
What fastness of Kithairon will not echo them?
And that bridal-descant of yours—you'll know it then,
220 The song they sang when you came here to Thebes
And found your misguided berthing.
All this, and more, that you can not guess at now,
Will bring you to yourself among your children.

Be angry, then. Curse Creon. Curse my words.
I tell you, no man that walks upon the earth
Shall be rooted out more horribly than you.

    OEDIPUS Am I to bear this from him?—Damnation
Take you! Out of this place! Out of my sight!

TEIRESIAS   I would not have come at all if you had not asked me.
230   OEDIPUS   Could I have told that you'd talk nonsense, that
You'd come here to make a fool of yourself, and of me?
TEIRESIAS   A fool? Your parents thought me sane enough.
OEDIPUS   My parents again!—Wait: who were my parents?
TEIRESIAS   This day will give you a father, and break your heart.
OEDIPUS   Your infantile riddles! Your damned abracadabra!
TEIRESIAS   You were a great man once at solving riddles.
OEDIPUS   Mock me with that if you like; you will find it true.
TEIRESIAS   It was true enough. It brought about your ruin.
OEDIPUS   But if it saved this town?
240   TEIRESIAS   Boy, give me your hand.   [*To the* PAGE]
OEDIPUS   Yes, boy; lead him away.
                              —While you are here
We can do nothing. Go; leave us in peace.
TEIRESIAS   I will go when I have said what I have to say.
How can you hurt me? And I tell you again:
The man you have been looking for all this time,
The damned man, the murderer of Laïos,
That man is in Thebes. To your mind he is foreign-born,
But it will soon be shown that he is a Theban,
250 A revelation that will fail to please.
                              A blind man,
Who has his eyes now; a penniless man, who is rich now;
And he will go tapping the strange earth with his staff.
To the children with whom he lives now he will be
Brother and father—the very same; to her
Who bore him, son and husband—the very same
Who came to his father's bed, wet with his father's blood.

Enough. Go think that over.
If later you find error in what I have said,
260 You may say that I have no skill in prophecy.

[*Exit* TEIRESIAS, *led by his* PAGE. OEDIPUS *goes into the palace.*]

Ode I

CHORUS   The Delphic stone of prophecies   [*Strophe 1*]
Remembers ancient regicide
And a still bloody hand.
That killer's hour of flight has come.
He must be stronger than riderless
Coursers of untiring wind,
For the son of Zeus armed with his father's thunder
Leaps in lightning after him;
And the Furies follow him, the sad Furies.

10 Holy Parnassos' peak of snow   *[Antistrophe 1]*
  Flashes and blinds that secret man,
  That all shall hunt him down:
  Though he may roam the forest shade
  Like a bull gone wild from pasture
  To rage through glooms of stone.
  Doom comes down on him; flight will not avail him;
  For the world's heart calls him desolate,
  And the immortal Furies follow, for ever follow.

  But now a wilder thing is heard—   *[Strophe 2]*
20 From the old man skilled at hearing Fate in the wingbeat of a bird.
  Bewildered as a blown bird, my soul hovers and can not find
  Foothold in this debate, or any reason or rest of mind.
  But no man ever brought—none can bring
  Proof of strife between Thebes' royal house,
  Labdakos' line, and the son of Polybos;
  And never until now has any man brought word
  Of Laïos' dark death staining Oedipus the King.

  Divine Zeus and Apollo hold   *[Antistrophe 2]*
  Perfect intelligence alone of all tales ever told;
30 And well though this diviner works, he works in his own night;
  No man can judge that rough unknown or trust in second sight,
  For wisdom changes hands among the wise.
  Shall I believe my great lord criminal
  At a raging word that a blind old man let fall?
  I saw him, when the carrion woman faced him of old,
  Prove his heroic mind! These evil words are lies.

Scene II

  CREON Men of Thebes:
I am told that heavy accusations
Have been brought against me by King Oedipus.

I am not the kind of man to bear this tamely.

If in these present difficulties
He holds me accountable for any harm to him
Through anything I have said or done—why, then,
I do not value life in this dishonor.
It is not as though this rumor touched upon
10 Some private indiscretion. The matter is grave.
The fact is that I am being called disloyal
To the State, to my fellow citizens, to my friends.
    CHORAGOS He may have spoken in anger, not from his mind.

CREON   But did you not hear him say I was the one
Who seduced the old prophet into lying?
    CHORAGOS   The thing was said; I do not know how seriously.
    CREON   But you were watching him! Were his eyes steady?
Did he look like a man in his right mind?
    CHORAGOS   I do not know.
20 I can not judge the behavior of great men.
But here is the King himself.   [*Enter* OEDIPUS]
    OEDIPUS   So you dared come back.
Why? How brazen of you to come to my house,
You murderer!
              Do you think I do not know
That you plotted to kill me, plotted to steal my throne?
Tell me, in God's name: am I coward, a fool,
That you should dream you could accomplish this?
A fool who could not see your slippery game?
30 A coward, not to fight back when I saw it?
You are the fool, Creon, are you not? hoping
Without support or friends to get a throne?
Thrones may be won or bought: you could do neither.
    CREON   Now listen to me. You have talked; let me talk, too.
You can not judge unless you know the facts.
    OEDIPUS   You speak well: there is one fact; but I find it hard
To learn from the deadliest enemy I have.
    CREON   That above all I must dispute with you.
    OEDIPUS   That above all I will not hear you deny.
40   CREON   If you think there is anything good in being stubborn
Against all reason, then I say you are wrong.
    OEDIPUS   If you think a man can sin against his own kind
And not be punished for it, I say you are mad.
    CREON   I agree. But tell me: what have I done to you?
    OEDIPUS   You advised me to send for that wizard, did you not?
    CREON   I did. I should do it again.
    OEDIPUS   Very well. Now tell me:
How long has it been since Laïos—
    CREON   What of Laïos?
50   OEDIPUS   Since he vanished in that onset by the road?
    CREON   It was long ago, a long time.
    OEDIPUS   And this prophet,
Was he practicing here then?
    CREON   He was; and with honor, as now.
    OEDIPUS   Did he speak of me at that time?
    CREON   He never did;
At least, not when I was present.
    OEDIPUS   But . . . the enquiry?
I suppose you held one?
60   CREON   We did, but we learned nothing.

OEDIPUS   Why did the prophet not speak against me then?

CREON   I do not know; and I am the kind of man

Who holds his tongue when he has no facts to go on.

OEDIPUS   There's one fact that you know, and you could tell it.

CREON   What fact is that? If I know it, you shall have it.

OEDIPUS   If he were not involved with you, he could not say

That it was I who murdered Laïos.

CREON   If he says that, you are the one that knows it!—

But now it is my turn to question you.

70   OEDIPUS   Put your questions. I am no murderer.

CREON   First, then: You married my sister?

OEDIPUS   I married your sister.

CREON   And you rule the kingdom equally with her?

OEDIPUS   Everything that she wants she has from me.

CREON   And I am the third, equal to both of you?

OEDIPUS   That is why I call you a bad friend.

CREON   No. Reason it out, as I have done.

Think of this first: Would any sane man prefer

Power, with all a king's anxieties,

80 To that same power and the grace of sleep?

Certainly not I.

I have never longed for the king's power—only his rights.

Would any wise man differ from me in this?

As matters stand, I have my way in everything

With your consent, and no responsibilities.

If I were king, I should be a slave to policy.

How could I desire a scepter more

Than what is now mine—untroubled influence?

No, I have not gone mad; I need no honors,

90 Except those with the perquisites I have now.

I am welcome everywhere; every man salutes me,

And those who want your favor seek my ear,

Since I know how to manage what they ask.

Should I exchange this ease for that anxiety?

Besides, no sober mind is treasonable.

I hate anarchy

And never would deal with any man who likes it.

Test what I have said. Go to the priestess

At Delphi, ask if I quoted her correctly.

100 And as for this other thing: if I am found

Guilty of treason with Teiresias,

Then sentence me to death! You have my word

It is a sentence I should cast my vote for—

But not without evidence!

                        You do wrong

When you take good men for bad, bad men for good.

A true friend thrown aside—why, life itself
Is not more precious!
                     In time you will know this well:
110 For time, and time alone, will show the just man,
Though scoundrels are discovered in a day.
      CHORAGOS   This is well said, and a prudent man would ponder it.
Judgments too quickly formed are dangerous.
      OEDIPUS   But is he not quick in his duplicity?
And shall I not be quick to parry him?
Would you have me stand still, hold my peace, and let
This man win everything, through my inaction?
      CREON   And you want—what is it, then? To banish me?
      OEDIPUS   No, not exile. It is your death I want,
120 So that all the world may see what treason means.
      CREON   You will persist, then? You will not believe me?
      OEDIPUS   How can I believe you?
      CREON   Then you are a fool.
      OEDIPUS   To save myself?
      CREON   In justice, think of me.
      OEDIPUS   You are evil incarnate.
      CREON   But suppose that you are wrong?
      OEDIPUS   Still I must rule.
      CREON   But not if you rule badly.
130   OEDIPUS   O city, city!
      CREON   It is my city, too!
      CHORAGOS   Now, my lords, be still. I see the Queen,
Iocastê, coming from her palace chambers;
And it is time she came, for the sake of you both.
This dreadful quarrel can be resolved through her.

[*Enter* IOCASTE]

      IOCASTE   Poor foolish men, what wicked din is this?
With Thebes sick to death, is it not shameful
That you should rake some private quarrel up?   [*To* OEDIPUS]
Come into the house.

140   —And you, Creon, go now:
Let us have no more of this tumult over nothing.
      CREON   Nothing? No, sister: what your husband plans for me
Is one of two great evils: exile or death.
      OEDIPUS   He is right.
               Why, woman I have caught him squarely
Plotting against my life.
      CREON   No! Let me die
Accurst if ever I have wished you harm!
      IOCASTE   Ah, believe it, Oedipus!

150 In the name of the gods, respect this oath of his
For my sake, for the sake of these people here!
    CHORAGOS Open your mind to her, my lord. Be ruled by her, I beg you!
                                                                     [*Strophe 1*]

    OEDIPUS What would you have me do?
    CHORAGOS Respect Creon's word. He has never spoken like a fool,
And now he has sworn an oath.
    OEDIPUS   You know what you ask?
    CHORAGOS   I do.
    OEDIPUS   Speak on, then.
    CHORAGOS A friend so sworn should not be baited so,
160 In blind malice, and without final proof.
    OEDIPUS You are aware, I hope, that what you say
Means death for me, or exile at the least.
    CHORAGOS No, I swear by Helios, first in Heaven   [*Strophe 2*]
    May I die friendless and accurst,
The worst of deaths, if ever I meant that!
      It is the withering fields
          That hurt my sick heart:
      Must we bear all these ills,
          And now your bad blood as well?
170   OEDIPUS Then let him go. And let me die, if I must,
Or be driven by him in shame from the land of Thebes.
It is your unhappiness, and not his talk,
That touches me.
               As for him—
Wherever he is, I will hate him as long as I live.
    CREON Ugly in yielding, as you were ugly in rage!
Natures like yours chiefly torment themselves.
    OEDIPUS Can you not go? Can you not leave me?
    CREON   I can.
180 You do not know me; but the city knows me,
And in its eyes I am just, if not in yours.   [*Exit* CREON]
    CHORAGOS Lady Iocastê, did you not ask the King to go to his chambers?
                                                      [*Antistrophe 1*]

    IOCASTE First tell me what has happened.
    CHORAGOS There was suspicion without evidence; yet it rankled
As even false charges will.
    IOCASTE   On both sides?
    CHORAGOS   On both.
    IOCASTE   But what was said?
    CHORAGOS Oh let it rest, let it be done with!
190 Have we not suffered enough?
    OEDIPUS You see to what your decency has brought you:
You have made difficulties where my heart saw none.
    CHORAGOS Oedipus, it is not once only I have told you—   [*Antistrophe 2*]
You must know I should count myself unwise

To the point of madness, should I now forsake you—
    You, under whose hand,
      In the storm of another time,
      Our dear land sailed out free.
        But now stand fast at the helm!

200   IOCASTE   In God's name, Oedipus, inform your wife as well:
Why are you so set in this hard anger?
    OEDIPUS   I will tell you, for none of these men deserves
My confidence as you do. It is Creon's work,
His treachery, his plotting against me.
    IOCASTE   Go on, if you can make this clear to me.
    OEDIPUS   He charges me with the murder of Laïos.
    IOCASTE   Has he some knowledge? Or does he speak from hearsay?
    OEDIPUS   He would not commit himself to such a charge,
But he has brought in that damnable soothsayer
210 To tell his story.
    IOCASTE   Set your mind at rest.
If it is a question of soothsayers, I tell you
That you will find no man whose craft gives knowledge
Of the unknowable.
              Here is my proof:

An oracle was reported to Laïos once
(I will not say from Phoibos himself, but from
His appointed ministers, at any rate)
That his doom would be death at the hands of his own son—
220 His son, born of his flesh and of mine!

Now, you remember the story: Laïos was killed
By marauding strangers where three highways meet;
But his child had not been three days in this world
Before the King had pierced the baby's ankles
And had him left to die on a lonely mountain.

Thus, Apollo never caused that child
To kill his father, and it was not Laïos' fate
To die at the hands of his son, as he had feared.
This is what prophets and prophecies are worth!
230 Have no dread of them.
             It is God himself
Who can show us what he wills, in his own way.
    OEDIPUS   How strange a shadowy memory crossed my mind,
Just now while you were speaking; it chilled my heart.
    IOCASTE   What do you mean? What memory do you speak of?
    OEDIPUS   If I understand you, Laïos was killed
At a place where three roads meet.
    IOCASTE   So it was said;
We have no later story.

240 OEDIPUS   Where did it happen?
     IOCASTE Phokis, it is called: at a place where the Theban Way
Divides into the roads toward Delphi and Daulia.
     OEDIPUS When?
     IOCASTE   We had the news not long before you came
And proved the right to your succession here.
     OEDIPUS Ah, what net has God been weaving for me?
     IOCASTE Oedipus! Why does this trouble you?
     OEDIPUS   Do not ask me yet.
First, tell me how Laïos looked, and tell me
250 How old he was.
     IOCASTE   He was tall, his hair just touched
With white; his form was not unlike your own.
     OEDIPUS I think that I myself may be accurst
By my own ignorant edict.
     IOCASTE   You speak strangely.
It makes me tremble to look at you, my King.
     OEDIPUS I am not sure that the blind man can not see.
But I should know better if you were to tell me—
     IOCASTE Anything—though I dread to hear you ask it.
260 OEDIPUS Was the King lightly escorted, or did he ride
With a large company, as a ruler should?
     IOCASTE There were five men with him in all: one was a herald;
And a single chariot, which he was driving.
     OEDIPUS Alas, that makes it plain enough!
                                        But who—
Who told you how it happened?
     IOCASTE   A household servant,
The only one to escape.
     OEDIPUS   And is he still
270 A servant of ours?
     IOCASTE   No; for when he came back at last
And found you enthroned in the place of the dead king,
He came to me, touched my hand with his, and begged
That I would send him away to the frontier district
Where only the shepherds go—
As far away from the city as I could send him.
I granted his prayer; for although the man was a slave,
He had earned more than this favor at my hands.
     OEDIPUS Can he be called back quickly?
280 IOCASTE   Easily.
But why?
     OEDIPUS I have taken too much upon myself
Without enquiry; therefore I wish to consult him.
     IOCASTE Then he shall come.
                        But am I not one also
To whom you might confide these fears of yours?

OEDIPUS   That is your right; it will not be denied you,
Now least of all; for I have reached a pitch
Of wild foreboding. Is there anyone
290 To whom I should sooner speak?
Polybos of Corinth is my father.
My mother is a Dorian: Meropê.
I grew up chief among the men of Corinth
Until a strange thing happened—
Not worth my passion, it may be, but strange.
At a feast, a drunken man maundering in his cups
Cries out that I am not my father's son!

I contained myself that night, though I felt anger
And a sinking heart. The next day I visited
300 My father and mother, and questioned them. They stormed,
Calling it all the slanderous rant of a fool;
And this relieved me. Yet the suspicion
Remained always aching in my mind;
I knew there was talk; I could not rest;
And finally, saying nothing to my parents,
I went to the shrine at Delphi.
The god dismissed my question without reply;
He spoke of other things.
                              Some were clear,
310 Full of wretchedness, dreadful, unbearable:
As, that I should lie with my own mother, breed
Children from whom all men would turn their eyes;
And that I should be my father's murderer.

I heard all this, and fled. And from that day
Corinth to me was only in the stars
Descending in that quarter of the sky,
As I wandered farther and farther on my way
To a land where I should never see the evil
Sung by the oracle. And I came to this country
320 Where, so you say, King Laïos was killed.

I will tell you all that happened there, my lady.

There were three highways
Coming together at a place I passed;
And there a herald came towards me, and a chariot
Drawn by horses, with a man such as you describe
Seated in it. The groom leading the horses
Forced me off the road at his lord's command;
But as this charioteer lurched over towards me
I struck him in my rage. The old man saw me

330 And brought his double goad down upon my head
    As I came abreast.

                        He was paid back, and more!
    Swinging my club in this right hand I knocked him
    Out of his car, and he rolled on the ground.

                                        I killed him.

    I killed them all.
    Now if that stranger and Laïos were—kin,
    Where is a man more miserable than I?
    More hated by the gods? Citizen and alien alike
340 Must never shelter me or speak to me—
    I must be shunned by all.

                        And I myself
    Pronounced this malediction upon myself!

    Think of it: I have touched you with these hands,
    These hands that killed your husband. What defilement!

    Am I all evil, then? It must be so,
    Since I must flee from Thebes, yet never again
    See my own countrymen, my own country,
    For fear of joining my mother in marriage
350 And killing Polybos, my father.

                            Ah,
    If I was created so, born to this fate,
    Who could deny the savagery of God?

    O holy majesty of heavenly powers!
    May I never see that day! Never!
    Rather let me vanish from the race of men
    Than know the abomination destined me!
        CHORAGOS We too, my lord, have felt dismay at this.
    But there is hope: you have yet to hear the shepherd.
360   OEDIPUS Indeed, I fear no other hope is left me.
        IOCASTE What do you hope from him when he comes?
        OEDIPUS   This much:
    If his account of the murder tallies with yours,
    Then I am cleared.
        IOCASTE   What was it that I said
    Of such importance?
        OEDIPUS   Why, "marauders," you said,
    Killed the King, according to this man's story.
    If he maintains that still, if there were several,
370 Clearly the guilt is not mine: I was alone.
    But if he says one man, singlehanded, did it,
    Then the evidence all points to me.

IOCASTE   You may be sure that he said there were several;
And can he call back that story now? He can not.
The whole city heard it as plainly as I.
But suppose he alters some detail of it:
He can not ever show that Laïos death
Fulfilled the oracle: for Apollo said
My child was doomed to kill him; and my child—
380   Poor baby!—it was my child that died first.

No. From now on, where oracles are concerned,
I would not waste a second thought on any.
    OEDIPUS   You may be right.
                                        But come: let someone go
For the shepherd at once. This matter must be settled.
    IOCASTE   I will send for him.
I would not wish to cross you in anything,
And surely not in this.—Let us go in.   [Exeunt into the palace]

Ode II

    CHORUS   Let me be reverent in the ways of right,   [Strophe 1]
Lowly the paths I journey on;
Let all my words and actions keep
The laws of the pure universe
From highest Heaven handed down.
For Heaven is their bright nurse,
Those generations of the realms of light;
Ah, never of mortal kind were they begot,
Nor are they slaves of memory, lost in sleep:
10   Their Father is greater than Time, and ages not.

The tyrant is a child of Pride   [Antistrophe 1]
Who drinks from his great sickening cup
Recklessness and vanity,
Until from his high crest headlong
He plummets to the dust of hope.
That strong man is not strong.
But let no fair ambition be denied;
May God protect the wrestler for the State
In government, in comely policy,
20   Who will fear God, and on His ordinance wait.

Haughtiness and the high hand of disdain   [Strophe 2]
Tempt and outrage God's holy law;
And any mortal who dares hold
No immortal Power in awe
Will be caught up in a net of pain:

The price for which his levity is sold.
Let each man take due earnings, then,
And keep his hands from holy things,
And from blasphemy stand apart—
30 Else the crackling blast of heaven
Blows on his head, and on his desperate heart;
Though fools will honor impious men,
In their cities no tragic poet sings.

Shall we lose faith in Delphi's obscurities,   [*Antistrophe 2*]
We who have heard the world's core
Discredited, and the sacred wood
Of Zeus at Elis praised no more?
The deeds and the strange prophecies
Must make a pattern yet to be understood.
40 Zeus, if indeed you are lord of all,
Throned in light over night and day,
Mirror this in your endless mind:
Our masters call the oracle
Words on the wind, and the Delphic vision blind!
Their hearts no longer know Apollo,
And reverence for the gods has died away.

Scene III

[*Enter* IOCASTE]

IOCASTE   Princes of Thebes, it has occurred to me
To visit the altars of the gods, bearing
These branches as a suppliant, and this incense.
Our King is not himself: his noble soul
Is overwrought with fantasies of dread,
Else he would consider
The new prophecies in the light of the old.
He will listen to any voice that speaks disaster,
And my advice goes for nothing.

[*She approaches the altar, R.*]

10   To you, then, Apollo,
Lycean lord, since you are nearest, I turn in prayer.
Receive these offerings, and grant us deliverance
From defilement. Our hearts are heavy with fear
When we see our leader distracted, as helpless sailors
Are terrified by the confusion of their helmsman.

[*Enter* MESSENGER]

MESSENGER   Friends, no doubt you can direct me:
Where shall I find the house of Oedipus,
Or, better still, where is the King himself?
    CHORAGOS   It is this very place, stranger; he is inside.
20 This is his wife and mother of his children.
    MESSENGER   I wish her happiness in a happy house,
Blest in all the fulfillment of her marriage.
    IOCASTE   I wish as much for you: your courtesy
Deserves a like good fortune. But now, tell me:
Why have you come? What have you to say to us?
    MESSENGER   Good news, my lady, for your house and your husband.
    IOCASTE   What news? Who sent you here?
    MESSENGER   I am from Corinth.
The news I bring ought to mean joy for you,
30 Though it may be you will find some grief in it.
    IOCASTE   What is it? How can it touch us in both ways?
    MESSENGER   The people of Corinth, they say,
Intend to call Oedipus to be their king.
    IOCASTE   But old Polybos—is he not reigning still?
    MESSENGER   No. Death holds him in his sepulchre.
    IOCASTE   What are you saying? Polybos is dead?
    MESSENGER   If I am not telling the truth, may I die myself.
    IOCASTE   Go in, go quickly; tell this to your master.   [*To a* MAIDSERVANT]

O riddlers of God's will, where are you now!
40 This was the man whom Oedipus, long ago,
Feared so, fled so, in dread of destroying him—
But it was another fate by which he died.

[*Enter* OEDIPUS, *C.*]

    OEDIPUS   Dearest Iocastê, why have you sent for me?
    IOCASTE   Listen to what this man says, and then tell me
What has become of the solemn prophecies.
    OEDIPUS   Who is this man? What is his news for me?
    IOCASTE   He has come from Corinth to announce your father's death!
    OEDIPUS   Is it true, stranger? Tell me in your own words.
    MESSENGER   I can not say it more clearly: the King is dead.
50   OEDIPUS   Was it by treason? Or by an attack of illness?
    MESSENGER   A little thing brings old men to their rest.
    OEDIPUS   It was sickness, then?
    MESSENGER   Yes, and his many years.
    OEDIPUS   Ah!
Why should a man respect the Pythian hearth, or
Give heed to the birds that jangle above his head?
They prophesied that I should kill Polybos,
Kill my own father; but he is dead and buried,

And I am here—I never touched him, never,
60 Unless he died of grief for my departure,
And thus, in a sense, through me. No. Polybos
Has packed the oracles off with him underground.
They are empty words.
    IOCASTE   Had I not told you so?
    OEDIPUS You had; it was my faint heart that betrayed me.
    IOCASTE From now on never think of those things again.
    OEDIPUS And yet—must I not fear my mother's bed?
    IOCASTE Why should anyone in this world be afraid,
Since Fate rules us and nothing can be foreseen?
70 A man should live only for the present day.

Have no more fear of sleeping with your mother:
How many men, in dreams, have lain with their mothers!
No reasonable man is troubled by such things.
    OEDIPUS That is true; only—
If only my mother were not still alive!
But she is alive. I can not help my dread.
    IOCASTE Yet this news of your father's death is wonderful.
    OEDIPUS Wonderful. But I fear the living woman.
    MESSENGER Tell me, who is this woman that you fear?
80   OEDIPUS It is Meropê, man; the wife of King Polybos.
    MESSENGER Meropê? Why should you be afraid of her?
    OEDIPUS An oracle of the gods, a dreadful saying.
    MESSENGER Can you tell me about it or are you sworn to silence?
    OEDIPUS I can tell you, and I will.
Apollo said through his prophet that I was the man
Who should marry his own mother, shed his father's blood
With his own hands. And so, for all these years
I have kept clear of Corinth, and no harm has come—
Though it would have been sweet to see my parents again.
90   MESSENGER And is this the fear that drove you out of Corinth?
    OEDIPUS Would you have me kill my father?
    MESSENGER   As for that
You must be reassured by the news I gave you.
    OEDIPUS If you could reassure me, I would reward you.
    MESSENGER I had that in mind, I will confess: I thought
I could count on you when you returned to Corinth.
    OEDIPUS No: I will never go near my parents again.
    MESSENGER Ah, son, you still do not know what you are doing—
    OEDIPUS What do you mean? In the name of God tell me!
100   MESSENGER If these are your reasons for not going home.
    OEDIPUS I tell you, I fear the oracle may come true.
    MESSENGER And guilt may come upon you through your parents?
    OEDIPUS That is the dread that is always in my heart.
    MESSENGER Can you not see that all your fears are groundless?

OEDIPUS How can you say that? They are my parents, surely?

MESSENGER Polybos was not your father.

OEDIPUS   Not my father?

MESSENGER No more your father than the man speaking to you.

OEDIPUS But you are nothing to me!

110   MESSENGER   Neither was he.

OEDIPUS Then why did he call me son?

MESSENGER   I will tell you:

Long ago he had you from my hands, as a gift.

OEDIPUS Then how could he love me so, if I was not his?

MESSENGER He had no children, and his heart turned to you.

OEDIPUS What of you? Did you buy me? Did you find me by chance?

MESSENGER I came upon you in the crooked pass of Kithairon.

OEDIPUS And what were you doing there?

MESSENGER   Tending my flocks.

120   OEDIPUS A wandering shepherd?

MESSENGER   But your savior, son, that day.

OEDIPUS From what did you save me?

MESSENGER   Your ankles should tell you that.

OEDIPUS Ah, stranger, why do you speak of that childhood pain?

MESSENGER I cut the bonds that tied your ankles together.

OEDIPUS I have had the mark as long as I can remember.

MESSENGER That was why you were given the name you bear.

OEDIPUS God! Was it my father or my mother who did it?

Tell me!

130   MESSENGER I do not know. The man who gave you to me

Can tell you better than I.

OEDIPUS It was not you that found me, but another?

MESSENGER It was another shepherd gave you to me.

OEDIPUS Who was he? Can you tell me who he was?

MESSENGER I think he was said to be one of Laïos' people.

OEDIPUS You mean the Laïos who was king here years ago?

MESSENGER Yes; King Laïos; and the man was one of his herdsmen.

OEDIPUS Is he still alive? Can I see him?

MESSENGER   These men here

140 Know best about such things.

OEDIPUS   Does anyone here

Know this shepherd that he is talking about?

Have you seen him in the fields, or in the town?

If you have, tell me. It is time things were made plain.

CHORAGOS I think the man he means is that same shepherd

You have already asked to see. Iocastê perhaps

Could tell you something.

OEDIPUS   Do you know anything

About him, Lady? Is he the man we have summoned?

150 Is that the man this shepherd means?

IOCASTE   Why think of him?

Forget this herdsman. Forget it all.
This talk is a waste of time.
    OEDIPUS   How can you say that,
When the clues to my true birth are in my hands?
    IOCASTE   For God's love, let us have no more questioning!
Is your life nothing to you?
My own is pain enough for me to bear.
    OEDIPUS   You need not worry. Suppose my mother a slave,
160 And born of slaves: no baseness can touch you.
    IOCASTE   Listen to me, I beg you: do not do this thing!
    OEDIPUS   I will not listen; the truth must be made known.
    IOCASTE   Everything that I say is for your own good!
    OEDIPUS   My own good
Snaps my patience, then; I want none of it.
    IOCASTE   You are fatally wrong! May you never learn who you are!
    OEDIPUS   Go, one of you, and bring the shepherd here.
Let us leave this woman to brag of her royal name.
    IOCASTE   Ah, miserable!
170 That is the only word I have for you now.
That is the only word I can ever have.   *[Exit into the palace]*
    CHORAGOS   Why has she left us, Oedipus? Why has she gone
In such a passion of sorrow? I fear this silence:
Something dreadful may come of it.
    OEDIPUS   Let it come!
However base my birth, I must know about it.
The Queen, like a woman, is perhaps ashamed
To think of my low origin. But I
Am a child of Luck; I can not be dishonored.
180 Luck is my mother; the passing months, my brothers,
Have seen me rich and poor.
                      If this is so,
How could I wish that I were someone else?
How could I not be glad to know my birth?

Ode III

    CHORUS   If ever the coming time were known   *[Strophe]*
To my heart's pondering,
Kithairon, now by Heaven I see the torches
At the festival of the next full moon,
And see the dance, and hear the choir sing
A grace to your gentle shade:
Mountain where Oedipus was found,
O mountain guard of a noble race!
May the god who heals us lend his aid,
10 And let that glory come to pass
For our king's cradling-ground.

Of the nymphs that flower beyond the years,   [*Antistrophe*]
Who bore you, royal child,
To Pan of the hills or the timberline Apollo,
Cold in delight where the upland clears,
Or Hermês for whom Kyllenê's heights are piled?
Or flushed as evening cloud,
Great Dionysos, roamer of mountains,
He—was it he who found you there,
20 And caught you up in his own proud
Arms from the sweet god-ravisher
Who laughed by the Muses' fountains?

Scene IV

OEDIPUS   Sirs: though I do not know the man,
I think I see him coming, this shepherd we want:
He is old, like our friend here, and the men
Bringing him seem to be servants of my house.
But you can tell, if you have ever seen him.

[*Enter* SHEPHERD *escorted by servants*]

CHORAGOS   I know him, he was Laïos' man. You can trust him.
OEDIPUS   Tell me first, you from Corinth: is this the shepherd
We were discussing?
MESSENGER   This is the very man.
10   OEDIPUS   Come here. No, look at me. You must answer   [*To* SHEPHERD]
Everything I ask.—You belonged to Laïos?
SHEPHERD   Yes: born his slave, brought up in his house.
OEDIPUS   Tell me: what kind of work did you do for him?
SHEPHERD   I was a shepherd of his, most of my life.
OEDIPUS   Where mainly did you go for pasturage?
SHEPHERD   Sometimes Kithairon, sometimes the hills near-by.
OEDIPUS   Do you remember ever seeing this man out there?
SHEPHERD   What would he be doing there? This man?
OEDIPUS   This man standing here. Have you ever seen him before?
20   SHEPHERD   No. At least, not to my recollection.
MESSENGER   And that is not strange, my lord. But I'll refresh
His memory: he must remember when we two
Spent three whole seasons together, March to September,
On Kithairon or thereabouts. He had two flocks;
I had one. Each autumn I'd drive mine home
And he would go back with his to Laïos' sheepfold.—
Is this not true, just as I have described it?
SHEPHERD   True, yes; but it was all so long ago.
MESSENGER   Well, then: do you remember, back in those days,
30 That you gave me a baby boy to bring up as my own?

SHEPHERD   What if I did? What are you trying to say?

MESSENGER   King Oedipus was once that little child.

SHEPHERD   Damn you, hold your tongue!

OEDIPUS   No more of that!

It is your tongue needs watching, not this man's.

SHEPHERD   My King, my Master, what is it I have done wrong?

OEDIPUS   You have not answered his question about the boy.

SHEPHERD   He does not know . . . He is only making trouble . . .

OEDIPUS   Come, speak plainly, or it will go hard with you.

40   SHEPHERD   In God's name, do not torture an old man!

OEDIPUS   Come here, one of you; bind his arms behind him.

SHEPHERD   Unhappy king! What more do you wish to learn?

OEDIPUS   Did you give this man the child he speaks of?

SHEPHERD   I did.

And I would to God I had died that very day.

OEDIPUS   You will die now unless you speak the truth.

SHEPHERD   Yet if I speak the truth, I am worse than dead.

OEDIPUS   Very well; since you insist upon delaying—

SHEPHERD   No! I have told you already that I gave him the boy.

50   OEDIPUS   Where did you get him? From your house? From somewhere else?

SHEPHERD   Not from mine, no. A man gave him to me.

OEDIPUS   Is that man here? Do you know whose slave he was?

SHEPHERD   For God's love, my King, do not ask me any more!

OEDIPUS   You are a dead man if I have to ask you again.

SHEPHERD   Then . . . Then the child was from the palace of Laïos.

OEDIPUS   A slave child? or a child of his own line?

SHEPHERD   Ah, I am on the brink of dreadful speech!

OEDIPUS   And I of dreadful hearing. Yet I must hear.

SHEPHERD   If you must be told, then . . .

60   They said it was Laïos' child;

But it is your wife who can tell you about that.

OEDIPUS   My wife!—Did she give it to you?

SHEPHERD   My lord, she did.

OEDIPUS   Do you know why?

SHEPHERD   I was told to get rid of it.

OEDIPUS   An unspeakable mother!

SHEPHERD   There had been prophecies . . .

OEDIPUS   Tell me.

SHEPHERD   It was said that the boy would kill his own father.

70   OEDIPUS   Then why did you give him over to this old man?

SHEPHERD   I pitied the baby, my King,

And I thought that this man would take him far away

To his own country.

                            He saved him—but for what a fate!

For if you are what this man says you are,

No man living is more wretched than Oedipus.

OEDIPUS   Ah God!

It was true!
     All the prophecies!
80   —Now,
O Light, may I look on you for the last time!
I, Oedipus,
Oedipus, damned in his birth, in his marriage damned,
Damned in the blood he shed with his own hand!

[*He rushes into the palace*]

Ode IV

CHORUS   Alas for the seed of men.   [*Strophe 1*]

What measure shall I give these generations
That breathe on the void and are void
And exist and do not exist?

Who bears more weight of joy
Than mass of sunlight shifting in images,
Or who shall make his thoughts stay on
That down time drifts away?

Your splendor is all fallen.

10 O naked brow of wrath and tears,
    O change of Oedipus!
    I who saw your days call no man blest—
    Your great days like ghósts góne.

That mind was a strong bow.   [*Antistrophe 1*]

Deep, how deep you drew it then, hard archer,
At a dim fearful range,
And brought dear glory down!

You overcame the stranger—
The virgin with her hooking lion claws—
20 And though death sang, stood like a tower
   To make pale Thebes take heart.

Fortress against our sorrow!

Divine king, giver of laws,
Majestic Oedipus!

No prince in Thebes had ever such renown,
No prince won such grace of power.

And now of all men ever known   [*Strophe 2*]
Most pitiful is this man's story:
His fortunes are most changed, his state
30 Fallen to a low slave's
Ground under bitter fate.

O Oedipus, most royal one!
The great door that expelled you to the light
Gave at night—ah, gave night to your glory:
As to the father, to the fathering son.

All understood too late.

How could that queen whom Laïos won,
The garden that he harrowed at his height,
Be silent when that act was done?

40 But all eyes fail before time's eye,   [*Antistrophe 2*]
All actions come to justice there.
Though never willed, though far down the deep past,
Your bed, your dread sirings,
Are brought to book at last.
Child by Laïos doomed to die,
Then doomed to lose that fortunate little death,
Would God you never took breath in this air
That with my wailing lips I take to cry:

For I weep the world's outcast.

50 Blind I was, and can not tell why;
Asleep, for you had given ease of breath;
A fool, while the false years went by.

Éxodos

[*Enter, from the palace,* SECOND MESSENGER]

   SECOND MESSENGER   Elders of Thebes, most honored in this land,
What horrors are yours to see and hear, what weight
Of sorrow to be endured, if, true to your birth,
You venerate the line of Labdakos!
I think neither Istros nor Phasis, those great rivers,
Could purify this place of the corruption

It shelters now, or soon must bring to light—
Evil not done unconsciously, but willed.

The greatest griefs are those we cause ourselves.
10   CHORAGOS   Surely, friend, we have grief enough already;
What new sorrow do you mean?
        SECOND MESSENGER   The Queen is dead.
        CHORAGOS   Iocastê? Dead? But at whose hand?
        SECOND MESSENGER   Her own.
The full horror of what happened you can now know,
For you did not see it; but I, who did, will tell you
As clearly as I can how she met her death.

When she had left us,
In passionate silence, passing through the court,
20   She ran to her apartment in the house,
Her hair clutched by the fingers of both hands.
She closed the doors behind her; then, by that bed
Where long ago the fatal son was conceived—
That son who should bring about his father's death—
We heard her call upon Laïos, dead so many years,
And heard her wail for the double fruit of her marriage,
A husband by her husband, children by her child.

Exactly how she died I do not know:
For Oedipus burst in moaning and would not let us
30   Keep vigil to the end: it was by him
As he stormed about the room that our eyes were caught.
From one to another of us he went, begging a sword,
Cursing the wife who was not his wife, the mother
Whose womb had carried his own children and himself.
I do not know: it was none of us aided him,
But surely one of the gods was in control!
For with a dreadful cry
He hurled his weight, as though wrenched out of himself,
At the twin doors: the bolts gave, and he rushed in.
40   And there we saw her hanging, her body swaying
From the cruel cord she had noosed about her neck.
A great sob broke from him, heartbreaking to hear,
As he loosed the rope and lowered her to the ground.

I would blot out from my mind what happened next!
For the King ripped from her gown the golden brooches
That were her ornament, and raised them, and plunged them down
Straight into his own eyeballs, crying, "No more,
No more shall you look on the misery about me,
The horrors of my own doing! Too long you have known
50   The faces of those whom I should never have seen,

Too long been blind to those for whom I was searching!
From this hour, go in darkness!" And as he spoke,
He struck at his eyes—not once, but many times;
And the blood spattered his beard,
Bursting from his ruined sockets like red hail.

So from the unhappiness of two this evil has sprung,
A curse on the man and woman alike. The old
Happiness of the house of Labdakos
Was happiness enough: where is it today?
60 It is all wailing and ruin, disgrace, death—all
The misery of mankind that has a name—
And it is wholly and for ever theirs.
    CHORAGOS Is he in agony still? Is there no rest for him?
    SECOND MESSENGER He is calling for someone to lead him to the gates
So that all the children of Kadmos may look upon
His father's murderer, his mother's—no,
I can not say it!
              And then he will leave Thebes,
Self-exiled, in order that the curse
70 Which he himself pronounced may depart from the house.
He is weak, and there is none to lead him,
So terrible is his suffering.
              But you will see:
Look, the doors are opening; in a moment
You will see a thing that would crush a heart of stone.

[*The central door is opened:* OEDIPUS, *blinded, is led in.*]

    CHORAGOS Dreadful indeed for men to see.
Never have my own eyes
Looked on a sight so full of fear.

Oedipus!
80 What madness came upon you, what daemon
Leaped on your life with heavier
Punishment than a mortal man can bear?
No: I can not even
Look at you, poor ruined one.
And I would speak, question, ponder,
If I were able. No.
You make me shudder.
    OEDIPUS God. God.
Is there a sorrow greater?
90 Where shall I find harbor in this world?
My voice is hurled far on a dark wind.
What has God done to me?

CHORAGOS   Too terrible to think of, or to see.

OEDIPUS   O cloud of night,   *[Strophe 1]*
Never to be turned away: night coming on,
I can not tell how: night like a shroud!

My fair winds brought me here.
                                                O God. Again
The pain of the spikes where I had sight,
100 The flooding pain
Of memory, never to be gouged out.
      CHORAGOS   This is not strange.
You suffer it all twice over, remorse in pain,
Pain in remorse.

      OEDIPUS   Ah dear friend   *[Antistrophe 1]*
Are you faithful even yet, you alone?
Are you still standing near me, will you stay here,
Patient, to care for the blind?
                                    The blind man!
110 Yet even blind I know who it is attends me,
By the voice's tone—
Though my new darkness hide the comforter.
      CHORAGOS   Oh fearful act!
What god was it drove you to rake black
Night across your eyes?

      OEDIPUS   Apollo. Apollo. Dear   *[Strophe 2]*
Children, the god was Apollo.
He brought my sick, sick fate upon me.
But the blinding hand was my own!
120 How could I bear to see
When all my sight was horror everywhere?
      CHORAGOS   Everywhere; that is true.
      OEDIPUS   And now what is left?
Images? Love? A greeting even,
Sweet to the senses? Is there anything?
Ah, no, friends: lead me away.
Lead me away from Thebes.
                              Lead the great wreck
And hell of Oedipus, whom the gods hate.
130   CHORAGOS   Your fate is clear, you are not blind to that.
Would God you had never found it out!

      OEDIPUS   Death take the man who unbound   *[Antistrophe 2]*
My feet on that hillside
And delivered me from death to life! What life?
If only I had died,

This weight of monstrous doom
Could not have dragged me and my darlings down.
    CHORAGOS   I would have wished the same.
    OEDIPUS   Oh never to have come here
140 With my father's blood upon me! Never
To have been the man they call his mother's husband!
Oh accurst! Oh child of evil,
To have entered that wretched bed—
                        the selfsame one!
More primal than sin itself, this fell to me.
    CHORAGOS   I do not know how I can answer you.
You were better dead than alive and blind.
    OEDIPUS   Do not counsel me any more. This punishment
That I have laid upon myself is just.
150 If I had eyes,
I do not know how I could bear the sight
Of my father, when I came to the house of Death,
Or my mother: for I have sinned against them both
So vilely that I could not make my peace
By strangling my own life.
                Or do you think my children,
Born as they were born, would be sweet to my eyes?
Ah never, never! Nor this town with its high walls,
Nor the holy images of the gods.
160   For I,
Thrice miserable!—Oedipus, noblest of all the line
Of Kadmos, have condemned myself to enjoy
These things no more, by my own malediction
Expelling that man whom the gods declared
To be a defilement in the house of Laïos.
After exposing the rankness of my own guilt,
How could I look men frankly in the eyes?
No, I swear it,
If I could have stifled my hearing at its source,
170 I would have done it and made all this body
A tight cell of misery, blank to light and sound:
So I should have been safe in a dark agony
Beyond all recollection.
                Ah Kithairon!
Why did you shelter me? When I was cast upon you,
Why did I not die? Then I should never
Have shown the world my execrable birth.

Ah Polybos! Corinth, city that I believed
The ancient seat of my ancestors: how fair
180 I seemed, your child! And all the while this evil
Was cancerous within me!

                For I am sick
In my daily life, sick in my origin.

O three roads, dark ravine, woodland and way
Where three roads met: you, drinking my father's blood,
My own blood, spilled by my own hand: can you remember
The unspeakable things I did there, and the things
I went on from there to do?
                    O marriage, marriage!
190 The act that engendered me, and again the act
Performed by the son in the same bed—
                       Ah, the net
Of incest, mingling fathers, brothers, sons,
With brides, wives, mothers: the last evil
That can be known by men: no tongue can say
How evil!
          No. For the love of God, conceal me
Somewhere far from Thebes; or kill me; or hurl me
Into the sea, away from men's eyes for ever.

200 Come, lead me. You need not fear to touch me.
Of all men, I alone can bear this guilt.

[*Enter* CREON]

      CHORAGOS We are not the ones to decide; but Creon here
May fitly judge of what you ask. He only
Is left to protect the city in your place.
      OEDIPUS Alas, how can I speak to him? What right have I
To beg his courtesy whom I have deeply wronged?
      CREON I have not come to mock you, Oedipus,
Or to reproach you, either.

[*To* ATTENDANTS]

                  —You, standing there:
210 If you have lost all respect for man's dignity,
At least respect the flame of Lord Helios:
Do not allow this pollution to show itself
Openly here, an affront to the earth
And Heaven's rain and the light of day. No, take him
Into the house as quickly as you can.
For it is proper
That only the close kindred see his grief.
      OEDIPUS I pray you in God's name, since your courtesy
Ignores my dark expectation, visiting
220 With mercy this man of men most execrable:

Give me what I ask—for your good, not for mine.
    CREON And what is it that you would have me do?
    OEDIPUS Drive me out of this country as quickly as may be
To a place where no human voice can ever greet me.
    CREON I should have done that before now—only,
God's will had not been wholly revealed to me.
    OEDIPUS But his command is plain: the parricide
Must be destroyed. I am that evil man.
    CREON That is the sense of it, yes; but as things are,
230 We had best discover clearly what is to be done.
    OEDIPUS You would learn more about a man like me?
    CREON You are ready now to listen to the god.
    OEDIPUS I will listen. But it is to you
That I must turn for help. I beg you, hear me.

The woman in there—
Give her whatever funeral you think proper:
She is your sister.
                  —But let me go, Creon!
Let me purge my father's Thebes of the pollution
240 Of my living here, and go out to the wild hills,
To Kithairon, that has won such fame with me,
The tomb my mother and father appointed for me,
And let me die there, as they willed I should.
And yet I know
Death will not ever come to me through sickness
Or in any natural way: I have been preserved
For some unthinkable fate. But let that be.
As for my sons, you need not care for them.
They are men, they will find some way to live.
250 But my poor daughters, who have shared my table,
Who never before have been parted from their father—
Take care of them, Creon; do this for me.
And will you let me touch them with my hands
A last time, and let us weep together?
Be kind, my lord,
Great prince, be kind!
                        Could I but touch them,
They would be mine again, as when I had my eyes.

[*Enter* ANTIGONE *and* ISMENE, *attended*]

Ah, God!
260 Is it my dearest children I hear weeping?
Has Creon pitied me and sent my daughters?
    CREON Yes, Oedipus: I knew that they were dear to you
In the old days, and know you must love them still.

OEDIPUS May God bless you for this—and be a friendlier
Guardian to you than he has been to me!

Children, where are you?
Come quickly to my hands: they are your brother's—
Hands that have brought your father's once clear eyes
To this way of seeing—
270   Ah dearest ones,
I had neither sight nor knowledge then, your father
By the woman who was the source of his own life!
And I weep for you—having no strength to see you—,
I weep for you when I think of the bitterness
That men will visit upon you all your lives.
What homes, what festivals can you attend
Without being forced to depart again in tears?
And when you come to marriageable age,
Where is the man, my daughters, who would dare
280 Risk the bane that lies on all my children?
Is there any evil wanting? Your father killed
His father; sowed the womb of her who bore him;
Engendered you at the fount of his own existence!
That is what they will say of you.
                              Then, whom
Can you ever marry? There are no bridegrooms for you,
And your lives must wither away in sterile dreaming.

O Creon, son of Menoikeus!
You are the only father my daughters have,
290 Since we, their parents, are both of us gone for ever.
They are your own blood: you will not let them
Fall into beggary and loneliness;
You will keep them from the miseries that are mine!
Take pity on them; see, they are only children,
Friendless except for you. Promise me this,
Great Prince, and give me your hand in token of it.

[CREON *clasps his right hand*]

Children:
I could say much, if you could understand me,
But as it is, I have only this prayer for you:
300 Live where you can, be as happy as you can—
Happier, please God, than God has made your father!
    CREON Enough. You have wept enough. Now go within.
    OEDIPUS I must; but it is hard.
    CREON   Time eases all things.
    OEDIPUS But you must promise—

CREON   Say what you desire.

OEDIPUS   Send me from Thebes!

CREON   God grant that I may!

OEDIPUS   But since God hates me . . .

310   CREON   No, he will grant your wish.

OEDIPUS   You promise?

CREON   I can not speak beyond my knowledge.

OEDIPUS   Then lead me in.

CREON   Come now, and leave your children.

OEDIPUS   No! Do not take them from me!

CREON   Think no longer

That you are in command here, but rather think

How, when you were, you served your own destruction.

[Exeunt into the house all but the CHORUS; the CHORAGOS chants directly to the audience]

CHORAGOS   Men of Thebes: look upon Oedipus.

320   This is the king who solved the famous riddle

And towered up, most powerful of men.

No mortal eyes but looked on him with envy,

Yet in the end ruin swept over him.

Let every man in mankind's frailty

Consider his last day; and let none

Presume on his good fortune until he find

Life, at his death, a memory without pain.

Questions

1. On a sheet of paper, outline the plot of *Oedipus Rex* by summarizing what happens in each exchange of dialogue between two or more characters. (Count the chorus or the leader of the chorus as a character.) For instance:

   Chorus complains about plague; Oedipus consults oracle . . .

   Using your outline, summarize the conflicts and crises of the play.

2. How many reversals of intention can you discover? Recognitions? Moments of dramatic irony? (See definitions, page 753.)

3. After Teiresias first reveals Oedipus's guilt (to the audience if not to Oedipus), there is a moment of dialogue when it seems that Teiresias must be mistaken. Where is it? What purpose does this misdirection serve in the shape of the play?

4. Discuss coincidence and probability in *Oedipus Rex*. What is the effect of the accumulation of coincidence?

5. Does Iocastê understand what happened before Oedipus does? What does she know? How do we know that she knows?

6. After the guilt and punishment of this tragic hero, what will happen to Thebes? Does Sophocles prepare us for an enduring society? (You might like to know that *Creon* means "ruler" or "king.")

7. A servant describes Iocastê's hanging and Oedipus's self-mutilation. Would the play be better if these actions took place onstage?

8. How does Sophocles give us the character of Oedipus? How much do we learn from other characters when Oedipus is not on the stage? From other characters in the way they speak to Oedipus? From his own speech? From his gestures? From his actions?

9. How does the chorus represent the citizenry of Thebes? When is it most like a group, and when is it most like a particular person? How does it serve the action of the play?

10. After Oedipus's discovery and downfall, does his character change? How? Is there development? After his downfall, how is it possible to continue to speak of his greatness?

11. Why does Oedipus blind himself as he does? What instruments does he use and why?

12. The last lines of the play, uttered by the chorus, give a warning to the audience — which now includes you. Do you take this warning?

13. Discuss in class possible stagings of *Oedipus Rex.*

    If you performed the play in what you understand of the ancient Greek manner, how would you stage it? To answer the question, choose two or three pages of the play and consider the blocking and the entrances and exits for them. Remember that you are dealing with an all-male cast, wearing masks, in daylight, with limited scenery.

    How would you stage the same two or three pages in a contemporary theater with a picture stage? How would you use lighting? How realistic would you want to be, in costuming, makeup, properties?

    Discuss the differences in the productions.

14. To watch the play with understanding, how much would a contemporary audience need to know that an ancient audience would already have known? Could we make up for ignorance by staging? By other means?

15. Is this play out of date? Can you apply its thought to yourself, to your own life, to other twentieth-century American lives? Can you apply it to all people everywhere at any time?

CHAPTER FOUR

Elizabethan Drama and Shakespeare

In England during the reign of Elizabeth I (1558–1603), theater flourished as it had not for some centuries. Roman theater had followed and imitated the Greek, producing the great comedies of Plautus and Terence, who wrote in the third and second centuries B.C. In the Middle Ages, elements of theater survived in church ritual and in popular festivals. In tenth-century England, for example, we find the *Quem Quaeritis* (Latin: "Whom do you seek?"), a dialogue in which priests representing the three Marys, as part of a church service, approach another priest dressed in white, playing the role of an angel at the tomb of Jesus. The angel speaks from the tomb: "Whom do you seek?"; the three answer that they seek Jesus; the angel tells them "He has risen as He foretold," and the three Marys announce the Resurrection to the world—the worshipers in the church.

In this small enactment, theater had its rebirth. But six centuries elapsed between the *Quem Quaeritis* and the Elizabethan age. We are aware of the gradual growth of theater, and some medieval plays survive. A few old secular plays chronicle the adventures of Robin Hood, but most plays from the Middle Ages to the time of Elizabeth are religious. Perhaps the best known is the *Second Shepherds' Play;* although it is a drama that enacts Christ's birth, the anonymous playwright makes broad and bawdy comedy before he shows the birth in the manger. In the Renaissance, a revival of classical learning added the remains of ancient drama to existing religious plays. Drama expanded into the universities, aristocratic houses, the court, the law schools, and the inn yards. This same period saw the development of short secular plays called interludes and the beginning of professional acting companies. Drama gradually became a popular form of entertainment, and permanent theaters were built in the suburbs of London. The first generation of Elizabethan playwrights included Christopher Marlowe, Thomas Kyd, John Lyly, Robert Greene, and George Peele.

Christopher Marlowe (1564–1593), author of *The Tragical History of Doctor Faustus,* is the first great Elizabethan playwright. He developed for dramatic use the poetic line of iambic pentameter, or blank verse, that Shakespeare perfected. (For a discussion of blank verse, see page 490.) Ben Jonson (1572–1637), Shakespeare's greatest contemporary, was author of great comedies—*Volpone* (1606) and *The Alchemist* (1610), for example. (There is a poem by Christopher Marlowe on page 645; for two of Ben Jonson's poems, see pages 429 and 624.) Along with many other playwrights, Jonson lived from Elizabeth's time into the reign of James I. When Oliver Cromwell's Puritan revolution overthrew James's son Charles I, Cromwell, like a good Puritan, closed the theaters. About twenty years later, when Cromwell had died and the monarchy had been returned, the Restoration began a new era in English theater.

Elizabethan theater was a secular, popular art played by traveling troupes like the wandering players in *Hamlet* and by resident companies in London playhouses. The Globe, located across the Thames from London proper, was Shakespeare's theater. It was many-sided, almost round—the "wooden O" which Shakespeare describes in *Henry V.* Going inside, an Elizabethan could stand on the ground before the stage for a fee of one penny. For more money, the playgoer could sit in one of the galleries that ran for three stories around three-quarters of the building. Perhaps eight hundred people stood in the unroofed center—where they might be rained on—while fifteen hundred sat in the sheltered galleries. The stage itself thrust from a rear wall,

The Globe playhouse—Shakespeare's theater—stood on the Bankside, across the Thames from the walled city of London. Constructed in 1599, it burned during the performance of a play in June 1613. (This is a model reconstruction by John Cranford Adams.)

with entrances and exits at the sides and rear, where characters might hide or where they might be revealed by an opening curtain. Over the alcove, actors could perform on a balcony or gallery, as when Brabantio emerges from his bedroom in the first scene of *Othello.* At the front of the stage, a trapdoor allowed a ghost to rise or a damned soul to drop screaming into hell.

Elizabethan theater used little scenery and few props; an Elizabethan diary lists some of the props one company owned, including swords, pikes, daggers, scepters, broken staffs, scrolls, and torches. Gravediggers might carry shovels. Servants might bring tables and chairs on stage. For the most part, speeches described where the characters were and what they carried. In the first scene of *Othello,* Roderigo says to Iago "Here is her father's house," and we know where we are. Instead of lights rising pink to show us dawn, a character described the light of dawn in a poetic image. Lacking scenery, the staging required neither blackout nor curtain for changing scenery, and stage action for the Elizabethans was continuous, like the action of a modern film. Actors walked off, actors walked on—and we learned by their dialogue that the scene had shifted. Stimulated by language, the audience made a seacoast of a bare stage or by imagination turned the bare stage into the opulent dining hall of a great king. Modern editors have added stage directions to our texts of Shakespeare.

As we study the drama of the Greeks and the Elizabethans, one of the greatest differences appears to be the audience played to. Elizabethan society and theater were more secular and more diverse than the Greek. Both societies were prosperous, expanding, energetic, adventurous, imperialistic, but the society of Athens was more cohesive, more unified by religion and by social order. Elizabethan England was colorful, chaotic, and relatively lawless. Elizabethan tragedy is more diverse, various, and inclusive than Greek; less singular and uncompromising in its shape and purpose. An Elizabethan came to the theater expecting to be lifted from his seat by surprise, shock, shouting, outrage, and murder; he would be cajoled by fools, he would hear songs, he would laugh at puns and leer at sexual innuendoes. He probably knew how the story went, just as the Greeks did. (The plot of *Othello* comes from a story by an Italian writer of the sixteenth century, Giraldi Cinthio.) Although the protagonists Othello and Oedipus both act from the deepest psychic sources—both emblems of human nature, despite the centuries that separate them—details of the two tragedies reveal wide differences between the eras that produced them. Sophocles would never have introduced the bawdy banter between Iago and Emilia, or Emilia's defense of adultery at the end of Act IV. Sophocles would never have allowed tragic events to depend upon a lost handkerchief. Elizabethan drama was superabundant in energy and language and life; Greek drama found its magnificence not so much in abundance as in starkness. The Elizabethans were less interested in probability, more in particular color; the Greeks were more obsessed by the sense of inevitability. Two terms need special definition in connection with Elizabethan drama. Sometimes a character on the Elizabethan stage will speak an **aside** directed to the audience, which by convention the other characters on the stage are unable to hear. Its ironic utility is clear: the audience learns something from character A that character B knows nothing of—although the audience can see that A and B occupy the same stage. As an aside provides access to a character's mind, to his concealed or private thoughts, so does the **soliloquy**—a speech by an actor alone on the stage, like Hamlet's meditation on suicide beginning "To be or not to be. . . ." When playwrights have their characters think aloud on the stage, in asides or in soliloquies, they show not only a character's actions but a character's inward thoughts.

William Shakespeare

About William Shakespeare (1564–1616) we do not know as much as we would like. He was born in Stratford-upon-Avon, son of a glovemaker who became mayor of his town. Apparently Shakespeare attended school in Stratford, and in 1582 married Anne Hathaway, who was eight years his senior. They had three children; one son named Hamnet died in childhood. At some point in the decade after his marriage, Shakespeare moved to London alone and became an actor. (He continued acting after becoming a playwright; tradition has him playing Hamlet's father's ghost.) He began writing for the stage about 1590. He acted and wrote for the Lord Chamberlain's Men, later called the King's Men, which was the best company of his time and starred the great actor Richard Burbage, who took the original lead in *Othello*.

Other great Shakespearean tragedies include *Julius Caesar, Hamlet, Macbeth,* and *King Lear*. He excelled not only in tragedy but in comedy: *Love's Labour's Lost, The Taming of the Shrew, A Midsummer Night's Dream, The Tempest, Measure for Measure, Twelfth Night,* and many others. He excelled as well in writing the history play, a form of drama that recounted English history—reigns, rebellions, and wars. Over the centuries, however, when readers have looked for literature's highest moments, they have found them in tragedy, and in no tragedian more than in William Shakespeare. Although a given reader may prefer *King Lear* or *Hamlet, Othello* is the most engaging of tragedies—combining nobility and passion with psychological power.

After Shakespeare wrote his dark comedy *Measure for Measure,* his tragic imagination traveled south and he wrote about the Moor of Venice in *Othello*—the tale of a heroic black soldier who loves and marries a Venetian maiden. General Othello is vigorous, outward, brave, and generous—a naïve victim of the poison of Iago's malice.

Othello, The Moor of Venice   (1604?)

Edited by Alvin Kernan[1]

Dramatis Personae

OTHELLO, the Moor
BRABANTIO, father to Desdemona
CASSIO, an honorable lieutenant
IAGO, a villain
RODERIGO, a gulled gentleman
DUKE OF VENICE
SENATORS
MONTANO, Governor of Cyprus
GENTLEMEN OF CYPRUS

LODOVICO AND GRATIANO, two noble
   Venetians
SAILORS
CLOWN
DESDEMONA, wife to Othello
EMILIA, wife to Iago
BIANCA, a courtesan
[MESSENGER, HERALD, OFFICERS, GENTLEMEN,
     MUSICIANS, ATTENDANTS]

Scene. *Venice and Cyprus*

Act I, Scene I. [*Venice. A street.*]

RODERIGO   Tush! Never tell me? I take it much unkindly
That thou, Iago, who hast had my purse
As if the strings were thine, shouldst know of this.
    IAGO   'Sblood, but you'll not hear me! If ever I did dream
Of such a matter, abhor me.
    RODERIGO   Thou told'st me
Thou didst hold him in thy hate.
    IAGO   Despise me
If I do not. Three great ones of the city,
10 In personal suit to make me his lieutenant,
Off-capped[2] to him; and, by the faith of man,
I know my price; I am worth no worse a place.
But he, as loving his own pride and purposes,
Evades them with a bombast circumstance,[3]
Horribly stuffed with epithets of war;
Nonsuits[4] my mediators. For, "Certes," says he,

---

[1] This text of *Othello,* edited by Alvin Kernan, is based on that of the First Folio, or large collection, of Shakespeare's plays (1623). However, there are many differences between the Folio text and that of the play's first printing in the Quarto, or small volume, of 1621 (eighteen or nineteen years after the play's first performance). Some readings from the Quarto are included. Some material has been added by the editor (some indications of scene, some stage directions). Such additions are enclosed in brackets. Alvin Kernan's text and notes were prepared for the edition of *Othello* in the Signet Classic Shakespeare series (New York: New American Library, 1963), under the general editorship of Sylvan Barnet.

    Footnotes that gloss or translate a single word are in roman type. When the explanation covers more than one word, the relevant passage in Shakespeare precedes the explanation, in *italic* type.   [2] doffed their caps—as a mark of respect   [3] *bombast circumstance* stuffed, roundabout speech   [4] rejects

"I have already chose my officer." And what was he?
Forsooth, a great arithmetician,[5]
One Michael Cassio, a Florentine,
20 [A fellow almost damned in a fair wife][6]
That never set a squadron in the field,
Nor the division of a battle knows
More than a spinster; unless the bookish theoric,
Wherein the tonguèd[7] consuls can propose
As masterly as he. Mere prattle without practice
Is all his soldiership. But he, sir, had th' election;
And I, of whom his eyes had seen the proof
At Rhodes, at Cyprus, and on other grounds
Christian and heathen, must be belee'd and calmed
30 By debitor and creditor. This counter-caster,[8]
He, in good time, must his lieutenant be,
And I—God bless the mark!—his Moorship's ancient.[9]
    RODERIGO   By heaven, I rather would have been his hangman.
    IAGO   Why, there's no remedy. 'Tis the curse of service:
Preferment goes by letter and affection,[10]
And not by old gradation,[11] where each second
Stood heir to th' first. Now, sir, be judge yourself,
Whether I in any just term am affined[12]
To love the Moor.
40   RODERIGO   I would not follow him then.
    IAGO   O, sir, content you.
I follow him to serve my turn upon him.
We cannot all be masters, nor all masters
Cannot be truly followed. You shall mark
Many a duteous and knee-crooking[13] knave
That, doting on his own obsequious bondage,
Wears out his time, much like his master's ass,
For naught but provender; and when he's old, cashiered.
Whip me such honest knaves! Others there are
50 Who, trimmed in forms and visages of duty,
Keep yet their hearts attending on themselves,
And, throwing but shows of service on their lords,
Do well thrive by them, and when they have lined their coats,
Do themselves homage. These fellows have some soul;
And such a one do I profess myself. For, sir,

---

[5] theorist (rather than practical)   [6] *A . . . wife* (a much-disputed passage, probably best taken as a general sneer at Cassio as a dandy and a ladies' man. But in the story from which Shakespeare took his plot the counterpart of Cassio is married, and it may be that at the beginning of the play Shakespeare had decided to keep him married but later changed his mind)   [7] eloquent   [8] *countercaster* i.e., a bookkeeper who casts (reckons up) figures on a *counter* (abacus)   [9] standard-bearer; and under-officer   [10] *letter and affection* recommendations (from men of power) and personal preference   [11] *old gradation* seniority   [12] bound   [13] bowing

It is as sure as you are Roderigo,
Were I the Moor, I would not be Iago.
In following him, I follow but myself.
Heaven is my judge, not I for love and duty,
60 But seeming so, for my peculiar[14] end;
For when my outward action doth demonstrate
The native[15] act and figure of my heart
In complement extern,[16] 'tis not long after
But I will wear my heart upon my sleeve
For daws to peck at; I am not what I am.
    RODERIGO   What a full fortune does the thick-lips owe[17]
If he can carry't thus!
    IAGO   Call up her father,
Rouse him. Make after him, poison his delight,
70 Proclaim him in the streets, incense her kinsmen,
And though he in a fertile climate dwell,
Plague him with flies; though that his joy be joy,
Yet throw such chances of vexation on't
As it may lose some color.
    RODERIGO   Here is her father's house. I'll call aloud.
    IAGO   Do, with like timorous[18] accent and dire yell
As when, by night and negligence, the fire
Is spied in populous cities.
    RODERIGO   What, ho, Brabantio! Signior Brabantio, ho!
80   IAGO   Awake! What, ho, Brabantio! Thieves! Thieves!
Look to your house, your daughter, and your bags!
Thieves! Thieves!

BRABANTIO *above*[19] [*at a window*].

    BRABANTIO   What is the reason of this terrible summons?
What is the matter there?
    RODERIGO   Signior, is all your family within?
    IAGO   Are your doors locked?
    BRABANTIO   Why, wherefore ask you this?
    IAGO   Zounds, sir, y'are robbed! For shame. Put on your gown!
Your heart is burst, you have lost half your soul.
90 Even now, now, very now, an old black ram
Is tupping your white ewe. Arise, arise!
Awake the snorting citizens with the bell,
Or else the devil will make a grandsire of you.
Arise, I say!
    BRABANTIO   What, have you lost your wits?

---

[14] personal   [15] natural, innate   [16] *complement extern* outward appearance   [17] own   [18] frightening
[19] i.e., on the small upper stage above and to the rear of the main platform stage, which resembled the projecting upper story of an Elizabethan house

RODERIGO   Most reverend signior, do you know my voice?

BRABANTIO   Not I. What are you?

RODERIGO   My name is Roderigo.

BRABANTIO   The worser welcome!
100 I have charged thee not to haunt about my doors.
In honest plainness thou hast heard me say
My daughter is not for thee; and now, in madness,
Being full of supper and distemp'ring draughts,[20]
Upon malicious knavery dost thou come
To start[21] my quiet.

RODERIGO   Sir, sir, sir—

BRABANTIO   But thou must needs be sure
My spirits and my place[22] have in their power
To make this bitter to thee.
110   RODERIGO   Patience, good sir.

BRABANTIO   What tell'st thou me of robbing? This is Venice.
My house is not a grange.[23]

RODERIGO   Most grave Brabantio,
In simple and pure soul I come to you.

IAGO   Zounds, sir, you are one of those that will not serve God if the devil
bid you. Because we come to do you service and you think we are ruffians,
you'll have your daughter covered with a Barbary[24] horse, you'll have your
nephews[25] neigh to you, you'll have coursers for cousins,[26] and gennets for
germans.[27]

120   BRABANTIO   What profane wretch art thou?

IAGO   I am one, sir, that comes to tell you your daughter and the Moor are
making the beast with two backs.

BRABANTIO   Thou are a villain.

IAGO   You are—a senator.

BRABANTIO   This thou shalt answer. I know thee, Roderigo.

RODERIGO   Sir, I will answer anything. But I beseech you,
If't be your pleasure and most wise consent,
As partly I find it is, that your fair daughter,
At this odd-even[28] and dull watch o' the' night,
130 Transported, with no worse nor better guard
But with a knave of common hire, a gondolier,
To the gross clasps of a lascivious Moor—
If this be known to you, and your allowance,
We then have done you bold and saucy wrongs;
But if you know not this, my manners tell me
We have your wrong rebuke. Do not believe
That from the sense of all civility[29]

---

[20] *distemp'ring draughts* unsettling drinks   [21] disrupt   [22] rank, i.e., of senator   [23] isolated
house   [24] Arabian, i.e., Moorish   [25] i.e., grandsons   [26] relations   [27] *gennets for germans* Spanish
horses for blood relatives   [28] between night and morning   [29] *sense of all civility* feeling of what
is proper

I thus would play and trifle with your reverence.
Your daughter, if you have not given her leave,
140 I say again, hath made a gross revolt,
Tying her duty, beauty, wit, and fortunes
In an extravagant[30] and wheeling stranger
Of here and everywhere. Straight satisfy yourself.
If she be in her chamber, or your house,
Let loose on me the justice of the state
For thus deluding you.
    BRABANTIO   Strike on the tinder, ho!
Give me a taper! Call up all my people!
This accident[31] is not unlike my dream.
150 Belief of it oppresses me already.
Light, I say! Light!   *Exit* [*above*].
    IAGO   Farewell, for I must leave you.
It seems not meet, not wholesome to my place,
To be produced—as, if I stay, I shall—
Against the Moor. For I do know the State,
However this may gall him with some check,[32]
Cannot with safety cast[33] him; for he's embarked
With such loud reason to the Cyprus wars,
Which even now stands in act,[34] that for their souls
160 Another of his fathom[35] they have none
To lead their business; in which regard,
Though I do hate him as I do hell-pains,
Yet, for necessity of present life,
I must show out a flag and sign of love,
Which is indeed but sign. That you shall surely find him,
Lead to the Sagittary[36] that raisèd search:
And there will I be with him. So farewell.   [*Exit.*]

Enter BRABANTIO [*in his nightgown*], *with Servants and torches.*

    BRABANTIO It is too true an evil. Gone she is;
And what's to come of my despisèd time
170 Is naught but bitterness. Now, Roderigo,
Where didst thou see her?—O unhappy girl!—
With the Moor, say'st thou?—Who would be a father?—
How didst thou know 'twas she? O, she deceives me
Past thought!—What said she to you? Get moe[37] tapers!
Raise all my kindred!—Are they married, think you?
    RODERIGO Truly I think they are.
    BRABANTIO O heaven! How got she out? O treason of the blood!

---

[30] vagrant, wandering (Othello is not Venetian and thus may be considered a wandering
soldier of fortune) [31] happening [32] restraint [33] dismiss [34] *stands in act* takes place [35] ability
[36] (probably the name of an inn) [37] more

Fathers, from hence trust not your daughters' minds
By what you see them act.[38] Is there not charms
180 By which the property[39] of youth and maidhood
May be abused? Have you not read, Roderigo,
Of some such thing?
    RODERIGO   Yes, sir, I have indeed.
    BRABANTIO Call up my brother.—O, would you had had her!—
Some one way, some another.—Do you know
Where we may apprehend her and the Moor?
    RODERIGO I think I can discover him, if you please
To get good guard and go along with me.
    BRABANTIO Pray you lead on. At every house I'll call;
190 I may command at most.—Get weapons, ho!
And raise some special officers of night.—
On, good Roderigo; I will deserve your pains.[40]   [*Exeunt.*]

Scene II. [*A street.*]

Enter OTHELLO, IAGO, ATTENDANTS *with torches.*

    IAGO Though in the trade of war I have slain men,
Yet do I hold it very stuff[41] o' th' conscience
To do no contrived murder. I lack iniquity
Sometime to do me service. Nine or ten times
I had thought t' have jerked[42] him here, under the ribs.
    OTHELLO Tis better as it is.
    IAGO   Nay, but he prated,
And spoke such scurvy and provoking terms
Against your honor, that with the little godliness I have
10 I did full hard forbear him. But I pray you, sir,
Are you fast married? Be assured of this,
That the magnifico[43] is much beloved,
And hath in his effect a voice potential
As double as the Duke's.[44] He will divorce you,
Or put upon you what restraint or grievance
The law, with all his might to enforce it on,
Will give him cable.[45]
    OTHELLO   Let him do his spite.
My services which I have done the Signiory[46]
20 Shall out-tongue his complaints. 'Tis yet to know[47]—
Which when I know that boasting is an honor
I shall promulgate—I fetch my life and being
From men of royal siege,[48] and my demerits[49]

---

    [38] do   [39] true nature   [40] *deserve your pains* be worthy of (and reward) your efforts
[41] essence   [42] stabbed   [43] nobleman   [44] *hath . . . Duke's* i.e., can be as effective as the Duke
[45] range, scope   [46] the rulers of Venice   [47] *yet to know* unknown as yet   [48] rank   [49] deserts

May speak unbonneted to as proud a fortune
As this that I have reached.[50] For know, Iago,
But that I love the gentle Desdemona,
I would not my unhoused[51] free condition
Put into circumscription and confine
For the seas' worth. But look, what lights come yond?

Enter CASSIO, *with* [OFFICERS *and*] *torches.*

30   IAGO   Those are the raisèd father and his friends.
You were best go in.
        OTHELLO   Not I. I must be found.
My parts, my title, and my perfect soul[52]
Shall manifest me rightly. Is it they?
        IAGO   By Janus, I think no.
        OTHELLO   The servants of the Duke? And my lieutenant?
The goodness of the night upon you, friends.
What is the news?
        CASSIO   The Duke does greet you, general;
40 And he requires your haste-posthaste appearance
Even on the instant.
        OTHELLO   What is the matter, think you?
        CASSIO   Something from Cyprus, as I may divine.
It is a business of some heat. The galleys
Have sent a dozen sequent[53] messengers
This very night at one another's heels,
And many of the consuls, raised and met,
Are at the Duke's already. You have been hotly called for.
When, being not at your lodging to be found,
50 The Senate hath sent about three several[54] quests
To search you out.
        OTHELLO   'Tis well I am found by you.
I will but spend a word here in the house,
And go with you.   [*Exit.*]
        CASSIO   Ancient, what makes he here?
        IAGO   Faith, he tonight hath boarded a land carack.[55]
If it prove lawful prize, he's made forever.
        CASSIO   I do not understand.
        IAGO   He's married.
60   CASSIO   To who?

[*Enter* OTHELLO.]

        IAGO   Marry,[56] to—Come captain, will you go?

[50] *May . . . reached* i.e., are the equal of the family I have married into   [51] uncon-
fined   [52] *perfect soul* clear, unflawed conscience   [53] successive   [54] separate   [55] treasure ship
[56] By Mary (an interjection)

OTHELLO   Have with you.
CASSIO Here comes another troop to seek for you.

Enter BRABANTIO, RODERIGO, *with* OFFICERS *and torches.*

IAGO It is Brabantio. General, be advised.
He comes to bad intent.
OTHELLO   Holla! Stand there!
RODERIGO Signior, it is the Moor.
BRABANTIO   Down with him, thief! [*They draw swords.*]
IAGO You, Roderigo? Come, sir, I am for you.
70   OTHELLO Keep up your bright swords, for the dew will rust them.
Good signior, you shall more command with years
Than with your weapons.
BRABANTIO O thou foul thief, where hast thou stowed my daughter?
Damned as thou art, thou hast enchanted her!
For I'll refer me to all things of sense,[57]
If she in chains of magic were not bound,
Whether a maid so tender, fair, and happy,
So opposite to marriage that she shunned
The wealthy, curled darlings of our nation,
80   Would ever have, t'incur a general mock,[58]
Run from her guardage to the sooty bosom
Of such a thing as thou—to fear, not to delight.
Judge me the world if'tis not gross in sense[59]
That thou hast practiced[60] on her with foul charms,
Abused her delicate youth with drugs or minerals
That weaken motion.[61] I'll have't disputed on;
'Tis probable, and palpable to thinking.
I therefore apprehend and do attach[62] thee
For an abuser of the world, a practicer
90   Of arts inhibited and out of warrant.[63]
Lay hold upon him. If he do resist,
Subdue him at his peril.
OTHELLO   Hold your hands,
Both you of my inclining and the rest.
Were it my cue to fight, I should have known it
Without a prompter. Whither will you that I go
To answer this your charge?
BRABANTIO   To prison, till fit time
Of law and course of direct session
100   Call thee to answer.
OTHELLO   What if I do obey?

---

[57] *refer . . . sense* i.e., base (my argument) on all ordinary understanding of nature
[58] *general mock* public shame [59] *gross in sense* obvious [60] used tricks [61] thought, i.e., reason [62] arrest [63] *inhibited . . . warrant* prohibited and illegal (black magic)

How may the Duke be therewith satisfied,
Whose messengers are here about my side
Upon some present[64] business of the state
To bring me to him?
    OFFICER   'Tis true, most worthy signior.
The Duke's in council, and your noble self
I am sure is sent for.
    BRABANTIO   How? The Duke in council?
110 In this time of the night? Bring him away.
Mine's not an idle cause. The Duke himself,
Or any of my brothers[65] of the state,
Cannot but feel this wrong as 'twere their own;
For if such actions may have passage free,
Bondslaves and pagans shall our statesmen be.   *Exeunt.*

Scene III. [*A council chamber.*]

Enter DUKE, SENATORS, *and* OFFICERS [*set at a table, with lights and* ATTENDANTS].

    DUKE   There's no composition[66] in this news
That gives them credit.[67]
    FIRST SENATOR   Indeed, they are disproportioned.
My letters say a hundred and seven galleys.
    DUKE   And mine a hundred forty.
    SECOND SENATOR   And mine two hundred.
But though they jump[68] not on a just accompt[69] —
As in these cases where the aim[70] reports
'Tis oft with difference — yet do they all confirm
10 A Turkish fleet, and bearing up to Cyprus.
    DUKE   Nay, it is possible enough to judgment.[71]
I do not so secure me in error,
But the main article I do approve
In fearful sense.[72]
    SAILOR [*Within*]   What, ho! What, ho! What, ho!

Enter SAILOR.

    OFFICER   A messenger from the galleys.
    DUKE   Now? What's the business?
    SAILOR   The Turkish preparation makes for Rhodes.
So was I bid report here to the State
20 By Signior Angelo.

---

   [64] immediate   [65] i.e., the other senators   [66] agreement   [67] *gives them credit* makes them believable   [68] agree   [69] *just accompt* exact counting   [70] approximation   [71] *to judgment* when carefully considered   [72] *I do . . . sense* i.e., just because the numbers disagree in the reports, I do not doubt that the principal information (that the Turkish fleet is out) is fearfully true

DUKE   How say you by this change?

FIRST SENATOR   This cannot be

By no assay of reason. 'Tis a pageant[73]

To keep us in false gaze.[74] When we consider

Th' importancy of Cyprus to the Turk,

And let ourselves again but understand

That, as it more concerns the Turk than Rhodes,

So may he with more facile question[75] bear it,

For that it stands not in such warlike brace,[76]

30   But altogether lacks th' abilities

That Rhodes is dressed in. If we make thought of this,

We must not think the Turk is so unskillful

To leave that latest which concerns him first,

Neglecting an attempt to ease and gain

To wake and wage a danger profitless.

     DUKE   Nay, in all confidence he's not for Rhodes.

     OFFICER   Here is more news.

Enter a MESSENGER.

     MESSENGER   The Ottomites, reverend and gracious,

Steering with due course toward the isle of Rhodes,

40   Have there injointed them with an after[77] fleet.

     FIRST SENATOR   Ay, so I thought. How many, as you guess?

     MESSENGER   Of thirty sail; and now they do restem

Their backward course, bearing with frank appearance

Their purposes toward Cyprus. Signior Montano,

Your trusty and most valiant servitor,

With his free duty[78] recommends[79] you thus,

And prays you to believe him.

     DUKE   'Tis certain then for Cyprus.

Marcus Luccicos, is not he in town?

50   FIRST SENATOR   He's now in Florence.

     DUKE   Write from us to him; post-posthaste dispatch.

     FIRST SENATOR   Here comes Brabantio and the valiant Moor.

Enter BRABANTIO, OTHELLO, CASSIO, IAGO, RODERIGO, *and* OFFICERS.

     DUKE   Valiant Othello, we must straight[80] employ you

Against the general[81] enemy Ottoman.

[*To* BRABANTIO] I did not see you. Welcome, gentle signior.

We lacked your counsel and your help tonight.

     BRABANTIO   So did I yours. Good your grace, pardon me.

---

[73] show, pretense   [74] *in false gaze* looking the wrong way   [75] *facile question* easy struggle   [76] *warlike brace* "military posture"   [77] following   [78] *free duty* unlimited respect   [79] informs   [80] at once   [81] universal

Neither my place, nor aught I heard of business,
Hath raised me from my bed; nor doth the general care
60 Take hold on me; for my particular grief
Is of so floodgate and o'erbearing nature
That it engulfs and swallows other sorrows,
And it is still itself.

DUKE   Why, what's the matter?

BRABANTIO   My daughter! O, my daughter!

SENATORS   Dead?

BRABANTIO   Ay, to me.
She is abused, stol'n from me, and corrupted
By spells and medicines bought of mountebanks;
70 For nature so prepost'rously to err,
Being not deficient, blind, or lame of sense,
Sans[82] witchcraft could not.

DUKE   Whoe'er he be that in this foul proceeding
Hath thus beguiled your daughter of herself,
And you of her, the bloody book of law
You shall yourself read in the bitter letter
After your own sense; yea, though our proper[83] son
Stood in your action.[84]

BRABANTIO   Humbly I thank your Grace.
80 Here is the man—this Moor, whom now, it seems,
Your special mandate for the state affairs
Hath hither brought.

ALL   We are very sorry for't.

DUKE [*To* OTHELLO]   What in your own part can you say to this?

BRABANTIO   Nothing, but this is so.

OTHELLO   Most potent, grave, and reverend signiors,
My very noble and approved[85] good masters,
That I have ta'en away this old man's daughter,
It is most true; true I have married her.
90 The very head and front[86] of my offending
Hath this extent, no more. Rude am I in my speech,
And little blessed with the soft phrase of peace.
For since these arms of mine had seven years' pith[87]
Till now some nine moons wasted,[88] they have used
Their dearest[89] action in the tented field;
And little of this great world can I speak
More than pertains to feats of broils and battle;
And therefore little shall I grace my cause
In speaking for myself. Yet, by your gracious patience,
100 I will a round[90] unvarnished tale deliver

---

[82] without   [83] own   [84] *Stood in your action* were the accused in your suit   [85] tested, proven
by past performance   [86] *head and front* extreme form (*front* = forehead)   [87] strength   [88] past
[89] most important   [90] blunt

Of my whole course of love—what drugs, what charms,
What conjuration, and what mighty magic,
For such proceeding I am charged withal,
I won his daughter—
    BRABANTIO   A maiden never bold,
Of spirit so still and quiet that her motion
Blushed at herself,[91] and she, in spite of nature,
Of years, of country, credit, everything,
To fall in love with what she feared to look on!
110 It is a judgment maimed and most imperfect
That will confess perfection so could err
Against all rules of nature, and must be driven
To find out practices of cunning hell
Why this should be. I therefore vouch again
That with some mixtures pow'rful o'er the blood,
Or with some dram, conjured to this effect,
He wrought upon her.
    DUKE   To vouch this is no proof,
Without more wider and more overt test
120 Than these thin habits[92] and poor likelihoods
Of modern[93] seeming do prefer against him.
    FIRST SENATOR   But, Othello, speak.
Did you by indirect and forcèd courses
Subdue and poison this young maid's affections?
Or came it by request, and such fair question[94]
As soul to soul affordeth?
    OTHELLO   I do beseech you,
Send for the lady to the Sagittary
And let her speak of me before her father.
130 If you do find me foul in her report,
The trust, the office, I do hold of you
Not only take away, but let your sentence
Even fall upon my life.
    DUKE   Fetch Desdemona hither.
    OTHELLO   Ancient, conduct them; you best know the place.

                       [*Exit* IAGO, *with two or three* ATTENDANTS.]

And till she come, as truly as to heaven
I do confess the vices of my blood,
So justly to your grave ears I'll present
How I did thrive in this fair lady's love,
140 And she in mine.
    DUKE   Say it, Othello.

[91] *her motion/Blushed at herself* i.e., she was so modest that she blushed at every thought
(and movement)   [92] clothing   [93] trivial   [94] discussion

OTHELLO   Her father loved me; oft invited me;
Still[95] questioned me the story of my life
From year to year, the battle, sieges, fortune
That I have passed.
I ran it through, even from my boyish days
To th' very moment that he bade me tell it.
Wherein I spoke of most disastrous chances,
Of moving accidents by flood and field,
150 Of hairbreadth scapes i' th' imminent[96] deadly breach,
Of being taken by the insolent foe
And sold to slavery, of my redemption thence
And portance[97] in my travel's history,
Wherein of anters[98] vast and deserts idle,[99]
Rough quarries, rocks, and hills whose heads touch heaven,
It was my hint to speak. Such was my process.
And of the Cannibals that each other eat,
The Anthropophagi,[100] and men whose heads
Grew beneath their shoulders. These things to hear
160 Would Desdemona seriously incline;
But still the house affairs would draw her thence;
Which ever as she could with haste dispatch,
She'd come again, and with a greedy ear
Devour up my discourse. Which I observing,
Took once a pliant hour, and found good means
To draw from her a prayer of earnest heart
That I would all my pilgrimage dilate,[101]
Whereof by parcels she had something heard,
But not intentively.[102] I did consent,
170 And often did beguile her of her tears
When I did speak of some distressful stroke
That my youth suffered. My story being done,
She gave me for my pains a world of kisses.
She swore in faith 'twas strange, 'twas passing[103] strange;
'Twas pitiful, 'twas wondrous pitiful.
She wished she had not heard it; yet she wished
That heaven had made her such a man. She thanked me,
And bade me, if I had a friend that loved her,
I should but teach him how to tell my story,
180 And that would woo her. Upon this hint I spake.
She loved me for the dangers I had passed,
And I loved her that she did pity them.
This only is the witchcraft I have used.
Here comes the lady. Let her witness it.

---

[95] regularly   [96] threatening   [97] manner of acting   [98] caves   [99] empty, sterile   [100] maneaters
[101] relate in full   [102] at length and in sequence   [103] surpassing

Enter DESDEMONA, IAGO, ATTENDANTS.

DUKE I think this tale would win my daughter too.
Good Brabantio, take up this mangled matter at the best.[104]
Men do their broken weapons rather use
Than their bare hands.
BRABANTIO   I pray you hear her speak.
190 If she confess that she was half the wooer,
Destruction on my head if my bad blame
Light on the man. Come hither, gentle mistress.
Do you perceive in all this noble company
Where most you owe obedience?
DESDEMONA   My noble father,
I do perceive here a divided duty.
To you I am bound for life and education;
My life and education both do learn me
How to respect you. You are the lord of duty,
200 I am hitherto your daughter. But here's my husband,
And so much duty as my mother showed
To you, preferring you before her father,
So much I challenge[105] that I may profess
Due to the Moor my lord.
BRABANTIO   God be with you. I have done.
Please it your Grace, on to the state affairs.
I had rather to adopt a child than get[106] it.
Come hither, Moor.
I here do give thee that with all my heart
210 Which, but thou hast already, with all my heart
I would keep from thee. For your sake,[107] jewel,
I am glad at soul I have no other child,
For thy escape would teach me tyranny,
To hang clogs on them. I have done, my lord.
DUKE Let me speak like yourself and lay a sentence[108]
Which, as a grise[109] or step, may help these lovers.
When remedies are past, the griefs are ended
By seeing the worst, which late on hopes depended.[110]
To mourn a mischief that is past and gone
220 Is the next[111] way to draw new mischief on.
What cannot be preserved when fortune takes,
Patience her injury a mock'ry makes.
The robbed that smiles, steals something from the thief;
He robs himself that spends a bootless[112] grief.
BRABANTIO So let the Turk of Cyprus us beguile:

[104] *take . . . best* i.e., make the best of this disaster [105] claim as right [106] beget [107] *For your sake* because of you [108] *lay a sentence* provide a maxim [109] step [110] *late on hopes depended* was supported by hope (of a better outcome) until lately [111] closest, surest [112] valueless

We lose it not so long as we can smile.
He bears the sentence well that nothing bears
But the free comfort which from thence he hears;
But he bears both the sentence and the sorrow
230 That to pay grief must of poor patience borrow.
These sentences, to sugar, or to gall,
Being strong on both sides, are equivocal.
But words are words. I never yet did hear
That the bruisèd heart was piercèd[113] through the ear.
I humbly beseech you, proceed to th' affairs of state.

DUKE   The Turk with a most mightly preparation makes for Cyprus. Othello, the fortitude[114] of the place is best known to you; and though we have
there a substitute[115] of most allowed sufficiency,[116] yet opinion, a more sovereign mistress of effects, throws a more safer voice on you.[117] You must there-
240 fore be content to slubber[118] the gloss of your new fortunes with this more
stubborn and boisterous[119] expedition.

OTHELLO   The tyrant Custom, most grave senators,
Hath made the flinty and steel couch of war
My thrice-driven[120] bed of down. I do agnize[121]
A natural and prompt alacrity
I find in hardness and do undertake
These present wars against the Ottomites.
Most humbly, therefore, bending to your state,
I crave fit disposition for my wife,
250 Due reference of place, and exhibition,[122]
With such accommodation and besort
As levels with[123] her breeding.

DUKE   Why, at her father's.

BRABANTIO   I will not have it so.

OTHELLO   Nor I.

DESDEMONA   Nor would I there reside,
To put my father in impatient thoughts
By being in his eye. Most gracious Duke,
To my unfolding[124] lend your prosperous[125] ear,
260 And let me find a charter[126] in your voice,
T' assist my simpleness.

DUKE   What would you, Desdemona?

DESDEMONA   That I love the Moor to live with him,
My downright violence, and storm of fortunes,

---

[113] (some editors emend to *piecèd,* i.e., "healed." But *piercèd* makes good sense: Brabantio is
saying in effect that his heart cannot be further hurt [pierced] by the indignity of the useless,
conventional advice the Duke offers him. *Pierced* can also mean, however, "lanced" in the
medical sense, and would then mean "treated")   [114] fortification   [115] viceroy   [116] *most allowed
sufficiency* generally acknowledged capability   [117] *opinion . . . you* i.e., the general opinion,
which finally controls affairs, is that you would be the best man in this situation
[118] besmear   [119] *stubborn and boisterous* rough and violent   [120] i.e., softest   [121] know in myself
[122] grant of funds   [123] *levels with* is suitable to   [124] explanation   [125] flavoring   [126] permission

May trumpet to the world. My heart's subdued
Even to the very quality of my lord.[127]
I saw Othello's visage in his mind,
And to his honors and his valiant parts
Did I my soul and fortunes consecrate.
270 So that, dear lords, if I be left behind,
A moth of peace, and he go to the war,
The rites[128] for why I love him are bereft me,
And I a heavy interim shall support
By his dear absence. Let me go with him.
    OTHELLO   Let her have your voice.[129]
Vouch with me, heaven, I therefore beg it not
To please the palate of my appetite,
Nor to comply with heat[130]—the young affects[131]
In me defunct—and proper satisfaction;[132]
280 But to be free and bounteous to her mind;
And heaven defend[133] your good souls that you think
I will your serious and great business scant
When she is with me. No, when light-winged toys
Of feathered Cupid seel[134] with wanton[135] dullness
My speculative and officed instrument,[136]
That my disports corrupt and taint my business,
Let housewives make a skillet of my helm,
And all indign[137] and base adversities
Make head[138] against my estimation![139]—
290   DUKE   Be it as you shall privately determine,
Either for her stay or going. Th' affair cries haste,
And speed must answer it.
    FIRST SENATOR   You must away tonight.
    OTHELLO   With all my heart.
    DUKE   At nine i' th' morning here we'll meet again.
Othello, leave some officer behind,
And he shall our commission bring to you,
And such things else of quality and respect
As doth import you.
300   OTHELLO   So please your grace, my ancient;
A man he is of honesty and trust.
To his conveyance I assign my wife,
With what else needful your good grace shall think
To be sent after me.
    DUKE   Let it be so.
Good night to every one. [*To* BRABANTIO] And, noble signior,

---

[127] *My . . . lord* i.e., I have become one in nature and being with the man I married (therefore, I too would go to the wars like a soldier)   [128] (may refer either to the marriage rites or to the rites, formalities, of war)   [129] consent   [130] lust   [131] passions   [132] *proper satisfaction* i.e., consummation of the marriage   [133] forbid   [134] sew up   [135] lascivious   [136] *speculative . . . instrument* i.e., sight (and, by extension, the mind)   [137] unworthy   [138] *Make head* form an army, i.e., attack   [139] reputation

If virtue no delighted[140] beauty lack,
Your son-in-law is far more fair than black.
    FIRST SENATOR Adieu, brave Moor. Use Desdemona well.
310   BRABANTIO Look to her, Moor, if thou hast eyes to see:
She has deceived her father, and may thee.

[Exeunt DUKE, SENATORS, OFFICERS, *etc.]*

    OTHELLO My life upon her faith! Honest Iago,
My Desdemona must I leave to thee.
I prithee let thy wife attend on her,
And bring them after in the best advantage.[141]
Come, Desdemona, I have but an hour
Of love, or worldly matter, and direction
To spend with thee. We must obey the time.

Exit [MOOR *with* DESDEMONA].

    RODERIGO Iago?
320   IAGO What say'st thou, noble heart?
    RODERIGO What will I do, think'st thou?
    IAGO Why, go to bed and sleep.
    RODERIGO I will incontinently[142] drown myself.
    IAGO If thou dost, I shall never love thee after. Why, thou silly gentleman?
    RODERIGO It is silliness to live when to live is torment; and then have we a prescription to die when death is our physician.
    IAGO O villainous! I have looked upon the world for four times seven years, and since I could distinguish betwixt a benefit and an injury, I never found man that knew how to love himself. Ere I would say I would drown myself for
330 the love of a guinea hen, I would change my humanity with a baboon.
    RODERIGO What should I do? I confess it is my shame to be so fond, but it is not in my virtue[143] to amend it.
    IAGO Virtue? A fig! 'Tis in ourselves that we are thus, or thus. Our bodies are our gardens, to the which our wills are gardeners; so that if we will plant nettles or sow lettuce, set hyssop and weed up thyme, supply it with one gender of herbs or distract[144] it with many—either to have it sterile with idleness or manured with industry—why, the power and corrigible[145] authority of this lies in our wills. If the balance of our lives had not one scale of reason to poise another of sensuality, the blood and baseness of our natures
340 would conduct us to most prepost'rous conclusions.[146] But we have reason to cool our raging motions, our carnal sting or unbitted[147] lusts, whereof I take this that you call love to be a sect or scion.[148]
    RODERIGO It cannot be.
    IAGO It is merely a lust of the blood and a permission of the will. Come, be a man! Drown thyself? Drown cats and blind puppies! I have professed me

---

[140] delightful   [141] opportunity   [142] at once   [143] strength (Roderigo is saying that his nature controls him)   [144] vary   [145] corrective   [146] ends   [147] i.e., uncontrolled   [148] *sect or scion* off-shoot

thy friend, and I confess me knit to thy deserving with cables of perdurable toughness. I could never better stead[149] thee than now. Put money in thy purse. Follow thou the wars; defeat thy favor[150] with an usurped[151] beard. I say, put money in thy purse. It cannot be long that Desdemona should con-
350 tinue her love to the Moor. Put money in thy purse. Nor he his to her. It was a violent commencement in her and thou shalt see an answerable[152] sequestration—put but money in thy purse. These Moors are changeable in their wills—fill thy purse with money. The food that to him now is as luscious as locusts[153] shall be to him shortly as bitter as coloquintida.[154] She must change for youth; when she is sated with his body, she will find the errors of her choice. Therefore, put money in thy purse. If thou wilt needs damn thyself, do it a more delicate way than drowning. Make all the money thou canst. If sanctimony[155] and a frail vow betwixt an erring[156] barbarian and supersubtle Venetian be not too hard for my wits, and all the tribe of hell, thou shalt enjoy
360 her. Therefore, make money. A pox of drowning thyself, it is clean out of the way. Seek thou rather to be hanged in compassing[157] thy joy than to be drowned and go without her.

    RODERIGO   Wilt thou be fast to my hopes, if I depend on the issue?

    IAGO   Thou art sure of me. Go, make money. I have told thee often, and I retell thee again and again, I hate the Moor. My cause is hearted;[158] thine hath no less reason. Let us be conjunctive[159] in our revenge against him. If thou canst cuckold him, thou dost thyself a pleasure, me a sport. There are many events in the womb of time, which will be delivered. Traverse, go, provide thy money! We will have more of this tomorrow. Adieu.

370   RODERIGO   Where shall we meet i' th' morning?

    IAGO   At my lodging.

    RODERIGO   I'll be with thee betimes.

    IAGO   Go to, farewell. Do you hear, Roderigo?

    RODERIGO   I'll sell all my land.   *Exit.*

    IAGO   Thus do I ever make my fool my purse;
For I mine own gained knowledge[160] should profane
If I would time expend with such a snipe
But for my sport and profit. I hate the Moor,
And it is thought abroad that 'twixt my sheets
380 H'as done my office. I know not if't be true,
But I, for mere suspicion in that kind,
Will do, as if for surety.[161] He holds me well;
The better shall my purpose work on him.
Cassio's a proper[162] man. Let me see now:
To get his place, and to plume up my will[163]
In double knavery. How? How? Let's see.

[149] serve   [150] *defeat thy favor* disguise your face   [151] assumed   [152] similar   [153] a sweet fruit
[154] a purgative derived from a bitter apple   [155] sacred bond (of marriage)   [156] wandering
[157] encompassing, achieving   [158] deep-seated in the heart   [159] joined   [160] *gained knowledge*
i.e., practical, worldly wisdom   [161] certainty   [162] handsome   [163] *plume up my will* (many explanations have been offered for this crucial line, which in Q₁ reads "make up my will." The general sense is something like "to make more proud and gratify my ego")

After some time, to abuse Othello's ears
That he is too familiar with his wife.
He hath a person and a smooth dispose[164]

390 To be suspected—framed[165] to make women false.
The Moor is of a free and open nature
That thinks men honest that but seem to be so;
And will as tenderly be led by th' nose
As asses are.
I have't! It is engendered! Hell and night
Must bring this monstrous birth to the world's light.   [*Exit.*]

Act II, Scene I. [*Cyprus.*]

Enter MONTANO *and two* GENTLEMEN [*one above*].[166]

    MONTANO What from the cape can you discern at sea?
    FIRST GENTLEMAN Nothing at all, it is a high-wrought flood.
I cannot 'twixt the heaven and the main
Descry a sail.
    MONTANO Methinks the wind hath spoke aloud at land;
A fuller blast ne'er shook our battlements.
If it hath ruffianed so upon the sea,
What ribs of oak, when mountains melt on them,
Can hold the mortise? What shall we hear of this?

10   SECOND GENTLEMAN A segregation[167] of the Turkish fleet.
For do but stand upon the foaming shore,
The chidden billow seems to pelt the clouds;
The wind-shaked surge, with high and monstrous main,[168]
Seems to cast water on the burning Bear
And quench the guards of th' ever-fixèd pole.[169]
I never did like molestation view
On the enchafèd flood.
    MONTANO   If that the Turkish fleet
Be not ensheltered and embayed, they are drowned;

20 It is impossible to bear it out.

Enter a [*third*] GENTLEMAN.

    THIRD GENTLEMAN News, lads! Our wars are done.
The desperate tempest hath so banged the Turks
That their designment halts. A noble ship of Venice

---

[164] manner   [165] designed   [166] (the Folio arrangement of this scene requires that the First Gentleman stand above—on the upper stage—and act as a lookout reporting sights which cannot be seen by Montano standing below on the main stage)   [167] separation   [168] both "ocean" and "strength"   [169] *Seems . . . pole* (the constellation Ursa Minor contains two stars which are the *guards,* or companions, of the *pole,* or North Star)

Hath seen a grievous wrack and sufferance[170]
On most part of their fleet.
   MONTANO   How? Is this true?
   THIRD GENTLEMAN   The ship is here put in,
A Veronesa; Michael Cassio,
Lieutenant to the warlike Moor Othello,
30 Is come on shore; the Moor himself at sea,
And is in full commission here for Cyprus.
   MONTANO   I am glad on't. 'Tis a worthy governor.
   THIRD GENTLEMAN   But this same Cassio, though he speak of comfort
Touching the Turkish loss, yet he looks sadly
And prays the Moor be safe, for they were parted
With foul and violent tempest.
   MONTANO   Pray heavens he be;
For I have served him, and the man commands
Like a full soldier. Let's to the seaside, ho!
40 As well to see the vessel that's come in
As to throw out our eyes for brave Othello,
Even till we make the main and th' aerial blue
An indistinct regard.[171]
   THIRD GENTLEMAN   Come, let's do so;
For every minute is expectancy
Of more arrivancie.[172]

Enter CASSIO.

   CASSIO   Thanks, you the valiant of the warlike isle,
That so approve[173] the Moor. O, let the heavens
Give him defense against the elements,
50 For I have lost him on a dangerous sea.
   MONTANO   Is he well shipped?
   CASSIO   His bark is stoutly timbered, and his pilot
Of very expert and approved allowance;[174]
Therefore my hopes, not surfeited to death,[175]
Stand in bold cure.[176] [*Within:* A sail, a sail, a sail!]
   CASSIO   What noise?
   FIRST GENTLEMAN   The town is empty; on the brow o' th' sea
Stand ranks of people, and they cry, "A sail!"   [*A shot.*]
   CASSIO   My hopes do shape him for the governor.
60   SECOND GENTLEMAN   They do discharge their shot of courtesy:
Our friends at least.
   CASSIO   I pray you, sir, go forth
And give us truth who 'tis that is arrived.

---

[170] damage   [171] *the main . . . regard* i.e., the sea and sky become indistinguishable
[172] arrivals   [173] "honor" or, perhaps, "are as warlike and valiant as your governor"   [174] *approved allowance* known and tested   [175] *not surfeited to death* i.e., not so great as to be in danger
[176] *Stand in bold cure* i.e., are likely to be restored

SECOND GENTLEMAN   I shall.   [*Exit.*]
MONTANO   But, good lieutenant, is your general wived?
CASSIO   Most fortunately. He hath achieved a maid
That paragons[177] description and wild fame;[178]
One that excels the quirks of blazoning pens,[179]
And in th' essential vesture of creation[180]
70 Does tire the ingener.[181]

Enter [Second] GENTLEMAN.

                    How now? Who has put in?
SECOND GENTLEMAN   'Tis one Iago, ancient to the general.
CASSIO   H'as had most favorable and happy speed:
Tempests themselves, high seas, and howling winds,
The guttered[182] rocks and congregated[183] sands,
Traitors ensteeped[184] to enclog the guiltless keel,
As having sense[185] of beauty, do omit
Their mortal[186] natures, letting go safely by
The divine Desdemona.
80   MONTANO   What is she?
CASSIO   She that I spake of, our great captain's captain,
Left in the conduct of the bold Iago,
Whose footing[187] here anticipates our thoughts
A se'nnight's[188] speed. Great Jove, Othello guard,
And swell his sail with thine one pow'rful breath,
That he may bless this bay with his tall[189] ship,
Make love's quick pants in Desdemona's arms,
Give renewed fire to our extincted spirits.

Enter DESDEMONA, IAGO, RODERIGO, *and* EMILIA.

O, behold! The riches of the ship is come on shore!
90 You men of Cyprus, let her have your knees.   [*Kneeling.*]
Hail to thee, lady! and the grace of heaven,
Before, behind thee, and on every hand,
Enwheel thee round.
DESDEMONA   I thank you, valiant Cassio.
What tidings can you tell of my lord?
CASSIO   He is not yet arrived, nor know I aught
But that he's well and will be shortly here.
DESDEMONA   O but I fear. How lost you company?

---

[177] exceeds   [178] *wild fame* extravagant report   [179] *quirks of blazoning pens* ingenuities of
praising pens   [180] *essential vesture of creation* essential human nature as given by the Creator   [181] *tire the ingener* a difficult line that probably means something like "outdo the human
ability to imagine and picture"   [182] jagged   [183] gathered   [184] submerged   [185] awareness   [186] deadly
[187] landing   [188] week's   [189] brave

CASSIO   The great contention of sea and skies
100 Parted our fellowship. [*Within:* A sail, a sail!]   [*A shot.*]
                    But hark. A sail!
       SECOND GENTLEMAN   They give this greeting to the citadel;
This likewise is a friend.
       CASSIO   See for the news.   [*Exit* GENTLEMAN.]
Good ancient, you are welcome [*To* EMILIA] Welcome, mistress.
Let it not gall your patience, good Iago,
That I extend[190] my manners. 'Tis my breeding[191]
That gives me this bold show of courtesy.   [*Kisses* EMILIA.]
       IAGO   Sir, would she give you so much of her lips
110 As of her tongue she oft bestows on me,
You would have enough.
       DESDEMONA   Alas, she has no speech.
       IAGO   In faith, too much.
I find it still when I have leave to sleep.[192]
Marry, before your ladyship,[193] I grant,
She puts her tongue a little in her heart
And chides with thinking.
       EMILIA   You have little cause to say so.
       IAGO   Come on, come on! You are pictures[194] out of door,
120 Bells in your parlors, wildcats in your kitchens,
Saints in your injuries,[195] devils being offended,
Players in your housewifery,[196] and housewives in your beds.
       DESDEMONA   O, fie upon thee, slanderer!
       IAGO   Nay, it is true, or else I am a Turk:
You rise to play, and go to bed to work.
       EMILIA   You shall not write my praise.
       IAGO   No, let me not.
       DESDEMONA   What wouldst write of me, if thou shouldst praise me?
       IAGO   O gentle lady, do not put me to't.
130 For I am nothing if not critical.
       DESDEMONA   Come on, assay. There's one gone to the harbor?
       IAGO   Ay, madam.
       DESDEMONA [*Aside*]   I am not merry; but I do beguile
The thing I am by seeming otherwise.—
Come, how wouldst thou praise me?
       IAGO   I am about it; but indeed my invention
Comes from my pate as birdlime[197] does from frieze[198]—
It plucks out brains and all. But my Muse labors,

---

[190] stretch   [191] careful training in manners (Cassio is considerably more the polished gentleman than Iago, and aware of it)   [192] *still . . . sleep* i.e., even when she allows me to sleep she continues to scold   [193] *before your ladyship* in your presence   [194] models (of virtue)   [195] *in your injuries* when you injure others   [196] this word can mean "careful, economical household management," and Iago would then be accusing women of only pretending to be good housekeepers, while in bed they are either [1] economical of their favors, or more likely [2] serious and dedicated workers   [197] a sticky substance put on branches to catch birds   [198] rough cloth

And thus she is delivered:
140 If she be fair[199] and wise: fairness and wit,
The one's for use, the other useth it.
    DESDEMONA Well praised. How if she be black[200] and witty?
    IAGO If she be black, and thereto have a wit,
She'll find a white that shall her blackness fit.
    DESDEMONA Worse and worse!
    EMILIA How if fair and foolish?
    IAGO She never yet was foolish that was fair,
For even her folly helped her to an heir.
    DESDEMONA Those are old fond[201] paradoxes to make fools laugh i' th'
150 alehouse.
What miserable praise hast thou for her that's foul and foolish?
    IAGO There's none so foul, and foolish thereunto,
But does foul pranks which fair and wise ones do.
    DESDEMONA O heavy ignorance. Thou praisest the worst best. But what
praise couldst thou bestow on a deserving woman indeed—one that in the
authority of her merit did justly put on the vouch of very malice itself?[202]
    IAGO She that was ever fair, and never proud;
Had tongue at will, and yet was never loud;
Never lacked gold, and yet went never gay;
160 Fled from her wish, and yet said "Now I may";
She that being angered, her revenge being nigh,
Bade her wrong stay, and her displeasure fly;
She that in wisdom never was so frail
To change the cod's head for the salmon's tail;[203]
She that could think, and nev'r disclose her mind;
See suitors following, and not look behind:
She was a wight[204] [if ever such wights were]—
    DESDEMONA To do what?
    IAGO To suckle fools and chronicle small beer.[205]
170   DESDEMONA O most lame and impotent conclusion. Do not learn of him,
Emilia, though he be thy husband. How say you, Cassio? Is he not a most
profane and liberal[206] counselor?
    CASSIO He speaks home,[207] madam. You may relish him more in[208] the
soldier than in the scholar [*Takes* DESDEMONA*'s hand.*]
    IAGO [*Aside*] He takes her by the palm. Ay, well said, whisper! With as
little a web as this will I ensnare as great a fly as Cassio. Ay, smile upon her,
do! I will gyve[209] thee in thine own courtship.—You say true; 'tis so, indeed!
—If such tricks as these strip you out of your lieutenantry, it had been better
you had not kissed your three fingers so oft—which now again you are most

---

[199] light-complexioned [200] brunette [201] foolish [202] *one . . . itself* i.e., a woman so honest
and deserving that even malice would be forced to approve of her [203] *To . . . tail* i.e., to
exchange something valuable for something useless [204] person [205] *chronicle small beer* i.e.,
keep household accounts (the most trivial of occupations in Iago's opinion) [206] licentious
[207] *speaks home* thrusts deeply with his speech [208] *relish him more in* enjoy him more as
[209] bind

180 apt to play the sir[210] in. Very good! Well kissed! An excellent curtsy![211] 'Tis so,
indeed. Yet again your fingers to your lips? Would they were clyster pipes[212]
for your sake! [*Trumpets within.*] The Moor! I know his trumpet![213]

CASSIO 'Tis truly so.

DESDEMONA Let's meet him and receive him.

CASSIO Lo, where he comes.

OTHELLO O my fair warrior!

DESDEMONA   My dear Othello.

OTHELLO It gives me wonder great as my content
To see you here before me. O my soul's joy!
190 If after every tempest come such calms,
May the winds blow till they have wakened death.
And let the laboring bark climb hills of seas
Olympus-high, and duck again as low
As hell's from heaven. If it were now to die,
'Twere now to be most happy; for I fear
My soul hath her content so absolute
That not another comfort like to this
Succeeds in unknown fate.

DESDEMONA   The heavens forbid
200 But that our loves and comforts should increase
Even as our days do grow.

OTHELLO   Amen to that, sweet powers!
I cannot speak enough of this content:
It stops me here [*touches his heart*]; it is too much of joy.
And this, and this, the greatest discords be   [*They kiss.*]
That e'er our hearts shall make!

IAGO [*Aside*]   O, you are well tuned now!
But I'll set down the pegs[214] that make this music,
As honest as I am.

210   OTHELLO   Come, let us to the castle.
News, friends! Our wars are done; the Turks are drowned.
How does my old acquaintance of this isle?
Honey, you shall be well desired in Cyprus;
I have found great love amongst them. O my sweet,
I prattle out of fashion, and I dote
In mine own comforts. I prithee, good Iago,
Go to the bay and disembark my coffers.
Bring thou the master to the citadel;
He is a good one and his worthiness
220 Does challenge[215] much respect. Come, Desdemona,
Once more well met at Cyprus.

---

[210] *the sir* the fashionable gentleman   [211] courtsy, i.e., bow   [212] *clyster pipes* enema tubes
[213] *his trumpet* (great men had their own distinctive calls)   [214] *set down the pegs* loosen the
strings (to produce discord)   [215] require, exact

Exit OTHELLO *and* DESDEMONA [*and all but* IAGO *and* RODERIGO].

IAGO [*To an* ATTENDANT]   Do thou meet me presently at the harbor. [*To* RODERIGO] Come hither. If thou be'st valiant [as they say base men being in love have then a nobility in their natures more than is native to them], list me. The lieutenant tonight watches on the court of guard.[216] First, I must tell thee this: Desdemona is directly in love with him.

RODERIGO   With him? Why, 'tis not possible.

IAGO   Lay thy finger thus [*puts his finger to his lips*], and let thy soul be instructed. Mark me with what violence she first loved the Moor but for bragging and telling her fantastical lies. To love him still for prating? Let not
230 thy discreet heart think it. Her eye must be fed. And what delight shall she have to look on the devil? When the blood is made dull with the act of sport, there should be a game[217] to inflame it and to give satiety a fresh appetite, loveliness in favor,[218] sympathy in years,[219] manners, and beauties; all which the Moor is defective in. Now for want of these required conveniences,[220] her delicate tenderness will find itself abused, begin to heave the gorge,[221] dis-relish and abhor the Moor. Very nature will instruct her in it and compel her to some second choice. Now sir, this granted—as it is a most pregnant[222] and unforced position—who stands so eminent in the degree of this fortune as Cassio does? A knave very voluble; no further conscionable[223] than in putting
240 on the mere form of civil and humane[224] seeming for the better compass of his salt[225] and most hidden loose[226] affection. Why, none! Why, none! A slipper[227] and subtle knave, a finder of occasion, that has an eye can stamp and counterfeit advantages, though true advantage never present itself. A devilish knave. Besides, the knave is handsome, young, and hath all those requisites in him that folly and green minds look after. A pestilent complete knave, and the woman hath found him already.

RODERIGO   I cannot believe that in her; she's full of most blessed condition.

IAGO   Blessed fig's-end! The wine she drinks is made of grapes. If she had been blessed, she would never have loved the Moor. Blessed pudding! Didst
250 thou not see her paddle with the palm of his hand? Didst not mark that?

RODERIGO   Yes, that I did; but that was but courtesy.

IAGO   Lechery, by this hand! [*Extends his index finger*] An index[228] and obscure prologue to the history of lust and foul thoughts. They met so near with their lips that their breaths embraced together. Villainous thoughts, Roderigo. When these mutualities so marshal the way, hard at hand comes the master and main exercise, th' incorporate[229] conclusion: Pish! But, sir, be you ruled by me. I have brought you from Venice. Watch you tonight; for the command, I'll lay't upon you. Cassio knows you not. I'll not be far from you. Do you find some occasion to anger Cassio, either by speaking too loud, or
260 tainting[230] his discipline, or from what other course you please which the time shall more favorably minister.

---

[216] *court of guard* guardhouse   [217] sport (with the added sense of "gamey," "rank") [218] countenance, appearance   [219] *sympathy in years* sameness of age   [220] advantages   [221] *heave the gorge* vomit   [222] likely   [223] *no further conscionable* having no more conscience   [224] polite [225] lecherous   [226] immoral   [227] slippery   [228] pointer   [229] carnal   [230] discrediting

RODERIGO Well.

IAGO Sir, he's rash and very sudden in choler,[231] and haply may strike at you. Provoke him that he may; for even out of that will I cause these of Cyprus to mutiny, whose qualification shall come into no true taste[232] again but by the displanting of Cassio. So shall you have a shorter journey to your desires by the means I shall then have to prefer them; and the impediment most profitably removed without the which there were no expectation of our prosperity.

RODERIGO I will do this if you can bring it to any opportunity.

270   IAGO I warrant thee. Meet me by and by at the citadel. I must fetch his necessaries ashore. Farewell.

RODERIGO Adieu.   *Exit.*

IAGO That Cassio loves her, I do well believ't;
That she loves him, 'tis apt and of great credit.
The Moor, howbeit that I endure him not,
Is of a constant, loving, noble nature,
And I dare think he'll prove to Desdemona
A most dear[233] husband. Now I do love her too;
Not out of absolute[234] lust, though peradventure[235]
280 I stand accountant for as great a sin,
But partly led to diet[236] my revenge,
For that I do suspect the lusty Moor
Hath leaped into my seat; the thought whereof
Doth, like a poisonous mineral, gnaw my inwards;
And nothing can or shall content my soul
Till I am evened with him, wife for wife.
Or failing so, yet that I put the Moor
At least into a jealousy so strong
That judgment cannot cure. Which thing to do,
290 If this poor trash of Venice, whom I trace[237]
For his quick hunting, stand the putting on,
I'll have our Michael Cassio on the hip,
Abuse him to the Moor in the right garb[238]
[For I fear Cassio with my nightcap too],
Make the Moor thank me, love me, and reward me
For making him egregiously an ass
And practicing upon[239] his peace and quiet,
Even to madness. 'Tis here, but yet confused:
Knavery's plain face is never seen till used.   *Exit.*

---

[231] anger [232] *qualification* . . . *taste* i.e., appeasement will not be brought about (wine was "qualified" by adding water) [233] expensive [234] *out of absolute* absolutely out of [235] perchance [236] feed [237] most editors emend to "trash," meaning to hang weights on a dog to slow his hunting: but "trace" clearly means something like "put on the trace" or "set on the track" [238] *right garb* i.e., "proper fashion" [239] *practicing upon* scheming to destroy

Scene II. [*A street.*]

Enter OTHELLO'S HERALD, *with a proclamation.*

HERALD   It is Othello's pleasure, our noble and valiant general, that upon certain tidings now arrived importing the mere perdition[240] of the Turkish fleet, every man put himself into triumph. Some to dance, some to make bonfires, each man to what sport and revels his addition[241] leads him. For, besides these beneficial news, it is the celebration of his nuptial. So much was his pleasure should be proclaimed. All offices[242] are open, and there is full liberty of feasting from this present hour of five till the bell have told eleven. Bless the isle of Cyprus and our noble general Othello!   *Exit.*

Scene III. [*The citadel of Cyprus.*]

Enter OTHELLO, DESDEMONA, CASSIO, *and* ATTENDANTS.

OTHELLO   Good Michael, look you to the guard tonight.
Let's teach ourselves that honorable stop,
Not to outsport discretion.
CASSIO   Iago hath discretion what to do;
But notwithstanding, with my personal eye
Will I look to't.
OTHELLO   Iago is most honest.
Michael, good night. Tomorrow with your earliest
Let me have speech with you. [*To* DESDEMONA] Come, my dear love,
10   The purchase made, the fruits are to ensue.
That profit's yet to come 'tween me and you.
Good night.   *Exit* [OTHELLO *with* DESDEMONA *and* ATTENDANTS].

Enter IAGO.

CASSIO   Welcome, Iago. We must to the watch.
IAGO   Not this hour, lieutenant; 'tis not yet ten o' th' clock. Our general cast[243] us thus early for the love of his Desdemona; who let us not therefore blame. He hath not yet made wanton the night with her, and she is sport for Jove.
CASSIO   She's a most exquisite lady.
IAGO   And, I'll warrant her, full of game.
20   CASSIO   Indeed, she's a most fresh and delicate creature.
IAGO   What an eye she has! Methinks it sounds a parley to provocation.
CASSIO   An inviting eye; and yet methinks right modest.
IAGO   And when she speaks, is it not an alarum[244] to love?
CASSIO   She is indeed perfection.

[240] *mere perdition* absolute destruction   [241] rank   [242] kitchens and storerooms of food   [243] dismissed   [244] the call to action, "general quarters"

IAGO   Well, happiness to their sheets! Come, lieutenant, I have a stoup[245] of wine, and here without are a brace of Cyprus gallants that would fain have a measure to the health of black Othello.

CASSIO   Not tonight, good Iago. I have very poor and unhappy brains for drinking; I could well wish courtesy would invent some other custom of
30   entertainment.

IAGO   O they are our friends. But one cup! I'll drink for you.

CASSIO   I have drunk but one tonight, and that was craftily qualified[246] too; and behold what innovation it makes here. I am unfortunate in the infirmity and dare not task my weakness with any more.

IAGO   What, man! 'Tis a night of revels, the gallants desire it.

CASSIO   Where are they?

IAGO   Here, at the door. I pray you call them in.

CASSIO   I'll do't, but it dislikes me.   *Exit.*

IAGO   If I can fasten but one cup upon him
40 With that which he hath drunk tonight already,
He'll be as full of quarrel and offense
As my young mistress' dog. Now, my sick fool Roderigo,
Whom love hath turned almost the wrong side out,
To Desdemona hath tonight caroused
Potations pottle-deep;[247] and he's to watch.
Three else[248] of Cyprus, noble swelling spirits,
That hold their honors in a wary distance,[249]
The very elements of this warlike isle,
Have I tonight flustered with flowing cups,
50 And they watch too. Now, 'mongst this flock of drunkards
Am I to put our Cassio in some action
That may offend the isle. But here they come.

Enter CASSIO, MONTANO, *and* GENTLEMEN.

If consequence do but approve my dream
My boat sails freely, both with wind and stream.

CASSIO   Fore God, they have given me a rouse[250] already.

MONTANO   Good faith, a little one; not past a pint, as I am a soldier.

IAGO   Some wine, ho!
[*Sings*] And let me the canakin clink, clink;
          And let me the canakin clink.
60   A soldier's a man;
                  O man's life's but a span.
                  Why then, let a soldier drink.
Some wine, boys!

CASSIO   Fore God, an excellent song!

IAGO   I learned it in England, where indeed they are most potent in potting. Your Dane, your German, and your swag-bellied[251] Hollander—Drink,

---

[245] two-quart tankard   [246] diluted   [247] to the bottom of the cup   [248] others   [249] *hold* . . . *distance* are scrupulous in maintaining their honor   [250] drink   [251] pendulous-bellied

ho!—are nothing to your English.

CASSIO Is your Englishman so exquisite[252] in his drinking?

IAGO Why, he drinks you with facility your Dane dead drunk; he sweats
not to overthrow your Almain; he gives your Hollander a vomit ere the next
pottle can be filled.

CASSIO To the health of our general!

MONTANO I am for it, lieutenant, and I'll do you justice.

IAGO O sweet England!

[*Sings*] King Stephen was and a worthy peer;
     His breeches cost him but a crown;
     He held them sixpence all too dear,
     With that he called the tailor lown.[253]
     He was a wight of high renown,
     And thou art but of low degree:
     'Tis pride that pulls the country down;
     And take thine auld cloak about thee.

Some wine, ho!

CASSIO 'Fore God, this is a more exquisite song than the other.

IAGO Will you hear't again?

CASSIO No, for I hold him to be unworthy of his place that does those
things. Well, God's above all; and there be souls must be saved, and there be
souls must not be saved.

IAGO It's true, good lieutenant.

CASSIO For mine own part—no offense to the general, nor any man of
quality—I hope to be saved.

IAGO And so do I too, lieutenant.

CASSIO Ay, but, by your leave, not before me. The lieutenant is to be saved
before the ancient. Let's have no more of this; let's to our affairs.—God forgive
us our sins!—Gentlemen, let's look to our business. Do not think, gentlemen,
I am drunk. This is my ancient; this is my right hand, and this is my left. I am
not drunk now. I can stand well enough and I speak well enough.

GENTLEMEN Excellent well!

CASSIO Why, very well then. You must not think then that I am drunk. *Exit.*

MONTANO To th' platform, masters. Come, let's set the watch.

IAGO You see this fellow that is gone before.
He's a soldier fit to stand by Caesar
And give direction; and do but see his vice.
'Tis to his virtue a just equinox,[254]
The one as long as th' other. 'Tis pity of him.
I fear the trust Othello puts him in,
On some odd time of his infirmity,
Will shake this island.

MONTANO   But is he often thus?

IAGO 'Tis evermore his prologue to his sleep:
He'll watch the horologe a double set[255]

---

[252] superb [253] lout [254] *just equinox* exact balance (of dark and light) [255] *watch . . . set*
stay awake twice around the clock

If drink rock not his cradle.

MONTANO   It were well
The general were put in mind of it.
Perhaps he sees it not, or his good nature
Prizes the virtue that appears in Cassio
And looks not on his evils. Is not this true?

Enter RODERIGO.

IAGO [*Aside*]   How now, Roderigo?
I pray you after the lieutenant, go!   [*Exit* RODERIGO.]
120   MONTANO   And 'tis great pity that the noble Moor
Should hazard such a place as his own second
With one of an ingraft[256] infirmity.
It were an honest action to say so
To the Moor.
IAGO   Not I, for this fair island!
I do love Cassio well and would do much

[Help, Help! *Within.*]

To cure him of this evil.
                        But hark! What noise?

Enter CASSIO, *pursuing* RODERIGO.

CASSIO   Zounds, you rogue! You rascal!
130   MONTANO   What's the matter lieutenant?
CASSIO   A knave teach me my duty? I'll beat the knave into a twiggen[257]
bottle.
RODERIGO   Beat me?
CASSIO   Dost thou prate, rogue?   [*Strikes him.*]
MONTANO   Nay, good lieutenant! I pray you, sir, hold your hand.
                                            [*Stays him.*]
CASSIO   Let me go, sir, or I'll knock you oe'r the mazzard.[258]
MONTANO   Come, come, you're drunk!
CASSIO   Drunk?   [*They fight.*]
140   IAGO [*Aside to* RODERIGO]   Away, I say! Go out and cry a mutiny!

                                            [*Exit* RODERIGO.]

Nay, good lieutenant. God's will, gentlemen!
Help, ho! Lieutenant. Sir. Montano.
Help, masters! Here's a goodly watch indeed!   [*A bell rung.*]
Who's that which rings the bell? Diablo, ho!

---

[256] ingrained   [257] wicker-covered   [258] head

The town will rise. God's will, lieutenant,
You'll be ashamed forever.

Enter OTHELLO *and* ATTENDANTS.

 OTHELLO   What is the matter here?
 MONTANO Zounds, I bleed still. I am hurt to the death.
He dies.   [*He and* CASSIO *fight again.*]
150 OTHELLO Hold for your lives!
 IAGO Hold, ho! Lieutenant. Sir. Montano. Gentlemen!
Have you forgot all place of sense and duty?
Hold! The general speaks to you. Hold, for shame!
 OTHELLO Why, how now, ho? From whence ariseth this?
Are we turned Turks, and to ourselves do that
Which heaven hath forbid the Ottomites?[259]
For Christian shame put by this barbarous brawl!
He that stirs next to carve for his own rage
Holds his soul light;[260] he dies upon his motion.
160 Silence that dreadful bell! It frights the isle
From her propriety.[261] What is the matter, masters?
Honest Iago, that looks dead with grieving,
Speak. Who began this? On thy love, I charge thee.
 IAGO I do not know. Friends all, but now, even now,
In quarter[262] and in terms like bride and groom
Devesting them for bed; and then, but now—
As if some planet had unwitted men—
Swords out, and tilting one at other's breasts
In opposition bloody. I cannot speak
170 Any beginning to this peevish odds,[263]
And would in action glorious I had lost
These legs that brought me to a part of it!
 OTHELLO How comes it, Michael, you are thus forgot?
 CASSIO I pray you pardon me; I cannot speak.
 OTHELLO Worthy Montano, you were wont to be civil;
The gravity and stillness of your youth
The world hath noted, and your name is great
In mouths of wisest censure.[264] What's the matter
That you unlace[265] your reputation thus
180 And spend your rich opinion[266] for the name
Of a night-brawler? Give me answer to it.
 MONTANO Worthy Othello, I am hurt to danger.
Your officer, Iago, can inform you.
While I spare speech, which something now offends[267] me,

---

[259] *heaven . . . Ottomites* i.e., by sending the storm which dispersed the Turks [260] *Holds his soul light* values his soul lightly [261] proper order [262] *In quarter* on duty [263] quarrel [264] judgment [265] undo (the term refers specifically to the dressing of a wild boar killed in the hunt) [266] reputation [267] harms, hurts

Of all that I do know; nor know I aught
By me that's said or done amiss this night,
Unless self-charity be sometimes a vice,
And to defend ourselves it be a sin
When violence assails us.

190   OTHELLO   Now, by heaven,
My blood begins my safer guides to rule,
And passion, having my best judgment collied,[268]
Assays to lead the way. If I once stir
Or do but lift this arm, the best of you
Shall sink in my rebuke. Give me to know
How this foul rout began, who set it on;
And he that is approved in this offense,
Though he had twinned with me, both at a birth,
Shall lose me. What? In a town of war
200 Yet wild, the people's hearts brimful of fear,
To manage[269] private and domestic quarrel?
In night, and on the count and guard of safety?
'Tis monstrous. Iago, who began't?

    MONTANO   If partially affined, or leagued in office,[270]
Thou dost deliver more or less than truth,
Thou art no solider.

    IAGO   Touch me not so near.
I had rather have this tongue cut from my mouth
Than it should do offense to Michael Cassio.
210 Yet I persuade myself to speak the truth
Shall nothing wrong him. This it is, general.
Montano and myself being in speech,
There comes a fellow crying out for help,
And Cassio following him with determined sword
To execute upon him. Sir, this gentleman
Steps in to Cassio and entreats his pause.
Myself the crying fellow did pursue,
Lest by his clamor—as it so fell out—
The town might fall in fright. He, swift of foot,
220 Outran my purpose; and I returned then rather
For that I heard the clink and fall of swords,
And Cassio high in oath; which till tonight
I ne'er might say before. When I came back—
For this was brief—I found them close together
At blow and thrust, even as again they were
When you yourself did part them.
More of this matter cannot I report;
But men are men; the best sometimes forget.
Though Cassio did some little wrong to him,

---

[268] darkened   [269] conduct   [270] *If . . . office* if you are partial because you are related ("affined") or the brother officer (of Cassio)

230   As men in rage strike those that wish them best,
      Yet surely Cassio I believe received
      From him that fled some strange indignity,
      Which patience could not pass.[271]
           OTHELLO   I know, Iago,
      Thy honesty and love doth mince[272] this matter,
      Making it light to Cassio. Cassio, I love thee;
      But never more be officer of mine.

      Enter DESDEMONA, *attended.*

      Look if my gentle love be not raised up.
      I'll make thee an example.
240   DESDEMONA   What is the matter, dear?
           OTHELLO   All's well, sweeting; come away to bed.
      [To MONTANO] Sir, for your hurts, myself will be your surgeon.
      Lead him off.

                                        [MONTANO *led off.*]

      Iago, look with care about the town
      And silence those whom this vile brawl distracted.
      Come, Desdemona: 'tis the soldiers' life
      To have their balmy slumbers waked with strife.

                              Exit [*with all but* IAGO *and* CASSIO].

           IAGO   What, are you hurt, lieutenant?
           CASSIO   Ay, past all surgery.
250   IAGO   Marry, God forbid!
           CASSIO   Reputation, reputation, reputation! O, I have lost my reputation! I
      have lost the immortal part of myself, and what remains is bestial. My reputa-
      tion, Iago, my reputation.
           IAGO   As I am an honest man, I had thought you had received some bodily
      wound. There is more sense[273] in that than in reputation. Reputation is an idle
      and most false imposition,[274] oft got without merit and lost without deserving.
      You have lost no reputation at all unless you repute yourself such a loser. What,
      man, there are more ways to recover the general again. You are but now cast in
      his mood[275]—a punishment more in policy[276] than in malice—even so as one
260   would beat his offenseless dog to affright an imperious lion. Sue to him again,
      and he's yours.
           CASSIO   I will rather sue to be despised than to deceive so good a comman-
      der with so slight, so drunken, and so indiscreet an officer. Drunk! And speak
      parrot![277] And squabble! Swagger! Sweat! and discourse fustian[278] with one's

      ---

      [271] allow to pass [272] cut up (i.e., tell only part of) [273] physical feeling [274] external thing
      [275] *cast in his mood* dismissed because of his anger [276] *in policy* politically necessary [277] *speak
      parrot* gabble without sense [278] *discourse fustian* speak nonsense ("fustian" was a coarse
      cotton cloth used for stuffing)

own shadow! O thou invisible spirit of wine, if thou hast no name to be known by, let us call thee devil!

IAGO   What was he that you followed with your sword? What had he done to you?

CASSIO   I know not.

270   IAGO   Is't possible?

CASSIO   I remember a mass of things, but nothing distinctly: a quarrel, but nothing wherefore. O God, that men should put an enemy in their mouths to steal away their brains! that we should with joy, pleasance, revel, and applause transform ourselves into beasts!

IAGO   Why, but you are now well enough. How came you thus recovered?

CASSIO   It hath pleased the devil drunkenness to give place to the devil wrath. One unperfectness shows me another, to make me frankly despise myself.

IAGO   Come, you are too severe a moraler. As the time, the place, and the
280   condition of this country stands, I could heartily wish this had not befall'n; but since it is as it is, mend it for your own good.

CASSIO   I will ask him for my place again: he shall tell me I am a drunkard. Had I as many mouths as Hydra, such an answer would stop them all. To be now a sensible man, by and by a fool, and presently a beast! O strange! Every inordinate cup is unblest, and the ingredient is a devil.

IAGO   Come, come, good wine is a good familiar creature if it be well used. Exclaim no more against it. And, good lieutenant, I think you think I love you.

CASSIO   I have well approved it, sir. I drunk?

290   IAGO   You or any man living may be drunk at a time, man. I tell you what you shall do. Our general's wife is now the general. I may say so in this respect, for all he hath devoted and given up himself to the contemplation, mark, and devotement of her parts[279] and graces. Confess yourself freely to her; importune her help to put you in your place again. She is of so free, so kind, so apt, so blessed a disposition she holds it a vice in her goodness not to do more than she is requested. This broken joint between you and her husband entreat her to splinter;[280] and my fortunes against any lay[281] worth naming, this crack of your love shall grow stronger than it was before.

CASSIO   You advise me well.

300   IAGO   I protest, in the sincerity of love and honest kindness.

CASSIO   I think it freely; and betimes in the morning I will beseech the virtuous Desdemona to undertake for me. I am desperate of my fortunes if they check[282] me.

IAGO   You are in the right. Good night, lieutenant; I must to the watch.

CASSIO   Good night, honest Iago.   *Exit* CASSIO.

IAGO   And what's he then that says I play the villain,
When this advice is free[283] I give, and honest,
Probal to[284] thinking, and indeed the course

---

[279] *devotement of her parts* devotion to her qualities   [280] splint   [281] wager   [282] repulse
[283] generous and open   [284] *Probal to* provable by

To win the Moor again? For 'tis most easy
310 Th' inclining[285] Desdemona to subdue
In any honest suit; she's framed as fruitful[286]
As the free elements.[287] And then for her
To win the Moor—were't to renounce his baptism,
All seals and symbols of redeemèd sin—
His soul is so enfettered to her love
That she may make, unmake, do what she list,
Even as her appetite[288] shall play the god
With his weak function.[289] How am I then a villain
To counsel Cassio to this parallel course,
320 Directly to his good? Divinity of hell!
When devils will the blackest sins put on,[290]
They do suggest at first with heavenly shows,[291]
As I do now. For whiles this honest fool
Plies Desdemona to repair his fortune,
And she for him pleads strongly to the Moor,
I'll pour this pestilence into his ear:
That she repeals him[292] for her body's lust;
And by how much she strives to do him good,
She shall undo her credit with the Moor.
330 So will I turn her virtue into pitch,
And out of her own goodness make the net
That shall enmesh them all. How now, Roderigo?   *Enter* RODERIGO.

  RODERIGO I do not follow here in the chase, not like a hound that hunts,
but one that fills up the cry.[293] My money is almost spent; I have been tonight
exceedingly well cudgeled; and I think the issue will be, I shall have so
much experience for my pains; and so, with no money at all, and a little more
wit, return again to Venice.

  IAGO How poor are they that have not patience!
What wound did ever heal but by degrees?
340 Thou know'st we work by wit, and not by witchcraft;
And wit depends on dilatory time.
Does't not go well? Cassio hath beaten thee,
And thou by that small hurt hath cashiered Cassio.
Though other things grow fair against the sun,
Yet fruits that blossom first will first be ripe.
Content thyself awhile. By the mass, 'tis morning!
Pleasure and action make the hours seem short.
Retire thee, go where thou art billeted.
Away, I say! Thou shalt know more hereafter.
350 Nay, get thee gone!   *Exit* RODERIGO.

---

[285] inclined (to be helpful)   [286] *framed as fruitful* made as generous   [287] i.e., basic nature   [288] liking   [289] thought   [290] *put on* advance, further   [291] appearances   [292] *repeals him* asks
for (Cassio's reinstatement)   [293] *fills up the cry* makes up one of the hunting pack, adding to the
noise but not actually tracking

Two things are to be done:
My wife must move[294] for Cassio to her mistress;
I'll set her on;
Myself awhile[295] to draw the Moor apart
And bring him jump[296] when he may Cassio find
Soliciting his wife. Ay, that's the way!
Dull not device by coldness and delay.   *Exit.*

Act III, Scene I. [*A street.*]

Enter CASSIO [*and*] MUSICIANS.

CASSIO   Masters, play here. I will content your pains.[297]
Something that's brief; and bid "Good morrow, general." [*They play.*]

[*Enter* CLOWN.[298]]

CLOWN   Why, masters, have your instruments been in Naples[299] that they
speak i' th' nose thus?
MUSICIAN   How, sir, how?
CLOWN   Are these, I pray you, wind instruments?
MUSICIAN   Ay, marry, are they, sir.
CLOWN   O, thereby hangs a tale.
MUSICIAN   Whereby hangs a tale, sir?
10   CLOWN   Marry, sir, by many a wind instrument that I know. But, masters,
here's money for you; and the general so likes your music that he desires you,
for love's sake, to make no more noise with it.
MUSICIAN   Well, sir, we will not.
CLOWN   If you have any music that may not be heard, to't again. But, as
they say, to hear music the general does not greatly care.
MUSICIAN   We have none such, sir.
CLOWN   Then put up your pipes in your bag, for I'll away. Go, vanish into
air, away!   *Exit* MUSICIANS.
CASSIO   Dost thou hear me, mine honest friend?
20   CLOWN   No. I hear not your honest friend. I hear you.
CASSIO   Prithee keep up thy quillets.[300] There's a poor piece of gold for
thee. If the gentlewoman that attends the general's wife be stirring, tell her
there's one Cassio entreats her a little favor of speech. Wilt thou do this?
CLOWN   She is stirring, sir. If she will stir hither, I shall seem to notify unto
her.[301]   *Exit* CLOWN.

Enter IAGO.

[294] petition   [295] at the same time   [296] at the precise moment and place   [297] *content your
pains* reward your efforts   [298] fool   [299] this may refer either to the Neopolitan nasal tone, or to
syphilis—rife in Naples—which breaks down the nose   [300] puns   [301] *seem . . . her* (the Clown
is mocking Cassio's overly elegant manner of speaking)

CASSIO   In happy time, Iago.

IAGO   You have not been abed then?

CASSIO   Why no, the day had broke before we parted.
I have made bold, Iago, to send in to your wife;
30 My suit to her is that she will to virtuous Desdemona
Procure me some access.

IAGO   I'll send her to you presently,
And I'll devise a mean to draw the Moor
Out of the way, that your converse and business
May be more free.

CASSIO   I humbly thank you for't.   *Exit* [IAGO].
                                    I never knew
A Florentine[302] more kind and honest.

Enter EMILIA.

EMILIA   Good morrow, good lieutenant. I am sorry
40 For your displeasure;[303] but all will sure be well.
The general and his wife are talking of it,
And she speaks for you stoutly. The Moor replies
That he you hurt is of great fame in Cyprus
And great affinity,[304] and that in wholesome wisdom
He might not but refuse you. But he protests he loves you.
And needs no other suitor but his likings
To bring you in again.

CASSIO   Yet I beseech you,
If you think fit, or that it may be done,
50 Give me advantage of some brief discourse
With Desdemona alone.

EMILIA   Pray you come in.
I will bestow you where you shall have time
To speak your bosom[305] freely.

CASSIO   I am much bound to you.   *Exeunt.*

Scene II. [*The citadel.*]

Enter OTHELLO, IAGO, *and* GENTLEMEN.

OTHELLO   These letters give, Iago, to the pilot
And by him do my duties to the Senate.
That done, I will be walking on the works;
Repair[306] there to me.

IAGO   Well, my good lord, I'll do't.

OTHELLO   This fortification, gentlemen, shall we see't?

GENTLEMEN   We'll wait upon your lordship.   *Exeunt.*

---

[302] i.e., Iago is as kind as if he were from Cassio's home town, Florence   [303] discomforting
[304] family   [305] inmost thoughts   [306] go

Scene III. [*The citadel.*]

Enter DESDEMONA, CASSIO, *and* EMILIA.

DESDEMONA   Be thou assured, good Cassio, I will do
All my abilities in thy behalf.
   EMILIA   Good madam, do. I warrant it grieves my husband
As if the cause were his.
   DESDEMONA   O, that's an honest fellow. Do not doubt, Cassio,
But I will have my lord and you again
As friendly as you were.
   CASSIO   Bounteous madam,
Whatever shall become of Michael Cassio,
10 He's never anything but your true servant.
   DESDEMONA   I know't; I thank you. You do love my lord.
You have known him long, and be you well assured
He shall in strangeness stand no farther off
Than in a politic distance.[307]
   CASSIO   Ay, but, lady,
That policy may either last so long,
Or feed upon such nice[308] and waterish diet,
Or breed itself so out of circumstances,[309]
That, I being absent, and my place supplied,[310]
20 My general will forget my love and service.
   DESDEMONA   Do not doubt[311] that; before Emilia here
I give thee warrant of thy place. Assure thee,
If I do vow a friendship, I'll perform it
To the last article. My lord shall never rest;
I'll watch him tame[312] and talk him out of patience;
His bed shall seem a school, his board a shrift;[313]
I'll intermingle everything he does
With Cassio's suit. Therefore be merry, Cassio,
For thy solicitor shall rather die
30 Than give thy cause away.

Enter OTHELLO *and* IAGO [*at a distance*].

   EMILIA   Madam, here comes my lord.
   CASSIO   Madam, I'll take my leave.
   DESDEMONA   Why, stay, and hear me speak.
   CASSIO   Madam, not now. I am very ill at ease,
Unfit for mine own purposes.
   DESDEMONA   Well, do your discretion.   *Exit* CASSIO.
   IAGO   Ha! I like not that.

---

[307] *He . . . distance* i.e., he shall act no more distant to you than is necessary for political reasons   [308] trivial   [309] *Or . . . circumstances* i.e., or grow so on the basis of accidental happenings and political needs   [310] filled   [311] imagine   [312] *watch him tame* (animals were tamed by being kept awake)   [313] *board a shrift* table (seem) a confessional

OTHELLO   What dost thou say?

IAGO   Nothing, my lord; or if—I know not what.

40   OTHELLO   Was not that Cassio parted from my wife?

IAGO   Cassio, my lord? No, sure, I cannot think it

That he would steal away so guilty-like,

Seeing you coming.

OTHELLO   I do believe 'twas he.

DESDEMONA [*Coming to them*]   How now, my lord?

I have been talking with a suitor here,

A man that languishes in your displeasure.

OTHELLO   Who is't you mean?

DESDEMONA   Why, your lieutenant, Cassio. Good my lord,

50   If I have any grace or power to move you,

His present[314] reconciliation take.

For if he be not one that truly loves you,

That errs in ignorance, and not in cunning,

I have no judgment in an honest face.

I prithee call him back.

OTHELLO   Went he hence now?

DESDEMONA   I' sooth so humbled

That he hath left part of his grief with me

To suffer with him. Good love, call him back.

60   OTHELLO   Not now, sweet Desdemon; some other time.

DESDEMONA   But shall't be shortly?

OTHELLO   The sooner, sweet, for you.

DESDEMONA   Shall't be tonight at supper?

OTHELLO   No, not tonight.

DESDEMONA   Tomorrow dinner then?

OTHELLO   I shall not dine at home;

I meet the captains at the citadel.

DESDEMONA   Why then, tomorrow night, on Tuesday morn,

On Tuesday noon, or night, on Wednesday morn.

70   I prithee name the time, but let it not

Exceed three days. In faith, he's penitent;

And yet his trespass, in our common reason

[Save that, they say, the wars must make example

Out of her best], is not almost a fault

T' incur a private check.[315] When shall he come?

Tell me, Othello. I wonder in my soul

What you would ask me that I should deny

Or stand so mamm'ring[316] on. What? Michael Cassio,

That came awooing with you, and so many a time,

80   When I have spoke of you dispraisingly,

Hath ta'en your part—to have so much to do

To bring him in? By'r Lady, I could do much—

---

[314] immediate   [315] *is . . . check* is almost not serious enough for a private rebuke (let alone
a public disgrace)   [316] hesitating

OTHELLO   Prithee no more. Let him come when he will!
I will deny thee nothing.

DESDEMONA   Why, this is not a boon;
'Tis as I should entreat you wear your gloves,
Or feed on nourishing dishes, or keep you warm,
Or sue to you to do a peculiar profit[317]
To your own person. Nay, when I have a suit
90 Wherein I mean to touch your love indeed,
It shall be full of poise[318] and difficult weight,
And fearful to be granted.

OTHELLO   I will deny thee nothing!
Whereon I do beseech thee grant me this,
To leave me but a little to myself.

DESDEMONA   Shall I deny you? No. Farewell, my lord.

OTHELLO   Farewell, my Desdemona: I'll come to thee straight.[319]

DESDEMONA   Emilia, come. Be as your fancies teach you;
Whate'er you be, I am obedient.   *Exit [with* EMILIA].

100 OTHELLO   Excellent wretch! Perdition catch my soul
But I do love thee! And when I love thee not,
Chaos is come again.

IAGO   My noble lord—

OTHELLO   What dost thou say, Iago?

IAGO   Did Michael Cassio, when you wooed my lady,
Know of your love?

OTHELLO   He did, from first to last. Why dost thou ask?

IAGO   But for a satisfaction of my thought,
No further harm.

110 OTHELLO   Why of thy thought, Iago?

IAGO   I did not think he had been acquainted with her.

OTHELLO   O, yes, and went between us[320] very oft.

IAGO   Indeed?

OTHELLO   Indeed? Ay, indeed! Discern'st thou aught in that?
Is he not honest?

IAGO   Honest, my lord?

OTHELLO   Honest? Ay, honest.

IAGO   My lord, for aught I know.

OTHELLO   What dost thou think?

120 IAGO   Think, my lord?

OTHELLO   Think, my lord?
By heaven, thou echoest me,
As if there were some monster in thy thought
Too hideous to be shown. Thou dost mean something.
I heard thee say even now, thou lik'st not that,
When Cassio left my wife. What didst not like?
And when I told thee he was of my counsel[321]

---

[317] *peculiar profit* particularly personal good   [318] weight   [319] at once   [320] *between us* i.e., as
messenger   [321] *of my counsel* in my confidence

Of my whole course of wooing, thou cried'st "Indeed?"
And didst contract and purse thy brow together,
130 As if thou then hadst shut up in thy brain
Some horrible conceit.[322] If thou dost love me,
Show me thy thought.
    IAGO   My lord, you know I love you.
    OTHELLO   I think thou dost;
And, for I know thou'rt full of love and honesty
And weigh'st thy words before thou giv'st them breath,
Therefore these stops[323] of thine fright me the more;
For such things in a false disloyal knave
Are tricks of customs;[324] but in a man that's just
140 They're close dilations,[325] working from the heart
That passion cannot rule.
    IAGO   For Michael Cassio,
I dare be sworn, I think that he is honest.
    OTHELLO   I think so too.
    IAGO   Men should be what they seem;
Or those that be not, would they might seem none!
    OTHELLO   Certain, men should be what they seem.
    IAGO   Why then; I think Cassio's an honest man.
    OTHELLO   Nay, yet there's more in this?
150 I prithee speak to me as to thy thinkings,
As thou dost ruminate, and give thy worst of thoughts
The worst of words.
    IAGO   Good my lord, pardon me:
Though I am bound to every act of duty,
I am not bound to that all slaves are free to.
Utter my thoughts? Why, say they are vile and false,
As where's that palace whereinto foul things
Sometimes intrude not? Who has that breast so pure
But some uncleanly apprehensions
160 Keep leets and law days,[326] and in sessions sit
With meditations lawful?
    OTHELLO   Thou dost conspire against thy friend, Iago,
If thou but think'st him wronged, and mak'st this ear
A stranger to thy thoughts.
    IAGO   I do beseech you—
Though I perchance am vicious in my guess
[As I confess it is my nature's plague
To spy into abuses, and of my jealousy
Shape faults that are not], that your wisdom
170 From one that so imperfectly conceits
Would take no notice, nor build yourself a trouble

---

[322] thought   [323] interruptions   [324] *of custom* customary   [325] *close dilations* expressions of hidden thoughts   [326] *leets and law days* meetings of local courts

Out of his scattering and unsure observance.
It were not for your quiet nor your good,
Nor for my manhood, honesty, and wisdom,
To let you know my thoughts.
    OTHELLO   What dost thou mean?
    IAGO   Good name in man and woman, dear my lord,
Is the immediate jewel of their souls.
Who steals my purse steals trash; 'tis something, nothing;
180 'Twas mine, 'tis his, and has been slave to thousands;
But he that filches from me my good name
Robs me of that which not enriches him
And makes me poor indeed.
    OTHELLO   By heaven, I'll know thy thoughts!
    IAGO   You cannot, if my heart were in your hand;
Nor shall not whilst 'tis in my custody.
    OTHELLO   Ha!
    IAGO   O, beware, my lord, of jealousy!
It is the green-eyed monster, which doth mock
190 The meat it feeds on. That cuckold lives in bliss
Who, certain of his fate, loves not his wronger;
But O, what damnèd minutes tells[327] he o'er
Who dotes, yet doubts—suspects, yet fondly[328] loves!
    OTHELLO   O misery.
    IAGO   Poor and content is rich, and rich enough;
But riches fineless[329] is as poor as winter
To him that ever fears he shall be poor.
Good God the souls of all my tribe defend
From jealousy!
200   OTHELLO   Why? Why is this?
Think'st thou I'd make a life of jealousy,
To follow still[330] the changes of the moon
With fresh suspicions? No! To be once in doubt
Is to be resolved. Exchange me for a goat
When I shall turn the business of my soul
To such exsufflicate and blown[331] surmises,
Matching thy inference. 'Tis not to make me jealous
To say my wife is fair, feeds well, loves company,
Is free of speech, sings, plays, and dances;
210 Where virtue is, these are more virtuous.
Nor from mine own weak merits will I draw
The smallest fear or doubt of her revolt,
For she had eyes, and chose me. No, Iago;
I'll see before I doubt; when I doubt, prove;

---

[327] counts   [328] foolishly   [329] infinite   [330] *To follow still* to change always (as the phases of the
moon)   [331] *exsufflicate and blown* inflated and flyblown

And on the proof there is no more but this:
Away at once with love or jealousy!
    IAGO   I am glad of this; for now I shall have reason
To show the love and duty that I bear you
With franker spirit. Therefore, as I am bound,
220 Receive it from me. I speak not yet of proof.
Look to your wife; observe her well with Cassio;
Wear your eyes thus: not jealous nor secure.
I would not have your free and noble nature
Out of self-bounty[332] be abused. Look to't.
I know our country disposition well:
In Venice they do let heaven see the pranks
They dare not show their husbands; their best conscience
Is not to leave't undone, but kept unknown.[333]
    OTHELLO   Dost thou say so?
230   IAGO   She did deceive her father, marrying you;
And when she seemed to shake and fear your looks,
She loved them most.
    OTHELLO   And so she did.
    IAGO   Why, go to then!
She that so young could give out such a seeming
To seel[334] her father's eyes up close as oak[335]—
He thought 'twas witchcraft. But I am much to blame.
I humbly do beseech you of your pardon
For too much loving you.
240   OTHELLO   I am bound to thee forever.
    IAGO   I see this hath a little dashed your spirits.
    OTHELLO   Not a jot, not a jot.
    IAGO   Trust me, I fear it has.
I hope you will consider what is spoke
Comes from my love. But I do see y' are moved.
I am to pray you not to strain[336] my speech
To grosser issues nor to larger reach[337]
Than to suspicion.
    OTHELLO   I will not.
250   IAGO   Should you do so, my lord,
My speech should fall into such vile success
Which my thoughts aimed not. Cassio's my worthy friend—
My lord, I see y' are moved.
    OTHELLO   No, not much moved.
I do not think but Desdemona's honest.
    IAGO   Long live she so. And long live you to think so.
    OTHELLO   And yet, how nature erring from itself—

[332] innate kindness (which attributes his own motives to others) [333] *their . . . unknown* i.e., their morality does not forbid adultery, but it does forbid being found out [334] hoodwink [335] a close-grained wood [336] enlarge the meaning [337] meaning

IAGO   Ay, there's the point, as [to be bold with you]
Not to affect many proposèd matches
260 Of her own clime, complexion, and degree,[338]
Whereto we see in all things nature tends[339]—
Foh! One may smell in such a will most rank,
Foul disproportions, thoughts unnatural.
But, pardon me, I do not in position[340]
Distinctly[341] speak of her; though I may fear
Her will, recoiling to her better judgment,
May fall to match[342] you with her country forms,[343]
And happily[344] repent.
          OTHELLO   Farewell, farewell!
270 If more thou dost perceive, let me know more.
Set on thy wife to observe. Leave me, Iago.
          IAGO   My lord, I take my leave.   *Going.*
          OTHELLO   Why did I marry? This honest creature doubtless
Sees and knows more, much more, than he unfolds.
          IAGO [*Returns*]   My lord, I would I might entreat your honor
To scan this thing no farther. Leave it to time.
Although 'tis fit that Cassio have his place,
For sure he fills it up with great ability,
Yet, if you please to hold him off awhile,
280 You shall by that perceive him and his means.
Note if your lady strains his entertainment[345]
With any strong or vehement importunity;
Much will be seen in that. In the meantime
Let me be thought too busy in my fears
[As worthy cause I have to fear I am]
And hold her free, I do beseech your honor.
          OTHELLO   Fear not my government.[346]
          IAGO   I once more take my leave.   *Exit.*
          OTHELLO   This fellow's of exceeding honesty,
290 And knows all qualities,[347] with a learnèd spirit
Of human dealings. If I do prove her haggard,[348]
Though that her jesses[349] were my dear heartstrings,
I'd whistle her off and let her down the wind[350]
To prey at fortune. Haply for[351] I am black
And have not those soft parts[352] of conversation
That chamberers[353] have, or for I am declined

---

[338] social station   [339] *in . . . tends* i.e., all things in nature seek out their own kind
[340] general argument   [341] specifically   [342] *fall to match* happen to compare   [343] *country forms*
i.e., the familiar appearance of her countrymen   [344] by chance   [345] *strains his entertainment*
urge strongly that he be reinstated   [346] self-control   [347] natures, types of people   [348] a partly
trained hawk which has gone wild again   [349] straps which held the hawk's legs to the trainer's
wrist   [350] *I'd . . . wind* I would release her (like an untamable hawk) and let her fly
free   [351] *Haply for* it may be because   [352] *soft parts* gentle qualities and manners   [353] courtiers—
or, perhaps, accomplished seducers

Into the vale of years—yet that's not much—
She's gone. I am abused, and my relief
Must be to loathe her. O curse of marriage,
300 That we can call these delicate creatures ours,
And not their appetites! I had rather be a toad
And live upon the vapor of a dungeon
Than keep a corner in the thing I love
For others' uses. Yet 'tis the plague to great ones;
Prerogatived are they less than the base.
'Tis destiny unshunnable, like death.
Even then this forkèd[354] plague is fated to us
When we do quicken.[355] Look where she comes.

Enter DESDEMONA *and* EMILIA.

If she be false, heaven mocked itself!
310 I'll not believe't.
          DESDEMONA   How now, my dear Othello?
Your dinner, and the generous islanders
By you invited, do attend[356] your presence.
          OTHELLO   I am to blame.
          DESDEMONA   Why do you speak so faintly?
Are you not well?
          OTHELLO   I have a pain upon my forehead, here.[357]
          DESDEMONA   Why, that's with watching; 'twill away again,
Let me but bind it hard, within this hour
320 It will be well.
          OTHELLO   Your napkin[358] is too little;

[*He pushes the handkerchief away, and it falls.*]

Let it[359] alone. Come, I'll go in with you.
          DESDEMONA   I am very sorry that you are not well.   *Exit* [*with* OTHELLO].
          EMILIA   I am glad I have found this napkin;
This was her first remembrance from the Moor.
My wayward husband hath a hundred times
Wooed me to steal it; but she so loves the token
[For he conjured her she should ever keep it]
That she reserves it evermore about her
330 To kiss and talk to. I'll have the work ta'en out[360]
And give't Iago. What he will do with it,
Heaven knows, not I; I nothing[361] but to please his fantasy.[362]

---

[354] horned (the sign of the cuckold was horns)   [355] *do quicken* are born   [356] wait   [357] (he
points to his imaginary horns)   [358] elaborately worked handkerchief   [359] (it makes a considerable difference in the interpretation of later events whether this "it" refers to Othello's forehead
or to the handkerchief; nothing in the text makes the reference clear)   [360] *work ta'en out*
needlework copied   [361] *I nothing* I wish nothing   [362] fancy, whim

Enter IAGO.

IAGO   How now? What do you here alone?
EMILIA   Do not you chide; I have a thing for you.
IAGO   You have a thing for me? It is a common thing—
EMILIA   Ha?
IAGO   To have a foolish wife.
EMILIA   O, is that all? What will you give me now
For that same handkerchief?
340   IAGO   What handkerchief?
EMILIA   What handkerchief!
Why, that the Moor first gave to Desdemona,
That which so often you did bid me steal.
         IAGO   Hast stol'n it from her?
EMILIA   No, but she let it drop by negligence,
And to th' advantage,[363] I, being here, took't up.
Look, here 't is.
         IAGO   A good wench. Give it me.
EMILIA   What will you do with't, that you have been so earnest
350   To have me filch it?
         IAGO   Why, what is that to you?   [*Takes it.*]
EMILIA   If it be not for some purpose of import,[364]
Give't me again. Poor lady, she'll run mad
When she shall lack[365] it.
         IAGO   Be not acknown on't.[366]
I have use for it. Go, leave me.   *Exit* EMILIA.
I will in Cassio's lodging lose this napkin
And let him find it. Trifles light as air
Are to the jealous confirmations strong
360   As proofs of Holy Writ. This may do something.
The Moor already changes with my poison:
Dangerous conceits are in their natures poisons,
Which at the first are scarce found to distaste,[367]
But with a little,[368] act upon the blood,
Burn like the mines of sulfur. I did say so.

Enter OTHELLO.

Look where he comes! Not poppy nor mandragora,[369]
Nor all the drowsy syrups of the world,
Shall ever medicine thee to that sweet sleep
Which thou owedst[370] yesterday.
370   OTHELLO   Ha! ha! False to me?

---

[363] *to th' advantage* being lucky   [364] importance   [365] miss   [366] *Be not acknown on't* forget
you ever saw it   [367] *are scarce found to distaste* scarcely can be tasted   [368] *with a little* in a short
time   [369] *poppy nor mandragora* soporifics   [370] possessed

 IAGO Why, how now, general? No more of that.

 OTHELLO Avaunt! be gone! Thou hast set me on the rack.

I swear 'tis better to be much abused

Than but to know't a little.

 IAGO   How now, my lord?

 OTHELLO What sense had I of her stol'n hours of lust?

I saw't not, thought it not, it harmed not me;

I slept the next night well, fed well, was free and merry;

I found not Cassio's kisses on her lips.

380 He that is robbed, not wanting[371] what is stol'n,

Let him not know't, and he's not robbed at all.

 IAGO I am sorry to hear this.

 OTHELLO I had been happy if the general camp,

Pioners[372] and all, had tasted her sweet body,

So I had nothing known. O now, forever

Farewell the tranquil mind! Farewell content!

Farewell the plumèd troops, and the big wars

That make ambition virtue! O, farewell!

Farewell the neighing steed and the shrill trump,

390 The spirit-stirring drum, th' ear-piercing fife,

The royal banner, and all quality,

Pride, pomp, and circumstance[373] of glorious war!

And O you mortal engines[374] whose rude throats

Th' immortal Jove's dread clamors[375] counterfeit,

Farewell! Othello's occupation's gone!

 IAGO Is't possible, my lord?

 OTHELLO Villain, be sure thou prove my love a whore!

Be sure of it; give me the ocular proof;

Or, by the worth of mine eternal soul,

400 Thou hadst been better have been born a dog

Than answer my waked wrath!

 IAGO   Is't come to this?

 OTHELLO Make me to see't; or at the least so prove it

That the probation[376] bear no hinge nor loop

To hang a doubt on—or woe upon thy life!

 IAGO My noble lord—

 OTHELLO If thou dost slander her and torture me,

Never pray more; abandon all remorse;

On horror's head horrors accumulate;

410 Do deeds to make heaven weep, all earth amazed;

For nothing canst thou to damnation add

Greater than that.

 IAGO   O grace! O heaven forgive me!

Are you a man? Have you a soul or sense?

---

[371] missing [372] the basest manual laborers in the army, who dug trenches and mines
[373] pageantry [374] *mortal engines* lethal weapons, i.e., cannon [375] i.e., thunder [376] proof

God b' wi' you! Take mine office. O wretched fool,
That lov'st to make thine honesty a vice!
O monstrous world! Take note, take note, O world,
To be direct and honest is not safe.
I thank you for this profit, and from hence
420 I'll love no friend, sith[377] love breeds such offense.
    OTHELLO   Nay, stay. Thou shouldst be honest.
    IAGO   I should be wise; for honesty's a fool
And loses that it works for.
    OTHELLO   By the world,
I think my wife to be honest, and think she is not;
I think that thou art just, and think thou art not.
I'll have some proof. My name, that was as fresh
As Dian's[378] visage, is now begrimed and black
As mine own face. If there be cords, or knives,
430 Poison, or fire, or suffocating streams,
I'll not endure it. Would I were satisfied!
    IAGO   I see you are eaten up with passion.
I do repent me that I put it to you.
You would be satisfied?
    OTHELLO   Would? Nay, and I will.
    IAGO   And may; but how? How satisfied, my lord?
Would you, the supervisor,[379] grossly gape on?
Behold her topped?
    OTHELLO   Death and damnation! O!
440   IAGO   It were a tedious[380] difficulty, I think,
To bring them to that prospect.[381] Damn them then,
If ever mortal eyes do see them bolster[382]
More than their own! What then? How then?
What shall I say? Where's satisfaction?
It is impossible you should see this,
Were they as prime[383] as goats, as hot as monkeys,
As salt[384] as wolves in pride,[385] and fools as gross
As ignorance made drunk. But yet, I say,
If imputation and strong circumstances
450 Which lead directly to the door of truth
Will give you satisfaction, you might hav't.
    OTHELLO   Give me a living reason she's disloyal.
    IAGO   I do not like the office.[386]
But sith I am entered in this cause so far,
Pricked[387] to't by foolish honesty and love,
I will go on. I lay with Cassio lately,
And being troubled with a raging tooth,
I could not sleep.

---

[377] since   [378] Diana's (goddess of the moon and of chastity)   [379] onlooker   [380] hard to arrange
[381] sight (where they can be seen)   [382] go to bed with   [383], [384] *prime, salt* lustful   [385] heat
[386] duty   [387] spurred

There are a kind of men so loose of soul
460 That in their sleeps will mutter their affairs.
One of this kind is Cassio.
In sleep I heard him say, "Sweet Desdemona,
Let us be wary, let us hide our loves!"
And then, sir, would he gripe[388] and wring my hand,
Cry "O sweet creature!" Then kiss me hard,
As if he plucked up kisses by the roots
That grew upon my lips; laid his leg o'er my thigh,
And sigh, and kiss, and then cry, "Cursèd fate
That gave thee to the Moor!"

470   OTHELLO   O monstrous! monstrous!
       IAGO   Nay, this was but his dream.
       OTHELLO   But this denoted a foregone conclusion,[389]
'Tis a shrewd doubt,[390] though it be but a dream.
       IAGO   And this may help to thicken other proofs
That do demonstrate[391] thinly.
       OTHELLO   I'll tear her all to pieces!
       IAGO   Nay, yet be wise. Yet we see nothing done;
She may be honest yet. Tell me but this:
Have you not sometimes seen a handkerchief
480 Spotted with strawberries in your wife's hand?
       OTHELLO   I gave her such a one; 'twas my first gift.
       IAGO   I know not that; but such a handkerchief—
I am sure it was your wife's—did I today
See Cassio wipe his beard with.
       OTHELLO   If it be that—
       IAGO   If it be that or any that was hers,
It speaks against her with the other proofs.
       OTHELLO   O, that the slave had forty thousand lives!
One is too poor, too weak for my revenge.
490 Now do I see 'tis true. Look here, Iago:
All my fond love thus do I blow to heaven.
'Tis gone.
Arise, black vengeance, from the hollow hell!
Yield up, O love, thy crown and hearted[392] throne
To tyrannous hate! Swell, bosom, with thy fraught,[393]
For 'tis of aspics'[394] tongues.
       IAGO   Yet be content.[395]
       OTHELLO   O, blood, blood, blood!
       IAGO   Patience, I say. Your mind may change.
500   OTHELLO   Never, Iago. Like to the Pontic Sea,[396]
Whose icy current and compulsive course

---

[388] seize   [389] *foregone conclusion* consummated fact   [390] *shrewd doubt* penetrating guess
[391] show, appear   [392] seated in the heart   [393] burden   [394] asps   [395] patient, quiet   [396] *Pontic Sea*
the Black Sea (famous for the strong and constant current with which it flows through the
Bosporus into the Mediterranean, where the water level is lower)

Nev'r keeps retiring ebb, but keeps due on
To the Propontic and the Hellespont,
Even so my bloody thoughts, with violent pace,
Shall nev'r look back, nev'r ebb to humble love,
Till that a capable and wide[397] revenge
Swallow them up. [*He kneels.*] Now, by yond marble heaven,
In the due reverence of a sacred vow
I here engage my words.

510 IAGO   Do not rise yet.   [IAGO *kneels.*]
Witness, you ever-burning lights above,
Your elements that clip[398] us round about,
Witness that here Iago doth give up
The execution[399] of his wit, hands, heart
To wronged Othello's service! Let him command,
And to obey shall be in me remorse,[400]
What bloody business ever.[401]   [*They rise.*]
       OTHELLO   I greet thy love,
Not with vain thanks but with acceptance bounteous,[402]
520 And will upon the instant put thee to 't.[403]
Within these three days let me hear thee say
That Cassio's not alive.
       IAGO   My friend is dead. 'Tis done at your request.
But let her live.
       OTHELLO   Damn her, lewd minx! O, damn her! Damn her!
Come, go with me apart. I will withdraw
To furnish me with some swift means of death
For the fair devil. Now art thou my lieutenant.
       IAGO   I am your own forever.   *Exeunt.*

Scene IV. [*A street.*]

Enter DESDEMONA, EMILIA, *and* CLOWN.

       DESDEMONA   Do you know, sirrah, where Lieutenant Cassio lies?[404]
       CLOWN   I dare not say he lies anywhere.
       DESDEMONA   Why, man?
       CLOWN   He's a soldier, and for me to say a soldier lies, 'tis stabbing.
       DESDEMONA   Go to. Where lodges he?
       CLOWN   To tell you where he lodges is to tell you where I lie.
       DESDEMONA   Can anything be made of this?
       CLOWN   I know not where he lodges, and for me to devise a lodging, and
say he lies here or he lies there, were to lie in mine own throat.[405]
10   DESDEMONA   Can you enquire him out, and be edified[406] by report?

---

[397] *capable and wide* sufficient and far-reaching   [398] enfold   [399] workings, action   [400] pity
[401] soever   [402] absolute   [403] i.e., to the work you have said you are prepared to do   [404] lodges
[405] *lie in mine own throat* (to lie in the throat is to lie absolutely and completely)   [406] enlightened
(Desdemona mocks the Clown's overly elaborate diction)

CLOWN   I will catechize the world for him; that is, make questions, and by them answer.

DESDEMONA   Seek him, bid him come hither. Tell him I have moved[407] my lord on his behalf and hope all will be well.

CLOWN   To do this is within the compass[408] of man's wit, and therefore I will attempt the doing it.   *Exit* CLOWN.

DESDEMONA   Where should[409] I lose the handkerchief, Emilia?

EMILIA   I know not, madam.

DESDEMONA   Believe me, I had rather have lost my purse
20 Full of crusadoes.[410] And but my noble Moor
Is true of mind, and made of no such baseness
As jealous creatures are, it were enough
To put him to ill thinking.

EMILIA   Is he not jealous?

DESDEMONA   Who? He? I think the sun where he was born
Drew all such humors[411] from him.

EMILIA   Look where he comes.

Enter OTHELLO.

DESDEMONA   I will not leave now till Cassio
Be called to him. How is't with you, my lord?
30   OTHELLO   Well, my good lady. [*Aside*] O, hardness to
                            dissemble![412]—
How do you, Desdemona?

DESDEMONA   Well, my good lord.

OTHELLO   Give me your hand. This hand is moist,[413] my lady.

DESDEMONA   It hath felt no age nor known no sorrow.

OTHELLO   This argues[414] fruitfulness and liberal[415] heart.
Hot, hot, and moist. This hand of yours requires
A sequester[416] from liberty; fasting and prayer,
Much castigation; exercise devout;
40   For here's a young and sweating devil here
That commonly rebels. 'Tis a good hand,
A frank one.

DESDEMONA   You may, indeed, say so;
For 'twas that hand that gave away my heart.

OTHELLO   A liberal hand! The hearts of old gave hands,
But our new heraldry[417] is hands, not hearts.

DESDEMONA   I cannot speak of this. Come now, your promise!

---

[407] pleaded with   [408] reach   [409] might   [410] Portuguese gold coins   [411] characteristics
[412] *hardness to dissemble* (Othello may refer here either to the difficulty he has in maintaining his appearance of composure, or to what he believes to be Desdemona's hardened hypocrisy)
[413] (a moist, hot hand was taken as a sign of a lustful nature)   [414] suggests   [415] free, open (but also with a suggestion of "licentious"; from here on in this scene Othello's words bear a double meaning, seeming to be normal but accusing Desdemona of being unfaithful)   [416] separation
[417] heraldic symbolism

OTHELLO   What promise, chuck?
DESDEMONA   I have sent to bid Cassio come speak with you.
50   OTHELLO   I have a salt and sorry rheum[418] offends me.
Lend me thy handkerchief.
DESDEMONA   Here, my lord.
OTHELLO   That which I gave you.
DESDEMONA   I have it not about me.
OTHELLO   Not?
DESDEMONA   No, indeed, my lord.
OTHELLO   That's a fault.
That handkerchief
Did an Egyptian to my mother give.
60   She was a charmer,[419] and could almost read
The thoughts of people. She told her, while she kept it
'Twould make her amiable[420] and subdue my father
Entirely to her love; but if she lost it
Or made a gift of it, my father's eye
Should hold her loathèd, and his spirits should hunt
After new fancies. She, dying, gave it me,
And bid me, when my fate would have me wived,
To give it her. I did so; and take heed on't;
Make it a darling like your precious eye.
70   To lose't or give't away were such perdition
As nothing else could match.
DESDEMONA   Is't possible?
OTHELLO   'Tis true. There's magic in the web[421] of it.
A sibyl that had numbered in the world
The sun to course two hundred compasses,
In her prophetic fury[422] sewed the work;
The worms were hallowed that did breed the silk,
And it was dyed in mummy[423] which the skillful
Conserved of maidens' hearts.
80   DESDEMONA   Indeed? Is't true?
OTHELLO   Most veritable. Therefore look to't well.
DESDEMONA   Then would to God that I had never seen't!
OTHELLO   Ha! Wherefore?
DESDEMONA   Why do you speak so startingly and rash?
OTHELLO   Is't lost? Is't gone? Speak, is it out o' th' way?
DESDEMONA   Heaven bless us!
OTHELLO   Say you?
DESDEMONA   It is not lost. But what an if it were?
OTHELLO   How?
90   DESDEMONA   I say it is not lost.

---

[418] *a salt and sorry rheum* a heavy, running head cold   [419] magician   [420] desirable   [421] weaving   [422] *prophetic fury* seized by the spirit and able to prophesy   [423] liquid drained from embalmed bodies

OTHELLO Fetch't, let me see't!

DESDEMONA Why, so I can; but I will not now.
This is a trick to put me from my suit:
Pray you let Cassio be received again.

OTHELLO Fetch me the handkerchief! My mind misgives.

DESDEMONA Come, come!
You'll never meet a more sufficient[424] man—

OTHELLO The handkerchief!

DESDEMONA   A man that all his time
100 Hath founded his good fortunes on your love,
Shared dangers with you—

OTHELLO The handkerchief!

DESDEMONA I'faith, you are to blame.

OTHELLO Away!   *Exit* OTHELLO.

EMILIA Is not this man jealous?

DESDEMONA I nev'r saw this before.
Sure there's some wonder in this handkerchief;
I am most unhappy in the loss of it.

EMILIA 'Tis not a year or two shows us a man.
110 They are all but stomachs, and we all but food;
They eat us hungerly, and when they are full,
They belch us.

Enter IAGO *and* CASSIO.

              Look you, Cassio and my husband.

IAGO There is no other way; 'tis she must do't.
And lo the happiness! Go and importune her.

DESDEMONA How now, good Cassio? What's the news with you?

CASSIO Madam, my former suit. I do beseech you
That by your virtuous means I may again
Exist, and be a member of his love
120 Whom I with all the office[425] of my heart
Entirely honor. I would not be delayed.
If my offense be of such mortal kind
That nor my service past, nor present sorrows,
Nor purposed merit in futurity,
Can ransom me into his love again,
But to know so must be my benefit.[426]
So shall I clothe me in a forced content,
And shut myself up in some other course
To fortune's alms.

130   DESDEMONA   Alas, thrice-gentle Cassio,
My advocation[427] is not now in tune.
My lord is not my lord; nor should I know him

---

[424] complete, with all proper qualities   [425] duty   [426] good   [427] advocacy

Were he in favor[428] as in humor altered.
So help me every spirit sanctified
As I have spoken for you all my best
And stood within the blank[429] of his displeasure
For my free speech. You must awhile be patient.
What I can do I will; and more I will
Than for myself I dare. Let that suffice you.

140   IAGO   Is my lord angry?

    EMILIA   He went hence but now,
And certainly in strange unquietness.

    IAGO   Can he be angry? I have seen the cannon
When it hath blown his ranks into the air
And, like the devil, from his very arm
Puffed his own brother. And is he angry?
Something of moment[430] then. I will go meet him.
There's matter in't indeed if he be angry.

    DESDEMONA   I prithee do so.   *Exit* [IAGO].

150   Something sure of state,[431]
Either from Venice or some unhatched practice[432]
Made demonstrable here in Cyprus to him,
Hath puddled[433] his clear spirit; and in such cases
Men's natures wrangle with inferior things,
Though great ones are their object. 'Tis even so.
For let our finger ache, and it endues[434]
Our other, healthful members even to a sense
Of pain. Nay, we must think men are not gods,
Nor of them look for such observancy

160   As fits the bridal. Beshrew me much, Emilia,
I was, unhandsome warrior as I am,
Arraigning his unkindness with my soul;
But now I find I had suborned the witness,
And he's indicted falsely.

    EMILIA   Pray heaven it be
State matters, as you think, and no conception
Nor no jealous toy[435] concerning you.

    DESDEMONA   Alas the day! I never gave him cause.

    EMILIA   But jealous souls will not be answered so;

170   They are not ever jealous for the cause,
But jealous for they're jealous. It is a monster
Begot upon itself, born on itself.

    DESDEMONA   Heaven keep the monster from Othello's mind!

    EMILIA   Lady, amen.

    DESDEMONA   I will go seek him. Cassio, walk here about.
If I do find him fit,[436] I'll move your suit

---

[428] countenance   [429] bull's-eye of a target   [430] importance   [431] *of state* state affairs
[432] *unhatched practice* undisclosed plot   [433] muddied   [434] leads   [435] trifle   [436] receptive

And seek to effect it to my uttermost.
    CASSIO I humbly thank your ladyship.   *Exit* [DESDEMONA *with* EMILIA].

Enter BIANCA.

    BIANCA Save you, friend Cassio!

180   CASSIO   What make you from home?
How is't with you, my most fair Bianca?
I'faith, sweet love, I was coming to your house.
    BIANCA And I was going to your lodging, Cassio.
What, keep a week away? Seven days and nights?
Eightscore eight hours? And lovers' absent hours
More tedious than the dial eightscore times?
O weary reck'ning.[437]
    CASSIO   Pardon me, Bianca.
I have this while with leaden thoughts been pressed,
190 But I shall in a more continuate[438] time
Strike off this score[439] of absence. Sweet Bianca.

                      [*Gives her* DESDEMONA's *handkerchief.*]

Take me this work out.
    BIANCA   O Cassio, whence came this?
This is some token from a newer friend.
To the felt absence now I feel a cause.
Is't come to this? Well, well.
    CASSIO   Go to, woman!
Throw your vile guesses in the devil's teeth,
From whence you have them. You are jealous now
200 That this is from some mistress, some remembrance.
No, by my faith, Bianca.
    BIANCA   Why, whose is it?
    CASSIO I know not neither; I found it in my chamber.
I like the work well; ere it be demanded,[440]
As like enough it will, I would have it copied.
Take it and do't, and leave me for this time.
    BIANCA Leave you? Wherefore?
    CASSIO I do attend here on the general
And think it no addition, nor my wish,
210 To have him see me womaned.
    BIANCA   Why, I pray you?
    CASSIO Not that I love you not.
    BIANCA   But that you do not love me!

---

[437] addition   [438] uninterrupted   [439] *Strike off this score* i.e., pay this bill (the *score* being the account of drinks kept in a tavern)   [440] asked for (by the person who lost it)

I pray you bring[441] me on the way a little,
And say if I shall see you soon at night.
    CASSIO 'Tis but a little way that I can bring you,
For I attend here; but I'll see you soon.
    BIANCA 'Tis very good. I must be circumstanced.[442]   *Exeunt omnes.*

Act IV, Scene I. [*A street.*]

Enter OTHELLO *and* IAGO.

    IAGO Will you think so?
    OTHELLO   Think so, Iago?
    IAGO   What,
To kiss in private?
    OTHELLO   An unauthorized[443] kiss?
    IAGO Or to be naked with her friend in bed
An hour or more, not meaning any harm?
    OTHELLO Naked in bed, Iago, and not mean harm?
It is hypocrisy against the devil.
10 They that mean virtuously, and yet do so,
The devil their virtue tempts, and they tempt heaven.
    IAGO If they do nothing, 'tis a venial slip.
But if I give my wife a handkerchief—
    OTHELLO What then?
    IAGO Why, then 'tis hers, my lord; and being hers,
She may, I think, bestow't on any man.
    OTHELLO She is protectress of her honor too.
May she give that?
    IAGO Her honor is an essence that's not seen;
20 They have it very oft that have it not.
But for the handkerchief—
    OTHELLO By heaven, I would most gladly have forgot it!
Thou said'st—O, it comes o'er my memory
As doth the raven[444] o'er the infected house,
Boding to all—he had my handkerchief.
    IAGO Ay, what of that?
    OTHELLO   That's not so good now.
    IAGO What if I had said I had seen him do you wrong?
Or heard him say—as knaves be such abroad[445]
30 Who having, by their own importunate suit,
Or voluntary dotage[446] of some mistress,
Convincèd or supplied[447] them, cannot choose
But they must blab—

---

[441] accompany   [442] *be circumstanced* accept things as they are   [443] illicit   [444] (a harbinger of death)   [445] i.e., in the world   [446] *voluntary dotage* weakness of the will   [447] *Convincèd or supplied* persuaded or gratified (the mistress)

OTHELLO   Hath he said anything?

IAGO   He hath, my lord; but be you well assured,
No more than he'll unswear.

OTHELLO   What hath he said?

IAGO   Why, that he did—I know not what he did.

OTHELLO   What? what?

40   IAGO   Lie—

OTHELLO   With her?

IAGO   With her, on her; what you will.

OTHELLO   Lie with her? Lie on her?—We say lie on her when they belie her.—Lie with her! Zounds, that's fulsome.[448]—Handkerchief—confessions—handkerchief!—To confess, and be hanged for his labor—first to be hanged, and then to confess! I tremble at it. Nature would not invest herself in such shadowing passion without some instruction.[449] It is not words that shakes me thus.—Pish! Noses, ears, and lips? Is't possible?—Confess?—Handkerchief?—O devil!   *Falls in a trance.*

50   IAGO   Work on.
My med'cine works! Thus credulous fools are caught,
And many worthy and chaste dames even thus,
All guiltless, meet reproach.[450] What, ho! My lord!
My lord, I say! Othello!

Enter CASSIO.

                     How now, Cassio?

CASSIO   What's the matter?

IAGO   My lord is fall'n into an epilepsy.
This is his second fit; he had one yesterday.

CASSIO   Rub him about the temples.

60   IAGO   The lethargy[451] must have his quiet course.
If not, he foams at mouth, and by and by
Breaks out to savage madness. Look, he stirs.
Do you withdraw yourself a little while.
He will recover straight. When he is gone,
I would on great occasion[452] speak with you.   [*Exit* CASSIO.]
How is it, general? Have you not hurt your head?

OTHELLO   Dost thou mock[453] me?

IAGO   I mock you not, by heaven.
Would you would bear your fortune like a man.

70   OTHELLO   A hornèd man's a monster and a beast.

IAGO   There's many a beast then in a populous city,
And many a civil[454] monster.

---

[448] foul, repulsive   [449] *Nature . . . instruction* i.e., my mind would not become so darkened (with anger) unless there were something in this (accusation); (it should be remembered that Othello believes in the workings of magic and supernatural forces)   [450] shame [451] coma [452] *great occasion* very important matter   [453] (Othello takes Iago's comment as a reference to his horns—which it is)   [454] city-dwelling

OTHELLO   Did he confess it?

IAGO   Good, sir, be a man.
Think every bearded fellow that's but yoked
May draw[455] with you. There's millions now alive
That nightly lie in those unproper[456] beds
Which they dare swear peculiar.[457] Your case is better.
O, 'tis the spite of hell, the fiend's arch-mock,
80   To lip a wanton in a secure couch,
And to suppose her chaste. No, let me know;
And knowing what I am, I know what she shall be.

OTHELLO   O, thou art wise! 'Tis certain.

IAGO   Stand you awhile apart;
Confine yourself but in a patient list.[458]
Whilst you were here, o'erwhelmèd with your grief—
A passion most unsuiting such a man—
Cassio came hither. I shifted him away[459]
And laid good 'scuses upon your ecstasy,[460]
90   Bade him anon return, and here speak with me;
The which he promised. Do but encave[461] yourself
And mark the fleers,[462] the gibes, and notable[463] scorns
That dwell in every region of his face.
For I will make him tell the tale anew:
Where, how, how oft, how long ago, and when
He hath, and is again to cope your wife.
I say, but mark his gesture. Marry patience,
Or I shall say you're all in all in spleen,[464]
And nothing of a man.

100   OTHELLO   Dost thou hear, Iago?
I will be found most cunning in my patience;
But—dost thou hear?—most bloody.

IAGO   That's not amiss;
But yet keep time in all. Will you withdraw?

[OTHELLO *moves to one side, where his remarks are not audible to* CASSIO *and* IAGO.]

Now will I question Cassio of Bianca,
A huswife[465] that by selling her desires
Buys herself bread and cloth. It is a creature
That dotes on Cassio, as 'tis the strumpet's plague
To beguile many and be beguiled by one.
110   He, when he hears of her, cannot restrain
From the excess of laughter. Here he comes.

---

[455] i.e., like the horned ox   [456] i.e., not exclusively the husband's   [457] their own alone   [458] *a patient list* the bounds of patience   [459] *shifted him away* got rid of him by a strategem   [460] trance (the literal meaning, "outside oneself," bears on the meaning of the change Othello is undergoing)   [461] hide   [462] mocking looks or speeches   [463] obvious   [464] passion, particularly anger   [465] housewife (but with the special meaning here of "prostitute")

Enter CASSIO.

As he shall smile, Othello shall go mad:
And his unbookish[466] jealousy must conster[467]
Poor Cassio's smiles, gestures, and light behaviors
Quite in the wrong. How do you, lieutenant?

CASSIO   The worser that you give me the addition[468]
Whose want even kills me.

IAGO   Ply Desdemona well, and you are sure on't.
Now, if this suit lay in Bianca's power,
120 How quickly should you speed!

CASSIO   Alas, poor caitiff![469]

OTHELLO   Look how he laughs already!

IAGO   I never knew woman love man so.

CASSIO   Alas, poor rogue! I think, i'faith, she loves me.

OTHELLO   Now he denies it faintly, and laughs it out.

IAGO   Do you hear, Cassio?

OTHELLO   Now he importunes him
To tell it o'er. Go to! Well said, well said!

IAGO   She gives it out that you shall marry her.
130 Do you intend it?

CASSIO   Ha, ha, ha!

OTHELLO   Do ye triumph, Roman? Do you triumph?

CASSIO   I marry? What, a customer?[470] Prithee bear some charity to my wit;
do not think it so unwholesome. Ha, ha, ha!

OTHELLO   So, so, so, so. They laugh that win.

IAGO   Why, the cry goes that you marry her.

CASSIO   Prithee, say true.

IAGO   I am a very villain else.

OTHELLO   Have you scored[471] me? Well.
140   CASSIO   This is the monkey's own giving out. She is persuaded I will marry
her out of her own love and flattery, not out of my promise.

OTHELLO   Iago beckons me; now he begins the story.

[OTHELLO *moves close enough to hear.*]

CASSIO   She was here even now; she haunts me in every place. I was the
other day talking on the sea bank with certain Venetians, and thither comes
the bauble,[472] and falls me thus about my neck—

OTHELLO   Crying "O dear Cassio!" as it were. His gesture imports it.

CASSIO   So, hangs, and lolls, and weaps upon me; so shakes and pulls me!
Ha, ha, ha!

OTHELLO   Now he tells how she plucked him to my chamber. O, I see that
150 nose of yours, but not that dog I shall throw it to.

---

[466] ignorant   [467] construe   [468] title   [469] wretch   [470] one who sells, a merchant (here, a prostitute)   [471] marked, defaced   [472] plaything

CASSIO Well, I must leave her company.

IAGO Before me![473] Look where she comes.

Enter BIANCA.

CASSIO 'Tis such another fitchew![474] Marry a perfumed one? What do you mean by this haunting of me?

BIANCA Let the devil and his dam haunt you! What did you mean by that same handkerchief you gave me even now? I was a fine fool to take it. I must take out the work? A likely piece of work that you should find it in your chamber and know not who left it there! This is some minx's token, and I must take out the work? There! [*She throws down the handkerchief.*] Give it
160 your hobbyhorse.[475] Wheresoever you had it I'll take out no work on't.

CASSIO How now, my sweet Bianca? How now? how now?

OTHELLO By heaven, that should be my handkerchief!

BIANCA If you'll come to supper tonight, you may; if you will not, come when you are next prepared for.[476]   *Exit.*

IAGO After her, after her!

CASSIO Faith, I must; she'll rail in the streets else.

IAGO Will you sup there?

CASSIO Yes, I intend so.

IAGO Well, I may chance to see you, for I would very fain speak with you.
170 CASSIO Prithee come. Will you?

IAGO Go to, say no more.   [*Exit* CASSIO.]

OTHELLO [*Comes forward*] How shall I murder him, Iago?

IAGO Did you perceive how he laughed at his vice?

OTHELLO O Iago!

IAGO And did you see the handkerchief?

OTHELLO Was that mine?

IAGO Yours, by this hand! And to see how he prizes the foolish woman your wife! She gave it him, and he hath giv'n it his whore.

OTHELLO I would have him nine years a-killing!—A fine woman, a fair
180 woman, a sweet woman?

IAGO Nay, you must forget that.

OTHELLO Ay, let her rot, and perish, and be damned tonight; for she shall not live. No, my heart is turned to stone; I strike it, and it hurts my hand. O, the world hath not a sweeter creature! She might lie by an emperor's side and command him tasks.

IAGO Nay, that's not your way.[477]

OTHELLO Hang her! I do but say what she is. So delicate with her needle. An admirable musician. O, she will sing the savageness out of a bear! Of so high and plenteous wit and invention[478]—
190 IAGO She's the worse for all this.

---

[473] *Before me!* (an exclamation of surprise)   [474] polecat, i.e., strong-smelling creature
[475] prostitute   [476] *next prepared for* next expected—i.e., never   [477] proper course
[478] imagination

OTHELLO   O, a thousand, a thousand times. And then, of so gentle a condition?[479]

IAGO   Ay, too gentle.

OTHELLO   Nay, that's certain. But yet the pity of it, Iago. O Iago, the pity of it, Iago.

IAGO   If you are so fond over her iniquity, give her patent to offend; for if it touch[480] not you, it comes near nobody.

OTHELLO   I will chop her into messes![481] Cuckold me!

IAGO   O, 'tis foul in her.

200   OTHELLO   With mine officer!

IAGO   That's fouler.

OTHELLO   Get me some poison, Iago, this night. I'll not expostulate with her, lest her body and beauty unprovide my mind[482] again. This night, Iago!

IAGO   Do it not with poison. Strangle her in her bed, even the bed she hath contaminated.

OTHELLO   Good, good! The justice of it pleases. Very good!

IAGO   And for Cassio, let me be his undertaker.[483] You shall hear more by midnight.

OTHELLO   Excellent good!   [*A trumpet.*]

210   What trumpet is that same?

IAGO   I warrant something from Venice.

Enter LODOVICO, DESDEMONA, *and* ATTENDANTS.

                                          'Tis Lodovico.
This comes from the Duke. See, your wife's with him.

LODOVICO   God save you, worthy general.

OTHELLO   With[484] all my heart, sir.

LODOVICO   The Duke and the senators of Venice greet you.

                                          [*Gives him a letter.*]

OTHELLO   I kiss the instrument of their pleasures.

                                          [*Opens the letter and reads.*]

DESDEMONA   And what's the news, good cousin Lodovico?

IAGO   I am very glad to see you, signior.

220 Welcome to Cyprus.

LODOVICO   Thank you. How does Lieutenant Cassio?

IAGO   Lives, sir.

DESDEMONA   Cousin, there's fall'n between him and my lord
An unkind[485] breach; but you shall make all well.

---

[479] *gentle a condition* (1) well born (2) of a gentle nature   [480] affects   [481] bits   [482] *unprovide my mind* undo my resolution   [483] (not "burier" but "one who undertakes to do something")   [484] i.e., I greet you with   [485] unnatural

OTHELLO Are you sure of that?

DESDEMONA My lord?

OTHELLO [*Reads*] "This fail you not to do, as you will—"

LODOVICO He did not call; he's busy in the paper.

Is there division 'twixt my lord and Cassio?

230 DESDEMONA A most unhappy one. I would do much

T' atone[486] them, for the love I bear to Cassio.

OTHELLO Fire and brimstone!

DESDEMONA   My lord?

OTHELLO   Are you wise?

DESDEMONA What, is he angry?

LODOVICO   May be th' letter moved him;

For, as I think, they do command him home,

Deputing Cassio in his government.[487]

DESDEMONA Trust me, I am glad on't.

240 OTHELLO   Indeed?

DESDEMONA   My lord?

OTHELLO I am glad to see you mad.

DESDEMONA   Why, sweet Othello—

OTHELLO Devil!   [*Strikes her.*]

DESDEMONA I have not deserved this.

LODOVICO My lord, this would not be believed in Venice,

Though I should swear I saw't. 'Tis very much.

Make her amends; she weeps.

OTHELLO   O devil, devil!

250 If that the earth could teem[488] with woman's tears,

Each drop she falls[489] would prove a crocodile.[490]

Out of my sight!

DESDEMONA   I will not stay to offend you.   [*Going.*]

LODOVICO Truly, an obedient lady.

I do beseech your lordship call her back.

OTHELLO Mistress!

DESDEMONA   My lord?

OTHELLO   What would you with her, sir?

LODOVICO Who? I, my lord?

260 OTHELLO Ay! You did wish that I would make her turn.

Sir, she can turn, and turn, and yet go on

And turn again; and she can weep, sir, weep;

And she's obedient; as you say, obedient.

Very obedient. Proceed you in your tears.

Concerning this, sir—O Well-painted passion!

I am commanded home.—Get you away;

I'll send for you anon.—Sir, I obey the mandate

And will return to Venice.—Hence, avaunt!   [*Exit* DESDEMONA.]

---

[486] reconcile [487] office [488] conceive [489] drops [490] (the crocodile was supposed to shed false tears to lure its victims)

Cassio shall have my place. And, sir, tonight
270 I do entreat that we may sup together.
You are welcome, sir, to Cyprus.—Goats and monkeys!   *Exit.*
    LODOVICO   Is this the noble Moor whom our full Senate
Call all in all sufficient? Is this the nature
Whom passion could not shake? whose solid virtue
The shot of accident nor dart of chance
Could neither graze nor pierce?
    IAGO   He is much changed.
    LODOVICO   Are his wits safe? Is he not light of brain?
    IAGO   He's that he is; I may not breathe my censure.
280 What he might be [if, what he might, he is not]
I would to heaven he were!
    LODOVICO   What, strike his wife?
    IAGO   Faith, that was not so well; yet would I knew
That stroke would prove the worst.
    LODOVICO   Is it his use?[491]
Or did the letters work upon his blood[492]
And new-create his fault?
    IAGO   Alas, alas!
It is not honesty in me to speak
290 What I have seen and known. You shall observe him,
And his own courses[493] will denote him so
That I may save my speech. Do but go after
And mark how he continues.
    LODOVICO   I am sorry that I am deceived in him.   *Exeunt.*

Scene II. [*The citadel.*]

Enter OTHELLO *and* EMILIA.

    OTHELLO   You have seen nothing then?
    EMILIA   Nor ever heard, nor ever did suspect.
    OTHELLO   Yes, you have seen Cassio and she together.
    EMILIA   But then I saw no harm, and then I heard
Each syllable that breath made up[494] between them.
    OTHELLO   What, did they never whisper?
    EMILIA   Never, my lord.
    OTHELLO   Nor send you out o' th' way?
    EMILIA   Never.
10   OTHELLO   To fetch her fan, her gloves, her mask, nor nothing?
    EMILIA   Never, my lord.
    OTHELLO   That's strange.
    EMILIA   I durst, my lord, to wager she is honest,
Lay down my soul at stake.[495] If you think other,

---

[491] habit   [492] passion   [493] actions   [494] *that breath made up* spoken   [495] *at stake* as the wager

Remove your thought. It doth abuse your bosom.
If any wretch have put this in your head,
Let heaven requite it with the serpent's curse,[496]
For if she be not honest,[497] chaste, and true,
There's no man happy. The purest of their wives
20 Is foul as slander.

    OTHELLO   Bid her come hither. Go.   *Exit* EMILIA.
She says enough; yet she's a simple bawd[498]
That cannot say as much. This is a subtle whore,
A closet lock and key of villainous secrets,
And yet she'll kneel and pray; I have seen her do't.

Enter DESDEMONA *and* EMILIA.

    DESDEMONA My lord, what is your will?
    OTHELLO   Pray you, chuck, come hither.
    DESDEMONA What is your pleasure?
    OTHELLO   Let me see your eyes.
30 Look in my face.
    DESDEMONA   What horrible fancy's this?
    OTHELLO [*To* EMILIA] Some of your function,[499] mistress:
Leave procreants alone and shut the door;
Cough or cry hem if anybody come.
Your mystery,[500] your mystery! Nay, dispatch!   *Exit* EMILIA.
    DESDEMONA Upon my knee, what doth your speech import?
I understand a fury in your words.[501]
    OTHELLO Why, what art thou?
    DESDEMONA   Your wife, my lord; your true
40 And loyal wife.
    OTHELLO   Come, swear it, damn thyself;
Lest, being like one of heaven, the devils themselves
Should fear to seize thee. Therefore be doubledamned:
Swear thou art honest.
    DESDEMONA   Heaven doth truly know it.
    OTHELLO Heaven truly knows that thou art false as hell.
    DESDEMONA To whom, my lord? With whom? How am I false?
    OTHELLO Ah, Desdemon! Away! Away! Away!
    DESDEMONA Alas the heavy day! Why do you weep?
50 Am I the motive[502] of these tears, my lord?
If haply[503] you my father do suspect
An instrument of this your calling back,
Lay not your blame on me. If you have lost him,
I have lost him too.

---

[496] *serpent's curse* (God's curse on the serpent after the fall in Eden)   [497] chaste   [498] procuress
[499] *Some of your function* do your proper work (as the operator of a brothel)   [500] trade
[501] (Q1 adds to this line, "But not the words")   [502] cause   [503] by chance

OTHELLO   Had it pleased heaven
To try me with affliction, had they rained
All kinds of sores and shames on my bare head,
Steeped[504] me in poverty to the very lips,
Given to captivity me and my utmost hopes,
60 I should have found in some place of my soul
A drop of patience. But, alas, to make me
The fixèd figure for the time of scorn[505]
To point his slow and moving finger at.
Yet could I bear that too, well, very well.
But there where I have garnered up my heart,
Where either I must live or bear no life,
The fountain from the which my current runs
Or else dries up—to be discarded thence,
Or keep it as a cistern for foul toads
70 To knot and gender[506] in—turn thy complexion there,
Patience, thou young and rose-lipped cherubin!
I here look grim as hell![507]
　　DESDEMONA　I hope my noble lord esteems me honest.
　　OTHELLO　O, ay, as summer flies are in the shambles,[508]
That quicken even with blowing.[509] O thou weed,
Who art so lovely fair, and smell'st so sweet,
That the sense aches at thee, would thou hadst never been born!
　　DESDEMONA　Alas, what ignorant[510] sin have I committed?
　　OTHELLO　Was this fair paper, this most goodly book,
80 Made to write "whore" upon? What committed?
Committed? O thou public commoner,[511]
I should make very forges of my cheeks
That would to cinders burn up modesty,
Did I but speak thy deeds. What committed?
Heaven stops the nose at it, and the moon winks;[512]
The bawdy wind that kisses all it meets
Is hushed within the hollow mine of earth
And will not hear't. What committed?
　　DESDEMONA　By heaven, you do me wrong!
90　OTHELLO　Are you not a strumpet?
　　DESDEMONA　　　　　　　No, as I am a Christian!
If to preserve this vessel for my lord
From any other foul unlawful touch
Be not to be a strumpet, I am none.
　　OTHELLO　What, not a whore?

---

[504] submerged   [505] *The . . . scorn* the very image of scorn in our time   [506] *knot and gender* twist in bunches and procreate   [507] *turn . . . hell* (the rough sense would seem to be "even Patience would grow pale, turn complexion, at Desdemona's perfidy, but that Othello looks grimly on")   [508] abattoirs   [509] *quicken even with blowing* become impregnated as soon as they lay their eggs   [510] unknowing   [511] prostitute   [512] closes its eyes (the moon was the symbol of chastity)

DESDEMONA   No, as I shall be saved!
OTHELLO   Is't possible?
DESDEMONA   O, heaven forgive us!
OTHELLO   I cry you mercy[513] then.
100 I took you for that cunning whore of Venice
That married with Othello. [*Calling*] You, mistress,

Enter EMILIA.

That have the office opposite to Saint Peter
And keep the gate of hell! You, you, ay, you!
We have done our course; there's money for your pains.

                                        [*Throws her some coins.*]

I pray you turn the key and keep our counsel.   *Exit.*
    EMILIA   Alas, what does this gentleman conceive?
How do you, madam? How do you, my good lady?
    DESDEMONA   Faith, half asleep.
    EMILIA   Good madam, what's the matter with my lord?
110   DESDEMONA   With who?
    EMILIA   Why, with my lord, madam.
    DESDEMONA   Who is thy lord?
    EMILIA   He that is yours, sweet lady.
    DESDEMONA   I have none. Do not talk to me, Emilia.
I cannot weep, nor answers have I none
But what should go by water.[514] Prithee tonight
Lay on my bed my wedding sheets, remember;
And call thy husband hither.
    EMILIA   Here's a change indeed!   *Exit.*
120   DESDEMONA   'Tis meet I should be used so, very meet.
How have I been behaved, that he might stick
The small'st opinion on my least misuse?[515]

Enter IAGO *and* EMILIA.

    IAGO   What is your pleasure, madam? How is't with you?
    DESDEMONA   I cannot tell. Those that do teach young babes
Do it with gentle means and easy tasks.
He might have chid me so; for, in good faith,
I am a child to chiding.
    IAGO   What is the matter, lady?
    EMILIA   Alas, Iago, my lord hath so bewhored her,
130 Thrown such despite[516] and heavy terms upon her
That true hearts cannot bear it.

---

[513] *cry you mercy* ask your pardon   [514] tears   [515] *stick . . . misuse* base any doubt on my smallest fault   [516] abuse

DESDEMONA Am I that name, Iago?

IAGO   What name, fair lady?

DESDEMONA Such as she said my lord did say I was.

EMILIA He called her whore. A beggar in his drink
Could not have laid such terms upon his callet.[517]

IAGO Why did he so?

DESDEMONA I do not know; I am sure I am none such.

IAGO Do not weep, do not weep. Alas the day.

140   EMILIA Hath she forsook so many noble matches,
Her father and her country, and her friends,
To be called whore? Would it not make one weep?

DESDEMONA It is my wretched fortune.

IAGO   Beshrew[518] him for't!
How comes this trick upon him?

DESDEMONA   Nay, heaven doth know.

EMILIA I will be hanged if some eternal villain,
Some busy and insinuating rogue,
Some cogging,[519] cozening slave, to get some office,

150   Have not devised this slander. I will be hanged else.

IAGO Fie, there is no such man! It is impossible.

DESDEMONA If any such there be, heaven pardon him.

EMILIA A halter pardon him! And hell gnaw his bones!
Why should he call her whore? Who keeps her company?
What place? What time? What form? What likelihood?
The Moor's abused by some most villainous knave,
Some base notorious knave, some scurvy fellow.
O heavens, that such companions[520] thou'dst unfold,[521]
And put in every honest hand a whip

160   To lash the rascals naked through the world
Even from the east to th' west!

IAGO   Speak within door.[522]

EMILIA O, fie upon them! Some such squire[523] he was
That turned your wit the seamy side without
And made you to suspect me with the Moor.

IAGO You are a fool. Go to.

DESDEMONA   Alas, Iago,
What shall I do to win my lord again?
Good friend, go to him, for, by this light of heaven,

170   I know not how I lost him. Here I kneel:
If e'er my will did trespass 'gainst his love
Either in discourse of thought[524] or actual deed,
Or that mine eyes, mine ears, or any sense
Delighted them in any other form;
Or that I do not yet, and ever did,

---

[517] slut [518] curse [519] cheating [520] fellows, rogues [521] disclose [522] *within door* more quietly and moderately [523] a term of contempt [524] *discourse of thought* thinking

And ever will [though he do shake me off
To beggarly divorcement] love him dearly,
Comfort forswear me. Unkindness may do much,
And his unkindness may defeat[525] my life,
180 But never taint my love. I cannot say "whore."
It does abhor me now I speak the word;
To do the act that might the addition earn
Not the world's mass of vanity could make me.

    IAGO   I pray you be content. 'Tis but his humor.[526]
The business of the state does him offense.

    DESDEMONA   If 'twere no other.

    IAGO   It is but so, I warrant.   [*Trumpets within.*]
Hark how these instruments summon to supper.
The messengers of Venice stay the meat.[527]
190 Go in, and weep not. All things shall be well.

                            [*Exeunt* DESDEMONA *and* EMILIA.]

Enter RODERIGO.

How now, Roderigo?

    RODERIGO   I do not find that thou deal'st justly with me.

    IAGO   What in the contrary?

    RODERIGO   Every day thou daff'st[528] me with some device,[529] Iago, and rather, as it seems to me now, keep'st from me all conveniency[530] than suppliest me with the least advantage of hope. I will indeed no longer endure it; nor am I yet persuaded to put up[531] in peace what already I have foolishly suffered.

    IAGO   Will you hear me, Roderigo?

    RODERIGO   I have heard too much, and your words and performances are
200 no kin together.

    IAGO   You charge me most unjustly.

    RODERIGO   With naught but truth. I have wasted myself out of my means. The jewels you have had from me to deliver Desdemona would half have corrupted a votarist.[532] You have told me she hath received them, and returned me expectations and comforts of sudden respect[533] and acquaintance; but I find none.

    IAGO   Well, go to; very well.

    RODERIGO   Very well? Go to? I cannot go to, man; nor 'tis not very well. Nay, I think it is scurvy, and begin to find myself fopped[534] in it.
210   IAGO   Very well.

    RODERIGO   I tell you 'tis not very well. I will make myself known to Desdemona. If she will return me my jewels, I will give over my suit and repent my unlawful solicitation. If not, assure yourself I will seek satisfaction of you.

    IAGO   You have said now?

---

[525] destroy   [526] mood   [527] *stay the meat* await the meal   [528] put off   [529] scheme   [530] what is needful   [531] *put up* accept   [532] nun   [533] *sudden respect* immediate consideration   [534] duped

RODERIGO   Ay, and said nothing but what I protest[535] intendment of doing.

IAGO   Why, now I see there's mettle[536] in thee, and even from this instant do build on thee a better opinion than ever before. Give me thy hand, Roderigo. Thou has taken me a most just exception,[537] but yet I protest I have dealt most directly[538] in thy affair.

220   RODERIGO   It hath not appeared.

IAGO   I grant indeed it hath not appeared, and your suspicion is not without wit and judgment. But, Roderigo, if thou hast that in thee indeed which I have greater reason to believe now than ever—I mean purpose, courage, and valor—this night show it. If thou the next night following enjoy not Desdemona, take me from this world with treachery and devise engines for[539] my life.

RODERIGO   Well, what is it? Is it within reason and compass?[540]

IAGO   Sir, there is especial commission come from Venice to depute Cassio in Othello's place.

230   RODERIGO   Is that true? Why, then Othello and Desdemona return again to Venice.

IAGO   O, no; he goes into Mauritania and taketh away with him the fair Desdemona, unless his abode be lingered here by some accident; wherein none can be so determinate[541] as the removing of Cassio.

RODERIGO   How do you mean, removing him?

IAGO   Why, by making him uncapable of Othello's place—knocking out his brains.

RODERIGO   And that you would have me to do?

IAGO   Ay, if you dare do yourself a profit and a right. He sups tonight with 240 a harlotry,[542] and thither will I go to him. He knows not yet of his honorable fortune. If you will watch his going thence, which I will fashion to fall out[543] between twelve and one, you may take him at your pleasure. I will be near to second[544] your attempt, and he shall fall between us. Come, stand not amazed at it, but go along with me. I will show you such a necessity in his death that you shall think yourself bound to put it on him. It is now high supper time, and the night grows to waste. About it.

RODERIGO   I will hear further reason for this.

IAGO   And you shall be satisfied.   *Exeunt.*

Scene III. [*The citadel.*]

Enter OTHELLO, LODOVICO, DESDEMONA, EMILIA, *and* ATTENDANTS.

LODOVICO   I do beseech you, sir, trouble yourself no further.

OTHELLO   O, pardon me; 'twill do me good to walk.

LODOVICO   Madam, good night. I humbly thank your ladyship.

DESDEMONA   Your honor is most welcome.

OTHELLO   Will you walk, sir? O, Desdemona.

---

[535] aver   [536] spirit   [537] objective   [538] straightforwardly   [539] *engines for* schemes against [540] possibility   [541] effective   [542] female   [543] *fall out* occur   [544] support

DESDEMONA My lord?

OTHELLO Get you to bed on th' instant; I will be returned forthwith.
Dismiss your attendant there. Look 't be done.

DESDEMONA I will, my lord.

Exit [OTHELLO, *with* LODOVICO *and* ATTENDANTS].

10   EMILIA How goes it now? He looks gentler than he did.

DESDEMONA He says he will return incontinent,[545]
And hath commanded me to go to bed.
And bade me to dismiss you.

EMILIA   Dismiss me?

DESDEMONA It was his bidding; therefore, good Emilia,
Give me my nightly wearing, and adieu.
We must not now displease him.

EMILIA I would you had never seen him!

DESDEMONA So would not I. My love doth so approve him

20 That even his stubbornness, his checks,[546] his frowns—
Prithee unpin me—have grace and favor.

EMILIA I have laid these sheets you bade me on the bed.

DESDEMONA All's one.[547] Good Father, how foolish are our minds!
If I do die before, prithee shroud me
In one of these same sheets.

EMILIA   Come, come! You talk.

DESDEMONA My mother had a maid called Barbary.
She was in love; and he she loved proved mad
And did forsake her. She had a song of "Willow";

30 An old thing 'twas, but it expressed her fortune,
And she died singing it. That song tonight
Will not go from my mind; I have much to do
But to go hang my head all at one side
And sing it like poor Barbary. Prithee dispatch.

EMILIA Shall I go fetch your nightgown?

DESDEMONA No, unpin me here.
This Lodovico is a proper man.

EMILIA A very handsome man.

DESDEMONA He speaks well.

40   EMILIA I know a lady in Venice would have walked barefoot to Palestine
for a touch of his nether lip.

DESDEMONA [*Sings*]
"The poor soul sat singing by a sycamore tree,
    Sing all a green willow;
Her hand on her bosom, her head on her knee,
    Sing willow, willow, willow.
The fresh streams ran by her and murmured her moans;
    Sing willow, willow, willow;

---

[545] at once   [546] rebukes   [547] *All's one* no matter

Her salt tears fell from her, and soft'ned the stones—
50   Sing willow, willow, willow—"
Lay by these.   [*Gives* EMILIA *her clothes.*]
       "Willow, Willow"——
Prithee hie[548] thee; he'll come anon.[549]
       "Sing all a green willow must be my garland
       Let nobody blame him; his scorn I approve"——
Nay, that's not next. Hark! Who is't that knocks?
       EMILIA   It is the wind.
       DESDEMONA [*Sings*]
       "I called my love false love; but what said he then?
60   Sing willow, willow, willow:
       If I court moe[550] women, you'll couch with moe men."
So, get thee gone; good night. Mine eyes do itch.
Doth that bode weeping?
       EMILIA   'Tis neither here nor there.
       DESDEMONA   I have heard it said so. O, these men, these men.
Dost thou in conscience think, tell me, Emilia,
That there be women do abuse their husbands
In such gross kind?
       EMILIA   There be some such, no question.
70   DESDEMONA   Wouldst thou do such a deed for all the world?
       EMILIA   Why, would not you?
       DESDEMONA   No, by this heavenly light!
       EMILIA   Nor I neither by this heavenly light.
I might do't as well i' th' dark.
       DESDEMONA   Wouldst thou do such a deed for all the world?
       EMILIA   The world's a huge thing; it is a great price for a small vice.
       DESDEMONA   In troth, I think thou wouldst not.
       EMILIA   In troth, I think I should; and undo't when I had done. Marry, I
would not do such a thing for a joint-ring,[551] nor for measures of lawn,[552] nor
80 for gowns, petticoats, nor caps, nor any pretty exhibition,[553] but for all the
whole world? Why, who would not make her husband a cuckold to make him
a monarch? I should venture purgatory for't.
       DESDEMONA   Beshrew me if I would do such a wrong for the whole world.
       EMILIA   Why, the wrong is but a wrong i' th' world; and having the world for
your labor, 'tis a wrong in your own world, and you might quickly make it right.
       DESDEMONA   I do not think there is any such woman.
       EMILIA   Yes, a dozen; and as many to th' vantage as would store[554] the
world they played for.
But I do think it is their husbands' faults
90 If wives do fall. Say that they slack their duties
And pour our treasures into foreign[555] laps;
Or else break out in peevish jealousies,
Throwing restraint upon us; or say they strike us,

---

[548] hurry   [549] at once   [550] more   [551] a ring with two interlocking halves   [552] fine linen
[553] payment   [554] *to . . . store* in addition as would fill   [555] alien, i.e., other than the wife

Or scant our former having in despite[556]—
Why, we have galls; and though we have some grace,
Yet have we some revenge. Let husbands know
Their wives have sense like them. They see, and smell,
And have their palates both for sweet and sour,
As husbands have. What is it that they do
100 When they change[557] us for others? Is it sport?
I think it is. And doth affection[558] breed it?
I think it doth. Is't frailty that thus errs?
It is so too. And have not we affections?
Desires for sport? and frailty? as men have?
Then let them use us well; else let them know,
The ills we do, their ills instruct us so.[559]

  DESDEMONA   Good night, good night. Heaven me such uses[560] send,
Not to pick bad from bad, but by bad mend.   *Exeunt.*

Act V, Scene I. [*A street.*]

Enter IAGO *and* RODERIGO.

  IAGO   Here, stand behind this bulk;[561] straight will he come.
Wear thy good rapier bare, and put it home.
Quick, quick! Fear nothing; I'll be at thy elbow.
It makes us, or it mars us, think on that,
And fix most firm thy resolution.
  RODERIGO   Be near at hand; I may miscarry in't.
  IAGO   Here, at thy hand. Be bold, and take thy stand.   [*Moves to one side.*]
  RODERIGO   I have no great devotion to the deed,
And yet he hath given me satisfying reasons.
10 'Tis but a man gone. Forth my sword! He dies!
  IAGO   I have rubbed this young quat[562] almost to the sense,[563]
And he grows angry. Now, whether he kill Cassio,
Or Cassio him, or each do kill the other,
Every way makes my gain. Live Roderigo,
He calls me to a restitution large
Of gold and jewels that I bobbed[564] from him
As gifts to Desdemona.
It must not be. If Cassio do remain,
He hath a daily beauty in his life
20 That makes me ugly; and besides, the Moor
May unfold me to him; there stand I in much peril.
No, he must die. But so, I hear him coming.

Enter CASSIO.

[556] *scant . . . despite* reduce, in spite, our household allowance (?) [557] exchange [558] strong feeling, desire   [559] *instruct us so* teach us to do likewise   [560] practices   [561] projecting stall of a shop   [562] pimple   [563] *to the sense* raw   [564] swindled

RODERIGO   I know his gait. 'Tis he. Villain, thou diest!   [*Thrusts at* CASSIO.]
CASSIO   That thrust had been mine enemy indeed
But that my coat[565] is better than thou know'st.
I will make proof of thine.   [*Fights with* RODERIGO.]
RODERIGO   O, I am slain![566]
CASSIO   I am maimed forever. Help, ho! Murder! Murder!

Enter OTHELLO [*to one side*].

OTHELLO   The voice of Cassio, Iago keeps his word.
30   RODERIGO   O, villain that I am!
OTHELLO   It is even so.
CASSIO   O help, ho! Light! A surgeon!
OTHELLO   'Tis he. O brave Iago, honest and just,
That has such noble sense of thy friend's wrong!
Thou teachest me. Minion,[567] your dear lies dead,
And your unblest[568] fate hies.[569] Strumpet, I come.
Forth of my heart those charms, thine eyes, are blotted.
Thy bed, lust-stained, shall with lust's blood be spotted.   *Exit* OTHELLO.

Enter LODOVICO *and* GRATIANO.

CASSIO   What, ho? No watch? No passage?[570] Murder! Murder!
40   GRATIANO   'Tis some mischance. The voice is very direful.
CASSIO   O, help!
LODOVICO   Hark!
RODERIGO   O wretched villain!
LODOVICO   Two or three groan. 'Tis heavy night.
These may be counterfeits. Let's think't unsafe
To come into the cry without more help.
RODERIGO   Nobody come? Then shall I bleed to death.
LODOVICO   Hark!

Enter IAGO [*with a light*].

GRATIANO   Here's one comes in his shirt, with light and weapons.
50   IAGO   Who's there? Whose noise is this that cries on murder?
LODOVICO   We do not know.
IAGO   Do not you hear a cry?
CASSIO   Here, here! For heaven's sake, help me!
IAGO   What's the matter?

---

[565] i.e., a mail shirt or bulletproof vest   [566] Most editors add here a stage direction that has
Iago wounding Cassio in the leg from behind, but remaining unseen. However, nothing in the
text requires this, and Cassio's wound can be given him in the fight with Roderigo, for presumably when Cassio attacks Roderigo the latter would not simply accept the thrust but would
parry. Since Iago enters again at line 46, he must exit at some point after line 22   [567] hussy, i.e.,
Desdemona   [568] unsanctified   [569] approaches swiftly   [570] passersby

GRATIANO This is Othello's ancient, as I take it.
LODOVICO The same indeed, a very valiant fellow.
IAGO What are you here that cry so grievously?
CASSIO Iago? O, I am spoiled, undone by villains.
Give me some help.
60   IAGO O me, lieutenant! What villains have done this?
CASSIO I think that one of them is hereabout
And cannot make away.
    IAGO   O treacherous villains!
[*To* LODOVICO *and* GRATIANO] What are you there?
Come in, and give some help.
    RODERIGO O, help me here!
    CASSIO That's one of them.
    IAGO   O murd'rous slave! O villain!   [*Stabs* RODERIGO.]
    RODERIGO O damned Iago! O inhuman dog!
70   IAGO Kill me i' th' dark?—Where be these bloody thieves?—
How silent is this town!—Ho! Murder! Murder!—
What may you be? Are you of good or evil?
    LODOVICO As you shall prove us, praise us.
    IAGO Signior Lodovico?
    LODOVICO He, sir.
    IAGO I cry you mercy. Here's Cassio hurt by villains.
    GRATIANO Cassio?
    IAGO How is't, brother?
    CASSIO My leg is cut in two.
80   IAGO   Marry, heaven forbid!
Light, gentlemen. I'll bind it with my shirt.

Enter BIANCA.

    BIANCA What is the matter, ho? Who is't that cried?
    IAGO Who is't that cried?
    BIANCA O my dear Cassio! My sweet Cassio!
O Cassio, Cassio, Cassio!
    IAGO O notable strumpet!—Cassio, may you suspect
Who they should be that have thus mangled you?
    CASSIO No.
    GRATIANO I am sorry to find you thus. I have been to seek you.
90   IAGO Lend me a garter. So. O for a chair
To bear him easily hence.
    BIANCA Alas, he faints! O Cassio, Cassio, Cassio!
    IAGO Gentlemen all, I do suspect this trash
To be a party in this injury.—
Patience awhile, good Cassio.—Come, come.
Lend me a light. Know we this face or no?
Alas, my friend and my dear countryman
Roderigo? No.—Yes, sure.—Yes, 'tis Roderigo!

GRATIANO What, of Venice?

100 IAGO Even he, sir. Did you know him?

GRATIANO   Know him? Ay.

IAGO Signior Gratiano? I cry your gentle pardon.
These bloody accidents must excuse my manners
That so neglected you.

GRATIANO   I am glad to see you.

IAGO How do you, Cassio?—O, a chair, a chair!

GRATIANO Roderigo?

IAGO He, he, 'tis he! [*A chair brought in.*] O, that's well said;[571] the chair.
Some good man bear him carefully from hence.

110 I'll fetch the general's surgeon. [*To* BIANCA] For you, mistress,
Save you your labor. [*To* CASSIO] He that lies slain here, Cassio,
Was my dear friend. What malice was between you?

CASSIO None in the world; nor do I know the man.

IAGO What, look you pale?—O, bear him out o' th' air.

[CASSIO *is carried off.*]

Stay you, good gentlemen.—Look you pale, mistress?
Do you perceive the gastness[572] of her eye?
Nay, if you stare, we shall hear more anon.
Behold her well; I pray you look upon her.
Do you see, gentlemen? Nay, guiltiness will speak,

120 Though tongues were out of use.[573]

[*Enter* EMILIA.]

EMILIA Alas, what is the matter? What is the matter, husband?

IAGO Cassio hath here been set on in the dark
By Roderigo and fellows that are scaped.
He's almost slain, and Roderigo quite dead.

EMILIA Alas, good gentleman! Alas, good Cassio!

IAGO This is the fruits of whoring. Prithee, Emilia,
Go know of Cassio where he supped tonight.
[*To* BIANCA] What, do you shake at that?

BIANCA He supped at my house; but I therefore shake not.

130 IAGO O, did he so? I charge[574] you go with me.

EMILIA Oh fie upon thee, strumpet!

BIANCA I am no strumpet, but of life as honest
As you that thus abuse me.

EMILIA   As I? Fie upon thee!

IAGO Kind gentlemen, let's go see poor Cassio dressed.[575]
[*To* BIANCA] Come, mistress, you must tell's another tale.

---

[571] *well said* well done   [572] terror   [573] *tongues were out of use* men no longer spoke
[574] command   [575] bandaged

Emilia, run you to the citadel
And tell my lord and lady what hath happed.   [*Exit* EMILIA.]
Will you go on afore?   *Exeunt* [*all but* IAGO].
140   This is the night
That either makes me or fordoes me quite.[576]   [*Exit.*]

Scene II. [DESDEMONA *'s chamber*.]

Enter OTHELLO [*with a light*]; *and* DESDEMONA *in her bed.*

   OTHELLO   It is the cause, it is the cause, my soul.
Let me not name it to you, you chaste stars.
It is the cause. Yet I'll not shed her blood,
Nor scar that whiter skin of hers than snow
And smooth as monumental alabaster.
Yet she must die, else she'll betray more men.
Put out the light, and then put out the light.
If I quench thee, thou flaming minister,[577]
I can again thy former light restore,
10   Should I repent me; but once put out thy light,
Thou cunning'st[578] pattern of excelling nature,
I know not where is that Promethean heat[579]
That can thy light resume.[580] When I have plucked the rose,
I cannot give it vital[581] growth again;
It needs must wither. I'll smell thee on the tree.   [*He kisses her.*]
O balmy breath, that dost almost persuade
Justice to break her sword. One more, one more!
Be thus when thou art dead, and I will kill thee,
And love thee after. One more, and that's the last!
20   So sweet was ne'er so fatal. I must weep,
But they are cruel tears. This sorrow's heavenly;
It strikes where it doth love. She wakes.
   DESDEMONA   Who's there? Othello?
   OTHELLO   Ay, Desdemona.
   DESDEMONA   Will you come to bed, my lord?
   OTHELLO   Have you prayed tonight, Desdemon?
   DESDEMONA   Ay, my lord.
   OTHELLO   If you bethink yourself of any crime
Unreconciled as yet to heaven and grace,
30   Solicit for it straight.
   DESDEMONA   Alack, my lord, what may you mean by that?
   OTHELLO   Well, do it, and be brief; I will walk by.[582]
I would not kill thy unpreparèd spirit.

---

[576] *fordoes me quite* completely ruins me   [577] worker, servant   [578] most intricate and skill-
fully wrought (by nature excelling itself)   [579] *Promethean heat* divine fire (Prometheus is the
Titan who stole fire from heaven and gave it to man)   [580] relight   [581] living   [582] nearby

No, heavens forfend! I would not kill thy soul.
 DESDEMONA Talk you of killing?
 OTHELLO   Ay, I do.
 DESDEMONA   Then heaven
Have mercy on me!
 OTHELLO   Amen, with all my heart.
40 DESDEMONA If you say so, I hope you will not kill me.
 OTHELLO Humh.
 DESDEMONA And yet I fear you; for you're fatal then
When your eyes roll so. Why I should fear I know not,
Since guiltiness I know not; but yet I feel I fear.
 OTHELLO Think on thy sins.
 DESDEMONA   They are loves I bear to you.
 OTHELLO Ay, and for that thou diest.
 DESDEMONA That death's unnatural that kills for loving.
Alas, why gnaw you so your nether lip?
50 Some bloody passion shakes your very frame.
These are portents; but yet I hope, I hope,
They do not point on me.
 OTHELLO   Peace and be still.
 DESDEMONA I will so. What's the matter?
 OTHELLO That handkerchief which I so loved and gave thee,
That gav'st to Cassio.
 DESDEMONA   No, by my life and soul!
Send for the man and ask him.
 OTHELLO   Sweet soul, take heed,
60 Take heed of perjury; thou art on thy deathbed.
 DESDEMONA Ay, but not yet to die.
 OTHELLO   Presently.[583]
Therefore confess thee freely of thy sin,
For to deny each article[584] with oath
Cannot remove nor choke the strong conception
That I do groan withal. Thou art to die.
 DESDEMONA Then Lord have mercy on me.
 OTHELLO   I say, amen.
 DESDEMONA And have you mercy too. I never did
70 Offend you in my life; never loved Cassio
But with such general warranty[585] of heaven
As I might love. I never gave him token.
 OTHELLO By heaven, I saw my handkerchief in's hand!
O perjured woman! thou dost stone[586] my heart,
And mak'st me call what I intend to do
A murder, which I thought a sacrifice.
I saw the handkerchief.

---

[583] immediately [584] item (of the charge of adultery. Othello makes heavy use of legal terms
in this scene) [585] allowance [586] turn to stone

DESDEMONA   He found it then.
I never gave it him. Send for him hither.
80 Let him confess a truth.
OTHELLO   He hath confessed.
DESDEMONA What, my lord?
OTHELLO That he hath used thee.
DESDEMONA   How? Unlawfully?
OTHELLO   Ay.
DESDEMONA He will not say so.
OTHELLO   No, his mouth is stopped.
Honest Iago hath ta'en order for't.[587]
DESDEMONA O, my fear interprets. What, is he dead?
90 OTHELLO Had all his hairs been lives, my great revenge
Had stomach[588] for them all.
DESDEMONA Alas, he is betrayed, and I undone!
OTHELLO Out, strumpet! Weep'st thou for him to my face?
DESDEMONA O, banish me, my lord, but kill me not!
OTHELLO Down, strumpet!
DESDEMONA Kill me tomorrow; let me live tonight!
OTHELLO Nay, if you strive—
DESDEMONA But half an hour!
OTHELLO   Being done, there is no pause.
100 DESDEMONA But while I say one prayer!
OTHELLO   It is too late.   *Smothers her.*

EMILIA *at the door.*

EMILIA [*Calls within*]   My lord, my lord! What, ho, my lord, my lord!
OTHELLO What noise is this? Not dead? Not yet quite dead?
I that am cruel am yet merciful;
I would not have thee linger in thy pain.
EMILIA [*Within*] What, ho! My lord, my lord!
OTHELLO   So, so. Who's there?
EMILIA [*Within*]   O, good my lord, I would speak a word with you.
OTHELLO Yes, 'tis Emilia.—By and by.—She's dead.—
110 'Tis like she comes to speak of Cassio's death.
The noise was high.[589] Ha! No more moving?
Still as the grave.—Shall she come in? Were't good?—
I think she stirs again. No.—What's best to do?
If she come in, she'll sure speak to my wife.
My wife! My wife! What wife? I have no wife.
O, insupportable! O heavy hour!
Methinks[590] it should be now a huge eclipse

---

[587] *ta'en order for't* made sure of it   [588] appetite   [589] loud (Q1 reads "here")   [590] *Methinks*
. . . *alteration* (The Elizabethans believed that great changes in human affairs were reflected
by disorders in nature)

Of sun and moon, and that th' affrighted globe
Should yawn[591] at alteration.
120   EMILIA [*Within*]   I do beseech you
That I may speak with you, O good my lord!
    OTHELLO   I had forgot thee. O, come in, Emilia.
Soft, by and by.—Let me the curtains draw.—

               [*Draws the bed hangings and then opens the door.*]

Where art thou?

Enter EMILIA.

What's the matter with thee now?
    EMILIA   O my good lord, yonder's foul murders done!
    OTHELLO   What? Now?
    EMILIA   But now, my lord.
    OTHELLO   It is the very error[592] of the moon.
130 She comes more nearer earth than she was wont
And makes men mad.
    EMILIA   Cassio, my lord, hath killed a young Venetian
Called Roderigo.
    OTHELLO   Roderigo killed?
And Cassio killed?
    EMILIA   No, Cassio is not killed.
    OTHELLO   Not Cassio killed? Then murder's out of tune,
And sweet revenge grows harsh.
    DESDEMONA   O, falsely, falsely murdered!
140   EMILIA   O Lord! What cry is that?
    OTHELLO   That? What?
    EMILIA   Out and alas! that was my lady's voice.
Help! Help, ho! Help! O lady, speak again!
Sweet Desdemona! O sweet mistress, speak!
    DESDEMONA   A guiltless death I die.
    EMILIA   O, who hath done this deed?
    DESDEMONA   Nobody—I myself. Farewell.
Commend me to my kind lord. O, farewell!   [*She dies.*]
    OTHELLO   Why, how should she be murd'red?
150   EMILIA   Alas, who knows?
    OTHELLO   You heard her say herself, it was not I.
    EMILIA   She said so. I must needs report the truth.
    OTHELLO   She's like a liar gone to burning hell!
'Twas I that killed her.
    EMILIA   O, the more angel she,

---

[591] gape open (as in an earthquake)   [592] wandering out of regular course (disorders in the heavens were believed by some to cause disorders on earth, as well as vice versa)

And you the blacker devil!

OTHELLO She turned to folly, and she was a whore.

EMILIA Thou dost belie her, and thou art a devil.

OTHELLO She was false as water.

160 EMILIA   Thou art rash as fire to say

That she was false. O, she was heavenly true!

OTHELLO Cassio did top her. Ask thy husband else.

O, I were damned beneath all depth in hell

But that I did proceed upon just grounds

To this extremity. Thy husband knew it all.

EMILIA My husband?

OTHELLO   Thy husband.

EMILIA   That she was false to wedlock?

OTHELLO Ay, with Cassio. Had she been true,

170 If heaven would make me such another world

Of one entire and perfect chrysolite,[593]

I'd not have sold her for it.

EMILIA   My husband?

OTHELLO Ay, 'twas he that told me on her first.

An honest man he is, and hates the slime

That sticks on filthy deeds.

EMILIA   My husband?

OTHELLO What needs this iterance? Woman, I say thy husband.

EMILIA O mistress, villainy hath made mocks with love!

180 My husband say she was false?

OTHELLO   He, woman.

I say, thy husband. Dost understand the word?

My friend, thy husband; honest, honest Iago.

EMILIA If he say so, may his pernicious soul

Rot half a grain a day! He lies to th' heart.

She was too fond of her most filthy bargain.

OTHELLO Hah?

EMILIA Do thy worst.

This deed of thine is no more worthy heaven

190 Than thou wast worthy her.

OTHELLO   Peace, you were best.[594]

EMILIA Thou hast not half that pow'r to do me harm

As I have to be hurt. O gull! O dolt!

As ignorant as dirt! Thou hast done a deed—

[OTHELLO *moves to draw his sword.*]

I care not for thy sword; I'll make thee known,

Though I lost twenty lives. Help! Help! Ho! Help!

The Moor hath killed my mistress! Murder! murder!

[593] topaz   [594] *Peace, you were best* i.e., you had better be silent

Enter MONTANO, GRATIANO, *and* IAGO [*and* OTHERS].

    MONTANO What is the matter? How now, general?

    EMILIA O, are you come, Iago? You have done well,

200 That men must lay their murders on your neck.

    GRATIANO What is the matter?

    EMILIA Disprove this villain, if thou be'st a man.

He says thou told'st him that his wife was false.

I know thou didst not; thou'rt not such a villain.

Speak, for my heart is full.

    IAGO I told him what I thought, and told no more

Than what he found himself was apt and true.

    EMILIA But did you ever tell him she was false?

    IAGO I did.

210   EMILIA You told a lie, an odious damnèd lie!

Upon my soul, a lie! A wicked lie!

She false with Cassio? Did you say with Cassio?

    IAGO With Cassio, mistress. Go to, charm[595] your tongue.

    EMILIA I will not charm my tongue; I am bound to speak:

My mistress here lies murdered in her bed.

    ALL O heavens forfend!

    EMILIA And your reports have set the murder on.

    OTHELLO Nay, stare not, masters. It is true indeed.

    GRATIANO 'Tis a strange truth.

220   MONTANO O monstrous act!

    EMILIA   Villainy, villainy, villainy!

I think upon't—I think I smell't!—O villainy!

I thought so then.—I'll kill myself for grief.—

O villainy, villainy!

    IAGO What, are you mad? I charge you get you home.

    EMILIA Good gentlemen, let me have leave to speak.

'Tis proper I obey him, but not now.

Perchance, Iago, I will ne'er go home.

    OTHELLO O! O! O!

                                             [*Falls on the bed.*]

230   EMILIA   Nay, lay thee down and roar,

For thou hast killed the sweetest innocent

That e'er did lift up eye.

    OTHELLO   O, she was foul!   [*Rises.*]

I scarce did know you, uncle. There lies your niece,

Whose breath, indeed, these hands have newly stopped.

I know this act shows horrible and grim.

    GRATIANO Poor Desdemon! I am glad thy father's dead.

[595] control

Thy match was mortal to him, and pure grief
Shore his old thread in twain. Did he live now,
240 This sight would make him do a desperate turn;
Yea, curse his better angel from his side,
And fall to reprobation.[596]
    OTHELLO   'Tis pitiful; but yet Iago knows
That she with Cassio hath the act of shame
A thousand times committed. Cassio confessed it
And she did gratify his amorous works
With that recognizance and pledge of love,
Which I first gave her. I saw it in his hand.
It was a handkerchief, an antique token
250 My father gave my mother.
    EMILIA   O God! O heavenly God!
    IAGO   Zounds, hold your peace!
    EMILIA   'Twill out, 'twill out! I peace?
No, I will speak as liberal as the north.[597]
Let heaven and men and devils, let them all,
All, all, cry shame against me, yet I'll speak.
    IAGO   Be wise, and get you home.
    EMILIA   I will not.

                 [IAGO *draws and threatens* EMILIA.]

    GRATIANO   Fie! Your sword upon a woman?
260   EMILIA   O thou dull Moor, that handkerchief thou speak'st of
I found by fortune, and did give my husband;
For often with a solemn earnestness—
More than indeed belonged to such a trifle—
He begged of me to steal't.
    IAGO   Villainous whore!
    EMILIA   She give it Cassio? No, alas, I found it,
And I did give't my husband.
    IAGO   Filth, thou liest!
    EMILIA   By heaven, I do not, gentlemen.
270 O murd'rous coxcomb! What should such a fool
Do with so good a wife?
    OTHELLO   Are there no stones[598] in heaven
But what serves for the thunder? Precious villain!

[*The* MOOR *runs at* IAGO, *but is disarmed by* MONTANO. IAGO *kills his wife.*]

    GRATIANO   The woman falls. Sure he hath killed his wife.
    EMILIA   Ay, ay. O, lay me by my mistress' side.   [*Exit* IAGO.]

---

[596] damnation   [597] *liberal as the north* freely (and bitingly) as the north wind blows
[598] thunderbolts

GRATIANO He's gone, but his wife's killed.

MONTANO 'Tis a notorious[599] villain. Take you this weapon,
Which I have recovered from the Moor.
Come, guard the door without. Let him not pass,
280 But kill him rather. I'll after that same villain,
For 'tis a damnèd slave.   *Exit [with all but* OTHELLO *and* EMILIA].

OTHELLO   I am not valiant neither;
But every puny whipster[600] gets my sword.
But why should honor outlive honesty?
Let it go all.

EMILIA   What did thy song bode, lady?
Hark, canst thou hear me? I will play the swan,
And die in music. [*Sings*] "Willow, willow, willow."
Moor, she was chaste. She loved thee, cruel Moor,
290 So come my soul to bliss as I speak true.
So speaking as I think, alas, I die.   [*She dies.*]

OTHELLO I have another weapon in this chamber;
It was a sword of Spain, the ice-brook's temper.
O, here it is.—Uncle, I must come forth.

GRATIANO [*Within*]   If thou attempt it, it will cost thee dear.
Thou hast no weapon, and perforce must suffer.

OTHELLO Look in upon me then and speak with me,
Or, naked as I am, I will assault thee.

[*Enter* GRATIANO.]

GRATIANO What is the matter?

300   OTHELLO   Behold, I have a weapon;
A better never did itself sustain
Upon a soldier's thigh. I have seen the day
That with this little arm and this good sword
I have made my way through more impediments
Than twenty times your stop. But O vain boast!
Who can control his fate? 'Tis not so now.
Be not afraid, though you do see me weaponed.
Here is my journey's end, here is my butt,[601]
And very seamark of my utmost sail.[602]
310 Do you go back dismayed? 'Tis a lost fear.
Man but a rush[603] against Othello's breast.
And he retires. Where should Othello go?
Now, how dost thou look now? O ill-starred wench!
Pale as thy smock! When we shall meet at compt,[604]
This look of thine will hurl my soul from heaven,

---

[599] out-and-out   [600] *puny whipster* small top-whipping boy (?)   [601] target, stopping place
[602] *seamark of my utmost sail* maker of my furthest journey   [603] *Man but a rush* attack with only
a reed   [604] Judgment Day

And fiends will snatch at it. Cold, cold, my girl?
Even like thy chastity.
O cursèd, cursèd slave! Whip me, ye devils,
From the possession of[605] this heavenly sight!
320 Blow me about in winds! roast me in sulfur!
Wash me in steep-down gulfs of liquid fire!
O Desdemon! Dead Desdemon; dead. O! O!

Enter LODOVICO, CASSIO, MONTANO, *and* IAGO [*as prisoner*] *with* OFFICERS.

LODOVICO   Where is this rash and most unfortunate man?
OTHELLO   That's he that was Othello? Here I am.
LODOVICO   Where is that viper? Bring the villain forth.
OTHELLO   I look down towards his feet[606]—but that's a fable.
If that thou be'st a devil, I cannot kill thee.   [*Wounds* IAGO.]
LODOVICO   Wrench his sword from him.   [OTHELLO *is disarmed.*]
IAGO   I bleed, sir, but not killed.
330 OTHELLO   I am not sorry neither. I'd have thee live;
For in my sense, 'tis happiness to die.
LODOVICO   O thou Othello that was once so good,
Fall'n in the practice[607] of a cursèd slave,
What shall be said to thee?
OTHELLO   Why, anything:
An honorable murderer, if you will;
For naught I did in hate, but all in honor.
LODOVICO   This wretch hath part confessed his villainy.
Did you and he consent in Cassio's death?
340 OTHELLO   Ay.
CASSIO   Dear general, I never gave you cause.
OTHELLO   I do believe it, and I ask your pardon.
Will you, I pray, demand that demi-devil
Why he hath thus ensnared my soul and body?
IAGO   Demand me nothing. What you know, you know.
From this time forth I never will speak word.
LODOVICO   What, not to pray?
GRATIANO   Torments will ope your lips.
OTHELLO   Well, thou dost best.
350 LODOVICO   Sir, you shall understand what hath befall'n,
Which, as I think, you know not. Here is a letter
Found in the pocket of the slain Roderigo;
And here another. The one of them imports
The death of Cassio to be undertook
By Roderigo.
OTHELLO   O villain!

---

[605] *the possession of* being possessed by   [606] *towards his feet* i.e., for his cloven hoofs
[607] plotting

CASSIO   Most heathenish and most gross!

LODOVICO   Now here's another discontented paper
Found in his pocket too; and this, it seems,
360 Roderigo meant t' have sent this damnèd villain;
But that, belike, Iago in the interim
Came in and satisfied him.

OTHELLO   O thou pernicious caitiff!
How came you, Cassio, by that handkerchief
That was my wife's?

CASSIO   I found it in my chamber;
And he himself confessed it but even now
That there he dropped it for a special purpose
Which wrought to his desire.

370 OTHELLO   O fool! Fool! Fool!

CASSIO   There is besides in Roderigo's letter,
How he upbraids Iago that he made him
Brave me upon the watch; whereon it came
That I was cast; and even but now he spake,
After long seeming dead—Iago hurt him,
Iago set him on.

LODOVICO   You must forsake this room and go with us.
Your power and your command is taken off,
And Cassio rules in Cyprus. For this slave,
380 If there be any cunning cruelty
That can torment him much and hold him long,
It shall be his. You shall close prisoner rest
Till that the nature of your fault be known
To the Venetian state. Come, bring away.

OTHELLO   Soft you, a word or two before you go.
I have done the state some service and they know't.
No more of that. I pray you, in your letters,
When you shall these unlucky deeds relate,
Speak of me as I am. Nothing extenuate,
390 Nor set down aught in malice. Then must you speak
Of one that loved not wisely, but too well;
Of one not easily jealous, but, being wrought,
Perplexed in the extreme; of one whose hand,
Like the base Judean,[608] threw a pearl away
Richer than all his tribe; of one whose subdued eyes,
Albeit unusèd to the melting mood,
Drops tears as fast as the Arabian trees
Their med'cinable gum. Set you down this.
And say besides that in Aleppo once,
400 Where a malignant and a turbaned Turk

---

[608] Most editors use the Q1 reading, "Indian," here, but F is clear; both readings point toward
the infidel, the unbeliever.

Beat a Venetian and traduced the state,
I took by th' throat the circumcisèd dog
And smote him—thus.   *[He stabs himself.]*

    LODOVICO   O bloody period![609]

    GRATIANO   All that is spoke is marred.

    OTHELLO   I kissed thee ere I killed thee. No way but this,
Killing myself, to die upon a kiss.   *[He falls over* DESDEMONA *and dies.]*

    CASSIO   This did I fear, but thought he had no weapon;
For he was great of heart.

410   LODOVICO *[To* IAGO]   O Spartan dog,
More fell[610] than anguish, hunger, or the sea!
Look on the tragic loading of this bed.
This is thy work. The object poisons sight;
Let it be hid.   *[Bed curtains drawn.]*

        Gratiano, keep[611] the house,
And seize upon the fortunes of the Moor,
For they succeed on you. To you, lord governor,
Remains the censure of this hellish villain,
The time, the place, the torture. O, enforce it!

420 Myself will straight aboard, and to the state
This heavy act with heavy heart relate.   *Exeunt.*

Questions

1. Shakespeare builds his plot by scenes. Write a brief synopsis of each scene in the first act, indicating how each serves to advance plot.

2. In each scene of the first act, which actions and speeches contribute to our understanding of character? Iago's? Othello's? Desdemona's?

3. Iago is considered one of the direst villains of literature. Does Shakespeare present him as evil by nature—born to evil as others are born to wealth, good looks, talent, or imbecility? Or does he become evil for reasons or causes that explain, if they do not justify?

4. Although Iago is evil, he is the source of much of *Othello's* humor. Find examples. Does his humor make him appear less evil? More evil? Characterize his humor. Are you able to contrast it with Sophocles's humor?

5. Discuss social position or class in *Othello* and its relationship to motive and plot.

6. Discern the several separate and distinct devices by which Iago creates jealousy in Othello. Note the scenes by which each device is furthered.
   Does Iago's ongoing scheme make the unfolding of *Othello* seem as inevitable as *Oedipus?*

7. *Othello* is sometimes discussed in terms of contrasting pairs of characters. Find as many such pairs as you can. Can you find a group of three characters set in contrast?

8. How do the women differ? Do they resemble each other at all?

---

[609] end   [610] cruel   [611] remain in

9. Is there a role in *Othello* that resembles the part played by Creon in *Oedipus?*

10. If we look for a tragic flaw in Othello, what do we find? Is jealousy Othello's tragic flaw? What does Othello consider his error? Do you agree with his assessment?

11. Perhaps the final ingredient of Othello's wrath is supplied by the scene in which he overhears Cassio brag lightly of Bianca's love for him—while Othello supposes that Cassio speaks of Desdemona. Does this scene stretch your credulity? Should it? If you accept it without question, why are you unskeptical?

12. Aristotle says a hero must be a great man. Is Othello a great man?

13. How important to the play is Othello's blackness? Is racism one of the themes of the play? Can you conceive of an Othello not black but white, perhaps a successful military man risen from the ranks?
    Trace the development of black-and-white imagery in the play. How do the images work?

14. In this play, the words *honest* and *honesty* turn up again and again. Divide the class into five parts and let each group investigate these words in one act. Discuss the levels of irony in the repeated words. (Do not attempt to speak of these words without consulting the *Oxford English Dictionary.*)

15. Find animal images in *Othello.* What do they contribute?

16. In *Othello,* Shakespeare's characters, even the heroic protagonist, lapse into prose from time to time. In what circumstances does the author move from poetry to prose? What is accomplished?

17. Find a scene that allows scope for staging, and write an account of entrances, exits, and blocking as if you were using an Elizabethan theater. Use balcony, alcove, perhaps trapdoor. Be ingenious but probable.

18. Emilia's speech at the end of Act IV has been cited as evidence for Shakespeare's own special genius. What is unusual about it? Can you imagine critics for whom it would be an example of Shakespeare's faults?

19. Does the play leave you believing that Othello once cuckolded Iago? Why do you think so? Why is the suggestion made?

20. Write a scenario for a happy ending to *Othello.* How much would need to change? Who might expose Iago in the nick of time?

21. Make note of Shakespeare's exposition in *Othello.* How do we know what we need to know?

22. *Othello* has enough dramatic irony for three ordinary tragedies. See I, iii, 813–815, for instance. Find five more examples.

23. Othello says to Desdemona, "I've got good news and bad news. The bad news is that I have discovered your infidelity and you must die. The good news is I found that handkerchief you lost." Comment.

CHAPTER FIVE

Comedy and Wilde

Comedy makes us laugh and leaves us smiling, but that is not all it does. The tragic mask in Greek theater shows the downturned mouth, fitted to the role of the protagonist whose downfall is fated. If the comic mask shows a perpetual smile, we should not imagine that comedy is evenly comic or does not provoke tears and sober thoughts. Comedy is various in its mixture of feelings, frequently frightening in its crises, satiric, and cruel—but, by definition, in a comedy *things come out all right in the end.*

Like tragedy, comedy derived from the worship of Dionysus, the wine god of ancient Greece. Although the year must die each autumn into winter, passing inexorably underground, the year will be born again in spring—just as necessarily. The Greek word that becomes *comedy* means *revelry* and suggests the celebration of triumph over adversity. In tragedy, adversity overcomes a king. In comedy at its most typical, someone socially a little lower than a king faces adversity, overcomes it by good luck—and gets married. The hero's adversity may take the form of a villain, whose overthrow may be comic or satiric, or adversity may be a trick of fate, like a mixed-up set of identical twins and a shipwreck. In the ritual that lies behind comedy, adversity was winter and triumph was the green shoots of spring. Both comedy and the year's cycle lead to fruition: from the marriage that brings down the final curtain we can expect a green crop of children.

Aristotle's elements of theater can be applied to comedy as well as to tragedy. Comic plots move through conflicts and crises as the protagonist works to overcome adversity. Coincidence and improbable good luck aid the protagonist; scenes of recognition make our happy ending: long-lost wives and sons sold into slavery miraculously reappear; the beggar inherits a great fortune; the villain proves to be the heir's double and an imposter. Improbability of resolution, rather than displeasing us, seems essential to the comic view of the world. The counterpart to tragedy's unavoidable doom, comedy's happy ending is unavoidable. Improbability emphasizes the comic understanding: no matter how bad things look, something will turn up to save the day.

Characters in comedy tend to be types, as tragic characters tend to be individuals. Titles of comedies often name a characteristic, as in Molière's *The Misanthrope;* titles of tragedies like *Oedipus Rex* and *Othello* tend to be the names of tragic heroes. Wilde's *The Importance of Being Earnest* names a character (sort of), reminds us of plot, and makes the joke of suggesting its own opposite. "Earnestness" is a human characteristic—perhaps a characteristic not to be found in Wilde's play. It is common for a comic character to embody one human trait with a monstrous consistency: the miser is always and only a miser, the fop nothing but a fop. The ancient idea of **humors** portrayed human character according to the mixture of four bodily fluids, or humors: blood, phlegm, yellow bile, black bile—and a dominance of any one determined a person's character: sanguine, phlegmatic, choleric, or melancholy. In the comedy of humors, a character is wholly dominated by one characteristic trait or humor—rather like Dopey or Grumpy among Disney's Seven Dwarfs.

Exaggeration, of course, is a device of humor. By multiplying or expanding a trait to monstrosity, we expose it to laughter. Comedies use exaggerated stock characters to expose social foolishness as well as the foolishness of individuals. With types, and exaggerated types, we approach stereotypes (see page 740), which are common to comedy, less common in tragedy. Thus we have the classic stereotypes of the braggart and the artful slave. Even in Shakespearean comedy, and comedies of the modern theater, we find many expected roles: the young lovers, the scheming (for good or evil) servant, the kind parent and the wicked guardian, the drunk, the greedy landlord.

Thought in comedy runs the gamut from profundity to fatuousness. **Satiric comedy** is moral, and exposes foolishness to ridicule. As such, it can be said to benefit society by providing moral guidelines and allowing us to correct ourselves. In Molière's *Tartuffe,* for instance, the hypocrite named in the title wears a mask of pious morality in the endeavor to enrich himself. He is condemned by being revealed. But the play's moral endeavor condemns, not the hypocrite who is perfectly bad, but the naïve simpleton who believes in him. It is the credulous eyes that must be opened, the foolishness of naïveté that the play's satire condemns, exposes, and holds up to ridicule.

Even in satiric comedies, we usually find blameless young lovers to admire. Not all comedies, however, are satiric. Shakespeare's early comedies, like *As You Like It* or *Love's Labour's Lost,* while they include obvious silliness obviously corrected, entertain us first—and seldom bother to persuade us of moral ideas. We take from these plays a delight in their shape, their wit, their resolution: we are entertained. This is the **romantic comedy**, at which Shakespeare excelled; his rival Ben Jonson wrote satiric comedy, which takes a sharp view of human foibles. A romantic comedy is good-natured, optimistic, or accepting.

Language provides us another means for distinguishing types of comedy. In **high comedy**, the characters speak with verbal wit. Shakespeare's fools may tease puns for lines, his heroes may sum up a scene in an epigram; on Broadway, characters wisecrack at each other. In **low comedy**, we laugh at situations and pratfalls. A **farce** is low comedy, usually without pretension to satire or to profound thought, in which plotting makes situations that are inherently absurd. The variant **bedroom farce** may show us a woman stuffing one lover after another into closets, under beds, and onto balconies. In **slapstick**, the laughter comes from physical movement more than from situation, as characters slip and fall down, bang their heads on closet doors, and hit each other with anything handy.

There are many theories of laughter and its sources, and no consensus. The poet Baudelaire, the philosopher Bergson, the novelist George Meredith, and the psychologist Freud have all written famous essays on humor. Reading comedy, attending to its thoughts, action, and language, we find incongruity a comic constant. Perhaps we laugh feeling superior to characters on the stage, perceiving an incongruity between what we would do and what they have done. Perhaps we laugh because we see our suppressed desires acted out on the stage, our alienated characteristics exhibited, an incongruity between desire and performance. Perhaps we laugh to see our wishes fulfilled.

Wilde's comedy uses familiar plot devices, masks and impersonations, love and impediments to love, to construct a well-made play that amuses us and satisfies our sense of shape. In the golden world of romantic comedy, the lovers are attractive and love is irresistible; we know, always, that the lovers will find a way out of their impasse—and even the impasse, which frequently takes the shape of an elder relative, will prove at least moderately attractive and forgivable. In Wilde's play, the plot is perfectly silly, and genuinely funny, but the dialogue occasioned by the plot, while funny, is also serious: the paradoxes, the ten thousand reversals of commonplace, carry both sting and intelligence.

Tragicomedy and Mixed Forms

We have treated tragedy and comedy as if these forms of drama never touched upon each other. But few great plays are so pure: in Shakespeare's great tragedies, we have noticed comic routines and considerable laughter; in Shakespeare's comedy we have tears; and in a late comedy like *Measure for Measure* we have tragic figures and possible tragedy, turned aside into comedy. In modern theater, the mixture of laughter and tears has become the rule rather than the exception. Chekhov's comedies are funny and melancholy at once. In retrospect, modern readers have found that even the later Greek drama admitted some mixture; in Euripides's comedy *Alcestis* we see a tragedy averted by a comic turn of plot.

When in Shakespeare's *Macbeth,* after a dreadful murder a drunken porter delivers a comic, bawdy soliloquy, some critics have spoken of **comic relief**. Perhaps we feel in laughter a release of the tension that mounts as we witness evil. Other critics find the dramatic effect greater than mere relief; a conflict of modes in the play's form, they claim, adds to the play's complexity by providing dramatic contrast: while our hearts are still swollen with horror at the murder of an innocent and generous king, we are wrenched aside by a description of the effects of alcohol on sexual desire and potency. Presumably, a similar conflict has similar effects when a serious element enters a play that is mostly funny: our laughter and our lightness stand out against a black background.

Oscar Wilde

Oscar Wilde (1854–1900) was born in Dublin, where his father was a doctor and his mother a writer. As an undergraduate at Oxford, he won the Newdigate Prize for Poetry. A wit and a dandy, he originally attracted attention for his style as much as for his writing. He first published *Poems* (1881) and later a volume of tales written for his children. He published short stories and a novel called *The Picture of Dorian Gray* (1890); his critical intelligence, in *Intentions* (1891), is extraordinary. But his most successful work is four brilliant comedies: *Lady Windermere's Fan* (1892), *A Woman of No Importance* (1893), *An Ideal Husband* (1895), and *The Importance of Being Earnest* (1895). In Wilde's theater, frivolous, witty language is everything: appearances, disguises, reality subsumed; what is true? Only language is true, only the fine, fictive, balanced sentence is true. Style is everything, and we learn by his style the style of laughter.

The man himself was more complicated than his work. He was imprisoned as a homosexual in 1895, and died in France after his release.

The Importance of Being Earnest   (1895)

The Persons of the Play

JOHN WORTHING, J.P.   LADY BRACKNELL
ALGERNON MONCRIEFF   HON. GWENDOLEN FAIRFAX
REV. CANON CHASUBLE, D.D.   CECILY CARDEW
MERRIMAN, butler   MISS PRISM, governess
LANE, manservant

The Scenes of the Play

ACT   I   *Algernon Moncrieff's Flat in Half-Moon Street, W.*
ACT II   *The Garden at the Manor House, Woolton.*
ACT III   *Drawing-Room at the Manor House, Woolton.*

First Act

Scene. *Morning-room in* ALGERNON's *flat in Half-Moon Street. The room is luxuriously and artistically furnished. The sound of a piano is heard in the adjoining room.*

[LANE *is arranging afternoon tea on the table, and after the music has ceased,* ALGERNON *enters.*]

ALGERNON   Did you hear what I was playing, Lane?

LANE   I didn't think it polite to listen, sir.

ALGERNON   I'm sorry for that, for your sake. I don't play accurately—anyone can play accurately—but I play with wonderful expression. As far as the piano is concerned, sentiment is my forte. I keep science for life.

LANE   Yes, sir.

ALGERNON   And, speaking of the science of life, have you got the cucumber sandwiches cut for Lady Bracknell?

LANE   Yes, sir. [*Hands them on a salver.*]

10   ALGERNON [*Inspects them, takes two, and sits down on the sofa.*]   Oh! . . . by the way, Lane, I see from your book that on Thursday night, when Lord Shoreman and Mr. Worthing were dining with me, eight bottles of champagne are entered as having been consumed.

LANE   Yes, sir; eight bottles and a pint.

ALGERNON   Why is it that at a bachelor's establishment the servants invariably drink the champagne? I ask merely for information.

LANE   I attribute it to the superior quality of the wine, sir. I have often observed that in married households the champagne is rarely of a first-rate brand.

20   ALGERNON   Good Heavens! Is marriage so demoralizing as that?

LANE   I believe it *is* a very pleasant state, sir. I have had very little experience of it myself up to the present. I have only been married once. That was in consequence of a misunderstanding between myself and a young person.

ALGERNON [*Languidly.*]   I don't know that I am much interested in your family life, Lane.

LANE   No, sir; it is not a very interesting subject. I never think of it myself.

ALGERNON   Very natural, I am sure. That will do, Lane, thank you.

LANE   Thank you, sir.   [LANE *goes out.*]

ALGERNON   Lane's views on marriage seem somewhat lax. Really, if the
30 lower orders don't set us a good example, what on earth is the use of them? They seem, as a class, to have absolutely no sense of moral responsibility.

[*Enter* LANE.]

LANE   Mr. Ernest Worthing.

[*Enter* JACK.]   [LANE *goes out.*]

ALGERNON   How are you, my dear Ernest? What brings you up to town?

JACK   Oh, pleasure, pleasure! What else should bring one anywhere? Eating as usual, I see, Algy!

ALGERNON [*Stiffly.*]   I believe it is customary in good society to take some slight refreshment at five o'clock. Where have you been since last Thursday?

JACK [*Sitting down on the sofa.*]   In the country.

ALGERNON   What on earth do you do there?

40   JACK [*Pulling off his gloves.*]   When one is in town one amuses oneself. When one is in the country one amuses other people. It is excessively boring.

ALGERNON   And who are the people you amuse?

JACK [*Airily.*]   Oh, neighbours, neighbours.

ALGERNON   Got nice neighbours in your part of Shropshire?

JACK   Perfectly horrid! Never speak to one of them.

ALGERNON   How immensely you must amuse them! [*Goes over and takes sandwich.*] By the way, Shropshire is your county, is it not?

JACK   Eh? Shropshire? Yes, of course. Hallo! Why all these cups? Why cucumber sandwiches? Why such reckless extravagance in one so young? Who
50 is coming to tea?

ALGERNON   Oh! merely Aunt Augusta and Gwendolen.

JACK   How perfectly delightful!

ALGERNON   Yes, that is all very well; but I am afraid Aunt Augusta won't quite approve of your being here.

JACK   May I ask why?

ALGERNON   My dear fellow, the way you flirt with Gwendolen is perfectly disgraceful. It is almost as bad as the way Gwendolen flirts with you.

JACK   I am in love with Gwendolen. I have come up to town expressly to propose to her.

60   ALGERNON   I thought you had come up for pleasure? . . . I call that business.

JACK   How utterly unromantic you are!

ALGERNON   I really don't see anything romantic in proposing. It is very romantic to be in love. But there is nothing romantic about a definite proposal. Why, one may be accepted. One usually is, I believe. Then the excitement is all over. The very essence of romance is uncertainty. If ever I get married, I'll certainly try to forget the fact.

JACK   I have no doubt about that, dear Algy. The Divorce Court was specially invented for people whose memories are so curiously constituted.

70   ALGERNON   Oh! there is no use speculating on that subject. Divorces are made in Heaven—[JACK *puts out his hand to take a sandwich.* ALGERNON *at once interferes.*] Please don't touch the cucumber sandwiches. They are ordered specially for Aunt Augusta. [*Takes one and eats it.*]

JACK   Well, you have been eating them all the time.

ALGERNON   That is quite a different matter. She is my aunt. [*Takes plate from below.*] Have some bread and butter. The bread and butter is for Gwendolen. Gwendolen is devoted to bread and butter.

JACK [*Advancing to table and helping himself.*]   And very good bread and butter it is too.

80   ALGERNON   Well, my dear fellow, you need not eat as if you were going to eat it all. You behave as if you were married to her already. You are not married to her already, and I don't think you ever will be.

JACK   Why on earth do you say that?

ALGERNON   Well, in the first place girls never marry the men they flirt with. Girls don't think it right.

JACK   Oh, that is nonsense!

ALGERNON   It isn't. It is a great truth. It accounts for the extraordinary number of bachelors that one sees all over the place. In the second place, I don't give my consent.

90   JACK   Your consent!

ALGERNON   My dear fellow, Gwendolen is my first cousin. And before I allow you to marry her, you will have to clear up the whole question of Cecily. [*Rings bell.*]

JACK   Cecily! What on earth do you mean? What do you mean, Algy, by Cecily? I don't know anyone of the name of Cecily.

[*Enter* LANE.]

ALGERNON   Bring me that cigarette case Mr. Worthing left in the smoking-
room the last time he dined here.

LANE   Yes, sir.   [LANE goes out.]

JACK   Do you mean to say you have had my cigarette case all this time? I
100 wish to goodness you had let me know. I have been writing frantic letters to
Scotland Yard about it. I was very nearly offering a large reward.

ALGERNON   Well, I wish you would offer one. I happen to be more than
usually hard up.

JACK   There is no good offering a large reward now that the thing is found.

[Enter LANE with the cigarette case on a salver. ALGERNON takes it at once. LANE goes out.]

ALGERNON   I think that is rather mean of you, Ernest, I must say. [Opens
case and examines it.] However, it makes no matter, for, now that I look at
the inscription inside, I find that the thing isn't yours after all.

JACK   Of course it's mine. [Moving to him.] You have seen me with it a
hundred times, and you have no right whatsoever to read what is written
110 inside. It is a very ungentlemanly thing to read a private cigarette case.

ALGERNON   Oh! it is absurd to have a hard-and-fast rule about what one
should read and what one shouldn't. More than half of modern culture depends on what one shouldn't read.

JACK   I am quite aware of the fact, and I don't propose to discuss modern
culture. It isn't the sort of thing one should talk of in private. I simply want
my cigarette case back.

ALGERNON   Yes; but this isn't your cigarette case. This cigarette case is a
present from someone of the name of Cecily, and you said you didn't know
anyone of that name.

120 JACK   Well, if you want to know, Cecily happens to be my aunt.

ALGERNON   Your aunt!

JACK   Yes. Charming old lady she is, too. Lives at Tunbridge Wells. Just give
it back to me, Algy.

ALGERNON [Retreating to back of sofa.]   But why does she call herself Cecily
if she is your aunt and lives at Tunbridge Wells? [Reading.] "From little Cecily
with her fondest love."

JACK [Moving to sofa and kneeling upon it.]   My dear fellow, what on earth
is there in that? Some aunts are tall, some aunts are not tall. That is a matter that
surely an aunt may be allowed to decide for herself. You seem to think that
130 every aunt should be exactly like your aunt! That is absurd! For Heaven's sake
give me back my cigarette case. [Follows ALGERNON round the room.]

ALGERNON   Yes. But why does your aunt call you her uncle. "From little
Cecily, with her fondest love to her dear Uncle Jack." There is no objection, I
admit, to an aunt being a small aunt, but why an aunt, no matter what her size
may be, should call her own nephew her uncle, I can't quite make out.
Besides, your name isn't Jack at all; it is Ernest.

JACK   It isn't Ernest; it's Jack.

ALGERNON   You have always told me it was Ernest. I have introduced you to
everyone as Ernest. You answer to the name of Ernest. You look as if your name

140 was Ernest. You are the most earnest looking person I ever saw in my life. It is perfectly absurd your saying that your name isn't Ernest. It's on your cards. Here is one of them. [*Taking it from case.*] "Mr. Ernest Worthing, B. 4, The Albany." I'll keep this as a proof that your name is Ernest if ever you attempt to deny it to me, or to Gwendolen, or to anyone else. [*Puts the card in his pocket.*]

JACK Well, my name is Ernest in town and Jack in the country, and the cigarette case was given to me in the country.

ALGERNON Yes, but that does not account for the fact that your small Aunt Cecily, who lives at Tunbridge Wells, calls you her dear uncle. Come, old boy, you had much better have the thing out at once.

150 JACK My dear Algy, you talk exactly as if you were a dentist. It is very vulgar to talk like a dentist when one isn't a dentist. It produces a false impression.

ALGERNON Well, that is exactly what dentists always do. Now, go on! Tell me the whole thing. I may mention that I have always suspected you of being a confirmed and secret Bunburyist; and I am quite sure of it now.

JACK Bunburyist? What on earth do you mean by a Bunburyist?

ALGERNON I'll reveal to you the meaning of that incomparable expression as soon as you are kind enough to inform me why you are Ernest in town and Jack in the country.

JACK Well, produce my cigarette case first.

160 ALGERNON Here it is. [*Hands cigarette case.*] Now produce your explanation, and pray make it improbable. [*Sits on sofa.*]

JACK My dear fellow, there is nothing improbable about my explanation at all. In fact it's perfectly ordinary. Old Mr. Thomas Cardew, who adopted me when I was a little boy, made me in his will guardian to his granddaughter, Miss Cecily Cardew. Cecily, who addresses me as her uncle from motives of respect that you could not possibly appreciate, lives at my place in the country under the charge of her admirable governess, Miss Prism.

ALGERNON Where is that place in the country, by the way?

JACK That is nothing to you, dear boy. You are not going to be invited. . . .

170 I may tell you candidly that the place is not in Shropshire.

ALGERNON I suspected that, my dear fellow! I have Bunburyed all over Shropshire on two separate occasions. Now, go on. Why are you Ernest in town and Jack in the country?

JACK My dear Algy, I don't know whether you will be able to understand my real motives. You are hardly serious enough. When one is placed in the position of guardian, one has to adopt a very high moral tone on all subjects. It's one's duty to do so. And as a high moral tone can hardly be said to conduce very much to either one's health or one's happiness, in order to get up to town I have always pretended to have a younger brother of the name of

180 Ernest, who lives in the Albany, and gets into the most dreadful scrapes. That, my dear Algy, is the whole truth pure and simple.

ALGERNON The truth is rarely pure and never simple. Modern life would be very tedious if it were either, and modern literature a complete impossibility!

JACK That wouldn't be at all a bad thing.

ALGERNON Literary criticism is not your forte, my dear fellow. Don't try it. You should leave that to people who haven't been at a University. They do it so well in the daily papers. What you really are is a Bunburyist. I was quite right in saying you were a Bunburyist. You are one of the most advanced Bunburyists I know.

190   JACK   What on earth do you mean?

    ALGERNON   You have invented a very useful young brother called Ernest, in order that you may be able to come up to town as often as you like. I have invented an invaluable permanent invalid called Bunbury, in order that I may be able to go down into the country whenever I choose. Bunbury is perfectly invaluable. If it wasn't for Bunbury's extraordinary bad health, for instance, I wouldn't be able to dine with you at Willis's tonight, for I have been really engaged to Aunt Augusta for more than a week.

    JACK   I haven't asked you to dine with me anywhere tonight.

    ALGERNON   I know. You are absurdly careless about sending out invitations.
200 It is very foolish of you. Nothing annoys people so much as not receiving invitations.

    JACK   You had much better dine with your Aunt Augusta.

    ALGERNON   I haven't the smallest intention of doing anything of the kind. To begin with, I dined there on Monday, and once a week is quite enough to dine with one's own relations. In the second place, whenever I do dine there I am always treated as a member of the family, and sent down with either no woman at all, or two. In the third place, I know perfectly well whom she will place me next to, tonight. She will place me next Mary Farquhar, who always flirts with her own husband across the dinner-table. That is not very pleasant. Indeed, it
210 is not even decent . . . and that sort of thing is enormously on the increase. The amount of women in London who flirt with their own husbands is perfectly scandalous. It looks so bad. It is simply washing one's clean linen in public. Besides, now that I know you to be a confirmed Bunburyist, I naturally want to talk to you about Bunburying. I want to tell you the rules.

    JACK   I am not a Bunburyist at all. If Gwendolen accepts me, I am going to kill my brother, indeed I think I'll kill him in any case. Cecily is a little too much interested in him. It is rather a bore. So I am going to get rid of Ernest. And I strongly advise you to do the same with Mr. . . . with your invalid friend who has the absurd name.

220   ALGERNON   Nothing will induce me to part with Bunbury, and if you ever get married, which seems to me extremely problematic, you will be very glad to know Bunbury. A man who marries without knowing Bunbury has a very tedious time of it.

    JACK   That is nonsense. If I marry a charming girl like Gwendolen, and she is the only girl I ever saw in my life that I would marry, I certainly won't want to know Bunbury.

    ALGERNON   Then your wife will. You don't seem to realize, that in married life three is company and two is none.

    JACK [*Sententiously.*]   That, my dear young friend, is the theory that the
230 corrupt French Drama has been propounding for the last fifty years.

    ALGERNON   Yes; and that the happy English home has proved in half the time.

    JACK   For heaven's sake, don't try to be cynical. It's perfectly easy to be cynical.

ALGERNON   My dear fellow, it isn't easy to be anything nowadays. There's such a lot of beastly competition about. [*The sound of an electric bell is heard.*] Ah! that must be Aunt Augusta. Only relatives, or creditors, ever ring in that Wagnerian manner. Now, if I get her out of the way for ten minutes, so that you can have an opportunity for proposing to Gwendolen, may I dine with you tonight at Willis's?

240   JACK   I suppose so, if you want to.

ALGERNON   Yes, but you must be serious about it. I hate people who are not serious about meals. It is so shallow of them.

[*Enter* LANE.]

LANE   Lady Bracknell and Miss Fairfax.

[ALGERNON *goes forward to meet them. Enter* LADY BRACKNELL *and* GWENDOLEN]

LADY BRACKNELL   Good afternoon, dear Algernon, I hope you are behaving very well.

ALGERNON   I'm feeling very well, Aunt Augusta.

LADY BRACKNELL   That's not quite the same thing. In fact the two things rarely go together. [*Sees* JACK *and bows to him with icy coldness.*]

ALGERNON [*To* GWENDOLEN.]   Dear me, you are smart!

250   GWENDOLEN   I am always smart! Aren't I, Mr. Worthing?

JACK   You're quite perfect, Miss Fairfax.

GWENDOLEN   Oh! I hope I am not that. It would leave no room for develop-ments, and I intend to develop in many directions. [GWENDOLEN *and* JACK *sit down together in the corner.*]

LADY BRACKNELL   I'm sorry if we are a little late, Algernon, but I was obliged to call on dear Lady Harbury. I hadn't been there since her poor husband's death. I never saw a woman so altered; she looks quite twenty years younger. And now I'll have a cup of tea, and one of those nice cucumber sandwiches you promised me.

260   ALGERNON   Certainly, Aunt Augusta. [*Goes over to tea-table.*]

LADY BRACKNELL   Won't you come and sit here, Gwendolen?

GWENDOLEN   Thanks, Mamma, I'm quite comfortable where I am.

ALGERNON [*Picking up empty plate in horror.*]   Good heavens! Lane! Why are there no cucumber sandwiches? I ordered them specially.

LANE [*Gravely.*]   There were no cucumbers in the market this morning, sir. I went down twice.

ALGERNON   No cucumbers!

LANE   No, sir. Not even for ready money.

ALGERNON   That will do, Lane, thank you.

270   LANE   Thank you, sir.

ALGERNON   I am greatly distressed, Aunt Augusta, about there being no cucumbers, not even for ready money.

LADY BRACKNELL   It really makes no matter, Algernon. I had some crumpets with Lady Harbury, who seems to me to be living entirely for pleasure now.

ALGERNON   I hear her hair has turned quite gold from grief.

LADY BRACKNELL   It certainly has changed its colour. From what cause I, of course, cannot say. [ALGERNON *crosses and hands tea.*] Thank you. I've quite a treat for you tonight, Algernon. I am going to send you down with Mary Farquhar. She is such a nice woman, and so attentive to her husband. It's
280   delightful to watch them.

ALGERNON   I am afraid, Aunt Augusta, I shall have to give up the pleasure of dining with you tonight after all.

LADY BRACKNELL [*Frowning.*]   I hope not, Algernon. It would put my table completely out. Your uncle would have to dine upstairs. Fortunately he is accustomed to that.

ALGERNON   It is a great bore, and, I need hardly say, a terrible disappointment to me, but the fact is I have just had a telegram to say that my poor friend Bunbury is very ill again. [*Exchanges glances with* JACK.] They seem to think I should be with him.

290   LADY BRACKNELL   It is very strange. This Mr. Bunbury seems to suffer from curiously bad health.

ALGERNON   Yes; poor Bunbury is a dreadful invalid.

LADY BRACKNELL   Well, I must say, Algernon, that I think it is high time that Mr. Bunbury made up his mind whether he was going to live or to die. This shilly-shallying with the question is absurd. Nor do I in any way approve of the modern sympathy with invalids. I consider it morbid. Illness of any kind is hardly a thing to be encouraged in others. Health is the primary duty of life. I am always telling that to your poor uncle, but he never seems to take much notice . . . as far as any improvement in his ailments goes. I should
300   be obliged if you would ask Mr. Bunbury, from me, to be kind enough not to have a relapse on Saturday, for I rely on you to arrange my music for me. It is my last reception, and one wants something that will encourage conversation, particularly at the end of the season when everyone has practically said whatever they had to say, which, in most cases, was probably not much.

ALGERNON   I'll speak to Bunbury, Aunt Augusta, if he is still conscious, and I think I can promise you he'll be all right by Saturday. Of course the music is a great difficulty. You see, if one plays good music, people don't listen, and if one plays bad music, people don't talk. But I'll run over the programme I've drawn out, if you will kindly come into the next room for a moment.

310   LADY BRACKNELL   Thank you, Algernon. It is very thoughtful of you. [*Rising, and following* ALGERNON.] I'm sure the programme will be delightful, after a few expurgations. French songs I cannot possibly allow. People always seem to think that they are improper, and either look shocked, which is vulgar, or laugh, which is worse. But German sounds a thoroughly respectable language, and indeed, I believe is so. Gwendolen, you will accompany me.

GWENDOLEN   Certainly, Mamma.

[LADY BRACKNELL *and* ALGERNON *go into the music-room.* GWENDOLEN *remains behind.*]

JACK   Charming day it has been, Miss Fairfax.

GWENDOLEN   Pray don't talk to me about the weather, Mr. Worthing.

Whenever people talk to me about the weather, I always feel quite certain
320 that they mean something else. And that makes me so nervous.

JACK   I do mean something else.

GWENDOLEN   I thought so. In fact, I am never wrong.

JACK   And I would like to be allowed to take advantage of Lady Bracknell's
temporary absence. . . .

GWENDOLEN   I would certainly advise you to do so. Mamma has a way of
coming back suddenly into a room that I have often had to speak to her about.

JACK   [*Nervously.*]   Miss Fairfax, ever since I met you I have admired you
more than any girl . . . I have ever met since . . . I met you.

GWENDOLEN   Yes, I am quite aware of the fact. And I often wish that in
330 public, at any rate, you had been more demonstrative. For me you have
always had an irresistible fascination. Even before I met you I was far from
indifferent to you. [JACK *looks at her in amazement.*] We live, as I hope you
know, Mr. Worthing, in an age of ideals. The fact is constantly mentioned in
the more expensive monthly magazines, and has reached the provincial pulpits I am told: and my ideal has always been to love someone of the name of
Ernest. There is something in that name that inspires absolute confidence.
The moment Algernon first mentioned to me that he had a friend called
Ernest, I knew I was destined to love you.

JACK   You really love me, Gwendolen?

340 GWENDOLEN   Passionately!

JACK   Darling! You don't know how happy you've made me.

GWENDOLEN   My own Ernest!

JACK   But you don't really mean to say that you couldn't love me if my name
wasn't Ernest?

GWENDOLEN   But your name is Ernest.

JACK   Yes, I know it is. But supposing it was something else? Do you mean
to say you couldn't love me then?

GWENDOLEN   [*Glibly.*]   Ah! that is clearly a metaphysical speculation, and
like most metaphysical speculations has very little reference at all to the
350 actual facts of real life, as we know them.

JACK   Personally, darling, to speak quite candidly, I don't much care about
the name of Ernest . . . I don't think the name suits me at all.

GWENDOLEN   It suits you perfectly. It is a divine name. It has a music of its
own. It produces vibrations.

JACK   Well, really, Gwendolen, I must say that I think there are lots of
other much nicer names. I think Jack, for instance, a charming name.

GWENDOLEN   Jack? . . . No, there is very little music in the name Jack, if
any at all, indeed. It does not thrill. It produces absolutely no vibrations. . . .
I have known several Jacks, and they all, without exception, were more than
360 usually plain. Besides, Jack is a notorious domesticity for John! And I pity any
woman who is married to a man called John. She would probably never be
allowed to know the entrancing pleasure of a single moment's solitude. The
only really safe name is Ernest.

JACK   Gwendolen, I must get christened at once—I mean we must get
married at once. There is no time to be lost.

GWENDOLEN   Married, Mr. Worthing?

JACK [*Astounded.*]   Well . . . surely. You know that I love you, and you led me to believe, Miss Fairfax, that you were not absolutely indifferent to me.

GWENDOLEN   I adore you. But you haven't proposed to me yet. Nothing has
370 been said at all about marriage. The subject has not even been touched on.

JACK   Well . . . may I propose to you now?

GWENDOLEN   I think it would be an admirable opportunity. And to spare you any possible disappointment, Mr. Worthing, I think it only fair to tell you quite frankly beforehand that I am fully determined to accept you.

JACK   Gwendolen!

GWENDOLEN   Yes, Mr. Worthing, what have you got to say to me?

JACK   You know what I have got to say to you.

GWENDOLEN   Yes, but you don't say it.

JACK   Gwendolen, will you marry me? [*Goes on his knees.*]

380 GWENDOLEN   Of course I will, darling. How long you have been about it! I am afraid you have had very little experience in how to propose.

JACK   My own one, I have never loved anyone in the world but you.

GWENDOLEN   Yes, but men often propose for practice. I know my brother Gerald does. All my girl-friends tell me so. What wonderfully blue eyes you have, Ernest! They are quite, quite blue. I hope you will always look at me just like that, especially when there are other people present.

[*Enter* LADY BRACKNELL.]

LADY BRACKNELL   Mr. Worthing! Rise, sir, from this semi-recumbent posture. It is most indecorous.

GWENDOLEN   Mamma! [*He tries to rise; she restrains him.*] I must beg you
390 to retire. This is no place for you. Besides, Mr. Worthing has not quite finished yet.

LADY BRACKNELL   Finished what, may I ask?

GWENDOLEN   I am engaged to Mr. Worthing, Mamma. [*They rise together.*]

LADY BRACKNELL   Pardon me, you are not engaged to anyone. When you do become engaged to someone, I, or your father, should his health permit him, will inform you of the fact. An engagement should come on a young girl as a surprise, pleasant or unpleasant, as the case may be. It is hardly a matter that she could be allowed to arrange for herself. . . . And now I have a few questions to put to you, Mr. Worthing. While I am making these inquiries,
400 you, Gwendolen, will wait for me below in the carriage.

GWENDOLEN [*Reproachfully.*]   Mamma!

LADY BRACKNELL   In the carriage, Gwendolen! [GWENDOLEN *goes to the door. She and* JACK *blow kisses to each other behind* LADY BRACKNELL*'s back.* LADY BRACKNELL *looks vaguely about as if she could not understand what the noise was. Finally turns round.*] Gwendolen, the carriage!

GWENDOLEN   Yes, Mamma. [*Goes out, looking back at* JACK.]

LADY BRACKNELL [*Sitting down.*]   You can take a seat, Mr. Worthing.

[*Looks in her pocket for note-book and pencil.*]

JACK Thank you, Lady Bracknell, I prefer standing.

LADY BRACKNELL [*Pencil and note-book in hand.*] I feel bound to tell you
410 that you are not down on my list of eligible young men, although I have the
same list as the dear Duchess of Bolton has. We work together, in fact. However, I am quite ready to enter your name, should your answers be what a
really affectionate mother requires. Do you smoke?

JACK Well, yes, I must admit I smoke.

LADY BRACKNELL I am glad to hear it. A man should always have an occupation of some kind. There are far too many idle men in London as it is. How
old are you?

JACK Twenty-nine.

LADY BRACKNELL A very good age to be married at. I have always been of
420 opinion that a man who desires to get married should know either everything or nothing. Which do you know?

JACK [*After some hesitation.*] I know nothing, Lady Bracknell.

LADY BRACKNELL I am pleased to hear it. I do not approve of anything that
tampers with natural ignorance. Ignorance is like a delicate exotic fruit; touch
it and the bloom is gone. The whole theory of modern education is radically
unsound. Fortunately in England, at any rate, education produces no effect
whatsoever. If it did, it would prove a serious danger to the upper classes, and
probably lead to acts of violence in Grosvenor Square. What is your income?

JACK Between seven and eight thousand a year.

430 LADY BRACKNELL [*Makes a note in her book.*] In land, or in *investments?*

JACK In investments, chiefly.

LADY BRACKNELL That is satisfactory. What between the duties expected of
one during one's lifetime, and the duties exacted from one after one's death,
land has ceased to be either a profit or a pleasure. It gives one position, and
prevents one from keeping it up. That's all that can be said about land.

JACK I have a country house with some land, of course, attached to it,
about fifteen hundred acres, I believe; but I don't depend on that for my real
income. In fact, as far as I can make out, the poachers are the only people
who make anything out of it.

440 LADY BRACKNELL A country house! How many bedrooms? Well, that point
can be cleared up afterwards. You have a town house, I hope? A girl with a
simple, unspoiled nature, like Gwendolen, could hardly be expected to
reside in the country.

JACK Well, I own a house in Belgrave Square, but it is let by the year to Lady
Bloxham. Of course, I can get it back whenever I like, at six months' notice.

LADY BRACKNELL Lady Bloxham? I don't know her.

JACK Oh, she goes about very little. She is a lady considerably advanced in
years.

LADY BRACKNELL Ah, nowadays that is no guarantee of respectability of
450 character. What number in Belgrave Square?

JACK 149.

LADY BRACKNELL [*Shaking her head.*] The unfashionable side. I thought
there was something. However, that could easily be altered.

JACK Do you mean the fashion, or the side?

LADY BRACKNELL [*Sternly.*]   Both, if necessary, I presume. What are your politics?

JACK   Well, I am afraid I really have none. I am a Liberal Unionist.

LADY BRACKNELL   Oh, they count as Tories. They dine with us. Or come in the evening, at any rate. Now to minor matters. Are your parents living?

460   JACK   I have lost both my parents.

LADY BRACKNELL   Both? . . . That seems like carelessness. Who was your father? He was evidently a man of some wealth. Was he born in what the Radical papers call the purple of commerce, or did he rise from the ranks of aristocracy?

JACK   I am afraid I really don't know. The fact is, Lady Bracknell, I said I had lost my parents. It would be nearer the truth to say that my parents seem to have lost me. . . . I don't actually know who I am by birth. I was . . . well, I was found.

LADY BRACKNELL   Found!

470   JACK   The late Mr. Thomas Cardew, an old gentleman of a very charitable and kindly disposition, found me, and gave me the name of Worthing, because he happened to have a first-class ticket for Worthing in his pocket at the time. Worthing is a place in Sussex. It is a seaside resort.

LADY BRACKNELL   Where did the charitable gentleman who had a first-class ticket for this seaside resort find you?

JACK [*Gravely.*]   In a handbag.

LADY BRACKNELL   A handbag?

JACK [*Very seriously.*]   Yes, Lady Bracknell. I was in a handbag—a somewhat large, black leather handbag with handles to it—an ordinary handbag,
480   in fact.

LADY BRACKNELL   In what locality did this Mr. James, or Thomas, Cardew come across this ordinary handbag?

JACK   In the cloakroom at Victoria Station. It was given to him in mistake for his own.

LADY BRACKNELL   The cloakroom at Victoria Station?

JACK   Yes. The Brighton line.

LADY BRACKNELL   The line is immaterial. Mr. Worthing, I confess I feel somewhat bewildered by what you have just told me. To be born, or at any rate, bred in a handbag, whether it had handles or not, seems to me to display
490   a contempt for the ordinary decencies of family life that remind one of the worst excesses of the French Revolution. And I presume you know what that unfortunate movement led to? As for the particular locality in which the handbag was found, a cloakroom at a railway station might serve to conceal a social indiscretion—has probably, indeed, been used for that purpose before now—but it could hardly be regarded as an assured basis for a recognized position in good society.

JACK   May I ask you then what you would advise me to do? I need hardly say I would do anything in the world to ensure Gwendolen's happiness.

LADY BRACKNELL   I would strongly advise you, Mr. Worthing, to try and
500   acquire some relations as soon as possible, and to make a definite effort to produce at any rate one parent, of either sex, before the season is quite over.

JACK Well, I don't see how I could possibly manage to do that. I can produce the handbag at any moment. It is in my dressing-room at home. I really think that should satisfy you, Lady Bracknell.

LADY BRACKNELL Me, sir! What has it to do with me? You can hardly imagine that I and Lord Bracknell would dream of allowing our only daughter—a girl brought up with the utmost care—to marry into a cloakroom, and form an alliance with a parcel? Good morning, Mr. Worthing!

[LADY BRACKNELL *sweeps out in majestic indignation.*]

JACK Good morning! [ALGERNON, *from the other room, strikes up the* Wed-
510 ding March. JACK *looks perfectly furious, and goes to the door.*] For goodness' sake don't play that ghastly tune, Algy! How idiotic you are!

[*The music stops, and* ALGERNON *enters cheerily.*]

ALGERNON Didn't it go off all right, old boy? You don't mean to say Gwendolen refused you? I know it is a way she has. She is always refusing people. I think it is most ill-natured of her.

JACK Oh, Gwendolen is as right as a trivet. As far as she is concerned, we are engaged. Her mother is perfectly unbearable. Never met such a gorgon . . . I don't really know what a gorgon is like, but I am quite sure that Lady Bracknell is one. In any case, she is a monster, without being a myth, which is rather unfair . . . I beg your pardon, Algy, I suppose I shouldn't talk about your own
520 aunt in that way before you.

ALGERNON My dear boy, I love hearing my relations abused. It is the only thing that makes me put up with them at all. Relations are simply a tedious pack of people who haven't got the remotest knowledge of how to live, nor the smallest instinct about when to die.

JACK Oh, that is nonsense!

ALGERNON It isn't!

JACK Well, I won't argue about the matter. You always want to argue about things.

ALGERNON That is exactly what things were originally made for.
530 JACK Upon my word, if I thought that, I'd shoot myself. . . . [*A pause.*] You don't think there is any chance of Gwendolen becoming like her mother in about a hundred and fifty years, do you, Algy?

ALGERNON All women become like their mothers. That is their tragedy. No man does. That's his.

JACK Is that clever?

ALGERNON It is perfectly phrased! and quite as true as any observation in civilized life should be.

JACK I am sick to death of cleverness. Everybody is clever nowadays. You can't go anywhere without meeting clever people. The thing has become an
540 absolute public nuisance. I wish to goodness we had a few fools left.

ALGERNON We have.

JACK I should extremely like to meet them. What do they talk about?

ALGERNON   The fools! Oh! about the clever people, of course.

JACK   What fools!

ALGERNON   By the way, did you tell Gwendolen the truth about your being Ernest in town, and Jack in the country?

JACK [*In a very patronizing manner.*]   My dear fellow, the truth isn't quite the sort of thing one tells to a nice sweet refined girl. What extraordinary ideas you have about the way to behave to a woman!

550   ALGERNON   The only way to behave to a woman is to make love to her, if she is pretty, and to someone else if she is plain.

JACK   Oh, that is nonsense.

ALGERNON   What about your brother? What about the profligate Ernest?

JACK   Oh, before the end of the week I shall have got rid of him. I'll say he died in Paris of apoplexy. Lots of people die of apoplexy, quite suddenly, don't they?

ALGERNON   Yes, but it's hereditary, my dear fellow. It's a sort of thing that runs in families. You had much better say a severe chill.

JACK   You are sure a severe chill isn't hereditary, or anything of that kind?

560   ALGERNON   Of course it isn't!

JACK   Very well, then. My poor brother Ernest is carried off suddenly in Paris, by a severe chill. That gets rid of him.

ALGERNON   But I thought you said that . . . Miss Cardew was a little too much interested in your poor brother Ernest? Won't she feel his loss a good deal?

JACK   Oh, that is all right. Cecily is not a silly romantic girl, I am glad to say. She has got a capital appetite, goes long walks, and pays no attention at all to her lessons.

ALGERNON   I would rather like to see Cecily.

570   JACK   I will take very good care you never do. She is excessively pretty, and she is only just eighteen.

ALGERNON   Have you told Gwendolen yet that you have an excessively pretty ward who is only just eighteen?

JACK   Oh! one doesn't blurt these things out to people. Cecily and Gwendolen are perfectly certain to be extremely great friends. I'll bet you anything you like that half an hour after they have met, they will be calling each other sister.

ALGERNON   Women only do that when they have called each other a lot of other things first. Now, my dear boy, if we want to get a good table at Willis's,

580   we really must go and dress. Do you know it is nearly seven?

JACK [*Irritably.*]   Oh! It always is nearly seven.

ALGERNON   Well, I'm hungry.

JACK   I never knew you when you weren't. . . .

ALGERNON   What shall we do after dinner? Go to the theatre?

JACK   Oh no! I loathe listening.

ALGERNON   Well, let us go to the club?

JACK   Oh, no! I hate talking.

ALGERNON   Well, we might trot round to the Empire at ten?

JACK   Oh no! I can't bear looking at things. It is so silly.

590   ALGERNON Well, what shall we do?

JACK Nothing!

ALGERNON It is awfully hard work doing nothing. However, I don't mind hard work where there is no definite object of any kind.

[*Enter* LANE.]

LANE Miss Fairfax.

[*Enter* GWENDOLEN. LANE *goes out.*]

ALGERNON Gwendolen, upon my word!

GWENDOLEN Algy, kindly turn your back. I have something very particular to say to Mr. Worthing.

ALGERNON Really, Gwendolen, I don't think I can allow this at all.

GWENDOLEN Algy, you always adopt a strictly immoral attitude towards life.
600 You are not quite old enough to do that. [ALGERNON *retires to the fireplace.*]

JACK My own darling!

GWENDOLEN Ernest, we may never be married. From the expression on Mamma's face I fear we never shall. Few parents nowadays pay any regard to what their children say to them. The old-fashioned respect for the young is fast dying out. Whatever influence I ever had over Mamma, I lost at the age of three. But although she may prevent us from becoming man and wife, and I may marry someone else, and marry often, nothing that she can possibly do can alter my eternal devotion to you.

JACK Dear Gwendolen!

610   GWENDOLEN The story of your romantic origin, as related to me by Mamma, with unpleasing comments, has naturally stirred the deeper fibres of my nature. Your Christian name has an irresistible fascination. The simplicity of your character makes you exquisitely incomprehensible to me. Your town address at the Albany I have. What is your address in the country?

JACK The Manor House, Woolton, Hertfordshire.

[ALGERNON, *who has been carefully listening, smiles to himself, and writes the address on his shirt-cuff. Then picks up the Railway Guide.*]

GWENDOLEN There is a good postal service, I suppose? It may be necessary to do something desperate. That of course will require serious consideration. I will communicate with you daily.

JACK My own one!

620   GWENDOLEN How long do you remain in town?

JACK Till Monday.

GWENDOLEN Good! Algy, you may turn round now.

ALGERNON Thanks, I've turned round already.

GWENDOLEN You may also ring the bell.

JACK You will let me see you to your carriage, my own darling?

GWENDOLEN Certainly.

JACK [*To* LANE, *who now enters.*]   I will see Miss Fairfax out.
LANE   Yes, sir. [JACK *and* GWENDOLEN *go off.*]

[LANE *presents several letters on a salver to* ALGERNON. *It is to be surmised that they are bills, as* ALGERNON *after looking at the envelopes, tears them up.*]

ALGERNON   A glass of sherry, Lane.
630   LANE   Yes, sir.
ALGERNON   Tomorrow, Lane, I'm going Bunburying.
LANE   Yes, sir.
ALGERNON   I shall probably not be back till Monday. You can put up my dress clothes, my smoking jacket, and all the Bunbury suits. . . .
LANE   Yes, sir. [*Handing sherry.*]
ALGERNON   I hope tomorrow will be a fine day, Lane.
LANE   It never is, sir.
ALGERNON   Lane, you're a perfect pessimist.
LANE   I do my best to give satisfaction, sir.

[*Enter* JACK. LANE *goes off.*]

640   JACK   There's a sensible, intellectual girl! The only girl I ever cared for in my life. [ALGERNON *is laughing immoderately.*] What on earth are you so amused at?
ALGERNON   Oh, I'm a little anxious about poor Bunbury, that is all.
JACK   If you don't take care, your friend Bunbury will get you into a serious scrape some day.
ALGERNON   I love scrapes. They are the only things that are never serious.
JACK   Oh, that's nonsense, Algy. You never talk anything but nonsense.
ALGERNON   Nobody ever does.

[JACK *looks indignantly at him, and leaves the room.* ALGERNON *lights a cigarette, reads his shirt-cuff, and smiles.*]

Act-Drop.

Second Act

Scene. *Garden at the Manor House. A flight of grey stone steps leads up to the house. The garden, an old-fashioned one, full of roses. Time of year, July. Basket chairs, and a table covered with books, are set under a large yew tree.*
    [MISS PRISM *discovered seated at the table.* CECILY *is at the back watering flowers.*]

MISS PRISM [*Calling.*]   Cecily, Cecily! Surely such a utilitarian occupation as the watering of flowers is rather Moulton's duty than yours? Especially at a moment when intellectual pleasures await you. Your German grammar is on the table. Pray open it at page fifteen. We will repeat yesterday's lesson.

CECILY [*Coming over very slowly.*]   But I don't like German. It isn't at all a becoming language. I know perfectly well that I look quite plain after my German lesson.

MISS PRISM   Child, you know how anxious your guardian is that you should improve yourself in every way. He laid particular stress on your German, as
10 he was leaving for town yesterday. Indeed, he always lays stress on your German when he is leaving for town.

CECILY   Dear Uncle Jack is so very serious! Sometimes he is so serious that I think he cannot be quite well.

MISS PRISM [*Drawing herself up.*]   Your guardian enjoys the best of health, and his gravity of demeanour is especially to be commended in one so comparatively young as he is. I know no one who has a higher sense of duty and responsibility.

CECILY   I suppose that is why he often looks a little bored when we three are together.
20   MISS PRISM   Cecily! I am surprised at you. Mr. Worthing has many troubles in his life. Idle merriment and triviality would be out of place in his conversation. You must remember his constant anxiety about that unfortunate young man his brother.

CECILY   I wish Uncle Jack would allow that unfortunate young man, his brother, to come down here sometimes. We might have a good influence over him, Miss Prism. I am sure you certainly would. You know German, and Geology, and things of that kind influence a man very much. [CECILY *begins to write in her diary.*]

MISS PRISM [*Shaking her head.*]   I do not think that even I could produce
30 any effect on a character that according to his own brother's admission is irretrievably weak and vacillating. Indeed I am not sure that I would desire to reclaim him. I am not in favour of this modern mania for turning bad people into good people at a moment's notice. As a man sows so let him reap. You must put away your diary, Cecily. I really don't see why you should keep a diary at all.

CECILY   I keep a diary in order to enter the wonderful secrets of my life. If I didn't write them down I should probably forget all about them.

MISS PRISM   Memory, my dear Cecily, is the diary that we all carry about with us.
40   CECILY   Yes, but it usually chronicles the things that have never happened, and couldn't possibly have happened. I believe that memory is responsible for nearly all the three-volume novels that Mudie sends us.

MISS PRISM   Do not speak slightingly of the three-volume novel, Cecily. I wrote one myself in earlier days.

CECILY   Did you really, Miss Prism? How wonderfully clever you are! I hope it did not end happily? I don't like novels that end happily. They depress me so much.

MISS PRISM   The good ended happily, and the bad unhappily. That is what fiction means.
50   CECILY   I suppose so. But it seems very unfair. And was your novel ever published?

MISS PRISM   Alas! no. The manuscript unfortunately was abandoned. I use the word in the sense of lost or mislaid. To your work, child, these specula- tions are profitless.

CECILY [*Smiling.*]   But I see dear Dr. Chasuble coming up through the garden.

MISS PRISM [*Rising and advancing.*]   Dr. Chasuble! This is indeed a pleasure.

[*Enter* CANON CHASUBLE.]

CHASUBLE   And how are we this morning? Miss Prism, you are, I trust, well?

CECILY   Miss Prism has just been complaining of a slight headache. I think
60 it would do her so much good to have a short stroll with you in the Park, Dr. Chasuble.

MISS PRISM   Cecily, I have not mentioned anything about a headache.

CECILY   No, dear Miss Prism, I know that, but I felt instinctively that you had a headache. Indeed I was thinking about that, and not about my German lesson, when the Rector came in.

CHASUBLE   I hope, Cecily, you are not inattentive.

CECILY   Oh, I am afraid I am.

CHASUBLE   That is strange. Were I fortunate enough to be Miss Prism's pupil, I would hang upon her lips. [MISS PRISM *glares.*] I spoke metaphori-
70 cally.—My metaphor was drawn from bees. Ahem! Mr. Worthing, I suppose, has not returned from town yet?

MISS PRISM   We do not expect him till Monday afternoon.

CHASUBLE   Ah yes, he usually likes to spend his Sunday in London. He is not one of those whose sole aim is enjoyment, as, by all accounts, that unfortunate young man his brother seems to be. But I must not disturb Egeria and her pupil any longer.

MISS PRISM   Egeria? My name is Laetitia, Doctor.

CHASUBLE [*Bowing.*]   A classical allusion merely, drawn from the pagan authors. I shall see you both no doubt at Evensong?
80 MISS PRISM   I think, dear Doctor, I will have a stroll with you. I find I have a headache after all, and a walk might do it good.

CHASUBLE   With pleasure, Miss Prism, with pleasure. We might go as far as the schools and back.

MISS PRISM   That would be delightful. Cecily, you will read your Political Economy in my absence. The chapter on the Fall of the Rupee you may omit. It is somewhat too sensational. Even these metallic problems have their melodramatic side.

[*Goes down the garden with* DR. CHASUBLE.]

CECILY [*Picks up books and throws them back on table.*]   Horrid Political Economy! Horrid Geography! Horrid, horrid German!

[*Enter* MERRIMAN *with a card on a salver.*]

90   MERRIMAN   Mr. Ernest Worthing has just driven over from the station. He
has brought his luggage with him.

       CECILY [*Takes the card and reads it.*]   "Mr. Ernest Worthing, B. 4 The
Albany, W." Uncle Jack's brother! Did you tell him Mr. Worthing was in town?

       MERRIMAN   Yes, Miss. He seemed very much disappointed. I mentioned
that you and Miss Prism were in the garden. He said he was anxious to speak
to you privately for a moment.

       CECILY   Ask Mr. Ernest Worthing to come here. I suppose you had better
talk to the housekeeper about a room for him.

       MERRIMAN   Yes, Miss.   [MERRIMAN *goes off.*]

100   CECILY   I have never met any really wicked person before. I feel rather
frightened. I am so afraid he will look just like everyone else.

[*Enter* ALGERNON, *very gay and debonair.*]

He does!

       ALGERNON [*Raising his hat.*]   You are my little cousin Cecily, I'm sure.

       CECILY   You are under some strange mistake. I am not little. In fact, I
believe I am more than usually tall for my age. [ALGERNON *is rather taken
aback.*] But I am your cousin Cecily. You, I see from your card, are Uncle
Jack's brother, my cousin Ernest, my wicked cousin Ernest.

       ALGERNON   Oh! I am not really wicked at all, cousin Cecily. You mustn't
think that I am wicked.

110   CECILY   If you are not, then you have certainly been deceiving us all in a
very inexcusable manner. I hope you have not been leading a double life,
pretending to be wicked and being really good all the time. That would be
hypocrisy.

       ALGERNON   [*Looks at her in amazement.*]   Oh! Of course I have been
rather reckless.

       CECILY   I am glad to hear it.

       ALGERNON   In fact, now you mention the subject, I have been very bad in
my own small way.

       CECILY   I don't think you should be so proud of that, though I am sure it
120 must have been very pleasant.

       ALGERNON   It is much pleasanter being here with you.

       CECILY   I can't understand how you are here at all. Uncle Jack won't be
back till Monday afternoon.

       ALGERNON   That is a great disappointment. I am obliged to go up by the
first train on Monday morning. I have a business appointment that I am
anxious . . . to miss.

       CECILY   Couldn't you miss it anywhere but in London?

       ALGERNON   No; the appointment is in London.

       CECILY   Well, I know, of course, how important it is not to keep a business
130 engagement, if one wants to retain any sense of the beauty of life, but still
I think you had better wait till Uncle Jack arrives. I know he wants to speak to
you about your emigrating.

ALGERNON About my what?

CECILY Your emigrating. He has gone up to buy your outfit.

ALGERNON I certainly wouldn't let Jack buy my outfit. He has no taste in neckties at all.

CECILY I don't think you will require neckties. Uncle Jack is sending you to Australia.

ALGERNON Australia? I'd sooner die.

140   CECILY Well, he said at dinner on Wednesday night, that you would have to choose between this world, the next world, and Australia.

ALGERNON Oh, well! The accounts I have received of Australia and the next world are not particularly encouraging. This world is good enough for me, cousin Cecily.

CECILY Yes, but are you good enough for it?

ALGERNON I'm afraid I'm not that. That is why I want you to reform me. You might make that your mission, if you don't mind, cousin Cecily.

CECILY I'm afraid I've no time, this afternoon.

ALGERNON Well, would you mind my reforming myself this afternoon?

150   CECILY It is rather quixotic of you. But I think you should try.

ALGERNON I will. I feel better already.

CECILY You are looking a little worse.

ALGERNON That is because I am hungry.

CECILY How thoughtless of me. I should have remembered that when one is going to lead an entirely new life, one requires regular and wholesome meals. Won't you come in?

ALGERNON Thank you. Might I have a button-hole first? I never have any appetite unless I have a button-hole first.

CECILY A Maréchal Niel? [*Picks up scissors.*]

160   ALGERNON No, I'd sooner have a pink rose.

CECILY Why? [*Cuts a flower.*]

ALGERNON Because you are like a pink rose, cousin Cecily.

CECILY I don't think it can be right for you to talk to me like that. Miss Prism never says such things to me.

ALGERNON Then Miss Prism is a short-sighted old lady. [CECILY *puts the rose in his button-hole.*] You are the prettiest girl I ever saw.

CECILY Miss Prism says that all good looks are a snare.

ALGERNON They are a snare that every sensible man would like to be caught in.

170   CECILY Oh! I don't think I would care to catch a sensible man. I shouldn't know what to talk to him about.

[*They pass into the house.* MISS PRISM *and* DR. CHASUBLE *return.*]

MISS PRISM You are too much alone, dear Dr. Chasuble. You should get married. A misanthrope I can understand—a womanthrope, never!

CHASUBLE [*With a scholar's shudder.*] Believe me, I do not deserve so neologistic a phrase. The precept as well as the practice of the Primitive Church was distinctly against matrimony.

MISS PRISM [*Sententiously.*]   That is obviously the reason why the Primitive Church has not lasted up to the present day. And you do not seem to realize, dear Doctor, that by persistently remaining single, a man converts himself
180   into a permanent public temptation. Men should be more careful; this very celibacy leads weaker vessels astray.

CHASUBLE   But is a man not equally attractive when married?

MISS PRISM   No married man is ever attractive except to his wife.

CHASUBLE   And often, I've been told, not even to her.

MISS PRISM   That depends on the intellectual sympathies of the woman. Maturity can always be depended on. Ripeness can be trusted. Young women are green. [DR. CHASUBLE *starts.*] I spoke horticulturally. My metaphor was drawn from fruits. But where is Cecily?

CHASUBLE   Perhaps she followed us to the schools.

[*Enter* JACK *slowly from the back of the garden. He is dressed in the deepest mourning, with crape hatband and black gloves.*]

190   MISS PRISM   Mr. Worthing!

CHASUBLE   Mr. Worthing?

MISS PRISM   This is indeed a surprise. We did not look for you till Monday afternoon.

JACK [*Shakes* MISS PRISM's *hand in a tragic manner.*]   I have returned sooner than I expected. Dr. Chasuble, I hope you are well?

CHASUBLE   Dear Mr. Worthing, I trust this garb of woe does not betoken some terrible calamity?

JACK   My brother.

MISS PRISM   More shameful debts and extravagance?

200   CHASUBLE   Still leading his life of pleasure?

JACK [*Shaking his head.*]   Dead!

CHASUBLE   Your brother Ernest dead?

JACK   Quite dead.

MISS PRISM   What a lesson for him! I trust he will profit by it.

CHASUBLE   Mr. Worthing, I offer you my sincere condolence. You have at least the consolation of knowing that you were always the most generous and forgiving of brothers.

JACK   Poor Ernest! He had many faults, but it is a sad, sad blow.

CHASUBLE   Very sad indeed. Were you with him at the end?

210   JACK   No. He died abroad; in Paris, in fact. I had a telegram last night from the manager of the Grand Hotel.

CHASUBLE   Was the cause of death mentioned?

JACK   A severe chill, it seems.

MISS PRISM   As a man sows, so shall he reap.

CHASUBLE [*Raising his hand.*]   Charity, dear Miss Prism, charity! None of us are perfect. I myself am peculiarly susceptible to draughts. Will the interment take place here?

JACK   No. He seemed to have expressed a desire to be buried in Paris.

CHASUBLE In Paris! [*Shakes his head.*] I feat that hardly points to any very
220 serious state of mind at the last. You would no doubt wish me to make some
slight allusion to this tragic domestic affliction next Sunday. [JACK *presses his
hand convulsively.*] My sermon on the meaning of the manna in the
wilderness can be adapted to almost any occasion, joyful, or, as in the
present case, distressing. [*All* sigh.] I have preached it at harvest celebrations,
christenings, confirmations, on days of humiliation and festal days. The last
time I delivered it was in the Cathedral, as a charity sermon on behalf of the
Society for the Prevention of Discontent among the Upper Orders. The
Bishop, who was present, was much struck by some of the analogies I drew.

JACK Ah! that reminds me, you mentioned christenings, I think, Dr.
230 Chasuble? I suppose you know how to christen all right? [DR. CHASUBLE *looks
astounded.*] I mean, of course, you are continually christening, aren't you?

MISS PRISM It is, I regret to say, one of the Rector's most constant duties in
this parish. I have often spoken to the poorer classes on the subject. But they
don't seem to know what thrift is.

CHASUBLE But is there any particular infant in whom you are interested,
Mr. Worthing? Your brother was, I believe unmarried, was he not?

JACK Oh, yes.

MISS PRISM [*Bitterly.*]   People who live entirely for pleasure usually are.

JACK But it is not for any child, dear Doctor. I am very fond of children.
240 No! the fact is, I would like to be christened myself, this afternoon, if you
have nothing better to do.

CHASUBLE But surely, Mr. Worthing, you have been christened already?

JACK I don't remember anything about it.

CHASUBLE But have you any grave doubts on the subject?

JACK I certainly intend to have. Of course I don't know if the thing would
bother you in any way, or if you think I am a little too old now.

CHASUBLE Not at all. The sprinkling, and, indeed, the immersion of adults
is a perfectly canonical practice.

JACK Immersion!

250 CHASUBLE You need have no apprehensions. Sprinkling is all that is necessary, or indeed I think advisable. Our weather is so changeable. At what hour
would you wish the ceremony performed?

JACK Oh, I might trot round about five if that would suit you.

CHASUBLE Perfectly, perfectly! In fact I have two similar ceremonies to
perform at that time. A case of twins that occurred recently in one of the
outlying cottages on your own estate. Poor Jenkins the carter, a most hard-
working man.

JACK Oh! I don't see much fun in being christened along with other
babies. It would be childish. Would half-past five do?

260 CHASUBLE Admirably! Admirably! [*Takes out watch.*] And now, dear Mr.
Worthing, I will not intrude any longer into a house of sorrow. I would
merely beg you not to be too much bowed down by grief. What seems to us
bitter trials are often blessings in disguise.

MISS PRISM This seems to me a blessing of an extremely obvious kind.

[*Enter* CECILY *from the house.*]

CECILY   Uncle Jack! Oh, I am pleased to see you back. But what horrid clothes you have got on! Do go and change them.

MISS PRISM   Cecily!

CHASUBLE   My child! my child! [CECILY *goes towards* JACK; *he kisses her brow in a melancholy manner.*]

270   CECILY   What is the matter, Uncle Jack? Do look happy! You look as if you had a toothache, and I have got such a surprise for you. Who do you think is in the dining-room? Your brother!

JACK   Who?

CECILY   Your brother Ernest. He arrived about half an hour ago.

JACK   What nonsense! I haven't got a brother!

CECILY   Oh, don't say that. However badly he may have behaved to you in the past he is still your brother. You couldn't be so heartless as to disown him. I'll tell him to come out. And you will shake hands with him, won't you, Uncle Jack? [*Runs back into the house.*]

280   CHASUBLE   These are very joyful tidings.

MISS PRISM   After we had all been resigned to his loss, his sudden return seems to me peculiarly distressing.

JACK   My brother is in the dining-room? I don't know what it all means. I think it is perfectly absurd.

[*Enter* ALGERNON *and* CECILY *hand in hand. They come slowly up to* JACK.]

JACK   Good heavens! [*Motions* ALGERNON *away.*]

ALGERNON   Brother John, I have come down from town to tell you that I am very sorry for all the trouble I have given you, and that I intend to lead a better life in the future. [JACK *glares at him and does not take his hand.*]

CECILY   Uncle Jack, you are not going to refuse your own brother's hand?

290   JACK   Nothing will induce me to take his hand. I think his coming down here disgraceful. He knows perfectly well why.

CECILY   Uncle Jack, do be nice. There is some good in everyone. Ernest has just been telling me about his poor invalid friend Mr. Bunbury whom he goes to visit so often. And surely there must be much good in one who is kind to an invalid, and leaves the pleasures of London to sit by a bed of pain.

JACK   Oh! he has been talking about Bunbury, has he?

CECILY   Yes, he has told me all about poor Mr. Bunbury, and his terrible state of health.

JACK   Bunbury! Well, I won't have him talk to you about Bunbury or about

300   anything else. It is enough to drive one perfectly frantic.

ALGERNON   Of course I admit that the faults were all on my side. But I must say that I think that Brother John's coldness to me is peculiarly painful. I expected a more enthusiastic welcome, especially considering it is the first time I have come here.

CECILY   Uncle Jack, if you don't shake hands with Ernest, I will never forgive you.

JACK   Never forgive me?

CECILY   Never, never, never!

JACK   Well, this is the last time I shall ever do it.

[Shakes hands with ALGERNON *and glares.]*

310   CHASUBLE   It's pleasant, is it not, to see so perfect a reconciliation? I think we might leave the two brothers together.

MISS PRISM   Cecily, you will come with us.

CECILY   Certainly, Miss Prism. My little task of reconciliation is over.

CHASUBLE   You have done a beautiful action today, dear child.

MISS PRISM   We must not be premature in our judgments.

CECILY   I feel very happy. *[They all go off.]*

JACK   You young scoundrel, Algy, you must get out of this place as soon as possible. I don't allow any Bunburying here.

[Enter MERRIMAN.*]*

MERRIMAN   I have put Mr. Ernest's things in the room next to yours, sir. I
320   suppose that is all right?

JACK   What?

MERRIMAN   Mr. Ernest's luggage, sir. I have unpacked it and put it in the room next to your own.

JACK   His luggage?

MERRIMAN   Yes, sir. Three portmanteaus, a dressing-case, two hat boxes, and a large luncheon-basket.

ALGERNON   I am afraid I can't stay more than a week this time.

JACK   Merriman, order the dog-cart at once. Mr. Ernest has been suddenly called back to town.

330   MERRIMAN   Yes, sir. *[Goes back into the house.]*

ALGERNON   What a fearful liar you are, Jack. I have not been called back to town at all.

JACK   Yes, you have.

ALGERNON   I haven't heard anyone call me.

JACK   Your duty as a gentleman calls you back.

ALGERNON   My duty as a gentleman has never interfered with my pleasures in the smallest degree.

JACK   I can quite understand that.

ALGERNON   Well, Cecily is a darling.

340   JACK   You are not to talk of Miss Cardew like that. I don't like it.

ALGERNON   Well, I don't like your clothes. You look perfectly ridiculous in them. Why on earth don't you go up and change? It is perfectly childish to be in deep mourning for a man who is actually staying for a whole week with you in your house as a guest. I call it grotesque.

JACK   You are certainly not staying with me for a whole week as a guest or anything else. You have got to leave . . . by the four-five train.

ALGERNON   I certainly won't leave you so long as you are in mourning. It would be most unfriendly. If I were in mourning you would stay with me, I suppose. I should think it very unkind if you didn't.

350   JACK   Well, will you go if I change my clothes?

ALGERNON   Yes, if you are not too long. I never saw anybody take so long to dress, and with such little result.

JACK   Well, at any rate, that is better than being always overdressed as you are.

ALGERNON   If I am occasionally a little overdressed, I make up for it by being always immensely overeducated.

JACK   Your vanity is ridiculous, your conduct an outrage, and your presence in my garden utterly absurd. However, you have got to catch the four-five, and I hope you will have a pleasant journey back to town. This Bunburying, as you 360 call it, has not been a great success for you.   [*Goes into the house.*]

ALGERNON   I think it has been a great success. I'm in love with Cecily, and that is everything.

[*Enter* CECILY *at the back of the garden. She picks up the can and begins to water the flowers.*]

But I must see her before I go, and make arrangements for another Bunbury. Ah, there she is.

CECILY   Oh, I merely came back to water the roses. I thought you were with Uncle Jack.

ALGERNON   He's gone to order the dog-cart for me.

CECILY   Oh, is he going to take you for a nice drive?

ALGERNON   He's going to send me away.

370   CECILY   Then have we got to part?

ALGERNON   I am afraid so. It's very painful parting.

CECILY   It is always painful to part from people whom one has known for a very brief space of time. The absence of old friends one can endure with equanimity. But even a momentary separation from anyone to whom one has just been introduced is almost unbearable.

ALGERNON   Thank you.

[*Enter* MERRIMAN.]

MERRIMAN   The dog-cart is at the door, sir. [ALGERNON *looks appealingly at* CECILY.]

CECILY   It can wait, Merriman . . . for . . . five minutes.

380   MERRIMAN   Yes, Miss.   [*Exit* MERRIMAN.]

ALGERNON   I hope, Cecily, I shall not offend you if I state quite frankly and openly that you seem to me to be in every way the visible personification of absolute perfection.

CECILY   I think your frankness does you great credit, Ernest. If you will allow me I will copy your remarks into my diary. [*Goes over to table and begins writing in diary.*]

ALGERNON   Do you really keep a diary? I'd give anything to look at it. May I?

CECILY   Oh no. [*Puts her hand over it.*] You see, it is simply a very young girl's record of her own thoughts and impressions, and consequently meant 390 for publication. When it appears in volume form I hope you will order a copy. But pray, Ernest, don't stop. I delight in taking down from dictation. I have reached "absolute perfection." You can go on. I am quite ready for more.

ALGERNON [*Somewhat taken aback.*]   Ahem! Ahem!

CECILY   Oh, don't cough, Ernest. When one is dictating one should speak fluently and not cough. Besides, I don't know how to spell a cough.

[*Writes as* ALGERNON *speaks.*]

ALGERNON [*Speaking very rapidly.*]   Cecily, ever since I first looked upon your wonderful and incomparable beauty, I have dared to love you wildly, passionately, devotedly, hopelessly.

CECILY   I don't think that you should tell me that you love me wildly,
400 passionately, devotedly, hopelessly. Hopelessly doesn't seem to make much sense, does it?

ALGERNON   Cecily!

[*Enter* MERRIMAN.]

MERRIMAN   The dog-cart is waiting, sir.

ALGERNON   Tell it to come round next week, at the same hour.

MERRIMAN [*Looks at* CECILY, *who makes no sign.*]
Yes, sir.   [MERRIMAN *retires.*]

CECILY   Uncle Jack would be very much annoyed if he knew you were staying on till next week, at the same hour.

ALGERNON   Oh, I don't care about Jack. I don't care for anybody in the
410 whole world but you. I love you, Cecily. You will marry me, won't you?

CECILY   You silly boy! Of course. Why, we have been engaged for the last three months.

ALGERNON   For the last three months?

CECILY   Yes, it will be exactly three months on Thursday.

ALGERNON   But how did we become engaged?

CECILY   Well, ever since dear Uncle Jack first confessed to us that he had a younger brother who was very wicked and bad, you of course have formed the chief topic of conversation between myself and Miss Prism. And of course a man who is much talked about is always very attractive. One feels there
420 must be something in him after all. I daresay it was foolish of me, but I fell in love with you, Ernest.

ALGERNON   Darling! And when was the engagement actually settled?

CECILY   On the 14th of February last. Worn out by your entire ignorance of my existence, I determined to end the matter one way or the other, and after a long struggle with myself I accepted you under this dear old tree here. The next day I bought this little ring in your name, and this is the little bangle with the true lovers' knot I promised you always to wear.

ALGERNON   Did I give you this? It's very pretty, isn't it?

CECILY   Yes, you've wonderfully good taste, Ernest. It's the excuse I've al-
430 ways given for your leading such a bad life. And this is the box in which I keep all your dear letters. [*Kneels at table, opens box, and produces letters tied up with blue ribbon.*]

ALGERNON   My letters! But my own sweet Cecily, I have never written you any letters.

CECILY   You need hardly remind me of that, Ernest. I remember only too well that I was forced to write your letters for you. I always wrote three times a week, and sometimes oftener.

ALGERNON   Oh, do let me read them, Cecily?

CECILY   Oh, I couldn't possibly. They would make you far too conceited.
440 [*Replaces box.*] The three you wrote me after I had broken off the engagement are so beautiful, and so badly spelled, that even now I can hardly read them without crying a little.

ALGERNON   But was our engagement ever broken off?

CECILY   Of course it was. On the 22nd of March. You can see the entry if you like. [*Shows diary.*] "Today I broke off my engagement with Ernest. I feel it is better to do so. The weather still continues charming."

ALGERNON   But why on earth did you break it off? What had I done? I had done nothing at all. Cecily, I am very much hurt indeed to hear you broke it off. Particularly when the weather was so charming.
450   CECILY   It would hardly have been a really serious engagement if it hadn't been broken off at least once. But I forgave you before the week was out.

ALGERNON [*Crossing to her, and kneeling.*]   What a perfect angel you are, Cecily.

CECILY   You dear romantic boy. [*He kisses her, she puts her fingers through his hair.*] I hope your hair curls naturally, does it?

ALGERNON   Yes, darling, with a little help from others.

CECILY   I am so glad.

ALGERNON   You'll never break off our engagement again, Cecily?

CECILY   I don't think I could break it off now that I have actually met you.
460 Besides, of course, there is the question of your name.

ALGERNON   Yes, of course. [*Nervously.*]

CECILY   You must not laugh at me, darling, but it had always been a girlish dream of mine to love someone whose name was Ernest. [ALGERNON *rises.* CECILY *also.*] There is something in that name that seems to inspire absolute confidence. I pity any poor married woman whose husband is not called Ernest.

ALGERNON   But, my dear child, do you mean to say you could not love me if I had some other name?

CECILY   But what name?
470   ALGERNON   Oh, any name you like—Algernon—for instance. . . .

CECILY   But I don't like the name of Algernon.

ALGERNON   Well, my own dear, sweet, loving little darling, I really can't see why you should object to the name of Algernon. It is not at all a bad name. In fact, it is rather an aristocratic name. Half of the chaps who get into the Bankruptcy Court are called Algernon. But seriously, Cecily . . . [*Moving to her.*] . . . if my name was Algy, couldn't you love me?

CECILY [*Rising.*]   I might respect you, Ernest, I might admire your character, but I fear that I should not be able to give you my undivided attention.

ALGERNON   Ahem! Cecily! [*Picking up hat.*] Your Rector here is, I suppose,
480 thoroughly experienced in the practice of all the rites and ceremonials of the Church?

CECILY   Oh, yes. Dr. Chasuble is a most learned man. He has never written a single book, so you can imagine how much he knows.

ALGERNON   I must see him at once on a most important christening—I mean on most important business.

CECILY   Oh!

ALGERNON   I shan't be away more than half an hour.

CECILY   Considering that we have been engaged since February the 14th, and that I only met you today for the first time, I think it is rather hard that 490 you should leave me for so long a period as half an hour. Couldn't you make it twenty minutes?

ALGERNON   I'll be back in no time.

[Kisses her and rushes down the garden.]

CECILY   What an impetuous boy he is! I like his hair so much. I must enter his proposal in my diary.

[Enter MERRIMAN.*]*

MERRIMAN   A Miss Fairfax has just called to see Mr. Worthing. On very important business Miss Fairfax states.

CECILY   Isn't Mr. Worthing in his library?

MERRIMAN   Mr. Worthing went over in the direction of the Rectory some time ago.

500 CECILY   Pray ask the lady to come out here; Mr. Worthing is sure to be back soon. And you can bring tea.

MERRIMAN   Yes, Miss.   *[Goes out.]*

CECILY   Miss Fairfax! I suppose one of the many good elderly women who are associated with Uncle Jack in some of his philanthropic work in London. I don't quite like women who are interested in philanthropic work. I think it is so forward of them.

[Enter MERRIMAN.*]*

MERRIMAN   Miss Fairfax.

[Enter GWENDOLEN.*]*   *[Exit* MERRIMAN.*]*

CECILY *[Advancing to meet her.]*   Pray let me introduce myself to you. My name is Cecily Cardew.

510 GWENDOLEN   Cecily Cardew? *[Moving to her and shaking hands.]* What a very sweet name! Something tells me that we are going to be great friends. I like you already more than I can say. My first impressions of people are never wrong.

CECILY   How nice of you to like me so much after we have known each other such a comparatively short time. Pray sit down.

GWENDOLEN *[Still standing up.]*   I may call you Cecily, may I not?

CECILY With pleasure!

GWENDOLEN And you will always call me Gwendolen, won't you?

CECILY If you wish.

520 GWENDOLEN Then that is all quite settled, is it not?

CECILY I hope so. [*A pause. They both sit down together.*]

GWENDOLEN Perhaps this might be a favourable opportunity for my mentioning who I am. My father is Lord Bracknell. You have never heard of Papa, I suppose?

CECILY I don't think so.

GWENDOLEN Outside the family circle, Papa, I am glad to say, is entirely unknown. I think that is quite as it should be. The home seems to me to be the proper sphere for the man. And certainly once a man begins to neglect his domestic duties he becomes painfully effeminate, does he not? And I
530 don't like that. It makes men so very attractive. Cecily, Mamma, whose views on education are remarkably strict, has brought me up to be extremely short-sighted; it is part of her system; so do you mind my looking at you through my glasses?

CECILY Oh! not at all, Gwendolen. I am very fond of being looked at.

GWENDOLEN [*After examining* CECILY *carefully through a lorgnette.*] You are here on a short visit I suppose.

CECILY Oh no! I live here.

GWENDOLEN [*Severely.*] Really? Your mother, no doubt, or some female relative of advanced years, resides here also?

540 CECILY Oh no! I have no mother, nor, in fact, any relations.

GWENDOLEN Indeed?

CECILY My dear guardian, with the assistance of Miss Prism, has the arduous task of looking after me.

GWENDOLEN Your guardian?

CECILY Yes, I am Mr. Worthing's ward.

GWENDOLEN Oh! It is strange he never mentioned to me that he had a ward. How secretive of him! He grows more interesting hourly. I am not sure, however, that the news inspires me with feelings of unmixed delight. [*Rising and going to her.*] I am very fond of you, Cecily; I have liked you ever since I
550 met you! But I am bound to state that now that I know that you are Mr. Worthing's ward, I cannot help expressing a wish you were—well just a little older than you seem to be—and not quite so very alluring in appearance. In fact, if I may speak candidly—

CECILY Pray do! I think that whenever one has anything unpleasant to say, one should always be quite candid.

GWENDOLEN Well, to speak with perfect candour, Cecily, I wish that you were fully forty-two, and more than usually plain for your age. Ernest has a strong upright nature. He is the very soul of truth and honour. Disloyalty would be as impossible to him as deception. But even men of the noblest
560 possible moral character are extremely susceptible to the influence of the physical charms of others. Modern, no less than ancient history, supplies us with many most painful examples of what I refer to. If it were not so, indeed, history would be quite unreadable.

CECILY   I beg your pardon, Gwendolen, did you say Ernest?

GWENDOLEN   Yes.

CECILY   Oh, but it is not Mr. Ernest Worthing who is my guardian. It is his brother—his elder brother.

GWENDOLEN [*Sitting down again.*]   Ernest never mentioned to me that he had a brother.

570   CECILY   I am sorry to say they have not been on good terms for a long time.

GWENDOLEN   Ah! that accounts for it. And now that I think of it I have never heard any man mention his brother. The subject seems distasteful to most men. Cecily, you have lifted a load from my mind. I was growing almost anxious. It would have been terrible if any cloud had come across a friendship like ours, would it not? Of course you are quite, quite sure that it is not Mr. Ernest Worthing who is your guardian?

CECILY   Quite sure. [*A pause.*] In fact, I am going to be his.

GWENDOLEN [*Enquiringly.*]   I beg your pardon?

CECILY [*Rather shy and confidingly.*]   Dearest Gwendolen, there is no

580   reason why I should make a secret of it to you. Our little county newspaper is sure to chronicle the fact next week. Mr. Ernest Worthing and I are engaged to be married.

GWENDOLEN [*Quite politely, rising.*]   My darling Cecily, I think there must be some slight error. Mr. Ernest Worthing is engaged to me. The announcement will appear in the *Morning Post* on Saturday at the latest.

CECILY [*Very politely, rising.*]   I am afraid you must be under some misconception. Ernest proposed to me exactly ten minutes ago. [*Shows diary.*]

GWENDOLEN [*Examines diary through her lorgnette carefully.*]   It is certainly very curious, for he asked me to be his wife yesterday afternoon at

590   5:30. If you would care to verify the incident, pray do so. [*Produces diary of her own.*] I never travel without my diary. One should always have something sensational to read in the train. I am so sorry, dear Cecily, if it is any disappointment to you, but I am afraid *I* have the prior claim.

CECILY   It would distress me more than I can tell you, dear Gwendolen, if it caused you any mental or physical anguish, but I feel bound to point out that since Ernest proposed to you he clearly has changed his mind.

GWENDOLEN [*Meditatively.*]   If the poor fellow has been entrapped into any foolish promise I shall consider it my duty to rescue him at once, and with a firm hand.

600   CECILY [*Thoughtfully and sadly.*]   Whatever unfortunate entanglement my dear boy may have got into, I will never reproach him with it after we are married.

GWENDOLEN   Do you allude to me, Miss Cardew, as an entanglement? You are presumptuous. On an occasion of this kind it becomes more than a moral duty to speak one's mind. It becomes a pleasure.

CECILY   Do you suggest, Miss Fairfax, that I entrapped Ernest into an engagement? How dare you? This is no time for wearing the shallow mask of manners. When I see a spade I call it a spade.

GWENDOLEN [*Satirically.*]   I am glad to say that I have never seen a spade.

610   It is obvious that our social spheres have been widely different.

[*Enter* MERRIMAN, *followed by the footman. He carries a salver, table cloth, and plate stand.* CECILY *is about to retort. The presence of the servants exercises a restraining influence, under which both girls chafe.*]

MERRIMAN   Shall I lay tea here as usual, Miss?

CECILY [*Sternly, in a calm voice.*]   Yes, as usual. [MERRIMAN *begins to clear table and lay cloth. A long pause.* CECILY *and* GWENDOLEN *glare at each other.*]

GWENDOLEN   Are there many interesting walks in the vicinity, Miss Cardew?

CECILY   Oh! yes! a great many. From the top of one of the hills quite close one can see five counties.

GWENDOLEN   Five counties! I don't think I should like that. I hate crowds.

CECILY [*Sweetly.*]   I suppose that is why you live in town? [GWENDOLEN *bites her lip, and beats her foot nervously with her parasol.*]

620   GWENDOLEN [*Looking round.*]   Quite a well-kept garden this is, Miss Cardew.

CECILY   So glad you like it, Miss Fairfax.

GWENDOLEN   I had no idea there were any flowers in the country.

CECILY   Oh, flowers are as common here, Miss Fairfax, as people are in London.

GWENDOLEN   Personally I cannot understand how anybody manages to exist in the country, if anybody who is anybody does. The country always bores me to death.

CECILY   Ah! This is what the newspapers call agricultural depression, is it
630 not? I believe the aristocracy are suffering very much from it just at present. It is almost an epidemic amongst them, I have been told. May I offer you some tea, Miss Fairfax?

GWENDOLEN [*With elaborate politeness.*]   Thank you. [*Aside.*] Detestable girl! But I require tea!

CECILY [*Sweetly.*]   Sugar?

GWENDOLEN [*Superciliously.*]   No, thank you. Sugar is not fashionable any more. [CECILY *looks angrily at her, takes up the tongs and puts four lumps of sugar into the cup.*]

CECILY [*Severely.*]   Cake or bread and butter?

640   GWENDOLEN [*In a bored manner.*]   Bread and butter, please. Cake is rarely seen at the best houses nowadays.

CECILY [*Cuts a very large slice of cake, and puts it on the tray.*]   Hand that to Miss Fairfax.

[MERRIMAN *does so, and goes out with footman.* GWENDOLEN *drinks the tea and makes a grimace. Puts down cup at once, reaches out her hand to the bread and butter, looks at it, and finds it is cake. Rises in indignation.*]

GWENDOLEN   You have filled my tea with lumps of sugar, and though I asked most distinctly for bread and butter, you have given me cake. I am known for the gentleness of my disposition, and the extraordinary sweetness of my nature, but I warn you, Miss Cardew, you may go too far.

CECILY [*Rising.*]   To save my poor, innocent, trusting boy from the machi-
nations of any other girl there are no lengths to which I would not go.

650   GWENDOLEN   From the moment I saw you I distrusted you. I felt that you
were false and deceitful. I am never deceived in such matters. My first impressions of people are invariably right.

CECILY   It seems to me, Miss Fairfax, that I am trespassing on your valuable
time. No doubt you have many other calls of a similar character to make in
the neighbourhood.

[*Enter* JACK.]

GWENDOLEN [*Catching sight of him.*]   Ernest! My own Ernest!

JACK   Gwendolen! Darling! [*Offers to kiss her.*]

GWENDOLEN [*Drawing back.*]   A moment! May I ask if you are engaged to
be married to this young lady? [*Points to* CECILY.]

660   JACK [*Laughing.*]   To dear little Cecily! Of course not! What could have put
such an idea into your pretty little head?

GWENDOLEN   Thank you. You may! [*Offers her cheek.*]

CECILY [*Very sweetly.*]   I knew there must be some misunderstanding,
Miss Fairfax. The gentleman whose arm is at present round your waist is my
dear guardian, Mr. John Worthing.

GWENDOLEN   I beg your pardon?

CECILY   This is Uncle Jack.

GWENDOLEN [*Receding.*]   Jack! Oh!

[*Enter* ALGERNON.]

CECILY   Here is Ernest.

670   ALGERNON [*Goes straight over to* CECILY *without noticing anyone else.*]   My
own love! [*Offers to kiss her.*]

CECILY [*Drawing back.*]   A moment, Ernest! May I ask you—are you engaged to be married to this young lady?

ALGERNON [*Looking round.*]   To what young lady? Good heavens! Gwendolen!

CECILY   Yes! to good heavens, Gwendolen, I mean to Gwendolen.

ALGERNON [*Laughing.*]   Of course not! What could have put such an idea
into your pretty little head?

CECILY   Thank you. [*Presenting her cheek to be kissed.*] You may. [ALGERNON

680   *kisses her.*]

GWENDOLEN   I felt there was some slight error, Miss Cardew. The gentleman who is now embracing you is my cousin, Mr. Algernon Moncrieff.

CECILY [*Breaking away from* ALGERNON.]   Algernon Moncrieff! Oh! [*The
two girls move towards each other and put their arms round each other's
waists as if for protection.*]

CECILY   Are you called Algernon?

ALGERNON   I cannot deny it.

CECILY Oh!

GWENDOLEN Is your name really John?

690   JACK [*Standing rather proudly.*]   I could deny it if I liked. I could deny anything if I liked. But my name certainly is John. It has been John for years.

CECILY   [*To* GWENDOLEN.] A gross deception has been practised on both of us.

GWENDOLEN My poor wounded Cecily!

CECILY My sweet wronged Gwendolen!

GWENDOLEN [*Slowly and seriously.*]   You will call me sister, will you not? [*They embrace.* JACK *and* ALGERNON *groan and walk up and down.*]

CECILY [*Rather brightly.*]   There is just one question I would like to be allowed to ask my guardian.

700   GWENDOLEN An admirable idea! Mr. Worthing, there is just one question I would like to be permitted to put to you. Where is your brother Ernest? We are both engaged to be married to your brother Ernest, so it is a matter of some importance to us to know where your brother Ernest is at present.

JACK [*Slowly and hesitatingly.*]   Gwendolen—Cecily—it is very painful for me to be forced to speak the truth. It is the first time in my life that I have ever been reduced to such a painful position, and I am really quite inexperienced at doing anything of the kind. However I will tell you quite frankly that I have no brother Ernest. I have no brother at all. I never had a brother in my life, and I certainly have not the smallest intention of ever having one in the future.

710   CECILY [*Surprised.*]   No brother at all?

JACK [*Cheerily.*]   None!

GWENDOLEN [*Severely.*]   Had you never a brother of any kind?

JACK [*Pleasantly.*]   Never. Not even of any kind.

GWENDOLEN I am afraid it is quite clear, Cecily, that neither of us is engaged to be married to anyone.

CECILY It is not a very pleasant position for a young girl suddenly to find herself in. Is it?

GWENDOLEN Let us go into the house. They will hardly venture to come after us there.

720   CECILY No, men are so cowardly, aren't they?

[*They retire into the house with scornful looks.*]

JACK This ghastly state of things is what you call Bunburying, I suppose?

ALGERNON Yes, and a perfectly wonderful Bunbury it is. The most wonderful Bunbury I have ever had in my life.

JACK Well, you've no right whatsoever to Bunbury here.

ALGERNON That is absurd. One has a right to Bunbury anywhere one chooses. Every serious Bunburyist knows that.

JACK Serious Bunburyist! Good heavens!

ALGERNON Well, one must be serious about something, if one wants to have any amusement in life. I happen to be serious about Bunburying. What 730 on earth you are serious about I haven't got the remotest idea. About everything, I should fancy. You have such an absolutely trivial nature.

JACK   Well, the only small satisfaction I have in the whole of this wretched business is that your friend Bunbury is quite exploded. You won't be able to run down to the country quite so often as you used to do, dear Algy. And a very good thing too.

ALGERNON   Your brother is a little off colour, isn't he, dear Jack? You won't be able to disappear to London quite so frequently as your wicked custom was. And not a bad thing either.

740   JACK   As for your conduct towards Miss Cardew, I must say that your taking in a sweet, simple, innocent girl like that is quite inexcusable. To say nothing of the fact that she is my ward.

ALGERNON   I can see no possible defence at all for your deceiving a brilliant, clever, thoroughly experienced young lady like Miss Fairfax. To say nothing of the fact that she is my cousin.

JACK   I wanted to be engaged to Gwendolen, that is all. I love her.

ALGERNON   Well, I simply wanted to be engaged to Cecily. I adore her.

JACK   There is certainly no chance of your marrying Miss Cardew.

ALGERNON   I don't think there is much likelihood, Jack, of you and Miss Fairfax being united.

750   JACK   Well, that is no business of yours.

ALGERNON   If it was my business, I wouldn't talk about it. [*Begins to eat muffins.*] It is very vulgar to talk about one's business. Only people like stockbrokers do that, and then merely at dinner parties.

JACK   How you can sit there, calmly eating muffins when we are in this horrible trouble, I can't make out. You seem to me to be perfectly heartless.

ALGERNON   Well, I can't eat muffins in an agitated manner. The butter would probably get on my cuffs. One should always eat muffins quite calmly. It is the only way to eat them.

JACK   I say it's perfectly heartless your eating muffins at all, under the
760   circumstances.

ALGERNON   When I am in trouble, eating is the only thing that consoles me. Indeed, when I am in really great trouble, as anyone who knows me intimately will tell you, I refuse everything except food and drink. At the present moment I am eating muffins because I am unhappy. Besides, I am particularly fond of muffins. [*Rising.*]

JACK [*Rising.*]   Well, that is no reason why you should eat them all in that greedy way. [*Takes muffins from* ALGERNON.]

ALGERNON [*Offering tea-cake.*]   I wish you would have tea-cake instead. I don't like tea-cake.

770   JACK   Good heavens! I suppose a man may eat his own muffins in his own garden.

ALGERNON   But you have just said it was perfectly heartless to eat muffins.

JACK   I said it was perfectly heartless of you, under the circumstances. That is a very different thing.

ALGERNON   That may be. But the muffins are the same. [*He seizes the muffin-dish from* JACK.]

JACK   Algy, I wish to goodness you would go.

ALGERNON   You can't possibly ask me to go without having some dinner.

It's absurd. I never go without my dinner. No one ever does, except vegetari-
780 ans and people like that. Besides I have just made arrangements with Dr.
Chasuble to be christened at a quarter to six under the name of Ernest.

JACK   My dear fellow, the sooner you give up that nonsense the better. I
made arrangements this morning with Dr. Chasuble to be christened myself
at 5:30, and I naturally will take the name of Ernest. Gwendolen would wish
it. We can't both be christened Ernest. It's absurd. Besides, I have a perfect
right to be christened if I like. There is no evidence at all that I ever have
been christened by anybody. I should think it extremely probable I never
was, and so does Dr. Chasuble. It is entirely different in your case. You have
been christened already.

790 ALGERNON   Yes, but I have not been christened for years.

JACK   Yes, but you have been christened. That is the important thing.

ALGERNON   Quite so. So I know my constitution can stand it. If you are not
quite sure about your ever having been christened, I must say I think it rather
dangerous your venturing on it now. It might make you very unwell. You can
hardly have forgotten that someone very closely connected with you was very
nearly carried off this week in Paris by a severe chill.

JACK   Yes, but you said yourself that a severe chill was not hereditary.

ALGERNON   It usen't to be, I know—but I daresay it is now. Science is
always making wonderful improvements in things.

800 JACK [*Picking up the muffin-dish.*]   Oh, that is nonsense; you are always
talking nonsense.

ALGERNON   Jack, you are at the muffins again! I wish you wouldn't. There
are only two left. [*Takes them.*] I told you I was particularly fond of muffins.

JACK   But I hate tea-cake.

ALGERNON   Why on earth then do you allow tea-cake to be served up for
your guests? What ideas you have of hospitality!

JACK   Algernon! I have already told you to go. I don't want you here. Why
don't you go!

ALGERNON   I haven't quite finished my tea yet! and there is still one muffin
810 left. [JACK *groans, and sinks into a chair,* ALGERNON *still continues eating.*]

Act-Drop.

Third Act

Scene.   *Morning-room at the Manor House.*
[GWENDOLEN *and* CECILY *are at the window, looking out into the garden.*]

GWENDOLEN   The fact that they did not follow us at once into the house, as
anyone else would have done, seems to me to show that they have some
sense of shame left.

CECILY   They have been eating muffins. That looks like repentance.

GWENDOLEN [*After a pause.*]   They don't seem to notice us at all. Couldn't
you cough?

CECILY   But I haven't got a cough.

GWENDOLEN They're looking at us. What effrontery!

CECILY They're approaching. That's very forward of them.

10 GWENDOLEN Let us preserve a dignified silence.

CECILY Certainly. It's the only thing to do now.

[*Enter* JACK *followed by* ALGERNON. *They whistle some dreadful popular air from a British opera.*]

GWENDOLEN This dignified silence seems to produce an unpleasant effect.

CECILY A most distasteful one.

GWENDOLEN But we will not be the first to speak.

CECILY Certainly not.

GWENDOLEN Mr. Worthing, I have something very particular to ask you. Much depends on your reply.

CECILY Gwendolen, your common sense is invaluable. Mr. Moncrieff, kindly answer me the following question. Why did you pretend to be my

20 guardian's brother?

ALGERNON In order that I might have an opportunity of meeting you.

CECILY [*To* GWENDOLEN.] That certainly seems a satisfactory explanation, does it not?

GWENDOLEN Yes, dear, if you can believe him.

CECILY I don't. But that does not affect the wonderful beauty of his answer.

GWENDOLEN True. In matters of grave importance, style, not sincerity is the vital thing. Mr. Worthing, what explanation can you offer to me for pretending to have a brother? Was it in order that you might have an opportunity of coming up to town to see me as often as possible?

30 JACK Can you doubt it, Miss Fairfax?

GWENDOLEN I have the gravest doubts upon the subject. But I intend to crush them. This is not the moment for German scepticism. [*Moving to* CECILY.] Their explanations appear to be quite satisfactory, especially Mr. Worthing's. That seems to me to have the stamp of truth upon it.

CECILY I am more than content with what Mr. Moncrieff said. His voice alone inspires one with absolute credulity.

GWENDOLEN Then you think we should forgive them?

CECILY Yes. I mean no.

GWENDOLEN True! I had forgotten. There are principles at stake that one

40 cannot surrender. Which of us should tell them? The task is not a pleasant one.

CECILY Could we not both speak at the same time?

GWENDOLEN An excellent idea! I nearly always speak at the same time as other people. Will you take the time from me?

CECILY Certainly. [GWENDOLEN *beats time with uplifted finger.*]

GWENDOLEN AND CECILY [*Speaking together.*] Your Christian names are still an unsuperable barrier. That is all!

JACK AND ALGERNON [*Speaking together.*] Our Christian names! Is that all? But we are going to be christened this afternoon.

GWENDOLEN [*To* JACK.] For my sake you are prepared to do this terrible

50 thing?

JACK   I am.

CECILY [*To* ALGERNON.]   To please me you are ready to face this fearful ordeal?

ALGERNON   I am!

GWENDOLEN   How absurd to talk of the equality of the sexes! Where questions of self-sacrifice are concerned, men are infinitely beyond us.

JACK   We are. [*Clasps hands with* ALGERNON.]

CECILY   They have moments of physical courage of which we women know absolutely nothing.

60   GWENDOLEN [*To* JACK.]   Darling!

ALGERNON [*To* CECILY.]   Darling. [*They fall into each other's arms.*]

[*Enter* MERRIMAN. *When he enters he coughs loudly seeing the situation.*]

MERRIMAN   Ahem! Ahem! Lady Bracknell!

JACK   Good heavens!

[*Enter* LADY BRACKNELL. *The couples separate in alarm. Exit* MERRIMAN.]

LADY BRACKNELL   Gwendolen! What does this mean?

GWENDOLEN   Merely that I am engaged to be married to Mr. Worthing, Mamma.

LADY BRACKNELL   Come here. Sit down. Sit down immediately. Hesitation of any kind is a sign of mental decay in the young, of physical weakness in the old. [*Turns to* JACK.] Apprised, sir, of my daughter's sudden flight by her
70 trusty maid, whose confidence I purchased by means of a small coin, I followed her at once by a luggage train. Her unhappy father is, I am glad to say, under the impression that she is attending a more than usually lengthy lecture by the University Extension Scheme on the influence of a permanent income on thought. I do not propose to undeceive him. Indeed I have never undeceived him on any question. I would consider it wrong. But of course, you will clearly understand that all communication between yourself and my daughter must cease immediately from this moment. On this point, as indeed on all points, I am firm.

JACK   I am engaged to be married to Gwendolen, Lady Bracknell!

80   LADY BRACKNELL   You are nothing of the kind, sir. And now, as regards Algernon! . . . Algernon!

ALGERNON   Yes, Aunt Augusta.

LADY BRACKNELL   May I ask if it is in this house that your invalid friend Mr. Bunbury resides?

ALGERNON [*Stammering.*]   Oh! No! Bunbury doesn't live here. Bunbury is somewhere else at present. In fact, Bunbury is dead.

LADY BRACKNELL   Dead! When did Mr. Bunbury die? His death must have been extremely sudden.

ALGERNON [*Airily.*]   Oh! I killed Bunbury this afternoon. I mean poor Bun-
90 bury died this afternoon.

LADY BRACKNELL   What did he die of?

ALGERNON   Bunbury? Oh, he was quite exploded.

LADY BRACKNELL   Exploded! Was he the victim of a revolutionary outrage? I was not aware that Mr. Bunbury was interested in social legislation. If so, he is well punished for his morbidity.

ALGERNON   My dear Aunt Augusta, I mean he was found out! The doctors found out that Bunbury could not live, that is what I mean—so Bunbury died.

LADY BRACKNELL   He seems to have had great confidence in the opinion of his physicians. I am glad, however, that he made up his mind at the last to
100 some definite course of action, and acted under proper medical advice. And now that we have finally got rid of this Mr. Bunbury, may I ask, Mr. Worthing, who is that young person whose hand my nephew Algernon is now holding in what seems to me a peculiarly unnecessary manner?

JACK   That lady is Miss Cecily Cardew, my ward. [LADY BRACKNELL *bows coldly to* CECILY.]

ALGERNON   I am engaged to be married to Cecily, Aunt Augusta.

LADY BRACKNELL   I beg your pardon?

CECILY   Mr. Moncrieff and I are engaged to be married, Lady Bracknell.

LADY BRACKNELL [*With a shiver, crossing to the sofa and sitting down.*]   I do
110 not know whether there is anything peculiarly exciting in the air of this particular part of Hertfordshire, but the number of engagements that go on seems to me considerably above the proper average that statistics have laid down for our guidance. I think some preliminary enquiry on my part would not be out of place. Mr. Worthing, is Miss Cardew at all connected with any of the larger railway stations in London? I merely desire information. Until yesterday I had no idea that there were any families or persons whose origin was a Terminus. [JACK *looks perfectly furious, but restrains himself.*]

JACK [*In a clear, cold voice.*]   Miss Cardew is the granddaughter of the late Mr. Thomas Cardew of 149, Belgrave Square, S.W.; Gervase Park, Dorking,
120 Surrey; and the Sporran, Fifeshire, N.B.

LADY BRACKNELL   That sounds not unsatisfactory. Three addresses always inspire confidence, even in tradesmen. But what proof have I of their authenticity?

JACK   I have carefully preserved the Court Guides of the period. They are open to your inspection, Lady Bracknell.

LADY BRACKNELL [*Grimly.*]   I have known strange errors in that publication.

JACK   Miss Cardew's family solicitors are Messrs. Markby, Markby, and Markby.

LADY BRACKNELL   Markby, Markby, and Markby? A firm of the very highest
130 position in their profession. Indeed I am told that one of the Mr. Markbys is occasionally to be seen at dinner parties. So far I am satisfied.

JACK [*Very irritably.*]   How extremely kind of you, Lady Bracknell! I have also in my possession, you will be pleased to hear, certificates of Miss Cardew's birth, baptism, whooping cough, registration, vaccination, confirmation, and the measles; both the German and the English variety.

LADY BRACKNELL   Ah! A life crowded with incident, I see; though perhaps somewhat too exciting for a young girl. I am not myself in favour of premature experiences. [*Rises, looks at her watch.*] Gwendolen! the time approaches for

140 our departure. We have not a moment to lose. As a matter of form, Mr. Worthing,
I had better ask you if Miss Cardew has any little fortune?

JACK   Oh! about a hundred and thirty thousand pounds in the Funds. That
is all. Good-bye, Lady Bracknell. So pleased to have seen you.

LADY BRACKNELL   [*Sitting down again.*] A moment, Mr. Worthing. A hundred and thirty thousand pounds! And in the Funds! Miss Cardew seems to
me a most attractive young lady, now that I look at her. Few girls of the
present day have any really solid qualities, any of the qualities that last, and
improve with time. We live, I regret to say, in an age of surfaces. [*To* CECILY.]
Come over here, dear. [CECILY *goes across.*] Pretty child! your dress is sadly
simple, and your hair seems almost as nature might have left it. But we can
150 soon alter all that. A thoroughly experienced French maid produces a really
marvellous result in a very brief space of time. I remember recommending
one to young Lady Lancing, and after three months her own husband did not
know her.

JACK [*Aside.*]   And after six months nobody knew her.

LADY BRACKNELL [*Glares at* JACK *for a few moments. Then bends, with a practised smile, to* CECILY.]   Kindly turn round, sweet child. [CECILY *turns completely round.*] No, the side view is what I want. [CECILY *presents her profile.*]
Yes, quite as I expected. There are distinct social possibilities in your profile.
The two weak points in our age are its want of principle and its want of profile.
160 The chin a little higher, dear. Style largely depends on the way the chin is
worn. They are worn very high, just at present. Algernon!

ALGERNON   Yes, Aunt Augusta!

LADY BRACKNELL   There are distinct social possibilities in Miss Cardew's
profile.

ALGERNON   Cecily is the sweetest, dearest, prettiest girl in the whole
world. And I don't care twopence about social possibilities.

LADY BRACKNELL   Never speak disrespectfully of Society, Algernon. Only
people who can't get into it do that. [*To* CECILY.] Dear child, of course you
know that Algernon has nothing but his debts to depend upon. But I do not
170 approve of mercenary marriages. When I married Lord Bracknell I had no
fortune of any kind. But I never dreamed for a moment of allowing that to
stand in my way. Well, I suppose I must give my consent.

ALGERNON   Thank you, Aunt Augusta.

LADY BRACKNELL   Cecily, you may kiss me!

CECILY [*Kisses her.*]   Thank you, Lady Bracknell.

LADY BRACKNELL   You may also address me as Aunt Augusta for the future.

CECILY   Thank you, Aunt Augusta.

LADY BRACKNELL   The marriage, I think, had better take place quite soon.

ALGERNON   Thank you, Aunt Augusta.

180 CECILY   Thank you, Aunt Augusta.

LADY BRACKNELL   To speak frankly, I am not in favour of long engagements.
They give people the opportunity of finding out each other's character before marriage, which I think is never advisable.

JACK   I beg your pardon for interrupting you, Lady Bracknell, but this
engagement is quite out of the question. I am Miss Cardew's guardian, and

she cannot marry without my consent until she comes of age. That consent I absolutely decline to give.

LADY BRACKNELL Upon what grounds may I ask? Algernon is an extremely, I may almost say an ostentatiously, eligible young man. He has nothing, but
190 he looks everything. What more can one desire?

JACK It pains me very much to have to speak frankly to you, Lady Bracknell, about your nephew, but the fact is that I do not approve at all of his moral character. I suspect him of being untruthful. [ALGERNON *and* CECILY *look at him in indignant amazement.*]

LADY BRACKNELL Untruthful! My nephew Algernon? Impossible! He is an Oxonian.

JACK I fear there can be no possible doubt about the matter. This afternoon, during my temporary absence in London on an important question of romance, he obtained admission to my house by means of the false pretence
200 of being my brother. Under an assumed name he drank, I've just been informed by my butler, an entire pint bottle of my Perrier-Jouet, Brut, '89; a wine I was specially reserving for myself. Continuing his disgraceful deception, he succeeded in the course of the afternoon in alienating the affections of my only ward. He subsequently stayed to tea, and devoured every single muffin. And what makes his conduct all the more heartless is, that he was perfectly well aware from the first that I have no brother, that I never had a brother, and that I don't intend to have a brother, not even of any kind. I distinctly told him so myself yesterday afternoon.

LADY BRACKNELL Ahem! Mr. Worthing, after careful consideration I have
210 decided entirely to overlook my nephew's conduct to you.

JACK That is very generous of you, Lady Bracknell. My own decision, however, is unalterable. I decline to give my consent.

LADY BRACKNELL [*To* CECILY.] Come here, sweet child. [CECILY *goes over.*] How old are you, dear?

CECILY Well, I am really only eighteen, but I always admit to twenty when I go to evening parties.

LADY BRACKNELL You are perfectly right in making some slight alteration. Indeed, no woman should ever be quite accurate about her age. It looks so calculating. . . . [*In a meditative manner.*] Eighteen, but admitting to
220 twenty at evening parties. Well, it will not be very long before you are of age and free from the restraints of tutelage. So I don't think your guardian's consent is, after all, a matter of any importance.

JACK Pray excuse me, Lady Bracknell, for interrupting you again, but it is only fair to tell you that according to the terms of her grandfather's will Miss Cardew does not come legally of age till she is thirty-five.

LADY BRACKNELL That does not seem to me to be a grave objection. Thirty-five is a very attractive age. London society is full of women of the very highest birth who have, of their own free choice, remained thirty-five for years. Lady Dumbleton is an instance in point. To my own knowledge she
230 has been thirty-five ever since she arrived at the age of forty, which was many years ago now. I see no reason why our dear Cecily should not be even still more attractive at the age you mention than she is at present. There will be a large accumulation of property.

CECILY   Algy, could you wait for me till I was thirty-five?

ALGERNON   Of course I could, Cecily. You know I could.

CECILY   Yes, I felt it instinctively, but I couldn't wait all that time. I hate waiting even five minutes for anybody. It always makes me rather cross. I am not punctual myself, I know, but I do like punctuality in others, and waiting, even to be married, is quite out of the question.

240   ALGERNON   Then what is to be done, Cecily?

CECILY   I don't know, Mr. Moncrieff.

LADY BRACKNELL   My dear Mr. Worthing, as Miss Cardew states positively that she cannot wait till she is thirty-five—a remark which I am bound to say seems to me to show a somewhat impatient nature—I would beg of you to reconsider your decision.

JACK   But my dear Lady Bracknell, the matter is entirely in your own hands. The moment you consent to my marriage with Gwendolen, I will most gladly allow your nephew to form an alliance with my ward.

LADY BRACKNELL [*Rising and drawing herself up.*]   You must be quite aware
250   that what you propose is out of the question.

JACK   Then a passionate celibacy is all that any of us can look forward to.

LADY BRACKNELL   That is not the destiny I propose for Gwendolen. Algernon, of course, can choose for himself. [*Pulls out her watch.*] Come, dear; [GWENDOLEN *rises.*] we have already missed five, if not six, trains. To miss any more might expose us to comment on the platform.

[*Enter* DR. CHASUBLE.]

CHASUBLE   Everything is quite ready for the christenings.

LADY BRACKNELL   The christenings, sir! Is not that somewhat premature?

CHASUBLE [*Looking rather puzzled, and pointing to* JACK *and* ALGERNON.]   Both these gentlemen have expressed a desire for immediate baptism.

260   LADY BRACKNELL   At their age? The idea is grotesque and irreligious! Algernon, I forbid you to be baptized. I will not hear of such excesses. Lord Bracknell would be highly displeased if he learned that that was the way in which you wasted your time and money.

CHASUBLE   Am I to understand then that there are to be no christenings at all this afternoon?

JACK   I don't think that, as things are now, it would be of much practical value to either of us, Dr. Chasuble.

CHASUBLE   I am grieved to hear such sentiments from you, Mr. Worthing. They savour of the heretical views of the Anabaptists, views that I have
270   completely refuted in four of my unpublished sermons. However, as your present mood seems to be one peculiarly secular, I will return to the church at once. Indeed, I have just been informed by the pew-opener that for the last hour and a half Miss Prism has been waiting for me in the vestry.

LADY BRACKNELL [*Starting.*]   Miss Prism! Did I hear you mention a Miss Prism?

CHASUBLE   Yes, Lady Bracknell. I am on my way to join her.

LADY BRACKNELL   Pray allow me to detain you for a moment. This matter may prove to be one of vital importance to Lord Bracknell and myself. Is this Miss Prism a female of repellent aspect, remotely connected with education?

280   CHASUBLE [*Somewhat indignantly.*]   She is the most cultivated of ladies, and the very picture of respectability.

LADY BRACKNELL   It is obviously the same person. May I ask what position she holds in your household?

CHASUBLE [*Severely.*]   I am a celibate, madam.

JACK [*Interposing.*]   Miss Prism, Lady Bracknell, has been for the last three years Miss Cardew's esteemed governess and valued companion.

LADY BRACKNELL   In spite of what I hear of her, I must see her at once. Let her be sent for.

CHASUBLE [*Looking off.*]   She approaches; she is nigh.

[*Enter* MISS PRISM *hurriedly.*]

290   MISS PRISM   I was told you expected me in the vestry, dear Canon. I have been waiting for you there for an hour and three quarters. [*Catches sight of* LADY BRACKNELL *who has fixed her with a stony glare.* MISS PRISM *grows pale and quails. She looks anxiously round as if desirous to escape.*]

LADY BRACKNELL [*In a severe, judicial voice.*]   Prism! [MISS PRISM *bows her head in shame.*] Come here, Prism! [MISS PRISM *approaches in a humble manner.*] Prism! Where is that baby? [*General consternation. The* CANON *starts back in horror.* ALGERNON *and* JACK *pretend to be anxious to shield* CECILY *and* GWENDOLEN *from hearing the details of a terrible public scandal.*] Twenty-eight years ago, Prism, you left Lord Bracknell's house, Num-
300 ber 104, Upper Grosvenor Street, in charge of a perambulator that contained a baby, of the male sex. You never returned. A few weeks later, through the elaborate investigations of the Metropolitan police, the perambulator was discovered at midnight, standing by itself in a remote corner of Bayswater. It contained the manuscript of a three-volume novel of more than usually revolting sentimentality. [MISS PRISM *starts in involuntary indignation.*] But the baby was not there! [*Everyone looks at* MISS PRISM.] Prism! Where is that baby? [*A pause.*]

MISS PRISM   Lady Bracknell, I admit with shame that I do not know. I only wish I did. The plain facts of the case are these. On the morning of the day
310 you mention, a day that is for ever branded on my memory, I prepared as usual to take the baby out in its perambulator. I had also with me a somewhat old, but capacious handbag, in which I had intended to place the manuscript of a work of fiction that I had written during my few unoccupied hours. In a moment of mental abstraction, for which I never can forgive myself, I deposited the manuscript in the bassinette, and placed the baby in the handbag.

JACK [*Who has been listening attentively.*]   But where did you deposit the handbag?

MISS PRISM   Do not ask me, Mr. Worthing.

JACK   Miss Prism, this is a matter of no small importance to me. I insist on
320 knowing where you deposited the handbag that contained that infant.

MISS PRISM   I left it in the cloakroom of one of the larger railway stations in London.

JACK   What railway station?

MISS PRISM [*Quite crushed.*]   Victoria. The Brighton line. [*Sinks into a chair.*]
JACK   I must retire to my room for a moment. Gwendolen, wait here for me.
GWENDOLEN   If you are not too long, I will wait here for you all my life.

[*Exit* JACK *in great excitement.*]

CHASUBLE   What do you think this means, Lady Bracknell?
LADY BRACKNELL   I dare not even suspect, Dr. Chasuble. I need hardly tell
you that in families of high position strange coincidences are not supposed
330   to occur. They are hardly considered the thing.

[*Noises heard overhead as if someone was throwing trunks about. Everyone looks up.*]

CECILY   Uncle Jack seems strangely agitated.
CHASUBLE   Your guardian has a very emotional nature.
LADY BRACKNELL   This noise is extremely unpleasant. It sounds as if he was
having an argument. I dislike arguments of any kind. They are always vulgar,
and often convincing.
CHASUBLE [*Looking up.*]   It has stopped now. [*The noise is redoubled.*]
LADY BRACKNELL   I wish he would arrive at some conclusion.
GWENDOLEN   This suspense is terrible. I hope it will last.

[*Enter* JACK *with a handbag of black leather in his hand.*]

JACK [*Rushing over to* MISS PRISM.]   Is this the handbag, Miss Prism? Exam-
340   ine it carefully before you speak. The happiness of more than one life depends on your answer.
MISS PRISM [*Calmly.*]   It seems to be mine. Yes, here is the injury it received
through the upsetting of a Gower Street omnibus in younger and happier
days. Here is the stain on the lining caused by the explosion of a temperance
beverage, an incident that occurred at Leamington. And here, on the lock, are
my initials. I had forgotten that in an extravagant mood I had had them
placed there. The bag is undoubtedly mine. I am delighted to have it so
unexpectedly restored to me. It has been a great inconvenience being without it all these years.
350   JACK [*In a pathetic voice.*]   Miss Prism, more is restored to you than this
handbag. I was the baby you placed in it.
MISS PRISM [*Amazed.*]   You?
JACK [*Embracing her.*]   Yes . . . mother!
MISS PRISM [*Recoiling in indignant astonishment.*]   Mr. Worthing! I am
unmarried!
JACK   Unmarried! I do not deny that is a serious blow. But after all, who
has the right to cast a stone against one who has suffered? Cannot repentance
wipe out an act of folly? Why should there be one law for me, and another for
women? Mother, I forgive you. [*Tries to embrace her again.*]
360   MISS PRISM [*Still more indignant.*]   Mr. Worthing, there is some error.
[*Pointing to* LADY BRACKNELL.]   There is the lady who can tell you who you
really are.

JACK [*After a pause.*]   Lady Bracknell, I hate to seem inquisitive, but would you kindly inform me who I am?

LADY BRACKNELL   I am afraid that the news I have to give you will not altogether please you. You are the son of my poor sister, Mrs. Moncrieff, and consequently Algernon's elder brother.

JACK   Algy's elder brother! Then I have a brother after all. I knew I had a brother! I always said I had a brother! Cecily,—how could you have ever
370   doubted that I had a brother? [*Seizes hold of* ALGERNON.] Dr. Chasuble, my unfortunate brother. Miss Prism, my unfortunate brother. Gwendolen, my unfortunate brother. Algy, you young scoundrel, you will have to treat me with more respect in the future. You have never behaved to me like a brother in all your life.

ALGERNON   Well, not till today, old boy, I admit. I did my best, however, though I was out of practice. [*Shakes hands.*]

GWENDOLEN [*To* JACK.]   My own! But what own are you? What is your Christian name, now that you have become someone else?

JACK   Good heavens! . . . I had quite forgotten that point. Your decision
380   on the subject of my name is irrevocable, I suppose?

GWENDOLEN   I never change, except in my affections.

CECILY   What a noble nature you have, Gwendolen!

JACK   Then the question had better be cleared up at once. Aunt Augusta, a moment. At the time when Miss Prism left me in the handbag, had I been christened already?

LADY BRACKNELL   Every luxury that money could buy, including christening, had been lavished on you by your fond and doting parents.

JACK   Then I was christened! That is settled. Now, what name was I given? Let me know the worst.

390   LADY BRACKNELL   Being the eldest son you were naturally christened after your father.

JACK [*Irritably.*]   Yes, but what was my father's Christian name?

LADY BRACKNELL [*Meditatively.*]   I cannot at the present moment recall what the General's Christian name was. But I have no doubt he had one. He was eccentric, I admit. But only in later years. And that was the result of the Indian climate, and marriage, and indigestion, and other things of that kind.

JACK   Algy! Can't you recollect what our father's Christian name was?

ALGERNON   My dear boy, we were never even on speaking terms. He died before I was a year old.

400   JACK   His name would appear in the Army Lists of the period, I suppose, Aunt Augusta?

LADY BRACKNELL   The General was essentially a man of peace, except in his domestic life. But I have no doubt his name would appear in any military directory.

JACK   The Army Lists of the last forty years are here. These delightful records should have been my constant study. [*Rushes to bookcase and tears the books out.*] M. Generals . . . Mallam, Maxbohm, Magley, what ghastly names they have—Markby, Migsby, Mobbs, Moncrieff! Lieutenant 1840, Captain, Lieutenant-Colonel, Colonel, General 1869, Christian names, Ernest

410 JOHN. [*Puts book very quietly down and speaks quite calmly.*] I always told you, Gwendolen, my name was Ernest, didn't I? Well, it is Ernest after all. I mean it naturally is Ernest.

LADY BRACKNELL   Yes, I remember now that the General was called Ernest. I knew I had some particular reason for disliking the name.

GWENDOLEN   Ernest! My own Ernest! I felt from the first that you could have no other name!

JACK   Gwendolen, it is a terrible thing for a man to find out suddenly that all his life he has been speaking nothing but the truth. Can you forgive me?

GWENDOLEN   I can. For I feel that you are sure to change.

420 JACK   My own one!

CHASUBLE [*To* MISS PRISM.]   Laetitia! [*Embraces her.*]

MISS PRISM [*Enthusiastically.*]   Frederick! At last!

ALGERNON   Cecily! [*Embraces her.*] At last!

JACK   Gwendolen! [*Embraces her.*] At last!

LADY BRACKNELL   My nephew, you seem to be displaying signs of triviality.

JACK   On the contrary, Aunt Augusta, I've now realized for the first time in my life the vital Importance of Being Earnest.

Curtain.

Questions

1. In the first scene, what information does Wilde give you, necessary to the development of his plot? How does he avoid seeming merely to provide information?

2. Define "paradox." Find seven brilliant paradoxes in this play. Bring your list to class and be prepared to defend it.

3. What does the playwright tell us about marriage? What quality of human beings is most important to society in the world of this play? What other social observations does Wilde provide?

4. Why are characters named "Prism" and "Chasuble"? Are they important to the plot? In how many ways? When we see them at the end, how do they fit Wilde's comic world?

5. Outline plot structure establishing parallelism.

6. "Wilde's theater starts from the premise that what looks real is unreal, and what looks unreal is real. In this premise Wilde's theater resembles all theaters." Discuss.

CHAPTER SIX

Modern Drama, Realism, and Chekhov

The Idea of Realism

We call modern drama realistic when it uses theatrical conventions we accept as representing the world we live in. In realistic modern drama, we look at actors imitating actual people, speaking dialogue constructed to resemble people talking, among sets that resemble rooms or gardens. To understand why we call this theater realistic, we must look at it from the other side of history, and understand realism in the context of earlier drama. We must understand what modern realistic drama is *not:* people do not speak in rhymed couplets; people do not converse with ghosts or address the audience in asides or speak eloquent blank-verse meditations on empty stages; people are not kings fated to marry widowed queens who are their secret mothers. On the modern realistic stage, instead of kings, characters are salesmen, landowners, nurses, society matrons, politicians, real-estate developers. Instead of poetry they speak prose, and they interrupt and misunderstand each other. Their problems lie not in mysterious plagues but in diseases like tuberculosis. Instead of needing to avenge a king-father's murder, realistic heroes struggle to prevail over petty envy or to love and be loved, to find a job or keep a pension.

If we contrast *Oedipus Rex* with *Death of a Salesman,* the difference seems to justify the word *realistic,* yet the term is treacherous. After all, when we praise *Oedipus Rex* as true to nature, or *Othello* as psychologically profound, we are calling each of the plays *real*—if not realistic drama.

The movement toward realism on the stage began earlier than the mid-nineteenth century and arose from social and historical causes. Even on the stage of the Jacobean period, which succeeded the Elizabethan era in England, middle-class characters took over subplots; gradually, middle-class subplots weighed heavier than noble main plots. A rising middle class required mirrors of itself on the stage it patronized. Realism necessitated improved technology in lighting, stage machinery, sets, and sound effects. The

Act I of the first production of *The Cherry Orchard* at the Moscow Art Theater, January 1904.

same capitalist industrialism that enriched the middle class invented the phonograph and the electric light. By the late nineteenth century, a materialistic world view, which substituted neurosis for witchcraft and syphillis for fate, demanded from the theater plain talk and sophisticated technology.

For the great playwrights of the modern stage, drama was no mere plaything of the middle class or entertainment for tired capitalists. Their art was a representation of life as it actually was lived, viewed with attitudes ranging from indictment to affection. Henrik Ibsen (1828–1906) wrote realistic drama in the great middle period of his long artistic life (see "Henrik Ibsen and *Hedda Gabler*," page 986). A great British realist was George Bernard Shaw (1856–1950). Among other playwrights of the realistic stage, August Strindberg (1849–1912) in his early work carried realism on to naturalism— a variant that is concerned with the most sordid parts of reality, or, to use the title of a naturalist play by Maxim Gorki (1868–1936), *The Lower Depths.*

Contemporary Americans should understand the social background of Anton Chekhov's plays, perhaps most particularly of *The Cherry Orchard.* In fiction and in drama alike, Chekhov presents peasants and merchants and aristocrats with equal clarity, compassion, and humor. Reading *The Cherry Orchard,* we must realize that the serfs, who had been virtual slaves, had been only recently liberated; it became legal for landowners to free serfs in 1803, compulsory in 1861. Old Firs therefore acts as if he were still a serf. On the other hand, Lopakhin, like Chekhov, comes from a family of liberated serfs—and Lopakhin belongs to a rising class of entrepreneurs. We might expect Chekhov, because of his background, to make class war on Madame

Ranevskaya and her brother, but Chekhov's temperament is gentle and ironic, his artistic attitude objective. In *The Cherry Orchard,* liberated serfs and impoverished landowners associate with one another, and younger Russians of various backgrounds attempt to adjust to the new Russia. Many of the characters seem left over from an old life: others are visionaries of the future. The play may be dense with the texture of society, but it is by no means merely a social document. The historical context of *The Cherry Orchard* merely provides particulars for a view of the world—as human comedy— Chekhov was able to discover.

　The Cherry Orchard has survived seventy years of melancholy productions. Chekhov considered it a comedy almost as broad as farce, and recently the play has been acted for its humor. The best productions are nevertheless funny and sad at the same time. *The Cherry Orchard* varies emotional pitch continually, is by turns euphoric and miserable. Its realism lies not in its social particularity so much as in its psychological exactness; here is a silly, vain, affectionate woman; here is her ineffectual, optimistic, doomed brother; here is a shrewd, opportunistic peasant, at the same time shy, diffident; here are lovers, here are fools: *and each is unique.* Chekhov's stage is large enough to suggest the universe.

Anton Chekhov

One of the masters of dramatic realism was the Russian Anton Chekhov (1864–1904), a master as well of the short story (his "Gooseberries" appears on pages 136–143). Chekhov emerged from the rising merchant class in the late years of Tzarist Russia; his grandfather had been a serf and his father was a small shopkeeper. Chekhov trained to be a doctor, and while he was studying medicine wrote humorous short stories to make money. Ultimately, literature won out over medicine. When he turned to the theater after success in fiction, the first production of *The Sea Gull* was a disaster. Only when Konstantin Stanislavsky (see page 742), the great director of the Moscow Art Theater, produced *The Sea Gull* in 1898 did the play succeed. In the brief time remaining to him, Chekhov wrote *Uncle Vanya* (1899), *The Three Sisters* (1901), and *The Cherry Orchard* (1904).

The Cherry Orchard   (1904, tr. 1964)
Translated by Ann Dunnigan

A Comedy in Four Acts

Characters in the Play

RANEVSKAYA, LYUBOV ANDREYEVNA, a
   landowner
ANYA, her daughter, seventeen years old
VARYA, her adopted daughter,
   twenty-four years old
GAYEV, Leonid Andreyevich, Madame
   Ranevskaya's brother
LOPAKHIN, Yermolai Alekseyevich, a
   merchant
TROFIMOV, Pyotr Sergeyevich, a student
SEMYONOV-PISHCHIK, Boris Borisovich, a
   landowner

CHARLOTTA IVANOVNA, a governess
YEPIKHODOV, Semyon Panteleyevich, a
   clerk
DUNYASHA, a maid
FIRS, an old valet, eighty-seven years old
YASHA, a young footman
A STRANGER
THE STATIONMASTER
A POST-OFFICE CLERK
GUESTS, SERVANTS

The action takes place on Madame Ranevskaya's estate.

Act I

[*A room that is still called the nursery. One of the doors leads into* ANYA's *room. Dawn; the sun will soon rise. It is May, the cherry trees are in bloom, but it is cold in the orchard; there is a morning frost. The windows in the room are closed. Enter* DUNYASHA *with a candle, and* LOPAKHIN *with a book in his hands.*]

LOPAKHIN The train is in, thank God. What time is it?

DUNYASHA Nearly two. [*Blows out the candle.*] It's already light.

LOPAKHIN How late is the train, anyway? A couple of hours at least. [*Yawns and stretches.*] I'm a fine one! What a fool I've made of myself! Came here on purpose to meet them at the station, and then overslept. . . . Fell asleep in the chair. It's annoying. . . . You might have waked me.

DUNYASHA I thought you had gone. [*Listens.*] They're coming now, I think!

LOPAKHIN [*listens*] No . . . they've got to get the luggage and one thing and another. [*Pause*] Lyubov Andreyevna has lived abroad for five years, I
10 don't know what she's like now. . . . She's a fine person. Sweet-tempered, simple. I remember when I was a boy of fifteen, my late father—he had a shop in the village then—gave me a punch in the face and made my nose bleed. . . . We had come into the yard here for some reason or other, and he'd had a drop too much. Lyubov Andreyevna—I remember as if it were yesterday—still young, and so slender, led me to the washstand in this very room, the nursery. "Don't cry, little peasant," she said, "it will heal in time for your wedding. . . ." [*Pause*] Little peasant . . . my father was a peasant, it's true, and here I am in a white waistcoat and tan shoes. Like a pig in a

pastry shop. . . . I may be rich, I've made a lot of money, but if you think
20 about it, analyze it, I'm a peasant through and through. [*Turning pages of the book*] Here I've been reading this book, and I didn't understand a thing. Fell asleep over it. [*Pause*]

DUNYASHA   The dogs didn't sleep all night: they can tell that their masters are coming.

LOPAKHIN   What's the matter with you, Dunyasha, you're so . . .

DUNYASHA   My hands are trembling. I'm going to faint.

LOPAKHIN   You're much too delicate, Dunyasha. You dress like a lady, and do your hair like one, too. It's not right. You should know your place.

[*Enter* YEPIKHODOV *with a bouquet; he wears a jacket and highly polished boots that squeak loudly. He drops the flowers as he comes in.*]

YEPIKHODOV [*picking up the flowers*]   Here, the gardener sent these. He
30 says you're to put them in the dining room. [*Hands the bouquet to* DUNYASHA.]

LOPAKHIN   And bring me some kvas.

DUNYASHA   Yes, sir. [*Goes out.*]

YEPIKHODOV   There's a frost this morning—three degrees—and the cherry trees are in bloom. I cannot approve of our climate. [*Sighs.*] I cannot. Our climate is not exactly conducive. And now, Yermolai Alekseyevich, permit me to append: the day before yesterday I bought myself a pair of boots, which, I venture to assure you, squeak so that it's quite infeasible. What should I grease them with?

LOPAKHIN   Leave me alone. You make me tired.

40 YEPIKHODOV   Every day some misfortune happens to me. But I don't complain, I'm used to it, I even smile.

[DUNYASHA *enters, serves* LOPAKHIN *the kvas.*]

YEPIKHODOV   I'm going. [*Stumbles over a chair and upsets it.*] There! [*As if in triumph.*] Now you see, excuse the expression . . . the sort of circumstance, incidentally. . . . It's really quite remarkable! [*Goes out.*]

DUNYASHA   You know, Yermolai Alekseyich, I have to confess that Yepikhodov has proposed to me.

LOPAKHIN   Ah!

DUNYASHA   And I simply don't know. . . . He's a quiet man, but sometimes, when he starts talking, you can't understand a thing he says. It's nice,
50 and full of feeling, only it doesn't make sense. I sort of like him. He's madly in love with me. But he's an unlucky fellow: every day something happens to him. They tease him about it around here; they call him Two-and-twenty Troubles.

LOPAKHIN [*listening*]   I think I hear them coming . . .

DUNYASHA   They're coming! What's the matter with me? I'm cold all over.

LOPAKHIN   They're really coming. Let's go and meet them. Will she recognize me? It's five years since we've seen each other.

DUNYASHA [*agitated*]   I'll faint this very minute . . . oh, I'm going to faint!

[*Two carriages are heard driving up to the house.* LOPAKHIN *and* DUNYASHA *go out quickly. The stage is empty. There is a hubbub in the adjoining rooms.* FIRS *hurriedly crosses the stage leaning on a stick. He has been to meet* LYUBOV ANDREYEVNA *and wears old-fashioned livery and a high hat. He mutters something to himself, not a word of which can be understood. The noise offstage grows louder and louder. A voice: "Let's go through here. . . ." Enter* LYUBOV ANDREYEVNA, ANYA, CHARLOTTA IVANOVNA *with a little dog on a chain, all in traveling dress;* VARYA *wearing a coat and kerchief;* GAYEV, SEMYONOV-PISHCHIK, LOPAKHIN, DUNYASHA *with a bundle and parasol; servants with luggage—all walk through the room.*]

ANYA   Let's go this way. Do you remember, Mama, what room this is?

60   LYUBOV ANDREYEVNA [*joyfully, through tears*]   The nursery!

VARYA   How cold it is! My hands are numb. [*To* LYUBOV ANDREYEVNA] Your rooms, both the white one and the violet one, are just as you left them, Mama.

LYUBOV ANDREYEVNA   The nursery . . . my dear, lovely nursery. . . . I used to sleep here when I was little. . . . [*Weeps.*] And now, like a child, I . . .[*Kisses her brother,* VARYA, *then her brother again.*] Varya hasn't changed; she still looks like a nun. And I recognized Dunyasha. . . . [*Kisses* DUNYASHA.]

GAYEV   The train was two hours late. How's that? What kind of management is that?

CHARLOTTA [*to* PISHCHIK]   My dog even eats nuts.

70   PISHCHIK [*amazed*]   Think of that now!

[*They all go out except* ANYA *and* DUNYASHA.]

DUNYASHA   We've been waiting and waiting for you. . . . [*Takes off* ANYA*'s coat and hat.*]

ANYA   I didn't sleep for four nights on the road . . . now I feel cold.

DUNYASHA   It was Lent when you went away, there was snow and frost then, but now? My darling! [*Laughs and kisses her.*] I've waited so long for you, my joy, my precious . . . I must tell you at once, I can't wait another minute. . . .

ANYA [*listlessly*]   What now?

DUNYASHA   The clerk, Yepikhodov, proposed to me just after Easter.

80   ANYA   You always talk about the same thing. . . . [*Straightening her hair*] I've lost all my hairpins. . . . [*She is so exhausted she can hardly stand.*]

DUNYASHA   I really don't know what to think. He loves me—he loves me so!

ANYA [*looking through the door into her room, tenderly*]   My room, my windows . . . it's just as though I'd never been away. I am home! Tomorrow morning I'll get up and run into the orchard. . . . Oh, if I could only sleep! I didn't sleep during the entire journey, I was so tormented by anxiety.

DUNYASHA   Pyotr Sergeich arrived the day before yesterday.

ANYA [*joyfully*]   Petya!

DUNYASHA   He's asleep in the bathhouse, he's staying there. "I'm afraid of

90   being in the way," he said. [*Looks at her pocket watch.*] I ought to wake him up, but Varvara Mikhailovna told me not to. "Don't you wake him," she said.

[*Enter* VARYA *with a bunch of keys at her waist.*]

VARYA   Dunyasha, coffee, quickly . . . Mama's asking for coffee.

DUNYASHA   This very minute. [*Goes out.*]

VARYA   Thank God, you've come! You're home again. [*Caressing her.*] My little darling has come back! My pretty one is here!

ANYA   I've been through so much.

VARYA   I can imagine!

ANYA   I left in Holy Week, it was cold then. Charlotta never stopped talking and doing her conjuring tricks the entire journey. Why did you saddle me 100 with Charlotta?

VARYA   You couldn't have traveled alone, darling. At seventeen!

ANYA   When we arrived in Paris, it was cold, snowing. My French is awful. . . . Mama was living on the fifth floor, and when I got there, she had all sorts of Frenchmen and ladies with her, and an old priest with a little book, and it was full of smoke, dismal. Suddenly I felt sorry for Mama, so sorry. I took her head in my arms and held her close and couldn't let her go. Afterward she kept hugging me and crying. . . .

VARYA   [*through her tears*]   Don't talk about it, don't talk about it. . . .

ANYA   She had already sold her villa near Mentone, and she had nothing 110 left, nothing. And I hadn't so much as a kopeck left, we barely managed to get there. But Mama doesn't understand! When we had dinner in a station restaurant, she always ordered the most expensive dishes and tipped each of the waiters a ruble. Charlotta is the same. And Yasha also ordered a dinner, it was simply awful. You know, Yasha is Mama's footman; we brought him with us.

VARYA   I saw the rogue.

ANYA   Well, how are things? Have you paid the interest?

VARYA   How could we?

ANYA   Oh, my God, my God!

VARYA   In August the estate will be put up for sale.

120   ANYA   My God!

[LOPAKHIN *peeps in at the door and moo's like a cow.*]

LOPAKHIN   Moo-o-o! [*Disappears.*]

VARYA   [*through her tears*]   What I couldn't do to him! [*Shakes her fist.*]

ANYA   [*embracing* VARYA, *softly*]   Varya, has he proposed to you? [VARYA *shakes her head.*] But he loves you. . . . Why don't you come to an understanding, what are you waiting for?

VARYA   I don't think anything will ever come of it. He's too busy, he has no time for me . . . he doesn't even notice me. I've washed my hands of him, it makes me miserable to see him. . . . Everyone talks of our wedding, they all congratulate me, and actually there's nothing to it—it's all like a dream. . . . 130 [*In a different tone.*] You have a brooch like a bee.

ANYA   [*sadly*]   Mama bought it. [*Goes into her own room; speaks gaily, like a child.*] In Paris I went up in a balloon!

VARYA   My darling is home! My pretty one has come back!

[DUNYASHA *has come in with the coffeepot and prepares coffee.*]

VARYA [*stands at the door of* ANYA *'s room*]   You know, darling, all day long I'm busy looking after the house, but I keep dreaming. If we could marry you to a rich man I'd be at peace. I could go into a hermitage, then to Kiev, to Moscow, and from one holy place to another. . . . I'd go on and on. What a blessing!

ANYA   The birds are singing in the orchard. What time is it?

140   VARYA   It must be after two. Time you were asleep, darling. [*Goes into* ANYA'S *room.*] What a blessing!

[YASHA *enters with a lap robe and a traveling bag.*]

YASHA [*crosses the stage mincingly*]   May one go through here?

DUNYASHA   A person would hardly recognize you, Yasha. Your stay abroad has done wonders for you.

YASHA   Hm. . . . And who are you?

DUNYASHA   When you left here I was only that high—[*indicating with her hand*]. I'm Dunyasha, Fyodor Kozoyedov's daughter. You don't remember!

YASHA   Hm. . . . A little cucumber! [*Looks around, then embraces her; she cries out and drops a saucer. He quickly goes out.*]

150   VARYA [*in a tone of annoyance, from the doorway*]   What's going on here?

DUNYASHA [*tearfully*]   I broke a saucer.

VARYA   That's good luck.

ANYA   We ought to prepare Mama: Petya is here. . . .

VARYA   I gave orders not to wake him.

ANYA [*pensively*]   Six years ago Father died, and a month later brother Grisha drowned in the river . . . a pretty little seven-year-old boy. Mama couldn't bear it and went away . . . went without looking back. . . . [*Shudders.*] How I understand her, if she only knew! [*Pause*] And Petya Trofimov was Grisha's tutor, he may remind her. . . .

[*Enter* FIRS *wearing a jacket and a white waistcoat.*]

160   FIRS [*goes to the coffeepot, anxiously*]   The mistress will have her coffee here. [*Puts on white gloves.*] Is the coffee ready? [*To* DUNYASHA, *sternly.*] You! Where's the cream?

DUNYASIIA   Oh, my goodness! [*Quickly goes out.*]

FIRS [*fussing over the coffeepot*]   Ah, what an addlepate! [*Mutters to himself.*] They've come back from Paris. . . . The master used to go to Paris . . . by carriage. . . . [*Laughs.*]

VARYA   What is it, Firs?

FIRS   If you please? [*Joyfully*] My mistress has come home! At last! Now I can die. . . . [*Weeps with joy.*]

[*Enter* LYUBOV ANDREYEVNA, GAYEV, *and* SEMYONOV-PISHCHIK, *the last wearing a sleeveless peasant coat of fine cloth and full trousers,* GAYEV, *as he comes in, goes through the motions of playing billiards.*]

170   LYUBOV ANDREYEVNA   How does it go? Let's see if I can remember . . . cue ball into the corner! Double the rail to center table.

GAYEV   Cut shot into the corner! There was a time, sister, when you and I used to sleep here in this very room, and now I'm fifty-one, strange as it may seem. . . .

LOPAKHIN   Yes, time passes.

GAYEV   How's that?

LOPAKHIN   Time, I say, passes.

GAYEV   It smells of patchouli here.

ANYA   I'm going to bed. Good night, Mama. [*Kisses her mother.*]

180   LYUBOV ANDREYEVNA   My precious child. [*Kisses her hands.*] Are you glad to be home? I still feel dazed.

ANYA   Good night, Uncle.

GAYEV [*kisses her face and hands*]   God bless you. How like your mother you are! [*To his sister*] At her age you were exactly like her, Lyuba.

[ANYA *shakes hands with* LOPAKHIN *and* PISHCHIK *and goes out, closing the door after her.*]

LYUBOV ANDREYEVNA   She's exhausted.

PISHCHIK   Must have been a long journey.

VARYA   Well, gentlemen? It's after two, high time you were going.

LYUBOV ANDREYEVNA [*laughs*]   You haven't changed, Varya. [*Draws* VARYA *to her and kisses her.*] I'll just drink my coffee and then we'll all go. [FIRS *places*

190   *a cushion under her feet.*] Thank you, my dear. I've got used to coffee. I drink it day and night. Thanks, dear old man. [*Kisses him.*]

VARYA   I'd better see if all the luggage has been brought in.

LYUBOV ANDREYEVNA   Is this really me sitting here? [*Laughs.*] I feel like jumping about and waving my arms. [*Buries her face in her hands.*] What if it's only a dream! God knows I love my country, love it dearly. I couldn't look out the train window, I was crying so! [*Through tears*] But I must drink my coffee. Thank you, Firs, thank you, my dear old friend. I'm so glad you're still alive.

FIRS   The day before yesterday.

200   GAYEV   He's hard of hearing.

LOPAKHIN   I must go now, I'm leaving for Kharkov about five o'clock. It's so annoying! I wanted to have a good look at you, and have a talk. You're as splendid as ever.

PISHCHIK [*breathing heavily*]   Even more beautiful. . . . Dressed like a Parisienne. . . . There goes my wagon, all four wheels!

LOPAKHIN   Your brother here, Leonid Andreich, says I'm a boor, a money-grubber, but I don't mind. Let him talk. All I want is that you should trust me as you used to, and that your wonderful, touching eyes should look at me as they did then. Merciful God! My father was one of your father's serfs, and

210   your grandfather's, but you yourself did so much for me once, that I've forgotten all that and love you as if you were my own kin—more than my kin.

LYUBOV ANDREYEVNA   I can't sit still, I simply cannot. [*Jumps up and walks about the room in great excitement.*] I cannot bear this joy. . . . Laugh at me, I'm silly. . . . My dear little bookcase . . . [*Kisses bookcase.*] my little table . . .

GAYEV   Nurse died while you were away.

LYUBOV ANDREYEVNA [*sits down and drinks coffee*]   Yes, God rest her soul. They wrote me.

GAYEV   And Anastasy is dead. Petrushka Kosoi left me and is now with the
220 police inspector in town. [*Takes a box of hard candies from his pocket and begins to suck one.*]

PISHCHIK   My daughter, Dashenka . . . sends her regards . . .

LOPAKHIN   I wish I could tell you something very pleasant and cheering. [*Glances at his watch.*] I must go directly, there's no time to talk, but . . . well, I'll say it in a couple of words. As you know, the cherry orchard is to be sold to pay your debts. The auction is set for August twenty-second, but you need not worry, my dear, you can sleep in peace, there is a way out. This is my plan. Now, please listen! Your estate is only twenty versts from town, the railway runs close by, and if the cherry orchard and the land along the river
230 were cut up into lots and leased for summer cottages, you'd have, at the very least, an income of twenty-five thousand a year.

GAYEV   Excuse me, what nonsense!

LYUBOV ANDREYEVNA   I don't quite understand you, Yermolai Alekseich.

LOPAKHIN   You will get, at the very least, twenty-five rubles a year for a two-and-a-half-acre lot, and if you advertise now, I guarantee you won't have a single plot of ground left by autumn, everything will be snapped up. In short, I congratulate you, you are saved. The site is splendid, the river is deep. Only, of course, the ground must be cleared . . . you must tear down all the old outbuildings, for instance, and this house, which is worthless, cut
240 down the old cherry orchard—

LYUBOV ANDREYEVNA   Cut it down? Forgive me, my dear, but you don't know what you are talking about. If there is one thing in the whole province that is interesting, not to say remarkable, it's our cherry orchard.

LOPAKHIN   The only remarkable thing about this orchard is that it is very big. There's a crop of cherries every other year, and then you can't get rid of them, nobody buys them.

GAYEV   This orchard is even mentioned in the *Encyclopedia.*

LOPAKHIN [*glancing at his watch*]   If we don't think of something and come to a decision, on the twenty-second of August the cherry orchard, and
250 the entire estate, will be sold at auction. Make up your minds! There is no other way out, I swear to you. None whatsoever.

FIRS   In the old days, forty or fifty years ago, the cherries were dried, soaked, marinated, and made into jam, and they used to—

GAYEV   Be quiet, Firs.

FIRS   And they used to send cartloads of dried cherries to Moscow and Kharkov. And that brought in money! The dried cherries were soft and juicy in those days, sweet, fragrant. . . . They had a method then . . .

LYUBOV ANDREYEVNA   And what has become of that method now?

FIRS   Forgotten. Nobody remembers. . . .

260 PISHCHIK   How was it in Paris? What's it like there? Did you eat frogs?

LYUBOV ANDREYEVNA   I ate crocodiles.

PISHCHIK   Think of that now!

LOPAKHIN   There used to be only the gentry and the peasants living in the country, but now these summer people have appeared. All the towns, even the smallest ones, are surrounded by summer cottages. And it is safe to say that in another twenty years these people will multiply enormously. Now the summer resident only drinks tea on his porch, but it may well be that he'll take to cultivating his acre, and then your cherry orchard will be a happy, rich, luxuriant—

270   GAYEV [*indignantly*]   What nonsense!

[*Enter* VARYA *and* YASHA.]

VARYA   There are two telegrams for you, Mama. [*Picks out a key and with a jingling sound opens an old-fashioned bookcase.*] Here they are.

LYUBOV ANDREYEVNA   From Paris. [*Tears up the telegrams without reading them.*] That's all over. . . .

GAYEV   Do you know, Lyuba, how old this bookcase is? A week ago I pulled out the bottom drawer, and what do I see? Some figures burnt into it. The bookcase was made exactly a hundred years ago. What do you think of that? Eh? We could have celebrated its jubilee. It's an inanimate object, but nevertheless, for all that, it's a bookcase.

280   PISHCHIK   A hundred years . . . think of that now!

GAYEV   Yes . . . that is something. . . . [*Feeling the bookcase*] Dear, honored bookcase, I salute thy existence, which for over one hundred years has served the glorious ideals of goodness and justice; thy silent appeal to fruitful endeavor, unflagging in the course of a hundred years, tearfully sustaining through generations of our family, courage and faith in a better future, and fostering in us ideals of goodness and social consciousness. . . .

[*A pause*]

LOPAKHIN   Yes . . .

LYUBOV ANDREYEVNA   You are the same as ever, Lyonya.

GAYEV [*somewhat embarrassed*]   Carom into the corner, cut shot to center

290   table.

LOPAKHIN [*looks at his watch*]   Well, time for me to go.

YASHA [*hands medicine to* LYUBOV ANDREYEVNA]   Perhaps you will take your pills now.

PISHCHIK   Don't take medicaments, dearest lady, they do neither harm nor good. Let me have them, honored lady. [*Takes the pill box, shakes the pills into his hand, blows on them, puts them into his mouth, and washes them down with kvas.*] There!

LYUBOV ANDREYEVNA [*alarmed*]   Why, you must be mad!

PISHCHIK   I've taken all the pills.

300   LOPAKHIN   What a glutton!

[*Everyone laughs.*]

FIRS The gentleman stayed with us during Holy Week . . . ate half a bucket of pickles. . . . [*Mumbles.*]

LYUBOV ANDREYEVNA What is he saying?

VARYA He's been muttering like that for three years now. We've grown used to it.

YASHA He's in his dotage.

[CHARLOTTA IVANOVNA, *very thin, tightly laced, in a white dress with a lorgnette at her belt, crosses the stage.*]

LOPAKHIN Forgive me, Charlotta Ivanovna, I haven't had a chance to say how do you do to you. [*Tries to kiss her hand.*]

CHARLOTTA [*pulls her hand away*] If I permit you to kiss my hand you'll
310 be wanting to kiss my elbow next, then my shoulder.

LOPAKHIN I have no luck today. [*Everyone laughs.*] Charlotta Ivanovna, show us a trick!

LYUBOV ANDREYEVNA Charlotta, show us a trick!

CHARLOTTA No. I want to sleep. [*Goes out.*]

LOPAKHIN In three weeks we'll meet again. [*Kisses* LYUBOV ANDREYEVNA*'s hand.*] Good-bye till then. Time to go. [*To* GAYEV.] Good-bye. [*Kisses* PISHCHIK.] Good-bye. [*Shakes hands with* VARYA, *then with* FIRS *and* YASHA.] I don't feel like going. [*To* LYUBOV ANDREYEVNA] If you make up your mind about the summer cottages and come to a decision, let me know; I'll get you a loan
320 of fifty thousand or so. Think it over seriously.

VARYA [*angrily*] Oh, why don't you go!

LOPAKHIN I'm going, I'm going. [*Goes out.*]

GAYEV Boor. Oh, pardon. Varya's going to marry him, he's Varya's young man.

VARYA Uncle dear, you talk too much.

LYUBOV ANDREYEVNA Well, Varya, I shall be very glad. He's a good man.

PISHCHIK A man, I must truly say . . . most worthy. . . . And my Dashenka . . . says, too, that . . . says all sorts of things. [*Snores but wakes up at once.*] In any case, honored lady, oblige me . . . a loan of two hundred
330 and forty rubles . . . tomorrow the interest on my mortgage is due. . . .

VARYA [*in alarm*] We have nothing, nothing at all!

LYUBOV ANDREYEVNA I really haven't any money.

PISHCHIK It'll turn up. [*Laughs.*] I never lose hope. Just when I thought everything was lost, that I was done for, lo and behold—the railway line ran through my land . . . and they paid me for it. And before you know it, something else will turn up, if not today—tomorrow. . . . Dashenka will win two hundred thousand . . . she's got a lottery ticket.

LYUBOV ANDREYEVNA The coffee is finished, we can go to bed.

FIRS [*brushing* GAYEV*'s clothes, admonishingly*] You've put on the wrong
340 trousers again. What am I to do with you?

VARYA [*softly*] Anya's asleep. [*Quietly opens the window.*] The sun has risen, it's no longer cold. Look, Mama dear, what wonderful trees! Oh, Lord, the air! The starlings are singing!

GAYEV [*opens another window*]   The orchard is all white. You haven't forgotten, Lyuba? That long avenue there that runs straight—straight as a stretched-out strap; it gleams on moonlight nights. Remember? You've not forgotten?

LYUBOV ANDREYEVNA [*looking out the window at the orchard*]   Oh, my childhood, my innocence! I used to sleep in this nursery, I looked out from
350   here into the orchard, happiness awoke with me each morning, it was just as it is now, nothing has changed. [*Laughing with joy*] All, all white! Oh, my orchard! After the dark, rainy autumn and the cold winter, you are young again, full of happiness, the heavenly angels have not forsaken you. . . . If I could cast off this heavy stone weighing on my breast and shoulders, if I could forget my past!

GAYEV   Yes, and the orchard will be sold for our debts, strange as it may seem. . . .

LYUBOV ANDREYEVNA   Look, our dead mother walks in the orchard . . . in a white dress! [*Laughs with joy.*] It is she!
360   GAYEV   Where?

VARYA   God be with you, Mama dear.

LYUBOV ANDREYEVNA   There's no one there, I just imagined it. To the right, as you turn to the summerhouse, a slender white sapling is bent over . . . it looks like a woman.

[*Enter* TROFIMOV *wearing a shabby student's uniform and spectacles.*]

LYUBOV ANDREYEVNA   What a wonderful orchard! The white masses of blossoms, the blue sky—

TROFIMOV   Lyubov Andreyevna! [*She looks around at him.*] I only want to pay my respects, then I'll go at once. [*Kisses her hand ardently.*] I was told to wait until morning, but I hadn't the patience.

[LYUBOV ANDREYEVNA *looks at him, puzzled.*]

370   VARYA [*through tears*]   This is Petya Trofimov.

TROFIMOV   Petya Trofimov, I was Grisha's tutor. . . . Can I have changed so much?

[LYUBOV ANDREYEVNA *embraces him, quietly weeping.*]

GAYEV [*embarrassed*]   There, there, Lyuba.

VARYA [*crying*]   Didn't I tell you, Petya, to wait till tomorrow?

LYUBOV ANDREYEVNA   My Grisha . . . my little boy . . . Grisha . . . my son. . . .

VARYA   What can we do, Mama dear? It's God's will.

TROFIMOV [*gently, through tears*]   Don't, don't. . . .

LYUBOV ANDREYEVNA [*quietly weeping*]   My little boy dead, drowned. . . .
380 Why? Why, my friend? [*In a lower voice.*] Anya is sleeping in there, and I'm talking loudly . . . making all this noise. . . . But Petya, why do you look so bad? Why have you grown so old?

TROFIMOV A peasant woman in the train called me a mangy gentleman.

LYUBOV ANDREYEVNA You were just a boy then, a charming little student, and now your hair is thin—and spectacles! Is it possible you are still a student? [*Goes toward the door.*]

TROFIMOV I shall probably be an eternal student.

LYUBOV ANDREYEVNA [*kisses her brother, then* VARYA] Now, go to bed. . . . You've grown older too, Leonid.

390 PISHCHIK [*follows her*] Well, seems to be time to sleep. . . . Oh, my gout! I'm staying the night. Lyubov Andreyevna, my soul, tomorrow morning . . . two hundred and forty rubles. . . .

GAYEV He keeps at it.

PISHCHIK Two hundred and forty rubles . . . to pay the interest on my mortgage.

LYUBOV ANDREYEVNA I have no money, my friend.

PISHCHIK My dear, I'll pay it back. . . . It's a trifling sum.

LYUBOV ANDREYEVNA Well, all right, Leonid will give it to you. . . . Give it to him, Leonid.

400 GAYEV Me give it to him! . . . Hold out your pocket!

LYUBOV ANDREYEVNA It can't be helped, give it to him. . . . He needs it. . . . He'll pay it back.

[LYUBOV ANDREYEVNA, TROFIMOV, PISHCHIK, *and* FIRS *go out.* GAYEV, VARYA, *and* YASHA *remain.*]

GAYEV My sister hasn't yet lost her habit of squandering money. [*To* YASHA.] Go away, my good fellow, you smell of the henhouse.

YASHA [*with a smirk*] And you, Leonid Andreyevich, are just the same as ever.

GAYEV How's that? [*To* VARYA] What did he say?

VARYA Your mother has come from the village; she's been sitting in the servants' room since yesterday, waiting to see you. . . .

410 YASHA Let her wait, for God's sake!

VARYA Aren't you ashamed?

YASHA A lot I need her! She could have come tomorrow. [*Goes out.*]

VARYA Mama's the same as ever, she hasn't changed a bit. She'd give away everything, if she could.

GAYEV Yes. . . . [*A pause*] If a great many remedies are suggested for a disease, it means that the disease is incurable. I keep thinking, racking my brains, I have many remedies, a great many, and that means, in effect, that I have none. It would be good to receive a legacy from someone, good to marry our Anya to a very rich man, good to go to Yaroslav and try our luck
420 with our aunt, the Countess. She is very, very rich, you know.

VARYA [*crying*] If only God would help us!

GAYEV Stop bawling. Auntie's very rich, but she doesn't like us. In the first place, sister married a lawyer, not a nobleman . . . [ANYA *appears in the doorway.*] She married beneath her, and it cannot be said that she has conducted herself very virtuously. She is good, kind, charming, and I love her dearly, but no matter how much you allow for extenuating circumstances, you must admit she leads a sinful life. You feel it in her slightest movement.

VARYA [*in a whisper*]   Anya is standing in the doorway.

GAYEV   What? [*Pause*] Funny, something got into my right eye . . . I can't
430 see very well. And Thursday, when I was in the district court . . .

[ANYA *enters.*]

VARYA   Why aren't you asleep, Anya?

ANYA   I can't get to sleep. I just can't.

GAYEV   My little one! [*Kisses* ANYA's *face and hands*] My child. . . .
[*Through tears*] You are not my niece, you are my angel, you are everything to
me. Believe me, believe me.

ANYA   I believe you, Uncle. Everyone loves you and respects you, but,
Uncle dear, you must keep quiet, just keep quiet. What were you saying just
now about my mother, about your own sister? What made you say that?

GAYEV   Yes, yes. . . . [*Covers his face with her hand*] Really, it's awful! My
440 God! God help me! And today I made a speech to the bookcase . . . so
stupid! And it was only when I had finished that I realized it was stupid.

VARYA   It's true, Uncle dear, you ought to keep quiet. Just don't talk,
that's all.

ANYA   If you could keep from talking, it would make things easier for
you, too.

GAYEV   I'll be quiet. [*Kisses* ANYA's *and* VARYA's *hands.*] I'll be quiet. Only
this is about business. On Thursday I was in the district court, well, a group
of us gathered together and began talking about one thing and another, this
and that, and it seems it might be possible to arrange a loan on a promissory
450 note to pay the interest at the bank.

VARYA   If only God would help us!

GAYEV   On Tuesday I'll go and talk it over again. [*To* VARYA] Stop bawling.
[*To* ANYA] Your mama will talk to Lopakhin; he, of course, will not refuse
her. . . . And as soon as you've rested, you will go to Yaroslav to the
Countess your great-aunt. In that way we shall be working from three directions and our business is in the hat. We'll pay the interest I'm certain of
it. . . . [*Puts a candy in his mouth.*] On my honor, I'll swear by anything you
like, the estate shall not be sold. [*Excitedly.*] By my happiness, I swear it!
Here's my hand on it, call me a worthless, dishonorable man if I let it come to
460 auction! I swear by my whole being!

ANYA [*a calm mood returns to her, she is happy*]   How good you are,
Uncle, how clever! [*Embraces him.*] Now I am at peace! I'm at peace! I'm
happy!

[*Enter* FIRS.]

FIRS [*reproachfully*]   Leonid Andreich, have you no fear of God? When are
you going to bed?

GAYEV   Presently, presently. Go away, Firs. I'll . . . all right I'll undress
myself. Well, children, bye-bye. . . . Details tomorrow, and now go to sleep.
[*Kisses* ANYA *and* VARYA.] I am a man of the eighties. . . . They don't think much

of that period today, nevertheless, I can say that in the course of my life I have
470 suffered not a little for my convictions. It is not for nothing that the peasant
loves me. You have to know the peasant! You have to know from what—

ANYA There you go again, Uncle!

VARYA Uncle dear, do be quiet.

FIRS [*angrily*] Leonid Andreich!

GAYEV I'm coming, I'm coming. . . . Go to bed. A clean double rail shot
to center table. . . . [*Goes out;* FIRS *hobbles after him.*]

ANYA I'm at peace now. I would rather not go to Yaroslav, I don't like my
great-aunt, but still, I'm at peace, thanks to Uncle. [*She sits down.*]

VARYA We must get some sleep. I'm going now. Oh, something unpleasant
480 happened while you were away. In the old servants' quarters, as you know,
there are only the old people: Yefimushka, Polya, Yevstignei, and, of course,
Karp. They began letting in all sorts of rogues to spend the night—I didn't
say anything. But then I heard they'd been spreading a rumor that I'd given
an order for them to be fed nothing but dried peas. Out of stinginess, you
see. . . . It was all Yevstignei's doing. . . . Very well, I think, if that's how
it is, you just wait. I send for Yevstignei . . . [*yawning*] he comes. . . .
"How is it, Yevstignei," I say, "that you could be such a fool. . . ." [*Looks
at* ANYA.] She's fallen asleep. [*Takes her by the arm.*] Come to your little
bed. . . . Come along. [*Leading her*] My little darling fell asleep.
490 Come. . . . [*They go.*]

[*In the distance, beyond the orchard, a shepherd is playing on a reed pipe.* TROFIMOV
crosses the stage and, seeing VARYA *and* ANYA, *stops.*]

VARYA Sh! She's asleep . . . asleep. . . . Come along, darling.

ANYA [*softly, half-asleep*] I'm so tired. . . . Those bells . . . Uncle . . .
dear . . . Mama and Uncle . . .

VARYA Come, darling, come along. [*They go into* ANYA*'s room.*]

TROFIMOV [*deeply moved*] My sunshine! My spring!

Act II

[*A meadow. An old, lopsided, long-abandoned little chapel; near it a well, large
stones that apparently were once tombstones, and an old bench. A road to the* GAYEV
*manor house can be seen. On one side, where the cherry orchard begins, tall poplars
loom. In the distance a row of telegraph poles, and far, far away, on the horizon, the
faint outline of a large town, which is visible only in very fine, clear weather. The sun
will soon set.* CHARLOTTA, YASHA, *and* DUNYASHA *are sitting on the bench;* YEPIKHODOV
stands near playing something sad on the guitar. They are all lost in thought. CHAR-
LOTTA *wears an old forage cap; she has taken a gun from her shoulder and is adjusting the buckle on the sling.*]

CHARLOTTA [*reflectively*] I haven't got a real passport, I don't know how
old I am, but it always seems to me that I'm quite young. When I was a little
girl, my father and mother used to travel from one fair to another giving

performances—very good ones. And I did the *salto mortale* and all sorts of tricks. Then when Papa and Mama died, a German lady took me to live with her and began teaching me. Good. I grew up and became a governess. But where I come from and who I am—I do not know. . . . Who my parents were—perhaps they weren't even married—I don't know. [*Takes a cucumber out of her pocket and eats it.*] I don't know anything. [*Pause*] One wants
10 so much to talk, but there isn't anyone to talk to . . . I have no one.

YEPIKHODOV [*plays the guitar and sings*] "What care I for the clamorous world, what's friend or foe to me?" . . . How pleasant it is to play a mandolin!

DUNYASHA That's a guitar, not a mandolin. [*Looks at herself in a hand mirror and powders her face.*]

YEPIKHODOV To a madman, in love, it is a mandolin. . . . [*Sings.*] "Would that the heart were warmed by the flame of requited love . . ."

[YASHA *joins in.*]

CHARLOTTA How horribly these people sing! . . . Pfui! Like jackals!

DUNYASHA [*to* YASHA] Really, how fortunate to have been abroad!

YASHA Yes, to be sure. I cannot but agree with you there. [*Yawns, then*
20 *lights a cigar.*]

YEPIKHODOV It stands to reason. Abroad everything has long since been fully constituted.

YASHA Obviously.

YEPIKHODOV I am a cultivated man, I read all sorts of remarkable books, but I am in no way able to make out my own inclinations, what it is I really want, whether, strictly speaking, to live or to shoot myself; nevertheless, I always carry a revolver on me. Here it is. [*Shows revolver.*]

CHARLOTTA Finished. Now I'm going. [*Slings the gun over her shoulder.*] You're a very clever man, Yepikhodov, and quite terrifying; women must be
30 mad about you. Brrr! [*Starts to go.*] These clever people are all so stupid, there's no one for me to talk to. . . . Alone, always alone, I have no one . . . and who I am, and why I am, nobody knows. . . . [*Goes out unhurriedly.*]

YEPIKHODOV Strictly speaking, all else aside, I must state regarding myself, that fate treats me unmercifully, as a storm does a small ship. If, let us assume, I am mistaken, then why, to mention a single instance, do I wake up this morning, and there on my chest see a spider of terrifying magnitude? . . . Like that. [*Indicates with both hands.*] And likewise, I take up some kvas to quench my thirst, and there see something in the highest degree unseemly, like a cockroach. [*Pause.*] Have you read Buckle? [*Pause.*]
40 If I may trouble you, Avdotya Fedorovna, I should like to have a word or two with you.

DUNYASHA Go ahead.

YEPIKHODOV I prefer to speak with you alone. . . . [*Sighs.*]

DUNYASHA [*embarrassed*] Very well . . . only first bring me my little cape . . . you'll find it by the cupboard. . . . It's rather damp here. . . .

YEPIKHODOV Certainly, ma'am . . . I'll fetch it, ma'am. . . . Now I know what to do with my revolver. . . . [*Takes the guitar and goes off playing it.*]

YASHA   Two-and-twenty Troubles! Between ourselves, a stupid fellow. [*Yawns.*]

50 DUNYASHA   God forbid that he should shoot himself. [*Pause.*] I've grown so anxious, I'm always worried. I was only a little girl when I was taken into the master's house, and now I'm quite unused to the simple life, and my hands are white as can be, just like a lady's. I've become so delicate, so tender and ladylike, I'm afraid of everything. . . . Frightfully so. And, Yasha, if you deceive me, I just don't know what will become of my nerves.

YASHA [*kisses her*]   You little cucumber! Of course, a girl should never forget herself. What I dislike above everything is when a girl doesn't conduct herself properly.

DUNYASHA   I'm passionately in love with you; you're educated, you can 60 discuss anything. [*Pause*]

YASHA [*yawns*]   Yes. . . . As I see it, it's like this: if a girl loves somebody, that means she's immoral. [*Pause*] Very pleasant smoking a cigar in the open air. . . . [*Listens.*] Someone's coming this way. . . . It's the masters. [DUN-YASHA *impulsively embraces him.*] You go home, as if you'd been to the river to bathe; take that path, otherwise they'll see you and suspect me of having a rendezvous with you. I can't endure that sort of thing.

DUNYASHA [*with a little cough*]   My head is beginning to ache from your cigar. . . . [*Goes out.*]

[YASHA *remains, sitting near the chapel,* LYUBOV ANDREYEVNA, GAYEV, *and* LOPAKHIN *enter.*]

LOPAKHIN   You must make up your mind once and for all—time won't 70 stand still. The question, after all, is quite simple. Do you agree to lease the land for summer cottages or not? Answer in one word: yes or no? Only one word!

LYUBOV ANDREYEVNA   Who is it that smokes those disgusting cigars out here? [*Sits down.*]

GAYEV   Now that the railway line is so near, it's made things convenient. [*Sits down.*] We went to town and had lunch . . . cue ball to the center! I feel like going to the house first and playing a game.

LYUBOV ANDREYEVNA   Later.

LOPAKHIN   Just one word! [*Imploringly*] Do give me an answer!

80 GAYEV [*yawning*]   How's that?

LYUBOV ANDREYEVNA [*looks into her purse*]   Yesterday I had a lot of money, and today there's hardly any left. My poor Varya tries to economize by feeding everyone milk soup, and in the kitchen the old people get nothing but dried peas, while I squander money foolishly. . . . [*Drops the purse, scattering gold coins.*] There they go. . . . [*Vexed*]

YASHA   Allow me, I'll pick them up in an instant. [*Picks up the money.*]

LYUBOV ANDREYEVNA   Please do, Yasha. And why did I go to town for lunch? . . . That miserable restaurant of yours with its music, and table-cloths smelling of soap. . . . Why drink so much, Lyonya? Why eat so much? 90 Why talk so much? Today in the restaurant again you talked too much, and it was all so pointless. About the seventies, about the decadents. And to whom? Talking to waiters about the decadents!

LOPAKHIN Yes.

GAYEV [*waving his hand*] I'm incorrigible, that's evident. . . . [*Irritably to* YASHA] Why do you keep twirling about in front of me?

YASHA [*laughs*] I can't help laughing when I hear your voice.

GAYEV [*to his sister*] Either he or I—

LYUBOV ANDREYEVNA Go away, Yasha, run along.

YASHA [*hands* LYUBOV ANDREYEVNA *her purse*] I'm going, right away.
100 [*Hardly able to contain his laughter.*] This very instant. . . . [*Goes out.*]

LOPAKHIN That rich man, Deriganov, is prepared to buy the estate. They say he's coming to the auction himself.

LYUBOV ANDREYEVNA Where did you hear that?

LOPAKHIN That's what they're saying in town.

LYUBOV ANDREYEVNA Our aunt in Yaroslav promised to send us something, but when and how much, no one knows.

LOPAKHIN How much do you think she'll send? A hundred thousand? Two hundred?

LYUBOV ANDREYEVNA Oh . . . ten or fifteen thousand, and we'll be thank-
110 ful for that.

LOPAKHIN Forgive me, but I have never seen such frivolous, such queer, unbusinesslike people as you, my friends. You are told in plain language that your estate is to be sold, and it's as though you don't understand it.

LYUBOV ANDREYEVNA But what are we to do? Tell us what to do.

LOPAKHIN I tell you every day. Every day I say the same thing. Both the cherry orchard and the land must be leased for summer cottages, and it must be done now, as quickly as possible—the auction is close at hand. Try to understand! Once you definitely decide on the cottages, you can raise as much money as you like, and then you are saved.

120 LYUBOV ANDREYEVNA Cottages, summer people—forgive me, but it's so vulgar.

GAYEV I agree with you, absolutely.

LOPAKHIN I'll either burst into tears, start shouting, or fall into a faint! I can't stand it! You've worn me out! [*To* GAYEV] You're an old woman!

GAYEV How's that?

LOPAKHIN An old woman! [*Starts to go.*]

LYUBOV ANDREYEVNA [*alarmed*] No, don't go, stay, my dear. I beg you. Perhaps we'll think of something!

LOPAKHIN What is there to think of?

130 LYUBOV ANDREYEVNA Don't go away, please. With you here it's more cheer-ful somehow. . . . [*Pause.*] I keep expecting something to happen, like the house caving in on us.

GAYEV [*in deep thought*] Double rail shot into the corner. . . . Cross table to the center. . . .

LYUBOV ANDREYEVNA We have sinned so much. . . .

LOPAKHIN What sins could you have—

GAYEV [*puts a candy into his mouth*] They say I've eaten up my entire fortune in candies. . . . [*Laughs.*]

LYUBOV ANDREYEVNA Oh, my sins. . . . I've always squandered money
140 recklessly, like a madwoman, and I married a man who did nothing but amass debts. My husband died from champagne—he drank terribly—then, to my sorrow, I fell in love with another man, lived with him, and just at that time—that was my first punishment, a blow on the head—my little boy was drowned . . . here in the river. And I went abroad, went away for good, never to return, never to see this river. . . . I closed my eyes and ran, beside myself, and *he* after me . . . callously, without pity. I bought a villa near Mentone, because he fell ill there, and for three years I had no rest, day or night. The sick man wore me out, my soul dried up. Then last year, when the villa was sold to pay my debts, I went to Paris, and there he stripped me of
150 everything, and left me for another woman; I tried to poison myself. . . . So stupid, so shameful. . . . And suddenly I felt a longing for Russia, for my own country, for my little girl. . . . [*Wipes away her tears.*] Lord, Lord, be merciful, forgive my sins! Don't punish me any more! [*Takes a telegram out of her pocket.*] This came today from Paris. . . . He asks my forgiveness, begs me to return. . . . [*Tears up telegram.*] Do I hear music? [*Listens.*]

GAYEV That's our famous Jewish band. You remember, four violins, a flute and double bass.

LYUBOV ANDREYEVNA It's still in existence? We ought to send for them some time and give a party.

160 LOPAKHIN [*listens*] I don't hear anything. . . . [*Sings softly.*] "The Germans, for pay, will turn Russians into Frenchmen, they say." [*Laughs.*] What a play I saw yesterday at the theater—very funny!

LYUBOV ANDREYEVNA There was probably nothing funny about it. Instead of going to see plays you ought to look at yourselves a little more often. How drab your lives are, how full of futile talk!

LOPAKHIN That's true. I must say, this life of ours is stupid. . . . [*Pause*] My father was a peasant, an idiot; he understood nothing, taught me nothing; all he did was beat me when he was drunk, and always with a stick. As a matter of fact, I'm as big a blockhead and idiot as he was. I never learned
170 anything, my handwriting's disgusting, I write like a pig—I'm ashamed to have people see it.

LYUBOV ANDREYEVNA You ought to get married, my friend.

LOPAKHIN Yes . . . that's true.

LYUBOV ANDREYEVNA To our Varya. She's a nice girl.

LOPAKHIN Yes.

LYUBOV ANDREYEVNA She's a girl who comes from simple people, works all day long, but the main thing is she loves you. Besides, you've liked her for a long time now.

LOPAKHIN Well? I've nothing against it. . . . She's a good girl. [*Pause*]
180 GAYEV I've been offered a place in the bank. Six thousand a year. . . . Have you heard?

LYUBOV ANDREYEVNA How could you! You stay where you are. . . .

[FIRS *enters carrying an overcoat.*]

FIRS [*To* GAYEV]   If you please, sir, put this on, it's damp.

GAYEV [*puts on the overcoat*]   You're a pest, old man.

FIRS   Never mind. . . . You went off this morning without telling me. [*Looks him over.*]

LYUBOV ANDREYEVNA   How you have aged, Firs!

FIRS   What do you wish, madam?

LOPAKHIN   She says you've grown very old!

190   FIRS   I've lived a long time. They were arranging a marriage for me before your papa was born. . . . [*Laughs.*] I was already head footman when the Emancipation came. At that time I wouldn't consent to my freedom, I stayed with the masters. . . . [*Pause*] I remember, everyone was happy, but what they were happy about, they themselves didn't know.

LOPAKHIN   It was better in the old days. At least they flogged them.

FIRS [*not hearing*]   Of course. The peasants kept to the masters, the masters kept to the peasants; but now they have all gone their own ways, you can't tell about anything.

GAYEV   Be quiet, Firs. Tomorrow I must go to town. I've been promised an
200   introduction to a certain general who might let us have a loan.

LOPAKHIN   Nothing will come of it. And you can rest assured, you won't even pay the interest.

LYUBOV ANDREYEVNA   He's raving. There is no such general.

[*Enter* TROFIMOV, ANYA, *and* VARYA.]

GAYEV   Here come our young people.

ANYA   There's Mama.

LYUBOV ANDREYEVNA [*tenderly*]   Come, come along, my darlings. [*Embraces* ANYA *and* VARYA.] If you only knew how I love you both! Sit here beside me—there, like that.

[*They all sit down.*]

LOPAKHIN   Our eternal student is always with the young ladies.

210   TROFIMOV   That's none of your business.

LOPAKHIN   He'll soon be fifty, but he's still a student.

TROFIMOV   Drop your stupid jokes.

LOPAKHIN   What are you so angry about, you queer fellow?

TROFIMOV   Just leave me alone.

LOPAKHIN [*laughs*]   Let me ask you something: what do you make of me?

TROFIMOV   My idea of you, Yermolai Alekseich, is this: you're a rich man, you will soon be a millionaire. Just as the beast of prey, which devours everything that crosses its path, is necessary in the metabolic process, so are you necessary.

[*Everyone laughs.*]

220   VARYA Petya, you'd better tell us something about the planets.

LYUBOV ANDREYEVNA No, let's go on with yesterday's conversation.

TROFIMOV What was it about?

GAYEV About the proud man.

TROFIMOV We talked a long time yesterday, but we didn't get anywhere. In the proud man, in your sense of the word, there's something mystical. And you may be right from your point of view, but if you look at it simply, without being abstruse, why even talk about pride? Is there any sense in it if, physiologically, man is poorly constructed, if, in the vast majority of cases, he is coarse, ignorant, and profoundly unhappy? We should stop admiring
230   ourselves. We should just work, and that's all.

GAYEV You die, anyway.

TROFIMOV Who knows? And what does it mean—to die? It may be that man has a hundred senses, and at his death only the five that are known to us perish, and the other ninety-five go on living.

LYUBOV ANDREYEVNA How clever you are, Petya!

LOPAKHIN [*ironically*] Terribly clever!

TROFIMOV Mankind goes forward, perfecting its powers. Everything that is now unattainable will some day be comprehensible and within our grasp, only we must work, and help with all our might those who are seeking the
240   truth. So far, among us here in Russia, only a very few work. The great majority of the intelligentsia that I know seek nothing, do nothing, and as yet are incapable of work. They call themselves the intelligentsia, yet they belittle their servants, treat the peasants like animals, are wretched students, never read anything serious, and do absolutely nothing; they only talk about science and know very little about art. They all look serious, have grim expressions, speak of weighty matters, and philosophize; and meanwhile anyone can see that the workers eat abominably, sleep without pillows, thirty or forty to a room, and everywhere there are bedbugs, stench, dampness, and immorality. . . . It's obvious that all our fine talk is merely to delude
250   ourselves and others. Show me the day nurseries they are always talking about—and where are the reading rooms? They only write about them in novels, but in reality they don't exist. There is nothing but filth, vulgarity, asiaticism. . . . I'm afraid of those very serious countenances, I don't like them, I'm afraid of serious conversations. We'd do better to remain silent.

LOPAKHIN You know, I get up before five in the morning, and I work from morning to night; now, I'm always handling money, my own and other people's, and I see what people around me are like. You have only to start doing something to find out how few honest, decent people there are. Sometimes, when I can't sleep, I think: "Lord, Thou gavest us vast forests, boundless
260   fields, broad horizons, and living in their midst we ourselves ought truly to be giants. . . ."

LYUBOV ANDREYEVNA Now you want giants! They're good only in fairy tales, otherwise they're frightening.

[YEPIKHODOV *crosses at the rear of the stage, playing the guitar.*]

LYUBOV ANDREYEVNA [*pensively*] There goes Yepikhodov . . . .
ANYA [*pensively*] There goes Yepikhodov . . .
GAYEV The sun has set, ladies and gentlemen.
TROFIMOV Yes.
GAYEV [*in a low voice, as though reciting*] Oh, Nature, wondrous Nature,
you shine with eternal radiance, beautiful and indifferent; you, whom we call
270 mother, unite within yourself both life and death, giving life and taking it
away. . . .
VARYA [*beseechingly*] Uncle dear!
ANYA Uncle, you're doing it again!
TROFIMOV You'd better cue ball into the center.
GAYEV I'll be silent, silent.

[*All sit lost in thought. The silence is broken only by the subdued muttering of* FIRS.
*Suddenly a distant sound is heard, as if from the sky, like the sound of a snapped
string mournfully dying away.*]

LYUBOV ANDREYEVNA What was that?
LOPAKHIN I don't know. Somewhere far off in a mine shaft a bucket's
broken loose. But somewhere very far away.
GAYEV It might be a bird of some sort . . . like a heron.
280 TROFIMOV Or an owl . . .
LYUBOV ANDREYEVNA [*shudders*] It's unpleasant somehow. . . . [*Pause*]
FIRS The same thing happened before the troubles: an owl hooted and the
samovar hissed continually.
GAYEV Before what troubles?
FIRS Before the Emancipation.
LYUBOV ANDREYEVNA Come along, my friends, let us go, evening is falling.
[*To* ANYA] There are tears in your eyes—what is it, my little one?

[*Embraces her.*]

ANYA It's all right, Mama. It's nothing.
TROFIMOV Someone is coming.

[A STRANGER *appears wearing a shabby white forage cap and an overcoat. He is
slightly drunk.*]

290   STRANGER Permit me to inquire, can I go straight through here to the
station?
GAYEV You can. Follow the road.
STRANGER I am deeply grateful to you. [*Coughs.*] Splendid weather. . . .
[*Reciting*] "My brother, my suffering brother . . . come to the Volga, whose
groans" . . . [*To* VARYA] Mademoiselle, will you oblige a hungry Russian with
thirty kopecks?

[VARYA, *frightened, cries out.*]

LOPAKHIN [*angrily*]   There's a limit to everything.

LYUBOV ANDREYEVNA [*panic-stricken*]   Here you are—take this. . . . [*Fumbles in her purse.*] I have no silver. . . . Never mind, here's a gold piece
300   for you. . . .

STRANGER   I am deeply grateful to you. [*Goes off.*]

[*Laughter*]

VARYA [*frightened*]   I'm leaving . . . I'm leaving. . . . Oh, Mama, dear, there's nothing in the house for the servants to eat, and you give him a gold piece!

LYUBOV ANDREYEVNA   What's to be done with such a silly creature? When we get home I'll give you all I've got. Yermolai Alekseyevich, you'll lend me some more!

LOPAKHIN   At your service.

LYUBOV ANDREYEVNA   Come, my friends, it's time to go. Oh, Varya, we have
310   definitely made a match for you. Congratulations!

VARYA [*through tears*]   Mama, that's not something to joke about.

LOPAKHIN   "Aurelia, get thee to a nunnery . . ."

GAYEV   Look, my hands are trembling: it's a long time since I've played a game of billiards.

LOPAKHIN   "Aurelia, O Nymph, in thy orisons, be all my sins remember'd!"

LYUBOV ANDREYEVNA   Let us go, my friends, it will soon be suppertime.

VARYA   He frightened me. My heart is simply pounding.

LOPAKHIN   Let me remind you, ladies and gentlemen: on the twenty-second of August the cherry orchard is to be sold. Think about that!—Think!

[*All go out except* TROFIMOV *and* ANYA.]

320   ANYA [*laughs*]   My thanks to the stranger for frightening Varya, now we are alone.

TROFIMOV   Varya is so afraid we might suddenly fall in love with each other that she hasn't left us alone for days. With her narrow mind she can't understand that we are above love. To avoid the petty and the illusory, which prevent our being free and happy—that is the aim and meaning of life. Forward! We are moving irresistibly toward the bright star that burns in the distance! Forward! Do not fall behind, friends!

ANYA [*clasping her hands*]   How well you talk! [*Pause*] It's marvelous here today!

330   TROFIMOV   Yes, the weather is wonderful.

ANYA   What have you done to me, Petya, that I no longer love the cherry orchard as I used to? I loved it so tenderly, it seemed to me there was no better place on earth than our orchard.

TROFIMOV   All Russia is our orchard. It is a great and beautiful land, and there are many wonderful places in it. [*Pause*] Just think, Anya: your grandfather, your great-grandfather, and all your ancestors were serf-owners, possessors of living souls. Don't you see that from every cherry tree, from every

leaf and trunk, human beings are peering out at you? Don't you hear their voices? To possess living souls—that has corrupted all of you, those who
340 lived before and you who are living now, so that your mother, you, your uncle, no longer perceive that you are living in debt, at someone else's expense, at the expense of those whom you wouldn't allow to cross your threshold. . . . We are at least two hundred years behind the times, we have as yet absolutely nothing, we have no definite attitude toward the past, we only philosophize, complain of boredom, or drink vodka. Yet it's quite clear that to begin to live we must first atone for the past, be done with it, and we can atone for it only by suffering, only by extraordinary, unceasing labor. Understand this, Anya.

ANYA The house we live in hasn't really been ours for a long time, and I
350 shall leave it, I give you my word.

TROFIMOV If you have the keys of the household, throw them into the well and go. Be as free as the wind.

ANYA [*in ecstasy*] How well you put that!

TROFIMOV Believe me, Anya, believe me! I am not yet thirty, I am young, still a student, but I have already been through so much! As soon as winter comes, I am hungry, sick, worried, poor as a beggar, and—where has not fate driven me! Where have I not been? And yet always, every minute of the day and night, my soul was filled with inexplicable premonitions. I have a premonition of happiness, Anya, I can see it . . .

360 ANYA The moon is rising.

[YEPIKHODOV *is heard playing the same melancholy song on the guitar. The moon rises. Somewhere near the poplars* VARYA *is looking for* ANYA *and calling: "Anya, where are you?"*]

TROFIMOV Yes, the moon is rising. [*Pause*] There it is—happiness . . . it's coming, nearer and nearer, I can hear its footsteps. And if we do not see it, if we do not recognize it, what does it matter? Others will see it.

VARYA'S VOICE Anya! Where are you?

TROFIMOV That Varya again! [*Angrily*] It's revolting!

ANYA Well? Let's go down to the river. It's lovely there.

TROFIMOV Come on. [*They go.*]

VARYA'S VOICE Anya! Anya!

Act III

[*The drawing room, separated by an arch from the ballroom. The chandelier is lighted. The Jewish band that was mentioned in Act II is heard playing in the hall. It is evening. In the ballroom they are dancing a grand rond. The voice of* SEMYONOV-PISHCHIK: "Promenade à une paire!" *They all enter the drawing room.* PISHCHIK *and* CHARLOTTA IVANOVNA *are the first couple,* TROFIMOV *and* LYUBOV ANDREYEVNA *the second,* ANYA *and the* POST-OFFICE CLERK *the third,* VARYA *and the* STATIONMASTER *the fourth, etc.* VARYA, *quietly weeping, dries her tears as she dances.* DUNYASHA *is in the last couple. As they cross the drawing room* PISHCHIK *calls: "Grand rond, balancez!" and "Les cavaliers à genoux et remercier vos dames!"* FIRS, *wearing a dress coat, brings in a tray with seltzer water.* PISHCHIK *and* TROFIMOV *come into the drawing room.*]

PISHCHIK I'm a full-blooded man, I've already had two strokes, and dancing's hard work for me, but as they say, "If you run with the pack, you can bark or not, but at least wag your tail." At that, I'm as strong as a horse. My late father—quite a joker he was, God rest his soul—used to say, talking about our origins, that the ancient line of Semyonov-Pishchik was descended from the very horse that Caligula had seated in the Senate. . . . [*Sits down.*] But the trouble is—no money! A hungry dog believes in nothing but meat. . . . [*Snores but wakes up at once.*] It's the same with me—I can think of nothing but money. . . .

10   TROFIMOV You know, there really is something equine about your figure.
      PISHCHIK Well, a horse is a fine animal. . . . You can sell a horse.

[*There is the sound of a billiard game in the next room.* VARYA *appears in the archway.*]

      TROFIMOV [*teasing her*] Madame Lopakhina! Madame Lopakhina!
      VARYA [*angrily*] Mangy gentleman!
      TROFIMOV Yes, I am a mangy gentleman, and proud of it!
      VARYA [*reflecting bitterly*] Here we've hired musicians, and what are we going to pay them with? [*Goes out.*]
      TROFIMOV [*to* PISHCHIK] If the energy you have expended in the course of your life trying to find money to pay interest had gone into something else, ultimately, you might very well have turned the world upside down.
20   PISHCHIK Nietzsche . . . the philosopher . . . the greatest, most renowned . . . a man of tremendous intellect . . . says in his works that it is possible to forge banknotes.
      TROFIMOV And have you read Nietzsche?
      PISHCHIK Well . . . Dashenka told me. I'm in such a state now that I'm just about ready for forging. . . . The day after tomorrow I have to pay three hundred and ten rubles . . . I've got a hundred and thirty. . . . [*Feels in his pocket, grows alarmed.*] The money is gone! I've lost the money! [*Tearfully*] Where is my money? [*Joyfully*] Here it is, inside the lining. . . . I'm all in a sweat. . . .

[LYUBOV ANDREYEVNA *and* CHARLOTTA IVANOVNA *come in.*]

30   LYUBOV ANDREYEVNA [*humming a* LEZGINKA] Why does Leonid take so long? What is he doing in town? [*To* DUNYASHA] Dunyasha, offer the musicians some tea.
      TROFIMOV In all probability, the auction didn't take place.
      LYUBOV ANDREYEVNA It was the wrong time to have the musicians, the wrong time to give a dance. . . . Well, never mind. . . . [*Sits down and hums softly.*]
      CHARLOTTA [*gives* PISHCHIK *a deck of cards*] Here's a deck of cards for you. Think of a card.

PISHCHIK   I've thought of one.

40   CHARLOTTA   Now shuffle the pack. Very good. And now, my dear Mr. Pishchik, hand it to me. *Ein, zwei, drei!* Now look for it—it's in your side pocket.

PISHCHIK [*takes the card out of his side pocket*]   The eight of spades—absolutely right! [*Amazed*] Think of that, now!

CHARLOTTA [*holding the deck of cards in the palm of her hand, to* TROFIMOV] Quickly, tell me, which card is on top?

TROFIMOV   What? Well, the queen of spades.

CHARLOTTA   Right! [*To* PISHCHIK] Now which card is on top?

PISHCHIK   The ace of hearts.

50   CHARLOTTA   Right! [*Claps her hands and the deck of cards disappears.*] What lovely weather we're having today! [*A mysterious feminine voice, which seems to come from under the floor, answers her: "Oh, yes, splendid weather, madam."*] You are so nice, you're my ideal. . . . [*The voice: "And I'm very fond of you, too, madam."*]

STATIONMASTER [*applauding*]   Bravo, Madame Ventriloquist!

PISHCHIK [*amazed*]   Think of that, now! Most enchanting Charlotta Ivanovna . . . I am simply in love with you. . . .

CHARLOTTA   In love? [*Shrugs her shoulders.*] Is it possible that you can love? *Guter Mensch, aber schlechter Musikant.*

60   TROFIMOV [*claps* PISHCHIK *on the shoulder*]   You old horse, you!

CHARLOTTA   Attention, please! One more trick. [*Takes a lap robe from a chair.*] Here's a very fine lap robe; I should like to sell it. [*Shakes it out.*] Doesn't anyone want to buy it?

PISHCHIK [*amazed*]   Think of that, now!

CHARLOTTA   *Ein, zwei, drei!* [*Quickly raises the lap robe; behind it stands* ANYA, *who curtseys, runs to her mother, embraces her, and runs back into the ballroom amid the general enthusiasm.*]

LYUBOV ANDREYEVNA [*applauding*]   Bravo, bravo!

CHARLOTTA   Once again! *Ein, zwei, drei.* [*Raises the lap robe; behind it
70 stands* VARYA, *who bows.*]

PISHCHIK [*amazed*]   Think of that, now!

CHARLOTTA   The end! [*Throws the robe at* PISHCHIK, *makes a curtsey, and runs out of the room.*]

PISHCHIK [*hurries after her*]   The minx! . . . What a woman! What a woman! [*Goes out.*]

LYUBOV ANDREYEVNA   And Leonid still not here. What he is doing in town so long, I do not understand! It must be all over by now. Either the estate is sold, or the auction didn't take place—but why keep us in suspense so long!

VARYA [*trying to comfort her*]   Uncle has bought it, I am certain of that.

80   TROFIMOV [*mockingly*]   Yes.

VARYA   Great-aunt sent him power of attorney to buy it in her name and transfer the debt. She's doing it for Anya's sake. And I am sure, with God's help, Uncle will buy it.

LYUBOV ANDREYEVNA   Our great-aunt in Yaroslavl sent fifteen thousand to buy the estate in her name—she doesn't trust us—but that's not even enough to pay the interest. [*Covers her face with her hands.*] Today my fate will be decided, my fate . . .

TROFIMOV [*teasing* VARYA]   Madame Lopakhina!

VARYA [*angrily*]   Eternal student! Twice already you've been expelled
90   from the university.

LYUBOV ANDREYEVNA   Why are you so cross, Varya? If he teases you about Lopakhin, what of it? Go ahead and marry Lopakhin if you want to. He's a nice man, he's interesting. And if you don't want to, don't. Nobody's forcing you, my pet.

VARYA   To be frank, Mama dear, I regard this matter seriously. He is a good man, I like him.

LYUBOV ANDREYEVNA   Then marry him. I don't know what you're waiting for!

VARYA   Mama, I can't propose to him myself. For the last two years everyone's been talking to me about him; everyone talks, but he is either silent or
100   he jokes. I understand. He's getting rich, he's absorbed in business, he has no time for me. If I had some money, no matter how little, if it were only a hundred rubles, I'd drop everything and go far away. I'd go into a nunnery.

TROFIMOV   A blessing!

VARYA [*to* TROFIMOV]   A student ought to be intelligent! [*In a gentle tone, tearfully*] How homely you have grown, Petya, how old! [*To* LYUBOV ANDREYEVNA, *no longer crying*] It's just that I cannot live without work, Mama. I must be doing something every minute.

[YASHA *enters.*]

YASHA [*barely able to suppress his laughter*]   Yepikhodov has broken a billiard cue! [*Goes out.*]
110   VARYA   But why is Yepikhodov here? Who gave him permission to play billiards? I don't understand these people. . . . [*Goes out.*]

LYUBOV ANDREYEVNA   Don't tease her, Petya. You can see she's unhappy enough without that.

TROFIMOV   She's much too zealous, always meddling in other people's affairs. All summer long she's given Anya and me no peace—afraid a romance might develop. What business is it of hers? Besides, I've given no occasion for it, I am far removed from such banality. We are above love!

LYUBOV ANDREYEVNA   And I suppose I am beneath love. [*In great agitation*] Why isn't Leonid here? If only I knew whether the estate had been sold or
120   not! The disaster seems to me so incredible that I don't even know what to think, I'm lost. . . . I could scream this very instant . . . I could do something foolish. Save me, Petya. Talk to me, say something. . . .

TROFIMOV   Whether or not the estate is sold today—does it really matter? That's all done with long ago; there's no turning back, the path is overgrown. Be calm, my dear. One must not deceive oneself; at least once in one's life one ought to look the truth straight in the eye.

LYUBOV ANDREYEVNA   What truth? You can see where there is truth and where there isn't, but I seem to have lost my sight, I see nothing. You boldly settle all the important problems, but tell me, my dear boy, isn't it because

130   you are young and have not yet had to suffer for a single one of your problems? You boldly look ahead, but isn't it because you neither see nor expect
anything dreadful, since life is still hidden from your young eyes? You're
bolder, more honest, deeper than we are, but think about it, be just a little bit
magnanimous, and spare me. You see, I was born here, my mother and father
lived here, and my grandfather. I love this house, without the cherry orchard
my life has no meaning for me, and if it must be sold, then sell me with the
orchard. . . . [*Embraces* TROFIMOV *and kisses him on the forehead.*] And my
son was drowned here. . . . [*Weeps.*] Have pity on me, you good, kind man.

    TROFIMOV   You know I feel for you with all my heart.

140   LYUBOV ANDREYEVNA   But that should have been said differently, quite differently. . . . [*Takes out her handkerchief and a telegram falls to the floor.*]
My heart is heavy today, you can't imagine. It's so noisy here, my soul quivers
at every sound, I tremble all over, and yet I can't go to my room. When I am
alone the silence frightens me. Don't condemn me, Petya . . . I love you as
if you were my own. I would gladly let you marry Anya, I swear it, only you
must study, my dear, you must get your degree. You do nothing, fate simply
tosses you from place to place—it's so strange. . . . Isn't that true? Isn't
it? And you must do something about your beard, to make it grow somehow. . . . [*Laughs.*] You're so funny!

150   TROFIMOV [*picks up the telegram*]   I have no desire to be an Adonis.

    LYUBOV ANDREYEVNA   That's a telegram from Paris. I get them every day.
One yesterday, one today. That wild man has fallen ill again, he's in trouble
again. . . . He begs my forgiveness, implores me to come, and really, I
ought to go to Paris to be near him. Your face is stern, Petya, but what can one
do, my dear? What am I to do? He is ill, he's alone and unhappy, and who will
look after him there, who will keep him from making mistakes, who will give
him his medicine on time? And why hide it or keep silent, I love him, that's
clear. I love him, love him. . . . It's a millstone round my neck, I'm sinking
to the bottom with it, but I love that stone, I cannot live without it. [*Presses*
160   TROFIMOV'*s hand.*] Don't think badly of me, Petya, and don't say anything to
me, don't say anything. . . .

    TROFIMOV [*through tears*]   For God's sake, forgive my frankness: you know
that he robbed you!

    LYUBOV ANDREYEVNA   No, no, no, you mustn't say such things! [*Covers her
ears.*]

    TROFIMOV   But he's a scoundrel! You're the only one who doesn't know it!
He's a petty scoundrel, a nonentity—

    LYUBOV ANDREYEVNA [*angry, but controlling herself*]   —You are twenty-six
or twenty-seven years old, but you're still a schoolboy!

170   TROFIMOV   That may be!

    LYUBOV ANDREYEVNA   You should be a man, at your age you ought to under-
stand those who love. And you ought to be in love yourself. [*Angrily*] Yes, yes!
It's not purity with you, it's simply prudery, you're a ridiculous crank, a
freak—

    TROFIMOV [*horrified*]   What is she saying!

LYUBOV ANDREYEVNA   "I am above love!" You're not above love, you're just an addlepate, as Firs would say. Not to have a mistress at your age!

TROFIMOV [*in horror*]   This is awful! What is she saying! . . . [*Goes quickly toward the ballroom.*] This is awful . . . I can't . . . I won't stay
180   here. . . . [*Goes out, but immediately returns.*] All is over between us! [*Goes out to the hall.*]

LYUBOV ANDREYEVNA [*calls after him*]   Petya, wait! You absurd creature, I was joking! Petya!

[*In the hall there is the sound of someone running quickly downstairs and suddenly falling with a crash.* ANYA *and* VARYA *scream, but a moment later laughter is heard.*]

LYUBOV ANDREYEVNA   What was that?

[ANYA *runs in.*]

ANYA [*laughing*]   Petya fell down the stairs! [*Runs out.*]
LYUBOV ANDREYEVNA   What a funny boy that Petya is!

[*The* STATIONMASTER *stands in the middle of the ballroom and recites A. Tolstoy's "The Sinner." Everyone listens to him, but he has no sooner spoken a few lines than the sound of a waltz is heard from the hall and the recitation is broken off. They all dance.* TROFIMOV, ANYA, VARYA, *and* LYUBOV ANDREYEVNA *come in from the hall.*]

LYUBOV ANDREYEVNA   Come, Petya . . . come, you pure soul . . . please, forgive me. . . . Let's dance. . . . [*They dance.*]

[ANYA *and* VARYA *dance.* FIRS *comes in, puts his stick by the side door.* YASHA *also comes into the drawing room and watches the dancers.*]

YASHA   What is it, grandpa?
190   FIRS   I don't feel well. In the old days we used to have generals, barons, admirals, dancing at our balls, but now we send for the post-office clerk and the stationmaster, and even they are none too eager to come. Somehow I've grown weak. The late master, their grandfather, dosed everyone with sealing wax, no matter what ailed them. I've been taking sealing wax every day for twenty years or more; maybe that's what's kept me alive.

YASHA   You bore me, grandpa. [*Yawns.*] High time you croaked.
FIRS   Ah, you . . . addlepate! [*Mumbles.*]

[TROFIMOV *and* LYUBOV ANDREYEVNA *dance from the ballroom into the drawing room.*]

LYUBOV ANDREYEVNA   *Merci.* I'll sit down a while. [*Sits.*] I'm tired.

[ANYA *comes in.*]

ANYA [*excitedly*]   There was a man in the kitchen just now saying that the
200   cherry orchard was sold today.

LYUBOV ANDREYEVNA   Sold to whom?

ANYA   He didn't say. He's gone. [*Dances with* TROFIMOV; *they go into the
ballroom.*]

YASHA   That was just some old man babbling. A stranger.

FIRS   Leonid Andreich is not back yet, still hasn't come. And he's wearing
the light, between-seasons overcoat; like enough he'll catch cold. Ah, when
they're young they're green.

LYUBOV ANDREYEVNA   This is killing me. Yasha, go and find out who it was
sold to.

210   YASHA   But that old man left long ago. [*Laughs.*]

LYUBOV ANDREYEVNA [*slightly annoyed*]   Well, what are you laughing at?
What are you so happy about?

YASHA   That Yepikhodov is very funny! Hopeless! Two-and-twenty Troubles.

LYUBOV ANDREYEVNA   Firs, if the estate is sold, where will you go?

FIRS   Wherever you tell me to go, I'll go.

LYUBOV ANDREYEVNA   Why do you look like that? Aren't you well? You ought
to go to bed.

FIRS   Yes. . . . [*With a smirk.*] Go to bed, and without me who will serve,
who will see to things? I'm the only one in the whole house.

220   YASHA [*to* LYUBOV ANDREYEVNA]   Lyubov Andreyevna! Permit me to make a
request, be so kind! If you go back to Paris again, do me the favor of taking
me with you. It is positively impossible for me to stay here. [*Looking around,
then in a low voice*] There's no need to say it, you can see for yourself, it's an
uncivilized country, the people have no morals, and the boredom! The food
they give us in the kitchen is unmentionable, and besides, there's this Firs
who keeps walking about mumbling all sorts of inappropriate things. Take
me with you, be so kind!

[*Enter* PISHCHIK.]

PISHCHIK   May I have the pleasure of a waltz with you, fairest lady? [LYUBOV
ANDREYEVNA *goes with him.*] I really must borrow a hundred and eighty rubles
230   from you, my charmer . . . I really must. . . . [*Dancing.*] Just a hundred
and eighty rubles. . . . [*They pass into the ballroom.*]

YASHA [*softly sings*]   "Wilt thou know my soul's unrest . . ."

[*In the ballroom a figure in a gray top hat and checked trousers is jumping about,
waving its arms; there are shouts of "Bravo, Charlotta Ivanovna!"*]

DUNYASHA [*stopping to powder her face*]   The young mistress told me to
dance—there are lots of gentlemen and not enough ladies—but dancing
makes me dizzy, and my heart begins to thump. Firs Nikolayevich, the post-
office clerk just said something to me that took my breath away.

[*The music grows more subdued.*]

FIRS What did he say to you?

DUNYASHA "You," he said, "are like a flower."

YASHA [*yawns*] What ignorance. . . . [*Goes out.*]

240 DUNYASHA Like a flower. . . . I'm such a delicate girl, I just adore tender words.

FIRS You'll get your head turned.

[*Enter* YEPIKHODOV.]

YEPIKHODOV Avdotya Fyodorovna, you are not desirous of seeing me . . . I might almost be some sort of insect. [*Sighs.*] Ah, life!

DUNYASHA What is it you want?

YEPIKHODOV Indubitably, you may be right. [*Sighs.*] But, of course, if one looks at it from a point of view, then, if I may so express myself, and you will forgive my frankness, you have completely reduced me to a state of mind. I know my fate, every day some misfortune befalls me, but I have long since

250 grown accustomed to that; I look upon my fate with a smile. But you gave me your word, and although I—

DUNYASHA Please, we'll talk about it later, but leave me in peace now. Just now I'm dreaming. . . . [*Plays with her fan.*]

YEPIKHODOV Every day is misfortune, and yet, if I may so express myself, I merely smile, I even laugh.

[VARYA *enters from the ballroom.*]

VARYA Are you still here, Semyon? What a disrespectful man you are, really! [*To* DUNYASHA] Run along, Dunyasha. [*To* YEPIKHODOV] First you play billiards and break a cue, then you wander about the drawing room as though you were a guest.

260 YEPIKHODOV You cannot, if I may so express myself, penalize me.

VARYA I am not penalizing you, I'm telling you. You do nothing but wander from one place to another, and you don't do your work. We keep a clerk, but for what, I don't know.

YEPIKHODOV [*offended*] Whether I work, or wander about, or eat, or play billiards, these are matters to be discussed only by persons of discernment, and my elders.

VARYA You dare say that to me! [*Flaring up*] You dare? You mean to say I have no discernment? Get out of here! This instant!

YEPIKHODOV [*intimidated*] I beg you to express yourself in a more deli-

270 cate manner.

VARYA [*beside herself*] Get out, this very instant! Get out! [*He goes to the door, she follows him.*] Two-and-twenty Troubles! Don't let me set eyes on you again!

YEPIKHODOV [*goes out, his voice is heard behind the door*] I shall lodge a complaint against you!

VARYA Oh, you're coming back? [*Seizes the stick left near the door by* FIRS.] Come, come on. . . . Come, I'll show you. . . . Ah, so you're coming, are you? Then take that—[*Swings the stick just as* LOPAKHIN *enters.*]

LOPAKHIN   Thank you kindly.

280   VARYA [*angrily and mockingly*]   I beg your pardon.

LOPAKHIN   Not at all. I humbly thank you for your charming reception.

VARYA   Don't mention it. [*Walks away, then looks back and gently asks.*] I didn't hurt you, did I?

LOPAKHIN   No, it's nothing. A huge bump coming up, that's all.

[*Voices in the ballroom: "Lopakhin has come! Yermolai Alekseich!"* PISHCHIK *enters.*]

PISHCHIK   As I live and breathe! [*Kisses* LOPAKHIN.] There is a whiff of cognac about you, dear soul. And we've been making merry here, too.

[*Enter* LYUBOV ANDREYEVNA.]

LYUBOV ANDREYEVNA   Is that you, Yermolai Alekseich? What kept you so long? Where's Leonid?

LOPAKHIN   Leonid Andreich arrived with me, he's coming . . .

290   LYUBOV ANDREYEVNA [*agitated*]   Well, what happened? Did the sale take place? Tell me!

LOPAKHIN [*embarrassed, fearing to reveal his joy*]   The auction was over by four o'clock. . . . We missed the train, had to wait till half past nine. [*Sighing heavily*] Ugh! My head is swimming. . . .

[*Enter* GAYEV; *he carries his purchases in one hand and wipes away his tears with the other.*]

LYUBOV ANDREYEVNA   Lyonya, what happened? Well, Lyonya? [*Impatiently, through tears.*] Be quick, for God's sake!

GAYEV [*not answering her, simply waves his hand. To* FIRS, *weeping*] Here, take these. . . . There's anchovies, Kerch herrings. . . . I haven't eaten anything all day. . . . What I have been through! [*The click of billiard*

300   *balls is heard through the open door to the billiard room, and* YASHA's *voice: "Seven and eighteen!"* GAYEV's *expression changes, he is no longer weeping.*] I'm terribly tired. Firs, help me change. [*Goes through the ballroom to his own room, followed by* FIRS.]

PISHCHIK   What happened at the auction? Come on, tell us!

LYUBOV ANDREYEVNA   Is the cherry orchard sold?

LOPAKHIN   It's sold.

LYUBOV ANDREYEVNA   Who bought it?

LOPAKHIN   I bought it. [*Pause*]

[LYUBOV ANDREYEVNA *is overcome; she would fall to the floor if it were not for the chair and table near which she stands.* VARYA *takes the keys from her belt and throws them on the floor in the middle of the drawing room and goes out.*]

LOPAKHIN   I bought it! Kindly wait a moment, ladies and gentlemen, my

310   head is swimming. I can't talk. . . . [*Laughs.*] We arrived at the auction, Deriganov was already there. Leonid Andreich had only fifteen thousand,

and straight off Deriganov bid thirty thousand over and above the mortgage. I
saw how the land lay, so I got into the fight and bid forty. He bid forty-five.
I bid fifty-five. In other words, he kept raising it by five thousand, and I by
ten. Well, it finally came to an end. I bid ninety thousand above the mortgage, and it was knocked down to me. The cherry orchard is now mine! Mine!
[*Laughs uproariously.*] Lord! God in heaven! The cherry orchard is mine! Tell
me I'm drunk, out of my mind, that I imagine it. . . . [*Stamps his feet.*] Don't
laugh at me! If my father and my grandfather could only rise from their graves
320 and see all that has happened, how their Yermolai, their beaten, half-literate
Yermolai, who used to run about barefoot in winter, how that same Yermolai
has bought an estate, the most beautiful estate in the whole world! I bought
the estate where my father and grandfather were slaves, where they weren't
even allowed in the kitchen. I'm asleep, this is just some dream of mine, it
only seems to be. . . . It's the fruit of your imagination, hidden in the darkness of uncertainty. . . . [*Picks up the keys, smiling tenderly.*] She threw
down the keys, wants to show that she's not mistress here any more. . . .
[*Jingles the keys.*] Well, no matter. [*The orchestra is heard tuning up.*] Hey,
musicians, play, I want to hear you! Come on, everybody, and see how Yer-
330 molai Lopakhin will lay the ax to the cherry orchard, how the trees will fall to
the ground! We're going to build summer cottages, and our grandsons and
great-grandsons will see a new life here. . . . Music! Strike up!

[*The orchestra plays.* LYUBOV ANDREYEVNA *sinks into a chair and weeps bitterly.*]

LOPAKHIN [*reproachfully*]   Why didn't you listen to me, why? My poor
friend, there's no turning back now. [*With tears*] Oh, if only all this could be
over quickly, if somehow our discordant, unhappy life could be changed!
PISHCHIK [*takes him by the arm; speaks in an undertone*]   She's crying.
Let's go into the ballroom, let her be alone. . . . Come on. . . . [*Leads him
into the ballroom.*]
LOPAKHIN   What's happened? Musicians, play so I can hear you! Let every-
340 thing be as I want it! [*Ironically*] Here comes the new master, owner of the
cherry orchard! [*Accidentally bumps into a little table, almost upsetting the
candelabrum.*] I can pay for everything! [*Goes out with* PISHCHIK.]

[*There is no one left in either the drawing room or the ballroom except* LYUBOV
ANDREYEVNA, *who sits huddled up and weeping bitterly. The music plays softly.* ANYA
and TROFIMOV *enter hurriedly.* ANYA *goes to her mother and kneels before her.* TROFI-
MOV *remains in the doorway of the ballroom.*]

ANYA   Mama! . . . Mama, you're crying! Dear, kind, good Mama, my beautiful one, I love you . . . I bless you. The cherry orchard is sold, it's gone,
that's true, true, but don't cry, Mama, life is still before you, you still have your
good, pure soul. . . . Come with me, come, darling, we'll go away from
here! . . . We'll plant a new orchard, more luxuriant than this one. You will
see it and understand; and joy, quiet, deep joy, will sink into your soul, like the
evening sun, and you will smile, Mama! Come, darling, let us go. . . .

Act IV

[*The scene is the same as Act I. There are neither curtains on the windows nor pictures on the walls, and only a little furniture piled up in one corner, as if for sale. There is a sense of emptiness. Near the outer door, at the rear of the stage, suitcases, traveling bags, etc., are piled up. Through the open door on the left the voices of* VARYA *and* ANYA *can be heard.* LOPAKHIN *stands waiting.* YASHA *is holding a tray with little glasses of champagne. In the hall,* YEPIKHODOV *is tying up a box. Offstage, at the rear, there is a hum of voices. It is the peasants who have come to say good-bye.* GAYEV*'s voice: "Thanks, brothers, thank you."*]

YASHA The peasants have come to say good-bye. In my opinion, Yermolai Alekseich, peasants are good-natured, but they don't know much.

[*The hum subsides.* LYUBOV ANDREYEVNA *enters from the hall with* GAYEV. *She is not crying, but she is pale, her face twitches, and she cannot speak.*]

GAYEV You gave them your purse, Lyuba. That won't do! That won't do!

LYUBOV ANDREYEVNA I couldn't help it! I couldn't help it! [*They both go out.*]

LOPAKHIN [*in the doorway, calls after them*] Please, do me the honor of having a little glass at parting. I didn't think of bringing champagne from town, and at the station I found only one bottle. Please! What's the matter, friends, don't you want any? [*Walks away from the door.*] If I'd known that, I

10 wouldn't have bought it. Well, then I won't drink any either. [YASHA *carefully sets the tray down on a chair.*] At least you have a glass, Yasha.

YASHA To those who are departing! Good luck! [*Drinks.*] This champagne is not the real stuff, I can assure you.

LOPAKHIN Eight rubles a bottle. [*Pause*] It's devilish cold in here.

YASHA They didn't light the stoves today; it doesn't matter, since we're leaving. [*Laughs.*]

LOPAKHIN Why are you laughing?

YASHA Because I'm pleased.

LOPAKHIN It's October, yet it's sunny and still outside, like summer. Good

20 for building. [*Looks at his watch, then calls through the door.*] Bear in mind, ladies and gentlemen, only forty-six minutes till train time! That means leaving for the station in twenty minutes. Better hurry up!

[TROFIMOV *enters from outside wearing an overcoat.*]

TROFIMOV Seems to me it's time to start. The carriages are at the door. What the devil has become of my rubbers? They're lost. [*Calls through the door.*] Anya, my rubbers are not here. I can't find them.

LOPAKHIN I've got to go to Kharkov. I'm taking the same train you are. I'm going to spend the winter in Kharkov. I've been hanging around here with you, and I'm sick and tired of loafing. I can't live without work, I don't know

what to do with my hands; they dangle in some strange way, as if they didn't
30 belong to me.

TROFIMOV We'll soon be gone, then you can take up your useful labors
again.

LOPAKHIN Here, have a little drink.

TROFIMOV No, I don't want any.

LOPAKHIN So you're off for Moscow?

TROFIMOV Yes, I'll see them into town, and tomorrow I'll go to Moscow.

LOPAKHIN Yes. . . . Well, I expect the professors haven't been giving any
lectures: they're waiting for you to come!

TROFIMOV That's none of your business.

40   LOPAKHIN How many years is it you've been studying at the university?

TROFIMOV Can't you think of something new? That's stale and flat. [*Looks
for his rubbers.*] You know, we'll probably never see each other again, so
allow me to give you one piece of advice at parting: don't wave your arms
about! Get out of that habit—of arm-waving. And another thing, building
cottages and counting on the summer residents in time becoming independent farmers—that's just another form of arm-waving. Well, when all's said
and done, I'm fond of you anyway. You have fine, delicate fingers, like an
artist; you have a fine delicate soul.

LOPAKHIN [*embraces him*] Good-bye, my dear fellow. Thank you for ev-
50 erything. Let me give you some money for the journey, if you need it.

TROFIMOV What for? I don't need it.

LOPAKHIN But you haven't any!

TROFIMOV I have. Thank you. I got some money for a translation. Here it is
in my pocket. [*Anxiously*] But where are my rubbers?

VARYA [*from the next room*] Here, take the nasty things! [*Flings a pair of
rubbers onto the stage.*]

TROFIMOV What are you so cross about, Varya? Hm. . . . But these are not
my rubbers.

LOPAKHIN In the spring I sowed three thousand acres of poppies, and now
60 I've made forty thousand rubles clear. And when my poppies were in bloom,
what a picture it was! So, I'm telling you, I've made forty thousand, which
means I'm offering you a loan because I can afford to. Why turn up your
nose? I'm a peasant—I speak bluntly.

TROFIMOV Your father was a peasant, mine was a pharmacist—which
proves absolutely nothing. [LOPAKHIN *takes out his wallet.*] No, don't—even if
you gave me two hundred thousand I wouldn't take it. I'm a free man. And
everything that is valued so highly and held so dear by all of you, rich and
poor alike, has not the slightest power over me—it's like a feather floating in
the air. I can get along without you, I can pass you by, I'm strong and proud.
70 Mankind is advancing toward the highest truth, the highest happiness attain-
able on earth, and I am in the front ranks!

LOPAKHIN Will you get there?

TROFIMOV I'll get there. [*Pause*] I'll either get there or I'll show others the
way to get there.

[*The sound of axes chopping down trees is heard in the distance.*]

LOPAKHIN   Well, good-bye, my dear fellow. It's time to go. We turn up our noses at one another, but life goes on just the same. When I work for a long time without stopping, my mind is easier, and it seems to me that I, too, know why I exist. But how many there are in Russia, brother, who exist nobody knows why. Well, it doesn't matter, that's not what makes the wheels go round.
80 They say Leonid Andreich has taken a position in the bank, six thousand a year. . . . Only, of course, he won't stick it out, he's too lazy. . . .

ANYA [*in the doorway*]   Mama asks you not to start cutting down the cherry orchard until she's gone.

TROFIMOV   Yes, really, not to have had the tact . . . [*Goes out through the hall.*]

LOPAKHIN   Right away, right away. . . . Ach, what people. . . . [*Follows* TROFIMOV *out.*]

ANYA   Has Firs been taken to the hospital?

YASHA   I told them this morning. They must have taken him.

90   ANYA [*to* YEPIKHODOV, *who is crossing the room*]   Semyon Panteleich, please find out if Firs has been taken to the hospital.

YASHA [*offended*]   I told Yegor this morning. Why ask a dozen times?

YEPIKHODOV   It is my conclusive opinion that the venerable Firs is beyond repair; it's time he was gathered to his fathers. And I can only envy him. [*Puts a suitcase down on a hatbox and crushes it.*] There you are! Of course! I knew it! [*Goes out.*]

YASHA [*mockingly*]   Two-and-twenty Troubles!

VARYA [*through the door*]   Has Firs been taken to the hospital?

ANYA   Yes, he has.

100   VARYA   Then why didn't they take the letter to the doctor?

ANYA   We must send it on after them. . . . [*Goes out.*]

VARYA [*from the adjoining room*]   Where is Yasha? Tell him his mother has come to say good-bye to him.

YASHA [*waves his hand*]   They really try my patience.

[DUNYASHA *has been fussing with the luggage; now that* YASHA *is alone she goes up to him.*]

DUNYASHA   You might give me one little look, Yasha. You're going away . . . leaving me. . . . [*Cries and throws herself on his neck.*]

YASHA   What's there to cry about? [*Drinks champagne.*] In six days I'll be in Paris again. Tomorrow we'll take the express, off we go, and that's the last you'll see of us. I can hardly believe it. *Vive la France!* This place is not for
110 me, I can't live here. . . . It can't be helped. I've had enough of this ignorance—I'm fed up with it. [*Drinks champagne.*] What are you crying for? Behave yourself properly, then you won't cry.

DUNYASHA [*looks into a small mirror and powders her face*]   Send me a letter from Paris. You know, I loved you, Yasha, how I loved you! I'm such a tender creature, Yasha!

YASHA   Here they come. [*Busies himself with the luggage, humming softly.*]

[*Enter* LYUBOV ANDREYEVNA, GAYEV, CHARLOTTA IVANOVNA.]

GAYEV   We ought to be leaving. There's not much time now. [*Looks at* YASHA] Who smells of herring?

LYUBOV ANDREYEVNA   In about ten minutes we should be getting into the
120   carriages. [*Glances around the room.*] Good-bye, dear house, old grandfather. Winter will pass, spring will come, and you will no longer be here, they will tear you down. How much these walls have seen! [*Kisses her daughter warmly.*] My treasure, you are radiant, your eyes are sparkling like two diamonds. Are you glad? Very?

ANYA   Very! A new life is beginning, Mama!

GAYEV [*cheerfully*]   Yes, indeed, everything is all right now. Before the cherry orchard was sold we were all worried and miserable, but afterward, when the question was finally settled once and for all, everybody calmed down and felt quite cheerful. . . . I'm in a bank now, a financier . . . cue
130   ball into the center . . . and you, Lyuba, say what you like, you look better, no doubt about it.

LYUBOV ANDREYEVNA   Yes. My nerves are better, that's true. [*Her hat and coat are handed to her.*] I sleep well. Carry out my things, Yasha, it's time. [*To* ANYA] My little girl, we shall see each other soon. . . . I shall go to Paris and live there on the money your great-aunt sent to buy the estate—long live Auntie!—but that money won't last long.

ANYA   You'll come back soon, Mama, soon . . . won't you? I'll study hard and pass my high-school examinations, and then I can work and help you. We'll read all sorts of books together, Mama. . . . Won't we? [*Kisses her*
140   *mother's hand.*] We'll read in the autumn evenings, we'll read lots of books, and a new and wonderful world will open up before us. . . . [*Dreaming*] Mama, come back. . . .

LYUBOV ANDREYEVNA   I'll come, my precious. [*Embraces her.*]

[*Enter* LOPAKHIN. CHARLOTTA IVANOVNA *is softly humming a song.*]

GAYEV   Happy Charlotta: she's singing!

CHARLOTTA [*picks up a bundle and holds it like a baby in swaddling clothes*]   Bye, baby, bye. . . . [*A baby's crying is heard, "Wah! Wah!"*] Be quiet, my darling, my dear little boy. [*"Wah! Wah!"*] I'm so sorry for you! [*Throws the bundle down.*] You will find me a position, won't you? I can't go on like this.

150   LOPAKHIN   We'll find something, Charlotta Ivanovna, don't worry.

GAYEV   Everyone is leaving us, Varya's going away . . . all of a sudden nobody needs us.

CHARLOTTA   I have nowhere to go in town. I must go away. [*Hums.*] It doesn't matter . . .

[*Enter* PISHCHIK.]

LOPAKHIN   Nature's wonder!

PISCHIK [*panting*]   Ugh! Let me catch my breath. . . . I'm exhausted. . . . My esteemed friends. . . . Give me some water. . . .

GAYEV   After money, I suppose? Excuse me, I'm fleeing from temptation. . . . [*Goes out.*]

160   PISCHIK   It's a long time since I've been to see you . . . fairest lady. . . . [*To* LOPAKHIN] So you're here. . . . Glad to see you, you intellectual giant. . . . Here . . . take it . . . four hundred rubles . . . I still owe you eight hundred and forty . . .

LOPAKHIN [*shrugs his shoulders in bewilderment*]   I must be dreaming. . . . Where did you get it?

PISCHIK   Wait . . . I'm hot. . . . A most extraordinary event. Some Englishman came to my place and discovered some kind of white clay on my land. [*To* LYUBOV ANDREYEVNA] And four hundred for you . . . fairest, most wonderful lady. . . . [*Hands her the money.*] The rest later. [*Takes a drink of*
170   *water.*] Just now a young man in the train was saying that a certain . . . great philosopher recommends jumping off roofs. . . . "Jump!" he says, and therein lies the whole problem. [*In amazement*] Think of that, now! . . . Water!

LOPAKHIN   Who were those Englishmen?

PISCHIK   I leased them the tract of land with the clay on it for twenty-four years. . . . And now, excuse me, I have no time . . . I must be trotting along . . . I'm going to Znoikov's . . . to Kardamanov's . . . I owe everybody. [*Drinks.*] Keep well . . . I'll drop in on Thursday . . .

LYUBOV ANDREYEVNA   We're just moving into town, and tomorrow I go
180   abroad . . .

PISCHIK   What? [*Alarmed*] Why into town? That's why I see the furniture . . . suitcases. . . . Well, never mind. . . . [*Through tears*] Never mind. . . . Men of the greatest intellect, those Englishmen. . . . Never mind. . . . Be happy . . . God will help you. . . . Never mind. . . . Everything in this world comes to an end. . . . [*Kisses* LYUBOV ANDREYEVNA's *hand.*] And should the news reach you that my end has come, just remember this old horse, and say: "There once lived a certain Semyonov-Pishchik, God rest his soul." . . . Splendid weather. . . . Yes. . . . [*Goes out greatly disconcerted, but immediately returns and speaks from the doorway.*]
190   Dashenka sends her regards. [*Goes out.*]

LYUBOV ANDREYEVNA   Now we can go. I am leaving with two things on my mind. First—that Firs is sick. [*Looks at her watch.*] We still have about five minutes. . . .

ANYA   Mama, Firs has already been taken to the hospital. Yasha sent him there this morning.

LYUBOV ANDREYEVNA   My second concern is Varya. She's used to getting up early and working, and now, with no work to do, she's like a fish out of water. She's grown pale and thin, and cries all the time, poor girl. . . . [*Pause*] You know very well, Yermolai Alekseich, that I dreamed of marrying her to you,
200   and everything pointed to your getting married. [*Whispers to* ANYA, *who nods to* CHARLOTTA, *and they both go out.*] She loves you, you are fond of her, and I

don't know—I don't know why it is you seem to avoid each other. I can't understand it!

LOPAKHIN To tell you the truth, I don't understand it myself. The whole thing is strange, somehow. . . . If there's still time, I'm ready right now. . . . Let's finish it up—and *basta,* but without you I feel I'll never be able to propose to her.

LYUBOV ANDREYEVNA Splendid! After all, it only takes a minute. I'll call her in at once. . . .

210 LOPAKHIN And we even have the champagne. [*Looks at the glasses.*] Empty! Somebody's already drunk it. [YASHA *coughs.*] That's what you call lapping it up.

LYUBOV ANDREYEVNA [*animatedly*] Splendid! We'll leave you. . . . Yasha, *allez!* I'll call her. . . . [*At the door*] Varya, leave everything and come here. Come! [*Goes out with* YASHA.]

LOPAKHIN [*looking at his watch*] Yes. . . . [*Pause*]

[*Behind the door there is smothered laughter and whispering; finally* VARYA *enters.*]

VARYA [*looking over the luggage for a long time*] Strange, I can't seem to find it . . .

LOPAKHIN What are you looking for?

220 VARYA I packed it myself, and I can't remember . . . [*Pause*]

LOPAKHIN Where are you going now, Varya Mikhailovna?

VARYA I? To the Ragulins'. . . . I've agreed to go there to look after the house . . . as a sort of housekeeper.

LOPAKHIN At Yashnevo? That would be about seventy versts from here. [*Pause*] Well, life in this house has come to an end. . . .

VARYA [*examining the luggage*] Where can it be? . . . Perhaps I put it in the trunk. . . . Yes, life in this house has come to an end . . . there'll be no more . . .

LOPAKHIN And I'm off for Kharkov . . . by the next train. I have a lot to 230 do. I'm leaving Yepikhodov here . . . I've taken him on.

VARYA Really!

LOPAKHIN Last year at this time it was already snowing, if you remember, but now it's still and sunny. It's cold though. . . . About three degrees of frost.

VARYA I haven't looked. [*Pause*] And besides, our thermometer's broken. [*Pause*]

[*A voice from the yard calls:* "Yermolai Alekseich!"]

LOPAKHIN [*as if he had been waiting for a long time for the call*] Coming! [*Goes out quickly.*]

[VARYA *sits on the floor, lays her head on a bundle of clothes, and quietly sobs. The door opens and* LYUBOV ANDREYEVNA *enters cautiously.*]

LYUBOV ANDREYEVNA Well? [*Pause*] We must be going.

240   VARYA [*no longer crying, dries her eyes*] Yes, it's time, Mama dear. I can get to the Ragulins' today, if only we don't miss the train.

LYUBOV ANDREYEVNA [*in the doorway*] Anya, put your things on!

[*Enter* ANYA, *then* GAYEV *and* CHARLOTTA IVANOVNA. GAYEV *wears a warm overcoat with a hood. The servants and coachmen come in.* YEPIKHODOV *bustles about the luggage.*]

LYUBOV ANDREYEVNA Now we can be on our way.

ANYA [*joyfully*] On our way!

GAYEV My friends, my dear, cherished friends! Leaving this house forever, can I pass over in silence, can I refrain from giving utterance, as we say farewell, to those feelings that now fill my whole being—

ANYA [*imploringly*] Uncle!

VARYA Uncle dear, don't!

250   GAYEV [*forlornly*] Double the rail off the white to center table . . . yellow into the side pocket. . . . I'll be quiet. . . .

[*Enter* TROFIMOV, *then* LOPAKHIN.]

TROFIMOV Well, ladies and gentlemen, it's time to go!

LOPAKHIN Yepikhodov, my coat!

LYUBOV ANDREYEVNA I'll sit here just one more minute. It's as though I had never before seen what the walls of this house were like, what the ceilings were like, and now I look at them hungrily, with such tender love . . .

GAYEV I remember when I was six years old, sitting on this window sill on Whitsunday, watching my father going to church . . .

LYUBOV ANDREYEVNA Have they taken all the things?

260   LOPAKHIN Everything, I think. [*Puts on his overcoat.*] Yepikhodov, see that everything is in order.

YEPIKHODOV [*in a hoarse voice*] Rest assured, Yermolai Alekseich!

LOPAKHIN What's the matter with your voice?

YEPIKHODOV Just drank some water . . . must have swallowed something.

YASHA [*contemptuously*] What ignorance!

LYUBOV ANDREYEVNA When we go—there won't be a soul left here. . . .

LOPAKHIN Till spring.

VARYA [*pulls an umbrella out of a bundle as though she were going to hit someone;* LOPAKHIN *pretends to be frightened*] Why are you—I never

270   thought such a thing!

TROFIMOV Ladies and gentlemen, let's get into the carriages—it's time now! The train will soon be in!

VARYA Petya, there they are—your rubbers, by the suitcase. [*Tearfully*] And what dirty old things they are!

TROFIMOV [*putting on his rubbers*] Let's go, ladies and gentlemen!

GAYEV [*extremely upset, afraid of bursting into tears*] The train . . . the station. . . . Cross table to the center, double the rail . . . on the white into the corner.

LYUBOV ANDREYEVNA Let us go!

280   GAYEV Are we all here? No one in there? [*Locks the side door on the left.*] There are some things stored in there, we must lock up. Let's go!

ANYA Good-bye, house! Good-bye, old life!

TROFIMOV Hail to the new life! [*Goes out with* ANYA.]

[VARYA *looks around the room and slowly goes out.* YASHA *and* CHARLOTTA *with her dog go out.*]

LOPAKHIN And so, till spring. Come along, my friends. . . . Till we meet! [*Goes out.*]

[LYUBOV ANDREYEVNA *and* GAYEV *are left alone. As though they had been waiting for this, they fall onto each other's necks and break into quiet, restrained sobs, afraid of being heard.*]

GAYEV [*in despair*] My sister, my sister. . . .

LYUBOV ANDREYEVNA Oh, my dear, sweet, lovely orchard! . . . My life, my youth, my happiness, good-bye! . . . Good-bye!

ANYA'S VOICE [*gaily calling*] Mama!

290   TROFIMOV'S VOICE [*gay and excited*] Aa-oo!

LYUBOV ANDREYEVNA One last look at these walls, these windows. . . . Mother loved to walk about in this room. . . .

GAYEV My sister, my sister!

ANYA'S VOICE Mama!

TROFIMOV'S VOICE Aa-oo!

LYUBOV ANDREYEVNA We're coming! [*They go out.*]

[*The stage is empty. There is the sound of doors being locked, then of the carriages driving away. It grows quiet. In the stillness there is the dull thud of an ax on a tree, a forlorn, melancholy sound. Footsteps are heard. From the door on the right* FIRS *appears. He is dressed as always in a jacket and white waistcoat, and wears slippers. He is ill.*]

FIRS [*goes to the door and tries the handle*] Locked. They have gone. . . . [*Sits down on the sofa.*] They've forgotten me. . . . Never mind . . . I'll sit here awhile. . . . I expect Leonid Andreich hasn't put on his fur coat and

300 has gone off in his overcoat. [*Sighs anxiously.*] And I didn't see to it. . . . When they're young, they're green! [*Mumbles something which cannot be understood.*] I'll lie down awhile. . . . There's no strength left in you, nothing's left, nothing. . . . Ach, you . . . addlepate! [*Lies motionless.*]

[*A distant sound is heard that seems to come from the sky, the sound of a snapped string mournfully dying away. A stillness falls, and nothing is heard but the thud of the ax on a tree far away in the orchard.*]

Questions

1. Is there a villain in this play? If so, is Lopakhin the villain? Explain.

2. Chekhov's stage directions require the sound effects of trains. What other sound effects does the author specify? Follow sounds through *The Cherry Orchard* and see how they contribute to plot or character. How do these stage directions separate *The Cherry Orchard* from older drama?

3. Is Lopakhin a practical, decisive character? In what matters is he indecisive?

4. We think of masks as worn to delude other people. Do any of these characters wear masks to delude themselves? Describe them.

5. The cherry orchard itself has been called the tragic hero of this play. Comment. Discuss each character in terms of what the cherry orchard means to him or her.

6. Is it funny that Firs is locked in a deserted house at the end of the play? Could one argue that Firs death would make this play a tragedy? Discuss.

7. Do you sense that Chekhov's characters are not speaking to each other? Aren't hearing each other? Find an example. How would you block the scene you find so that spectacle reflected incomplete dialogue?

8. Look up *non sequitur* in the dictionary, if you do not know it. Are there non sequiturs in Chekhov's dialogue? Are there non sequiturs in the plot? Comment on this description of the play: "A monument to disconnectedness."

9. Try turning *The Cherry Orchard* into a California play, with *The Tomato Patch* threatened by a condominium developer. What problems do you encounter?

10. When the dying Chekhov saw *The Cherry Orchard* performed for the first time he was disappointed. He considered it broad comedy, and Stanislavsky had directed it as a melancholy play. Chekhov protested when he attended rehearsals but was too ill to press his arguments. "Stanislavsky has ruined my play," said the author.

    Write a dialogue between playwright and director on the subject of this play. Stanislavsky came from the landowning class; Chekhov did not.

11. Is it possible to imagine a comic production of *Hamlet? Oedipus?* Compare with Chekhov.

12. Chekhov wrote "The artist should be, not the judge of his characters and their conversations, but only an unbiased witness." Does Chekhov practice what he preaches in *The Cherry Orchard?*

13. Compare "Gooseberries" (pages 136–143) with *The Cherry Orchard.* Is Chekhov an "unbiased witness" in "Gooseberries"? In *The Cherry Orchard?* How do the two works remind you of each other?

    Compare point of view in the short story with dramatic form in the play. What can plays do that stories cannot? What can stories do that plays cannot? If you turned "Gooseberries" into a play, what would you lose? What might you gain?

CHAPTER SEVEN

Nonrealistic Modern Drama, Theater of the Absurd, and Samuel Beckett

Among the varieties of nonrealistic drama, the most contemporary is theater of the absurd. Luigi Pirandello anticipated this type of theater with his public doubts about reality and identity. To define absurdity in the theater, we must first mention existentialism, a modern philosophic doctrine that derives from the writings of Søren Kierkegaard (1813–1855). Kierkegaard was a religious thinker who felt that God and humanity were utterly distinct, and human life inherently absurd. Kierkegaard made "a leap of faith" to Christianity, but the later German philosopher Martin Heidegger (1889–1976) and the French philosopher, novelist, and playwright Jean Paul Sartre (1905–1980) affirmed absurdity while they denied divinity. Another French philosopher, novelist, and playwright, Albert Camus (1913–1960), wrote a collection of essays called *The Myth of Sisyphus* (1942) that set forth literary existentialist notions of absurdity. In existentialist thought, humans are distinguished from the rest of nature by their consciousness and their will. Human character has no innate form, but is self-created against the nothingness and meaninglessness out of which people are born and into which they die.

Absurdist playwrights need not subscribe to existentialist philosophy, but they share the notions that human life lacks discernible meaning or purpose, that we make up our own characters as we go along, that we act without rules or with rules which make no sense, that our consciousness is dominated only by certain death, that our existence, in a word, is *absurd*. If absurdity makes for comedy, it is hardly happy; the smile on the comic mask of absurdist theater is sometimes sardonic, sometimes wild with graveyard gaiety; it is never placid. When we speak of absurdist plays as tragicomedies, we speak of a mixture of laughter and anxiety, melancholy and farce—not of elements found in the classic definitions of either tragedy or comedy.

Human beings have always been prone to visions of life's absurdity, and we can point to pre-absurdist writers from Aristophanes to Oscar Wilde who anticipate these later playwrights. In France, the playwright Alfred Jarry (1873–1907) wrote *Ubu Roi* (1898), a zany, meaningless, very funny play that anticipated both surrealism and absurdity. But the true originator of absurdism is surely Samuel Beckett (1906–1989), an Irishman living in Paris and writing in French. In his *Waiting for Godot* (1953), which inaugurated absurdist theater, two tramps who resemble clowns occupy the stage, attended by a servant-slave who is worse off than they are. They wait for the mysterious and powerful Godot, who will come and set things right—and who never arrives. These two tramps are antiheroes, far from the noble souls of high estate that Aristotle prescribed for tragedy. Beckett subtitles his play a tragicomedy, and the comedy is indeed broad and farcical, featuring bits of slapstick that may remind us of The Three Stooges. We laugh, we feel dread, we sympathize and emphathize—and we laugh again. Among other Beckett dramas, *Endgame* (1957) sums up humanity in a blind, paralyzed hero who lives, like his father and mother, in a garbage can. In *Krapp's Last Tape* (1958), a single actor playing an old man talks to himself, and listens to tape recordings made in years past. Other leading playwrights of the absurd include Eugène Ionesco, who was born in Romania in 1912 and writes in French, and the Englishmen Harold Pinter (1930–   ) and Tom Stoppard (1937–   ).

Samuel Beckett

Samuel Beckett (1906–1989) was born and brought up in Ireland, and moved to Paris as a young man. He met James Joyce there, wrote an essay on him, and helped Joyce by acting as his secretary. Beckett published poems and stories, then novels: *Murphy* (1938) and *Watt* (1953) were written in English. Later, he wrote novels in French, some of which he translated into English; among them is *Malone Dies* (French, 1951; English, 1958). His greatest work was for the theater. *Waiting for Godot* (1952; English, 1955) is perhaps his best-known play. His was the greatest imagination in the theater of the absurd, of which *Endgame* (1957) and *Krapp's Last Tape* (1958) are further examples. He received the Nobel Prize for Literature in 1969.

Krapp's Last Tape   (1958)

A late evening in the future.

KRAPP*'s den.*

Front centre a small table, the two drawers of which open towards the audience.

Sitting at the table, facing front, i.e. across from the drawers, a wearish old man: KRAPP.

Rusty black narrow trousers too short for him. Rusty black sleeveless waistcoat, four capacious pockets. Heavy silver watch and chain. Grimy white shirt open at neck, no collar. Surprising pair of dirty white boots, size ten at least, very narrow and pointed.

White face. Purple nose. Disordered grey hair. Unshaven.

Very near-sighted (but unspectacled). Hard of hearing.

Cracked voice. Distinctive intonation.

Laborious walk.

On the table a tape-recorder with microphone and a number of cardboard boxes containing reels of recorded tapes.

Table and immediately adjacent area in strong white light. Rest of stage in darkness.

KRAPP *remains a moment motionless, heaves a great sigh, looks at his watch, fumbles in his pockets, takes out an envelope, puts it back, fumbles, takes out a small bunch of keys, raises it to his eyes, chooses a key, gets up and moves to front of table. He stoops, unlocks first drawer, peers into it, feels about inside it, takes out a reel of tape, peers at it, puts it back, locks drawer, unlocks second drawer, peers into it, feels about inside it, takes out a large banana, peers at it, locks drawer, puts keys back in his pocket. He turns, advances to edge of stage, halts, strokes banana, peels it, drops skin at his feet, puts end of banana in his mouth and remains motionless, staring vacuously before him. Finally he bites off the end, turns aside and begins pacing to and fro at edge of stage, in the light, i.e. not more than four or five paces either way, meditatively eating banana. He treads on skin, slips, nearly falls, recovers himself, stoops and peers at skin and finally pushes it, still stooping, with his foot over edge of stage into pit. He resumes his pacing, finishes banana, returns to table, sits down, remains a moment motionless, heaves a great sigh, takes keys from his pockets, raises them to his eyes, chooses key, gets up and moves to front of table, unlocks second drawer, takes out a second large banana, peers at it, locks drawer, puts back keys in his pocket, turns, advances to edge of stage, halts, strokes banana, peels it, tosses skin into pit, puts end of banana in his mouth and remains motionless, staring vacuously before him. Finally he has an idea, puts banana in his waistcoat pocket, the end emerging, and goes with all the speed he can muster backstage into darkness. Ten seconds. Loud pop of cork. Fifteen seconds. He comes back into light carrying an old ledger and sits down at table. He lays ledger on table, wipes his mouth, wipes his hands on the front of his waistcoat, brings them smartly together and rubs them.*

KRAPP   [*Briskly.*]. Ah! [*He bends over ledger, turns the pages, finds the entry he wants, reads.*] Box . . . threee . . . spool . . . five. [*He raises his head and stares front, with relish.*] Spool! [*Pause.*] Spooool! [*Happy smile.*

Pause. He bends over table, starts peering and poking at the boxes.]
Box . . . thrree . . . thrree . . . four . . . two . . . [*with surprise*] nine!
good God! . . . seven . . . ah! the little rascal! [*He takes up box, peers at it.*]
Box thrree. [*He lays it on table, opens it and peers at spools inside.*]
Spool . . . [*he peers at ledger*] . . . five . . . [*he peers at spools*] . . .
five . . . five . . . ah! the little scoundrel! [*He takes out a spool, peers at it.*]
10 Spool five. [*He lays it on table, closes box three, puts it back with the others,
takes up the spool.*] Box thrree, spool five. [*He bends over the machine, looks
up. With relish.*] Spooool! [*Happy smile. He bends, loads spool on machine,
rubs his hands.*] Ah! [*He peers at ledger, reads entry at foot of page.*] Mother
at rest at last. . . . Hm. . . . The black ball. . . . [*He raises his head, stares
blankly front. Puzzled.*] Black ball? . . . [*He peers again at ledger, reads.*]
The dark nurse. . . . [*He raises his head, broods, peers again at ledger,
reads.*] Slight improvement in bowel condition. . . . Hm. . . . Memorable. . . . what? [*He peers closer.*] Equinox, memorable equinox. [*He raises
his head, stares blankly front. Puzzled.*] Memorable equinox? . . . [*Pause.
20 He shrugs his shoulders, peers again at ledger, reads.*] Farewell to—[*he turns
page*]—love.

[*He raises his head, broods, bends over machine, switches on and assumes listening
posture, i.e. leaning forward, elbows on table, hand cupping ear towards machine,
face front.*]

TAPE [*Strong voice, rather pompous, clearly* KRAPP'*s at a much earlier
time.*] Thirty-nine today, sound as a—[*Settling himself more comfortably he
knocks one of the boxes off the table, curses, switches off, sweeps boxes and
ledger violently to the ground, winds tape back to beginning, switches on,
resumes posture.*] Thirty-nine today, sound as a bell, apart from my old
weakness, and intellectually I have now every reason to suspect at the
. . . [*hesitates*] . . . crest of the wave—or thereabouts. Celebrated the awful occasion, as in recent years, quietly at the Winehouse. Not a soul. Sat
30 before the fire with closed eyes, separating the grain from the husks. Jotted
down a few notes, on the back of an envelope. Good to be back in my den, in
my old rags. Have just eaten I regret to say three bananas and only with
difficulty refrained from a fourth. Fatal things for a man with my condition.
[*Vehemently.*] Cut'em out! [*Pause.*] The new light above my table is a great
improvement. With all this darkness round me I feel less alone. [*Pause.*] In a
way. [*Pause.*] I love to get up and move about in it, then back here to . . .
[*hesitates*] . . . me. [*Pause.*] Krapp.

[*Pause.*]

The grain, now what I wonder do I mean by that, I mean . . . [*hesitates*]
. . . I suppose I mean those things worth having when all the dust has—
40 when all *my* dust has settled. I close my eyes and try and imagine them.

[*Pause.* KRAPP *closes his eyes briefly.*]

Extraordinary silence this evening, I strain my ears and do not hear a sound. Old Miss McGlome always sings at this hour. But not tonight. Songs of her girlhood, she says. Hard to think of her as a girl. Wonderful woman though. Connaught, I fancy. [*Pause.*] Shall I sing when I am her age, if I ever am? No. [*Pause.*] Did I sing as a boy? No. [*Pause.*] Did I ever sing? No.

[*Pause.*]

Just been listening to an old year, passages at random. I did not check in the book, but it must be at least ten or twelve years ago. At that time I think I was still living on and off with Bianca in Kedar Street. Well out of that, Jesus yes! Hopeless business. [*Pause.*] Not much about her, apart from a tribute to her
50 eyes. Very warm. I suddenly saw them again. [*Pause.*] Incomparable! [*Pause.*] Ah well. . . . [*Pause.*] These old P.M.s are gruesome, but I often find them— [KRAPP *switches off, broods, switches on.*]—a help before embarking on a new . . . [*hesitates*] . . . retrospect. Hard to believe I was ever that young whelp. The voice! Jesus! And the aspirations! [*Brief laugh in which* KRAPP *joins.*] And the resolutions! [*Brief laugh in which* KRAPP *joins.*] To drink less, in particular. [*Brief laugh of* KRAPP *alone.*] Statistics. Seventeen hundred hours, out of the preceding eight thousand odd, consumed on licensed premises alone. More than 20 per cent, say 40 per cent of his waking life. [*Pause.*] Plans for a less . . . [*hesitates*] . . . engrossing sexual life. Last
60 illness of his father. Flagging pursuit of happiness. Unattainable laxation. Sneers at what he calls his youth and thanks to God that it's over. [*Pause.*] False ring there. [*Pause.*] Shadows of the opus . . . magnum. Closing with a—[*brief laugh*]—yelp to Providence. [*Prolonged laugh in which* KRAPP *joins.*] What remains of all that misery? A girl in a shabby green coat, on a railway-station platform? No?

[*Pause.*]

When I look—

[KRAPP *switches off, broods, looks at his watch, gets up, goes backstage into darkness. Ten seconds. Pop of cork. Ten seconds. Second cork. Ten seconds. Third cork. Ten seconds. Brief burst of quavering song.*]

    KRAPP [*Sings.*] Now the day is over,
                   Night is drawing nigh-igh,
                   Shadows—

[*Fit of coughing. He comes back into light, sits down, wipes his mouth, switches on, resumes his listening posture.*]

70 TAPE —back on the year that is gone, with what I hope is perhaps a glint of the old eye to come, there is of course the house on the canal where mother lay a-dying, in the late autumn, after her long viduity [KRAPP *gives a*

start] and the—[KRAPP *switches off, winds back tape a little, bends his ear closer to machine, switches on*]—a-dying, after her long viduity, and the—

[KRAPP *switches off, raises his head, stares blankly before him. His lips move in the syllables of 'viduity.' No sound. He gets up, goes backstage into darkness, comes back with an enormous dictionary, lays it on table, sits down and looks up the word.*]

KRAPP   [*Reading from dictionary.*] State—or condition—of being—or remaining—a widow—or widower. [*Looks up. Puzzled.*] Being—or remaining? . . . [*Pause. He peers again at dictionary. Reading.*] 'Deep weeds of viduity'. . . . Also of an animal, especially a bird . . . the vidua or weaver-bird. . . . Black plumage of male. . . . [*He looks up. With relish.*] The
80 vidua-bird!

[*Pause. He closes dictionary, switches on, resumes listening posture.*]

TAPE   —bench by the weir from where I could see her window. There I sat, in the biting wind, wishing she were gone. [*Pause.*] Hardly a soul, just a few regulars, nursemaids, infants, old men, dogs. I got to know them quite well—oh by appearance of course I mean! One dark young beauty I recollect particularly, all white and starch, incomparable bosom, with a big black hooded perambulator, most funereal thing. Whenever I looked in her direction she had her eyes on me. And yet when I was bold enough to speak to her—not having been introduced—she threatened to call a policeman. As if I had designs on her virtue! [*Laugh. Pause.*] The face she had! The eyes!
90 Like . . . [*hesitates*] . . . chrysolite! [*Pause.*] Ah well. . . . [*Pause.*] I was there when—[KRAPP *switches off, broods, switches on again.*]—the blind went down, one of those dirty brown roller affairs, throwing a ball for a little white dog as chance would have it. I happened to look up and there it was. All over and done with, at last. I sat on for a few moments with the ball in my hand and the dog yelping and pawing at me. [*Pause.*] Moments. Her moments, my moments. [*Pause.*] The dog's moments. [*Pause.*] In the end I held it out to him and he took it in his mouth, gently, gently. A small, old, black, hard, solid rubber ball. [*Pause.*] I shall feel it, in my hand, until my dying day. [*Pause.*] I might have kept it. [*Pause.*] But I gave it to the dog.

[*Pause.*]

100 Ah well. . . .

[*Pause.*]

Spiritually a year of profound gloom and indigence until that memorable night in March, at the end of the jetty, in the howling wind, never to be forgotten, when suddenly I saw the whole thing. The vision at last. This I fancy is what I have chiefly to record this evening, against the day when my work will be done and perhaps no place left in my memory, warm or cold, for

the miracle that . . . [*hesitates*] . . . for the fire that set it alight. What I suddenly saw then was this, that the belief I had been going on all my life, namely—[KRAPP *switches off impatiently, winds tape forward, switches on again*]—great granite rocks the foam flying up in the light of the lighthouse
110 and the wind-gauge spinning like a propeller, clear to me at last that the dark I have always struggled to keep under is in reality my most—[KRAPP *curses, switches off, winds tape forward, switches on again*]—unshatterable association until my dissolution of storm and night with the light of the understanding and the fire—[KRAPP *curses louder, switches off, winds tape forward, switches on again*]—my face in her breasts and my hand on her. We lay there without moving. But under us all moved, and moved us, gently, up and down, and from side to side.

[*Pause.*]

Past midnight. Never knew such silence. The earth might be uninhabited.

[*Pause.*]

Here I end—[KRAPP *switches off, winds tape back, switches on again.*]—
120 upper lake, with the punt, bathed off the bank, then pushed out into the stream and drifted. She lay stretched out on the floorboards with her hands under her head and her eyes closed. Sun blazing down, bit of a breeze, water nice and lively. I noticed a scratch on her thigh, and asked her how she came by it. Picking gooseberries, she said. I said again I thought it was hopeless and no good going on and she agreed, without opening her eyes. [*Pause.*] I asked her to look at me and after a few moments—[*Pause.*]—after a few moments she did, but the eyes just slits, because of the glare. I bent over her to get them in the shadow and they opened. [*Pause. Low.*] Let me in. [*Pause.*] We drifted in among the flags and stuck. The way they went down, sighing,
130 before the stem! [*Pause.*] I lay down across her with my face in her breasts and my hand on her. We lay there without moving. But under us all moved, and moved us, gently, up and down, and from side to side.

[*Pause.*]

Past midnight. Never knew—

[KRAPP *switches off, broods. Finally he fumbles in his pockets, encounters the banana, takes it out, peers at it, puts it back, fumbles, brings out envelope, fumbles, puts back envelope, looks at his watch, gets up and goes backstage into darkness. Ten seconds. Sound of bottle against glass, then brief siphon. Ten seconds. Bottle against glass alone. Ten seconds. He comes back a little unsteadily into light, goes to front of table, takes out keys, raises them to his eyes, chooses key, unlocks first drawer, peers into it, feels about inside, takes out reel, peers at it, locks drawer, puts keys back in his pocket, goes and sits down, takes reel off machine, lays it on dictionary, loads virgin reel on machine, takes envelope from his pocket, consults back of it, lays it on table, switches on, clears his throat and begins to record.*]

KRAPP Just been listening to that stupid bastard I took myself for thirty years ago, hard to believe I was ever as bad as that. Thank God that's all done with anyway. [*Pause.*] The eyes she had! [*Broods, realizes he is recording silence, switches off, broods. Finally.*] Everything there, everything, all the— [*Realizes this is not being recorded, switches on.*] Everything there, everything on this old muckball, all the light and dark and famine and feasting
140   of . . . [*hesitates*] . . . the ages! [*In a shout.*] Yes! [*Pause.*] Let that go! Jesus! Take his mind off his homework! Jesus! [*Pause. Weary.*] Ah well, maybe he was right. [*Pause.*] Maybe he was right. [*Broods. Realizes. Switches off. Consults envelope.*] Pah! [*Crumples it and throws it away. Broods. Switches on.*] Nothing to say, not a squeak. What's a year now? The sour cud and the iron stool. [*Pause.*] Revelled in the word spool. [*With relish.*] Spooool! Happiest moment of the past half million. [*Pause.*] Seventeen copies sold, of which eleven at trade price to free circulating libraries beyond the seas. Getting known. [*Pause.*] One pound six and something, eight I have little doubt. [*Pause.*] Crawled out once or twice, before the summer was cold. Sat shiver-
150   ing in the park, drowned in dreams and burning to be gone. Not a soul. [*Pause.*] Last fancies. [*Vehemently.*] Keep 'em under! [*Pause.*] Scalded the eyes out of me reading *Effie* again, a page a day, with tears again. Effie. . . . [*Pause.*] Could have been happy with her, up there on the Baltic, and the pines, and the dunes. [*Pause.*] Could I? [*Pause.*] And she? [*Pause.*] Pah! [*Pause.*] Fanny came in a couple of times. Bony old ghost of a whore. Couldn't do much, but I suppose better than a kick in the crutch. The last time wasn't so bad. How do you manage it, she said, at your age? I told her I'd been saving up for her all my life. [*Pause.*] Went to Vespers once, like when I was in short trousers. [*Pause. Sings.*]
160   Now the day is over,
        Night is drawing nigh-igh,
        Shadows—[*coughing, then almost inaudible*]—
           of the evening
        Steal across the sky.
[*Gasping.*] Went to sleep and fell off the pew. [*Pause.*] Sometimes wondered in the night if a last effort mightn't—[*Pause.*] Ah finish your booze now and get to your bed. Go on with this drivel in the morning. Or leave it at that. [*Pause.*] Leave it at that. [*Pause.*] Lie propped up in the dark—and wander. Be again in the dingle on a Christmas Eve, gathering holly, the red-berried.
170   [*Pause.*] Be again on Croghan on a Sunday morning, in the haze, with the bitch, stop and listen to the bells. [*Pause.*] And so on. [*Pause.*] Be again, be again. [*Pause.*] All that old misery. [*Pause.*] Once wasn't enough for you. [*Pause.*] Lie down across her. [*Long pause. He suddenly bends over machine, switches off, wrenches off tape, throws it away, puts on the other, winds it forward to the passage he wants, switches on, listens staring front.*]
TAPE —gooseberries, she said. I said again I thought it was hopeless and no good going on and she agreed, without opening her eyes. [*Pause.*] I asked her to look at me and after a few moments—[*Pause.*]—after a few moments she did, but the eyes just slits, because of the glare. I bent over to get them in
180   the shadow and they opened. [*Pause. Low.*] Let me in. [*Pause.*] We drifted in

among the flags and stuck. The way they went down, sighing, before the stem! [*Pause.*] I lay down across her with my face in her breasts and my hand on her. We lay there without moving. But under us all moved, and moved us, gently, up and down, and from side to side.

[*Pause.* KRAPP*'s lips move. No sound.*]

Past midnight. Never knew such silence. The earth might be uninhabited.

[*Pause.*]

Here I end this reel. Box—[*Pause.*]—three, spool—[*Pause.*]—five. [*Pause.*] Perhaps my best years are gone. When there was a chance of happiness. But I wouldn't want them back. Not with the fire in me now. No, I wouldn't want them back.

[KRAPP *motionless staring before him. The tape runs on in silence.*]

Curtain

Questions

1. Consider the stage directions for this play. How important are its stage directions, as opposed to its dialogue? Are stage directions more important in this play than in most plays? Why?

2. Why is this play set "in the future"?

3. Everyone has seen farce—old Three Stooges films, the Marx Brothers, even cartoons on Saturday morning. Are there elements of farce in this play? Are there elements of absurdity in Bart Simpson? In Charlie Chaplin? In Roadrunner?

4. Discuss bananas in the theater of Samuel Beckett, at least as you come upon them in *Krapp's Last Tape*.

5. "Absurd" is not necessarily "meaningless." What is *Krapp's Last Tape* about? Is this a serious play? Is it a funny play? Is it tragicomedy?

6. How many characters are there in *Krapp's Last Tape?* Is there any sense in this apparently stupid question?

7. Look up reviews or other accounts of productions of *Krapp's Last Tape* and bring them to class for discussion.

Plays for Further Reading

Henrik Ibsen

The work of Henrik Ibsen (1828–1906) anticipates the variety of modern theater. His best-known plays are realistic, but he began as a poet and ended as a symbolist. Ibsen started young; he wrote his first play in 1850 and continued his apprenticeship with a series of romantic and historical plays. At the same time, he learned stagecraft by working as a resident with several theatrical companies. In 1866, he wrote the dramatic poem *Brand,* and followed it two years later with the poetic drama *Peer Gynt.*

In his great middle period, from about 1875 to 1890, Ibsen wrote his most famous plays, in the style of dramatic realism. *Pillars of Society* (1877) attacked bourgeois conventions. A series of plays, of which *A Doll's House* (1879) is best known, explored the hazards of domestic life. *Ghosts* (1883) was shocking because the plot turned on the subject of venereal disease. *An Enemy of the People* (1883), *The Wild Duck* (1885), and *Rosmersholm* (1887) all dealt with contemporary society; all were tightly constructed, informed by passion and compassion. Toward the end of his life, Ibsen returned to a symbolic, less realistic theater—with considerable success—in *The Master Builder* (1893), *John Gabriel Borkman* (1897), and *When We Dead Awaken* (1900).

The realistic drama *Hedda Gabler* was first performed in Munich in 1891. The protagonist is an unusual woman married to a conventional man; she is fierce, proud, neurotic, and unable to direct her intelligence and energy toward an acceptable goal. *Hedda Gabler* shows affinities with feminist thinking, for Ibsen understood the anger and despair of his heroine, denied power by a patriarchal society. The play has dramatic power separate from its political morality, and its conclusion remains ambiguous.

Henrik Ibsen

Hedda Gabler   (1890; tr. 1891)
Translated by Edmund Gosse and William Archer

Cast

GEORGE TESMAN

HEDDA TESMAN, his wife

MISS JULIANA TESMAN, his aunt

MRS. ELVSTED

JUDGE BRACK

EILERT LÖVBORG

BERTA, servant at the Tesmans'

Scene. *The action is at Tesman's villa, in the west end of Christiania*

Act I

Scene. *A spacious, handsome, and tastefully furnished drawing room, decorated in dark colors. In the back, a wide doorway with curtains drawn back, leading into a smaller room decorated in the same style as the drawing room. In the righthand wall of the front room, a folding door leading out to the hall. In the opposite wall, on the left, a glass door, also with curtains drawn back. Through the panes can be seen part of a veranda outside, and trees covered with autumn foliage. An oval table, with a cover on it, and surrounded by chairs, stands well forward. In front, by the wall on the right, a wide stove of dark porcelain, a high-backed armchair, a cushioned footrest, and two footstools. A settee, with a small round table in front of it, fills the upper right-hand corner. In front, on the left, a little way from the wall, a sofa. Farther back than the glass door, a piano. On either side of the doorway at the back a whatnot with terra-cotta and majolica ornaments. Against the back wall of the inner room a sofa, with a table, and one or two chairs. Over the sofa hangs the portrait of a handsome elderly man in a General's uniform. Over the table a hanging lamp, with an opal glass shade. A number of bouquets are arranged about the drawing room, in vases and glasses. Others lie upon the tables. The floors in both rooms are covered with thick carpets. Morning light. The sun shines in through the glass door.*

MISS JULIANA TESMAN, *with her bonnet on and carrying a parasol, comes in from the hall, followed by* BERTA, *who carries a bouquet wrapped in paper.* MISS TESMAN *is a comely and pleasant-looking lady of about sixty-five. She is nicely but simply dressed in a gray walking costume.* BERTA *is a middle-aged woman of plain and rather countrified appearance.*

MISS TESMAN [*stops close to the door, listens, and says softly*] Upon my word, I don't believe they are stirring yet!

BERTA [*also softly*] I told you so, Miss. Remember how late the steamboat got in last night. And then, when they got home!—good Lord, what a lot the young mistress had to unpack before she could get to bed.

MISS TESMAN   Well, well—let them have their sleep out. But let us see that they get a good breath of the fresh morning air when they do appear. [*She goes to the glass door and throws it open.*]

BERTA [*beside the table, at a loss what to do with the bouquet in her hand*]
10 I declare, there isn't a bit of room left. I think I'll put it down here, Miss. [*She places it on the piano.*]

MISS TESMAN   So you've got a new mistress now, my dear Berta. Heaven knows it was a wrench to me to part with you.

BERTA [*on the point of weeping*]   And do you think it wasn't hard for me, too, Miss? After all the blessed years I've been with you and Miss Rina.

MISS TESMAN   We must make the best of it, Berta. There was nothing else to be done. George can't do without you, you see—he absolutely can't. He has had you to look after him ever since he was a little boy.

BERTA   Ah, but, Miss Julia, I can't help thinking of Miss Rina lying helpless
20 at home there, poor thing. And with only that new girl, too! She'll never learn to take proper care of an invalid.

MISS TESMAN   Oh, I shall manage to train her. And, of course, you know I shall take most of it upon myself. You needn't be uneasy about my poor sister, my dear Berta.

BERTA   Well, but there's another thing, Miss. I'm so mortally afraid I shan't be able to suit the young mistress.

MISS TESMAN   Oh, well—just at first there may be one or two things.

BERTA   Most like she'll be terrible grand in her ways.

MISS TESMAN   Well, you can't wonder at that—General Gabler's daughter!
30 Think of the sort of life she was accustomed to in her father's time. Don't you remember how we used to see her riding down the road along with the General? In that long black habit—and with feathers in her hat?

BERTA   Yes, indeed—I remember well enough!—But, good Lord, I should never have dreamt in those days that she and Master George would make a match of it.

MISS TESMAN   Nor I. But by the by, Berta—while I think of it: in future you mustn't say Master George. You must say Dr. Tesman.

BERTA   Yes, the young mistress spoke of that, too—last night—the moment they set foot in the house. Is it true then, Miss?
40 MISS TESMAN   Yes, indeed it is. Only think, Berta—some foreign university has made him a doctor—while he has been abroad, you understand. I hadn't heard a word about it, until he told me himself upon the pier.

BERTA   Well, well, he's clever enough for anything, he is. But I didn't think he'd have gone in for doctoring people, too.

MISS TESMAN   No, no, it's not that sort of doctor he is. [*Nods significantly*] But let me tell you, we may have to call him something still grander before long.

BERTA   You don't say so! What can that be, Miss?

MISS TESMAN [*smiling*]   H'm—wouldn't you like to know! [*With emotion*]
50 Ah, dear, dear—if my poor brother could only look up from his grave now, and see what his little boy has grown into! [*Looks around*] But bless me, Berta—why have you done this? Taken the chintz covers off all the furniture?

BERTA The mistress told me to. She can't abide covers on the chairs, she says.

MISS TESMAN Are they going to make this their everyday sitting room then?

BERTA Yes, that's what I understood—from the mistress. Master George—the doctor—he said nothing.

GEORGE TESMAN *comes from the right into the inner room, humming to himself, and carrying an unstrapped empty portmanteau. He is a middle-sized, young-looking man of thirty-three, rather stout, with a round, open, cheerful face, fair hair and beard. He wears spectacles, and is somewhat carelessly dressed in comfortable indoor clothes.*

MISS TESMAN Good morning, good morning, George.

TESMAN [*in the doorway between the rooms*] Aunt Julia! Dear Aunt Julia!
60 [*Goes up to her and shakes hands warmly*] Come all this way—so early! Eh?

MISS TESMAN Why, of course I had to come and see how you were getting on.

TESMAN In spite of your having had no proper night's rest?

MISS TESMAN Oh, that makes no difference to me.

TESMAN Well, I suppose you got home all right from the pier? Eh?

MISS TESMAN Yes, quite safely, thank goodness. Judge Brack was good enough to see me right to my door.

TESMAN We were so sorry we couldn't give you a seat in the carriage. But you saw what a pile of boxes Hedda had to bring with her.

MISS TESMAN Yes, she had certainly plenty of boxes.

70 BERTA [*to TESMAN*] Shall I go in and see if there's anything I can do for the mistress?

TESMAN No thank you, Berta—you needn't. She said she would ring if she wanted anything.

BERTA [*going towards the right*] Very well.

TESMAN But look here—take this portmanteau with you.

BERTA [*taking it*] I'll put it in the attic. [*She goes out by the hall door.*]

TESMAN Fancy, Auntie—I had the whole of that portmanteau chock full of copies of documents. You wouldn't believe how much I have picked up from all the archives I have been examining—curious old details that no one has
80 had any idea of . . .

MISS TESMAN Yes, you don't seem to have wasted your time on your wedding trip, George.

TESMAN No, that I haven't. But do take off your bonnet, Auntie. Look here! Let me untie the strings—eh?

MISS TESMAN [*while he does so*] Well, well—this is just as if you were still at home with us.

TESMAN [*with the bonnet in his hand; looks at it from all sides*] Why, what a gorgeous bonnet you've been investing in!

MISS TESMAN I bought it on Hedda's account.

90 TESMAN On Hedda's account? Eh?

MISS TESMAN Yes, so that Hedda needn't be ashamed of me if we happened to go out together.

TESMAN [*patting her cheek*]   You always think of everything, Aunt Julia.
[*Lays the bonnet on a chair beside the table*] And now, look here—suppose
we sit comfortably on the sofa and have a little chat, till Hedda comes. [*They
seat themselves. She places her parasol in the corner of the sofa.*]

MISS TESMAN [*takes both his hands and look at him*]   What a delight it is to
have you again, as large as life, before my very eyes, George! My George—
my poor brother's own boy!

100   TESMAN   And it's a delight for me, too, to see you again, Aunt Julia! You,
who have been father and mother in one to me.

MISS TESMAN   Oh, yes, I know you will always keep a place in your heart for
your old aunts.

TESMAN   And what about Aunt Rina? No improvement—eh?

MISS TESMAN   Oh no—we can scarcely look for any improvement in her
case, poor thing. There she lies, helpless, as she has lain for all these years.
But heaven grant I may not lose her yet awhile. For if I did, I don't know what
I should make of my life, George—especially now that I haven't you to look
after any more.

110   TESMAN [*patting her back*]   There, there, there . . . !

MISS TESMAN [*suddenly changing her tone*]   And to think that here you are a
married man, George! And that you should be the one to carry off Hedda
Gabler—the beautiful Hedda Gabler! Only think of it—she, that was so beset
with admirers!

TESMAN [*hums a little and smiles complacently*]   Yes, I fancy I have several
good friends about town who would like to stand in my shoes—eh?

MISS TESMAN   And then this fine long wedding tour you have had! More than
five—nearly six months . . .

TESMAN   Well, for me it has been a sort of tour of research as well. I have
120 had to do so much grubbing among old records—and to read no end of
books too, Auntie.

MISS TESMAN   Oh yes, I suppose so. [*More confidentially, and lowering her
voice a little*] But listen now, George—have you nothing—nothing special to
tell me?

TESMAN   As to our journey?

MISS TESMAN   Yes.

TESMAN   No, I don't know of anything except what I have told you in my
letters. I had a doctor's degree conferred on me—but that I told you yesterday.

MISS TESMAN   Yes, yes, you did. But what I mean is—haven't you any—
130 any—expectations . . . ?

TESMAN   Expectations?

MISS TESMAN   Why you know, George—I'm your old auntie!

TESMAN   Why, of course I have expectations.

MISS TESMAN   Ah!

TESMAN   I have every expectation of being a professor one of these days.

MISS TESMAN   Oh yes, a professor . . .

TESMAN   Indeed, I may say I am certain of it. But my dear Auntie—you
know all about that already!

MISS TESMAN [*laughing to herself*]   Yes, of course I do. You are quite right

140 there. [*Changing the subject*] But we were talking about your journey. It must have cost a great deal of money, George?

TESMAN   Well, you see—my handsome traveling scholarship went a good way.

MISS TESMAN   But I can't understand how you can have made it go far enough for two.

TESMAN   No, that's not so easy to understand—eh?

MISS TESMAN   And especially traveling with a lady—they tell me that makes it ever so much more expensive.

TESMAN   Yes, of course—it makes it a little more expensive. But Hedda
150 had to have this trip, Auntie! She really had to. Nothing else would have done.

MISS TESMAN   No, no, I suppose not. A wedding tour seems to be quite indispensable nowadays. But tell me now—have you gone thoroughly over the house yet.

TESMAN   Yes, you may be sure I have. I have been afoot ever since daylight.

MISS TESMAN   And what do you think of it all?

TESMAN   I'm delighted! Quite delighted! Only I can't think what we are to do with the two empty rooms between this inner parlor and Hedda's bedroom.

MISS TESMAN [*laughing*]   Oh my dear George, I daresay you may find some use for them—in the course of time.

160 TESMAN   Why of course you are quite right, Aunt Julia! You mean as my library increases—eh?

MISS TESMAN   Yes, quite so, my dear boy. It was your library I was thinking of.

TESMAN   I am specially pleased on Hedda's account. Often and often, before we were engaged, she said that she would never care to live anywhere but in Secretary Falk's villa.

MISS TESMAN   Yes, it was lucky that this very house should come into the market, just after you had started.

TESMAN   Yes, Aunt Julia, the luck was on our side, wasn't it—eh?

MISS TESMAN   But the expense, my dear George! You will find it very ex-
170 pensive, all this.

TESMAN [*looks at her, a little cast down*]   Yes, I suppose I shall, Aunt!

MISS TESMAN   Oh, frightfully!

TESMAN   How much do you think? In round numbers?—Eh?

MISS TESMAN   Oh, I can't even guess until all the accounts come in.

TESMAN   Well, fortunately, Judge Brack has secured the most favorable terms for me—so he said in a letter to Hedda.

MISS TESMAN   Yes, don't be uneasy my dear boy. Besides, I have given security for the furniture and all the carpets.

TESMAN   Security! You! My dear Aunt Julia—what sort of security could you
180 give?

MISS TESMAN   I have given a mortgage on our annuity.

TESMAN [*jumps up*]   What! On your—and Aunt Rina's annuity!

MISS TESMAN   Yes, I knew of no other plan, you see.

TESMAN [*placing himself before her*]   Have you gone out of your senses, Auntie! Your annuity—it's all that you and Aunt Rina have to live upon.

MISS TESMAN   Well, well—don't get so excited about it. It's only a matter of

form you know—Judge Brack assured me of that. It was he that was kind
enough to arrange the whole affair for me. A mere matter of form, he said.

TESMAN   Yes, that may be all very well. But nevertheless . . .

190   MISS TESMAN   You will have your own salary to depend upon now. And,
good heavens, even if we did have to pay up a little . . . ! To eke things out a
bit at the start . . . ! Why, it would be nothing but a pleasure to us.

TESMAN   Oh Auntie—will you never be tired of making sacrifices for me!

MISS TESMAN [*rises and lays her hands on his shoulders*]   Have I any other
happiness in this world except to smooth your way for you, my dear boy? You,
who have had neither father nor mother to depend on. And now we have
reached the goal, George! Things have looked black enough for us, sometimes; but, thank heaven, now you have nothing to fear.

TESMAN   Yes, it is really marvelous how everything has turned out for the
200   best.

MISS TESMAN   And the people who opposed you—who wanted to bar the
way for you—now you have them at your feet. They have fallen, George. Your
most dangerous rival—his fall was the worst. And now he has to lie on the
bed he has made for himself—poor misguided creature.

TESMAN   Have you heard anything of Eilert? Since I went away, I mean.

MISS TESMAN   Only that he is said to have published a new book.

TESMAN   What! Eilert Lövborg! Recently—eh?

MISS TESMAN   Yes, so they say. Heaven knows whether it can be worth anything! Ah, when your new book appears—that will be another story, George!
210   What is it to be about?

TESMAN   It will deal with the domestic industries of Brabant during the
Middle Ages.

MISS TESMAN   Fancy—to be able to write on such a subject as that!

TESMAN   However, it may be some time before the book is ready. I have all
these collections to arrange first, you see.

MISS TESMAN   Yes, collecting and arranging—no one can beat you at that.
There you are my poor brother's own son.

TESMAN   I am looking forward eagerly to setting to work at it; especially
now that I have my own delightful home to work in.

220   MISS TESMAN   And, most of all, now that you have got a wife of your heart,
my dear George.

TESMAN [*embracing her*]   Oh yes, yes, Aunt Julia. Hedda—she is the best
part of it all! [*Looks towards the doorway*] I believe I hear her coming—eh?

HEDDA *enters from the left through the inner room. She is a woman of nine-and-
twenty. Her face and figure show refinement and distinction. Her complexion is pale
and opaque. Her steel-gray eyes express a cold, unruffled repose. Her hair is of an
agreeable medium brown, but not particularly abundant. She is dressed in a tasteful, somewhat loose-fitting morning gown.*

MISS TESMAN [*going to meet* HEDDA]   Good morning, my dear Hedda! Good
morning, and a hearty welcome!

HEDDA [*holds out her hand*]   Good morning, dear Miss Tesman! So early a call! That is kind of you.

MISS TESMAN [*with some embarrassment*]   Well—has the bride slept well in her new home?

230   HEDDA   Oh yes, thanks. Passably.

TESMAN [*laughing*]   Passably! Come, that's good, Hedda! You were sleeping like a stone when I got up.

HEDDA   Fortunately. Of course, one has always to accustom one's self to new surroundings, Miss Tesman—little by little. [*Looking towards the left*] Oh—there the servant has gone and opened the veranda door, and let in a whole flood of sunshine.

MISS TESMAN [*going towards the door*]   Well, then we will shut it.

HEDDA   No, no, not that! Tesman, please draw the curtains. That will give a softer light.

240   TESMAN [*at the door*]   All right—all right. There now, Hedda, now you have both shade and fresh air.

HEDDA   Yes, fresh air we certainly must have, with all these stacks of flowers . . . But—won't you sit down, Miss Tesman?

MISS TESMAN   No, thank you. Now that I have seen that everything is all right here—thank heaven!—I must be getting home again. My sister is lying longing for me, poor thing.

TESMAN   Give her my very best love, Auntie; and say I shall look in and see her later in the day.

MISS TESMAN   Yes, yes, I'll be sure to tell her. But by the by, George—
250   [*feeling in her dress pocket*]—I had almost forgotten—I have something for you here.

TESMAN   What is it, Auntie? Eh?

MISS TESMAN [*produces a flat parcel wrapped in newspaper and hands it to him*]   Look here, my dear boy.

TESMAN [*opening the parcel*]   Well, I declare! Have you really saved them for me, Aunt Julia! Hedda! Isn't this touching—eh?

HEDDA [*beside the whatnot on the right*]   Well, what is it?

TESMAN   My old morning shoes! My slippers.

HEDDA   Indeed. I remember you often spoke of them while we were
260   abroad.

TESMAN   Yes, I missed them terribly. [*Goes up to her*] Now you shall see them, Hedda!

HEDDA [*going towards the stove*]   Thanks, I really don't care about it.

TESMAN [*following her*]   Only think—ill as she was, Aunt Rina embroidered these for me. Oh you can't think how many associations cling to them.

HEDDA [*at the table*]   Scarcely for me.

MISS TESMAN   Of course not for Hedda, George.

TESMAN   Well, but now that she belongs to the family, I thought . . .

HEDDA [*interrupting*]   We shall never get on with this servant, Tesman.

270   MISS TESMAN   Not get on with Berta?

TESMAN   Why, dear, what puts that in your head? Eh?

HEDDA [*pointing*]   Look there! She has left her old bonnet lying about on a chair.

TESMAN [*in consternation, drops the slippers on the floor*]   Why, Hedda . . .

HEDDA   Just fancy, if any one should come in and see it!

TESMAN   But Hedda—that's Aunt Julia's bonnet.

HEDDA   Is it!

MISS TESMAN [*taking up the bonnet*]   Yes, indeed it's mine. And, what's more, it's not old, Madam Hedda.

280   HEDDA   I really did not look closely at it, Miss Tesman.

MISS TESMAN [*trying on the bonnet*]   Let me tell you it's the first time I have worn it—the very first time.

TESMAN   And a very nice bonnet it is too—quite a beauty!

MISS TESMAN   Oh, it's no such great thing, George. [*Looks around her*] My parasol . . . ? Ah, here. [*Takes it*] For this is mine too—[*mutters*]—not Berta's.

TESMAN   A new bonnet and a new parasol! Only think, Hedda!

HEDDA   Very handsome indeed.

TESMAN   Yes, isn't it? Eh? But Auntie, take a good look at Hedda before you go! See how handsome she is!

290   MISS TESMAN   Oh, my dear boy, there's nothing new in that. Hedda was always lovely. [*She nods and goes towards the right.*]

TESMAN [*following*]   Yes, but have you noticed what splendid condition she is in? How she has filled out on the journey?

HEDDA [*crossing the room*]   Oh, do be quiet . . . !

MISS TESMAN [*who has stopped and turned*]   Filled out?

TESMAN   Of course you don't notice it so much now that she has that dress on. But I, who can see. . . .

HEDDA [*at the glass door, impatiently*]   Oh, you can't see anything.

TESMAN   It must be the mountain air in the Tyrol . . .

300   HEDDA [*curtly, interrupting*]   I am exactly as I was when I started.

TESMAN   So you insist; but I'm quite certain you are not. Don't you agree with me, Auntie?

MISS TESMAN [*who has been gazing at her with folded hands*]   Hedda is lovely—lovely—lovely. [*Goes up to her, takes her head between both hands, draws it downwards, and kisses her hair*] God bless and preserve Hedda Tesman—for George's sake.

HEDDA [*gently freeing herself*]   Oh—! Let me go.

MISS TESMAN [*in quiet emotion*]   I shall not let a day pass without coming to see you.

310   TESMAN   No you won't, will you, Auntie? Eh?

MISS TESMAN   Good-bye—good-bye!

She goes out by the hall door. TESMAN *accompanies her. The door remains half open.* TESMAN *can be heard repeating his message to* AUNT RINA *and his thanks for the slippers. In the meantime,* HEDDA *walks about the room, raising her arms and clenching her hands as if in desperation. Then she flings back the curtains from the glass door, and stands there looking out. Presently* TESMAN *returns and closes the door behind him.*

TESMAN [*picks up the slippers from the floor*]   What are you looking at, Hedda?

HEDDA [*once more calm and mistress of herself*]   I am only looking at the leaves. They are so yellow—so withered.

TESMAN [*wraps up the slippers and lays them on the table*]   Well you see, we are well into September now.

HEDDA [*again restless*]   Yes, to think of it! Already in—in September.

TESMAN   Don't you think Aunt Julia's manner was strange, dear? Almost
320   solemn? Can you imagine what was the matter with her? Eh?

HEDDA   I scarcely know her, you see. Is she not often like that?

TESMAN   No, not as she was today.

HEDDA [*leaving the glass door*]   Do you think she was annoyed about the bonnet?

TESMAN   Oh, scarcely at all. Perhaps a little, just at the moment . . .

HEDDA   But what an idea, to pitch her bonnet about in the drawing room! No one does that sort of thing.

TESMAN   Well you may be sure Aunt Julia won't do it again.

HEDDA   In any case, I shall manage to make my peace with her.
330   TESMAN   Yes, my dear, good Hedda, if you only would.

HEDDA   When you call this afternoon, you might invite her to spend the evening here.

TESMAN   Yes, that I will. And there's one thing more you could do that would delight her heart.

HEDDA   What is it?

TESMAN   If you could only prevail on yourself to say *du*[1] to her. For my sake, Hedda? Eh?

HEDDA   No, no, Tesman—you really mustn't ask that of me. I have told you so already. I shall try to call her "Aunt"; and you must be satisfied with that.
340   TESMAN   Well, well. Only I think now that you belong to the family, you . . .

HEDDA   H'm—I can't in the least see why . . . [*She goes up towards the middle doorway.*]

TESMAN [*after a pause*]   Is there anything the matter with you, Hedda? Eh?

HEDDA   I'm only looking at my old piano. It doesn't go at all well with all the other things.

TESMAN   The first time I draw my salary, we'll see about exchanging it.

HEDDA   No, no—no exchanging. I don't want to part with it. Suppose we put it there in the inner room, and then get another here in its place. When it's convenient, I mean.
350   TESMAN [*a little taken aback*]   Yes—of course we could do that.

HEDDA [*takes up the bouquet from the piano*]   These flowers were not here last night when we arrived.

TESMAN   Aunt Julia must have brought them for you.

HEDDA [*examining the bouquet*]   A visiting card. [*Takes it out and reads*] "Shall return later in the day." Can you guess whose card it is?

TESMAN   No, whose? Eh?

---

[1] *Du*, the second person singular, implies intimacy.

HEDDA   The name is "Mrs. Elvsted."

TESMAN   Is it really? Sheriff Elvsted's wife? Miss Rysing that was.

HEDDA   Exactly. The girl with the irritating hair, that she was always show-
360 ing off. An old flame of yours I've been told.

TESMAN [*laughing*]   Oh, that didn't last long; and it was before I knew you,
Hedda. But fancy her being in town!

HEDDA   It's odd that she should call upon us. I have scarcely seen her since
we left school.

TESMAN   I haven't seen her either for—heaven knows how long. I wonder
how she can endure to live in such an out-of-the-way hole—eh?

HEDDA [*after a moment's thought, says suddenly*]   Tell me, Tesman—isn't
it somewhere near there that he—that—Eilert Lövborg is living?

TESMAN   Yes, he is somewhere in that part of the country.

BERTA *enters by the hall door.*

370   BERTA   That lady, ma'am, that brought some flowers a little while ago, is
here again. [*Pointing*] The flowers you have in your hand, ma'am.

HEDDA   Ah, is she? Well, please show her in.

BERTA *opens the door for* MRS. ELVSTED, *and goes out herself*—MRS. ELVSTED *is a woman
of fragile figure, with pretty, soft features. Her eyes are light blue, large, round, and
somewhat prominent, with a startled, inquiring expression. Her hair is remarkably
light, almost flaxen, and unusually abundant and wavy. She is a couple of years
younger than* HEDDA. *She wears a dark visiting dress, tasteful, but not quite in the
latest fashion.*

HEDDA [*receives her warmly*]   How do you do, my dear Mrs. Elvsted? It's
delightful to see you again.

MRS. ELVSTED [*nervously, struggling for self-control*]   Yes, it's a very long
time since we met.

TESMAN [*gives her his hand*]   And we too—eh?

HEDDA   Thanks for your lovely flowers . . .

MRS. ELVSTED   Oh, not at all . . . I would have come straight here yester-
380 day afternoon; but I heard that you were away . . .

TESMAN   Have you just come to town? Eh?

MRS. ELVSTED   I arrived yesterday, about midday. Oh, I was quite in despair
when I heard that you were not at home.

HEDDA   In despair! How so?

TESMAN   Why, my dear Mrs. Rysing—I mean Mrs. Elvsted . . .

HEDDA   I hope that you are not in any trouble?

MRS. ELVSTED   Yes, I am. And I don't know another living creature here that
I can turn to.

HEDDA [*laying the bouquet on the table*]   Come—let us sit here on the
390 sofa . . .

MRS. ELVSTED   Oh, I am too restless to sit down.

HEDDA   Oh no, you're not. Come here. [*She draws* MRS. ELVSTED *down upon
the sofa and sits at her side.*]

TESMAN   Well? What is it, Mrs. Elvsted . . . ?

HEDDA   Has anything particular happened to you at home?

MRS. ELVSTED   Yes—and no. Oh—I am so anxious you should not misunderstand me . . .

HEDDA   Then your best plan is to tell us the whole story, Mrs. Elvsted.

TESMAN   I suppose that's what you have come for—eh?

400   MRS. ELVSTED   Yes, yes—of course it is. Well then, I must tell you, if you don't already know, that Eilert Lövborg is in town, too.

HEDDA   Lövborg . . . !

TESMAN   What! Has Eilert Lövborg come back? Fancy that, Hedda!

HEDDA   Well, well—I hear it.

MRS. ELVSTED   He has been here a week already. Just fancy—a whole week! In this terrible town, alone! With so many temptations on all sides.

HEDDA   But, my dear Mrs. Elvsted—how does he concern you so much?

MRS. ELVSTED [looks at her with a startled air, and says rapidly]   He was the children's tutor.

410   HEDDA   Your children's?

MRS. ELVSTED   My husband's. I have none.

HEDDA   Your stepchildren's, then?

MRS. ELVSTED   Yes.

TESMAN [somewhat hesitatingly]   Then was he—I don't know how to express it—was he—regular enough in his habits to be fit for the post? Eh?

MRS. ELVSTED   For the last two years his conduct has been irreproachable.

TESMAN   Has it indeed? Fancy that, Hedda!

HEDDA   I hear it.

MRS. ELVSTED   Perfectly irreproachable, I assure you! In every respect. But

420   all the same—now that I know he is here—in this great town—and with a large sum of money in his hands—I can't help being in mortal fear for him.

TESMAN   Why did he not remain where he was? With you and your husband? Eh?

MRS. ELVSTED   After his book was published he was too restless and unsettled to remain with us.

TESMAN   Yes, by the by, Aunt Julia told me he had published a new book.

MRS. ELVSTED   Yes, a big book, dealing with the march of civilization—in broad outline, as it were. It came out about a fortnight ago. And since it has sold so well, and been so much read—and made such a sensation . . .

430   TESMAN   Has it indeed? It must be something he has had lying by since his better days.

MRS. ELVSTED   Long ago, you mean?

TESMAN   Yes.

MRS. ELVSTED   No, he has written it all since he has been with us—within the last year.

TESMAN   Isn't that good news, Hedda? Think of that.

MRS. ELVSTED   Ah yes, if only it would last!

HEDDA   Have you seen him here in town?

MRS. ELVSTED   No, not yet. I have had the greatest difficulty in finding out

440   his address. But this morning I discovered it at last.

HEDDA [*looks searchingly at her*]   Do you know, it seems to me a little odd of your husband—h'm . . .

MRS. ELVSTED [*starting nervously*]   Of my husband! What?

HEDDA   That he should send you to town on such an errand—that he does not come himself and look after his friend.

MRS. ELVSTED   Oh no, no—my husband has no time. And besides, I—I had some shopping to do.

HEDDA [*with a slight smile*]   Ah, that is a different matter.

MRS. ELVSTED [*rising quickly and uneasily*]   And now I beg and implore
450 you, Mr. Tesman—receive Eilert Lövborg kindly if he comes to you! And that he is sure to do. You see you were such great friends in the old days. And then you are interested in the same studies—the same branch of science—so far as I can understand.

TESMAN   We used to be, at any rate.

MRS. ELVSTED   That is why I beg so earnestly that you—you too—will keep a sharp eye upon him. Oh, you will promise me that, Mr. Tesman—won't you?

TESMAN   With the greatest of pleasure, Mrs. Rysing . . .

HEDDA   Elvsted.

TESMAN   I assure you I shall do all I possibly can for Eilert. You may rely
460 upon me.

MRS. ELVSTED   Oh, how very, very kind of you! [*Presses his hands*] Thanks, thanks, thanks! [*Frightened*] You see, my husband is so very fond of him!

HEDDA [*rising*]   You ought to write to him, Tesman. Perhaps he may not care to come to you of his own accord.

TESMAN   Well, perhaps it would be the right thing to do, Hedda? Eh?

HEDDA   And the sooner the better. Why not at once?

MRS. ELVSTED [*imploringly*]   Oh, if you only would!

TESMAN   I'll write this moment. Have you his address, Mrs.—Mrs. Elvsted?

MRS. ELVSTED   Yes. [*Takes a slip of paper from her pocket, and hands it to
470 him*] Here it is.

TESMAN   Good, good. Then I'll go in . . . [*Looks about him*] By the by— my slippers? Oh, here. [*Takes the packet, and is about to go*]

HEDDA   Be sure you write him a cordial, friendly letter. And a good long one too.

TESMAN   Yes, I will.

MRS. ELVSTED   But please, please don't say a word to show that I have suggested it.

TESMAN   No, how could you think I would? Eh? [*He goes out to the right, through the inner room.*]

480 HEDDA [*goes up to* MRS. ELVSTED, *smiles and says in a low voice*] There! We have killed two birds with one stone.

MRS. ELVSTED   What do you mean?

HEDDA   Could you not see that I wanted him to go?

MRS. ELVSTED   Yes, to write the letter . . .

HEDDA   And that I might speak to you alone.

MRS. ELVSTED [*confused*]   About the same thing?

HEDDA   Precisely.

MRS. ELVSTED [*apprehensively*] But there is nothing more, Mrs. Tesman! Absolutely nothing!

490   HEDDA Oh yes, but there is. There is a great deal more—I can see that. Sit here—and we'll have a cozy, confidential chat. [*She forces* MRS. ELVSTED *to sit in the easy-chair beside the stove, and seats herself on one of the footstools.*]

MRS. ELVSTED [*anxiously, looking at her watch*] But, my dear Mrs. Tesman—I was really on the point of going.

HEDDA Oh, you can't be in such a hurry. Well? Now tell me something about your life at home.

MRS. ELVSTED Oh, that is just what I care least to speak about.

HEDDA But to me, dear . . . ? Why, weren't we schoolfellows?

MRS. ELVSTED Yes, but you were in the class above me. Oh, how dreadfully
500 afraid of you I was then!

HEDDA Afraid of me?

MRS. ELVSTED Yes, dreadfully. For when we met on the stairs you used always to pull my hair.

HEDDA Did I, really?

MRS. ELVSTED Yes, and once you said you would burn it off my head.

HEDDA Oh, that was all nonsense, of course.

MRS. ELVSTED Yes, but I was so silly in those days. And since then, too—we have drifted so far—far apart from each other. Our circles have been so entirely different.

510 HEDDA Well then, we must try to drift together again. Now listen! At school we said *du* to each other; and we called each other by our Christian names . . .

MRS. ELVSTED No, I am sure you must be mistaken.

HEDDA No, not at all! I can remember quite distinctly. So now we are going to renew our old friendship. [*Draws the footstool closer to* MRS. ELVSTED] There now! [*Kisses her cheek*] You must say *du* to me and call me Hedda.

MRS. ELVSTED [*presses and pats her hands*] Oh, how good and kind you are! I am not used to such kindness.

HEDDA There, there, there! And I shall say *du* to you, as in the old days,
520 and call you my dear Thora.

MRS. ELVSTED My name is Thea.

HEDDA Why, of course! I meant Thea. [*Looks at her compassionately*] So you are not accustomed to goodness and kindness, Thea? Not in your own home?

MRS. ELVSTED Oh, if I only had a home! But I haven't any; I have never had a home.

HEDDA [*looks at her for a moment*] I almost suspected as much.

MRS. ELVSTED [*gazing helplessly before her*] Yes—yes—yes.

HEDDA I don't quite remember—was it not as housekeeper that you first
530 went to Mr. Elvsted's?

MRS. ELVSTED I really went as governess. But his wife—his late wife—was an invalid, and rarely left her room. So I had to look after the housekeeping as well.

HEDDA And then—at last—you became mistress of the house.

MRS. ELVSTED [*sadly*]   Yes, I did.

HEDDA   Let me see—about how long ago was that?

MRS. ELVSTED   My marriage?

HEDDA   Yes.

MRS. ELVSTED   Five years ago.

540   HEDDA   To be sure; it must be that.

MRS. ELVSTED   Oh those five years . . . ! Or at all events the last two or three of them! Oh, if you[2] could only imagine . . .

HEDDA [*giving her a little slap on the hand*]   De? Fie, Thea!

MRS. ELVSTED   Yes, yes, I will try . . . Well, if—you could only imagine and understand . . .

HEDDA [*lightly*]   Eilert Lövborg has been in your neighborhood about three years, hasn't he?

MRS. ELVSTED [*looks at her doubtfully*]   Eilert Lövborg? Yes—he has.

HEDDA   Had you known him before, in town here?

550   MRS. ELVSTED   Scarcely at all. I mean—I knew him by name of course.

HEDDA   But you saw a good deal of him in the country?

MRS. ELVSTED   Yes, he came to us every day. You see, he gave the children lessons; for in the long run I couldn't manage it all myself.

HEDDA   No, that's clear.—And your husband—? I suppose he is often away from home?

MRS. ELVSTED   Yes. Being sheriff, you know, he has to travel about a good deal in his district.

HEDDA [*leaning against the arm of the chair*]   Thea—my poor, sweet Thea—now you must tell me everything—exactly as it stands.

560   MRS. ELVSTED   Well then, you must question me.

HEDDA   What sort of a man is your husband, Thea? I mean—you know—in everyday life. Is he kind to you?

MRS. ELVSTED [*evasively*]   I am sure he means well in everything.

HEDDA   I should think he must be altogether too old for you. There is at last twenty years' difference between you, is there not?

MRS. ELVSTED [*irritably*]   Yes, that is true, too. Everything about him is repellent to me! We have not a thought in common. We have no single point of sympathy—he and I.

HEDDA   But he is not fond of you all the same? In his own way?

570   MRS. ELVSTED   Oh I really don't know. I think he regards me simply as a useful property. And then it doesn't cost much to keep me. I am not expensive.

HEDDA   That is stupid of you.

MRS. ELVSTED [*shakes her head*]   It cannot be otherwise—not with him. I don't think he really cares for any one but himself—and perhaps a little for the children.

HEDDA   And for Eilert Lövborg, Thea.

MRS. ELVSTED [*looking at her*]   For Eilert Lövborg? What puts that into your head?

HEDDA   Well, my dear—I should say, when he sends you after him all the

---

[2] Mrs. Elvsted uses the formal *de* (for *you*) instead of the intimate *du*.

580 way to town . . . [*Smiling almost imperceptibly*] And besides, you said so
yourself, to Tesman.

MRS. ELVSTED [*with a little nervous twitch*]   Did I? Yes, I suppose I did.
[*Vehemently, but not loudly*] No—I may just as well make a clean breast of it
at once! For it must all come out in any case.

HEDDA   Why, my dear Thea . . . ?

MRS. ELVSTED   Well, to make a long story short: My husband did not know
that I was coming.

HEDDA   What! Your husband didn't know it!

MRS. ELVSTED   No, of course not. For that matter, he was away from home
590 himself—he was traveling. Oh, I could bear it no longer, Hedda! I couldn't
indeed—so utterly alone as I should have been in future.

HEDDA   Well? And then?

MRS. ELVSTED   So I put together some of my things—what I needed most—
as quietly as possible. And then I left the house.

HEDDA   Without a word?

MRS. ELVSTED   Yes—and took the train straight to town.

HEDDA   Why, my dear, good Thea—to think of you daring to do it!

MRS. ELVSTED [*rises and moves about the room*]   What else could I possibly
do?

600   HEDDA   But what do you think your husband will say when you go home
again?

MRS. ELVSTED [*at the table, looks at her*]   Back to him?

HEDDA   Of course.

MRS. ELVSTED   I shall never go back to him again.

HEDDA [*rising and going towards her*]   Then you have left your home—for
good and all?

MRS. ELVSTED   Yes. There was nothing else to be done.

HEDDA   But then—to take flight so openly.

MRS. ELVSTED   Oh, it's impossible to keep things of that sort secret.

610   HEDDA   But what do you think people will say to you, Thea?

MRS. ELVSTED   They may say what they like, for aught *I* care, [*Seats herself
wearily and sadly on the sofa*] I have done nothing but what I had to do.

HEDDA [*after a short silence*]   And what are your plans now? What do you
think of doing?

MRS. ELVSTED   I don't know yet. I only know that, that I must live here,
where Eilert Lövborg is—if I am to live at all.

HEDDA [*takes a chair from the table, seats herself beside her, and strokes her
hands*]   My dear Thea—how did this—this friendship—between you and
Eilert Lövborg come about?

620   MRS. ELVSTED   Oh it grew up gradually. I gained a sort of influence over him.

HEDDA   Indeed?

MRS. ELVSTED   He gave up his old habits. Not because I asked him to, for I
never dared to do that. But of course he saw how repulsive they were to me;
and so he dropped them.

HEDDA [*concealing an involuntary smile of scorn*]   Then you have reclaimed him—as the saying goes—my little Thea.

MRS. ELVSTED So he says himself, at any rate. And he, on his side, has made a real human being of me—taught me to think, and to understand so many things.

630   HEDDA Did he give you lessons too, then?

MRS. ELVSTED No, not exactly lessons. But he talked to me—talked about such an infinity of things. And then came the lovely, happy time when I began to share in his work—when he allowed me to help him!

HEDDA Oh he did, did he?

MRS. ELVSTED Yes! He never wrote anything without my assistance.

HEDDA You were two good comrades, in fact?

MRS. ELVSTED [*eagerly*] Comrades! Yes, fancy, Hedda—that is the very word he used! Oh, I ought to feel perfectly happy; and yet I cannot; for I don't know how long it will last.

640   HEDDA Are you no surer of him than that?

MRS. ELVSTED [*gloomily*] A woman's shadow stands between Eilert Lövborg and me.

HEDDA [*looks at her anxiously*] Who can that be?

MRS. ELVSTED I don't know. Some one he knew in his—in his past. Some one he has never been able wholly to forget.

HEDDA What has he told you—about this?

MRS. ELVSTED He has only once—quite vaguely—alluded to it.

HEDDA Well! And what did he say?

MRS. ELVSTED He said that when they parted, she threatened to shoot him

650 with a pistol.

HEDDA [*with cold composure*] Oh, nonsense! No one does that sort of thing here.

MRS. ELVSTED No. And that is why I think it must have been that red-haired singing woman whom he once . . .

HEDDA Yes, very likely.

MRS. ELVSTED For I remember they used to say of her that she carried loaded firearms.

HEDDA Oh—then of course it must have been she.

MRS. ELVSTED [*wringing her hands*] And now just fancy, Hedda—I hear

660 that this singing woman—that she is in town again! Oh, I don't know what to do . . .

HEDDA [*glancing towards the inner room*] Hush! Here comes Tesman. [*Rises and whispers*] Thea—all this must remain between you and me.

MRS. ELVSTED [*springing up*] Oh yes—yes! For heaven's sake . . . !

GEORGE TESMAN, *with a letter in his hand, comes from the right through the inner room.*

TESMAN There now—the epistle is finished.

HEDDA That's right. And now Mrs. Elvsted is just going. Wait a moment—I'll go with you to the garden gate.

TESMAN Do you think Berta could post the letter, Hedda dear?

HEDDA [*takes it*] I will tell her to.

[BERTA *enters from the hall.*]

670   BERTA   Judge Brack wishes to know if Mrs. Tesman will receive him.
      HEDDA   Yes, ask Judge Brack to come in. And look here—put this letter in
the post.
      BERTA [*taking the letter*]   Yes, Ma'am.

She opens the door for JUDGE BRACK *and goes out herself.* BRACK *is a man of forty-five;
thickset, but well built and elastic in his movements. His face is roundish with an
aristocratic profile. His hair is short, still almost black, and carefully dressed. His
eyes are lively and sparkling. His eyebrows thick. His mustaches are also thick, with
short-cut ends. He wears a well-cut walking suit, a little too youthful for his age. He
uses an eyeglass, which he now and then lets drop.*

      JUDGE BRACK [*with his hat in his hand, bowing*]   May one venture to call so
early in the day?
      HEDDA   Of course one may.
      TESMAN [*presses his hand*]   You are welcome at any time. [*introducing
him*] Judge Brack—Miss Rysing . . .
      HEDDA   Oh . . . !
680   BRACK [*bowing*]   Ah—delighted . . .
      HEDDA [*looks at him and laughs*]   It's nice to have a look at you by day-
light, Judge!
      BRACK   Do you find me—altered?
      HEDDA   A little younger, I think.
      BRACK   Thank you so much.
      TESMAN   But what do you think of Hedda—eh? Doesn't she look flourish-
ing? She has actually . . .
      HEDDA   Oh, do leave me alone. You haven't thanked Judge Brack for all the
trouble he has taken . . .
690   BRACK   Oh, nonsense—it was a pleasure to me . . .
      HEDDA   Yes, you are a friend indeed. But here stands Thea all impatience
to be off—so *au revoir*, Judge. I shall be back again presently.

Mutual salutations. MRS. ELVSTED *and* HEDDA *go out by the hall door.*

      BRACK   Well, is your wife tolerably satisfied . . .
      TESMAN   Yes, we can't thank you sufficiently. Of course she talks of a little
rearrangement here and there; and one or two things are still wanting. We
shall have to buy some additional trifles.
      BRACK   Indeed!
      TESMAN   But we won't trouble you about these things. Hedda says she
herself will look after what is wanting. Shan't we sit down? Eh?
700   BRACK   Thanks, for a moment. [*Seats himself beside the table*] There is
something I wanted to speak to you about, my dear Tesman.
      TESMAN   Indeed? Ah, I understand! [*Seating himself*] I suppose it's the
serious part of the frolic that is coming now. Eh?

BRACK Oh, the money question is not so very pressing; though, for that matter, I wish we had gone a little more economically to work.

TESMAN But that would never have done, you know! Think of Hedda, my dear fellow! You, who know her so well . . . I couldn't possibly ask her to put up with a shabby style of living!

BRACK No, no—that is just the difficulty.

710 TESMAN And then—fortunately—it can't be long before I receive my appointment.

BRACK Well, you see—such things are often apt to hang fire for a time.

TESMAN Have you heard anything definite? Eh?

BRACK Nothing exactly definite . . . [*Interrupting himself*] But by the by—I have one piece of news for you.

TESMAN Well?

BRACK Your old friend, Eilert Lövborg, has returned to town.

TESMAN I know that already.

BRACK Indeed! How did you learn it?

720 TESMAN From that lady who went out with Hedda.

BRACK Really? What was her name? I didn't quite catch it.

TESMAN Mrs. Elvsted.

BRACK Aha—Sheriff Elvsted's wife? Of course—he has been living up in their regions.

TESMAN And fancy—I'm delighted to hear that he is quite a reformed character!

BRACK So they say.

TESMAN And then he has published a new book—eh?

BRACK Yes, indeed he has.

730 TESMAN And I hear it has made some sensation!

BRACK Quite an unusual sensation.

TESMAN Fancy—isn't that good news! A man of such extraordinary talents . . . I felt so grieved to think that he had gone irretrievably to ruin.

BRACK That was what everybody thought.

TESMAN But I cannot imagine what he will take to now! How in the world will he be able to make his living? Eh?

During the last words, HEDDA *has entered by the hall door.*

HEDDA [*to* BRACK *laughing with a touch of scorn*] Tesman is for ever worrying about how people are to make their living.

TESMAN Well you see, dear—we were talking about poor Eilert Lövborg.

740 HEDDA [*glancing at him rapidly*] Oh, indeed? [*Seats herself in the armchair beside the stove and asks indifferently*] What is the matter with him?

TESMAN Well—no doubt he has run through all his property long ago; and he can scarcely write a new book every year—eh? So I really can't see what is to become of him.

BRACK Perhaps I can give you some information on that point.

TESMAN Indeed!

BRACK   You must remember that his relations have a good deal of influence.

TESMAN   Oh, his relations, unfortunately, have entirely washed their hands of him.

750   BRACK   At one time they called him the hope of the family.

TESMAN   At one time, yes! But he has put an end to all that.

HEDDA   Who knows? [*With a slight smile*] I hear they have reclaimed him up at Sheriff Elvsted's . . .

BRACK   And then this book that he has published . . .

TESMAN   Well, well, I hope to goodness they may find something for him to do. I have just written to him. I asked him to come and see us this evening, Hedda dear.

BRACK   But my dear fellow, you are booked for my bachelors' party this evening. You promised on the pier last night.

760   HEDDA   Had you forgotten, Tesman?

TESMAN   Yes, I had utterly forgotten.

BRACK   But it doesn't matter, for you may be sure he won't come.

TESMAN   What makes you think that? Eh?

BRACK [*with a little hesitation, rising and resting his hands on the back of his chair*]   My dear Tesman—and you, too, Mrs. Tesman—I think I ought not to keep you in the dark about something that—that . . .

TESMAN   That concerns Eilert . . . ?

BRACK   Both you and him.

TESMAN   Well, my dear Judge, out with it.

770   BRACK   You must be prepared to find your appointment deferred longer than you desired or expected.

TESMAN [*jumping up uneasily*]   Is there some hitch about it? Eh?

BRACK   The nomination may perhaps be made conditional on the result of a competition . . .

TESMAN   Competition! Think of that, Hedda!

HEDDA [*leans further back in the chair*]   Aha—aha!

TESMAN   But who can my competitor be? Surely not . . . ?

BRACK   Yes, precisely, Eilert Lövborg.

TESMAN [*clasping his hands*]   No, no—it's quite inconceivable! Quite im-
780   possible! Eh?

BRACK   H'm—that is what it may come to, all the same.

TESMAN   Well but, Judge Brack—it would show the most incredible lack of consideration for me. [*Gesticulates with his arms*] For—just think—I'm a married man! We have married on the strength of these prospects, Hedda and I; and run deep into debt; and borrowed money from Aunt Julia too. Good heavens, they had as good as promised me the appointment. Eh?

BRACK   Well, well, well—no doubt you will get it in the end; only after a contest.

HEDDA [*immovable in her armchair*]   Fancy, Tesman, there will be a sort
790   of sporting interest in that.

TESMAN   Why, my dearest Hedda, how can you be so indifferent about it?

HEDDA [*as before*]   I am not at all indifferent. I am most eager to see who wins.

BRACK   In any case, Mrs. Tesman, it is best that you should know how matters stand. I mean—before you set about the little purchases I hear you are threatening.

HEDDA   This can make no difference.

BRACK   Indeed! Then I have no more to say. Good-bye! [*To* TESMAN] I shall look in on my way back from my afternoon walk, and take you home with me.

800   TESMAN   Oh, yes, yes—your news has quite upset me.

HEDDA [*reclining, holds out her hand*]   Good-bye, Judge; and be sure you call in the afternoon.

BRACK   Many thanks. Good-bye, good-bye!

TESMAN [*accompanying him to the door*]   Good-bye, my dear Judge! You must really excuse me . . .

JUDGE BRACK *goes out by the hall door.*

TESMAN [*crosses the room*]   Oh Hedda—one should never rush into adventures. Eh?

HEDDA [*looks at him, smiling*]   Do you do that?

TESMAN   Yes, dear—there is no denying—it was adventurous to go and
810   marry and set up house upon mere expectations.

HEDDA   Perhaps you are right there.

TESMAN   Well—at all events, we have our delightful home, Hedda! Fancy, the home we both dreamed of—the home we were in love with, I may almost say. Eh?

HEDDA [*rising slowly and wearily*]   It was part of our compact that we were to go into society—to keep open house.

TESMAN   Yes, if you only knew how I had been looking forward to it! Fancy—to see you as hostess—in a select circle! Eh? Well, well, well—for the present we shall have to get on without society, Hedda—only to invite Aunt
820   Julia now and then. Oh, I intended you to lead such an utterly different life, dear . . . !

HEDDA   Of course I cannot have my man in livery just yet.

TESMAN   Oh no, unfortunately. It would be out of the question for us to keep a footman, you know.

HEDDA   And the saddle horse I was to have had . . .

TESMAN [*aghast*]   The saddle horse!

HEDDA   . . . I suppose I must not think of that now.

TESMAN   Good heavens, no!—that's as clear as daylight.

HEDDA [*goes up the room*]   Well, I shall have one thing at least to kill time
830   with in the meanwhile.

TESMAN [*beaming*]   Oh thank heaven for that! What is it, Hedda? Eh?

HEDDA [*in the middle doorway, looks at him with covert scorn*]   My pistols, George.

TESMAN [*in alarm*]   Your pistols!

HEDDA [*with cold eyes*]   General Gabler's pistols. [*She goes out through the inner room, to the left.*]

TESMAN [*rushes up to the middle doorway and calls after her*]   No, for heaven's sake, Hedda darling—don't touch those dangerous things! For my sake, Hedda! Eh?

Act II

Scene.   *The room at the* TESMANS' *as in the first act, except that the piano has been removed, and an elegant little writing table with bookshelves put in its place. A smaller table stands near the sofa on the left. Most of the bouquets have been taken away.* MRS. ELVSTED*'s bouquet is upon the large table in front. It is afternoon.* HEDDA, *dressed to receive callers, is alone in the room. She stands by the open glass door, loading a revolver. The fellow to it lies in an open pistol case on the writing table.*

HEDDA [*looks down the garden, and calls*]   So you are here again, Judge!
BRACK [*is heard calling from a distance*]   As you see, Mrs. Tesman!
HEDDA [*raises the pistol and points*]   Now I'll shoot you, Judge Brack!
BRACK [*calling unseen*]   No, no, no! Don't stand aiming at me!
HEDDA   This is what comes of sneaking in by the back way. [*She fires.*]
BRACK [*nearer*]   Are you out of your senses! . . .
HEDDA   Dear me—did I happen to hit you?
BRACK [*still outside*]   I wish you would let these pranks alone!
HEDDA   Come in then, Judge.

JUDGE BRACK, *dressed as though for a men's party, enters by the glass door. He carries a light overcoat over his arm.*

10   BRACK   What the deuce—haven't you tired of that sport, yet? What are you shooting at?
HEDDA   Oh, I am only firing in the air.
BRACK [*gently takes the pistol out of her hand*]   Allow me, Madam! [*Looks at it*] Ah—I know this pistol well! [*Looks around*] Where is the case? Ah, here it is. [*Lays the pistol in it, and shuts it*] Now we won't play at that game any more today.
HEDDA   Then what in heaven's name would you have me do with myself?
BRACK   Have you had no visitors?
HEDDA [*closing the glass door*]   Not one. I suppose all our set are still out 20 of town.
BRACK   And is Tesman not at home either?
HEDDA [*at the writing table, putting the pistol case in a drawer which she shuts*]   No. He rushed off to his aunt's directly after lunch; he didn't expect you so early.
BRACK   H'm—how stupid of me not to have thought of that!
HEDDA [*turning her head to look at him*]   Why stupid?
BRACK   Because if I had thought of it I should have come a little—earlier.
HEDDA [*crossing the room*]   Then you would have found no one to receive you; for I have been in my room changing my dress ever since lunch.

30   BRACK And is there no sort of little chink that we could hold a parley through?

HEDDA You have forgotten to arrange one.

BRACK That was another piece of stupidity.

HEDDA Well, we must just settle down here—and wait. Tesman is not likely to be back for some time yet.

BRACK Never mind; I shall not be impatient.

HEDDA *seats herself in the corner of the sofa.* BRACK *lays his overcoat over the back of the nearest chair, and sits down, but keeps his hat on his hand. A short silence. They look at each other.*

HEDDA Well?

BRACK [*in the same tone*] Well?

HEDDA I spoke first.

40   BRACK [*bending a little forward*] Come, let us have a cozy little chat, Mrs. Hedda.

HEDDA [*leaning further back in the sofa*] Does it not seem like a whole eternity since our last talk? Of course I don't count those few words yesterday evening and this morning.

BRACK You mean since our last confidential talk? Our last *tête-à-tête*?

HEDDA Well, yes—since you put it so.

BRACK Not a day has passed but I have wished that you were home again.

HEDDA And I have done nothing but wish the same thing.

BRACK You? Really, Mrs. Hedda? And I thought you had been enjoying
50 your tour so much!

HEDDA Oh, yes, you may be sure of that!

BRACK But Tesman's letters spoke of nothing but happiness.

HEDDA Oh, Tesman! You see, he thinks nothing so delightful as grubbing in libraries and making copies of old parchments, or whatever you call them.

BRACK [*with a spice of malice*] Well, that is his vocation in life—or part of it at any rate.

HEDDA Yes, of course, and no doubt when it's your vocation . . . But *I*! Oh, my dear Mr. Brack, how mortally bored I have been.

BRACK [*sympathetically*] Do you really say so? In downright earnest?

60   HEDDA Yes, you can surely understand it . . . ! To go for six whole months without meeting a soul that knew anything of our circle, or could talk about the things we are interested in.

BRACK Yes, yes—I, too, should feel that a deprivation.

HEDDA And then, what I found most intolerable of all . . .

BRACK Well?

HEDDA . . . was being everlastingly in the company of—one and the same person . . .

BRACK [*with a nod of assent*] Morning, noon, and night, yes—at all possible times and seasons.

70   HEDDA I said "everlastingly."

BRACK   Just so. But I should have thought, with our excellent Tesman, one could . . .

HEDDA   Tesman is—a specialist, my dear Judge.

BRACK   Undeniably.

HEDDA   And specialists are not at all amusing to travel with. Not in the long run at any rate.

BRACK   Not even—the specialist one happens to love?

HEDDA   Faugh—don't use that sickening word!

BRACK [*taken aback*]   What do you say, Mrs. Hedda?

80   HEDDA [*half laughingly, half irritated*]   You should just try it! To hear of nothing but the history of civilization morning, noon, and night . . .

BRACK   Everlastingly.

HEDDA   Yes, yes, yes! And then all this about the domestic industry of the Middle Ages . . . ! That's the most disgusting part of it!

BRACK [*looks searchingly at her*]   But tell me—in that case, how am I to understand your . . . ? H'm . . .

HEDDA   My accepting George Tesman, you mean?

BRACK   Well, let us put it so.

HEDDA   Good heavens, do you see anything so wonderful in that?

90   BRACK   Yes and no—Mrs. Hedda.

HEDDA   I had positively danced myself tired, my dear Judge. My day was done . . . [*With a slight shudder*] Oh, no—I won't say that; nor think it, either!

BRACK   You have assuredly no reason to.

HEDDA   Oh, reasons . . . [*Watching him closely*] And George Tesman— after all, you must admit that he is correctness itself.

BRACK   His correctness and respectability are beyond all question.

HEDDA   And I don't see anything absolutely ridiculous about him. Do you?

BRACK   Ridiculous? N—no—I shouldn't exactly say so . . .

100   HEDDA   Well—and his powers of research, at all events, are untiring. I see no reason why he should not one day come to the front, after all.

BRACK [*looks at her hesitatingly*]   I thought that you, like every one else, expected him to attain the highest distinction.

HEDDA [*with an expression of fatigue*]   Yes, so I did—And then, since he was bent, at all hazards, on being allowed to provide for me—I really don't know why I should not have accepted his offer.

BRACK   No—if you look at it in that light . . .

HEDDA   It was more than any other adorers were prepared to do for me, my dear Judge.

110   BRACK [*laughing*]   Well, I can't answer for all the rest; but as for myself, you know quite well that I have always entertained a—a certain respect for the marriage tie—for marriage as an institution, Mrs. Hedda.

HEDDA [*jestingly*]   Oh, I assure you I have never cherished any hopes with respect to you.

BRACK   All I require is a pleasant and intimate interior, where I can make myself useful in every way, and am free to come and go as—as a trusted friend . . .

HEDDA   Of the master of the house, do you mean?

BRACK [*bowing*]   Frankly—of the mistress first of all; but, of course, of the
120 master, too, in the second place. Such a triangular friendship—if I may call it
so—is really a great convenience for all parties, let me tell you.

HEDDA   Yes, I have many a time longed for some one to make a third on our
travels. Oh—those railway-carriage *tête-à-têtes* . . . !

BRACK   Fortunately your wedding journey is over now.

HEDDA [*shaking her head*]   Not by a long—long way. I have only arrived at
a station on the line.

BRACK   Well, then the passengers jump out and move about a little, Mrs.
Hedda.

HEDDA   I never jump out.

130 BRACK   Really?

HEDDA   No—because there is always some one standing by to . . .

BRACK [*laughing*]   To look at your legs, do you mean?

HEDDA   Precisely.

BRACK   Well, but, dear me . . .

HEDDA [*with a gesture of repulsion*]   I won't have it. I would rather keep
my seat where I happen to be—and continue the *tête-à-tête*.

BRACK   But suppose a third person were to jump in and join the couple.

HEDDA   Ah—that is quite another matter!

BRACK   A trusted, sympathetic friend . . .

140 HEDDA   . . . with a fund of conversation of all sorts of lively topics . . .

BRACK   . . . and not the least bit of a specialist!

HEDDA [*with an audible sigh*]   Yes, that would be a relief, indeed.

BRACK [*hears the front door open, and glances in that direction*]   The
triangle is completed.

HEDDA [*half aloud*]   And on goes the train.

GEORGE TESMAN, *in a gray walking suit, with a soft felt hat, enters from the hall. He has
a number of unbound books under his arm and in his pockets.*

TESMAN [*goes up to the table beside the corner settee*]   Ouf—what a load
for a warm day—all these books. [*Lays them on the table*] I'm positively
perspiring, Hedda. Hallo—are you there already, my dear Judge? Eh? Berta
didn't tell me.

150 BRACK [*rising*]   I came in through the garden.

HEDDA   What books have you got there?

TESMAN [*stands looking them through*]   Some new books on my special
subjects—quite indispensable to me.

HEDDA   Your special subjects?

BRACK   Yes, books on his special subjects, Mrs. Tesman.

BRACK *and* HEDDA *exchange a confidential smile.*

HEDDA   Do you need still more books on your special subjects?

TESMAN   Yes, my dear Hedda, one can never have too many of them. Of
course, one must keep up with all that is written and published.

HEDDA   Yes, I suppose one must.

160   TESMAN [*searching among his books*]   And look here—I have got hold of Eilert Lövborg's new book, too. [*Offering it to her*] Perhaps you would like to glance through it—Hedda? Eh?

HEDDA   No, thank you. Or rather—afterwards perhaps.

TESMAN   I looked into it a little on the way home.

BRACK   Well, what do you think of it—as a specialist?

TESMAN   I think it shows quite remarkable soundness of judgment. He never wrote like that before. [*Putting the books together*] Now I shall take all these into my study. I'm longing to cut the leaves . . . ! And then I must change my clothes. [*To* BRACK] I suppose we needn't start just yet? Eh?

170   BRACK   Oh, dear, no—there is not the slightest hurry.

TESMAN   Well, then, I will take my time. [*Is going with his books, but stops in the doorway and turns*] By the by, Hedda—Aunt Julia is not coming this evening.

HEDDA   Not coming? Is it that affair of the bonnet that keeps her away?

TESMAN   Oh, not at all. How could you think such a thing of Aunt Julia? Just fancy . . . ! The fact is, Aunt Rina is very ill.

HEDDA   She always is.

TESMAN   Yes, but today she is much worse than usual, poor dear.

HEDDA   Oh, then it's only natural that her sister should remain with her. I
180   must bear my disappointment.

TESMAN   And you can't imagine, dear, how delighted Aunt Julia seemed to be—because you had come home looking so flourishing!

HEDDA [*half aloud, rising*]   Oh, those everlasting aunts!

TESMAN   What?

HEDDA [*going to the glass door*]   Nothing.

TESMAN   Oh, all right. [*He goes through the inner room, out to the right.*]

BRACK   What bonnet were you talking about?

HEDDA   Oh, it was a little episode with Miss Tesman this morning. She had laid down her bonnet on the chair there—[*looks at him and smiles*]—and I
190   pretended to think it was the servant's.

BRACK [*shaking his head*]   Now, my dear Mrs. Hedda, how could you do such a thing? To that excellent old lady, too!

HEDDA [*nervously crossing the room*]   Well, you see—these impulses come over me all of a sudden; and I cannot resist them. [*Throws herself down in the easy-chair by the stove*] Oh, I don't know how to explain it.

BRACK [*behind the easy-chair*]   You are not really happy—that is at the bottom of it.

HEDDA [*Looking straight before her*]   I know of no reason why I should be—happy. Perhaps you can give me one?

200   BRACK   Well—amongst other things, because you have got exactly the home you had set your heart on.

HEDDA [*looks up at him and laughs*]   Do you, too, believe in that legend?

BRACK   Is there nothing in it, then?

HEDDA   Oh, yes, there is something in it.

BRACK   Well?

HEDDA   There is this in it, that I made use of Tesman to see me home from
evening parties last summer . . .

BRACK   I, unfortunately, had to go quite a different way.

HEDDA   That's true. I know you were going a different way last summer.

210   BRACK [*laughing*]   Oh fie, Mrs. Hedda! Well, then—you and Tesman . . . ?

HEDDA   Well, we happened to pass here one evening; Tesman, poor fellow, was writhing in the agony of having to find conversation; so I took pity
on the learned man . . .

BRACK [*smiles doubtfully*]   You took pity? H'm . . .

HEDDA   Yes, I really did. And so—to help him out of his torment—I happened to say, in pure thoughtlessness, that I should like to live in this villa.

BRACK   No more than that?

HEDDA   Not that evening.

BRACK   But afterwards?

220   HEDDA   Yes, my thoughtlessness had consequences, my dear Judge.

BRACK   Unfortunately that too often happens, Mrs. Hedda.

HEDDA   Thanks! So you see it was this enthusiasm for Secretary Falk's villa
that first constituted a bond of sympathy between George Tesman and me.
From that came our engagement and our marriage, and our wedding journey,
and all the rest of it. Well, well, my dear Judge—as you make your bed so you
must lie, I could almost say.

BRACK   This is exquisite! And you really cared not a rap about it all the
time?

HEDDA   No, heaven knows I didn't.

230   BRACK   But now? Now that we have made it so homelike for you?

HEDDA   Ugh—the rooms all seem to smell of lavender and dried rose-
leaves. But perhaps it's Aunt Julia that has brought that scent with her.

BRACK [*laughing*]   No, I think it must be a legacy from the late Mrs. Secretary Falk.

HEDDA   Yes, there is an odor of mortality about it. It reminds me of a
bouquet—the day after the ball. [*Clasps her hands behind her head, leans
back in her chair and looks at him*] Oh, my dear Judge—you cannot imagine
how horribly I shall bore myself here.

BRACK   Why should not you, too, find some sort of vocation in life, Mrs.
240 Hedda?

HEDDA   A vocation—what should attract me?

BRACK   If possible, of course.

HEDDA   Heaven knows what sort of a vocation that could be. I often wonder whether . . . [*Breaking off*] But that would never do, either.

BRACK   Who can tell? Let me hear what it is.

HEDDA   Whether I might not get Tesman to go into politics, I mean.

BRACK [*laughing*]   Tesman? No, really now, political life is not the thing
for him—not at all in his line.

HEDDA   No, I daresay not. But if I could get him into it all the same?

250   BRACK   Why—what satisfaction could you find in that? If he is not fitted for
that sort of thing, why should you want to drive him into it?

HEDDA   Because I am bored, I tell you! [*After a pause*] So you think it quite out of the question that Tesman should ever get into the ministry?

BRACK   H'm—you see, my dear Mrs. Hedda—to get into the ministry, he would have to be a tolerably rich man.

HEDDA [*rising impatiently*]   Yes, there we have it! It is this genteel poverty I have managed to drop into . . . ! [*Crosses the room*] That is what makes life so pitiable! So utterly ludicrous!—For that's what it is.

BRACK   Now I should say the fault lay elsewhere.

260   HEDDA   Where, then?

BRACK   You have never gone through any really stimulating experience.

HEDDA   Anything serious, you mean?

BRACK   Yes, you may call it so. But now you may perhaps have one in store.

HEDDA [*tossing her head*]   Oh, you're thinking of the annoyances about this wretched professorship! But that must be Tesman's own affair. I assure you I shall not waste a thought upon it.

BRACK   No, no, I daresay not. But suppose now that what people call—in elegant language—a solemn responsibility were to come upon you? [*Smiling*] A new responsibility, Mrs. Hedda?

270   HEDDA [*angrily*]   Be quiet! Nothing of that sort will ever happen!

BRACK [*warily*]   We will speak of this again a year hence—at the very outside.

HEDDA [*curtly*]   I have no turn for anything of the sort, Judge Brack. No responsibilities for me!

BRACK   Are you so unlike the generality of women as to have no turn for duties which . . . ?

HEDDA [*beside the glass door*]   Oh, be quiet, I tell you! I often think there is only one thing in the world I have any turn for.

BRACK [*drawing near to her*]   And what is that, if I may ask?

280   HEDDA [*stands looking out*]   Boring myself to death. Now you know it. [*Turns, looks towards the inner room, and laughs*] Yes, as I thought! Here comes the Professor.

BRACK [*softly, in a tone of warning*]   Come, come, come, Mrs. Hedda!

GEORGE TESMAN, *dressed for the party, with his gloves and hat in his hand, enters from the right through the inner room.*

TESMAN   Hedda, has no message come from Eilert Lövborg? Eh?

HEDDA   No.

TESMAN   Then you'll see he'll be here presently.

BRACK   Do you really think he will come?

TESMAN   Yes, I am almost sure of it. For what you were telling us this morning must have been a mere floating rumor.

290   BRACK   You think so?

TESMAN   At any rate, Aunt Julia said she did not believe for a moment that he would ever stand in my way again. Fancy that!

BRACK   Well, then, that's all right.

TESMAN [*placing his hat and gloves on a chair on the right*]   Yes, but you must really let me wait for him as long as possible.

BRACK   We have plenty of time yet. None of my guests will arrive before seven or half-past.

TESMAN   Then meanwhile we can keep Hedda company, and see what happens. Eh?

300   HEDDA [*placing* BRACK*'s hat and overcoat upon the corner settee*]   And at the worst Mr. Lövborg can remain here with me.

BRACK [*offering to take his things*]   Oh, allow me, Mrs. Tesman! What do you mean by "at the worst"?

HEDDA   If he won't go with you and Tesman.

TESMAN [*looks dubiously at her*]   But, Hedda, dear—do you think it would quite do for him to remain with you? Eh? Remember, Aunt Julia can't come.

HEDDA   No, but Mrs. Elvsted is coming. We three can have a cup of tea together.

TESMAN   Oh, yes, that will be all right.

310   BRACK [*smiling*]   And that would perhaps be the safest plan for him.

HEDDA   Why so?

BRACK   Well, you know, Mrs. Tesman, how you used to jeer at my little bachelor parties. You declared they were adapted only for men of the strictest principles.

HEDDA   But no doubt Mr. Lövborg's priniciples are strict enough now. A converted sinner . . .

BERTA *appears at the hall door.*

BERTA   There's a gentleman asking if you are at home, ma'am . . .

HEDDA   Well, show him in.

TESMAN [*softly*]   I'm sure it is he! Fancy that!

EILERT LÖVBORG *enters the hall. He is slim and lean; of the same age as* TESMAN, *but looks older and somewhat worn-out. His hair and beard are of a blackish brown, his face long and pale, but with patches of color on the cheekbones. He is dressed in a well-cut black visiting suit, quite new. He has dark gloves and a silk hat. He stops near the door, and makes a rapid bow, seeming somewhat embarrassed.*

320   TESMAN [*goes up to him and shakes him warmly by the hand*]   Well, my dear Eilert—so at last we meet again!

EILERT LÖVBORG [*speaks in a subdued voice*]   Thanks for your letter, Tesman. [*Approaching* HEDDA] Will you, too, shake hands with me, Mrs. Tesman?

HEDDA [*taking his hand*]   I am glad to see you, Mr. Lövborg. [*With a motion of her hand*] I don't know whether you two gentlemen . . . ?

LÖVBORG [*bowing slightly*]   Judge Brack, I think.

BRACK [*doing likewise*]   Oh, yes—in the old days . . .

TESMAN [*to* LÖVBORG, *with his hands on his shoulders*]   And now you must make yourself entirely at home, Eilert! Mustn't he, Hedda—For I hear you

330 are going to settle in town again? Eh?

LÖVBORG   Yes, I am.

TESMAN   Quite right, quite right. Let me tell you, I have got hold of your new book; but I haven't had time to read it yet.

LÖVBORG You may spare yourself the trouble.

TESMAN Why so?

LÖVBORG Because there is very little in it.

TESMAN Just fancy—how can you say so?

BRACK But it has been very much praised, I hear.

LÖVBORG That was what I wanted; so I put nothing into the book but what
340 every one would agree with.

BRACK Very wise of you.

TESMAN Well, but, my dear Eilert . . . !

LÖVBORG For now I mean to win myself a position again—to make a fresh
start.

TESMAN [*a little embarrassed*] Ah, that is what you wish to do? Eh?

LÖVBORG [*smiling, lays down his hat, and draws a packet, wrapped in
paper, from his coat pocket*] But when this one appears, George Tesman,
you will have to read it. For this is the real book—the book I have put my true
self into.

350 TESMAN Indeed? And what is it?

LÖVBORG It is the continuation.

TESMAN The continuation? Of what?

LÖVBORG Of the book.

TESMAN Of the new book?

LÖVBORG Of course.

TESMAN Why, my dear Eilert—does it not come down to our own days?

LÖVBORG Yes, it does; and this one deals with the future.

TESMAN With the future! But, good heavens, we know nothing of the future!

LÖVBORG No; but there is a thing or two to be said about it all the same.
360 [*Opens the packet*] Look here . . .

TESMAN Why, that's not your handwriting.

LÖVBORG I dictated it. [*Turning over the pages*] It falls into two sections.
The first deals with the civilizing forces of the future. And here is the second—[*running through the pages towards the end*]—forecasting the probable line of development.

TESMAN How odd now! I should never have thought of writing anything of
that sort.

HEDDA [*at the glass door, drumming on the pane*] H'm . . . I daresay not.

LÖVBORG [*replacing the manuscript in its paper and laying the packet on
370 the table*] I brought it, thinking I might read you a little of it this evening.

TESMAN That was very good of you, Eilert. But this evening . . . ? [*Looking at* BRACK] I don't quite see how we can manage it . . .

LÖVBORG Well, then, some other time. There is no hurry.

BRACK I must tell you, Mr. Lövborg—there is a little gathering at my house
this evening—mainly in honor of Tesman, you know . . .

LÖVBORG [*looking for his hat*] Oh—then I won't detain you . . .

BRACK No, but listen—will you not do me the favor of joining us?

LÖVBORG [*curtly and decidedly*] No, I can't—thank you very much.

BRACK Oh, nonsense—do! We shall be quite a select little circle. And I
380 assure you we shall have a "lively time," as Mrs. Hed—as Mrs. Tesman says.

LÖVBORG   I have no doubt of it. But nevertheless . . .

BRACK   And then you might bring your manuscript with you, and read it to Tesman at my house. I could give you a room to yourselves.

TESMAN   Yes, think of that, Eilert—why shouldn't you? Eh?

HEDDA [*interposing*]   But, Tesman, if Mr. Lövborg would really rather not! I am sure Mr. Lövborg is much more inclined to remain here and have supper with me.

LÖVBORG [*looking at her*]   With you, Mrs. Tesman?

HEDDA   And with Mrs. Elvsted.

390   LÖVBORG   Ah . . . [*lightly*] I saw her for a moment this morning.

HEDDA   Did you? Well, she is coming this evening. So you see you are almost bound to remain, Mr. Lövborg, or she will have no one to see her home.

LÖVBORG   That's true. Many thanks, Mrs. Tesman—in that case I will remain.

HEDDA   Then I have one or two orders to give the servant . . .

She goes to the hall door and rings. BERTA *enters.* HEDDA *talks to her in a whisper, and points towards the inner room.* BERTA *nods and goes out again.*

TESMAN [*at the same time, to* LÖVBORG]   Tell me, Eilert—is it this new subject—the future—that you are going to lecture about?

LÖVBORG   Yes.

TESMAN   They told me at the bookseller's that you are going to deliver a course of lectures this autumn.

400   LÖVBORG   That is my intention. I hope you won't take it ill, Tesman.

TESMAN   Oh no, not in the least! But . . . ?

LÖVBORG   I can quite understand that it must be disagreeable to you.

TESMAN [*cast down*]   Oh, I can't expect you, out of consideration for me, to . . .

LÖVBORG   But I shall wait till you have received your appointment.

TESMAN   Will you wait? Yes, but—yes, but—are you not going to compete with me? Eh?

LÖVBORG   No; it is only the moral victory I care for.

TESMAN   Why, bless me—then Aunt Julia was right after all! Oh, yes—I 410 knew it! Hedda! Just fancy—Eilert Lövborg is not going to stand in our way!

HEDDA [*curtly*]   Our way? Pray leave me out of the question.

She goes up towards the inner room, where BERTA *is placing a tray with decanters and glasses on the table.* HEDDA *nods approval, and comes forward again.* BERTA *goes out.*

TESMAN [*at the same time*]   And you, Judge Brack—what do you say to this? Eh?

BRACK   Well, I say that a moral victory—h'm—may be all very fine . . .

TESMAN   Yes, certainly. But all the same . . .

HEDDA [*looking at* TESMAN *with a cold smile*]   You stand there looking as if you were thunderstruck . . .

TESMAN   Yes—so I am—I almost think . . .

BRACK   Don't you see, Mrs. Tesman, a thunderstorm has just passed over?

420   HEDDA [*pointing towards the inner room*]   Will you not take a glass of cold punch, gentlemen?

BRACK [*looking at his watch*]   A stirrup cup? Yes, it wouldn't come amiss.

TESMAN   A capital idea, Hedda! Just the thing! Now that the weight has been taken off my mind . . .

HEDDA   Will you not join them, Mr. Lövborg?

LÖVBORG [*with a gesture of refusal*]   No, thank you. Nothing for me.

BRACK   Why bless me—cold punch is surely not poison.

LÖVBORG   Perhaps not for every one.

HEDDA   I will keep Mr. Lövborg company in the meantime.

430   TESMAN   Yes, yes, Hedda dear, do.

He and BRACK *go into the inner room, seat themselves, drink punch, smoke cigarettes, and carry on a lively conversation during what follows,* EILERT LÖVBORG *remains standing beside the stove.* HEDDA *goes to the writing table.*

HEDDA [*raising her voice a little*]   Do you care to look at some photographs, Mr. Lövborg? You know Tesman and I made a tour in the Tyrol on our way home?

She takes up an album, and places it on the table beside the sofa, in the further corner of which she seats herself. EILERT LÖVBORG *approaches, stops, and looks at her. Then he takes a chair and seats himself to her left, with his back towards the inner room.*

HEDDA [*opening the album*]   Do you see this range of mountains, Mr. Lövborg? It's the Ortler group. Tesman has written the name underneath. Here it is: "The Ortler group near Meram."

LÖVBORG [*who has never taken his eyes off her, says softly and slowly*] Hedda—Gabler!

HEDDA [*glancing hastily at him*]   Ah! Hush!

440   LÖVBORG [*repeats softly*]   Hedda Gabler!

HEDDA [*looking at the album*]   That was my name in the old days—when we two knew each other.

LÖVBORG   And I must teach myself never to say Hedda Gabler again—never, as long as I live.

HEDDA [*still turning over the pages*]   Yes, you must. And I think you ought to practice in time. The sooner the better, I should say.

LÖVBORG [*in a tone of indignation*]   Hedda Gabler married? And married to—George Tesman!

HEDDA   Yes—so the world goes.

450   LÖVBORG   Oh, Hedda, Hedda—how could you[3] throw yourself away!

HEDDA [*looks sharply at him*]   What? I can't allow this!

LÖVBORG   What do you mean?

TESMAN *comes into the room and goes toward the sofa.*

[3] *du*

HEDDA [*hears him coming and says in an indifferent tone*]   And this is a view from the Val d'Ampezzo, Mr. Lövborg. Just look at these peaks! [*Looks affectionately up at* TESMAN] What's the name of these curious peaks, dear?

TESMAN   Let me see. Oh, those are the Dolomites.

HEDDA   Yes, that's it! Those are the Dolomites, Mr. Lövborg.

TESMAN   Hedda, dear, I only wanted to ask whether I shouldn't bring you a little punch after all? For yourself, at any rate—eh?

460   HEDDA   Yes, do, please; and perhaps a few biscuits.

TESMAN   No cigarettes?

HEDDA   No.

TESMAN   Very well.

He goes into the inner room and out to the right. BRACK *sits in the inner room, and keeps an eye from time to time on* HEDDA *and* LÖVBORG.

LÖVBORG [*softly, as before*]   Answer me, Hedda—how could you go and do this?

HEDDA [*apparently absorbed in the album*]   If you continue to say *du* to me I won't talk to you.

LÖVBORG   May I not say *du* even when we are alone?

HEDDA   No. You may think it; but you mustn't say it.

470   LÖVBORG   Ah, I understand. It is an offense against George Tesman, whom you[4] love.

HEDDA [*glances at him and smiles*]   Love? What an idea!

LÖVBORG   You don't love him then!

HEDDA   But I won't hear of any sort of unfaithfulness! Remember that.

LÖVBORG   Hedda—answer me one thing . . .

HEDDA   Hush!

TESMAN *enters with a small tray from the inner room.*

TESMAN   Here you are! Isn't this tempting?

He puts the tray on the table.

HEDDA   Why do you bring it yourself?

TESMAN [*filling the glasses*]   Because I think it's such fun to wait upon you,
480   Hedda.

HEDDA   But you have poured out two glasses. Mr. Lövborg said he wouldn't have any . . .

TESMAN   No, but Mrs. Elvsted will soon be here, won't she?

HEDDA   Yes, by the by—Mrs. Elvsted . . .

TESMAN   Had you forgotten her? Eh?

HEDDA   We were so absorbed in these photographs. [*Shows him a picture*] Do you remember this little village?

---

[4] *du*

TESMAN   Oh, it's that one just below the Brenner Pass. It was there we passed the night . . .

490   HEDDA   . . . and met that lively party of tourists.

TESMAN   Yes, that was the place. Fancy—if we could only have had you with us, Eilert! Eh?

He returns to the inner room and sits beside BRACK.

LÖVBORG   Answer me this one thing, Hedda . . .

HEDDA   Well?

LÖVBORG   Was there no love in your friendship for me, either? Not a spark—not a tinge of love in it?

HEDDA   I wonder if there was? To me it seems as though we were two good comrades—two thoroughly intimate friends. [*Smilingly*] You especially were frankness itself.

500   LÖVBORG   It was you that made me so.

HEDDA   As I look back upon it all, I think there was really something beautiful, something fascinating—something daring—in—in that secret intimacy—that comradeship which no living creature so much as dreamed of.

LÖVBORG   Yes, yes, Hedda! Was there not?—When I used to come to your father's in the afternoon—and the General sat over at the window reading his papers—with his back towards us . . .

HEDDA   And we two on the corner sofa . . .

LÖVBORG   Always with the same illustrated paper before us . . .

HEDDA   For want of an album, yes.

510   LÖVBORG   Yes, Hedda, and when I made my confessions to you—told you about myself, things that at that time no one else knew! There I would sit and tell you of my escapades—my days and nights of devilment. Oh, Hedda—what was the power in you that forced me to confess these things?

HEDDA   Do you think it was any power in me?

LÖVBORG   How else can I explain it? And all those—those roundabout questions you used to put to me . . .

HEDDA   Which you understood so particularly well . . .

LÖVBORG   How could you sit and question me like that? Question me quite frankly . . .

520   HEDDA   In roundabout terms, please observe.

LÖVBORG   Yes, but frankly nevertheless. Cross-question me about—all that sort of thing?

HEDDA   And how could you answer, Mr. Lövborg?

LÖVBORG   Yes, that is just what I can't understand—in looking back upon it. But tell me now, Hedda—was there not love at the bottom of our friendship? On your side, did you not feel as though you might purge my stains away—if I made you my confessor? Was it not so?

HEDDA   No, not quite.

LÖVBORG   What was your motive, then?

530   HEDDA   Do you think it quite incomprehensible that a young girl—when it can be done—without any one knowing . . .

LÖVBORG Well?

HEDDA . . . should be glad to have a peep, now and then, into a world which . . .

LÖVBORG Which . . . ?

HEDDA . . . which she is forbidden to know anything about?

LÖVBORG So that was it?

HEDDA Partly. Partly—I almost think.

LÖVBORG Comradeship in the thirst for life. But why should not that, at any
540 rate, have continued?

HEDDA The fault was yours.

LÖVBORG It was you that broke with me.

HEDDA Yes, when our friendship threatened to develop into something
more serious. Shame upon you, Eilert Lövborg! How could you think of
wronging your—your frank comrade?

LÖVBORG [*clenching his hands*] Oh, why did you not carry out your threat?
Why did you not shoot me down?

HEDDA Because I have such a dread of scandal.

LÖVBORG Yes, Hedda, you are a coward at heart.

550 HEDDA A terrible coward. [*Changing her tone*] But it was a lucky thing for
you. And now you have found ample consolation at the Elvsteds'.

LÖVBORG I know what Thea has confided to you.

HEDDA And perhaps you have confided to her something about us?

LÖVBORG Not a word. She is too stupid to understand anything of that sort.

HEDDA Stupid?

LÖVBORG She is stupid about matters of that sort.

HEDDA And I am cowardly. [*Bends over towards him, without looking him
in the face, and says more softly*] But now I will confide something to you.

LÖVBORG [*eagerly*] Well?

560 HEDDA The fact that I dared not shoot you down . . .

LÖVBORG Yes!

HEDDA . . . that was not my most arrant cowardice—that evening.

LÖVBORG [*looks at her a moment, understands and whispers passionately*]
Oh, Hedda! Hedda Gabler! Now I begin to see a hidden reason beneath our
comradeship! You[5] and I . . . ! After all, then, it was your craving for life . . .

HEDDA [*softly, with a sharp glance*] Take care! Believe nothing of the sort!

Twilight has begun to fall. The hall door is opened from without by BERTA.

HEDDA [*closes the album with a bang and calls smilingly*] Ah, at last! My
darling Thea—come along!

MRS. ELVSTED *enters from the hall. She is in evening dress. The door is closed behind her.*

HEDDA [*on the sofa, stretches out her arms towards her*] My sweet Thea—
570 you can't think how I have been longing for you!

[5] Back to *du*: Hedda continues to say *de*.

MRS. ELVSTED, *in passing, exchanges slight salutations with the gentlemen in the inner room, then goes up to the table and gives* HEDDA *her hand,* EILERT LÖVBORG *has risen. He and* MRS. ELVSTED *greet each other with a silent nod.*

MRS. ELVSTED   Ought I to go in and talk to your husband for a moment?

HEDDA   Oh, not at all. Leave those two alone. They will soon be going.

MRS. ELVSTED   Are they going out?

HEDDA   Yes, to a supper party.

MRS. ELVSTED [*quickly, to* LÖVBORG]   Not you?

LÖVBORG   No.

HEDDA   Mr. Lövborg remains with us.

MRS. ELVSTED [*takes a chair and is about to seat herself at his side*]   Oh, how nice it is here!

580   HEDDA   No, thank you, my little Thea! Not there! You'll be good enough to come over here to me. I will sit between you.

MRS. ELVSTED   Yes, just as you please.

She goes round the table and seats herself on the sofa on HEDDA'*s right.* LÖVBORG *reseats himself on his chair.*

LÖVBORG [*after a short pause, to* HEDDA]   Is not she lovely to look at?

HEDDA [*lightly stroking her hair*]   Only to look at?

LÖVBORG   Yes. For we two—she and I—we are two real comrades. We have absolute faith in each other; so we can sit and talk with perfect frankness . . .

HEDDA   Not roundabout, Mr. Lövborg?

LÖVBORG   Well . . .

MRS. ELVSTED [*softly clinging close to* HEDDA]   Oh, how happy I am, Hedda!

590   For, only think, he says I have inspired him, too.

HEDDA [*looks at her with a smile*]   Ah! Does he say that, dear?

LÖVBORG   And then she is so brave, Mrs. Tesman!

MRS. ELVSTED   Good heavens—am I brave?

LÖVBORG   Exceedingly—where your comrade is concerned.

HEDDA   Ah, yes—courage! If one only had that!

LÖVBORG   What then? What do you mean?

HEDDA   Then life would perhaps be livable, after all. [*With a sudden change of tone*] But now, my dearest Thea, you really must have a glass of cold punch.

600   MRS. ELVSTED   No, thanks—I never take anything of that kind.

HEDDA   Well, then, you, Mr. Lövborg.

LÖVBORG   Nor I, thank you.

MRS. ELVSTED   No, he doesn't, either.

HEDDA [*looks fixedly at him*]   But if I say you shall?

LÖVBORG   It would be no use.

HEDDA [*laughing*]   Then I, poor creature, have no sort of power over you?

LÖVBORG   Not in that respect.

HEDDA   But seriously, I think you ought to—for your own sake.

MRS. ELVSTED   Why, Hedda . . . !

610 LÖVBORG   How so?

HEDDA   Or rather on account of other people.

LÖVBORG   Indeed?

HEDDA   Otherwise people might be apt to suspect that—in your heart of hearts—you did not feel quite secure—quite confident in yourself.

MRS. ELVSTED [*softly*]   Oh, please, Hedda . . . !

LÖVBORG   People may suspect what they like—for the present.

MRS. ELVSTED [*joyfully*]   Yes, let them!

HEDDA   I saw it plainly in Judge Brack's face a moment ago.

LÖVBORG   What did you see?

620 HEDDA   His contemptuous smile, when you dared not go with them into the inner room.

LÖVBORG   Dared not? Of course I preferred to stop here and talk to you.

MRS. ELVSTED   What could be more natural, Hedda?

HEDDA   But the Judge could not guess that. And I saw, too, the way he smiled and glanced at Tesman when you dared not accept his invitation to this wretched little supper party of his.

LÖVBORG   Dared not? Do you say I dared not?

HEDDA   *I* don't say so. But that was how Judge Brack understood it.

LÖVBORG   Well, let him.

630 HEDDA   Then you are not going with them?

LÖVBORG   I will stay here with you and Thea.

MRS. ELVSTED   Yes, Hedda—how can you doubt that?

HEDDA [*smiles and nods approvingly to* LÖVBORG]   Firm as a rock! Faithful to your principles, now and forever! Ah, that is how a man should be! [*Turns to* MRS. ELVSTED *and caresses her*] Well, now, what did I tell you, when you came to us this morning in such a state of distraction . . .

LÖVBORG [*surprised*]   Distraction!

MRS. ELVSTED [*terrified*]   Hedda—oh, Hedda . . . !

HEDDA   You can see for yourself! You haven't the slightest reason to be in
640 such mortal terror . . . [*Interrupting herself*] There! Now we can all three enjoy ourselves!

LÖVBORG [*who has given a start*]   Ah—what is all this, Mrs. Tesman?

MRS. ELVSTED   Oh, my God, Hedda! What are you saying? What are you doing?

HEDDA   Don't get excited! That horrid Judge Brack is sitting watching you.

LÖVBORG   So she was in mortal terror! On my account!

MRS. ELVSTED [*softly and piteously*]   Oh, Hedda—now you have ruined everything!

LÖVBORG [*looks fixedly at her for a moment. His face is distorted.*]   So that
650 was my comrade's frank confidence in me?

MRS. ELVSTED [*imploringly*]   Oh, my dearest friend—only let me tell you . . .

EILERT LÖVBORG [*takes one of the glasses of punch, raises it to his lips, and says in a low, husky voice*]   Your health, Thea!

He empties the glass, puts it down, and takes the second.

MRS. ELVSTED [*softly*]   Oh, Hedda—how could you do this?

HEDDA   *I* do it? *I?* Are you crazy?

LÖVBORG   Here's to your health, too, Mrs. Tesman. Thanks for the truth. Hurrah for the truth!

He empties the glass and is about to refill it.

HEDDA [*lays her hand on his arm*]   Come, come—no more for the present. Remember you are going out to supper.

660   MRS. ELVSTED   No, no, no!

HEDDA   Hush! They are sitting watching you.

LÖVBORG [*putting down the glass*]   Now, Thea—tell me the truth . . .

MRS. ELVSTED   Yes.

LÖVBORG   Did your husband know that you had come after me?

MRS. ELVSTED [*wringing her hands*]   Oh, Hedda—do you hear what he is asking?

LÖVBORG   Was it arranged between you and him that you were to come to town and look after me? Perhaps it was the Sheriff himself that urged you to come? Aha, my dear—no doubt he wanted my help in his office. Or was it at

670   the card table that he missed me?

MRS. ELVSTED [*softly, in agony*]   Oh, Lövborg, Lövborg . . . !

LÖVBORG [*seizes a glass and is on the point of filling it*]   Here's a glass for the old Sheriff, too!

HEDDA [*preventing him*]   No more just now. Remember, you have to read your manuscript to Tesman.

LÖVBORG [*calmly, putting down the glass*]   It was stupid of me all this, Thea—to take it in this way, I mean. Don't be angry with me, my dear, dear comrade. You shall see—both you and the others—that if I was fallen once— now I have risen again! Thanks to you, Thea.

680   MRS. ELVSTED [*radiant with joy*]   Oh, heaven be praised . . . !

BRACK *has in the meantime looked at his watch. He and* TESMAN *rise and come into the drawing room.*

BRACK [*takes his hat and overcoat*]   Well, Mrs. Tesman, our time has come.

HEDDA   I suppose it has.

LÖVBORG [*rising*]   Mine too, Judge Brack.

MRS. ELVSTED [*softly and imploringly*]   Oh, Lövborg, don't do it!

HEDDA [*pinching her arm*]   They can hear you!

MRS. ELVSTED [*with a suppressed shriek*]   Ow!

LÖVBORG [*to* BRACK]   You were good enough to invite me.

BRACK   Well, are you coming after all?

LÖVBORG   Yes, many thanks.

690   BRACK   I'm delighted . . .

LÖVBORG [*to* TESMAN, *putting the parcel of MS. in his pocket*]   I should like to show you one or two things before I send it to the printers.

TESMAN   Fancy—that will be delightful. But, Hedda dear, how is Mrs. Elvsted to get home? Eh?

HEDDA   Oh, that can be managed somehow.

LÖVBORG [*looking towards the ladies*]   Mrs. Elvsted? Of course, I'll come again and fetch her. [*Approaching*] At ten or thereabouts, Mrs. Tesman? Will that do?

HEDDA   Certainly. That will do capitally.

700   TESMAN   Well, then, that's all right. But you must not expect me so early, Hedda.

HEDDA   Oh, you may stop as long—as long as ever you please.

MRS. ELVSTED [*trying to conceal her anxiety*]   Well, then, Mr. Lövborg—I shall remain here until you come.

LÖVBORG [*with his hat in his hand*]   Pray do, Mrs. Elvsted.

BRACK   And now off goes the excursion train, gentlemen! I hope we shall have a lively time, as a certain fair lady puts it.

HEDDA   Ah, if only the fair lady could be present unseen . . . !

BRACK   Why unseen?

710   HEDDA   In order to hear a little of your liveliness at first hand, Judge Brack.

BRACK [*laughing*]   I should not advise the fair lady to try it.

TESMAN [*also laughing*]   Come, you're a nice one, Hedda! Fancy that!

BRACK   Well, good-bye, good-bye, ladies.

LÖVBORG [*bowing*]   About ten o'clock, then.

BRACK, LÖVBORG, *and* TESMAN *go out by the hall door. At the same time.* BERTA *enters from the inner room with a lighted lamp, which she places on the drawing room table; she goes out by the way she came.*

MRS. ELVSTED [*who has risen and is wandering restlessly about the room*] Hedda—Hedda—what will come of all this?

HEDDA   At ten o'clock—he will be here. I can see him already—with vine leaves[6] in his hair—flushed and fearless . . .

MRS. ELVSTED   Oh, I hope he may.

720   HEDDA   And then, you see—then he will have regained control over himself. Then he will be a free man for all his days.

MRS. ELVSTED   Oh, God!—if he would only come as you see him now!

HEDDA   He will come as I see him—so, and not otherwise! [*Rises and approaches* THEA] You may doubt him as long as you please; *I* believe in him. And now we will try . . .

MRS. ELVSTED   You have some hidden motive in this, Hedda!

HEDDA   Yes, I have. I want for once in my life to have power to mold a human destiny.

MRS. ELVSTED   Have you not the power?

730   HEDDA   I have not—and have never had it.

MRS. ELVSTED   Not your husband's?

HEDDA   Do you think that is worth the trouble? Oh, if you could only understand how poor I am. And fate has made you so rich! [*Clasps her passionately in her arms*] I think I must burn your hair off, after all.

---

[6] In classical mythology the Roman god Bacchus—the Greek Dionysus—was pictured with a wreath of bay (vine) leaves in his hair.

MRS. ELVSTED   Let me go! Let me go! I am afraid of you, Hedda.

BERTA [*in the middle doorway*]   Tea is laid in the dining room, ma'am.

HEDDA   Very well. We are coming.

MRS. ELVSTED   No, no, no! I would rather go home alone! At once!

HEDDA   Nonsense? First you shall have a cup of tea, you little stupid. And
740   then—at ten o'clock—Eilert Lövborg will be here—with vine leaves in his
hair.

She drags MRS. ELVSTED *almost by force towards the middle doorway.*

Act III

Scene. *The room at the* TESMANS'. *The curtains are drawn over the middle doorway,
and also over the glass door. The lamp, half turned down, and with a shade over it, is
burning on the table. In the stove, the door of which stands open, there has been a
fire, which is now nearly burnt out.* MRS. ELVSTED, *wrapped in a large shawl, and with
her feet upon a foot-rest, sits close to the stove, sunk back in the armchair.* HEDDA, *fully
dressed, lies sleeping upon the sofa, with a sofa-blanket over her.*

MRS. ELVSTED [*after a pause, suddenly sits up in her chair, and listens eagerly. Then she sinks back again wearily, moaning to herself*]   Not yet!—Oh
God—oh God—not yet!

BERTA *slips in by the hall door. She has a letter in her hand.*

MRS. ELVSTED [*turns and whispers eagerly*]   Well—has anyone come?

BERTA [*softly*]   Yes, a girl has just brought this letter.

MRS. ELVSTED [*quickly, holding out her hand*]   A letter! Give it to me!

BERTA   No, it's for Dr. Tesman, ma'am.

MRS. ELVSTED   Oh, indeed.

BERTA   It was Miss Tesman's servant that brought it. I'll lay it here on the
10   table.

MRS. ELVSTED   Yes, do.

BERTA [*laying down the letter*]   I think I had better put out the lamp. It's
smoking.

MRS. ELVSTED   Yes, put it out. It must soon be daylight now.

BERTA [*putting out the lamp*]   It is daylight already, ma'am.

MRS. ELVSTED   Yes, broad day! And no one come back yet . . . !

BERTA   Lord bless you, ma'am—I guessed how it would be.

MRS. ELVSTED   You guessed?

BERTA   Yes, when I saw that a certain person had come back to town—and
20   that he went off with them. For we've heard enough about that gentleman
before now.

MRS. ELVSTED   Don't speak so loud. You will waken Mrs. Tesman.

BERTA [*looks towards the sofa and sighs*]   No, no—let her sleep, poor thing.
Shan't I put some wood on the fire?

MRS. ELVSTED   Thanks, not for me.

BERTA   Oh, very well.

She goes softly out by the hall door.

HEDDA [*is awakened by the shutting of the door, and looks up*]   What's that . . . ?

MRS. ELVSTED   It was only the servant . . .

30   HEDDA [*looking about her*]   Oh, we're here . . . ! Yes, now I remember. [*Sits erect upon the sofa, stretches herself, and rubs her eyes*] What o'clock is it, Thea?

MRS. ELVSTED [*looks at her watch*]   It's past seven.

HEDDA   When did Tesman come home?

MRS. ELVSTED   He has not come.

HEDDA   Not come home yet?

MRS. ELVSTED [*rising*]   No one has come.

HEDDA   Think of our watching and waiting here till four in the morning . . .

MRS. ELVSTED [*wringing her hands*]   And how I watched and waited for him!

40   HEDDA [*yawns, and says with her hand before her mouth*]   Well, well—we might have spared ourselves the trouble.

MRS. ELVSTED   Did you get a little sleep?

HEDDA   Oh, yes; I believe I have slept pretty well. Have you not?

MRS. ELVSTED   Not for a moment. I couldn't, Hedda!—not to save my life.

HEDDA [*rises and goes towards her*]   There, there, there! There's nothing to be so alarmed about. I understand quite well what has happened.

MRS. ELVSTED   Well, what do you think? Won't you tell me?

HEDDA   Why, of course, it has been a very late affair at Judge Brack's . . .

MRS. ELVSTED   Yes, yes—that is clear enough. But all the same . . .

50   HEDDA   And then, you see, Tesman hasn't cared to come home and ring us up in the middle of the night. [*Laughing*] Perhaps he wasn't inclined to show himself either—immediately after a jollification.

MRS. ELVSTED   But in that case—where can he have gone?

HEDDA   Of course, he has gone to his aunts' and slept there. They have his old room ready for him.

MRS. ELVSTED   No, he can't be with them; for a letter has just come for him from Miss Tesman. There it lies.

HEDDA   Indeed? [*Looks at the address*] Why, yes, it's addressed in Aunt Julia's own hand. Well, then, he has remained at Judge Brack's. And as for Eilert

60   Lövborg—he is sitting, with vine leaves in his hair, reading his manuscript.

MRS. ELVSTED   Oh, Hedda, you are just saying things you don't believe a bit.

HEDDA   You really are a little blockhead, Thea.

MRS. ELVSTED   Oh, yes, I suppose I am.

HEDDA   And how mortally tired you look.

MRS. ELVSTED   Yes, I am mortally tired.

HEDDA   Well, then, you must do as I tell you. You must go into my room and lie down for a little while.

MRS. ELVSTED   Oh, no, no—I shouldn't be able to sleep.

HEDDA   I am sure you would.

70   MRS. ELVSTED Well, but your husband is certain to come soon now; and then I want to know at once . . .

HEDDA   I shall take care to let you know when he comes.

MRS. ELVSTED Do you promise me, Hedda?

HEDDA   Yes, rely upon me. Just you go in and have a sleep in the meantime.

MRS. ELVSTED Thanks; then I'll try to.

She goes off through the inner room. HEDDA *goes up to the glass door and draws back the curtains. The broad daylight streams into the room. Then she takes a little hand glass from the writing table, looks at herself in it and arranges her hair. Next she goes to the hall door and presses the bell button.* BERTA *presently appears at the hall door.*

BERTA   Did you want anything, ma'am?

HEDDA   Yes; you must put some more wood in the stove. I am shivering.

BERTA   Bless me—I'll make up the fire at once. [*She rakes the embers together and lays a piece of wood upon them; then stops and listens*] That was
80 a ring at the front door, ma'am.

HEDDA   Then go to the door. I will look after the fire.

BERTA   It'll soon burn up.

She goes out by the hall door. HEDDA *kneels on the footrest and lays some more pieces of wood in the stove. After a short pause,* GEORGE TESMAN *enters from the hall. He looks tired and rather serious. He steals on tiptoe towards the middle doorway and is about to slip through the curtains.*

HEDDA [*at the stove, without looking up*]   Good morning.

TESMAN [*turns*] Hedda! [*Approaching her*] Good heavens—are you up so early? Eh?

HEDDA   Yes, I am up very early this morning.

TESMAN   And I never doubted you were still sound asleep! Fancy that, Hedda!

HEDDA   Don't speak so loud. Mrs. Elvsted is resting in my room.
90   TESMAN   Has Mrs. Elvsted been here all night?

HEDDA   Yes, since no one came to fetch her.

TESMAN   Ah, to be sure.

HEDDA [*closes the door of the stove and rises*] Well, did you enjoy yourselves at Judge Brack's?

TESMAN   Have you been anxious about me? Eh?

HEDDA   No. I should never think of being anxious. But I asked if you had enjoyed yourself.

TESMAN   Oh, yes—for once in a way. Especially the beginning of the evening; for then Eilert read me part of his book. We arrived more than an hour
100 too early—fancy that! And Brack had all sorts of arrangements to make—so Eilert read to me.

HEDDA [*seating herself by the table on the right*] Well? Tell me, then . . .

TESMAN [*sitting on a footstool near the stove*] Oh, Hedda, you can't conceive what a book that is going to be! I believe it is one of the most remarkable things that have ever been written. Fancy that!

HEDDA   Yes, yes; I don't care about that . . .

TESMAN   I must make a confession to you, Hedda. When he had finished reading—a horrid feeling came over me.

HEDDA   A horrid feeling?

110   TESMAN   I felt jealous of Eilert for having had it in him to write such a book. Only think, Hedda!

HEDDA   Yes, yes, I am thinking!

TESMAN   And then how pitiful to think that he—with all his gifts—should be irreclaimable, after all.

HEDDA   I suppose you mean that he has more courage than the rest?

TESMAN   No, not at all—I mean that he is incapable of taking his pleasures in moderation.

HEDDA   And what came of it all—in the end?

TESMAN   Well, to tell the truth, I think it might best be described as an
120   orgy, Hedda.

HEDDA   Had he vine leaves in his hair?

TESMAN   Vine leaves? No, I saw nothing of the sort. But he made a long, rambling speech in honor of the woman who had inspired him in his work— that was the phrase he used.

HEDDA   Did he name her?

TESMAN   No, he didn't; but I can't help thinking he meant Mrs. Elvsted. You may be sure he did.

HEDDA   Well—where did you part from him?

TESMAN   On the way to town. We broke up—the rest of us at any rate—all
130   together, and Brack came with us to get a breath of fresh air. And then, you see, we agreed to take Eilert home; for he had had far more than was good for him.

HEDDA   I daresay.

TESMAN   But now comes the strange part of it, Hedda; or, I should rather say, the melancholy part of it. I declare I am almost ashamed—on Eilert's account—to tell you . . .

HEDDA   Oh, go on . . . !

TESMAN   Well, as we were getting near town, you see, I happened to drop a little behind the others. Only for a minute or two-fancy that!

140   HEDDA   Yes, yes, yes, but . . . ?

TESMAN   And then, as I hurried after them—what do you think I found by the wayside? Eh?

HEDDA   Oh, how should I know!

TESMAN   You mustn't speak of it to a soul, Hedda! Do you hear? Promise me, for Eilert's sake. [*Draws a parcel, wrapped in paper, from his coat pocket*] Fancy, dear—I found this.

HEDDA   Is not that the parcel he had with him yesterday?

TESMAN   Yes, it is the whole of his precious, irreplaceable manuscript! And he had gone and lost it, and knew nothing about it. Only fancy, Hedda! So
150   deplorably . . .

HEDDA   But why did you not give him back the parcel at once?

TESMAN   I didn't dare to—in the state he was then in . . .

HEDDA   Did you not tell any of the others that you had found it?

TESMAN   Oh, far from it! You can surely understand that for Eilert's sake, I wouldn't do that.

HEDDA   So no one knows that Eilert Lövborg's manuscript is in your possession?

TESMAN   No. And no one must know it.

HEDDA   Then what did you say to him afterwards?

160   TESMAN   I didn't talk to him again at all; for when we got in among the streets, he and two or three of the others gave us the slip and disappeared. Fancy that!

HEDDA   Indeed! They must have taken him home then.

TESMAN   Yes, so it would appear. And Brack, too, left us.

HEDDA   And what have you been doing with yourself since?

TESMAN   Well, I and some of the others went home with one of the party, a jolly fellow, and took our morning coffee with him; or perhaps I should rather call it our night coffee—eh? But now, when I have rested a little, and given Eilert, poor fellow, time to have his sleep out, I must take this back
170   to him.

HEDDA [*holds out her hand for the packet*]   No—don't give it to him! Not in such a hurry, I mean. Let me read it first.

TESMAN   No, my dearest Hedda, I mustn't, I really mustn't.

HEDDA   You must not?

TESMAN   No—for you can imagine what a state of despair he will be in when he wakens and misses the manuscript. He has no copy of it, you must know! He told me so.

HEDDA [*looking searchingly at him*]   Can such a thing not be reproduced? Written over again?

180   TESMAN   No, I don't think that would be possible. For the inspiration, you see . . .

HEDDA   Yes, yes—I suppose it depends on that . . . [*Lightly*] But, by the by—here is a letter for you.

TESMAN   Fancy . . . !

HEDDA [*handing it to him*]   It came early this morning.

TESMAN   It's from Aunt Julia! What can it be? [*He lays the packet on the other footstool, opens the letter, runs his eye through it, and jumps up*] Oh, Hedda—she says that poor Aunt Rina is dying!

HEDDA   Well, we were prepared for that.

190   TESMAN   And that if I want to see her again, I must make haste. I'll run in to them at once.

HEDDA [*suppressing a smile*]   Will you run?

TESMAN   Oh, my dearest Hedda—if you could only make up your mind to come with me! Just think!

HEDDA [*rises and says wearily, repelling the idea*]   No, no, don't ask me. I will not look upon sickness and death. I loathe all sorts of ugliness.

TESMAN   Well, well, then . . . ! [*Bustling around*] My hat . . . ? My overcoat . . . ? Oh, in the hall . . . I do hope I mayn't come too late, Hedda! Eh?

HEDDA   Oh, if you run . . .

BERTA *appears at the hall door.*

200   BERTA   Judge Brack is at the door, and wishes to know if he may come in.
       TESMAN   At this time! No, I can't possibly see him.
       HEDDA   But I can. [*To* BERTA] Ask Judge Brack to come in.

BERTA *goes out.*

       HEDDA [*quickly, whispering*]   The parcel, Tesman!

She snatches it up from the stool.

       TESMAN   Yes, give it to me!
       HEDDA   No, no, I will keep it till you come back.

She goes to the writing table and places it in the bookcase. TESMAN *stands in a flurry
of haste, and cannot get his gloves on.* JUDGE BRACK *enters from the hall.*

       HEDDA [*nodding to him*]   You are an early bird, I must say.
       BRACK   Yes, don't you think so? [*To* TESMAN] Are you on the move, too?
       TESMAN   Yes, I must rush off to my aunts'. Fancy—the invalid one is lying
at death's door, poor creature.
210   BRACK   Dear me, is she indeed? Then on no account let me detain you. At
such a critical moment . . .
       TESMAN   Yes, I must really rush . . . Good-bye! Good-bye!

He hastens out by the hall door.

       HEDDA [*approaching*]   You seem to have made a particularly lively night of
it at your rooms, Judge Brack.
       BRACK   I assure you I have not had my clothes off, Mrs. Hedda.
       HEDDA   Not you, either?
       BRACK   No, as you may see. But what has Tesman been telling you of the
night's adventures?
       HEDDA   Oh, some tiresome story. Only that they went and had coffee
220 somewhere or other.
       BRACK   I have heard about that coffee party already. Eilert Lövborg was not
with them, I fancy?
       HEDDA   No, they had taken him home before that.
       BRACK   Tesman too?
       HEDDA   No, but some of the others, he said.
       BRACK [*smiling*]   George Tesman is really an ingenuous creature, Mrs.
Hedda.
       HEDDA   Yes, heaven knows he is. Then is there something behind all this?
       BRACK   Yes, perhaps there may be.
230   HEDDA   Well then, sit down, my dear Judge, and tell your story in comfort.

She seats herself to the left of the table. BRACK *sits near her, at the long side of the table.*

HEDDA   Now then?

BRACK   I had special reasons for keeping track of my guests—or rather of some of my guests—last night.

HEDDA   Of Eilert Lövborg among the rest, perhaps?

BRACK   Frankly—yes.

HEDDA   Now you make me really curious . . .

BRACK   Do you know where he and one or two of the others finished the night, Mrs. Hedda?

HEDDA   If it is not quite unmentionable, tell me.

240   BRACK   Oh no, it's not at all unmentionable. Well, they put in an appearance at a particularly animated *soirée*.[7]

HEDDA   Of the lively kind?

BRACK   Of the very liveliest . . .

HEDDA   Tell me more of this, Judge Brack . . .

BRACK   Lövborg, as well as the others, had been invited in advance. I knew all about it. But he had declined the invitation; for now, as you know, he has become a new man.

HEDDA   Up at the Elvsteds', yes. But he went after all, then?

BRACK   Well, you see, Mrs. Hedda—unhappily the spirit moved him at my
250   rooms last evening—

HEDDA   Yes, I hear he found inspiration.

BRACK   Pretty violent inspiration. Well, I fancy, that altered his purpose; for we men folk are unfortunately not always so firm in our principles as we ought to be.

HEDDA   Oh, I am sure you are an exception, Judge Brack. But as to Lövborg—?

BRACK   To make a long story short—he landed at last in Mademoiselle Diana's rooms.

HEDDA   Mademoiselle Diana's?

260   BRACK   It was Mademoiselle Diana that was giving the soirée to a select circle of her admirers and her lady friends.

HEDDA   Is she a red-haired woman?

BRACK   Precisely.

HEDDA   A sort of a—singer?

BRACK   Oh yes—in her leisure moments. And moreover a mighty huntress—of men—Mrs. Hedda. You have no doubt heard of her. Eilert Lövborg was one of her most enthusiastic protectors—in the days of his glory.

HEDDA   And how did all this end?

BRACK   Far from amicably, it appears. After a most tender meeting, they
270   seem to have come to blows—

HEDDA   Lövborg and she?

---

[7] An evening party.

BRACK   Yes. He accused her or her friends of having robbed him. He declared that his pocket-book had disappeared—and other things as well. In short, he seems to have made a furious disturbance.

HEDDA   And what came of it all?

BRACK   It came to a general scrimmage, in which the ladies as well as the gentlemen took part. Fortunately the police at last appeared on the scene.

HEDDA   The police too?

BRACK   Yes. I fancy it will prove a costly frolic for Eilert Lövborg, crazy
280 being that he is.

HEDDA   How so?

BRACK   He seems to have made a violent resistance—to have hit one of the constables on the head and torn the coat off his back. So they had to march him off to the police station with the rest.

HEDDA   How have you learnt all this?

BRACK   From the police themselves.

HEDDA [*gazing straight before her*]   So that is what happened. Then he had no vine leaves in his hair.

BRACK   Vine leaves, Mrs. Hedda?

290 HEDDA [*changing her tone*]   But tell me now, Judge—what is your real reason for tracking out Eilert Lövborg's movements so carefully?

BRACK   In the first place, it could not be entirely indifferent to me if it should appear in the police court that he came straight from my house.

HEDDA   Will the matter come into court then?

BRACK   Of course. However, I should scarcely have troubled so much about that. But I thought that, as a friend of the family, it was my duty to supply you and Tesman with a full account of his nocturnal exploits.

HEDDA   Why so, Judge Brack?

BRACK   Why, because I have a shrewd suspicion that he intends to use you
300 as a sort of blind.

HEDDA   Oh, how can you think such a thing!

BRACK   Good heavens, Mrs. Hedda—we have eyes in our head. Mark my words! This Mrs. Elvsted will be in no hurry to leave town again.

HEDDA   Well, even if there should be anything between them, I suppose there are plenty of other places where they could meet.

BRACK   Not a single home. Henceforth, as before, every respectable house will be closed against Eilert Lövborg.

HEDDA   And so ought mine to be, you mean?

BRACK   Yes. I confess it would be more than painful to me if this person-
310 age were to be made free of your house. How superfluous, how intrusive, he would be, if he were to force his way into . . .

HEDDA   . . . into the triangle?

BRACK   Precisely. It would simply mean that I should find myself homeless.

HEDDA [*looks at him with a smile*]   So you want to be the one cock in the basket—that is your aim.

BRACK [*nods slowly and lower his voice*]   Yes, that is my aim. And for that I will fight—with every weapon I can command.

HEDDA [*her smile vanishing*]   I see you are a dangerous person—when it comes to the point.

320   BRACK Do you think so?

HEDDA I am beginning to think so. And I am exceedingly glad to think—that you have no sort of hold over me.

BRACK [*laughing equivocally*]   Well, well, Mrs. Hedda—perhaps you are right there. If I had, who knows what I might be capable of?

HEDDA Come, come now, Judge Brack! That sounds almost like a threat.

BRACK [*rising*]   Oh, not at all! The triangle, you know, ought, if possible, to be spontaneously constructed.

HEDDA There I agree with you.

BRACK Well, now I have said all I had to say; and I had better be getting
330 back to town. Good-bye, Mrs. Hedda. [*He goes towards the glass door.*]

HEDDA [*rising*]   Are you going through the garden?

BRACK Yes, it's a short cut for me.

HEDDA And then it is a back way, too.

BRACK Quite so. I have no objection to back ways. They may be piquant enough at times.

HEDDA When there is shooting practice going on, you mean?

BRACK [*in the doorway, laughing to her*]   Oh, people don't shoot their tame poultry, I fancy.

HEDDA [*also laughing*]   Oh no, when there is only one cock in the bas-
340 ket . . .

They exchange laughing nods of farewell. He goes. She closes the door behind him.
HEDDA, *who has become quite serious, stands for a moment looking out. Presently she goes and peeps through the curtain over the middle doorway. Then she goes to the writing table, takes* LÖVBORG'*s packet out of the bookcase, and is on the point of looking through its contents.* BERTA *is heard speaking loudly in the hall.* HEDDA *turns and listens. Then she hastily locks up the packet in the drawer, and lays the key on the inkstand.* EILERT LÖVBORG *with his greatcoat on and his hat in his hand, tears open the hall door. He looks somewhat confused and irritated.*

LÖVBORG [*looking towards the hall*]   And I tell you I must and will come in! There!

He closes the door, turns, sees HEDDA *at once regains his self-control, and bows.*

HEDDA [*at the writing table*]   Well, Mr. Lövborg, this is rather a late hour to call for Thea.

LÖVBORG You mean rather an early hour to call on you. Pray pardon me.

HEDDA How do you know that she is still here?

LÖVBORG They told me at her lodgings that she had been out all night.

HEDDA [*going to the oval table*]   Did you notice anything about the people of the house when they said that?

350   LÖVBORG [*looks inquiringly at her*]   Notice anything about them?

HEDDA   I mean, did they seem to think it odd?

LÖVBORG [*suddenly understanding*]   Oh yes, of course! I am dragging her down with me! However, I didn't notice anything.—I suppose Tesman is not up yet?

HEDDA   No—I think not . . .

LÖVBORG   When did he come home?

HEDDA   Very late.

LÖVBORG   Did he tell you anything?

HEDDA   Yes, I gathered that you had had an exceedingly jolly evening at
360 Judge Brack's.

LÖVBORG   Nothing more?

HEDDA   I don't think so. However, I was so dreadfully sleepy . . .

MRS. ELVSTED *enters through the curtains of the middle doorway.*

MRS. ELVSTED [*going towards him*]   Ah, Lövborg! At last . . . !

LÖVBORG   Yes, at last. And too late!

MRS. ELVSTED [*looks anxiously at him*]   What is too late?

LÖVBORG   Everything is too late now. It is all over with me.

MRS. ELVSTED   Oh no, no—don't say that!

LÖVBORG   You will say the same when you hear . . .

MRS. ELVSTED   I won't hear anything!

370 HEDDA   Perhaps you would prefer to talk to her alone? If so, I will leave you.

LÖVBORG   No, stay—you too. I beg you to stay.

MRS. ELVSTED   Yes, but I won't hear anything, I tell you.

LÖVBORG   It is not last night's adventures that I want to talk about.

MRS. ELVSTED   What is it then . . . ?

LÖVBORG   I want to say that now our ways must part.

MRS. ELVSTED   Part!

HEDDA [*involuntarily*]   I knew it!

LÖVBORG   You can be of no more service to me, Thea.

MRS. ELVSTED   How can you stand there and say that! No more service to you!
380 Am I not to help you now, as before? Are we not to go on working together?

LÖVBORG   Henceforward I shall do no work.

MRS. ELVSTED [*despairingly*]   Then what am I to do with my life?

LÖVBORG   You must try to live your life as if you had never known me.

MRS. ELVSTED   But you know I cannot do that!

LÖVBORG   Try if you cannot, Thea. You must go home again . . .

MRS. ELVSTED [*in vehement protest*]   Never in this world! Where you are, there will I be also! I will not let myself be driven away like this! I will remain here! I will be with you when the book appears.

HEDDA [*half aloud, in suspense*]   Ah yes—the book!

390 LÖVBORG [*looks at her*]   My book and Thea's; for that is what it is.

MRS. ELVSTED   Yes, I feel that it is. And that is why I have a right to be with you when it appears! I will see with my own eyes how respect and honor pour in upon you afresh. And the happiness—the happiness—oh, I must share it with you!

LÖVBORG   Thea—our book will never appear.

HEDDA Ah!

MRS. ELVSTED Never appear!

LÖVBORG Can never appear.

MRS. ELVSTED [*in agonized foreboding*] Lövborg—what have you done with
400 the manuscript?

HEDDA [*looks anxiously at him*] Yes, the manuscript . . .

MRS. ELVSTED Where is it?

LÖVBORG Oh, Thea—don't ask me about it!

MRS. ELVSTED Yes, yes, I will know. I demand to be told at once.

LÖVBORG The manuscript . . . Well then—I have torn the manuscript into
a thousand pieces.

MRS. ELVSTED [*shrieks*] Oh no, no . . . !

HEDDA [*involuntarily*] But that's not . . .

LÖVBORG [*looks at her*] Not true, you think?

410 HEDDA [*collecting herself*] Oh well, of course—since you say so. But it
sounded so improbable . . .

LÖVBORG It is true, all the same.

MRS. ELVSTED [*wringing her hands*] Oh God—oh God, Hedda—torn his
own work to pieces!

LÖVBORG I have torn my own life to pieces. So why should I not tear my
lifework too . . . ?

MRS. ELVSTED And you did this last night?

LÖVBORG Yes, I tell you! Tore it into a thousand pieces—and scattered
them on the fjord—far out. There there is a cool sea water at any rate—let
420 them drift upon it—drift with the current and the wind. And then presently
they will sink—deeper and deeper—as I shall, Thea.

MRS. ELVSTED Do you know, Lövborg, that what you have done with the
book—I shall think of it to my dying day as though you had killed a little
child.

LÖVBORG Yes, you are right. It is a sort of child murder.

MRS. ELVSTED How could you, then . . . ! Did not the child belong to me,
too?

HEDDA [*almost inaudibly*] Ah, the child . . .

MRS. ELVSTED [*breathing heavily*] It is all over then. Well, well, now I will
430 go, Hedda.

HEDDA But you are not going away from town?

MRS. ELVSTED Oh, I don't know what I shall do. I see nothing but darkness
before me. [*She goes out by the hall door.*]

HEDDA [*stands waiting for a moment*] So you are not going to see her
home, Mr. Lövborg?

LÖVBORG I? Through the streets? Would you have people see her walking
with me?

HEDDA Of course I don't know what else may have happened last night.
But is it so utterly irretrievable?

440 LÖVBORG It will not end with last night—I know that perfectly well. And
the thing is that now I have no taste for that sort of life either. I won't begin it
anew. She has broken my courage and my power of braving life out.

HEDDA [*looking straight before her*]   So that pretty little fool has had her fingers in a man's destiny. [*Looks at him*] But all the same, how could you treat her so heartlessly?

LÖVBORG   Oh, don't say that it was heartless!

HEDDA   To go and destroy what has filled her whole soul for months and years! You do not call that heartless!

LÖVBORG   To you I can tell the truth, Hedda.

450   HEDDA   The truth?

LÖVBORG   First promise me—give me your word—that what I now confide to you Thea shall never know.

HEDDA   I give you my word.

LÖVBORG   Good. Then let me tell you that what I said just now was untrue.

HEDDA   About the manuscript?

LÖVBORG   Yes. I have not torn it to pieces—nor thrown it into the fjord.

HEDDA   No, no . . . But—where is it then?

LÖVBORG   I have destroyed it none the less—utterly destroyed it, Hedda!

HEDDA   I don't understand.

460   LÖVBORG   Thea said that what I had done seemed to her like a child murder.

HEDDA   Yes, so she said.

LÖVBORG   But to kill his child—that is not the worst thing a father can do to it.

HEDDA   Not the worst?

LÖVBORG   No. I wanted to spare Thea from hearing the worst.

HEDDA   Then what is the worst?

LÖVBORG   Suppose now, Hedda, that a man—in the small hours of the morning—came home to his child's mother after a night of riot and debauchery, and said: "Listen—I have been here and there—in this place and in that.

470   And I have taken our child with me—to this place and to that. And I have lost the child—utterly lost it. The devil knows into what hands it may have fallen—who may have had their clutches on it."

HEDDA   Well—but when all is said and done, you know—this was only a book . . .

LÖVBORG   Thea's pure soul was in that book.

HEDDA   Yes, so I understand.

LÖVBORG   And you can understand, too, that for her and me together no future is possible.

HEDDA   What path do you mean to take then?

480   LÖVBORG   None. I will only try to make an end of it all—the sooner the better.

HEDDA [*a step nearer him*]   Eilert Lövborg—listen to me. Will you not try to—to do it beautifully?

LÖVBORG   Beautifully? [*Smiling*] With vine leaves in my hair, as you used to dream in the old days . . . ?

HEDDA   No, no. I have lost my faith in the vine leaves. But beautifully nevertheless! For once in a way! Good-bye! You must go now—and do not come here any more.

LÖVBORG   Good-bye, Mrs. Tesman. And give George Tesman my love. [*He*
490 *is on the point of going.*]
     HEDDA   No, wait! I must give you a memento to take with you.

She goes to the writing table and opens the drawer and the pistol case; then returns to
LÖVBORG *with one of the pistols.*

     LOVBORG [*looks at her*]   This? Is this the memento?
     HEDDA [*nodding slowly*]   Do you recognize it? It was aimed at you once.
     LÖVBORG   You should have used it then.
     HEDDA   Take it—and do you use it now.
     LOVBORG [*puts the pistol in his breast pocket*]   Thanks!
     HEDDA   And beautifully, Eilert Lövborg. Promise me that!
     LÖVBORG   Good-bye, Hedda Gabler.

He goes out by the hall door. HEDDA *listens for a moment at the door. Then she goes up
to the writing table, takes out the packet of manuscript, peeps under the cover, draws
a few of the sheets half out, and looks at them. Next she goes over and seats herself in
the armchair beside the stove, with the packet in her lap. Presently she opens the stove
door, and then the packet.*

     HEDDA [*throws one of the quires into the fire and whispers to herself*]   Now
500 I am burning your child, Thea!—Burning it, curly-locks! [*Throwing one or
     two more quires into the stove*] Your child and Eilert Lövborg's. [*Throws the
     rest in*] I am burning—I am burning your child.

Act IV

Scene. *The same rooms at the* TESMAN's. *It is evening. The drawing room is in darkness. The back room is lighted by the hanging lamp over the table. The curtains over
the glass door are drawn close.* HEDDA, *dressed in black, walks to and fro in the dark
room. Then she goes into the back room and disappears for a moment to the left. She
is heard to strike a few chords on the piano. Presently she comes in sight again, and
returns to the drawing room.* BERTA *enters from the right, through the inner room,
with a lighted lamp, which she places on the table in front of the corner settee in the
drawing room. Her eyes are red with weeping, and she has black ribbon in her cap.
She goes quietly and circumspectly out to the right.* HEDDA *goes up to the glass door,
lifts the curtain a little aside, and looks out into the darkness. Shortly afterwards,*
MISS TESMAN, *in mourning, with a bonnet and veil on, comes in from the hall.* HEDDA
goes towards her and holds out her hand.

     MISS TESMAN   Yes, Hedda, here I am, in mourning and forlorn; for now my
poor sister has at last found peace.
     HEDDA   I have heard the news already, as you see. Tesman sent me a card.
     MISS TESMAN   Yes, he promised me he would. But nevertheless I thought
that to Hedda—here in the house of life—I ought myself to bring the tidings
of death.

HEDDA   That was very kind of you.

MISS TESMAN   Ah, Rina ought not to have left us just now. This is not the time for Hedda's house to be a house of mourning.

10   HEDDA [*changing the subject*]   She died quite peacefully, did she not, Miss Tesman?

MISS TESMAN   Oh, her end was so calm, so beautiful. And then she had the unspeakable happiness of seeing George once more—and bidding him good-bye. Has he not come home yet?

HEDDA   No. He wrote that he might be detained. But won't you sit down?

MISS TESMAN   No thank you, my dear, dear Hedda. I should like to, but I have so much to do. I must prepare my dear one for her rest as well as I can. She shall go to her grave looking her best.

HEDDA   Can I not help you in any way?

20   MISS TESMAN   Oh, you must not think of it! Hedda Tesman must have no hand in such mournful work. Nor let her thoughts dwell on it, either—not at this time.

HEDDA   One is not always mistress of one's thoughts . . .

MISS TESMAN [*continuing*]   Ah, yes, it is the way of the world. At home we shall be sewing a shroud; and here there will soon be sewing too, I suppose—but of another sort, thank God!

GEORGE TESMAN *enters by the hall door.*

HEDDA   Ah, you have come at last!

TESMAN   You here, Aunt Julia? With Hedda? Fancy that!

MISS TESMAN   I was just going, my dear boy. Well, have you done all you 30   promised?

TESMAN   No; I'm really afraid I have forgotten half of it. I must come to you again tomorrow. Today my brain is all in a whirl. I can't keep my thoughts together.

MISS TESMAN   Why, my dear George, you mustn't take it in this way.

TESMAN   Mustn't . . . ? How do you mean?

MISS TESMAN   Even in your sorrow you must rejoice, as I do—rejoice that she is at rest.

TESMAN   Oh yes, yes—you are thinking of Aunt Rina.

HEDDA   You will feel lonely now, Miss Tesman.

40   MISS TESMAN   Just at first, yes. But that will not last very long, I hope. I daresay I shall soon find an occupant for poor Rina's little room.

TESMAN   Indeed? Who do you think will take it? Eh?

MISS TESMAN   Oh, there's always some poor invalid or other in want of nursing, unfortunately.

HEDDA   Would you really take such a burden upon you again?

MISS TESMAN   A burden! Heaven forgive you, child—it has been no burden to me.

HEDDA   But suppose you had a total stranger on your hands . . .

MISS TESMAN   Oh, one soon makes friends with sick folk; and it's such an

50 absolute necessity for me to have some one to live for. Well, heaven be praised, there may soon be something in *this* house, too, to keep an old aunt busy.

HEDDA   Oh, don't trouble about anything here.

TESMAN   Yes, just fancy what a nice time we three might have together, if . . . ?

HEDDA   If . . . ?

TESMAN [*uneasily*]   Oh, nothing. It will all come right. Let us hope so—eh?

MISS TESMAN   Well, well, I daresay you two want to talk to each other. [*Smiling*] And perhaps Hedda may have something to tell you too, George. Good-bye! I must go home to Rina. [*Turning at the door*] How strange it is to
60 think that now Rina is with me and with my poor brother as well!

TESMAN   Yes, fancy that, Aunt Julia! Eh? [MISS TESMAN *goes out by the hall door.*]

HEDDA [*follows* TESMAN *coldly and searchingly with her eyes*]   I almost believe your Aunt Rina's death affects you more than it does your Aunt Julia.

TESMAN   Oh, it's not that alone. It's Eilert I am so terribly uneasy about.

HEDDA [*quickly*]   Is there anything new about him?

TESMAN   I looked in at his rooms this afternoon, intending to tell him the manuscript was in safe keeping.

HEDDA   Well, did you not find him?

70 TESMAN   No. He wasn't at home. But afterwards I met Mrs. Elvsted, and she told me that he had been here early this morning.

HEDDA   Yes, directly after you had gone.

TESMAN   And he said that he had torn his manuscript to pieces—eh?

HEDDA   Yes, so he declared.

TESMAN   Why, good heavens, he must have been completely out of his mind! And I suppose you thought it best not to give it back to him, Hedda?

HEDDA   No, he did not get it.

TESMAN   But of course you told him that we had it?

HEDDA   No. [*Quickly*] Did you tell Mrs. Elvsted?

80 TESMAN   No; I thought I had better not. But you ought to have told him. Fancy if, in desperation, he should go and do himself some injury! Let me have the manuscript, Hedda! I will take it to him at once. Where is it?

HEDDA [*cold and immovable, leaning on the armchair*]   I have not got it.

TESMAN   Have not got it? What in the world do you mean?

HEDDA   I have burnt it—every line of it.

TESMAN [*with a violent movement of terror*]   Burnt! Burnt Eilert's manuscript!

HEDDA   Don't scream so. The servant might hear you.

TESMAN   Burnt! Why, good God . . . ! No, no, no! It's impossible!

90 HEDDA   It is so, nevertheless.

TESMAN   Do you know what you have done, Hedda? It's unlawful appropriation of lost property. Fancy that! Just ask Judge Brack, and he'll tell you what it is.

HEDDA   I advise you not to speak of it—either to Judge Brack, or to any one else.

TESMAN   But how could you do anything so unheard of? What put it into your head? What possessed you? Answer me that—eh?

HEDDA [*suppressing an almost imperceptible smile*]   I did it for your sake, George.

100   TESMAN   For my sake!

HEDDA   This morning, when you told me about what he had read to you . . .

TESMAN   Yes, yes—what then?

HEDDA   You acknowledged that you envied him his work.

TESMAN   Oh, of course I didn't mean that literally.

HEDDA   No matter—I could not bear the idea that any one should throw you into the shade.

TESMAN [*in an outburst of mingled doubt and joy*]   Hedda! Oh, is this true? But—but—I never knew you to show your love like that before. Fancy that!

HEDDA   Well, I may as well tell you that—just at this time . . .
110   [*Impatiently, breaking off*] No, no; you can ask Aunt Julia. She will tell you, fast enough.

TESMAN   Oh, I almost think I understand you, Hedda! [*Clasps his hands together*] Great heavens! Do you really mean it? Eh?

HEDDA   Don't shout so. The servant might hear.

TESMAN [*laughing in irrepressible glee*]   The servant! Why, how absurd you are, Hedda. It's only my old Berta! Why, I'll tell Berta myself.

HEDDA [*clenching her hands together in desperation*]   Oh, it is killing me— it is killing me, all this!

TESMAN   What is, Hedda? Eh?

120   HEDDA [*coldly, controlling herself*]   All this—absurdity—George.

TESMAN   Absurdity! Do you see anything absurd in my being overjoyed at the news! But after all—perhaps I had better not say anything to Berta.

HEDDA   Oh . . . why not that too?

TESMAN   No, no, not yet! But I must certainly tell Aunt Julia. And then that you have begun to call me George too! Fancy that! Oh, Aunt Julia will be so happy—so happy!

HEDDA   When she hears that I have burnt Eilert Lövborg's manuscript—for your sake?

TESMAN   No, by the by—that affair of the manuscript—of course nobody
130   must know about that. But that you love me so much, Hedda—Aunt Julia must really share my joy in that! I wonder, now, whether this sort of thing is usual in young wives? Eh?

HEDDA   I think you had better ask Aunt Julia that question too.

TESMAN   I will indeed, some time or other. [*Looks uneasy and downcast again*] And yet the manuscript—the manuscript! Good God! It is terrible to think what will become of poor Eilert now.

MRS. ELVSTED, *dressed as in the first act, with hat and cloak, enters by the hall door.*

MRS. ELVSTED [*greets them hurriedly, and says in evident agitation*]   Oh, dear Hedda, forgive my coming again.

HEDDA   What is the matter with you, Thea?

140   TESMAN   Something about Eilert Lövborg again—eh?

MRS. ELVSTED   Yes! I am dreadfully afraid some misfortune has happened to him.

HEDDA [*seizes her arm*]   Ah—do you think so?

TESMAN   Why, good Lord—what makes you think that, Mrs. Elvsted?

MRS. ELVSTED   I heard them talking at my boardinghouse—just as I came in. Oh, the most incredible rumors are afloat about him today.

TESMAN   Yes, fancy, so I heard too! And I can bear witness that he went straight home to bed last night. Fancy that!

HEDDA   Well, what did they say at the boardinghouse?

150   MRS. ELVSTED   Oh, I couldn't make out anything clearly. Either they knew nothing definite, or else . . . They stopped talking when they saw me; and I did not dare to ask.

TESMAN [*moving about uneasily*]   We must hope—we must hope that you misunderstood them, Mrs. Elvsted.

MRS. ELVSTED   No, no; I am sure it was of him they were talking. And I heard something about the hospital or . . .

TESMAN   The hospital?

HEDDA   No—surely that cannot be!

MRS. ELVSTED   Oh, I was in such mortal terror! I went to his lodgings and

160   asked for him there.

HEDDA   You could make up your mind to that, Thea!

MRS. ELVSTED   What else could I do? I really could bear the suspense no longer.

TESMAN   But you didn't find him either—eh?

MRS. ELVSTED   No. And the people knew nothing about him. He hadn't been home since yesterday afternoon, they said.

TESMAN   Yesterday! Fancy, how could they say that?

MRS. ELVSTED   Oh, I am sure something terrible must have happened to him.

TESMAN   Hedda, dear—how would it be if I were to go and make in-

170   quiries . . . ?

HEDDA   No, no—don't mix yourself up in this affair.

JUDGE BRACK, *with his hat in his hand, enters by the hall door, which* BERTA *opens, and closes behind him. He looks grave and bows in silence.*

TESMAN   Oh, is that you, my dear Judge? Eh?

BRACK   Yes. It was imperative I should see you this evening.

TESMAN   I can see you have heard the news about Aunt Rina?

BRACK   Yes, that among other things.

TESMAN   Isn't it sad—eh?

BRACK   Well, my dear Tesman, that depends on how you look at it.

TESMAN [*looks doubtfully at him*]   Has anything else happened?

BRACK   Yes.

180   HEDDA [*in suspense*]   Anything sad, Judge Brack?

BRACK   That too, depends on how you look at it, Mrs. Tesman.

MRS. ELVSTED [*unable to restrain her anxiety*]   Oh! It is something about Eilert Lövborg!

BRACK [*with a glance at her*]   What makes you think that, Madam? Perhaps you have already heard something . . . ?

MRS. ELVSTED [*in confusion*]   No, nothing at all, but . . .

TESMAN   Oh, for heaven's sake, tell us!

BRACK [*shrugging his shoulders*]   Well, I regret to say Eilert Lövborg has been taken to the hospital. He is lying at the point of death.

190   MRS. ELVSTED [*shrieks*]   Oh God! oh God . . . !

TESMAN   To the hospital! And at the point of death!

HEDDA [*involuntarily*]   So soon after . . .

MRS. ELVSTED [*wailing*]   And we parted in anger, Hedda!

HEDDA [*whispers*]   Thea—Thea—be careful!

MRS. ELVSTED [*not heeding her*]   I must go to him! I must see him alive!

BRACK   It is useless, Madam. No one will be admitted.

MRS. ELVSTED   Oh, at least tell me what has happened to him? What is it?

TESMAN   You don't mean to say that he has himself . . . Eh?

HEDDA   Yes, I am sure he has.

200   TESMAN   Hedda, how can you . . . ?

BRACK [*keeping his eyes fixed upon her*]   Unfortunately you have guessed quite correctly, Mrs. Tesman.

MRS. ELVSTED   Oh, how horrible!

TESMAN   Himself, then! Fancy that!

HEDDA   Shot himself!

BRACK   Rightly guessed again, Mrs. Tesman.

MRS. ELVSTED [*with an effort at self-control*]   When did it happen, Mr. Brack?

BRACK   This afternoon—between three and four.

TESMAN   But, good Lord—where did he do it? Eh?

210   BRACK [*with some hesitation*]   Where? Well—I suppose at his lodgings.

MRS. ELVSTED   No, that cannot be; for I was there between six and seven.

BRACK   Well then, somewhere else. I don't know exactly. I only know that he was found . . . He had shot himself—in the breast.

MRS. ELVSTED   Oh, how terrible! That he should die like that!

HEDDA [*to* BRACK]   Was it in the breast?

BRACK   Yes—as I told you.

HEDDA   Not in the temple?

BRACK   In the breast, Mrs. Tesman.

HEDDA   Well, well—the breast is a good place, too.

220   BRACK   How do you mean, Mrs. Tesman?

HEDDA [*evasively*]   Oh, nothing—nothing.

TESMAN   And the wound is dangerous, you say—eh?

BRACK   Absolutely mortal. The end has probably come by this time.

MRS. ELVSTED   Yes, yes, I feel it. The end! The end! Oh, Hedda . . . !

TESMAN   But tell me, how have you learnt all this?

BRACK [*curtly*]   Through one of the police. A man I had some business with.

HEDDA [*in a clear voice*]   At last a deed worth doing!

TESMAN [*terrified*]   Good heavens, Hedda! what are you saying?

HEDDA   I say there is beauty in this.

230   BRACK   H'm, Mrs. Tesman . . .

TESMAN   Beauty! Fancy that!

MRS. ELVSTED   Oh, Hedda, how can you talk of beauty in such an act!

HEDDA   Eilert Lövborg has himself made up his account with life. He has had the courage to do—the one right thing.

MRS. ELVSTED   No, you must never think that was how it happened! It must have been in delirium that he did it.

TESMAN   In despair!

HEDDA   That he did not. I am certain of that.

MRS. ELVSTED   Yes, yes! In delirium! Just as when he tore up our manuscript.

240   BRACK [*starting*]   The manuscript? Has he torn that up?

MRS. ELVSTED   Yes, last night.

TESMAN [*whispers softly*]   Oh, Hedda, we shall never get over this.

BRACK   H'm, very extraordinary.

TESMAN [*moving about the room*]   To think of Eilert going out of the world in this way! And not leaving behind him the book that would have immortalized his name . . .

MRS. ELVSTED   Oh, if only it could be put together again!

TESMAN   Yes, if it only could! I don't know what I would not give . . .

MRS. ELVSTED   Perhaps it can, Mr. Tesman.

250   TESMAN   What do you mean?

MRS. ELVSTED [*searches in the pocket of her dress*]   Look here. I have kept all the loose notes he used to dictate from.

HEDDA [*a step forward*]   Ah . . . !

TESMAN   You have kept them, Mrs. Elvsted! Eh?

MRS. ELVSTED   Yes, I have them here. I put them in my pocket when I left home. Here they still are . . .

TESMAN   Oh, do let me see them!

MRS. ELVSTED [*hands him a bundle of papers*]   But they are in such disorder—all mixed up.

260   TESMAN   Fancy, if we could make something out of them, after all! Perhaps if we two put our heads together . . .

MRS. ELVSTED   Oh yes, at least let us try . . .

TESMAN   We will manage it! We must! I will dedicate my life to this task.

HEDDA   You, George? Your life?

TESMAN   Yes, or rather all the time I can spare. My own collections must wait in the meantime. Hedda—you understand, eh? I owe this to Eilert's memory.

HEDDA   Perhaps.

TESMAN   And so, my dear Mrs. Elvsted, we will give our whole minds to it.
270 There is no use in brooding over what can't be undone—eh? We must try to control our grief as much as possible, and . . .

MRS. ELVSTED   Yes, yes, Mr. Tesman, I will do the best I can.

TESMAN   Well then, come here. I can't rest until we have looked through the notes. Where shall we sit? No, in there, in the back room. Excuse me, my dear Judge. Come with me, Mrs. Elvsted.

MRS. ELVSTED   Oh, if only it were possible!

TESMAN *and* MRS. ELVSTED *go into the back room. She takes off her hat and cloak. They both sit at the table under the hanging lamp, and are soon deep in an eager examination of the papers.* HEDDA *crosses to the stove and sits in the armchair. Presently* BRACK *goes up to her.*

HEDDA [*in a low voice*]   Oh, what a sense of freedom it gives one, this act of Eilert Lövborg's.

BRACK   Freedom, Mrs. Hedda? Well, of course, it is a release for him . . .

280   HEDDA   I mean for me. It gives me a sense of freedom to know that a deed of deliberate courage is still possible in this world—a deed of spontaneous beauty.

BRACK [*smiling*]   H'm—my dear Mrs. Hedda . . .

HEDDA   Oh, I know what you are going to say. For you are a kind of specialist, too, like—you know!

BRACK [*looking hard at her*]   Eilert Lövborg was more to you than perhaps you are willing to admit to yourself. Am I wrong?

HEDDA   I don't answer such questions. I only know that Eilert Lövborg has had the courage to live his life after his own fashion. And then—the last great

290   act, with its beauty! Ah! that he should have the will and the strength to turn away from the banquet of life—so early.

BRACK   I am sorry, Mrs. Hedda, but I fear I must dispel an amiable illusion.

HEDDA   Illusion?

BRACK   Which could not have lasted long in any case.

HEDDA   What do you mean?

BRACK   Eilert Lövborg did not shoot himself—voluntarily.

HEDDA   Not voluntarily!

BRACK   No. The thing did not happen exactly as I told it.

HEDDA [*in suspense*]   Have you concealed something? What is it?

300   BRACK   For poor Mrs. Elvsted's sake I idealized the facts a little.

HEDDA   What are the facts?

BRACK   First, that he is already dead.

HEDDA   At the hospital?

BRACK   Yes—without regaining consciousness.

HEDDA   What more have you concealed?

BRACK   This—the event did not happen at his lodgings.

HEDDA   Oh, that can make no difference.

BRACK   Perhaps it may. For I must tell you—Eilert Lövborg was found shot in—in Mademoiselle Diana's boudoir.

310   HEDDA [*makes a motion as if to rise, but sinks back again*]   That is impossible, Judge Brack! He cannot have been there again today.

BRACK   He was there this afternoon. He went there, he said, to demand the return of something, which they had taken from him. Talked wildly about a lost child . . .

HEDDA   Ah—so that was why . . .

BRACK   I thought probably he meant his manuscript; but now I hear he destroyed that himself. So I suppose it must have been his pocketbook.

HEDDA   Yes, no doubt. And there—there he was found?

BRACK   Yes, there. With a pistol in his breast pocket, discharged. The ball
320   had lodged in a vital part.

HEDDA   In the breast—yes.

BRACK   No—in the bowels.

HEDDA [*looks up at him with an expression of loathing*]   That, too! Oh,
what a curse is it that makes everything I touch turn ludicrous and mean?

BRACK   There is one point more, Mrs. Hedda—another disagreeable feature in the affair.

HEDDA   And what is that?

BRACK   The pistol he carried . . .

HEDDA [*breathless*]   Well? What of it?

330   BRACK   He must have stolen it.

HEDDA [*leaps up*]   Stolen it! That is not true! He did not steal it!

BRACK   No other explanation is possible. He must have stolen it . . . . Hush!

TESMAN *and* MRS. ELVSTED *have risen from the table in the back room, and come into
the drawing room.*

TESMAN [*with the papers in both his hands*]   Hedda, dear, it is almost
impossible to see under that lamp. Think of that!

HEDDA   Yes, I am thinking.

TESMAN   Would you mind our sitting at your writing table—eh?

HEDDA   If you like. [*Quickly*] No, wait! Let me clear it first!

TESMAN   Oh, you needn't trouble, Hedda. There is plenty of room.

HEDDA   Oh, no, let me clear it, I say! I will take these things in and put
340   them on the piano. There!

*She has drawn out an object, covered with sheet music, from under the bookcase,
places several other pieces of music upon it, and carries the whole into the inner
room, to the left.* TESMAN *lays the scraps of paper on the writing table, and moves the
lamp there from the corner table. He and* MRS. ELVSTED *sit down and proceed with
their work.* HEDDA *returns.*

HEDDA [*behind* MRS. ELVSTED'*s chair, gently ruffling her hair*]   Well, my
sweet Thea, how goes it with Eilert Lövborg's monument?

MRS. ELVSTED [*looks dispiritedly up at her*]   Oh, it will be terribly hard to
put in order.

TESMAN   We must manage it. I am determined. And arranging other people's papers is just the work for me.

HEDDA *goes over to the stove, and seats herself on one of the footstools.* BRACK *stands
over her, leaning on the armchair.*

HEDDA [*whispers*]   What did you say about the pistol?

BRACK [*softly*]   That he must have stolen it.

HEDDA   Why stolen it?

350   BRACK   Because every other explanation ought to be impossible, Mrs.
Hedda.

HEDDA Indeed?

BRACK [*glances at her*] Of course, Eilert Lövborg was here this morning.
Was he not?

HEDDA Yes.

BRACK Were you alone with him?

HEDDA Part of the time.

BRACK Did you not leave the room whilst he was here?

HEDDA No.

360 BRACK Try to recollect. Were you not out of the room a moment?

HEDDA Yes, perhaps just a moment—out in the hall.

BRACK And where was your pistol case during that time?

HEDDA I had it locked up in . . .

BRACK Well, Mrs. Hedda?

HEDDA The case stood there on the writing table.

BRACK Have you looked since, to see whether both the pistols are there?

HEDDA No.

BRACK Well, you need not. I saw the pistol found in Lövborg's pocket, and
I knew it at once as the one I had seen yesterday—and before, too.

370 HEDDA Have you it with you?

BRACK No, the police have it.

HEDDA What will the police do with it?

BRACK Search till they find the owner.

HEDDA Do you think they will succeed?

BRACK [*bends over her and whispers*] No, Hedda Gabler—not so long as I
say nothing.

HEDDA [*looks frightened at him*] And if you do not say nothing—what then?

BRACK [*shrugs his shoulders*] There is always the possibility that pistol
was stolen.

380 HEDDA [*firmly*] Death rather than that.

BRACK [*smiling*] People say such things—but they don't do them.

HEDDA [*without replying*] And supposing the pistol was not stolen, and
the owner is discovered? What then?

BRACK Well, Hedda—then comes the scandal.

HEDDA The scandal!

BRACK Yes, the scandal—of which you are so mortally afraid. You will, of
course, be brought before the court—both you and Mademoiselle Diana. She
will have to explain how the thing happened—whether it was an accidental
shot or murder. Did the pistol go off as he was trying to take it out of his
390 pocket, to threaten her with? Or did she tear the pistol out of his hand, shoot
him, and push it back into his pocket? That would be quite like her; for she is
an able-bodied young person, this same Mademoiselle Diana.

HEDDA But *I* have nothing to do with all this repulsive business.

BRACK No. But you will have to answer the question: Why did you give
Eilert Lövborg the pistol? And what conclusions will people draw from the
fact that you did give it to him?

HEDDA [*lets her head sink*] That is true. I did not think of that.

BRACK Well, fortunately, there is no danger, so long as I say nothing.

HEDDA [*looks up at him*]   So I am in your power, Judge Brack. You have me
400 at your beck and call, from this time forward.

BRACK [*whispers softly*]   Dearest Hedda—believe me—I shall not abuse
my advantage.

HEDDA   I am in your power none the less. Subject to your will and your
demands. A slave, a slave then! [*Rises impetuously*] No, I cannot endure the
thought of that! Never!

BRACK [*looks half-mockingly at her*]   People generally get used to the
inevitable.

HEDDA [*returns his look*]   Yes, perhaps. [*She crosses to the writing table.
Suppressing an involuntary smile, she imitates* TESMAN'*s intonations.*] Well?
410 Are you getting on, George? Eh?

TESMAN   Heaven knows, dear. In any case it will be the work of months.

HEDDA [*as before*]   Fancy that! [*Passes her hands softly through* MRS.
ELVSTED'*s hair*] Doesn't it seem strange to you, Thea? Here you are sitting
with Tesman—just as you used to sit with Eilert Lövborg?

MRS. ELVSTED   Ah, if I could only inspire your husband in the same way!

HEDDA   Oh, that will come, too—in time.

TESMAN   Yes, do you know, Hedda—I really think I begin to feel something of the sort. But won't you go and sit with Brack again?

HEDDA   Is there nothing I can do to help you two?

420 TESMAN   No, nothing in the world. [*Turning his head*] I trust to you to keep
Hedda company, my dear Brack.

BRACK [*with a glance at* HEDDA]   With the very greatest of pleasure.

HEDDA   Thanks. But I am tired this evening. I will go in and lie down a
little on the sofa.

TESMAN   Yes, do, dear—eh?

HEDDA *goes into the back room and draws the curtains. A short pause. Suddenly she is
heard playing a wild dance on the piano.*

MRS. ELVSTED [*starts from her chair*]   Oh—what is that?

TESMAN [*runs to the doorway*]   Why, my dearest Hedda—don't play dance
music tonight! Just think of Aunt Rina! And of Eilert, too!

HEDDA [*puts her head out between the curtains*]   And of Aunt Julia. And of
430 all the rest of them. After this, I will be quiet. [*Closes the curtains again*]

TESMAN [*at the writing table*]   It's not good for her to see us at this distressing work. I'll tell you what, Mrs. Elvsted—you shall take the empty room
at Aunt Julia's, and then I will come over in the evenings, and we can sit and
work there—eh?

HEDDA [*in the inner room*]   I hear what you are saying, Tesman. But how
am *I* to get through the evenings out here?

TESMAN [*turning over the papers*]   Oh, I daresay Judge Brack will be so
kind as to look in now and then, even though I am out.

BRACK [*in the armchair, calls out gaily*]   Every blessed evening, with all
440 the pleasure in life, Mrs. Tesman! We shall get on capitally together, we two!

HEDDA [*speaking loud and clear*]   Yes, don't you flatter yourself we will, Judge Brack? Now that you are the one cock in the basket . . .

A shot is heard within. TESMAN, MRS. ELVSTED, *and* BRACK *leap to their feet.*

TESMAN   Oh, now she is playing with those pistols again.

He throws back the curtains and runs in, followed by MRS. ELVSTED. HEDDA *lies stretched on the sofa, lifeless. Confusion and cries.* BERTA *enters in alarm from the right.*

TESMAN [*shrieks to* BRACK]   Shot herself! Shot herself in the temple! Fancy that!

BRACK [*half-fainting in the armchair*]   Good God!—people don't do such things.

Arthur Miller

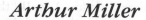

Arthur Miller (1915–) is an American playwright whose tragic vision remains unreconciled to the inevitability of doom. Finding human nature alterable, he looks at society with a prophet's fierceness, analyzing with compassion, denouncing with energy, deploring, and understanding. His first successful play, *All My Sons* (1947), attacked war profiteering. *Death of a Salesman* followed a year later, an attempt to write the tragedy not of a king but of a traveling salesman, a relatively low man named Willy Loman. Miller has written, "I believe that the common man is as apt a subject for tragedy . . . as kings were. . . . " This protagonist experiences tragic recognition when he is able to see with clarity the implications of his past life. Willy Loman does not discover that he killed his father and married his mother, but what he recognizes shatters him as much as Oedipus is shattered. ". . . The tragic feeling," wrote Miller, "is evoked in us when we are in the presence of a character who is ready to lay down his life . . . to secure . . . his sense of personal dignity."

In 1952, Miller wrote *The Crucible,* based upon the Salem witch trials of the seventeenth century. The play was courageous; it took the metaphor of witch hunts, used to describe the punitive investigation of Senator Joseph McCarthy, and let the analogy work itself out on the stage. Miller has followed with *A View from the Bridge* (1955), *After the Fall* (1964), *Incident at Vichy* (1964), and *The Price* (1968).

Death of a Salesman   (1948)
Certain Private Conversations in Two Acts and a Requiem

Characters

WILLY LOMAN

LINDA, his wife

BIFF ⎱

HAPPY ⎰ his sons

UNCLE BEN

CHARLEY

BERNARD

THE WOMAN

HOWARD WAGNER

JENNY

STANLEY

MISS FORSYTHE

LETTA

The action takes place in WILLY LOMAN*'s house and yard and in various places he visits in the New York and Boston of today.*

Act I

A melody is heard, played upon a flute. It is small and fine, telling of grass and trees and the horizon. The curtain rises.

Before us is the Salesman's house. We are aware of towering, angular shapes behind it, surrounding it on all sides. Only the blue light of the sky falls upon the house and forestage; the surrounding area shows an angry glow of orange. As more light appears, we see a solid vault of apartment houses around the small, fragile-seeming home. An air of the dream clings to the place, a dream rising out of reality. The kitchen at center seems actual enough, for there is a kitchen table with three chairs, and a refrigerator. But no other fixtures are seen. At the back of the kitchen there is a draped entrance, which leads to the living-room. To the right of the kitchen, on a level raised two feet, is a bedroom furnished only with a brass bedstead and a straight chair. On a shelf over the bed a silver athletic trophy stands. A window opens onto the apartment house at the side.

Behind the kitchen, on a level raised six and a half feet, is the boys' bedroom, at present barely visible. Two beds are dimly seen, and at the back of the room a dormer window. [This bedroom is above the unseen living-room.] At the left a stairway curves up to it from the kitchen.

The entire setting is wholly or, in some places, partially transparent. The roof-line of the house is one-dimensional; under and over it we see the apartment buildings. Before the house lies an apron, curving beyond the forestage into the orchestra. This forward area serves as the back yard as well as the locale of all WILLY*'s imaginings and of his city scenes. Whenever the action is in the present the actors observe the imaginary wall-lines, entering the house only through the door at the left. But in the scenes of the past these boundaries are broken, and characters enter or leave a room by stepping "through" a wall onto the forestage.*

[From the right, WILLY LOMAN, *the Salesman, enters, carrying two large sample cases. The flute plays on. He hears but is not aware of it. He is past sixty years of age, dressed quietly. Even as he crosses the stage to the doorway of the house, his exhaustion is*

Scene from a CBS television production of *Death of a Salesman* starring Dustin Hoffman.

apparent. He unlocks the door, comes into the kitchen, and thankfully lets his bur-
den down, feeling the soreness of his palms. A word-sigh escapes his lips—it might be
"Oh, boy, oh, boy." He closes the door, then carries his cases out into the living-room,
through the draped kitchen doorway.]

[LINDA, *his wife, has stirred in her bed at the right. She gets out and puts on a robe,*
listening. Most often jovial, she has developed an iron repression of her exceptions to
WILLY's *behavior—she more than loves him, she admires him, as though his mercurial*
nature, his temper, his massive dreams and little cruelties, served her only as sharp
reminders of the turbulent longings within him, longings which she shares but lacks
the temperament to utter and follow to their end.]

    LINDA [*bearing* WILLY *outside the bedroom, calls with some trepidation*]
Willy!

    WILLY   It's all right. I came back.

    LINDA   Why? What happened? [*Sight pause*] Did something happen, Willy?

    WILLY   No, nothing happened.

    LINDA   You didn't smash the car, did you?

    WILLY [*with casual irritation*]   I said nothing happened. Didn't you hear
me?

    LINDA   Don't you feel well?

10   WILLY   I am tired to the death. [*The flute has faded away. He sits on the bed
beside her, a little numb.*] I couldn't make it. I just couldn't make it, Linda.

Scene from a CBS television production of *Death of a Salesman* starring Dustin Hoffman.

LINDA [*very carefully, delicately*] Where were you all day? You look terrible.

WILLY I got as far as a little above Yonkers. I stopped for a cup of coffee. Maybe it was the coffee.

LINDA What?

WILLY [*after a pause*] I suddenly couldn't drive any more. The car kept going onto the shoulder, y'know?

LINDA [*helpfully*] Oh. Maybe it was the steering again. I don't think An-
20 gelo knows the Studebaker.

WILLY No, it's me, it's me. Suddenly I realize I'm goin' sixty miles an hour and I don't remember the last five minutes. I'm—I can't seem to—keep my mind to it.

LINDA Maybe it's your glasses. You never went for your new glasses.

WILLY No, I see everything. I came back ten miles an hour. It took me nearly four hours from Yonkers.

LINDA [*resigned*] Well, you'll just have to take a rest, Willy, you can't continue this way.

WILLY I just got back from Florida.

30 LINDA But you didn't rest your mind. Your mind is overactive, and the mind is what counts, dear.

WILLY I'll start out in the morning. Maybe I'll feel better in the morning. [*She is taking off his shoes.*] These goddam arch supports are killing me.

LINDA   Take an aspirin. Should I get you an aspirin? It'll soothe you.

WILLY [*with wonder*]   I was driving along, you understand? And I was fine. I was even observing the scenery. You can imagine, me looking at scenery, on the road every week of my life. But it's so beautiful up there, Linda, the trees are so thick, and the sun is warm. I opened the windshield and just let the warm air bathe over me. And then all of a sudden I'm goin' off the road!

40   I'm tellin' ya, I absolutely forgot I was driving. If I'd've gone the other way over the white line I might've killed somebody. So I went on again—and five minutes later I'm dreamin' again, and I nearly—[*He presses two fingers against his eyes.*] I have such thoughts, I have such strange thoughts.

LINDA   Willy, dear. Talk to them again. There's no reason why you can't work in New York.

WILLY   They don't need me in New York. I'm the New England man. I'm vital in New England.

LINDA   But you're sixty years old. They can't expect you to keep traveling every week.

50   WILLY   I'll have to send a wire to Portland. I'm supposed to see Brown and Morrison tomorrow morning at ten o'clock to show the line. Goddammit, I could sell them! [*He starts putting on his jacket.*]

LINDA [*taking the jacket from him*]   Why don't you go down to the place tomorrow and tell Howard you've simply got to work in New York? You're too accommodating, dear.

WILLY   If old man Wagner was alive I'd a been in charge of New York now! That man was a prince, he was a masterful man. But that boy of his, that Howard, he don't appreciate. When I went north the first time, the Wagner Company didn't know where New England was!

60   LINDA   Why don't you tell those things to Howard, dear?

WILLY [*encouraged*]   I will, I definitely will. Is there any cheese?

LINDA   I'll make you a sandwich.

WILLY   No, go to sleep. I'll take some milk. I'll be up right away. The boys in?

LINDA   They're sleeping. Happy took Biff on a date tonight.

WILLY [*interested*]   That so?

LINDA   It was so nice to see them shaving together, one behind the other, in the bathroom. And going out together. You notice? The whole house smells of shaving lotion.

70   WILLY   Figure it out. Work a lifetime to pay off a house. You finally own it, and there's nobody to live in it.

LINDA   Well, dear, life is a casting off. It's always that way.

WILLY   No, no, some people—some people accomplish something. Did Biff say anything after I went this morning?

LINDA   You shouldn't have criticized him, Willy, especially after he just got off the train. You mustn't lose your temper with him.

WILLY   When the hell did I lose my temper? I simply asked him if he was making any money. Is that a criticism?

LINDA   But, dear, how could he make any money?

80   WILLY [*worried and angered*]   There's such an undercurrent in him. He became a moody man. Did he apologize when I left this morning?

LINDA   He was crestfallen, Willy. You know how he admires you. I think if he finds himself, then you'll both be happier and not fight any more.

WILLY   How can he find himself on a farm? Is that a life? A farmhand? In the beginning, when he was young, I thought, well, a young man, it's good for him to tramp around, take a lot of different jobs. But it's more than ten years now and he has yet to make thirty-five dollars a week!

LINDA   He's finding himself, Willy.

WILLY   Not finding yourself at the age of thirty-four is a disgrace!

90   LINDA   Shh!

WILLY   The trouble is he's lazy, goddammit!

LINDA   Willy, please!

WILLY   Biff is a lazy bum!

LINDA   They're sleeping. Get something to eat. Go on down.

WILLY   Why did he come home? I would like to know what brought him home.

LINDA   I don't know. I think he's still lost, Willy. I think he's very lost.

WILLY   Biff Loman is lost. In the greatest country in the world a young man with such—personal attractiveness, gets lost. And such a hard worker.

100   There's one thing about Biff—he's not lazy.

LINDA   Never.

WILLY   [with pity and resolve]   I'll see him in the morning. I'll have a nice talk with him. I'll get him a job selling. He could be big in no time. My God! Remember how they used to follow him around in high school? When he smiled at one of them their faces lit up. When he walked down the street . . . [He loses himself in reminiscences.]

LINDA   [trying to bring him out of it]   Willy, dear, I got a new kind of American-type cheese today. It's whipped.

WILLY   Why do you get American when I like Swiss?

110   LINDA   I just thought you'd like a change—

WILLY   I don't want a change! I want Swiss cheese. Why am I always being contradicted?

LINDA   [with a covering laugh]   I thought it would be a surprise.

WILLY   Why don't you open a window in here, for God's sake?

LINDA   [with infinite patience]   They're all open, dear.

WILLY   The way they boxed us in here. Bricks and windows, windows and bricks.

LINDA   We should've bought the land next door.

WILLY   The street is lined with cars. There's not a breath of fresh air in the

120   neighborhood. The grass don't grow any more, you can't raise a carrot in the back yard. They should've had a law against apartment houses. Remember those two beautiful elm trees out there? When I and Biff hung the swing between them?

LINDA   Yeah, like being a million miles from the city.

WILLY   They should've arrested the builder for cutting those down. They massacred the neighborhood. [Lost] More and more I think of those days, Linda. This time of year it was lilac and wisteria. And then the peonies would come out, and the daffodils. What fragrance in this room!

LINDA   Well, after all, people had to move somewhere.

130   WILLY   No, there's more people now.

LINDA   I don't think there's more people. I think—

WILLY   There's more people! That's what's ruining this country! Population is getting out of control. The competition is maddening! Smell the stink from that apartment house! And another one the other side . . . How can they whip cheese?

On WILLY's *last line,* BIFF *and* HAPPY *raise themselves up in their beds, listening.*

LINDA   Go down, try it. And be quiet.

WILLY [*turning to* LINDA, *guiltily*]   You're not worried about me, are you, sweetheart?

BIFF   What's the matter?

140   HAPPY   Listen!

LINDA   You've got too much on the ball to worry about.

WILLY   You're my foundation and my support, Linda.

LINDA   Just try to relax, dear. You make mountains out of molehills.

WILLY   I won't fight with him any more. If he wants to go back to Texas, let him go.

LINDA   He'll find his way.

WILLY   Sure. Certain men just don't get started till later in life. Like Thomas Edison, I think. Or B. F. Goodrich. One of them was deaf. [*He starts for the bedroom doorway.*] I'll put my money on Biff.

150   LINDA   And Willy—if it's warm Sunday we'll drive in the country. And we'll open the windshield, and take lunch.

WILLY   No, the windshields don't open on the new cars.

LINDA   But you opened it today.

WILLY   Me? I didn't. [*He stops.*] Now isn't that peculiar! Isn't that a remarkable—[*He breaks off in amazement and fright as the flute is heard distantly.*]

LINDA   What, darling?

WILLY   That is the most remarkable thing.

LINDA   What, dear?

WILLY   I was thinking of the Chevvy. [*Slight pause*] Nineteen twenty-eight

160   . . . when I had that red Chevvy—[*Breaks off*] That funny? I coulda sworn I was driving that Chevvy today.

LINDA   Well, that's nothing. Something must've reminded you.

WILLY   Remarkable. Ts. Remember those days? The way Biff used to simonize that car? The dealer refused to believe there was eighty-thousand miles on it. [*He shakes his head.*] Heh! [*To* LINDA] Close your eyes, I'll be right up. [*He walks out of the bedroom.*]

HAPPY [*to* BIFF]   Jesus, maybe he smashed up the car again!

LINDA [*calling after* WILLY]   Be careful on the stairs, dear! The cheese is on the middle shelf! [*She turns, goes over to the bed, takes his jacket, and goes*

170   *out of the bedroom.*]

Light has risen on the boys' room. Unseen, WILLY *is heard talking to himself, "Eighty thousand miles," and a little laugh.* BIFF *gets out of bed, comes downstage a bit, and*

stands attentively. BIFF *is two years older than his brother* HAPPY, *well built, but in these days bears a worn air and seems less self-assured. He has succeeded less, and his dreams are stronger and less acceptable than* HAPPY'*s.* HAPPY *is tall, powerfully made. Sexuality is like a visible color on him, or a scent that many women have discovered. He, like his brother, is lost, but in a different way, for he has never allowed himself to turn his face toward defeat and is thus more confused and hard-skinned, although seemingly more content.*

HAPPY [*getting out of bed*]   He's going to get his license taken away if he keeps that up. I'm getting nervous about him, y'know, Biff?

BIFF   His eyes are going.

HAPPY   No, I've driven with him. He sees all right. He just doesn't keep his mind on it. I drove into the city with him last week. He stops at a green light and then it turns red and he goes. [*He laughs.*]

BIFF   Maybe he's color-blind.

HAPPY   Pop? Why he's got the finest eye for color in the business. You know that.

180   BIFF [*sitting down on his bed*]   I'm going to sleep.

HAPPY   You're not still sour on Dad, are you, Biff?

BIFF   He's all right, I guess.

WILLY [*underneath them, in the living-room*]   Yes, sir, eighty thousand miles—eighty-two thousand!

BIFF   You smoking?

HAPPY [*holding out a pack of cigarettes*]   Want one?

BIFF [*taking a cigarette*]   I can never sleep when I smell it.

WILLY   What a simonizing job, heh!

HAPPY [*with deep sentiment*]   Funny, Biff, y'know? Us sleeping in here
190 again? The old beds. [*He pats his bed affectionately.*] All the talk that went across those two beds, huh? Our whole lives.

BIFF   Yeah. Lotta dreams and plans.

HAPPY [*with a deep and masculine laugh*]   About five hundred women would like to know what was said in this room.

They share a soft laugh.

BIFF   Remember that big Betsy something—what the hell was her name— over on Bushwick Avenue?

HAPPY [*combing his hair*]   With the collie dog!

BIFF   That's the one. I got you in there, remember?

HAPPY   Yeah, that was my first time—I think. Boy, there was a pig! [*They
200 laugh, almost crudely.*] You taught me everything I know about women. Don't forget that.

BIFF   I bet you forgot how bashful you used to be. Especially with girls.

HAPPY   Oh, I still am, Biff.

BIFF   Oh, go on.

HAPPY   I just control it, that's all. I think I got less bashful and you got more so. What happened, Biff? Where's the old humor, the old confidence?

[*He shakes* BIFF's *knee.* BIFF *gets up and moves restlessly about the room.*]
What's the matter?

BIFF   Why does Dad mock me all the time?

210   HAPPY   He's not mocking you, he—

BIFF   Everything I say there's a twist of mockery on his face. I can't get near him.

HAPPY   He just wants you to make good, that's all. I wanted to talk to you about Dad for a long time, Biff. Something's—happening to him. He—talks to himself.

BIFF   I noticed that this morning. But he always mumbled.

HAPPY   But not so noticeable. It got so embarrassing I sent him to Florida. And you know something? Most of the time he's talking to you.

BIFF   What's he say about me?

220   HAPPY   I can't make it out.

BIFF   What's he say about me?

HAPPY   I think the fact that you're not settled, that you're still kind of up in the air . . .

BIFF   There's one or two other things depressing him, Happy.

HAPPY   What do you mean?

BIFF   Never mind. Just don't lay it all to me.

HAPPY   But I think if you just got started—I mean—is there any future for you out there?

BIFF   I tell ya, Hap, I don't know what the future is. I don't know—what

230   I'm supposed to want.

HAPPY   What do you mean?

BIFF   Well, I spent six or seven years after high school trying to work myself up. Shipping clerk, salesman, business of one kind or another. And it's a measly manner of existence. To get on that subway on the hot mornings in summer. To devote your whole life to keeping stock, or making phone calls, or selling or buying. To suffer fifty weeks of the year for the sake of a two-week vacation, when all you really desire is to be outdoors, with your shirt off. And always to have to get ahead of the next fella. And still—that's how you build a future.

240   HAPPY   Well, you really enjoy it on a farm? Are you content out there?

BIFF [*with rising agitation*]   Hap, I've had twenty or thirty different kinds of jobs since I left home before the war, and it always turns out the same. I just realized it lately. In Nebraska when I herded cattle, and the Dakotas, and Arizona, and now in Texas. It's why I came home now, I guess, because I realized it. This farm I work on, it's spring there now, see? And they've got about fifteen new colts. There's nothing more inspiring or—beautiful than the sight of a mare and a new colt. And it's cool there now, see? Texas is cool now, and it's spring. And whenever spring comes to where I am, I suddenly get the feeling, my God, I'm not gettin' anywhere! What the hell am I doing,

250   playing around with horses, twenty-eight dollars a week! I'm thirty-four years old, I oughta be makin' my future. That's when I come running home. And now, I get here, and I don't know what to do with myself. [*After a pause*] I've always made a point of not wasting my life, and everytime I come back here I know that all I've done is to waste my life.

HAPPY   You're a poet, you know that, Biff? You're a—you're an idealist!

BIFF   No, I'm mixed up very bad. Maybe I oughta get married. Maybe I oughta get stuck into something. Maybe that's my trouble. I'm like a boy. I'm not married, I'm not in business, I just—I'm like a boy. Are you content, Hap? You're a success, aren't you? Are you content?

260   HAPPY   Hell, no!

BIFF   Why? You're making money, aren't you?

HAPPY   [*moving about with energy, expressiveness*]   All I can do now is wait for the merchandise manager to die. And suppose I get to be merchandise manager? He's a good friend of mine, and he just built a terrific estate on Long Island. And he lived there about two months and sold it, and now he's building another one. He can't enjoy it once it's finished. And I know that's just what I would do. I don't know what the hell I'm workin' for. Sometimes I sit in my apartment—all alone. And I think of the rent I'm paying. And it's crazy. But then, it's what I always wanted. My own apartment, a car, and

270   plenty of women. And still, goddammit, I'm lonely.

BIFF   [*with enthusiasm*]   Listen, why don't you come out West with me?

HAPPY   You and I, heh?

BIFF   Sure, maybe we could buy a ranch. Raise cattle, use our muscles. Men built like we are should be working out in the open.

HAPPY   [*avidly*]   The Loman Brothers, heh?

BIFF   [*with vast affection*]   Sure, we'd be known all over the counties!

HAPPY   [*enthralled*]   That's what I dream about, Biff. Sometimes I want to just rip my clothes off in the middle of the store and outbox that goddam merchandise manager. I mean I can outbox, outrun, and outlift anybody in

280   that store, and I have to take orders from those common, petty sons-of-bitches till I can't stand it any more.

BIFF   I'm tellin' you, kid, if you were with me I'd be happy out there.

HAPPY   [*enthused*]   See, Biff, everybody around me is so false that I'm constantly lowering my ideals . . .

BIFF   Baby, together we'd stand up for one another, we'd have someone to trust.

HAPPY   If I were around you—

BIFF   Hap, the trouble is we weren't brought up to grub for money. I don't know how to do it.

290   HAPPY   Neither can I!

BIFF   Then let's go!

HAPPY   The only thing is—what can you make out there?

BIFF   But look at your friend. Builds an estate and then hasn't the peace of mind to live in it.

HAPPY   Yeah, but when he walks into the store the waves part in front of him. That's fifty-two thousand dollars a year coming through the revolving door, and I got more in my pinky finger than he's got in his head.

BIFF   Yeah, but you just said—

HAPPY   I gotta show some of those pompous, self-important executives

300   over there that Hap Loman can make the grade. I want to walk into the store the way he walks in. Then I'll go with you, Biff. We'll be together yet, I swear. But take those two we had tonight. Now weren't they gorgeous creatures?

BIFF   Yeah, yeah, most gorgeous I've had in years.

HAPPY   I get that any time I want, Biff. Whenever I feel disgusted. The only trouble is, it gets like bowling or something. I just keep knockin' them over and it doesn't mean anything. You still run around a lot?

BIFF   Naa. I'd like to find a girl—steady, somebody with substance.

HAPPY   That's what I long for.

BIFF   Go on! You'd never come home.

310   HAPPY   I would! Somebody with character, with resistance! Like Mom, y'know? You're gonna call me a bastard when I tell you this. That girl Charlotte I was with tonight is engaged to be married in five weeks. [*He tries on his new hat.*]

BIFF   No kiddin'!

HAPPY   Sure, the guy's in line for the vice-presidency of the store. I don't know what gets into me, maybe I just have an overdeveloped sense of competition or something, but I went and ruined her, and furthermore I can't get rid of her. And he's the third executive I've done that to. Isn't that a crummy characteristic? And to top it all, I go to their weddings! [*Indignantly, but*

320   *laughing*] Like I'm not supposed to take bribes. Manufacturers offer me a hundred-dollar bill now and then to throw an order their way. You know how honest I am, but it's like this girl, see. I hate myself for it. Because I don't want the girl, and, still, I take it and—I love it!

BIFF   Let's go to sleep.

HAPPY   I guess we didn't settle anything, heh?

BIFF   I just got one idea that I think I'm going to try.

HAPPY   What's that?

BIFF   Remember Bill Oliver?

HAPPY   Sure, Oliver is very big now. You want to work for him again?

330   BIFF   No, but when I quit he said something to me. He put his arm on my shoulder, and he said, "Biff, if you ever need anything, come to me."

HAPPY   I remember that. That sounds good.

BIFF   I think I'll go to see him. If I could get ten thousand or even seven or eight thousand dollars I could buy a beautiful ranch.

HAPPY   I bet he'd back you. 'Cause he thought highly of you, Biff. I mean, they all do. You're well liked, Biff. That's why I say to come back here, and we both have the apartment. And I'm telln' you, Biff, any babe you want . . .

BIFF   No, with a ranch I could do the work I like and still be something. I just wonder though. I wonder if Oliver still thinks I stole that carton of

340   basketballs.

HAPPY   Oh, he probably forgot that long ago. It's almost ten years. You're too sensitive. Anyway, he didn't really fire you.

BIFF   Well, I think he was going to. I think that's why I quit. I was never sure whether he knew or not. I know he thought the world of me, though. I was the only one he'd let lock up the place.

WILLY [*below*]   You gonna wash the engine, Biff?

HAPPY   Shh!

BIFF *looks at* HAPPY, *who is gazing down, listening.* WILLY *is mumbling in the parlor.*

HAPPY   You hear that?

They listen. WILLY *laughs warmly.*

BIFF [*growing angry*]   Doesn't he know Mom can hear that?
350   WILLY   Don't get your sweater dirty, Biff!

A look of pain crosses BIFF*'s face.*

HAPPY   Isn't that terrible? Don't leave again, will you? You'll find a job
here. You gotta stick around. I don't know what to do about him, it's getting
embarrassing.
WILLY   What a simonizing job!
BIFF   Mom's hearing that!
WILLY   No kiddin', Biff, you got a date? Wonderful!
HAPPY   Go on to sleep. But talk to him in the morning, will you?
BIFF [*reluctantly getting into bed*]   I wish you'd have a good talk with him.

The light on their room begins to fade.

BIFF [*to himself in bed*]   That selfish, stupid . . .
360   HAPPY   Sh . . . Sleep, Biff.

Their light is out. Well before they have finished speaking, WILLY*'s form is dimly seen
below in the darkened kitchen. He opens the refrigerator, searches in there, and takes
out a bottle of milk. The apartment houses are fading out, and the entire house and
surroundings become covered with leaves. Music insinuates itself as the leaves appear.*

WILLY   Just wanna be careful with those girls, Biff, that's all. Don't make
any promises. No promises of any kind. Because a girl, y'know, they always
believe what you tell 'em, and you're very young, Biff, you're too young to be
talking seriously to girls.

Light rises on the kitchen. WILLY, *talking, shuts the refrigerator door and comes
downstage to the kitchen table. He pours milk into a glass. He is totally immersed in
himself, smiling faintly.*

WILLY   Too young entirely, Biff. You want to watch your schooling first.
Then when you're all set, there'll be plenty of girls for a boy like you. [*He
smiles broadly at a kitchen chair.*] That so? The girls pay for you? [*He laughs.*]
Boy, you must really be makin' a hit.

WILLY *is gradually addressing—physically—a point offstage, speaking through the
wall of the kitchen, and his voice has been rising in volume to that of a normal
conversation.*

WILLY   I been wondering why you polish the car so careful. Ha! Don't
370   leave the hubcaps, boys. Get the chamois to the hubcaps. Happy, use paper

on the windows, it's the easiest thing. Show him how to do it, Biff! You see, Happy? Pad it up, use it like a pad. That's it, that's it, good work. You're doin' all right, Hap. [*He pauses, then nods in approbation for a few seconds, then looks upward.*] Biff, first thing we gotta do when we get time is clip that big branch over the house. Afraid it's gonna fall in a storm and hit the roof. Tell you what. We get a rope and sling her around, and then we climb up there with a couple of saws and take her down. Soon as you finish the car, boys, I wanna see ya. I got a surprise for you, boys.

    BIFF [*offstage*]   Whatta ya got, Dad?

380   WILLY   No, you finish first. Never leave a job till you're finished—remember that. [*Looking toward the "big trees"*] Biff, up in Albany I saw a beautiful hammock. I think I'll buy it next trip, and we'll hang it right between those two elms. Wouldn't that be something? Just swingin' there under those branches. Boy, that would be . . .

YOUNG BIFF *and* YOUNG HAPPY *appear from the direction* WILLY *was addressing.* HAPPY *carries rags and a pail of water.* BIFF, *wearing a sweater with a block "S," carries a football.*

    BIFF [*pointing in the direction of the car offstage*]   How's that, Pop, professional?

    WILLY   Terrific. Terrific job, boys. Good work, Biff.

    HAPPY   Where's the surprise, Pop?

    WILLY   In the back seat of the car.

390   HAPPY   Boy! [*He runs off.*]

    BIFF   What is it, Dad? Tell me, what'd you buy?

    WILLY [*laughing, cuffs him*]   Never mind, something I want you to have.

    BIFF [*turns and starts off*]   What is it, Hap?

    HAPPY [*offstage*]   It's a punching bag!

    BIFF   Oh, Pop!

    WILLY   It's got Gene Tunney's signature on it!

HAPPY *runs onstage with a punching bag.*

    BIFF   Gee, how'd you know we wanted a punching bag?

    WILLY   Well, it's the finest thing for the timing.

    HAPPY [*lies down on his back and pedals with his feet*]   I'm losing weight,
400 you notice, Pop?

    WILLY [*to* HAPPY]   Jumping rope is good too.

    BIFF   Did you see the new football I got?

    WILLY [*examining the ball*]   Where'd you get a new ball?

    BIFF   The coach told me to practice my passing.

    WILLY   That so? And he gave you the ball, heh?

    BIFF   Well, I borrowed it from the locker room. [*He laughs confidentially.*]

    WILLY [*laughing with him at the theft*]   I want you to return that.

    HAPPY   I told you he wouldn't like it!

    BIFF [*angrily*]   Well, I'm bringing it back!

410   WILLY [*stopping the incipient argument, to* HAPPY]   Sure, he's gotta practice with a regulation ball, doesn't he? [*To* BIFF] Coach'll probably congratulate you on your initiative!

BIFF   Oh, he keeps congratulating my initiative all the time, Pop.

WILLY   That's because he likes you. If somebody else took that ball there'd be an uproar. So what's the report, boys, what's the report?

BIFF   Where'd you go this time, Dad? Gee we were lonesome for you.

WILLY [*pleased, puts an arm around each boy and they come down to the apron*]   Lonesome, heh?

BIFF   Missed you every minute.

420   WILLY   Don't say? Tell you a secret, boys. Don't breathe it to a soul. Someday I'll have my own business, and I'll never have to leave home any more.

HAPPY   Like Uncle Charley, heh?

WILLY   Bigger than Uncle Charley! Because Charley is not—liked. He's liked, but he's not—well liked.

BIFF   Where'd you go this time, Dad?

WILLY   Well, I got on the road, and I went north to Providence. Met the Mayor.

BIFF   The Mayor of Providence!

WILLY   He was sitting in the hotel lobby.

430   BIFF   What'd he say?

WILLY   He said, "Morning!" And I said, "You got a fine city here, Mayor." And then he had coffee with me. And then I went to Waterbury. Waterbury is a fine city. Big clock city, the famous Waterbury clock. Sold a nice bill there. And then Boston—Boston is the cradle of the Revolution. A fine city. And a couple of other towns in Mass., and on to Portland and Bangor and straight home!

BIFF   Gee, I'd love to go with you sometime, Dad.

WILLY   Soon as summer comes.

HAPPY   Promise?

WILLY   You and Hap and I, and I'll show you all the towns. America is full
440 of beautiful towns and fine, upstanding people. And they know me, boys, they know me up and down New England. The finest people. And when I bring you fellas up, there'll be open sesame for all of us, 'cause one thing, boys: I have friends. I can park my car in any street in New England, and the cops protect it like their own. This summer, heh?

BIFF AND HAPPY [*together*]   Yeah! You bet!

WILLY   We'll take our bathing suits.

HAPPY   We'll carry your bags, Pop!

WILLY   Oh, won't that be something! Me comin' into the Boston stores with you boys carryin' my bags. What a sensation!

BIFF *is prancing around, practicing passing the ball.*

450   WILLY   You nervous, Biff, about the game?

BIFF   Not if you're gonna be there.

WILLY   What do they say about you in school, now that they made you captain?

HAPPY   There's a crowd of girls behind him everytime the classes change.

BIFF [*taking* WILLY *'s hand*]   This Saturday, Pop, this Saturday—just for you, I'm going to break through for a touchdown.

HAPPY   You're supposed to pass.

BIFF   I'm takin' one play for Pop. You watch me, Pop, and when I take off my helmet, that means I'm breakin' out. Then you watch me crash through
460   that line!

WILLY [*kisses* BIFF]   Oh, wait'll I tell this in Boston!

BERNARD *enters in knickers. He is younger than* BIFF, *earnest and loyal, a worried boy.*

BERNARD   Biff, where are you? You're supposed to study with me today.

WILLY   Hey, looka Bernard. What're you lookin' so anemic about, Bernard?

BERNARD   He's gotta study, Uncle Willy. He's got Regents next week.

HAPPY [*tauntingly, spinning* BERNARD *around*]   Let's box, Bernard!

BERNARD   Biff! [*He gets away from* HAPPY.] Listen, Biff, I heard Mr. Birnbaum say that if you don't start studyin' math he's gonna flunk you, and you won't graduate. I heard him!

WILLY   You better study with him, Biff. Go ahead now.

470   BERNARD   I heard him!

BIFF   Oh, Pop, you didn't see my sneakers! [*He holds up a foot for* WILLY *to look at.*]

WILLY   Hey, that's a beautiful job of printing!

BERNARD [*wiping his glasses*]   Just because he printed University of Virginia on his sneakers doesn't mean they've got to graduate him, Uncle Willy!

WILLY [*angrily*]   What're you talking about? With scholarships to three universities they're gonna flunk him?

BERNARD   But I heard Mr. Birnbaum say—

WILLY   Don't be a pest, Bernard! [*To his boys*] What an anemic!

480   BERNARD   Okay, I'm waiting for you in my house, Biff.

BERNARD *goes off. The* LOMANS *laugh.*

WILLY   Bernard is not well liked, is he?

BIFF   He's liked, but he's not well liked.

HAPPY   That's right, Pop.

WILLY   That's just what I mean. Bernard can get the best marks in school, y'understand, but when he gets out in the business world, y'understand, you are going to be five times ahead of him. That's why I thank Almighty God you're both built like Adonises. Because the man who makes an appearance in the business world, the man who creates personal interest, is the man who gets ahead. Be liked and you will never want. You take me, for instance. I never
490   have to wait in line to see a buyer. "Willy Loman is here!" That's all they have to know, and I go right through.

BIFF   Did you knock them dead, Pop?

WILLY   Knocked 'em cold in Providence, slaughtered 'em in Boston.

HAPPY [*on his back, pedaling again*]   I'm losing weight, you notice, Pop?

LINDA *enters, as of old, a ribbon in her hair, carrying a basket of washing.*

LINDA [*with youthful energy*]   Hello, dear!

WILLY   Sweetheart!

LINDA   How'd the Chevvy run?

WILLY   Chevrolet, Linda, is the greatest car ever built. [*To the boys*] Since when do you let your mother carry wash up the stairs?

500   BIFF   Grab hold there, boy!

HAPPY   Where to, Mom?

LINDA   Hang them up on the line. And you better go down to your friends, Biff. The cellar is full of boys. They don't know what to do with themselves.

BIFF   Ah, when Pop comes home they can wait!

WILLY [*laughs appreciatively*]   You better go down and tell them what to do, Biff.

BIFF   I think I'll have them sweep out the furnace room.

WILLY   Good work, Biff.

BIFF [*goes through wall-line of kitchen to doorway at back and calls*
510   *down*]   Fellas! Everybody sweep out the furnace room! I'll be right down!

VOICES   All right! Okay, Biff.

BIFF   George and Sam and Frank, come out back! We're hangin' up the wash! Come on, Hap, on the double! [*He and* HAPPY *carry out the basket.*]

LINDA   The way they obey him!

WILLY   Well, that's training, the training. I'm tellin' you, I was sellin' thousands and thousands, but I had to come home.

LINDA   Oh, the whole block'll be at that game. Did you sell anything?

WILLY   I did five hundred gross in Providence and seven hundred gross in Boston.

520   LINDA   No! Wait a minute, I've got a pencil. [*She pulls pencil and paper out of her apron pocket.*] That makes your commission . . . Two hundred—my God! Two hundred and twelve dollars!

WILLY   Well, I didn't figure it yet, but . . .

LINDA   How much did you do?

WILLY   Well, I—I did—about a hundred and eighty gross in Providence. Well, no—it came to—roughly two hundred gross on the whole trip.

LINDA [*without hesitation*]   Two hundred gross. That's . . . [*She figures.*]

WILLY   The trouble was that three of the stores were half closed for inventory in Boston. Otherwise I woulda broke records.

530   LINDA   Well, it makes seventy dollars and some pennies. That's very good.

WILLY   What do we owe?

LINDA   Well, on the first there's sixteen dollars on the refrigerator—

WILLY   Why sixteen?

LINDA   Well, the fan belt broke, so it was a dollar eighty.

WILLY   But it's brand new.

LINDA   Well, the man said that's the way it is. Till they work themselves in, y'know.

They move through the wall-line into the kitchen.

WILLY   I hope we didn't get stuck on that machine.

LINDA   They got the biggest ads of any of them!

540   WILLY   I know, it's a fine machine. What else?

LINDA   Well, there's nine-sixty for the washing machine. And for the vacuum cleaner there's three and a half due on the fifteenth. Then the roof, you got twenty-one dollars remaining.

WILLY   It don't leak, does it?

LINDA   No, they did a wonderful job. Then you owe Frank for the carburetor.

WILLY   I'm not going to pay that man! That goddam Chevrolet, they ought to prohibit the manufacture of that car!

LINDA   Well, you owe him three and a half. And odds and ends, comes to around a hundred and twenty dollars by the fifteenth.

550   WILLY   A hundred and twenty dollars! My God, if business don't pick up I don't know what I'm gonna do!

LINDA   Well, next week you'll do better.

WILLY   Oh, I'll knock 'em dead next week. I'll go to Hartford. I'm very well liked in Hartford. You know, the trouble is, Linda, people don't seem to take to me.

They move onto the forestage.

LINDA   Oh, don't be foolish.

WILLY   I know it when I walk in. They seem to laugh at me.

LINDA   Why? Why would they laugh at you? Don't talk that way, Willy.

WILLY *moves to the edge of the stage.* LINDA *goes into the kitchen and starts to darn stockings.*

WILLY   I don't know the reason for it, but they just pass me by. I'm not

560   noticed.

LINDA   But you're doing wonderful, dear. You're making seventy to a hundred dollars a week.

WILLY   But I gotta be at it ten, twelve hours a day. Other men—I don't know—they do it easier. I don't know why—I can't stop myself—I talk too much. A man oughta come in with a few words. One thing about Charley. He's a man of few words, and they respect him.

LINDA   You don't talk too much, you're just lively.

WILLY [*smiling*]   Well, I figure, what the hell, life is short, a couple of jokes. [*To himself*] I joke too much! [*The smile goes.*]

570   LINDA   Why? You're—

WILLY   I'm fat. I'm very—foolish to look at, Linda. I didn't tell you, but Christmas time I happened to be calling on F. H. Stewarts, and a salesman I know, as I was going in to see the buyer I heard him say something about—walrus. And I—I cracked him right across the face. I won't take that. I simply will not take that. But they do laugh at me. I know that.

LINDA   Darling . . .

WILLY   I gotta overcome it. I know I gotta overcome it. I'm not dressing to advantage, maybe.

LINDA   Willy, darling, you're the handsomest man in the world—
580   WILLY   Oh, no, Linda.
LINDA   To me you are. [*Slight pause*] The handsomest.

From the darkness is heard the laughter of a woman. WILLY *doesn't turn to it, but it continues through* LINDA*'s lines.*

LINDA   And the boys, Willy. Few men are idolized by their children the way you are.

Music is heard as behind a scrim, to the left of the house, THE WOMAN, *dimly seen, is dressing.*

WILLY [*with great feeling*]   You're the best there is, Linda, you're a pal, you know that? On the road—on the road I want to grab you sometimes and just kiss the life outa you.

The laughter is loud now, and he moves into a brightening area at the left, where THE WOMAN *has come from behind the scrim and is standing, putting on her hat, looking into a "mirror" and laughing.*

WILLY   'Cause I get so lonely—especially when business is bad and there's nobody to talk to. I get the feeling that I'll never sell anything again, that I won't make a living for you, or a business, a business for the boys. [*He*
590   *talks through* THE WOMAN*'s subsiding laughter;* THE WOMAN *primps at the "mirror."*] There's so much I want to make for—
THE WOMAN   Me? You didn't make me, Willy. I picked you.
WILLY [*pleased*]   You picked me?
THE WOMAN [*who is quite proper looking,* WILLY*'s age*]   I did. I've been sitting at that desk watching all the salesmen go by, day in, day out. But you've got such a sense of humor, and we do have such a good time together, don't we?
WILLY   Sure, sure. [*He takes her in his arms.*] Why do you have to go now?
THE WOMAN   It's two o'clock . . .
600   WILLY   No, come on in! [*He pulls her.*]
THE WOMAN   . . . My sisters'll be scandalized. When'll you be back?
WILLY   Oh, two weeks about. Will you come up again?
THE WOMAN   Sure thing. You do make me laugh. It's good for me. [*She squeezes his arm, kisses him.*] And I think you're a wonderful man.
WILLY   You picked me, heh?
THE WOMAN   Sure. Because you're so sweet. And such a kidder.
WILLY   Well, I'll see you next time I'm in Boston.
THE WOMAN   I'll put you right through to the buyers.
WILLY [*slapping her bottom*]   Right. Well, bottoms up!
610   THE WOMAN [*slaps him gently and laughs*]   You just kill me, Willy. [*He suddenly grabs her and kisses her roughly.*] You kill me. And thanks for the stockings. I love a lot of stockings. Well, good night.

WILLY   Good night. And keep your pores open!
THE WOMAN   Oh, Willy!

THE WOMAN *bursts out laughing, and* LINDA*'s laughter blends in.* THE WOMAN *disappears into the dark. Now the area at the kitchen table brightens.* LINDA *is sitting where she was at the kitchen table, but now is mending a pair of her silk stockings.*

LINDA   You are, Willy. The handsomest man. You've got no reason to feel that—
WILLY [*coming out of* THE WOMAN*'s dimming area and going over to* LINDA] I'll make it all up to you, Linda, I'll—
LINDA   There's nothing to make up, dear. You're doing fine, better than—
620   WILLY [*noticing her mending*]   What's that?
LINDA   Just mending my stockings. They're so expensive—
WILLY [*angrily, taking them from her*]   I won't have you mending stockings in this house! Now throw them out!

LINDA *puts the stockings in her pocket.*

BERNARD [*entering on the run*]   Where is he? If he doesn't study!
WILLY [*moving to the forestage, with great agitation*]   You'll give him the answers!
BERNARD   I do, but I can't on a Regents! That's a state exam! They're liable to arrest me!
WILLY   Where is he? I'll whip him, I'll whip him!
630   LINDA   And he'd better give back that football, Willy, it's not nice.
WILLY   Biff! Where is he? Why is he taking everything?
LINDA   He's too tough with the girls, Willy. All the mothers are afraid of him!
WILLY   I'll whip him!
BERNARD   He's driving the car without a license!

THE WOMAN*'s laugh is heard.*

WILLY   Shut up!
LINDA   All the mothers—
WILLY   Shut up!
BERNARD [*backing quietly away and out*]   Mr. Birnbaum says he's stuck up.
640   WILLY   Get outa here!
BERNARD   If he doesn't buckle down he'll flunk math! [*He goes off.*]
LINDA   He's right, Willy, you've gotta—
WILLY [*exploding at her*]   There's nothing the matter with him! You want him to be a worm like Bernard? He's got spirit, personality . . .

As he speaks, LINDA, *almost in tears, exits into the living-room.* WILLY *is alone in the kitchen, wilting and staring. The leaves are gone. It is night again, and the apartment houses look down from behind.*

WILLY   Loaded with it. Loaded! What is he stealing? He's giving it back, isn't he? Why is he stealing? What did I tell him? I never in my life told him anything but decent things.

HAPPY *in pajamas has come down the stairs;* WILLY *suddenly becomes aware of* HAPPY*'s presence.*

HAPPY   Let's go now, come on.
WILLY [*sitting down at the kitchen table*]   Huh! Why did she have to wax
650 the floors herself? Everytime she waxes the floors she keels over. She knows that!
HAPPY   Shh! Take it easy. What brought you back tonight?
WILLY   I got an awful scare. Nearly hit a kid in Yonkers. God! Why didn't I go to Alaska with my brother Ben that time! Ben! That man was a genius, that man was success incarnate! What a mistake! He begged me to go.
HAPPY   Well, there's no use in—
WILLY   You guys! There was a man started with the clothes on his back and ended up with diamond mines!
HAPPY   Boy, someday I'd like to know how he did it.
660 WILLY   What's the mystery? The man knew what he wanted and went out and got it! Walked into a jungle, and comes out, the age of twenty-one, and he's rich! The world is an oyster, but you don't crack it open on a mattress!
HAPPY   Pop, I told you I'm gonna retire you for life.
WILLY   You'll retire me for life on seventy goddam dollars a week? And your women and your car and your apartment, and you'll retire me for life! Christ's sake, I couldn't get past Yonkers today! Where are you guys, where are you? The woods are burning! I can't drive a car!

CHARLEY *has appeared in the doorway. He is a large man, slow of speech, laconic, immovable. In all he says, despite what he says, there is pity, and now, trepidation. He has a robe over his pajamas, slippers on his feet. He enters the kitchen.*

CHARLEY   Everything all right?
HAPPY   Yeah, Charley, everything's . . .
670 WILLY   What's the matter?
CHARLEY   I heard some noise. I thought something happened. Can't we do something about the walls? You sneeze in here, and in my house hats blow off.
HAPPY   Let's go to bed, Dad. Come on.

CHARLEY *signals to* HAPPY *to go.*

WILLY   You go ahead, I'm not tired at the moment.
HAPPY [*to* WILLY]   Take it easy, huh? [*He exits.*]
WILLY   What're you doin' up?
CHARLEY [*sitting down at the kitchen table opposite* WILLY]   Couldn't sleep good. I had a heartburn.

680   WILLY   Well, you don't know how to eat.

CHARLEY   I eat with my mouth.

WILLY   No, you're ignorant. You gotta know about vitamins and things like that.

CHARLEY   Come on, let's shoot. Tire you out a little.

WILLY [*hesitantly*]   All right. You got cards?

CHARLEY [*taking a deck from his pocket*]   Yeah, I got them. Someplace. What is it with those vitamins?

WILLY [*dealing*]   They build up your bones. Chemistry.

CHARLEY   Yeah, but there's no bones in a heartburn.

690   WILLY   What are you talkin' about? Do you know the first thing about it?

CHARLEY   Don't get insulted.

WILLY   Don't talk about something you don't know anything about.

They are playing. Pause.

CHARLEY   What're you doin' home?

WILLY   A little trouble with the car.

CHARLEY   Oh. [*Pause*] I'd like to take a trip to California.

WILLY   Don't say.

CHARLEY   You want a job?

WILLY   I got a job, I told you that. [*After a slight pause*] What the hell are you offering me a job for?

700   CHARLEY   Don't get insulted.

WILLY   Don't insult me.

CHARLEY   I don't see no sense in it. You don't have to go on this way.

WILLY   I got a good job. [*Slight pause*] What do you keep comin' in here for?

CHARLEY   You want me to go?

WILLY [*after a pause, withering*]   I can't understand it. He's going back to Texas again. What the hell is that?

CHARLEY   Let him go.

WILLY   I got nothin' to give him, Charley, I'm clean, I'm clean.

710   CHARLEY   He won't starve. None a them starve. Forget about him.

WILLY   Then what have I got to remember?

CHARLEY   You take it too hard. To hell with it. When a deposit bottle is broken you don't get your nickel back.

WILLY   That's easy enough for you to say.

CHARLEY   That ain't easy for me to say.

WILLY   Did you see the ceiling I put up in the living-room?

CHARLEY   Yeah, that's a piece of work. To put up a ceiling is a mystery to me. How do you do it?

WILLY   What's the difference?

720   CHARLEY   Well, talk about it.

WILLY   You gonna put up a ceiling?

CHARLEY   How could I put up a ceiling?

WILLY   Then what the hell are you bothering me for?

CHARLEY   You're insulted again.

WILLY   A man who can't handle tools is not a man. You're disgusting.

CHARLEY   Don't call me disgusting, Willy.

UNCLE BEN, *carrying a valise and an umbrella, enters the forestage from around the right corner of the house. He is a stolid man, in his sixties, with a mustache and an authoritative air. He is utterly certain of his destiny, and there is an aura of far places about him. He enters exactly as* WILLY *speaks.*

WILLY   I'm getting awfully tired, Ben.

BEN *'s music is heard.* BEN *looks around at everything.*

CHARLEY   Good, keep playing; you'll sleep better. Did you call me Ben?

BEN *looks at his watch.*

WILLY   That's funny. For a second there you reminded me of my brother
730 Ben.

BEN   I only have a few minutes. [*He strolls, inspecting the place.* WILLY *and* CHARLEY *continue playing.*]

CHARLEY   You never heard from him again, heh? Since that time?

WILLY   Didn't Linda tell you? Couple of weeks ago we got a letter from his wife in Africa. He died.

CHARLEY   That so.

BEN [*chuckling*]   So this is Brooklyn, eh?

CHARLEY   Maybe you're in for some of his money.

WILLY   Naa, he had seven sons. There's just one opportunity I had with
740 that man . . .

BEN   I must make a train, William. There are several properties I'm look-ing at in Alaska.

WILLY   Sure, sure! If I'd gone with him to Alaska that time, everything would've been totally different.

CHARLEY   Go on, you'd froze to death up there.

WILLY   What're you talking about?

BEN   Opportunity is tremendous in Alaska, William. Surprised you're not up there.

WILLY   Sure, tremendous.

750 CHARLEY   Heh?

WILLY   There was the only man I ever met who knew the answers.

CHARLEY   Who?

BEN   How are you all?

WILLY [*taking a pot, smiling*]   Fine, fine.

CHARLEY   Pretty sharp tonight.

BEN   Is Mother living with you?

WILLY   No, she died a long time ago.

CHARLEY   Who?

BEN   That's too bad. Fine specimen of a lady, Mother.
760   WILLY [*to* CHARLEY]   Heh?
BEN   I'd hoped to see the old girl.
CHARLEY   Who died?
BEN   Heard anything from Father, have you?
WILLY [*unnerved*]   What do you mean, who died?
CHARLEY [*taking a pot*]   What're you talkin' about?
BEN [*looking at his watch*]   William, it's half-past eight!
WILLY [*as though to dispel his confusion he angrily stops* CHARLEY*'s hand.*]
That's my build!
CHARLEY   I put the ace—
770   WILLY   If you don't know how to play the game I'm not gonna throw my
money away on you!
CHARLEY [*rising*]   It was my ace, for God's sake!
WILLY   I'm through, I'm through!
BEN   When did Mother die?
WILLY   Long ago. Since the beginning you never knew how to play cards.
CHARLEY [*picks up the cards and goes to the door*]   All right! Next time I'll
bring a deck with five aces.
WILLY   I don't play that kind of game!
CHARLEY [*turning to him*]   You ought to be ashamed of yourself!
780   WILLY   Yeah?
CHARLEY   Yeah! [*He goes out.*]
WILLY [*slamming the door after him*]   Ignoramus!
BEN [*as* WILLY *comes toward him through the wall-line of the kitchen*]   So
you're William.
WILLY [*shaking* BEN*'s hand*]   Ben! I've been waiting for you so long! What's
the answer? How did you do it?
BEN   Oh, there's a story in that.

LINDA *enters the forestage, as of old, carrying the wash basket.*

LINDA   Is this Ben?
BEN [*gallantly*]   How do you do, my dear.
790   LINDA   Where've you been all these years? Willy's always wondered why
you—
WILLY [*pulling* BEN *away from her impatiently*]   Where is Dad? Didn't you
follow him? How did you get started?
BEN   Well, I don't know how much you remember.
WILLY   Well, I was just a baby, of course, only three or four years old—
BEN   Three years and eleven months.
WILLY   What a memory, Ben!
BEN   I have many enterprises, William, and I have never kept books.
WILLY   I remember I was sitting under the wagon in—was it Nebraska?
800   BEN   It was South Dakota, and I gave you a bunch of wild flowers.
WILLY   I remember you walking away down some open road.
BEN [*laughing*]   I was going to find Father in Alaska.

WILLY   Where is he?

BEN   At that age I had a very faulty view of geography, William. I discovered after a few days that I was heading due south, so instead of Alaska, I ended up in Africa.

LINDA   Africa!

WILLY   The Gold Coast!

BEN   Principally diamond mines.

810   LINDA   Diamond mines!

BEN   Yes, my dear. But I've only a few minutes—

WILLY   No! Boys! Boys! [*Young* BIFF *and* HAPPY *appear.*] Listen to this. This is your Uncle Ben, a great man! Tell my boys, Ben!

BEN   Why, boys, when I was seventeen I walked into the jungle, and when I was twenty-one I walked out. [*He laughs.*] And by God I was rich.

WILLY [*to the boys*]   You see what I been talking about? The greatest things can happen!

BEN [*glancing at his watch*]   I have an appointment in Ketchikan Tuesday week.

820   WILLY   No, Ben! Please tell about Dad. I want my boys to hear. I want them to know the kind of stock they spring from. All I remember is a man with a big beard, and I was in Mamma's lap, sitting around a fire, and some kind of high music.

BEN   His flute. He played the flute.

WILLY   Sure, the flute, that's right!

New music is heard, a high, rollicking tune.

BEN   Father was a very great and a very wild-hearted man. We would start in Boston, and he'd toss the whole family into the wagon, and then he'd drive the team right across the country; through Ohio, and Indiana, Michigan, Illinois, and all the Western states. And we'd stop in the towns and sell the

830   flutes that he'd made on the way. Great inventor, Father. With one gadget he made more in a week than a man like you could make in a lifetime.

WILLY   That's just the way I'm bringing them up, Ben—rugged, well liked, all-around.

BEN   Yeah? [*To Biff*] Hit that, boy—hard as you can. [*He pounds his stomach.*]

BIFF   Oh, no, sir!

BEN [*taking boxing stance*]   Come on, get to me! [*He laughs.*]

BIFF   Okay! [*He cocks his fist and starts in.*]

LINDA [*to* WILLY]   Why must he fight, dear?

840   BEN [*sparring with* BIFF]   Good boy! Good boy!

WILLY   How's that, Ben, heh?

HAPPY   Give him the left, Biff!

LINDA   Why are you fighting?

BEN   Good boy! [*Suddenly comes in, trips* BIFF, *and stands over him, the point of his umbrella poised over* BIFF*'s eye*]

LINDA   Look out, Biff!

BIFF   Gee!

BEN [*patting* BIFF *'s knee*]   Never fight fair with a stranger, boy. You'll never get out of the jungle that way. [*Taking* LINDA*'s hand and bowing*] It was
850 an honor and a pleasure to meet you, Linda.

LINDA [*withdrawing her hand coldly, frightened*]   Have a nice—trip.

BEN [*to* WILLY]   And good luck with your—what do you do?

WILLY   Selling.

BEN   Yes. Well . . . [*He raises his hand in farewell to all.*]

WILLY   No, Ben, I don't want you to think . . . [*He takes* BEN*'s arm to show him.*] It's Brooklyn, I know, but we hunt too.

BEN   Really, now.

WILLY   Oh, sure, there's snakes and rabbits and—that's why I moved out here. Why, Biff can fell any one of these trees in no time! Boys! Go right
860 over to where they're building the apartment house and get some sand. We're gonna rebuild the entire front stoop right now! Watch this, Ben!

BIFF   Yes, sir! On the double, Hap!

HAPPY [*as he and* BIFF *run off*]   I lost weight, Pop, you notice?

CHARLEY *enters in knickers, even before the boys are gone.*

CHARLEY   Listen, if they steal any more from that building the watchman'll put the cops on them!

LINDA [*to* WILLY]   Don't let Biff . . .

BEN *laughs lustily.*

WILLY   You shoulda seen the lumber they brought home last week. At least a dozen six-by-tens worth all kinds a money.

CHARLEY   Listen, if that watchman—
870 WILLY   I gave them hell, understand. But I got a couple of fearless characters there.

CHARLEY   Willy, the jails are full of fearless characters.

BEN [*clapping* WILLY *on the back, with a laugh at* CHARLEY]   And the stock exchange, friend!

WILLY [*joining in* BEN*'s laughter*]   Where are the rest of your pants?

CHARLEY   My wife bought them.

WILLY   Now all you need is a golf club and you can go upstairs and go to sleep. [*To* BEN] Great athlete! Between him and his son Bernard they can't hammer a nail!
880 BERNARD [*rushing in*]   The watchman's chasing Biff!

WILLY [*angrily*]   Shut up! He's not stealing anything!

LINDA [*alarmed, hurrying off left*]   Where is he? Biff, dear! [*She exits.*]

WILLY [*moving toward the left, away from* BEN]   There's nothing wrong. What's the matter with you?

BEN   Nervy boy. Good!

WILLY [*laughing*]   Oh, nerves of iron, that Biff!

CHARLEY   Don't know what it is. My New England man comes back and he's bleedin', they murdered him up there.

WILLY   It's contacts, Charley, I got important contacts!

890   CHARLEY [*sarcastically*]   Glad to hear it, Willy. Come in later, we'll shoot a little casino. I'll take some of your Portland money. [*He laughs at* WILLY *and exits.*]

WILLY [*turning to* BEN]   Business is bad, it's murderous. But not for me, of course.

BEN   I'll stop by on my way back to Africa.

WILLY [*longingly*]   Can't you stay a few days? You're just what I need, Ben, because I—I have a fine position here, but I—well, Dad left when I was such a baby and I never had a chance to talk to him and I still feel—kind of temporary about myself.

900   BEN   I'll be late for my train.

They are at opposite ends of the stage.

WILLY   Ben, my boys—can't we talk? They'd go into the jaws of hell for me, see, but I—

BEN   William, you're being first-rate with your boys. Outstanding, manly chaps!

WILLY [*hanging on to his words*]   Oh, Ben, that's good to hear! Because sometimes I'm afraid that I'm not teaching them the right kind of—Ben, how should I teach them?

BEN [*giving great weight to each word, and with a certain vicious audacity*]   William, when I walked into the jungle, I was seventeen. When I

910   walked out I was twenty-one. And, by God, I was rich! [*He goes off into darkness around the right corner of the house.*]

WILLY   . . . was rich! That's just the spirit I want to imbue them with! To walk into a jungle! I was right! I was right! I was right!

BEN *is gone, but* WILLY *is still speaking to him as* LINDA, *in nightgown and robe, enters the kitchen, glances around for* WILLY, *then goes to the door of the house, looks out and sees him. Comes down to his left. He looks at her.*

LINDA   Willy, dear? Willy?

WILLY   I was right!

LINDA   Did you have some cheese? [*He can't answer.*] It's very late, darling. Come to bed, heh?

WILLY [*looking straight up*]   Gotta break your neck to see a star in this yard.

LINDA   You coming in?

920   WILLY   Whatever happened to that diamond watch fob? Remember? When Ben came from Africa that time? Didn't he give me a watch fob with a diamond in it?

LINDA   You pawned it, dear. Twelve, thirteen years ago. For Biff's radio correspondence course.

WILLY   Gee, that was a beautiful thing. I'll take a walk.

LINDA   But you're in your slippers.

WILLY [*starting to go around the house at the left*]   I was right! I was! [*Half to* LINDA, *as he goes, shaking his head.*] What a man! There was a man worth talking to. I was right!

930   LINDA [*calling after* WILLY]   But in your slippers, Willy!

WILLY *is almost gone when* BIFF, *in his pajamas, comes down the stairs and enters the kitchen.*

BIFF   What is he doing out there?

LINDA   Sh!

BIFF   God Almighty, Mom, how long has he been doing this?

LINDA   Don't, he'll hear you.

BIFF   What the hell is the matter with him?

LINDA   It'll pass by morning.

BIFF   Shouldn't we do anything?

LINDA   Oh, my dear, you should do a lot of things, but there's nothing to do, so go to sleep.

HAPPY *comes down the stairs and sits on the steps.*

940   HAPPY   I never heard him so loud, Mom.

LINDA   Well, come around more often; you'll hear him. [*She sits down at the table and mends the lining of* WILLY's *jacket.*]

BIFF   Why didn't you ever write me about this, Mom?

LINDA   How would I write to you? For over three months you had no address.

BIFF   I was on the move. But you know I thought of you all the time. You know that, don't you, pal?

LINDA   I know, dear, I know. But he likes to have a letter. Just to know that there's still a possibility for better things.

BIFF   He's not like this all the time, is he?

950   LINDA   It's when you come home he's always the worst.

BIFF   When I come home?

LINDA   When you write you're coming, he's all smiles, and talks about the future, and—he's just wonderful. And then the closer you seem to come, the more shaky he gets, and then, by the time you get here, he's arguing, and he seems angry at you. I think it's just that maybe he can't bring himself to—to open up to you. Why are you so hateful to each other? Why is that?

BIFF [*evasively*]   I'm not hateful, Mom.

LINDA   But you no sooner come in the door than you're fighting!

BIFF   I don't know why. I mean to change. I'm tryin', Mom, you understand?

960   LINDA   Are you home to stay now?

BIFF   I don't know. I want to look around, see what's doin'.

LINDA   Biff, you can't look around all your life, can you?

BIFF   I just can't take hold, Mom. I can't take hold of some kind of a life.

LINDA   Biff, a man is not a bird, to come and go with the springtime.

BIFF   Your hair . . . [*He touches her hair.*] Your hair got so gray.

LINDA   Oh, it's been gray since you were in high school. I just stopped dyeing it, that's all.

BIFF   Dye it again, will ya? I don't want my pal looking old. [*He smiles.*]

LINDA   You're such a boy! You think you can go away for a year and . . .

970   You've got to get it into your head now that one day you'll knock on this door and there'll be strange people here—

BIFF   What are you talking about? You're not even sixty, Mom.

LINDA   But what about your father?

BIFF [*lamely*]   Well, I meant him too.

HAPPY   He admires Pop.

LINDA   Biff, dear, if you don't have any feeling for him, then you can't have any feeling for me.

BIFF   Sure I can, Mom.

LINDA   No. You can't just come to see me, because I love him. [*With a*
980   *threat, but only a threat, of tears*] He's the dearest man in the world to me, and I won't have anyone making him feel unwanted and low and blue. You've got to make up your mind now, darling, there's no leeway any more. Either he's your father and you pay him that respect, or else you're not to come here. I know he's not easy to get along with—nobody knows that better than me—but . . .

WILLY [*from the left, with a laugh*]   Hey, hey, Biffo!

BIFF [*starting to go out after* WILLY]   What the hell is the matter with him? [HAPPY *stops him.*]

LINDA   Don't—don't go near him!

990   BIFF   Stop making excuses for him! He always, always wiped the floor with you. Never had an ounce of respect for you.

HAPPY   He's always had respect for—

BIFF   What the hell do you know about it?

HAPPY [*surlily*]   Just don't call him crazy!

BIFF   He's got no character—Charley wouldn't do this. Not in his own house—spewing out that vomit from his mind.

HAPPY   Charley never had to cope with what he's got to.

BIFF   People are worse off than Willy Loman. Believe me, I've seen them!

LINDA   Then make Charley your father, Biff. You can't do that, can you? I
1000   don't say he's a great man. Willy Loman never made a lot of money. His name was never in the paper. He's not the finest character that ever lived. But he's a human being, and a terrible thing is happening to him. So attention must be paid. He's not to be allowed to fall into his grave like an old dog. Attention, attention must be finally paid to such a person. You called him crazy—

BIFF   I didn't mean—

LINDA   No, a lot of people think he's lost his—balance. But you don't have to be very smart to know what his trouble is. The man is exhausted.

HAPPY   Sure!

LINDA   A small man can be just as exhausted as a great man. He works for a
1010   company thirty-six years this March, opens up unheard-of territories to their trademark, and now in his old age they take his salary away.

HAPPY [*indignantly*]   I didn't know that, Mom.

LINDA   You never asked, my dear! Now that you get your spending money someplace else you don't trouble your mind with him.

HAPPY   But I gave you money last—

LINDA   Christmas time, fifty dollars! To fix the hot water it cost ninety-seven fifty! For five weeks he's been on straight commission, like a beginner, an unknown!

BIFF   Those ungrateful bastards!

1020   LINDA   Are they any worse than his sons? When he brought them business, when he was young, they were glad to see him. But now his old friends, the old buyers that loved him so and always found some order to hand him in a pinch—they're all dead, retired. He used to be able to make six, seven calls a day in Boston. Now he takes his valises out of the car and puts them back and takes them out again and he's exhausted. Instead of walking he talks now. He drives seven hundred miles, and when he gets there no one knows him any more, no one welcomes him. And what goes through a man's mind, driving seven hundred miles home without having earned a cent? Why shouldn't he talk to himself? Why? When he has to go to Charley and borrow

1030 fifty dollars a week and pretend to me that it's his pay? How long can that go on? How long? You see what I'm sitting here and waiting for? And you tell me he has no character? The man who never worked a day but for your benefit? When does he get the medal for that? Is this his reward—to turn around at the age of sixty-three and find his sons, who he loved better than his life, one a philandering bum—

HAPPY   Mom!

LINDA   That's all you are, my baby! [*To* BIFF] And you! What happened to the love you had for him? You were such pals! How you used to talk to him on the phone every night! How lonely he was till he could come home to you!

1040   BIFF   All right, Mom. I'll live here in my room, and I'll get a job. I'll keep away from him, that's all.

LINDA   No, Biff. You can't stay here and fight all the time.

BIFF   He threw me out of this house, remember that.

LINDA   Why did he do that? I never knew why.

BIFF   Because I know he's a fake and he doesn't like anybody around who knows!

LINDA   Why a fake? In what way? What do you mean?

BIFF   Just don't lay it all at my feet. It's between me and him—that's all I have to say. I'll chip in from now on. He'll settle for half my pay check. He'll

1050 be all right. I'm going to bed. [*He starts for the stairs.*]

LINDA   He won't be all right.

BIFF [*turning on the stairs, furiously*]   I hate this city and I'll stay here. Now what do you want?

LINDA   He's dying, Biff.

HAPPY *turns quickly to her, shocked.*

BIFF [*after a pause*]   Why is he dying?

LINDA   He's been trying to kill himself.

BIFF [*with great horror*]   How?

LINDA   I live from day to day.

BIFF   What're you talking about?

1060   LINDA   Remember I wrote you that he smashed up the car again? In February?

BIFF   Well?

LINDA   The insurance inspector came. He said that they have evidence. That all these accidents in the last year—weren't—weren't—accidents.

HAPPY   How can they tell that? That's a lie.

LINDA   It seems there's a woman . . . [*She takes a breath as*]

{ BIFF [*sharply but contained*]   What woman?
{ LINDA [*simultaneously*]   . . . and this woman . . .

LINDA   What?

1070   BIFF   Nothing. Go ahead.

LINDA   What did you say?

BIFF   Nothing. I just said what woman?

HAPPY   What about her?

LINDA   Well, it seems she was walking down the road and saw his car. She says that he wasn't driving fast at all, and that he didn't skid. She says he came to that little bridge, and then deliberately smashed into the railing, and it was only the shallowness of the water that saved him.

BIFF   Oh, no, he probably just fell asleep again.

LINDA   I don't think he fell asleep.

1080   BIFF   Why not?

LINDA   Last month . . . [*With great difficulty*] Oh, boys, it's so hard to say a thing like this! He's just a big stupid man to you, but I tell you there's more good in him than in many other people. [*She chokes, wipes her eyes.*] I was looking for a fuse. The lights blew out, and I went down the cellar. And behind the fuse box—it happened to fall out—was a length of rubber pipe— just short.

HAPPY   No kidding?

LINDA   There's a little attachment on the end of it. I knew right away. And sure enough, on the bottom of the water heater there's a new little nipple on 1090 the gas pipe.

HAPPY [*angrily*]   That—jerk.

BIFF   Did you have it taken off?

LINDA   I'm—I'm ashamed to. How can I mention it to him? Every day I go down and take away that little rubber pipe. But, when he comes home, I put it back where it was. How can I insult him that way? I don't know what to do. I live from day to day, boys. I tell you, I know every thought in his mind. It sounds so old-fashioned and silly, but I tell you he put his whole life into you and you've turned your backs on him. [*She is bent over in the chair, weeping, her face in her hands.*] Biff, I swear to God! Biff, his life is in your hands!

1100   HAPPY [*to* BIFF]   How do you like that damned fool!

BIFF [*kissing her*]   All right, pal, all right. It's all settled now. I've been remiss. I know that, Mom. But now I'll stay, and I swear to you, I'll apply myself. [*Kneeling in front of her, in a fever of self-reproach*] It's just—you see, Mom, I don't fit in business. Not that I won't try. I'll try, and I'll make good.

HAPPY   Sure you will. The trouble with you in business was you never tried to please people.

BIFF   I know, I—

HAPPY   Like when you worked for Harrison's. Bob Harrison said you were tops, and then you go and do some damn fool thing like whistling whole
1110   songs in the elevator like a comedian.

BIFF [*against* HAPPY]   So what? I like to whistle sometimes.

HAPPY   You don't raise a guy to a responsible job who whistles in the elevator!

LINDA   Well, don't argue about it now.

HAPPY   Like when you'd go off and swim in the middle of the day instead of taking the line around.

BIFF [*his resentment rising*]   Well, don't you run off? You take off sometimes, don't you? On a nice summer day?

HAPPY   Yeah, but I cover myself!
1120   LINDA   Boys!

HAPPY   If I'm going to take a fade the boss can call any number where I'm supposed to be and they'll swear to him that I just left. I'll tell you something that I hate to say, Biff, but in the business world some of them think you're crazy.

BIFF [*angered*]   Screw the business world!

HAPPY   All right, screw it! Great, but cover yourself!

LINDA   Hap, Hap!

BIFF   I don't care what they think! They've laughed at Dad for years, and you know why? Because we don't belong in this nuthouse of a city! We
1130   should be mixing cement on some open plain, or—or carpenters. A carpenter is allowed to whistle!

WILLY *walks in from the entrance of the house, at left.*

WILLY   Even your grandfather was better than a carpenter. [*Pause. They watch him.*] You never grew up. Bernard does not whistle in the elevator, I assure you.

BIFF [*as though to laugh* WILLY *out of it*]   Yeah, but you do, Pop.

WILLY   I never in my life whistled in an elevator! And who in the business world thinks I'm crazy?

BIFF   I didn't mean it like that, Pop. Now don't make a whole thing out of it, will ya?
1140   WILLY   Go back to the West! Be a carpenter, a cowboy, enjoy yourself!

LINDA   Willy, he was just saying—

WILLY   I heard what he said!

HAPPY [*trying to quiet* WILLY]   Hey, Pop, come on now . . .

WILLY [*continuing over* HAPPY's *line*]   They laugh at me, heh? Go to Filene's, go to the Hub, go to Slattery's, Boston. Call out the name Willy Loman and see what happens! Big shot!

BIFF   All right, Pop.

WILLY   Big!

BIFF   All right!

1150   WILLY   Why do you always insult me?

BIFF   I didn't say a word. [*To* LINDA] Did I say a word?

LINDA   He didn't say anything, Willy.

WILLY [*going to the doorway of the living-room*]   All right, good night, good night.

LINDA   Willy, dear, he just decided . . .

WILLY [*to* BIFF]   If you get tired hanging around tomorrow, paint the ceiling I put up in the living room.

BIFF   I'm leaving early tomorrow.

HAPPY   He's going to see Bill Oliver, Pop.

1160   WILLY [*interestedly*]   Oliver? For what?

BIFF [*with reserve, but trying, trying*]   He always said he'd stake me. I'd like to go into business, so maybe I can take him up on it.

LINDA   Isn't that wonderful?

WILLY   Don't interrupt. What's wonderful about it? There's fifty men in the City of New York who'd stake him. [*To* BIFF] Sporting goods?

BIFF   I guess so. I know something about it and—

WILLY   He knows something about it! You know sporting goods better than Spalding, for God's sake! How much is he giving you?

BIFF   I don't know, I didn't even see him yet, but—

1170   WILLY   Then what're you talkin' about?

BIFF [*getting angry*]   Well, all I said was I'm gonna see him, that's all!

WILLY [*turning away*]   Ah, you're counting your chickens again.

BIFF [*starting left for the stairs*]   Oh, Jesus, I'm going to sleep!

WILLY [*calling after him*]   Don't curse in this house!

BIFF [*turning*]   Since when did you get so clean?

HAPPY [*trying to stop them*]   Wait a . . .

WILLY   Don't use that language to me! I won't have it!

HAPPY [*grabbing* BIFF, *shouts*]   Wait a minute! I got an idea. I got a feasible idea. Come here, Biff, let's talk this over now, let's talk some sense here. When
1180 I was down in Florida last time, I thought of a great idea to sell sporting goods. It just came back to me. You and I, Biff—we have a line, the Loman Line. We train a couple of weeks, and put on a couple of exhibitions, see?

WILLY   That's an idea!

HAPPY   Wait! We form two basketball teams, see? Two waterpolo teams. We play each other. It's a million dollars' worth of publicity. Two brothers, see? The Loman Brothers. Displays in the Royal Palms—all the hotels. And banners over the ring and the basketball court: "Loman Brothers." Baby, we could sell sporting goods!

WILLY   That is a one-million-dollar idea!

1190   LINDA   Marvelous!

BIFF   I'm in great shape as far as that's concerned.

HAPPY   And the beauty of it is, Biff, it wouldn't be like a business. We'd be out playin' ball again . . .

BIFF [*enthused*]   Yeah, that's . . .

WILLY   Million-dollar . . .

HAPPY   And you wouldn't get fed up with it, Biff. It'd be the family again. There'd be the old honor, and comradeship, and if you wanted to go off for a swim or somethin'—well, you'd do it! Without some smart cooky gettin' up ahead of you!

1200   WILLY   Lick the world! You guys together could absolutely lick the civilized world.

BIFF   I'll see Oliver tomorrow. Hap, if we could work that out . . .

LINDA   Maybe things are beginning to—

WILLY [*wildly enthused, to* LINDA]   Stop interrupting! [*To* BIFF] But don't wear sport jacket and slacks when you see Oliver.

BIFF   No, I'll—

WILLY   A business suit, and talk as little as possible, and don't crack any jokes.

BIFF   He did like me. Always liked me.

1210   LINDA   He loved you!

WILLY [*to* LINDA]   Will you stop! [*To* BIFF] Walk in very serious. You are not applying for a boy's job. Money is to pass. Be quiet, fine, and serious. Everybody likes a kidder, but nobody lends him money.

HAPPY   I'll try to get some myself, Biff. I'm sure I can.

WILLY   I can see great things for you kids, I think your troubles are over. But remember, start big and you'll end big. Ask for fifteen. How much you gonna ask for?

BIFF   Gee, I don't know—

WILLY   And don't say "Gee." "Gee" is a boy's word. A man walking in for
1220   fifteen thousand dollars does not say "Gee!"

BIFF   Ten, I think, would be top though.

WILLY   Don't be so modest. You always started too low. Walk in with a big laugh. Don't look worried. Start off with a couple of your good stories to lighten things up. It's not what you say, it's how you say it—because personality always wins the day.

LINDA   Oliver always thought the highest of him—

WILLY   Will you let me talk?

BIFF   Don't yell at her, Pop, will ya?

WILLY [*angrily*]   I was talking, wasn't I?

1230   BIFF   I don't like you yelling at her all the time, and I'm tellin' you, that's all.

WILLY   What're you, takin' over this house?

LINDA   Willy—

WILLY [*turning on her*]   Don't take his side all the time, goddammit!

BIFF [*furiously*]   Stop yelling at her!

WILLY [*suddenly pulling on his cheek, beaten down, guilt ridden*]   Give my best to Bill Oliver—he may remember me.

He exits through the livingroom doorway.

LINDA [*her voice subdued*]   What'd you have to start that for? [BIFF *turns away.*] You see how sweet he was as soon as you talked hopefully? [*She goes over to* BIFF.] Come up and say good night to him. Don't let him go to bed that
1240   way.

HAPPY   Come on, Biff, let's buck him up.

LINDA   Please, dear. Just say good night. It takes so little to make him happy. Come. [*She goes through the living-room doorway, calling upstairs from within the living-room.*] Your pajamas are hanging in the bathroom, Willy!

HAPPY [*looking toward where* LINDA *went out*]   What a woman! They broke the mold when they made her. You know that, Biff?

BIFF   He's off salary. My God, working on commission!

HAPPY   Well, let's face it: he's no hot-shot selling man. Except that some-times, you have to admit, he's a sweet personality.

1250   BIFF [*deciding*]   Lend me ten bucks, will ya? I want to buy some new ties.

HAPPY   I'll take you to a place I know. Beautiful stuff. Wear one of my striped shirts tomorrow.

BIFF   She got gray. Mom got awful old. Gee, I'm gonna go in to Oliver tomorrow and knock him for a—

HAPPY   Come on up. Tell that to Dad. Let's give him a whirl. Come on.

BIFF [*steamed up*]   You know, with ten thousand bucks, boy!

HAPPY [*as they go into the living-room*]   That's the talk, Biff, that's the first time I've heard the old confidence out of you! [*From within the living-room, fading off*] You're gonna live with me, kid, and any babe you want just say the

1260   word . . . [*The last lines are hardly heard. They are mounting the stairs to their parents' bedroom.*]

LINDA [*entering her bedroom and addressing* WILLY, *who is in the bath-room. She is straightening the bed for him.*]   Can you do anything about the shower? It drips.

WILLY [*from the bathroom*]   All of a sudden everything falls to pieces! Goddam plumbing, oughta be sued, those people. I hardly finished putting it in and the thing . . . [*His words rumble off.*]

LINDA   I'm just wondering if Oliver will remember him. You think he might?

WILLY [*coming out of the bathroom in his pajamas*]   Remember him? What's

1270   the matter with you, you crazy? If he'd've stayed with Oliver he'd be on top by now! Wait'll Oliver gets a look at him. You don't know the average caliber any more. The average young man today—[*He is getting into bed.*]—is got a cal-iber of zero. Greatest thing in the world for him was to bum around.

BIFF *and* HAPPY *enter the bedroom. Slight pause.*

WILLY [*stops short, looking at* BIFF]   Glad to hear it, boy.

HAPPY   He wanted to say good night to you, sport.

WILLY [*to* BIFF]   Yeah. Knock him dead, boy. What'd you want to tell me?

BIFF   Just take it easy, Pop. Good night. [*He turns to go.*]

WILLY [*unable to resist*]   And if anything falls off the desk while you're talking to him—like a package or something—don't you pick it up. They

1280   have office boys for that.

LINDA   I'll make a big breakfast—

WILLY   Will you let me finish? [*To* BIFF] Tell him you were in the business in the West. Not farm work.

BIFF   All right, Dad.

LINDA   I think everything—

WILLY [*going right through her speech*]   And don't undersell yourself. No less than fifteen thousand dollars.

BIFF [*unable to bear him*]   Okay. Good night, Mom. [*He starts moving.*]

WILLY   Because you got a greatness in you, Biff, remember that. You got all
1290   kinds a greatness . . . [*He lies back, exhausted.*]

BIFF *walks out.*

LINDA [*calling after* BIFF]   Sleep well, darling!

HAPPY   I'm gonna get married, Mom. I wanted to tell you.

LINDA   Go to sleep, dear.

HAPPY [*going*]   I just wanted to tell you.

WILLY   Keep up the good work. [HAPPY *exits.*] God . . . remember that Ebbets Field game? The championship of the city?

LINDA   Just rest. Should I sing to you?

WILLY   Yeah. Sing to me. [LINDA *hums a soft lullaby.*] When that team came out—he was the tallest, remember?

1300   LINDA   Oh, yes. And in gold.

BIFF *enters the darkened kitchen, takes a cigarette, and leaves the house. He comes downstage into a golden pool of light. He smokes, staring at the night.*

WILLY   Like a young god. Hercules—something like that. And the sun, the sun all around him. Remember how he waved to me? Right up from the field, with the representatives of three colleges standing by? And the buyers I brought, and the cheers when he came out—Loman, Loman, Loman! God Almighty, he'll be great yet. A star like that, magnificent, can never really fade away!

The light on WILLY *is fading. The gas heater begins to glow through the kitchen wall, near the stairs, a blue flame beneath red coils.*

LINDA [*timidly*]   Willy, dear, what has he got against you?

WILLY   I'm so tired. Don't talk any more.

BIFF *slowly returns to the kitchen. He stops, stares toward the heater.*

LINDA   Will you ask Howard to let you work in New York?

1310   WILLY   First thing in the morning. Everything'll be alright.

BIFF *reaches behind the heater and draws out a length of rubber tubing. He is horrified and turns his head toward* WILLY*'s room, still dimly lit, from which the strains of* LINDA*'s desperate but monotonous humming rise.*

WILLY [*staring through the window into the moonlight*]   Gee, look at the moon moving between the buildings!

BIFF *wraps the tubing around his hand and quickly goes up the stairs.*

Act II

Music is heard, gay and bright. The curtain rises as the music fades away. WILLY, *in shirt sleeves, is sitting at the kitchen table, sipping coffee, his hat in his lap.* LINDA *is filling his cup when she can.*

WILLY   Wonderful coffee. Meal in itself.

LINDA   Can I make you some eggs?

WILLY   No. Take a breath.

LINDA   You look so rested, dear.

WILLY   I slept like a dead one. First time in months. Imagine, sleeping till ten on a Tuesday morning. Boys left nice and early, heh?

LINDA   They were out of here by eight o'clock.

WILLY   Good work!

LINDA   It was so thrilling to see them leaving together. I can't get over the
10 shaving lotion in this house!

WILLY [*smiling*]   Mmm—

LINDA   Biff was very changed this morning. His whole attitude seemed to be hopeful. He couldn't wait to get downtown to see Oliver.

WILLY   He's heading for a change. There's no question, there simply are certain men that take longer to get—solidified. How did he dress?

LINDA   His blue suit. He's so handsome in that suit. He could be a— anything in that suit!

WILLY *gets up from the table.* LINDA *holds his jacket for him.*

WILLY   There's no question, no question at all. Gee, on the way home tonight I'd like to buy some seeds.

20 LINDA [*laughing*]   That'd be wonderful. But not enough sun gets back there. Nothing'll grow any more.

WILLY   You wait, kid, before it's all over we're gonna get a little place out in the country, and I'll raise some vegetables, a couple of chickens . . .

LINDA   You'll do it yet, dear.

WILLY *walks out of his jacket.* LINDA *follows him.*

WILLY   And they'll get married, and come for a weekend. I'd build a little guest house. 'Cause I got so many fine tools, all I'd need would be a little lumber and some peace of mind.

LINDA [*joyfully*]   I sewed the lining . . .

WILLY   I could build two guest houses, so they'd both come. Did he de-
30 cide how much he's going to ask Oliver for?

LINDA [*getting him into the jacket*]   He didn't mention it, but I imagine ten or fifteen thousand. You going to talk to Howard today?

WILLY   Yeah. I'll put it to him straight and simple. He'll just have to take me off the road.

LINDA   And Willy, don't forget to ask for a little advance, because we've got the insurance premium. It's the grace period now.

WILLY   That's a hundred . . . ?

LINDA   A hundred and eight, sixty-eight. Because we're a little short again.

WILLY   Why are we short?

40   LINDA   Well, you had the motor job on the car . . .

WILLY   That goddam Studebaker!

LINDA   And you got one more payment on the refrigerator . . .

WILLY   But it just broke again!

LINDA   Well, it's old, dear.

WILLY   I told you we should've bought a well-advertised machine. Charley bought a General Electric and it's twenty years old and it's still good, that son-of-a-bitch.

LINDA   But, Willy—

WILLY   Whoever heard of a Hastings refrigerator? Once in my life I would 50 like to own something outright before it's broken! I'm always in a race with the junkyard! I just finished paying for the car and it's on its last legs. The refrigerator consumes belts like a goddam maniac. They time those things. They time them so when you finally paid for them, they're used up.

LINDA [*buttoning up his jacket as he unbuttons it*]   All told, about two hundred dollars would carry us, dear. But that includes the last payment on the mortgage. After this payment, Willy, the house belongs to us.

WILLY   It's twenty-five years!

LINDA   Biff was nine years old when we bought it.

WILLY   Well, that's a great thing. To weather a twenty-five year mortgage 60 is—

LINDA   It's an accomplishment.

WILLY   All the cement, the lumber, the reconstruction I put in this house! There ain't a crack to be found in it any more.

LINDA   Well, it served its purpose.

WILLY   What purpose? Some stranger'll come along, move in, and that's that. If only Biff would take this house, and raise a family . . . [*He starts to go.*] Goodby, I'm late.

LINDA [*suddenly remembering*]   Oh, I forgot! You're supposed to meet them for dinner.

70   WILLY   Me?

LINDA   At Frank's Chop House on Forty-eighth near Sixth Avenue.

WILLY   Is that so! How about you?

LINDA   No, just the three of you. They're gonna blow you to a big meal!

WILLY   Don't say! Who thought of that?

LINDA   Biff came to me this morning, Willy, and he said, "Tell Dad, we want to blow him to a big meal." Be there six o'clock. You and your two boys are going to have dinner.

WILLY   Gee whiz! That's really somethin'. I'm gonna knock Howard for a loop, kid. I'll get an advance, and I'll come home with a New York job. 80 Goddammit, now I'm gonna do it!

LINDA   Oh, that's the spirit, Willy!

WILLY   I will never get behind a wheel the rest of my life!

LINDA   It's changing, Willy, I can feel it changing!

WILLY   Beyond a question. G'by, I'm late. [*He starts to go again.*]

LINDA [*calling after him as she runs to the kitchen table for a handkerchief*]   You got your glasses?

WILLY [*feels for them, then comes back in*]   Yeah, yeah, got my glasses.

LINDA [*giving him the handkerchief*]   And a handkerchief.

WILLY   Yeah, handkerchief.

90   LINDA   And your saccharine?

WILLY   Yeah, my saccharine.

LINDA   Be careful on the subway stairs.

She kisses him, and a silk stocking is seen hanging from her hand. WILLY *notices it.*

WILLY   Will you stop mending stockings? At least while I'm in the house. It gets me nervous. I can't tell you. Please.

LINDA *hides the stocking in her hand as she follows* WILLY *across the forestage in front of the house.*

LINDA   Remember, Frank's Chop House.

WILLY [*passing the apron*]   Maybe beets would grow out there.

LINDA [*laughing*]   But you tried so many times.

WILLY   Yeah. Well, don't work hard today. [*He disappears around the right corner of the house.*]

100   LINDA   Be careful!

As WILLY *vanishes,* LINDA *waves to him. Suddenly the phone rings. She runs across the stage and into the kitchen and lifts it.*

LINDA   Hello? Oh, Biff! I'm so glad you called, I just . . . Yes, sure, I just told him. Yes, he'll be there for dinner at six o'clock, I didn't forget. Listen, I was just dying to tell you. You know that little rubber pipe I told you about? That he connected to the gas heater? I finally decided to go down the cellar this morning and take it away and destroy it. But it's gone! Imagine? He took it away himself, it isn't there! [*She listens.*] When? Oh, then you took it. Oh—nothing, it's just that I'd hoped he'd taken it away himself. Oh, I'm not worried, darling, because this morning he left in such high spirits, it was like the old days! I'm not afraid any more. Did Mr. Oliver see you? . . . Well, you

110   wait there then. And make a nice impression on him, darling. Just don't perspire too much before you see him. And have a nice time with Dad. He may have big news too! . . . That's right, a New York job. And be sweet to him tonight, dear. Be loving to him. Because he's only a little boat looking for a harbor. [*She is trembling with sorrow and joy.*] Oh, that's wonderful, Biff, you'll save his life. Thanks, darling. Just put your arm around him when he comes into the restaurant. Give him a smile. That's the boy . . . Good-by, dear. . . . You got your comb? . . . That's fine. Good-by, Biff dear.

In the middle of her speech, HOWARD WAGNER, *thirty-six, wheels on a small typewriter table on which is a wire-recording machine and proceeds to plug it in. This is on the left forestage. Light slowly fades on* LINDA *as it rises on* HOWARD. HOWARD *is intent on thread-ing the machine and only glances over his shoulder as* WILLY *appears.*

WILLY   Pst! Pst!

HOWARD   Hello, Willy, come in.

120   WILLY   Like to have a little talk with you, Howard.

HOWARD   Sorry to keep you waiting. I'll be with you in a minute.

WILLY   What's that, Howard?

HOWARD   Didn't you ever see one of these? Wire recorder.

WILLY   Oh. Can we talk a minute?

HOWARD   Records things. Just got delivery yesterday. Been driving me crazy, the most terrific machine I ever saw in my life. I was up all night with it.

WILLY   What do you do with it?

HOWARD   I bought it for dictation, but you can do anything with it. Listen to this. I had it home last night. Listen to what I picked up. The first one is my

130   daughter. Get this. [*He flicks the switch and "Roll out the Barrel" is heard being whistled.*] Listen to that kid whistle.

WILLY   That is lifelike, isn't it?

HOWARD   Seven years old. Get that tone.

WILLY   Ts, ts. Like to ask a little favor if you . . .

The whistling breaks off, and the voice of HOWARD'S DAUGHTER *is heard.*

HIS DAUGHTER   "Now you, Daddy."

HOWARD   She's crazy for me! [*Again the same song is whistled.*] That's me! Ha! [*He winks.*]

WILLY   You're very good!

The whistling breaks off again. The machine runs silent for a moment.

HOWARD   Sh! Get this now, this is my son.

140   HIS SON   "The capital of Alabama is Montgomery; the capital of Arizona is Phoenix; the capital of Arkansas is Little Rock; the capital of California is Sacramento . . ." [*And on, and on*]

HOWARD [*holding up five fingers*]   Five years old, Willy!

WILLY   He'll make an announcer some day!

HIS SON [*continuing*]   "The capital . . ."

HOWARD   Get that—alphabetical order! [*The machine breaks off sud-denly.*] Wait a minute. The maid kicked the plug out.

WILLY   It certainly is a—

HOWARD   Sh, for God's sake!

150   HIS SON   "It's nine o'clock, Bulova watch time. So I have to go to sleep."

WILLY   That really is—

HOWARD   Wait a minute! The next is my wife.

They wait.

HOWARD'S VOICE   "Go on, say something." [*Pause*] "Well, you gonna talk?"

HIS WIFE   "I can't think of anything."

HOWARD'S VOICE   "Well, talk—it's turning."

HIS WIFE [*shyly, beaten*]   "Hello." [*Silence*] "Oh, Howard, I can't talk into this . . ."

HOWARD [*snapping the machine off*]   That was my wife.

WILLY   That is a wonderful machine. Can we—

160   HOWARD   I tell you, Willy, I'm gonna take my camera, and my bandsaw, and all my hobbies, and out they go. This is the most fascinating relaxation I ever found.

WILLY   I think I'll get one myself.

HOWARD   Sure, they're only a hundred and a half. You can't do without it. Supposing you wanna hear Jack Benny, see? But you can't be at home at that hour. So you tell the maid to turn the radio on when Jack Benny comes on, and this automatically goes on with the radio . . .

WILLY   And when you come home you . . .

HOWARD   You can come home twelve o'clock, one o'clock, any time you
170   like, and you get yourself a Coke and sit yourself down, throw the switch, and there's Jack Benny's program in the middle of the night!

WILLY   I'm definitely going to get one. Because lots of time I'm on the road, and I think to myself, what I must be missing on the radio!

HOWARD   Don't you have a radio in the car?

WILLY   Yeah, but who ever thinks of turning it on?

HOWARD   Say, aren't you supposed to be in Boston?

WILLY   That's what I want to talk to you about, Howard. You got a minute?

He draws a chair in from the wing.

HOWARD   What happened? What're you doing here?

WILLY   Well . . .

180   HOWARD   You didn't crack up again, did you?

WILLY   Oh, no. No . . .

HOWARD   Geez, you had me worried there for a minute. What's the trouble?

WILLY   Well, to tell you the truth, Howard, I've come to the conclusion that I'd rather not travel any more.

HOWARD   Not travel! Well, what'll you do?

WILLY   Remember, Christmas time, when you had the party here? You said you'd try to think of some spot for me here in town.

HOWARD   With us?

WILLY   Well, sure.

190   HOWARD   Oh, yeah, yeah. I remember. Well, I couldn't think of anything for you, Willy.

WILLY   I tell ya, Howard. The kids are all grown up, y'know. I don't need much any more. If I could take home—well, sixty-five dollars a week, I could swing it.

HOWARD   Yeah, but Willy, see I—

WILLY   I tell ya why, Howard. Speaking frankly and between the two of us, y'know—I'm just a little tired.

HOWARD   Oh, I could understand that, Willy. But you're a road man, Willy, and we do a road business. We've only got a half-dozen salesmen on the floor
200 here.

WILLY   God knows, Howard, I never asked a favor of any man. But I was with the firm when your father used to carry you up here in his arms.

HOWARD   I know that, Willy, but—

WILLY   Your father came to me the day you were born and asked me what I thought of the name of Howard, may he rest in peace.

HOWARD   I appreciate that, Willy, but there just is no spot here for you. If I had a spot I'd slam you right in, but I just don't have a single, solitary spot.

He looks for his lighter. WILLY *has picked it up and gives it to him. Pause.*

WILLY [*with increasing anger*]   Howard, all I need to set my table is fifty dollars a week.
210 HOWARD   But where am I going to put you, kid?

WILLY   Look, it isn't a question of whether I can sell merchandise, is it?

HOWARD   No, but it's a business, kid, and everybody's gotta pull his own weight.

WILLY [*desperately*]   Just let me tell you a story, Howard—

HOWARD   'Cause you gotta admit, business is business.

WILLY [*angrily*]   Business is definitely business, but just listen for a minute. You don't understand this. When I was a boy—eighteen, nineteen—I was already on the road. And there was a question in my mind as to whether selling had a future for me. Because in those days I had a yearning to go to Alaska.
220 See, there were three gold strikes in one month in Alaska, and I felt like going out. Just for the ride, you might say.

HOWARD [*barely interested*]   Don't say.

WILLY   Oh, yeah, my father lived many years in Alaska. He was an adventurous man. We've got quite a little streak of self-reliance in our family. I thought I'd go out with my older brother and try to locate him, and maybe settle in the North with the old man. And I was almost decided to go, when I met a salesman in the Parker House. His name was Dave Singleman. And he was eighty-four years old, and he'd drummed merchandise in thirty-one states. And old Dave, he'd go up to his room, y'understand, put on his green
230 velvet slippers—I'll never forget—and pick up his phone and call the buyers, and without ever leaving his room, at the age of eighty-four, he made his living. And when I saw that, I realized that selling was the greatest career a man could want. 'Cause what could be more satisfying than to be able to go, at the age of eighty-four, into twenty or thirty different cities, and pick up a phone, and be remembered and loved and helped by so many different people? Do you know? when he died—and by the way he died the death of a salesman, in his green velvet slippers in the smoker of the New York, New Haven and Hartford, going into Boston—when he died, hundreds of

salesmen and buyers were at his funeral. Things were sad on a lotta trains for
240 months after that. [*He stands up.* HOWARD *has not looked at him.*] In those
days there was personality in it, Howard. There was respect, and comradeship, and gratitude in it. Today, it's all cut and dried, and there's no chance
for bringing friendship to bear—or personality. You see what I mean? They
don't know me any more.

HOWARD [*moving away, to the right*]   That's just the thing, Willy.

WILLY   If I had forty dollars a week—that's all I'd need. Forty dollars,
Howard.

HOWARD   Kid, I can't take blood from a stone, I—

WILLY [*desperation is on him now*]   Howard, the year Al Smith was nomi-
250 nated, your father came to me and—

HOWARD [*starting to go off*]   I've got to see some people, kid.

WILLY [*stopping him*]   I'm talking about your father! There were promises
made across this desk! You mustn't tell me you've got people to see—I put
thirty-four years into this firm, Howard, and now I can't pay my insurance!
You can't eat the orange and throw the peel away—a man is not a piece of
fruit! [*After a pause*] Now pay attention. Your father—in 1928 I had a big year.
I averaged a hundred and seventy dollars a week in commissions.

HOWARD [*impatiently*]   Now, Willy, you never averaged—

WILLY [*banging his hand on the desk*]   I averaged a hundred and seventy
260 dollars a week in the year of 1928! And your father came to me—or rather, I
was in the office here—it was right over this desk—and he put his hand on
my shoulder—

HOWARD [*getting up*]   You'll have to excuse me, Willy, I gotta see some
people. Pull yourself together. [*Going out*] I'll be back in a little while.

On HOWARD'*s exit, the light on his chair grows very bright and strange.*

WILLY   Pull myself together! What the hell did I say to him? My God, I was
yelling at him! How could I! [WILLY *breaks off, staring at the light, which
occupies the chair, animating it.*] Frank, Frank, don't you remember what
you told me that time? How you put your hand on my shoulder, and
Frank . . . [*He leans on the desk and as he speaks the dead man's name he
270 accidentally switches on the recorder, and instantly*]

HOWARD'S SON   ". . . of New York is Albany. The capital of Ohio is Cincin-
nati, the capital of Rhode Island is . . ." [*The recitation continues.*]

WILLY [*leaping away with fright, shouting*]   Ha! Howard! Howard! Howard!

HOWARD [*rushing in*]   What happened?

WILLY [*pointing at the machine, which continues nasally, childishly, with
the capital cities*]   Shut it off! Shut it off!

HOWARD [*pulling the plug out*]   Look, Willy . . .

WILLY [*pressing his hands to his eyes*]   I gotta get myself some coffee. I'll
get some coffee . . .

WILLY *starts to walk out.* HOWARD *stops him.*

280   HOWARD [*rolling up the cord*]   Willy, look . . .

WILLY   I'll go to Boston.

HOWARD   Willy, you can't go to Boston for us.

WILLY   Why can't I go?

HOWARD   I don't want you to represent us. I've been meaning to tell you for a long time now.

WILLY   Howard, are you firing me?

HOWARD   I think you need a good long rest, Willy.

WILLY   Howard—

HOWARD   And when you feel better, come back, and we'll see if we can

290 work something out.

WILLY   But I gotta earn money, Howard. I'm in no position—

HOWARD   Where are your sons? Why don't your sons give you a hand?

WILLY   They're working on a very big deal.

HOWARD   This is no time for false pride, Willy. You go to your sons and you tell them that you're tired. You've got two great boys, haven't you?

WILLY   Oh, no question, no question, but in the meantime . . .

HOWARD   Then that's that, heh?

WILLY   All right, I'll go to Boston tomorrow.

HOWARD   No, no.

300 WILLY   I can't throw myself on my sons. I'm not a cripple!

HOWARD   Look, kid, I'm busy this morning.

WILLY [*grasping* HOWARD*'s arm*]   Howard, you've got to let me go to Boston!

HOWARD [*hard, keeping himself under control*]   I've got a line of people to see this morning. Sit down, take five minutes, and pull yourself together, and then go home, will ya? I need the office, Willy. [*He starts to go, turns, remembering the recorder, starts to push off the table holding the recorder.*] Oh, yeah. Whenever you can this week, stop by and drop off the samples. You'll feel better, Willy, and then come back and we'll talk. Pull yourself together, kid, there's people outside.

HOWARD *exits, pushing the table off left.* WILLY *stares into space, exhausted. Now the music is heard—* BEN*'s music—first distantly, then closer, closer. As* WILLY *speaks,* BEN *enters from the right. He carries valise and umbrella.*

310   WILLY   Oh, Ben, how did you do it? What is the answer? Did you wind up the Alaska deal already?

BEN   Doesn't take much time if you know what you're doing. Just a short business trip. Boarding ship in an hour. Wanted to say good-by.

WILLY   Ben, I've got to talk to you.

BEN [*glancing at his watch*]   Haven't much time, William.

WILLY [*crossing the apron to Ben*]   Ben, nothing's working out. I don't know what to do.

BEN   Now, look here, William. I've bought timberland in Alaska and I need a man to look after things for me.

320   WILLY   God, timberland! Me and my boys in those grand outdoors!

BEN   You've a new continent at your doorstep, William. Get out of these cities, they're full of talk and time payments and courts of law. Screw on your fists and you can fight for a fortune up there.

WILLY   Yes, yes! Linda, Linda!

LINDA *enters as of old, with the wash.*

LINDA   Oh, you're back?

BEN   I haven't much time.

WILLY   No, wait! Linda, he's got a proposition for me in Alaska.

LINDA   But you've got—[*To* BEN] He's got a beautiful job here.

WILLY   But in Alaska, kid, I could—

330   LINDA   You're doing well enough, Willy!

BEN [*to* LINDA]   Enough for what, my dear?

LINDA [*frightened of* BEN *and angry at him*]   Don't say those things to him! Enough to be happy right here, right now. [*To* WILLY, *while* BEN *laughs*] Why must everybody conquer the world? You're well liked, and the boys love you, and someday—[*To* BEN]—why old man Wagner told him just the other day that if he keeps it up he'll be a member of the firm, didn't he, Willy?

WILLY   Sure, sure. I am building something with this firm, Ben, and if a man is building something he must be on the right track, mustn't he?

BEN   What are you building? Lay your hand on it. Where is it?

340   WILLY [*hesitantly*]   That's true, Linda, there's nothing.

LINDA   Why? [*To* BEN] There's a man eighty-four years old—

WILLY   That's right, Ben, that's right. When I look at that man I say, what is there to worry about?

BEN   Bah!

WILLY   It's true, Ben. All he has to do is go into any city, pick up the phone, and he's making his living and you know why?

BEN [*picking up his valise*]   I've got to go.

WILLY [*holding* BEN *back*]   Look at this boy!

BIFF, *in his high school sweater, enters carrying suitcase.* HAPPY *carries* BIFF*'s shoulder guards, gold helmet, and football pants.*

WILLY   Without a penny to his name, three great universities are begging
350 for him, and from there the sky's the limit, because it's not what you do, Ben. It's who you know and the smile on your face! It's contacts, Ben, contacts! The whole wealth of Alaska passes over the lunch table at the Commodore Hotel, and that's the wonder, the wonder of this country, that a man can end with diamonds here on the basis of being liked! [*He turns to* BIFF.] And that's why when you get out on that field today it's important. Because thousands of people will be rooting for you and loving you. [*To* BEN, *who has again begun to leave*] And Ben! when he walks into a business office his name will sound out like a bell and all the doors will open to him! I've seen it, Ben, I've seen it a thousand times! You can't feel it with your hand like timber, but
360 it's there!

BEN   Good-by, William.

WILLY   Ben, am I right? Don't you think I'm right? I value your advice.

BEN   There's a new continent at your doorstep, William. You could walk out rich. Rich! [*He is gone.*]

WILLY   We'll do it here, Ben! You hear me? We're gonna do it here!

Young BERNARD *rushes in. The gay music of the Boys is heard.*

BERNARD   Oh, gee, I was afraid you left already!

WILLY   Why? What time is it?

BERNARD   It's half-past one!

WILLY   Well, come on, everybody! Ebbets Field next stop! Where's the
370   pennants? [*He rushes through the wall-line of the kitchen and out into the living-room.*]

LINDA [*to* BIFF]   Did you pack fresh underwear?

BIFF [*who has been limbering up*]   I want to go!

BERNARD   Biff, I'm carrying your helmet, ain't I?

HAPPY   No, I'm carrying the helmet.

BERNARD   Oh, Biff, you promised me.

HAPPY   I'm carrying the helmet.

BERNARD   How am I going to get in the locker room?

LINDA   Let him carry the shoulder guards. [*She puts her coat and hat on in*
380   *the kitchen.*]

BERNARD   Can I, Biff? 'Cause I told everybody I'm going to be in the locker room.

HAPPY   In Ebbets Field it's the clubhouse.

BERNARD   I meant the clubhouse, Biff!

HAPPY   Biff!

BIFF [*grandly, after a slight pause*]   Let him carry the shoulder guards.

HAPPY [*as he gives* BERNARD *the shoulder guards*]   Stay close to us now.

WILLY *rushes in with the pennants.*

WILLY [*handing them out*]   Everybody wave when Biff comes out on the field. [HAPPY *and* BERNARD *run off.*] You set now, boy?

The music has died away.

390   BIFF   Ready to go, Pop. Every muscle is ready.

WILLY [*at the edge of the apron*]   You realize what this means?

BIFF   That's right, Pop.

WILLY [*feeling* BIFF*'s muscles*]   You're comin' home this afternoon captain of the All-Scholastic Championship Team of the City of New York.

BIFF   I got it, Pop. And remember, pal, when I take off my helmet, that touchdown is for you.

WILLY   Let's go! [*He is starting out, with his arm around* BIFF, *when* CHARLEY *enters, as of old, in knickers.*] I got no room for you, Charley.

CHARLEY   Room? For what?

400   WILLY   In the car.

CHARLEY   You goin' for a ride? I wanted to shoot some casino.

WILLY [*furiously*]   Casino! [*Incredulously*] Don't you realize what today is?

LINDA   Oh, he knows, Willy. He's just kidding you.

WILLY   That's nothing to kid about!

CHARLEY   No, Linda, what's goin' on?

LINDA   He's playing in Ebbets Field.

CHARLEY   Baseball in this weather?

WILLY   Don't talk to him. Come on, come on! [*He is pushing them out.*]

CHARLEY   Wait a minute, didn't you hear the news?

410   WILLY   What?

CHARLEY   Don't you listen to the radio? Ebbets Field just blew up.

WILLY   You go to hell! [CHARLEY *laughs. Pushing them out*] Come on, come on! We're late.

CHARLEY [*as they go*]   Knock a homer, Biff, knock a homer!

WILLY [*the last to leave, turning to* CHARLEY]   I don't think that was funny, Charley. This is the greatest day of his life.

CHARLEY   Willy, when are you going to grow up?

WILLY   Yeah, heh? When this game is over, Charley, you'll be laughing out the other side of your face. They'll be calling him another Red Grange.
420 Twenty-five thousand a year.

CHARLEY [*kidding*]   Is that so?

WILLY   Yeah, that's so.

CHARLEY   Well, then, I'm sorry, Willy. But tell me something.

WILLY   What?

CHARLEY   Who is Red Grange?

WILLY   Put up your hands. Goddam you, put up your hands!

CHARLEY, *chuckling, shakes his head and walks away, around the left corner of the stage.* WILLY *follows him. The music rises to a mocking frenzy.*

WILLY   Who the hell do you think you are, better than everybody else? You don't know everything, you big, ignorant, stupid . . . Put up your hands!

Light rises, on the right side of the forestage, on a small table in the reception room of CHARLEY's *office. Traffic sounds are heard.* BERNARD, *now mature, sits whistling to himself. A pair of tennis rackets and an overnight bag are on the floor beside him.*

WILLY [*offstage*]   What are you walking away for? Don't walk away! If
430 you're going to say something say it to my face! I know you laugh at me behind my back. You'll laugh out of the other side of your goddam face after this game. Touchdown! Touchdown! Eighty thousand people! Touchdown! Right between the goal posts.

BERNARD *is a quiet, earnest, but self-assured young man.* WILLY's *voice is coming from right upstage now.* BERNARD *lowers his feet off the table and listens.* JENNY, *his father's secretary, enters.*

JENNY [*distressed*]   Say, Bernard, will you go out in the hall?

BERNARD   What is that noise? Who is it?

JENNY   Mr. Loman. He just got off the elevator.

BERNARD [*getting up*]   Who's he arguing with?

JENNY   Nobody. There's nobody with him. I can't deal with him any more, and your father gets all upset everytime he comes. I've got a lot of typing to
440 do, and your father's waiting to sign it. Will you see him?

WILLY [*entering*]   Touchdown! Touch—[*He sees* JENNY.] Jenny, Jenny, good to see you. How're ya? Workin'? Or still honest?

JENNY   Fine. How've you been feeling?

WILLY   Not much any more, Jenny. Ha, ha! [*He is surprised to see the rackets.*]

BERNARD   Hello, Uncle Willy.

WILLY [*almost shocked*]   Bernard! Well, look who's here! [*He comes quickly, guiltily, to* BERNARD *and warmly shakes his hand.*]

BERNARD   How are you? Good to see you.
450 WILLY   What are you doing here?

BERNARD   Oh, just stopped off to see Pop. Get off my feet till my train leaves. I'm going to Washington in a few minutes.

WILLY   Is he in?

BERNARD   Yes, he's in his office with the accountants. Sit down.

WILLY [*sitting down*]   What're you going to do in Washington?

BERNARD   Oh, just a case I've got there, Willy.

WILLY   That so? [*indicating the rackets*] You going to play tennis there?

BERNARD   I'm staying with a friend who's got a court.

WILLY   Don't say. His own tennis court. Must be fine people, I bet.
460 BERNARD   They are, very nice. Dad tells me Biff's in town.

WILLY [*with a big smile*]   Yeah, Biff's in. Working on a very big deal, Bernard.

BERNARD   What's Biff doing?

WILLY   Well, he's been doing very big things in the West. But he decided to establish himself here. Very big. We're having dinner. Did I hear your wife had a boy?

BERNARD   That's right. Our second.

WILLY   Two boys! What do you know!

BERNARD   What kind of a deal has Biff got?
470 WILLY   Well, Bill Oliver—very big sporting-goods man—he wants Biff very badly. Called him in from the West. Long distance, carte blanche, special deliveries. Your friends have their own private tennis court?

BERNARD   You still with the old firm, Willy?

WILLY [*after a pause*]   I'm—I'm overjoyed to see how you made the grade, Bernard, overjoyed. It's an encouraging thing to see a young man really—really—Looks very good for Biff—very—[*He breaks off, then*] Bernard—[*He is so full of emotion, he breaks off again.*]

BERNARD   What is it, Willy?

WILLY [*small and alone*]   What—what's the secret?
480 BERNARD   What secret?

WILLY   How—how did you? Why didn't he ever catch on?

BERNARD   I wouldn't know that, Willy.

WILLY [*confidentially, desperately*]   You were his friend, his boyhood friend. There's something I don't understand about it. His life ended after that Ebbets Field game. From the age of seventeen, nothing good ever happened to him.

BERNARD   He never trained himself for anything.

WILLY   But he did, he did. After high school he took so many correspond-ence courses. Radio mechanics; television; God knows what, and never made

490   the slightest mark.

BERNARD [*taking off his glasses*]   Willy, do you want to talk candidly?

WILLY [*rising, faces Bernard*]   I regard you as a very brilliant man, Bernard. I value your advice.

BERNARD   Oh, the hell with the advice, Willy. I couldn't advise you. There's just one thing I've always wanted to ask you. When he was supposed to graduate, and the math teacher flunked him—

WILLY   Oh, that son-of-a-bitch ruined his life.

BERNARD   Yeah, but, Willy, all he had to do was go to summer school and make up that subject.

500   WILLY   That's right, that's right.

BERNARD   Did you tell him not to go to summer school?

WILLY   Me? I begged him to go. I ordered him to go!

BERNARD   Then why wouldn't he go?

WILLY   Why? Why! Bernard, that question has been trailing me like a ghost for the last fifteen years. He flunked the subject, and laid down and died like a hammer hit him!

BERNARD   Take it easy, kid.

WILLY   Let me talk to you—I got nobody to talk to. Bernard, Bernard, was it my fault? Y'see? It keeps going around in my mind, maybe I did something

510   to him. I got nothing to give him.

BERNARD   Don't take it so hard.

WILLY   Why did he lay down? What is the story there? You were his friend!

BERNARD   Willy, I remember, it was June, and our grades came out. And he'd flunked math.

WILLY   That son-of-a-bitch!

BERNARD   No, it wasn't right then. Biff just got very angry, I remember, and he was ready to enroll in summer school.

WILLY [*surprised*]   He was?

BERNARD   He wasn't beaten by it at all. But then, Willy, he disappeared

520   from the block for almost a month. And I got the idea that he'd gone up to New England to see you. Did he have a talk with you then?

WILLY *stares in silence.*

BERNARD   Willy?

WILLY [*with a strong edge of resentment in his voice*]   Yeah, he came to Boston. What about it?

BERNARD   Well, just that when he came back—I'll never forget this, it always mystifies me. Because I'd thought so well of Biff, even though he'd always taken advantage of me. I loved him, Willy, y'know? And he came back after that month and took his sneakers—remember those sneakers with "University of Virginia" printed on them? He was so proud of those, wore them
530 every day. And he took them down in the cellar, and burned them up in the furnace. We had a fist fight. It lasted at least half an hour. Just the two of us, punching each other down the cellar, and crying right through it. I've often thought of how strange it was that I knew he'd given up his life. What happened in Boston, Willy?

WILLY *looks at him as at an intruder.*

BERNARD   I just bring it up because you asked me.
WILLY [*angrily*]   Nothing. What do you mean, "What happened?" What's that got to do with anything?
BERNARD   Well, don't get sore.
WILLY   What are you trying to do, blame it on me? If a boy lays down is that
540 my fault?
BERNARD   Now, Willy, don't get—
WILLY   Well, don't—don't talk to me that way! What does that mean, "What happened?"

CHARLEY *enters. He is in his vest, and he carries a bottle of bourbon.*

CHARLEY   Hey, you're going to miss that train. [*He waves the bottle.*]
BERNARD   Yeah, I'm going. [*He takes the bottle.*] Thanks, Pop. [*He picks up his rackets and bag.*] Good-by, Willy, and don't worry about it. You know, "If at first you don't succeed . . ."
WILLY   Yes, I believe in that.
BERNARD   But sometimes, Willy, it's better for a man just to walk away.
550 WILLY   Walk away?
BERNARD   That's right.
WILLY   But if you can't walk away?
BERNARD [*after a slight pause*]   I guess that's when it's tough. [*Extending his hand*] Good-by, Willy.
WILLY [*shaking* BERNARD*'s hand*]   Good-by, boy.
CHARLEY [*an arm on* BERNARD*'s shoulder*]   How do you like this kid? Gonna argue a case in front of the Supreme Court.
BERNARD [*protesting*]   Pop!
WILLY [*genuinely shocked, pained, and happy*]   No! The Supreme Court!
560 BERNARD   I gotta run. 'By, Dad!
CHARLEY   Knock 'em dead, Bernard!

BERNARD *goes off.*

WILLY [*as* CHARLEY *takes out his wallet*]   The Supreme Court! And he didn't even mention it!

CHARLEY [*counting out money on the desk*]   He don't have to—he's gonna do it.

WILLY   And you never told him what to do, did you? You never took any interest in him.

CHARLEY   My salvation is that I never took any interest in anything. There's some money—fifty dollars. I got an accountant inside.

570   WILLY   Charley, look . . . [*With difficulty*] I got my insurance to pay. If you can manage it—I need a hundred and ten dollars.

CHARLEY *doesn't reply for a moment; merely stops moving.*

WILLY   I'd draw it from my bank but Linda would know, and I . . .

CHARLEY   Sit down, Willy.

WILLY [*moving toward the chair*]   I'm keeping an account of everything, remember. I'll pay every penny back. [*He sits.*]

CHARLEY   Now listen to me, Willy.

WILLY   I want you to know I appreciate . . .

CHARLEY [*sitting down on the table*]   Willy, what're you doin'? What the hell is goin' on in your head?

580   WILLY   Why? I'm simply . . .

CHARLEY   I offered you a job. You can make fifty dollars a week. And I won't send you on the road.

WILLY   I've got a job.

CHARLEY   Without pay? What kind of a job is a job without pay? [*He rises.*] Now, look, kid, enough is enough. I'm no genius but I know when I'm being insulted.

WILLY   Insulted!

CHARLEY   Why don't you want to work for me?

WILLY   What's the matter with you? I've got a job.

590   CHARLEY   Then what're you walkin' in here every week for?

WILLY [*getting up*]   Well, if you don't want me to walk in here—

CHARLEY   I am offering you a job.

WILLY   I don't want your goddam job!

CHARLEY   When the hell are you going to grow up?

WILLY [*furiously*]   You big ignoramus, if you say that to me again I'll rap you one! I don't care how big you are! [*He's ready to fight.*]

Pause.

CHARLEY [*kindly, going to him*]   How much do you need, Willy?

WILLY   Charley, I'm strapped. I'm strapped. I don't know what to do. I was just fired.

600   CHARLEY   Howard fired you?

WILLY   That snotnose. Imagine that? I named him. I named him Howard.

CHARLEY   Willy, when're you gonna realize that them things don't mean anything? You named him Howard, but you can't sell that. The only thing you got in this world is what you can sell. And the funny thing is that you're a salesman, and you don't know that.

WILLY   I've tried to think otherwise, I guess. I always felt that if a man was impressive, and well liked, that nothing—

CHARLEY   Why must everybody like you? Who liked J. P. Morgan? Was he impressive? In a Turkish bath he'd look like a butcher. But with his pockets 610 on he was very well liked. Now listen, Willy, I know you don't like me, and nobody can say I'm in love with you, but I'll give you a job because—just for the hell of it, put it that way. Now what do you say?

WILLY   I—I just can't work for you, Charley.

CHARLEY   What're you, jealous of me?

WILLY   I can't work for you, that's all, don't ask me why.

CHARLEY [*angered, takes out more bills*]   You been jealous of me all your life, you damned fool! Here, pay your insurance. [*He puts the money in* WILLY'*s hand.*]

WILLY   I'm keeping strict accounts.

620 CHARLEY   I've got some work to do. Take care of yourself. And pay your insurance.

WILLY [*moving to the right*]   Funny, y'know? After all the highways, and the trains, and the appointments, and the years, you end up worth more dead than alive.

CHARLEY   Willy, nobody's worth nothin' dead. [*After a slight pause*] Did you hear what I said?

WILLY *stands still, dreaming.*

CHARLEY   Willy!

WILLY   Apologize to Bernard for me when you see him. I didn't mean to argue with him. He's a fine boy. They're all fine boys, and they'll end up 630 big—all of them. Someday they'll all play tennis together. Wish me luck, Charley. He saw Bill Oliver today.

CHARLEY   Good luck.

WILLY [*on the verge of tears*]   Charley, you're the only friend I got. Isn't that a remarkable thing? [*He goes out.*]

CHARLEY   Jesus!

CHARLEY *stares after him a moment and follows. All light blacks out. Suddenly raucous music is heard, and a red glow rises behind the screen at right.* STANLEY, *a young waiter, appears, carrying a table, followed by* HAPPY, *who is carrying two chairs.*

STANLEY [*putting the table down*]   That's all right, Mr. Loman, I can handle it myself. [*He turns and takes the chairs from* HAPPY *and places them at the table.*]

HAPPY [*glancing around*]   Oh, this is better.

640 STANLEY   Sure, in the front there you're in the middle of all kinds of noise. Whenever you got a party, Mr. Loman, you just tell me and I'll put you back here. Y'know, there's a lotta people they don't like it private, because when they go out they like to see a lotta action around them because they're sick and tired to stay in the house by theirself. But I know you, you ain't from Hackensack. You know what I mean?

HAPPY [*sitting down*]   So, how's it coming, Stanley?

STANLEY   Ah, it's a dog's life. I only wish during the war they'd a took me in the Army. I coulda been dead by now.

HAPPY   My brother's back, Stanley.

650   STANLEY   Oh, he come back, heh? From the Far West.

HAPPY   Yeah, big cattle man, my brother, so treat him right. And my father's coming too.

STANLEY   Oh, your father too!

HAPPY   You got a couple of nice lobsters?

STANLEY   Hundred per cent, big.

HAPPY   I want them with claws.

STANLEY   Don't worry, I don't give you no mice. [HAPPY *laughs.*] How about some wine? It'll put a head on the meal.

HAPPY   No. You remember, Stanley, that recipe I brought you from over-

660 seas? With the champagne in it?

STANLEY   Oh, yeah, sure. I still got it tacked up yet in the kitchen. But that'll have to cost a buck apiece anyways.

HAPPY   That's all right.

STANLEY   What'd you, hit a number or somethin'?

HAPPY   No, it's a little celebration. My brother is—I think he pulled off a big deal today. I think we're going into business together.

STANLEY   Great! That's the best for you. Because a family business, you know what I mean?—that's the best.

HAPPY   That's what I think.

670   STANLEY   'Cause what's the difference? Somebody steals? It's in the family. Know what I mean? [*Sotto voce*] Like this bartender here. The boss is goin' crazy what kinda leak he's got in the cash register. You put it in but it don't come out.

HAPPY [*raising his head*]   Sh!

STANLEY   What?

HAPPY   You notice I wasn't lookin' right or left, was I?

STANLEY   No.

HAPPY   And my eyes are closed.

STANLEY   So what's the—

680   HAPPY   Strudel's comin'.

STANLEY [*catching on, looks around*]   Ah, no, there's no—

He breaks off as a furred, lavishly dressed GIRL *enters and sits at the next table. Both follow her with their eyes.*

STANLEY   Geez, how'd ya know?

HAPPY   I got radar or something. [*Staring directly at her profile*] Oooooooo . . . Stanley.

STANLEY   I think that's for you, Mr. Loman.

HAPPY   Look at that mouth. Oh God. And the binoculars.

STANLEY   Geez, you got a life, Mr. Loman.

HAPPY   Wait on her.

STANLEY [*going to the* GIRL*'s table*]   Would you like a menu, ma'am?

690   GIRL   I'm expecting someone, but I'd like a—

HAPPY   Why don't you bring her—excuse me, miss, do you mind? I sell champagne, and I'd like you to try my brand. Bring her a champagne, Stanley.

GIRL   That's awfully nice of you.

HAPPY   Don't mention it. It's all company money. [*He laughs.*]

GIRL   That's a charming product to be selling, isn't it?

HAPPY   Oh, gets to be like everything else. Selling is selling, y'know.

GIRL   I suppose.

HAPPY   You don't happen to sell, do you?

GIRL   No, I don't sell.

700   HAPPY   Would you object to a compliment from a stranger? You ought to be on a magazine cover.

GIRL   [*looking at him a little archly*]   I have been.

STANLEY *comes in with a glass of champagne.*

HAPPY   What'd I say before, Stanley? You see? She's a cover girl.

STANLEY   Oh, I could see, I could see.

HAPPY   [*to the* GIRL]   What magazine?

GIRL   Oh, a lot of them. [*She takes the drink.*] Thank you.

HAPPY   You know what they say in France, don't you? "Champagne is the drink of the complexion"—Hya, Biff!

BIFF *has entered and sits with* HAPPY.

BIFF   Hello, kid. Sorry I'm late.

710   HAPPY   I just got here. Uh, Miss—?

GIRL   Forsythe.

HAPPY   Miss Forsythe, this is my brother.

BIFF   Is Dad here?

HAPPY   His name is Biff. You might've heard of him. Great football player.

GIRL   Really? What team?

HAPPY   Are you familiar with football?

GIRL   No, I'm afraid I'm not.

HAPPY   Biff is quarterback with the New York Giants.

GIRL   Well, that is nice, isn't it? [*She drinks.*]

720   HAPPY   Good health.

GIRL   I'm happy to meet you.

HAPPY   That's my name. Hap. It's really Harold, but at West Point they called me Happy.

GIRL   [*now really impressed*]   Oh, I see. How do you do? [*She turns her profile.*]

BIFF   Isn't Dad coming?

HAPPY   You want her?

BIFF   Oh, I could never make that.

HAPPY   I remember the time that idea would never come into your head.

730 Where's the old confidence, Biff?

BIFF   I just saw Oliver—

HAPPY   Wait a minute. I've got to see that old confidence again. Do you want her? She's on call.

BIFF   Oh, no. [*He turns to look at the* GIRL.]

HAPPY   I'm telling you. Watch this. [*Turning to the* GIRL.] Honey? [*She turns to him.*] Are you busy?

GIRL   Well, I am . . . but I could make a phone call.

HAPPY   Do that, will you, honey? And see if you can get a friend. We'll be here for a while. Biff is one of the greatest football players in the country.

740   GIRL [*standing up*]   Well, I'm certainly happy to meet you.

HAPPY   Come back soon.

GIRL   I'll try.

HAPPY   Don't try, honey, try hard.

The GIRL *exits.* STANLEY *follows, shaking his head in bewildered admiration.*

HAPPY   Isn't that a shame now? A beautiful girl like that? That's why I can't get married. There's not a good woman in a thousand. New York is loaded with them, kid!

BIFF   Hap, look—

HAPPY   I told you she was on call!

BIFF [*strangely unnerved*]   Cut it out, will ya? I want to say something to 750 you.

HAPPY   Did you see Oliver?

BIFF   I saw him all right. Now look, I want to tell Dad a couple of things and I want you to help me.

HAPPY   What? Is he going to back you?

BIFF   Are you crazy? You're out of your goddam head, you know that?

HAPPY   Why? What happened?

BIFF [*breathlessly*]   I did a terrible thing today, Hap. It's been the strangest day I ever went through. I'm all numb, I swear.

HAPPY   You mean he wouldn't see you?

760   BIFF   Well, I waited six hours for him, see? All day. Kept sending my name in. Even tried to date his secretary so she'd get me to him, but no soap.

HAPPY   Because you're not showin' the old confidence, Biff. He remembered you, didn't he?

BIFF [*stopping* HAPPY *with a gesture*]   Finally, about five o'clock, he comes out. Didn't remember who I was or anything. I felt like such an idiot, Hap.

HAPPY   Did you tell him my Florida idea?

BIFF   He walked away. I saw him for one minute. I got so mad I could've torn the walls down! How the hell did I ever get the idea I was a salesman there? I even believed myself that I'd been a salesman for him! And then he 770 gave me one look and—I realized what a ridiculous lie my whole life has been! We've been talking in a dream for fifteen years, I was a shipping clerk.

HAPPY   What'd you do?

BIFF [*with great tension and wonder*]   Well, he left, see. And the secretary went out. I was all alone in the waiting-room. I don't know what came over me, Hap. The next thing I know I'm in his office—paneled walls, everything. I can't explain it. I—Hap, I took his fountain pen.

HAPPY   Geez, did he catch you?

BIFF   I ran out. I ran down all eleven flights. I ran and ran and ran.

HAPPY   That was an awful dumb—what'd you do that for?

780   BIFF [*agonized*]   I don't know, I just—wanted to take something, I don't know. You gotta help me, Hap. I'm gonna tell Pop.

HAPPY   You crazy? What for?

BIFF   Hap, he's got to understand that I'm not the man somebody lends that kind of money to. He thinks I've been spiting him all these years and it's eating him up.

HAPPY   That's just it. You tell him something nice.

BIFF   I can't.

HAPPY   Say you got a lunch date with Oliver tomorrow.

BIFF   So what do I do tomorrow?

790   HAPPY   You leave the house tomorrow and come back at night and say Oliver is thinking it over. And he thinks it over for a couple of weeks, and gradually it fades away and nobody's the worse.

BIFF   But it'll go on forever!

HAPPY   Dad is never so happy as when he's looking forward to something!

WILLY *enters.*

HAPPY   Hello, scout!

WILLY   Gee, I haven't been here in years!

STANLEY *has followed* WILLY *in and sets a chair for him.* STANLEY *starts off but* HAPPY *stops him.*

HAPPY   Stanley!

STANLEY *stands by, waiting for an order.*

BIFF [*going to* WILLY *with guilt, as to an invalid*]   Sit down, Pop. You want a drink?

800   WILLY   Sure, I don't mind.

BIFF   Let's get a load on.

WILLY   You look worried.

BIFF   N-no. [*To* STANLEY.] Scotch all around. Make it doubles.

STANLEY   Doubles, right. [*He goes.*]

WILLY   You had a couple already, didn't you?

BIFF   Just a couple, yeah.

WILLY   Well, what happened, boy? [*Nodding affirmatively, with a smile*] Everything go all right?

BIFF [*takes a breath, then reaches out and grasps* WILLY*'s hand*]   Pal . . .

810   [*He is smiling bravely, and* WILLY *is smiling too.*] I had an experience today.

HAPPY   Terrific, Pop.

WILLY   That so? What happened?

BIFF [*high, slightly alcoholic, above the earth*]   I'm going to tell you everything from first to last. It's been a strange day. [*Silence. He looks around, composes himself as best he can, but his breath keeps breaking the rhythm of his voice.*] I had to wait quite a while for him, and—

WILLY   Oliver?

BIFF   Yeah, Oliver. All day, as a matter of cold fact. And a lot of—instances—facts, Pop, facts about my life came back to me. Who was it, Pop? Who ever said

820   I was a salesman with Oliver?

WILLY   Well, you were.

BIFF   No, Dad, I was a shipping clerk.

WILLY   But you were practically—

BIFF [*with determination*]   Dad, I don't know who said it first, but I was never a salesman for Bill Oliver.

WILLY   What're you talking about?

BIFF   Let's hold on to the facts tonight, Pop. We're not going to get anywhere bullin' around. I was a shipping clerk.

WILLY [*angrily*]   All right, now listen to me—

830   BIFF   Why don't you let me finish?

WILLY   I'm not interested in stories about the past or any crap of that kind because the woods are burning, boys, you understand? There's a big blaze going on all around. I was fired today.

BIFF [*shocked*]   How could you be?

WILLY   I was fired, and I'm looking for a little good news to tell your mother, because the woman has waited and the woman has suffered. The gist of it is that I haven't got a story left in my head, Biff. So don't give me a lecture about facts and aspects. I am not interested. Now what've you got to say to me?

STANLEY *enters with three drinks. They wait until he leaves.*

840   WILLY   Did you see Oliver?

BIFF   Jesus, Dad!

WILLY   You mean you didn't go up there?

HAPPY   Sure he went up there.

BIFF   I did.—I saw him. How could they fire you?

WILLY [*on the edge of his chair*]   What kind of a welcome did he give you?

BIFF   He won't even let you work on commission?

WILLY   I'm out! [*Driving*] So tell me, he gave you a warm welcome?

HAPPY   Sure, Pop, sure!

850   BIFF [*driven*]   Well, it was kind of—

WILLY   I was wondering if he'd remember you. [*To* HAPPY] Imagine, man doesn't see him for ten, twelve years and gives him that kind of a welcome!

HAPPY   Damn right!

BIFF [*trying to return to the offensive*]   Pop, look—

WILLY   You know why he remembered you, don't you? Because you impressed him in those days.

BIFF   Let's talk quietly and get this down to the facts, huh?

WILLY [*as though* BIFF *had been interrupting*]   Well, what happened?
860 It's great news, Biff. Did he take you into his office or'd you talk in the
waiting-room?

BIFF   Well, he came in, see, and—

WILLY [*with a big smile*]   What'd he say? Betcha he threw his arm around
you.

BIFF   Well, he kinda—

WILLY   He's a fine man. [*To* HAPPY] Very hard man to see, y'know.

HAPPY [*agreeing*]   Oh, I know.

WILLY [*to* BIFF]   Is that where you had the drinks?

BIFF   Yeah, he gave me a couple of—no, no!

870 HAPPY [*cutting in*]   He told him my Florida idea.

WILLY   Don't interrupt. [*To* BIFF] How'd he react to the Florida idea?

BIFF   Dad, will you give me a minute to explain?

WILLY   I've been waiting for you to explain since I sat down here! What
happened? He took you into his office and what?

BIFF   Well—I talked. And—and he listened, see.

WILLY   Famous for the way he listens, y'know. What was his answer?

BIFF   His answer was—[*He breaks off, suddenly angry.*] Dad, you're not
letting me tell you what I want to tell you!

WILLY [*accusing, angered*]   You didn't see him, did you?

880 BIFF   I did see him!

WILLY   What'd you insult him or something? You insulted him, didn't you?

BIFF   Listen, will you let me out of it, will you just let me out of it!

HAPPY   What the hell!

WILLY   Tell me what happened!

BIFF [*to* HAPPY]   I can't talk to him!

*A single trumpet note jars the ear. The light of green leaves stains the house, which
holds the air of night and a dream.* YOUNG BERNARD *enters and knocks on the door of
the house.*

YOUNG BERNARD [*frantically*]   Mrs. Loman, Mrs. Loman!

HAPPY   Tell him what happened!

BIFF [*to* HAPPY]   Shut up and leave me alone!

890 WILLY   No, no! You had to go and flunk math!

BIFF   What math? What're you talking about?

YOUNG BERNARD   Mrs. Loman, Mrs. Loman!

LINDA *appears in the house, as of old.*

WILLY [*wildly*]   Math, math, math!

BIFF   Take it easy, Pop!

YOUNG BERNARD   Mrs. Loman!

WILLY [*furiously*]   If you hadn't flunked you'd've been set by now!

BIFF   Now, look, I'm gonna tell you what happened, and you're going to listen to me.

YOUNG BERNARD   Mrs. Loman!

900   BIFF   I waited six hours—

HAPPY   What the hell are you saying?

BIFF   I kept sending in my name but he wouldn't see me. So finally he . . .

He continues unheard as light fades low on the restaurant.

YOUNG BERNARD   Biff flunked math!

LINDA   No!

YOUNG BERNARD   Birnbaum flunked him! They won't graduate him!

LINDA   But they have to. He's gotta go to the university. Where is he? Biff! Biff!

YOUNG BERNARD   No, he left. He went to Grand Central.

910   LINDA   Grand—You mean he went to Boston!

YOUNG BERNARD   Is Uncle Willy in Boston?

LINDA   Oh, maybe Willy can talk to the teacher. Oh, the poor, poor boy!

Light on house area snaps out.

BIFF [*at the table, now audible, holding up a gold fountain pen*]   . . . so I'm washed up with Oliver, you understand? Are you listening to me?

WILLY [*at a loss*]   Yeah, sure. If you hadn't flunked—

BIFF   Flunked what? What're you talking about?

WILLY   Don't blame everything on me! I didn't flunk math—you did! What pen?

HAPPY   That was awful dumb, Biff, a pen like that is worth—

920   WILLY [*seeing the pen for the first time*]   You took Oliver's pen?

BIFF [*weakening*]   Dad, I just explained it to you.

WILLY   You stole Bill Oliver's fountain pen!

BIFF   I didn't exactly steal it! That's just what I've been explaining to you!

HAPPY   He had it in his hand and just then Oliver walked in, so he got nervous and stuck it in his pocket!

WILLY   My God, Biff!

BIFF   I never intended to do it, Dad!

OPERATOR'S VOICE   Standish Arms, good evening!

WILLY [*shouting*]   I'm not in my room!

930   BIFF [*frightened*]   Dad, what's the matter? [*He and* HAPPY *stand up.*]

OPERATOR   Ringing Mr. Loman for you!

WILLY   I'm not there, stop it!

BIFF [*horrified, gets down on one knee before* WILLY]   Dad, I'll make good, I'll make good. [WILLY *tries to get to his feet.* BIFF *holds him down.*] Sit down now.

WILLY   No, you're no good, you're no good for anything.

BIFF   I am, Dad, I'll find something else, you understand? Now don't worry about anything. [*He holds up* WILLY*'s face.*] Talk to me, Dad.

OPERATOR   Mr. Loman does not answer. Shall I page him?

940   WILLY [*attempting to stand, as though to rush and silence the* OPERATOR] No, no, no!

HAPPY   He'll strike something, Pop.

WILLY   No, no . . .

BIFF [*desperately, standing over* WILLY]   Pop, listen! Listen to me! I'm telling you something good. Oliver talked to his partner about the Florida idea. You listening? He—he talked to his partner, and he came to me . . . I'm going to be all right, you hear? Dad, listen to me, he said it was just a question of the amount!

WILLY   Then you . . . got it?

950   HAPPY   He's gonna be terrific, Pop!

WILLY [*trying to stand*]   Then you got it, haven't you? You got it! You got it!

BIFF [*agonized, holds* WILLY *down*]   No, no. Look, Pop. I'm supposed to have lunch with them tomorrow. I'm just telling you this so you'll know that I can still make an impression, Pop. And I'll make good somewhere, but I can't go tomorrow, see?

WILLY   Why not? You simply—

BIFF   But the pen, Pop!

WILLY   You give it to him and tell him it was an oversight!

HAPPY   Sure, have lunch tomorrow!

960   BIFF   I can't say that—

WILLY   You were doing a crossword puzzle and accidentally used his pen!

BIFF   Listen, kid, I took those balls years ago, now I walk in with his fountain pen? That clinches it, don't you see? I can't face him like that! I'll try elsewhere.

PAGE'S VOICE   Paging Mr. Loman!

WILLY   Don't you want to be anything?

BIFF   Pop, how can I go back?

WILLY   You don't want to be anything, is that what's behind it?

BIFF [*now angry at* WILLY *for not crediting his sympathy*]   Don't take it that
970   way! You think it was easy walking into that office after what I'd done to him? A team of horses couldn't have dragged me back to Bill Oliver!

WILLY   Then why'd you go?

BIFF   Why did I go? Why did I go! Look at you! Look at what's become of you!

Off left, THE WOMAN *laughs.*

WILLY   Biff, you're going to go to that lunch tomorrow, or—

BIFF   I can't go. I've got no appointment!

HAPPY   Biff, for . . . !

WILLY   Are you spiting me?

BIFF   Don't take it that way! Goddammit!

980   WILLY [*strikes* BIFF *and falters away from the table*] You rotten little
louse! Are you spiting me?

THE WOMAN   Someone's at the door, Willy!

BIFF   I'm no good, can't you see what I am?

HAPPY [*separating them*]   Hey, you're in a restaurant! Now cut it out, both
of you! [*The girls enter.*] Hello, girls, sit down.

THE WOMAN *laughs, off left.*

MISS FORSYTHE   I guess we might as well. This is Letta.

THE WOMAN   Willy, are you going to wake up?

BIFF [*ignoring* WILLY]   How're ya, miss, sit down. What do you drink?

MISS FORSYTHE   Letta might not be able to stay long.

990   LETTA   I gotta get up very early tomorrow. I got jury duty. I'm so excited!
Were you fellows ever on a jury?

BIFF   No, but I been in front of them! [*The girls laugh.*] This is my father.

LETTA   Isn't he cute? Sit down with us, Pop.

HAPPY   Sit him down, Biff!

BIFF [*going to him*]   Come on, slugger, drink us under the table. To hell
with it! Come on, sit down, pal.

On BIFF*'s last insistence,* WILLY *is about to sit.*

THE WOMAN [*now urgently*]   Willy, are you going to answer the door!

THE WOMAN*'s call pulls* WILLY *back. He starts right, befuddled.*

BIFF   Hey, where are you going?

WILLY   Open the door.

1000   BIFF   The door?

WILLY   The washroom . . . the door . . . where's the door?

BIFF [*leading* WILLY *to the left*]   Just go straight down.

WILLY *moves left.*

THE WOMAN   Willy, Willy, are you going to get up, get up, get up, get up?

WILLY *exits left.*

LETTA   I think it's sweet you bring your daddy along.

MISS FORSYTHE   Oh, he isn't really your father!

BIFF [*at left, turning to her resentfully*]   Miss Forsythe, you've just seen a
prince walk by. A fine, troubled prince. A hard-working, unappreciated
prince. A pal, you understand? A good companion. Always for his boys.

LETTA   That's so sweet.

1010   HAPPY   Well, girls, what's the program? We're wasting time. Come on, Biff.
Gather round. Where would you like to go?

BIFF   Why don't you do something for him?

HAPPY   Me!

BIFF   Don't you give a damn for him, Hap?

HAPPY   What're you talking about? I'm the one who—

BIFF   I sense it, you don't give a good goddam about him. [*He takes the rolled-up hose from his pocket and puts it on the table in front of* HAPPY.] Look what I found in the cellar, for Christ's sake. How can you bear to let it go on?

HAPPY   Me? Who goes away? Who runs off and—

1020   BIFF   Yeah, but he doesn't mean anything to you. You could help him—I can't! Don't you understand what I'm talking about? He's going to kill him-self, don't you know that?

HAPPY   Don't I know it! Me!

BIFF   Hap, help him! Jesus . . . help him . . . Help me, help me, I can't bear to look at his face! [*Ready to weep, he hurries out, up right.*]

HAPPY [*starting after him*]   Where are you going?

MISS FORSYTHE   What's he so mad about?

HAPPY   Come on, girls, we'll catch up with him.

MISS FORSYTHE [*as* HAPPY *pushes her out*]   Say, I don't like that temper of his!

1030   HAPPY   He's just a little overstrung, he'll be all right!

WILLY [*off left, as* THE WOMAN *laughs*]   Don't answer! Don't answer!

LETTA   Don't you want to tell your father—

HAPPY   No, that's not my father. He's just a guy. Come on, we'll catch Biff, and, honey, we're going to paint this town! Stanley, where's the check! Hey, Stanley!

They exit. STANLEY *looks toward left.*

STANLEY [*calling to* HAPPY *indignantly*]   Mr. Loman! Mr. Loman!

STANLEY *picks up a chair and follows them off. Knocking is heard off left.* THE WOMAN *enters, laughing.* WILLY *follows her. She is in a black slip; he is buttoning his shirt. Raw, sensuous music accompanies their speech.*

WILLY   Will you stop laughing? Will you stop?

THE WOMAN   Aren't you going to answer the door? He'll wake the whole hotel.

1040   WILLY   I'm not expecting anybody.

THE WOMAN   Whyn't you have another drink, honey, and stop being so damn self-centered?

WILLY   I'm so lonely.

THE WOMAN   You know you ruined me, Willy? From now on, whenever you come to the office, I'll see that you go right through to the buyers. No waiting at my desk any more, Willy. You ruined me.

WILLY   That's nice of you to say that.

THE WOMAN   Gee, you are self-centered! Why so sad? You are the saddest, self-centeredest soul I ever did see-saw. [*She laughs.*] [*He kisses her.*] Come 1050   on inside, drummer boy. It's silly to be dressing in the middle of the night. [*As knocking is heard*] Aren't you going to answer the door?

WILLY   They're knocking on the wrong door.

THE WOMAN   But I felt the knocking. And he heard us talking in here. Maybe the hotel's on fire!

WILLY [*his terror rising*]   It's a mistake.

THE WOMAN   Then tell him to go away!

WILLY   There's nobody there.

THE WOMAN   It's getting on my nerves, Willy. There's somebody standing out there and it's getting on my nerves!

1060   WILLY [*pushing her away from him*]   All right, stay in the bathroom here, and don't come out. I think there's a law in Massachusetts about it, so don't come out. It may be that new room clerk. He looked very mean. So don't come out. It's a mistake, there's no fire.

The knocking is heard again. He takes a few steps away from her, and she vanishes into the wing. The light follows him, and now he is facing YOUNG BIFF, *who carries a suitcase.* BIFF *steps toward him. The music is gone.*

BIFF   Why didn't you answer?

WILLY   Biff! What are you doing in Boston?

BIFF   Why didn't you answer? I've been knocking for five minutes, I called you on the phone—

WILLY   I just heard you. I was in the bathroom and had the door shut. Did anything happen home?

1070   BIFF   Dad—I let you down.

WILLY   What do you mean?

BIFF   Dad . . .

WILLY   Biffo, what's this about? [*Putting his arm around* BIFF] Come on, let's go downstairs and get you a malted.

BIFF   Dad, I flunked math.

WILLY   Not for the term?

BIFF   The term. I haven't got enough credits to graduate.

WILLY   You mean to say Bernard wouldn't give you the answers?

BIFF   He did, he tried, but I only got a sixty-one.

1080   WILLY   And they wouldn't give you four points?

BIFF   Birnbaum refused absolutely. I begged him, Pop, but he won't give me those points. You gotta talk to him before they close the school. Because if he saw the kind of man you are, and you just talked to him in your way, I'm sure he'd come through for me. The class came right before practice, see, and I didn't go enough. Would you talk to him? He'd like you, Pop. You know the way you could talk.

WILLY   You're on. We'll drive right back.

BIFF   Oh, Dad, good work! I'm sure he'll change it for you!

WILLY   Go downstairs and tell the clerk I'm checkin' out. Go right down.

1090   BIFF   Yes, Sir! See, the reason he hates me, Pop—one day he was late for class so I got up at the blackboard and imitated him. I crossed my eyes and talked with a lithp.

WILLY [*laughing*]   You did? The kids like it?

BIFF   They nearly died laughing!

WILLY   Yeah? What'd you do?

BIFF   The thquare root of thixthy twee is . . . [WILLY *bursts out laughing;* BIFF *joins him.*] And in the middle of it he walked in!

WILLY *laughs and* THE WOMAN *joins in offstage.*

WILLY [*without hesitation*]   Hurry downstairs and—

BIFF   Somebody in there?

1100   WILLY   No, that was next door.

BIFF   Somebody got in your bathroom!

THE WOMAN *laughs offstage.*

WILLY   No, it's the next room, there's a party—

THE WOMAN [*enters, laughing. She lisps this.*]   Can I come in? There's something in the bathtub, Willy, and it's moving!

WILLY *looks at* BIFF, *who is staring open-mouthed and horrified at* THE WOMAN.

WILLY   Ah—you better go back to your room. They must be finished painting by now. They're painting her room so I let her take a shower here. Go back, go back . . . [*He pushes her.*]

THE WOMAN [*resisting*]   But I've got to get dressed, Willy, I can't—

WILLY   Get out of here! Go back, go back . . . [*Suddenly striving for the* 1110 *ordinary*] This is Miss Francis, Biff, she's a buyer. They're painting her room. Go back, Miss Francis, go back . . .

THE WOMAN   But my clothes, I can't go out naked in the hall!

WILLY [*pushing her offstage*]   Get outa here! Go back, go back!

BIFF *slowly sits down on his suitcase as the argument continues offstage.*

THE WOMAN   Where's my stockings? You promised me stockings, Willy!

WILLY   I have no stockings here!

THE WOMAN   You had two boxes of size nine sheers for me, and I want them!

WILLY   Here, for God's sake, will you get outa here!

THE WOMAN [*enters holding a box of stockings*]   I just hope there's nobody 1120 in the hall. That's all I hope. [*To* BIFF] Are you football or baseball?

BIFF   Football.

THE WOMAN [*angry, humiliated*]   That's me too. G'night. [*She snatches her clothes from* WILLY, *and walks out.*]

WILLY [*after a pause*]   Well, better get going. I want to get to the school first thing in the morning. Get my suits out of the closet. I'll get my valise. [BIFF *doesn't move.*] What's the matter? [BIFF *remains motionless, tears falling.*] She's a buyer. Buys for J. H. Simmons. She lives down the hall—they're painting. You don't imagine—[*He breaks off. After a pause*] Now listen, pal, she's just a buyer. She sees merchandise in her room and they have to keep it

1130 looking just so . . . [*Pause. Assuming command*] All right, get my suits. [BIFF *doesn't move.*] Now stop crying and do as I say. I gave you an order. Biff, I gave you an order! Is that what you do when I give you an order? How dare you cry! [*Putting his arm around* BIFF] Now look, Biff, when you grow up you'll under-stand about these things. You mustn't—you mustn't overemphasize a thing like this. I'll see Birnbaum first thing in the morning.

BIFF   Never mind.

WILLY [*getting down beside* BIFF]   Never mind! He's going to give you those points. I'll see to it.

BIFF   He wouldn't listen to you.

1140   WILLY   He certainly will listen to me. You need those points for the U. of Virginia.

BIFF   I'm not going there.

WILLY   Heh? If I can't get him to change that mark you'll make it up in summer school. You've got all summer to—

BIFF [*his weeping breaking from him*]   Dad . . .

WILLY [*infected by it*]   Oh, my boy . . .

BIFF   Dad . . .

WILLY   She's nothing to me, Biff. I was lonely, I was terribly lonely.

BIFF   You—you gave her Mama's stockings! [*His tears break through and*
1150 *he rises to go.*]

WILLY [*grabbing for* BIFF]   I gave you an order!

BIFF   Don't touch me, you—liar!

WILLY   Apologize for that!

BIFF   You fake! You phony little fake! You fake! [*Overcome, he turns quickly and weeping fully goes out with his suitcase.* WILLY *is left on the floor on his knees.*]

WILLY   I gave you an order! Biff, come back here or I'll beat you! Come back here! I'll whip you!

STANLEY *comes quickly in from the right and stands in front of* WILLY.

WILLY [*shouts at* STANLEY]   I gave you an order . . .
1160   STANLEY   Hey, let's pick it up, pick it up, Mr. Loman. [*He helps* WILLY *to his feet.*] Your boys left with the chippies. They said they'll see you home.

A SECOND WAITER *watches some distance away.*

WILLY   But we were supposed to have dinner together.

Music is heard, WILLY*'s theme.*

STANLEY   Can you make it?

WILLY   I'll—sure, I can make it. [*Suddenly concerned about his clothes*] Do I—I look all right?

STANLEY   Sure, you look all right. [*He flicks a speck off* WILLY*'s lapel.*]

WILLY   Here—here's a dollar.

STANLEY   Oh, your son paid me. It's all right.

WILLY [*putting it in* STANLEY'*s hand*]   No, take it. You're a good boy.

1170   STANLEY   Oh, no, you don't have to . . .

WILLY   Here—here's some more, I don't need it any more. [*After a slight pause*] Tell me—is there a seed store in the neighborhood?

STANLEY   Seeds? You mean like to plant?

As WILLY *turns,* STANLEY *slips the money back into his jacket pocket.*

WILLY   Yes. Carrots, peas . . .

STANLEY   Well, there's hardware stores on Sixth Avenue, but it may be too late now.

WILLY [*anxiously*]   Oh, I'd better hurry. I've got to get some seeds. [*He starts off to the right.*] I've got to get some seeds, right away. Nothing's planted. I don't have a thing in the ground.

WILLY *hurries out as the light goes down.* STANLEY *moves over to the right after him, watches him off. The other waiter has been staring at* WILLY.

1180   STANLEY [*to the* WAITER]   Well, whatta you looking at?

The WAITER *picks up the chairs and moves off right.* STANLEY *takes the table and follows him. The light fades on this area. There is a long pause, the sound of the flute coming over. The light gradually rises on the kitchen, which is empty.* HAPPY *appears at the door of the house, followed by* BIFF. HAPPY *is carrying a large bunch of long-stemmed roses. He enters the kitchen, looks around for* LINDA. *Not seeing her, he turns to* BIFF, *who is just outside the house door, and makes a gesture with his hands, indicating "Not here, I guess." He looks into the living-room and freezes. Inside,* LINDA, *unseen, is seated,* WILLY'*s coat on her lap. She rises ominously and quietly and moves toward Happy, who backs up into the kitchen, afraid.*

HAPPY   Hey, what're you doing up? [LINDA *says nothing but moves toward him implacably.*] Where's Pop? [*He keeps backing to the right, and now* LINDA *is in full view in the doorway to the living-room.*] Is he sleeping?

LINDA   Where were you?

HAPPY [*trying to laugh it off*]   We met two girls, Mom, very fine types. Here, we brought you some flowers. [*Offering them to her*] Put them in your room, Ma.

She knocks them to the floor at BIFF'*s feet. He has now come inside and closed the door behind him. She stares at* BIFF, *silent.*

HAPPY   Now what'd you do that for? Mom, I want you to have some flowers—

1190   LINDA [*cutting* HAPPY *off, violently to* BIFF]   Don't you care whether he lives or dies?

HAPPY [*going to the stairs*]   Come upstairs, Biff.

BIFF [*with a flare of disgust, to* HAPPY]   Go away from me! [*To* LINDA] What do you mean, lives or dies? Nobody's dying around here, pal.

LINDA   Get out of my sight! Get out of here!

BIFF   I wanna see the boss.

LINDA   You're not going near him!

BIFF   Where is he? [*He moves into the living-room and* LINDA *follows.*]

1200   LINDA [*shouting after* BIFF]   You invite him for dinner. He looks forward to it all day—[BIFF *appears in his parents' bedroom, looks around, and exits*]—and then you desert him there. There's no stranger you'd do that to!

HAPPY   Why? He had a swell time with us. Listen, when I—[LINDA *comes back into the kitchen.*]—desert him I hope I don't outlive the day!

LINDA   Get out of here!

HAPPY   Now look, Mom . . .

LINDA   Did you have to go to women tonight? You and your lousy rotten whores!

BIFF *re-enters the kitchen.*

HAPPY   Mom, all we did was follow Biff around trying to cheer him up! [*To* BIFF] Boy, what a night you gave me!

1210   LINDA   Get out of here, both of you, and don't come back! I don't want you tormenting him any more. Go on now, get your things together! [*To* BIFF] You can sleep in his apartment. [*She starts to pick up the flowers and stops herself.*] Pick up this stuff, I'm not your maid any more. Pick it up, you bum, you!

HAPPY *turns his back to her in refusal.* BIFF *slowly moves over and gets down on his knees, picking up the flowers.*

LINDA   You're a pair of animals! Not one, not another living soul would have had the cruelty to walk out on that man in a restaurant!

BIFF [*not looking at her*]   Is that what he said?

LINDA   He didn't have to say anything. He was so humiliated he nearly limped when he came in.

HAPPY   But, Mom, he had a great time with us—

1220   BIFF [*cutting him off violently*]   Shut up!

Without another word, HAPPY *goes upstairs.*

LINDA   You! You didn't even go in to see if he was all right!

BIFF [*still on the floor in front of* LINDA, *the flowers in his hand; with self-loathing*]   No. Didn't. Didn't do a damned thing. How do you like that, heh? Left him babbling in a toilet.

LINDA   You louse. You . . .

BIFF   Now you hit it on the nose! [*He gets up, throws the flowers in the wastebasket.*] The scum of the earth, and you're looking at him!

LINDA   Get out of here!

BIFF   I gotta talk to the boss, Mom. Where is he?

1230   LINDA   You're not going near him. Get out of this house!

BIFF [*with absolute assurance, determination*]   No. We're gonna have an abrupt conversation, him and me.

LINDA   You're not talking to him!

Hammering is heard from outside the house, off right. BIFF *turns toward the noise.*

LINDA [*suddenly pleading*]   Will you please leave him alone?

BIFF   What's he doing out there?

LINDA   He's planting the garden!

BIFF [*quietly*]   Now? Oh, my God!

BIFF *moves outside,* LINDA *following. The light dies down on them and comes up on the center of the apron as* WILLY *walks into it. He is carrying a flashlight, a hoe, and a handful of seed packets. He raps the top of the hoe sharply to fix it firmly, and then moves to the left, measuring off the distance with his foot. He holds the flashlight to look at the seed packets, reading off the instructions. He is in the blue of night.*

WILLY   Carrots . . . quarter-inch apart. Rows . . . one-foot rows. [*He measures it off.*] One foot. [*He puts down a package and measures off.*]
1240   Beets. [*He puts down another package and measures again.*] Lettuce. [*He reads the package, puts it down.*] One foot—[*He breaks off as* BEN *appears at the right and moves slowly down to him.*] What a proposition, ts, ts. Terrific, terrific. 'Cause she's suffered, Ben, the woman has suffered. You understand me? A man can't go out the way he came in, Ben, a man has got to add up to something. You can't, you can't—[BEN *moves toward him as though to interrupt.*] You gotta consider, now. Don't answer so quick. Remember, it's a guaranteed twenty-thousand-dollar proposition. Now look, Ben, I want you to go through the ins and outs of this thing with me. I've got nobody to talk to, Ben, and the woman has suffered, you hear me?
1250   BEN [*standing still, considering*]   What's the proposition?

WILLY   It's twenty thousand dollars on the barrelhead. Guaranteed, gilt-edged, you understand?

BEN   You don't want to make a fool of yourself. They might not honor the policy.

WILLY   How can they dare refuse? Didn't I work like a coolie to meet every premium on the nose? And now they don't pay off? Impossible!

BEN   It's called a cowardly thing, William.

WILLY   Why? Does it take more guts to stand here the rest of my life ringing up a zero?
1260   BEN [*yielding*]   That's a point, William. [*He moves, thinking, turns.*] And twenty thousand—that *is* something one can feel with the hand, it is there.

WILLY [*now assured, with rising power*]   Oh, Ben, that's the whole beauty of it! I see it like a diamond, shining in the dark, hard and rough, that I can pick up and touch in my hand. Not like—like an appointment! This would not be another damned-fool appointment, Ben, and it changes all the aspects. Because he thinks I'm nothing, see, and so he spites me. But the

funeral—[*Straightening up*] Ben, that funeral will be massive! They'll come
from Maine, Massachusetts, Vermont, New Hampshire! All the old-timers
with the strange license plates—that boy will be thunder-struck, Ben, be-
1270 cause he never realized—I am known! Rhode Island, New York, New
Jersey—I am known, Ben, and he'll see it with his eyes once and for all. He'll
see what I am, Ben! He's in for a shock, that boy!

    BEN [*coming down to the edge of the garden*]   He'll call you a coward.

    WILLY [*suddenly fearful*]   No, that would be terrible.

    BEN   Yes. And a damned fool.

    WILLY   No, no, he mustn't, I won't have that! [*He is broken and desperate.*]

    BEN   He'll hate you, William.

The gay music of the Boys is heard.

    WILLY   Oh, Ben, how do we get back to all the great times? Used to be so
full of light, and comradeship, the sleigh-riding in winter, and the ruddiness
1280 on his cheeks. And always some kind of good news coming up, always something nice coming up ahead. And never even let me carry the valises in the
house, and simonizing, simonizing that little red car! Why, why can't I give
him something and not have him hate me?

    BEN   Let me think about it. [*He glances at his watch.*] I still have a little
time. Remarkable proposition, but you've got to be sure you're not making a
fool of yourself.

BEN *drifts off upstage and goes out of sight.* BIFF *comes down from the left.*

    WILLY [*suddenly conscious of* BIFF, *turns and looks up at him, then begins
picking up the packages of seeds in confusion*]   Where the hell is that seed?
[*Indignantly*] You can't see nothing out here! They boxed in the whole
1290 goddam neighborhood!

    BIFF   There are people all around here. Don't you realize that?

    WILLY   I'm busy. Don't bother me.

    BIFF [*taking the hoe from* WILLY]   I'm saying good-by to you, Pop. [WILLY
looks at him, silent, unable to move.] I'm not coming back any more.

    WILLY   You're not going to see Oliver tomorrow?

    BIFF   I've got no appointment, Dad.

    WILLY   He put his arm around you, and you've got no appointment?

    BIFF   Pop, get this now, will you? Everytime I've left it's been a fight that
sent me out of here. Today I realized something about myself and I tried to
1300 explain it to you and I—I think I'm just not smart enough to make any sense
out of it for you. To hell with whose fault it is or anything like that. [*He takes*
WILLY*'s arm.*] Let's just wrap it up, heh? Come on in, we'll tell Mom. [*He
gently tries to pull* WILLY *to the left.*]

    WILLY [*frozen, immobile, with guilt in his voice*]   No, I don't want to see her.

    BIFF   Come on! [*He pulls again, and* WILLY *tries to pull away.*]

    WILLY [*highly nervous*]   No, no, I don't want to see her.

    BIFF [*tries to look into* WILLY*'s face, as if to find the answer there*]   Why don't
you want to see her?

WILLY [*more harshly now*]   Don't bother me, will you?

1310   BIFF   What do you mean, you don't want to see her? You don't want them calling you yellow, do you? This isn't your fault; it's me, I'm a bum. Now come inside! [WILLY *strains to get away.*] Did you hear what I said to you?

WILLY *pulls away and quickly goes by himself into the house.* BIFF *follows.*

LINDA [*to* WILLY]   Did you plant, dear?

BIFF [*at the door, to* LINDA]   All right, we had it out. I'm going and I'm not writing any more.

LINDA [*going to* WILLY *in the kitchen*]   I think that's the best way, dear. 'Cause there's no use drawing it out, you'll just never get along.

WILLY *doesn't respond.*

BIFF   People ask where I am and what I'm doing, you don't know, and you don't care. That way it'll be off your mind and you can start brightening up 1320   again. All right? That clears it, doesn't it? [WILLY *is silent, and* BIFF *goes to him.*] You gonna wish me luck, scout? [*He extends his hand.*] What do you say?

LINDA   Shake his hand, Willy.

WILLY [*turning to her, seething with hurt*]   There's no necessity to mention the pen at all, y'know.

BIFF [*gently*]   I've got no appointment, Dad.

WILLY [*erupting fiercely*]   He put his arm around . . . ?

BIFF   Dad, you're never going to see what I am, so what's the use of arguing? If I strike oil I'll send you a check. Meantime forget I'm alive.

WILLY [*to* LINDA]   Spite, see?

1330   BIFF   Shake hands, Dad.

WILLY   Not my hand.

BIFF   I was hoping not to go this way.

WILLY   Well, this is the way you're going. Good-by.

BIFF *looks at him a moment, then turns sharply and goes to the stairs.*

WILLY [*stops him with*]   May you rot in hell if you leave this house!

BIFF [*turning*]   Exactly what is it that you want from me?

WILLY   I want you to know, on the train, in the mountains, in the valleys, wherever you go, that you cut down your life for spite!

BIFF   No, no.

WILLY   Spite, spite, is the word of your undoing! And when you're down 1340   and out, remember what did it. When you're rotting somewhere beside the railroad tracks, remember, and don't you dare blame it on me!

BIFF   I'm not blaming it on you!

WILLY   I won't take the rap for this, you hear?

HAPPY *comes down the stairs and stands on the bottom step, watching.*

BIFF   That's just what I'm telling you!

WILLY [*sinking into a chair at the table, with full accusation*]   You're trying to put a knife in me—don't think I don't know what you're doing!

BIFF   All right, phony! Then let's lay it on the line. [*He whips the rubber tube out of his pocket and puts it on the table.*]

HAPPY   You crazy—

1350   LINDA   Biff! [*She moves to grab the hose, but* BIFF *holds it down with his hand.*]

BIFF   Leave it there! Don't move it!

WILLY [*not looking at it*]   What is that?

BIFF   You know goddam well what that is.

WILLY [*caged, wanting to escape*]   I never saw that.

BIFF   You saw it. The mice didn't bring it into the cellar! What is this supposed to do, make a hero out of you? This supposed to make me sorry for you?

WILLY   Never heard of it.

BIFF   There'll be no pity for you, you hear it? No pity!

1360   WILLY [*to* LINDA]   You hear the spite!

BIFF   No, you're going to hear the truth—what you are and what I am!

LINDA   Stop it!

WILLY   Spite!

HAPPY [*coming down toward* BIFF]   You cut it now!

BIFF [*to* HAPPY]   The man don't know who we are! The man is gonna know! [*To* WILLY] We never told the truth for ten minutes in this house!

HAPPY   We always told the truth!

BIFF [*turning on him*]   You big blow, are you the assistant buyer? You're one of the two assistants to the assistant, aren't you?

1370   HAPPY   Well, I'm practically—

BIFF   You're practically full of it! We all are! And I'm through with it. [*To* WILLY] Now hear this, Willy, this is me.

WILLY   I know you!

BIFF   You know why I had no address for three months? I stole a suit in Kansas City and I was in jail. [*To* LINDA, *who is sobbing*] Stop crying. I'm through with it.

LINDA *turns away from them, her hands covering her face.*

WILLY   I suppose that's my fault!

BIFF   I stole myself out of every good job since high school!

WILLY   And whose fault is that?

1380   BIFF   And I never got anywhere because you blew me so full of hot air I could never stand taking orders from anybody! That's whose fault it is!

WILLY   I hear that!

LINDA   Don't, Biff!

BIFF   It's goddam time you heard that! I had to be boss big shot in two weeks, and I'm through with it!

WILLY   Then hang yourself! For spite, hang yourself!

BIFF   No! Nobody's hanging himself, Willy! I ran down eleven flights with a pen in my hand today. And suddenly I stopped, you hear me? And in the middle of that office building, do you hear this? I stopped in the middle of
1390 that building and I saw—the sky. I saw the things that I love in this world. The work and the food and time to sit and smoke. And I looked at the pen and said to myself, what the hell am I grabbing this for? Why am I trying to become what I don't want to be? What am I doing in an office, making a contemptuous, begging fool of myself, when all I want is out there, waiting for me the minute I say I know who I am! Why can't I say that, Willy?

He tries to make WILLY *face him, but* WILLY *pulls away and moves to the left.*

WILLY [*with hatred, threateningly*]   The door of your life is wide open!
BIFF   Pop! I'm a dime a dozen, and so are you!
WILLY [*turning on him now in an uncontrolled outburst*]   I am not a dime a dozen! I am Willy Loman, and you are Biff Loman!

BIFF *starts for* WILLY, *but is blocked by* HAPPY. *In his fury,* BIFF *seems on the verge of attacking his father.*

1400   BIFF   I am not a leader of men, Willy, and neither are you. You were never anything but a hard-working drummer who landed in the ash can like all the rest of them! I'm one dollar an hour, Willy! I tried seven states and couldn't raise it. A buck an hour! Do you gather my meaning? I'm not bringing home any prizes any more, and you're going to stop waiting for me to bring them home!
WILLY [*directly to* BIFF]   You vengeful, spiteful mut!

BIFF *breaks from* HAPPY. WILLY, *in fright, starts up the stairs.* BIFF *grabs him.*

BIFF [*at the peak of his fury*]   Pop, I'm nothing! I'm nothing, Pop. Can't you understand that? There's no spite in it any more. I'm just what I am, that's all.

BIFF*'s fury has spent itself, and he breaks down, sobbing, holding on to* WILLY, *who dumbly fumbles for* BIFF*'s face.*

1410   WILLY [*astonished*]   What're you doing? What're you doing? [*To* LINDA] Why is he crying?
BIFF [*crying, broken*]   Will you let me go, for Christ's sake? Will you take that phony dream and burn it before something happens? [*Struggling to contain himself, he pulls away and moves to the stairs.*] I'll go in the morning. Put him—put him to bed. [*Exhausted,* BIFF *moves up the stairs to his room.*]
WILLY [*after a long pause, astonished, elevated*]   Isn't that—isn't that remarkable? Biff—he likes me!
LINDA   He loves you, Willy!
HAPPY [*deeply moved*]   Always did, Pop.

1420   WILLY   Oh, Biff! [*Staring wildly*] He cried! Cried to me. [*He is choking with his love, and now cries out his promise.*] That boy—that boy is going to be magnificent!

BEN *appears in the light just outside the kitchen.*

BEN   Yes, outstanding, with twenty thousand behind him.

LINDA [*sensing the racing of his mind, fearfully, carefully*]   Now come to bed, Willy. It's all settled now.

WILLY [*finding it difficult not to rush out of the house*]   Yes, we'll sleep. Come on. Go to sleep, Hap.

BEN   And it does take a great kind of man to crack the jungle.

In accents of dread, BEN's *idyllic music starts up.*

HAPPY [*his arm around* LINDA]   I'm getting married, Pop, don't forget it.
1430 I'm changing everything. I'm gonna run that department before the year is up. You'll see, Mom. [*He kisses her.*]

BEN   The jungle is dark but full of diamonds, Willy.

WILLY *turns, moves, listening to* BEN.

LINDA   Be good. You're both good boys, just act that way, that's all.

HAPPY   'Night, Pop. [*He goes upstairs.*]

LINDA [*to* WILLY]   Come, dear.

BEN [*with greater force*]   One must go in to fetch a diamond out.

WILLY [*to* LINDA, *as he moves slowly along the edge of the kitchen, toward the door*]   I just want to get settled down, Linda. Let me sit alone for a little.

LINDA [*almost uttering her fear*]   I want you upstairs.

1440   WILLY [*taking her in his arms*]   In a few minutes, Linda. I couldn't sleep right now. Go on, you look awful tired. [*He kisses her.*]

BEN   Not like an appointment at all. A diamond is rough and hard to the touch.

WILLY   Go on now. I'll be right up.

LINDA   I think this is the only way, Willy.

WILLY   Sure, it's the best thing.

BEN   Best thing!

WILLY   The only way. Everything is gonna be—go on, kid, get to bed. You look so tired.

1450   LINDA   Come right up.

WILLY   Two minutes.

LINDA *goes into the living-room, then reappears in her bedroom.* WILLY *moves just outside the kitchen door.*

WILLY   Loves me. [*Wonderingly*] Always loved me. Isn't that a remarkable thing? Ben, he'll worship me for it!

BEN [*with promise*]   It's dark there, but full of diamonds.

WILLY   Can you imagine that magnificence with twenty thousand dollars in his pocket?

LINDA [*calling from her room*]   Willy! Come up!

WILLY [*calling from the kitchen*]   Yes! Yes. Coming! It's very smart, you realize that, don't you, sweetheart? Even Ben sees it. I gotta go, baby. 'By!
1460 By! [*Going over to* BEN, *almost dancing*] Imagine? When the mail comes he'll be ahead of Bernard again!

BEN   A perfect proposition all around.

WILLY   Did you see how he cried to me? Oh, if I could kiss him, Ben!

BEN   Time, William, time!

WILLY   Oh, Ben, I always knew one way or another we were gonna make it, Biff and I!

BEN [*looking at his watch*]   The boat. We'll be late. [*He moves slowly off into the darkness.*]

WILLY [*elegiacally, turning to the house*]   Now when you kick off, boy, I
1470 want a seventy-yard boot, and get right down the field under the ball, and when you hit, hit low and hit hard, because it's important, boy. [*He swings around and faces the audience.*] There's all kinds of important people in the stands, and the first thing you know . . . [*Suddenly, realizing he is alone*] Ben! Ben, where do I . . . ? [*He makes a sudden movement of search.*] Ben, how do I . . . ?

LINDA [*calling*]   Willy, you coming up?

WILLY [*uttering a gasp of fear, whirling about as if to quiet her*]   Sh! [*He turns around as if to find his way; sounds, faces, voices, seem to be swarming in upon him and he flicks at them, crying*] Sh! Sh! [*Suddenly music, faint
1480 and high, stops him. It rises in intensity, almost to an unbearable scream. He goes up and down on his toes, and rushes off around the house.*] Shhh!

LINDA   Willy?

There is no answer. LINDA *waits.* BIFF *gets up off his bed. He is still in his clothes.* HAPPY *sits up.* BIFF *stands listening.*

LINDA [*with real fear*]   Willy, answer me! Willy!

There is the sound of a car starting and moving away at full speed.

LINDA   No!

BIFF [*rushing down the stairs*]   Pop!

As the car speeds off, the music crashes down in a frenzy of sound, which becomes the soft pulsation of a single cello string. BIFF *slowly returns to his bedroom. He and* HAPPY *gravely don their jackets.* LINDA *slowly walks out of her room. The music has developed into a dead march. The leaves of day are appearing over everything.* CHARLEY *and* BERNARD, *somberly dressed, appear and knock on the kitchen door.* BIFF *and* HAPPY *slowly descend the stairs to the kitchen as* CHARLEY *and* BERNARD *enter. All stop a moment when* LINDA, *in clothes of mourning, bearing a little bunch of roses, comes through the draped doorway into the kitchen. She goes to* CHARLEY *and takes his arm. Now all move toward the audience, through the wall-line of the kitchen. At the limit of the apron,* LINDA *lays down the flowers, kneels, and sits back on her heels. All stare down at the grave.*

Requiem

CHARLEY   It's getting dark, Linda.

LINDA *doesn't react. She stares at the grave.*

BIFF   How about it, Mom? Better get some rest, heh? They'll be closing the gate soon.

LINDA *makes no move. Pause.*

HAPPY [*deeply angered*]   He had no right to do that. There was no necessity for it. We would've helped him.
CHARLEY [*grunting*]   Hmmm.
BIFF   Come along, Mom.
LINDA   Why didn't anybody come?
CHARLEY   It was a very nice funeral.
10   LINDA   But where are all the people he knew? Maybe they blame him.
CHARLEY   Naa. It's a rough world, Linda. They wouldn't blame him.
LINDA   I can't understand it. At this time especially. First time in thirty-five years we were just about free and clear. He only needed a little salary. He was even finished with the dentist.
CHARLEY   No man only needs a little salary.
LINDA   I can't understand it.
BIFF   There were a lot of nice days. When he'd come home from a trip; or on Sundays, making the stoop; finishing the cellar; putting on the new porch; when he built the extra bathroom; and put up the garage. You know some-
20   thing, Charley, there's more of him in that front stoop than in all the sales he ever made.
CHARLEY   Yeah. He was a happy man with a batch of cement.
LINDA   He was so wonderful with his hands.
BIFF   He had the wrong dreams. All, all, wrong.
HAPPY [*almost ready to fight* BIFF]   Don't say that!
BIFF   He never knew who he was.
CHARLEY [*stopping* HAPPY'*s movement and reply. To* BIFF]   Nobody dast blame this man. You don't understand. Willy was a salesman. And for a salesman, there is no rock bottom to the life. He don't put a bolt to a nut, he don't
30   tell you the law or give you medicine. He's a man out there in the blue, riding on a smile and a shoeshine. And when they start not smiling back—that's an earthquake. And then you get yourself a couple of spots on your hat, and you're finished. Nobody dast blame this man. A salesman is got to dream, boy. It comes with the territory.

BIFF   Charley, the man didn't know who he was.

HAPPY [*infuriated*]   Don't say that!

BIFF   Why don't you come with me, Happy?

HAPPY   I'm not licked that easily. I'm staying right in this city, and I'm gonna beat this racket! [*He looks at* BIFF, *his chin set.*] The Loman Brothers!

40   BIFF   I know who I am, kid.

HAPPY   All right, boy. I'm gonna show you and everybody else that Willy Loman did not die in vain. He had a good dream. It's the only dream you can have—to come out number-one man. He fought it out here, and this is where I'm gonna win it for him.

BIFF [*with a hopeless glance at* HAPPY, *bends toward his mother*]   Let's go, Mom.

LINDA   I'll be with you in a minute. Go on, Charley. [*He hesitates*] I want to, just for a minute. I never had a chance to say good-by.

CHARLEY *moves away, followed by* HAPPY. BIFF *remains a slight distance up and left of* LINDA. *She sits there, summoning herself. The flute begins, not far away, playing behind her speech.*

LINDA   Forgive me, dear. I can't cry. I don't know what it is, but I can't cry.
50   I don't understand it. Why did you ever do that? Help me, Willy, I can't cry. It seems to me that you're just on another trip. I keep expecting you. Willy, dear, I can't cry. Why did you do it? I search and search and I search, and I can't understand it, Willy. I made the last payment on the house today. Today, dear. And there'll be nobody home. [*A sob rises in her throat.*] We're free and clear. [*Sobbing more fully, released*] We're free. [BIFF *comes slowly toward her.*] We're free . . . We're free . . .

BIFF *lifts her to her feet and moves out up right with her in his arms.* LINDA *sobs quietly.* BERNARD *and* CHARLEY *come together and follow them, followed by* HAPPY. *Only the music of the flute is left on the darkening stage as over the house the hard towers of the apartment buildings rise into sharp focus, and*

The Curtain Falls

Marsha Norman

Marsha Norman (1947–   ) produced her first play, *Getting Out,* in 1977 in Louisville, Kentucky. Later, it ran off-Broadway at the Theater de Lys and won a number of awards. Five years later, in December 1982, *'night, Mother* opened at the American Repertory Theater in Cambridge, Massachusetts, and it moved to Broadway in March of the next year. Marsha Norman won the 1983 Pulitzer Prize for Drama for *'night, Mother.*

'night Mother   (1982)

Characters

JESSIE CATES, in her late thirties or early forties, is pale and vaguely unsteady physically. It is only in the last year that Jessie has gained control of her mind and body, and tonight she is determined to hold on to that control. She wears pants and a long black sweater with deep pockets, which contain scraps of paper, and there may be a pencil behind her ear or a pen clipped to one of the pockets of the sweater.

As a rule, Jessie doesn't feel much like talking. Other people have rarely found her quirky sense of humor amusing. She has a peaceful energy on this night, a sense of purpose, but is clearly aware of the time passing moment by moment. Oddly enough, Jessie has never been as communicative or as enjoyable as she is on this evening, but we must know she has not always been this way. There is a familiarity between these two women that comes from having lived together for a long time. There is a shorthand to the talk and a sense of routine comfort in the way they relate to each other physically. Naturally, there are also routine aggravations.

THELMA CATES, "MAMA," is Jessie's mother, in her late fifties or early sixties. She has begun to feel her age and so takes it easy when she can, or when it serves her purpose to let someone help her. But she speaks quickly and enjoys talking. She believes that things *are* what she says they are. Her sturdiness is more a mental quality than a physical one, finally. She is chatty and nosy, and this is *her* house.

The play takes place in a relatively new house built way out on a country road, with a living room and connecting kitchen, and a center hall that leads off to the bedrooms. A pull cord in the hall ceiling releases a ladder which leads to the attic. One of these bedrooms opens directly onto the hall, and its entry should be visible to everyone in the audience. It should be, in fact, the focal point of the entire set, and the lighting should make it disappear completely at times and draw the entire set into it at others. It is a point of both threat and promise. It is an ordinary door that opens onto absolute nothingness. That door is the point of all the action, and the utmost care should be given to its design and construction.

The living room is cluttered with magazines and needlework catalogues, ashtrays and candy dishes. Examples of MAMA *'s needlework are everywhere—pillows, afghans, and quilts, doilies and rugs, and they are quite nice examples. The house is more comfortable than messy, but there is quite a lot to keep in place here. It is more personal than charming. It is not quaint. Under no circumstances should the set and its dressing make a judgment about the intelligence or taste of* JESSIE *and* MAMA. *It should simply indicate that they are very specific real people who happen to live in a particular part of the country. Heavy accents, which would further distance the audience from* JESSIE *and* MAMA *are also wrong.*

The time is the present, with the action beginning about 8:15. Clocks onstage in the kitchen and on a table in the living room should run throughout the performance and be visible to the audience.

There will be no intermission.

MAMA *stretches to reach the cupcakes in a cabinet in the kitchen. She can't see them, but she can feel around for them, and she's eager to have one, so she's working pretty hard at it. This may be the most serious exercise* MAMA *ever gets. She finds a cupcake, the coconut-covered, raspberry-and-marshmallow-filled kind known as a snowball, but sees that there's one missing from the package. She calls to* JESSIE *who is apparently somewhere else in the house.*

MAMA [*Unwrapping the cupcake*]   Jessie, it's the last snowball, sugar. Put it on the list, O.K.? And we're out of Hershey bars, and where's that peanut brittle? I think maybe Dawson's been in it again. I ought to put a big mirror on the refrigerator door. That'll keep him out of my treats, won't it? You hear me, honey? [*Then more to herself*] I hate it when the coconut falls off. Why does the coconut fall off?

[JESSIE *enters from her bedroom, carrying a stack of newspapers*]

JESSIE   We got any old towels?

MAMA   There you are!

JESSIE [*Holding a towel that was on the stack of newspapers*]   Towels you
10 don't want anymore. [*Picking up* MAMA *'s snowball wrapper*] How about this swimming towel Loretta gave us? Beach towel, that's the name of it. You want it? [MAMA *shakes her head no*]

MAMA   What have you been doing in there?

JESSIE   And a big piece of plastic like a rubber sheet or something. Garbage bags would do if there's enough.

MAMA   Don't go making a big mess, Jessie. It's eight o'clock already.

JESSIE   Maybe an old blanket or towels we got in a soap box sometime?

MAMA   I said don't make a mess. Your hair is black enough, hon.

JESSIE [*Continuing to search the kitchen cabinets, finding two or three*
20 *more towels to add to her stack*]   It's not for my hair, Mama. What about some old pillows anywhere, or a foam cushion out of a yard chair would be real good.

MAMA   You haven't forgot what night it is, have you? [*Holding up her fingernails*] They're all chipped, see? I've been waiting all week, Jess. It's Saturday night, sugar.

JESSIE   I know. I got it on the schedule.

MAMA [*Crossing to the living room*]   You want me to wash 'em now or are you making your mess first? [*Looking at the snowball*] We're out of these. Did I say that already?

30   JESSIE   There's more coming tomorrow. I ordered you a whole case.

MAMA [*Checking the* TV Guide]   A whole case will go stale, Jessie.

JESSIE   They can go in the freezer till you're ready for them. Where's Daddy's gun?

MAMA   In the attic.

JESSIE   Where in the attic? I looked your whole nap and couldn't find it anywhere.

MAMA   One of his shoeboxes, I think.

JESSIE   Full of shoes. I looked already.

MAMA   Well, you didn't look good enough, then. There's that box from the
40 ones he wore to the hospital. When he died, they told me I could have them back, but I never did like those shoes.

JESSIE [*Pulling them out of her pocket*]   I found the bullets. They were in an old milk can.

MAMA [*As* JESSIE *starts for the hall*]   Dawson took the shotgun, didn't he? Hand me that basket, hon.

JESSIE [*Getting the basket for her*]   Dawson better not've taken that pistol.

MAMA [*Stopping her again*]   Now my glasses, please. [JESSIE *returns to get the glasses*] I told him to take those rubber boots, too, but he said they were for fishing. I told him to take up fishing.

[JESSIE *reaches for the cleaning spray, and cleans* MAMA*'s glasses for her*]

50   JESSIE   He's just too lazy to climb up there, Mama. Or maybe he's just being smart. That floor's not very steady.

MAMA [*Getting out a piece of knitting*]   It's not a floor at all, hon, it's a board now and then. Measure this for me. I need six inches.

JESSIE [*As she measures*]   Dawson could probably use some of those clothes up there. Somebody should have them. You ought to call the Salvation Army before the whole thing falls in on you. Six inches exactly.

MAMA   It's plenty safe! As long as you don't go up there.

JESSIE [*Turning to go again*]   I'm careful.

MAMA   What do you want the gun for, Jess?

60   JESSIE [*Not returning this time. Opening the ladder in the hall*]   Protection. [*She steadies the ladder as* MAMA *talks*]

MAMA   You take the TV way too serious, hon. I've never seen a criminal in my life. This is way too far to come for what's out here to steal. Never seen a one.

JESSIE [*Taking her first step up*]   Except for Ricky.

MAMA   Ricky is mixed up. That's not a crime.

JESSIE   Get your hands washed. I'll be right back. And get'em real dry. You dry your hands till I get back or it's no go, all right?

MAMA   I thought Dawson told you not to go up those stairs.

70   JESSIE [*Going up*]   He did.

MAMA   I don't like the idea of a gun, Jess.

JESSIE [*Calling down from the attic*]   Which shoebox, do you remember?

MAMA   Black.

JESSIE   The box was black?

MAMA   The shoes were black.

JESSIE   That doesn't help much, Mother.

MAMA   I'm not trying to help, sugar. [*No answer*] We don't have anything anybody'd want, Jessie. I mean, I don't even want what we got, Jessie.

JESSIE   Neither do I. Wash your hands. [MAMA *gets up and crosses to stand*
80 *under the ladder*]

MAMA   You come down from there before you have a fit. I can't come up and get you, you know.

JESSIE   I know.

MAMA   We'll just hand it over to them when they come, how's that? Whatever they want, the criminals.

JESSIE   That's a good idea, Mama.

MAMA   Ricky will grow out of this and be a real fine boy, Jess. But I have to tell you, I wouldn't want Ricky to know we had a gun in the house.

JESSIE   Here it is. I found it.

90   MAMA   It's just something Ricky's going through. Maybe he's in with some bad people. He just needs some time, sugar. He'll get back in school or get a job or one day you'll get a call and he'll say he's sorry for all the trouble he's caused and invite you out for supper someplace dress-up.

JESSIE [*Coming back down the steps*]   Don't worry. It's not for him, it's for me.

MAMA   I didn't think you would shoot your own boy, Jessie. I know you've felt like it, well, we've all felt like shooting somebody, but we don't do it. I just don't think we need . . .

JESSIE [*Interrupting*]   Your hands aren't washed. Do you want a manicure
100 or not?

MAMA   Yes, I do, but . . .

JESSIE [*Crossing to the chair*]   Then wash your hands and don't talk to me any more about Ricky. Those two rings he took were the last valuable things *I* had, so now he's started in on other people, door to door. I hope they put him away sometime. I'd turn him in myself if I knew where he was.

MAMA   You don't mean that.

JESSIE   Every word. Wash your hands and that's that last time I'm telling you.

[JESSIE *sits down with the gun and starts cleaning it, pushing the cylinder out, checking to see that the chambers and barrel are empty, then putting some oil on a small patch of cloth and pushing it through the barrel with the push rod that was in the box.* MAMA *goes to the kitchen and washes hands, as instructed, trying not to show her concern about the gun*]

MAMA   I shoulda got you to bring down that milk can. Agnes Fletcher sold
110 hers to somebody with a flea market for forty dollars apiece.

JESSIE   I'll go back and get it in a minute. There's a wagon wheel up there, too. There's even a churn. I'll get it all if you want.

MAMA [*Coming over, taking over now*]   What are you doing?

JESSIE   The barrel has to be clean, Mama. Old powder, dust gets in it . . .

MAMA   What for?

JESSIE   I told you.

MAMA [*Reaching for the gun*]   And I told you, we don't get criminals out here.

JESSIE [*Quickly pulling it to her*]   And I told you . . . [*Then trying to be
120 calm*] The gun is for me.

MAMA   Well, you can have it if you want. When I die, you'll get it all, anyway.

JESSIE   I'm going to kill myself, Mama.

MAMA [*Returning to the sofa*]   Very funny. Very funny.

JESSIE   I am.

MAMA   You are not! Don't even say such a thing, Jessie.

JESSIE   How would you know if I didn't say it? You want it to be a surprise? You're lying there in your bed or maybe you're just brushing your teeth and you hear this . . . noise down the hall?

130 MAMA   Kill yourself.

JESSIE   Shoot myself. In a couple of hours.

MAMA   It must be time for your medicine.

JESSIE   Took it already.

MAMA   What's the matter with you?

JESSIE   Not a thing. Feel fine.

MAMA   You feel fine. You're just going to kill yourself.

JESSIE   Waited until I felt good enough, in fact.

MAMA   Don't make jokes, Jessie. I'm too old for jokes.

JESSIE   It's not a joke, Mama.

[MAMA *watches for a moment in silence*]

140 MAMA   That gun's no good, you know. He broke it right before he died. He dropped it in the mud one day.

JESSIE   Seems O.K. [*She spins the chamber, cocks the pistol, and pulls the trigger. The gun is not yet loaded, so all we hear is the click, but it will definitely work. It's also obvious that* JESSIE *knows her way around a gun,* MAMA *cannot speak*] I had Cecil's all ready in there, just in case I couldn't find this one, but I'd rather use Daddy's.

MAMA   Those bullets are at least fifteen years old.

JESSIE [*Pulling out another box*]   These are from last week.

MAMA   Where did you get those?

150 JESSIE   Feed store Dawson told me about.

MAMA   Dawson!

JESSIE   I told him I was worried about prowlers. He said he thought it was a good idea. He told me what kind to ask for.

MAMA   If he had any idea . . .

JESSIE   He took it as a compliment. He thought I might be taking an interest in things. He got through telling me all about the bullets and then he said we ought to talk like this more often.

MAMA   And where was I while this was going on?

JESSIE   On the phone with Agnes. About the milk can, I guess. Anyway, I 160 asked Dawson if he thought they'd send me some bullets and he said he'd just call for me, because he knew they'd send them if he told them to. And he was absolutely right. Here they are.

MAMA   How could he do that?

JESSIE   Just trying to help, Mama.

MAMA   And then I told you where the gun was.

JESSIE [*Smiling, enjoying this joke*]   See? Everybody's doing what they can.

MAMA   You told me it was for protection!

JESSIE   It *is!* I'm still doing your nails, though. Want to try that new China-berry color?

170 MAMA   Well, I'm calling Dawson right now. We'll just see what he has to say about this little stunt.

JESSIE   Dawson doesn't have any more to do with this.

MAMA   He's your brother.

JESSIE   And that's all.

MAMA [*Stands up, moves toward the phone*]   Dawson will put a stop to this. Yes he will. He'll take the gun away.

JESSIE   If you call him, I'll just have to do it before he gets here. Soon as you hang up the phone, I'll just walk in the bedroom and lock the door. Dawson will get here just in time to help you clean up. Go ahead, call him. 180 Then call the police. Then call the funeral home. Then call Loretta and see if *she'll* do your nails.

MAMA   You will not! This is crazy talk, Jessie!

[MAMA *goes directly to the telephone and starts to dial, but* JESSIE *is fast, coming up behind her and taking the receiver out of her hand, putting it back down*]

JESSIE [*Firm and quiet*]   I said no. This is private. Dawson is not invited.

MAMA   Just me.

JESSIE   I don't want anybody else over here. Just you and me. If Dawson comes over, it'll make me feel stupid for not doing it ten years ago.

MAMA   I think we better call the doctor. Or how about the ambulance. You like that one driver, I know. What's his name, Timmy? Get you somebody to talk to.

190   JESSIE [*Going back to her chair*]   I'm through talking, Mama. You're it. No more.

MAMA   We're just going to sit around like every other night in the world and then you're going to kill yourself? [JESSIE *doesn't answer*] You'll miss. [*Again there is no response*] You'll just wind up a vegetable. How would you like that? Shoot your ear off? You know what the doctor said about getting excited. You'll cock the pistol and have a fit.

JESSIE   I think I can kill myself, Mama.

MAMA   You're not going to kill yourself, Jessie. You're not even upset! [JESSIE *smiles, or laughs quietly, and* MAMA *tries a different approach*] People
200   don't really kill themselves, Jessie. No, mam, doesn't make sense, unless you're retarded or deranged, and you're as normal as they come, Jessie, for the most part. We're all *afraid* to die.

JESSIE   I'm not, Mama. I'm cold all the time, anyway.

MAMA   That's ridiculous.

JESSIE   It's exactly what I want. It's dark and quiet.

MAMA   So is the back yard, Jessie! Close your eyes. Stuff cotton in your ears. Take a nap! It's quiet in your room. I'll leave the TV off all night.

JESSIE   So quiet I don't know it's quiet. So nobody can get me.

MAMA   You don't know what dead is like. It might not be quiet at all. What
210   if it's like an alarm clock, and you can't wake up so you can't shut it off. Ever.

JESSIE   Dead is everybody and everything I ever knew, gone. Dead is dead quiet.

MAMA   It's a sin. You'll go to hell.

JESSIE   Uh-huh.

MAMA   You will!

JESSIE   Jesus was a suicide, if you ask me.

MAMA   You'll go to hell just for saying that. Jessie!

JESSIE [*With genuine surprise*]   I didn't know I thought that.

MAMA   Jessie!

[JESSIE *doesn't answer. She puts the now-loaded gun back in the box and crosses to the kitchen. But* MAMA *is afraid she's headed for the bedroom*]

220   MAMA [*In a panic*]   You can't use my towels! They're my towels. I've had them for a long time. I like my towels.

JESSIE   I asked you if you wanted that swimming towel and you said you didn't.

MAMA   And you can't use your father's gun, either. It's mine now, too. And you can't do it in my house.

JESSIE   Oh, come on.

MAMA   No. You can't do it. I won't let you. The house is in my name.

JESSIE   I have to go in the bedroom and lock the door behind me so they won't arrest you for killing me. They'll probably test your hands for gunpow-
230   der, anyway, but you'll pass.

MAMA   Not in my house!

JESSIE   If I'd known you were going to act like this, I wouldn't have told you.

MAMA   How am I supposed to act? Tell you to go ahead? O.K. by me, sugar? Might try it myself. What took you so long?

JESSIE   There's just no point in fighting me over it, that's all. Want some coffee?

MAMA   Your birthday's coming up, Jessie. Don't you want to know what we got you?

240   JESSIE   You got me dusting powder, Loretta got me a new housecoat, pink probably, and Dawson got me new slippers, too small, but they go with the robe, he'll say. [MAMA *cannot speak*] Right? [*Apparently* JESSIE *is right*] Be back in a minute.

[JESSIE *takes the gun box, puts it on top of the stack of towels and garbage bags, and takes them into her bedroom.* MAMA, *alone for a moment, goes to the phone, picks up the receiver, looks toward the bedroom, starts to dial, and then replaces the receiver in its cradle as* JESSIE *walks back into the room.* JESSIE *wonders, silently. They have lived together for so long there is very rarely any reason for one to ask what the other was about to do*]

MAMA   I started to, but I didn't. I didn't call him.

JESSIE   Good. Thank you.

MAMA [*Starting over, a new approach*]   What's this all about, Jessie?

JESSIE   About?

[JESSIE *now begins the next task she had "on the schedule," which is refilling all the candy jars, taking the empty papers out of the boxes of chocolates, etc.* MAMA *generally snitches when* JESSIE *does this. Not tonight, though. Nevertheless,* JESSIE *offers*]

MAMA   What did I do?

JESSIE   Nothing. Want a caramel?

250   MAMA [*Ignoring the candy*]   You're mad at me.

JESSIE   Not a bit. I am worried about you, but I'm going to do what I can before I go. We're not just going to sit around tonight. I made a list of things.

MAMA   What things?

JESSIE   How the washer works. Things like that.

MAMA   I know how the washer works. You put the clothes in. You put the soap in. You turn it on. You wait.

JESSIE   You do something else. You don't just wait.

MAMA   Whatever else you find to do, you're still mainly waiting. The waiting's the worst part of it. The waiting's what you pay somebody else to do, if 260   you can.

JESSIE [*Nodding*]   O.K. Where do we keep the soap?

MAMA   I could find it.

JESSIE   See?

MAMA   If you're mad about doing the wash, we can get Loretta to do it.

JESSIE   Oh now, that might be worth staying to see.

MAMA   She'd never in her life, would she?

JESSIE   Nope.

MAMA   What's the matter with her?

JESSIE   She thinks she's better than we are. She's not.

270   MAMA   Maybe if she didn't wear that yellow all the time.

JESSIE   The washer repair number is on a little card taped to the side of the machine.

MAMA   Loretta doesn't ever have to come over here again. Dawson can just leave her at home when he comes. And we don't ever have to see Dawson either if he bothers you. Does he bother you?

JESSIE   Sure he does. Be sure you clean out the lint tray every time you use the dryer. But don't ever put your house shoes in, it'll melt the soles.

MAMA   What does Dawson do, that bothers you?

JESSIE   He just calls me Jess like he knows who he's talking to. He's always

280   wondering what I do all day. I mean, I wonder that myself, but it's my day, so it's mine to wonder about, not his.

MAMA   Family is just accident, Jessie. It's nothing personal, hon. They don't mean to get on your nerves. They don't even mean to be your family, they just are.

JESSIE   They know too much.

MAMA   About what?

JESSIE   They know things about you, and they learned it before you had a chance to say whether you wanted them to know it or not. They were there when it happened and it don't belong to them, it belongs to you, only they

290   got it. Like my mail-order bra got delivered to their house.

MAMA   By accident!

JESSIE   All the same . . . they opened it. They saw the little rosebuds on it. [*Offering her another candy*] Chewy mint?

MAMA [*Shaking her head no*]   What do they know about you? I'll tell them never to talk about it again. Is it Ricky or Cecil or your fits or your hair is falling out or you drink too much coffee or you never go out of the house or what?

JESSIE   I just don't like their talk. The account at the grocery is in Dawson's name when you call. The number's on a whole list of numbers on the back cover of the phone book.

300   MAMA   Well! Now we're getting somewhere. They're none of them ever setting foot in this house again.

JESSIE   It's not them, Mother. I wouldn't kill myself just to get away from them.

MAMA   You leave the room when they come over, anyway.

JESSIE   I stay as long as I can. Besides, it's you they come to see.

MAMA   That's because I stay in the room when they come.

JESSIE   It's not them.

MAMA   Then what is it?

JESSIE [*Checking the list on her note pad*]   The grocery won't deliver on

310   Saturday anymore. And if you want your order the same day, you have to call before ten. And they won't deliver less than fifteen dollars' worth. What I do is tell them what we need and tell them to add on cigarettes until it gets to fifteen dollars.

MAMA   It's Ricky. You're trying to get through to him.

JESSIE   If I thought I could do that, I would stay.

MAMA   Make him sorry he hurt you, then. That's it, isn't it?

JESSIE   He's hurt me, I've hurt him. We're about even.

MAMA   You'll be telling him killing is O.K. with you, you know. Want him to start killing next? Nothing wrong with it. Mom did it.

320   JESSIE   Only a matter of time, anyway, Mama. When the call comes, you let Dawson handle it.

MAMA   Honey, nothing says those calls are always going to be some new trouble he's into. You could get one that he's got a job, that he's getting married, or how about he's joined the army, wouldn't that be nice?

JESSIE   If you call the Sweet Tooth before you call the grocery, that Susie will take your fudge next door to the grocery and it'll all come out together. Be sure you talk to Susie, though. She won't let them put it in the bottom of a sack like that one time, remember?

MAMA   Ricky could come over, you know. What if he calls us?

330   JESSIE   It's not Ricky, Mama.

MAMA   Or anybody could call us, Jessie.

JESSIE   Not on Saturday night, Mama.

MAMA   Then what is it? Are you sick? If your gums are swelling again, we can get you to the dentist in the morning.

JESSIE   No. Can you order your medicine or do you want Dawson to? I've got a note to him. I'll add that to it if you want.

MAMA   Your eyes don't look right. I thought so yesterday.

JESSIE   That was just the ragweed. I'm not sick.

MAMA   Epilepsy is sick, Jessie.

340   JESSIE   It won't kill me. [A pause] If it would, I wouldn't have to.

MAMA   You don't *have* to.

JESSIE   No, I don't. That's what I like about it.

MAMA   Well, I won't let you!

JESSIE   It's not up to you.

MAMA   Jessie!

JESSIE   I want to hang a big sign around my neck, like Daddy's on the barn. GONE FISHING.

MAMA   You don't like it here.

JESSIE [Smiling]   Exactly.

350   MAMA   I meant here in my house.

JESSIE   I know you did.

MAMA   You never should have moved back in here with me. If you'd kept your little house or found another place when Cecil left you, you'd have made some new friends at least. Had a life to lead. Had your own things around you. Give Ricky a place to come see you. You never should've come here.

JESSIE   Maybe.

MAMA   But I didn't force you, did I?

JESSIE   If it was a mistake, we made it together. You took me in. I appreciate that.

360   MAMA   You didn't have any business being by yourself right then, but I can see how you might want a place of your own. A grown woman should . . .

JESSIE   Mama . . . I'm just not having a very good time and I don't have any reason to think it'll get anything but worse. I'm tired. I'm hurt. I'm sad. I feel used.

MAMA   Tired of what?

JESSIE   It all.

MAMA   What does that mean?

JESSIE   I can't say it any better.

370   MAMA   Well, you'll have to say it better because I'm not letting you alone till you do. What were those other things? Hurt . . . [*Before* JESSIE *can answer*] You had this all ready to say to me, didn't you? Did you write this down? How long have you been thinking about this?

JESSIE   Off and on, ten years. On all the time, since Christmas.

MAMA   What happened at Christmas?

JESSIE   Nothing.

MAMA   So why Christmas?

JESSIE   That's it. On the nose.

[*A pause.* MAMA *knows exactly what* JESSIE *means. She was there, too, after all*]

JESSIE   [*Putting the candy sacks away*]   See where all this is? Red hots up front, sour balls and horehound mixed together in this one sack. New pack-
380   ages of toffee and licorice right in back there.

MAMA   Go back to your list. You're hurt by what?

JESSIE   [MAMA *knows perfectly well*]   Mama . . .

MAMA   O.K. Sad about what? There's nothing real sad going on right now. If it was after your divorce or something, that would make sense.

JESSIE   [*Looking at her list, then opening the drawer*]   Now, this drawer has everything in it that there's no better place for. Extension cords, batteries for the radio, extra lighters, sandpaper, masking tape, Elmer's glue, thumbtacks, that kind of stuff. The mousetraps are under the sink, but you call Dawson if you've got one and let him do it.

390   MAMA   Sad about what?

JESSIE   The way things are.

MAMA   Not good enough. What things?

JESSIE   Oh, everything from you and me to Red China.

MAMA   I think we can leave the Chinese out of this.

JESSIE   [*Crosses back into the living room*]   There's extra light bulbs in a box in the hall closet. And we've got a couple of packages of fuses in the fuse box. There's candles and matches in the top of the broom closet, but if the lights go out, just call Dawson and sit tight. But don't open the refrigerator door. Things will stay cool in there as long as you keep the door shut.

400   MAMA   I asked you a question.

JESSIE   I read the paper. I don't like how things are. And they're not any better out there than they are here.

MAMA   If you're doing this because of the newspapers, I can sure fix that!

JESSIE   There's just more of it on TV.

MAMA   [*Kicking the television set*]   Take it out, then!

JESSIE You wouldn't do that.

MAMA Watch me.

JESSIE What would you do all day?

MAMA [*Desperately*] Sing. [JESSIE *laughs*] I would, too. You want to watch?
410 I'll sing till morning to keep you alive, Jessie, please!

JESSIE No. [*Then affectionately*] It's a funny idea, though. What do you sing?

MAMA [*Has no idea how to answer this*] We've got a good life here!

JESSIE [*Going back into the kitchen*] I called this morning and canceled the papers, except for Sunday, for your puzzles; you'll still get that one.

MAMA Let's get another dog, Jessie! You liked a big dog, now, didn't you? That King dog, didn't you?

JESSIE [*Washing her hands*] I did like that King dog, yes.

MAMA I'm so dumb. He's the one run under the tractor.

JESSIE That makes him dumb, not you.

420 MAMA For bringing it up.

JESSIE It's O.K. Handi-Wipes and sponges under the sink.

MAMA We could get a new dog and keep him in the house. Dogs are cheap!

JESSIE [*Getting big pill jars out of the cabinet*] No.

MAMA Something for you to take care of.

JESSIE I've had you, Mama.

MAMA [*Frantically starting to fill pill bottles*] You do too much for me. I can fill pill bottles all day, Jessie, and change the shelf paper and wash the floor when I get through. You just watch me. You don't have to do another thing in this house if you don't want to. You don't have to take care of me, Jessie.

430 JESSIE I know that. You've just been letting me do it so I'll have something to do, haven't you?

MAMA [*Realizing this was a mistake*] I don't do it as well as you. I just meant if it tires you out or makes you feel used . . .

JESSIE Mama, I know you used to ride the bus. Riding the bus and it's hot and bumpy and crowded and too noisy and more than anything in the world you want to get off and the only reason in the world you don't get off is it's still fifty blocks from where you're going? Well, I can get off right now if I want to, because even if I ride fifty more years and get off then, it's the same place when I step down to it. Whenever I feel like it, I can get off. As soon as
440 I've had enough, it's my stop. I've had enough.

MAMA You're feeling sorry for yourself!

JESSIE The plumber's helper is under the sink, too.

MAMA You're not having a good time! Whoever promised you a good time? Do you think I've had a good time?

JESSIE I think you're pretty happy, yeah. You have things you like to do.

MAMA Like what?

JESSIE Like crochet.

MAMA I'll teach you to crochet.

JESSIE I can't do any of that nice work, Mama.

450 MAMA Good time don't come looking for you, Jessie. You could work some puzzles or put in a garden or go to the store. Let's call a taxi and go to the A&P!

JESSIE   I shopped you up for about two weeks already. You're not going to need toilet paper till Thanksgiving.

MAMA [*Interrupting*]   You're acting like some little brat, Jessie. You're mad and everybody's boring and you don't have anything to do and you don't like me and you don't like going out and you don't like staying in and you never talk on the phone and you don't watch TV and you're miserable and it's your own sweet fault.

JESSIE   And it's time I did something about it.

460   MAMA   Not something like killing yourself. Something like . . . buying us all new dishes! I'd like that. Or maybe the doctor would let you get a driver's license now, or I know what let's do right this minute, let's rearrange the furniture.

JESSIE   I'll do that. If you want. I always thought if the TV was somewhere else, you wouldn't get such a glare on it during the day. I'll do whatever you want before I go.

MAMA [*Badly frightened by those words*]   You could get a job!

JESSIE   I took that telephone sales job and I didn't even make enough money to pay the phone bill, and I tried to work at the gift shop at the hospital and

470   they said I made people real uncomfortable smiling at them the way I did.

MAMA   You could keep books. You kept your dad's books.

JESSIE   But nobody ever checked them.

MAMA   When he died, they checked them.

JESSIE   And that's when they took the books away from me.

MAMA   That's because without him there wasn't any business, Jessie!

JESSIE [*Putting the pill bottles away*]   You know I couldn't work. I can't do anything. I've never been around people my whole life except when I went to the hospital. I could have a seizure any time. What good would a job do? The kind of job I could get would make me feel worse.

480   MAMA   Jessie!

JESSIE   It's true!

MAMA   It's what you think is true!

JESSIE [*Struck by the clarity of that*]   That's right. It's what I think is true.

MAMA [*Hysterically*]   But I can't do anything about that!

JESSIE [*Quietly*]   No. You can't. [MAMA *slumps, if not physically, at least emotionally*] And I can't do anything either, about my life, to change it, make it better, make me feel better about it. Like it better, make it work. But I can stop it. Shut it down, turn it off like the radio when there's nothing on I want to listen to. It's all I really have that belongs to me and I'm going to say what

490   happens to it. And it's going to stop. And I'm going to stop it. So. Let's just have a good time.

MAMA   Have a good time.

JESSIE   We can't go on fussing all night. I mean, I could ask you things I always wanted to know and you could make me some hot chocolate. The old way.

MAMA [*In despair*]   It takes cocoa, Jessie.

JESSIE [*Gets it out of the cabinet*]   I bought cocoa, Mama. And I'd like to have a caramel apple and do your nails.

MAMA   You didn't eat a bit of supper.
500   JESSIE   Does that mean I can't have a caramel apple?
MAMA   Of course not. I mean . . . [*Smiling a little*] Of course you can
have a caramel apple.
JESSIE   I thought I could.
MAMA   I make the best caramel apples in the world.
JESSIE   I know you do.
MAMA   Or used to. And you don't get cocoa like mine anywhere anymore.
JESSIE   It takes time, I know, but . . .
MAMA   The salt is the trick.
JESSIE   Trouble and everything.
510   MAMA [*Backing away toward the stove*]   It's no trouble. What trouble? You
put it in the pan and stir it up. All right. Fine. Caramel apples. Cocoa. O.K.

[JESSIE *walks to the counter to retrieve her cigarettes as* MAMA *looks for the right pan.
There are brief near-smiles, and maybe* MAMA *clears her throat. We have a truce, for
the moment. A genuine but nevertheless uneasy one.* JESSIE, *who has been in constant
motion since the beginning, now seems content to sit.*

MAMA *starts looking for a pan to make the cocoa, getting out all the pans in the
cabinets in the process. It looks like she's making a mess on purpose so* JESSIE *will have
to put them all away again.* MAMA *is buying time, or trying to, and entertaining*]

JESSIE   You talk to Agnes today?
MAMA   She's calling me from a pay phone this week. God only knows why.
She has a perfectly good Trimline at home.
JESSIE [*Laughing*]   Well, how is she?
MAMA   How is she every day, Jessie? Nuts.
JESSIE   Is she really crazy or just silly?
MAMA   No, she's really crazy. She was probably using the pay phone be-
cause she had another little fire problem at home.
520   JESSIE   Mother . . .
MAMA   I'm serious! Agnes Fletcher's burned down every house she ever
lived in. Eight fires, and she's due for a new one any day now.
JESSIE [*Laughing*]   No!
MAMA   Wouldn't surprise me a bit.
JESSIE [*Laughing*]   Why didn't you tell me this before? Why isn't she locked
up somewhere?
MAMA   'Cause nobody ever got hurt, I guess. Agnes woke everybody up to
watch the fires as soon as she set 'em. One time she set out porch chairs and
served lemonade.
530   JESSIE [*Shaking her head*]   Real lemonade?
MAMA   The houses they lived in, you knew they were going to fall down
anyway, so why wait for it, is all I could ever make out about it. Agnes likes a
feeling of accomplishment.
JESSIE   Good for her.
MAMA [*Finding the pan she wants*]   Why are you asking about Agnes? One
cup or two?
JESSIE   One. She's your friend. No marshmallows.

MAMA [*Getting the milk, etc.*]   You have to have marshmallows. That's the old way, Jess. Two or three? Three is better.

540   JESSIE   Three, then. Her whole house burns up? Her clothes and pillows and everything? I'm not sure I believe this.

MAMA   When she was a girl, Jess, not now. Long time ago. But she's still got it in her, I'm sure of it.

JESSIE   She wouldn't burn her house down now. Where would she go? She can't get Buster to build her a new one, he's dead. How could she burn it up?

MAMA   Be exciting, though if she did. You never know.

JESSIE   You do too know, Mama. She wouldn't do it.

MAMA [*Forced to admit, but reluctant*]   I guess not.

JESSIE   What else? Why does she wear all those whistles around her neck?

550   MAMA   Why does she have a house full of birds?

JESSIE   I didn't know she had a house full of birds!

MAMA   Well, she does. And she says they just follow her home. Well, I know for a fact that she's still paying on the last parrot she bought. You gotta keep your life filled up, she says. She says a lot of stupid things. [JESSIE *laughs*, MAMA *continues, convinced she's getting somewhere*] It's all that okra she eats. You can't just willy-nilly eat okra two meals a day and expect to get away with it. Made her crazy.

JESSIE   She really eats okra twice a day? Where does she get it in the winter?

MAMA   Well, she eats it a lot. Maybe not two meals but . . .

560   JESSIE   More than the average person.

MAMA [*Beginning to get irritated*]   I don't know how much okra the average person eats.

JESSIE   Do you know how much okra Agnes eats?

MAMA   No.

JESSIE   How many birds does she have?

MAMA   Two.

JESSIE   Then what are the whistles for?

MAMA   They're not real whistles. Just little plastic ones on a necklace she won playing Bingo, and I only told you about it because I thought I might get

570   a laugh out of you for once even if it wasn't the truth, Jessie. Things don't have to be true to talk about 'em, you know.

JESSIE   Why won't she come over here?

[MAMA *is suddenly quiet, but the cocoa and milk are in the pan now, so she lights the stove and starts stirring*]

MAMA   Well now, what a good idea. We should've had more cocoa. Cocoa is perfect.

JESSIE   Except you don't like milk.

MAMA [*Another attempt, but not as energetic*]   I hate milk. Coats your throat as bad as okra. Something just downright disgusting about it.

JESSIE   It's because of me, isn't it?

MAMA   No, Jess.

580   JESSIE   Yes, Mama.

MAMA   O.K. Yes, then, but she's crazy. She's as crazy as they come. She's a lunatic.

JESSIE   What is it exactly? Did I say something, sometime? Or did she see me have a fit and's afraid I might have another one if she came over, or what?

MAMA   I guess.

JESSIE   You guess what? What's she ever said? She must've given you some reason.

MAMA   Your hands are cold.

JESSIE   What difference does that make?

590   MAMA   "Like a corpse," she says, "and I'm gonna be one soon enough as it is."

JESSIE   That's crazy.

MAMA   That's Agnes. "Jessie's shook the hand of death and I can't take the chance it's catching, Thelma, so I ain't comin' over, and you can understand or not, but I ain't comin'. I'll come up the driveway, but that's as far as I go."

JESSIE [*Laughing, relieved*]   I thought she didn't like me! She's scared of me! How about that! Scared of me.

MAMA   I could make her come over here, Jessie. I could call her up right now and she could bring the birds and come visit. I didn't know you ever
600   thought about her at all. I'll tell her she just has to come and she'll come, all right. She owes me one.

JESSIE   No, that's all right. I just wondered about it. When I'm in the hospital, does she come over here?

MAMA   Her kitchen is just a tiny thing. When she comes over here, she feels like . . . [*Toning it down a little*] Well, we all like a change of scene, don't we.

JESSIE [*Playing along*]   Sure we do. Plus there's no birds diving around.

MAMA   I hate those birds. She says I don't understand them. What's there to understand about birds?

610   JESSIE   Why Agnes likes them, for one thing. Why they stay with her when they could be outside with the other birds. What their singing means. How they fly. What they think Agnes is.

MAMA   Why do you have to know so much about things, Jessie? There's just not that much *to* things that I could ever see.

JESSIE   That you could ever *tell,* you mean. You didn't have to lie to me about Agnes.

MAMA   I didn't lie. You never asked before!

JESSIE   You lied about setting fire to all those houses and about how many birds she has and how much okra she eats and why she won't come over here.
620   If I have to keep dragging the truth out of you, this is going to take all night.

MAMA   That's fine with me. I'm not a bit sleepy.

JESSIE   Mama . . .

MAMA   All right. Ask me whatever you want. Here.

[*They come to an awkward stop, as the cocoa is ready and* MAMA *pours it into the cups* JESSIE *has set on the table*]

JESSIE [*As* MAMA *takes her first sip*]   Did you love Daddy?

MAMA   No.

JESSIE [*Pleased that* MAMA *understands the rules better now*]   I didn't think so. Were you really fifteen when you married him?

MAMA   The way he told it? I'm sitting in the mud, he comes along, drags me in the kitchen, "She's been there ever since"?

630   JESSIE   Yes.

MAMA   No. It was a big fat lie, the whole thing. He just thought it was funnier that way. God, this milk in here.

JESSIE   The cocoa helps.

MAMA [*Pleased that they agree on this, at least*]   Not enough, though, does it? You can still taste it, can't you?

JESSIE   Yeah, it's pretty bad. I thought it was my memory that was bad, but it's not. It's the milk, all right.

MAMA   It's a real waste of chocolate. You don't have to finish it.

JESSIE [*Putting her cup down*]   Thanks, though.

640   MAMA   I should've known not to make it. I knew you wouldn't like it. You never did like it.

JESSIE   You didn't ever love him, or he did something and you stopped loving him, or what?

MAMA   He felt sorry for me. He wanted a plain country woman and that's what he married, and then he held it against me the rest of my life like I was supposed to change and surprise him somehow. Like I remember this one day he was standing on the porch and I told him to get a shirt on and he went in and got one and then he said, real peaceful, but to the point, "You're right, Thelma. If God had meant for people to go around without any clothes on, 650   they'd have been born that way."

JESSIE [*Sees* MAMA*'s hurt*]   He didn't mean anything by that, Mama.

MAMA   He never said a word he didn't have to, Jessie. That was probably all he'd said to me all day, Jessie. So if he said it, there was something to it, but I never did figure that one out. What did that mean?

JESSIE   I don't know. I liked him better than you did, but I didn't know him any better.

MAMA   How could I love him, Jessie. I didn't have a thing he wanted. [JESSIE *doesn't answer*] He got his share, though. You loved him enough for both of us. You followed him around like some . . . Jessie, all the man ever 660   did was farm and sit . . . and try to think of somebody to sell the farm to.

JESSIE   Or make me a boyfriend out of pipe cleaners and sit back and smile like the stick man was about to dance and wasn't I going to get a kick out of that. Or sit up with a sick cow all night and leave me a chain of sleepy stick elephants on my bed in the morning.

MAMA   Or just sit.

JESSIE   I liked him sitting. Big old faded blue man in the chair. Quiet.

MAMA   Agnes gets more talk out of her birds than I got from the two of you. He could've had that GONE FISHING sign around his neck in that chair. I saw him stare off at the water. I saw him look at the weather rolling in. I got

670 where I could practically see the boat myself. But you, you knew what he was thinking about and you're going to tell me.

JESSIE I don't know, Mama! His life, I guess. His corn. His boots. Us. Things. You know.

MAMA No, I don't know, Jessie! You had those quiet little conversations after supper every night. What were you whispering about?

JESSIE We weren't whispering, you were just across the room.

MAMA What did you talk about?

JESSIE We talked about why black socks are warmer than blue socks. Is that something to go tell Mother? You were just jealous because I'd rather talk to
680 him than wash the dishes with you.

MAMA I was jealous because you'd rather talk to him than anything! [JESSIE *reaches across the table for the small clock and starts to wind it*] If I had died instead of him, he wouldn't have taken you in like I did.

JESSIE I wouldn't have expected him to.

MAMA Then what would you have done?

JESSIE Come visit.

MAMA Oh, I see. He died and left you stuck with me and you're mad about it.

JESSIE [*Getting up from the table*] Not anymore. He didn't mean to. I
690 didn't have to come here. We've been through this.

MAMA He felt sorry for you, too, Jessie, don't kid yourself about that. He said you were a runt and he said it from the day you were born and he said you didn't have a chance.

JESSIE [*Getting the canister of sugar and starting to refill the sugar bowl*] I know he loved me.

MAMA What if he did? It didn't change anything.

JESSIE It didn't have to. I miss him.

MAMA He never really went fishing, you know. Never once. His tackle box was full of chewing tobacco and all he ever did was drive out to the lake and
700 sit in his car. Dawson told me. And Bennie at the bait shop, he told Dawson. They all laughed about it. And he'd come back from fishing and all he'd have to show for it was . . . a whole pipe-cleaner *family*—chickens, pigs, a dog with a bad leg—it was creepy strange. It made me sick to look at them and I hid his pipe cleaners a couple of times but he always had more somewhere.

JESSIE I thought it might be better for you after he died. You'd get interested in things. Breathe better. Change somehow.

MAMA Into what? The Queen? A clerk in a shoe store? Why should I? Because he said to? Because you said to? [JESSIE *shakes her head*] Well I wasn't here for his entertainment and I'm not here for yours either, Jessie. I don't
710 know what I'm here for, but then I don't think about it. [*Realizing what all this means*] But I bet you wouldn't be killing yourself if he were still alive. That's a fine thing to figure out, isn't it?

JESSIE [*Filling the honey jar now*] That's not true.

MAMA Oh no? Then what were you asking about him for? Why did you want to know if I loved him?

JESSIE I didn't think you did, that's all.

MAMA   Fine then. You were right. Do you feel better now?

JESSIE [*Cleaning the honey jar carefully*]   It feels good to be right about it.

MAMA   It didn't matter whether I loved him. It didn't matter to me and it
720 didn't matter to him. And it didn't mean we didn't get along. It wasn't important. We didn't talk about it. [*Sweeping the pots off the cabinet*] Take all these
pots out to the porch!

JESSIE   What for?

MAMA   Just leave me this one pan. [*She jerks the silverware drawer open*]
Get me one knife, one fork, one big spoon, and the can opener, and put them
out where I can get them. [*Starts throwing knives and forks in one of the pans*]

JESSIE   Don't do that! I just straightened that drawer!

MAMA [*Throwing the pan in the sink*]   And throw out all the plates and
cups. I'll use paper. Loretta can have what she wants and Dawson can sell
730 the rest.

JESSIE [*Calmly*]   What are you doing?

MAMA   I'm not going to cook. I never liked it, anyway. I like candy.
Wrapped in plastic or coming in sacks. And tuna. I like tuna. I'll eat tuna,
thank you.

JESSIE [*Taking the pan out of the sink*]   What if you want to make apple
butter? You can't make apple butter in that little pan. What if you leave carrots
on cooking and burn up that pan?

MAMA   I don't like carrots.

JESSIE   What if the strawberries are good this year and you want to go
740 picking with Agnes.

MAMA   I'll tell her to bring a pan. You said you would do whatever I
wanted! I don't want a bunch of pans cluttering up my cabinets I can't get
down to, anyway. Throw them out. Every last one.

JESSIE [*Gathering up the pots*]   I'm putting them all back in. I'm not taking
them to the porch. If you want them, they'll be here. You'll bend down and
get them, like you got the one for the cocoa. And if somebody else comes
over here to cook, they'll have something to cook in, and that's the end of it!

MAMA   Who's going to come cook here?

JESSIE   Agnes.

750   MAMA   In my pots. Not on your life.

JESSIE   There's no reason why the two of you couldn't just live here together. Be cheaper for both of you and somebody to talk to. And if the birds
bothered you, well, one day when Agnes is out getting her hair done, you
could take them all for a walk!

MAMA [*As* JESSIE *straightens the silverware*]   So that's why you're pestering
me about Agnes. You think you can rest easy if you get me a new babysitter?
Well, I don't want to live with Agnes. I barely want to talk with Agnes. She's
just around. We go back, that's all. I'm not letting Agnes near this place. You
don't get off as easy as that, child.

760   JESSIE   O.K., then. It's just something to think about.

MAMA   I don't like things to think about. I like things to go on.

JESSIE [*Closing the silverware drawer*]   I want to know what Daddy said to
you the night he died. You came storming out of his room and said I could

wait it out with him if I wanted to, but you were going to watch *Gunsmoke*. What did he say to you?

MAMA   He didn't have *anything* to say to me, Jessie. That's why I left. He didn't say a thing. It was his last chance not to talk to me and he took full advantage of it.

770 JESSIE [*After a moment*]   I'm sorry you didn't love him. Sorry for you, I mean. He seemed like a nice man.

MAMA [*As* JESSIE *walks to the refrigerator*]   Ready for your apple now?

JESSIE   Soon as I'm through here, Mama.

MAMA   You won't like the apple, either. It'll be just like the cocoa. You never liked eating at all, did you? Any of it! What have you been living on all these years, toothpaste?

JESSIE [*As she starts to clean out the refrigerator*]   Now, you know the milkman comes on Wednesdays and Saturdays, and he leaves the order blank in an egg box, and you give the bills to Dawson once a month.

MAMA   Do they still make that orangeade?

780 JESSIE   It's not orangeade, it's just orange.

MAMA   I'm going to get some. I thought they stopped making it. You just stopped ordering it.

JESSIE   You should drink milk.

MAMA   Not anymore, I'm not. That hot chocolate was the last. Hooray.

JESSIE [*Getting the garbage can from under the sink*]   I told them to keep delivering a quart a week no matter what you said. I told them you'd run out of Cokes and you'd have to drink it. I told them I knew you wouldn't pour it on the ground . . .

MAMA [*Finishing her sentence*]   And you told them you weren't going to 790 be ordering anymore?

JESSIE   I told them I was taking a little holiday and to look after you.

MAMA   And they didn't think something was funny about that? You who doesn't go to the front steps? You, who only sees the driveway looking down from a stretcher passed out cold?

JESSIE [*Enjoying this, but not laughing*]   They said it was about time, but why didn't I take you with me? And I said I didn't think you'd want to go, and they said, "Yeah, everybody's got their own idea of vacation."

MAMA   I guess you think that's funny.

JESSIE [*Pulling jars out of the refrigerator*]   You know there never was any 800 reason to call the ambulance for me. All they ever did for me in the emergency room was let me wake up. I could've done that here. Now, I'll just call them out and you say yes or no. I know you like pickles. Ketchup?

MAMA   Keep it.

JESSIE   We've had this since last Fourth of July.

MAMA   Keep the ketchup. Keep it all.

JESSIE   Are you going to drink ketchup from the bottle or what? How can you want your food and not want your pots to cook it in? This stuff will all spoil in here, Mother.

MAMA   Nothing I ever did was good enough for you and I want to know why.

810 JESSIE   That's not true.

MAMA   And I want to know why you've lived here this long feeling the way you do.

JESSIE   You have no earthly idea how I feel.

MAMA   Well, how could I? You're real far back there, Jessie.

JESSIE   Back where?

MAMA   What's it like over there, where you are? Do people always say the right thing or get whatever they want, or what?

JESSIE   What are you talking about?

MAMA   Why do you read the newspaper? Why don't you wear that sweater I
820   made for you? Do you remember how I used to look, or am I just any old woman now? When you have a fit, do you see stars or what? How did you fall off the horse, really? Why did Cecil leave you? Where did you put my old glasses?

JESSIE [*Stunned by* MAMA*'s intensity*]   They're in the bottom drawer of your dresser in an old Milk of Magnesia box. Cecil left me because he made me choose between him and smoking.

MAMA   Jessie, I know he wasn't that dumb.

JESSIE   I never understood why he hated it so much when it's so good. Smoking is the only thing I know that's always just what you think it's going to be.
830   Just like it was the last time, right there when you want it and real quiet.

MAMA   Your fits made him sick and you know it.

JESSIE   Say seizures, not fits. Seizures.

MAMA   It's the same thing. A seizure in the hospital is a fit at home.

JESSIE   They didn't bother him at all. Except he did feel responsible for it. It *was* his idea to go horseback riding that day. It was his idea I could do *anything* if I just made up my mind to. I fell off the horse because I didn't know how to hold on. Cecil left for pretty much the same reason.

MAMA   He had a girl, Jessie. I walked right in on them in the toolshed.

JESSIE [*After a moment*]   O.K. That's fair. [*Lighting another cigarette*] Was
840   she very pretty?

MAMA   She was Agnes's girl, Carlene. Judge for yourself.

JESSIE [*As she walks to the living room*]   I guess you and Agnes had a good talk about that, huh?

MAMA   I never thought he was good enough for you. They moved here from Tennessee, you know.

JESSIE   What are you talking about? You liked him better than I did. You flirted him out here to build your porch or I'd never even met him at all. You thought maybe he'd help you out around the place, come in and get some coffee and talk to you. God knows what you thought. All that curly hair.

850   MAMA   He's the best carpenter I ever saw. That little house of yours will still be standing at the end of the world, Jessie.

JESSIE   You didn't need a porch, Mama.

MAMA   All right! I wanted you to have a husband.

JESSIE   And I couldn't get one on my own, of course.

MAMA   How were you going to get husband never opening your mouth to a living soul?

JESSIE   So I was quiet about it, so what?

MAMA   So I should have let you just sit here? Sit like your daddy? Sit here?

JESSIE   Maybe.

860   MAMA   Well, I didn't think so.

JESSIE   Well, what did you know?

MAMA   I never said I knew much. How was I supposed to learn anything living out here? I didn't know enough to do half the things I did in my life. Things happen. You do what you can about them and you see what happens next. I married you off to the wrong man, I admit that. So I took you in when he left. I'm sorry.

JESSIE   He wasn't the wrong man.

MAMA   He didn't love you, Jessie, or he wouldn't have left.

JESSIE   He wasn't the wrong man, Mama. I loved Cecil so much. And I tried
870   to get more exercise and I tried to stay awake. I tried to learn to ride a horse. And I tried to stay outside with him, but he always knew I was trying, so it didn't work.

MAMA   He was a selfish man. He told me once he hated to see people move into his houses after he built them. He knew they'd mess them up.

JESSIE   I loved that bridge he built over the creek in back of the house. It didn't have to be anything special, a couple of boards would have been just fine, but he used that yellow pine and rubbed it so smooth . . . .

MAMA   He had responsibilities here. He had a wife and son here and he failed you.

880   JESSIE   Or that baby bed he built for Ricky. I told him he didn't have to spend so much time on it, but he said it had to last, and the thing ended up weighing two hundred pounds and I couldn't move it. I said, "How long does a baby bed have to last, anyway?" But maybe he thought if it was strong enough, it might keep Ricky a baby.

MAMA   Ricky is too much like Cecil.

JESSIE   He is not. Ricky is as much like me as it's possible for any human to be. We even wear the same size pants. These are his, I think.

MAMA   That's just the same size. That's not you're the same person.

JESSIE   I see it on his face. I hear it when he talks. We look out at the world
890   and we see the same thing: Not Fair. And the only difference between us is Ricky's out there trying to get even. And he knows not to trust anybody and he got it straight from me. And he knows not to try to get work, and guess where he got that. He walks around like there's loose boards in the floor, and you know who laid that floor, I did.

MAMA   Ricky isn' through yet. You don't know how he'll turn out!

JESSIE   [*Going back to the kitchen*]   Yes I do and so did Cecil. Ricky is the two of us together for all time in too small a space. And we're tearing each other apart, like always, inside that boy, and if you don't see it, then you're just blind.

900   MAMA   Give him time, Jess.

JESSIE   Oh, he'll have plenty of that. Five years for forgery, ten years for armed assault . . .

MAMA   [*Furious*]   Stop that! [*Then pleading*] Jessie, Cecil might be ready to try it again, honey, that happens sometimes. Go downtown. Find him. Talk to him. He didn't know what he had in you. Maybe he sees things different now, but you're not going to know that till you go see him. Or call him up! Right now! He might be home.

JESSIE And say what? Nothing's changed, Cecil, I'd just like to look at you, if you don't mind? He loved me, Mama. He just didn't know how things fall down
910 around me like they do. I think he did the right thing. He gave himself another chance, that's all. But I did beg him to take me with him. I did tell him I would leave Ricky and you and everything I loved out here if only he would take me with him, but he couldn't and I understood that. [*Pause*] I wrote that note I showed you. I wrote it. Not Cecil. I said "I'm sorry, Jessie, I can't fix it all for you." I said I'd always love me, not Cecil. But that's how he felt.

MAMA Then he should've taken you with him!

JESSIE [*Picking up the garbage bag she has filled*] Mama, you don't pack your garbage when you move.

MAMA You will not call yourself garbage, Jessie.

920 JESSIE [*Taking the bag to the big garbage can near the back door*] Just a way of saying it, Mama. Thinking about my list, that's all. [*Opening the can, putting the garbage in, then securing the lid*] Well, a little more than that, I was trying to say it's all right that Cecil left. It was . . . a relief in a way. I never was what he wanted to see, so it was better when he wasn't looking at me all the time.

MAMA I'll make your apple now.

JESSIE No thanks. You get the manicure stuff and I'll be right there.

[JESSIE *ties up the big garbage bag in the can and replaces the small garbage bag under the sink, all the time trying desperately to regain her calm.* MAMA *watches, from a distance, her hand reaching unconsciously for the phone. Then she has a better idea. Or rather she thinks of the only other thing left and is willing to try it. Maybe she is even convinced it will work*]

MAMA Jessie, I think your daddy had little . . .

JESSIE [*Interrupting her*] Garbage night is Tuesday. Put it out as late as you can. The Davis's dogs get in it if you don't. [*Replacing the garbage bag in*
930 *the can under the sink*] And keep ordering the heavy black bags. It doesn't pay to buy the cheap ones. And I've got all the ties here with the hammers and all. Take them out of the box as soon as you open a new one and put them in this drawer. They'll get lost if you don't, and rubber bands or something else won't work.

MAMA I think your daddy had fits, too. I think he sat in his chair and had little fits. I read this a long time ago in a magazine, how little fits go, just little blackouts where maybe their eyes don't even close and people just call them "thinking spells."

JESSIE [*Getting the slipcover out of the laundry basket*] I don't think you
940 want this manicure we've been looking forward to. I washed this cover for the sofa, but it'll take both of us to get it back on.

MAMA I watched his eyes. I know that's what it was. The magazine said some people don't even know they've had one.

JESSIE   Daddy would've known if he'd had fits, Mama.

MAMA   The lady in this story had kept track of hers and she'd had eighty thousand of them in the last eleven years.

JESSIE   Next time you wash this cover, it'll dry better if you put it on wet.

MAMA   Jessie, listen to what I'm telling you. This lady had anywhere between five and five hundred fits a day and they lasted maybe fifteen seconds
950 apiece, so that out of her life, she'd only lost about two weeks altogether, and she had a fulltime secretary job and an IQ of 120.

JESSIE [*Amused by* MAMA*'s approach*]   You want to talk about fits, is that it?

MAMA   Yes. I do. I want to say . . .

JESSIE [*Interrupting*]   Most of the time I wouldn't even know I'd had one, except I wake up with different clothes on, feeling like I've been run over. Sometimes I feel my head start to turn around or hear myself scream. And sometimes there *is* this dizzy stupid feeling a little before it, but if the TV's on, well, it's easy to miss.

[*As* JESSIE *and* MAMA *replace the slipcover on the sofa and the afghan on the chair, the physical struggle somehow mirrors the emotional one in the conversation*]

MAMA   I can tell when you're about to have one. Your eyes get this big!
960 But, Jessie, you haven't . . .

JESSIE [*Taking charge of this*]   What do they look like? The seizures.

MAMA [*Reluctant*]   Different each time, Jess.

JESSIE   O.K. Pick one, then. A good one. I think I want to know now.

MAMA   There's not much to tell. You just . . . crumple, in a heap, like a puppet and somebody cut the strings all at once, or like the firing squad in some Mexican movie, you just slide down the wall, you know. You don't know what happens? How can you not know what happens?

JESSIE   I'm busy.

MAMA   That's not funny.

970 JESSIE   I'm not laughing. My head turns around and I fall down and then what?

MAMA   Well, your chest squeezes in and out, and you sound like you're gagging, sucking air in and out like you can't breathe.

JESSIE   Do it for me. Make the sound for me.

MAMA   I will not. It's awful-sounding.

JESSIE   Yeah. It felt like it might be. What's next?

MAMA   Your mouth bites down and I have to get your tongue out of the way fast, so you don't bite yourself.

JESSIE   Or you. I bite you, too, don't I?

980 MAMA   You got me once real good. I had to get a tetanus! But I know what to watch for now. And then you turn blue and the jerks start up. Like I'm standing there poking you with a cattle prod or you're sticking your finger in a light socket as fast as you can . . .

JESSIE   Foaming like a mad dog the whole time.

MAMA   It's bubbling, Jess, not foam like the washer overflowed, for God's sake; it's bubbling like a baby spitting up. I go get a wet washcloth, that's all.

And then the jerks slow down and you wet yourself and it's over. Two minutes tops.

JESSIE How do I get to the bed?

990 MAMA How do you think?

JESSIE I'm too heavy for you now. How do you do it?

MAMA I call Dawson. But I get you cleaned up before he gets here and I make him leave before you wake up.

JESSIE You could just leave me on the floor.

MAMA I want you to wake up someplace nice, O.K.? [*Then making a real effort*] But, Jessie, and this is the reason I even brought this up! You haven't had a seizure for a solid year. A whole year, do you realize that?

JESSIE Yeah, the phenobarb's about right now, I guess.

MAMA You bet it is. You might never have another one, ever! You might be

1000 through with it for all time!

JESSIE Could be.

MAMA You are. I know you are!

JESSIE I sure am feeling good. I really am. The double vision's gone and my gums aren't swelling. No rashes or anything. I'm feeling as good as I ever felt in my life. I'm even feeling like worrying or getting mad and I'm not afraid it will start a fit if I do, I just go ahead.

MAMA Of course you do! You can even scream at me, if you want to. I can take it. You don't have to act like you're just visiting here, Jessie. This is your house, too.

1010 JESSIE The best part is, my memory's back.

MAMA Your memory's always been good. When couldn't you remember things? You're always reminding me what . . .

JESSIE Because I've made lists for everything. But now I remember what things mean on my lists. I see "dish towels," and I used to wonder whether I was supposed to wash them, buy them, or look for them because I wouldn't remember where I put them after I washed them, but now I know it means wrap them up, they're a present for Loretta's birthday.

MAMA [*Finished with the sofa now*] You used to go looking for your lists, too. I've noticed that. You always know where they are now! [*Then suddenly*

1020 *worried*] Loretta's birthday isn't coming up, is it?

JESSIE I made a list of all the birthdays for you. I even put yours on it. [*A small smile*] So you can call Loretta and remind her.

MAMA Let's take Loretta to Howard Johnson's and have those fried clams. I *know* you love that clam roll.

JESSIE [*Slight pause*] I won't be here, Mama.

MAMA What have we just been talking about? You'll be here. You're well, Jessie. You're starting all over. You said it yourself. You're remembering things and . . .

JESSIE I won't be here. If I'd ever had a year like this, to think straight and

1030 all, before now, I'd be gone already.

MAMA [*Not pleading, commanding*] No. Jessie.

JESSIE [*Folding the rest of the laundry*] Yes, Mama. Once I started remembering, I could see what it all added up to.

MAMA   The fits are over!

JESSIE   It's not the fits, Mama.

MAMA   Then it's me for giving them to you, but I didn't do it!

JESSIE   It's not the fits! You said it yourself, the medicine takes care of the fits.

1040   MAMA [*Interrupting*]   Your daddy gave you those fits, Jessie. He passed it down to you like your green eyes and your straight hair. It's not my fault!

JESSIE   So what if he had little fits? It's not inherited. I fell off the horse. It was an accident.

MAMA   The horse wasn't the first time, Jessie. You had a fit when you were five years old.

JESSIE   I did not.

MAMA   You did! You were eating a popsicle and down you went. He gave it to you. It's *his* fault, not mine.

JESSIE   Well, you took your time telling me.

MAMA   How do you tell that to a five-year-old?

1050   JESSIE   What did the doctor say?

MAMA   He said kids have them all the time. He said there wasn't anything to do but wait for another one.

JESSIE   But I didn't have another one.

[*Now there is a real silence*]

JESSIE   You mean to tell me I had fits all the time as a kid and you just told me I fell down or something and it wasn't till I had the fit when Cecil was looking that anybody bothered to find out what was the matter with me?

MAMA   It wasn't *all the time,* Jessie. And they changed when you started to school. More like your daddy's. Oh, that was some swell time, sitting here with the two of you turning off and on like light bulbs some nights.

1060   JESSIE   How many fits did I have?

MAMA   You never hurt yourself. I never let you out of my sight. I caught you every time.

JESSIE   But you didn't tell anybody.

MAMA   It was none of their business.

JESSIE   You were ashamed.

MAMA   I didn't want anybody to know. Least of all you.

JESSIE   Least of all me. Oh, right. That was mine to know, Mama, not yours. Did Daddy know?

MAMA   He thought you were . . . you fell down a lot. That's what he
1070   thought. You were careless. Or maybe he thought I beat you. I don't know what he thought. He didn't think about it.

JESSIE   Because you didn't tell him!

MAMA   If I told him about you, I'd have to tell him about him!

JESSIE   I don't like this. I don't like this one bit.

MAMA   I didn't think you'd like it. That's why I didn't tell you.

JESSIE   If I'd known I was an epileptic, Mama, I wouldn't have ridden any horses.

MAMA Make you feel like a freak, is that what I should have done?

JESSIE Just get the manicure tray and sit down!

1080   MAMA [*Throwing it to the floor*] I don't want a manicure!

JESSIE Doesn't look like you do, no.

MAMA Maybe I did drop you, you don't know.

JESSIE If you say you didn't, you didn't.

MAMA [*Beginning to break down*] Maybe I fed you the wrong thing. Maybe you had a fever sometime and I didn't know it soon enough. Maybe it's a punishment.

JESSIE For what?

MAMA I don't know. Because of how I felt about your father. Because I didn't want any more children. Because I smoked too much or didn't eat

1090   right when I was carrying you. It has to be something I did.

JESSIE It does not. It's just a sickness, not a curse. Epilepsy doesn't mean anything. It just is.

MAMA I'm not talking about the fits here, Jessie! I'm talking about this killing yourself. It has to be me that's the matter here. You wouldn't be doing this if it wasn't. I didn't tell you things or I married you off to the wrong man or I took you in and let your life get away from you or all of it put together. I don't know what I did, but I did it, I know this is all my fault, Jessie, but I don't know what to do about it now!

JESSIE [*Exasperated at having to say this again*] It doesn't have anything

1100   to do with you!

MAMA Everything you do has to do with me, Jessie. You can't do *anything,* wash your face or cut your finger, without doing it to me. That's right! You might as well kill me as you, Jessie, it's the same thing. This has to do with me, Jessie.

JESSIE Then what if it does! What if it has everything to do with you! What if you are all I have and you're not enough? What if I could take all the rest of it if only I didn't have you here? What if the only way I can get away from you for good is to kill myself? What if it is? I can *still* do it!

MAMA [*In desperate tears*] Don't leave me, Jessie! [JESSIE *stands for a*

1110   *moment, then turns for the bedroom*] No! [*She grabs* JESSIE *'s arm*]

JESSIE [*Carefully taking her arm away*] I have a box of things I want people to have. I'm just going to go get it for you. You . . . just rest a minute.

[JESSIE *is gone.* MAMA *heads for the telephone, but she can't even pick up the receiver this time and, instead, stoops to clean up the bottles that have spilled out of the manicure tray*

JESSIE *returns, carrying a box that groceries were delivered in. It probably says Hershey Kisses or Starkist Tuna.* MAMA *is still down on the floor cleaning up, hoping that maybe if she just makes it look nice enough,* JESSIE *will stay*]

MAMA Jessie, how can I live here without you? I need you! You're supposed to tell me to stand up straight and say how nice I look in my pink dress, and drink my milk. You're supposed to go around and lock up so I know we're safe for the night, and when I wake up, you're supposed to be out there

making the coffee and watching me get older every day, and you're supposed to help me die when the time comes. I can't do that by myself, Jessie. I'm not like you, Jessie. I hate the quiet and I don't want to die and I don't want you
1120 to go, Jessie. How can I . . . [*Has to stop a moment*] How can I get up every day knowing you had to kill yourself to make it stop hurting and I was here all the time and I never even saw it. And then you gave me this chance to make it better, convince you to stay alive, and I couldn't do it. How can I live with myself after this, Jessie?

JESSIE   I only told you so I could explain it, so you wouldn't blame your-self, so you wouldn't feel bad. There wasn't anything you could say to change my mind. I didn't want you to save me. I just wanted you to know.

MAMA   Stay with me just a little longer. Just a few more years. I don't have that many more to go, Jessie. And as soon as I'm dead, you can do whatever
1130 you want. Maybe with me gone, you'll have all the quiet you want, right here in the house. And maybe one day you'll put in some begonias up the walk and get just the right rain for them all summer. And Ricky will be married by then and he'll bring your grandbabies over and you can sneak them a piece of candy when their daddy's not looking and then be real glad when they've gone home and left you to your quiet again.

JESSIE   Don't you see, Mama, everything I do winds up like this. How could I think you would understand? How could I think you would want a mani-cure? We could hold hands for an hour and then I could go shoot myself? I'm sorry about tonight, Mama, but it's exactly why I'm doing it.

1140   MAMA   If you've got the guts to kill yourself, Jessie, you've got the guts to stay alive.

JESSIE   I know that. So it's really just a matter of where I'd rather be.

MAMA   Look, maybe I can't think of what you should do, but that doesn't mean there isn't something that would help. *You* find it. *You* think of it. You can keep trying. You can get brave and try some more. You don't have to give up!

JESSIE   I'm *not* giving up! This *is* the other thing I'm trying. And I'm sure there are some other things that might work, but *might* work isn't good enough anymore. I need something that *will* work. *This* will work. That's why I picked it.

1150   MAMA   But something might happen. Something that could change every-thing. Who knows what it might be, but it might be worth waiting for! [JESSIE *doesn't respond*] Try it for two more weeks. We could have more talks like tonight.

JESSIE   No, Mama.

MAMA   I'll pay more attention to you. Tell the truth when you ask me. Let you have your say.

JESSIE   No, Mama! We wouldn't have more talks like tonight, because it's this next part that's made this last part so good, Mama. No, Mama. *This* is how I have my say. This is how I say what I thought about it *all* and I say no. To
1160 Dawson and Loretta and the Red Chinese and epilepsy and Ricky and Cecil and you. And me. And hope. I say no! [*Then going to Mama on the sofa*] Just let me go easy, Mama.

MAMA   How can I let you go?

JESSIE   You can because you have to. It's what you've always done.

MAMA   You are my child!

JESSIE   I am what became of your child. [MAMA *cannot answer*] I found an old baby picture of me. And it was somebody else, not me. It was somebody pink and fat who never heard of sick or lonely, somebody who cried and got fed, and reached up and got held and kicked but didn't hurt anybody, and
1170   slept whenever she wanted to, just by closing her eyes. Somebody who mainly just laid there and laughed at the colors waving around over her head and chewed on a polka-dot whale and woke up knowing some new trick nearly every day, and rolled over and drooled on the sheet and felt your hand pulling my quilt back up over me. That's who I started out and this is who is left. [*There is no self-pity here*] That's what this is about. It's somebody I lost, all right, it's my own self. Who I never was. Or who I tried to be and never got there. Somebody I waited for who never came. And never will. So, see, it doesn't much matter what else happens in the world or in this house, even. I'm what was worth waiting for and I didn't make it. Me . . . who might have
1180   made a difference to me . . . I'm not going to show up, so there's no reason to stay, except to keep you company, and that's . . . not reason enough because I'm not . . . very good company. [*Pause*] Am I.

MAMA [*Knowing she must tell the truth*]   No. And neither am I.

JESSIE   I had this strange little thought, well, maybe it's not so strange. Anyway, after Christmas, after I decided to do this, I would wonder, sometimes, what might keep me here, what might be worth staying for, and you know what it was? It was maybe if there was something I really liked, like maybe if I really liked rice pudding or cornflakes for breakfast or something, that might be enough.

1190   MAMA   Rice pudding is good.

JESSIE   Not to me.

MAMA   And you're not afraid?

JESSIE   Afraid of what?

MAMA   I'm afraid of it, for me, I mean. When my time comes. I know it's coming, but . . .

JESSIE   You don't know when. Like in a scary movie.

MAMA   Yeah, sneaking up on me like some killer on the loose, hiding out in the back yard just waiting for me to have my hands full someday and how am I supposed to protect myself anyhow when I don't know what he looks
1200   like and I don't know how he sounds coming up behind me like that or if it will hurt or take very long or what I don't get done before it happens.

JESSIE   You've got plenty of time left.

MAMA   I forget what for, right now.

JESSIE   For whatever happens, I don't know. For the rest of your life. For Agnes burning down one more house or Dawson losing his hair or . . .

MAMA [*Quickly*]   Jessie. I can't just sit here and say O.K., kill yourself if you want to.

JESSIE   Sure you can. You just did. Say it again.

MAMA [*Really startled*]   Jessie! [*Quiet horror*] How dare you! [*Furious*]
1210   How dare you! You think you can just leave whenever you want, like you're

watching television here? No, you can't, Jessie. You make me feel like a fool for being alive, child, and you are so wrong! I like it here, and I will stay here until they make me go, until they drag me screaming and I mean screeching into my grave, and you're real smart to get away before then because, I mean, honey, you've never heard noise like that in your life. [JESSIE *turns away*] Who am I talking to? You're gone already, aren't you? I'm looking right through you! I can't stop you because you're already gone! I guess you think they'll all have to talk about you now! I guess you think this will really confuse them. Oh yes, ever since Christmas you've been laughing to yourself
1220 and thinking, "Boy, are they all in for a surprise." Well, nobody's going to be a bit surprised, sweetheart. This is just like you. Do it the hard way, that's my girl, all right. [JESSIE *gets up and goes into the kitchen, but* MAMA *follows her*] You know who they're going to feel sorry for? Me! How about that! Not you, me! They're going to be *ashamed* of you. Yes. *Ashamed!* If somebody asks Dawson about it, he'll change the subject as fast as he can. He'll talk about how much he has to pay to park his car these days.

JESSIE Leave me alone.

MAMA It's the truth!

JESSIE I should've just left you a note!

1230 MAMA [*Screaming*] Yes! [*Then suddenly understanding what she has said, nearly paralyzed by the thought of it, she turns slowly to face* JESSIE, *nearly whispering*] No. No. I . . . might not have thought of all the things you've said.

JESSIE It's O.K., Mama.

[MAMA *is nearly unconscious from the emotional devastation of these last few moments. She sits down at the kitchen table, hurt and angry and desperately afraid. But she looks almost numb. She is so far beyond what is known as pain that she is virtually unreachable and* JESSIE *knows this, and talks quietly, watching for signs of recovery*]

JESSIE [*Washes her hands in the sink*] I remember you liked that preacher who did Daddy's, so if you want to ask him to the service, that's O.K. with me.

MAMA [*Not an answer, just a word*] What.

JESSIE [*Putting on hand lotion as she talks*] And pick some songs you like or let Agnes pick, she'll know exactly which ones. Oh, and I had your dress
1240 cleaned that you wore to Daddy's. You looked real good in that.

MAMA I don't remember, hon.

JESSIE And it won't be so bad once your friends start coming to the funeral home. You'll probably see people you haven't seen for years, but I thought about what you should say to get you over that nervous part when they first come in.

MAMA [*Simply repeating*] Come in.

JESSIE Take them up to see their flowers, they'd like that. And when they say, "I'm so sorry, Thelma," you just say, "I appreciate your coming, Connie." And then ask how their garden was this summer or what they're doing for
1250 Thanksgiving or how their children . . .

MAMA   I don't think I should ask about their children. I'll talk about what they have on, that's always good. And I'll have some crochet work with me.

JESSIE   And Agnes will be there, so you might not have to talk at all.

MAMA   Maybe if Connie Richards does come, I can get her to tell me where she gets that Irish yarn, she calls it. I know it doesn't come from Ireland. I think it just comes with a green wrapper.

JESSIE   And be sure to invite enough people home afterward so you get enough food to feed them all and have some left for you. But don't let anybody take anything home, especially Loretta.

1260   MAMA   Loretta will get all the food set up, honey. It's only fair to let her have some macaroni or something.

JESSIE   No, Mama. You have to be more selfish from now on. [*Sitting at the table with* MAMA] Now, somebody's bound to ask you why I did it and you just say you don't know. That you loved me and you know I loved you and we just sat around tonight like every other night of our lives, and then I came over and kissed you and said, "'Night, Mother," and you heard me close my bedroom door and the next thing you heard was the shot. And whatever reasons I had, well, you guess I just took them with me.

MAMA [*Quietly*]   It was something personal.

1270   JESSIE   Good. That's good, Mama.

MAMA   That's what I'll say, then.

JESSIE   Personal. Yeah.

MAMA   Is that what I tell Dawson and Loretta, too? We sat around, you kissed me, "'Night, Mother"? They'll want to know more, Jessie. They won't believe it.

JESSIE   Well, then, tell them what we did. I filled up the candy jars. I cleaned out the refrigerator. We made some hot chocolate and put the cover back on the sofa. You had no idea. All right? I really think it's better that way. If they knew we talked about it, they really won't understand how you let me go.

1280   MAMA   I guess not.

JESSIE   It's private. Tonight is private, yours and mine, and I don't want anybody else to have any of it.

MAMA   O.K., then.

JESSIE [*Standing behind* MAMA *now, holding her shoulders*]   Now, when you hear the shot, I don't want you to come in. First of all, you won't be able to get in by yourself, but I don't want you trying. Call Dawson, then call the police, and then call Agnes. And then you'll need something to do till somebody gets here, so wash the hot-chocolate pan. You wash that pan till you hear the doorbell ring and I don't care if it's an hour, you keep washing that pan.

1290   MAMA   I'll make my calls and then I'll just sit. I won't need something to do. What will the police say?

JESSIE   They'll do that gunpowder test, I guess, and ask you what happened, and by that time, the ambulance will be here and they'll come in and get me and you know how that goes. You stay out here with Dawson and Loretta. You keep Dawson out here. I want the police in the room first, not Dawson, O.K.?

MAMA   What if Dawson and Loretta want me to go home with them?

JESSIE [*Returning to the living room*]   That's up to you.

MAMA   I think I'll stay here. All they've got is Sanka.

JESSIE   Maybe Agnes could come stay with you for a few days.

1300   MAMA [*Standing up, looking into the living room*]   I'd rather be by myself, I think. [*Walking toward the box* JESSIE *brought in earlier*] You want me to give people those things?

JESSIE [*They sit down on the sofa,* JESSIE *holding the box on her lap*]   I want Loretta to have my little calculator. Dawson bought it for himself, you know, but then he saw one he liked better and he couldn't bring both of them home with Loretta counting every penny the way she does, so he gave the first one to me. Be funny for her to have it now, don't you think? And all my house slippers are in a sack for her in my closet. Tell her I know they'll fit and I've never worn any of them, and make sure Dawson hears you tell her that. I'm glad he loves
1310   Loretta so much, but I wish he knew not everybody has her size feet.

MAMA [*Taking the calculator*]   O.K.

JESSIE [*Reaching into the box again*]   This letter is for Dawson, but it's mostly about you, so read it if you want. There's a list of presents for you for at least twenty more Christmases and birthdays, so if you want anything special you better add it to this list before you give it to him. Or if you want to be surprised, just don't read that page. This Christmas, you're getting mostly stuff for the house, like a new rug in your bathroom and needlework, but next Christmas, you're really going to cost him next Christmas. I think you'll like
it a lot and you'd never think of it.

1320   MAMA   And you think he'll go for it?

JESSIE   I think he'll feel like a real jerk if he doesn't. Me telling him to, like this and all. Now, this number's where you call Cecil. I called it last week and he answered, so I know he still lives there.

MAMA   What do you want me to tell him?

JESSIE   Tell him we talked about him and I only had good things to say about him, but mainly tell him to find Ricky and tell him what I did, and tell Ricky you have something for him, out here, from me, and to come get it. [*Pulls a sack out of the box*]

MAMA [*The sack feels empty*]   What is it?

1330   JESSIE [*Taking it off*]   My watch. [*Putting it in the sack and taking a ribbon out of the sack to tie around the top of it*]

MAMA   He'll sell it!

JESSIE   That's the idea. I appreciate him not stealing it already. I'd like to buy him a good meal.

MAMA   He'll buy dope with it!

JESSIE   Well, then, I hope he gets some good dope with it, Mama. And the rest of this is for you. [*Handing* MAMA *the box now.* MAMA *picks up the things and looks at them*]

MAMA [*Surprised and pleased*]   When did you do all this? During my naps,
1340   I guess.

JESSIE   I guess. I tried to be quiet about it. [*As* MAMA *is puzzled by the presents*] Those are just little presents. For whenever you need one. They're not bought presents, just things I thought you might like to look at, pictures or things you think you've lost. Things you didn't know you had, even. You'll see.

MAMA I'm not sure I want them. They'll make me think of you.

JESSIE No they won't. They're just things, like a free tube of toothpaste I found hanging on the door one day.

MAMA Oh. All right, then.

JESSIE Well, maybe there's one nice present in there somewhere. It's 1350 Granny's ring she gave me and I thought you might like to have it, but I didn't think you'd wear it if I gave it to you right now.

MAMA [*Taking the box to a table nearby*] No. Probably not. [*Turning back to face her*] I'm ready for my manicure, I guess. Want me to wash my hands again?

JESSIE [*Standing up*] It's time for me to go, Mama.

MAMA [*Starting for her*] No, Jessie, you've got all night!

JESSIE [*As* MAMA *grabs her*] No, Mama.

MAMA It's not even ten o'clock.

JESSIE [*Very calm*] Let me go, Mama.

1360 MAMA I can't. You can't go. You can't do this. You didn't say it would be so soon, Jessie. I'm scared. I love you.

JESSIE [*Takes her hands away*] Let go of me, Mama. I've said everything I had to say.

MAMA [*Standing still a minute*] You said you wanted to do my nails.

JESSIE [*Taking a small step backward*] I can't. It's too late.

MAMA It's not too late!

JESSIE I don't want you to wake Dawson and Loretta when you call. I want them to still be up and dressed so they can get right over.

MAMA [*As* JESSIE *backs up,* MAMA *moves in on her, but carefully*] They wake 1370 up fast, Jessie, if they have to. They don't matter here, Jessie. You do. I do. We're not through yet. We've got a lot of things to take care of here. I don't know where my prescriptions are and you didn't tell me what to tell Dr. Davis when he calls or how much you want me to tell Ricky or who I call to rake the leaves or . . .

JESSIE Don't try and stop me, Mama, you can't do it.

MAMA [*Grabbing her again, this time hard*] I can too! I'll stand in front of this hall and you can't get past me. [*They struggle*] You'll have to knock me down to get away from me, Jessie. I'm not about to let you . . .

[MAMA *struggles with* JESSIE *at the door and in the struggle* JESSIE *gets away from her and—*

JESSIE [*Almost a whisper*] 'Night, Mother. [*She vanishes into her bedroom* 1380 *and we hear the door lock just as* MAMA *gets to it*]

MAMA [*Screams*] Jessie! [*Pounding on the door*] Jessie, you let me in there. Don't you do this, Jessie. I'm not going to stop screaming until you open this door, Jessie. Jessie! Jessie! What if I don't do any of the things you told me to do! I'll tell Cecil what a miserable man he was to make you feel the way he did and I'll give Ricky's watch to Dawson if I feel like it and the only way you can make sure I do what you want is you come out here and make me, Jessie! [*Pounding again*] Jessie! Stop this! I didn't know! I was here with you all the time. How could I know you were so alone?

[*And* MAMA *stops for a moment, breathless and frantic, putting her ear to the door, and when she doesn't hear anything, she stands up straight again and screams once more*]

Jessie! Please!

[*And we hear the shot, and it sounds like an answer, it sounds like No.*
   MAMA *collapses against the door, tears streaming down her face, but not scream-ing anymore. In shock now*]

1390 Jessie, Jessie, child . . . Forgive me. [*Pause*] I thought you were mine.

[*And she leaves the door and makes her way through the living room, around the furniture, as though she didn't know where it was, not knowing what to do. Finally, she goes to the stove in the kitchen and picks up the hot-chocolate pan and carries it with her to the telephone, and holds on to it while she dials the number. She looks down at the pan, holding it tight like her life depended on it. She hears Loretta answer*]

MAMA Loretta, let me talk to Dawson, honey.

Tennessee Williams

Tennessee Williams (1911–1983) was born in Mississippi and grew up in Mississippi and Missouri. He began writing for the theater when he was in his twenties, and *The Glass Menagerie* was his first success in 1944. *A Streetcar Named Desire* came in 1947, followed by *Summer and Smoke* (1948), *The Rose Tattoo* (1950), *Camino Real* (1953), *Cat on a Hot Tin Roof* (1955), *Suddenly Last Summer* (1958), and many other plays. He also wrote short stories, poetry, and his *Memoirs* (1975). Many lovers of the theater prefer *The Glass Menagerie* above his other successes. Autobiographical, written in poetic language, it is a memory play of sympathy and compassion.

The Glass Menagerie (1944)

The Characters

AMANDA WINGFIELD [*the mother*]

A little woman of great but confused vitality clinging frantically to another time and place. Her characterization must be carefully created, not copied from type. She is not paranoiac, but her life is paranoia. There is much to admire in Amanda, and as much to love and pity as there is to laugh at. Certainly she has endurance and a kind of heroism, and though her foolishness makes her unwittingly cruel at times, there is tenderness in her slight person.

LAURA WINGFIELD [*her daughter*]

Amanda, having failed to establish contact with reality, continues to live vitally in her illusions, but Laura's situation is even graver. A childhood illness has left her crippled, one leg slightly shorter than the other, and held in a brace. This defect need not be more than suggested on the stage. Stemming from this, Laura's separation increases till she is like a piece of her own glass collection, too exquisitely fragile to move from the shelf.

TOM WINGFIELD [*her son*]

And the narrator of the play. A poet with a job in a warehouse. His nature is not remorseless, but to escape from a trap he has to act without pity.

JIM O'CONNOR [*the gentleman caller*]

A nice, ordinary, young man.

Scene One

The Wingfield apartment is in the rear of the building, one of those vast hive-like conglomerations of cellular living-units that flower as warty growths in overcrowded urban centers of lower middle-class population and are symptomatic of the impulse of this largest and fundamentally enslaved section of American society to avoid fluidity and differentiation and to exist and function as one interfused mass of automatism.

The apartment faces an alley and is entered by a fire escape, a structure whose name is a touch of accidental poetic truth, for all of these huge buildings are always burning with the slow and implacable fires of human desperation. The fire escape is part of what we see — that is, the landing of it and steps descending from it.

The scene is memory and is therefore nonrealistic. Memory takes a lot of poetic license. It omits some details; others are exaggerated, according to the emotional value of the articles it touches, for memory is seated predominantly in the heart. The interior is therefore rather dim and poetic.

At the rise of the curtain, the audience is faced with the dark, grim rear wall of the Wingfield tenement. This building is flanked on both sides by dark, narrow alleys which run into murky canyons of tangled clotheslines, garbage cans, and the sinister latticework of neighboring fire escapes. It is up and down these side alleys that exterior entrances and exits are made during the play. At the end of TOM's *opening commentary, the dark tenement wall slowly becomes transparent and reveals the interior of the ground-floor Wingfield apartment.*

Nearest the audience is the living room, which also serves as a sleeping room for LAURA, *the sofa unfolding to make her bed. Just beyond, separated from the living room by a wide arch or second proscenium with transparent faded portieres [or second curtain], is the dining room. In an old-fashioned whatnot in the living room are seen scores of transparent glass animals. A blown-up photograph of the father hangs on the wall of the living room, to the left of the archway. It is the face of a very handsome young man in a doughboy's First World War cap. He is gallantly smiling, ineluctably smiling, as if to say "I will be smiling forever."*

Also hanging on the wall, near the photograph, are a typewriter keyboard chart and a Gregg shorthand diagram. An upright typewriter on a small table stands beneath the charts.

The audience hears and sees the opening scene in the dining room through both the transparent fourth wall of the building and the transparent gauze portieres of the dining-room arch. It is during this revealing scene that the fourth wall slowly ascends, out of sight. This transparent exterior wall is not brought down again until the very end of the play, during TOM'*s final speech.*

The narrator is an undisguised convention of the play. He takes whatever license with dramatic convention is convenient to his purposes.

TOM *enters, dressed as a merchant sailor, and strolls across to the fire escape. There he stops and lights a cigarette. He addresses the audience.*

TOM   Yes, I have tricks in my pocket, I have things up my sleeve. But I am the opposite of a stage magician. He gives you illusion that has the appearance of truth. I give you truth in the pleasant disguise of illusion.

To begin with, I turn back time. I reverse it to that quaint period, the thirties, when the huge middle class of America was matriculating in a school for the blind. Their eyes had failed them, or they had failed their eyes, and so they were having their fingers pressed forcibly down on the fiery Braille alphabet of a dissolving economy.

In Spain there was revolution. Here there was only shouting and confu-
10 sion. In Spain there was Guernica. Here there were disturbances of labor, sometimes pretty violent, in otherwise peaceful cities such as Chicago, Cleveland, Saint Louis . . . This is the social background of the play.

[*Music begins to play.*]

The play is memory. Being a memory play, it is dimly lighted, it is sentimental, it is not realistic. In memory everything seems to happen to music. That explains the fiddle in the wings.

I am the narrator of the play, and also a character in it. The other characters are my mother, Amanda, my sister, Laura, and a gentleman caller who appears in the final scenes. He is the most realistic character in the play, being an emissary from the world of reality that we were somehow set apart
20 from. But since I have a poet's weakness for symbols, I am using this character also as a symbol, he is the long-delayed but always expected something that we live for.

There is a fifth character in the play who doesn't appear except in this larger-than-life photograph over the mantel. This is our father who left us a long time ago. He was a telephone man who fell in love with long distances; he gave up his job with the telephone company and skipped the light fantastic out of town . . . The last we heard of him was a picture postcard from Mazutlan, on the Pacific coast of Mexico, containing a message of two words: "Hello—Goodbye!" and no address.

30   I think the rest of the play will explain itself. . . .

[AMANDA's *voice becomes audible through the portieres.*]

[*Legend on screen:* "Ou sont les neiges."]

[TOM *divides the portieres and enters the dining room.* AMANDA *and* LAURA *are seated at a drop-leaf table. Eating is indicated by gestures without food or utensils.* AMANDA *faces the audience.* TOM *and* LAURA *are seated in profile. The interior has lit up softly and through the scrim we see* AMANDA *and* LAURA *seated at the table.*]

AMANDA [*calling*]   Tom?
TOM   Yes, Mother.
AMANDA   We can't say grace until you come to the table!
TOM   Coming, Mother. [*He bows slightly and withdraws, reappearing a few moments later in his place at the table.*]
AMANDA [*to her son*]   Honey, don't *push* with your *fingers*. If you have to push with something, the thing to push with is a crust of bread, and chew— chew! Animals have secretions in their stomachs which enable them to digest food without mastication, but human beings are supposed to chew their food
40   before they swallow it down. Eat food leisurely, son, and really enjoy it. A well-cooked meal has lots of delicate flavors that have to be held in the mouth for appreciation. So chew your food and give your salivary glands a chance to function!

[TOM *deliberately lays his imaginary fork down and pushes his chair back from the table.*]

TOM   I haven't enjoyed one bite of this dinner because of your constant directions on how to eat it. It's you that make me rush through meals with your hawklike attention to every bite I take. Sickening—spoils my appetite—all this discussion of—animals' secretion—salivary glands—mastication!
AMANDA [*lightly*]   Temperament like a Metropolitan star!

[TOM *rises and walks toward the living room.*]

You're not excused from the table.
50   TOM   I'm getting a cigarette.
AMANDA   You smoke too much.

[LAURA *rises.*]

LAURA   I'll bring in the blanc mange.

[TOM *remains standing with his cigarette by the portieres.*]

AMANDA [*rising*]   No, sister, no, sister—you be the lady this time and I'll
be the darky.
LAURA   I'm already up.
AMANDA   Resume your seat, little sister—I want you to stay fresh and
pretty—for gentlemen callers!
LAURA [*sitting down*]   I'm not expecting any gentlemen callers.
AMANDA [*crossing out to the kitchenette, airily*]   Sometimes they come
60 when they are least expected! Why, I remember one Sunday afternoon in
Blue Mountain—

[*She enters the kitchenette.*]

TOM   I know what's coming!
LAURA   Yes. But let her tell it.
TOM   Again?
LAURA   She loves to tell it.

[AMANDA *returns with a bowl of dessert.*]

AMANDA   One Sunday afternoon in Blue Mountain—your mother received—
seventeen!—gentlemen callers! Why, sometimes there weren't chairs enough
to accommodate them all. We had to send the nigger over to bring in folding
chairs from the parish house.
70   TOM [*remaining at the portieres*]   How did you entertain those gentlemen
callers?
AMANDA   I understood the art of conversation!
TOM   I bet you could talk.
AMANDA   Girls in those days *knew* how to talk, I can tell you.
TOM   Yes?

[*Image on screen:* AMANDA *as a girl on a porch, greeting callers.*]

AMANDA   They knew how to entertain their gentlemen callers. It wasn't
enough for a girl to be possessed of a pretty face and a graceful figure—
although I wasn't slighted in either respect. She also needed to have a nim-
ble wit and a tongue to meet all occasions.
80   TOM   What did you talk about?
AMANDA   Things of importance going on in the world! Never anything
coarse or common or vulgar.

[*She addresses* TOM *as though he were seated in the vacant chair at the table though
he remains by the portieres. He plays this scene as though reading from a script.*]

My callers were gentlemen—all! Among my callers were some of the most
prominent young planters of the Mississippi Delta—planters and sons of
planters!

[TOM *motions for music and a spot of light on* AMANDA. *Her eyes lift, her face glows, her
voice becomes rich and elegiac.*]

[*Screen legend:* "Où sont les neiges d'antan?"]

There was young Champ Laughlin who later became vice-president of the
Delta Planters Bank. Hadley Stevenson who was drowned in Moon Lake and
left his widow one hundred and fifty thousand in Government bonds. There
were the Cutrere brothers, Wesley and Bates. Bates was one of my bright
90 particular beaux! He got in a quarrel with that wild Wainwright boy. They
shot it out on the floor of Moon Lake Casino. Bates was shot through the
stomach. Died in the ambulance on his way to Memphis. His widow was also
well provided-for, came into eight or ten thousand acres, that's all. She married him on the rebound—never loved her—carried my picture on him the
night he died! And there was that boy that every girl in the Delta had set her
cap for! That beautiful, brilliant, young Fitzhugh boy from Greene County!
    TOM What did he leave his widow?
    AMANDA He never married! Gracious, you talk as though all of my old
admirers had turned up their toes to the daisies!
100   TOM Isn't this the first you've mentioned that still survives?
    AMANDA That Fitzhugh boy went North and made a fortune—came to be
known as the Wolf of Wall Street! He had the Midas touch, whatever he
touched turned to gold! And I could have been Mrs. Duncan J. Fitzhugh,
mind you! But—I picked your *father!*
    LAURA [*rising*] Mother, let me clear the table.
    AMANDA No, dear, you go in front and study your typewriter chart. Or prac-
tice your shorthand a little. Stay fresh and pretty!—It's almost time for our
gentlemen callers to start arriving. [*She flounces girlishly toward the kitchenette.*] How many do you suppose we're going to entertain this afternoon?

[TOM *throws down the paper and jumps up with a groan.*]

110   LAURA [*alone in the dining room*] I don't believe we're going to receive
any, Mother.
    AMANDA [*reappearing, airily*] What? No one—not one? You must be joking!

[LAURA *nervously echoes her laugh. She slips in a fugitive manner through the half-
open portieres and draws them gently behind her. A shaft of very clear light is thrown
on her face against the faded tapestry of the curtains. Faintly the music of "The Glass
Menagerie" is heard as she continues, lightly:*]

Not one gentleman caller? It can't be true! There must be a flood, there must
have been a tornado!

LAURA   It isn't a flood, it's not a tornado, Mother. I'm just not popular like you were in Blue Mountain. . . .

[TOM *utters another groan.* LAURA *glances at him with a faint, apologetic smile. Her voice catches a little:*]

Mother's afraid I'm going to be an old maid.

[*The scene dims out with the "Glass Menagerie" music.*]

Scene Two

On the dark stage the screen is lighted with the image of blue roses. Gradually LAURA*'s figure becomes apparent and the screen goes out. The music subsides.*
   LAURA *is seated in the delicate ivory chair at the small claw-foot table. She wears a dress of soft violet material for a kimono—her hair is tied back from her forehead with a ribbon. She is washing and polishing her collection of glass.* AMANDA *appears on the fire escape steps. At the sound of her ascent,* LAURA *catches her breath, thrusts the bowl of ornaments away, and seats herself stiffly before the diagram of the typewriter keyboard as though it held her spellbound. Something has happened to* AMANDA. *It is written in her face as she climbs to the landing: a look that is grim and hopeless and a little absurd. She has on one of those cheap or imitation velvety-looking cloth coats with imitation fur collar. Her hat is five or six years old, one of those dreadful cloche hats that were worn in the late Twenties, and she is clutching an enormous black patent-leather pocketbook with nickel clasps and initials. This is her full-dress outfit, the one she usually wears to the D.A.R. Before entering she looks through the door. She purses her lips, opens her eyes very wide, rolls them upward and shakes her head. Then she slowly lets herself in the door. Seeing her mother's expression* LAURA *touches her lips with a nervous gesture.*]

   LAURA   Hello, Mother, I was—[*She makes a nervous gesture toward the chart on the wall.* AMANDA *leans against the shut door and stares at* LAURA *with a martyred look.*]
   AMANDA   Deception? Deception? [*She slowly removes her hat and gloves, continuing the sweet suffering stare. She lets the hat and gloves fall on the floor—a bit of acting.*]
   LAURA [*shakily*]   How was the D.A.R. meeting?

[AMANDA *slowly opens her purse and removes a dainty white handkerchief which she shakes out delicately and delicately touches to her lips and nostrils.*]

Didn't you go to the D.A.R. meeting, Mother?
   AMANDA [*faintly, almost inaudibly*]   —No.—No. [*then more forcibly:*] I
10 did not have the strength—to go to the D.A.R. In fact, I did not have the courage! I wanted to find a hole in the ground and hide myself in it forever!
[*She crosses slowly to the wall and removes the diagram of the typewriter keyboard. She holds it in front of her for a second, staring at it sweetly and*

sorrowfully—then bites her lips and tears it in two pieces.]
　　LAURA [*faintly*]   Why did you do that, Mother?

[AMANDA *repeats the same procedure with the chart of the Gregg Alphabet.*]

Why are you—
　　AMANDA   Why? Why? How old are you, Laura?
　　LAURA   Mother, you know my age.
　　AMANDA   I thought that you were an adult; it seems that I was mistaken.
20 [*She crosses slowly to the sofa and sinks down and stares at* LAURA.]
　　LAURA   Please don't stare at me, Mother.

[AMANDA *closes her eyes and lowers her head. There is a ten-second pause.*]

　　AMANDA   What are we going to do, what is going to become of us, what is the future?

[*There is another pause.*]

　　LAURA   Has something happened, Mother?

[AMANDA *draws a long breath, takes out the handkerchief again, goes through the dabbing process.*]

Mother, has—something happened?
　　AMANDA   I'll be all right in a minute, I'm just bewildered—[*She hesitates.*]—by life. . . .
　　LAURA   Mother, I wish that you would tell me what's happened!
　　AMANDA   As you know, I was supposed to be inducted into my office at the
30 D.A.R. this afternoon.

[*Screen image:* A swarm of typewriters.]

But I stopped off at Rubicam's Business College to speak to your teachers about your having a cold and ask them what progress they thought you were making down there.
　　LAURA   Oh. . . .
　　AMANDA   I went to the typing instructor and introduced myself as your mother. She didn't know who you were. "Wingfield," she said. "We don't have any such student enrolled at the school!"
　　I assured her she did, that you had been going to classes since early in January.
40 　"I wonder," she said. "If you could be talking about that terribly shy little girl who dropped out of school after only a few days' attendance?" "No," I said, "Laura, my daughter, has been going to school every day for the past six weeks!"
　　"Excuse me," she said. She took the attendance book out and there was your name, unmistakably printed, and all the dates you were absent until they decided that you had dropped out of school.

I still said, "No, there must have been some mistake! There must have been some mix-up in the records!"

And she said, "No—I remember her perfectly now. Her hands shook so that
50 she couldn't hit the right keys! The first time we gave a speed test, she broke down completely—was sick at the stomach and almost had to be carried into the wash room! After that morning she never showed up any more. We phoned the house but never got any answer"—While I was working at Famous and Barr, I suppose, demonstrating those—

[*She indicates a brassiere with her hands.*]

Oh! I felt so weak I could barely keep on my feet! I had to sit down while they got me a glass of water! Fifty dollars' tuition, all of our plans—my hopes and ambitions for you—just gone up the spout, just gone up the spout like that.

[LAURA *draws a long breath and gets awkwardly to her feet. She crosses to the Victrola and winds it up.*]

What are you doing?

LAURA   Oh! [*She releases the handle and returns to her seat.*]
60   AMANDA   Laura, where have you been going when you've gone out pretending that you were going to business college?

LAURA   I've just been going out walking.

AMANDA   That's not true.

LAURA   It is. I just went walking.

AMANDA   Walking? Walking? In winter? Deliberately courting pneumonia in that light coat? Where did you walk to, Laura?

LAURA   All sorts of places—mostly in the park.

AMANDA   Even after you'd started catching that cold?

LAURA   It was the lesser of two evils, Mother.

[*Screen image:* Winter scene in a park.]

70 I couldn't go back there. I—threw up—on the floor!

AMANDA   From half past seven till after five every day you mean to tell me you walked around in the park, because you wanted to make me think that you were still going to Rubicam's Business College?

LAURA   It wasn't as bad as it sounds. I went inside places to get warmed up.

AMANDA   Inside where?

LAURA   I went in the art museum and the bird houses at the Zoo. I visited the penguins every day! Sometimes I did without lunch and went to the movies. Lately I've been spending most of my afternoons in the Jewel Box, that big glass house where they raise the tropical flowers.
80   AMANDA   You did all this to deceive me, just for deception?

[LAURA *looks down.*] Why?

LAURA Mother, when you're disappointed, you get that awful suffering look on your face, like the picture of Jesus' mother in the museum!

AMANDA Hush!

LAURA I couldn't face it.

[*There is a pause. A whisper of strings is heard. Legend on screen:* "The Crust of Humility."]

AMANDA [*hopelessly fingering the huge pocketbook*] So what are we going to do the rest of our lives? Stay home and watch the parades go by? Amuse ourselves with the glass menagerie, darling? Eternally play those worn-out phonograph records your father left as a painful reminder of him? We won't have a business career—we've given that up because it gave us nervous
90 indigestion! [*She laughs wearily.*] What is there left but dependency all our lives? I know so well what becomes of unmarried women who aren't prepared to occupy a position. I've seen such pitiful cases in the South—barely tolerated spinsters living upon the grudging patronage of sister's husband or brother's wife!—stuck away in some little mousetrap of a room—encouraged by one in-law to visit another—little birdlike women without any nest— eating the crust of humility all their life!

Is that the future that we've mapped out for ourselves? I swear it's the only alternative I can think of! [*She pauses.*] It isn't a very pleasant alternative, is it? [*She pauses again.*] Of course—some girls *do marry.*

[LAURA *twists her hands nervously.*]

100 Haven't you ever liked some boy?

LAURA Yes. I liked one once. [*She rises.*] I came across his picture a while ago.

AMANDA [*with some interest*] He gave you his picture?

LAURA No, it's in the yearbook.

AMANDA [*disappointed*] Oh—a high school boy.

[*Screen image:* JIM as the high school hero bearing a silver cup.]

LAURA Yes. His name was Jim. [*She lifts the heavy annual from the claw-foot table.*] Here he is in *The Pirates of Penzance.*

AMANDA [*absently*] The what?

LAURA The operetta the senior class put on. He had a wonderful voice and
110 we sat across the aisle from each other Mondays, Wednesdays and Fridays in the Aud. Here he is with the silver cup for debating! See his grin?

AMANDA [*absently*] He must have had a jolly disposition.

LAURA He used to call me—Blue Roses.

[*Screen image:* Blue roses.]

AMANDA Why did he call you such a name as that?

LAURA When I had that attack of pleurosis—he asked me what was the matter when I came back. I said pleurosis—he thought that I said Blue Roses! So that's what he always called me after that. Whenever he saw me, he'd holler, "Hello, Blue Roses!" I didn't care for the girl that he went out with. Emily Meisenbach. Emily was the best-dressed girl at Soldan. She never
120 struck me, though, as being sincere . . . It says in the Personal Section—they're engaged. That's—six years ago! They must be married by now.

AMANDA Girls that aren't cut out for business careers usually wind up married to some nice man. [*She gets up with a spark of revival.*] Sister, that's what you'll do!

[LAURA *utters a startled, doubtful laugh. She reaches quickly for a piece of glass.*]

LAURA But, Mother—

AMANDA Yes? [*She goes over to the photograph.*]

LAURA [*in a tone of frightened apology*] I'm—crippled!

AMANDA Nonsense! Laura, I've told you never, never to use that word. Why, you're not crippled, you just have a little defect—hardly noticeable,
130 even! When people have some slight disadvantage like that, they cultivate other things to make up for it—develop charm—and vivacity—and—*charm!* That's all you have to do!

[*She turns again to the photograph.*] One thing your father had *plenty of*—was *charm!*

[*The scene fades out with music.*]

Scene Three

Legend on screen: "After the fiasco—"

TOM *speaks from the fire escape landing.*

TOM After the fiasco at Rubicam's Business College, the idea of getting a gentleman caller for Laura began to play a more and more important part in Mother's calculations. It became an obsession. Like some archetype of the universal unconscious, the image of the gentleman caller haunted our small apartment. . . .

[*Screen image:* A young man at the door of a house with flowers.]

An evening at home rarely passed without some allusion to this image, this specter, this hope. . . . Even when he wasn't mentioned, his presence hung in Mother's preoccupied look and in my sister's frightened, apologetic manner—hung like a sentence passed upon the Wingfields! Mother was a woman
10 of action as well as words. She began to take logical steps in the planned

direction. Late that winter and in the early spring—realizing that extra money would be needed to properly feather the nest and plume the bird—she conducted a vigorous campaign on the telephone, roping in subscribers to one of those magazines for matrons called *The Homemaker's Companion,* the type of journal that features the serialized sublimations of ladies of letters who think in terms of delicate cuplike breasts, slim, tapering waists, rich, creamy thighs, eyes like wood smoke in autumn, fingers that soothe and caress like strains of music, bodies as powerful as Etruscan sculpture.

[*Screen image:* The cover of a glamor magazine.]

[AMANDA *enters with the telephone on a long extension cord. She is spotlighted in the dim stage.*]

AMANDA   Ida Scott? This is Amanda Wingfield! We *missed* you at the D.A.R.
20 last Monday! I said to myself: She's probably suffering with that sinus condition! How is that sinus condition?

Horrors! Heaven have mercy!—You're a Christian martyr, yes, that's what you are, a Christian martyr!

Well, I just now happened to notice that your subscription to the *Companion*'s about to expire! Yes, it expires with the next issue, honey!—just when that wonderful new serial by Bessie Mae Hopper is getting off to such an exciting start. Oh, honey, it's something that you can't miss! You remember how *Gone with the Wind* took everybody by storm? You simply couldn't go out if you hadn't read it. All everybody *talked* was Scarlett O'Hara. Well, this
30 is a book that critics already compare to *Gone with the Wind.* It's the *Gone with the Wind* of the post-World-War generation!—What?—Burning?—Oh, honey, don't let them burn, go take a look in the oven and I'll hold the wire! Heavens—I think she's hung up!

[*The scene dims out.*]

[*Legend on screen:* "You think I'm in love with Continental Shoemakers?"]

[*Before the lights come up again, the violent voices of* TOM *and* AMANDA *are heard. They are quarreling behind the portieres. In front of them stands* LAURA *with clenched hands and panicky expression. A clear pool of light is on her figure throughout this scene.*]

TOM   What in Christ's name am I—
AMANDA [*shrilly*]   Don't you use that—
TOM   —supposed to do!
AMANDA   —expression! Not in my—
TOM   Ohhh!
AMANDA   —presence! Have you gone out of your senses?
40 TOM   I have, that's true, *driven* out!
AMANDA   What is the matter with you, you—big—big—IDIOT!
TOM   Look!—I've got *no thing,* no single thing—

AMANDA   Lower your voice!
TOM   —in my life here that I can call my OWN! Everything is—
AMANDA   Stop that shouting!
TOM   Yesterday you confiscated my books! You had the nerve to—
AMANDA   I took that horrible novel back to the library—yes! That hideous
book by that insane Mr. Lawrence.

[TOM *laughs wildly.*]

I cannot control the output of diseased minds or people who cater to them—

[TOM *laughs still more wildly.*]

50   BUT I WON'T ALLOW SUCH FILTH BROUGHT INTO MY HOUSE! No, no, no, no, no!
TOM   House, house! Who pays rent on it, who makes a slave of himself to—
AMANDA   [*fairly screeching*]   Don't you DARE to—
TOM   No, no, *I* mustn't say things! *I've* got to just—
AMANDA   Let me tell you—
TOM   I don't want to hear any more!

[*He tears the portieres open. The dining-room area is lit with a turgid smoky red glow.
Now we see* AMANDA: *her hair is in metal curlers and she is wearing a very old
bathrobe, much too large for her slight figure, a relic of the faithless Mr. Wingfield.
The upright typewriter now stands on the drop-leaf table, along with a wild disarray
of manuscripts. The quarrel was probably precipitated by* AMANDA's *interruption of*
TOM's *creative labor. A chair lies overthrown on the floor. Their gesticulating shadows are cast on the ceiling by the fiery glow.*]

AMANDA   You *will* hear more, you—
TOM   No, I won't hear more, I'm going out!
AMANDA   You come right back in—
TOM   Out, out, out! Because I'm—
60   AMANDA   Come back here, Tom Wingfield! I'm not through talking to you!
TOM   Oh, go—
LAURA [*desperately*]   —Tom!
AMANDA   You're going to listen, and no more insolence from you! I'm at
the end of my patience!

[*He comes back toward her.*]

TOM   What do you think I'm at? Aren't I supposed to have any patience to
reach the end of, Mother? I know, I know. It seems unimportant to you, what
I'm *doing*—what I *want* to do—having a little *difference* between them! You
don't think that—
AMANDA   I think you've been doing things that you're ashamed of. That's
70   why you act like this. I don't believe that you go every night to the movies.
Nobody goes to the movies night after night. Nobody in their right minds

goes to the movies as often as you pretend to. People don't go to the movies
at nearly midnight, and movies don't let out at two A.M. Come in stumbling.
Muttering to yourself like a maniac! You get three hours' sleep and then go to
work. Oh, I can picture the way you're doing down there. Moping, doping,
because you're in no condition.

AMANDA What right have you got to jeopardize your job? Jeopardize the
security of us all? How do you think we'd manage if you were—

TOM [*wildly*]   No, I'm in no condition!

80   TOM   Listen! You think I'm crazy about the *warehouse?* [*He bends fiercely
toward her slight figure.*] You think I'm in love with the Continental Shoemakers? You think I want to spend fifty-five *years* down there in that—
celotex interior! with—*fluorescent—tubes!* Look! I'd rather somebody
picked up a crowbar and battered out my brains—than go back mornings! I
go! Every time you come in yelling that Goddamn *"Rise and Shine!" "Rise and
Shine!"* I say to myself, "How *lucky dead* people are!" But I get up. I *go!* For
sixty-five dollars a month I give up all that I dream of doing and being *ever!*
And you say self—*self's* all I ever think of. Why, listen, if self is what I thought
of, Mother, I'd be where he is—GONE! [*He points to his father's picture.*] As
90   far as the system of transportation reaches! [*He starts past her. She grabs his
arm.*] Don't grab at me, Mother!

AMANDA   Where are you going?

TOM   I'm going to the *movies!*

AMANDA   I don't believe that lie!

[TOM *crouches toward her, overtowering her tiny figure. She backs away, gasping.*]

TOM   I'm going to opium dens! Yes, opium dens, dens of vice and criminals' hangouts, Mother. I've joined the Hogan Gang, I'm a hired assassin. I
carry a tommy gun in a violin case! I run a string of cat houses in the Valley!
They call me Killer, Killer Wingfield, I'm leading a double-life, a simple,
honest warehouse worker by day, by night a dynamic *czar* of the *under-*
100   *world, Mother.* I go to gambling casinos, I spin away fortunes on the roulette
table! I wear a patch over one eye and a false mustache, sometimes I put on
green whiskers. On those occasions they call me—*El Diablo!* Oh, I could tell
you many things to make you sleepless! My enemies plan to dynamite this
place. They're going to blow us all sky-high some night! I'll be glad, very
happy, and so will you! You'll go up, up on a broomstick, over Blue Mountain
with seventeen gentlemen callers! you ugly—babbling old—*witch.* . . .
[*He goes through a series of violent, clumsy movements, seizing his overcoat,
lunging to the door, pulling it fiercely open. The women watch him, aghast.
His arm catches in the sleeve of the coat as he struggles to pull it on. For a
110   moment he is pinioned by the bulky garment. With an outraged groan he
tears the coat off again, splitting the shoulder of it, and hurls it across the
room. It strikes against the shelf of* LAURA's *glass collection, and there is a
tinkle of shattering glass.* LAURA *cries out as if wounded.*]

[*Music.*]

[*Screen legend:* "The Glass Menagerie."]

LAURA [*shrilly*] My glass!—menagerie. . . . [*She covers her face and turns away.*]

[*But* AMANDA *is still stunned and stupefied by the "ugly witch" so that she barely notices this occurrence. Now she recovers her speech.*]

AMANDA [*in an awful voice*] I won't speak to you—until you apologize!

[*She crosses through the portieres and draws them together behind her.* TOM *is left with* LAURA. LAURA *clings weakly to the mantel with her face averted.* TOM *stares at her stupidly for a moment. Then he crosses to the shelf. He drops awkwardly on his knees to collect the fallen glass, glancing at* LAURA *as if he would speak but couldn't.*]

[*"The Glass Menagerie" music steals in as the scene dims out.*]

Scene Four

The interior of the apartment is dark. There is a faint light in the alley. A deep-voiced bell in a church is tolling the hour of five.

TOM *appears at the top of the alley. After each solumn boom of the bell in the tower, he shakes a little noisemaker or rattle as if to express the tiny spasm of man in contrast to the sustained power and dignity of the Almighty. This and the unsteadiness of his advance make it evident that he has been drinking. As he climbs the few steps to the fire escape landing light steals up inside.* LAURA *appears in the front room in a nightdress. She notices that* TOM'S *bed is empty.* TOM *fishes in his pockets for his door key, removing a motley assortment of articles in the search, including a shower of movie ticket stubs and an empty bottle. At last he finds the key, but just as he is about to insert it, it slips from his fingers. He strikes a match and crouches below the door.*

TOM [*bitterly*] One crack—and it falls through!

[LAURA *opens the door.*]

LAURA Tom! Tom, what are you doing?
TOM Looking for a door key.
LAURA Where have you been all this time?
TOM I have been to the movies.
LAURA All this time at the movies?
TOM There was a very long program. There was a Garbo picture and a Mickey Mouse and a travelogue and a newsreel and a preview of coming attractions. And there was an organ solo and a collection for the Milk Fund—
10 simultaneously—which ended up in a terrible fight between a fat lady and an usher!
LAURA [*innocently*] Did you have to stay through everything?

TOM   Of course! And, oh, I forgot! There was a big stage show! The headliner on this stage show was Malvolio the Magician. He performed wonderful tricks, many of them, such as pouring water back and forth between pitchers. First it turned to wine and then it turned to beer and then it turned to whiskey. I know it was whisky it finally turned into because he needed somebody to come up out of the audience to help him, and I came up—both shows! It was Kentucky Straight Bourbon. A very generous fellow, he gave

20   souvenirs. [*He pulls from his back pocket a shimmering rainbow-colored scarf.*] He gave me this. This is his magic scarf. You can have it, Laura. You wave it over a canary cage and you get a bowl of goldfish. You wave it over the goldfish bowl and they fly away canaries. . . . But the wonderfullest trick of all was the coffin trick. We nailed him into a coffin and he got out of the coffin without removing one nail. [*He has come inside.*] There is a trick that would come in handy for me—get me out of this two-by-four situation! [*He flops onto the bed and starts removing his shoes.*]

LAURA   Tom—shhh!

TOM   What're you shushing me for?

30   LAURA   You'll wake up Mother.

TOM   Goody, goody! Pay'er back for all those "Rise an' Shines." [*He lies down, groaning.*] You know it don't take much intelligence to get yourself into a nailed-up coffin, Laura. But who in hell ever got himself out of one without removing one nail?

[*As if in answer, the father's grinning photograph lights up. The scene dims out.*]

[*Immediately following, the church bell is heard striking six. At the sixth stroke the alarm clock goes off in* AMANDA*'s room, and after a few moments we hear her calling: "Rise and Shine! Rise and Shine!* LAURA, *go tell your brother to rise and shine!"*]

TOM [*sitting up slowly*]   I'll rise—but I won't shine.

[*The light increases.*]

AMANDA   Laura, tell your brother his coffee is ready.

[LAURA *slips into the front room.*]

LAURA   Tom!—It's nearly seven. Don't make Mother nervous.

[*He stares at her stupidly.*]

[*beseechingly*]   Tom, speak to Mother this morning. Make up with her, apologize, speak to her!

40   TOM   She won't to me. It's her that started not speaking.

LAURA   If you just say you're sorry she'll start speaking.

TOM   Her not speaking—is that such a tragedy?

LAURA   Please—please!

AMANDA [*calling from the kitchenette*] Laura, are you going to do what I asked you to do, or do I have to get dressed and go out myself?

LAURA Going, going—soon as I get on my coat!

[*She pulls on a shapeless felt hat with a nervous, jerky movement, pleadingly glancing at* TOM. *She rushes awkwardly for her coat. The coat is one of* AMANDA's, *inaccurately made-over, the sleeves too short for* LAURA.]

Butter and what else?

AMANDA [*entering from the kitchenette*] Just butter. Tell them to charge it.

LAURA Mother, they make such faces when I do that.

50 AMANDA Sticks and stones can break our bones, but the expression on Mr. Garfinkel's face won't harm us! Tell your brother his coffee is getting cold.

LAURA [*at the door*] Do what I asked you, will you, will you, Tom?

[*He looks sullenly away.*]

AMANDA Laura, go now or just don't go at all!

LAURA [*rushing out*] Going—going!

[*A second later she cries out.* TOM *springs up and crosses to the door.* TOM *opens the door.*]

TOM Laura?

LAURA I'm all right. I slipped, but I'm all right.

AMANDA [*peering anxiously after her*] If anyone breaks a leg on those fire-escape steps, the landlord ought to be sued for every cent he possesses! [*She shuts the door. Now she remembers she isn't speaking to* TOM *and re-*
60 *turns to the other room.*]

[*As* TOM *comes listlessly for his coffee, she turns her back to him and stands rigidly facing the window on the gloomy gray vault of the areaway. Its light on her face with its aged but childish features is cruelly sharp, satirical as a Daumier print.*]

[*The music of "Ave Maria," is heard softly.*]

[TOM *glances sheepishly but sullenly at her averted figure and slumps at the table. The coffee is scalding hot: he sips it and gasps and spits it back in the cup. At his gasp,* AMANDA *catches her breath and half turns. Then she catches herself and turns back to the window.* TOM *blows on his coffee, glancing sidewise at his mother. She clears her throat.* TOM *clears his. He starts to rise, sinks back down again, scratches his head, clears his throat again.* AMANDA *coughs.* TOM *raises his cup in both hands to blow on it, his eyes staring over the rim of it at his mother for several moments. Then he slowly sets the cup down and awkwardly and hesitantly rises from the chair.*]

TOM [*hoarsely*] Mother. I—I apologize, Mother.

[AMANDA *draws a quick, shuddering breath. Her face works grotesquely. She breaks into childlike tears.*]

I'm sorry for what I said, for everything that I said, I didn't mean it.

AMANDA [*sobbingly*]   My devotion has made me a witch and so I make myself hateful to my children!

TOM   *No,* you *don't.*

AMANDA   I worry so much, don't sleep, it makes me nervous!

TOM [*gently*]   I understand that.

AMANDA   I've had to put up a solitary battle all these years. But you're my righthand bower! Don't fall down, don't fail!

70   TOM [*gently*]   I try, Mother.

AMANDA [*with great enthusiasm*]   Try and you will *succeed!* [*The notion makes her breathless.*] Why, you—you're just *full* of natural endowments! Both of my children—they're *unusual* children! Don't you think I know it? I'm so—*proud!* Happy and—feel I've—so much to be thankful for but— promise me one thing, son!

TOM   What, Mother?

AMANDA   Promise, son, you'll—never be a drunkard!

TOM [*turns to her grinning*]   I will never be a drunkard, Mother.

AMANDA   That's what frightened me so, that you'd be drinking! Eat a bowl
80   of Purina!

TOM   Just coffee, Mother.

AMANDA   Shredded wheat biscuit?

TOM   No. No, Mother, just coffee.

AMANDA   You can't put in a day's work on an empty stomach. You've got ten minutes—don't gulp! Drinking too-hot liquids makes cancer of the stomach. . . . Put cream in.

TOM   No, thank you.

AMANDA   To cool it.

TOM   No! No, thank you, I want it black.

90   AMANDA   I know, but it's not good for you. We have to do all that we can to build ourselves up. In these trying times we live in, all that we have to cling to is—each other. . . . That's why it's so important to—Tom, I—I sent out your sister so I could discuss something with you. If you hadn't spoken I would have spoken to you. [*She sits down.*]

TOM [*gently*]   What is it, Mother, that you want to discuss?

AMANDA   *Laura!*

[TOM *puts his cup down slowly.*]

[*Legend on screen:* "Laura." *Music:* "The Glass Menagerie."]

TOM   —Oh.—Laura . . .

AMANDA [*touching his sleeve*]   You know how Laura is. So quiet but—still water runs deep! She notices things and I think she—broods about them.

[TOM *looks up.*]

100 A few days ago I came in and she was crying.

    TOM   What about?

    AMANDA   You.

    TOM   Me?

    AMANDA   She has an idea that you're not happy here.

    TOM   What gave her that idea?

    AMANDA   What gives her any idea? However, you do act strangely. I—I'm not criticizing, understand *that!* I know your ambitions do not lie in the warehouse, that like everybody in the whole wide world—you've had to—make sacrifices, but—Tom—Tom—life's not easy, it calls for—Spartan en-
110 durance! There's so many things in my heart that I cannot describe to you! I've never told you but I—*loved* your father. . . .

    TOM [*gently*]   I know that, Mother.

    AMANDA   And you—when I see you taking after his ways! Staying out late—and—well, you *had* been drinking the night you were in that—terrifying condition! Laura says that you hate the apartment and that you go out nights to get away from it! Is that true, Tom?

    TOM   No. You say there's so much in your heart that you can't describe to me. That's true of me, too. There's so much in my heart that I can't describe to *you!* So let's respect each other's—
120   AMANDA   But, why—*why,* Tom—are you always so *restless?* Where do you *go* to, nights?

    TOM   I—go to the movies.

    AMANDA   Why do you go to the movies so much, Tom?

    TOM   I go to the movies because—I like adventure. Adventure is something I don't have much of at work, so I go to the movies.

    AMANDA   But, Tom, you go to the movies *entirely too much!*

    TOM   I like a lot of adventure.

[AMANDA *looks baffled, then hurt. As the familiar inquisition resumes,* TOM *becomes hard and impatient again.* AMANDA *slips back into her querulous attitude toward him.*]

[*Image on screen:* A sailing vessel with Jolly Roger.]

    AMANDA   Most young men find adventure in their careers.

    TOM   Then most young men are not employed in a warehouse.
130   AMANDA   The world is full of young men employed in warehouses and offices and factories.

    TOM   Do all of them find adventure in their careers?

    AMANDA   They do or they do without it! Not everybody has a craze for adventure.

    TOM   Man is by instinct a lover, a hunter, a fighter, and none of those instincts are given much play at the warehouse!

    AMANDA   Man is by instinct! Don't quote instinct to me! Instinct is something that people have got away from! It belongs to animals! Christian adults don't want it!
140   TOM   What do Christian adults want, then, Mother?

AMANDA Superior things! Things of the mind and the spirit! Only animals have to satisfy instincts! Surely your aims are somewhat higher than theirs! Than monkeys—pigs—

TOM I reckon they're not.

AMANDA You're joking. However, that isn't what I wanted to discuss.

TOM [*rising*] I haven't much time.

AMANDA [*pushing his shoulders*] Sit down.

TOM You want me to punch in red at the warehouse, Mother?

AMANDA You have five minutes. I want to talk about Laura.

[*Screen legend:* "Plans and Provisions."]

150   TOM All right! What about Laura?

AMANDA We have to be making some plans and provisions for her. She's older than you, two years, and nothing has happened. She just drifts along doing nothing. It frightens me terribly how she just drifts along.

TOM I guess she's the type that people call home girls.

AMANDA There's no such type, and if there is, it's a pity! That is unless the home is hers, with a husband!

TOM What?

AMANDA Oh, I can see the handwriting on the wall as plain as I see the nose in front of my face! It's terrifying! More and more you remind me of your
160 father! He was out all hours without explanation!—Then *left! Goodbye!* And me with the bag to hold. I saw that letter you got from the Merchant Marine. I know what you're dreaming of. I'm not standing here blindfolded. [*She pauses.*] Very well, then. Then *do* it! But not till there's somebody to take your place.

TOM What do you mean?

AMANDA I mean that as soon as Laura has got somebody to take care of her, married, a home of her own, independent—why, then you'll be free to go wherever you please, on land, on sea, whichever way the wind blows you! But until that time you've got to look out for your sister. I don't say me because I'm
170 old and don't matter! I say for your sister because she's young and dependent.

I put her in business college—a dismal failure! Frightened her so it made her sick at the stomach. I took her over to the Young People's League at the church. Another fiasco. She spoke to nobody, nobody spoke to her. Now all she does is fool with those pieces of glass and play those worn-out records. What kind of a life is that for a girl to lead?

TOM What can I do about it?

AMANDA Overcome selfishness! Self, self, self is all that you ever think of!

[TOM *springs up and crosses to get his coat. It is ugly and bulky. He pulls on a cap with earmuffs.*]

Where is your muffler? Put your wool muffler on!

[*He snatches it angrily from the closet, tosses it around his neck and pulls both ends tight.*]

Tom! I haven't said what I had in mind to ask you.

180   TOM   I'm too late to—

AMANDA [*catching his arm—very importunately: then shyly*]   Down at the warehouse, aren't there some—nice young men?

TOM   No!

AMANDA   There *must* be—*some* . . .

TOM   Mother—[*He gestures.*]

AMANDA   Find out one that's clean-living—doesn't drink and ask him out for sister!

TOM   What?

AMANDA   For *sister!* To *meet!* Get *acquainted!*

190   TOM [*stamping to the door*]   Oh, my *go-osh!*

AMANDA   Will you?

[*He opens the door. She says, imploringly:*]

Will you?

[*He starts down the fire escape.*]

Will you? *Will* you, dear?

TOM [*calling back*]   Yes!

[AMANDA *closes the door hesitantly and with a troubled but faintly hopeful expression.*]

[*Screen image:* The cover of a glamor magazine.]

[*The spotlight picks up* AMANDA *at the phone.*]

AMANDA   Ella Cartwright? This is Amanda Wingfield!
How are you, honey?
How is that kidney condition?

[*There is a five-second pause.*]

Horrors!

[*There is another pause.*]

You're a Christian martyr, yes, honey, that's what you are, a Christian martyr!
200 Well, I just now happened to notice in my little red book that your subscription to the *Companion* has just run out! I knew that you wouldn't want to miss out on the wonderful serial starting in this new issue. It's by Bessie Mae Hopper, the first thing she's written since *Honeymoon for Three.* Wasn't that a strange and interesting story? Well, this one is even lovelier, I believe. It has a sophisticated, society background. It's all about the horsey set on Long Island!

[*The light fades out.*]

Scene Five

Legend on the screen: "Annunciation."

Music is heard as the light slowly comes on.

It is early dusk of a spring evening. Supper has just been finished in the Wingfield apartment. AMANDA *and* LAURA, *in light-colored dresses, are removing dishes from the table in the dining room, which is shadowy, their movements formalized almost as a dance or ritual, their moving forms as pale and silent as moths.* TOM, *in white shirt and trousers, rises from the table and crosses toward the fire escape.*

> AMANDA [*as he passes her*]   Son, will you do me a favor?
> TOM   What?
> AMANDA   Comb your hair! You look so pretty when your hair is combed!

[TOM *slouches on the sofa with the evening paper. Its enormous headline reads:* "Franco Triumphs."]

There is only one respect in which I would like you to emulate your father.
> TOM   What respect is that?
> AMANDA   The care he always took of his appearance. He never allowed himself to look untidy.

[*He throws down the paper and crosses to the fire escape.*]

Where are you going?
> TOM   I'm going out to smoke.
10   AMANDA   You smoke too much. A pack a day at fifteen cents a pack. How much would that amount to in a month? Thirty times fifteen is how much, Tom? Figure it out and you will be astounded at what you could save. Enough to give you a night-school course in accounting at Washington U.! Just think what a wonderful thing that would be for you, son!

[TOM *is unmoved by the thought.*]

> TOM   I'd rather smoke. [*He steps out on the landing, letting the screen door slam.*]
> AMANDA [*sharply*]   I know! That's the tragedy of it. . . . [*Alone, she turns to look at her husband's picture.*]

[*Dance music:* "The World Is Waiting for the Sunrise!"]

> TOM [*to the audience*]   Across the alley from us was the Paradise Dance
20 Hall. On evenings in spring the windows and doors were open and the music came outdoors. Sometimes the lights were turned out except for a large glass sphere that hung from the ceiling. It would turn slowly about and filter the

dusk with delicate rainbow colors. Then the orchestra played a waltz or a tango, something that had a slow and sensuous rhythm. Couples would come outside, to the relative privacy of the alley. You could see them kissing behind ash pits and telephone poles. This was the compensation for lives that passed like mine, without any change or adventure. Adventure and change were imminent in this year. They were waiting around the corner for all these kids. Suspended in the mist over Berchtesgaden, caught in the folds of
30 Chamberlain's umbrella. In Spain there was Guernica! But here there was only hot swing music and liquor, dance halls, bars, and movies, and sex that hung in the gloom like a chandelier and flooded the world with brief, deceptive rainbows. . . . All the world was waiting for bombardments!

[AMANDA *turns from the picture and comes outside.*]

AMANDA [*sighing*]   A fire escape landing's a poor excuse for a porch. [*She spreads a newspaper on a step and sits down, gracefully and demurely as if she were settling into a swing on a Mississippi veranda.*] What are you looking at?

TOM   The moon.

AMANDA   Is there a moon this evening?

40   TOM   It's rising over Garfinkel's Delicatessen.

AMANDA   So it is! A little silver slipper of a moon. Have you made a wish on it yet?

TOM   Um-hum.

AMANDA   What did you wish for?

TOM   That's a secret.

AMANDA   A secret, huh? Well, I won't tell mine either. I will be just as mysterious as you.

TOM   I bet I can guess what yours is.

AMANDA   Is my head so transparent?

50   TOM   You're not a sphinx.

AMANDA   No, I don't have secrets. I'll tell you what I wished for on the moon. Success and happiness for my precious children! I wish for that whenever there's a moon, and when there isn't a moon, I wish for it, too.

TOM   I thought perhaps you wished for a gentleman caller.

AMANDA   Why do you say that?

TOM   Don't you remember asking me to fetch one?

AMANDA   I remember suggesting that it would be nice for your sister if you brought home some nice young man from the warehouse. I think that I've made that suggestion more than once.

60   TOM   Yes, you have made it repeatedly.

AMANDA   Well?

TOM   We are going to have one.

AMANDA   *What?*

TOM   A gentleman caller!

[*The annunciation is celebrated with music.*]

[AMANDA *rises.*]

[*Image on screen:* A caller with a bouquet.]

AMANDA You mean you have asked some nice young man to come over?

TOM Yep. I've asked him to dinner.

AMANDA You really did?

TOM I did!

AMANDA You did, and did he—*accept?*

70 TOM He did!

AMANDA Well, well—well, well! That's—lovely!

TOM I thought that you would be pleased.

AMANDA It's definite then?

TOM Very definite.

AMANDA Soon?

TOM Very soon.

AMANDA For heaven's sake, stop putting on and tell me some things, will you?

TOM What things do you want me to tell you?

80 AMANDA *Naturally* I would like to know when he's *coming!*

TOM He's coming tomorrow.

AMANDA *Tomorrow?*

TOM Yep. Tomorrow.

AMANDA But, Tom!

TOM Yes, Mother?

AMANDA Tomorrow gives me no time!

TOM Time for what?

AMANDA Preparations! Why didn't you phone me at once, as soon as you asked him, the minute that he accepted? Then, don't you see, I could have 90 been getting ready!

TOM You don't have to make any fuss.

AMANDA Oh, Tom, Tom, Tom, of course I have to make a fuss! I want things nice, not sloppy! Not thrown together. I'll certainly have to do some fast thinking, won't I?

TOM I don't see why you have to think at all.

AMANDA You just don't know. We can't have a gentleman caller in a pigsty! All my wedding silver has to be polished, the monogrammed table linen ought to be laundered! The windows have to be washed and fresh curtains put up. And how about clothes? We have to *wear* something, don't we?

100 TOM Mother, this boy is no one to make a fuss over!

AMANDA Do you realize he's the first young man we've introduced to your sister? It's terrible, dreadful, disgraceful that poor little sister has never received a single gentleman caller! Tom, come inside! [*She opens the screen door.*]

TOM What for?

AMANDA I want to ask you some things.

TOM   If you're going to make such a fuss, I'll call it off, I'll tell him not to come!

AMANDA   You certainly won't do anything of the kind. Nothing offends peo-
110 ple worse than broken engagements. It simply means I'll have to work like a Turk! We won't be brilliant, but we will pass inspection. Come on inside.

[TOM *follows her inside, groaning.*]

Sit down.

TOM   Any particular place you would like me to sit?

AMANDA   Thank heavens I've got that new sofa! I'm also making payments on a floor lamp I'll have sent out! And put the chintz covers on, they'll brighten things up! Of course I'd hoped to have these walls re-papered. . . . What is the young man's name?

TOM   His name is O'Connor.

AMANDA   That, of course, means fish—tomorrow is Friday! I'll have that
120 salmon loaf—with Durkee's dressing! What does he do? He works at the warehouse?

TOM   Of course! How else would I—

AMANDA   Tom, he—doesn't drink?

TOM   Why do you ask me that?

AMANDA   Your father *did!*

TOM   Don't get started on that!

AMANDA   He *does* drink, then?

TOM   Not that I know of!

AMANDA   Make sure, be certain! The last thing I want for my daughter's a
130 boy who drinks!

TOM   Aren't you being a little bit premature? Mr. O'Connor has not yet appeared on the scene!

AMANDA   But will tomorrow. To meet your sister, and what do I know about his character? Nothing! Old maids are better off than wives of drunkards!

TOM   Oh, my God!

AMANDA   Be still!

TOM [*leaning forward to whisper*]   Lots of fellows meet girls whom they don't marry!

AMANDA   Oh, talk sensibly, Tom—and don't be sarcastic! [*She has gotten a*
140 *hairbrush.*]

TOM   What are you doing?

AMANDA   I'm brushing that cowlick down! [*She attacks his hair with the brush.*] What is this young man's position at the warehouse?

TOM [*submitting grimly to the brush and the interrogation*]   This young man's position is that of a shipping clerk, Mother.

AMANDA   Sounds to me like a fairly responsible job, the sort of a job *you* would be in if you just had more *get-up.* What is his salary? Have you any idea?

TOM   I would judge it to be approximately eighty-five dollars a month.

AMANDA   Well—not princely, but—

150   TOM   Twenty more than I make.

AMANDA   Yes, how well I know! But for a family man, eighty-five dollars a month is not much more than you can just get by on. . . .

TOM   Yes, but Mr. O'Connor is not a family man.

AMANDA   He might be, mightn't he? Some time in the future?

TOM   I see. Plans and provisions.

AMANDA   You are the only young man that I know of who ignores the fact that the future becomes the present, the present the past, and the past turns into everlasting regret if you don't plan for it!

TOM   I will think that over and see what I can make of it.

160   AMANDA   Don't be supercilious with your mother! Tell me some more about this—what do you call him?

TOM   James D. O'Connor. The D. is for Delaney.

AMANDA   Irish on *both* sides! *Gracious!* And doesn't drink?

TOM   Shall I call him up and ask him right this minute?

AMANDA   The only way to find out about those things is to make discreet inquiries at the proper moment. When I was a girl in Blue Mountain and it was suspected that a young man drank, the girl whose attentions he had been receiving, if any girl *was,* would sometimes speak to the minister of his church, or rather her father would if her father was living, and sort of feel him

170   out on the young man's character. That is the way such things are discreetly handled to keep a young woman from making a tragic mistake!

TOM   Then how did you happen to make a tragic mistake?

AMANDA   That innocent look of your father's had everyone fooled! He *smiled*—the world was *enchanted!* No girl can do worse than put herself at the mercy of a handsome appearance! I hope that Mr. O'Connor is not too good-looking.

TOM   No, he's not too good-looking. He's covered with freckles and hasn't too much of a nose.

AMANDA   He's not right-down homely, though?

180   TOM   Not right-down homely. Just medium homely, I'd say.

AMANDA   Character's what to look for in a man.

TOM   That's what I've always said, Mother.

AMANDA   You've never said anything of the kind and I suspect you would never give it a thought.

TOM   Don't be so suspicious of me.

AMANDA   At least I hope he's the type that's up and coming.

TOM   I think he really goes in for self-improvement.

AMANDA   What reason have you to think so?

TOM   He goes to night school.

190   AMANDA [*beaming*]   Splendid! What does he do, I mean study?

TOM   Radio engineering and public speaking!

AMANDA   Then he has visions of being advanced in the world! Any young man who studies public speaking is aiming to have an executive job some day! And radio engineering? A thing for the future! Both of these facts are very illuminating. Those are the sort of things that a mother should know concerning any young man who comes to call on her daughter. Seriously or—not.

TOM   One little warning. He doesn't know about Laura. I didn't let on that we had dark ulterior motives. I just said, why don't you come and have dinner with us? He said okay and that was the whole conversation.

200   AMANDA   I bet it was! You're eloquent as an oyster. However, he'll know about Laura when he gets here. When he sees how lovely and sweet and pretty she is, he'll thank his lucky stars he was asked to dinner.

TOM   Mother, you mustn't expect too much of Laura.

AMANDA   What do you mean?

TOM   Laura seems all those things to you and me because she's ours and we love her. We don't even notice she's crippled any more.

AMANDA   Don't say crippled! You know that I never allow that word to be used!

TOM   But face facts, Mother. She is and—that's not all—

210   AMANDA   What do you mean "not all"?

TOM   Laura is very different from other girls.

AMANDA   I think the difference is all to her advantage.

TOM   Not quite all—in the eyes of others—strangers—she's terribly shy and lives in a world of her own and those things make her seem a little peculiar to people outside the house.

AMANDA   Don't say peculiar.

TOM   Face the facts. She is.

[*The dance hall music changes to a tango that has a minor and somewhat ominous tone.*]

AMANDA   In what way is she peculiar—may I ask?

TOM [*gently*]   She lives in a world of her own—a world of little glass
220 ornaments, Mother. . . .

[*He gets up,* AMANDA *remains holding the brush, looking at him, troubled.*]

She plays old phonograph records and—that's about all—[*He glances at himself in the mirror and crosses to the door.*]

AMANDA [*sharply*]   Where are you going?

TOM   I'm going to the movies. [*He goes out the screen door.*]

AMANDA   Not to the movies, every night to the movies! [*She follows quickly to the screen door.*] I don't believe you always go to the movies!

[*He is gone.* AMANDA *looks worriedly after him for a moment. Then vitality and optimism return and she turns from the door, crossing to the portieres.*]

Laura! Laura!

[LAURA *answers from the kitchenette.*]

LAURA   Yes, Mother.

AMANDA   Let those dishes go and come in front!

[LAURA *appears with a dish towel.* AMANDA *speaks to her gaily.*]

230 Laura, come here and make a wish on the moon!

[*Screen image:* The Moon.]

LAURA [*entering*] Moon—moon?
AMANDA A little silver slipper of a moon. Look over your left shoulder, Laura, and make a wish!

[LAURA *looks faintly puzzled as if called out of sleep.* AMANDA *seizes her shoulders and turns her at an angle by the door.*]

Now! Now, darling, *wish!*
LAURA What shall I wish for, Mother?
AMANDA [*her voice trembling and her eyes suddenly filling with tears*] Happiness! Good fortune!

[*The sound of the violin rises and the stage dims out.*]

Scene Six

The light comes up on the fire escape landing. TOM *is leaning against the grill, smoking.*

[*Screen image:* The high school hero.]

TOM And so the following evening I brought Jim home to dinner. I had known Jim slightly in high school. In high school Jim was a hero. He had tremendous Irish good nature and vitality with the scrubbed and polished look of white chinaware. He seemed to move in a continual spotlight. He was a star in basketball, captain of the debating club, president of the senior class and the glee club and he sang the male lead in the annual light operas. He was always running or bounding, never just walking. He seemed always at the point of defeating the law of gravity. He was shooting with such velocity through his adolescence that you would logically expect him to arrive at
10 nothing short of the White House by the time he was thirty. But Jim apparently ran into more interference after his graduation from Soldan. His speed had definitely slowed. Six years after he left high school he was holding a job that wasn't much better than mine.

[*Screen image:* The Clerk.]

He was the only one at the warehouse with whom I was on friendly terms. I was valuable to him as someone who could remember his former glory, who had seen him win basketball games and the silver cup in debating. He knew of my secret practice of retiring to a cabinet of the washroom to work on poems when business was slack in the warehouse. He called me Shakespeare. And

while the other boys in the warehouse regarded me with suspicious hostility,
20 Jim took a humorous attitude toward me. Gradually his attitude affected the
others, their hostility wore off and they also began to smile at me as people
smile at an oddly fashioned dog who trots across their path at some distance.
    I knew that Jim and Laura had known each other at Soldan, and I had
heard Laura speak admiringly of his voice. I didn't know if Jim remembered
her or not. In high school Laura had been as unobtrusive as Jim had been
astonishing. If he did remember Laura, it was not as my sister, for when I
asked him to dinner, he grinned and said, "You know, Shakespeare, I never
thought of you as having folks!" He was about to discover that I did. . . .

[*Legend on screen:* "The accent of a coming foot."]

[*The light dims out on* TOM *and comes up in the Wingfield living room—a delicate
lemony light. It is about five on a Friday evening of late spring which comes "scattering
poems in the sky."*]

[AMANDA *has worked like a Turk in preparation for the gentleman caller. The results
are astonishing. The new floor lamp with its rose silk shade is in place, a colored
paper lantern conceals the broken light fixture in the ceiling, new billowing white
curtains are at the windows, chintz covers are on the chairs and sofa, a pair of new
sofa pillows make their initial appearance. Open boxes and tissue paper are scattered on the floor.*]

[LAURA *stands in the middle of the room with lifted arms while* AMANDA *crouches
before her, adjusting the hem of a new dress, devout and ritualistic. The dress is
colored and designed by memory. The arrangement of* LAURA's *hair is changed: it is
softer and more becoming. A fragile, unearthly prettiness has come out in* LAURA: *she
is like a piece of translucent glass touched by light, given a momentary radiance, not
actual, not lasting.*]

AMANDA [*impatiently*]   Why are you trembling?
30 LAURA   Mother, you've made me so nervous!
    AMANDA   How have I made you nervous?
    LAURA   By all this fuss! You make it seem so important!
    AMANDA   I don't understand you, Laura. You couldn't be satisfied with just
sitting home, and yet whenever I try to arrange something for you, you seem
to resist it. [*She gets up.*] Now take a look at yourself. No, wait! Wait just a
moment—I have an idea!
    LAURA   What is it now?

[AMANDA *produces two powder puffs which she wraps in handkerchiefs and stuffs into*
LAURA's *bosom.*]

    LAURA   Mother, what are you doing?
    AMANDA   They call them "Gay Deceivers"!
40 LAURA   I won't wear them!

AMANDA You will!
LAURA Why should I?
AMANDA Because, to be painfully honest, your chest is flat.
LAURA You make it seem like we were setting a trap.
AMANDA All pretty girls are a trap, a pretty trap, and men expect them to be.

[*Legend on screen:* "A pretty trap."]

Now look at yourself, young lady. This is the prettiest you will ever be! [*She stands back to admire* LAURA.] I've got to fix myself now! You're going to be surprised by your mother's appearance!

[AMANDA *crosses through the portieres, humming gaily.* LAURA *moves slowly to the long mirror and stares solemnly at herself. A wind blows the white curtains inward in a slow, graceful motion and with a faint, sorrowful sighing.*]

AMANDA [*from somewhere behind the portieres*]   It isn't dark enough yet.

[LAURA *turns slowly before the mirror with a troubled look.*]

[*Legend on screen:* "This is my sister: Celebrate her with strings!" *Music plays.*]

50   AMANDA [*laughing, still not visible*]   I'm going to show you something. I'm going to make a spectacular appearance!
    LAURA What is it, Mother?
    AMANDA Possess your soul in patience—you will see! Something I've resurrected from that old trunk! Styles haven't changed so terribly much after all. . . . [*She parts the portieres.*] Now just look at your mother! [*She wears a girlish frock of yellowed voile with a blue silk sash. She carries a bunch of jonquils—the legend of her youth is nearly revived. Now she speaks feverishly.*] This is the dress in which I led the cotillion. Won the cakewalk twice at Sunset Hill, wore one Spring to the Governor's Ball in Jackson! See how I
60 sashayed around the ballroom, Laura? [*She raises her skirt and does a mincing step around the room.*] I wore it on Sundays for my gentlemen callers! I had it on the day I met your father. . . . I had malaria fever all that Spring. The change of climate from East Tennessee to the Delta—weakened resistance. I had a little temperature all the time—not enough to be serious—just enough to make me restless and giddy! Invitations poured in—parties all over the Delta! "Stay in bed," said Mother, "you have a fever!"—but I just wouldn't. I took quinine but kept on going, going! Evenings, dances! Afternoons, long, long rides! Picnics—lovely! So lovely, that country in May—all lacy with dogwood, literally flooded with jonquils! That was the Spring I had
70 the craze for jonquils. Jonquils became an absolute obsession. Mother said, "Honey, there's no more room for jonquils." And still I kept on bringing in more jonquils. Whenever, wherever I saw them, I'd say, "Stop! Stop! I see jonquils!" I made the young men help me gather the jonquils! It was a joke, Amanda and her jonquils. Finally there were no more vases to hold them,

every available space was filled with jonquils. No vases to hold them? All right, I'll hold them myself! And then I—[*She stops in front of the picture. Music plays.*] met your father! Malaria fever and jonquils and then—this—boy. . . . [*She switches on the rose-colored lamp.*] I hope they get here before it starts to rain. [*She crosses the room and places the jonquils in a bowl on* 80 *the table.*] I gave your brother a little extra change so he and Mr. O'Connor could take the service car home.

    LAURA [*with an altered look*]   What did you say his name was?

    AMANDA   O'Connor.

    LAURA   What is his first name?

    AMANDA   I don't remember. Oh, yes, I do. It was—Jim!

[LAURA *sways slightly and catches hold of a chair.*]

[*Legend on screen:* "Not Jim!"]

    LAURA [*faintly*]   Not—Jim!

    AMANDA   Yes, that was it, it was Jim! I've never known a Jim that wasn't nice!

[*The music becomes ominous.*]

    LAURA   Are you sure his name is Jim O'Connor?

    AMANDA   Yes. Why?

90   LAURA   Is he the one that Tom used to know in high school?

    AMANDA   He didn't say so. I think he just got to know him at the warehouse.

    LAURA   There was a Jim O'Connor we both knew in high school—[*then, with effort*] If that is the one that Tom is bringing to dinner—you'll have to excuse me, I won't come to the table.

    AMANDA   What sort of nonsense is this?

    LAURA   You asked me once if I'd ever liked a boy. Don't you remember I showed you this boy's picture?

    AMANDA   You mean the boy you showed me in the yearbook?

    LAURA   Yes, that boy.

100   AMANDA   Laura, Laura, were you in love with that boy?

    LAURA   I don't know, Mother. All I know is I couldn't sit at the table if it was him!

    AMANDA   It won't be him! It isn't the least bit likely. But whether it is or not, you will come to the table. You will not be excused.

    LAURA   I'll have to be, Mother.

    AMANDA   I don't intend to humor your silliness, Laura. I've had too much from you and your brother, both! So just sit down and compose yourself till they come. Tom has forgotten his key so you'll have to let them in, when they arrive.

110   LAURA [*panicky*]   Oh, Mother—*you* answer the door!

    AMANDA [*lightly*]   I'll be in the kitchen—busy!

    LAURA   Oh, Mother, please answer the door, don't make me do it!

AMANDA [*crossing into the kitchenette*]   I've got to fix the dressing for the salmon. Fuss, fuss—silliness!—over a gentleman caller!

[*The door swings shut.* LAURA *is left alone.*]

[*Legend on screen:* "Terror!"]

[*She utters a low moan and turns off the lamp—sits stiffly on the edge of the sofa, knotting her fingers together.*]

[*Legend on screen:* "The Opening of a Door!"]

[TOM *and* JIM *appear on the fire escape steps and climb to the landing. Hearing their approach,* LAURA *rises with a panicky gesture. She retreats to the portieres. The door-bell rings.* LAURA *catches her breath and touches her throat. Low drums sound.*]

AMANDA [*calling*]   Laura, sweetheart! The door!

[LAURA *stares at it without moving.*]

JIM   I think we just beat the rain.
TOM   Uh-huh. [*He rings again, nervously.* JIM *whistles and fishes for a cigarette.*]
AMANDA [*very, very gaily*]   Laura, that is your brother and Mr. O'Connor! Will you let them in, darling?

[LAURA *crosses toward the kitchenette door.*]

120   LAURA [*breathlessly*]   Mother—you go to the door!

[AMANDA *steps out of the kitchenette and stares furiously at* LAURA. *She points imperiously at the door.*]

LAURA   Please, please!
AMANDA [*in a fierce whisper*]   What is the matter with you, you silly thing?
LAURA [*desperately*]   Please, you answer it, *please!*
AMANDA   I told you I wasn't going to humor you, Laura. Why have you chosen this moment to lose your mind?
LAURA   Please, please, please, you go!
AMANDA   You'll have to go to the door because I can't!
LAURA [*despairingly*]   I can't either!
AMANDA   Why?
130   LAURA   I'm *sick!*
AMANDA   I'm sick, too—of your nonsense! Why can't you and your brother be normal people? Fantastic whims and behavior!

[TOM *gives a long ring.*]

Preposterous goings on! Can you give me one reason—[*She calls out lyrically.*] *Coming! Just one second!*—why you should be afraid to open a door? Now you answer it, Laura!

LAURA   Oh, oh, oh . . . [*She returns through the portieres, darts to the Victrola, winds it frantically and turns it on.*]

AMANDA   Laura Wingfield, you march right to that door!

LAURA   Yes—yes, Mother!

[*A faraway, scratchy rendition of "Dardenella" softens the air and gives her strength to move through it. She slips to the door and draws it cautiously open.* TOM *enters with the caller,* JIM O'CONNOR.]

140   TOM   Laura, this is Jim. Jim, this is my sister, Laura.

JIM [*stepping inside*]   I didn't know that Shakespeare had a sister!

LAURA [*retreating, stiff and trembling, from the door*]   How—how do you do?

JIM [*heartily, extending his hand*]   Okay!

[LAURA *touches it hesitantly with hers.*]

JIM   Your hand's *cold,* Laura!

LAURA   Yes, well—I've been playing the Victrola. . . .

JIM   Must have been playing classical music on it! You ought to play a little hot swing music to warm you up!

LAURA   Excuse me—I haven't finished playing the Victrola. . . . [*She*
150   *turns awkwardly and hurries into the front room. She pauses a second by the Victrola. Then she catches her breath and darts through the portieres like a frightened deer.*]

JIM [*grinning*]   What was the matter?

TOM   Oh—with Laura? Laura is—terribly shy.

JIM   Shy, huh? It's unusual to meet a shy girl nowadays. I don't believe you ever mentioned you had a sister.

TOM   Well, now you know. I have one. Here is the *Post Dispatch.* You want a piece of it?

JIM   Uh-huh.

160   TOM   What piece? The comics?

JIM   Sports! [*He glances at it.*] Ole Dizzy Dean is on his bad behavior.

TOM [*uninterested*]   Yeah? [*He lights a cigarette and goes over to the fire-escape door.*]

JIM   Where are *you* going?

TOM   I'm going out on the terrace.

JIM [*going after him*]   You know, Shakespeare—I'm going to sell you a bill of goods!

TOM   What goods?

JIM   A course I'm taking.

170   TOM   Huh?

JIM   In public speaking! You and me, we're not the warehouse type.

TOM   Thanks—that's good news. But what has public speaking got to do with it?

JIM   It fits you for—executive positions!

TOM   Awww.

JIM   I tell you it's done a helluva lot for me.

[*Image on screen:* Executive at his desk.]

TOM   In what respect?

JIM   In every! Ask yourself what is the difference between you an' me and men in the office down front? Brains?—No!—Ability?—No! Then what? Just
180 one little thing—

TOM   What is that one little thing?

JIM   Primarily it amounts to—social poise! Being able to square up to people and hold your own on any social level!

AMANDA [*from the kitchenette*]   Tom?

TOM   Yes, Mother?

AMANDA   Is that you and Mr. O'Connor?

TOM   Yes, Mother.

AMANDA   Well, you just make yourselves comfortable in there.

TOM   Yes, Mother.

190   AMANDA   Ask Mr. O'Connor if he would like to wash his hands.

JIM   Aw, no—no—thank you—I took care of that at the warehouse. Tom—

TOM   Yes?

JIM   Mr. Mendoza was speaking to me about you.

TOM   Favorably?

JIM   What do you think?

TOM   Well—

JIM   You're going to be out of a job if you don't wake up.

TOM   I am waking up—

JIM   You show no signs.

200   TOM   The signs are interior.

[*Image on screen:* The sailing vessel with the Jolly Roger again.]

TOM   I'm planning to change. [*He leans over the fire-escape rail, speaking with quiet exhilaration. The incandescent marquees and signs of the first-run movie houses light his face from across the alley. He looks like a voyager.*] I'm right at the point of committing myself to a future that doesn't include the warehouse and Mr. Mendoza or even a night-school course in public speaking.

JIM   What are you gassing about?

TOM   I'm tired of the movies.

JIM   Movies!

TOM   Yes, movies! Look at them—[*a wave toward the marvels of Grand*
210 *Avenue*] All of those glamorous people—having adventures—hogging it all, gobbling the whole thing up! You know what happens? People go to the *movies* instead of *moving!* Hollywood characters are supposed to have all the

adventures for everybody in America, while everybody in America sits in a
dark room and watches them have them! Yes, until there's a war. That's when
adventure becomes available to the masses! *Everyone's* dish, not only
Gable's! Then the people in the dark room come out of the dark room to have
some adventures themselves—goody, goody! It's our turn now, to go to the
South Sea Island—to make a safari—to be exotic, far-off! But I'm not patient.
I don't want to wait till then. I'm tired of the *movies* and I am *about to move!*
220   JIM [*incredulously*]   Move?
       TOM   Yes.
       JIM   When?
       TOM   Soon!
       JIM   Where? Where?

[*The music seems to answer the question, while* TOM *thinks it over. He searches in his
pockets.*]

       TOM   I'm starting to boil inside. I know I seem dreamy, but inside—well,
I'm boiling! Whenever I pick up a shoe, I shudder a little thinking how short
life is and what I am doing! Whatever that means, I know it doesn't mean
shoes—except as something to wear on a traveler's feet! [*He finds what he
has been searching for in his pockets and holds out a paper to* JIM.] Look—
230   JIM   What?
       TOM   I'm a member.
       JIM [*reading*]   The Union of Merchant Seamen.
       TOM   I paid my dues this month, instead of the light bill.
       JIM   You will regret it when they turn the lights off.
       TOM   I won't be here.
       JIM   How about your mother?
       TOM   I'm like my father. The bastard son of a bastard! Did you notice how
he's grinning in his picture in there? And he's been absent going on sixteen
years!
240   JIM   You're just talking, you drip. How does your mother feel about it?
       TOM   Shhh! Here comes Mother! Mother is not acquainted with my plans!
       AMANDA [*coming through the portieres*]   Where are you all?
       TOM   On the terrace, Mother.

[*They start inside. She advances to them.* TOM *is distinctly shocked at her appearance.
Even* JIM *blinks a little. He is making his first contact with girlish Southern vivacity and
in spite of the night-school course in public speaking is somewhat thrown off the beam
by the unexpected outlay of social charm. Certain responses are attempted by* JIM *but
are swept aside by* AMANDA*'s gay laughter and chatter.* TOM *is embarrassed but after the
first shock* JIM *reacts very warmly. He grins and chuckles, is altogether won over.*]

[*Image on screen:* Amanda as a girl.]

       AMANDA [*coyly smiling, shaking her girlish ringlets*]   Well, well, well, so
this is Mr. O'Connor. Introductions entirely unnecessary. I've heard so much

about you from my boy. I finally said to him, Tom—good gracious!—why
don't you bring this paragon to supper? I'd like to meet this nice young man
at the warehouse!—instead of just hearing him sing your praises so much! I
don't know why my son is so stand-offish—that's not Southern behavior!

250   Let's sit down and—I think we could stand a little more air in here! Tom,
leave the door open. I felt a nice fresh breeze a moment ago. Where has it
gone to? Mmm, so warm already! And not quite summer, even. We're going to
burn up when summer really gets started. However, we're having—we're
having a very light supper. I think light things are better fo' this time of year.
The same as light clothes are. Light clothes an' light food are what warm
weather calls fo'. You know our blood gets so thick during th' winter—it
takes a while fo' us to *adjust* ou'selves!—when the season changes . . . It's
come so quick this year. I wasn't prepared. All of a sudden—heavens! Already summer! I ran to the trunk an' pulled out this light dress—terribly old!

260 Historical almost! But feels so good—so good an' co-ol, y'know. . . .
      TOM Mother—
      AMANDA Yes, honey?
      TOM How about—supper?
      AMANDA Honey, you go ask Sister if supper is ready! You know that Sister
is in full charge of supper! Tell her you hungry boys are waiting for it. [*to* JIM]
Have you met Laura?
      JIM She—
      AMANDA Let you in? Oh, good, you've met already! It's rare for a girl as
sweet an' pretty as Laura to be domestic! But Laura is, thank heavens, not only

270 pretty but also very domestic. I'm not at all. I never was a bit. I never could
make a thing but angel-food cake. Well, in the South we had so many servants. Gone, gone, gone. All vestige of gracious living! Gone completely! I
wasn't prepared for what the future brought me. All of my gentlemen callers
were sons of planters and so of course I assumed that I would be married to
one and raise my family on a large piece of land with plenty of servants. But
man proposes—and woman accepts the proposal! To vary that old, old saying
a little bit—I married no planter! I married a man who worked for the telephone company! That gallantly smiling gentleman over there! [*She points to
the picture.*] A telephone man who—fell in love with long-distance! Now he

280 travels and I don't even know where! But what am I going on for about my—
tribulations? Tell me yours—I hope you don't have any! Tom?
      TOM [*returning*] Yes, Mother?
      AMANDA Is supper nearly ready?
      TOM It looks to me like supper is on the table.
      AMANDA Let me look—[*She rises prettily and looks through the portieres.*]
Oh, lovely! But where is Sister?
      TOM Laura is not feeling well and she says that she thinks she'd better not
come to the table.
      AMANDA What? Nonsense! Laura? Oh, Laura!

290   LAURA [*from the kitchenette, faintly*] Yes, Mother.
      AMANDA You really must come to the table. We won't be seated until you
come to the table! Come in, Mr. O'Connor. You sit over there, and I'll. . . .

Laura? Laura Wingfield! You're keeping us waiting, honey! We can't say grace until you come to the table!

[*The kitchenette door is pushed weakly open and* LAURA *comes in. She is obviously quite faint, her lips trembling, her eyes wide and staring. She moves unsteadily toward the table.*]

[*Screen legend:* "Terror!"]

[*Outside a summer storm is coming on abruptly. The white curtains billow inward at the windows and there is a sorrowful murmur from the deep blue dusk.*]

[LAURA *suddenly stumbles; she catches at a chair with a faint moan.*]

>   TOM Laura!
>   AMANDA Laura!

[*There is a clap of thunder.*]

[*Screen legend:* "Ah!"]

[*despairingly*]   Why, Laura, you *are* ill, darling! Tom, help your sister into the living room, dear! Sit in the living room, Laura—rest on the sofa. Well! [*to* JIM *as* TOM *helps his sister to the sofa in the living room*] Standing over the hot
300 stove made her ill! I told her that it was just too warm this evening, but—

[TOM *comes back to the table.*]

Is Laura all right now?
>   TOM Yes.
>   AMANDA What is that? Rain? A nice cool rain has come up! [*She gives* JIM *a frightened look.*] I think we may—have grace—now . . .

[TOM *looks at her stupidly.*] Tom, honey—you say grace!

>   TOM Oh . . . "For these and all thy mercies—"

[*They bow their heads,* AMANDA *stealing a nervous glance at* JIM. *In the living room* LAURA, *stretched on the sofa, clenches her hand to her lips, to hold back a shuddering sob.*]

God's Holy Name be praised—

[*The scene dims out.*[1]]

Scene Seven

It is half an hour later. Dinner is just being finished in the dining room. LAURA *is still huddled upon the sofa, her feet drawn under her, her head resting on a pale blue pillow, her eyes wide and mysteriously watchful. The new floor lamp with its shade of rose-colored silk gives a soft, becoming light to her face, bringing out the fragile, unearthly prettiness which usually escapes attention. From outside there is a steady murmur of rain, but it is slackening and soon stops: the air outside becomes pale and luminous as the moon breaks through the clouds. A moment after the curtain rises, the lights in both rooms flicker and go out.*

JIM   Hey, there, Mr. Light Bulb!

[AMANDA *laughs nervously.*]

[*Legend on screen:* "Suspension of a public service."]

AMANDA   Where was Moses when the lights went out? Ha-ha. Do you know the answer to that one, Mr. O'Connor?
JIM   No, Ma'am, what's the answer?
AMANDA   In the dark!

[JIM *laughs appreciatively.*]

Everybody sit still. I'll light the candles. Isn't it lucky we have them on the table? Where's a match? Which of you gentlemen can provide a match?
JIM   Here.
AMANDA   Thank you, Sir.
10   JIM   Not at all, Ma'am!
AMANDA [*as she lights the candles*]   I guess the fuse has burnt out. Mr. O'Connor, can you tell a burnt-out fuse? I know I can't and Tom is a total loss when it comes to mechanics.

[*They rise from the table and go into the kitchenette, from where their voices are heard.*]

Oh, be careful you don't bump into something. We don't want our gentleman caller to break his neck. Now wouldn't that be a fine howdy-do?
JIM   Ha-ha! Where is the fuse-box?
AMANDA   Right here next to the stove. Can you see anything?
JIM   Just a minute.
AMANDA   Isn't electricity a mysterious thing? Wasn't it Benjamin Franklin
20 who tied a key to a kite? We live in such a mysterious universe, don't we? Some people say that science clears up all the mysteries for us. In my opinion it only creates more! Have you found it yet?
JIM   No, Ma'am. All these fuses look okay to me.
AMANDA   Tom!
TOM   Yes, Mother?
AMANDA   That light bill I gave you several days ago. The one I told you we got the notices about?

[*Legend on screen:* "Ha!"]

TOM   Oh—yeah.

AMANDA   You didn't neglect to pay it by any chance?

30   TOM   Why, I—

AMANDA   Didn't! I might have known it!

JIM   Shakespeare probably wrote a poem on that light bill, Mrs. Wingfield.

AMANDA   I might have known better than to trust him with it! There's such a high price for negligence in this world!

JIM   Maybe the poem will win a ten-dollar prize.

AMANDA   We'll just have to spend the remainder of the evening in the nineteenth century, before Mr. Edison made the Mazda lamp!

JIM   Candlelight is my favorite kind of light.

AMANDA   That shows you're romantic! But that's no excuse for Tom. Well,
40 we got through dinner. Very considerate of them to let us get through dinner before they plunged us into everlasting darkness, wasn't it, Mr. O'Connor?

JIM   Ha-ha!

AMANDA   Tom, as a penalty for your carelessness you can help me with the dishes.

JIM   Let me give you a hand.

AMANDA   Indeed you will not!

JIM   I ought to be good for something.

AMANDA   Good for something? [*Her tone is rhapsodic.*] *You?* Why, Mr. O'Connor, nobody, *nobody's* given me this much entertainment in years—as
50 you have!

JIM   Aw, now, Mrs. Wingfield!

AMANDA   I'm not exaggerating, not one bit! But Sister is all by her lone-some. You go keep her company in the parlor! I'll give you this lovely old candelabrum that used to be on the altar at the Church of the Heavenly Rest. It was melted a little out of shape when the church burnt down. Lightning struck it one spring. Gypsy Jones was holding a revival at the time and he intimated that the church was destroyed because the Episcopalians gave card parties.

JIM   Ha-ha.

60   AMANDA   And how about your coaxing Sister to drink a little wine? I think it would be good for her! Can you carry both at once?

JIM   Sure. I'm Superman!

AMANDA   Now, Thomas, get into this apron!

[JIM *comes into the dining room, carrying the candelabrum, its candles lighted, in one hand and a glass of wine in the other. The door of the kitchenette swings closed on* AMANDA*'s gay laughter; the flickering light approaches the portieres.* LAURA *sits up nervously as* JIM *enters. She can hardly speak from the almost intolerable strain of being alone with a stranger.*]

[*Screen legend:* "I don't suppose you remember me at all!"]

[*At first, before* JIM*'s warmth overcomes her paralyzing shyness,* LAURA*'s voice is thin and breathless, as though she had just run up a steep flight of stairs.* JIM*'s attitude is* *gently humorous. While the incident is apparently unimportant, it is to* LAURA *the climax of her secret life.*]

JIM   Hello there, Laura.
LAURA [*faintly*]   Hello.

[*She clears her throat.*]

JIM   How are you feeling now? Better?
LAURA   Yes. Yes, thank you.
JIM   This is for you. A little dandelion wine. [*He extends the glass toward her with extravagant gallantry.*]
70   LAURA   Thank you.
JIM   Drink it—but don't get drunk!

[*He laughs heartily.* LAURA *takes the glass uncertainly; she laughs shyly.*]

Where shall I set the candles?
LAURA   Oh—oh, anywhere . . .
JIM   How about here on the floor? Any objections?
LAURA   No.
JIM   I'll spread a newspaper under to catch the drippings. I like to sit on the floor. Mind if I do?
LAURA   Oh, no.
JIM   Give me a pillow?
80   LAURA   What?
JIM   A pillow!
LAURA   Oh . . . [*She hands him one quickly.*]
JIM   How about you? Don't you like to sit on the floor?
LAURA   Oh—yes.
JIM   Why don't you, then?
LAURA   I—will.
JIM   Take a pillow!

[LAURA *does. She sits on the floor on the other side of the candelabrum.* JIM *crosses his legs and smiles engagingly at her.*] I can't hardly see you sitting
90   way over there.

LAURA   I can—see you.
JIM   I know, but that's not fair, I'm in the limelight.

[LAURA *moves her pillow closer.*]

Good! Now I can see you! Comfortable?
LAURA   Yes.
JIM   So am I. Comfortable as a cow! Will you have some gum?
LAURA   No, thank you.

JIM   I think that I will indulge, with your permission. [*He musingly unwraps a stick of gum and holds it up.*] Think of the fortune made by the guy that invented the first piece of chewing gum. Amazing, huh? The Wrigley
100   Building is one of the sights of Chicago—I saw it when I went up to the Century of Progress. Did you take in the Century of Progress?

LAURA   No, I didn't.

JIM   Well, it was quite a wonderful exposition. What impressed me most was the Hall of Science. Gives you an idea of what the future will be in America, even more wonderful than the present time is! [*There is a pause.* JIM *smiles at her.*] Your brother tells me you're shy. Is that right, Laura?

LAURA   I—don't know.

JIM   I judge you to be an old-fashioned type of girl. Well, I think that's a pretty good type to be. Hope you don't think I'm being too personal—do you?
110   LAURA   [*hastily, out of embarrassment*]   I believe I *will* take a piece of gum, if you—don't mind. [*clearing her throat*] Mr. O'Connor, have you—kept up with your singing?

JIM   Singing? Me?

LAURA   Yes. I remember what a beautiful voice you had.

JIM   When did you hear me sing?

[LAURA *does not answer, and in the long pause which follows a man's voice is heard singing offstage.*]

VOICE
O blow, ye winds, heigh-ho,
A-roving I will go!
     I'm off to my love

120

     With a boxing glove—
Ten thousand miles away!

JIM   You say you've heard me sing?

LAURA   Oh, yes! Yes, very often . . . I—don't suppose—you remember me—at all?

JIM   [*smiling doubtfully*]   You know I have an idea I've seen you before. I had that idea as soon as you opened the door. It seemed almost like I was about to remember your name. But the name that I started to call you—wasn't a name! And so I stopped myself before I said it.

LAURA   Wasn't it—Blue Roses?
130   JIM   [*springing up, grinning*]   Blue Roses! My gosh, yes—Blue Roses! That's what I had on my tongue when you opened the door! Isn't it funny what tricks your memory plays? I didn't connect you with high school somehow or other. But that's where it was; it was high school. I didn't even know you were Shakespeare's sister! Gosh, I'm sorry.

LAURA   I didn't expect you to. You—barely knew me!

JIM   But we did have a speaking acquaintance, huh?

LAURA   Yes, we—spoke to each other.

JIM   When did you recognize me?

LAURA   Oh, right away!

140   JIM   Soon as I came in the door?

LAURA   When I heard your name I thought it was probably you. I knew that Tom used to know you a little in high school. So when you came in the door—well, then I was—sure.

JIM   Why didn't you *say* something, then?

LAURA [*breathlessly*]   I didn't know what to say, I was—too surprised!

JIM   For goodness' sakes! You know, this sure is funny!

LAURA   Yes! Yes, isn't it, though . . . .

JIM   Didn't we have a class in something together?

LAURA   Yes, we did.

150   JIM   What class was that?

LAURA   It was—singing—chorus!

JIM   Aw!

LAURA   I sat across the aisle from you in the Aud.

JIM   Aw.

LAURA   Mondays, Wednesdays, and Fridays.

JIM   Now I remember—you always came in late.

LAURA   Yes, it was so hard for me, getting upstairs. I had that brace on my leg—it clumped so loud!

JIM   I never heard any clumping.

160   LAURA [*wincing at the recollection*]   To me it sounded like—thunder!

JIM   Well, well, well, I never even noticed.

LAURA   And everybody was seated before I came in. I had to walk in front of all those people. My seat was in the back row. I had to go clumping all the way up the aisle with everyone watching!

JIM   You shouldn't have been self-conscious.

LAURA   I know, but I was. It was always such a relief when the singing started.

JIM   Aw, yes, I've placed you now! I used to call you Blue Roses. How was it that I got started calling you that?

170   LAURA   I was out of school a little while with pleurosis. When I came back you asked me what was the matter. I said I had pleurosis—you thought I said *Blue Roses.* That's what you always called me after that!

JIM   I hope you didn't mind.

LAURA   Oh, no—I liked it. You see, I wasn't acquainted with many—people. . . .

JIM   As I remember you sort of stuck by yourself.

LAURA   I—I—never have had much luck at—making friends.

JIM   I don't see why you wouldn't.

LAURA   Well, I—started out badly.

180   JIM   You mean being—

LAURA   Yes, it sort of—stood between me—

JIM   You shouldn't have let it!

LAURA   I know, but it did, and—

JIM   You were shy with people!

LAURA   I tried not to be but never could—

JIM   Overcome it?

LAURA   No, I—I never could!

JIM   I guess being shy is something you have to work out of kind of gradually.

190   LAURA [*sorrowfully*]   Yes—I guess it—

JIM   Takes time!

LAURA   Yes—

JIM   People are not so dreadful when you know them. That's what you have to remember! And everybody has problems, not just you, but practically everybody has got some problems. You think of yourself as having the only problems, as being the only one who is disappointed. But just look around you and you will see lots of people as disappointed as you are. For instance, I hoped when I was going to high school that I would be further along at this time, six years later, than I am now. You remember that wonderful write-up I

200   had in *The Torch?*

LAURA   Yes! [*She rises and crosses to the table.*]

JIM   It said I was bound to succeed in anything I went into!

[LAURA *returns with the high school yearbook.*]

Holy Jeez! *The Torch!*

[*He accepts it reverently. They smile across the book with mutual wonder.* LAURA *crouches beside him and they begin to turn the pages.* LAURA*'s shyness is dissolving in his warmth.*]

LAURA   Here you are in *The Pirates of Penzance!*

JIM [*wistfully*]   I sang the baritone lead in that operetta.

LAURA [*raptly*]   So—*beautifully!*

JIM [*protesting*]   Aw—

LAURA   Yes, yes—beautifully—beautifully!

JIM   You heard me?

210   LAURA   All three times!

JIM   No!

LAURA   Yes!

JIM   All three performances?

LAURA [*looking down*]   Yes.

JIM   Why?

LAURA   I—wanted to ask you to—autograph my program. [*She takes the program from the back of the yearbook and shows it to him.*]

JIM   Why didn't you ask me to?

LAURA   You were always surrounded by your own friends so much that I

220   never had a chance to.

JIM   You should have just—

LAURA   Well, I—thought you might think I was—

JIM   Thought I might think you was—what?

LAURA   Oh—

JIM [*with reflective relish*]   I was beleaguered by females in those days.

LAURA   You were terribly popular!

JIM   Yeah—

LAURA   You had such a—friendly way—

JIM   I was spoiled in high school.

230   LAURA   Everybody—liked you!

JIM   Including you?

LAURA   I—yes, I—did, too—[*She gently closes the book in her lap.*]

JIM   Well, well, well! Give me that program, Laura.

[*She hands it to him. He signs it with a flourish.*]

There you are—better late than never!

LAURA   Oh, I—what a—surprise!

JIM   My signature isn't worth very much right now. But some day—maybe—it will increase in value! Being disappointed is one thing and being discouraged is something else. I am disappointed but I am not discouraged. I'm twenty-three years old. How old are you?

240   LAURA   I'll be twenty-four in June.

JIM   That's not old age!

LAURA   No, but—

JIM   You finished high school?

LAURA [*with difficulty*]   I didn't go back.

JIM   You mean you dropped out?

LAURA   I made bad grades in my final examinations. [*She rises and replaces the book and the program on the table. Her voice is strained.*] How is—Emily Meisenbach getting along?

JIM   Oh, that kraut-head!

250   LAURA   Why do you call her that?

JIM   That's what she was.

LAURA   You're not still—going with her?

JIM   I never see her.

LAURA   It said in the "Personal" section that you were—engaged!

JIM   I know, but I wasn't impressed by that—propaganda!

LAURA   It wasn't—the truth?

JIM   Only in Emily's optimistic opinion!

LAURA   Oh—

[*Legend:* "What have you done since high school?"]

[JIM *lights a cigarette and leans indolently back on his elbows smiling at* LAURA *with a warmth and charm which lights her inwardly with altar candles. She remains by the table, picks up a piece from the glass menagerie collection, and turns it in her hands to cover her tumult.*]

JIM [*after several reflective puffs on his cigarette*]   What have you done

260 since high school?

[*She seems not to hear him.*]

Huh?

[LAURA *looks up.*]

I said what have you done since high school, Laura?

LAURA   Nothing much.

JIM   You must have been doing something these six long years.

LAURA   Yes.

JIM   Well, then, such as what?

LAURA   I took a business course at business college—

JIM   How did that work out?

LAURA   Well, not very—well—I had to drop out, it gave me—indigestion—

[JIM *laughs gently.*]

270   JIM   What are you doing now?

LAURA   I don't do anything—much. Oh, please don't think I sit around doing nothing! My glass collection takes up a good deal of time. Glass is something you have to take good care of.

JIM   What did you say—about glass?

LAURA   Collection I said—I have one—[*She clears her throat and turns away again, acutely shy.*]

JIM [*abruptly*]   You know what I judge to be the trouble with you? Inferiority complex! You know what that is? That's what they call it when someone low-rates himself! I understand it because I had it, too. Although my case was
280   not so aggravated as yours seems to be. I had it until I took up public speaking, developed my voice, and learned that I had an aptitude for science. Before that time I never thought of myself as being outstanding in any way whatsoever! Now I've never made a regular study of it, but I have a friend who says I can analyze people better than doctors that make a profession of it. I don't claim that to be necessarily true, but I can sure guess a person's psychology, Laura! [*He takes out his gum.*] Excuse me, Laura. I always take it out when the flavor is gone. I'll use this scrap of paper to wrap it in. I know how it is to get it stuck on a shoe. [*He wraps the gum in paper and puts it in his pocket.*] Yes—that's what I judge to be your principal trouble. A lack of
290   confidence in yourself as a person. You don't have the proper amount of faith in yourself. I'm basing that fact on a number of your remarks and also on certain observations I've made. For instance that clumping you thought was so awful in high school. You say that you even dreaded to walk into class. You see what you did? You dropped out of school, you gave up an education because of a clump, which as far as I know was practically non-existent! A little physical defect is what you have. Hardly noticeable even! Magnified thousands of times by imagination! You know what my strong advice to you is? Think of yourself as *superior* in some way!

LAURA   In what way would I think?

300   JIM   Why, man alive, Laura! Just look about you a little. What do you see? A
world full of common people! All of 'em born and all of 'em going to die!
Which of them has one-tenth of your good points! Or mine! Or anyone else's,
as far as that goes—gosh! Everybody excels in some one thing. Some in
many! [*He unconsciously glances at himself in the mirror.*] All you've got to
do is discover in *what!* Take me, for instance. [*He adjusts his tie at the
mirror.*] My interest happens to lie in electro-dynamics. I'm taking a course
in radio engineering at night school, Laura, on top of a fairly responsible job
at the warehouse. I'm taking that course and studying public speaking.
        LAURA   Ohhhh.
310   JIM   Because I believe in the future of television! [*turning his back to her*]
I wish to be ready to go up right along with it. Therefore I'm planning to get
in on the ground floor. In fact I've already made the right connections and all
that remains is for the industry itself to get under way! Full steam—[*His eyes
are starry.*] *Knowledge*—Zzzzzp! *Money*—Zzzzzzp!—*Power!* That's the cycle democracy is built on!

[*His attitude is convincingly dynamic.* LAURA *stares at him, even her shyness eclipsed
in her absolute wonder. He suddenly grins.*]

I guess you think I think a lot of myself!
        LAURA   No—o-o-o, I—
        JIM   Now how about you? Isn't there something you take more interest in
than anything else?
320   LAURA   Well, I do—as I said—have my—glass collection—

[*A peal of girlish laughter rings from the kitchenette.*]

        JIM   I'm not right sure I know what you're talking about. What kind of glass
is it?
        LAURA   Little articles of it, they're ornaments mostly! Most of them are
little animals made out of glass, the tiniest little animals in the world. Mother
calls them a glass menagerie! Here's an example of one, if you'd like to see it!
This one is one of the oldest. It's nearly thirteen.

[*Music: "The Glass Menagerie."*]

[*He stretches out his hand.*]

Oh, be careful—if you breathe, it breaks!
        JIM   I'd better not take it. I'm pretty clumsy with things.
        LAURA   Go on, I trust you with him! [*She places the piece in his palm.*]
330 There now—you're holding him gently! Hold him over the light, he loves the
light! You see how the light shines through him?
        JIM   It sure does shine!
        LAURA   I shouldn't be partial, but he is my favorite one.
        JIM   What kind of a thing is this one supposed to be?

LAURA   Haven't you noticed the single horn on his forehead?

JIM   A unicorn, huh?

LAURA   Mmmmm-hmmm!

JIM   Unicorns—aren't they extinct in the modern world?

LAURA   I know!

340   JIM   Poor little fellow, he must feel sort of lonesome.

LAURA [*smiling*]   Well, if he does, he doesn't complain about it. He stays on a shelf with some horses that don't have horns and all of them seem to get along nicely together.

JIM   How do you know?

LAURA [*lightly*]   I haven't heard any arguments among them!

JIM [*grinning*]   No arguments, huh? Well, that's a pretty good sign! Where shall I set him?

LAURA   Put him on the table. They all like a change of scenery once in a while!

350   JIM   Well, well, well, well—[*He places the glass piece on the table, then raises his arms and stretches.*] Look how big my shadow is when I stretch!

LAURA   Oh, oh, yes—it stretches across the ceiling!

JIM [*crossing to the door*]   I think it's stopped raining. [*He opens the fire-escape door and the background music changes to a dance tune.*] Where does the music come from?

LAURA   From the Paradise Dance Hall across the alley.

JIM   How about cutting the rug a little, Miss Wingfield?

LAURA   Oh, I—

JIM   Or is your program filled up? Let me have a look at it [*He grasps an*
360   *imaginary card.*] Why, every dance is taken! I'll just have to scratch some out.

[*Waltz music: "La Golondrina."*]

Ahhh, a waltz! [*He executes some sweeping turns by himself, then holds his arms toward* LAURA.]

LAURA [*breathlessly*]   I—can't dance!

JIM   There you go, that inferiority stuff!

LAURA   I've never danced in my life!

JIM   Come on, try!

LAURA   Oh, but I'd step on you!

JIM   I'm not made out of glass.

LAURA   How—how—how do we start?

370   JIM   Just leave it to me. You hold your arms out a little.

LAURA   Like this?

JIM [*taking her in his arms*]   A little bit higher. Right. Now don't tighten up, that's the main thing about it—relax.

LAURA [*laughing breathlessly*]   It's hard not to.

JIM   Okay.

LAURA   I'm afraid you can't budge me.

JIM   What do you bet I can't? [*He swings her into motion.*]

LAURA   Goodness, yes, you can!

JIM Let yourself go, now, Laura, just let yourself go.

380 LAURA I'm—

JIM Come on!

LAURA —trying!

JIM Not so stiff—easy does it!

LAURA I know but I'm—

JIM Loosen th' backbone! There now, that's a lot better.

LAURA Am I?

JIM Lots, lots better! [*He moves her about the room in a clumsy waltz.*]

LAURA Oh, my!

JIM Ha-ha!

390 LAURA Oh, my goodness!

JIM Ha-ha-ha!

[*They suddenly bump into the table, and the glass piece on it falls to the floor.* JIM *stops the dance.*]

What did we hit on?

LAURA Table.

JIM Did something fall off it? I think—

LAURA Yes.

JIM I hope that it wasn't the little glass horse with the horn!

LAURA Yes. [*She stoops to pick it up.*]

JIM Aw, aw, aw. Is it broken?

LAURA Now it is just like all the other horses.

400 JIM It's lost its—

LAURA Horn! It doesn't matter. Maybe it's a blessing in disguise.

JIM You'll never forgive me. I bet that that was your favorite piece of glass.

LAURA I don't have favorites much. It's no tragedy, Freckles. Glass breaks so easily. No matter how careful you are. The traffic jars the shelves and things fall off them.

JIM Still I'm awfully sorry that I was the cause.

LAURA [*smiling*] I'll just imagine he had an operation. The horn was removed to make him feel less—freakish!

[*They both laugh.*]

Now he will feel more at home with the other horses, the ones that don't

410 have horns. . . .

JIM Ha-ha, that's very funny! [*Suddenly he is serious.*] I'm glad to see that you have a sense of humor. You know—you're—well—very different! Surprisingly different from anyone else I know! [*His voice becomes soft and hesitant with a genuine feeling.*] Do you mind me telling you that?

[LAURA *is abashed beyond speech.*]

I mean it in a nice way—

[LAURA *nods shyly, looking away.*]

You make me feel sort of—I don't know how to put it! I'm usually pretty good at expressing things, but—this is something that I don't know how to say!

[LAURA *touches her throat and clears it—turns the broken unicorn in her hands. His voice becomes softer.*]

Has anyone ever told you that you were pretty?

[*There is a pause, and the music rises slightly.* LAURA *looks up slowly, with wonder, and shakes her head.*]

420   Well, you are! In a very different way from anyone else. And all the nicer because of the difference, too.

[*His voice becomes low and husky.* LAURA *turns away, nearly faint with the novelty of her emotions.*]

I wish that you were my sister. I'd teach you to have some confidence in yourself. The different people are not like other people, but being different is nothing to be ashamed of. Because other people are not such wonderful people. They're one hundred times one thousand. You're one times one! They walk all over the earth. You just stay here. They're common as—weeds, but—you—well, you're—*Blue Roses!*

[*Image on screen:* Blue Roses.]

[*The music changes.*]

   LAURA   But blue is wrong for—roses. . . .
   JIM   It's right for you! You're—pretty!
430   LAURA   In what respect am I pretty?
   JIM   In all respects—believe me! Your eyes—your hair—are pretty! Your hands are pretty! [*He catches hold of her hand.*] You think I'm making this up because I'm invited to dinner and have to be nice. Oh, I could do that! I could put on an act for you, Laura, and say lots of things without being very sincere. But this time I am. I'm talking to you sincerely. I happened to notice you had this inferiority complex that keeps you from feeling comfortable with people. Somebody needs to build your confidence up and make you proud instead of shy and turning away and—blushing. Somebody—ought to—*kiss* you, Laura!

[*His hand slips slowly up her arm to her shoulder as the music swells tumultuously. He suddenly turns her about and kisses her on the lips. When he releases her,* LAURA *sinks on the sofa with a bright, dazed look.* JIM *backs away and fishes in his pocket for a cigarette.*]

[*Legend on screen:* "A souvenir."]

440   Stumblejohn!

[*He lights the cigarette, avoiding her look. There is a peal of girlish laughter from* AMANDA *in the kitchenette.* LAURA *slowly raises and opens her hand. It still contains the little broken glass animal. She looks at it with a tender, bewildered expression.*]

Stumblejohn! I shouldn't have done that—that was way off the beam. You don't smoke, do you?

[*She looks up, smiling, not hearing the question. He sits beside her rather gingerly. She looks at him speechlessly—waiting. He coughs decorously and moves a little farther aside as he considers the situation and senses her feelings, dimly, with perturbation. He speaks gently.*]

Would you—care for a—mint?

[*She doesn't seem to hear him but her look grows brighter even.*]

Peppermint? Life Saver? My pocket's a regular drugstore—wherever I go. . . . [*He pops a mint in his mouth. Then he gulps and decides to make a clean breast of it. He speaks slowly and gingerly.*] Laura, you know if I had a sister like you, I'd do the same thing as Tom. I'd bring out fellows and— introduce her to them. The right type of boys—of a type to—appreciate her. Only—well—he made a mistake about me. Maybe I've got no call to be
450   saying this. That may not have been the idea in having me over. But what if it was? There's nothing wrong about that. The only trouble is that in my case— I'm not in a situation to—do the right thing. I can't take down your number and say I'll phone. I can't call up next week and—ask for a date. I thought I had better explain the situation in case you—misunderstood it and—I hurt your feelings. . . .

[*There is a pause. Slowly, very slowly,* LAURA*'s look changes, her eyes returning slowly from his to the glass figure in her palm.* AMANDA *utters another gay laugh in the kitchenette.*]

LAURA [*faintly*] You—won't—call again?
JIM No, Laura, I can't. [*He rises from the sofa.*] As I was just explaining, I've—got strings on me. Laura, I've—been going steady! I go out all the time with a girl named Betty. She's a home-girl like you, and Catholic, and Irish,
460   and in a great many ways we—get along fine. I met her last summer on a moonlight boat trip up the river to Alton, on the *Majestic.* Well—right away from the start it was—love!

[*Legend:* Love!]

[LAURA *sways slightly forward and grips the arm of the sofa. He fails to notice, now enrapt in his own comfortable being.*]

Being in love has made a new man of me!

[*Leaning stiffly forward, clutching the arm of the sofa,* LAURA *struggles visibly with her storm. But Jim is oblivious; she is a long way off.*]

The power of love is really pretty tremendous! Love is something that—changes the whole world, Laura!

[*The storm abates a little and* LAURA *leans back. He notices her again.*]

It happened that Betty's aunt took sick, she got a wire and had to go to Centralia. So Tom—when he asked me to dinner—I naturally just accepted the invitation, not knowing that you—that he—that I—[*He stops awkwardly.*] Huh—I'm a stumblejohn!

[*He flops back on the sofa. The holy candles on the altar of* LAURA's *face have been snuffed out. There is a look of almost infinite desolation.* JIM *glances at her uneasily.*]

470   I wish that you would—say something.

[*She bites her lip which was trembling and then bravely smiles. She opens her hand again on the broken glass figure. Then she gently takes his hand and raises it level with her own. She carefully places the unicorn in the palm of his hand, then pushes his fingers closed upon it.*]

What are you—doing that for? You want me to have him? Laura?

[*She nods.*]

What for?
LAURA   A—souvenir. . . .

[*She rises unsteadily and crouches beside the Victrola to wind it up.*]

[*Legend on screen:* "Things have a way of turning out so badly!" *Or image:* "Gentleman caller waving goodbye—gaily."]

[*At this moment* AMANDA *rushes brightly back into the living room. She bears a pitcher of fruit punch in an old-fashioned cut-glass pitcher, and a plate of macaroons. The plate has a gold border and poppies painted on it.*]

AMANDA   Well, well, well! Isn't the air delightful after the shower? I've made you children a little liquid refreshment.

[*She turns gaily to Jim.*] Jim, do you know that song about lemonade?

"Lemonade, lemonade
Made in the shade and stirred with a spade—
Good enough for any old maid!"

480   JIM [*uneasily*]   Ha-ha! No—I never heard it.

AMANDA   Why, Laura! You look so serious!

JIM   We were having a serious conversation.

AMANDA   Good! Now you're better acquainted!

JIM [*uncertainly*]   Ha-ha! Yes.

AMANDA   You modern young people are much more serious-minded than my generation. I was so gay as a girl!

JIM   You haven't changed, Mrs. Wingfield.

AMANDA   Tonight I'm rejuvenated! The gaiety of the occasion, Mr. O'Connor! [*She tosses her head with a peal of laughter, spilling some lemon-*
490   *ade.*] Oooo! I'm baptizing myself!

JIM   Here—let me—

AMANDA [*setting the pitcher down*]   There now. I discovered we had some maraschino cherries. I dumped them in, juice and all!

JIM   You shouldn't have gone to that trouble, Mrs. Wingfield.

AMANDA   Trouble, trouble? Why, it was loads of fun! Didn't you hear me cutting up in the kitchen? I bet your ears were burning! I told Tom how out-done with him I was for keeping you to himself so long a time! He should have brought you over much, much sooner! Well, now that you've found your way, I want you to be a very frequent caller! Not just occasional but all the time. Oh,
500   we're going to have a lot of gay times together! I see them coming! Mmm, just breathe that air! So fresh, and the moon's so pretty! I'll skip back out—I know where my place is when young folks are having a—serious conversation!

JIM   Oh, don't go out, Mrs. Wingfield. The fact of the matter is I've got to be going.

AMANDA   Going, now? You're joking? Why, it's only the shank of the evening, Mr. O'Connor.

JIM   Well, you know how it is.

AMANDA   You mean you're a young workingman and have to keep working-men's hours. We'll let you off early tonight. But only on the condition that
510   next time you stay later. What's the best night for you? Isn't Saturday night the best night for you workingmen?

JIM   I have a couple of time-clocks to punch, Mrs. Wingfield. One at morn-ing, another one at night!

AMANDA   My, but you *are* ambitious! You work at night, too?

JIM   No, Ma'am, not work but—Betty!

[*He crosses deliberately to pick up his hat. The band at the Paradise Dance Hall goes into a tender waltz.*]

AMANDA   Betty? Betty? Who's—Betty!

[*There is an ominous cracking sound in the sky.*]

JIM   Oh, just a girl. The girl I go steady with!

[*He smiles charmingly. The sky falls.*]

[*Legend:* "The Sky Falls."]

AMANDA [*a long-drawn exhalation*]   Ohhhh . . . Is it a serious romance, Mr. O'Connor?

520   JIM   We're going to be married the second Sunday in June.

AMANDA   Ohhhh—how nice! Tom didn't mention that you were engaged to be married.

JIM   The cat's not out of the bag at the warehouse yet. You know how they are. They call you Romeo and stuff like that. [*He stops at the oval mirror to put on his hat. He carefully shapes the brim and the crown to give a discreetly dashing effect.*] It's been a wonderful evening, Mrs. Wingfield. I guess this is what they mean by Southern hospitality.

AMANDA   It really wasn't anything at all.

JIM   I hope it don't seem like I'm rushing off. But I promised Betty I'd
530 pick her up at the Wabash depot, an' by the time I get my jalopy down there her train'll be in. Some women are pretty upset if you keep 'em waiting.

AMANDA   Yes, I know—the tyranny of women! [*She extends her hand.*] Good-bye, Mr. O'Connor. I wish you luck—and happiness—and success! All three of them, and so does Laura! Don't you, Laura?

LAURA   Yes!

JIM [*taking Laura's hand*]   Goodbye, Laura. I'm certainly going to treasure that souvenir. And don't you forget the good advice I gave you. [*He raises his voice to a cheery shout.*] So long, Shakespeare! Thanks again, ladies. Good night!

[*He grins and ducks jauntily out. Still bravely grimacing,* AMANDA *closes the door on the gentleman caller. Then she turns back to the room with a puzzled expression. She and* LAURA *don't dare to face each other.* LAURA *crouches beside the Victrola to wind it.*]

540   AMANDA [*faintly*]   Things have a way of turning out so badly. I don't believe that I would play the Victrola. Well, well—well! Our gentleman caller was engaged to be married! [*She raises her voice.*] Tom!

TOM [*from the kitchenette*]   Yes, Mother?

AMANDA   Come in here a minute. I want to tell you something awfully funny.

TOM [*entering with a macaroon and a glass of the lemonade*]   Has the gentleman caller gotten away already?

AMANDA   The gentleman caller has made an early departure. What a wonderful joke you played on us!

TOM   How do you mean?

550   AMANDA   You didn't mention that he was engaged to be married.

TOM   Jim? Engaged?

AMANDA   That's what he just informed us.

TOM   I'll be jiggered! I didn't know about that.

AMANDA That seems very peculiar.

TOM What's peculiar about it?

AMANDA Didn't you call him your best friend down at the warehouse?

TOM He is, but how did I know?

AMANDA It seems extremely peculiar that you wouldn't know your best friend was going to be married!

560 TOM The warehouse is where I work, not where I know things about people!

AMANDA You don't know things anywhere! You live in a dream, you manufacture illusions!

[*He crosses to the door.*]

Where are you going?

TOM I'm going to the movies.

AMANDA That's right, now that you've had us make such fools of ourselves. The effort, the preparations, all the expense! The new floor lamp, the rug, the clothes for Laura! All for what? To entertain some other girl's fiancé! Go to the movies, go! Don't think about us, a mother deserted, an unmarried 570 sister who's crippled and has no job! Don't let anything interfere with your selfish pleasure! Just go, go, go—to the movies!

TOM All right, I will! The more you shout about my selfishness to me the quicker I'll go, and I won't go to the movies!

AMANDA Go, then! Go to the moon—you selfish dreamer!

[TOM *smashes his glass on the floor. He plunges out on the fire escape, slamming the door.* LAURA *screams in fright. The dance-hall music becomes louder.* TOM *stands on the fire escape, gripping the rail. The moon breaks through the storm clouds, illuminating his face.*]

[*Legend on screen:* "And so goodbye . . ."]

[TOM'*s closing speech is timed with what is happening inside the house. We see, as though through soundproof glass, that* AMANDA *appears to be making a comforting speech to* LAURA, *who is huddled upon the sofa. Now that we cannot hear the mother's speech, her silliness is gone and she has dignity and tragic beauty.* LAURA'*s hair hides her face until, at the end of the speech, she lifts her head to smile at her mother.* AMANDA'*s gestures are slow and graceful, almost dancelike, as she comforts her daughter. At the end of her speech she glances a moment at the father's picture— then withdraws through the portieres. At the close of* TOM'*s speech,* LAURA *blows out the candles, ending the play.*]

TOM I didn't go to the moon, I went much further—for time is the longest distance between two places. Not long after that I was fired for writing a poem on the lid of a shoe-box. I left Saint Louis. I descended the steps of this fire escape for a last time and followed, from then on, in my father's footsteps, attempting to find in motion what was lost in space. I traveled around a

580 great deal. The cities swept about me like dead leaves, leaves that were brightly colored but torn away from the branches. I would have stopped, but I was pursued by something. It always came upon me unawares, taking me altogether by surprise. Perhaps it was a familiar bit of music. Perhaps it was only a piece of transparent glass. Perhaps I am walking along a street at night, in some strange city, before I have found companions. I pass the lighted window of a shop where perfume is sold. The window is filled with pieces of colored glass, tiny transparent bottles in delicate colors, like bits of a shattered rainbow. Then all at once my sister touches my shoulder. I turn around and look into her eyes. Oh, Laura, Laura, I tried to leave you behind
590 me, but I am more faithful than I intended to be! I reach for a cigarette, I cross the street, I run into the movies or a bar, I buy a drink, I speak to the nearest stranger—anything that can blow your candles out!

[LAURA *bends over the candles.*]

For nowadays the world is lit by lightning! Blow out your candles, Laura—and so goodbye. . . .

[*She blows the candles out.*]

August Wilson

August Wilson (1945–   ) is considered by most theater critics the best among new American dramatists. He grew up on The Hill in Pittsburgh, an African-American neighborhood that resembles the setting of *Fences.* Leaving school in the ninth grade, he educated himself by eclectic reading while working menial jobs. In 1968, he helped to start a local drama group, Black Horizons Theater, which staged plays by black playwrights. In the 1980s, Lloyd Richards of the Yale University School of Drama put on a series of Wilson's plays which then moved to New York. *Ma Rainey's Black Bottom* (1985) won an award from the New York Drama Critics Circle. *Fences* (1987), which won the Pulitzer Prize, was followed by *Joe Turner's Come and Gone* (1988), and by *The Piano Lesson* (1989), which won August Wilson another Pulitzer.

Fences   (1987)

Characters

TROY MAXSON	
JIM BONO	TROY *'s friend*
ROSE	TROY *'s wife*
LYONS	TROY *'s oldest son by previous marriage*
GABRIEL	TROY *'s brother*
CORY	TROY *and* ROSE *'s son*
RAYNELL	TROY *'s daughter*

Setting

The setting is the yard which fronts the only entrance to the MAXSON *household, an ancient two-story brick house set back off a small alley in a big-city neighborhood. The entrance to the house is gained by two or three steps leading to a wooden porch badly in need of paint.*

A relatively recent addition to the house and running its full width, the porch lacks congruence. It is a sturdy porch with a flat roof. One or two chairs of dubious value sit at one end where the kitchen window opens onto the porch. An old-fashioned icebox stands silent guard at the opposite end.

The yard is a small dirt yard, partially fenced, except for the last scene, with a wooden sawhorse, a pile of lumber, and other fence-building equipment set off to the side. Opposite is a tree from which hangs a ball made of rags. A baseball bat leans against the tree. Two oil drums serve as garbage receptacles and sit near the house at right to complete the setting.

The Play

Near the turn of the century, the destitute of Europe sprang on the city with tenacious claws and an honest and solid dream. The city devoured them. They swelled its belly until it burst into a thousand furnaces and sewing machines, a thousand butcher shops and bakers' ovens, a thousand churches and hospitals and funeral parlors and money-lenders. The city grew. It nourished itself and offered each man a partnership limited only by his talent, his guile, and his willingness and capacity for hard work. For the immigrants of Europe, a dream dared and won true.

The descendants of African slaves were offered no such welcome or participation. They came from places called the Carolinas and the Virginias, Georgia, Alabama, Mississippi, and Tennessee. They came strong, eager, searching. The city rejected them and they fled and settled along the riverbanks and under bridges in shallow, ramshackle houses made of sticks and tar-paper. They collected rags and wood. They sold the use of their muscles and their bodies. They cleaned houses and washed clothes, they shined shoes, and in quiet desperation and vengeful pride, they stole, and lived in pursuit of their own dream. That they could breathe free, finally, and stand to meet life with the force of dignity and whatever eloquence the heart could call upon.

By 1957, the hard-won victories of the European immigrants had solidified the industrial might of America. War had been confronted and won with new energies that used loyalty and patriotism as its fuel. Life was rich, full, and flourishing. The Milwaukee Braves won the World Series, and the hot winds of change that would make the sixties a turbulent, racing, dangerous, and provocative decade had not yet begun to blow full.

Act One

Scene One

It is 1957. TROY *and* BONO *enter the yard, engaged in conversation.* TROY *is fifty-three years old, a large man with thick, heavy hands; it is this largeness that he strives to fill out and make an accommodation with. Together with his blackness, his largeness informs his sensibilities and the choices he has made in his life.*

Of the two men, BONO *is obviously the follower. His commitment to their friendship of thirty-odd years is rooted in his admiration of* TROY*'s honesty, capacity for hard work, and his strength, which* BONO *seeks to emulate.*

It is Friday night, payday, and the one night of the week the two men engage in a ritual of talk and drink. TROY *is usually the most talkative and at times he can be crude and almost vulgar, though he is capable of rising to profound heights of expression. The men carry lunch buckets and wear or carry burlap aprons and are dressed in clothes suitable to their jobs as garbage collectors.*

> BONO   Troy, you ought to stop that lying!
>
> TROY   I ain't lying! The nigger had a watermelon this big.

[*He indicates with his hands.*]

Talking about . . . "What watermelon, Mr. Rand?" I liked to fell out! "What watermelon, Mr. Rand?" . . . And it sitting there big as life.

> BONO   What did Mr. Rand say?
>
> TROY   Ain't said nothing. Figure if the nigger too dumb to know he carrying a watermelon, he wasn't gonna get much sense out of him. Trying to hide that great big old watermelon under his coat. Afraid to let the white man see him carry it home.

10   BONO   I'm like you . . . I ain't got no time for them kind of people.

> TROY   Now what he look like getting mad cause he see the man from the union talking to Mr. Rand?
>
> BONO   He come to me talking about . . . "Maxson gonna get us fired." I told him to get away from me with that. He walked away from me calling you a troublemaker. What Mr. Rand say?
>
> TROY   Ain't said nothing. He told me to go down the Commissioner's office next Friday. They called me down there to see them.
>
> BONO   Well, as long as you got your complaint filed, they can't fire you. That's what one of them white fellows tell me.

20   TROY   I ain't worried about them firing me. They gonna fire me cause I asked a question? That's all I did. I went to Mr. Rand and asked him, "Why?" Why you got the white mens driving and the colored lifting?" Told him, "what's the matter, don't I count? You think only white fellows got sense enough to drive a truck. That ain't no paper job! Hell, anybody can drive a truck. How come you got all whites driving and the colored lifting? He told me "take it to the union." Well, hell, that's what I done! Now they wanna come up with this pack of lies.

BONO   I told Brownie if the man come and ask him any questions . . . just tell the truth! It ain't nothing but something they done trumped up on you
30   cause you filed a complaint on them.

TROY   Brownie don't understand nothing. All I want them to do is change the job description. Give everybody a chance to drive the truck. Brownie can't see that. He ain't got that much sense.

BONO   How you figure he be making out with that gal be up at Taylors' all the time . . . that Alberta gal?

TROY   Same as you and me. Getting just as much as we is. Which is to say nothing.

BONO   It is, huh? I figure you doing a little better than me . . . and I ain't saying what I'm doing.
40   TROY   Aw, nigger, look here . . . I know you. If you had got anywhere near that gal, twenty minutes later you be looking to tell somebody. And the first one you gonna tell . . . that you gonna want to brag to . . . is gonna be me.

BONO   I ain't saying that. I see where you be eyeing her.

TROY   I eye all the women. I don't miss nothing. Don't never let nobody tell you Troy Maxson don't eye the women.

BONO   You been doing more than eyeing her. You done bought her a drink or two.

TROY   Hell yeah, I bought her a drink! What that mean? I bought you one, too. What that mean cause I buy her a drink? I'm just being polite.
50   BONO   It's alright to buy her one drink. That's what you call being polite. But when you wanna be buying two or three . . . that's what you call eyeing her.

TROY   Look here, as long as you known me . . . you ever known me to chase after women?

BONO   Hell yeah! Long as I done known you. You forgetting I knew you when.

TROY   Naw, I'm talking about since I been married to Rose?

BONO   Oh, not since you been married to Rose. Now, that's the truth, there. I can say that.
60   TROY   Alright then! Case closed.

BONO   I see you be walking up around Alberta's house. You supposed to be at Taylors' and you be walking up around there.

TROY   What you watching where I'm walking for? I ain't watching after you.

BONO   I seen you walking around there more than once.

TROY   Hell, you liable to see me walking anywhere! That don't mean nothing cause you see me walking around there.

BONO   Where she come from anyway? She just kinda showed up one day.

TROY   Tallahassee. You can look at her and tell she one of them Florida
gals. They got some big healthy women down there. Grow them right up out
70 the ground. Got a little bit of Indian in her. Most of them niggers down in
Florida got some Indian in them.

BONO   I don't know about that Indian part. But she damn sure big and
healthy. Woman wear some big stockings. Got them great big old legs and
hips as wide as the Mississippi River.

TROY   Legs don't mean nothing. You don't do nothing but push them out
of the way. But them hips cushion the ride!

BONO   Troy, you ain't got no sense.

TROY   It's the truth! Like you riding on Goodyears!

[ROSE *enters from the house. She is ten years younger than* TROY, *her devotion to him
stems from her recognition of the possibilities of her life without him: a succession of
abusive men and their babies, a life of partying and running the streets, the Church,
or aloneness with its attendant pain and frustration. She recognizes* TROY*'s spirit as
a fine and illuminating one and she either ignores or forgives his faults, only some of
which she recognizes. Though she doesn't drink, her presence is an integral part of
the Friday night rituals. She alternates between the porch and the kitchen, where
supper preparations are under way.*]

ROSE   What you all out here getting into?

80 TROY   What you worried about what we getting into for? This is men talk,
woman.

ROSE   What I care what you all talking about? Bono, you gonna stay for
supper?

BONO   No, I thank you, Rose. But Lucille say she cooking up a pot of pigfeet.

TROY   Pigfeet! Hell, I'm going home with you! Might even stay the night if
you got some pigfeet. You got something in there to top them pigfeet, Rose?

ROSE   I'm cooking up some chicken. I got some chicken and collard
greens.

TROY   Well, go on back in the house and let me and Bono finish what we
90 was talking about. This is men talk. I got some talk for you later. You know
what kind of talk I mean. You go on and powder it up.

ROSE   Troy Maxson, don't you start that now!

TROY [*Puts his arm around her.*]   Aw, woman . . . come here. Look here,
Bono . . . when I met this woman . . . I got out that place, say, "Hitch up
my pony, saddle up my mare . . . there's a woman out there for me somewhere. I looked here. Looked there. Saw Rose and latched on to her." I latched
on to her and told her—I'm gonna tell you the truth—I told her, "Baby, I don't
wanna marry, I just wanna be your man." Rose told me . . . tell him what you
told me, Rose.

100 ROSE   I told him if he wasn't the marrying kind, then move out the way so
the marrying kind could find me.

TROY   That's what she told me. "Nigger, you in my way. You blocking the
view! Move out the way so I can find me a husband." I thought it over two or
three days. Come back—

ROSE Ain't no two or three days nothing. You was back the same night.

TROY Come back, told her . . . "Okay, baby . . . but I'm gonna buy me a banty rooster and put him out there in the backyard . . . and when he see a stranger come, he'll flap his wings and crow . . ." Look here, Bono, I could watch the front door by myself . . . it was that back door I was worried about.

110 ROSE Troy, you ought not talk like that. Troy ain't doing nothing but telling a lie.

TROY Only thing is . . . when we first got married . . . forget the rooster . . . we ain't had no yard!

BONO I hear you tell it. Me and Lucille was staying down there on Logan Street. Had two rooms with the outhouse in the back. I ain't mind the outhouse none. But when that goddamn wind blow through there in the winter . . . that's what I'm talking about! To this day I wonder why in the hell I ever stayed down there for six long years. But see, I didn't know I could do no better. I thought only white folks had inside toilets and things.

120 ROSE There's a lot of people don't know they can do no better than they doing now. That's just something you got to learn. A lot of folks still shop at Bella's.

TROY Ain't nothing wrong with shopping at Bella's. She got fresh food.

ROSE I ain't said nothing about if she got fresh food. I'm talking about what she charge. She charge ten cents more than the A&P.

TROY The A&P ain't never done nothing for me. I spends my money where I'm treated right. I go down to Bella, say, "I need a loaf of bread, I'll pay you Friday." She give it to me. What sense that make when I got money to go and spend it somewhere else and ignore the person who done right by 130 me? That ain't in the Bible.

ROSE We ain't talking about what's in the Bible. What sense it make to shop there when she overcharge?

TROY You shop where you want to. I'll do my shopping where the people been good to me.

ROSE Well, I don't think it's right for her to overcharge. That's all I was saying.

BONO Look here . . . I got to get on. Lucille going be raising all kind of hell.

TROY Where you going, nigger? We ain't finished this pint. Come here, 140 finish this pint.

BONO Well, hell, I am . . . if you ever turn the bottle loose.

TROY [*Hands him the bottle.*] The only thing I say about the A&P is I'm glad Cory got that job down there. Help him take care of his school clothes and things. Gabe done moved out and things getting tight around here. He got that job . . . He can start to look out for himself.

ROSE Cory done went and got recruited by a college football team.

TROY I told that boy about that football stuff. The white man ain't gonna let him get nowhere with that football. I told him when he first come to me with it. Now you come telling me he done went and got more tied up in it. He 150 ought to go and get recruited in how to fix cars or something where he can make a living.

ROSE   He ain't talking about making no living playing football. It's just something the boys in school do. They gonna send a recruiter by to talk to you. He'll tell you he ain't talking about making no living playing football. It's a honor to be recruited.

TROY   It ain't gonna get him nowhere. Bono'll tell you that.

BONO   If he be like you in the sports . . . he's gonna be alright. Ain't but two men ever played baseball as good as you. That's Babe Ruth and Josh Gibson. Them's the only two men ever hit more home runs than you.

160   TROY   What it ever get me? Ain't got a pot to piss in or a window to throw it out of.

ROSE   Times have changed since you was playing baseball, Troy. That was before the war. Times have changed a lot since then.

TROY   How in hell they done changed?

ROSE   They got lots of colored boys playing ball now. Baseball and football.

BONO   You right about that, Rose. Times have changed, Troy. You just come along too early.

TROY   There ought not never have been no time called too early! Now you
170   take that fellow . . . what's that fellow they had playing right field for the Yankees back then? You know who I'm talking about, Bono. Used to play right field for the Yankees.

ROSE   Selkirk?

TROY   Selkirk! That's it! Man batting .269, understand? .269. What kind of sense that make? I was hitting .432 with thirty-seven home runs! Man batting .269 and playing right field for the Yankees! I saw Josh Gibson's daughter yesterday. She walking around with raggedy shoes on her feet. Now I bet you Selkirk's daughter ain't walking around with raggedy shoes on her feet! I bet you that!

180   ROSE   They got a lot of colored baseball players now. Jackie Robinson was the first. Folks had to wait for Jackie Robinson.

TROY   I done seen a hundred niggers play baseball better than Jackie Robinson. Hell, I know some teams Jackie Robinson couldn't even make! What you talking about Jackie Robinson. Jackie Robinson wasn't nobody. I'm talking about if you could play ball then they ought to have let you play. Don't care what color you were. Come telling me I come along too early. If you could play . . . then they ought to have let you play.

[TROY *takes a long drink from the bottle.*]

ROSE   You gonna drink yourself to death. You don't need to be drinking like that.

190   TROY   Death ain't nothing. I done seen him. Done wrassled with him. You can't tell me nothing about death. Death ain't nothing but a fastball on the outside corner. And you know what I'll do to that! Lookee here, Bono . . . am I lying? You get one of them fastballs, about waist high, over the outside corner of the plate where you can get the meat of the bat on it . . . and good god! You can kiss it goodbye. Now, am I lying?

BONO   Naw, you telling the truth there. I seen you do it.

TROY   If I'm lying . . . that 450 feet worth of lying!

[*Pause.*]

That's all death is to me. A fastball on the outside corner.

ROSE   I don't know why you want to get on talking about death.

200   TROY   Ain't nothing wrong with talking about death. That's part of life. Everybody gonna die. You gonna die, I'm gonna die. Bono's gonna die. Hell, we all gonna die.

ROSE   But you ain't got to talk about it. I don't like to talk about it.

TROY   You the one brought it up. Me and Bono was talking about baseball . . . you tell me I'm gonna drink myself to death. Ain't that right, Bono? You know I don't drink this but one night out of the week. That's Friday night. I'm gonna drink just enough to where I can handle it. Then I cuts it loose. I leave it alone. So don't you worry about me drinking myself to death. 'Cause I ain't worried about Death. I done seen him. I done wrestled with him.

210   Look here, Bono . . . I looked up one day and Death was marching straight at me. Like Soldiers on Parade! The Army of Death was marching straight at me. The middle of July, 1941. It got real cold just like it be winter. It seem like Death himself reached out and touched me on the shoulder. He touch me just like I touch you. I got cold as ice and Death standing there grinning at me.

ROSE   Troy, why don't you hush that talk.

TROY   I say . . . What you want, Mr. Death? You be wanting me? You done brought your army to be getting me? I looked him dead in the eye. I wasn't fearing nothing. I was ready to tangle. Just like I'm ready to tangle now. The

220   Bible say be ever vigilant. That's why I don't get but so drunk. I got to keep watch.

ROSE   Troy was right down there in Mercy Hospital. You remember he had pneumonia? Laying there with a fever talking plumb out of his head.

TROY   Death standing there staring at me . . . carrying that sickle in his hand. Finally he say, "You want bound over for another year?" See, just like that . . . "You want bound over for another year?" I told him, "Bound over hell! Let's settle this now!"

It seem like he kinda fell back when I said that, and all the cold went out of me. I reached down and grabbed that sickle and threw it just as far as I could

230   throw it . . . and me and him commenced to wrestling.

We wrestled for three days and three nights. I can't say where I found the strength from. Every time it seemed like he was gonna get the best of me, I'd reach way down deep inside myself and find the strength to do him one better.

ROSE   Every time Troy tell that story he find different ways to tell it. Different things to make up about it.

TROY   I ain't making up nothing. I'm telling you the facts of what happened. I wrestled with Death for three days and three nights and I'm standing here to tell you about it.

[*Pause.*]

Alright. At the end of the third night we done weakened each other to where
240 we can't hardly move. Death stood up, throwed on his robe . . . had him a
white robe with a hood on it. He threwed on that robe and went off to look
for his sickle. Say, "I'll be back." Just like that. "I'll be back." I told him, say,
"Yeah, but . . . you gonna have to find me!" I wasn't no fool. I wasn't going
looking for him. Death ain't nothing to play with. And I know he's gonna get
me. I know I got to join his army . . . his camp followers. But as long as I
keep my strength and see him coming . . . as long as I keep up my vigilance . . . he's gonna have to fight to get me. I ain't going easy.

   BONO   Well, look here, since you got to keep up your vigilance . . . let
me have the bottle.

250 TROY   Aw hell, I shouldn't have told you that part. I should have left out
that part.

   ROSE   Troy be talking that stuff and half the time don't even know what he
be talking about.

   TROY   Bono know me better than that.

   BONO   That's right. I know you. I know you got some Uncle Remus in your
blood. You got more stories than the devil got sinners.

   TROY   Aw hell, I done seen him too! Done talked with the devil.

   ROSE   Troy, don't nobody wanna be hearing all that stuff.

[LYONS *enters the yard from the street. Thirty-four years old,* TROY*'s son by a previous
marriage, he sports a neatly trimmed goatee, sport coat, white shirt, tieless and
buttoned at the collar. Though he fancies himself a musician, he is more caught up in
the rituals and "idea" of being a musician than in the actual practice of the music.
He has come to borrow money from* TROY, *and while he knows he will be successful, he
is uncertain as to what extent his lifestyle will be held up to scrutiny and ridicule.*]

   LYONS   Hey, Pop.
260 TROY   What you come "Hey, Popping" me for?
   LYONS   How you doing, Rose?

[*He kisses her.*]

Mr. Bono. How you doing?

   BONO   Hey, Lyons . . . how you been?

   TROY   He must have been doing alright. I ain't seen him around here last
week.

   ROSE   Troy, leave your boy alone. He come by to see you and you wanna
start all that nonsense.

   TROY   I ain't bothering Lyons.

[*Offers him the bottle.*]

Here . . . get you a drink. We got an understanding. I know why he come by
270 to see me and he know I know.

   LYONS   Come on, Pop . . . I just stopped by to say hi . . . see how you
was doing.

TROY   You ain't stopped by yesterday.

ROSE   You gonna stay for supper, Lyons? I got some chicken cooking in the oven.

LYONS   No, Rose . . . thanks. I was just in the neighborhood and thought I'd stop by for a minute.

TROY   You was in the neighborhood alright, nigger. You tell the truth there. You was in the neighborhood cause it's my payday.

280   LYONS   Well, hell, since you mentioned it . . . let me have ten dollars.

TROY   I'll be damned! I'll die and go to hell and play blackjack with the devil before I give you ten dollars.

BONO   That's what I wanna know about . . . that devil you done seen.

LYONS   What . . . Pop done seen the devil? You too much, Pops.

TROY   Yeah, I done seen him. Talked to him too!

ROSE   You ain't seen no devil. I done told you that man ain't had nothing to do with the devil. Anything you can't understand, you want to call it the devil.

TROY   Look here, Bono . . . I went down to see Hertzberger about some furniture. Got three rooms for two-ninety-eight. That what it say on the radio.

290   "Three rooms . . . two-ninety-eight." Even made up a little song about it. Go down there . . . man tell me I can't get no credit. I'm working every day and can't get no credit. What to do? I got an empty house with some raggedy furniture in it. Cory ain't got no bed. He's sleeping on a pile of rags on the floor. Working every day and can't get no credit. Come back here—Rose'll tell you—madder than hell. Sit down . . . try to figure what I'm gonna do. Come a knock on the door. Ain't been living here but three days. Who know I'm here? Open the door . . . devil standing there bigger than life. White fellow . . . got on good clothes and everything. Standing there with a clip-board in his hand. I ain't had to say nothing. First words come out of his

300   mouth was . . . "I understand you need some furniture and can't get no credit." I liked to fell over. He say "I'll give you all the credit you want, but you got to pay the interest on it." I told him, "Give me three rooms worth and charge whatever you want." Next day a truck pulled up here and two men unloaded them three rooms. Man what drove the truck give me a book. Say send ten dollars, first of every month to the address in the book and every-thing will be alright. Say if I miss a payment the devil was coming back and it'll be hell to pay. That was fifteen years ago. To this day . . . the first of the month I send my ten dollars, Rose'll tell you.

ROSE   Troy lying.

310   TROY   I ain't never seen that man since. Now you tell me who else that could have been but the devil? I ain't sold my soul or nothing like that, you understand. Naw, I wouldn't have truck with the devil about nothing like that. I got my furniture and pays my ten dollars the first of the month just like clockwork.

BONO   How long you say you been paying this ten dollars a month?

TROY   Fifteen years!

BONO   Hell, ain't you finished paying for it yet? How much the man done charged you.

TROY   Aw hell, I done paid for it. I done paid for it ten times over! The fact

320   is I'm scared to stop paying it.

ROSE   Troy lying. We got that furniture from Mr. Glickman. He ain't paying no ten dollars a month to nobody.

TROY   Aw hell, woman. Bono know I ain't that big a fool.

LYONS   I was just getting ready to say . . . I know where there's a bridge for sale.

TROY   Look here, I'll tell you this . . . it don't matter to me if he was the devil. It don't matter if the devil give credit. Somebody has got to give it.

ROSE   It ought to matter. You going around talking about having truck with the devil . . . God's the one you gonna have to answer to. He's the one
330 gonna be at the Judgment.

LYONS   Yeah, well, look here, Pop . . . let me have that ten dollars. I'll give it back to you. Bonnie got a job working at the hospital.

TROY   What I tell you, Bono? The only time I see this nigger is when he wants something. That's the only time I see him.

LYONS   Come on, Pop, Mr. Bono don't want to hear all that. Let me have the ten dollars. I told you Bonnie working.

TROY   What that mean to me? "Bonnie working." I don't care if she working. Go ask her for the ten dollars if she working. Talking about "Bonnie working." Why ain't you working?
340 LYONS   Aw, Pop, you know I can't find no decent job. Where am I gonna get a job at? You know I can't get no job.

TROY   I told you I know some people down there. I can get you on the rubbish if you want to work. I told you that the last time you came by here asking me for something.

LYONS   Naw, Pop . . . thanks. That ain't for me. I don't wanna be carrying nobody's rubbish. I don't wanna be punching nobody's time clock.

TROY   What's the matter, you too good to carry people's rubbish? Where you think that ten dollars you talking about come from? I'm just supposed to haul people's rubbish and give my money to you cause you too lazy to work.
350 You too lazy to work and wanna know why you ain't got what I got.

ROSE   What hospital Bonnie working at? Mercy?

LYONS   She's down at Passavant working in the laundry.

TROY   I ain't got nothing as it is. I give you that ten dollars and I got to eat beans the rest of the week. Naw . . . you ain't getting no ten dollars here.

LYONS   You ain't got to be eating no beans. I don't know why you wanna say that.

TROY   I ain't got no extra money. Gabe done moved over to Miss Pearl's paying her the rent and things done got tight around here. I can't afford to be giving you every payday.
360 LYONS   I ain't asked you to give me nothing. I asked you to loan me ten dollars. I know you got ten dollars.

TROY   Yeah, I got it. You know why I got it? Cause I don't throw my money away out there in the streets. You living the fast life . . . wanna be a musician . . . running around in them clubs and things . . . then, you learn to take care of yourself. You ain't gonna find me going and asking nobody for nothing. I done spent too many years without.

LYONS   You and me is two different people, Pop.

TROY   I done learned my mistake and learned to do what's right by it. You still trying to get something for nothing. Life don't owe you nothing. You owe
370 it to yourself. Ask Bono. He'll tell you I'm right.

LYONS   You got your way of dealing with the world . . . I got mine. The only thing that matters to me is the music.

TROY   Yeah, I can see that! It don't matter how you gonna eat . . . where your next dollar is coming from. You telling the truth there.

LYONS   I know I got to eat. But I got to live too. I need something that gonna help me to get out of the bed in the morning. Make me feel like I belong in the world. I don't bother nobody. I just stay with my music cause that's the only way I can find to live in the world. Otherwise there ain't no telling what I might do. Now I don't come criticizing you and how you live. I
380 just come by to ask you for ten dollars. I don't wanna hear all that about how I live.

TROY   Boy, your mama did a hell of a job raising you.

LYONS   You can't change me, Pop. I'm thirty-four years old. If you wanted to change me, you should have been there when I was growing up. I come by to see you . . . ask for ten dollars and you want to talk about how I was raised. You don't know nothing about how I was raised.

ROSE   Let the boy have ten dollars, Troy.

TROY [*To* LYONS]   What the hell you looking at me for? I ain't got no ten dollars. You know what I do with my money.

[*To* ROSE.]

390 Give him ten dollars if you want him to have it.

ROSE   I will. Just as soon as you turn it loose.

TROY [*Handing* ROSE *the money.*]   There it is. Seventy-six dollars and forty-two cents. You see this, Bono? Now, I ain't gonna get but six of that back.

ROSE   You ought to stop telling that lie. Here, Lyons.

[*She hands him the money.*]

LYONS   Thanks, Rose. Look . . . I got to run . . . I'll see you later.

TROY   Wait a minute. You gonna say, "thanks, Rose" and ain't gonna look to see where she got that ten dollars from? See how they do me, Bono?

LYONS   I know she got it from you, Pop. Thanks. I'll give it back to you.

TROY   There he go telling another lie. Time I see that ten dollars . . . he'll
400 be owing me thirty more.

LYONS   See you, Mr. Bono.

BONO   Take care, Lyons!

LYONS   Thanks, Pop. I'll see you again.

[LYONS *exits the yard.*]

TROY   I don't know why he don't go and get him a decent job and take care of that woman he got.

BONO He'll be alright, Troy. The boy is still young.

TROY The *boy* is thirty-four years old.

ROSE Let's not get off into all that.

BONO Look here . . . I got to be going. I got to be getting on. Lucille
410 gonna be waiting.

TROY [*Puts his arm around* ROSE.] See this woman, Bono? I love this
woman. I love this woman so much it hurts. I love her so much . . . I done
run out of ways of loving her. So I got to go back to basics. Don't you come by
my house Monday morning talking about time to go to work . . . 'cause I'm
still gonna be stroking!

ROSE Troy! Stop it now!

BONO I ain't paying him no mind, Rose. That ain't nothing but gin-talk. Go
on, Troy. I'll see you Monday.

TROY Don't you come by my house, nigger! I done told you what I'm
420 gonna be doing.

[*The lights go down to black.*]

Act One

Scene Two

The lights come up on ROSE *hanging up clothes. She hums and sings softly to herself. It
is the following morning.*

> ROSE [*Sings*] Jesus, be a fence all around me every day
> Jesus, I want you to protect me as I travel on my way.
> Jesus, be a fence all around me every day.

[TROY *enters from the house*]

> ROSE [*continued*] Jesus, I want you to protect me
> As I travel on my way.

[*To* TROY]

'Morning. You ready for breakfast? I can fix it soon as I finish hanging up
these clothes?

TROY I got the coffee on. That'll be alright. I'll just drink some of that this
morning.

10 ROSE That 651 hit yesterday. That's the second time this month. Miss Pearl
hit for a dollar . . . seem like those that need the least always get lucky. Poor
folks can't get nothing.

TROY Them numbers don't know nobody. I don't know why you fool with
them. You and Lyons both.

ROSE It's something to do.

TROY You ain't doing nothing but throwing your money away.

ROSE Troy, you know I don't play foolishly. I just play a nickel here and a nickel there.

TROY That's two nickels you done thrown away.

20   ROSE Now I hit sometimes . . . that makes up for it. It always comes in handy when I do hit. I don't hear you complaining then.

TROY I ain't complaining now. I just say it's foolish. Trying to guess out of six hundred ways which way the number gonna come. If I had all the money niggers, these Negroes, throw away on numbers for one week—just one week—I'd be a rich man.

ROSE Well, you wishing and calling it foolish ain't gonna stop folks from playing numbers. That's one thing for sure. Besides . . . some good things come from playing numbers. Look where Pope done bought him that restaurant off of numbers.

30   TROY I can't stand niggers like that. Man ain't had two dimes to rub together. He walking around with his shoes all run over bumming money for cigarettes. Alright. Got lucky there and hit the numbers . . .

ROSE Troy, I know all about it.

TROY Had good sense, I'll say that for him. He ain't throwed his money away. I seen niggers hit the numbers and go through two thousand dollars in four days. Man brought him that restaurant down there . . . fixed it up real nice . . . and then didn't want nobody to come in it! A Negro go in there and can't get no kind of service. I seen a white fellow come in there and order a bowl of stew. Pope picked all the meat out the pot for him. Man ain't had nothing but a bowl of meat! Negro come behind him and ain't got nothing but the potatoes and carrots. Talking about what numbers do for people, you picked a wrong example. Ain't done nothing but make a worser fool out of him than he was before.

ROSE Troy, you ought to stop worrying about what happened at work yesterday.

TROY I ain't worried. Just told me to be down there at the Commissioner's office on Friday. Everybody think they gonna fire me. I ain't worried about them firing me. You ain't got to worry about that.

[*Pause.*]

Where's Cory? Cory in the house? [*Calls*] Cory?

50   ROSE He gone out.

TROY Out, huh? He gone out 'cause he know I want him to help me with this fence. I know how he is. That boy scared of work.

[GABRIEL *enters. He comes halfway down the alley and, hearing* TROY *'s voice, stops.*]

TROY [*continues*] He ain't done a lick of work in his life.

ROSE He had to go to football practice. Coach wanted them to get in a little extra practice before the season start.

TROY I got his practice . . . running out of here before he get his chores done.

ROSE Troy, what is wrong with you this morning? Don't nothing set right with you. Go on back in there and go to bed . . . get up on the other side.

60   TROY Why something got to be wrong with me? I ain't said nothing wrong with me.

ROSE You got something to say about everything. First it's the numbers . . . then it's the way the man runs his restaurant . . . then you done got on Cory. What's it gonna be next? Take a look up there and see if the weather suits you . . . or is it gonna be how you gonna put up the fence with the clothes hanging in the yard.

TROY You hit the nail on the head then.

ROSE I know you like I know the back of my hand. Go on in there and get you some coffee . . . see if that straighten you up. 'Cause you ain't right this

70 morning.

[TROY *starts into the house and sees* GABRIEL. GABRIEL *starts singing.* TROY*'s brother, he is seven years younger than* TROY. *Injured in World War II, he has a metal plate in his head. He carries an old trumpet tied around his waist and believes with every fiber of his being that he is the Archangel Gabriel. He carries a chipped basket with an assortment of discarded fruits and vegetables he has picked up in the strip district and which he attempts to sell.*]

GABRIEL [*Singing.*]
Yes, ma'am, I got plums
You ask me how I sell them
Oh ten cents apiece
Three for a quarter
Come and buy now
'Cause I'm here today
And tomorrow I'll be gone

[GABRIEL *enters.*]

Hey, Rose!

80   ROSE How you doing, Gabe?
GABRIEL There's Troy . . . Hey, Troy!
TROY Hey, Gabe.

[*Exit into kitchen.*]

ROSE [*To* GABRIEL] What you got there?
GABRIEL You know what I got, Rose. I got fruits and vegetables.
ROSE [*Looking in basket.*] Where's all these plums you talking about?
GABRIEL I ain't got no plums today, Rose. I was just singing that. Have some tomorrow. Put me in a big order for plums. Have enough plums tomorrow for St. Peter and everybody.

[TROY *re-enters from kitchen, crosses to steps.*]

[*To* ROSE.]

Troy's mad at me.

90   TROY   I ain't mad at you. What I got to be mad at you about? You ain't done nothing to me.

GABRIEL   I just moved over to Miss Pearl's to keep out from in your way. I ain't mean no harm by it.

TROY   Who said anything about that? I ain't said anything about that.

GABRIEL   You ain't mad at me, is you?

TROY   Naw . . . I ain't mad at you, Gabe. If I was mad at you I'd tell you about it.

GABRIEL   Got me two rooms. In the basement. Got my own door too. Wanna see my key?

[*He holds up a key.*]

100   That's my own key! Ain't nobody else got a key like that. That's my key! My two rooms!

TROY   Well, that's good, Gabe. You got your own key . . . that's good.

ROSE   You hungry, Gabe? I was just fixing to cook Troy his breakfast.

GABRIEL   I'll take some biscuits. You got some biscuits? Did you know when I was in heaven . . . every morning me and St. Peter would sit down by the gate and eat some big fat biscuits? Oh, yeah! We had us a good time. We'd sit there and eat us them biscuits and then St. Peter would go off to sleep and tell me to wake him up when it's time to open the gates for the judgment.

ROSE   Well, come on . . . I'll make up a batch of biscuits.

[ROSE *exits into the house.*]

110   GABRIEL   Troy . . . St. Peter got your name in the book. I seen it. It say . . . Troy Maxson. I say . . . I know him! He got the same name like what I got. That's my brother!

TROY   How many times you gonna tell me that, Gabe?

GABRIEL   Ain't got my name in the book. Don't have to have my name. I done died and went to heaven. He got your name though. One morning St. Peter was looking at his book . . . marking it up for the judgment . . . and he let me see your name. Got it in there under M. Got Rose's name . . . I ain't seen it like I seen yours . . . but I know it's in there. He got a great big book. Got everybody's name what was ever been born. That's what he told

120   me. But I seen your name. Seen it with my own eyes.

TROY   Go on in the house there. Rose going to fix you something to eat.

GABRIEL   Oh, I ain't hungry. I done had breakfast with Aunt Jemimah. She come by and cooked me up a whole mess of flapjacks. Remember how we used to eat them flapjacks?

TROY   Go on in the house and get you something to eat now.

GABRIEL   I got to go sell my plums. I done sold some tomatoes. Got me two quarters. Wanna see?

[*He shows* TROY *his quarters.*]

I'm gonna save them and buy me a new horn so St. Peter can hear me when it's time to open the gates.

[GABRIEL *stops suddenly. Listens.*]

130   Hear that? That's the hellhounds. I got to chase them out of here. Go on get out of here! Get out!

[GABRIEL *exits singing.*]

Better get ready for the judgment
Better get ready for the judgment
My Lord is coming down

[ROSE *enters from the house.*]

TROY   He gone off somewhere.
GABRIEL [*Offstage*]
Better get ready for the judgment
Better get ready for the judgment morning
Better get ready for the judgment
140   My God is coming down
ROSE   He ain't eating right. Miss Pearl say she can't get him to eat nothing.
TROY   What you want me to do about it, Rose? I done did everything I can for the man. I can't make him get well. Man got half his head blown away . . . what you expect?
ROSE   Seem like something ought to be done to help him.
TROY   Man don't bother nobody. He just mixed up from that metal plate he got in his head. Ain't no sense for him to go back into the hospital.
ROSE   Least he be eating right. They can help him take care of himself.
TROY   Don't nobody wanna be locked up, Rose. What you wanna lock him
150   up for? Man go over there and fight the war . . . messin' around with them Japs, get half his head blown off . . . and they give him a lousy three thousand dollars. And I had to swoop down on that.
ROSE   Is you fixing to go into that again?
TROY   That's the only way I got a roof over my head . . . . cause of that metal plate.
ROSE   Ain't no sense you blaming yourself for nothing. Gabe wasn't in no condition to manage that money. You done what was right by him. Can't nobody say you ain't done what was right by him. Look how long you took care of him . . . till he wanted to have his own place and moved over there
160   with Miss Pearl.
TROY   That ain't what I'm saying, woman! I'm just stating the facts. If my brother didn't have that metal plate in his head . . . I wouldn't have a pot to piss in or a window to throw it out of. And I'm fifty-three years old. Now see if you can understand that!

[TROY *gets up from the porch and starts to exit the yard.*]

ROSE   Where you going off to? You been running out of here every Saturday for weeks. I thought you was gonna work on this fence?

TROY   I'm gonna walk down to Taylors'. Listen to the ball game. I'll be
back in a bit. I'll work on it when I get back.

[*He exits the yard. The lights go to black.*]

Act One

Scene Three

The lights come up on the yard. It is four hours later. ROSE *is taking down the clothes
from the line.* CORY *enters carrying his football equipment.*

ROSE   Your daddy like to had a fit with you running out of here this morning without doing your chores.

CORY   I told you I had to go to practice.

ROSE   He say you were supposed to help him with this fence.

CORY   He been saying that the last four or five Saturdays, and then he don't
never do nothing, but go down to Taylors'. Did you tell him about the recruiter?

ROSE   Yeah, I told him.

CORY   What he say?

10   ROSE   He ain't said nothing too much. You get in there and get started on
your chores before he gets back. Go on and scrub down them steps before he
gets back here hollering and carrying on.

CORY   I'm hungry. What you got to eat, Mama?

ROSE   Go on and get started on your chores. I got some meat loaf in there.
Go on and make you a sandwich . . . and don't leave no mess in there.

[CORY *exits into house.* ROSE *continues to take down the clothes.* TROY *enters the yard
and sneaks up and grabs her from behind.*]

Troy! Go on, now. You liked to scared me to death. What was the score of the
game? Lucille had me on the phone and I couldn't keep up with it.

TROY   What I care about the game? Come here, woman. [*He tries to kiss her.*]

ROSE   I thought you went down Taylors' to listen to the game. Go on, Troy!

20   You supposed to be putting up this fence.

TROY [*Attempting to kiss her again.*]   I'll put it up when I finish with what
is at hand.

ROSE   Go on, Troy. I ain't studying you.

TROY [*Chasing after her.*]   I'm studying you . . . fixing to do my homework!

ROSE   Troy, you better leave me alone.

TROY   Where's Cory? That boy brought his butt home yet?

ROSE He's in the house doing his chores.

TROY [*Calling.*]   Cory! Get your butt out here, boy!

[ROSE *exits into the house with the laundry.* TROY *goes over to the pile of wood, picks up a board, and starts sawing.* CORY *enters from the house.*]

30   TROY You just now coming in here from leaving this morning?

CORY Yeah, I had to go to football practice.

TROY Yeah, what?

CORY Yessir.

TROY I ain't but two seconds off you noway. The garbage sitting in there overflowing . . . you ain't done none of your chores . . . and you come in here talking about "Yeah."

CORY I was just getting ready to do my chores now, Pop . . .

TROY Your first chore is to help me with this fence on Saturday. Everything else come after that. Now get that saw and cut them boards.

[CORY *takes the saw and begins cutting the boards.* TROY *continues working. There is a long pause.*]

40   CORY Hey, Pop . . . why don't you buy a TV?

TROY What I want with a TV? What I want one of them for?

CORY Everybody got one. Earl, Ba Bra . . . Jesse!

TROY I ain't asked you who had one. I say what I want with one?

CORY So you can watch it. They got lots of things on TV. Baseball games and everything. We could watch the World Series.

TROY Yeah . . . and how much this TV cost?

CORY I don't know. They got them on sale for around two hundred dollars.

TROY Two hundred dollars, huh?

CORY That ain't that much, Pop.

50   TROY Naw, it's just two hundred dollars. See that roof you got over your head at night? Let me tell you something about that roof. It's been over ten years since that roof was last tarred. See now . . . the snow come this winter and sit up there on that roof like it is . . . and it's gonna seep inside. It's just gonna be a little bit . . . ain't gonna hardly notice it. Then the next thing you know, it's gonna be leaking all over the house. Then the wood rot from all that water and you gonna need a whole new roof. Now, how much you think it cost to get that roof tarred?

CORY I don't know.

TROY Two hundred and sixty-four dollars . . . cash money. While you
60 thinking about a TV, I got to be thinking about the roof . . . and whatever else go wrong around here. Now if you had two hundred dollars, what would you do . . . fix the roof or buy a TV?

CORY I'd buy a TV. Then when the roof started to leak . . . when it needed fixing . . . I'd fix it.

TROY Where you gonna get the money from? You done spent it for a TV. You gonna sit up and watch the water run all over your brand new TV.

CORY Aw, Pop. You got money. I know you do.

TROY   Where I got it at, huh?

CORY   You got it in the bank.

70   TROY   You wanna see my bankbook? You wanna see that seventy-three dollars and twenty-two cents I got sitting up in there.

CORY   You ain't got to pay for it all at one time. You can put a down payment on it and carry it on home with you.

TROY   Not me. I ain't gonna owe nobody nothing if I can help it. Miss a payment and they come and snatch it right out your house. Then what you got? Now, soon as I get two hundred dollars clear, then I'll buy a TV. Right now, as soon as I get two hundred and sixty-four dollars, I'm gonna have this roof tarred.

CORY   Aw . . . Pop!

80   TROY   You go on and get you two hundred dollars and buy one if ya want it. I got better things to do with my money.

CORY   I can't get no two hundred dollars. I ain't never seen two hundred dollars.

TROY   I'll tell you what . . . you get you a hundred dollars and I'll put the other hundred with it.

CORY   Alright, I'm gonna show you.

TROY   You gonna show me how you can cut them boards right now.

[CORY *begins to cut the boards. There is long pause.*]

CORY   The Pirates won today. That makes five in a row.

TROY   I ain't thinking about the Pirates. Got an all-white team. Got that
90   boy . . . that Puerto Rican boy . . . Clemente. Don't even half-play him. That boy could be something if they give him a chance. Play him one day and sit him on the bench the next.

CORY   He gets a lot of chances to play.

TROY   I'm talking about playing regular. Playing every day so you can get your timing. That's what I'm talking about.

CORY   They got some white guys on the team that don't play every day. You can't play everybody at the same time.

TROY   If they got a white fellow sitting on the bench . . . you can bet your last dollar he can't play! The colored guy got to be twice as good before he
100 get on the team. That's why I don't want you to get all tied up in them sports. Man on the team and what it get him? They got colored on the team and don't use them. Same as not having them. All them teams the same.

CORY   The Braves got Hank Aaron and Wes Covington. Hank Aaron hit two home runs today. That makes forty-three.

TROY   Hank Aaron ain't nobody. That's what you supposed to do. That's how you supposed to play the game. Ain't nothing to it. It's just a matter of timing . . . getting the right follow-through. Hell, I can hit forty-three home runs right now!

CORY   Not off no major-league pitching, you couldn't.

110 TROY   We had better pitching in the Negro leagues. I hit seven home runs off of Satchel Paige. You can't get no better than that!

CORY   Sandy Koufax. He's leading the league in strikeouts.

TROY   I ain't thinking of no Sandy Koufax.

CORY   You got Warren Spahn and Lew Burdette. I bet you couldn't hit no home runs off of Warren Spahn.

TROY   I'm through with it now. You go on and cut them boards.

[*Pause.*]

Your mama tell me you done got recruited by a college football team? Is that right?

CORY   Yeah. Coach Zellman say the recruiter gonna be coming by to talk to
120 you. Get you to sign the permission papers.

TROY   I thought you supposed to be working down there at the A&P. Ain't you supposed to be working down there after school?

CORY   Mr. Stawicki say he gonna hold my job for me until after the football season. Say starting next week I can work weekends.

TROY   I thought we had an understanding about this football stuff? You suppose to keep up with your chores and hold that job down at the A&P. Ain't been around here all day on a Saturday. Ain't none of your chores done . . . and now you telling me you done quit your job.

CORY   I'm gonna be working weekends.

130 TROY   You damn right you are! And ain't no need for nobody coming around here to talk to me about signing nothing.

CORY   Hey, Pop . . . you can't do that. He's coming all the way from North Carolina.

TROY   I don't care where he coming from. The white man ain't gonna let you get nowhere with that football noway. You go on and get your book-learning so you can work yourself up in that A&P or learn how to fix cars or build houses or something, get you a trade. That way you have something can't nobody take away from you. You go on and learn how to put your hands to some good use. Besides hauling people's garbage.

140 CORY   I get good grades, Pop. That's why the recruiter wants to talk with you. You got to keep up your grades to get recruited. This way I'll be going to college. I'll get a chance . . .

TROY   First you gonna get your butt down there to the A&P and get your job back.

CORY   Mr. Stawicki done already hired somebody else 'cause I told him I was playing football.

TROY   You a bigger fool than I thought . . . to let somebody take away your job so you can play some football. Where you gonna get your money to take out your girlfriend and whatnot? What kind of foolishness is that to let
150 somebody take away your job?

CORY   I'm still gonna be working weekends.

TROY   Naw . . . naw. You getting your butt out of here and finding you another job.

CORY   Come on, Pop! I got to practice. I can't work after school and play football too. The team needs me. That's what Coach Zellman say . . .

TROY   I don't care what nobody else say. I'm the boss . . . you understand? I'm the boss around here. I do the only saying what counts.
    CORY   Come on, Pop!
    TROY   I asked you . . . did you understand?
160   CORY   Yeah . . .
    TROY   What?!
    CORY   Yessir.
    TROY   You go on down there to that A&P and see if you can get your job
back. If you can't do both . . . then you quit the football team. You've got to
take the crookeds with the straights.
    CORY   Yessir.

[*Pause.*]

Can I ask you a question?
    TROY   What the hell you wanna ask me? Mr. Stawicki the one you got the
questions for.
170   CORY   How come you ain't never liked me?
    TROY   Liked you? Who the hell say I got to like you? What law is there say I
got to like you? Wanna stand up in my face and ask a damn fool-ass question
like that. Talking about liking somebody. Come here, boy, when I talk to you.

[CORY *comes over to where* TROY *is working. He stands slouched over and* TROY *shoves
him on his shoulder.*]

Straighten up, goddammit! I asked you a question . . . what law is there say
I got to like you?
    CORY   None.
    TROY   Well, alright then! Don't you eat every day?

[*Pause.*]

Answer me when I talk to you! Don't you eat every day?
    CORY   Yeah.
180   TROY   Nigger, as long as you in my house, you put that sir on the end of it
when you talk to me!
    CORY   Yes . . . sir.
    TROY   You eat every day.
    CORY   Yessir!
    TROY   Got a roof over your head.
    CORY   Yessir!
    TROY   Got clothes on your back.
    CORY   Yessir.
    TROY   Why you think that is?
190   CORY   Cause of you.
    TROY   Aw, hell I know it's 'cause of me . . . but why do you think that is?
    CORY [*Hesitant.*]   Cause you like me.

TROY   Like you? I go out of here every morning . . . bust my butt . . . putting up with them crackers every day . . . cause I like you? You about the biggest fool I ever saw.

[*Pause.*]

It's my job. It's my responsibility! You understand that? A man got to take care of his family. You live in my house . . . sleep you behind on my bedclothes . . . fill you belly up with my food . . . cause you my son. You my flesh and blood. Not 'cause I like you! Cause it's my duty to take care of you. I owe a
200   responsibility to you! Let's get this straight right here . . . before it go along any further . . . I ain't got to like you. Mr. Rand don't give me my money come payday cause he likes me. He gives me cause he owe me. I done give you everything I had to give you. I gave you your life! Me and your mama worked that out between us. And liking your black ass wasn't part of the bargain. Don't you try and go through life worrying about if somebody like you or not. You best be making sure they doing right by you. You understand what I'm saying, boy?
      CORY   Yessir.
      TROY   Then get the hell out of my face, and get on down to that A&P.

[ROSE *has been standing behind the screen door for much of the scene. She enters as* CORY *exits.*]

210   ROSE   Why don't you let the boy go ahead and play football, Troy? Ain't no harm in that. He's just trying to be like you with the sports.
      TROY   I don't want him to be like me! I want him to move as far away from my life as he can get. You the only decent thing that ever happened to me. I wish him that. But I don't wish him a thing else from my life. I decided seventeen years ago that boy wasn't getting involved in no sports. Not after what they did to me in the sports.
      ROSE   Troy, why don't you admit you was too old to play in the major leagues? For once . . . why don't you admit that?
      TROY   What do you mean too old? Don't come telling me I was too old. I
220   just wasn't the right color. Hell, I'm fifty-three years old and can do better than Selkirk's .269 right now!
      ROSE   How's was you gonna play ball when you were over forty? Some-times I can't get no sense out of you.
      TROY   I got good sense, woman. I got sense enough not to let my boy get hurt over playing no sports. You been mothering that boy too much. Worried about if people like him.
      ROSE   Everything that boy do . . . he do for you. He wants you to say "Good job, son." That's all.
      TROY   Rose, I ain't got time for that. He's alive. He's healthy. He's got to
230   make his own way. I made mine. Ain't nobody gonna hold his hand when he get out there in that world.

ROSE Times have changed from when you was young, Troy. People change. The world's changing around you and you can't even see it.

TROY [*Slow, methodical.*] Woman . . . I do the best I can do. I come in here every Friday. I carry a sack of potatoes and a bucket of lard. You all line up at the door with your hands out. I give you the lint from my pockets. I give you my sweat and my blood. I ain't got no tears. I done spent them. We go upstairs in that room at night . . . and I fall down on you and try to blast a hole into forever. I get up Monday morning . . . find my lunch on the table. I go out.
240 Make my way. Find my strength to carry me through to the next Friday.

[*Pause.*]

That's all I got, Rose. That's all I got to give. I can't give nothing else.

[TROY *exits into the house. The lights go down to black.*]

Act One

Scene Four

It is Friday. Two weeks later. CORY *starts out of the house with his football equipment. The phone rings.*

CORY [*Calling.*] I got it!

[*He answers the phone and stands in the screen door talking.*]

Hello? Hey, Jesse. Naw . . . I was just getting ready to leave now.

ROSE [*Calling.*] Cory!

CORY I told you, man, them spikes is all tore up. You can use them if you want, but they ain't no good. Earl got some spikes.

ROSE [*Calling.*] Cory!

CORY [*Calling to* ROSE.] Mam? I'm talking to Jesse.

[*Into phone.*]

When she say that? [*Pause.*] Aw, you lying man. I'm gonna tell her you said
10 that.

ROSE [*Calling.*] Cory, don't you go nowhere!

CORY I got to go to the game, Ma!

[*Into the phone.*]

Yeah, hey, look, I'll talk to you later. Yeah, I'll meet you over Earl's house. Later. Bye, Ma.

[CORY *exits the house and starts out the yard.*]

ROSE Cory, where you going off to? You got that stuff all pulled out and thrown all over your room.

CORY [*In the yard.*]   I was looking for my spikes. Jesse wanted to borrow my spikes.

20   ROSE   Get up there and get that cleaned up before your daddy get back in here.

CORY   I got to go to the game! I'll clean it up *when I get back.*

[CORY *exits.*]

ROSE   That's all he need to do is see that room all messed up.

[ROSE *exits into the house.* TROY *and* BONO *enter the yard.* TROY *is dressed in clothes other than his work clothes.*]

BONO   He told him the same thing he told you. Take it to the union.

TROY   Brownie ain't got that much sense. Man wasn't thinking about nothing. He wait until I confront them on it . . . then he wanna come crying seniority.

[*Calls.*]

Hey, Rose!

BONO   I wish I could have seen Mr. Rand's face when he told you.

30   TROY   He couldn't get it out of his mouth! Liked to bit his tongue! When they called me down there to the Commissioner's office . . . he thought they was gonna fire me. Like everybody else.

BONO   I didn't think they was gonna fire you. I thought they was gonna put you on the warning paper.

TROY   Hey, Rose!

[*To* BONO.]

Yeah, Mr. Rand like to bit his tongue.

[TROY *breaks the seal on the bottle, takes a drink, and hands it to* BONO.]

BONO   I see you run right down to Taylors' and told that Alberta gal.

TROY [*Calling.*]   Hey Rose! [*To* BONO.] I told everybody. Hey, Rose! I went down there to cash my check.

40   ROSE [*Entering from the house.*]   Hush all that hollering, man! I know you out here. What they say down there at the Commissioner's office?

TROY   You supposed to come when I call you, woman. Bono'll tell you that.

[*To* BONO.]

Don't Lucille come when you call her?

ROSE   Man, hush your mouth. I ain't no dog . . . talk about "come when you call me."

TROY [*Puts his arm around* ROSE.]   You hear this, Bono? I had me an old dog used to get uppity like that. You say, "C'mere, Blue!" . . . and he just lay
50 there and look at you. End up getting a stick and chasing him away trying to make him come.

ROSE   I ain't studying you and your dog. I remember you used to sing that old song.

TROY [*He sings.*]   Hear it ring! Hear it ring!
I had a dog his name was Blue.

ROSE   Don't nobody wanna hear you sing that old song.

TROY [*Sings.*]   You know Blue was mighty true.

ROSE   Used to have Cory running around here singing that song.

BONO   Hell, I remember that song myself.

60 TROY [*Sings.*]   You know Blue was a good old dog.
                    Blue treed a possum in a hollow log.
That was my daddy's song. My daddy made up that song.

ROSE   I don't care who made it up. Don't nobody wanna hear you sing it.

TROY [*Makes a song like calling a dog.*]   Come here, woman.

ROSE   You come in here carrying on, I reckon they ain't fired you. What they say down there at the Commissioner's office?

TROY   Look here, Rose . . . Mr. Rand called me into his office today when I got back from talking to them people down there . . . it come from up top . . . he called me in and told me they was making me a driver.

70 ROSE   Troy, you kidding!

TROY   No I ain't. Ask Bono.

ROSE   Well, that's great, Troy. Now you don't have to hassle them people no more.

[LYONS *enters from the street.*]

TROY   Aw hell, I wasn't looking to see you today. I thought you was in jail. Got it all over the front page of the *Courier* about them raiding Sefus' place . . . where you be hanging out with all them thugs.

LYONS   Hey, Pop . . . that ain't got nothing to do with me. I don't go down there gambling. I go down there to sit in with the band. I ain't got nothing to do with the gambling part. They got some good music down there.

80 TROY   They got some rogues . . . is what they got.

LYONS   How you been, Mr. Bono? Hi, Rose.

BONO   I see where you playing down at the Crawford Grill tonight.

ROSE   How come you ain't brought Bonnie like I told you. You should have brought Bonnie with you, she ain't been over in a month of Sundays.

LYONS   I was just in the neighborhood . . . thought I'd stop by.

TROY   Here he come . . .

BONO   Your daddy got a promotion on the rubbish. He's gonna be the first colored driver. Ain't got to do nothing but sit up there and read the paper like them white fellows.

90 LYONS   Hey, Pop . . . if you knew how to read you'd be alright.

BONO Naw . . . naw . . . you mean if the nigger knew how to *drive* he'd be all right. Been fighting with them people about driving and ain't even got a license. Mr. Rand know you ain't got no driver's license?

TROY Driving ain't nothing. All you do is point the truck where you want it to go. Driving ain't nothing.

BONO Do Mr. Rand know you ain't got no driver's license? That's what I'm talking about. I ain't asked if driving was easy. I asked if Mr. Rand know you ain't got no driver's license.

TROY He ain't got to know. The man ain't got to know my business. Time
100 he find out, I have two or three driver's licenses.

LYONS [*Going into his pocket.*] Say, look here, Pop . . .

TROY I knew it was coming. Didn't I tell you, Bono? I know what kind of "Look here, Pop" that was. The nigger fixing to ask me for some money. It's Friday night. It's my payday. All them rogues down there on the avenue . . . the ones that ain't in jail . . . and Lyons is hopping in his shoes to get down there with them.

LYONS See, Pop . . . if you give somebody else a chance to talk some-time, you'd see that I was fixing to pay you back your ten dollars like I told you. Here . . . I told you I'd pay you when Bonnie got paid.

110 TROY Naw . . . you go ahead and keep that ten dollars. Put it in the bank. The next time you feel like you wanna come by here and ask me for some-thing . . . you go on down there and get that.

LYONS Here's your ten dollars, Pop. I told you I don't want you to give me nothing. I just wanted to borrow ten dollars.

TROY Naw . . . you go on and keep that for the next time you want to ask me.

LYONS Come on, Pop . . . here go your ten dollars.

ROSE Why don't you go on and let the boy pay you back, Troy?

LYONS Here you go, Rose. If you don't take it I'm gonna have to hear about
120 it for the next six months.

[*He hands her the money.*]

ROSE You can hand yours over here too, Troy.

TROY You see this, Bono. You see how they do me.

BONO Yeah, Lucille do me the same way.

[GABRIEL *is heard singing offstage. He enters.*]

GABRIEL Better get ready for the Judgment! Better get ready for . . . Hey! . . . Hey! . . . There's Troy's boy!

LYONS How you doing, Uncle Gabe?

GABRIEL Lyons . . . The King of the Jungle! Rose . . . hey, Rose. Got a flower for you.

[*He takes a rose from his pocket.*]

Picked it myself. That's the same rose like you is!

130   ROSE   That's right nice of you, Gabe.

   LYONS   What you been doing, Uncle Gabe?

   GABRIEL   Oh, I been chasing hellhounds and waiting on the time to tell St. Peter to open the gates.

   LYONS   You been chasing hellhounds, huh? Well . . . you doing the right thing, Uncle Gabe. Somebody got to chase them.

   GABRIEL   Oh, yeah . . . I know it. The devil's strong. The devil ain't no pushover. Hellhounds snipping at everybody's heels. But I got my trumpet waiting on the judgment time.

   LYONS   Waiting on the Battle of Armageddon, huh?

140   GABRIEL   Ain't gonna be too much of a battle when God get to waving that Judgment sword. But the people's gonna have a hell of a time trying to get into heaven if them gates ain't open.

   LYONS   [*Putting his arm around* GABRIEL.]   You hear this, Pop. Uncle Gabe, you alright!

   GABRIEL   [*Laughing with* LYONS.]   Lyons! King of the Jungle.

   ROSE   You gonna stay for supper, Gabe. Want me to fix you a plate?

   GABRIEL   I'll take a sandwich, Rose. Don't want no plate. Just wanna eat with my hands. I'll take a sandwich.

   ROSE   How about you, Lyons? You staying? Got some short ribs cooking.

150   LYONS   Naw, I won't eat nothing till after we finished playing.

[*Pause.*]

You ought to come down and listen to me play, Pop.

   TROY   I don't like that Chinese music. All that noise.

   ROSE   Go on in the house and wash up, Gabe . . . . I'll fix you a sandwich.

   GABRIEL   [*To* LYONS, *as he exits.*]   Troy's mad at me.

   LYONS   What you mad at Uncle Gabe for, Pop.

   ROSE   He thinks Troy's mad at him cause he moved over to Miss Pearl's.

   TROY   I ain't mad at the man. He can live where he want to live at.

   LYONS   What he move over there for? Miss Pearl don't like nobody.

   ROSE   She don't mind him none. She treats him real nice. She just don't
160   allow all that singing.

   TROY   She don't mind that rent he be paying . . . that's what she don't mind.

   ROSE   Troy, I ain't going through that with you no more. He's over there cause he want to have his own place. He can come and go as he please.

   TROY   Hell, he could come and go as he please here. I wasn't stopping him. I ain't put no rules on him.

   ROSE   It ain't the same thing, Troy. And you know it.

[GABRIEL *comes to the door.*]

Now, that's the last I wanna hear about that. I don't wanna hear nothing else about Gabe and Miss Pearl. And next week . . .

   GABRIEL   I'm ready for my sandwich, Rose.

170   ROSE   And next week . . . when that recruiter come from that school . . . I want you to sign that paper and go on and let Cory play football. Then that'll be the last I have to hear about that.

TROY   [*To* ROSE *as she exits into the house.*]   I ain't thinking about Cory nothing.

LYONS   What . . . Cory got recruited? What school he going to?

TROY   That boy walking around here smelling his piss . . . thinking he's grown. Thinking he's gonna do what he want, irrespective of what I say. Look here, Bono . . . I left the Commissioner's office and went down to the A&P . . . that boy ain't working down there. He lying to me. Telling me he got his
180   job back . . . telling me he working weekends . . . telling me he working after school . . . Mr. Stawicki tell me he ain't working down there at all!

LYONS   Cory just growing up. He's just busting at the seams trying to fill our your shoes.

TROY   I don't care what he's doing. When he get to the point where he wanna disobey me . . . then it's time for him to move on. Bono'll tell you that. I bet he ain't never disobeyed his daddy without paying the consequences.

BONO   I ain't never had a chance. My daddy came on through . . . but I ain't never knew him to see him . . . or what he had on his mind or where he went. Just moving on through. Searching out the New Land. That's what the
190   old folks used to call it. See a fellow moving around from place to place . . . woman to woman . . . called it searching out the New Land. I can't say if he ever found it. I come along, didn't want no kids. Didn't know if I was gonna be in one place long enough to fix on them right as their daddy. I figured I was going searching too. As it turned out I been hooked up with Lucille near about as long as your daddy been with Rose. Going on sixteen years.

TROY   Sometimes I wish I hadn't known my daddy. He ain't cared nothing about no kids. A kid to him wasn't nothing. All he wanted was for you to learn how to walk so he could start you to working. When it come time for eating . . . he ate first. If there was anything left over, that's what you got. Man
200   would sit down and eat two chickens and give you the wing.

LYONS   You ought to stop that, Pop. Everybody feed their kids. No matter how hard times is . . . everybody care about their kids. Make sure they have something to eat.

TROY   The only thing my daddy cared about was getting them bales of cotton in to Mr. Lubin. That's the only thing that mattered to him. Sometimes I used to wonder why he was living. Wonder why the devil hadn't come and got him. "Get them bales of cotton in to Mr. Lubin" and find out he owe him money . . .

LYONS   He should have just went on and left when he saw he couldn't get
210   nowhere. That's what I would have done.

TROY   How he gonna leave with eleven kids? And where he gonna go? He ain't knew how to do nothing but farm. No, he was trapped and I think he knew it. But I'll say this for him . . . he felt a responsibility toward us. Maybe he ain't treated us the way I felt he should have . . . but without that responsibility he could have walked off and left us . . . made his own way.

BONO A lot of them did. Back in those days what you talking about . . . they walk out their front door and just take on down one road or another and keep on walking.

LYONS There you go! That's what I'm talking about.

220 BONO Just keep on walking till you come to something else. Ain't you never heard of nobody having the walking blues? Well, that's what you call it when you just take off like that.

TROY My daddy ain't had them walking blues! What you talking about? He stayed right there with his family. But he was just as evil as he could be. My mama couldn't stand him. Couldn't stand that evilness. She run off when I was about eight. She sneaked off one night after he had gone to sleep. Told me she was coming back for me. I ain't never seen her no more. All his women run off and left him. He wasn't good for nobody.

When my turn come to head out, I was fourteen and got to sniffing around
230 Joe Canewell's daughter. Had us an old mule we called Greyboy. My daddy sent me out to do some plowing and I tied up Greyboy and went to fooling around with Joe Canewell's daughter. We done found us a nice little spot, got real cozy with each other. She about thirteen and we done figured we was grown anyway . . . so we down there enjoying ourselves . . . ain't thinking about nothing. We didn't know Greyboy had got loose and wandered back to the house and my daddy was looking for me. We down there by the creek enjoying ourselves when my daddy come up on us. Surprised us. He had them leather straps off the mule and commenced to whupping me like there was no tomorrow. I jumped up, mad and embarrassed. I was scared of
240 my daddy. When he commenced to whupping on me . . . quite naturally I run to get out of the way.

[*Pause.*]

Now I thought he was mad cause I ain't done my work. But I see where he was chasing me off so he could have the gal for himself. When I see what the matter of it was, I lost all fear of my daddy. Right there is where I become a man . . . at fourteen years of age.

[*Pause.*]

Now it was my turn to run him off. I picked up them same reins that he had used on me. I picked up them reins and commenced to whupping on him. The gal jumped up and run off . . . and when my daddy turned to face me, I could see why the devil had never come to get him . . . cause he was the
250 devil himself. I don't know what happened. When I woke up, I was laying right there by the creek, and Blue . . . this old dog we had . . . was licking my face. I thought I was blind. I couldn't see nothing. Both my eyes were swollen shut. I layed there and cried. I didn't know what I was gonna do. The only thing I knew was the time had come for me to leave my daddy's house. And right there the world suddenly got big. And it was a long time before I could cut it down to where I could handle it.

Part of that cutting down was when I got to the place where I could feel him kicking in my blood and knew that the only thing that separated us was the matter of a few years.

[GABRIEL *enters from the house with a sandwich.*]

260 LYONS What you got there, Uncle Gabe?

GABRIEL Got me a ham sandwich. Rose gave me a ham sandwich.

TROY I don't know what happened to him. I done lost touch with everybody except Gabriel. But I hope he's dead. I hope he found some peace.

LYONS That's a heavy story, Pop. I didn't know you left home when you was fourteen.

TROY And didn't know nothing. The only part of the world I knew was the forty-two acres of Mr. Lubin's land. That's all I knew about life.

LYONS Fourteen's kinda young to be out on your own. [*Phone rings.*] I
270 don't even think I was ready to be out on my own at fourteen. I don't know what I would have done.

TROY I got up from the creek and walked on down to Mobile. I was through with farming. Figured I could do better in the city. So I walked the two hundred miles to Mobile.

LYONS Wait a minute . . . you ain't walked no two hundred miles, Pop. Ain't nobody gonna walk no two hundred miles. You talking about some walking there.

BONO That's the only way you got anywhere back in them days.

LYONS Shhh. Damn if I wouldn't have hitched a ride with somebody!

TROY Who you gonna hitch it with? They ain't had no cars and things like
280 they got now. We talking about 1918.

ROSE [*Entering.*] What you all out here getting into?

TROY [*To* ROSE.] I'm telling Lyons how good he got it. He don't know nothing about this I'm talking.

ROSE Lyons, that was Bonnie on the phone. She say you supposed to pick her up.

LYONS Yeah, okay, Rose.

TROY I walked on down to Mobile and hitched up with some of them fellows that was heading this way. Got up here and found out . . . not only couldn't you get a job . . . you couldn't find no place to live. I thought I was
290 in freedom. Shhh. Colored folks living down there on the riverbanks in whatever kind of shelter they could find for themselves. Right down there under the Brady Street Bridge. Living in shacks made of sticks and tarpaper. Messed around there and went from bad to worse. Started stealing. First it was food. Then I figured, hell, if I steal money I can buy me some food. Buy me some shoes too! One thing led to another. Met your mama. I was young and anxious to be a man. Met your mama and had you. What I do that for? Now I got to worry about feeding you and her. Got to steal three times as much. Went out one day looking for somebody to rob . . . that's what I was, a robber. I'll tell you the truth. I'm ashamed of it today. But it's the truth.
300 Went to rob this fellow . . . pulled out my knife . . . and he pulled out a

gun. Shot me in the chest. It felt just like somebody had taken a hot branding iron and laid it on me. When he shot me I jumped at him with my knife. They told me I killed him and they put me in the penitentiary and locked me up for fifteen years. That's where I met Bono. That's where I learned how to play baseball. Got out that place and your mama had taken you and went on to make life without me. Fifteen years was a long time for her to wait. But that fifteen years cured me of that robbing stuff. Rose'll tell you. She asked me when I met her if I had gotten all that foolishness out of my system. And I told her, "Baby, it's you and baseball all what count with me." You hear me,
310 Bono? I meant it too. She say, "Which one comes first?" I told her, "Baby, ain't no doubt it's baseball . . . but you stick and get old with me and we'll both outlive this baseball." Am I right, Rose? And it's true.

ROSE Man, hush your mouth. You ain't said no such thing. Talking about, "Baby, you know you'll always be number one with me." That's what you was talking.

TROY You hear that, Bono. That's why I love her.

BONO Rose'll keep you straight. You get off the track, she'll straighten you up.

ROSE Lyons, you better get on up and get Bonnie. She waiting on you.

320 LYONS [*Gets up to go.*] Hey, Pop, why don't you come on down to the Grill and hear me play?

TROY I ain't going down there. I'm too old to be sitting around in them clubs.

BONO You got to be good to play down at the Grill.

LYONS Come on, Pop . . .

TROY I got to get up in the morning.

LYONS You ain't got to stay long.

TROY Naw, I'm gonna get my supper and go on to bed.

LYONS Well, I got to go. I'll see you again.

330 TROY Don't you come around my house on my payday.

ROSE Pick up the phone and let somebody know you coming. And bring Bonnie with you. You know I'm always glad to see her.

LYONS Yeah, I'll do that, Rose. You take care now. See you, Pop. See you, Mr. Bono. See you, Uncle Gabe.

GABRIEL Lyons! King of the Jungle!

[LYONS *exits.*]

TROY Is supper ready, woman? Me and you got some business to take care of. I'm gonna tear it up too.

ROSE Troy, I done told you now!

TROY [*Puts his arm around* BONO.] Aw hell, woman . . . this is Bono.
340 Bono like family. I done known this nigger since . . . how long I done know you?

BONO It's been a long time.

TROY I done known this nigger since Skippy was a pup. Me and him done been through some times.

BONO   You sure right about that.

TROY   Hell, I done know him longer than I known you. And we still stand-ing shoulder to shoulder. Hey, look here, Bono . . . a man can't ask for no more than that.

[*Drinks to him.*]

I love you, nigger.

350   BONO   Hell, I love you too . . . but I got to get home see my woman. You got yours in hand. I got to go get mine.

[BONO *starts to exit as* CORY *enters the yard, dressed in his football uniform. He gives* TROY *a hard, uncompromising look.*]

CORY   What you do that for, Pop?

[*He throws his helmet down in the direction of* TROY.]

ROSE   What's the matter? Cory . . . what's the matter?

CORY   Papa done went up to the school and told Coach Zellman I can't play football no more. Wouldn't even let me play the game. Told him to tell the recruiter not to come.

ROSE   Troy . . .

TROY   What you Troying me for. Yeah, I did it. And the boy know why I did it.

360   CORY   Why you wanna do that to me? That was the one chance I had.

ROSE   Ain't nothing wrong with Cory playing football, Troy.

TROY   The boy lied to me. I told the nigger if he wanna play football . . . to keep up his chores and hold down that job at the A&P. That was the conditions. Stopped down there to see Mr. Stawicki . . .

CORY   I can't work after school during the football season, Pop! I tried to tell you that Mr. Stawicki's holding my job for me. You don't never want to listen to nobody. And then you wanna go and do this to me!

TROY   I ain't done nothing to you. You done it to yourself.

CORY   Just cause you didn't have a chance! You just scared I'm gonna be

370   better than you, that's all.

TROY   Come here.

ROSE   Troy . . .

[CORY *reluctantly crosses over to* TROY.]

TROY   Alright! See. You done made a mistake.

CORY   I didn't even do nothing!

TROY   I'm gonna tell you what your mistake was. See . . . you swung at the ball and didn't hit it. That's strike one. See, you in the batter's box now. You swung and you missed. That's strike one. Don't you strike out!

[*Lights fade to black.*]

Act Two

Scene One

The following morning. CORY *is at the tree hitting the ball with the bat. He tries to mimic* TROY, *but his swing is awkward, less sure.* ROSE *enters from the house.*

ROSE   Cory, I want you to help me with this cupboard.

CORY   I ain't quitting the team. I don't care what Poppa say.

ROSE   I'll talk to him when he gets back. He had to go see about your Uncle Gabe. The police done arrested him. Say he was disturbing the peace. He'll be back directly. Come on in here and help me clean out the top of this cupboard.

[CORY *exits into the house.* ROSE *sees* TROY *and* BONO *coming down the alley.*]

Troy . . . what they say down there?

TROY   Ain't said nothing. I give them fifty dollars and they let him go. I'll talk to you about it. Where's Cory?

10   ROSE   He's in there helping me clean out these cupboards.

TROY   Tell him to get his butt out here.

[TROY *and* BONO *go over to the pile of wood.* BONO *picks up the saw and begins sawing.*]

TROY [*To* BONO.]   All they want is the money. That makes six or seven times I done went down there and got him. See me coming they stick out their *hands*.

BONO   Yeah. I know what you mean. That's all they care about . . . that money. They don't care about what's right.

[*Pause.*]

Nigger, why you got to go and get some hard wood? You ain't doing nothing but building a little old fence. Get you some soft pine wood. That's all you need.

20   TROY   I know what I'm doing. This is outside wood. You put pine wood inside the house. Pine wood is inside wood. This here is outside wood. Now you tell me where the fence is gonna be?

BONO   You don't need this wood. You can put it up with pine wood and it'll stand as long as you gonna be here looking at it.

TROY   How you know how long I'm gonna be here, nigger? Hell, I might just live forever. Live longer than old man Horsely.

BONO   That's what Magee used to say.

TROY   Magee's a damn fool. Now you tell me who you ever heard of gonna pull their own teeth with a pair of rusty pliers.

30   BONO   The old folks . . . my granddaddy used to pull his teeth with pliers. They ain't had no dentists for the colored folks back then.

TROY   Get clean pliers! You understand? Clean pliers! Sterilize them! Besides we ain't living back then. All Magee had to do was walk over to Doc Goldblums.

BONO   I see where you and that Tallahassee gal . . . that Alberta . . . I see where you all done got tight.

TROY   What you mean "got tight"?

BONO   I see where you be laughing and joking with her all the time.

TROY   I laughs and jokes with all of them, Bono. You know me.

40   BONO   That ain't the kind of laughing and joking I'm talking about.

[CORY *enters from the house.*]

CORY   How you doing, Mr. Bono?

TROY   Cory? Get that saw from Bono and cut some wood. He talking about the wood's too hard to cut. Stand back there, Jim, and let that young boy show you how it's done.

BONO   He's sure welcome to it.

[CORY *takes the saw and begins to cut the wood.*]

Whew-e-e! Look at that. Big old strong boy. Look like Joe Louis. Hell, must be getting old the way I'm watching that boy whip through that wood.

CORY   I don't see why Mama want a fence around the yard noways.

TROY   Damn if I know either. What the hell she keeping out with it? She
50   ain't got nothing nobody want.

BONO   Some people build fences to keep people out . . . and other people build fences to keep people in. Rose wants to hold on to you all. She loves you.

TROY   Hell, nigger, I don't need nobody to tell me my wife loves me, Cory . . . go on in the house and see if you can find that other saw.

CORY   Where's it at?

TROY   I said find it! Look for it till you find it!

[CORY *exits into the house.*]

What's that supposed to mean? Wanna keep us in?

BONO   Troy . . . I done known you seem like damn near my whole life.
60   You and Rose both. I done know both of you all for a long time. I remember when you met Rose. When you was hitting them baseball out the park. A lot of them old gals was after you then. You had the pick of the litter. When you picked Rose, I was happy for you. That was the first time I knew you had any sense. I said . . . My man Troy knows what he's doing . . . I'm gonna follow this nigger . . . he might take me somewhere. I been following you too. I done learned a whole heap of things about life watching you. I done learned how to tell where the shit lies. How to tell it from the alfalfa. You done learned me a lot of things. You showed me how to not make the same mistakes . . . to take life as it comes along and keep putting one foot in
70   front of the other.

[*Pause.*]

Rose a good woman, Troy.

TROY   Hell, nigger, I know she a good woman. I been married to her for eighteen years. What you got on your mind, Bono?

BONO   I just say she a good woman. Just like I say anything. I ain't got to have nothing on my mind.

TROY   You just gonna say she a good woman and leave it hanging out there like that? Why you telling me she a good woman?

BONO   She loves you, Troy. Rose loves you.

TROY   You saying I don't measure up. That's what you trying to say. I don't
80 measure up cause I'm seeing this other gal. I know what you trying to say.

BONO   I know what Rose means to you, Troy. I'm just trying to say I don't want to see you mess up.

TROY   Yeah, I appreciate that, Bono. If you was messing around on Lucille I'd be telling you the same thing.

BONO   Well, that's all I got to say. I just say that because I love you both.

TROY   Hell, you know me . . . I wasn't out there looking for nothing. You can't find a better woman than Rose. I know that. But seems like this woman just stuck onto me where I can't shake her loose. I done wrestled with it, tried to throw her off me . . . but she just stuck on tighter. Now she's stuck
90 on for good.

BONO   You's in control . . . that's what you tell me all the time. You responsible for what you do.

TROY   I ain't ducking the responsibility of it. As long as it sets right in my heart . . . then I'm okay. Cause that's all I listen to. It'll tell me right from wrong every time. And I ain't talking about doing Rose no bad turn. I love Rose. She done carried me a long ways and I love and respect her for that.

BONO   I know you do. That's why I don't want to see you hurt her. But what you gonna do when she find out? What you got then? If you try and juggle both of them . . . sooner or later you gonna drop one of them. That's
100 common sense.

TROY   Yeah, I hear what you saying, Bono. I been trying to figure a way to work it out.

BONO   Work it out right, Troy. I don't want to be getting all up between you and Rose's business . . . but work it so it come out right.

TROY   Aw hell, I get all up between you and Lucille's business. When you gonna get that woman that refrigerator she been wanting? Don't tell me you ain't got no money now. I know who your banker is. Mellon don't need that money bad as Lucille want that refrigerator. I'll tell you that.

BONO   Tell you what I'll do . . . when you finish building this fence for
110 Rose . . . I'll buy Lucille that refrigerator.

TROY   You done stuck your foot in your mouth now!

[TROY *grabs up a board and begins to saw.* BONO *starts to walk out the yard.*]

Hey, nigger . . . where you going?

BONO   I'm going home. I know you don't expect me to help you now. I'm protecting my money. I wanna see you put that fence up by yourself. That's what I want to see. You'll be here another six months without me.

TROY   Nigger, you ain't right.

BONO   When it comes to my money . . . I'm right as fireworks on the Fourth of July.

TROY   Alright, we gonna see now. You better get out your bankbook.

[BONO *exits, and* TROY *continues to work.* ROSE *enters from the house.*]

120   ROSE   What they say down there? What's happening with Gabe?

TROY   I went down there and got him out. Cost me fifty dollars. Say he was disturbing the peace. Judge set up a hearing for him in three weeks. Say to show cause why he shouldn't be re-committed.

ROSE   What was he doing that cause them to arrest him?

TROY   Some kids was teasing him and he run them off home. Say he was howling and carrying on. Some folks seen him and called the police. That's all it was.

ROSE   Well, what's you say? What'd you tell the judge?

TROY   Told him I'd look after him. It didn't make no sense to recommit the
130   man. He stuck out his big greasy palm and told me to give him fifty dollars and take him on home.

ROSE   Where's he at now? Where'd he go off to?

TROY   He's gone on about his business. He don't need nobody to hold his hand.

ROSE   Well, I don't know. Seem like that would be the best place for him if they did put him into the hospital. I know what you're gonna say. But that's what I think would be best.

TROY   The man done had his life ruined fighting for what? And they wanna take and lock him up. Let him be free. He don't bother nobody.

140   ROSE   Well, everybody got their own way of looking at it I guess. Come on and get your lunch. I got a bowl of lima beans and some cornbread in the oven. Come on get something to eat. Ain't no sense you fretting over Gabe.
[*Rose turns to go into the house.*]

TROY   Rose . . . got something to tell you.

ROSE   Well, come on . . . wait till I get this food on the table.

TROY   Rose!

[*She stops and turns around.*]

I don't know how to say this.

[*Pause.*]

I can't explain it none. It just sort of grows on you till it gets out of hand. It starts out like a little bush . . . and the next think you know it's a whole forest.
150   ROSE   Troy . . . what is you talking about?

TROY I'm talking, woman, let me talk. I'm trying to find a way to tell you . . . I'm gonna be a daddy. I'm gonna be somebody's daddy.

ROSE Troy . . . you're not telling me this? You're gonna be . . . what?

TROY Rose . . . now . . . see . . .

ROSE You telling me you gonna be somebody's daddy? You telling your *wife* this?

[GABRIEL *enters from the street. He carries a rose in his hand.*]

GABRIEL Hey, Troy! Hey, Rose!

ROSE I have to wait eighteen years to hear something like this.

GABRIEL Hey, Rose . . . I got a flower for you.

[*He hands it to her.*]

160 That's a rose. Same rose like you is.

ROSE Thanks, Gabe.

GABRIEL Troy, you ain't mad at me is you? Them bad mens come and put me away. You ain't mad at me is you?

TROY Naw, Gabe, I ain't mad at you.

ROSE Eighteen years and you wanna come with this.

GABRIEL [*Takes a quarter out of his pocket.*] See what I got? Got a brand new quarter.

TROY Rose . . . it's just . . .

ROSE Ain't nothing you can say, Troy. Ain't no way of explaining that.

170 GABRIEL Fellow that give me this quarter had a whole mess of them. I'm gonna keep this quarter till it stop shining.

ROSE Gabe, go on in the house there. I got some watermelon in the frigidaire. Go on and get you a piece.

GABRIEL Say, Rose . . . you know I was chasing hellhounds and them bad mens come and get me and take me away. Troy helped me. He come down there and told them they better let me go before he beat them up. Yeah, he did!

ROSE You go on and get you a piece of watermelon, Gabe. Them bad mens is gone now.

GABRIEL Okay, Rose . . . gonna get me some watermelon. The kind with 180 the stripes on it.

[GABRIEL *exits into the house.*]

ROSE Why, Troy? Why? After all these years to come dragging this in to me now. It don't make no sense at your age. I could have expected this ten or fifteen years ago, but not now.

TROY Age ain't got nothing to do with it, Rose.

ROSE I done tried to be everything a wife should be. Everything a wife could be. Been married eighteen years and I got to live to see the day you tell me you been seeing another woman and done fathered a child by her. And you know I ain't never wanted no half nothing in my family. My whole family

is half. Everybody got different fathers and mothers . . . my two sisters and
190   my brother. Can't hardly tell who's who. Can't never sit down and talk about
Papa and Mama. It's your papa and your mama and my papa and my
mama . . .

TROY   Rose . . . stop it now.

ROSE   I ain't never wanted that for none of my children. And now you
wanna drag your behind in here and tell me something like this.

TROY   You ought to know. It's time for you to know.

ROSE   Well, I don't want to know, goddamn it!

TROY   I can't just make it go away. It's done now. I can't wish the circumstance of the thing away.

200   ROSE   And you don't want to either. Maybe you want to wish me and my
boy away. Maybe that's what you want? Well, you can't wish us away. I've got
eighteen years of my life invested in you. You ought to have stayed upstairs in
my bed where you belong.

TROY   Rose . . . now listen to me . . . we can get a handle on this thing.
We can talk this out . . . come to an understanding.

ROSE   All of a sudden it's "we." Where was "we" at when you was down
there rolling around with some god-forsaken woman? "We" should have come
to an understanding before you started making a damn fool of yourself. You're
a day late and a dollar short when it comes to an understanding with me.

210   TROY   It's just . . . She gives me a different idea . . . a different understanding about myself. I can step out of this house and get away from the
pressures and problems . . . be a different man. I ain't got to wonder how
I'm gonna pay the bills or get the roof fixed. I can just be a part of myself that
I ain't never been.

ROSE   What I want to know . . . is do you plan to continue seeing her.
That's all you can say to me.

TROY   I can sit up in her house and laugh. Do you understand what I'm
saying. I can laugh out loud . . . and it feels good. It reaches all the way
down to the bottom of my shoes.

[*Pause.*]

220   Rose, I can't give that up.

ROSE   Maybe you ought to go on and stay down there with her . . . if she a
better woman than me.

TROY   It ain't about nobody being a better woman or nothing. Rose, you
ain't the blame. A man couldn't ask for no woman to be a better wife than
you've been. I'm responsible for it. I done locked myself into a pattern trying
to take care of you all that I forgot about myself.

ROSE   What the hell was I there for? That was my job, not somebody else's.

TROY   Rose, I done tried all my life to live decent . . . to live a clean . . .
hard . . . useful life. I tried to be a good husband to you. In every way I
230   knew how. Maybe I come into the world backwards, I don't know. But . . .
you born with two strikes on you before you come to the plate. You got to
guard it closely . . . always looking for the curve-ball on the inside corner.

You can't afford to let none get past you. You can't afford a call strike. If you going down . . . you going down swinging. Everything lined up against you. What you gonna do. I fooled them, Rose. I bunted. When I found you and Cory and a halfway decent job . . . I was safe. Couldn't nothing touch me. I wasn't gonna strike out no more. I wasn't going back to the penitentiary. I wasn't gonna lay in the streets with a bottle of wine. I was safe. I had me a family. A job. I wasn't gonna get that last strike. I was on first looking for
240 one of them boys to knock me in. To get me home.

ROSE   You should have stayed in my bed, Troy.

TROY   Then when I saw that gal . . . she firmed up my backbone. And I got to thinking that if I tried . . . I just might be able to steal second. Do you understand after eighteen years I wanted to steal second.

ROSE   You should have held me tight. You should have grabbed me and held on.

TROY   I stood on first base for eighteen years and I thought . . . well, goddamn it . . . go on for it!

ROSE   We're not talking about baseball! We're talking about you going off
250 to lay in bed with another woman . . . and then bring it home to me. That's what we're talking about. We ain't talking about no baseball.

TROY   Rose, you're not listening to me. I'm trying the best I can to explain it to you. It's not easy for me to admit that I been standing in the same place for eighteen years.

ROSE   I been standing with you! I been right here with you, Troy. I got a life too. I gave eighteen years of my life to stand in the same spot with you. Don't you think I ever wanted other things? Don't you think I had dreams and hopes? What about my life? What about me. Don't you think it ever crossed my mind to want to know other men? That I wanted to lay up somewhere and
260 forget about my responsibilities? That I wanted someone to make me laugh so I could feel good? You not the only one who's got wants and needs. But I held on to you, Troy. I took all my feelings, my wants and needs, my dreams . . . and I buried them inside you. I planted a seed and watched and prayed over it. I planted myself inside you and waited to bloom. And it didn't take me no eighteen years to find out the soil was hard and rocky and it wasn't never gonna bloom.

But I held on to you, Troy. I held you tighter. You was my husband. I owed you everything I had. Every part of me I could find to give you. And upstairs in that room . . . with the darkness falling in on me . . . I gave everything
270 I had to try and erase the doubt that you wasn't the finest man in the world. And wherever you was going . . . I wanted to be there with you. Cause you was my husband. Cause that's the only way I was gonna survive as your wife. You always talking about what you give . . . and what you don't have to give. But you take too. You take . . . and don't even know nobody's giving!

[ROSE *turns to exit into the house;* TROY *grabs her arm.*]

TROY   You say I take and don't give!

ROSE   Troy! You're hurting me!

TROY   You say I take and don't give.

ROSE   Troy . . . you're hurting my arm! Let go!

TROY   I done give you everything I got. Don't you tell that lie on me.

280   ROSE   Troy!

TROY   Don't you tell that lie on me!

[CORY *enters from the house.*]

CORY   Mama!

ROSE   Troy. You're hurting me.

TROY   Don't you tell me about no taking and giving.

[CORY *comes up behind* TROY *and grabs him.* TROY, *surprised, is thrown off balance just as* CORY *throws a glancing blow that catches him on the chest and knocks him down.* TROY *is stunned, as is* CORY.]

ROSE   Troy. Troy. No!

[TROY *gets to his feet and starts at* CORY.]

Troy . . . . no. Please! Troy!

[ROSE *pulls on* TROY *to hold him back.* TROY *stops himself.*]

TROY [*To* CORY]   Alright. That's strike two. You stay away from around me, boy. Don't you strike out. You living with a full count. Don't you strike out.

[TROY *exits out the yard as the lights go down.*]

Act Two

Scene Two

It is six months later, early afternoon. TROY *enters from the house and starts to exit the yard.* ROSE *enters from the house.*

ROSE   Troy, I want to talk to you.

TROY   All of a sudden, after all this time, you want to talk to me, huh? You ain't wanted to talk to me for months. You ain't wanted to talk to me last night. You ain't wanted no part of me then. What you wanna talk to me about now?

ROSE   Tomorrow's Friday.

TROY   I know what day tomorrow is. You think I don't know tomorrow's Friday? My whole life I ain't done nothing but look to see Friday coming and you got to tell me it's Friday.

ROSE   I want to know if you're coming home.

10   TROY   I always come home, Rose. You know that. There ain't never been a night I ain't come home.

ROSE   That ain't what I mean . . . and you know it. I want to know if you're coming straight home after work.

TROY   I figure I'd cash my check . . . hang out at Taylors' with the boys . . . maybe play a game of checkers . . .

ROSE   Troy, I can't live like this. I won't live like this. You livin' on borrowed time with me. It's been going on six months now you ain't been coming home.

TROY   I be here every night. Every night of the year. That's 365 days.

ROSE   I want you to come home tomorrow after work.

20   TROY   Rose . . . I don't mess up my pay. You know that now. I take my pay and I give it to you. I don't have no money but what you give me back. I just want to have a little time to myself . . . a little time to enjoy life.

ROSE   What about me? When's my time to enjoy life?

TROY   I don't know what to tell you, Rose. I'm doing the best I can.

ROSE   You ain't been home from work but time enough to change your clothes and run out . . . and you wanna call that the best you can do?

TROY   I'm going over to the hospital to see Alberta. She went into the hospital this afternoon. Look like she might have the baby early. I won't be gone long.

30   ROSE   Well, you ought to know. They went over to Miss Pearl's and got Gabe today. She said you told them to go ahead and lock him up.

TROY   I ain't said no such thing. Whoever told you that is telling a lie. Pearl ain't doing nothing but telling a big fat lie.

ROSE   She ain't had to tell me. I read it on the papers.

TROY   I ain't told them nothing of the kind.

ROSE   I saw it right there on the papers.

TROY   What it say, huh?

ROSE   It said you told them to take him.

TROY   Then they screwed that up, just the way they screw up everything. I
40   ain't worried about what they got on the paper.

ROSE   Say the government send part of his check to the hospital and the other part to you.

TROY   I ain't got nothing to do with that if that's the way it works. I ain't made up the rules about how it work.

ROSE   You did Gabe just like you did Cory. You wouldn't sign the paper for Cory . . . but you signed for Gabe. You signed that paper.

[*The telephone is heard ringing inside the house.*]

TROY   I told you I ain't signed nothing, woman! The only thing I signed was the release form. Hell, I can't read, I don't know what they had on that paper! I ain't signed nothing about sending Gabe away.

50   ROSE   I said send him to the hospital . . . you said let him be free . . . now you done went down there and signed him to the hospital for half his money. You went back on yourself, Troy. You gonna have to answer for that.

TROY   See now . . . you been over there talking to Miss Pearl. She done got mad cause she ain't getting Gabe's rent money. That's all it is. She's liable to say anything.

ROSE   Troy, I seen where you signed the paper.

TROY   You ain't seen nothing I signed. What she doing got papers on my brother anyway? Miss Pearl telling a big fat lie. And I'm gonna tell her about it too! You ain't seen nothing I signed. Say . . . you ain't seen nothing I
60 signed.

[ROSE *exits into the house to answer the telephone. Presently she returns*].

ROSE   Troy . . . that was the hospital. Alberta had the baby.

TROY   What she have? What is it?

ROSE   It's a girl.

TROY   I better get on down to the hospital to see her.

ROSE   Troy . . .

TROY   Rose . . . I got to go see her now. That's only right . . . what's the matter . . . the baby's alright, ain't it?

ROSE   Alberta died having the baby.

TROY   Died . . . you say she's dead? Alberta's dead?

70 ROSE   They said they done all they could. They couldn't do nothing for her.

TROY   The baby? How's the baby?

ROSE   They say it's healthy. I wonder who's gonna bury her.

TROY   She had family, Rose. She wasn't living in the world by herself.

ROSE   I know she wasn't living in the world by herself.

TROY   Next thing you gonna want to know if she had any insurance.

ROSE   Troy, you ain't got to talk like that.

TROY   That's the first thing that jumped out your mouth. "Who's gonna bury her?" Like I'm fixing to take on that task for myself.

ROSE   I am your wife. Don't push me away.

80 TROY   I ain't pushing nobody away. Just give me some space. That's all. Just give me some room to breathe.

[ROSE *exits into the house.* TROY *walks about the yard.*]

TROY [*With a quiet rage that threatens to consume him.*]   Alright . . . Mr. Death. See now . . . I'm gonna tell you what I'm gonna do. I'm gonna take and build me a fence around this yard. See? I'm gonna build me a fence around what belongs to me. And then I want you to stay on the other side. See? You stay over there until you're ready for me. Then you come on. Bring your army. Bring your sickle. Bring your wrestling clothes. I ain't gonna fall down on my vigilance this time. You ain't gonna sneak up on me no more. When you ready for me . . . when the top of your list say Troy Maxson . . .
90 that's when you come around here. You come up and knock on the front door. Ain't nobody else got nothing to do with this. This is between you and me. Man to man. You stay on the other side of that fence until you ready for me. Then you come up and knock on the front door. Anytime you want. I'll be ready for you.

[*The lights go down to black.*]

Act Two

Scene Three

The lights come up on the porch. It is late evening three days later. ROSE *sits listening to the ball game waiting for* TROY. *The final out of the game is made and* ROSE *switches off the radio.* TROY *enters the yard carrying an infant wrapped in blankets. He stands back from the house and calls.*

[ROSE *enters and stands on the porch. There is a long, awkward silence, the weight of which grows heavier with each passing second.*]

TROY   Rose . . . I'm standing here with my daughter in my arms. She ain't but a wee bittie little old thing. She don't know nothing about grownups' business. She innocent . . . and she ain't got no mama.

ROSE   What you telling me for, Troy?

[*She turns and exits into the house.*]

TROY   Well . . . . I guess we'll just sit out here on the porch.

[*He sits down on the porch. There is an awkward indelicateness about the way he handles the baby. His largeness engulfs and seems to swallow it. He speaks loud enough for* ROSE *to hear.*]

A man's got to do what's right for him. I ain't sorry for nothing I done. It felt right in my heart.

[*To the baby.*]

What you smiling at? Your daddy's a big man. Got these great big old hands. But sometimes he's scared. And right now your daddy's scared cause we
10 sitting out here and ain't got no home. Oh, I been homeless before. I ain't had no little baby with me. But I been homeless. You just be out on the road by your lonesome and you see one of them trains coming and you just kinda go like this . . .

[*He sings as a lullaby.*]

Please, Mr. Engineer let a man ride the line
Please, Mr. Engineer let a man ride the line
I ain't got no ticket please let me ride the blinds

[ROSE *enters from the house.* TROY *hearing her steps behind him, stands and faces her.*]

She's my daughter, Rose. My own flesh and blood. I can't deny her no more than I can deny them boys.

[*Pause.*]

You and them boys is my family. You and them and this child is all I got in the
20 world. So I guess what I'm saying is . . . I'd appreciate it if you'd help me
take care of her.

ROSE   Okay, Troy . . . you're right. I'll take care of your baby for you . . .
cause . . . like you say . . . she's innocent . . . and you can't visit the sins
of the father upon the child. A motherless child has got a hard time.

[*She takes the baby from him.*]

From right now . . . this child got a mother. But you a womanless man.

[ROSE *turns and exits into the house with the baby. Lights go down to black.*]

Act Two

Scene Four

It is two months later. LYONS *enters from the street. He knocks on the door and calls*

LYONS   Hey, Rose! [*Pause.*] Rose!
ROSE [*From inside the house.*]   Stop that yelling. You gonna wake up
Raynell. I just got her to sleep.
LYONS   I just stopped by to pay Papa this twenty dollars I owe him. Where's
Papa at?
ROSE   He should be here in a minute. I'm getting ready to go down to the
church. Sit down and wait on him.
LYONS   I got to go pick up Bonnie over her mother's house.
ROSE   Well, sit it down there on the table. He'll get it.
10   LYONS [*Enters the house and sets the money on the table.*]   Tell Papa I said
thanks. I'll see you again.
ROSE   Alright, Lyons. We'll see you.

[LYONS *starts to exit as* CORY *enters.*]

CORY   Hey, Lyons.
LYONS   What's happening, Cory. Say man, I'm sorry I missed your gradua-
tion. You know I had a gig and couldn't get away. Otherwise, I would have
been there, man. So what you doing?
CORY   I'm trying to find a job.
LYONS   Yeah I know how that go, man. It's rough out here. Jobs are scarce.
CORY   Yeah, I know.
20   LYONS   Look here, I got to run. Talk to Papa . . . he know some people.
He'll be able to help get you a job. Talk to him . . . see what he say.
CORY   Yeah . . . alright, Lyons.
LYONS   You take care. I'll talk to you soon. We'll find some time to talk.

[LYONS *exits the yard.* CORY *wanders over to the tree, picks up the bat and assumes a batting stance. He studies an imaginary pitcher and swings. Dissatisfied with the result, he tries again.* TROY *enters. They eye each other for a beat.* CORY *puts the bat down and exits the yard.* TROY *starts into the house as* ROSE *exits with* RAYNELL. *She is carrying a cake.*]

TROY   I'm coming in and everybody's going out.

ROSE   I'm taking this cake down to the church for the bakesale. Lyons was by to see you. He stopped by to pay you your twenty dollars. It's laying in there on the table.

TROY [*Going into his pocket.*]   Well . . . here go this money.

ROSE   Put it in there on the table, Troy. I'll get it.

30   TROY   What time you coming back?

ROSE   Ain't no use in you studying me. It don't matter what time I come back.

TROY   I just asked you a question, woman. What's the matter . . . can't I ask you a question?

ROSE   Troy, I don't want to go into it. Your dinner's in there on the stove. All you got to do is heat it up. And don't you be eating the rest of them cakes in there. I'm coming back for them. We having a bakesale at the church tomorrow.

[ROSE *exits the yard.* TROY *sits down on the steps, takes a pint bottle from his pocket, opens it and drinks. He begins to sing.*]

TROY
Hear it ring! Hear it ring!
40   Had an old dog his name was Blue
You know Blue was mighty true
You know Blue as a good old dog
Blue trees a possum in a hollow log
You know from that he was a good old dog

[BONO *enters the yard.*]

BONO   Hey, Troy.

TROY   Hey, what's happening, Bono?

BONO   I just thought I'd stop by to see you.

TROY   What you stop by and see me for? You ain't stopped by in a month of Sundays. Hell, I must owe you money or something.

50   BONO   Since you got your promotion I can't keep up with you. Used to see you everyday. Now I don't even know what route you working.

TROY   They keep switching me around. Got me out in Greentree now . . . hauling white folks' garbage.

BONO   Greentree, huh? You lucky, at least you ain't got to be lifting them barrels. Damn if they ain't getting heavier. I'm gonna put in my two years and call it quits.

TROY   I'm thinking about retiring myself.

BONO   You got it easy. You can *drive* for another five years.

TROY   It ain't the same, Bono. It ain't like working the back of the truck.
60 Ain't got nobody to talk to . . . feel like you working by yourself. Naw, I'm
thinking about retiring. How's Lucille?

BONO   She alright. Her arthritis get to acting up on her sometime. Saw
Rose on my way in. She going down to the church, huh?

TROY   Yeah, she took up going down there. All them preachers looking for
somebody to fatten their pockets.

[*Pause.*]

Got some gin here.

BONO   Naw, thanks. I just stopped by to say hello.

TROY   Hell, nigger . . . you can take a drink. I ain't never known you to
say no to a drink. You ain't got to work tomorrow.

70   BONO   I just stopped by. I'm fixing to go over to Skinner's. We got us a
domino game going over his house every Friday.

TROY   Nigger, you can't play no dominoes. I used to whup you four games
out of five.

BONO   Well, that learned me. I'm getting better.

TROY   Yeah? Well, that's alright.

BONO   Look here . . . I got to be getting on. Stop by sometime, huh?

TROY   Yeah, I'll do that, Bono. Lucille told Rose you bought her a new
refrigerator.

BONO   Yeah, Rose told Lucille you had finally built your fence . . . so I
80 figured we'd call it even.

TROY   I knew you would.

BONO   Yeah . . . okay. I'll be talking to you.

TROY   Yeah, take care, Bono. Good to see you. I'm gonna stop over.

BONO   Yeah. Okay, Troy.

[BONO *exits.* TROY *drinks from the bottle.*]

TROY
Old Blue died and I dig his grave
Let him down with a golden chain
Every night when I hear old Blue bark
I know Blue treed a possum in Noah's Ark.
90 Hear it ring! Hear it ring!

[CORY *enters the yard. They eye each other for a beat.* TROY *is sitting in the middle of
the steps.* CORY *walks over.*]

CORY   I got to get by.

TROY   Say what? What's you say?

CORY   You in my way. I got to get by.

TROY   You got to get by where? This is my house. Bought and paid for. In full. Took me fifteen years. And if you wanna go in my house and I'm sitting on the steps . . . you say excuse me. Like your mama taught you.

CORY   Come on, Pop . . . I got to get by.

[CORY *starts to maneuver his way past* TROY. TROY *grabs his leg and shoves him back.*]

TROY   You just gonna walk over top of me?

CORY   I live here too!

100   TROY [*Advancing toward him.*]   You just gonna walk over top of me in my own house?

CORY   I ain't scared of you.

TROY   I ain't asked if you was scared of me. I asked you if you was fixing to walk over top of me in my own house? That's the question. You ain't gonna say excuse me? You just gonna walk over top of me?

CORY   If you wanna put it like that.

TROY   How else am I gonna put it?

CORY   I was walking by you to go into the house cause you sitting on the steps drunk, singing to yourself. You can put it like that.

110   TROY   Without saying excuse me???

[CORY *doesn't respond.*]

I asked you a question. Without saying excuse me???

CORY   I ain't got to say excuse me to you. You don't count around here no more.

TROY   Oh, I see . . . I don't count around here no more. You ain't got to say excuse me to your daddy. All of a sudden you done got so grown that your daddy don't count around here no more . . . Around here in his own house and yard that he done paid for with the sweat of his brow. You done got so grown to where you gonna take over. You gonna take over my house. Is that right? You gonna wear my pants. You gonna go in there and stretch out on my 120 bed. You ain't got to say excuse me cause I don't count around here no more. Is that right?

CORY   That's right. You always talking this dumb stuff. Now, why don't you just get out of my way.

TROY   I guess you got someplace to sleep and something to put in your belly. You got that, huh? You got that? That's what you need. You got that, huh?

CORY   You don't know what I got. You ain't got to worry about what I got.

TROY   You right! You one hundred percent right! I done spent the last seventeen years worrying about what you got. Now it's your turn, see? I'll tell you what to do. You grown . . . we done established that. You a man. Now, 130 let's see you act like one. Turn your behind around and walk out this yard. And when you get out there in the alley . . . you can forget about this house. See? Cause this is my house. You go on and be a man and get your own house. You can forget about this. 'Cause this is mine. You go on and get yours cause I'm through with doing for you.

CORY   You talking about what you did for me . . . what'd you ever give me?

TROY   Them feet and bones! That pumping heart, nigger! I give you more than anybody else is ever gonna give you.

CORY   You ain't never gave me nothing! You ain't never done nothing but hold me back. Afraid I was gonna be better than you. All you ever did was try

140 and make me scared of you. I used to tremble every time you called my name. Every time I heard your footsteps in the house. Wondering all the time . . . what's Papa gonna say if I do this? . . . What's he gonna say if I do that? . . . What's Papa gonna say if I turn on the radio? And Mama, too . . . she tries . . . but she's scared of you.

TROY   You leave your mama out of this. She ain't got nothing to do with this.

CORY   I don't know how she stand you . . . after what you did to her.

TROY   I told you to leave your mama out of this!

[*He advances toward* CORY.]

CORY   What you gonna do . . . give me a whupping? You can't whup me no more. You're too old. You just an old man.

150 TROY [*Shoves him on his shoulder.*]   Nigger! That's what you are. You just another nigger on the street to me!

CORY   You crazy! You know that?

TROY   Go on now! You got the devil in you. Get on away from me!

CORY   You just a crazy old man . . . talking about I got the devil in me.

TROY   Yeah, I'm crazy! If you don't get on the other side of that yard . . . I'm gonna show you how crazy I am! Go on . . . get the hell out of my yard.

CORY   It ain't your yard. You took Uncle Gabe's money he got from the army to buy this house and then you put him out.

TROY [TROY *advances on* CORY.]   Get your black ass out of my yard!

[TROY*'s advance backs* CORY *up against the tree.* CORY *grabs up the bat.*]

160 CORY   I ain't going nowhere! Come on . . . put me out! I ain't scared of you.

TROY   That's my bat!

CORY   Come on!

TROY   Put my bat down!

CORY   Come on, put me out.

[CORY *swings at* TROY, *who backs across the yard.*]

What's the matter? You so bad . . . put me out!

[TROY *advances toward* CORY.]

CORY [*Backing up.*]   Come on! Come on!

TROY   You're gonna have to use it! You wanna draw that bat back on me . . . you're gonna have to use it.

CORY   Come on! . . . Come on!

[CORY *swings the bat at* TROY *a second time. He misses.* TROY *continues to advance toward him.*]

170   TROY You're gonna have to kill me! You wanna draw that bat back on me. You're gonna have to kill me.

[CORY, *backed up against the tree, can go no farther.* TROY *taunts him. He sticks out his head and offers him a target.*]

Come on! Come on!

[CORY *is unable to swing the bat.* TROY *grabs it.*]

TROY Then I'll show you.

[CORY *and* TROY *struggle over the bat. The struggle is fierce and fully engaged.* TROY *ultimately is the stronger, and takes the bat from* CORY *and stands over him ready to swing. He stops himself.*]

Go on and get away from around my house.

[CORY, *stung by his defeat, picks himself up, walks slowly out of the yard and up the alley.*]

CORY Tell Mama I'll be back for my things.
TROY They'll be on the other side of that fence.

[CORY *exits.*]

TROY I can't taste nothing. Helluljah! I can't taste nothing no more. [TROY *assumes a batting posture and begins to taunt Death, the fastball in the outside corner.*] Come on! It's between you and me now! Come on! Anytime
180 you want! Come on! I be ready for you . . . but I ain't gonna be easy.

[*The lights go down on the scene.*]

Act Two

Scene Five

The time is 1965. The lights come up in the yard. It is the morning of TROY'*s funeral. A funeral plaque with a light hangs beside the door. There is a small garden plot off to the side. There is noise and activity in the house as* ROSE, GABRIEL *and* BONO *have gathered. The door opens and* RAYNELL, *seven years old, enters dressed in a flannel nightgown. She crosses to the garden and pokes around with a stick.* ROSE *calls from the house.*

ROSE Raynell!
RAYNELL Mam?

ROSE   What you doing out there?
RAYNELL   Nothing.

[ROSE *comes to the door.*]

ROSE   Girl, get in here and get dressed. What you doing?
RAYNELL   Seeing if my garden growed.
ROSE   I told you it ain't gonna grow overnight. You got to wait.
RAYNELL   It don't look like it never gonna grow. Dag!
ROSE   I told you a watched pot never boils. Get in here and get dressed.
10   RAYNELL   This ain't even no pot, Mama.
ROSE   You just have to give it a chance. It'll grow. Now you come on and do what I told you. We got to be getting ready. This ain't no morning to be playing around. You hear me?
RAYNELL   Yes, mam.

[ROSE *exits into the house.* RAYNELL *continues to poke at her garden with a stick.* CORY *enters. He is dressed in a Marine corporal's uniform, and carries a duffel bag. His posture is that of a military man, and his speech has a clipped sternness.*]

CORY [*To* RAYNELL.]   Hi.

[*Pause.*]

I bet your name is Raynell.
RAYNELL   Uh huh.
CORY   Is your mama home?

[RAYNELL *runs up on the porch and calls through the screendoor.*]

RAYNELL   Mama . . . there's some man out here. Mama?

[ROSE *comes to the door.*]

20   ROSE   Cory? Lord have mercy! Look here, you all!

[ROSE *and* CORY *embrace in a tearful reunion as* BONO *and* LYONS *enter from the house dressed in funeral clothes.*]

BONO   Aw, looka here . . .
ROSE   Done got all grown up!
CORY   Don't cry, Mama. What you crying about?
ROSE   I'm just so glad you made it.
CORY   Hey Lyons. How you doing, Mr. Bono.

[LYONS *goes to embrace* CORY.]

LYONS   Look at you, man. Look at you. Don't he look good, Rose. Got them Corporal stripes.

ROSE   What took you so long.

CORY   You know how the Marines are, Mama. They got to get all their
30 paperwork straight before they let you do anything.

ROSE   Well, I'm sure glad you made it. They let Lyons come. Your Uncle Gabe's still in the hospital. They don't know if they gonna let him out or not. I just talked to them a little while ago.

LYONS   A Corporal in the United States Marines.

BONO   Your daddy knew you had it in you. He used to tell me all the time.

LYONS   Don't he look good, Mr. Bono?

BONO   Yeah, he remind me of Troy when I first met him.

[*Pause.*]

Say, Rose, Lucille's down at the church with the choir. I'm gonna go down and get the pallbearers lined up. I'll be back to get you all.

40 ROSE   Thanks, Jim.

CORY   See you, Mr. Bono.

LYONS   [*With his arm around* RAYNELL.]   Cory . . . look at Raynell. Ain't she precious? She gonna break a whole lot of hearts.

ROSE   Raynell, come and say hello to your brother. This is your brother, Cory. You remember Cory.

RAYNELL   No, Mam.

CORY   She don't remember me, Mama.

ROSE   Well, we talk about you. She heard us talk about you.
[*To* RAYNELL.] This is your brother, Cory. Come on and say hello.

50 RAYNELL   Hi.

CORY   Hi. So you're Raynell. Mama told me a lot about you.

ROSE   You all come on into the house and let me fix you some breakfast. Keep up your strength.

CORY   I ain't hungry, Mama.

LYONS   You can fix me something, Rose. I'll be in there in a minute.

ROSE   Cory, you sure you don't want nothing. I know they ain't feeding you right.

CORY   No, Mama . . . thanks. I don't feel like eating. I'll get something later.

60 ROSE   Raynell . . . get on upstairs and get that dress on like I told you.

[ROSE *and* RAYNELL *exit into the house.*]

LYONS   So . . . I hear you thinking about getting married.

CORY   Yeah, I done found the right one, Lyons. It's about time.

LYONS   Me and Bonnie been split up about four years now. About the time Papa retired. I guess she just got tired of all them changes I was putting her through.

[*Pause.*]

I always knew you was gonna make something out yourself. Your head was always in the right direction. So . . . you gonna stay in . . . make it a career . . . put in your twenty years?

CORY I don't know. I got six already, I think that's enough.

70   LYONS Stick with Uncle Sam and retire early. Ain't nothing out here. I guess Rose told you what happened with me. They got me down the work-house. I thought I was being slick cashing other people's checks.

CORY How much time you doing?

LYONS They give me three years. I got that beat now. I ain't got but nine more months. It ain't so bad. You learn to deal with it like anything else. You got to take the crookeds with the straights. That's what Papa used to say. He used to say that when he struck out. I seen him strike out three times in a row . . . and the next time up he hit the ball over the grandstand. Right out there in Homestead Field. He wasn't satisfied hitting in the seats . . . he

80 want to hit it over everything! After the game he had two hundred people standing around waiting to shake his hand. You got to take the crookeds with the straights. Yeah, Papa was something else.

CORY You still playing?

LYONS Cory . . . you know I'm gonna do that. There's some fellows down there we got us a band . . . we gonna try and stay together when we get out . . . but yeah, I'm still playing. It still helps me to get out of bed in the morning. As long as it do that I'm gonna be right there playing and trying to make some sense out of it.

ROSE [*Calling.*] Lyons, I got these eggs in the pan.

90   LYONS Let me go and get these eggs, man. Get ready to go bury Papa.

[*Pause.*]

How you doing? You doing alright?

[CORY *nods.* LYONS *touches him on the shoulder and they share a moment of silent grief.* LYONS *exits into the house.* CORY *wanders about the yard.* RAYNELL *enters.*]

RAYNELL Hi.

CORY Hi.

RAYNELL Did you used to sleep in my room?

CORY Yeah . . . that used to be my room.

RAYNELL That's what Papa call it. "Cory's room." It got your football in the closet.

[ROSE *comes to the door.*]

ROSE Raynell, get in there and get them good shoes on.

RAYNELL Mama, can't I wear these. Them other one hurt my feet.

100   ROSE Well, they just gonna have to hurt your feet for a while. You ain't said they hurt your feet when you went down to the store and got them.

RAYNELL They didn't hurt then. My feet done got bigger.

ROSE Don't you give me no backtalk now. You get in there and get them shoes on.

[RAYNELL *exits into the house.*]

Ain't too much changed. He still got that piece of rag tied to that tree. He was out here swinging that bat. I was just ready to go back in the house. He swung that bat and bat and then he just fell over. Seem like he swung it and stood there with this grin on his face . . . and then he just fell over. They carried him on down to the hospital, but I knew there wasn't no need . . . why
110 don't you come on in the house?

CORY Mama . . . I got something to tell you. I don't know how to tell you this . . . but I've got to tell you . . . I'm not going to Papa's funeral.

ROSE Boy, hush your mouth. That's your daddy you talking about. I don't want hear that kind of talk this morning. I done raised you to come to this? You standing there all healthy and grown talking about you ain't going to your daddy's funeral?

CORY Mama . . . listen . . .

ROSE I don't want to hear it, Cory. You just get that thought out of your head.

CORY I can't drag Papa with me everywhere I go. I've got to say no to him.
120 One time in my life I've got to say no.

ROSE Don't nobody have to listen to nothing like that. I know you and your daddy ain't seen eye to eye, but I ain't got to listen to that kind of talk this morning. Whatever was between you and your daddy . . . the time has come to put it aside. Just take it and set it over there on the shelf and forget about it. Disrespecting your daddy ain't gonna make you a man, Cory. You got to find a way to come to that on your own. Not going to your daddy's funeral ain't gonna make you a man.

CORY The whole time I was growing up . . . living in his house . . . Papa was like a shadow that followed you everywhere. It weighed on you and
130 sunk into your flesh. It would wrap around you and lay there until you couldn't tell which one was you anymore. That shadow digging in your flesh. Trying to crawl in. Trying to live through you. Everywhere I looked, Troy Maxson was staring back at me . . . hiding under the bed . . . in the closet. I'm just saying I've got to find a way to get rid of that shadow, Mama.

ROSE You just like him. You got him in you good.

CORY Don't tell me that, Mama.

ROSE You Troy Maxson all over again.

CORY I don't want to be Troy Maxson. I want to be me.

ROSE You can't be nobody but who you are, Cory. That shadow wasn't
140 nothing but you growing into yourself. You either got to grow into it or cut it down to fit you. But that's all you got to make life with. That's all you got to measure yourself against that world out there. Your daddy wanted you to be everything he wasn't . . . and at the same time he tried to make you into everything he was. I don't know if he was right or wrong . . . but I do know he meant to do more good than he meant to do harm. He wasn't always right. Sometimes when he touched he bruised. And sometimes when he took me in his arms he cut.

When I first met your daddy I thought . . . Here is a man I can lay down with and make a baby. That's the first thing I thought when I seen him. I was 150 thirty years old and had done seen my share of men. But when he walked up to me and said, "I can dance a waltz that'll make you dizzy," I thought, Rose Lee, here is a man that you can open yourself up to and be filled to bursting. Here is a man that can fill all them empty spaces you been tipping around the edges of. One of them empty spaces was being somebody's mother.

I married your daddy and settled down to cooking his supper and keeping clean sheets on the bed. When your daddy walked through the house he was so big he filled it up. That was my first mistake. Not to make him leave some room for me. For my part in the matter. But at that time I wanted that. I wanted a house that I could sing in. And that's what your daddy gave me. I didn't know 160 to keep up his strength I had to give up little pieces of mine. I did that. I took on his life as mine and mixed up the pieces so that you couldn't hardly tell which was which anymore. It was my choice. It was my life and I didn't have to live it like that. But that's what life offered me in the way of being a woman and I took it. I grabbed hold of it with both hands.

By the time Raynell came into the house, me and your daddy had done lost touch with one another. I didn't want to make my blessing off of nobody's misfortune . . . but I took on to Raynell like she was all them babies I had wanted and never had.

[*The phone rings.*]

Like I'd been blessed to relive a part of my life. And if the Lord see fit to keep 170 up my strength . . . I'm gonna do her just like your daddy did you . . . I'm gonna give her the best of what's in me.

RAYNELL [*Entering, still with her old shoes.*] Mama . . . Reverend Tollivier on the phone.

[ROSE *exits into the house.*]

RAYNELL   Hi.

CORY   Hi.

RAYNELL   You in the Army or the Marines?

CORY   Marines.

RAYNELL   Papa said it was the Army. Did you know Blue?

CORY   Blue? Who's Blue?

180   RAYNELL   Papa's dog what he sing about all the time.

CORY [*Singing.*]   Hear it ring! Hear it ring!
I had a dog his name was Blue
You know Blue was mighty true
You know Blue was a good old dog
Blue treed a possum in a hollow log
You know from that he was a good old dog.
Hear it ring! Hear it ring!

[RAYNELL *joins in singing.*]

CORY *and* RAYNELL Blue treed a possum out on a limb
Blue looked at me and I looked at him
190 Grabbed that possum and put him in a sack
Blue stayed there till I came back
Old Blue's feets was big and round
Never allowed a possum to touch the ground.
Old Blue died and I dug his grave
I dug his grave with a silver spade
Let him down with a golden chain
And every night I call his name
Go on Blue, you good dog you
Go on Blue, you good dog you
200   RAYNELL Blue laid down and died like a man
Blue laid down and died . . .
      BOTH Blue laid down and died like a man
Now he's treeing possums in the Promised Land
I'm gonna tell you this to let you know
Blue's gone where the good dogs go
When I hear old Blue bark
When I hear old Blue bark
Blue treed a possum in Noah's Ark
Blue treed a possum in Noah's Ark.

[ROSE *comes to the screen door.*]

210   ROSE Cory, we gonna be ready to go in a minute.
      CORY [*To* RAYNELL.]   You go on in the house and change them shoes like
Mama told you so we can go to Papa's funeral.
      RAYNELL Okay, I'll be back.

[RAYNELL *exits into the house.* CORY *gets up and crosses over to the tree.* ROSE *stands in
the screen door watching him.* GABRIEL *enters from the alley.*]

      GABRIEL [*Calling.*]   Hey, Rose!
      ROSE Gabe?
      GABRIEL I'm here, Rose. Hey Rose, I'm here!

[ROSE *enters from the house.*]

      ROSE Lord . . . Look here, Lyons!
      LYONS See, I told you, Rose . . . I told you they'd let him come.
      CORY How you doing, Uncle Gabe?
220   LYONS How you doing, Uncle Gabe?

GABRIEL   Hey, Rose. It's time. It's time to tell St. Peter to open the gates. Troy, you ready? You ready, Troy. I'm gonna tell St. Peter to open the gates. You get ready now.

[GABRIEL, *with great fanfare, braces himself to blow. The trumpet is without a mouthpiece. He puts the end of it into his mouth and blows with great force, like a man who has been waiting some twenty-odd years for this single moment. No sound comes out of the trumpet. He braces himself and blows again with the same result. A third time he blows. There is a weight of impossible description that falls away and leaves him bare and exposed to a frightful realization. It is a trauma that a sane and normal mind would be unable to withstand. He begins to dance. A slow, strange dance, eerie and life-giving. A dance of atavistic signature and ritual.* LYONS *attempts to embrace him.* GABRIEL *pushes* LYONS *away. He begins to howl in what is an attempt at song, or perhaps a song turning back into itself in an attempt at speech. He finishes his dance and the gates of heaven stand open as wide as God's closet.*]

That's the way that go!

[*BLACKOUT.*]

TO WRITE ABOUT

Writing

One way to study something is to write about it.

It is both useful and important, when studying literature, to test an experience of reading stories, poems, and plays by writing essays about them—essays that explain or argue or compare or describe or discover or evaluate. Writing a paper, we clarify our ideas to ourselves; we explain to ourselves how we arrive at judgment; *but it is essential that we do not merely talk to ourselves.* We must address ourselves to others, in order to certify the clarity of our exposition. The paradox is familiar: in order to understand a subject ourselves, we need *first* to explain it to someone else. If our goal in studying literature is to arrive at sound taste and just discrimination, the purpose of paper writing is to examine and clarify the means by which we arrive at our judgments.

CHAPTER ONE

Ways of Attack, Methods of Approach, Common Pitfalls

The first general advice is this: use your intelligence. Maybe this advice sounds obvious, but many people need it when they begin to write about literature; they believe that, although it is appropriate to use intelligence in writing about history or psychology, the reasonable mind goes into suspense when it approaches literature. When these people begin to write about literature, they feel that they should show themselves responding, usually by intensity of feeling ("I cried when I finished the story"), instead of applying their brains and looking closely at the words in front of them. If you testify to your response, you write about yourself and not about the work in front of you. Probably most people would rather write about themselves than about anything else, but it is not the way to study literature. So, first of all, use your intelligence.

Second, be forthright in stating opinion; be brave. You learn by making a thesis and defending it, even if later you change your mind or discover that you have erred. A noncommittal paper usually has less to say (and is always more boring) than a paper that is vigorous but mistaken.

Third, while writing and revising a paper, continually question whether your writing serves the work that you write about. Do not digress into subjects that lead away from the work into the outside world; avoid personal anecdotes or responses that explore your inside world. Writing about Marsha Norman's *'night, Mother,* one student attacked American attitudes toward obesity; writing about Theodore Roethke's poem, "The Rose," another student recorded her botanic research into the flower. None of these students served the literary work itself by discussing something that the work suggested.

Use your brains; be candid in stating an opinion; keep your eye on the text.

Concentrate on the Text, the Words

Explicate

To *explicate* originally meant "to unfold." When we explicate a literary work we unfold its intricate layers of theme and form, showing its construction, understanding its lay-out—as if we spread a map out upon a table. We explicate to explain work that is dense and concentrated. We unfold a poem word by word or line by line, explaining as we go—giving reasons for each word, meanings, interpreting the interlocking relationships among words.

Some passages of fiction and drama, as well as poems, lend themselves to explication: one speech of Othello may reflect in miniature the complexity of the whole play. Or a paragraph of Flannery O'Connor may illuminate the author's methods of characterization. But, most often, you will use explication not so much for fiction or drama as for a brief poem or a portion of a longer poem—literature at its most concentrated, words at their most folded-up.

Remember that the goal of explication is not only close paraphrase of theme or content. Unfold structure as well as ideas. Pay attention not only to words in their meanings but words in their rhythms, sounds, tones, points of view, symbolism, and form as a whole. The goal of explication is to lay out in critical prose everything that an author has done in a brief passage or short poem; the best explication goes furthest toward this goal.

Explication does not move outside the work on the page. It does not concern itself with the author's life or times, but treats the work of art almost as if it were anonymous and timeless. The author's historical period, however, may determine the definitions of words. If a work is a hundred years old or older, it is almost certain that some of the words will have changed in their meanings, from the time when the author wrote to the time when the work is read. The explicator's task is to make explicit what an author may possibly have done in a work. Do not assume conscious intentions because you can never be aware of anyone else's intent. Limit your interpretation to what was possible in the author's time. An explicator must keep in mind the date of the work and the altering definitions of words. When an eighteenth-century writer like Alexander Pope speaks of "science," the word means something like "general knowledge" and not a curriculum of courses in chemistry, physics, and biology.

History may determine more than the definition of a word; it may determine its value or tone. When kings cut off people's heads, the word "king" meant something considerably different from the word in our ears today—when it is most likely to mean a long cigarette or a large bed. To investigate the meanings of words in different eras, it is useful to consult the *Oxford English Dictionary*. (For a reminder about the *OED* and how it works, look again at page 424.) Papers of explication, with their myopic attention to language, frequently quote dictionaries, and especially the *OED*.

Use common sense when you explicate. Some critics are tempted to go too far, to follow particular words down rabbit holes into Wonderland, using their ingenuity more than they use their intelligence. One student explicated a couplet by Robert Frost:

The old dog barks backward without getting up.
I can remember when he was a pup.

Desperate to write at least four hundred words about two lines—and having chosen the wrong poem to write four hundred words about—the student noticed that Frost had elsewhere written about Sirius the Dog Star, and that *dog* was "God" spelled backward, and wrote four hundred words to infuse astrology and theology into a pair of lines about aging and the passage of time. Some professional critics, with less excuse, have made careers out of ingenious explication no more sensible than this student's. Be sensible when you use your brains. Write so that you make sense of the whole work considered; do not lose yourself in fascinating improbabilities.

Other faults are probably more common. Fearing that she would not find enough to say, one student decided to write an eight-hundred-word theme explicating Walt Whitman's "Out of the Cradle Endlessly Rocking," which is itself considerably more than eight hundred words. To *explicate* the long Whitman poem, you would need to write a book, and a thin or watery explication is no explication at all. Do not write a summary and call it an explication. Pick something you can handle in the space you must fill. As with writing assignments in all courses of study, choice of topic is crucial to performance. If you make a sensible decision about your subject, the job of writing is half accomplished.

A student's explication of a poem is printed in "Writing about Poems," pages 1296–1298. "To Read a Poem" begins with a chapter that explicates—at greater length than students are expected to do—poems by Robert Frost and William Carlos Williams (pages 409 and 417).

Analyze

To analyze something is to separate it into parts in order to understand it. Explication deals exhaustively with something small; analysis deals with a part of something—perhaps the use of offstage noises during Chekhov's *The Cherry Orchard* or the repetition of certain phrases in D. H. Lawrence's "The Rocking Horse Winner" or Robert Frost's characterization in "The Death of the Hired Man." Attending to one part of a play, story, or poem, the analyst must relate that part to the work as a whole. Analysis uses summary or paraphrase to establish the whole, of which a part is analyzed. If an analysis fails to relate the part to the whole, the paper will seem pointless. Analysis may reveal that the poet repeats the word *blue* twenty-seven times in thirty-nine lines, but what does this repetition accomplish in the poem?

When you write about literary works of any length, analysis allows you to limit your topic. Never try to analyze a whole long work, any more than you would try to explicate a whole long work. Find ways to limit your topic by analysis—by the isolation of parts. No one can write a decent six-hundred-word theme on the whole of *The Death of Ivan Ilych.* Nor would an analysis of the characterization in that short novel be possible without a treatise of several thousand words. Analysis discovers part within part. It would be possible to analyze the characterization of Gerasim and relate Gerasim's character to the rest of the story.

When you consider writing an analytical paper, begin by thinking analytically about what you have read. Perhaps you have read Flannery O'Connor's "A Good Man Is Hard to Find" and find yourself fascinated and horrified by the character of The Misfit. Thinking analytically, you can separate the many ways in which you learned about The Misfit: by his actions, as reported by others; by implication, through the responses of other people to him; through his own speech; by his actions, as you watch him. As an example, you might find a disparity between your expectations before you meet him and the character you meet. You might write a paper that analyzes "The Misfit: Rumor and Reality." Looking at several poems by Robert Frost and fascinated by "Design," with its white flower that should have been blue, you might analyze "Color in Three Poems by Robert Frost."

When you write an analytical paper, always use the device of a *thesis* to hold the paper together, to give it coherence and design. An analytical paper asserts and defends an idea or thesis that can be reduced to a single sentence. A thesis is not the same as a topic: a topic is an area to investigate and a *thesis summarizes the result of an investigation*. A topic might be "Tolstoy's Characterization of Gerasim"; a thesis, derived from studying Tolstoy's characterization, makes a statement about the character, about the *result* of the characterization. A thesis summarizes the relationship of the analyzed part to the story as a whole; for example, "The character of Gerasim, as presented in action and dialogue by the author, relieves the dying Ivan Ilych by simple goodness." "For Robert Frost, in these poems, color disguises reality and suggests malignancy of matter or maker." "Showing The Misfit from afar and up close, Flannery O'Connor indicates the difference between terror, public and private."

Note that a thesis usually builds a topic into a clear assertion; it states a conviction about the topic which the author has won by study and thought. The paper's progress must support and demonstrate the validity of the thesis-assertion. It will achieve this goal by selection of detail and by reasoning. Using detail, the paper will quote or summarize action from the story or play, or quote an image from the poem, and interpret the function of the detail cited.

When you write an analytic paper, move from the general to the particular, then to the more particular, imitating a series of concentric circles. The biggest circle is the work itself, *The Death of Ivan Ilych.* Then the topic narrows, but remains broad: characterization, relation of character to theme. The topic narrows further to focus on Gerasim's character and its function in Tolstoy's story.

A student's analysis appears in "One Student's Paper from Start to Finish," pages 1287–1291. In "To Read a Story," the chapters about parts of the genre—tone and setting and theme and character—introduced the art of fiction by analysis of its component parts.

Compare and Contrast

A third kind of paper compares and contrasts two texts, usually in connection with a theme, or a formal device, or a technical element of the genre. For instance, a teacher might invite a comparison of Shakespeare's use of the sonnet form with Robert Frost's. (Comparison of two objects makes note of their likeness and unlikeness; henceforth we will speak only of comparing, but the word implies contrast.) A teacher might ask for a comparison of symbolism in two short stories, or of flashback in two plays. Because the terminus of a work of art is always important, a teacher might ask for a comparison of the endings or "curtains" of plays, or of the endings of poems, sometimes called "poetic cloture." Few teachers would ask students to compare the end of a poem with the end of a play. Although they are both literary works, it would be difficult to establish an area of similarity.

The process of comparison requires analysis of each work and notation of similarities and differences in matters covered.

Structure can be a problem in writing comparison and contrast. Read this passage from a student's draft:

> In the sonnet by Shakespeare every four lines is a whole separate idea, then the last two lines is another unit that is complete to itself. In Milton's the first part is eight lines and the second is six, without further subdivision. Shakespeare's rhyming separates the parts, not just the ideas. Milton's rhyming is more difficult, using just two rhymes in the octave (ABBAABBA) but therefore making the eight lines a smooth whole. Shakespeare . . .

These rapid oscillations are nervous; the reader's head snaps back and forth, as if watching a ping-pong game. Which poet is which, and who has the serve?

To be subjects for comparison and contrast, two works must share common ground. You would lack the basis to compare, say, a Keats poem with a Tolstoy novel, or a play with a sonnet sequence. Usually, you should compare works within the same genre, of similar length and quality. There are exceptions: you might compare two works by one author in different genres, perhaps a play and a short story by Chekhov. You might compare good and bad to illuminate criteria for judgment; or long and short, or genre with genre, to reveal strengths and weaknesses of different shapes and genres.

Mostly, finding the differences between two works starts with finding obvious similarities: two sonnets are each fourteen lines long, each within iambic pentameter, each rhymed throughout—and then the differences begin: structure of thought, rhyme, rhythm, metaphor, diction. One paper might end by asserting that, despite all the differences between them, the two sonnets share many qualities. Another might, with equal justice, argue that the differences outweigh the similarities. The conclusions will supply the writers' theses.

In a short paper of comparison, a writer may be able to write a paragraph or two on similarities, a paragraph or two on dissimilarities, and then reach a conclusion in the final paragraph. Such simplicity of structure is rare. More likely, the paper will need a structure something like this:

1. Statement of comparability
2. First similarity
   Work A
   Work B
3. Second similarity
   Work A
   Work B
4. First dissimilarity
   Work A
   Work B
5. Second dissimilarity
   Work A
   Work B
6. Conclusion based on evidence: thesis

Sometimes the grammar of a complex sentence can avoid the ping-pong monotony of compounds that flick our heads back and forth on our necks. Instead of saying "Work A is seven chapters which makes 110 pages and Work B is nine chapters which makes 131 pages," the writing can be more various: "While Work A compacts its seven chapters into 110 pages, Work B finds 131 pages sufficient for its nine."

A different structure takes a topic and then looks at each work two ways:

First item (like the use of a symbolic protagonist)
    Similarities between Works A and B
    Dissimilarities between Works A and B
Second item (like the means used for indicating symbolism)
    Similarities between Works A and B
    Dissimilarities between Works A and B

The material you collect for a paper determines its best form. Always decide on a thesis before writing. If you start writing in the sweet hope that a thesis will solidify from the air of your prose, you will write a disorganized paper.

Concentrate on Context

In studying literature, and in writing papers about it, you might concentrate not so much on the text as on the context of the work of art—the historical, personal, or literary backgrounds out of which the work came. This kind of criticism usually suggests cause and effect: the work has characteristics that derive from causes or sources in the author's society, personal life, or reading. To establish these characteristics, a critic must usually analyze or explicate; but then, having described these characteristics, the critic will shift emphasis from text to context.

History and Society

Whatever people do, they express the times they live in. When authors write, they reflect their own era by deploring it, be celebrating it, or even by writing to escape it. Social criticism sometimes supports philosophical positions. Some critics find literary form and content dominated and determined by economics; this criticism draws a line of causation from economic force to literary result. Other social criticism relates literature to theories of nationality and national history. Often, a social or historical critic tries to illuminate meaning by understanding the social and historical conditions under which older work was written, helping the modern reader to understand how it seemed to its contemporaries. Readers of ancient literature would be ignorant if they identified a queen as a figure resembling Queen Elizabeth II. Historical information can supply some notion of what it meant for Oedipus to be a king and of the somewhat different meaning of being a king, for Hamlet's father and Hamlet's uncle.

Because this sort of criticism requires historical knowledge, a student writing about the historical sources of a text must do research. In the library you can find what critics and historians have discovered about the relationship of Greek society to Greek drama or of Elizabethan culture to the sonnet sequence. Books are available to give backgrounds to different literary periods, setting forth the dominating philosophical, political, and religious ideas of an era. Basil Willey's *Eighteenth Century Background* is an example.

You need not write about remote times when you write social or historical papers. Writing about Carol Bly's "After the Baptism," one student made good use of a book studied for a sociology class, Christopher Lasch's *The Culture of Narcissism:* another relied on the "Living" section in a daily newspaper. Or, receding just a little further in time, a student could connect some poems by William Butler Yeats with the political situation of Yeats's Ireland by reading about the history of modern Ireland.

Biography

If a work of art cannot help but reflect its era, equally it cannot help but reflect the life of the man or woman who wrote it.

This statement is easy enough to make, but it is often difficult to demonstrate the connection between life and work: things are subtler than they seem. For instance, a poet may speak of himself overtly—Yeats wrote the line, "I, the poet William Yeats . . ."—yet make statements that are not historically true. If readers take the poet's word, they are often deceived. Writers frequently make up a self to speak from, and make great literature out of this fabrication. Walt Whitman constructed a character called "Walt Whitman" who was rough, manly, vigorous, brave, noisy; apparently the man himself was shy, and when he read his poems aloud spoke so softly that no one could hear him past the first row. T. S. Eliot proclaimed the impersonality of the artist, said that literature was a flight from personality, and proclaimed these doctrines when he had written "The Waste Land," which critics have begun to understand as the most personal of poems. By noticing disparities between the poets' proclamations and realities, students can begin to investigate the biographical context.

If you undertake biographical criticism, take warning. Perhaps no other approach to literature requires more sophistication. Like historical criticism, biographical criticism requires research as well as subtlety, psychological acumen, and modesty. The last quality may be the most urgent; you may suspect a biographical connection and suggest it by inference, but you seldom *know*. You know only the obvious. Reading a biography of Joseph Conrad, you can derive his writing about the sea from his experience as a sailor; but if you derive his ideas of evil from a childhood experience, you must be very careful.

In a college or university library, you can find many biographies of authors studied in this book. To name only a few, there is Richard Ellman's classic biography of James Joyce, published by the Oxford University Press as *James Joyce;* or William Pritchard's short biography of Robert Frost, *Robert Frost: A Literary Life Reconsidered*. There are several excellent biographies of John Keats, especially one by Walter Jackson Bate. Scholars don't know enough about Shakespeare and Sophocles to write genuine biographies of them, but there are many life stories of more recent playwrights, like Oscar Wilde and Tennessee Williams.

The Literary History

If a literary work is a big river, many of its tributaries have names. There is the language an author grows up speaking, the common speech of the time known and the place inhabited. There are the politics, economics, and social structures of an author's historical period. There are an author's personal psyche, upbringing, relationships with parents and siblings, even inheritance of characteristics. Another large tributary is the literature that the author has learned from.

Everything a writer has read—like everything that has happened in his or her life—can contribute to the work done. As athletes learn their moves from watching other athletes, as a guitar player learns chords from another musician, writers learn their craft from observing, analyzing, and loving earlier literary work. For this reason, literature has a history—a sequence if not a progress. (Progress would imply that literature was getting better all the time, a proposition difficult to support.)

To write a paper in literary history, the critic must know earlier literature. A reader of Conan Doyle's short stories about Sherlock Holmes may look for the influence of Edgar Allan Poe, who in "The Murders in the Rue Morgue" and other stories invented the modern detective story. You may try to discover what younger playwrights learned from their elders, or reverse the focus and write about the influence of earlier plays on later ones.

Although this discussion has separated these approaches to literature's context in order to describe them, they are not mutually exclusive. Before you write about influence on Keats, read his letters and consult his biographers.

Use explication and analysis, within the historical or biographical or literary methods, to establish claims about the text you discuss. It is most important to know what you are doing when you are doing it, and not to confuse your methods.

Common Pitfalls in Writing about Literature

A few common errors of method occur again and again.

The Personal Error

Many of the pitfalls that will threaten you when you write about literature take one shape: disregarding the work itself or its context, in favor of some irrelevant matter from the outside. One of the most frequent irrelevancies is our personal histories and beliefs.

To write a theme about one's personal experience can be a fine thing, but such a theme is *not* about literature. Perhaps because it seems easier to write out of personal experience, many people fall into the personal error. Taking the subject of D. H. Lawrence's "The Rocking Horse Winner," they tell about their own experience as a child with a rocking horse. Writing about Robert Frost's "Stopping by Woods on a Snowy Evening," they confide that they respond to this poem with special pleasure because they are so fond of horses. Writing about August Wilson's *Fences,* they speak of an uncle who played baseball in the minor leagues.

Even without personal narrative, there is danger of sanctifying personal response. It is a commonly held notion in the modern world that one person's opinion is as good as anybody else's. The defense of misreading is usually a smug "That is how *I* see it, and people are entitled to their own opinion." Democratic and egalitarian as the idea appears, it is an idea people hold to only so long as it conveniences them. The same student who holds that his opinion of Plato is as worthy as his philosophy professor's is unlikely to consider his professor's opinion of automobile repair as good as his own. Although there are many possible ways to understand a piece of literature, it is demonstrable that some interpretations are wrong; the text denies them. No one should go to jail for having a wrong opinion—but *opinions can be wrong*.

Literature is not a series of cloud shapes into which we can imagine all sorts of castles. Be governed by the text. Learn to submit to the text, to test all ideas and interpretations to the scrutiny of the text, and discard ideas that do not fit. This attitude requires humility before the fact of literature and expels or denies that conceit which says "Whatever *I* discover in the text is right for *me*." There is more of I/me in such reading than there is of literature.

Historical and Biographical Errors

A less egotistical fallacy is an equal impediment to good reading: the biographical or historical error that looks past an imaginary work to find events in the author's life or times of which the work is a representation or to which it responds. This error uses the text as a pretext for discourse, not about the work of art but about history or biography. Good criticism legitimately connects the work and the life, and the work and the times. However, too many readers pick on some portion of a story or a poem or a play, trust it as a piece of reality, and run away from literature to speak of history or biography. Yeats's poem "The Second Coming" (page 726) speaks of a time of chaos and turbulence, when "the center does not hold. / Mere anarchy is loosed upon the world. . . ." One student, noticing Yeats's dates (1865–1939) decided that Yeats was referring to the Great War of 1914–1918, and wrote:

> As Yeats predicted, the great empires came apart, the German and especially the Austro-Hungarian, but really it was not "mere anarchy" because out of parts of these empires Czechoslovakia was created, and the Treaty of Versailles which followed the war determined exactly who had authority over what territory. It is true that the League of Nations . . .

Here the historical error has run away with the paper, and the student has taken a few lines from the poem as a text for a summary of world history. Information is used not to illuminate the poem but to escape from it. As a matter of fact, this poem was written after World War I at the time of the Civil War in Ireland.

A similar error, biographical rather than historical, hurt a student's paper on Tillie Olsen's "I Stand Here Ironing." In the story, a mother ruminates about a daughter; the mother is a single parent who had lived through the Depression of the 1930s. In a biographical note before the story, the student learned that Tillie Olsen was of an age to live through the 1930s, that she had children, that she had been divorced. The student wrote:

> Tillie Olsen thinks these thoughts as she is ironing, remembering how her husband left her and she brought up her daughter and other kids by herself. Probably the sad experiences led her to becoming a writer, because she has so much to say about single parenting . . .

This student confuses the *I* of the short story with the author who wrote it, confuses the art of fiction with the facts of biography. It is tempting to make such a mishmash, when what you know of an author fits with the author's work. Avoid the temptation. Uninformed guesses are as likely to be wrong as right. When a writer undertakes a work, some of the material doubtless comes from the author's experience and observation, as true as a photograph or a verbatim account; and doubtless some of the material is imagined, made up in the services of a truth-telling broader than representation. For the most part, you cannot determine what is imagined and what is reported, and it does not matter. Your job as a reader is not to determine the one from the other but to read the whole as a work of art.

For some reason, readers make this error more often when they read poems than when they read stories. They read Robert Frost's "Stopping by Woods on a Snowy Evening." Making an assumption, they write: "When Robert Frost paused on a road in the woods to watch the snow fall . . . ." This particular notion may cause little trouble, but similar assumptions about all poems are foolish mistakes. For all we know, this poem may have started when Frost looked out his window to see a farmer or a Rural Free Delivery-man pausing to enjoy snow, and wrote the poem using what might be called an *Alien I.* No one knows. It is sensible, when you write criticism, to refer to "the speaker of the poem," although it is an awkward phrase, in order to avoid the mind-habit that thinks "Robert Frost" or "Elizabeth Bishop" or "Robert Browning." Robert Browning wrote dozens of monologues spoken by Renaissance painters and historical figures. Was he confessing to being Fra Lippa Lippi or a dying bishop? About as much as Shakespeare was confessing to being Othello.

Even in lyrics, there may be an Alien I. Even when a poet writes in his or her own name ("I, the poet William Yeats"), the name may be a fictional construction—or at any rate not an easy connection to any biographical facts that readers happen to know.

The Error of Influence

The error of influence blights some papers in literary history. There is a logical fallacy for which there is a Latin phrase, *post hoc ergo propter hoc:* "after the fact, therefore on account of the fact," describing the human tendency to mistake sequence for cause and effect. Many poor themes assume an influence on tenuous evidence. Even when the influence is genuine, it is not always important. It may be useful to notice that Hemingway's prose style derives from earlier authors, or to claim that without Ibsen's realistic theater we would not have the different, realistic theater of George Bernard Shaw. In each case, the causes are clear and the effects significant. But it does not follow that every literary phenomenon can usefully be discussed in terms of literary genealogy. Walt Whitman's style was a shock to the literary world it assaulted. We have learned that it derives partly from old Hebrew poetry translated by the scholars of the King James version of the Bible. Yet, for the most part, Whitman's style remains Whitman's invention. Anyone asserting literary influence ought to ask the question: If what I assert is true, what of it? It seems true enough, for instance, that the style of D. H. Lawrence's poetry altered after he had read Walt Whitman . . . but what of it? One student, noticing not only the influence but the background suggested by Whitman's style, came up with a notion of connection:

> Lawrence's rhythm and his use of parallel constructions changed only after he had studied Whitman in order to write his celebrated essay upon him. Such a fact, true enough, is merely a detail of influence. Whitman's rhythms apparently unleashed something in Lawrence, but what did they unleash? I want to suggest a connection which I cannot demonstrate. We know that much of Whitman's grammar, and therefore rhythm, came from the translations of Hebrew poetry, in its parallel syntactic structures, as rendered by the King James translators of the seventeenth century. We know from Lawrence's fiction and essays that he grew up listening to Bible readings and biblical oratory. Especially in his late work about the Book of Revelation, he reveals how essential to his emotional youth were the accents of prophecy. I suggest that Whitman affected Lawrence's poetry by way of the Bible. Whitman's rhythms showed Lawrence how to tap a source of feeling in himself.

Notice that this student takes a subject that has a factual base, and that the student uses biographical information and inference. We know that Lawrence read Whitman with great attention, because Lawrence wrote a famous essay about him. Sometimes influence-hunters have argued the influence of X on Y where it has been virtually certain that Y was wholly unaware of X, or could not possibly have read more than a story or two. Even more embarrassing, on occasion a critic has described the influence of A on B—when B died before A was born.

People will inevitably notice the genealogy of influence and write about it, without realizing that, because the study of influence is complex, it requires much knowledge, background, and experience of literature. Except in well-defined cases, the beginning student does best to avoid writing about influence or literary history.

Reading the Critics

If you are asked to write about history, biography, or literary influence, you are expected to use the library, to read historians, biographers, critics, and scholars.

If you explicate or analyze only—neither requires background information—how much should you use the library, how much should you refer to critics who have published analyses and explications of the works you are writing about?

Some teachers find it useful to ask their students to check out the critics, to test their own notions against the published work of professionals. Other teachers ask their students *not* to consult critics; some even forbid the practice. Many teachers feel that reading professional criticism inhibits their students and keeps them from developing their own ideas, from making mistakes and learning to correct their mistakes, from finding their own ways to evaluate and interpret. With an exaggerated respect for the printed word, these teachers argue, students become passive when they read critics; they assume that published work must be correct and they parrot it back in their own papers. On the other hand, students doing their own work without help or interference from professional critics, knowing that fellow students also work alone, do their best work.

Teachers differ, and their differing purposes lead to different agenda for writing about literature. If a teacher assigns a paper out of library research into critical work, the student must supply a list of works cited, and notes on the sources used. (See pages 1283–1286.) The student will wish to avoid any use of the ideas or language of others without acknowledgement. Unacknowledged appropriation is plagiarism—or literary theft. Never represent an idea or phrase as your own if you have come across it in anyone else's work.

CHAPTER TWO

To Write the Theme

Whether your topic is assigned or free, you need to gather ideas at the first stage of the paper-writing process, long before beginning your first draft.

Generally, you will know which works you are to write about. If you have a choice, you should pick the work that fascinates you most, even if you feel you do not understand it thoroughly. It is a deadly mistake to pick something uninteresting because you think it is simple or easy. If you are not interested, you will never write well about it. After the story, poem, or play is chosen, you must then undertake a series of thorough readings, pencil in hand. If the book is your own, you can write in the margins or underline. (If the book belongs to a library or to someone else, *do not make a mark on it.*) Some notes will spill over the page; keep a notebook beside the chair you read in. At first, you should not look for anything in particular, but take note of everything that strikes you—a pun, a piece of wit, a gesture that makes character, a rhyme, an ambiguity, a curious tone, a word to look up, a striking image, a puzzling repetition. You should make note not only of what you enjoy but of what puzzles or annoys you. You should read aggressively, demanding of each word or sentence that it reveal its function and usefulness. You should note big and note little, note outside and inside. If a short story occurs entirely in dialogue, or without dialogue, you should not neglect the fact. If a poem is fourteen lines long, you should remember that it can be embarrassing to write five pages on a brief poem without having mentioned that it is a sonnet.

You should read, taking notes, for one long session, then put the theme out of your mind for a day before you return to read again. It is astonishing how much thinking you do when you do not know you are thinking.

Any good composition text includes suggestions about the process of writing; these can help you when you write a paper on any subject. If you have taken a composition course, refresh your mind by glancing again at the remarks on process in your textbook. In Chapter 3 of *Writing Well,* by Donald Hall and Sven Birkerts, the authors suggest Brainstorming (taking rapid and undisciplined notes around a topic), Sprinting (writing rapidly to expand notes, generating further ideas), Cross-examining (asking, of one's own writing: Who? What? When? Where? Why? How? in order to expand and clarify), and invoking The Critic Inside (self-scrutiny, one part of the brain finding fault with another).

The next stage is to organize notes toward a conclusion. If you are writing an explication, you may use all the notes that continue to look sensible, that contribute to understanding and elucidating the meaning and form of the text. If you are writing analysis, you will need to narrow the topic, which will probably mean discarding many notes. Look for a topic large enough to be worth the time and effort, small enough to be handled in the space assigned. Analyzing the use of a single set in Marsha Norman's 'night Mother, you can discard your notes on characterization by diction, the prevalence of cliché, and religious symbolism.

Writing and Revising

Notes make a blueprint for constructing the paper. It helps to make an informal outline, a recognition of what needs to follow what, in order to demonstrate a thesis. These notes can be numbered in a notebook, or transferred to three-by-five-inch cards and stacked in order, or cut from long sheets and piled in appropriate piles. Probably, many notes will refer to pages and lines of the text; the heart of literary criticism is intelligent quotation. No amount of good argument—about characterization in Chekhov, or dialogue in Katherine Anne Porter—will persuade the reader so much as a brief, accurate example. Any paper will need to assert a thesis, list occasions, and exemplify.

You should always try to spend at least one day away from your paper, between a draft and a revision. Revising, you should check for good, complete sentences, fresh language, logic, accurate quotation, and correct spelling. Try for conciseness. We all use too many adjectives; you may find that you can drop a whole paragraph here and there. If you leave big margins in typing a first draft, or type it triple-space, you will be grateful for the correcting space. Fill out paragraphs that remain thin; find more reasons, more examples, and bolster your points. Examine the order of ideas, arguments, and examples.

See "One Student's Paper from Start to Finish" (1287–1291) for an example of one student's process in writing a paper.

Manuscript Form

Teachers sometimes require particular form for papers. In the absence of other directions, the notes that follow should serve in most circumstances.

Paper, Margins, etc.
Use 8½-by-11-inch paper.

Type, if you can, double space. Avoid erasable typing paper; it smudges. If you write by hand, use paper with deep lines, or use every other line on narrow-lined paper. Use only one side of any piece of paper.

Put your name, your teacher's name, your class and section number, and the date in the upper right-hand corner of your paper.

Leave margins of $1^{1}/_{4}$ inches at top, bottom, and sides. Always make a copy—a carbon or a photocopy—before you hand your paper in.

Number your pages.

Staple your pages together in the upper left-hand corner.

Titles

Underline the titles of books and plays (*The Old Man and the Sea, Othello*). Put quotation marks around titles of short stories ("A Worn Path") and poems shorter than book length ("Stopping by Woods on a Snowy Evening"). A book-length poem's title is underlined (*The Iliad*). Note that titles underlined in papers will be *italicized* in print.

Quotations

Use quotation marks around excerpts from literature that you quote within sentence and paragraph:

> When William Carlos Williams looked at a primitive piece of farm machinery, he saw something which he made important through the power of his seeing; he saw it "glazed with rain / water . . ." He saw it "beside the white / chickens . . ." But seeing was not the only sense the doctor . . .

(Use a /, when quoting a poem, to indicate a linebreak.) When you separate a quotation from sentence and paragraph—indenting it and typing it single space—do not use quotation marks. The spacings of the typography indicate that it is a quotation.

> When William Carlos Williams looked at a primitive piece of farm machinery, he saw something important because of the power of his seeing:
>
>> glazed with rain
>> water
>>
>> beside the white
>> chickens
>
> But seeing was not the only sense that the doctor employed in making his poems. . . .

These two ways of quoting are appropriate to different lengths of quotation. When you are quoting only a few words, include the quotation within the paragraph, and put quotation marks around it. When you quote more than a few words, indent the quotation, single-space it, and omit quotation marks—except when the quoted passage itself has already used quotation marks.

Notes

Use parenthetical notes in your papers to acknowledge your sources, whenever you quote or paraphrase from a poet, storywriter, playwright, critic, scholar, biographer, historian—or even from the *Encyclopedia Britannica*. You must take full notes as you read for a paper, researching or preparing; you must remain scrupulous in noting the sources of your ideas or words. If you do this, no one will ever accuse you of plagiarism, which is stealing, borrowing, or otherwise appropriating other people's ideas or sentences.

When you clearly quote from the text you are discussing, and there is no ambiguity as to the source of your quotation (usually true in an explication) there is no point in giving a parenthetical note about the source of a text. But when there is any vagueness about the source of something quoted, identify the source in a note inside parentheses.

It is pleasant or elegant to give the source of a quotation unobtrusively, in the text of the paper, without obvious notation. In the flow of a sentence, you can give the information that "Not until the fifth line does Robert Frost use an image of sight," instead of placing parentheses after the quoted image, saying "(Frost, line 5)." But if it is awkward to include such information in the flow of your sentences, use parentheses. Footnotes are the old-fashioned way—little figures raised above the line of the text, coded to small-print notes at the bottom of the page. Current style is to make notes in parentheses, within paragraphs, where they are easier to read: "Early in Othello, (I, iii, 74–84), we discover that . . . ."

When quoting, be sure to copy the quotation accurately; put quotation marks around the words quoted, and, in parentheses, identify the source of the quotation. Use the same system of parentheses when acknowledging the source of facts or opinions rather than direct quotation. At the end of a paper, include in a list of works cited the bibliographical material that readers will need if they want to consult sources. (See the next section.) In the notes to your text, to make reading smoother and quicker, use only the last name of an author, editor, or translator; or a short title and appropriate page numbers. A note in the text may be as brief as "(Tregear 22)" or "(*Country Journal* 34)."

When you mention an author's name in a sentence, you need not repeat it in the note:

In Perelman's discussion of the poetic line (82–83), she . . .

Here, page numbers are sufficient. If you refer to a whole work, you may eliminate the need for a note by quoting the author's name within your sentence:

All through *Workbook,* Perelman makes constant reference to Saussure's distinction.

A curious reader, wanting to consult Perelman, can discover the identity of this work in the list of works cited. If you refer to more than one book by the same author, you will need to identify the specific title in the sentence or in the parenthetical note.

When you have something long to say, parentheses would interrupt the text at too great a length. You may need a long note, to comment on or to qualify something that you have said in your text, or to mention information that you need to include but that is not important enough to interrupt the text. You may need to list a series of references, simply because the parenthetical statement inside the text would become too long and would disrupt the reader's attention. In such a case, use footnotes, or notes at the end of the paper, with a superscribed number.

For additional advice on notation, consult the new *MLA Handbook*. It is important to keep notes simple and concise. Here are some samples:

A book with one author: (Perelman 22)
A book with two or three authors: (Cordell and Matson 148)
A book with more than three authors: (Leavitt et al. 15)
A book with an editor: (Henderson 126)
An article from an edited book: (Lish 235)
A translated book: (Schulz 53)
One volume of a multi-volume: (Johnson 2: 929–940)
The whole volume: (Johnson Vol. 2)
A periodical article: (Mumford 198)

Some abbreviations frequently used in notes and lists of works cited include:

cf.	compare (not "see")
ch., chs., chap.	chapter(s)
ed.	edited by, editor
e.g.	for example
et al.	and others
i.e.	that is
illus	illustrated
ms., mss.	manuscript(s)
n., nn.	note(s)
n.d.	no date of publication given in book
n.p.	no place of publication or no publisher given
rev.	revised
trans	translated by translator
viz	namely (however, avoid using)
rpt.	reprinted by, reprint
U.P.	university press; used in documentation

List of Works Cited

In the new MLA system of notes, as described above, the list of works cited is more important than it used to be. Notes are briefer, filled out by the list. It is important to include all required information in the correct order.

When you have consulted books or magazines in order to write a paper, you must mention everything you have looked at, on a separate sheet at the end of the paper; this makes your bibliography or list of works cited. You should list materials consulted even if you have not made conscious use of them. Arrange the list alphabetically by the author's last name, or anonymous works alphabetically by title, beginning with the first word after an article.

When you do library work, preparatory to a paper, you should always remember that you will need bibliographical information. Keep a record of *everything* looked at—book, magazine article, encyclopedia—on a separate three-by-five-inch card. This record should include the information that you require for your list of works cited, in this order: author, title, publication information. Start with the author's last name, comma, and first name (Norman, Marsha). Then, after a period, include the full title and subtitle (underlined), place of publication (only the first place, if there is more than one), publisher, and date of publication. Generally, publishers are listed by the first proper noun of their names: *Random House* becomes *Random*. When the first noun is a first name, this becomes an exception; *William Morrow & Co.* becomes *Morrow,* not *William.* Include in the list of works cited any special information acquired from the book's title page. Is it a second edition? Twelfth? Is it a reprint? If it is a translation, who is the translator? Is there more than one volume? Which volume is cited?

For a periodical article, record the author, if one is named. Put the title of the article in quotation marks, and underline the title of the periodical; add the volume number if there is one, the date of the journal issue, and the page numbers that you have consulted.

Here are some sample citations. Please notice punctuation.

A book with one author:
Newman, Edwin. Strictly Speaking New York: Warner, 1975.

A book with two or three authors:
Cordell, Richard A. and Lowell Matson. The Off-Broadway Theater
    New York: Random, 1959.

A book with more than three authors:
Leavitt, Emily Stewart, et al. Animals and Their Legal Rights
    3rd ed. Washington, DC: Animal Welfare Institute, 1978.

A book with an editor:
Henderson, Bill, ed. The Art of Literary Publishing Yonkers:
    Pushcart, 1980.

An article from an edited book:
Lish, Gordon. "True Confessions of a Failed Reader." The Art of
    Literary Publishing Ed. Bill Henderson. Yonkers: Pushcart,
    1980. 230-238.

A translated book:
Schulz, Bruno. The Street of Crocodiles Trans. Celina
    Wieniewska. New York: Penguin, 1977.

An article in a magazine:
Pistorius, Alan. "A Berry Collection." Country Journal XIII no.
    2 Feb. 1986: 16-18.

CHAPTER THREE

One Student's Paper from Start to Finish

In a course introducing literature, an instructor assigned a paper on fiction, asking students to write on one of three stories: Kate Chopin's "The Story of an Hour," Alice Mattison's "The Middle Ages," or Kurt Vonnegut, Jr.'s "Harrison Bergeron." A student named Ralph Giannello chose to write about "Harrison Bergeron." The assignment called for analysis in five hundred words: find a topic, elaborate it into a thesis, and prove the thesis.

Ralph liked the story, but at first had no notion of what to say about it. He reread the story, making checks in the margin when something caught his attention, not searching for a particular topic. Then he read it again, more slowly, and took notes in his notebook, naming the points of interest. Here is the first page of notes he took:

```
unusual name? Harrison President of U.S.? (Two)--Bergeron?
2081--sig. to date?
"finally equal" first sentence starts theme of story?
"equal" in first three sentences
Handicapper--look up
brains equal unfair advantage
buzzer
ballerinas with weights--horses--"handicap"
milk bottle/hammer
Diana Moon Glompers--?name
gunfire
47 lbs bird shot
all talk is clichés
siren
ANTI-UTOPIA
Harrison's "handicaps," appearance
auto-collision
"I am the Emperor"? crazy?
```

```
dance/music/art
law-land/gravity
suspended in air? fantasy?
sadness/"forget sad things"
riveting gun
say that again--old joke
```

When Ralph looked up "handicap," he confirmed his suspicion that the word meant first a forced or assumed disadvantage, as in a horse race. The dictionary listed "physical disability"—a meaning with which Ralph was more familiar—as secondary. In a horse race, he read, a horse may be handicapped by weights added to its saddle, making it equal to horses normally less swift.

Looking over his list, thinking of the story, Ralph decided that the author's topic was equality. "But"—he wrote in a note—"it's not equality like people being born with equal rights before the law. It's a kind of equality which makes everybody exactly the same. Not equal but average ability and achievement. Bright and beautiful handicapped down to average brains and average looks." He had noted that Vonnegut's story was an "anti-utopia," set in a future that exaggerated a social idea into a horrid reality.

Trying to formulate a thesis, Ralph wrote at the bottom of his notes, "Vonnegut imagines a future where everybody is forced to be average regardless of ability." True enough, he thought, but this thesis was obvious and uninteresting, and omitted much of the story. He tried again: "George and Helen Bergeron have a genius son named Harrison, driven crazy by . . ." He stopped, reminding himself that a thesis was not a plot summary.

He looked back over his notes. He drew lines through some of them, because they led nowhere, and put additional question marks where he was unsure. Then he put letters beside items that seemed to go together.

```
A    "Finally equal" first sentence starts theme of story?

A    "equal" in first three sentences

C    Handicapper--look up

A    brains equal unfair advantage

B    buzzer

C    ballerinas with weights--horses--"handicap"

B    milk bottle/hammer

C    Diana Moon Glompers--?name

B    gunfire

C    47 lbs bird shot

D    all talk is clichés

B    siren

!!! ANTI-UTOPIA
```

```
C   Harrison's "handicaps," appearance

B   auto-collision

A?  law-land/gravity

D   sadness/"forget sad things"

B   riveting gun

D   say that again--old joke
```

Then he noticed something about the notes he had labeled B. All of the noises that entered George's head are noises that we live with today; we needn't wait until 2081 for them. Ralph had heard the phrase "noise pollution" to describe the racket of daily life in cities, on highways, at shopping centers, and on college campuses. George's intelligence and concentration span is limited by things that we all live with: buzzers, hammerings, gunfire, sirens, collisions, and riveting guns. This anti-utopia, Ralph saw, was not just Vonnegut's vision of a bad future; it was also his satire of a bad present.

Not sure just how much to make of this idea, Ralph decided to write a rapid paragraph about it, to see what he could generate. He had tried this technique, called Sprinting, when he took composition in the autumn of his freshman year: you were supposed to relax and write quickly without worrying about structure or correctness. On a fresh sheet of paper he wrote:

```
In a science-fiction story usually the noises would be coming
out of green zappers fired by punk androids at houseflies that
are big as elephants but in this story the noises that bug
everybody aren't science-fiction noises, I mean their things
that you see around us all the time like my roommate's
typewriter that drives me crazy right now and in the story its
stuff like hammers and gunshots. So this isn't science-fiction
exactly or it is but what you look at or get bothered by is
stuff right around you so that's the point not worrying about
the future. The thing with the future is politics not science.
```

When he finished, he derived another note from his Sprinting, and began to develop a theme for his paper: that "Harrison Bergeron" was satire of present-day conditions.

This notion added something to his thesis: "Although Kurt Vonnegut, Jr.'s science-fiction story 'Harrison Bergeron' is an anti-utopia attacking the idea that equality means being the same, it is also a satire of present conditions which prevent individuals from exercising their brains and talents." It was too long a thesis sentence, he decided, but he used it tentatively, as a map, when he read the story again, underlining and making check marks.

He wrote a draft, let it sit overnight, and rewrote it; he omitted a discussion of whether Harrison was crazy or pretending to be crazy when he declared himself emperor, and whether he really floated in the air or the author exaggerated to show how graceful the dancing was. These speculations did not advance his thesis, nor was it essential to deal with them in order to construct his paper. (If he had talked about everything he thought of, his paper would have lacked focus.) He expanded his remarks on the nature of the handicapping, which he felt was needed for his critical argument. He rewrote the paper, corrected it again for spelling, paragraphing, and sentence structure, typed a fresh copy, and handed it in. The last thing he thought of was a title.

Ralph Giannello
English 102, sec. 4
Dr. Carmichael
April 10, 1991

THE FUTURE NOW

Kurt Vonnegut, Jr.'s "Harrison Bergeron" is science fiction because it is set in the future, but it is not a future of space travel, time warps, or little people with green brains. It is a future of political oppression, in the name of equality, enforced by gadgets. The story's theme is philosophical or political, and by making an anti-utopia in the future Vonnegut criticizes present-day society.

In the world of 2081 which Vonnegut imagines, the United States has made it illegal, by "the 211th, 212th and 213th Amendments to the Constitution," to be anything but average. Being average is called being equal. The author makes his premise clear at the very beginning of the story, when he writes that now

> . . . everybody was finally equal. They weren't only equal before God and the law, they were equal every which way. Nobody was smarter than anybody else. Nobody was better looking than anybody else.

The author shows us how the government enforces equality by means of handicaps. The strong carry weights, like a fast horse handicapped in a race to make it average in strength and speed. Beauty is disguised to look ordinary, and brains are befuddled by the constant interruption of noise.

The story's events hold up to ridicule this idea of equality as sameness. We watch graceful dancers made to dance badly, and musicians prevented from making beautiful music. Because he shows us good things prevented, the author clearly indicates that he disagrees with an interpretation of equality which hinders excellence. When the author says, in the passage quoted, "They weren't only equal before God and the law," I think that he shows us the true ideal of equality, the ideal from the old Constitution before these amendments.

At the story's end the author gives us no hope for the future. The revolution attempted by Harrison Bergeron, seven-foot genius and son of the story's main characters, fails when he is killed by the United States Handicapper General, who is in charge of enforcing equality-as-averageness. But I feel that the story is not so much a prediction of the future as a criticism of the present world.

First, George and Hazel Bergeron talk exactly like ordinary people right now. Hazel talks in clichés and bad grammar that make her sound like a character in a television show. "You been so tired lately--kind of wore out." "He tried to do the best he could with what God gave him." The story ends with Hazel repeating one of the oldest jokes in the world. George says, "You can say that again," and so she says it again. Either she repeats an old joke or she is dumb enough to think he actually wants her to repeat herself.

George talks in clichés too, and seems to believe in enforced mediocrity, but Vonnegut shows him struggling more than Hazel does. George keeps starting to have a thought, but his chief handicap-gadget is a radio in his car which keeps blasting noise so that he cannot think consistently. As Vonnegut tells it, George's attention span is destroyed, not by futuristic noises of 2081, but by things which blast our eardrums every day right now--by the noises of a buzzer, for instance, or of an automobile collision, or of a riveting gun. Vonnegut shows us that his dreaded world of the future, where noise pollution prevents us from thinking consecutive thoughts, is already here--or at least beginning. He suggests that noise pollution has the effect of making us all average in our brains, and suggests that maybe some people like it that way.

CHAPTER FOUR

To Write on Each Genre

The nature of each genre suggests special advice. The first part of this appendix is a general prologue to approaching each category of reading covered in the book.

Writing About Fiction

Explicating Fiction

Because explication is line-by-line explanation, it would take too long to explicate a whole work of fiction. Sometimes, however, you can explicate a paragraph or a few lines of a work of fiction, relating it to the whole. In teaching James Joyce's huge novel *Ulysses,* some teachers have found it useful to assign one paragraph, asking students to explain everything in it and relate it to the rest of the novel. In a less demanding version of that assignment, a teacher may assign explication of one significant passage from a short story. A passage of description or setting may relate to a protagonist's character, the way Faulkner's description of the town's architecture in "A Rose for Emily" applies to Miss Emily herself. Or, a writer may explicate the last few lines of a story—including perhaps dialogue, narrative, and description—word by word, and reveal the whole story by explaining its conclusion.

If most fiction does not lend itself to explication so well as most poetry, this distinction reveals something about the two genres. As you think about writing a paper on a short story, if the work allows you to consider explication at all, you may realize something about its style: that it is written with some of the density and verbal cross-reference that is usually associated with poetry. Such an observation applies to works by James Joyce, Ernest Hemingway, and William Faulkner—all of whom published poetry before they published fiction.

Analyzing Fiction

In the analysis of fiction, separate it into parts and examine one part. In analyzing "Harrison Bergeron," Ralph isolated elements of theme. (If you look back at Ralph's essay, think of it not only as a model but as an example subject to improvement.) For a reminder of the elements of fiction, look again at the chapter headings of "To Read a Story"—plot, character, setting, and the rest. Remember that not every story contains all elements; many stories, for instance, do not deal in symbols.

For an analysis of plot, look at the first chapter of "To Read a Story," where several pages about "A Rose for Emily" analyze Faulkner's manipulation of plot. Because these pages intend to describe the story as a whole, they also include remarks on characterization, setting, and other elements. Analyzing plot in particular, the writer will want to understand the plot function of everything reported; if an episode seems out of place, what in fact is its use to the story, and why does it seem out of place? If sequence is other than chronological—if there is a flashback, for instance—what purpose does the sequence serve? Does the plot's action surprise? Why? Is there foreshadowing? What is the climax? The dénouement? In analyzing any element of fiction, you will do well to reread the chapter about the element you are analyzing, before writing your paper.

Often, a useful subject for analysis in fiction is the characterization of one important character. Writing an analysis of characterization, you should try to note *everything* in the story that gives an impression of the character chosen. Such impressions may derive from the character's major actions, from minor gestures of hands and eyebrows, from the character's speech or dialogue and other characters' response to it, from others' speech and actions in the character's absence, from the setting, if it is described to suggest something about the character, and sometimes from the author's outright statements, tone, and point of view.

Point of view is itself subject to analysis, especially when it undergoes subtle change, as it does in Chekhov's "Gooseberries," or when it is especially important to theme. Any of fiction's elements may be subject to analysis.

Examples of analysis, in writing about fiction, occur in each chapter of "To Read a Story." Look back at these chapters for reminders of how to analyze fiction.

Comparison and Contrast in Writing About Fiction

When you use comparison and contrast for papers in fiction, you are often comparing thematic matters, usually not the entire theme of stories but parts of themes. For instance, Eudora Welty in "A Worn Path" and Flannery O'Connor in "A Good Man Is Hard to Find" write about old women. A comparison and contrast might be "The Aging of Opposites." Or, a theme about two sorts of female endurance might combine "A Worn Path" with Tillie Olsen's "I Stand Here Ironing."

Comparisons and contrasts of fiction's technical elements can provide excellent subjects. Compare, for instance, the use of the first-person narrator in "I Stand Here Ironing" and Alice Munro's "Friend of my Youth." Compare the use of setting in Raymond Carver's "A Small Good Thing" and Carol Bly's "After the Baptism."

By and large, papers in comparison require two analyses followed by a point-by-point comparison and contrast of the fictional techniques the analyses have supplied. Sometimes the similarities and sometimes the differences will take the greater attention: You might compare two stories using the same point of view; you might contrast two stories using different points of view.

Sample Topics in Writing about Fiction

D. H. Lawrence's Use of Repetition in "The Rocking Horse Winner"
"I" and "I" in Olsen and Munro
Two Viewpoints: "He" and "I" in Carver and Munro
The Characterization of The Misfit
Gerasim's Part in Tolstoy's Whole
Themes of Two Cultures: "Jasmine" and "Storyteller"
Tone in Thurber: Who Loathes What and Why?
A Grandmother's Role—Character and Theme in a story by Flannery
    O'Connor
Uses of setting in Frank O'Connor
Joyce to the World: Adverbs in "Counterparts"
Imagery in a Story: Ace's Last Dance
Repetition in Lawrence and Hemingway: A Contrast
Tone of Dialogue in Porter
A Good Man's Faith: Theme in an Allegory
Barthelme and the Cliché

Things to Avoid When Writing About Fiction

A pitfall in writing about fiction is plot summary. We have all grown up listening to friends make forty-five-minute summaries of thirty-minute television shows. Unless instructed otherwise, assume that the reader knows what happens in the story, and refer only to those events that are germane to the thesis of the paper. Do not summarize except in the service of explanation. Anything else is padding.

Remember as well to avoid both the personal and the biographical errors. If you write about stories by Joyce or Frank O'Connor, it is irrelevant that your grandfather is Irish, or that you spent a summer in Dublin. If you write about Erdrich's "The Leap," it is irrelevant to speak of an aunt who worked in a circus.

Writing About Poetry

At first glance, it may seem easier or harder to write about poems than about stories—easier because poems tend to be shorter, harder because poems have the reputation of being difficult to understand. Although they are usually short, poems are complex and require a dense and attentive reading. Yet, if you write about a poem that you respond to, one that pleases you in its sound and its wisdom, you can find writing about it a pleasure as compact and shapely as the poem itself. With a short poem, you can have the pleasure of saying everything you know about it, which you cannot do with a story or a play. Writing about poems tests your ability, most of all, to respond to the words writers use, to their association and connections, to their connotations and denotations, to their rhythms and their sounds.

Explicating Poems

For an example of explication, look again at the poems explained in the first chapter of "To Read a Poem"—Frost's "Stopping by Woods on a Snowy Evening" and Williams's "so much depends." These explications are longer and more detailed than most teachers will expect from students beginning a study of literature, but they give notions of method and range. Remember that when you explain a poem or a passage in poetry, you should attend to form as well as to content; you must not simply indicate intellectual understanding by paraphrase, but account for the shape and sound of a poem as well as its paraphrasable content.

Paraphrase is a necessary *part* of explication; it is not the whole thing. Many critics beginning an explication find it useful to summarize the action and theme of the poem as a prelude, giving a brief account of the whole before concentrating on the parts. This summary is like the beginning of a speech in a debate, which tells us the general conclusion the argument will lead to. With explication as with argument, the proof is in the pudding. The step-by-step explanation of the use and function of particular words is the pudding of explication.

To write a paper of explication, you should always pick a poem that pleases you, one that you find fascinating. It will not serve to choose something you do not respond to, or something about which you find little that is intriguing. It is all right (it is possibly even good tactics) if something in the poem either displeases you or remains puzzling. When you have chosen a poem to write about, or narrowed your choice down to a few, you should read and reread. Read with a pencil or pen in hand, taking notes both of observations about the poem and about puzzlements. After many readings, with note-taking, it is wise to refresh your mind about the elements of poetry and reread the poem again, to notice matters possibly ignored. Everyone is naturally more sensitive to certain elements than to others. Perhaps you find yourself sensitive to the poem's structure as argument, if it is a poem that structures an argument. Perhaps you need to look harder to pick up the poem's images and their connections. Use the elements of poetry, as noted in the chapters of this text, as a checklist suggesting what to look for. Not all poems will satisfy all items on the checklist of chapters. But it is your task as explicator to make yourself aware of everything that is there.

Here is a paper by a student named Mary Lois Goldberg, who picked a short poem by Robert Frost for explication.

Mary Lois Goldberg
English 102, Sec. 1
Dr. Smith
March 2, 1991

MISTAKING SNOW

Only eight lines long, Robert Frost's "A Patch of Old Snow"
appears as slight as it is brief. Close reading of the poem,
however, reveals that its off-hand manner or tone conceals
something more serious than first appears. In this disparity
between appearance and reality, between apparent lightness and
real seriousness, we see a poem typical of Frost.

The title gives us no problem, because the poem's primary
subject is simply "a patch of old snow." Somebody might try to
work something out of the dictionary definition of "patch" as a
"piece of material used to mend or cover a hole or a weak
spot."[1] Perhaps the poem in its playful tone acts as a
concealment of its own seriousness--but really I don't think
the title expresses an idea of hiding. The snow is "a patch"
because it is smaller than the earth it lies on.

One of the first things I noticed about this poem was its
rhyme, which is really good! They are rhymes which you would
never expect. First, a verb with a -ed ending--"guessed,"
which we pronounce the same as "guest" really--is rhymed with
the noun "rest." Just because they are spelled differently,
and maybe because they are different parts of speech, they seem
as if they should not go together, but they do. Then the
second rhyme is a rhyme of two syllables, which is unusual in
itself: "overspread it" and "read it." Although the parts of
speech are the same--a verb followed by a pronoun object--the
first of the verbs has three syllables and the second has one.
This difference contributes to the surprise of the rhyme, and
the surprise gives part of the poem's pleasure.

The poem is written not only in rhyme but in meter. The
first and third lines of each stanza have three feet and the
second and fourth have two. (Trimeter and dimeter.) Some of
the feet are three-syllable ($\smile\smile-$) and some are two-syllable
($\smile-$). I don't know whether to call the meter anapestic or
iambic. Here is my scansion:

Thĕre's ă pátch | ŏf olď snów | ĭn ă córnĕr
   Thăt Ĭ shóuld | hăve guéssed
Wăs ă blów | ăwăy páp | ĕr thĕ wínd
   Hăd bróught | to rést.

[1] "patch," <u>Webster's New Collegiate Dictionary</u>, 1981 ed.

Ĭt ĭs spéck | lĕd wĭth gríme | ăs íf
    Smăll prínt | ŏvĕrspréad ĭt
Thĕ néws | ŏf ă dáy | I've fŏrgóttĕn--
    Ĭf Ĭ év | ĕr reád ĭt.

Thirteen of the twenty feet are anapestic and seven are iambic;
maybe we should call the meter anapestic with iambic
tendencies. Of the eight lines, half have feminine endings,
including the last line of the poem.

Having written all this about meter, I am not sure what to
say about it. I wonder if the tentativeness or uncertainty of
the meter--all those extra syllables, or all those syllables
cut away--might combine with the surprise of the rhyme to pull
you along feeling that you are not just sure where you are
going. But with the direct (if surprising) rhyme, and the
foot-numbers staying the same, when you come to the end you
know that this is the only place you could have come to.

Each stanza is composed of one sentence, and each sentence
also seems tentative or uncertain at first, and finally
conclusive. Frost built the sentences so that they stick
together (which is like the direct rhyme and count of feet) but
so that it's hard to see how they stick together (which is
like the witty rhymes and mixed feet). The "I should have
guessed" in the second line is an interruption to "that . . .
was"--except that without the interruption the sentence would
not make any sense because it would mix present and past
tenses. Therefore the sentence looks at first as if it were
careless or off-hand, but when you put it together, you see
that all the parts fit and are necessary.

Finally I want to talk about the meaning or theme in the
poem, and I come to it only now because I think that the poem
needs its own sound-shape and sentence-shape to say what it
has to say. The statement of the poem is easy enough to
paraphrase: I see a piece of snow and at first I think it is
a piece of newspaper because it looks like one, but it is a
small matter anyhow. But the poem seems to me to imply
something more.

There are two things I want to notice, one in each stanza.
First is "paper," which could be wrapping paper or waxpaper but
turns out to be newspaper. I think that the delay in
discovering the kind of paper is a teasing which is like the
surprise of the rhymes. Then in the second stanza, "speckled
with grime" is an accurate image for old snow--and when I
notice this I suddenly realize that this poem about something
visible has hardly any images in it. The title, "A Patch of
Old Snow," is an image, but not a vivid one. If this poem
does not end in description, then what does it end in?

> I think this poem is about a casual, unremarkable visual
> mistake--and then it says, "So what; it doesn't matter." At
> first the poet reports that he "would have guessed" that a
> clump of old snow was a piece of paper. We give easy assent
> to the comparison: yes, in April a piece of dirty snow does
> look like a newspaper. Then in the second stanza Frost
> explains that grime is speckled on snow as print overspreads
> paper, almost as if he needs to say: look; this mistake was
> easy to make! Then, as if he felt that he had protested too
> much, he says that the newspaper (which does not exist except
> as a mental error) probably did not have any news important
> to him anyway, because he would have forgotten it. As his
> withdrawal seems complete, he withdraws further: "If I ever
> read it." He has made a mistake and explained, and then said
> it's not worth worrying about, but at the same time he has
> shown himself worrying about it--a lot!

Another student in the same class decided that *patch* was a key word, that it implied diminishment, concealment, and repair in the poem—and wrote a good paper to defend her ideas.

Analyzing Poems

Analysis of a poem isolates a part, identifies it, and relates the part to the whole. Where explication unfolds a poem or passage, analysis deals with one element, usually in a longer poem or part of a poem. In the text of "To Read a Poem," many poems or passages are analyzed for one element—for the use of language, imagery, metaphor, allusion, symbolism, rhythm, assonance, alliteration, and meter. For examples, look at the metaphorical analysis of a Shakespearean sonnet on page 497, or the analysis of allusion in Louise Bogan's epigram on page 460.

Students writing analytical papers often limit their topics by concentrating on one part of an element. Theodore Roethke's "The Meadow Mouse" (page 680) includes so many images that "Imagery in 'The Meadow Mouse'" would make a long paper; we could narrow it to "'My Thumb of a Child': Images of Infancy in Roethke's 'Meadow Mouse.'" Writing about Frost's "Stopping by Woods on a Snowy Evening," a student might analyze "The Tone of Frost's Speaker," or "Frost's Smart Horse in 'Stopping by Woods . . . ,'" or "Images of Cold and Comfort." Dealing with a longer poem, a writer might isolate one character: "The Characterization of the Hired Man in Frost's 'Death of the Hired Man'"; or analyze a part of theme: "Definitions of 'Home' in Frost's 'Death of the Hired Man.'"

Writing analysis, you must remain aware that everything is related to everything else. If you speak of images, it is hard not to mention metaphor, because many images make metaphors. Discussing the metaphorical structure of a sonnet, you will notice that some of the linkage among metaphors is accomplished by images. Sometimes you may lose track of a topic by noticing too closely the interrelationships of many elements. You need, sometimes, to mention a rhyme when you are discussing characterization, if the rhyme makes a point of character. But you should not be sidetracked into a discussion of rhyme just because the subject comes up. You must keep watch, as you write, that you do not lose track. A clear thesis can be the North Star that guides you through the wilderness of analysis.

In making a thesis, it is best to look for an element that has relevance to the whole poem. Beware of falling into an analysis that records accurately some facts about a poem but stops short of showing the relevance of these facts. A formal analysis of a sonnet that only discloses the existence of a sonnet form would be trivial, too elementary for the name of analysis. However, a good analytical paper could be written to show how sonnet form reflects itself in the poem's shapely argument, sorting itself out into the quatrains (if the sonnet is Shakespearean) and into octave and sestet.

Comparison and Contrast in Writing About Poems

Illustrate analyzed elements of poems by comparing and contrasting them. You may find within one poet's work a habit of writing or thinking. "Emily Dickinson's Imagery of Animals," might compare and contrast parts of three or four Dickinson poems, to investigate her use of animal images. Not only images, but structural devices, recurrent symbols, and themes may provide material for comparative analysis.

You might also contrast two or more poets. "Poets and Flowers: Two Strategies in Roethke and Frost" compares Frost's "Design" with Roethke's "Cuttings." Any comparison and contrast, within one poet's work or between two poets, will require separate analyses or small explications, and judgment on likeness or difference. Note the remarks on the structure of such papers, pages 1273–1275.

Topics in Writing About Poems

Almost any poem brief enough can be subject to explication.

> The Tone of Tenses: Three Poems by Emily Dickinson
> Imagery in Dickinson's "After Great Pain . . ."
> Love and Love of God: Dickinson's "I Cannot Live with You . . ."
> Grief in "Home Burial" and "'Out, Out . . .'"
> The Shape of Apples: The Form of "After Apple Picking"
> Imagery in "To Earthward"
> Ballads Anonymous and Literary: "Edward, Edward," and "La Belle Dame Sans Merci"
> Autumn's Noises in John Keats
> Larkin's "Aubade"—a Range of Feeling
> Themes for Images in Auden's "Musée des Beaux Arts"

Things to Avoid When Writing About Poems

In writing about poetry, you can frequently fail by becoming too personal, by emphasizing your response or your connections with the poet's subject matter. For some reason, people tend to commit this kind of error more often in writing about poems than in writing about the other genres.

Do not confuse the speaker of the poem with the poet as a person. Stick to your thesis. Do not let the interrelatedness of a poem's elements lead you into a disorganized paper.

Writing About Drama

Usually, you will be asked to write about a play you have read rather than a performance you have witnessed. Reviewing a performance is different; for notes on reviewing, see page 1301–1302.

When you write about modern plays, remember that the author provides stage directions, and often interprets characters' feelings; these indicators are as much the play as the dialogue is, and help to stage the play in readers' mental theater.

For older plays, readers supply the scene and understand the characters from the spoken words of dialogue, sometimes with the help of modern editors and commentators. Because the historical context of older dramas supplies the limits of mental theater, even in the shape of the physical stages, you should consult background information while studying the play you write about.

Explicating Drama

Explication of a whole play, or even of an act, is out of the question. You might explicate a brief scene, no longer than a page, or, better still, a key speech by a key character. Writing about a sufficiently important speech, however, you are apt to feel that, in order to explain it thoroughly, everything in the play must be accounted for. As with fiction, be careful to stick to your topic and to avoid plot summary. Refer to other acts and scenes by using a Roman numeral capital for the act, and a lower-case Roman numeral for the scene: II, iii or V, iv.

Analyzing Drama

Analysis is the most common method in writing about drama. Analysis limits a topic. Noticing the importance of stage business in Chekhov's *The Cherry Orchard,* you may be tempted to isolate this element as "Stage Directions in *The Cherry Orchard,*" but, unless you are called upon for a long term paper, you need to narrow your topic. "Firs's Business: The Servant on Chekhov's Stage" would make a manageable topic. You would need to spend most of your time seeing what Chekhov's stage directions tell Firs to do, and deciding what you can learn of Firs's physical actions from dialogue. Then, as part of your topic, you would briefly relate Firs's business to the play as a whole.

The theme of a play is too large a subject, but you can analyze theme into parts. Defining all the uses to which the play puts the cherry orchard would be too much; you could instead define the orchard's meaning to one or two characters. By analyzing the use of trains in that play (references in dialogue, offstage whistles), you could touch on the play's structure and theme. Whatever element attracts you as you reread the play with an eye to writing about it, you must be alert to subdivide it into smaller parts for analysis.

Many of the elements discussed in relation to fiction or poetry can sustain analysis in writing about drama, if you narrow them sufficiently; plot, character, setting, tone, symbolism, imagery, metaphor. Aristotle's six elements provide another way to look at a play's components. It might be wise to glance again at the headings of "To Read a Play."

Comparison and Contrast in Writing About Drama

Different playwrights may be contrasted for any elements, for construction and characterization and dialogue. But focus must narrow. Do not attempt to compare and contrast the characters of Othello and Oedipus. It would be possible, nevertheless, to compare and contrast recognition scenes, in which each protagonist recognizes an inevitable horror. It is possible to contrast scenes of comic and tragic unmasking.

This book has many rewarding pairs of works for comparison and contrast. The more suggestive these comparisons, the more difficult it becomes to narrow the topic. Only hard thinking can do it.

A Paper on Staging

Another kind of paper, which some instructors assign, asks the student to imagine and describe how to stage a small segment of a play. Taking one scene of *Othello,* for instance, a student might stage it as it might have been played at Shakespeare's Globe Theater, using the possibilities and limitations of the Elizabethan stage, indicating props, blocking, and the use of different areas of the stage. Another student might write an account of the same scene produced on a modern stage. Such a paper, depending on the instructor's wishes, may include indications of spectacle, from lighting to makeup to costuming, and on down to the director's indications for actors' interpretation.

Reviewing a Performance

When you review a new performance of an old play, you should reread the play's text before attending the performance, establishing in your mind a range of possibilities for production. You should be ready to be surprised by a director's original, valid interpretation. Be ready as well to indicate in your review the nature of that interpretation, to estimate its validity, and to evaluate specifics of the production. It helps if you have seen other productions of the same play, to make comparison and contrast.

When you review a new play, you set yourself the considerable task of making an intellectual separation between the play's text, which you have experienced only as a performance, and the performance of that text. You will want to report on the value of the play at the same time as you evaluate the jobs done by director, scene designer, costumer, and actors. Such a separation may prove more than difficult, but you should attempt it. It will help to consult some reviews of recent openings, usually in New York, in the pages of *The New York Times, The New Yorker, Time, Newsweek,* and other publications. Often, critics attempt this separation, saying that a new play is thin and trite, but that one or two superb performances almost save the evening; or that, despite a promising script, miscasting or poor direction has left the performance a shambles.

Reviewing sounds like an impossible task; it is not as easy one. However, writing a play review is an excellent exercise in trying to investigate the complexities of theater—the play itself as well as the variable particulars of performance.

When writing a review, keep your readers in mind. If you write for a newspaper, you may need to summarize the play's plot, even if it is *Othello,* to reach readers whom you cannot assume to have read the text. You must account for the play's text *and* for the director's interpretation. You must list actors by name, and report on their competence; you must judge stage design, and even costuming and lighting.

Sample Topics in Writing About Drama

> Oedipus Rex and Necessary Shape: The Opening Chorus
> The Chorus Sees Oedipus: Beginning Characterization
> Why Othello Believes Iago: Plot and Character in One Scene
> Hedda Gabler as Feminism: The Conclusion
> Dramatic Irony in a Scene from Ibsen
> Wilde's Wild Suspense
> August Wilson's Play of Generations
> Death of a Salesman: Politics of Plot
> Three Tragic Flaws: Sophocles, Shakespeare, and Miller
> Staging Oedipus: The Last Scene
> Recognition Scenes in Othello and Oedipus
> Playwright as Director: Stage Directions in *'night, Mother.*

Things to Avoid When Writing About Drama

When you write about drama, you need especially to concentrate on narrowing your focus, because the length and variety of good drama will tempt you to wander, to lose track, to write diffusely.

Beware of plot summary, except when it is essential to the particulars of statement.

Sample Paper on a Play

Here is a paper written by a sophomore named Margerie Lux.

Margarie Lux
English 204
Dr. Brown
October 15, 1990

GETTING STARTED: Exposition in Marsha Norman's 'night, Mother.

As we read the text of Marsha Norman's 'night, Mother, we gather much information about the author's characters before we hear them speak. I intend to write about Norman's exposition in dialogue, but I need to begin by acknowledging that the

reader first becomes aware of these characters by reading a
little essay called "Characters," then a description of the set
which also conveys character: ". . . house more comfortable
than messy." I find her comments almost obtrusive, as if
Shakespeare wrote at the beginning of his play that Othello
was "a large black soldier who is naive in the way of the
world, confident because of bravery and military success, but
unable to distinguish subtle manipulation." What is left for
me to supply?

Of course these notes bring the play, for a reader of the
text, a little closer to the short story. I suppose that they
are intended to provide suggestions for (or to control) a
director and two actresses. When she writes stage directions
later in the play, Norman continually gives information to
reader and to cast, editorial comments on her characters: "MAMA
stretches to reach the cupcakes . . . This may be the most
serious exercise MAMA ever gets." Of course these comments are
also exposition.

When dialogue begins the characters reveal themselves by
their speeches. At first our attention fastens on the comedy
of eccentricity, but while our attention is gathered by humor,
we gradually discover information that we must have. We learn
about a brother, about Ricky who is a thief, and most
importantly about a prop, as central to our plot as a
character: we learn about Jessie's dead father's pistol.

Slowly we discover the importance of this object. The notion
that Jessie wants to kill herself builds in us over the first
few minutes of the play. The play is 30 pages in our printed
text, and we discover this information on the third page.
Because Norman does not hint at suicide in her notes on
"Characters," the pistol's use dawns on the reader as it does
on the audience.

When dialogue begins, it becomes clear that Jessie is
stocking her mother's larder as if she were preparing for a
blizzard; she is fixing things up for her mother, to hold her
for a while. Then Jessie says, as it seems casually, "Where's
Daddy's gun?" Discussion on where it might be found, which is
comic in its particularity, is interrupted by Jessie's "I found
the bullets." We begin to take notice, even to feel a little
fear, but now the dialogue slides off to Dawson (Jessie's
brother) and we have almost forgotten the gun when, on the
second page of the text, Mama asks the question that may have
appeared in the audience's mind: "What do you want the gun for,
Jess?" Jess's one-word answer is devious, and in the end
ironic: "Protection."

Mama in her ignorance or innocence, and in her suspiciousness,
acts now like an audience or even a chorus. She takes this
answer as a misdirection, as she is supposed to do, while Jessie

continues to search for her father's pistol. After more
dialogue she has found it--"It's for me"--and continued with her
preparations which include cleaning the gun. "What are you
doing?" says Mama. "The barrel has to be cleaned, Mama." It is
not for another page that Jessie says the words that, by now,
both Mama and the audience are afraid they will hear: "I'm going
to kill myself, Mama."

   Now the play is ready to begin. In many ways the two
characters speak--now that the cat is out of the bag--just the
way they spoke before. Their characters do not change, nor
their relationship, but by now the central tension or fact of
the play is out in the open, allowed to disseminate, carefully
and subtly and comically, by the playwright's shrewd and
gradual release of information--like a spansule dripping
anti-histamine gradually into the bloodstream.

Acknowledgments

Chinua Achebe, "The Madman" from *Girls at War and Other Stories* by Chinua Achebe. Copyright © 1972, 1973 by Chinua Achebe. Reprinted by permission of Bantam, Doubleday, Dell, Inc.

The American Bible Association, "The Lord is My Shepherd" from *The Good News Bible, The Bible in Today's English Version.* Copyright © 1966, 1971, 1976 by and reprinted by permission of The American Bible Association.

A. R. Ammons, "Working with Tools" from *Briefings: Poems Small and Easy* by A. R. Ammons. Copyright © by A. R. Ammons. Reprinted by permission of W. W. Norton & Company, Inc.

John Ashbery, "Rivers and Mountains" from *Rivers and Mountains* by John Ashbery. Copyright © 1962, 1963, 1964, 1966 by John Ashbery. Reprinted by permission of Georges Borschardt, Inc.

Margaret Atwood, "Dancing Girls" from *Dancing Girls* by Margaret Atwood. Copyright © 1977, 1982 by O. W. Toad, Ltd. and by McClelland & Stewart. Reprinted by permission of Simon & Schuster, Inc., (USA)/McClelland & Stewart, (CAN). "You Are Happy" from *You Are Happy* by Margaret Atwood. Copyright © 1974 by Margaret Atwood. Reprinted by permission of Phoebe Laramore, Inc.

W. H. Auden, "In Memory of W. B. Yeats," "Musee Des Beaux Arts" and "The Unknown Citizen" from *W. H. Auden: Collected Poems,* by W. H. Auden, compiled and edited by Edward Mendelson. Copyright 1940, renewed 1968 by W. H. Auden. Reprinted by permission of Random House, Inc.

Jimmy Santiago Baca "Perfecto Flores" from *Black Mesa Poems* by Jimmy Santiago Baca. Copyright © 1989 by Jimmy Santiago Baca. Reprinted by permission of Curbstone Press.

Toni Cade Bambara, "The Lesson" from *Gorilla, My Love* by Toni Cade Bambara. Copyright © 1960, 1963, 1965, 1968, 1970–1972 by Toni Cade Bambara. Reprinted by permission of Random House, Inc.

Imamu Amiri Baraka, "Careers" from *Selected Poetry of Imamu Amiri Baraka/ Leroy Jones* by Imamu Amiri Baraka. Copyright © 1979 by Imamu Amiri Baraka. Reprinted by permission of William Morrow & Company.

Donald Barthelme, "Some of Us Had Been Threatening Our Friend Colby" *Amateurs* by Donald Barthelme. Copyright © 1973, 1976 by Donald Barthelme. Reprinted by permission of Farrar, Straus & Giroux, Inc.

Samuel Beckett, *Krapp's Last Tape* by Samuel Beckett. Copyright © 1958 by Samuel Beckett. Reprinted by permission of Grove Weidenfeld, Inc.

Wendell Berry, "The Wild Geese" from *The Country of Marriage* by Wendell Berry. Copyright © 1971 by Wendell Berry. Reprinted by permission of Harcourt Brace Jovanovich, Inc.

John Berryman, "Dream Song #16," and "Dream Song #312" from *The Dream Songs* by John Berryman. Copyright © 1959, 1962–1969, by John Berryman. Reprinted by permission of HarperCollins.

Elizabeth Bishop, "The Monument" and "The Fish" from *The Complete Poems, 1927–1979* by Elizabeth Bishop. Copyright © 1939 by Elizabeth Bishop. Copyright © 1979, 1983 by Alice Helen Methfessel. Reprinted by permission of Farrar, Straus and Giroux, Inc.

Carol Bly, "After the Baptism" by Carol Bly from *The Western Humanities Review,* 1988. Copyright © 1988 by Carol Bly. Reprinted by permission of The Western Humanities Review, English Dept., University of Utah, Salt Lake City, Utah.

Robert Bly, "Hunting Pheasants in a Cornfield" from *Silence in the Snowy Fields,* by Robert Bly. Published by Wesleyan University Press. Copyright © 1962 by and reprinted by permission of Robert Bly.

Louise Bogan, "Cartography" and "To an Artist, to Take Heart" from *The Blue Estuaries* by Louise Bogan. Copyright © 1937, 1964, 1965, 1968 by Louise Bogan. Reprinted by permission of Farrar Straus and Giroux, Inc.

Jorge Luis Borges, "The Secret Miracle" from *Labyrinths* by Jorge Luis Borges. Copyright © 1962, 1966 by and reprinted by permission of New Directions Publishing Corporation.

Gwendolyn Brooks, "The Bean Eaters" and "We Real Cool" from *The Blacks* by Gwendolyn Brooks. Copyright © 1987 by Gwendolyn Brooks. Published by The David Company, Chicago. Reprinted by permission of Gwendolyn Brooks.

David Budbill, "What I Heard at the Discount Department Store" from *Judevine: The Complete Poems* by David Budbill. Copyright © 1991 by and reprinted by permission of David Budbill.

Raymond Carver, "A Small Good Thing" from *Cathedral* by Raymond Carver. Copyright © 1983 by Raymond Carver. Reprinted by permission of Alfred A. Knopf, Inc.

John Cheever, "The Chaste Clarissa" from *The Stories of John Cheever* by John Cheever. Copyright © 1952 by John Cheever. Reprinted by permission of Alfred A. Knopf, Inc./Random House, Inc.

Anton Chekhov, *The Cherry Orchard* by Anton Chekhov, translated by Stark Young. Copyright © by Stark Young. Reprinted by permission of Flora Roberts, Inc. "Gooseberries" by Anton Chekhov and translated by Avrahm Yarmolinsky, from THE PORTABLE CHEKHOV by Avrahm Yarmolinsky, editor. Copyright © 1947, 1968 by Viking Penguin, Inc. Renewed copyright © 1975 by Avrahm Yarmolinsky. Reprinted by permission of Viking Penguin, a division of Penguin Books USA.

Tom Clark, "Poem" from *Stones* by Tom Clark. Copyright © by and reprinted by permission of Tom Clark.

Michelle Cliff, "A Hanged Man" from *Bodies of Water* by Michelle Cliff, pp. 45–52. Copyright © and reprinted by permission of Michelle Cliff, represented by Faith Childs Literary Agency, New York.

Lucille Clifton, "good times," "my dream about the cows" and "my dream about the poet" from *Good Woman: Poems and A Memoir, 1969–1980,* by Lucille Clifton. Copyright © 1987 by Lucille Clifton. Reprinted by permission of Boa Editions, Ltd.

Hart Crane, from "The Bridge," and "Voyages I and II" from *The Complete Poems and Selected Prose and Poetry of Hart Crane* by Hart Crane. Copyright © 1933, 1958, 1966 by and reprinted by permission of Liveright Publishing Corporation.

Robert Creeley, "The Hill" and "The Rain" from *Collected Poems of Robert Creeley, 1945–1975,* by Robert Creeley. Copyright © 1983 by The Regents of the University of California. Reprinted by permission of The University of California Press.

Countee Cullen, "For a Lady I Know" from *On These I Stand* by Countee Cullen. Copyright © 1925 by Harper & Brothers, renewed 1953 by Ida M. Cullen. Reprinted by permission of GRM Associates, Inc., Agents for the Estate of Ida M. Cullen.

e.e. cummings, "l)a" from *Complete Poems 1913–1962* by e.e. cummings. Copyright © 1958 by e.e. cummings. Reprinted by permission of Harcourt Brace Jovanovich, Inc. "Poem, or Beauty Hurts Mr. Vinal" from *Is 5 Poems* by c.e. cummings. Copyright © 1926 by Boni Liveright, renewed 1953 by e.e. Cummings. Reprinted by permission of Liveright Publishing Corporation.

J.V. Cunningham, Two epigrams by J.V. Cunningham. Copyright © by J.V. Cunningham. Reprinted by permission of Ohio University Press, Athens.

James Dickey, "The Heaven of Animals" from *Drowning with Others* by James Dickey. Copyright © 1961 by James Dickey. Originally published in *The New Yorker.* Reprinted by permission of Wesleyan University Press.

Emily Dickinson, "After great pain, a formal feeling comes—," "The first Day's Night had come—," "Me from Myself—to banish—," "My Life had stood—A Loaded Gun—," "The Province of the Saved," and "A still—Volcano—Life—" from *The Complete Poems of Emily Dickinson,* by Emily Dickinson, edited by Thomas H. Johnson. Copyright 1914, 1929, 1935, 1942 by Martha Dickinson Bianchi, renewed 1957, 1963 by Mary L. Hampson. Reprinted by permission of Little Brown and Company. "Because I could not stop for Death—," "He fumbles at your Soul—," "He put the Belt around my life—," "I cannot live with You—," "I'm ceded—I've stopped being Theirs—," "I felt a Cleaving in my Mind—," "I heard a Fly buzz—when I died—," "I would not paint—a picture—," "A narrow Fellow in the Grass" "Much Madness is divinest Sense—," "Severer Service of myself," "The Soul has Bandaged moments—," from *The Poems of Emily Dickinson,* by Emily Dickinson, edited by Thomas H. Johnson, Cambridge, Mass. Copyright © 1951, 1955, 1979, 1983 by the President and Fellows of Harvard College. Reprinted by permission of Belknap, Harvard University Press/The Trustees of Amherst College.

David Dooley, "How I Wrote It" from *The Volcano Inside* by David Dooley. Copyright © 1988 by and reprinted by permission of David Dooley.

H. D., "Heat" and "Sea Rose" from *Selected Poems of H. D.,* by H. D. (Hilda Doolittle). Copyright © 1957 by Norman Holmes Pearson. Reprinted by permission of New Directions Publishing Corporation.

Edward Dorn, "On the Debt My Mother Owed to Sears Roebuck" by Edward Dorn. Copyright © by and reprinted by permission of Edward Dorn.

Rita Dove, "Horse and Tree" and "Lint" from *Grace Notes, Poems* by Rita Dove. Copyright © 1989 by Rita Dove. Reprinted by permission of W. W. Norton, Inc.

Alan Dugan, "On Hurricane Jackson" from *New and Collected Poems: 1961–1983* by Alan Dugan. Copyright © 1961 by Alan Dugan. Reprinted by permission of The Ecco Press.

Robert Duncan, "Poetry, A Natural Thing" from *The Opening of the Field* by Robert Duncan. Copyright © 1960 by Robert Duncan. Reprinted by permission of New Directions Publishing.

Richard Eberhart, "The Groundhog" from *Collected Poems 1930–1976* by Richard Eberhart. Copyright © 1960 by Richard Eberhart. Reprinted by permission of Oxford University Press.

Russell Edson, "Bringing a Dead Man Back to Life" from *The Intuitive Journey and Other Works* by Russell Edson. Copyright © 1976 by Russell Edson. Reprinted by permission of HarperCollins, Inc.

T. S. Eliot, "The Love Song of J. Alfred Prufrock" and "Journey of the Magi" from *Collected Poems 1909–1962* by T. S. Eliot. Copyright © by T. S. Eliot. Reprinted by permission of Harcourt Brace Jovanovich, Inc./Faber and Faber, Ltd.

Ralph Ellison, "Battle Royal" from *Invisible Man* by Ralph Ellison. Copyright 1948 by Ralph Ellison. Reprinted by permission of Random House, Inc.

Louise Erdrich, "The Leap" by Louise Erdrich. Copyright © 1990 by *Harper's Magazine,* March, 1990. All rights reserved. Reprinted by special permission of Harper's Magazine. "Owl" from *Baptism of Desire* by Louise Erdrich. Copyright © 1989 by Louise Erdrich. Reprinted by permission of HarperCollins.

Martin Espada, "Latin Night at the Pawnshop" and "The Savior is Abducted in Puerto Rico" from *Rebellion is the Circle of a Lover's Hands* by Martin Espada. Copyright © 1990 by Martin Espada. Reprinted by permission of Curbstone Press.

William Faulkner, "A Rose For Emily" from *Collected Stories of William Faulkner* by William Faulkner. Copyright © 1930 by William Faulkner. Reprinted by permission of Random House.

Ian Hamilton Finlay, "Homage to Malevich" from *Poems to Hear and See* by Ian Hamilton Finlay. Copyright © 1971 by Ian Hamilton Finlay. Reprinted by permission of Macmillan Publishing Co., Inc.

Robert Francis, "Hogwash" and "Three Woodchoppers" from *Robert Francis Collected Poems, 1936–1975* by Robert Francis. Copyright © 1944, 1965, 1972, 1976 by Robert Francis. Reprinted by permission of University of Massachusetts Press, Amherst.

Robert Frost, "Acquainted with the Night," "After Apple-Picking," "Birches," "Design," "To Earthward," "Home Burial," "The Most of It," "Mowing," "The Need of Being Versed in Country Things," "Once by the Pacific," "The Pasture," "The Road Not Taken," "The Silken Tent" and "The Gift Outright" from *The Poetry of Robert Frost,* by Robert Frost, edited by Edward Connery Lathem. Copyright 1923, © 1969 by Holt, Rinehart and Winston, Inc.; 1936, 1951 by Robert Frost; and 1964 by Lesley Frost Ballentine. Reprinted by permission of Henry Holt and Company, Inc. "The Draft Horse" from *The Poetry of Robert Frost,* by Robert Frost, edited by Edward Connery Lathem. Copyright 1923, 1928, 1930, 1934, 1939, © 1967, 1969, by Holt, Rinehart and Winston. Copyright 1935, 1942, 1951, © 1956, 1958, 1962 by Robert Frost. Copyright © 1964, 1967, 1970 by Lesley Frost Ballantine. Reprinted by permission of Henry Holt, and Company, Inc. "In White" from *The Dimensions of Robert Frost* by Robert Frost, edited by Reginald L. Cook. Copyright © 1958 by Robert Frost/Reginald Cook. Reprinted by permission of Henry Holt and Company, Inc. "Out, Out" from *The Poetry of Robert Frost* by Robert Frost, edited by Edward Connery Latham. Copyright 1916, 1944 by Robert Frost, renewed © 1969 by Holt, Rinehart and Winston, Inc. Reprinted by permission of Henry Holt and Company, Inc. "Stopping by Woods on a Snowy Evening" from *The Poetry of Robert Frost,* by Robert Frost, edited by Edward Connery Lathem. Copyright 1923, renewed 1951 by Robert Frost. Reprinted by permission of Holt, Rinehart and Winston, Inc.

Allen Ginsberg, "America" by Allen Ginsberg. Copyright © 1956, 1959 by Allen Ginsberg. "First Party at Ken Kesey's with Hell's Angels" from *Collected Poems, 1947–1980,* by Allen Ginsberg. Copyright © 1965, 1984 by Allen Ginsberg. Reprinted by permission of HarperCollins.

Louise Gluck, "Gratitude" from *The House on Marshland* by Louise Gluck. Copyright © 1971–1975 by Louise Gluck. Reprinted by permission of The Ecco Press.

Nadine Gordimer, "The Train from Rhodesia" from *The Soft Voice of The Serpent* by Nadine Gordimer. Copyright © 1952, renewed 1980 by Nadine Gordimer. Reprinted by permission of Russell & Volkening, Inc.

Edward Gorey, From "The Listing Attic" from *Amphigory* by Edward Gorey. Copyright © 1972 by Edward Gorey. Reprinted by permission of Candida Donadio & Associates, Inc.

Robert Graves, "In Broken Images" from *Robert Graves: Collected Poems 1975* by Robert Graves. Copyright © 1975 by Robert Graves. Reprinted by permission of A.P. Watt Ltd., and the Executors of the Estate of Robert Graves.

John Haines, From "And When The Green Man Comes" from *Winter News* by John Haines. Copyright © 1961, 1964 by John Haines. Reprinted by permission of Wesleyan University Press/University Press of New England.

Thomas Hardy, "During Wind and Rain," "Epitaph on a Pessimist," "The Oxen" and "Transformations" from *The Complete Poems of Thomas Hardy,* by Thomas Hardy, edited by James Gibson. Published by MacMillan, 1978.

Robert Hayden, "Middle Passage" from *Angle of Ascent, New and Selected Poems* by Robert Hayden. Copyright © 1970, 1972, 1975 by Robert Hayden. Reprinted by permission of Liveright Publishing Corporation.

Seamus Heaney, "A Drink of Water" and "Song" from *Field Work* by Seamus Heaney. Copyright © 1976, 1979 by Seamus Heaney. "Iron Spike" from "Shelf of Life" from *Station Island* by Seamus Heaney. Copyright © 1985 by Seamus Heaney. Reprinted by permission of Farrar Straus & Giroux, Inc.

Anthony Hecht, "The Dover Bitch: A Criticism of Life" from *The Hard Hours* by Anthony Hecht. Copyright © 1967 by Anthony Hecht. Reprinted by permission of Atheneum Publishers, Inc.

Ernest Hemingway, "A Clean, Well-Lighted Place" from *Winner Take Nothing* by Ernest Hemingway. Copyright © 1933 by Charles Scribner's Sons; copyright renewal © 1961 by Mary Hemingway. Reprinted with permission of Charles Scribner's sons, an imprint of Macmillan Publishing Company.

Geoffrey Hill, "Merlin" and "Orpheus and Euridice" from *Somewhere Is Such a Kingdom* by Geoffrey Hill. Copyright © 1975 by Geoffrey Hill. Reprinted by permission of Andre Deutsch Ltd.

Linda Hogan, "The Rainy Season" by Linda Hogan. Copyright © by and reprinted by permission of Linda Hogan.

Garrett Hongo, "The Legend" from *The River of Heaven* by Garrett Hongo. Copyright © 1988 by Garrett Hongo. Reprinted by permission of Alfred A. Knopf, Inc.

Langston Hughes, "Bad Luck Card," "Homecoming" and "Hope" from *Selected Poems of Langston Hughes,* by Langston Hughes. "Bad Luck Card," copyright © 1927 by Alfred A. Knopf, Inc.; "Homecoming," copyright © 1959 by Langston Hughes; and "Hope," copyright 1942 by Alfred A. Knopf, Inc., and renewed 1970 by Anna Bontemps and George Houston Bass. Reprinted by permission of Alfred A. Knopf, Inc. "On the Road" from *Laughing to Keep from Crying* by Langston Hughes. Copyright © 1952 by Langston Hughes. Copyright renewed 1980 by George Houston Bass. Reprinted by permission of Harold Ober Associates, Inc.

Ted Hughes, "Thrushes" from *New Selected Poems* and from *Lupercal* by Ted Hughes. Copyright © 1959 by Ted Hughes. Reprinted by permission of HarperCollins/Faber and Faber Ltd.

Richard Hugo, "Degrees of Gray in Philipsburg" from *The Lady in Kicking Horse Reservoir, Poems by Richard Hugo,* by Richard Hugo. Copyright © 1973 by Richard Hugo. Reprinted by permission of W. W. Norton & Company, Inc.

Randall Jarrell, "Eighth Air Force" from *Selected Poems* by Randall Jarrell. Copyright © 1947, 1967 by Mrs. Randall Jarrell. Reprinted by permission of Farrar Straus Giroux, Inc.

James Joyce, "Counterparts," from *Dubliners* by James Joyce. Copyright 1916 by B. W. Heubsch. Definitive text copyright © 1967 by the Estate of James Joyce. Reprinted by permission of Viking Penguin, a division of Penguin Books USA Inc.

Franz Kafka, "A Hunger Artist" from *The Metamorphosis, The Penal Colony and Other Stories* by Franz Kafka, translated by Willa and Edwin Muir. Copyright 1948 and renewed 1975 by Schocken Books, Inc. Reprinted by permission of Schocken Books, published by Pantheon Books, a division of Random House, Inc.

Jamaica Kincaid, "What I Have Been Doing Lately" from *At The Bottom of the River* by Jamaica Kincaid. Copyright © 1981, 1983 by Jamaica Kincaid. Reprinted by permission of Farrar, Straus and Giroux, Inc.

X. J. Kennedy, "In a Prominent Bar in Seraucus One Day" by X. J. Kennedy. Copyright © and reprinted by permission of X. J. Kennedy.

Galway Kinnell, "The Bear" from *Body Rags* by Galway Kinnell. Copyright © 1967 by Galway Kinnell. Reprinted by permission of Houghton Mifflin Company.

Etheridge Knight, "Hard Rock Returns to Prison from the Hospital of the Criminally Insane" from *Poems from Prison* by Etheridge Knight. Copyright © 1968 by Etheridge Knight. Reprinted by permission of Broadside/Crummell Press.

Robinson Jeffers, "Hurt Hawks" from *The Selected Poetry of Robinson Jeffers,* by Robinson Jeffers. Copyright 1928, renewed 1956 by Robinson Jeffers. Reprinted by permission of Random House, Inc.

Donald Justice, "Counting the Mad" from *The Summer Anniversaries* by Donald Justice. Copyright © 1957 by Donald Justice. Reprinted by permission of Wesleyan University Press.

Yusef Komunyakaa, "Facing It" from *Dien Cai Dau* by Yusef Komunyakaa. Copyright © 1988 by Yusef Komunyakaa. Reprinted by permission of Wesleyan University Press/University Press of New England.

Philip Larkin, "Aubade" and "Mr. Bleaney" from *The Whitsun Weddings* by Philip Larkin. Copyright © by the Estate of Philip Larkin. Reprinted by permission of Faber and Faber Ltd.

D. H. Lawrence, "Bavarian Gentians" and "The Song of a Man Who Has Come Through" from *The Complete Poems of D. H. Lawrence,* collected and edited by Vivian de Sola Pinto and F. Warren Roberts. Copyright © 1964, 1971 by Angelo Ravagli and C. Montague Weekley, Executors of the Estate of Frieda Lawrence Ravagli. Reprinted by permission of Viking Penguin, a Division of Penguin USA. "The Rocking Horse Winner" from *The Complete Short Stories of D. H. Lawrence* by D. H. Lawrence. Copyright © 1933 by the Estate of D. H. Lawrence, renewed © 1961 by Angelo Ravagli and C.Montague Weekley, Executors of the Estate of Frieda Lawrence Ravagli. Reprinted by permission of Viking Penguin, a division of Penguin USA Inc.

Philip Levine, "Salami" from *They Feed They Lion* by Philip Levine, published by Atheneum. Copyright © 1972 by and reprinted by permission of Philip Levine.

Li-Young Lee, "Eating Alone" from *Rose* by Li-Young Lee. Copyright © 1986 by Li-Young Lee. Reprinted by permission of Boa Editions, Ltd. "From Blossoms" from *Rose* by Li-Young Lee. Copyright © 1986 by Li-Young Lee. Reprinted by permission of BOA Editions, Ltd.

Denise Levertov, "October" and "The World Outside" from *Poems 1960–1967* by Denise Levertov. Copyright © 1962, 1964 by Denise Levertov Goodman. Reprinted by permission of New Directions Publishing Corporation.

Vachel Lindsay, "The Flower-Fed Buffaloes" from *Going to the Stars* by Vachel Lindsay. Copyright © 1926, renewed 1954 by Elizabeth C. Lindsay. Reprinted by permission of Hawthorn Books, Inc.

John Logan, "The Picnic" from *Only The Dreamer Can Change the Dream* by John Logan. Copyright © 1981 by John Logan. Reprinted by permission of John Logan/The Ecco Press.

Audre Lorde, "Hanging Fire" *The Black Unicorn* by Audre Lorde. Copyright © by Audre Lorde. Reprinted by permission of W. W. Norton, Inc.

Robert Lowell, "After the Surprising Conversions" and "New Year's Day" from *Lord Weary's Castle* by Robert Lowell. Copyright 1946, 1974 by Robert Lowell. Reprinted by permission of Harcourt Brace Jovanovich, Inc. "For the Union Dead" from *For The Union Dead* by Robert Lowell. Copyright © 1960 by Robert Lowell. Reprinted by permission of Farrar Straus & Giroux. "Skunk Hour" from *Life Studies* by Robert Lowell. Copyright © 1956 by Robert Lowell. Reprinted by permission of Farrar Straus & Giroux.

Archibald MacLeish, "You, Andrew Marvell" from *New and Collected Poems 1917–1976* by Archibald MacLeish. Copyright © 1976 by Archibald MacLeish. Reprinted by permission of Archibald MacLeish.

Louis MacNeice, "The Sunlight on the Garden" from *The Collected Poems of Louis MacNeice* by Louis MacNeice. Copyright © by Louis MacNeice. Reprinted by permission of Faber and Faber Ltd.

Derek Mahon, "The Chinese Restaurant in Portrush" from *Poems 1962–1978* by Derek Mahon. Copyright © 1979 by Derek Mahon. Reprinted by permission of Oxford University Press.

Alice Mattison, "The Middle Ages" from *The Great Wits* by Alice Mattison. Copyright © 1988 by Alice Mattison. Reprinted by permission of William Morrow & Company, Inc.

National Council of Churches of Christ, "The Lord Is My Shepherd" from *The Bible, Revised Standard Version*. Copyright © 1946, 1952, 1971 by the Division of Christian Education of the National Council of the Churches of Christ in U.S.A.

Wesley McNair, "Mina Bell's Cows" from *The Faces of Americans in 1853* by Wesley McNair. Copyright © 1983 by and reprinted by permission of Wesley McNair. "Where I Live" from *The Faces of Americans in 1853* by Wesley McNair. Copyright © 1983 by and reprinted by permission of Wesley McNair.

James Merrill, "After Greece" from *Water Street* by James Merrill. Copyright © 1962 by James Merrill. Reprinted by permission of Atheneum Publishers, Inc.

Arthur Miller, *Death of a Salesman* by Arthur Miller. Copyright © 1949, and renewed 1977 by Arthur Miller. Reprinted by permission of Viking Penguin, a division of Penguin Books USA Inc. This play in its printed form is designed for the reading public only. All dramatic rights in it are fully protected by copyright, and no public or private performance, professional or amateur, may be given without the author and the payment of royalty. As the courts have also ruled that the public reading of a play constitutes a public performance, no such reading may be given except under the conditions stated above. Communication should be addressed to the author's representative, International Creative Management, Inc.

Marianne Moore, "A Grave" and "Silence" from *Collected Poems* by Marianne Moore. Copyright © 1935 by Marianne Moore, renewed 1963 by Marianne Moore and T. S. Eliot. Reprinted by permission of Macmillan Publishing Co., Inc.

Thylias Moss, "November and Aunt Jemima" and "Sunrise Comes to Second Avenue" from *At Redbones* by Thylias Moss. Copyright © by Thylias Moss. Reprinted by permission of Thylias Moss/Cleveland State University Poetry Center.

Edwin Muir, "The Horses" from *The Collected Poems of Edwin Muir* by Edwin Muir. Copyright © by Edwin Muir. Reprinted by permission of Faber and Faber Ltd.

Bharati Mukherjee, "Jasmine" from *Middleman and Other Stories* by Bharati Mukherjee. Copyright © 1988 by Bharati Mukherjee. Reprinted by permission of Grove Press.

Alice Munro, "Friend of My Youth" from *Friend of My Youth* by Alice Munro. Copyright © 1990 by Alice Munro. Originally published in *The New Yorker.* Reprinted by permission of Alfred A. Knopf, Inc., Random House, Inc./Virginia Barber Literary Agency, Inc.

David Mura, "Grandfather and Grandmother in Love" from *After We Lost Our Way* by David Mura. Copyright © 1989 by David Mura. Reprinted by permission of E. P. Dutton, an imprint of New American Library, a division of Penguin Books USA Inc.

Pablo Neruda, "Ode to My Socks" from *Neruda and Valejo: Selected Poems,* edited and translated by Robert Bly. Published by Beacon Press. Copyright © 1967, 1976 by and reprinted by permission of Robert Bly.

Howard Norman, "The Wrong-Chill Windigo" from *Northern Tales* by Howard Norman. Copyright © 1990 by Howard Norman. Reprinted by permission of Pantheon Books, a division of Random House, Inc.

Marsha Norman, *'night, Mother* by Marsha Norman. Copyright © 1983 by Marsha Norman. Reprinted by permission of Hill and Wang, a division of Farrar Straus & Giroux, Inc. Caution: professionals and amateurs are hereby warned that *'night, Mother,* being fully protected under the Copyright Laws of The United States of America and all other countries of the Berne and Universal Copyright Conventions, is subject to a royalty. All rights including, but not limited to, professional, amateur, recording, motion picture, recitation, lecturing, public reading, radio and television broadcasting and the rights of translation in foreign languages are expressly reserved. All inquiries concerning rights, (other than stock and amateur rights), should be addressed to the author's agent, The William Morris Agency, Inc., 1350 Avenue of the Americas, NY NY 10019. The stock and amateur production rights for *'night, Mother* are controlled exclusively by The Dramatists Play Service, Inc., 440 Park Avenue South, NY, NY 10016. No amateur performance of the play may be given without obtaining in advance the written permission of the Dramatists Play Service Inc. and paying the requisite fee.

Flannery O'Connor, "A Good Man is Hard to Find" from *A Good Man is Hard to Find and Other Stories.* Copyright © 1953 by Flannery O'Connor and renewed 1981 by Regina O'Connor, reprinted by permission of Harcourt Brace Jovanovich.

Frank O'Connor, "Guests of the Nation" from *Collected Stories* by Frank O'Connor. Copyright © 1981 by Harriet O'Donovan Sheehy, Executrix of the Estate of Frank O'Connor. Reprinted by permission of Alfred A. Knopf/Joan Daves, Inc.

Frank O'Hara, "The Day Lady Died" from *Lunch Poems* by Frank O'Hara. Copyright © 1964 by Frank O'Hara. Reprinted by permission of City Lights, Inc.

Sharon Olds, "Sex Without Love" from *The Dead and The Living* by Sharon Olds. Copyright © 1983 by Sharon Olds. Reprinted by permission of Alfred A. Knopf, Inc.

Charles Olson, "Maximus, to Gloucester, Sunday, July 19" from *The Maximus Poems* by Charles Olson. Copyright © 1960 by Charles Olson. Reprinted by permission of Corinth Books, Inc.

Tillie Olson, "I Stand Here Ironing," from *Tell Me a Riddle* by Tillie Olsen. Copyright © 1956, 1957, 1960, 1961 by Tillie Olsen. Used by permission of Delacorte Press/ Seymour Lawrence, a division of Bantam Doubleday Dell Publishing Group, Inc.

Gregory Orr, "All Morning" and "The Sweater" from *Gathering The Bones Together* by Gregory Orr. Copyright © 1975 by and reprinted by permission of Gregory Orr. "Washing My Face" from *Burning the Empty Nests* by Gregory Orr. Copyright © 1973 by and reprinted by permission of Gregory Orr.

Joyce Peseroff, "The Hardness Scale" from *The Hardness Scale* by Joyce Peseroff. Copyright © by Joyce Peseroff. Reprinted by permission of The Alice James Poetry Cooperative, Inc.

Sylvia Plath, "Lady Lazarus" from *The Collected Poems of Sylvia Plath,* edited by Ted Hughes. Copyright © 1963 by Ted Hughes. Reprinted by permission of Harper-Collins.

Katherine Anne Porter, "Rope" from *Flowering Judas and Other Stories* by Katherine Anne Porter. Copyright © by Katherine Anne Porter, reprinted by permission of Harcourt Brace Jovanovich, Inc.

Ezra Pound, "The Bath Tub," "Hugh Selwyn Mauberly," "The Return" and "The River-Merchant's Wife: A Letter" from *Personae* by Ezra Pound. Copyright © 1926 by Ezra Pound. Reprinted by permission of New Directions Publishing Corporation.

John Crow Ransom, "Captain Carpenter" from *The Selected Poetry of John Crow Ransom,* Third Edition, by John Crow Ransom. Copyright © 1924 by John Crow Ransom. Reprinted by permission of Alfred A. Knopf, Inc.

Liam Rector, "Showing" from *The Sorrows of Architecture* by Liam Rector. Copyright © 1984 by Liam Rector. Reprinted by permission of Dragon Gate, Inc.

Kenneth Rexroth, "Proust's Madeleine" and "The Signature of All Things" from *Collected Shorter Poems* by Kenneth Rexroth. Copyright © 1949, 1963 by Kenneth Rexroth. Reprinted by permission of New Directions Publishing Corporation.

Charles Reznikoff, "Holding the Stem" from *The Complete Poems 1937–1975* by Charles Reznikoff. Copyright © 1941 by Charles Reznikoff. Reprinted with permission of Black Sparrow Press, Inc.

Adrienne Rich, "Aunt Jennifer's Tigers," "Living Memory," "After Twenty Years," "From an Old House in America," "Women," and II and XII from *Twenty-One Love Poems* by Adrienne Rich. Copyright © 1981, 1984 by Adrienne Rich. Reprinted by permission of W. W. Norton & Company, Inc.

Edwin Arlington Robinson, "Eros Turannos" and "Mr. Flood's Party" from *Collected Poems* by Edwin Arlington Robinson. Copyright © 1916 by Edwin Arlington Robinson, renewed 1944 by Ruth Nivison. Reprinted by permission of Macmillan Publishing Co.

Theodore Roethke, "My Papa's Waltz," "The Meadow Mouse" and "The Rose" from *The Collected Poems of Theodore Roethke* by Theodore Roethke. "My Papa's Waltz," copyright © 1972 by Hearst Magazines Inc., "The Rose" and "The Meadow Mouse," copyright © 1963 by Beatrice Roethke, Administratrix of the Estate of Theodore Roethke. Reprinted by permission of Doubleday, a division of Bantam Doubleday Dell Publishing Group, Inc.

David Rosenberg, "Psalm 23" from *Blues of the Sky* by David Rosenberg. Copyright © 1976 by David Rosenberg. Reprinted by permission of HarperCollins.

Carl Sandburg, "Chicago" from *Chicago Poems* by Carl Sandburg. Copyright © 1916 by Holt, Rinehart and Winston, copyright 1944 by Carl Sandburg. Reprinted by permission of Harcourt Brace Jovanovich, Inc.

Yvonne Sapia, "Valentino's Hair" from *Valentino's Hair* by Yvonne Sapia. Copyright © 1987 by Yvonne Sapia. Reprinted by permission of Northeastern University Press, Boston.

Vikram Seth, "God's Love" from *All you Who Sleep Tonight* by Vikram Seth. Copyright © 1990 by Vikram Seth. Reprinted by permission of Faber & Faber, Inc.

Anne Sexton, "Wanting to Die" from *Live or Die* by Anne Sexton. Copyright © 1966 by Anne Sexton. Reprinted by permission of Houghton Mifflin Company.

William Shakespeare, *The Tragedy of Othello* by William Shakespeare, edited by Alvin Kernan. Copyright © 1963 by Alvin Kernan. Reprinted by permission of New American Library.

Leslie Marmon Silko, "Storyteller" from *Storyteller* by Leslie Marmon Silko. Copyright © 1981 by and reprinted by permission of Leslie Marmon Silko. "When Mountain Lion Lay Down with Deer" by Leslie Marmon Silko. Copyright © by and reprinted by permission of Leslie Marmon Silko.

Charles Simic, "Fork" from *Dismantling the Silence* by Charles Simic. Copyright © by Charles Simic. Reprinted by permission of George Braziller, Inc. "Shelley" from *The Book of Gods and Devils* by Charles Simic. Copyright © 1990 by Charles Simic. Reprinted by permission of Harcourt Brace Jovanovich, Inc.

Louis Simpson, "Early in the Morning" from *The Good News of Death and Other Poems* by Louis Simpson. Copyright 1950, 1951, 1952, 1953, 1953, 1954, 1955 by Louis Simpson. Reprinted by permission of Charles Scribner's Sons. "In the Suburbs" and "Walt Whitman at Bear Mountain" from *At the End of the Open Road* by Louis Simpson. Copyright © by Louis Simpson. Reprinted by permission of Wesleyan University Press/University Press of New England. "To the Western World" from *A Dream of Governors* by Louis Simpson. Copyright © by Louis Simpson. Reprinted by permission of Wesleyan University Press/University Press of New England.

W. D. Snodgrass, "Lobsters in the Window" from *After Experience* by W. D. Snodgrass. Copyright © 1963 by W. D. Snodgrass. Reprinted by permission of Soho Press.

Gary Snyder, "Above Pate Valley" and "Hay for the Horses" from *Riprap* by Gary Snyder. Copyright © 1959, 1965 by Gary Snyder. Published by North Point Press. Reprinted by permission of Farrar Straus & Giroux, Inc.

Isaac Bashevis Singer, "Gimpel the Fool" from *A Treasury of Yiddish Stories* by Irving Howe and Eliezer Greenberg. Copyright 1953 by The Parisan Review, renewed © 1981 by Isaac Bashevis Singer. Reprinted by permission of Viking Penguin, a division of Penguin Books USA Inc.

Cathy Song, "A Small Light" from *Frameless Windows, Squares of Light* by Cathy Song. Copyright © by Cathy Song. Reprinted by permission of W. W. Norton, Inc.

William Stafford, "Travelling Through the Dark" from *Stories That Could Be True* by William Stafford. Copyright © 1960 by William Stafford. Reprinted by permission of HarperCollins.

John Steinbeck, "The Chrysanthemums" from *The Long Valley* by John Steinbeck. Copyright 1937, renewed © 1965 by John Steinbeck. Reprinted by permission of Viking Penguin, a division of Penguin Books USA Inc.

Wallace Stevens, "Disillusionment at Ten O'Clock," "The Emperor of Ice-Cream," "The Snow Man" and "Sunday Morning" from *The Collected Poems of Wallace Stevens* by Wallace Stevens. Copyright © 1923, renewed 1951 by Wallace Stevens. Reprinted by permission of Alfred A. Knopf, Inc.

Mark Strand, "Always" and "The End" from *The Continuous Life* by Mark Strand. Copyright © 1990 by Mark Strand. Reprinted by permission of Alfred A. Knopf, Inc.

Amy Tan, "Two Kinds" from *The Joy Luck Club* by Amy Tan. Copyright © 1989 by Amy Tan. Reprinted by permission of The Putnam Publishing Group, Inc.

Dylan Thomas, "Do Not Go Gently into That Good Night," "Fern Hill," and "This Bread I Break" from *Poems of Dylan Thomas* by Dylan Thomas. Copyright © 1945 by The Trustees for The Copyrights of Dylan Thomas. Reprinted by permission of New Directions Publishing Corporation/David Higham Associates Limited.

Edward Thomas, "The Owl" from *Collected Poems* by Edward Thomas. Copyright © 1974 by Edward Thomas. Reprinted by permission W. W. Norton & Company, Inc.

James Thurber, "The Catbird Seat" from *The Thurber Carnival* by James Thurber. Copyright © 1945 by James Thurber. Copyright © 1973 by Helen W. Thurber and Rosemary Thurber. Published by HarperCollins, Inc.

Leo Tolstoy, "The Death of Ivan Ilych" from *The Death of Ivan Ilych and Other Stories* by Leo Tolstoy, translated by Louise and Aylmer Maude. Published by Oxford University Press.

Charles Tomlinson, "Paring the Apple" from *Seeing is Believing* by Charles Tomlinson. Copyright © 1958, 1960 by Charles Tomlinson. Published by McDowell Oglesby, OUP. Reprinted by permission of Charles Tomlinson, Gloustershire, England.

Jean Toomer, "Reapers" from *Cane* by Jean Toomer. Copyright © 1923 by Boni & Liveright, renewed 1951 by Jean Toomer. Reprinted by permission of Liveright Publishing Corporation.

John Updike, "Ace in the Hole" from *The Same Door* by John Updike. Copyright 1955 by John Updike. Reprinted by permission of Alfred Knopf, Inc., a Division of Random House, Inc. "Ex-Basketball Players" from *The Carpentered Hen and Other Tame Creatures* by John Updike. Copyright © 1957, 1982 by John Updike. Reprinted by permission of Alfred A. Knopf, Inc., a Division of Random House, Inc.

Kurt Vonnegut, Jr., "Harrison Bergeron" from *Welcome To The Monkey House* by Kurt Vonnegut, Jr. Copyright © 1961 by Kurt Vonnegut. Originally published in *Fantasy and Science Fiction.* Reprinted by permission of Delacorte Press/Seymour Lawrence, a division of Bantam, Doubleday, Dell, Inc.

Derek Walcott, "Sea Grapes" from *Sea Grapes* by Derek Walcott. Copyright © 1976 by Derek Walcott. Reprinted by permission of Farrar Straus & Giroux, Inc.

Alice Walker, "Nineteen Fifty-Five" from *You Can't Keep a Good Woman Down,* by Alice Walker. Copyright © 1981 by Alice Walker. Reprinted by permission of Harcourt Brace Jovanovich, Inc.

Robert Penn Warren, "Gold Glade" from *Promises: Poems 1954–1956* by Robert Penn Warren. Copyright © 1957 by Robert Penn Warren. Reprinted by permission of Random House, Inc.

Eudora Welty, "A Worn Path" from *A Curtain of Green and Other Stories* by Eudora Welty. Copyright © 1941 and renewed 1969 by Eudora Welty. Reprinted by permission of Harcourt Brace Jovanovich, Inc.

Richard Wilbur, "Museum Piece," "Still, Citizen Sparrow" and "Tywater" from *Ceremony and Other Poems.* Copyright © 1950 and renewed 1978 by Richard Wilbur, reprinted by permission of Harcourt Brace Jovanovich, Inc.

Tennessee Williams, *Glass Menagerie* by Tennessee Williams. Copyright 1945 by Tennessee Williams and Edwina D. Williams, renewed 1973 by Tennessee Williams. Reprinted by permission of Random House, Inc.

William Carlos Williams, "Nantucket," "Poem" ("as the Cat"), "The Red Wheelbarrow," "Spring and All" and "This is Just to Say" from *Collected Earlier Poems* by William Carlos Williams. Copyright 1938 by and reprinted by permission of New Directions Publishing Corporation.

August Wilson, *Fences* by August Wilson. Copyright © 1986 by August Wilson. Reprinted by permission of Penguin Books USA Inc.

James Wright, "The First Days" from *To a Blossoming Pear Tree* by James Wright. Copyright © 1974, 1979 by James Wright. Reprinted by permission of Farrar Straus & Giroux, Inc. "Lying in a Hammock at William Duffy's Farm in Pine Island, Minnesota" from *Collected Poems* by James Wright. Copyright © 1961 by James Wright. Reprinted by permission of Wesleyan University Press/University Press of New England.

Jay Wright, "Meta-A and A of Absolutes" from *Selected Poems of Jay Wright,* pp. 175–176, by Jay Wright, edited by R. B. Stepto. Copyright © 1987 by Jay Wright. Reprinted by permission of Princeton University Press.

William Butler Yeats, "The Apparitions," "Among School Children," four versions of "Cradle Song," "Crazy Jane Talks with the Bishop," "Leda and the Swan," "The Magi,"

"Sailing to Byzantium," and "Second Coming," from *The Poems of W. B. Yeats: A New Edition* by William Butler Yeats, edited by Richard J. Finneran. Copyright © 1940 by Georgie Yeats, renewed 1968 by and reprinted by permission of Bertha Georgie Yeats, Michael Butler Yeats and Anne Yeats/Macmillan, London, Ltd.,/A. P. Watt, Ltd.

Louis Zukofsky, "In Arizona" from *Collected Short Poems 1923–1964* by Louis Zukofsky. Copyright © 1971 by Louis Zukofsky. Reprinted by permission of Paul Zukofsky, CZ Publications, Inc.

Photo Credits

William Faulkner (p. 4)/Wide World Photos; **Flannery O'Connor** (p. 38)/Wide World Photos; **Eudora Welty** (p. 67)/Wide World Photos; **Carol Bly** (p. 74)/by Larel Cazin. Copyright © 1991 by HarperCollins; **Alice Munro** (p. 99)/by Jerry Bauer. Copyright © 1991 by Alfred A. Knopf, Inc./Virginia Barber Agency; **John Cheever** (p. 121)/Wide World Photos; **Ernest Hemingway** (p. 154)/Wide World Photos; **Leo Tolstoy** (p. 204)/Bettmanns; **Chinua Achebe** (p. 246)/ Wide World Photos; **Ralph Ellison** (p. 281)/Pictorial Parade; **Nadine Gordimer** (p. 292), **Alice Walker** (p. 396)/Wide World Photos; **Jamaica Kincaid** (p. 300)/James A. Parcell/The Washington Post; **Bharati Mukherjee** (p. 317)/Tom Victor; **Leslie Marmon Silko** (p. 357)/Gus Nitsche; **Amy Tan** (p. 387)/Robert Foothorap Co. 199. Copyright © by G. P. Putnam's Sons; **John Keats** (p. 525), **Emily Dickinson** (p. 530), **Robert Frost** (p. 536)/Bettmanns; **Adrienne Rich** (p. 545)/Wide World Photos; **David Dooley** (p. 586)/courtesy of the author; **Rita Dove** (p. 588)/Wide World Photos; **Linda Hogan** (p. 615)/courtesy of the author; **Garrett Hongo** (p. 616)/Gary Tepfer and Charles Flowers; **Derek Walcott** (p. 708)/Wide World Photos; **Greek Theatre at Epidaurus** (p. 750)/Bettmanns; **Globe Playhouse** (p. 796)/Folger Shakespeare Library, Washington, D.C.; **William Shakespeare** (p. 798)/Bettmanns; **Anton Chekhov** (p. 936)/Bettmanns; ***Cherry Orchard*** (p. 935)/New York Times Picture Services; **Samuel Beckett** (p. 978)/Wide World Photos; **Arthur Miller** (p. 1048)/Wide World Photos; ***Death of A Salesman*** (pp. 1050 and 1051)/CBS Picture Services; **Marsha Norman** (p. 1123)/New York Time Picture Services, Inc.

Index

Page numbers in italic type show location of biographical information.

A Guide to Literary Terms

These are basic literary terms and important words from the genres of fiction, poetry, and drama. The page numbers will guide you quickly to definitions. To find these words elsewhere in the text, check the index. When more than two citations appear, the term is used in connection with more than one sort of literature: *conflict,* for example, is discussed in relation to fiction on page 29 and to drama on page 741.